HALSBURY'S
Laws of England

FIFTH EDITION
2015

Volume 97

This is volume 97 of the Fifth Edition of Halsbury's Laws of England, containing the titles TELECOMMUNICATIONS, TIME, TORT and TRADE AND INDUSTRY.

These titles replace the TELECOMMUNICATIONS, TIME, TORT and TRADE AND INDUSTRY titles contained in volume 97 (2010). The title TORT also replaces the Additional Materials booklet *Tort (Conversion and Wrongful Interference with Goods)*.

Volume 97 (2010) and the Additional Materials booklet *Tort (Conversion and Wrongful Interference with Goods)* may now be archived.

For a full list of volumes comprised in a current set of Halsbury's Laws of England please see overleaf.

Fifth Edition volumes:

1 (2008), 2 (2008), 3 (2011), 4 (2011), 5 (2013), 6 (2011), 7 (2015), 8 (2015), 9 (2012), 10 (2012), 11 (2009), 12 (2009), 13 (2009), 14 (2009), 15 (2009), 16 (2011), 17 (2011), 18 (2009), 19 (2011), 20 (2014), 21 (2011), 22 (2012), 23 (2013), 24 (2010), 25 (2010), 26 (2010), 27 (2010), 28 (2010), 29 (2014), 30 (2012), 31 (2012), 32 (2012), 33 (2013), 34 (2011), 35 (2011), 36 (2011), 37 (2013), 38 (2013), 38A (2013), 39 (2014), 40 (2014), 41 (2014), 41A (2014), 42 (2011), 43 (2011), 44 (2011), 45 (2010), 46 (2010), 47 (2014), 47A (2014), 48 (2008), 49 (2008), 50 (2008), 51 (2013), 52 (2014), 53 (2014), 54 (2008), 55 (2012), 56 (2011), 57 (2012), 58 (2014), 58A (2014), 59 (2014), 59A (2014), 60 (2011), 61 (2010), 62 (2012), 63 (2012), 64 (2012), 65 (2015), 66 (2015), 67 (2008), 68 (2008), 69 (2009), 70 (2012), 71 (2013), 72 (2015), 73 (2015), 74 (2011), 75 (2013), 76 (2013), 77 (2010), 78 (2010), 79 (2014), 80 (2013), 81 (2010), 82 (2010), 83 (2010), 84 (2013), 84A (2013), 85 (2012), 86 (2013), 87 (2012), 88 (2012), 88A (2013), 89 (2011), 90 (2011), 91 (2012), 92 (2010), 93 (2008), 94 (2008), 95 (2013), 96 (2012), 97 (2015), 97A (2014), 98 (2013), 99 (2012), 100 (2009), 101 (2009), 102 (2010), 103 (2010), 104 (2014)

Additional Materials:

Sentencing and Disposition of Offenders (*Release and Recall of Prisoners*) containing vol **92** (2010) paras 761–820

Consolidated Index and Tables:

2015 Consolidated Index (A–E), 2015 Consolidated Index (F–O), 2015 Consolidated Index (P–Z), 2015 Consolidated Table of Statutes, 2015 Consolidated Table of Statutory Instruments, etc, 2015 Consolidated Table of Cases (A–G), 2015 Consolidated Table of Cases (H–Q), 2015 Consolidated Table of Cases (R–Z, ECJ Cases)

Updating and ancillary materials:

2015 Annual Cumulative Supplement; Monthly Current Service; Annual Abridgments 1974–2014

July 2015

HALSBURY'S
Laws of England

Volume 97

2015

Members of the LexisNexis Group worldwide

United Kingdom	LexisNexis, a Division of Reed Elsevier (UK) Ltd, Lexis House, 30 Farringdon Street, LONDON, EC4A 4HH, and 9–10, St Andrew Square, EDINBURGH, EH2 2AF
Australia	Reed International Books Australia Pty Ltd trading as LexisNexis, Chatswood, New South Wales
Austria	LexisNexis Verlag ARD Orac GmbH & Co KG, Vienna
Benelux	LexisNexis Benelux, Amsterdam
Canada	LexisNexis Canada, Markham, Ontario
China	LexisNexis China, Beijing and Shanghai
France	LexisNexis SA, Paris
Germany	LexisNexis GmbH, Dusseldorf
Hong Kong	LexisNexis Hong Kong, Hong Kong
India	LexisNexis India, New Delhi
Italy	Giuffrè Editore, Milan
Japan	LexisNexis Japan, Tokyo
Malaysia	Malayan Law Journal Sdn Bhd, Kuala Lumpur
New Zealand	LexisNexis New Zealand Ltd, Wellington
Singapore	LexisNexis Singapore, Singapore
South Africa	LexisNexis, Durban
USA	LexisNexis, Dayton, Ohio

FIRST EDITION	*Published in 31 volumes between 1907 and 1917*
SECOND EDITION	*Published in 37 volumes between 1931 and 1942*
THIRD EDITION	*Published in 43 volumes between 1952 and 1964*
FOURTH EDITION	*Published in 56 volumes between 1973 and 1987, with reissues between 1988 and 2008*
FIFTH EDITION	*Published between 2008 and 2014, with reissues from 2014*

A CIP Catalogue record for this book is available from the British Library.

ISBN 13 (complete set, standard binding): 9781405734394

ISBN 13: 9781405798594

ISBN 978-1-4057-9859-4

9 781405 798594

Typeset by Letterpart Limited, Caterham on the Hill, Surrey CR3 5XL
Printed and bound by CPI Group (UK) Ltd, Croydon, CR0 4YY
Visit LexisNexis at www.lexisnexis.co.uk

TELECOMMUNICATIONS

Title Adviser
ROBERT WELLS
a Solicitor of the Senior Courts of England and Wales;
Principal Legal Adviser, Ofcom

TIME

prepared by the Halsbury's Laws of England editorial team

TORT

Consultant Editor
CHRISTIAN A WITTING, BEc LLB (Hons) SJD,
Barrister and Solicitor (High Court of Australia);
Professor of Law, University of Exeter

Contributor: Part 6, Wrongful Interference with Goods
SIMON DOUGLAS, LLB (Hons), BCL, DPhil, MA (Oxon);
Associate Professor, Jesus College, University of Oxford

TRADE AND INDUSTRY

prepared by the Halsbury's Laws of England editorial team

The law stated in this volume is in general that in force on 1 June 2015, although subsequent changes have been included wherever possible.

Any future updating material will be found in the Current Service and annual Cumulative Supplement to Halsbury's Laws of England.

TABLE OF CONTENTS

Volume 97

TELECOMMUNICATIONS

TIME

TORT

TRADE AND INDUSTRY

HOW TO USE HALSBURY'S LAWS
OF ENGLAND

Volumes

Each text volume of Halsbury's Laws of England contains the law on the titles contained in it as at a date stated at the front of the volume (the operative date).

Information contained in Halsbury's Laws of England may be accessed in several ways.

First, by using the tables of contents.

Each volume contains both a general Table of Contents, and a specific Table of Contents for each title contained in it. From these tables you will be directed to the relevant part of the work.

Readers should note that the current arrangement of titles can be found in the Current Service.

Secondly, by using tables of statutes, statutory instruments, cases or other materials.

If you know the name of the Act, statutory instrument or case with which your research is concerned, you should consult the Consolidated Tables of statutes, cases and so on (published as separate volumes) which will direct you to the relevant volume and paragraph.

(Each individual text volume also includes tables of those materials used as authority in that volume.)

Thirdly, by using the indexes.

If you are uncertain of the general subject area of your research, you should go to the Consolidated Index (published as separate volumes) for reference to the relevant volume(s) and paragraph(s).

(Each individual text volume also includes an index to the material contained therein.)

Updating publications

The text volumes of Halsbury's Laws should be used in conjunction with the annual Cumulative Supplement and the monthly Noter-Up.

The annual Cumulative Supplement

The Supplement gives details of all changes between the operative date of the text volume and the operative date of the Supplement. It is arranged in the same volume, title and paragraph order as the text volumes. Developments affecting particular points of law are noted to the relevant paragraph(s) of the text volumes.

For narrative treatment of material noted in the Cumulative Supplement, go to the Annual Abridgment volume for the relevant year.

Destination Tables

In certain titles in the annual *Cumulative Supplement*, reference is made to Destination Tables showing the destination of consolidated legislation. Those Destination Tables are to be found either at the end of the titles within the annual *Cumulative Supplement*, or in a separate *Destination Tables* booklet provided from time to time with the *Cumulative Supplement*.

The Noter-Up

The Noter-Up is contained in the Current Service Noter-Up booklet, issued monthly and noting changes since the publication of the annual Cumulative Supplement. Also arranged in the same volume, title and paragraph order as the text volumes, the Noter-Up follows the style of the Cumulative Supplement.

For narrative treatment of material noted in the Noter-Up, go to the relevant Monthly Review.

REFERENCES AND ABBREVIATIONS

ACT	Australian Capital Territory
A-G	Attorney General
Admin	Administrative Court
Admlty	Admiralty Court
Adv-Gen	Advocate General
affd	affirmed
affg	affirming
Alta	Alberta
App	Appendix
art	article
Aust	Australia
B	Baron
BC	British Columbia
C	Command Paper (of a series published before 1900)
c	chapter number of an Act
CA	Court of Appeal
CAC	Central Arbitration Committee
CA in Ch	Court of Appeal in Chancery
CB	Chief Baron
CCA	Court of Criminal Appeal
CCR	County Court Rules 1981 (as subsequently amended)
CCR	Court for Crown Cases Reserved
CJEU	Court of Justice of the European Union
C-MAC	Courts-Martial Appeal Court
CO	Crown Office
COD	Crown Office Digest
CPR	Civil Procedure Rules
Can	Canada
Cd	Command Paper (of the series published 1900–18)
Cf	compare
Ch	Chancery Division
ch	chapter
cl	clause
Cm	Command Paper (of the series published 1986 to date)

Cmd	Command Paper (of the series published 1919–56)
Cmnd	Command Paper (of the series published 1956–86)
Comm	Commercial Court
Comr	Commissioner
Court Forms (2nd Edn)	Atkin's Encyclopaedia of Court Forms in Civil Proceedings, 2nd Edn. See note 2 post.
CrimPR	Criminal Procedure Rules
DC	Divisional Court
DPP	Director of Public Prosecutions
EAT	Employment Appeal Tribunal
EC	European Community
ECJ	Court of Justice of the European Community (before the Treaty of Lisbon (OJ C306, 17.12.2007, p 1) came into force on 1 December 2009); European Court of Justice (after the Treaty of Lisbon (OJ C306, 17.12.2007, p 1) came into force on 1 December 2009)
EComHR	European Commission of Human Rights
ECSC	European Coal and Steel Community
ECtHR Rules of Court	Rules of Court of the European Court of Human Rights
EEC	European Economic Community
EFTA	European Free Trade Association
EGC	European General Court
EWCA Civ	Official neutral citation for judgments of the Court of Appeal (Civil Division)
EWCA Crim	Official neutral citation for judgments of the Court of Appeal (Criminal Division)
EWHC	Official neutral citation for judgments of the High Court
Edn	Edition
Euratom	European Atomic Energy Community
EU	European Union
Ex Ch	Court of Exchequer Chamber
ex p	ex parte
Fam	Family Division
Fed	Federal
Forms & Precedents (5th Edn)	Encyclopaedia of Forms and Precedents other than Court Forms, 5th Edn. See note 2 post.
GLC	Greater London Council
HC	High Court
HC	House of Commons

HK	Hong Kong
HL	House of Lords
IAT	Immigration Appeal Tribunal
ILM	International Legal Materials
INLR	Immigration and Nationality Law Reports
IRC	Inland Revenue Commissioners
Ind	India
Int Rels	International Relations
Ir	Ireland
J	Justice
JA	Judge of Appeal
Kan	Kansas
LA	Lord Advocate
LC	Lord Chancellor
LCC	London County Council
LCJ	Lord Chief Justice
LJ	Lord Justice of Appeal
LoN	League of Nations
MR	Master of the Rolls
Man	Manitoba
n	note
NB	New Brunswick
NI	Northern Ireland
NS	Nova Scotia
NSW	New South Wales
NY	New York
NZ	New Zealand
OHIM	Office for Harmonisation in the Internal Market
OJ	The Official Journal of the European Community published by the Office for Official Publications of the European Community
Ont	Ontario
P	President
PC	Judicial Committee of the Privy Council
PEI	Prince Edward Island
Pat	Patents Court
q	question
QB	Queen's Bench Division
QBD	Queen's Bench Division of the High Court
Qld	Queensland
Que	Quebec
r	rule

RDC	Rural District Council
RPC	Restrictive Practices Court
RSC	Rules of the Supreme Court 1965 (as subsequently amended)
reg	regulation
Res	Resolution
revsd	reversed
Rly	Railway
s	section
SA	South Africa
S Aust	South Australia
SC	Supreme Court
SI	Statutory Instruments published by authority
SR & O	Statutory Rules and Orders published by authority
SR & O Rev 1904	Revised Edition comprising all Public and General Statutory Rules and Orders in force on 31 December 1903
SR & O Rev 1948	Revised Edition comprising all Public and General Statutory Rules and Orders and Statutory Instruments in force on 31 December 1948
SRNI	Statutory Rules of Northern Ireland
STI	Simon's Tax Intelligence (1973–1995); Simon's Weekly Tax Intelligence (1996-current)
Sask	Saskatchewan
Sch	Schedule
Sess	Session
Sing	Singapore
TCC	Technology and Construction Court
TS	Treaty Series
Tanz	Tanzania
Tas	Tasmania
UDC	Urban District Council
UKHL	Official neutral citation for judgments of the House of Lords
UKPC	Official neutral citation for judgments of the Privy Council
UN	United Nations
V-C	Vice-Chancellor
Vict	Victoria
W Aust	Western Australia
Zimb	Zimbabwe

NOTE 1. A general list of the abbreviations of law reports and other sources used in this work can be found at the beginning of the Consolidated Table of Cases.

NOTE 2. Where references are made to other publications, the volume number precedes and the page number follows the name of the publication; eg the reference '12 Forms & Precedents (5th Edn) 44' refers to volume 12 of the Encyclopaedia of Forms and Precedents, page 44.

NOTE 3. An English statute is cited by short title or, where there is no short title, by regnal year and chapter number together with the name by which it is commonly known or a description of its subject matter and date. In the case of a foreign statute, the mode of citation generally follows the style of citation in use in the country concerned with the addition, where necessary, of the name of the country in parentheses.

NOTE 4. A statutory instrument is cited by short title, if any, followed by the year and number, or, if unnumbered, the date.

TABLE OF STATUTES

TABLE OF STATUTORY INSTRUMENTS

TABLE OF CIVIL PROCEDURE

Civil Procedure Rules 1998, SI 1998/3132 (CPR)

Practice Directions supplementing CPR

TABLE OF EUROPEAN
UNION LEGISLATION

TABLE OF CONVENTIONS

TABLE OF CASES

X

Y

Z

Decisions of the European Court of Justice are listed below numerically. These decisions are also included in the preceding alphabetical list.

TELECOMMUNICATIONS

1. REGULATION OF COMMUNICATIONS

(1) INTRODUCTION TO THE REGULATORY REGIME FOR COMMUNICATIONS

1. Communications regulation. The regulation of communications is governed by the Office of Communications Act 2002, which established the Office of Communications ('OFCOM')[1], and by the Communications Act 2003, which makes provision with respect to:

(1)   the functions of OFCOM[2];

(2)   networks, services and the radio spectrum[3];

(3)   television and radio services[4];

(4)   the licensing of television reception[5];

(5)   on-demand programme services[6]; and

(6)   competition in communications markets[7].

This has been the result of the implementation in the United Kingdom of five Directives (the 'EC Communications Directives'), which set out a package of measures for a common regulatory framework for electronic communications networks and services[8]. These Directives are:

(a)   the Framework Directive[9];

(b)   the Authorisation Directive[10];

(c)   the Access Directive[11];

(d)   the Universal Service Directive[12]; and

(e)   the Privacy and Electronic Communications Directive[13].

Provisions of the Radio Spectrum Decision[14], the Competition Directive[15], the Directive on competition in the markets in telecommunications terminal equipment[16], the Regulation on unbundled access to the local loop[17], the Regulation on roaming on public mobile telephone networks within the Community[18], and the Regulation establishing BEREC and the Office[19], have also had some impact.

The Communications Act 2003 implements a significant proportion of the regulatory package[20]. The Digital Economy Act 2010 includes provisions relating to OFCOM reports, online infringement of copyright, powers in relation to internet domain registries, regulation of television services and radio services, regulation of the use of the electromagnetic spectrum and public lending rights in relation to electronic publications[21].

1   See PARA 2 et seq. As to the former regulators see PARA 14 note 2.
2   See PARA 14 et seq; and INFORMATION TECHNOLOGY LAW vol 57 (2012) PARA 526.
3   See PARAS 54, 81 et seq; and BROADCASTING vol 4 (2011) PARA 504.
4   See BROADCASTING vol 4 (2011) PARA 504.
5   See BROADCASTING vol 4 (2011) PARA 504.
6   See BROADCASTING vol 4 (2011) PARA 785 et seq.
7   See PARA 38; and BROADCASTING vol 4 (2011) PARA 504.
8   European Parliament and the Council of Ministers, February 2002.
9   Ie European Parliament and Council Directive (EC) 2002/21 (OJ L108, 24.4.2002, p 33) on a common regulatory framework for electronic communications networks and services; European Parliament and Council Regulation (EC) 544/2009 (OJ L167, 29.6.2009, p 12); and European Parliament and Council Directive (EC) 2009/140 (OJ L337, 18.12.2009, p 37)). See also Commission Implementing Regulation (EU) 1203/2012 (OJ L347, 15.12.2012, p 1) on the separate sale of regulated retail roaming services within the European Union (with application from 1 July 2014 to 30 June 2022). See further PARA 68.
10   Ie European Parliament and Council Directive (EC) 2002/20 (OJ L108, 24.4.2002, p 21) on the authorisation of electronic communications networks and services.

11 Ie European Parliament and Council Directive (EC) 2002/19 (OJ L108, 24.4.2002, p 7) on access to, and interconnection of, electronic communications networks and associated facilities.
12 Ie European Parliament and Council Directive (EC) 2002/22 (OJ L108, 24.4.2002, p 51) on universal service and users' rights relating to electronic communications networks and services.
13 Ie European Parliament and Council Directive (EC) 2002/58 (OJ L201, 31.7.2002, p 37) concerning the processing of personal data and the protection of privacy in the electronic communications sector; and European Parliament and Council Directive (EC) 2009/136 (OJ L337, 18.12.2009, p 11).
14 Ie European Parliament and Council Decision (EC) 676/2002 (OJ L108, 24.4.2002, p 1) on a regulatory framework for radio spectrum policy in the European Union. See also Commission Decision (EU) 2010/166 (OJ L72, 20.3.2010, p 38) on harmonised conditions of use of radio spectrum for mobile communication services on board vessels (MCV services) in the European Union; European Parliament and Council Decision (EU) 243/2012 (OJ L81, 21.3.2012, p 7) establishing a multi-annual radio spectrum policy programme; Commission Implementing Decision (EU) 2013/195 (OJ L113, 25.4.2013, p 18) defining the practical arrangements, uniform formats and a methodology in relation to the radio spectrum inventory established by Decision 243/2012; Commission Implementing Decision (EU) 2014/641 (OJ L263, 3.9.2014, p 29) on harmonised technical conditions of radio spectrum use by wireless audio programme making and special events equipment in the EU.
15 Ie Commission Directive (EC) 2002/77 (OJ L249, 17.9.2002, p 21) on competition in the markets for electronic communications networks and services.
16 Ie Commission Directive (EC) 2008/63 (OJ L162, 21.6.2008, p 20) on competition in the markets in telecommunications terminal equipment.
17 Ie European Parliament and Council Regulation (EC) 2887/2000 (OJ L336, 30.12.2000, p 4) on unbundled access to the local loop.
18 Ie European Parliament and Council Regulation (EC) 531/2012 (OJ L172, 30.6.2012, p 10) on roaming on public mobile telephone networks within the Union which replaces the European Parliament and Council Regulation (EC) 717/2007 (OJ L171, 29.6.2007, p 32).
19 Ie European Parliament and Council Regulation (EC) 1211/2009 (OJ L337, 18.12.2009, p 1) establishing the Body of European Regulators for Electronic Communications (BEREC) and the Office. As to BEREC see PARA 58.
20 As to European Union legislation relating to telecommunications see further PARA 68.
21 As to the communications infrastructure see the Communications Act 2003 ss 134A, 134B; and PARA 150. As to broadcasting see BROADCASTING; and as to copyright see COPYRIGHT vol 23 (2013) PARA 601 et seq.

(2) THE OFFICE OF COMMUNICATIONS ('OFCOM')

(i) Establishment, Membership, etc of OFCOM

2.   Establishment of OFCOM. The Office of Communications Act 2002 established a body corporate, known as the Office of Communications ('OFCOM')[1]. OFCOM consists of such number of members as the Secretary of State[2] may determine, but he must not determine a membership for OFCOM of less than three or more than ten, which numbers may be modified by order[3]. The membership of OFCOM comprises a chairman appointed by the Secretary of State, such number of other members appointed by the Secretary of State as he may determine, and the executive members[4]. The Secretary of State may, by a direction to OFCOM, set a maximum and a minimum number for the executive members of OFCOM[5], and must exercise his powers to secure that the number of executive members of OFCOM is, so far as practicable, at all times less than the number of other members[6].

OFCOM must, in managing its affairs, have regard:

(1)   to such general guidance concerning the management of the affairs of public bodies as it considers appropriate[7]; and

(2)   subject to any such guidance and only to the extent that they may

reasonably be regarded as applicable in relation to a statutory corporation, to generally accepted principles of good corporate governance[8].

OFCOM is not treated for any purposes as a body exercising functions on behalf of the Crown, and, accordingly, no person is to be treated as a servant of the Crown by reason only of his membership of, or employment by, OFCOM[9]. Its members are disqualified for membership of the House of Commons[10].

1   Office of Communications Act 2002 s 1(1). See also the Wireless Telegraphy Act 2006 s 115(1); the Communications Act 2003 s 405(1); the Radio Equipment and Telecommunications Terminal Equipment Regulations 2000, SI 2000/730, reg 2(1); the Privacy and Electronic Communications (EC Directive) Regulations 2003, SI 2003/2426, reg 2(1); and the *Agreement between Her Majesty's Secretary of State for National Heritage and the British Broadcasting Corporation* (Cm 3152) (1996) cl 1.1 (definition as added).

     OFCOM was established in 2002, when the relevant provisions of the Office of Communications Act 2002 came into force (ie 1 July 2002: see the Office of Communications Act 2002 (Commencement No 1) Order 2002, SI 2002/1483); it took over most of its regulatory functions on 29 December 2003, although it did not take responsibility for television licences and television receivers until 1 April 2004 (see the Office of Communications Act 2002 (Commencement No 3) and Communications Act 2003 (Commencement No 2) Order 2003, SI 2003/3142, arts 3, 4(2), Sch 1, Sch 2). As to OFCOM's functions see PARA 14 et seq.

     As to provision for the making of schemes for the transfer of property, rights and liabilities from pre-commencement regulators to OFCOM see the Communications Act 2003 s 30, Sch 2. As to the meaning of 'pre-commencement regulator' see PARA 14 note 2.

2   As to the Secretary of State see PARA 76 note 1.

3   Office of Communications Act 2002 s 1(2), (7) (modified by SI 2005/2718). A statutory instrument containing an order under the Office of Communications Act 2002 s 1(7) is subject to annulment in pursuance of a resolution of either House of Parliament; and the power to make such an order includes power to make such incidental, supplemental, consequential and transitional provision as the Secretary of State think fit: s 1(8).

4   Office of Communications Act 2002 s 1(3). The executive members of OFCOM comprise the chief executive of OFCOM, and such other persons (if any) as may be appointed to membership of OFCOM from among its employees: s 1(4). It is for the members of OFCOM, after consulting the chief executive of OFCOM, to determine whether there should be any executive members and, subject to s 1(2), (6)(a), how many, and to make any appointments of executive members required for the purposes of any such determination: see s 1(5).

5   Office of Communications Act 2002 s 1(6)(a).

6   Office of Communications Act 2002 s 1(6)(b).

7   Office of Communications Act 2002 s 3(a).

8   Office of Communications Act 2002 s 3(b).

9   Office of Communications Act 2002 s 1(9).

10   House of Commons Disqualification Act 1975 s 1(1), Sch 1 Pt II (amended by the Office of Communications Act 2002 s 1(10), Schedule para 21). See PARLIAMENT vol 78 (2010) PARA 908.

3.   Non-executive members of OFCOM.   Before appointing a person to be the chairman or another non-executive member of OFCOM[1], the Secretary of State[2] must satisfy himself that that person will have no such financial or other interest as is likely to affect prejudicially the carrying out by him of his functions as a member of OFCOM[3]. The Secretary of State must also satisfy himself from time to time with respect to the chairman and every other non-executive member of OFCOM that that member has no such interest[4]. Every person who is a person whom the Secretary of State proposes to appoint to be the chairman or another non-executive member of OFCOM, or who is the chairman or another non-executive member of OFCOM, must, whenever requested by the Secretary of State to do so, furnish him with such information as the Secretary of State considers necessary for the performance by him of his duties under these provisions[5].

The chairman and every other non-executive member of OFCOM will each hold and vacate office in accordance with the terms of his appointment[6]. A person's appointment to be the chairman or another non-executive member of OFCOM must state the period for which the appointment is made; but a person is eligible for re-appointment at the end of any such period[7]. The chairman and every other non-executive member of OFCOM may at any time resign his office by notice in writing to the Secretary of State[8]. If the Secretary of State is satisfied that the chairman or another non-executive member of OFCOM:

(1) is an undischarged bankrupt or a person in relation to whom a moratorium period under a debt relief order applies[9] or has had his estate sequestrated without being discharged[10];

(2) has made an arrangement with his creditors, or has entered into a trust deed for creditors, or has made a composition contract with his creditors[11];

(3) has such a financial or other interest as is likely to affect prejudicially the carrying out by him of his functions as a member of OFCOM[12];

(4) has been guilty of misbehaviour[13]; or

(5) is otherwise incapable of carrying out, or unfit to carry out, the functions of his office[14],

the Secretary of State may by notice in writing remove him from office[15]. At the time of removing a person from office[16] the Secretary of State must make public the decision to remove the person[17]. The Secretary of State must give the person a statement of reasons for the removal and if so requested by the person, publish the statement[18].

OFCOM may pay to the chairman and other non-executive members of OFCOM such remuneration and allowances as the Secretary of State may determine[19]. OFCOM may pay, or make provision for paying, to or in respect of the chairman and other non-executive members of OFCOM, such sums by way of pensions, allowances or gratuities as the Secretary of State may determine[20]. Where a person ceases, otherwise than on the expiry of his term of office, to be the chairman or to be a non-executive member other than the chairman, and it appears to the Secretary of State that there are special circumstances which make it right for him to receive compensation, OFCOM may make a payment to him of such amount as the Secretary of State may determine[21]. If any non-executive member of OFCOM is a participant in any pension scheme applicable to his membership of OFCOM, and on ceasing to be a non-executive member of OFCOM, becomes an employee[22] of OFCOM or both such an employee and an executive member, he may, if the Secretary of State so determines, be treated for the purposes of the pension scheme as if his service (after ceasing to be a non-executive member of OFCOM) as an employee or executive member of OFCOM were service as a non-executive member of OFCOM[23].

The Secretary of State may appoint any member of OFCOM who is a non-executive member to be the deputy chairman of OFCOM[24]. A person appointed to be the deputy chairman ceases to be the deputy chairman if he ceases to be a member of OFCOM; but otherwise holds and vacates that office in accordance with the terms of his appointment[25]. The deputy chairman of OFCOM is entitled to carry out the functions of the chairman in such cases and in such manner as may be determined by or in accordance with any directions given by the chairman or the Secretary of State[26].

1   As to the establishment of OFCOM see PARA 2. As to the chairman see PARA 2. 'Non-executive
    member', in relation to OFCOM, means a member of OFCOM who is not an executive
    member: Office of Communications Act 2002 s 1(10), Schedule para 24(1). As to members of
    OFCOM see also PARA 2.
2   As to the Secretary of State see PARA 76 note 1.
3   Office of Communications Act 2002 Schedule para 1(1).
4   Office of Communications Act 2002 Schedule para 1(2).
5   Office of Communications Act 2002 Schedule para 1(3).
6   Office of Communications Act 2002 Schedule para 2(1).
7   Office of Communications Act 2002 Schedule para 2(2).
8   Office of Communications Act 2002 Schedule para 2(3).
9   Ie under the Insolvency Act 1986 Pt 7A (ss 251A–251X): see BANKRUPTCY AND INDIVIDUAL
    INSOLVENCY vol 5 (2013) PARA 101.
10 Office of Communications Act 2002 Schedule para 2(4)(a) (amended by SI 2012/204).
11 Office of Communications Act 2002 Schedule para 2(4)(b).
12 Office of Communications Act 2002 Schedule para 2(4)(c).
13 Office of Communications Act 2002 Schedule para 2(4)(d).
14 Office of Communications Act 2002 Schedule para 2(4)(e).
15 Office of Communications Act 2002 Schedule para 2(4).
16 Ie under the Office of Communications Act 2002 Schedule para 2(4).
17 Office of Communications Act 2002 Schedule para 2(5) (Schedule para 2(5), (6) added by
    SI 2011/1210).
18 Office of Communications Act 2002 Schedule para 2(6) (as added: see note 17).
19 Office of Communications Act 2002 Schedule para 3(1).
20 Office of Communications Act 2002 Schedule para 3(2). References to pensions, allowances or
    gratuities include references to any similar benefits provided on death or retirement; and
    references to the payment of pensions, allowances or gratuities to or in respect of any persons
    includes a reference to the making of payments towards the provision of the payment of
    pensions, allowances or gratuities to or in respect of those persons: Schedule para 24(2).
21 Office of Communications Act 2002 Schedule para 3(3).
22 'Employee', in relation to OFCOM, includes the chief executive: Office of Communications
    Act 2002 Schedule para 24(1).
23 Office of Communications Act 2002 Schedule para 3(4).
24 Office of Communications Act 2002 Schedule para 4(1).
25 Office of Communications Act 2002 Schedule para 4(2).
26 Office of Communications Act 2002 Schedule para 4(3).

4.   Executive members of OFCOM.   There is to be a chief executive of
OFCOM[1], who must be appointed by the chairman and other non-executive
members[2] of OFCOM with the approval of the Secretary of State[3]. OFCOM
may appoint such other employees as it may determine and make such other
arrangements for the staffing of OFCOM as it thinks fit[4].

The chief executive is to be appointed to hold his office, and the other
executive members of OFCOM are to be appointed as executive members and
employed by OFCOM, on such terms and conditions, including terms and
conditions as to remuneration, as the chairman and other non-executive
members may determine[5]. If the chairman and other non-executive members of
OFCOM so determine in the case of any of the employees of OFCOM who are
executive members, OFCOM must pay, to or in respect of those employees, such
pensions, allowances or gratuities, or provide and maintain for them such
pension schemes (whether contributory or not), as the chairman and the other
non-executive members may determine[6].

If any employee of OFCOM who is an executive member is a participant in
any pension scheme applicable to his employment, and becomes a non-executive
member of OFCOM, he may, if the Secretary of State so determines, be treated
for the purposes of the pension scheme as if his service as a non-executive
member were service as an employee of OFCOM[7]. If any employee of OFCOM
who is an executive member is a participant in any pension scheme applicable to

his membership of OFCOM, and ceases to be an executive member without ceasing to be an employee of OFCOM, he may, if the Secretary of State so determines, be treated for the purposes of the pension scheme as if his service (after ceasing to be an executive member) as an employee of OFCOM were service as an executive member of OFCOM[8].

1   Office of Communications Act 2002 s 1(10), Schedule para 5(1). This provision does not apply in relation to any time before such date as the Secretary of State may notify to OFCOM as the date from which it is required to have a chief executive; and the membership of OFCOM is not required at any time before that date to include any executive member: Schedule para 5(4). As to the establishment of OFCOM see PARA 2.
2   As to the chairman see PARA 2. As to the non-executive members see PARA 3. As to the meaning of 'non-executive member' see PARA 3 note 1.
3   Office of Communications Act 2002 Schedule para 5(2). As to the Secretary of State see PARA 76 note 1.
4   Office of Communications Act 2002 Schedule para 5(3). As to the meaning of 'employee' see PARA 3 note 22.
5   Office of Communications Act 2002 Schedule para 6(1).
6   Office of Communications Act 2002 Schedule para 6(2). As to the payment of pensions, allowances or gratuities see PARA 3 note 20.
7   Office of Communications Act 2002 Schedule para 6(3).
8   Office of Communications Act 2002 Schedule para 6(4).

5.   Other employees of OFCOM.

The employees[1] of OFCOM[2] who are not executive members[3] are to be appointed to and hold their employments on such terms and conditions, including terms and conditions as to remuneration, as OFCOM may determine[4]. If OFCOM so determines in the case of any of the employees of OFCOM who are not executive members, OFCOM must pay to or in respect of those employees such pensions, allowances or gratuities, or provide and maintain for them such pension schemes (whether contributory or not), as OFCOM may determine[5]. If any employee of OFCOM is a participant in any pension scheme applicable to his employment, and becomes an executive member or a non-executive member[6] of OFCOM, he may, if the Secretary of State[7] so determines, be treated for the purposes of the pension scheme as if his service as a member of OFCOM were service as an employee of OFCOM[8].

1   As to the meaning of 'employee' see PARA 3 note 22.
2   As to the establishment of OFCOM see PARA 2.
3   As to the executive members see PARAS 2, 4.
4   Office of Communications Act 2002 s 1(10), Schedule para 7(1).
5   Office of Communications Act 2002 Schedule para 7(2). As to the payment of pensions, allowances or gratuities see PARA 3 note 20.
6   As to the meaning of 'non-executive member' see PARA 3 note 1. As to the non-executive members see PARAS 2–3.
7   As to the Secretary of State see PARA 76 note 1.
8   Office of Communications Act 2002 Schedule para 7(3).

6.   Finances of OFCOM.

It is the duty of OFCOM[1] so to conduct its affairs as to secure that its revenues so far as they:

  (1)   derive from the exercise of powers to impose charges or fees in respect of the carrying out of particular functions[2]; and
  (2)   do not fall to be paid into the Consolidated Fund of the United Kingdom or of Northern Ireland[3],

are at least sufficient to enable OFCOM to meet the costs of carrying out the functions to which the revenues relate[4]. Any excess of OFCOM's revenues for any financial year over the sums required by it for that year for meeting its obligations and carrying out its functions must be applied by OFCOM in such manner as the Secretary of State[5], after consultation with OFCOM, may direct[6]. Such a direction may require the whole or any part of any such excess to be paid to the Secretary of State[7]. The Secretary of State must pay any sums so received by him into the Consolidated Fund[8].

The Secretary of State may, with the consent of the Treasury, make grants to OFCOM of such sums as he may think fit for the purpose of enabling OFCOM to incur or meet liabilities in respect of capital and revenue expenditure[9]. Such grants must be paid out of money provided by Parliament[10]. The Secretary of State may also make advances to OFCOM out of money provided by Parliament[11]. Any sums advanced under this provision must be repaid to the Secretary of State at such times and by such methods, and interest on those sums must be paid to him at such times and at such rates, as he may from time to time direct[12].

OFCOM must keep proper accounts and proper records in relation to the accounts, and prepare in respect of each financial year a statement of accounts in such form as the Secretary of State may direct[13]. OFCOM must, within such period after the end of the financial year[14] to which it relates as the Secretary of State may direct, send copies of every such statement to the Secretary of State and the Comptroller and Auditor General[15]. The Comptroller and Auditor General must examine, certify and report on every statement so sent to him and lay a copy of the statement and of his report before each House of Parliament[16].

1   As to the establishment of OFCOM see PARA 2.
2   Office of Communications Act 2002 s 1(10), Schedule para 8(1)(a) (substituted by the Communications Act 2003 s 406(1), Sch 17 para 172(1), (3)). References to functions of OFCOM include references to functions conferred by any enactment or subordinate legislation at any time after the passing of the Office of Communications Act 2002: s 1(10), Schedule para 24(3). As to the functions of OFCOM see PARA 14 et seq.
3   Office of Communications Act 2002 Schedule para 8(1)(b) (Schedule para 8(1) as substituted: see note 2). As to the requirement to pay into the Consolidated Fund see PARA 41. As to the Consolidated Fund see CONSTITUTIONAL AND ADMINISTRATIVE LAW vol 20 (2014) PARA 480 et seq; PARLIAMENT vol 78 (2010) PARAS 1028–1031.
4   Office of Communications Act 2002 Schedule para 8(1) (as substituted: see note 2).
5   As to the Secretary of State see PARA 76 note 1.
6   Office of Communications Act 2002 Schedule para 8(2).
7   Office of Communications Act 2002 Schedule para 8(3).
8   Office of Communications Act 2002 Schedule para 8(4).
9   Office of Communications Act 2002 Schedule para 9(1). As to the Treasury see CONSTITUTIONAL AND ADMINISTRATIVE LAW vol 20 (2014) PARAS 262–265.
10 Office of Communications Act 2002 Schedule para 9(2).
11 Office of Communications Act 2002 Schedule para 10(1).
12 Office of Communications Act 2002 Schedule para 10(2).
13 Office of Communications Act 2002 Schedule para 11(1).
14 'Financial year' means:
    (1)   the period of not more than 12 months beginning with the date on which OFCOM is established under the Office of Communications Act 2002 (see PARA 2 note 1) and ending with 31 March; and
    (2)   every subsequent period of 12 months ending with 31 March: Schedule para 24(1).
15 Office of Communications Act 2002 Schedule para 11(2). The 'Comptroller and Auditor General' means the Comptroller-General of the receipt and issue of Her Majesty's Exchequer and Auditor-General of Public Accounts: Interpretation Act 1978 s 5, Sch 1 (amended by the Budget Responsibility and National Audit Act 2011 Sch 5 para 12). As to the Comptroller and Auditor General see CONSTITUTIONAL AND ADMINISTRATIVE LAW vol 20 (2014) PARA 494 et seq.
16 Office of Communications Act 2002 Schedule para 11(3).

7. Annual report of OFCOM. As soon as possible after the end of each financial year[1], OFCOM[2] must prepare and send to the Secretary of State[3] a report of the carrying out of its functions[4] during that financial year[5]. Every such report must incorporate:

(1) a report of OFCOM's proceedings during that year[6];

(2) a report about OFCOM's performance, during that year, of their duty to secure provision of universal postal service[7]; and

(3) such information relating to the financial position of OFCOM, and to any other matters that he considers appropriate, as the Secretary of State may direct[8].

The Secretary of State must lay a copy of every such report sent to him before each House of Parliament[9].

1   As to the meaning of 'financial year' see PARA 6 note 14.
2   As to the establishment of OFCOM see PARA 2.
3   As to the Secretary of State see PARA 76 note 1.
4   As to references to OFCOM's functions see PARA 6 note 2.
5   Office of Communications Act 2002 s 1(10), Schedule para 12(1).
6   Office of Communications Act 2002 Schedule para 12(2)(a) (amended by the Postal Services Act 2011 Sch 12 para 168).
7   Office of Communications Act 2002 Schedule para 12(2)(aa) (added by the Postal Services Act 2011 Sch 12 para 168). The duty to secure provision of universal postal service is under the Postal Services Act 2011 s 29 (see POSTAL SERVICES vol 85 (2012) PARA 250): Office of Communications Act 2002 s 1(10), Schedule para 12(2)(aa) (as so added).
8   Office of Communications Act 2002 Schedule para 12(2)(b).
9   Office of Communications Act 2002 Schedule para 12(3).

8. Authentication of OFCOM's seal. The application of OFCOM's seal[1] must be authenticated by the signature of the chairman[2] or another member of OFCOM or of any other person authorised by OFCOM (whether generally or specially) for the purpose[3]. A document purporting to be duly executed under the seal of OFCOM or to be signed on behalf of OFCOM must be received in evidence and, except to the extent that the contrary is shown, taken to be duly so executed or signed[4].

1   As to the establishment of OFCOM see PARA 2.
2   As to the chairman see PARA 2.
3   Office of Communications Act 2002 s 1(10), Schedule para 13(1).
4   Office of Communications Act 2002 Schedule para 13(2).

9. Committees of OFCOM and advisory committees. OFCOM[1] may make such arrangements as it thinks fit for the carrying out of any of its functions[2] by committees established by it[3], and for committees established by OFCOM to give advice to it about matters relating to the carrying out of OFCOM's functions[4]. The committees established by OFCOM may include committees the membership of which comprises or includes persons (including persons constituting a majority of the committee) who are neither members nor employees[5] of OFCOM[6]. Except where the committee is established for the sole purpose of advising OFCOM on matters relating to the carrying out of its functions, and is not authorised[7] to carry out functions on behalf of OFCOM, the membership of every committee established by OFCOM must contain at least one person who is either a member or an employee of OFCOM, or who is both[8].

Where a person who is neither a member nor an employee of OFCOM is a member of any committee, OFCOM may pay to that person such remuneration and expenses as it may determine[9].

The committees established by OFCOM include the Content Board[10], the Advisory Committee for England, the Advisory Committee for Northern Ireland, the Advisory Committee for Scotland, the Advisory Committee for Wales, and the Advisory Committee on Older and Disabled People[11].

1   As to the establishment of OFCOM see PARA 2.
2   As to references to OFCOM's functions see PARA 6 note 2.
3   Office of Communications Act 2002 s 1(10), Schedule para 14(1)(a). See the text and notes 10–11.
4   Office of Communications Act 2002 Schedule para 14(1)(b).
5   As to the meaning of 'employee' see PARA 3 note 22.
6   Office of Communications Act 2002 Schedule para 14(2).
7   Ie under Office of Communications Act 2002 Schedule para 18: see PARA 11.
8   Office of Communications Act 2002 Schedule para 14(3). This has effect in the case of a committee of OFCOM which is not the Content Board (see PARA 24), but which has functions that are confined to functions falling within the Communications Act 2003 s 13(2) (functions within the Content Board's remit: see PARA 25), as if the reference in the Office of Communications Act 2002 Schedule para 14(3) to a member of OFCOM included a reference to a member of the Content Board who is not a member of OFCOM: Schedule para 14(3A) (added by the Communications Act 2003 s 406(1), Sch 17 para 172(1), (4)).
9   Office of Communications Act 2002 Schedule para 14(4).
10   As to the Content Board see PARAS 24–25.
11   As to the advisory committees for the different parts of the United Kingdom see PARA 30; and as to the Advisory Committee on Older and Disabled People see PARA 31. Other committees include the Finance Committee, the Audit and Risk Committee, the Remuneration Committee, the Radio Licensing Committee, the Content Sanctions Committee, and the Fairness Committee. There is also a Consumer Panel: see PARAS 28–29.

10.   Proceedings of OFCOM and its committees. OFCOM[1] may make such other arrangements for regulating its own procedure, and such arrangements for regulating the procedure of the committees established by it[2], as it thinks fit[3]. The procedure for the carrying out of the separate functions which are conferred[4] on the chairman and non-executive members of OFCOM[5] must be in accordance with such arrangements as may be determined by a majority of the non-executive members[6]. The arrangements may include arrangements as to quorums and as to the making of decisions by a majority[7]. OFCOM must publish, in such manner as it considers appropriate, any arrangements which it makes under these provisions[8].

OFCOM must make arrangements for the keeping of proper records:

(1)   of its proceedings[9];

(2)   of the proceedings of any committee established by it[10];

(3)   of the proceedings at any meeting of the chairman and other non-executive members of OFCOM[11]; and

(4)   of anything done by an employee[12] or member of OFCOM under a power delegated[13] to him[14].

1   As to the establishment of OFCOM see PARA 2.
2   As to committees of OFCOM see PARA 9.
3   Office of Communications Act 2002 s 1(10), Schedule para 15(1). Schedule para 15 has effect subject to Schedule para 17 (see PARA 12): Schedule para 15(5).
4   Ie under Office of Communications Act 2002 Schedule.
5   As to the chairman see PARA 2. As to the non-executive members see PARAS 2–3. As to the meaning of 'non-executive member' see PARA 3 note 1.
6   Office of Communications Act 2002 Schedule para 15(2).
7   Office of Communications Act 2002 Schedule para 15(3).

8 Office of Communications Act 2002 Schedule para 15(4).
9 Office of Communications Act 2002 Schedule para 16(a).
10 Office of Communications Act 2002 Schedule para 16(b).
11 Office of Communications Act 2002 Schedule para 16(c).
12 As to the meaning of 'employee' see PARA 3 note 22.
13 Ie under the Office of Communications Act 2002 Schedule para 18(a): see PARA 11.
14 Office of Communications Act 2002 Schedule para 16(d).

11. Delegation of OFCOM functions. Anything that is authorised or required by or under any enactment to be done by OFCOM[1] may be done on its behalf[2] by:

(1)   any employee or member of OFCOM[3] who has been authorised by OFCOM (whether generally or specially) for the purpose[4]; or

(2)   any committee established by OFCOM[5] which has been so authorised[6].

1 As to the establishment of OFCOM see PARA 2.
2 Office of Communications Act 2002 s 1(10), Schedule para 18.
3 As to the meaning of 'employee' see PARA 3 note 22. As to members of OFCOM see PARAS 2–4.
4 Office of Communications Act 2002 Schedule para 18(1)(a) (Schedule para 18(1) renumbered by the Enterprise and Regulatory Reform Act 2013 Sch 15 para 40). Heads (1) and (2) in the text are subject to provision in rules made under the Competition Act 1998 s 51 by virtue of Sch 9 para 1A in respect of the exercise of a function under Pt 1 (ss 1–60) (see COMPETITION vol 18 (2009) PARA 144): Office of Communications Act 2002 Schedule para 18(2) (added by the Enterprise and Regulatory Reform Act 2013 Sch 15 para 40).
5 As to committees established by OFCOM see PARA 9.
6 Office of Communications Act 2002 Schedule para 18(1)(b) (as renumbered: see note 4).

12. Disqualification of OFCOM member for acting in relation to certain matters. The following provisions apply if at any meeting of:

(1)   OFCOM[1];

(2)   the chairman[2] and other non-executive members[3] of OFCOM; or

(3)   any committee established by OFCOM[4],

any member of OFCOM or, as the case may be, of the committee has any form of direct or indirect interest in any matter falling to be considered at that meeting[5].

The person with the interest must declare it and the declaration must be recorded in the minutes of the meeting[6]. The person with the interest must not take part in any discussion or decision relating to the matter in which he has an interest, unless[7]:

(a)   in the case of a meeting of OFCOM or of the chairman and other non-executive members of OFCOM, the other members of OFCOM who are present when the discussion or decision falls to take place or is made have resolved unanimously that the interest is to be disregarded[8]; or

(b)   in any other case, the other members of the committee who are present when the discussion or decision falls to take place or is made have so resolved in the manner authorised by OFCOM[9].

It is the duty of OFCOM, in granting authorisations for the purposes of head (b) above, to secure that a resolution for those purposes does not allow a person to take part in a discussion or decision at a meeting of a committee established to carry out OFCOM's functions[10] unless at least the following requirements are met[11]:

(i)   the number of other members of the committee in favour of the resolution is not less than two thirds of those who are both present and entitled to vote on the resolution[12]; and

(ii)   the number of other members of the committee in favour of the resolution is not less than its quorum[13].

For these purposes, a general notification given at or sent to a meeting of OFCOM, of the chairman and other non-executive members of OFCOM, or of a committee established by OFCOM, that a person is a member of a company or firm and is to be regarded as interested in any matter involving that company or firm, is to be regarded[14] as compliance in relation to any such matter with the requirement to declare and record the interest[15] for the purposes of that meeting and any subsequent meeting of OFCOM, of the chairman and other non-executive members of OFCOM, or of the committee established by OFCOM, which is held while the notification is in force[16].

Such a notification:

(A)   remains in force until it is withdrawn[17]; and

(B)   if given at or sent to a meeting of the chairman and other non-executive members of OFCOM or to a committee is to have effect in relation only to meetings of the chairman and other non-executive members or, as the case may be, to meetings of that committee[18].

A person required to make a declaration for the purposes of these provisions in relation to any meeting is not required to attend the meeting, but is to be taken to have complied with the requirements if he takes reasonable steps to secure that notice of his interest is read out at, and taken into consideration at, the meeting in question[19].

1   As to the establishment of OFCOM see PARA 2.
2   As to the appointment of the chairman see PARA 2.
3   As to the meaning of 'non-executive member' see PARA 3 note 1. As to the non-executive members see PARAS 2–3.
4   As to committees established by OFCOM see PARA 9.
5   Office of Communications Act 2002 s 1(10), Schedule para 17(1).
6   Office of Communications Act 2002 Schedule para 17(2).
7   Office of Communications Act 2002 Schedule para 17(3).
8   Office of Communications Act 2002 Schedule para 17(3)(a).
9   Office of Communications Act 2002 Schedule para 17(3)(b).
10   Ie by virtue of the Office of Communications Act 2002 Schedule para 14(1)(a): see PARA 9 text to notes 1–3.
11   Office of Communications Act 2002 Schedule para 17(4).
12   Office of Communications Act 2002 Schedule para 17(4)(a).
13   Office of Communications Act 2002 Schedule para 17(4)(b).
14   Ie subject to the Office of Communications Act 2002 Schedule para 17(6)(b): see the text to notes 17, 18.
15   Ie the requirement in the Office of Communications Act 2002 Schedule para 17(2): see the text and note 6.
16   Office of Communications Act 2002 Schedule para 17(5).
17   Office of Communications Act 2002 Schedule para 17(6)(a).
18   Office of Communications Act 2002 Schedule para 17(6)(b).
19   Office of Communications Act 2002 Schedule para 17(7).

13.   Validity of proceedings of OFCOM. The validity of any proceedings of OFCOM[1], of the chairman[2] and other non-executive members[3] of OFCOM, or of any committee established by OFCOM[4], is not to be affected by[5]:

(1)   any vacancy in the membership of OFCOM or of such a committee[6];

(2)   any defect in the appointment of the chairman, deputy chairman or any other member of OFCOM[7];

(3)   any failure of the Secretary of State[8] to comply with the requirement[9] to secure that the number of executive members of OFCOM is, so far as practicable, at all times less than the number of other members[10]; or

(4) any failure to comply with any arrangements for regulating OFCOM's procedure[11] or with any of the requirements[12] relating to disqualification for acting[13].

However, nothing in head (4) above is to validate any proceedings of a meeting which (apart from any matter falling within head (2) or head (3) above) is inquorate[14].

1 As to the establishment of OFCOM see PARA 2.
2 As to the appointment of the chairman see PARA 2.
3 As to the meaning of 'non-executive member' see PARA 3 note 1. As to the non-executive members see PARAS 2–3.
4 As to committees established by OFCOM see PARA 9.
5 Office of Communications Act 2002 s 1(10), Schedule para 19(1).
6 Office of Communications Act 2002 Schedule para 19(1)(a).
7 Office of Communications Act 2002 Schedule para 19(1)(b).
8 As to the Secretary of State see PARA 84 note 1.
9 Ie the requirements of the Office of Communications Act 2002 s 1(6)(b): see PARA 2.
10 Office of Communications Act 2002 Schedule para 19(1)(c).
11 Ie under the Office of Communications Act 2002 Schedule para 15: see PARA 10.
12 Ie the requirements of the Office of Communications Act 2002 Schedule para 17: see PARA 12.
13 Office of Communications Act 2002 Schedule para 19(1)(d).
14 Office of Communications Act 2002 Schedule para 19(2).

(ii) Functions and Duties of OFCOM

A. GENERAL DUTIES AND FUNCTIONS

14. Functions transferred or assigned to OFCOM. OFCOM[1] has the following functions:
(1) the functions transferred to it[2]; and
(2) such other functions as may be conferred on it by or under any enactment[3] (including the Communications Act 2003)[4].

OFCOM also has any functions in relation to telephone numbers[5] that are conferred on it by the law of the Isle of Man or of any of the Channel Islands[6].

OFCOM may do anything which appears to it to be incidental or conducive to the carrying out of its functions, including the borrowing of money[7]. However, OFCOM must not borrow money except with the consent of the Secretary of State[8], or in accordance with a general authorisation given by him[9].

1 'OFCOM' means the Office of Communications: Communications Act 2003 s 405(1). As to the establishment of OFCOM see PARA 2.
2 Communications Act 2003 s 1(1)(a). The functions transferred to OFCOM included functions of the Secretary of State and of the pre-commencement regulators and those functions have now become functions of OFCOM: Communications Act 2003 s 2(1). See also the Office of Communications Act 2002 (Commencement No 3) and Communications Act 2003 (Commencement No 2) Order 2003, SI 2003/3142, arts 3, 4, Sch 1, Sch 2 (art 4 amended by SI 2004/454; SI 2004/697; and SI 2004/1492; Office of Communications Act 2002 (Commencement No 3) and Communications Act 2003 (Commencement No 2) Order 2003, SI 2003/3142, Sch 2 amended by SI 2004/454; and SI 2004/697). As to the functions transferred see the Communications Act 2003 Sch 1 (amended by the Wireless Telegraphy Act 2006 s 125(1), Sch 9 Pt 1). References in any enactment to a person who is a person from whom functions are transferred by virtue of the Communications Act 2003 s 2 are to have effect, so far as necessary for the purposes of the transfers, as references to OFCOM: Communications Act 2003 s 2(2). 'Person' includes a body of persons corporate or unincorporate: Interpretation Act 1978 s 5, Sch 1.
   The functions of OFCOM include the carrying out of the transferred functions, at times after the time when they became functions of OFCOM, in relation to anything occurring before that time: Communications Act 2003 s 2(3). Section 2 has effect subject to:

(1)   the modifications made by the Communications Act 2003 of the enactments relating to the transferred functions (s 2(4)(a)); and

(2)   any express transitional or consequential provisions made by or under the Communications Act 2003 in relation to those enactments (s 2(4)(b)).

'Modification' includes omissions, alterations and additions; and cognate expressions are to be construed accordingly: s 405(1).

The pre-commencement regulators had a duty to take all steps necessary or expedient for ensuring that OFCOM was able effectively to carry out its functions from the time when those functions were vested in it: see s 31(1)–(3).

'Pre-commencement regulator' is defined by s 405(1) so as to mean any of the following:

(a)   the Broadcasting Standards Commission (see BROADCASTING vol 4 (2011) PARA 872);

(b)   the Director General of Telecommunications (see below);

(c)   the Independent Television Commission (see BROADCASTING vol 4 (2011) PARA 507);

(d)   the Radio Authority (see BROADCASTING vol 4 (2011) PARA 507).

For the purposes of s 30 and Sch 2 (transfers of property etc from pre-commencement regulators: see PARA 2 note 1) each reference to a pre-commencement regulator includes the Postal Services Commission: Postal Services Act 2011 s 64(2).

The Communications Act 2003 provided for the abolition of the office of the Director General of Telecommunications and the Broadcasting Standards Commission, the Independent Television Commission and the Radio Authority: Communications Act 2003 s 31(4). The Communications Act 2003 also provided for the abolition of the advisory bodies established under the Telecommunications Act 1984 s 54 (now repealed) on such day as the Secretary of State may by order appoint: Communications Act 2003 s 31(5). Different days may be appointed under s 31 for the Director General of Telecommunications and for each of the other bodies mentioned: s 31(6). At the date at which this volume states the law, no such day had been appointed. However, for all intents and purposes the former regulators ceased to exist as from 29 December 2003, when OFCOM assumed its full statutory powers: see e g OFCOM Annual Report 2003–04 Section B *Operating and Financial Review*, available at the date at which this volume states the law on the OFCOM website. The Telecommunications Act 1984 made provision for the appointment of the Director General of Telecommunications, his staff and his functions: see ss 1, 55, 106(1), Sch 1 (prospectively repealed by the Communications Act 2003 s 406(7), Sch 19). At the date at which this volume states the law, no day had been appointed for the commencement for these purposes of the repealing provisions.

3   References in the Communications Act 2003 to OFCOM's functions under an enactment include references to its power to do anything which appears to it to be incidental or conducive to the carrying out of its functions under that enactment: s 405(3). 'Enactment' includes any enactment comprised in an Act of the Scottish Parliament or in any Northern Ireland legislation: s 405(1).

4   Communications Act 2003 s 1(1)(b).

The Deregulation and Contracting Out Act 1994 Pt II (ss 69–79) (see LOCAL GOVERNMENT vol 69 (2009) PARA 407 et seq) has effect in relation to the functions conferred on OFCOM by or under any enactment as if:

(1)   OFCOM were an office holder within the meaning of Pt II (Communications Act 2003 s 1(7)(a)); and

(2)   a power of OFCOM to make subordinate legislation were excluded from The Deregulation and Contracting Out Act 1994 s 69 to the extent only that it is exercisable by statutory instrument: (Communications Act 2003 s 1(7)(b)).

'Subordinate legislation' means:

(a)   any subordinate legislation within the meaning of the Interpretation Act 1978; or

(b)   any statutory rules (within the meaning of the Statutory Rules (Northern Ireland) Order 1979, SI 1979/1573 (NI 12) (Communications Act 2003 s 405(1)).

As to the contracting out of functions relating to broadcast advertising see the Contracting Out (Functions relating to Broadcast Advertising) and Specification of Relevant Functions Order 2004, SI 2004/1975 (amended by SI 2008/1277; and SI 2012/1916).

5   For the purposes of the Communications Act 2003 s 1, 'telephone numbers' has the same meaning as in Pt 2 Ch 1 (ss 32–151) (see PARA 100 note 4): s 1(8).

6   Communications Act 2003 s 1(2).

7   Communications Act 2003 s 1(3). OFCOM's powers under s 1(3) include, in particular:

(1)   power to undertake research and development work in connection with any matter in relation to which it has functions (s 1(5)(a));

(2)   power to promote the carrying out of such research and development by others, or otherwise to arrange for it to be carried out by others (s 1(5)(b));

(3) power to institute and carry on criminal proceedings in England and Wales or Northern Ireland for an offence relating to a matter in relation to which it has functions (s 1(5)(c)); and

(4) power, in such cases and in such circumstances as it may think fit, to make payments (where no legal liability arises) to persons adversely affected by the carrying out by OFCOM of any of its functions (s 1(5)(d)).

In exercise of its powers under s 1(3), OFCOM must establish and maintain separate offices in England, Wales, Scotland; and Northern Ireland: see s 1(6). 'United Kingdom' means Great Britain and Northern Ireland: Interpretation Act 1978 s 5, Sch 1. 'Great Britain' means England, Scotland and Wales: Union with Scotland Act 1706, preamble art I; Interpretation Act 1978 s 22(1), Sch 2 para 5(a). Neither the Isle of Man nor the Channel Islands are within the United Kingdom. 'England' means, subject to any alteration of the boundaries of local government areas, the areas consisting of the counties established by the Local Government Act 1972 s 1 (see LOCAL GOVERNMENT vol 69 (2009) PARAS 5, 24), and Greater London and the Isles of Scilly: see the Interpretation Act 1978 s 5, Sch 1. As to local government areas in England see LOCAL GOVERNMENT vol 69 (2009) PARA 22 et seq; and as to boundary changes see LOCAL GOVERNMENT vol 69 (2009) PARA 54 et seq. As to Greater London see LONDON GOVERNMENT vol 71 (2013) PARA 14 et seq. 'Wales' means the combined areas of the counties created by the Local Government Act 1972 s 20 (as originally enacted) (see LOCAL GOVERNMENT vol 69 (2009) PARAS 5, 37), but subject to any alteration made under s 73 (consequential alteration of boundary following alteration of watercourse: see LOCAL GOVERNMENT vol 69 (2009) PARA 90): see the Interpretation Act 1978 Sch 1 (definition substituted by the Local Government (Wales) Act 1994 s 1(3), Sch 2 para 9). See further CONSTITUTIONAL AND ADMINISTRATIVE LAW vol 20 (2014) PARAS 3, 75.

8 As to the Secretary of State see PARA 76 note 1.
9 Communications Act 2003 s 1(4).

15. Functions and duties in relation to communications and broadcasting.
The duties and functions of OFCOM[1] encompass duties relating to the regulation of electronic communications networks and services[2], the regulation and licensing of wireless telegraphy and spectrum use[3], and the regulation of broadcasting[4], including functions in relation to the British Broadcasting Corporation[5], and independent television[6] and radio services[7].

1 As to the meaning of 'OFCOM' see PARA 14 note 1; and as to the establishment of OFCOM see PARA 2.
2 See PARA 92 et seq.
3 See BROADCASTING vol 4 (2011) PARA 514 et seq.
4 See BROADCASTING vol 4 (2011) PARA 504 et seq.
5 See BROADCASTING vol 4 (2011) PARA 854 et seq.
6 See BROADCASTING vol 4 (2011) PARA 504.
7 See BROADCASTING vol 4 (2011) PARA 723 et seq.

16. General duties of OFCOM.
It is the principal duty of OFCOM[1], in carrying out its functions:

(1) to further the interests of citizens[2] in relation to communications matters[3]; and

(2) to further the interests of consumers[4] in relevant markets[5], where appropriate by promoting competition[6].

The things which[7] OFCOM is required to secure in the carrying out of its functions include, in particular, each of the following[8]:

(a) the optimal use for wireless telegraphy[9] of the electro-magnetic spectrum[10];

(b) the availability throughout the United Kingdom of a wide range of electronic communications services[11];

(c) the availability throughout the United Kingdom of a wide range of television and radio services[12] which (taken as a whole) are both of high quality and calculated to appeal to a variety of tastes and interests[13];

(d)   the maintenance of a sufficient plurality of providers of different television and radio services[14];

(e)   the application, in the case of all television and radio services, of standards that provide adequate protection to members of the public from the inclusion of offensive and harmful material in such services[15];

(f)   the application, in the case of all television and radio services, of standards that provide adequate protection to members of the public and all other persons from both unfair treatment in programmes included in such services and unwarranted infringements of privacy resulting from activities carried on for the purposes of such services[16].

In performing its duties[17], OFCOM must have regard, in all cases, to the principles under which regulatory activities should be transparent, accountable, proportionate, consistent and targeted only at cases in which action is needed; and any other principles appearing to OFCOM to represent the best regulatory practice[18].

OFCOM must also have regard, in performing those duties, to such of the following as appear to it to be relevant in the circumstances[19]:

(i)   the desirability of promoting the fulfilment of the purposes of public service television broadcasting in the United Kingdom[20];

(ii)   the desirability of promoting competition in relevant markets[21];

(iii)   the desirability of promoting and facilitating the development and use of effective forms of self-regulation[22];

(iv)   the desirability of encouraging investment and innovation in relevant markets[23];

(v)   the desirability of encouraging the availability and use of high speed data transfer services throughout the United Kingdom[24];

(vi)   the different needs and interests, so far as the use of the electro-magnetic spectrum for wireless telegraphy is concerned, of all persons who may wish to make use of it[25];

(vii)   the need to secure that the application in the case of television and radio services of standards falling within heads (e) and (f) above is in the manner[26] that best guarantees an appropriate level of freedom of expression[27];

(viii)   the vulnerability of children and of others whose circumstances appear to OFCOM to put them in need of special protection[28];

(ix)   the needs of persons with disabilities, of the elderly and of those on low incomes[29];

(x)   the desirability of preventing crime and disorder[30];

(xi)   the opinions of consumers in relevant markets and of members of the public generally[31];

(xii)   the different interests of persons in the different parts of the United Kingdom, of the different ethnic communities within the United Kingdom and of persons living in rural and in urban areas[32];

(xiii)   the extent to which, in the circumstances of the case, the furthering or securing of the matters mentioned above[33] is reasonably practicable[34].

Where it appears to OFCOM that any of its general duties[35] conflict with each other in a particular case, it must secure that the conflict is resolved in the manner it thinks best in the circumstances[36]. Where OFCOM resolves a conflict in an important case[37] between its duties under heads (1) and (2) above, it must publish a statement setting out:

(A)   the nature of the conflict[38];

(B)   the manner in which it has decided to resolve it[39]; and

(C)   the reasons for its decision to resolve it in that manner[40].

Every report[41] for a financial year must contain a summary of the manner in which, in that year, OFCOM resolved conflicts arising in important cases between its general duties[42].

1   As to the meaning of 'OFCOM' see PARA 14 note 1; and as to the establishment of OFCOM see PARA 2.

2   For the purposes of the Communications Act 2003 s 3, 'citizens' means all members of the public in the United Kingdom: s 3(14). As to the meaning of 'United Kingdom' see PARA 14 note 7.

3   Communications Act 2003 s 3(1)(a). For the purposes of the Communications Act 2003 s 3, 'communications matters' means the matters in relation to which OFCOM has functions: s 3(14).

4   In performing its duty under the Communications Act 2003 s 3 of furthering the interests of consumers, OFCOM must have regard, in particular, to the interests of those consumers in respect of choice, price, quality of service and value for money: s 3(5). For the purposes of the Communications Act 2003, persons are consumers in a market for a service, facility or apparatus, if they are:

    (1)   persons to whom the service, facility or apparatus is provided, made available or supplied (whether in their personal capacity or for the purposes of, or in connection with, their businesses);

    (2)   persons for whose benefit the service, facility or apparatus is provided, made available or supplied or for whose benefit persons falling within head (1) arrange for it to be provided, made available or supplied;

    (3)   persons whom the person providing the service or making the facility available, or the supplier of the apparatus, is seeking to make into persons falling within head (1) or head (2); or

    (4)   persons who wish to become persons falling within head (1) or head (2) or who are likely to seek to become persons falling within one or both of those heads: s 405(1), (5).

'Apparatus' includes any equipment, machinery or device and any wire or cable and the casing or coating for any wire or cable: s 405(1). 'Business' includes any trade or profession: s 405(1).

5   For the purposes of the Communications Act 2003 s 3, 'relevant markets' means markets for any of the services, facilities, apparatus or directories in relation to which OFCOM has functions: s 3(14). References in the Communications Act 2003 to services in relation to which OFCOM has functions include references to any services in relation to which OFCOM is required to set standards under s 319 (see BROADCASTING vol 4 (2011) PARA 897): s 405(6).

6   Communications Act 2003 s 3(1)(b). Section 3 is subject to ss 370(11), 371(11) (see PARA 44) and to the Enterprise Act 2002 s 119A(4) (which applies to functions conferred on OFCOM by the Communications Act 2003 Pt 5 Ch 2 (ss 373–389)) (media mergers): s 3(13).

7   Ie by virtue of the Communications Act 2003 s 3(1).

8   Communications Act 2003 s 3(2).

9   'Wireless telegraphy' has the same meaning as in the Wireless Telegraphy Act 2006: Communications Act 2003 s 405(1) (definition substituted by the Wireless Telegraphy Act 2006 s 123, Sch 7 paras 25, 34(1), (3)). In the Wireless Telegraphy Act 2006, 'wireless telegraphy' means the emitting or receiving, over paths that are not provided by any material substance constructed or arranged for the purpose, of energy to which s 116(2) applies: s 116(1). Section 116(2) applies to electromagnetic energy of a frequency not exceeding 3,000 gigahertz that:

    (1)   serves for conveying messages, sound or visual images (whether or not the messages, sound or images are actually received by anyone), or for operating or controlling machinery or apparatus (s 116(2)(a)); or

    (2)   is used in connection with determining position, bearing or distance, or for gaining information as to the presence, absence, position or motion of an object or of a class of objects (s 116(2)(b)).

The Secretary of State may by order modify the definition of 'wireless telegraphy' by substituting a different frequency for the frequency that is for the time being specified in s 116(2): s 116(3). No order is to be made containing provision authorised by s 116(3) unless a draft of the order has been laid before Parliament and approved by a resolution of each House: s 116(4). At the date at which this volume states the law, no such order has been made.

10   Communications Act 2003 s 3(2)(a).

11 Communications Act 2003 s 3(2)(b). As to the meaning of 'electronic communications service' see PARA 53.

12 'Television and radio services' means:

    (1)   programme services apart from those provided by the BBC; and

    (2)   services provided by the BBC in relation to which OFCOM has functions; and 'the BBC' means the British Broadcasting Corporation (Communications Act 2003 s 405(1)).

As to the BBC see BROADCASTING vol 4 (2011) PARAS 603–626. As to services provided by the BBC in relation to which OFCOM has functions see BROADCASTING vol 4 (2011) PARA 854 et seq.

    'Programme service' means:

    (a)   a television programme service;

    (b)   the public teletext service;

    (c)   an additional television service;

    (d)   a digital additional television service;

    (e)   a radio programme service; or

    (f)   a sound service provided by the BBC; and

expressions used in this definition and in Pt 3 (ss 198–362) have the same meanings in this definition as in Pt 3 (television and radio services: see BROADCASTING vol 4 (2011) PARA 504 et seq): s 405(1).

    'Television programme' means any programme (with or without sounds) which:

    (i)   is produced wholly or partly to be seen on television; and

    (ii)   consists of moving or still images or of legible text or of a combination of those things: s 405(1).

    'Programme' includes an advertisement and, in relation to a service, anything included in that service: s 405(1). As to the meaning of 'television programme service' see BROADCASTING vol 4 (2011) PARA 790 note 5; as to the meaning of 'public teletext service' see BROADCASTING vol 4 (2011) PARA 697 note 3; as to the meaning of 'additional television service' see BROADCASTING vol 4 (2011) PARA 857 note 8; as to the meaning of 'digital additional television service' see BROADCASTING vol 4 (2011) PARA 857 note 11; and as to the meaning of 'radio programme service' see BROADCASTING vol 4 (2011) PARA 899 note 3.

13 Communications Act 2003 s 3(2)(c).

14 Communications Act 2003 s 3(2)(d).

15 Communications Act 2003 s 3(2)(e).

16 Communications Act 2003 s 3(2)(f).

17 Ie its duties under the Communications Act 2003 s 3(1): see heads (1), (2) in the text.

18 Communications Act 2003 s 3(3). See also *British Telecommunication plc (Appellant) v Telefonica O2 Ltd (Respondent)* [2014] UKSC 42, [2014] 4 All ER 907, [2014] 2 All ER (Comm) 877 (Supreme Court upheld the Competition Appeal Tribunal's assessment that BT was contractually entitled to introduce new regime of charges but this within limits which were fixed by the objectives of the European Parliament and Council Directive (EC) 2002/21 (OJ L108, 24.4.2002, p 33) on a common regulatory framework for electronic communications networks and services (Framework Directive), art 8).

19 Communications Act 2003 s 3(4).

20 Communications Act 2003 s 3(4)(a). The purposes of public service television broadcasting in the United Kingdom are:

    (1)   the provision of relevant television services which secure that programmes dealing with a wide range of subject-matters are made available for viewing (see ss 264(4)(a), 405(1));

    (2)   the provision of relevant television services in a manner which (having regard to the days on which they are shown and the times of day at which they are shown) is likely to meet the needs and satisfy the interests of as many different audiences as practicable (see ss 264(4)(b), 405(1));

    (3)   the provision of relevant television services which (taken together and having regard to the same matters) are properly balanced, so far as their nature and subject-matters are concerned, for meeting the needs and satisfying the interests of the available audiences (see ss 264(4)(c), 405(1)); and

    (4)   the provision of relevant television services which (taken together) maintain high general standards with respect to the programmes included in them, and, in particular with respect to the contents of the programmes, the quality of the programme making and the professional skill and editorial integrity applied in the making of the programmes (see ss 264(4)(d), 405(1)).

When determining the extent to which any of the purposes of public service television broadcasting in the United Kingdom are fulfilled, OFCOM must have regard to the desirability of those purposes being fulfilled in a manner which ensures:

(a) that the relevant television services (taken together) comprise a public service for the dissemination of information and for the provision of education and entertainment (see ss 264(5), (6)(a), 405(1));

(b) that cultural activity in the United Kingdom, and its diversity, are reflected, supported and stimulated by the representation in those services (taken together) of drama, comedy and music, by the inclusion of feature films in those services and by the treatment of other visual and performing arts (see ss 264(5), (6)(b), 405(1));

(c) that those services (taken together) provide, to the extent that is appropriate for facilitating civic understanding and fair and well-informed debate on news and current affairs, a comprehensive and authoritative coverage of news and current affairs in, and in the different parts of, the United Kingdom and from around the world (see ss 264(5), (6)(c), 405(1));

(d) that those services (taken together) satisfy a wide range of different sporting and other leisure interests (see ss 264(5), (6)(d), 405(1));

(e) that those services (taken together) include what appears to OFCOM to be a suitable quantity and range of programmes on educational matters, of programmes of an educational nature and of other programmes of educative value (see ss 264(5), (6)(e), 405(1));

(f) that those services (taken together) include what appears to OFCOM to be a suitable quantity and range of programmes dealing with each of the following, science, religion and other beliefs, social issues, matters of international significance or interest and matters of specialist interest (see ss 264(5), (6)(f), 405(1));

(g) that the programmes included in those services that deal with religion and other beliefs include programmes providing news and other information about different religions and other beliefs, programmes about the history of different religions and other beliefs and programmes showing acts of worship and other ceremonies and practices (including some showing acts of worship and other ceremonies in their entirety) (see ss 264(5), (6)(g), 405(1));

(h) that those services (taken together) include what appears to OFCOM to be a suitable quantity and range of high quality and original programmes for children and young people (ss 264(5), (6)(h), 405(1));

(i) that those services (taken together) include what appears to OFCOM to be a sufficient quantity of programmes that reflect the lives and concerns of different communities and cultural interests and traditions within the United Kingdom, and locally in different parts of the United Kingdom (see ss 264(5), (6)(i), 405(1));

(j) that those services (taken together), so far as they include programmes made in the United Kingdom, include what appears to OFCOM to be an appropriate range and proportion of programmes made outside the M25 area (see ss 264(5), (6)(j), 405(1)).

See also **BROADCASTING** vol 4 (2011) PARA 788.

21 Communications Act 2003 s 3(4)(b).

22 Communications Act 2003 s 3(4)(c).

23 Communications Act 2003 s 3(4)(d).

24 Communications Act 2003 s 3(4)(e).

25 Communications Act 2003 s 3(4)(f).

26 Any power under the Communications Act 2003 to provide for the manner in which anything is to be done includes power to provide for the form in which it is to be done: s 405(2).

27 Communications Act 2003 s 3(4)(g).

28 Communications Act 2003 s 3(4)(h).

29 Communications Act 2003 s 3(4)(i).

30 Communications Act 2003 s 3(4)(j).

31 Communications Act 2003 s 3(4)(k).

32 Communications Act 2003 s 3(4)(l).

33 Ie mentioned in the Communications Act 2003 s 3(1), (2): see the text and notes 1–16.

34 Communications Act 2003 s 3(4)(m).

35 For the purposes of the Communications Act 2003 s 3, 'general duties', in relation to OFCOM, means:

(1) its duties under s 3(1)–(5) (see the text and notes 1–34); and

(2) the duty which, under s 107(5) (see PARA 156), is to rank equally for the purposes of s 3(6), (7) (see the text and note 36) with its duties under s 3: s 3(14).

36 Communications Act 2003 s 3(7). Where it appears to OFCOM, in relation to the carrying out of any of the functions mentioned in s 4(1) (see PARA 17), that any of its general duties conflict with one or more of its duties under ss 4, 24 and 25 (see PARAS 17, 34), priority must be given to its duties under those provisions: s 3(6). Where it appears to OFCOM, in relation to the carrying out of any of their functions in relation to postal services, that any of their general duties conflict with their duty under the Postal Services Act 2011 s 29 (duty to secure provision of universal postal service), priority must be given to their duty under s 29: Communications Act 2003 s 3(6A) (added by the Postal Services Act 2011 Sch 12 para 57).

37 A case is an important case for the purposes of the Communications Act 2003 s 3(8) or (10) only if:
  (1) it involved one or more of the following matters:
    (a) a major change in the activities carried on by OFCOM (s 3(11)(a), (12)(a));
    (b) matters likely to have a significant impact on persons carrying on businesses in any of the relevant markets (s 3(11)(a), (12)(b)); or
    (c) matters likely to have a significant impact on the general public in the United Kingdom or in a part of the United Kingdom (s 3(11)(a), (12)(c)); or
  (2) it otherwise appears to OFCOM to have been of unusual importance (s 3(11)(b)).

38 Communications Act 2003 s 3(8)(a). Where OFCOM is required to publish a statement under s 3(8), it must:
  (1) publish it as soon as possible after making its decision but not while it would (apart from a statutory requirement to publish) be subject to an obligation not to publish a matter that needs to be included in the statement (s 3(9)(a)); and
  (2) so publish it in such manner as it considers appropriate for bringing it to the attention of the persons who, in OFCOM's opinion, are likely to be affected by the matters to which the decision relates (s 3(9)(b)).

39 Communications Act 2003 s 3(8)(b). See note 38.

40 Communications Act 2003 s 3(8)(c). See note 38.

41 Ie under the Office of Communications Act 2002 Schedule para 12 (OFCOM's annual report: see PARA 7).

42 Communications Act 2003 s 3(10). See further note 37.

17. Duties for the purpose of fulfilling EU obligations. It is the duty of OFCOM[1], in carrying out any of the following functions, namely:

(1) its functions relating to electronic communications networks[2] and services[3];

(2) its functions under the enactments relating to the management of the radio spectrum[4];

(3) its functions[5] in relation to disputes referred to it[6];

(4) its functions[7] so far as they relate to information[8] required for purposes connected with matters in relation to which functions specified in heads (1) to (3) above and head (5) below are conferred on OFCOM[9]; and

(5) its functions[10] so far as they are carried out for the purpose of making information available to specified persons[11],

to act in accordance with the six European Union (EU) requirements[12].

The first EU requirement is a requirement to promote competition:

(a) in relation to the provision of electronic communications networks and electronic communications services[13];

(b) in relation to the provision and making available of services and facilities that are provided or made available in association with the provision of electronic communications networks or electronic communications services[14]; and

(c) in relation to the supply of directories capable of being used in connection with the use of electronic communications networks or electronic communications services[15].

The second EU requirement is a requirement to secure that OFCOM's activities contribute to the development of the European internal market[16].

The third EU requirement is a requirement to promote the interests of all persons who are citizens of the European Union[17].

The fourth EU requirement is a requirement to take account of the desirability of OFCOM's carrying out its functions in a manner which, so far as practicable, does not favour one form of electronic communications network, electronic communications service or associated facility[18], or one means of providing or making available such a network, service or facility, over another[19].

The fifth EU requirement is a requirement to encourage, to such extent as OFCOM considers appropriate for the specified purpose[20], the provision of network access[21] and service interoperability[22]. That purpose is the purpose of securing efficiency and sustainable competition, efficient investment and innovation and the maximum benefit for the persons who are customers[23] of communications providers and of persons who make associated facilities available[24].

The sixth EU requirement is a requirement to encourage such compliance with specified standards[25] as is necessary for facilitating service interoperability and securing freedom of choice for the customers of communications providers[26].

Where it appears to OFCOM that any of the EU requirements conflict with each other, it must secure that the conflict is resolved in the manner it thinks best in the circumstances[27].

In carrying out any of the functions mentioned in heads (1)–(5) above, OFCOM must take due account of all applicable recommendations issued[28] by the European Commission[29], and where OFCOM decides not to follow such a recommendation it must notify the Commission of its decision, and of the reasons for it[30].

1   As to the meaning of 'OFCOM' see PARA 14 note 1; and as to the establishment of OFCOM see PARA 2.
2   As to the meaning of 'electronic communications network' see PARA 53.
3   Communications Act 2003 s 4(1)(a). The functions referred to in head (1) in the text are those under the Communications Act 2003 Pt 2 Ch 1 (ss 32–151: see PARA 81 et seq): s 4(1)(a).
4   Communications Act 2003 s 4(1)(b). 'Enactments relating to the management of the radio spectrum' means the Wireless Telegraphy Act 2006 and the provisions of the Communications Act 2003 so far as relating to that Act: Communications Act 2003 s 405(1) (definition amended by the Wireless Telegraphy Act 2006 s 123, Sch 7 paras 25, 34(1), (2)). As to wireless telegraphy see BROADCASTING vol 4 (2011) PARA 509 et seq.
5   Ie under the Communications Act 2003 Pt 2 Ch 3 (ss 185–197): see PARA 217 et seq.
6   Communications Act 2003 s 4(1)(c). The disputes are referred to them under the Communications Act 2003 s 185: see PARA 217.
7   Ie under the Communications Act 2003 ss 24, 25: see PARA 34.
8   'Information' includes accounts, estimates and projections and any document: Communications Act 2003 s 405(1).
9   Communications Act 2003 s 4(1)(d).
10   Ie under the Communications Act 2003 s 26: see PARA 34.
11   Communications Act 2003 s 4(1)(e). The persons referred to in the text are those mentioned in s 26(2)(a)–(c): see PARA 34 heads (1)–(3).
12   Communications Act 2003 s 4(2). Those requirements give effect, among other things, to the requirements of the Framework Directive art 8 and are to be read accordingly: Communications Act 2003 s 4(2). For the purposes of ss 4, 4A and 5, 'Framework Directive' has the same meaning as in Pt 2 Ch 1 (ss 32–151) (see PARA 97 note 21): s 4(13) (added by SI 2011/1210). See further PARA 68.
13   Communications Act 2003 s 4(3)(a). 'Provide' and cognate expressions, in relation to an electronic communications network, electronic communications service or associated facilities, are to be construed in accordance with s 32(4) (see PARA 53 note 9): s 405(1).
14   Communications Act 2003 s 4(3)(b). See note 13.
15   Communications Act 2003 s 4(3)(c). See note 13.
16   Communications Act 2003 s 4(4).

17 Ie within the meaning of the Treaty on the Functioning of the European Union (Rome, 25 March 1957; TS 1 (1973); Cmnd 5179) ('TFEU') art 20: Communications Act 2003 s 4(5) (amended by SI 2012/1809). The Treaty was formerly known as the Treaty Establishing the European Community; it has been renamed by the Treaty of Lisbon (ie the Treaty of Lisbon Amending the Treaty Establishing the European Union and the Treaty Establishing the European Community (Lisbon, 13 December 2007; ECS 13 (2007); Cm 7294)) and its provisions renumbered by virtue of the Treaty of Amsterdam (ie the Treaty of Amsterdam amending the Treaty on European Union, the Treaties establishing the European Communities and related acts (Amsterdam, 2 October 1997; TS 52 (1999); Cm 4434; ECS 14 (1997); Cm 3780) (OJ C340, 10.11.1997, p 1)) and by the Treaty of Lisbon (see EUROPEAN UNION vol 47A (2014) PARA 1 et seq).

18 As to the meaning of 'associated facility' see PARA 53.

19 Communications Act 2003 s 4(6). The fourth EU requirement does not apply to:
    (1)   the imposition, in relation to a wireless telegraphy licence, of a limitation of a kind falling within the Wireless Telegraphy Act 2006 s 9ZA(1) (Communications Act 2003 s 4(6A)(a) (added by SI 2011/1210)); or
    (2)   the review, variation or removal of such a limitation (Communications Act 2003 s 4(6A)(b) (as so added)).

20 Ie the purpose mentioned in the Communications Act 2003 s 4(8): see the text to note 24.

21 'Network access' has the same meaning as in the Communications Act 2003 Pt 2 Ch 1 (ss 32–151) (see PARA 98 note 5): s 4(12).

22 Communications Act 2003 s 4(7). 'Service interoperability' has the same meaning as in Pt 2 Ch 1 (see PARA 98 note 4): s 4(12).

23 'Customers', in relation to a communications provider or a person who makes an associated facility available, means the following (including any of them whose use or potential use of the network, service or facility is for the purposes of, or in connection with, a business):
    (1)   the persons to whom the network, service or facility is provided or made available in the course of any business carried on as such by the provider or person who makes it available;
    (2)   the persons to whom the communications provider or person making the facility available is seeking to secure that the network, service or facility is so provided or made available;
    (3)   the persons who wish to be so provided with the network or service, or to have the facility so made available, or who are likely to seek to become persons to whom the network, service or facility is so provided or made available: Communications Act 2003 s 405(1).
    'Communications provider' means a person who (within the meaning of s 32(4) (see PARA 53 note 9)) provides an electronic communications network or an electronic communications service: s 405(1). See also note 13.

24 Communications Act 2003 s 4(8) (amended by SI 2011/1210).

25 Ie the standards mentioned in the Communications Act 2003 s 4(10). Those standards are:
    (1)   standards or specifications from time to time drawn up and published in accordance with the Framework Directive art 17 (Communications Act 2003 s 4(10)(a));
    (2)   the standards and specifications from time to time adopted by:
        (a)   the European Committee for Standardisation (s 4(10)(b)(i));
        (b)   the European Committee for Electrotechnical Standardisation (s 4(10)(b)(ii)); and
        (c)   the European Telecommunications Standards Institute (s 4(10)(b)(iii)); and
    (3)   the international standards and recommendations from time to time adopted by:
        (a)   the International Telecommunication Union (see PARA 59) (s 4(10)(c)(i));
        (b)   the International Organisation for Standardisation (s 4(10)(c)(ii));
        (c)   the European Conference of Postal and Telecommunications Administrations (s 4(10)(c)(iia) (added by SI 2011/1210)); and
        (d)   the International Electrotechnical Committee (Communications Act 2003 s 4(10)(c)(iii)).

26 Communications Act 2003 s 4(9).

27 Communications Act 2003 s 4(11).

28 Ie whether before or after the coming into force of the Communications Act 2003 s 4A (ie 26 May 2011: see the Electronic Communications and Wireless Telegraphy Regulations 2011, SI 2011/1210).

29 Ie under the Framework Directive art 19(1).

30 Commmunications Act 2003 s 4A (added by SI 2011/1210).

18. Directions in respect of networks and spectrum functions. It is the duty of OFCOM[1] to carry out the following functions, namely:

(1) its functions under Part 2 of the Communications Act 2003[2]; and

(2) its functions under the enactments relating to the management of the radio spectrum that are not contained in Part 2[3],

in accordance with such general or specific directions as may be given to it by the Secretary of State[4].

The Secretary of State's power to give directions under these provisions[5] is confined to a power to give directions for one or more of the following purposes:

(a) in the interests of national security[6];

(b) in the interests of relations with the government of a country or territory outside the United Kingdom[7];

(c) for the purpose of securing compliance with international obligations of the United Kingdom[8];

(d) in the interests of the safety of the public or of public health[9].

The Secretary of State is not entitled by virtue of any of these provisions to direct OFCOM to suspend or restrict:

(i) a person's entitlement to provide an electronic communications network or electronic communications service[10]; or

(ii) a person's entitlement to make available associated facilities[11].

The Secretary of State may not give a direction under these provisions[12] in respect of a function that OFCOM is required[13] to exercise without seeking or taking instructions from any other body[14].

Before giving a direction under these provisions, the Secretary of State must take due account of the desirability of not favouring:

(A) one form of electronic communications network, electronic communications service or associated facility[15]; or

(B) one means of providing or making available such a network, service or facility[16],

over another[17].

The Secretary of State must publish a direction under these provisions in such manner as appears to him to be appropriate for bringing it to the attention of the persons who, in his opinion, are likely to be affected by it[18].

1   As to the meaning of 'OFCOM' see PARA 14 note 1; and as to the establishment of OFCOM see PARA 2.

2   Ie the Communications Act 2003 ss 32–197, Schs 3–8.

3   Communications Act 2003 s 5(1). As to the meaning of 'enactments relating to the management of the radio spectrum' see PARA 17 note 4.

4   Communications Act 2003 s 5(2). As to the Secretary of State see PARA 76 note 1.

5   Ie under the Communications Act 2003 s 5.

6   Communications Act 2003 s 5(3)(a).

7   Communications Act 2003 s 5(3)(b). As to the meaning of 'United Kingdom' see PARA 14 note 7.

8   Communications Act 2003 s 5(3)(c).

9   Communications Act 2003 s 5(3)(d).

10   Communications Act 2003 s 5(4)(a). Section 5(4) does not affect the Secretary of State's powers under s 132 (see PARA 151): s 5(7). As to the meanings of 'electronic communications network' and 'electronic communications service' see PARA 53.

11   Communications Act 2003 s 5(4)(b). As to the meaning of 'associated facilities' see PARA 53. See note 10.

12   Ie under the Communications Act 2003 s 5.

13   Ie by the Framework Directive art 3(3a). As to the meaning of 'Framework Directive' see PARA 17 note 12.

14   Communications Act 2003 s 5(3A) (added by SI 2011/1210).

15   Communications Act 2003 s 5(4A)(a) (added by SI 2011/1210).

16   Communications Act 2003 s 5(4A)(b) (as added: see note 15).
17   Communications Act 2003 s 5(4A) (as added: see note 15).
18   Communications Act 2003 s 5(5). The Secretary of State is not required by s 5(5) to publish a direction, and he may exclude matter from a direction he does publish, if he considers the publication of the direction or matter to be:
    (1)   against the interests of national security (s 5(6)(a)); or
    (2)   against the interests of relations with the government of a country or territory outside the United Kingdom (s 5(6)(b)).

19.   Duties to review regulatory burdens.   OFCOM must keep the carrying out of its functions under review with a view to securing that regulation by OFCOM does not involve:

(1)   the imposition of burdens which are unnecessary[1]; or

(2)   the maintenance of burdens which have become unnecessary[2].

In reviewing its functions under these provisions[3] it is the duty of OFCOM:

(a)   to have regard to the extent to which the matters which it is required[4] to further or to secure are already furthered or secured, or are likely to be furthered or secured, by effective self-regulation[5]; and

(b)   in the light of that, to consider to what extent it would be appropriate to remove or reduce regulatory burdens imposed by OFCOM[6].

In determining for the purposes of these provisions whether procedures for self-regulation are effective, OFCOM must consider, in particular:

(i)   whether those procedures are administered by a person who is sufficiently independent of the persons who may be subjected to the procedures[7]; and

(ii)   whether adequate arrangements are in force for funding the activities of that person in relation to those procedures[8].

OFCOM must, from time to time, publish a statement setting out how it proposes, during the period for which the statement is made, to secure that regulation by OFCOM does not involve the imposition or maintenance of unnecessary burdens[9]. It is the duty of OFCOM, in carrying out its functions at times during a period for which such a statement is in force, to have regard to that statement[10]. OFCOM may, if it thinks fit, revise a statement at any time before or during the period for which it is made[11]. Where OFCOM revises a statement, it must publish the revision as soon as practicable[12]. The publication of a statement, or of a revision of a statement, must be in such manner as OFCOM considers appropriate for bringing it to the attention of the persons who, in its opinion, are likely to be affected by the matters to which it relates[13].

1   Communications Act 2003 s 6(1)(a). As to the meaning of 'OFCOM' see PARA 14 note 1; and as to the establishment of OFCOM see PARA 2.
2   Communications Act 2003 s 6(1)(b).
3   Ie under the Communications Act 2003 s 6.
4   Ie under the Communications Act 2003 s 3: see PARA 16.
5   Communications Act 2003 s 6(2)(a).
6   Communications Act 2003 s 6(2)(b).
7   Communications Act 2003 s 6(3)(a).
8   Communications Act 2003 s 6(3)(b).
9   Communications Act 2003 s 6(4).
    The first statement:
    (1)   must be published as soon as practicable after the commencement of s 6 (ie 29 December 2003: see the Office of Communications Act 2002 (Commencement No 3) and Communications Act 2003 (Commencement No 2) Order 2003, SI 2003/3142) (Communications Act 2003 s 6(5)(a); and
    (2)   must be a statement for the period of 12 months beginning with the day of its publication (s 6(5)(b)).

A subsequent statement:
(a)   must be published during the period to which the previous statement related (s 6(6)(a)); and
(b)   must be a statement for the period of 12 months beginning with the end of the previous period (s 6(6)(b)).

10 Communications Act 2003 s 6(7).
11 Communications Act 2003 s 6(8).
12 Communications Act 2003 s 6(9).
13 Communications Act 2003 s 6(10).

20.   Duty to carry out impact assessments. The following provisions apply where:

(1)   OFCOM[1] is proposing to do anything for the purposes of, or in connection with, the carrying out of its functions[2]; and

(2)   it appears to it that the proposal is important[3],

but they do not apply if it appears to OFCOM that the urgency of the matter makes it impracticable or inappropriate for it to comply with the requirements of the provisions[4].

Before implementing its proposal, OFCOM must either:

(a)   carry out and publish an assessment of the likely impact of implementing the proposal[5]; or

(b)   publish a statement setting out its reasons for thinking that it is unnecessary for it to carry out an assessment[6].

An assessment carried out under these provisions[7] may take such form, and must relate to such matters, as OFCOM considers appropriate[8]. In determining the matters to which an assessment should relate, OFCOM must have regard to such general guidance relating to the carrying out of impact assessments as it considers appropriate[9].

Where OFCOM publishes an assessment:

(i)   it must provide an opportunity of making representations[10] to it about its proposal to members of the public and other persons who, in OFCOM's opinion, are likely to be affected to a significant extent by its implementation[11];

(ii)   the published assessment must be accompanied by a statement setting out how representations may be made[12]; and

(iii)   OFCOM is not to implement its proposal unless the period for making representations about it has expired and it has considered all the representations that were made in that period[13].

Where OFCOM is required[14] to consult about a proposal to which these provisions apply, or to give a person an opportunity of making representations about it, the requirements of these provisions are in addition to, but may be performed contemporaneously with, the other requirements[15].

Every annual report[16] prepared by OFCOM must set out:

(A)   a list of the assessments carried out during the financial year to which the report relates[17]; and

(B)   a summary of the decisions taken during that year in relation to proposals to which assessments carried out in that year or previous financial years relate[18].

The publication of anything under the provisions described above must be in such manner as OFCOM considers appropriate for bringing it to the attention of the persons who, in OFCOM's opinion, are likely to be affected if its proposal is implemented[19].

1   As to the meaning of 'OFCOM' see PARA 14 note 1; and as to the establishment of OFCOM see PARA 2.
2   Communications Act 2003 s 7(1)(a).
3   Communications Act 2003 s 7(1)(b). A proposal is important for the purposes of the Communications Act 2003 s 7 only if its implementation would be likely to do one or more of the following:
      (1)   involve a major change in the activities carried on by OFCOM (s 7(2)(a));
      (2)   have a significant impact on persons carrying on businesses in the markets for any of the services, facilities, apparatus or directories in relation to which OFCOM has functions (s 7(2)(b)); or
      (3)   have a significant impact on the general public in the United Kingdom or in a part of the United Kingdom (s 7(2)(c)).
    As to the meaning of 'United Kingdom' see PARA 14 note 7.
4   Communications Act 2003 s 7(1)(b).
5   Communications Act 2003 s 7(3)(a).
6   Communications Act 2003 s 7(3)(b). An assessment under head (a) in the text must set out how, in OFCOM's opinion, the performance of its general duties (within the meaning of s 3 (see PARA 16)) is secured or furthered by or in relation to what it proposes: s 7(4).
7   Ie under the Communications Act 2003 s 7.
8   Communications Act 2003 s 7(5).
9   Communications Act 2003 s 7(6).
10   'Representation', in relation to a proposal or the contents of any notice or notification, includes an objection to the proposal or (as the case may be) to the whole or any part of those contents: Communications Act 2003 s 405(1).
11   Communications Act 2003 s 7(7)(a).
12   Communications Act 2003 s 7(7)(b).
13   Communications Act 2003 s 7(7)(c).
14   Ie apart from the Communications Act 2003 s 7.
15   Communications Act 2003 s 7(8).
16   As to OFCOM's annual report see the Office of Communications Act 2002 Schedule para 12; and PARA 7.
17   Communications Act 2003 s 7(9)(a).
18   Communications Act 2003 s 7(9)(b).
19   Communications Act 2003 s 7(10).

21. Duty to publish and meet promptness standards. It is the duty of OFCOM[1] to publish a statement setting out the standards it is proposing to meet with respect to promptness in:

(1)   the carrying out of its different functions; and
(2)   the transaction of business for purposes connected with the carrying out of those functions[2].

These provisions[3] do not require standards to be set out with respect to anything which is required[4] to be done by a time, or within a period, provided for by or under an enactment[5]. OFCOM may, if it thinks fit, at any time revise the statement for the time being in force[6]. It is the duty of OFCOM in carrying out its functions, and in transacting business for purposes connected with the carrying out of its functions, to have regard to the statement for the time being in force[7]. Where OFCOM revises a statement, it must publish the revision as soon as practicable[8]. The publication of a statement, or of a revision of a statement, must be in such manner as OFCOM considers appropriate for bringing it to the attention of the persons who, in its opinion, are likely to be affected by the matters to which it relates[9]. OFCOM's report[10] for each financial year must contain a statement by OFCOM summarising the extent to which it has complied during that year with the standards set out under these provisions[11].

Where the Secretary of State[12] considers that the statement published by OFCOM is not adequate for securing that it meets satisfactory promptness standards[13], he may give OFCOM a notification to that effect[14]. If the period of three months after the date of the giving of such a notification expires without OFCOM taking steps which the Secretary of State is satisfied remedy the situation, he may give it a direction requiring OFCOM to issue a new or revised statement in accordance with the direction[15]. Before giving such a direction, the Secretary of State must give OFCOM an opportunity of making representations to him about his proposed direction and have regard to any representations made to him by OFCOM[16]. Where the Secretary of State gives such a direction to OFCOM, he must publish a copy of it in such manner as he considers appropriate for bringing it to the attention of persons who, in his opinion, are likely to be affected by OFCOM's promptness standards[17]. It is the duty of OFCOM to revise its statement in accordance with any direction of the Secretary of State[18].

1 As to the meaning of 'OFCOM' see PARA 14 note 1; and as to the establishment of OFCOM see PARA 2.
2 Communications Act 2003 s 8(1).
3 Ie the Communications Act 2003 s 8.
4 Ie apart from the Communications Act 2003 s 8.
5 Communications Act 2003 s 8(2).
6 Communications Act 2003 s 8(3).
7 Communications Act 2003 s 8(4).
8 Communications Act 2003 s 8(5).
9 Communications Act 2003 s 8(6).
10 As to OFCOM's annual report see the Office of Communications Act 2002 Schedule para 12; and PARA 7.
11 Communications Act 2003 s 8(7).
12 As to the Secretary of State see PARA 76 note 1.
13 For these purposes, 'promptness standards' means standards of promptness in:
    (1)   the carrying out by OFCOM of its different functions (Communications Act 2003 s 9(7)(a)); and
    (2)   the transaction by OFCOM of business for purposes connected with the carrying out of those functions (s 9(7)(b)).
14 Communications Act 2003 s 9(1). No notification was to be given under s 9(1) at any time in the period of 12 months beginning with the commencement of s 8 (ie 29 December 2003: see the Office of Communications Act 2002 (Commencement No 3) and Communications Act 2003 (Commencement No 2) Order 2003, SI 2003/3142): Communications Act 2003 s 9(8).
15 Communications Act 2003 s 9(2), (3).
16 Communications Act 2003 s 9(4).
17 Communications Act 2003 s 9(5).
18 Communications Act 2003 s 9(6).

B. ACCESSIBLE DOMESTIC COMMUNICATIONS APPARATUS

22. Duty to encourage availability of easily usable apparatus. It is the duty of OFCOM[1] to take such steps, and to enter into such arrangements, as appear to it calculated to encourage others to secure:

(1)   that domestic electronic communications apparatus[2] is developed which is capable of being used with ease, and without modification, by the widest possible range of individuals (including those with disabilities)[3]; and

(2)   that domestic electronic communications apparatus which is capable of being so used is as widely available as possible for acquisition by those wishing to use it[4].

It is the duty of OFCOM from time to time to review whether it needs to take further steps, or to enter into further arrangements, for the purpose of performing its duty under these provisions[5]. OFCOM must not do anything under these provisions that would be inconsistent with the European Union (EU) requirements[6].

1   As to the meaning of 'OFCOM' see PARA 14 note 1; and as to the establishment of OFCOM see PARA 2.
2   For the purposes of the Communications Act 2003 s 10, 'electronic communications apparatus' means apparatus that is designed or adapted for a use which consists of or includes the sending or receiving of communications or other signals that are transmitted by means of an electronic communications network: s 10(4). 'Signal' includes:
     (1)   anything comprising speech, music, sounds, visual images or communications or data of any description (s 10(6)(a)); and
     (2)   signals serving for the impartation of anything between persons, between a person and a thing or between things, or for the actuation or control of apparatus (s 10(6)(b)).
     For the purposes of s 10, electronic communications apparatus is domestic electronic communications apparatus except to the extent that it is designed or adapted for use solely for the purposes of, or in connection with, a business: s 10(5). As to the meaning of 'electronic communications network' see PARA 53.
3   Communications Act 2003 s 10(1)(a).
4   Communications Act 2003 s 10(1)(b).
5   Ie under the Communications Act 2003 s 10: s 10(2).
6   Communications Act 2003 s 10(3). As to the EU requirements see s 4; and PARA 17.

C. MEDIA LITERACY

23. Duty to promote media literacy. It is the duty of OFCOM[1] to take such steps, and to enter into such arrangements, as appear to it calculated:

     (1)   to bring about, or to encourage others to bring about, a better public understanding of the nature and characteristics of material published by means of the electronic media[2];

     (2)   to bring about, or to encourage others to bring about, a better public awareness and understanding of the processes by which such material is selected, or made available, for publication by such means[3];

     (3)   to bring about, or to encourage others to bring about, the development of a better public awareness of the available systems by which access[4] to material published by means of the electronic media is or can be regulated[5];

     (4)   to bring about, or to encourage others to bring about, the development of a better public awareness of the available systems by which persons to whom such material is made available may control what is received and of the uses to which such systems may be put[6]; and

     (5)   to encourage the development and use of technologies and systems for regulating access to such material, and for facilitating control over what material is received, that are both effective and easy to use[7].

1   As to the meaning of 'OFCOM' see PARA 14 note 1; and as to the establishment of OFCOM see PARA 2.
2   Communications Act 2003 s 11(1)(a). References in the Communications Act 2003 s 11 (and in ss 13, 14: see PARAS 25, 26) to the publication of anything by means of the electronic media are references to its being:
     (1)   broadcast so as to be available for reception by members of the public or of a section of the public; or
     (2)   distributed by means of an electronic communications network to members of the public or of a section of the public: ss 11(2), 13(7), 14(8).
     'Broadcast' means broadcast by wireless telegraphy; and cognate expressions are to be construed accordingly: s 405(1). 'Distribute', in relation to a service, does not include broadcast; and cognate expressions are to be construed accordingly: s 405(1).
3   Communications Act 2003 s 11(1)(b).

4   References in the Communications Act 2003 to access in relation to an electronic
    communications network or electronic communications service, are references to the
    opportunity of making use of the network or service: s 405(4)(a). As to the meanings of
    'electronic communications network' and 'electronic communications service' see PARA 53.
5   Communications Act 2003 s 11(1)(c).
6   Communications Act 2003 s 11(1)(d).
7   Communications Act 2003 s 11(1)(e).

D. CONTENT BOARD

24.   Duty to establish and maintain Content Board.   It is the duty of OFCOM[1]
to exercise its powers[2] to establish and maintain a committee, known as the
'Content Board'[3]. The Content Board is to consist of:

(1)   a chairman appointed by OFCOM[4]; and
(2)   such number of other members appointed by OFCOM as OFCOM
       thinks fit[5].

The chairman of the Content Board must be a non-executive member of
OFCOM but is not to be the chairman of OFCOM[6]. At least one of the other
members of the Content Board must also be a non-executive member of
OFCOM other than the chairman of OFCOM[7]. In appointing persons to be
members of the Content Board, OFCOM must secure that, for each of the
following parts of the United Kingdom:

(a)   England,
(b)   Scotland,
(c)   Wales, and
(d)   Northern Ireland,

there is a different member of the Content Board capable of representing the
interests and opinions of persons living in that part of the United Kingdom[8].

It is the duty of OFCOM when appointing members of the Content Board to
secure, so far as practicable, that a majority of the members of the Content
Board (counting the chairman) consists of persons who are neither members nor
employees of OFCOM[9].

The following are disqualified from being the chairman or another member of
the Content Board:

(i)   governors and employees of the BBC[10];
(ii)   members and employees of the Welsh Authority[11]; and
(iii)   members and employees of C4C[12].

Before appointing a person to be the chairman or another member of the
Content Board, OFCOM must satisfy itself that he will not have any financial or
other interest which would be likely prejudicially to affect the carrying out by
him of any of his functions as chairman or member of the Content Board[13]. A
person is not to be taken to have such an interest by reason only that he is or will
be a member or employee of OFCOM[14].

In addition to paying remuneration and expenses[15], OFCOM may:

(A)   pay to, or in respect of, any member of the Content Board who is not a
       member or employee of OFCOM, such sums by way of pensions,
       allowances or gratuities as OFCOM may determine[16]; and
(B)   provide for the making of such payments to or in respect of any such
       member of the Content Board[17].

1   As to the meaning of 'OFCOM' see PARA 14 note 1; and as to the establishment of OFCOM see
    PARA 2.
2   Ie its powers under the Office of Communications Act 2002 Schedule para 14: see PARA 9.

3   Communications Act 2003 s 12(1). For the purposes of the Communications Act 2003, 'Content Board' means the committee of OFCOM established and maintained under s 12: s 405(1).
4   Communications Act 2003 s 12(2)(a).
5   Communications Act 2003 s 12(2)(b).
6   Communications Act 2003 s 12(3).
7   Communications Act 2003 s 12(4).
8   See the Communications Act 2003 s 12(5). As to the meaning of 'United Kingdom' see PARA 14 note 7. In appointing a person for the purposes of England, OFCOM must have regard to the desirability of ensuring that the person appointed is able to represent the interests and opinions of persons living in all the different regions of England: see s 12(6). The validity of any proceedings of the Content Board is not affected by any failure by OFCOM to comply with s 12(5) or (6): s 12(7).
9   Communications Act 2003 s 12(8).
10 Communications Act 2003 s 12(9)(a). As to the meaning of 'the BBC' see PARA 16 note 12.
11 Communications Act 2003 s 12(9)(b). The 'Welsh Authority' is the authority whose name is, by virtue of the Broadcasting Act 1990 s 56(1), Sianel Pedwar Cymru (see BROADCASTING vol 4 (2011) PARA 644 et seq): Communications Act 2003 s 405(1). As to the Welsh Authority see BROADCASTING vol 4 (2011) PARA 644 et seq.
12 Communications Act 2003 s 12(9)(c). 'C4C' means the Channel Four Television Corporation: s 405(1). As to the Channel Four Television Corporation see BROADCASTING vol 4 (2011) PARA 644 et seq.
13 Communications Act 2003 s 12(10). Every person whom OFCOM proposes to appoint to be the chairman or another member of the Content Board, must, whenever requested to do so by OFCOM, furnish OFCOM with any information it considers necessary for the performance of its duty under s 12(10): s 12(12).
14 Communications Act 2003 s 12(11).
15 Ie under the Office of Communications Act 2002 Schedule para 14(4): see PARA 9.
16 Communications Act 2003 s 12(13)(a).
17 Communications Act 2003 s 12(13)(b). In s 12(13), the reference to pensions, allowances and gratuities includes a reference to similar benefits payable on death or retirement; and the reference to providing for the payment of a pension, allowance or gratuity to, or in respect of, a person includes a reference to the making of payments towards the provision or payment of a pension, allowance or gratuity, or of any such similar benefits, to or in respect of that person: s 12(14).

25. Functions of the Content Board. The Content Board has such functions as OFCOM[1], in exercise of its powers[2], may confer on it[3]. The functions conferred on the Content Board include, to such extent and subject to such restrictions and approvals as OFCOM may determine, the carrying out on OFCOM's behalf of:

(1)   functions in relation to matters that concern the contents of anything which is or may be broadcast or otherwise transmitted by means of electronic communications networks[4]; and

(2)   functions in relation to the promotion of public understanding or awareness of matters relating to the publication of matter by means of the electronic media[5].

In determining what functions to confer on the Content Board, OFCOM must have particular regard to the desirability of securing that the Content Board has at least a significant influence on decisions which:

(a)   relate to the matters mentioned above[6]; and

(b)   involve the consideration of different interests and other factors as respects different parts of the United Kingdom[7].

It is the duty of the Content Board to ensure, in relation to:

(i)   the carrying out of OFCOM's functions[8];

(ii)   the matters with respect to which functions are conferred on the Content Board[9]; and

(iii)   such other matters[10] as OFCOM may determine[11],

that OFCOM is aware of the different interests and other factors which, in the Content Board's opinion, need to be taken into account as respects the different parts of the United Kingdom in relation to the carrying out of OFCOM's functions[12].

The power of OFCOM to determine the Content Board's functions includes power to authorise the Content Board to establish committees and panels to advise the Content Board on the carrying out of some or all of its functions[13]. The power of OFCOM to authorise the establishment of a committee or panel by the Content Board includes power to authorise the establishment of a committee or panel that includes persons who are not members of the Content Board[14].

1   As to the establishment of the Content board see PARA 24. As to the meaning of 'OFCOM' see PARA 14 note 1; and as to the establishment of OFCOM see PARA 2.
2   Ie under the Office of Communications Act 2002 Schedule: see PARA 3 et seq.
3   Communications Act 2003 s 13(1).
4   Communications Act 2003 s 13(2)(a).
5   Communications Act 2003 s 13(2)(b). As to references to the publication of anything by means of the electronic media see PARA 23 note 2.
6   Communications Act 2003 s 13(3)(a). The matters referred to in the text are matters referred in the Communications Act 2003 s 13(2): see heads (1) and (2) in the text.
7   Communications Act 2003 s 13(3)(b). As to the meaning of 'United Kingdom' see PARA 14 note 7.
8   Communications Act 2003 s 13(4)(a). The functions referred to in the text are those under the Communications Act 2003 Pt 3 (ss 198–362), the Broadcasting Act 1990 Pt I (ss 3–71), Pt III (ss 85–126), and the Broadcasting Act 1996 Pt I (ss 1–39), Pt II (ss 40–72).
9   Communications Act 2003 s 13(4)(b).
10 Ie the matters mentioned in the Communications Act 2003 s 13(2): see heads (1) and (2) in the text.
11 Communications Act 2003 s 13(4)(c).
12 Communications Act 2003 s 13(4).
13 Communications Act 2003 s 13(5).
14 Communications Act 2003 s 13(6).

E. PROTECTION OF CONSUMERS

26.   Consumer research. OFCOM[1] must make arrangements for ascertaining:
  (1)   the state of public opinion from time to time about the manner in which electronic communications networks[2] and electronic communications services[3] are provided[4];
  (2)   the state of public opinion from time to time about the manner in which associated facilities[5] are made available[6];
  (3)   the experiences of consumers[7] in the markets for electronic communications services and associated facilities, in relation to the manner in which electronic communications networks and electronic communications services are provided and associated facilities made available[8];
  (4)   the experiences of such consumers in relation to the handling, by communications providers and by persons making such facilities available, of complaints made to them by such consumers[9];
  (5)   the experiences of such consumers in relation to the resolution of disputes with communications providers or with persons making associated facilities available[10]; and
  (6)   the interests and experiences of such consumers in relation to other matters that are incidental to, or are otherwise connected with, their

experiences of the provision of electronic communications networks and electronic communications services or of the availability of associated facilities[11].

The matters to which the arrangements must relate do not include the incidence or investigation of interference[12] with wireless telegraphy[13]; nor do they include[14] public opinion with respect to the contents of anything broadcast or otherwise published by means of an electronic communications network or with respect to the experiences or interests of consumers in any market for electronic communications services with respect to anything so broadcast or published[15].

OFCOM must make arrangements for ascertaining:

(a)   the state of public opinion from time to time concerning programmes included in television and radio services[16];

(b)   any effects of such programmes, or of other material published by means of the electronic media[17], on the attitudes or behaviour of persons who watch, listen to or receive the programmes or material[18];

(c)   so far as necessary[19], the types of programmes that members of the public would like to see included in television and radio services[20].

(d)   the state of public opinion from time to time about the way in which postal services are provided[21];

(e)   the experiences of consumers in the markets for postal services, in relation to the way in which those services are provided[22];

(f)   the experiences of such consumers in relation to the handling, by persons providing postal services, of complaints made to them by such consumers[23];

(g)   the experiences of such consumers in relation to the resolution of disputes with persons providing postal services[24];

(h)   the interests and experiences of such consumers in relation to matters that are incidental to or otherwise connected with their experiences of the provision of postal services[25].

OFCOM must make arrangements for the carrying out of research into the following:

(i)   matters relating to media literacy[26];

(ii)   matters relating to, or connected with, the setting of programme and fairness standards[27];

(iii) matters relating to, or connected with, the observance of those standards by persons providing television and radio services[28];

(iv)   matters relating to, or connected with, the prevention of unjust or unfair treatment in programmes included in such services[29]; and

(v)   matters relating to, or connected with, the prevention of unwarranted infringements of privacy resulting from activities carried on for the purposes of such services[30].

Arrangements made by OFCOM for these purposes[31] may include arrangements for the carrying out of research in one or more of the following ways:

(A)   by members or employees of OFCOM[32];

(B)   by the Content Board[33];

(C)   in accordance with arrangements made by the Content Board[34];

(D)   by persons who are neither members nor employees of OFCOM[35].

The provisions described above do not restrict OFCOM's power to make any arrangements it considers to be incidental or conducive to the carrying out of any of its functions[36].

1 As to the meaning of 'OFCOM' see PARA 14 note 1; and as to the establishment of OFCOM see PARA 2.
2 As to the meaning of 'electronic communications network' see PARA 53.
3 As to the meaning of 'electronic communications service' see PARA 53.
4 Communications Act 2003 s 14(1)(a).
5 As to the meaning of 'associated facilities' see PARA 53.
6 Communications Act 2003 s 14(1)(b).
7 As to the meaning of 'consumer' see PARA 16 note 4.
8 Communications Act 2003 s 14(1)(c).
9 Communications Act 2003 s 14(1)(d).
10 Communications Act 2003 s 14(1)(e).
11 Communications Act 2003 s 14(1)(f).
12 As to the meaning of 'interference' see the Wireless Telegraphy Act 2006 s 115(1), (3); and BROADCASTING vol 4 (2011) PARA 541 note 2.
13 Communications Act 2003 s 14(2) (amended by the Wireless Telegraphy Act 2006 s 123, Sch 7 paras 25, 26).
14 Ie except so far as authorised or required by the Communications Act 2003 s 14(4)–(6): see the text and notes 16–20, 26–30.
15 Communications Act 2003 s 14(3).
16 Communications Act 2003 s 14(4)(a).
17 As to references to the publication of anything by means of the electronic media see PARA 23 note 2.
18 Communications Act 2003 s 14(4)(b).
19 Ie for the purpose mentioned in the Communications Act 2003 s 14(5), ie the carrying out by OFCOM of its functions under Pt 3 Ch 4 (ss 263–347) (regulatory provisions: see BROADCASTING vol 4 (2011) PARA 504 et seq): s 14(5).
20 Communications Act 2003 s 14(4)(c).
21 Communications Act 2003 s 14(6A)(a) (added by the Postal Services Act 2011 Sch 12 para 58).
22 Communications Act 2003 s 14(6A)(b) (as added: see note 21).
23 Communications Act 2003 s 14(6A)(c) (as added: see note 21).
24 Communications Act 2003 s 14(6A)(d) (as added: see note 21).
25 Communications Act 2003 s 14(6A)(e) (as added: see note 21).
26 Communications Act 2003 s 14(6)(a). The matters referred to in head (i) in the text is as mentioned in the Communications Act 2003 s 11(1) (see PARA 23): s 14(6)(a).
27 Communications Act 2003 s 14(6)(b). As to the setting of these standards see the Communications Act 2003 s 319; and BROADCASTING vol 4 (2011) PARA 897.
28 Communications Act 2003 s 14(6)(c).
29 Communications Act 2003 s 14(6)(d).
30 Communications Act 2003 s 14(6)(e).
31 Ie for the purposes of the Communications Act 2003 s 14.
32 Communications Act 2003 s 14(7)(a).
33 Communications Act 2003 s 14(7)(b).
34 Communications Act 2003 s 14(7)(b).
35 Communications Act 2003 s 14(7)(cd).
36 Communications Act 2003 s 14(9).

27. Duty to publish and take account of research. It is the duty of OFCOM[1]:

(1) to publish the results of any research carried out by it or on its behalf[2]; and

(2) to consider and, to such extent as it thinks fit, to take account of the results of such research in the carrying out of its functions[3].

OFCOM is not required under these provisions[4]:

(a) to publish any matter that is confidential[5]; or

(b) to publish anything that it would not be reasonably practicable to publish without disclosing such a matter[6].

The publication of research under these provisions must be in such manner as OFCOM considers appropriate[7].

1   As to the meaning of 'OFCOM' see PARA 14 note 1; and as to the establishment of OFCOM see PARA 2.
2   Communications Act 2003 s 15(1)(a). The research referred to in head (1) is research carried out under the Communications Act 2003 s 14 (see PARA 26): s 15(1)(a).
3   Communications Act 2003 s 15(1)(b).
4   Ie under the Communications Act 2003 s 15.
5   Communications Act 2003 s 15(2)(a). A matter is confidential if:
    (1)   it relates specifically to the affairs of a particular body (Communications Act 2003 s 15(3)(a)); and
    (2)   publication of that matter would or might, in OFCOM's opinion, seriously and prejudicially affect the interests of that body (s 15(3)(b)).
    'Body' (without more) means any body or association of persons, whether corporate or unincorporate, including a firm: s 405(1).
    A matter is also confidential if:
    (a)   it relates to the private affairs of an individual (s 15(4)(a)); and
    (b)   publication of that matter would or might, in OFCOM's opinion, seriously and prejudicially affect the interests of that individual (s 15(4)(b)).
6   Communications Act 2003 s 15(2)(b).
7   Communications Act 2003 s 15(5).

28.   Consumer consultation.   It is the duty of OFCOM[1] to establish and maintain effective arrangements for consultation about the carrying out of its functions with:

(1)   consumers in the markets for the services and facilities in relation to which OFCOM has functions[2];

(2)   consumers in the markets for apparatus used in connection with any such services or facilities (other than postal services)[3];

(3)   consumers in the markets for directories capable of being used in connection with the use of an electronic communications network or electronic communications service[4].

The arrangements must include the establishment and maintenance of a panel of persons (the 'Consumer Panel') with the function of advising both OFCOM and such other persons as the Consumer Panel thinks fit[5]. The arrangements must secure that the matters about which the Consumer Panel is able to give advice include the interests of domestic and small business consumers[6] in relation to the following matters:

(a)   the provision of electronic communications networks[7];

(b)   the provision and making available of certain services and facilities[8];

(c)   the supply of apparatus designed or adapted for use in connection with any such services or facilities[9];

(d)   the supply of directories capable of being used in connection with the use of an electronic communications network or electronic communications service[10];

(e)   the financial and other terms on which such services or facilities are provided or made available, or on which such apparatus or such a directory is supplied[11];

(f)   standards of service, quality and safety for such services, facilities, apparatus and directories[12];

(g)   the handling of complaints made by persons who are consumers in the markets for such services, facilities, apparatus or directories to the persons who provide the services or make the facilities available, or who are suppliers of the apparatus or directories[13];

(h)   the resolution of disputes between such consumers and the persons who provide such services or make such facilities available, or who are suppliers of such apparatus or directories[14];

(i)   the provision of remedies and redress in respect of matters that form the subject matter of such complaints or disputes[15];

(j)   the information about service standards and the rights of consumers that is made available by persons who provide or make available such services or facilities, or who are suppliers of such apparatus or directories[16];

(k)   any other matter appearing to the Consumer Panel to be necessary for securing effective protection for persons who are consumers in the markets for any such services, facilities, apparatus or directories[17].

The matters about which the Consumer Panel is to be able to give advice do not include any matter that concerns the contents of anything which is or may be broadcast or otherwise transmitted by means of electronic communications networks[18]. The arrangements made by OFCOM under these provisions must also secure that the Consumer Panel is able, in addition to giving advice on the matters mentioned above[19], to do each of the following:

(i)   at the request of OFCOM, to carry out research for it in relation to any of the matters in relation to which OFCOM has functions[20];

(ii)   to make arrangements for the carrying out of research into such other matters appearing to the Consumer Panel to be relevant to the carrying out of the Consumer Panel's functions as it thinks fit[21];

(iii)   to give advice to OFCOM in relation to any matter referred to the Consumer Panel by OFCOM for advice[22];

(iv)   to publish such information as the Consumer Panel thinks fit about the advice it gives, about the carrying out of its other functions and about the results of research carried out by it or on its behalf[23].

It is the duty of OFCOM, in the carrying out of its functions, to consider and, to such extent as it thinks appropriate, to have regard to any advice given to it by the Consumer Panel and any results notified to it of any research undertaken by the Consumer Panel[24].

It is the duty of OFCOM[25]:

(A)   to provide the Consumer Panel with all such information as, having regard, in particular, to the need to preserve commercial confidentiality, it considers appropriate to disclose to the Consumer Panel for the purpose of enabling the Consumer Panel to carry out its functions[26]; and

(B)   to provide the Consumer Panel with all such further information as the Consumer Panel may require[27].

It is the duty of OFCOM, in the case of any advice or opinion received from and published by the Consumer Panel which OFCOM proposes to disregard in whole or in part, or with which OFCOM disagrees in whole or in part, to ensure that the Consumer Panel knows OFCOM's reasons for disregarding or disagreeing with the advice or opinion; and to ensure that those reasons are or have been published in such manner as OFCOM considers appropriate for bringing them to the attention of persons who are aware of the Consumer Panel's advice or opinion[28].

As from 29 December 2003[29], the Consumer Panel, must as soon as practicable after the end of the period of 12 months, and as soon as practicable after the end of each subsequent period of 12 months, prepare a report on the carrying out of its functions in that period[30].

1   As to the meaning of 'OFCOM' see PARA 14 note 1; and as to the establishment of OFCOM see PARA 2.

2   Communications Act 2003 s 16(1)(a).

3   Communications Act 2003 s 16(1)(b).

4   Communications Act 2003 s 16(1)(c). As to the meaning of 'consumer' see PARA 16 note 4. As to the meanings of 'electronic communications network' and 'electronic communications service' see PARA 53.

5   Communications Act 2003 s 16(2). For the purposes of the Communications Act 2003, the 'Consumer Panel' means the panel established under s 16: s 405(1). As to membership, committees and procedure of the Consumer Panel see PARA 29.

6   For the purposes of the Communications Act 2003 s 16, 'domestic and small business consumer' means a person who:

    (1)   is a consumer in the market for services or facilities mentioned in s 16(4) (see note 8) or for apparatus designed or adapted for use in connection with any such services or facilities; but

    (2)   is neither:

        (a)   a communications provider (see PARA 17 note 23) or a person who makes associated facilities (see PARA 53) available; nor

        (b)   a person who is a consumer in the market in respect of an undertaking carried on by him for which more than ten individuals work (whether as employees or volunteers or otherwise): s 16(13).

7   Communications Act 2003 s 16(3)(a). The Secretary of State may by order modify s 16(3) so as to add to the matters about which the Consumer Panel is required to be able to give advice: see s 19(1). Before making such an order the Secretary of State must consult OFCOM and such other persons as he thinks fit: s 19(2). No order is to be made containing provision authorised by s 19 unless a draft of the order has been laid before Parliament and approved by a resolution of each House: s 19(3). The power to amend or revoke an order under s 19 does not include power to provide for a matter to cease to be a matter about which the Consumer Panel is required to be able to give advice: s 19(4). At the date at which this volume states the law, no such order has been made. As to the power of the Secretary of State to make orders under the Communications Act 2003 see s 402; and PARA 74. As to the Secretary of State see PARA 76 note 1.

8   Communications Act 2003 s 16(3)(b). Those services and facilities are:

    (1)   electronic communications services (s 16(4)(a));

    (2)   associated facilities (s 16(4)(b));

    (3)   directory enquiry facilities (s 16(4)(c));

    (4)   a service consisting in the supply of information for use in responding to directory enquiries or of an electronic programme guide (s 16(4)(d) (amended by the Postal Services Act 2011 Sch 12 para 59); and

    (5)   every service or facility not falling within any of the preceding heads which is provided or made available to members of the public:

        (a)   by means of an electronic communications network (Communications Act 2003 s 16(4)(e)(i)); and

        (b)   in pursuance of agreements entered into between the person by whom the service or facility is provided or made available and each of those members of the public (s 16(4)(e)(ii));

    (6)   postal services (s 16(4)(f) (added by the Postal Services Act 2011 Sch 12 para 59)).

'Electronic programme guide' means a service which consists of:

    (i)   the listing or promotion, or both the listing and the promotion, of some or all of the programmes included in any one or more programme services the providers of which are or include persons other than the provider of the guide; and

    (ii)   a facility for obtaining access, in whole or in part, to the programme service or services listed or promoted in the guide: Communications Act 2003 s 16(13).

References in the Communications Act 2003 to access in relation to a programme service are references to the opportunity of viewing in an intelligible form the programmes included in the service or (as the case may be) of listening to them in such a form: s 405(4)(b). For the purposes of the Communications Act 2003, something is not to be regarded as in an intelligible form if it cannot readily be understood without being decrypted or having some comparable process applied to it: s 405(9). For the purposes of the Communications Act 2003, the fact that a service

is not in an intelligible form will be disregarded, except where express provision is made to the contrary, in determining whether it has been provided:
    (A)   for general reception (s 405(8)(a));
    (B)   for reception by particular persons (s 405(8)(b)); or
    (C)   for reception at a particular place or in a particular area (s 405(8)(c)). See note 7.

9   Communications Act 2003 s 16(3)(c) (amended by the Postal Services Act 2011 Sch 12 para 59). As to the services or facilities see note 8. See note 7.

10 Communications Act 2003 s 16(3)(d). See note 7.

11 Communications Act 2003 s 16(3)(e) (amended by the Postal Services Act 2011 Sch 12 para 59). As to the services or facilities see note 8. See note 7.

12 Communications Act 2003 s 16(3)(f). See note 7.

13 Communications Act 2003 s 16(3)(g). See note 7.

14 Communications Act 2003 s 16(3)(h). See note 7.

15 Communications Act 2003 s 16(3)(i). See note 7.

16 Communications Act 2003 s 16(3)(j). See note 7.

17 Communications Act 2003 s 16(3)(k). See note 7.

18 Communications Act 2003 s 16(5).

19 Ie mentioned in the Communications Act 2003 s 16(3): see heads (a)–(k) in the text.

20 Communications Act 2003 s 16(6)(a). The functions referred to in head (i) in the text to this note are those under s 14 (see PARA 26): s 16(6)(a).

21 Communications Act 2003 s 16(6)(b).

22 Communications Act 2003 s 16(6)(c).

23 Communications Act 2003 s 16(6)(d).

24 Communications Act 2003 s 16(7).

25 Ie subject to the Communications Act 2003 s 16(9): see note 27.

26 Communications Act 2003 s 16(8)(a).

27 Communications Act 2003 s 16(8)(b). OFCOM is not required to provide information by virtue of head (B) in the text if, having regard to:
    (1)   the need to preserve commercial confidentiality; and
    (2)   any other matters that appear to OFCOM to be relevant,
    it is reasonable for OFCOM to refuse to disclose it to the Consumer Panel: s 16(9).

28 Communications Act 2003 s 16(10).

29 Ie the commencement of the Communications Act 2003 s 16 (see the Office of Communications Act 2002 (Commencement No 3) and Communications Act 2003 (Commencement No 2) Order 2003, SI 2003/3142).

30 Communications Act 2003 s 16(11). The Consumer Panel must publish each report as soon as practicable after its preparation is complete and in such manner as it considers appropriate: s 16(12).

29. The Consumer Panel. The members of the Consumer Panel[1] are to be appointed by OFCOM[2] and comprise a chairman and such other members as OFCOM may determine[3]. The approval of the Secretary of State[4] is required for the appointment of a person to be the chairman or to be another member of the Panel[5].

In appointing persons to be members of the Consumer Panel, OFCOM must secure that, for each of the following parts of the United Kingdom:
    (1)   England,
    (2)   Scotland,
    (3)   Wales and
    (4)   Northern Ireland,
there is a different member of the Panel capable of representing the interests and opinions of persons living in that part of the United Kingdom[6].

In appointing persons to be members of the Consumer Panel, OFCOM must secure, so far as practicable, that the Panel is able to give informed advice about matters referable to each of the following:
    (a)   the interests of persons living in rural areas[7];
    (b)   the interests of persons living in urban areas[8];
    (c)   the interests of small businesses[9];

(d)   the interests of disadvantaged persons, persons with low incomes and persons with disabilities[10]; and

(e)   the interests of the elderly[11].

The Secretary of State may direct OFCOM to appoint as a member of the Consumer Panel a person specified by the Secretary of State who is an employee of the National Association of Citizens Advice Bureaux ('Citizens Advice')[12] or as the case may be, Citizens Advice Scotland, and is nominated for this purpose by Citizens Advice or as the case may be, Citizens Advice Scotland, after consultation with OFCOM[13].

The validity of any proceedings of the Consumer Panel is not affected by any failure by OFCOM to comply with the statutory requirements[14] as to the qualification of members to be appointed[15].

It is the duty of the Consumer Panel, in carrying out its functions, to have regard to the following interests:

(i)   the interests of persons from the different parts of the United Kingdom[16]; and

(ii)   the interests specified in heads (a) to (e) above[17].

The Consumer Panel may make such arrangements as it thinks fit for committees established by the Panel to give advice to it about matters relating to the carrying out of the Panel's functions[18] and may make such other arrangements for regulating its own procedure, and for regulating the procedure of the committees established by it, as it thinks fit[19]. The committees established by the Panel may include committees the membership of which includes persons (including persons constituting a majority of the committee) who are not members of the Panel[20], but the membership of every committee established by the Consumer Panel must contain at least one person who is a member of the Panel[21].

1   As to the meaning of 'Consumer Panel' see PARA 28 note 5.

2   As to the meaning of 'OFCOM' see PARA 14 note 1; and as to the establishment of OFCOM see PARA 2.

3   Communications Act 2003 s 17(1). A person is disqualified from being the chairman or a member of the Consumer Panel if he is a member or employee of OFCOM: s 17(7). As to members and employees of OFCOM see PARAS 3–5. The chairman and every member of the Consumer Panel:

     (1)   is be appointed for a fixed period specified in the terms of his appointment but is eligible for re-appointment at the end of that period (s 17(8)(a)); and

     (2)   may at any time be removed from the Panel by a notice given by OFCOM with the approval of the Secretary of State (s 17(8)(b)).

     OFCOM may pay to the chairman and to any other member of the Consumer Panel such remuneration and allowances as OFCOM consider appropriate: s 17(9).

4   As to the Secretary of State see PARA 76 note 1.

5   Communications Act 2003 s 17(2).

6   Communications Act 2003 s 17(3). As to the meaning of 'United Kingdom' see PARA 14 note 7.

7   Communications Act 2003 s 17(4)(a).

8   Communications Act 2003 s 17(4)(b).

9   Communications Act 2003 s 17(4)(c).

10   Communications Act 2003 s 17(4)(d).

11   Communications Act 2003 s 17(4)(e).

12   As to the National Association of Citizens Advice Bureaux see CONSUMER PROTECTION vol 21 (2011) PARA 770.

13   Communications Act 2003 s 17(4A), (4BA) (s 17(4A) added by the Consumers, Estate Agents and Redress Act 2007 s 40 and substituted by SI 2014/631; Communications Act 2003 s 17(4BA) added by SI 2014/631). Only one person may, at any time, be a member of the Consumer Panel appointed in accordance with a direction under the Communications Act 2003 s 17(4A); but that does not prevent OFCOM appointing as a member of the Consumer Panel any person who is also an employee of Citizens Advice or as the case may be, Citizens Advice

Scotland: s 17(4B), (4BB) (s 17(4B) added by the Consumers, Estate Agents and Redress Act 2007 s 40 and amended by SI 2014/631; Communications Act 2003 s 17(4BB) added by SI 2014/631). A person appointed in accordance with a direction under the Communications Act 2003 s 17(4A) or (4BA) ceases to be a member of the Panel:

    (1)   on ceasing to be an employee of Citizens Advice or, as the case may be, Citizens Advice Scotland (s 17(4C)(a) (s 17(4C) added by the Consumers, Estate Agents and Redress Act 2007 s 40 and amended by SI 2014/631));

    (2)   if Citizens Advice or, as the case may be, Citizens Advice Scotland decide that the person is no longer to be on the Consumer Panel (Communications Act 2003 s 17(4C)(b) (as so added and amended)).

14 Ie the Communications Act 2003 s 17(3)–(4A), (4BA).

15 Communications Act 2003 s 17(5) (amended by the Consumers, Estate Agents and Redress Act 2007 s 40(b); and SI 2014/631).

16 Communications Act 2003 s 17(6)(a).

17 Communications Act 2003 s 17(6)(b).

18 Communications Act 2003 s 18(1).

19 Communications Act 2003 s 18(2). Those arrangements may include arrangements as to quorums and as to the making of decisions by a majority: s 18(3).

20 Communications Act 2003 s 18(4). Where a person who is not a member of the Consumer Panel is a member of a committee established by the Panel, OFCOM may pay to that person such remuneration and expenses as OFCOM may determine: s 18(6).

21 Communications Act 2003 s 18(5).

F. ADVISORY COMMITTEES

30. Advisory committees for different parts of the United Kingdom. It is the duty of OFCOM[1], to exercise its powers[2] to establish and maintain a committee for each of the following parts of the United Kingdom;

    (1)   England;

    (2)   Wales;

    (3)   Scotland; and

    (4)   Northern Ireland[3].

Each committee is to consist of:

    (a)   a chairman appointed by OFCOM[4]; and

    (b)   such number of other members appointed by OFCOM as OFCOM thinks fit[5].

In appointing a person in accordance with these provisions[6] to be a member of a committee, OFCOM must have regard to the desirability of ensuring that the person appointed is able to represent the interests and opinions, in relation to communications matters[7], of persons living in the part of the United Kingdom for which the committee has been established[8]. The function of each committee is to provide advice to OFCOM (including other committees established by OFCOM) about the interests and opinions, in relation to communications matters, of persons living in the part of the United Kingdom for which the committee has been established[9]. A committee established under these provisions may also, at the request of the Consumer Panel[10], provide advice about those interests and opinions to the Consumer Panel[11].

1 As to the meaning of 'OFCOM' see PARA 14 note 1; and as to the establishment of OFCOM see PARA 2.

2 Ie under the Office of Communications Act 2002 Schedule para 14 (committees of OFCOM: see PARA 9).

3 Communications Act 2003 s 20(1). As to the meaning of 'United Kingdom' see PARA 14 note 7.

4 Communications Act 2003 s 20(2)(a).

5 Communications Act 2003 s 20(2)(b).

6 Ie in accordance with the Communications Act 2003 s 20.

7 For the purposes of the Communications Act 2003 s 20, 'communications matters' has the same meaning as in s 3 (see PARA 16 note 3): s 20(7).
8 Communications Act 2003 s 20(3).
9 Communications Act 2003 s 20(4).
10 As to the Consumer Panel see PARAS 28–29.
11 Communications Act 2003 s 20(5). The consent of OFCOM is required for the giving of advice under s 20(5): s 20(6).

31. Advisory committee on elderly and disabled persons. It is the duty of OFCOM[1], to exercise its powers[2] to establish and maintain a committee to provide the specified advice[3].

The committee is to consist of:
(1)   a chairman appointed by OFCOM[4]; and
(2)   such number of other members appointed by OFCOM as OFCOM thinks fit[5].

In appointing persons to be members of the committee, OFCOM must have regard to the desirability of ensuring that the members of the committee include:
(a)   persons who are familiar with the needs of the elderly[6]; and
(b)   persons who are familiar with the needs of persons with disabilities[7].

The function of the committee is to provide advice to OFCOM (including other committees established by OFCOM) about the interests, in relation to communications matters[8], of:
(i)   the elderly[9]; and
(ii)   persons with disabilities[10].

The committee may also, at the request of the Consumer Panel, provide advice about those interests to the Consumer Panel[11].

1 As to the meaning of 'OFCOM' see PARA 14 note 1; and as to the establishment of OFCOM see PARA 2.
2 Ie under the Office of Communications Act 2002 Schedule para 14 (committees of OFCOM: see PARA 9).
3 Ie specified in the Communications Act 2003 s 21: s 21(1). See the text and notes 6–8.
4 Communications Act 2003 s 21(2)(a).
5 Communications Act 2003 s 21(2)(b).
6 Communications Act 2003 s 21(3)(a).
7 Communications Act 2003 s 21(3)(b).
8 For the purposes of the Communications Act 2003 s 21, 'communications matters' has the same meaning as in s 3 (see PARA 16 note 3): s 21(7).
9 Communications Act 2003 s 21(4)(a).
10 Communications Act 2003 s 21(4)(b).
11 Communications Act 2003 s 21(5). As to the Consumer Panel see PARAS 28–29. The consent of OFCOM is required for the giving of advice under s 21(5): s 21(6).

G. INTERNATIONAL MATTERS

32. Representation on international and other bodies. It is the duty of OFCOM[1] to do, as respects the United Kingdom[2], such of the following things as it is required to do by the Secretary of State[3]:
(1)   provide representation on behalf of Her Majesty's government in the United Kingdom on international and other bodies having communications functions[4];
(2)   become or serve as a member of an international or other body having such functions[5];
(3)   subscribe to such a body[6];
(4)   provide representation on behalf of Her Majesty's government in the United Kingdom at international meetings about communications[7].

OFCOM also has the power, if requested to do so by the Secretary of State, to do one or more of those things as respects any of the Channel Islands, the Isle of Man or a British overseas territory[8]. It is the duty of OFCOM to carry out its functions under these provisions[9] in accordance with such general or specific directions as may be given to it by the Secretary of State[10].

1   As to the meaning of 'OFCOM' see PARA 14 note 1; and as to the establishment of OFCOM see PARA 2.
2   As to the meaning of 'United Kingdom' see PARA 14 note 7.
3   As to the Secretary of State see PARA 76 note 1.
4   Communications Act 2003 s 22(1)(a). For the purposes of the Communications Act 2003 s 22, 'communications functions' means:
    (1)   functions relating to the use of the electro-magnetic spectrum for wireless telegraphy;
    (2)   functions relating to the regulation of television or radio broadcasting or the provision of television and radio services;
    (3)   functions relating to postal services; and
    (4)   any other function which relates to, or is connected with, a matter in respect of which OFCOM has functions: s 22(5) (amended by the Postal Services Act 2011 Sch 12 para 60).
    In relation to:
    (a)   a part of the British Islands outside the United Kingdom; or
    (b)   a British overseas territory,
the references in the Communications Act 2003 s 22(5) to matters in respect of which OFCOM has functions include references to matters corresponding, in the case of that part of those Islands or of that territory, to matters in respect of which OFCOM's functions are confined to the United Kingdom: s 22(6).
    For the purposes of s 22(5), 'television or radio broadcasting' includes the provision by means other than broadcasting of services similar to those provided by television or radio broadcasts: s 22(7). 'British Islands' means the United Kingdom, the Channel Islands and the Isle of Man: Interpretation Act 1978 s 5, Sch 1. As to British overseas territories see COMMONWEALTH vol 13 (2009) PARA 702.
5   Communications Act 2003 s 22(1)(b).
6   Communications Act 2003 s 22(1)(c).
7   Communications Act 2003 s 22(1)(d). 'International meetings about communications' means international meetings relating to, or to matters connected with, one or more of the following:
    (1)   the use of the electro-magnetic spectrum for wireless telegraphy;
    (2)   the regulation of television or radio broadcasting or of the provision of television and radio services;
    (3)   the regulation of postal services;
    (4)   any other matter in respect of which OFCOM has functions: s 22(5) (amended by the Postal Services Act 2011 Sch 12 para 60).
8   Communications Act 2003 s 22(2).
9   Ie under the Communications Act 2003 s 22.
10   Communications Act 2003 s 22(3). The Secretary of State is not entitled to direct OFCOM to comply with a request made under s 22(2) (see the text and note 8), but may give directions about how OFCOM is to carry out any representative role that it undertakes in accordance with such a request: s 22(4).

33. Directions for international purposes in respect of broadcasting functions.
The following provisions[1] apply to:
    (1)   OFCOM's functions under the enactments relating to broadcasting[2]; and
    (2)   the matters in relation to which those functions are conferred[3].
It is the duty of OFCOM:
    (a)   to carry out those functions in accordance with any general or specific directions given to it by the Secretary of State for the purpose mentioned below[4]; and
    (b)   to carry out such other functions in relation to the matters to which these provisions[5] apply as it is required to carry out by any general or specific directions so given[6].

The Secretary of State must not give a direction under these provisions except for the purpose of securing compliance, in relation to a matter to which these provisions apply, with an international obligation of the United Kingdom[7]. A direction under these provisions must be contained in an order made by the Secretary of State[8].

1   Ie the Communications Act 2003 s 23.
2   Communications Act 2003 s 23(1)(a). For the purposes of the Communications Act 2003 s 23, 'enactments relating to broadcasting' means:
    (1)   the Broadcasting Act 1990;
    (2)   the Broadcasting Act 1996;
    (3)   the Communications Act 2003 Pt 3 (ss 198–362); and
    (4)   the other provisions of the Communications Act 2003 so far as relating to the Broadcasting Act 1990, the Broadcasting Act 1996 or the Communications Act 2003 Pt 3: ss 23(5), 405(1).
    As to broadcasting see BROADCASTING vol 4 (2011) PARA 504 et seq. As to the meaning of 'OFCOM' see PARA 14 note 1; and as to the establishment of OFCOM see PARA 2.
3   Communications Act 2003 s 23(1)(b).
4   Communications Act 2003 s 23(2)(a). The purpose referred to in the text is the purpose mentioned in the Communications Act 2003 s 23(3): see the text and note 7. As to the Secretary of State see PARA 76 note 1.
5   Ie the Communications Act 2003 s 23.
6   Communications Act 2003 s 23(2)(b).
7   Communications Act 2003 s 23(3). 'International obligation of the United Kingdom' includes any EU obligation and any obligation which will or may arise under any international agreement or arrangements to which the United Kingdom is a party: s 405(1). As to the meaning of 'United Kingdom' see PARA 14 note 7.
8   Communications Act 2003 s 23(4). As to the power of the Secretary of State to make orders under the Communications Act 2003 see s 402; and PARA 74.

H. INFORMATION

34. General information functions. It is the duty of OFCOM[1] to comply with a direction by the Secretary of State[2] to provide him with any information reasonably required by him for the purpose of enabling him to secure compliance with an international obligation of the United Kingdom[3].

OFCOM is under a duty to comply with a requirement to provide the European Commission[4] with information for the purpose of enabling it to perform any of its functions in relation to electronic communications networks or services or associated facilities[5], and must also provide information requested by the Body of European Regulators for Electronic Communications ('BEREC') and its supporting Office[6].

OFCOM must arrange for the publication of information and advice[7] for[8]:

(1)   the customers of communications providers[9];

(2)   the customers of persons who make associated facilities available[10];

(3)   any person affected by the application of the electronic communications code[11];

(4)   persons who use electronic communications networks, electronic communications services or associated facilities[12]; and

(5)   persons to whom radio and television services are provided or who are otherwise able or likely to take advantage of any of those services[13];

(6)   the customers of persons who provide postal services[14].

1   As to the meaning of 'OFCOM' see PARA 14 note 1; and as to the establishment of OFCOM see PARA 2.
2   As to the Secretary of State see PARA 76 note 1.

3   See the Communications Act 2003 s 24(1), (2). Information that is required to be provided by a
    direction under s 24 must be provided in such manner and at such times as may be required by
    the direction: s 24(3). As to the meaning of 'international obligation of the United Kingdom' see
    PARA 33 note 7. As to the meaning of 'United Kingdom' see PARA 14 note 7.
4   As to the European Commission see EUROPEAN UNION vol 47A (2014) PARAS 48, 49.
5   See the Communications Act 2003 s 25(1), (2). If information provided to the European
    Commission under s 25 has been obtained by OFCOM from a person who is or, at the time the
    information was obtained from him, was a communications provider or a person making
    associated facilities available, OFCOM must notify him that it has provided the information to
    the Commission: s 25(3). It is for OFCOM to determine the manner in which such a notification
    is given: s 25(4). As to the meanings of 'electronic communications network', 'electronic
    communications service' and 'associated facilities' see PARA 53. As to the meaning of
    'communications provider' see PARA 17 note 23.
6   See European Parliament and Council Regulation (EC) 1211/2009 establishing the Body of
    European Regulators for Electronic Communications (BEREC) and the Office (OJ L337, 18.
    12.2009, p 1) art 19. As to BEREC see PARA 58.
7   Ie about matters in relation to which it has functions as it appears to it to be appropriate to
    make available to the persons mentioned in heads (1)–(6) in the text: Communications Act 2003
    s 26(1) (amended by SI 2011/1210).
8   Communications Act 2003 s 26(1) (as amended: see note 7). The publication of information or
    advice under s 26 must be in such manner as OFCOM considers appropriate: s 26(6). In
    arranging for the publication of information or advice under s 26, OFCOM must have regard to
    the need to exclude from publication, so far as that is practicable, matters which are
    confidential: s 26(3). A matter is confidential if:
    (1)   it relates specifically to the affairs of a particular body (s 26(4)(a)); and
    (2)   publication of that matter would or might, in OFCOM's opinion, seriously and
          prejudicially affect the interests of that body (s 26(4)(b)).
    A matter is also confidential if:
    (a)   it relates to the private affairs of an individual (s 26(5)(a)); and
    (b)   publication of that matter would or might, in OFCOM's opinion, seriously and
          prejudicially affect the interests of that individual (s 26(5)(b)).
9   Communications Act 2003 s 26(2)(a).
10 Communications Act 2003 s 26(2)(b).
11 Communications Act 2003 s 26(2)(ba) (added by SI 2011/1210). As to the meaning of
    'electronic communications code' see the Telecommunications Act 1984 Sch 2; and PARA 155
    note 1; definition applied by the Communications Act 2003 s 26(2)(ba), 106(1) (s 26(2)(ba) (as
    so added)).
12 Communications Act 2003 s 26(2)(c) (amended by the Postal Services Act 2011 Sch 12 para 61).
13 Communications Act 2003 s 26(2)(d).
14 Communications Act 2003 s 26(2)(e). The reference to customers of persons who provide postal
    services includes persons who wish to be provided with such services, persons who are likely to
    seek to be provided with such services and addressees: s 26(2A) (added by the Postal Services
    Act 2011 Sch 12 para 61).

I. EMPLOYMENT IN BROADCASTING

35.   Training and equality of opportunity. It is the duty of OFCOM[1] to take
all such steps as it considers appropriate for promoting the development of
opportunities for the training and retraining of persons:
  (1)   for employment by persons providing television and radio services[2]; and
  (2)   for work in connection with the provision of such services otherwise
         than as an employee[3].
It is the duty of OFCOM to take all such steps as it considers appropriate for
promoting equality of opportunity[4] in relation to both:
  (a)   employment by those providing television and radio services[5]; and
  (b)   the training and retraining of persons for such employment[6].
It is also the duty of OFCOM, in relation to such employment, training and
retraining, to take all such steps as it considers appropriate for promoting the
equalisation of opportunities for disabled[7] persons[8].

1   As to the meaning of 'OFCOM' see PARA 14 note 1; and as to the establishment of OFCOM see PARA 2.
2   Communications Act 2003 s 27(1)(a). As to the provision of television and radio services see BROADCASTING vol 4 (2011) PARA 504 et seq.
3   Communications Act 2003 s 27(1)(b).
4   The reference in the Communications Act 2003 s 27(2) to equality of opportunity is a reference to equality of opportunity:
    (1)   between men and women (s 27(4)(a)); and
    (2)   between persons of different racial groups (s 27(4)(b)).
    For the purposes of s 27, 'racial group' has the same meaning as in the Equality Act 2010 (see DISCRIMINATION vol 33 (2013) PARA 61): Communications Act 2003 s 27(5) (amended by the Equality Act 2010 Sch 26 para 54). The Secretary of State may by order amend the Communications Act 2003 s 27(4) by adding any other form of equality of opportunity that he considers appropriate: s 27(6). No order is to be made containing provision authorised by s 27(6) unless a draft of the order has been laid before Parliament and approved by a resolution of each House: s 27(7). At the date at which this volume states the law, no such order has been made. As to the Secretary of State see PARA 76 note 1. As to the power of the Secretary of State to make orders under the Communications Act 2003 see s 402; and PARA 74.
5   Communications Act 2003 s 27(2)(a).
6   Communications Act 2003 s 27(2)(b).
7   For the purposes of the Communications Act 2003 s 27, 'disabled' has the same meaning as in the Equality Act 2010 (see DISCRIMINATION vol 33 (2013) PARA 50 et seq): Communications Act 2003 s 27(5).
8   Communications Act 2003 s 27(3).

J. CHARGING

36.   General power to charge for services.   OFCOM[1] may provide a service[2] to which these provisions[3] apply to any person on such terms as to the making of payments to OFCOM as it may determine in advance or as may be agreed between that person and OFCOM[4]. These provisions apply to a service which is provided by OFCOM to a person in the course of carrying out its functions and is neither:

(1)   a service which OFCOM is under a duty to provide to that person[5]; nor

(2)   one in respect of which express provision is made by or under an enactment for authorising or forbidding the payment of fees or charges[6].

1   As to the meaning of 'OFCOM' see PARA 14 note 1; and as to the establishment of OFCOM see PARA 2.
2   In the Communications Act 2003 s 28, references to providing a service to a person include references to a service consisting in:
    (1)   the giving of advice to that person (s 28(3)(a));
    (2)   the entry of his particulars in a register or other record kept by OFCOM otherwise than in pursuance of an express statutory duty to keep the register or record (s 28(3)(b)); or
    (3)   the taking of steps for the purposes of determining whether to grant an application for an entry in a register or record so kept (s 28(3)(c)).
3   Ie the Communications Act 2003 s 28.
4   Communications Act 2003 s 28(1).
5   Communications Act 2003 s 28(2)(a).
6   Communications Act 2003 s 28(2)(b).

K. GUARANTEES

37.   Guarantees by Secretary of State for OFCOM borrowing.   The Secretary of State[1] may guarantee:

(1)   the repayment of the principal of any borrowing by OFCOM[2];

(2)   the payment of interest on any such borrowing[3]; and

(3) the discharge of other financial obligations incurred by OFCOM in connection with any such borrowing[4].

The power of the Secretary of State to give such a guarantee is a power[5] to give it in such manner and on such conditions as he thinks fit[6]. The Secretary of State must not give a guarantee under these provisions if the aggregate of:

(a) the amounts that he may be required to pay for fulfilling that guarantee[7]; and

(b) the amounts that he may be required to pay for fulfilling other guarantees previously given under these provisions and still in force[8],

exceeds £5 million[9].

Immediately after a guarantee is given under these provisions, the Secretary of State must lay a statement of the guarantee before each House of Parliament[10]. Where any sum is paid by the Secretary of State under a guarantee given under these provisions, he must lay a statement relating to that sum before each House of Parliament as soon as practicable after the end of each of the financial years beginning with the one in which the sum is paid and ending with the one in which OFCOM's liabilities[11] in respect of that sum are finally discharged[12]. If sums are paid by the Secretary of State in fulfilment of a guarantee, OFCOM must pay him such amounts in or towards the repayment to him of those sums as he may direct, and interest at such rates as he may determine on amounts outstanding under this provision[13].

1 As to the Secretary of State see PARA 76 note 1.
2 Communications Act 2003 s 29(1)(a). As to the meaning of 'OFCOM' see PARA 14 note 1; and as to the establishment of OFCOM see PARA 2.
3 Communications Act 2003 s 29(1)(b).
4 Communications Act 2003 s 29(1)(c).
5 Ie subject to the Communications Act 2003 s 29(3): see the text and notes 7–9.
6 Communications Act 2003 s 29(2).
7 Communications Act 2003 s 29(3)(a).
8 Communications Act 2003 s 29(3)(b).
9 Communications Act 2003 s 29(3). The Secretary of State may by order substitute another amount for the amount for the time being specified in s 29(3): s 29(4). No order is to be made containing provision authorised by s 29(4) unless a draft of the order has been laid before Parliament and approved by a resolution of the House of Commons: s 29(5). At the date at which this volume states the law, no such order has been made. As to the power of the Secretary of State to make orders under the Communications Act 2003 see s 402; and PARA 74.
10 Communications Act 2003 s 29(6).
11 Ie under the Communications Act 2003 s 29(8): see the text and note 13.
12 Communications Act 2003 s 29(7).
13 Communications Act 2003 s 29(8). Payments to the Secretary of State under s 29(8) must be made at such times and in such manner as he may determine: s 29(9).

L. COMPETITION

38. Functions of OFCOM under competition legislation. The functions of the Competition and Markets Authority relating to market studies and market investigations[1] so far as those functions are exercisable by the Competition and Markets Authority Board[2] and relate to commercial activities connected with communications matters[3], are concurrent functions of OFCOM and the Competition and Markets Authority[4]. Before the Competition and Markets Authority or OFCOM first exercises in relation to any matter functions which are exercisable concurrently by virtue of these provisions, it must consult the other[5]. Neither the Competition and Markets Authority nor OFCOM may exercise in relation to any matter functions which are exercisable concurrently by virtue of these provisions if functions which are so exercisable have been exercised in relation to that matter by the other[6].

It is the duty of OFCOM, for the purpose of assisting a Competition and Markets Authority group[7] in carrying out an investigation on a market investigation reference made by OFCOM[8], to give to the group:

(1)   any information which is in OFCOM's possession and relates to matters falling within the scope of the investigation and which:

      (a)   is requested by the group for that purpose[9]; or

      (b)   is information which, in OFCOM's opinion, it would be appropriate for that purpose to give to the group without any such request[10]; and

(2)   any other assistance which the group may require, and which it is within OFCOM's power to give, in relation to any such matters[11],

and the group, for the purposes of carrying out any such investigation, must take into account any information given to it for that purpose[12].

If any question arises as to whether, by virtue of these provisions, any functions fall to be, or are capable of being, carried out by OFCOM in relation to any particular case, that question must be referred to and determined by the Secretary of State[13].

No objection may be taken to anything done under the functions relating to market studies and market investigations[14] by or in relation to OFCOM on the ground that it should have been done by or in relation to the Competition and Markets Authority[15].

Provision is also made with respect to OFCOM's functions under the Competition Act 1998[16]. Specified functions[17] under the Competition Act 1998 are concurrent functions of OFCOM and the Competition and Markets Authority[18]. OFCOM may carry out, in respect of activities connected with communications matters and concurrently with the Competition and Markets Authority, specified functions[19] of the Competition and Markets Authority[20]. If any question arises as to whether, by virtue of these provisions, any functions fall to be, or are capable of being, carried out by OFCOM in relation to a particular case, that question must be referred to and determined by the Secretary of State[21]. No objection may be taken to anything done under by or in relation to OFCOM under the Competition Act 1998 on the ground that it should have been done by or in relation to the Competition and Markets Authority[22]. The statutory requirements as to the general duties of OFCOM[23] and the duty to secure provision of universal postal service[24] do not apply in relation to anything done by OFCOM in the carrying out of its functions by virtue of the above provisions[25], but in the carrying out of any functions by virtue of the above provisions OFCOM may nevertheless have regard to any of the matters in respect of which a duty is imposed on it[26] if it is a matter to which the Competition and Markets Authority is entitled to have regard in the carrying out of those functions[27].

1   Ie under the Enterprise Act 2002 Pt 4 (ss 130A–184) (market studies and market investigations: see COMPETITION vol 18 (2009) PARA 276 et seq), other than ss 166, 171, 174E: Communications Act 2003 s 370(2) (amended by SI 2014/892). See note 4. As to the Competition and Markets Authority see COMPETITION vol 18 (2009) PARA 23A. In the Communications Act 2003 s 370(2), (3A), the reference to activities connected with communications matters, so far as they are reference to activities connected with any apparatus falling within s 369(1)(d) (see note 3 head (4)), includes a reference to the supply and export of any such apparatus and the production or acquisition of any such apparatus for supply or export: s 370(4).

2   Ie within the meaning of the Enterprise and Regulatory Reform Act 2013 Sch 4 (see COMPETITION vol 18 (2009) PARA 23A): Communications Act 2003 s 370(2) (as amended: see note 1). See note 4.

3   In the Communications Act 2003 Pt 5 Ch 1 (ss 369–372), references to communications matters are references to any one or more of the following:

(1)   the provision of electronic communications networks (s 369(1)(a));
(2)   the provision of electronic communications services (s 369(1)(b));
(3)   the provision or making available of services or facilities which are provided or made available:

(a)   by means of, or in association with the provision (by the same person or another) of, an electronic communications network or electronic communications service (s 369(1)(c)(i))); or

(b)   for the purpose of facilitating the use of any such network or service (whether provided by the same person or another) (s 369(1)(c)(ii));

(4)   apparatus used for providing or making available anything mentioned in heads (1)–(3) (s 369(1)(d));
(5)   broadcasting and related matters (s 369(1)(e));
(6)   the provision of postal services (s 369(1)(f) (added by the Postal Services Act 2011 Sch 12 para 62)).

As to the meaning of 'electronic communications network' see PARA 53. As to the meaning of 'electronic communications service' see PARA 53.

The Secretary of State may by order make such amendments of the Communications Act 2003 s 369(1) as he may consider appropriate for the purpose of modifying the description of activities in respect of which any of the provisions of Pt 5 (ss 369–389):

(i)   confer functions on OFCOM under the Competition Act 1998 Pt I or relate to the carrying out by OFCOM of those functions (Communications Act 2003 s 369(2)(a)); or

(ii)   confer functions on OFCOM under the Enterprise Act 2002 Pt 4 or relate to the carrying out by OFCOM of those functions (Communications Act 2003 s 369(2)(b)).

No order is to be made containing provision authorised by s 369 unless a draft of the order has been laid before Parliament and approved by a resolution of each House: s 369(3). At the date at which this volume states the law, no such order has been made. As to the Secretary of State see PARA 76 note 1. As to the power of the Secretary of State to make orders under the Communications Act 2003 see s 402; and PARA 74. As to the meaning of 'OFCOM' see PARA 14 note 1; and as to the establishment of OFCOM see PARA 2.

4   Communications Act 2003 s 370(1) (amended by SI 2014/892). So far as necessary for the purposes of, or in connection with, the Communications Act 2003 s 370(1), (2), references in the Enterprise Act 2002 Pt 4 to the Competition and Markets Authority (including references in provisions of the Enterprise Act 2002 applied by Pt 4) are to be construed as including references to OFCOM except in ss 166, 171, 174E and where the context otherwise requires: Communications Act 2003 s 370(3) (amended by SI 2014/892).

Where OFCOM:

(1)   is proposing to fulfil its duties under the Communications Act 2003 s 3(1) by obtaining, compiling and keeping under review information in relation to a matter for the purposes of considering the extent to which a matter in relation to commercial activities connected with communications matters (within the meaning given by s 369(1): see note 3) has or may have effects adverse to the interests of consumers and assessing the extent to which steps can and should be taken to remedy, mitigate or prevent any such adverse effects; and

(2)   considers that the matter is one in respect of which it would be appropriate for it to exercise its powers under the Enterprise Act 2002 s 174 (investigation) in connection with deciding whether to make a reference under s 131,

OFCOM must publish a notice under the Enterprise Act 2002 s 130A ('market study notice'): see the Communications Act 2003 s 370(3A); Enterprise Act 2002 s 130A(1), (2); (Communications Act 2003 s 370(3A) added by SI 2014/892; Enterprise Act 2002 s 130A added by the Enterprise and Regulatory Reform Act 2013 Sch 12 para 1). See also note 1.

5   Communications Act 2003 s 370(5) (amended by SI 2014/892).

6   Communications Act 2003 s 370(6) (amended by SI 2014/892).

7   In the Communications Act 2003 s 370(7), 'CMA group' has the same meaning as in the Enterprise and Regulatory Reform Act 2013 Sch 4: Communications Act 2003 s 370(7A) (added by SI 2014/892).

8   Ie under the Enterprise Act 2002 s 131 by virtue of the Communications Act 2003 s 370(1).

9   Communications Act 2003 s 370(7)(a)(i) (s 370(7) amended by SI 2014/892).

10   Communications Act 2003 s 370(7)(a)(ii) (as amended: see note 9).

11 Communications Act 2003 s 370(7)(b) (as amended: see note 9).
12 Communications Act 2003 s 370(7) (as amended: see note 9). The purpose referred to in the text is that under the Communications Act 2003 s 370(7): s 370(7).
13 Communications Act 2003 s 370(8).
14 Ie under the Enterprise Act 2002 Pt 4 (ss 130A–184) (market studies and market investigations: see COMPETITION vol 18 (2009) PARA 276 et seq).
15 Communications Act 2003 s 370(9) (amended by SI 2014/892). The Enterprise Act 2002 s 117 (offences of supplying false or misleading information: see COMPETITION vol 18 (2009) PARA 134) as applied by s 180 has effect so far as relating to functions exercisable by OFCOM by virtue of the Communications Act 2003 s 370 as if the references in the Enterprise Act 2002 s 117(1)(a), (2) to the Competition and Markets Authority included references to OFCOM: Communications Act 2003 s 370(10) (amended by SI 2014/892). Subject to the Communications Act 2003 s 370(12), the provisions of s 3 (see PARA 16) and the Postal Services Act 2011 s 29 (duty to secure provision of universal postal service: see POSTAL SERVICES vol 85 (2012) PARA 250) do not apply in relation to anything done by OFCOM in the carrying out of its functions by virtue of the Communications Act 2003 s 370: s 370(11) (amended by the Postal Services Act 2011 Sch 12 para 63). In the carrying out of any functions by virtue of the Communications Act 2003 s 370, OFCOM may nevertheless have regard to any of the matters in respect of which a duty is imposed by s 3(1)–(4) or the Postal Services Act 2011 s 29 if it is a matter to which the Competition and Markets Authority is entitled to have regard in the carrying out of those functions: Communications Act 2003 s 370(12) (amended by the Postal Services Act 2011 Sch 12 para 63; and SI 2014/982).
16 See the Communications Act 2003 s 371; and text and notes 17–27.
17 Ie the functions of the Competition and Markets Authority which relate to activities connected with communications matters under the provisions of the Competition Act 1998 Pt I (ss 1–60) (other than ss 31D(1)–(6), 38(1)–(6), 40B(1)–(4) and 51), so far as relating to
    (1)   agreements, decisions or concerted practices of the kind mentioned in s 2(1) (see COMPETITION vol 18 (2009) PARA 116) (s 371(2)(a) (s 371(2) substituted by SI 2004/1261; and amended by the Enterprise and Regulatory Reform Act 2013 Sch 15 para 46; and SI 2014/892);
    (2)   conduct of the kind mentioned in the Competition Act 1998 s 18(1) (see COMPETITION vol 18 (2009) PARA 125) (s 371(2)(b) (as so substituted and amended));
    (3)   agreements, decisions or concerted practices of the kind mentioned in the Treaty on the Functioning of the European Union (Rome, 25 March 1957; TS 1 (1973); Cmnd 5179) art 101(1) (Communications Act 2003 s 371(2(c) (as so substituted and amended; s 371(2)(c) further amended by SI 2012/1809));
    (4)   conduct which amounts to abuse of the kind mentioned in the Treaty on the Functioning of the European Union (Rome, 25 March 1957; TS 1 (1973); Cmnd 5179) art 102 (Communications Act 2003 s 371(2)(d) (as so substituted and amended; s 371(2)(d) further amended by SI 2012/1809)).
The Treaty was formerly known as the Treaty Establishing the European Community; it has been renamed and its provisions renumbered: see PARA 17 note 17; and EUROPEAN UNION vol 47A (2014) PARA 3 et seq. The reference to activities connected with communications matters, so far as it is a reference to activities connected with any apparatus falling the Communications Act 2003 s 369(1)(d) (see note 3 head (4)), includes a reference to the supply and export of any such apparatus and the production or acquisition of any such apparatus for supply or export: s 371(4).
18 Communications Act 2003 s 371(1) (amended by SI 2014/892). So far as necessary for the purposes of, or in connection with, the provisions of the Communications Act 2003 s 371(1) and (2), references to the Competition and Markets Authority in the Competition Act 1998 Pt I are to be read as including references to OFCOM, except in ss 31D(1)–(6), 38(1)–(6), 40B(1)–(4), 51, 52(6), (8) and 54; and where the context otherwise requires (Communications Act 2003 s 371(3) (amended by the Enterprise and Regulatory Reform Act 2013 Sch 15 para 46; SI 2004/1261; and SI 2014/892)), and specified further amendments are made for these purposes to the Competition Act 1998 ss 54(1)(a), (4), 59(1), Sch 2 para 5(2), (3) (Communications Act 2003 s 371(5)–(7) (s 371(5) amended by SI 2014/892).
19 Ie functions under any of the Competition Act 1998 Sch 13 paras 3, 7, 19(3), 36–39 (transitional provisions).
20 Communications Act 2003 s 371(8) (amended by SI 2014/892).
21 Communications Act 2003 s 371(9).
22 Communications Act 2003 s 371(10) (amended by SI 2014/892).
23 Ie the Communications Act 2003 s 3: see PARA 16.
24 Ie the Postal Services Act 2011 s 29.

25 Communications Act 2003 s 371(11) (amended by the Postal Services Act 2011 Sch 12 para 64).
26 Ie by the Communications Act 2003 s 3(1)–(4) (see PARA 16 text and notes 1–34) or the Postal Services Act 2011 s 29.
27 Communications Act 2003 s 371(12) (amended by the Postal Services Act 2011 Sch 12 para 64; and SI 2014/892).

(iii) Administrative Provisions

39. Regulations and orders made by OFCOM. Where any power of OFCOM[1] to make regulations or to make an order or scheme is one to which these provisions[2] are expressly applied, the power is exercisable by statutory instrument, and the Statutory Instruments Act 1946[3] is to apply in relation to those powers as if OFCOM were a Minister of the Crown[4]. Where an instrument made under a power to which these provisions apply falls to be laid before Parliament, OFCOM must, immediately after it is made, send it to the Secretary of State[5] for laying by him[6]. Before making any regulations or order under a power to which these provisions apply, OFCOM must[7]:

(1) give a notice[8] of its proposal to do so to such persons representative of the persons appearing to OFCOM to be likely to be affected by the implementation of the proposal as OFCOM thinks fit[9];

(2) publish notice of its proposal in such manner as it considers appropriate for bringing it to the attention of the persons who, in its opinion, are likely to be affected by it and are not given notice by virtue of head (1) above[10]; and

(3) consider any representations that are made to OFCOM, before the time specified in the notice[11].

Every power of OFCOM to which these provisions apply includes power[12]:

(a) to make different provision for different cases (including different provision in respect of different areas)[13];

(b) to make provision subject to such exemptions and exceptions as OFCOM thinks fit[14]; and

(c) to make such incidental, supplemental, consequential and transitional provision as OFCOM thinks fit[15].

1 As to the meaning of 'OFCOM' see PARA 14 note 1; and as to the establishment of OFCOM see PARA 2.
2 Ie the Communications Act 2003 s 403.
3 As to the Statutory Instruments Act 1946 see STATUTES AND LEGISLATIVE PROCESS vol 96 (2012) PARA 1045 et seq.
4 Communications Act 2003 s 403(1), (2). In addition, the Documentary Evidence Act 1868 (proof of orders and regulations etc) (see CIVIL PROCEDURE vol 11 (2009) PARAS 892–894) is to have effect as if OFCOM were included in the first column of the Schedule to that Act, and OFCOM and persons authorised to act on its behalf were mentioned in the second column of that Schedule: Communications Act 2003 s 403(8).
5 As to the Secretary of State see PARA 76 note 1.
6 Communications Act 2003 s 403(3).
7 Communications Act 2003 s 403(4).
8 A notice for the purposes of the Communications Act 2003 s 403(4) must:
    (1) state that OFCOM proposes to make the regulations or order in question (s 403(5)(a));
    (2) set out the general effect of the regulations or order (s 403(5)(b));
    (3) specify an address from which a copy of the proposed regulations or order may be obtained (s 403(5)(c)); and
    (4) specify a time before which any representations with respect to the proposal must be made to OFCOM (s 403(5)(d)).
The time specified for the purpose of representations must be no earlier than the end of the period of one month beginning with the day after the latest day on which the notice is given or published: s 403(6).

9   Communications Act 2003 s 403(4)(a).
10 Communications Act 2003 s 403(4)(b).
11 Communications Act 2003 s 403(4)(c).
12 Communications Act 2003 s 403(7).
13 Communications Act 2003 s 403(7)(a).
14 Communications Act 2003 s 403(7)(b).
15 Communications Act 2003 s 403(7)(c).

40. Penalties imposed by OFCOM. It is the duty of OFCOM[1] to prepare and publish a statement containing the guidelines it proposes to follow in determining the amount of penalties imposed by it under provisions contained in the Communications Act 2003 or any other enactment apart from the Competition Act 1998[2]. OFCOM may from time to time revise that statement as it thinks fit[3]. Where OFCOM makes or revises its statement, it must publish the statement or (as the case may be) the revised statement in such manner as it considers appropriate for bringing it to the attention of the persons who, in its opinion, are likely to be affected by it[4]. Before publishing such a statement or revised statement OFCOM must consult both the Secretary of State[5] and such other persons as it considers appropriate about the guidelines it is proposing to include in the statement[6]. Before determining how to publish such a statement or revised statement OFCOM must consult the Secretary of State[7].

It is the duty of OFCOM, in determining the amount of any penalty to be imposed by it under the Communications Act 2003 or any other enactment (apart from the Competition Act 1998) to have regard to the guidelines contained in the statement for the time being in force under these provisions[8].

1   As to the meaning of 'OFCOM' see PARA 14 note 1; and as to the establishment of OFCOM see PARA 2.
2   Communications Act 2003 s 392(1). References in s 392 to penalties imposed by OFCOM under provisions contained in the Communications Act 2003 include references to penalties which the BBC is liable to pay to OFCOM by virtue of s 198(3) (see BROADCASTING vol 4 (2011) PARA 854): s 392(7). As to the meaning of 'the BBC' see PARA 16 note 12.
3   Communications Act 2003 s 392(2).
4   Communications Act 2003 s 392(3). As to the meaning of 'person' see PARA 14 note 2.
5   As to the Secretary of State see PARA 76 note 1.
6   Communications Act 2003 s 392(4).
7   Communications Act 2003 s 392(5).
8   Communications Act 2003 s 392(6).

41. Destination of licence fees and penalties. Where OFCOM[1] receives an amount to which these provisions[2] apply, it must be paid into the appropriate Consolidated Fund[3]; but this does not apply to an amount which is required by OFCOM for making an adjustment in respect of an overpayment[4]. The requirement applies[5] to:

(1) an amount paid to OFCOM in respect of a penalty imposed by it[6] (including a penalty imposed[7] in relation to failure to provide information in connection with a dispute)[8];

(2) so much of an amount paid to OFCOM under numbering conditions[9] in respect of an allocation of telephone numbers as is an amount determined by reference to an indication given in response to an invitation to persons to indicate the payments each would be willing to make to OFCOM if allocated the numbers[10];

(3) an amount paid to OFCOM in pursuance of an obligation imposed by or under provisions in the Wireless Telegraphy Act 2006 relating to wireless telegraphy licences[11] or grants of recognised spectrum access[12];

(4)   an amount paid to OFCOM in respect of a penalty imposed by it[13] for a contravention by a multiplex licence holder[14];

(5)   a cash bid amount[15] paid to OFCOM under a Broadcasting Act licence for the first year falling within the period for which the licence is in force[16];

(6)   an amount paid to OFCOM under such a licence for a subsequent year as the amount equal to a cash bid amount increased by the appropriate percentage[17];

(7)   an amount paid to OFCOM under such a licence as an amount representing a percentage of relevant revenue[18] for an accounting period[19];

(8)   an amount paid to OFCOM in respect of a penalty imposed by it under provisions in the Broadcasting Act 1990 relating to independent television services[20] or independent radio services[21], in the Broadcasting Act 1996 relating to digital terrestrial television broadcasting[22] or to digital terrestrial sound broadcasting[23] or in the Communications Act 2003 relating to television and radio services[24];

(9)   an amount paid to OFCOM in respect of a penalty imposed by them under provisions in the Postal Services Act 2011 relating to the regulation of postal services[25].

OFCOM must, in respect of each financial year[26], prepare an account[27] showing:

(a)   the amounts to which these provisions apply that have been received by it during that year[28];

(b)   the sums paid into the Consolidated Funds of the United Kingdom and Northern Ireland respectively under these provisions in respect of those amounts[29];

(c)   the aggregate amount of the sums received by it during that year that is retained in accordance with a statement of principles[30] for meeting the costs of carrying out certain of OFCOM's functions under the enactments relating to the management of the radio spectrum[31] during that year[32];

(d)   the aggregate amount that it estimates will fall to be so retained out of amounts due to it and likely to be paid or recovered[33]; and

(e)   the cost to OFCOM of carrying out during that year the functions in respect of which amounts are or are to be retained in accordance with such a statement[34].

OFCOM must send that account to the Comptroller and Auditor General not later than the end of the month of November following the financial year to which it relates[35]. The Comptroller and Auditor General must examine, certify and report on the account and lay copies of it, together with his report, before each House of Parliament[36].

1   As to the meaning of 'OFCOM' see PARA 14 note 1; and as to the establishment of OFCOM see PARA 2.

2   Ie the Communications Act 2003 s 400: see the text and notes 3–36.

3   The reference to the payment of an amount into the appropriate Consolidated Fund:

    (1)   in the case of an amount received in respect of matters appearing to OFCOM to have no connection with Northern Ireland, is a reference to the payment of the amount into the Consolidated Fund of the United Kingdom (Communications Act 2003 s 400(3)(a));

    (2)   in the case of an amount received in respect of matters appearing to OFCOM to have a connection with Northern Ireland but no connection with the rest of the United Kingdom, is a reference to the payment of the amount into the Consolidated Fund of Northern Ireland (s 400(3)(b)); and

(3)   in any other case, is a reference to the payment of the amount, in such proportions as OFCOM considers appropriate, into each of those Funds (s 400(3)(c)).

As to the meaning of 'United Kingdom' see PARA 14 note 7. As to the Consolidated Fund see CONSTITUTIONAL AND ADMINISTRATIVE LAW vol 20 (2014) PARA 480 et seq; PARLIAMENT vol 78 (2010) PARAS 1028–1031.

4   Communications Act 2003 s 400(2).

5   Ie subject to the Communications Act 2003 s 401 (not yet in force) (power of OFCOM to retain costs of carrying out spectrum functions: see BROADCASTING vol 4 (2011) PARA 539): s 400(1).

6   Ie under the Communications Act 2003 Pt 2 Ch 1 (ss 32–151).

7   Ie by virtue of the Communications Act 2003 s 191(5): see PARA 223.

8   Communications Act 2003 s 400(1)(a).

9   'Numbering conditions' means conditions the setting of which is authorised by the Communications Act 2003 s 58 or s 59 (see PARA 100): s 400(8).

10   Communications Act 2003 s 400(1)(b). The reference to an invitation to persons to indicate the payments each would be willing to make in the text is under the Communications Act 2003 s 58(5)(a) (see PARA 100 note 4): s 400(1)(b). As to the meaning of 'person' see PARA 14 note 2.

11   Ie under the Wireless Telegraphy Act 2006 Pt 2 Ch 1 (ss 8–17) (wireless telegraphy licences).

12   Communications Act 2003 s 400(1)(c) (amended by the Wireless Telegraphy Act 2006 s 123, Sch 7 paras 25, 32(a)). The provisions relating to grants of recognised spectrum access are the Wireless Telegraphy Act 2006 Pt 2 Ch 2 (ss 18–26) (grants of recognised spectrum access). As to such amounts see BROADCASTING vol 4 (2011) PARA 520.

13   Ie under the Wireless Telegraphy Act 2006 s 42 or 43A: see BROADCASTING vol 4 (2011) PARA 528.

14   Communications Act 2003 s 400(1)(d) (amended by the Wireless Telegraphy Act 2006 Sch 7 para 32(b); and the Digital Economy Act 2010 s 39(3)). As to multiplex licences see BROADCASTING vol 4 (2011) PARA 690 et seq.

15   'Cash bid amount' means an amount specified in a cash bid for a Broadcasting Act licence or the amount determined by OFCOM for the purposes of any provision of the Broadcasting Act 1990 or the Communications Act 2003 Pt 6 (ss 390–411) to be what would have been the amount of a cash bid for a licence: s 400(8). As to Broadcasting Act licences see BROADCASTING.

16   Communications Act 2003 s 400(1)(e).

17   Communications Act 2003 s 400(1)(f). 'Appropriate percentage' has the same meaning as in the Broadcasting Act 1990 s 19 (see BROADCASTING vol 4 (2011) PARA 674): Communications Act 2003 s 400(8).

18   'Relevant revenue' means any of the following:
   (1)   the amount which for the purposes of the Broadcasting Act 1990 s 19, s 52(1), s 102(1) or s 118(1) (see BROADCASTING) is the amount of qualifying revenue for an accounting period;
   (2)   the amount which for the purposes of the Broadcasting Act 1996 s 13(1) or s 55(1) (see BROADCASTING vol 4 (2011) PARAS 690, 754) is the amount of multiplex revenue for an accounting period; or
   (3)   an amount which for the purposes of the Communications Act 2003 Sch 10 para 7 (payments to be made in respect of the public teletext service: see BROADCASTING vol 4 (2011) PARA 686) is the amount of qualifying revenue for an accounting period: s 400(8).

19   Communications Act 2003 s 400(1)(g).

20   Ie the Broadcasting Act 1990 Pt I (ss 3–71) (see BROADCASTING vol 4 (2011) PARAS 673, 865).

21   Ie the Broadcasting Act 1990 Pt III (ss 85–126) (see BROADCASTING vol 4 (2011) PARAS 733, 746, 778).

22   Ie the Broadcasting Act 1996 Pt I (ss 1–39) (see BROADCASTING).

23   Ie the Broadcasting Act 1996 Pt II (ss 40–72) (see BROADCASTING).

24   Communications Act 2003 s 400(1)(h). The reference to provisions in the Communications Act 2003 relating to television and radio services in the text are the Communications Act 2003 Pt 3 (ss 198–362) (see BROADCASTING vol 4 (2011) PARA 862). References in s 400 to penalties imposed by OFCOM under the Communications Act 2003 Pt 3 include references to penalties which the BBC is liable to pay to OFCOM by virtue of s 198(3) (see BROADCASTING vol 4 (2011) PARA 854): s 400(7). As to the meaning of 'the BBC' see PARA 16 note 12; and as to the BBC see BROADCASTING vol 4 (2011) PARAS 603–626.

25   Communications Act 2003 s 400(1)(i) (added by the Postal Services Act 2011 Sch 12 para 66). The reference to provisions in the Postal Services Act 2011 relating to the regulation of postal services in the text is the Postal Services Act 2011 Pt 3 (ss 27–67).

26   'Financial year' has the same meaning as in the Office of Communications Act 2002 Schedule (see PARA 6 note 14): Communications Act 2003 s 400(8).

27 Communications Act 2003 s 400(4).
28 Communications Act 2003 s 400(4)(a).
29 Communications Act 2003 s 400(4)(b).
30 Ie a statement of principles under the Communications Act 2003 s 401 (not yet in force): see
    BROADCASTING vol 4 (2011) PARA 540).
31 Ie the functions mentioned in the Communications Act 2003 s 401(4): see BROADCASTING vol 4
    (2011) PARA 540. As to the meaning of 'enactments relating to the management of the radio
    spectrum' see PARA 17 note 4.
32 Communications Act 2003 s 400(4)(c).
33 Communications Act 2003 s 400(4)(d).
34 Communications Act 2003 s 400(4)(e).
35 Communications Act 2003 s 400(5). As to the Comptroller and Auditor General see PARA 6 note
    15.
36 Communications Act 2003 s 400(6).

42. Disclosure of information obtained under the Telecommunications Act 1984. Subject to certain exceptions[1], no information with respect to any particular business which has been obtained under or by virtue of the provisions of the Telecommunications Act 1984 and which relates to the private affairs of any individual or to any particular business must, during the lifetime of that individual or so long as that business continues to be carried on, be disclosed without the consent of that individual or the person for the time being carrying on that business[2]. This restriction does not apply to any disclosure of information which is made:

(1)   for the purpose of facilitating the performance of any functions assigned to the Secretary of State or OFCOM by or under that Act[3];

(2)   for the purpose of facilitating the performance of any functions of any minister, any Northern Ireland department, the head of any such department, the Competition and Markets Authority, the Water Services Regulation Authority, the Gas and Electricity Markets Authority, the Director General of Electricity Supply for Northern Ireland, the Director General of Gas for Northern Ireland, the Office of Rail Regulation, OFCOM, the Civil Aviation Authority or a local weights and measures authority in Great Britain under certain enactments or subordinate legislation[4];

(3)   for the purpose of facilitating the carrying out by the Comptroller and Auditor General of any of his functions under any enactment[5];

(4)   in connection with the investigation of any criminal offence or for the purposes of any criminal proceedings[6];

(5)   for the purpose of any civil proceedings brought under or by virtue of the Telecommunications Act 1984, or of any of certain enactments or subordinate legislation[7]; or

(6)   in pursuance of a European Union (EU) obligation[8].

Any person who discloses information in contravention of these provisions is guilty of an offence[9].

There are similar provisions restricting disclosure of information obtained in exercise of a power conferred by the Communications Act 2003[10].

1 Ie subject to the Telecommunications Act 1984 s 101(2), (3): see the text and notes 3–9.
2 Telecommunications Act 1984 s 101(1) (amended by the Communications Act 2003 s 406(1),
   Sch 17 para 72(1), (2); and the Wireless Telegraphy Act 2006 s 125(1), Sch 9 Pt 1).
3 Telecommunications Act 1984 s 101(2)(a) (amended by the Communications Act 2003 s 406(7),
   Sch 17 para 72(3), Sch 19; and the Wireless Telegraphy Act 2006 Sch 9 Pt 1). As to the Secretary
   of State see PARA 76 note 1. As to the functions of the Secretary of State under the
   Telecommunications Act 1984 see PARA 76. As to the meaning of 'OFCOM' see PARA 14 note 1;
   and as to the general functions and duties of OFCOM see PARA 14 et seq.

4   Telecommunications Act 1984 s 101(2)(b) (amended by the Electricity Act 1989 s 112(1), Sch 16 para 29; the Water Act 1989 s 190, Sch 25 para 68; the Railways Act 1993 s 152, Sch 12 para 13(1); the Utilities Act 2000 s 3(2); the Enterprise Act 2002 s 278(1), Sch 25 para 13(1), (9)(a); the Communications Act 2003 Sch 17 para 72(4); the Railways and Transport Safety Act 2003 s 16(5), Sch 2 Pt 2 para 19(g); the Water Act 2003 s 101(1), Sch 7 Pt 2 para 23(a); and by SI 1988/915; SI 1992/231; SI 1996/275; SI 1999/506; SI 2001/4050; and SI 2014/892). As to the Office of Fair Trading and the Competition Commission see COMPETITION vol 18 (2009) PARAS 6–8, 9–12; as to the Director General of Water Services see WATER AND WATERWAYS vol 100 (2009) PARAS 13, 109 et seq; as to the Gas and Electricity Markets Authority see ENERGY AND CLIMATE CHANGE vol 42 (2011) PARA 202 et seq; as to the Office of Rail Regulation see RAILWAYS AND TRAMWAYS vol 86 (2013) PARA 51 et seq; as to the Civil Aviation Authority see AIR LAW vol 2 (2008) PARA 50 et seq; and as to local weights and measures authorities see WEIGHTS AND MEASURES vol 99 (2012) PARA 519. As to the meaning of 'Great Britain' see PARA 14 note 7.

      The enactments referred to in the text are: the Trade Descriptions Act 1968, the Fair Trading Act 1973, the Consumer Credit Act 1974, the Estate Agents Act 1979, the Competition Act 1980, the Consumer Protection Act 1987, the Water Act 1989, the Water Industry Act 1991 (or any of the other consolidation Acts within the meaning of s 206, namely, the Water Resources Act 1991, the Statutory Water Companies Act 1991, the Land Drainage Act 1991 and the Water Consolidation (Consequential Provisions) Act 1991: see WATER AND WATERWAYS), or the Water Act 2003, the Electricity Act 1989, the Railways Act 1993, the Competition Act 1998, the Transport Act 2000 Pt I (ss 1–107), the Enterprise Act 2002, the Communications Act 2003, the Railways Act 2005, the Business Protection from Misleading Marketing Regulations 2008, SI 2008/1276 (see COMPETITION vol 18 (2009) PARA 336A); the Consumer Protection from Unfair Trading Regulations 2008, SI 2008/1277; and the Enterprise and Regulatory Reform Act 2013 Pt 3 (ss 25–28) and Pt 4 (ss 29–58): see the Telecommunications Act 1984 s 101(3) (amended by the Consumer Protection Act 1987 s 48, Sch 4; the Electricity Act 1989 s 112(1), Sch 16 para 29; the Water Act 1989 s 190, Sch 25 para 68; the Water Consolidation (Consequential Provisions) Act 1991 s 2, Sch 1 para 38(2); the Railways Act 1993 s 152, Sch 12 para 13(2); the Competition Act 1998 ss 54(3), 74(3), Sch 10 para 9(7), Sch 14 Pt I; the Enterprise Act 2002 Sch 25 para 13(9)(b); the Communications Act 2003 Sch 17 para 72; the Water Act 2003 s 101(1), Sch 7 Pt 2 para 23(b); the Railways Act 2005 s 59(1), Sch 12 para 7; the Wireless Telegraphy Act 2006 Sch 9 Pt 1; and by SI 1988/915; SI 2001/4050; SI 2008/1277; and SI 2014/892).

5   Telecommunications Act 1984 s 101(2)(bb) (added by the Competition and Service (Utilities) Act 1992 s 56(6), Sch 1 para 3(a)). As to the Comptroller and Auditor General see PARA 6 note 15.

6   Telecommunications Act 1984 s 101(2)(c).

7   Telecommunications Act 1984 s 101(2)(d) (amended by SI 1988/915). The enactments referred to are those listed in note 4.

8   Telecommunications Act 1984 s 101(2)(e) (amended by SI 2011/1043).

9   Telecommunications Act 1984 s 101(5). He is liable on summary conviction to a fine not exceeding the statutory maximum (s 101(5)(a)), or on conviction on indictment to imprisonment for a term not exceeding two years or to a fine or both (s 101(5)(b)). As to the statutory maximum see SENTENCING AND DISPOSITION OF OFFENDERS vol 92 (2010) PARA 140.

      Information obtained by OFCOM in the exercise of functions which are exercisable concurrently with the Competition and Markets Authority under the Competition Act 1998 Pt I (ss 1–60) (see COMPETITION vol 18 (2009) PARA 115 et seq) is subject to the Enterprise Act 2002 Pt 9 (ss 237–247) (information: see COMPETITION vol 18 (2009) PARA 326 et seq) and not to the Telecommunications Act 1984 s 101(1)–(5): s 101(6) (added by the Competition Act 1998 s 54(3), Sch 10 para 9(8); and amended by the Enterprise Act 2002 Sch 25 para 13(9)(c); the Communications Act 2003 Sch 17 para 72(7); and SI 2014/982).

10 See the Communications Act 2003 s 393; and PARA 43.

43. Disclosure of information obtained under the Communications Act 2003, the Broadcasting Act 1990 or the Broadcasting Act 1996.
Information with respect to a particular business which has been obtained in exercise of a power conferred by the Communications Act 2003, the Broadcasting Act 1990 or the Broadcasting Act 1996, is not, so long as that business continues to be carried

on, to be disclosed without the consent of the person[1] for the time being carrying on that business[2]. This does not apply to any disclosure of information which is made:

(1)　for the purpose of facilitating the carrying out by OFCOM of any of its functions[3];

(2)　for the purpose of facilitating the carrying out by any relevant person[4] of any relevant function[5];

(3)　for the purpose of facilitating the carrying out by the Comptroller and Auditor General of any of his functions[6];

(4)　for any specified purpose in the Anti-terrorism, Crime and Security Act 2001 relating to criminal proceedings and investigations[7];

(5)　for the purpose of any civil proceedings brought under or by virtue of the Communications Act 2003 or any of specified enactments or instruments[8]; or

(6)　for the purpose of securing compliance with an international obligation of the United Kingdom[9].

Any person who discloses information in contravention of these provisions is guilty of an offence[10].

1　As to the meaning of 'person' see PARA 14 note 2.
2　Communications Act 2003 s 393(1) (amended by the Wireless Telegraphy Act 2006 s 125(1), Sch 9 Pt 1). Nothing in the Communications Act 2003 s 393:

(1)　limits the matters that may be published under s 15 (research for the benefit of consumers: see PARA 27), s 26 (information and advice: see PARA 34), s 390 (annual report on the functions of the Secretary of State: see PARA 78) (s 393(6)(a));

(2)　limits the information that may be made available under s 76A (see PARA 104) (s 393(6)(aa) (added by SI 2011/1210));

(3)　limits the matters that may be included in, or made public as part of, a report made by OFCOM by virtue of a provision of the Communications Act 2003 or the Office of Communications Act 2002 (Communications Act 2003 s 393(6)(b));

(4)　prevents the disclosure of anything for the purposes of a report of legal proceedings in which it has been publicly disclosed (s 393(6)(c));

(5)　applies to information that has been published or made public as mentioned in heads (1)–(4) (s 393(6)(d)).

For the purposes of s 393, 'legal proceedings' means civil or criminal proceedings in or before any court, or proceedings before any tribunal established by or under any enactment: s 393(12). As to OFCOM see PARA 2 et seq.

　　Nothing in s 393 applies to information obtained in exercise of the powers of entry and search conferred by the Broadcasting Act 1990 s 196 (see BROADCASTING vol 4 (2011) PARA 596): Communications Act 2003 s 393(7).

3　Communications Act 2003 s 393(2)(a).
4　Each of the following is a relevant person for the purposes of the Communications Act 2003 s 393:

(1)　a Minister of the Crown and the Treasury (s 393(3)(a));

(2)　the Scottish Executive (s 393(3)(b));

(3)　a Northern Ireland department (s 393(3)(c));

(4)　the Competition and Markets Authority (s 393(3)(d) (amended by SI 2014/892));

(5)　the Consumer Panel (Communications Act 2003 s 393(3)(f));

(6)　the Welsh Authority (s 393(3)(g));

(7)　a local weights and measures authority in Great Britain (s 393(3)(h));

(8)　any other person specified for the purposes of s 393(3) in an order made by the Secretary of State (s 393(3)(i)).

No order is to be made containing provision authorised by s 393(3) unless a draft of the order has been laid before Parliament and approved by a resolution of each House: s 393(11). As to orders which have been made see the Communications Act 2003 (Disclosure of Information) Order 2010, SI 2010/282; and the Communications Act 2003 (Disclosure of Information) Order 2014, SI 2014/1825. As to the Secretary of State see PARA 76 note 1. As to the Treasury see CONSTITUTIONAL AND ADMINISTRATIVE LAW vol 20 (2014) PARAS 262–265. As to the Competition and Markets Authority see COMPETITION vol 18 (2009) PARA 23A. As to the

Consumer Panel see PARAS 28–29. The 'Welsh Authority' is the authority whose name is, by virtue of the Broadcasting Act 1990 s 56(1), Sianel Pedwar Cymru (see BROADCASTING vol 4 (2011) PARA 644 et seq): Communications Act 2003 s 405(1). As to the Welsh Authority see PARA 24 note 11; and BROADCASTING vol 4 (2011) PARA 644 et seq. As to local weights and measures authorities see WEIGHTS AND MEASURES vol 99 (2012) PARA 519.

5   Communications Act 2003 s 393(2)(b). The following are relevant functions for the purposes of s 393:
    (1)   any function conferred by or under the Communications Act 2003 (s 393(4)(a));
    (2)   any function conferred by or under any enactment or instrument mentioned s 393(5) (see note 8) (s 393(4)(b));
    (3)   any other function specified for the purposes of s 393(4) in an order made by the Secretary of State (s 393(4)(c)).
    No order is to be made containing provision authorised by s 393(4) unless a draft of the order has been laid before Parliament and approved by a resolution of each House: s 393(11). As to orders that have been made under s 393(4) see the Contracting Out (Functions relating to Broadcast Advertising) and Specification of Relevant Functions Order 2004, SI 2004/1975 (amended by SI 2008/1277; and SI 2012/1916); the Communications Act 2003 (Maximum Penalty and Disclosure of Information) Order 2005, SI 2005/3469; and the Communications Act 2003 (Disclosure of Information) Order 2014, SI 2014/1825.

6   Communications Act 2003 s 393(2)(c). As to the Comptroller and Auditor General see PARA 6 note 15.

7   Communications Act 2003 s 393(2)(d). The text refers to purposes specified in the Anti-terrorism, Crime and Security Act 2001 s 17(2)(a)–(d) (see CRIMINAL LAW vol 25 (2010) PARA 384). Section 18 (restriction on disclosure of information for overseas purposes) has effect in relation to a disclosure by virtue of the Communications Act 2003 s 393(2)(d) as it applies in relation to a disclosure in exercise of a power to which the Anti-terrorism, Crime and Security Act 2001 s 17 applies: Communications Act 2003 s 393(9).

8   Communications Act 2003 s 393(2)(e). The enactments and instruments referred to in s 393(2), (4) are the Trade Descriptions Act 1968; the Fair Trading Act 1973; the Consumer Credit Act 1974; the Competition Act 1980; the Telecommunications Act 1984; the Consumer Protection Act 1987; the Broadcasting Act 1990; the Broadcasting Act 1996; the Competition Act 1998; the Enterprise Act 2002; the Wireless Telegraphy Act 2006; the Consumer Protection (Northern Ireland) Order 1987, SI 1987/2049 (NI 20); the Business Protection from Misleading Marketing Regulations 2008, SI 2008/1276 (see COMPETITION vol 18 (2009) PARA 336A); the Consumer Protection from Unfair Trading Regulations 2008, SI 2008/1277; and Enterprise and Regulatory Reform Act 2013 Pt 3 (ss 25–28) and Pt 4 (ss 29–58): Communications Act 2003 s 393(5) (amended by the Wireless Telegraphy Act 2006 ss 123, 125(1), Sch 7 para 31, Sch 9 Pt 1; the Enterprise and Regulatory Reform Act 2013 Sch 21 para 2; and by SI 2008/1277).

9   Communications Act 2003 s 393(2)(f). As to the meaning of 'international obligation of the United Kingdom' see PARA 33 note 7. As to the meaning of 'United Kingdom' see PARA 14 note 7.

10 Communications Act 2003 s 393(10). He is liable on summary conviction to a fine not exceeding the statutory maximum (s 393(10)(a)) or on conviction on indictment to imprisonment for a term not exceeding two years or to a fine, or to both (s 393(10)(b)). As to the statutory maximum see SENTENCING AND DISPOSITION OF OFFENDERS vol 92 (2010) PARA 140.
    Information obtained by OFCOM in exercise of functions which are exercisable by it concurrently with the Competition and Markets Authority under the Competition Act 1998 Pt I (ss 1–60) (see COMPETITION vol 18 (2009) PARA 115 et seq) is subject to the Enterprise Act 2002 Pt 9 (ss 237–247) (information: see COMPETITION vol 18 (2009) PARA 326 et seq), and not to the Communications Act 2003 s 393(1)–(7): s 393(8) (amended by SI 2014/892).

44.   Service of notifications and other documents. These provisions[1] apply where provision made (in whatever terms) by or under an enactment specified below authorises or requires a notification[2] to be given to any person[3] or a document[4] of any other description (including a copy of a document) to be sent to any person[5]. The specified enactments are:
    (1)   the Communications Act 2003[6];
    (2)   the Office of Communications Act 2002[7];
    (3)   Schedule 2 to the Telecommunications Act 1984[8];
    (4)   the Broadcasting Act 1990[9];

(5)   the Broadcasting Act 1996[10]; and

(6)   Part 3 of the Postal Services Act 2011[11].

The notification or document may be given or sent to the person in question:

(a)   by delivering it to him[12];

(b)   by leaving it at his proper address[13]; or

(c)   by sending it by post to him at that address[14].

The notification or document may be given or sent to a body corporate by being given or sent to the secretary or clerk of that body[15]. The notification or document may be given or sent to a firm by being given or sent to a partner in the firm or a person having the control or management of the partnership business[16]. The notification or document may be given or sent to an unincorporated body or association by being given or sent to a member of the governing body of the body or association[17].

1   Ie the Communications Act 2003 s 394.
2   'Notification' includes notice: Communications Act 2003 s 394(9).
3   As to the meaning of 'person' see PARA 14 note 2.
4   'Document' includes anything in writing: Communications Act 2003 s 394(9).
5   Communications Act 2003 s 394(1). References in s 394 to giving or sending a notification or other document to a person include references to transmitting it to him and to serving it on him: s 394(9). The provisions of s 394 are subject to s 395 (see PARA 45): s 394(10).
6   Communications Act 2003 s 394(2)(a).
7   Communications Act 2003 s 394(2)(b).
8   Communications Act 2003 s 394(2)(d).
9   Communications Act 2003 s 394(2)(e) (amended by the Postal Services Act 2011 Sch 12 para 65).
10 Communications Act 2003 s 394(2)(f).
11 Communications Act 2003 s 394(2)(g) (added by the Postal Services Act 2010 Sch 12 para 65).
12 Communications Act 2003 s 394(3)(a).
13 Communications Act 2003 s 394(3)(b). For the purposes of the Communications Act 2003 s 394 and of the Interpretation Act 1978 s 7 (service of documents by post) in its application to that provision, the proper address of a person is:
    (1)   in the case of body corporate, the address of the registered or principal office of the body (Communications Act 2003 s 394(7)(a));
    (2)   in the case of a firm, unincorporated body or association, the address of the principal office of the partnership, body or association (s 394(7)(b));
    (3)   in the case of a person to whom the notification or other document is given or sent in reliance on any of the provisions of the Communications Act 2003 s 394(4)–(6), the proper address of the body corporate, firm or (as the case may be) other body or association in question (s 394(7)(c)); and
    (4)   in any other case, the last known address of the person in question (s 394(7)(d)).
    In the case of:
    (a)   a company registered outside the United Kingdom;
    (b)   a firm carrying on business outside the United Kingdom; or
    (c)   an unincorporated body or association with offices outside the United Kingdom,
    the references in s 394(7) to its principal office include references to its principal office within the United Kingdom (if any): s 394(8).
    As to the meaning of 'United Kingdom' see PARA 14 note 7.
14 Communications Act 2003 s 394(3)(c).
15 Communications Act 2003 s 394(4).
16 Communications Act 2003 s 394(5).
17 Communications Act 2003 s 394(6).

45.   Notifications and documents in electronic form. These provisions[1] apply where the Communications Act 2003[2] authorises the giving or sending of a notification[3] or other document[4] by its delivery to a particular person[5] (the 'recipient') and the notification or other document is transmitted to the recipient by means of an electronic communications network[6] or by other means but in a form that nevertheless requires the use of apparatus by the recipient to render it intelligible[7]. The transmission has effect for the purposes of the specified enactments[8] as a delivery of the notification or other document to the recipient, but only if the requirements imposed by or under these provisions are complied with[9].

Where the recipient is OFCOM[10]:

(1)   it must have indicated its willingness to receive the notification or other document in a manner mentioned above[11];

(2)   the transmission must be made in such manner and satisfy such other conditions as OFCOM may require[12]; and

(3)   the notification or other document must take such form as OFCOM may require[13].

Where the person making the transmission is OFCOM, it may (subject to the willingness of the recipient[14]) determine the manner in which the transmission is made and the form in which the notification or other document is transmitted[15].

Where the recipient is a person other than OFCOM:

(a)   the recipient[16]; or

(b)   the person on whose behalf the recipient receives the notification or other document[17],

must have indicated to the person making the transmission the recipient's willingness to receive notifications or documents transmitted in the form and manner used[18]. An indication to any person for this purpose:

(i)   must be given to that person in such manner as he may require[19];

(ii)   may be a general indication or one that is limited to notifications or documents of a particular description[20];

(iii)   must state the address to be used and must be accompanied by such other information as that person requires for the making of the transmission[21]; and

(iv)   may be modified or withdrawn at any time by a notice given to that person in such manner as he may require[22].

An indication, requirement or determination given, imposed or made by OFCOM for the purposes of these provisions is to be given, imposed or made by being published in such manner as OFCOM considers appropriate for bringing it to the attention of the persons who, in its opinion, are likely to be affected by it[23].

The Secretary of State[24] may by order make provision specifying, for the purposes of the specified enactments[25]:

(A)   the manner of determining the times at which things done under those enactments by means of electronic communications networks are done[26]; and

(B)   the places at which such things are so done, and at which things transmitted by means of such networks are received[27].

Such provision may include provision as to the country or territory in which an electronic address is to be treated as located[28]. An order made by the Secretary of State may also make provision about the manner of proving in any legal proceedings that something done by means of an electronic communications network satisfies the requirements of the specified enactments for the doing of that thing and the matters mentioned in heads (A) and (B) above[29]. An order may provide for such presumptions to apply (whether conclusive or not) as the Secretary of State considers appropriate[30].

1   Ie the Communications Act 2003 s 395.
2   Ie the Communications Act 2003 s 394: see PARA 44.

3   As to the meaning of 'notification' see PARA 44 note 2; definition applied by the
    Communications Act 2003 s 395(8).
4   As to the meaning of 'document' see PARA 44 note 4; definition applied by the Communications
    Act 2003 s 395(8).
5   Communications Act 2003 s 395(1)(a). As to the meaning of 'person' see PARA 14 note 2.
6   As to the meaning of 'electronic communications network' see PARA 53.
7   Communications Act 2003 s 395(1)(b).
8   Ie the enactments specified in the Communications Act 2003 s 394(2): see PARA 44 heads
    (1)–(6).
9   Communications Act 2003 s 395(2).
10 As to OFCOM see PARA 2 et seq.
11 Communications Act 2003 s 395(3)(a). The manner referred to in the text is that in the
    Communications Act 2003 s 395(1)(b): see the text to note 7.
12 Communications Act 2003 s 395(3)(b).
13 Communications Act 2003 s 395(3)(c).
14 Ie subject to the Communications Act 2003 s 395(5): see the text to notes 16–18.
15 Communications Act 2003 s 395(4).
16 Communications Act 2003 s 395(5)(a).
17 Communications Act 2003 s 395(5)(b).
18 Communications Act 2003 s 395(5). Section 395(5), (6) (see text and notes 19–22) do not apply
    in relation to a notification or other document given by OFCOM under Pt 1 (ss 1–31) or
    Pt 2 Ch 1 (ss 32–151) to the European Commission, Body of European Regulators for
    Electronic Communications ('BEREC') or the regulatory authorities of member state (within the
    meaning of that Pt 2 Ch 1: see s 151(5); and PARA 92 note 6): s 395(6A) (added by
    SI 2011/1210). As to BEREC see PARA 58. As to the European Commission see EUROPEAN
    UNION vol 47A (2014) PARAS 48, 49.
19 Communications Act 2003 s 395(6)(a). See note 18.
20 Communications Act 2003 s 395(6)(b). See note 18.
21 Communications Act 2003 s 395(6)(c). See note 18.
22 Communications Act 2003 s 395(6)(d). See note 18.
23 Communications Act 2003 s 395(7).
24 As to the Secretary of State see PARA 76 note 1.
25 Ie the enactments specified in the Communications Act 2003 s 394(2): see PARA 49 heads
    (1)–(6).
26 Communications Act 2003 s 396(1)(a).
27 Communications Act 2003 s 396(1)(b).
28 Communications Act 2003 s 396(2).
29 Communications Act 2003 s 396(3).
30 Communications Act 2003 s 396(4). At the date at which this volume states the law, no order
    had been made under s 396.

2. TELECOMMUNICATIONS

(1) INTRODUCTION TO TELECOMMUNICATIONS

(i) Historical Background to Telecommunications

46. Development of the telegraph. In 1837 Wheatstone and Cooke patented a method of communication by means of electromagnetic impulses carried over wires and shortly afterwards conducted successful experiments between two London railway stations. By 1844 telegraphs were in use on a number of railways, and it was in that connection that they first became the subject of legislation[1]. At this stage telegraphs were mainly privately owned and operated, and in 1863 Parliament introduced a general code to regulate the exercise of the powers which the private telegraph companies derived from their various special Acts of Parliament[2]. In 1868 and 1869 the Postmaster General[3] was authorised[4] to purchase these private undertakings, except those engaged in transmitting telegrams[5] to or from places outside the United Kingdom[6]. At the same time he was given the exclusive privilege of transmitting telegrams[7], a monopoly which was subsequently held to extend to the telephone[8]. Within a short time the undertakings of all the private telegraph companies had become vested in him[9]. In 1969 the monopoly was abolished along with the office of Postmaster General, and in its place the Post Office was given the exclusive privilege of running the telecommunication systems throughout the British Islands[10], a privilege which passed to British Telecommunications in 1981[11] but which was abolished in 1984[12].

1   See the Railway Regulation Act 1844 ss 13, 14 (repealed), which provided for the establishment of telegraphs for Her Majesty's service on land adjoining railways and the throwing open to the public of all railway telegraphs. This is not the first reference to telegraphy in a statute: the Admiralty (Signals Stations) Act 1815 (repealed) authorised the compulsory acquisition of land for signal and telegraph stations. However, the reference was to visual telegraphs and not to electric telegraphs.

2   See the Telegraph Act 1863 (largely repealed). 'Telegraph' was defined for the purposes of the Telegraph Acts, and the definition may still be of importance in construing other old Acts or in understanding old cases.

    In the Telegraph Acts, 'telegraph' meant:
    (1)   any wire, cable, tube, pipe or other thing whatsoever used or intended to be used for the purpose of transmitting telegraphic messages or maintaining telegraphic communication;
    (2)   any casing, coating, tube, pipe or other thing whatsoever enclosing or intending to enclose the same; and
    (3)   any apparatus connected with anything falling within head (1) and used or intended to be used for the purpose there mentioned (Telegraph Act 1863 s 3 (repealed); British Telecommunications Act 1981 s 80(1) (repealed));
and included any apparatus for transmitting messages and other communications by means of electric signals (Telegraph Act 1869 s 3 (repealed)).

    The definition was wide enough to include a system of electric signals with or without wires, and a system of wires worked by hand if arranged so as to constitute a code of signals: *A-G v Edison Telephone Co of London Ltd* (1880) 6 QBD 244. The fact that a particular method of telegraphy was not invented or contemplated at the time when the definition was enacted did not prevent that method from falling within the terms of the definition: *A-G v Edison Telephone Co of London Ltd* (1880) 6 QBD 244. Thus it included telephones, wireless telegraphy, broadcasting, and, to the extent of the territorial limits of the relevant legislation, submarine cables: see *A-G v Edison Telephone Co of London Ltd* (1880) 6 QBD 244; *Re Regulation and Control of Radio Communication in Canada* [1932] AC 304 at 315–316, PC (where it was said that although in everyday speech 'telegraph' was used almost exclusively to denote the electrical instrument which by means of a wire connecting that instrument with another makes it possible to communicate signals or words of any kind, the original meaning of the word was broader, and denoted an apparatus for transmitting messages to a distance). As to broadcasting see BROADCASTING vol 4 (2011) PARA 504 et seq. As to submarine cables see PARAS 48, 212 et seq.

The Telegraph Acts 1863 to 1962 comprised the Telegraph Acts 1863, 1868, 1869, 1870, 1878, 1885, 1892, 1899, 1954 and 1962; the Telegraph Act Amendment Act 1866; the Telegraph (Isle of Man) Act 1889; the Telegraph (Construction) Acts 1908, 1911 and 1916; the Telegraph (Arbitration) Act 1909; the Telephone Transfer Act 1911; and so much of the Post Office and Telegraph Act 1940 as related to telegraphy. All these Acts have been repealed apart from a few provisions of the Acts of 1863, 1868 and 1870: see PARA 69 note 2.

3 As to the former office of Postmaster General see POSTAL SERVICES vol 85 (2012) PARA 208.
4 Ie by the Telegraph Act 1868 and the Telegraph Act 1869.
5 'Telegram' meant any message or other communication transmitted or intended for transmission by a telegraph: Telegraph Act 1869 s 3 (repealed).
6 Telegraph Act 1869 s 9 (repealed). As to the meaning of 'United Kingdom' see PARA 14 note 7.
7 Telegraph Act 1869 s 4 (repealed). Certain exemptions were set out in s 5 (repealed). As to the exclusive privilege see further PARA 49.
8 *A-G v Edison Telephone Co of London Ltd* (1880) 6 QBD 244.
9 This transfer did not include either the companies engaged in overseas communications as mentioned in the text to note 6, or telephone companies: see PARA 47.
10 Post Office Act 1969 s 24(1) (repealed). See PARA 56. For these purposes, 'British Islands' meant the United Kingdom, the Isle of Man and the Channel Islands: see s 86(1) (repealed); and see also PARA 32 note 4.
11 British Telecommunications Act 1981 s 12 (repealed).
12 See the Telecommunications Act 1984 s 2 (repealed); and PARA 49.

47. Development of the telephone. Patent rights in the United Kingdom[1] for their telephone inventions were secured by Bell in 1876 and by Edison in 1877, and in 1878 the first of a number of private companies was formed to exploit these patents. The development of this medium by private enterprise suffered a setback, however, when the court decided in 1880 that their activities were an infringement of the exclusive privilege of the Postmaster General of transmitting telegrams[2]. Thereafter private companies could carry on business only under written licence from the Postmaster General[3]. For the next 20 years, however, the telephone services continued to be for the most part in the hands of the private companies, but by the end of the century the National Telephone Company had absorbed all the other companies and its only rival was the comparatively small service operated by the Postmaster General[4]. However, in 1902 the Postmaster General entered the field as a serious competitor and in 1905 agreed to acquire the whole of the assets of the National Telephone Company[5]. In 1969 the Post Office was granted the exclusive privilege of running telecommunication systems throughout the British Islands[6], a privilege which passed to British Telecommunications in 1981 but which was abolished in 1984[7].

1 As to the meaning of 'United Kingdom' see PARA 14 note 7.
2 *A-G v Edison Telephone Co of London Ltd* (1880) 6 QBD 244. As to the exclusive privilege see PARA 56. See also PARA 46. As to the former office of Postmaster General see POSTAL SERVICES vol 85 (2012) PARA 208.
3 Telegraph Act 1869 s 5 (repealed).
4 In addition, licences were issued to six municipal corporations between 1900 and 1912, but of these only Kingston upon Hull City Council has continued to provide a public telephone service. The Secretary of State granted a licence under the Telecommunications Act 1984 s 7 (repealed) to that council on 25 June 1984 and the systems specified in that licence were designated as public telecommunication systems by the Public Telecommunication System Designation (Kingston upon Hull City Council and Kingston Communications (Hull) PLC) Order 1987, SI 1987/2094. The States of Jersey and the States of Guernsey also provided public telephone services under licence from the Postmaster General, and now provide them under licence from the Secretary of State: see PARA 69 note 5. As to the Secretary of State see PARA 76 note 1.

5   See the Telephone Transfer Act 1911 (repealed); the Telephone Transfer Amendment Act 1911 (repealed); *Postmaster-General v National Telephone Co Ltd* [1909] AC 269, HL; *National Telephone Co Ltd v HM Postmaster-General* [1913] 2 KB 614, CA (affd [1913] AC 546, HL). As to the rights and liabilities after transfer by agreement see also *Dublin County Council v Postmaster-General* [1914] 2 IR 208; and cf *Postmaster-General v Liverpool Corpn* [1923] AC 587, HL.

6   As to the meaning of 'British Islands' for these purposes see PARA 46 note 10.

7   See the Telecommunications Act 1984 s 2 (repealed); and PARA 49.

48.   Development of submarine cables.   In 1847 Siemens devised a successful process for insulating the wires in underwater cables. Cables were laid between England and France in 1851, between England and Ireland in 1853, and the first transatlantic cable came into use in 1866. The need for international co-operation to provide protection for submarine cables from shipping and other hazards resulted in 1884 in the Convention for the Protection of Submarine Cables[1].

1   Convention for the Protection of Submarine Cables (Paris, 14 March 1884; 75 BFSP 356; C 5910). The Convention was carried into effect in the United Kingdom by the Submarine Telegraph Act 1885: see PARA 212. The Convention is set out in the Schedule to the Act.

49.   Exclusive privilege with respect to telecommunications.   The Telegraph Act 1869 conferred on the Postmaster General the exclusive privilege of transmitting telegrams[1] and of performing all the incidental services of receiving, collecting or delivering them[2], so that, subject to certain exceptions[3], no one could lawfully conduct a telegraphic business otherwise than as his licensee, agent or lessee. Upon the abolition in 1969 of the office of Postmaster General[4], the Post Office acquired throughout the British Islands[5] the exclusive privilege of running systems for the conveyance, through the agency of electric, magnetic, electromagnetic, electrochemical or electromechanical energy, of:

(1)   speech, music and other sounds[6];

(2)   visual images[7];

(3)   signals serving for the impartation, whether as between persons and persons, things and things, or persons and things, of any matter otherwise than in the form of sound or visual images[8]; and

(4)   signals serving for the actuation or control of machinery or apparatus[9]. This exclusive privilege of transmitting telegrams described above passed in 1981 to British Telecommunications[10], but as from 5 August 1984 the privilege ceased to exist[11]. Although initially there was only one other company licensed to offer services, the market was later opened to full competition[12].

1   As to the meaning of 'telegram' see PARA 46 note 5.

2   Telegraph Act 1869 s 4 (repealed). See also PARA 46. As to the former office of Postmaster General, and as to the distribution of his functions, see POSTAL SERVICES vol 85 (2012) PARA 208.

3   See the Telegraph Act 1869 s 5 (repealed).

4   A Minister of Posts and Telecommunications was appointed: see the Post Office Act 1969 s 2 (as originally enacted); and POSTAL SERVICES vol 85 (2012) PARA 208. See note 11.

5   See the Post Office Act 1969 s 21(1), (2) (repealed); and PARA 50. As to the meaning of 'British Islands' for these purposes see PARA 46 note 10.

6   Post Office Act 1969 s 24(1)(a) (repealed). For exemptions see s 25 (repealed). Infringement was a criminal offence: see s 24(2) (repealed).

7   Post Office Act 1969 s 24(1)(b) (repealed).

8   Post Office Act 1969 s 24(1)(c) (repealed).

9   Post Office Act 1969 s 24(1)(d) (repealed).

10   See the British Telecommunications Act 1981 s 12 (repealed), which was in similar terms to the Post Office Act 1969 s 24 (repealed).

11 Telecommunications Act 1984 s 2 (repealed); Telecommunications Act 1984 (Appointed Day) (No 2) Order 1984, SI 1984/876, art 3. The property, rights and liabilities of British Telecommunications were transferred on 6 August 1984 to British Telecommunications plc: see the Telecommunications Act 1984 s 60 (repealed); and PARA 50. The Ministry of Posts and Telecommunications (see note 4) was dissolved in 1974 and the minister's functions were transferred to the Secretary of State: see eg the Ministry of Posts and Telecommunications (Dissolution) Order 1974, SI 1974/691.

12 Ie following the publication of the White Paper *Competition and Choice: Telecommunications Policy for the 1990s* (Cmnd 1461) (1991).

50. Transfer of telecommunications property, rights and liabilities. In 1969 the rights and liabilities under the Telegraph Acts 1863 to 1916[1] which were then enjoyed by and incumbent on the Postmaster General became those of the Post Office[2]. Before 1 October 1981[3] the Post Office was required to take steps to separate from the remainder of its undertaking the part of it concerned with the provision of telecommunication and data processing services[4], and on that day all the property, rights and liabilities of the Post Office which immediately before that day were comprised in that part of its undertaking were transferred to and vested in British Telecommunications[5]. The property, rights and liabilities of British Telecommunications were transferred on 6 August 1984 to British Telecommunications plc[6]. Nevertheless, the Post Office retained for a time power to provide, at post offices, services provided by means of telecommunication systems[7].

1 As to these Acts see PARA 46.

2 Post Office Act 1969 s 21(1), (2) (repealed). As to the former office of Postmaster General, and as to the distribution of his functions, see POSTAL SERVICES vol 85 (2012) PARA 208.

3 Ie the appointed day under the British Telecommunications Act 1981 s 1(2) (repealed): British Telecommunications Act 1981 (Appointed Day) Order 1981, SI 1981/1274 (lapsed).

4 British Telecommunications Act 1981 s 10(1).

5 British Telecommunications Act 1981 s 10(2). For detailed provisions as to the transfer see s 10(7), Sch 2. See also *British Telecommunications plc v Royal Mail Group Ltd* [2010] EWHC 8 (QB), [2010] All ER (D) 10 (Jan). There was power to exclude by agreement specified property, rights and liabilities (see the British Telecommunications Act 1981 s 10(3)), and to transfer other property, rights and liabilities to the corporation or to transfer specified property, rights and liabilities back to the Post Office (see s 10(4), (6)), although if an employee's contract of employment was concerned the employee had to be a party to the agreement (see s 10(5)).

6 See the Telecommunications Act 1984 s 60 (repealed); and PARA 51.

7 See the Post Office Act 1969 s 7 (repealed by the Postal Services Act 2000 s 127(6), Sch 9). As to telecommunications systems see PARA 52.

51. British Telecommunications. British Telecommunications was established as a body corporate by the British Telecommunications Act 1981[1]. It had the exclusive privilege of running telecommunication systems throughout the British Islands[2]. As from 5 August 1984[3] this exclusive privilege ceased to exist[4]. On 6 August 1984[5] all the property, rights and liabilities[6], other than excepted liabilities[7], to which British Telecommunications was entitled or subject immediately before that date became property, rights and liabilities of the successor company[8].

The successor company was to be a company nominated by the Secretary of State[9] for the purposes of receiving the property, rights and liabilities transferred from British Telecommunications[10]. The Secretary of State nominated British Telecommunications plc for this purpose[11]. The liability of British Telecommunications plc in respect of the principal of any transferred loan[12] was extinguished[13].

British Telecommunications continued to exist for a transitional period, but was dissolved on 6 September 1994[14]. Provision was made for agreements made with British Telecommunications, and for certain statutory references to British Telecommunications, to have effect as if they were made with, or referred to, the successor company[15].

1 British Telecommunications Act 1981 s 1, Sch 1 para 1 (repealed). As to the transfer to British Telecommunications of the part of the Post Office concerned with the provision of telecommunication and data processing services see s 10, Sch 2; and PARA 50.
2 See the British Telecommunications Act 1981 s 12(1) (repealed). As to infringement of the privilege see ss 12(2)–(4), 13, 14 (all repealed). For these purposes, 'British Islands' meant the United Kingdom and the Isle of Man: s 57(1) (repealed). As to the meaning of 'United Kingdom' see PARA 14 note 7.
3 Ie the appointed day: see the Telecommunications Act 1984 s 2 (repealed); and the Telecommunications Act 1984 (Appointed Day) (No 2) Order 1984, SI 1984/876, art 3.
4 Telecommunications Act 1984 s 2 (repealed); Telecommunications Act 1984 (Appointed Day) (No 2) Order 1984, SI 1984/876, art 3. See also PARA 49.
5 Ie the transfer date: see the Telecommunications Act 1984 s 60(1) (repealed), s 106(1); and the Telecommunications Act 1984 (Appointed Day) (No 2) Order 1984, SI 1984/876, art 5.
6 'Property, rights and liabilities of British Telecommunications' meant all such property, rights and liabilities, whether or not capable of being transferred or assigned by British Telecommunications: Telecommunications Act 1984 s 60(4) (repealed). 'Property of British Telecommunications' meant property of British Telecommunications whether situated in the United Kingdom or elsewhere; and 'rights and liabilities of British Telecommunications' meant rights to which British Telecommunications was entitled or, as the case may be, liabilities to which British Telecommunications was subject, whether under the law of the United Kingdom or of any part of the United Kingdom or under the law of any country or territory outside the United Kingdom: s 60(5) (repealed).
7 'Excepted liabilities' meant the liabilities subsisting by virtue of a deed of covenant dated 22 November 1978 and made between the Post Office and the then trustees of the Post Office Staff Superannuation Scheme: Telecommunications Act 1984 s 60(2) (repealed), s 106(1).
8 Telecommunications Act 1984 s 60(1) (repealed).
9 As to the Secretary of State see PARA 76 note 1.
10 See the Telecommunications Act 1984 s 60(1) (repealed), s 106(1). An order nominating a company could be varied or revoked by a subsequent order at any time before any property, rights or liabilities vested in any company by virtue of s 60 (repealed): s 73(2) (repealed).
   The successor company is to be treated for all purposes of corporation tax as if it were the same person as British Telecommunications: s 72(1) (amended by the Communications Act 2003 s 406(7), Sch 19). As to the treatment of payments by the successor company to an occupational pension scheme with a view to the provision of relevant benefits for persons who are employees of the Post Office see the Telecommunications Act 1984 s 72(3) (substituted by SI 2006/745).
11 See the Telecommunications Act 1984 s 60(3) (repealed); and the Telecommunications Act 1984 (Nominated Company) Order 1984, SI 1984/886, art 2 (lapsed). The company nominated had to be a company which on the transfer date was limited by shares and was wholly owned by the Crown: see the Telecommunications Act 1984 s 60(3) (repealed). A company was for this purpose regarded as wholly owned by the Crown at any time when all the issued shares in the company were held by or on behalf of the Crown: s 73(3) (repealed).
12 'Transferred loan' means any sum borrowed or treated as borrowed by British Telecommunications the liability to repay which vested in British Telecommunications plc by virtue of the Telecommunications Act 1984 s 60 (repealed): British Telecommunications plc (Extinguishment of Loans) Order 1984, SI 1984/992, art 2(1) (lapsed).
13 See the Telecommunications Act 1984 s 62(1) (repealed), s 104(1); and the British Telecommunications plc (Extinguishment of Loans) Order 1984, SI 1984/992, art 2(1) (lapsed). For the power to extinguish loans and the consequences of so doing see the Telecommunications Act 1984 s 62 (repealed). On a winding up of the successor company, the Secretary of State remains liable for any outstanding liabilities of the successor company for the payment of pensions which vested in it by virtue of s 60 (repealed): see s 68(2) (amended by the Communications Act 2003 s 398(1), (3)). As to the liability of the Secretary of State in respect of liabilities vesting in the successor company see the Telecommunications Act 1984 s 68 (amended by the Insolvency Act 1986 s 439(2), Sch 14; and the Communications Act 2003 s 398(3)).
14 See the Telecommunications Act 1984 s 69(2) (repealed); and the British Telecommunications (Dissolution) Order 1994, SI 1994/2162 (lapsed).

15 Where immediately before 6 August 1984 there was in force an agreement which conferred or imposed on British Telecommunications any rights or liabilities which vested in the successor company (ie by virtue of the Telecommunications Act 1984 s 60 (repealed)) and referred, in whatever terms and whether expressly or by implication, to a member or officer of British Telecommunications, that agreement has effect, in relation to anything falling to be done on or after that date, as if for that reference there were substituted a reference to such person as that company may appoint or, in default of appointment, to the officer of that company who corresponds as nearly as may be to the member or officer of British Telecommunications in question: s 109(4), Sch 5 para 35 (Sch 5 para 35 repealed).

Except as otherwise provided (see Sch 5 paras 20–35 (Sch 5 paras 20–33, 35 repealed)), any agreement made, transaction effected or other thing done by, to or in relation to British Telecommunications which was in force or effective immediately before 6 August 1984 had effect from that date as if made, effected or done by, to or in relation to the successor company, in all respects as if the successor company were the same person, in law, as British Telecommunications: Sch 5 para 36(1). Accordingly, references to British Telecommunications in:

(1) any agreement (whether or not in writing) and in any deed, bond or instrument (Sch 5 para 36(1)(a));

(2) any process or other document issued, prepared or employed for the purpose of any proceeding before any court or other tribunal or authority (Sch 5 para 36(1)(b)); and

(3) any other document whatsoever (other than an enactment) relating to or affecting any property, right or liability of British Telecommunications which vests in the successor company (Sch 5 para 36(1)(c)),

are to be taken as referring to the successor company (Sch 5 para 36(1)). Nothing in Sch 5 para 36(1) applies in relation to the deed of covenant by virtue of which the excepted liabilities subsist (see note 7): Sch 5 para 36(2).

The effect of the vesting of the property, rights and liabilities of British Telecommunications in the successor company (ie under s 60 (repealed)) in relation to any contract of employment with British Telecommunications in force immediately before 6 August 1984 is merely to modify the contract, as from that date, by substituting the successor company as the employer, and not to terminate the contract or vary it in any other way (Sch 5 para 37(1)(a)); and to vest the rights and liabilities of British Telecommunications under any agreement or arrangement for the payment of pensions, allowances or gratuities in the successor company along with all other rights and liabilities of British Telecommunications (Sch 5 para 37(1)(b)). Accordingly, for the purposes of any such agreement or arrangement any period of employment with British Telecommunications counts as employment with the successor company or a wholly owned subsidiary of it: see Sch 5 para 37(1). Nothing in Sch 5 para 37(1) applies in relation to the excepted liabilities (see note 7) or to the deed of covenant by virtue of which those liabilities subsist: Sch 5 para 37(2).

Where, by virtue of anything done before 6 August 1984, any enactment amended by the Telecommunications Act 1984 s 109(1), Sch 4 has effect in relation to British Telecommunications, then, on and after that date, any such enactment has effect in relation to the successor company as if that company were the same person, in law, as British Telecommunications: Sch 5 para 45.

52. Meaning of 'telecommunication system' and related expressions.

'Telecommunication system' in the Telecommunications Act 1984 meant a system for the conveyance[1], through the agency of electric, magnetic, electromagnetic, electrochemical or electromechanical energy[2], of:

(1) speech, music and other sounds[3];

(2) visual images[4];

(3) signals serving for the impartation (whether as between persons and persons, things and things or persons and things) of any matter otherwise than in the form of sounds or visual images[5]; or

(4) signals serving for the actuation or control of machinery or apparatus[6].

Telecommunication apparatus which was situated in the United Kingdom[7] and was connected to but not comprised in a telecommunication system, or was connected to and comprised in a telecommunication system which extended beyond the United Kingdom, was to be regarded as a telecommunication system, and any person who controlled the apparatus was to be regarded as running the system[8].

Except where the extended definition in the telecommunications code applied[9], 'telecommunication apparatus' meant apparatus constructed or adapted for use:

(a)   in transmitting or receiving anything falling within heads (1) to (4) above which was to be or had been conveyed[10] by means of a telecommunication system; or

(b)   in conveying for the purpose of such a system anything falling within those heads[11].

'Telecommunication service' meant any of the following:

(i)   a service consisting in the conveyance by means of a telecommunication system of anything falling within heads (1) to (4) above[12];

(ii)   a directory information service[13]; and

(iii)   a service consisting in the installation, maintenance, adjustment, repair, alteration, moving, removal or replacement of apparatus which was or was to be connected to a telecommunication system[14].

A telecommunication system was connected to another telecommunication system if it was being used, or was installed or connected for use, in conveying anything falling within heads (1) to (4) above which was to be or had been conveyed by means of that other system[15]. Apparatus was connected[16] to a telecommunication system if it was being used or was installed or connected for use:

(A)   in transmitting or receiving anything falling within heads (1) to (4) above which was to be or had been conveyed by means of that system[17]; or

(B)   in conveying, for the purposes of that system, anything falling within those heads[18].

1   For the purposes of the Telecommunications Act 1984 s 4(1) (repealed), 'conveyance' did not have the extended meaning set out in note 10: s 4(7) (repealed).

2   Telecommunications Act 1984 s 4(1) (repealed). No definitions were given for the various forms of energy mentioned in the text.

3   Telecommunications Act 1984 s 4(1)(a) (repealed).

4   Telecommunications Act 1984 s 4(1)(b) (repealed).

5   Telecommunications Act 1984 s 4(1)(c) (repealed). As to the meaning of 'person' see PARA 14 note 2.

6   Telecommunications Act 1984 s 4(1)(d) (repealed).

7   As to the meaning of 'United Kingdom' see PARA 14 note 7.

8   Telecommunications Act 1984 s 4(2) (repealed).

9   'Telecommunications code' meant the code contained in the Telecommunications Act 1984 Sch 2 (see PARA 166 et seq): s 10(1) (repealed). An extended definition of 'telecommunication apparatus' for the purposes of the telecommunications code was given in the Telecommunications Act 1984 Sch 2 para 1(1) (definition repealed).

10   In the Telecommunications Act 1984 s 4 (repealed) (except in s 4(1) (repealed): see the text and notes 1–6), 'convey' included transmit, switch or receive; and cognate expressions were to be construed accordingly: s 4(7) (repealed).

11   Telecommunications Act 1984 s 4(3) (repealed).

12   Telecommunications Act 1984 s 4(3)(a) (repealed).

13   Telecommunications Act 1984 s 4(3)(b) (repealed). 'Directory information service' meant a service consisting in the provision by means of a telecommunication system of directory information for the purpose of facilitating the use of a service falling within head (i) in the text and provided by means of that system: s 4(3)(b) (repealed).

14   Telecommunications Act 1984 s 4(3)(c) (repealed).

15   Telecommunications Act 1984 s 4(4) (repealed). The connection to a telecommunication system of any other telecommunication system or any apparatus was not to be regarded as a connection

if that other telecommunication system or that apparatus would not have been so connected but for its connection to another telecommunication system: s 4(6) (repealed).

16 See note 15.

17 Telecommunications Act 1984 s 4(5)(a) (repealed). References to anything falling within heads (1)–(4) in the text included references to energy of any kind there mentioned: s 4(5) (repealed).

18 Telecommunications Act 1984 s 4(5)(b) (repealed).

53. Meaning of 'electronic communications network' and related expressions.
The term 'electronic communications network' replaces the term 'telecommunication system', which was first introduced into legislation in 1981[1] and was continued in use by the legislation regulating telecommunications[2] until the replacement of that legislation by the Communications Act 2003[3].

'Electronic communications network' means[4]:

(1)   a transmission system[5] for the conveyance[6], by the use of electrical, magnetic or electro-magnetic energy, of signals[7] of any description[8]; and

(2)   such of the following as are used, by the person providing the system[9] and in association with it, for the conveyance of the signals:

(a)   apparatus comprised in the system[10];

(b)   apparatus used for the switching or routing of the signals[11];

(c)   software and stored data[12]; and

(d)   other resources[13], including network elements which are not active[14].

'Electronic communications service' means a service consisting in, or having as its principal feature, the conveyance by means of an electronic communications network of signals, except in so far as it is a content service[15].

'Associated facility' means a facility, element or service which is available for use, or has the potential to be used, in association with the use of an electronic communications network or electronic communications service (whether or not one provided by the person making the facility, element or service available) for the purpose of[16]:

(i)   making the provision of that network or service possible[17];

(ii)   making possible the provision of other services provided by means of that network or service[18]; or

(iii)   supporting the provision of such other services[19].

1   See the British Telecommunications Act 1981 s 12 (repealed); and cf the Post Office Act 1969 s 24 (repealed), where the same definition was used in relation to the granting to the Post Office of the exclusive privilege of running systems (see POSTAL SERVICES vol 85 (2012) PARA 208).

2   Ie the Telecommunications Act 1984, where the term was defined in s 4 (repealed), s 106(1): see PARA 52.

3   See PARA 1.

4   Communications Act 2003 ss 32(1), 405(1) (s 32(1) amended by SI 2011/1210). See also the Telecommunications Act 1984 Sch 2 para 1(1) (definition added by the Communications Act 2003 s 106(2), Sch 3 para 2(2)).

5   The reference in the Communications Act 2003 s 32(1) to a transmission system includes a reference to a transmission system consisting of no more than a transmitter used for the conveyance of signals: s 32(6).

6   In the Communications Act 2003 s 32, references to the conveyance of signals include references to the transmission or routing of signals or of parts of signals and to the broadcasting of signals for general reception: s 32(8).

7   'Signal' includes anything comprising speech, music, sounds, visual images or communications or data of any description and signals serving for the impartation of anything between persons, between a person and a thing or between things, or for the actuation or control of apparatus: Communications Act 2003 s 32(10).

8   Communications Act 2003 s 32(1)(a).

9   In the Communications Act 2003:

(1)   references to the provision of an electronic communications network include references to its establishment, maintenance or operation (s 32(4)(a));

(2)   references, where one or more persons are employed or engaged to provide the network or service under the direction or control of another person, to the person by whom an electronic communications network or electronic communications service is provided are confined to references to that other person (s 32(4)(b)); and

(3)   references, where one or more persons are employed or engaged to make facilities available under the direction or control of another person, to the person by whom any associated facilities are made available are confined to references to that other person (s 32(4)(c)).

Heads (1) and (2) apply in relation to references in s 32(1) to the provision of a transmission system as they apply in relation to references in the Communications Act 2003 to the provision of an electronic communications network: s 32(5).

10   Communications Act 2003 s 32(1)(b)(i).

11   Communications Act 2003 s 32(1)(b)(ii) (amended by SI 2011/1210).

12   Communications Act 2003 s 32(1)(b)(iii). For the purposes of the Communications Act 2003 s 32, the cases in which software and stored data are to be taken as being used for a particular purpose include cases in which they have been installed or stored in order to be used for that purpose and are available to be so used: s 32(9).

13   Ie except for the purposes of the Communications Act 2003 ss 125–127 (offences relating to networks and services: see PARAS 207, 208).

14   Communications Act 2003 s 32(1)(b)(iv) (added by SI 2011/1210).

15   Communications Act 2003 s 32(2), 405(1). In s 32(2), a 'content service' means so much of any service as consists in one or both of the following:

(1)   the provision of material with a view to its being comprised in signals conveyed by means of an electronic communications network (s 32(7)(a));

(2)   the exercise of editorial control over the contents of signals conveyed by means of such a network (s 32(7)(b)).

16   Communications Act 2003 ss 32(3), 405(1) (s 32(3) substituted by SI 2011/1210).

17   Communications Act 2003 ss 32(3)(a) (as substituted: see note 16).

18   Communications Act 2003 ss 32(3)(b) (as substituted: see note 16).

19   Communications Act 2003 ss 32(3)(c) (as substituted: see note 16).

(ii) International Aspects

54. Satellite telecommunications. The United Kingdom[1] has been party to the development of satellite communications since the launching of the first experimental communications satellite, TELSTAR 1, in 1962. Satellite communications have now established themselves as a significant and indispensable element in the provision of global telecommunications networks and services.

The main statute regulating the launching and operation of a satellite for the provision of telecommunications services[2] is the Outer Space Act 1986[3]. The Outer Space Act 1986 confers powers upon the Secretary of State[4] to secure compliance with the United Kingdom's international obligations[5] with respect to launching, or procuring the launch, of a space object, operating a space object, and any other activity in outer space[6].

There is European legislation concerning the selection and authorisation of systems providing mobile satellite services[7], which has been implemented in the United Kingdom by regulations making it a criminal offence to use certain frequency bands for the provision of mobile satellite services without an authorisation from OFCOM[8].

1   As to the meaning of 'United Kingdom' see PARA 14 note 7.

2   As to the meaning of 'telecommunication services' see PARA 52.

3   See INTERNATIONAL RELATIONS LAW vol 61 (2010) PARA 211.

4   As to the Secretary of State see PARA 76 note 1.

5   See the Treaty on Principles Governing the Activities of States in the Exploration and Use of Outer Space, including the Moon and Other Celestial Bodies (London, Moscow and

Washington, 27 January 1967; TS 10 (1968); Cmnd 3519). The Instrument of Ratification was deposited in London on 10 October 1967 and the Treaty entered into force on that date. See also the Convention on International Liability for Damage caused by Space Objects (London, Moscow and Washington, 29 March 1972; TS 16 (1974); Cmnd 5551). The United Kingdom's instruments of ratification were deposited on 9 October 1973 and the Treaty entered into force for the United Kingdom on that date. See also the Convention on Registration of Objects launched into Outer Space (New York, 14 January 1975; TS 70 (1978); Cmnd 7271). The United Kingdom instrument of ratification was deposited and the Convention entered into force for the United Kingdom on 30 May 1978. See also INTERNATIONAL RELATIONS LAW vol 61 (2010) PARA 207.

6   See the Outer Space Act 1986 s 1; and INTERNATIONAL RELATIONS LAW vol 61 (2010) PARA 211.

7   See European Parliament and Council Decision (EC) 626/2008 (OJ L172, 02.07.2008, p 15) on the selection and authorisation of systems providing mobile satellite services; and Commission Decision (EC) 2009/449 (OJ L149, 12.06.2009, p 65) on the selection of operators of pan-European systems providing mobile satellite services. See also Commission Decision (EU) 2011/667 (OJ L265, 11.10.2011, p 25) on modalities for co-ordinated application of the rules on enforcement with regard to mobile satellite services pursuant to Decision 626/2008 art 9(3).

8   A person commits an offence if that person uses the frequency bands 1980 to 2010MHz and 2170 to 2200MHz or any part of those bands for the provision of mobile satellite services except under and in accordance with an authorisation granted under the Authorisation of Frequency Use for the Provision of Mobile Satellite Services (European Union) Regulations 2010, SI 2010/672 by OFCOM: Authorisation of Frequency Use for the Provision of Mobile Satellite Services (European Union) Regulations 2010, SI 2010/672 (amended by SI 2013/174); and BROADCASTING vol 4 (2011) PARA 564 et seq. As to the meaning of 'OFCOM' see PARA 14 note 1; and as to the establishment of OFCOM see PARA 2.

55. INTELSAT. The United Kingdom was a founder member of the International Telecommunications Satellite Organisation, known as 'INTELSAT', which was set up in 1964 under an inter-governmental agreement establishing interim arrangements for a global commercial communications satellite system[1].

A plenipotentiary conference on definitive arrangements for INTELSAT opened in Washington DC in February 1969. In May 1971 agreement was reached on the text of the definitive Inter-governmental and Operating Agreements[2]. The United Kingdom signed the Inter-governmental Agreement in August 1971. The Post Office as the then designated telecommunications entity for the United Kingdom signed the Operating Agreement. British Telecommunications plc is now the designated signatory for the United Kingdom[3].

INTELSAT became a private company on 18 July 2001 and is now INTELSAT General Corporation, a US company, registered in Delaware and headquartered in Bethesda, Maryland. It provides government and industry customers from all parts of the world with satellite bandwidth, customised services and applications, end-to-end communications solutions and hosted payloads through its global telecommunications network[4].

1   See the Agreement establishing Interim Arrangements for a Global Commercial Communications Satellite System (Washington, 20 August 1964 to 20 February 1965; TS 12 (1966); Cmnd 2940). As to the meaning of 'United Kingdom' see PARA 14 note 7.

2   See the Agreement relating to the International Telecommunications Satellite Organisation 'INTELSAT' (with Operating Agreement) (Washington, 20 August 1971; TS 80 (1973); Cmnd 5416). The United Kingdom instrument of ratification was deposited with INTELSAT on 16 February 1972 and the Agreement and the Operating Agreement entered into force on 12 February 1973. It is not apparent that the treaty agreement is any longer valid since the privatisation of INTELSAT.

3   Although British Telecommunications plc is the designated signatory, over 20 other United Kingdom operators are designated as additional 'investing entities'.

4   See the INTELSAT General website which at the date this volume states the law is at www.intelsatgeneral.com.

56. INMARSAT. In 1979, the United Kingdom signed and ratified the Convention on the International Maritime Satellite Organisation (INMARSAT)[1]. Its purpose was to make provision for the space segment necessary for organising maritime communications, thereby assisting in improving distress communications and safety of life at sea communications, efficiency and management of ships, maritime public correspondence services and radio determination capabilities. INMARSAT has a similar structure and operating arrangements to INTELSAT. However, in 1999, INMARSAT became a private operating company (INMARSAT plc) as well as an inter-governmental organisation[2].

1   See the Convention on the International Maritime Satellite Organisation (INMARSAT) (with Operating Agreement) (London, 3 September 1976; TS 94 (1979); Cmnd 7722). The United Kingdom instrument of ratification was deposited on 30 April 1979 and the Convention came into force on 16 July 1979. The United Kingdom signed the Operating Agreement on 20 March 1979. As to the meaning of 'United Kingdom' see PARA 14 note 7.

    The title of INMARSAT was amended to the International Mobile Satellite Organisation by the Assembly of INMARSAT on 9 December 1994: see Amendments to the Convention on the International Maritime Satellite Organisation (Inmarsat) Cm 3069 (January 1996); Amendments to the Operating Agreement on the International Maritime Satellite Organisation (Inmarsat) Cm 3070 (January 1996); and the International Mobile Satellite Organisation (Immunities and Privileges) Order 1999, SI 1999/1125 (amended by virtue of the British Overseas Territories Act 2002 s 2(3)).

2   With effect from 15 April 1999, INMARSAT as an organisation created by treaty continues to exist as a legal entity but primarily to oversee the provision of the Global Maritime Distress and Safety System. See Amendments to the Convention and the operating agreement relating to the International Mobile Satellite Organisation (Inmarsat) (Cm 3995) (1998).

57. Eutelsat. The United Kingdom has signed and ratified the Convention establishing the European Telecommunications Satellite Organisation (Eutelsat)[1]. The prime objective of Eutelsat is the provision of the space segment required for international public telecommunication services in Europe. Where Eutelsat is operating in the exercise of its official activities, it has immunity from suit and legal process[2]. In the context of the general liberalisation of the telecommunications sector in Europe, Eutelsat's operations and activities were transferred to a private company called Eutelsat SA in July 2001. In April 2005, a new entity (Eutelsat Communications) was formed, which is now the holding company of the group, based in Paris[3].

1   See the Convention establishing the European Telecommunications Satellite Organisation (EUTELSAT) (Paris, 15 July 1982; TS 15 (1990); Cm 956) (amended by a Protocol of 15 December 1983; Cm 9154). The United Kingdom instrument of ratification of the Convention was deposited on 21 February 1985 and the Convention, Operating Agreement and Protocol entered into force on 1 September 1985.

2   See the EUTELSAT (Immunities and Privileges) Order 1988, SI 1988/1299, art 6. This order revokes the EUTELSAT (Immunities and Privileges) Order 1984, SI 1984/1980, and implements the Protocol on the Privileges and Immunities of the European Telecommunications Satellite Organisation (EUTELSAT) (Paris, 13 February 1987; TS 46 (1990); Cm 1106). The order is still in force notwithstanding the privatisation of EUTELSAT.

3   See the Eutelsat SA website which at the date this volume states the law is at www.eutelsat.com.

58. BEREC. The Body of European Regulators for Electronic Communications ('BEREC') was established to act as an exclusive forum for cooperation among the national regulatory authorities for electronic communications networks and services[1] and between the national regulatory authorities and the European Commission[2]. It replaced the European Regulators Group for electronic communications networks and services. BEREC provides assistance to the national regulatory authorities in the implementation of the EU regulatory framework[3]. The national regulatory authorities and the Commission must take account of any opinion, recommendation, guidelines, advice or regulatory best practice adopted by BEREC[4].

1   As to the current list of national regulatory authorities for electronic communications networks and services see the BEREC website, which at the date this volume states the law is available at www.berec.europa.eu. OFCOM is the national regulatory authority for the United Kingdom for these purposes. As to the meaning of 'OFCOM' see PARA 14 note 1; and as to OFCOM see PARA 2 et seq.

2   BEREC was established by the European Parliament and Council Regulation (EC) 1211/2009 (OJ L337, 18.12.2009, p 1).

3   See further the BEREC website and note 1.

4   See PARAS 92, 95, 108, 221.

59.   The International Telecommunication Union.   The International Telecommunication Union was founded in 1932[1]. It exists to further the development of telegraph, telephone and radio services, to promote international co-operation for the use of telecommunications and the development of technical facilities, and to allocate radio frequencies. The basic principles for the conduct of international telecommunication services, the basis for membership of the International Telecommunication Union and its organisation and permanent organs, are now contained in the Constitution and Convention of the International Telecommunication Union, to which the United Kingdom is a party[2].

1   See INTERNATIONAL RELATIONS LAW vol 61 (2010) PARA 533. It replaced the former International Telegraph Union, which was established in 1865.

2   See the Final Acts of the Plenipotentiary Conference of the International Telecommunication Union with Instruments amending the Constitution and Convention of the International Telecommunication Union, Decision, Resolutions and Recommendations (Kyoto, 14 October 1994; TS 65 (1997); Cm 3779). The amendments entered into force for the United Kingdom on deposit of the Instrument of Ratification on 11 February 1997.

60.   World Trade Organisation.   The World Trade Organisation was established in 1994[1]. The function of the World Trade Organisation is to facilitate the implementation, administration and operation of multilateral trade agreements[2], including the General Agreement on Trade in Services ('GATS')[3]. The GATS contains an annex on telecommunications[4] and a Protocol establishing commitments in basic telecommunications[5]. These agreements require member signatories to open up their telecommunication markets to competition from foreign operators.

1   See the Agreement establishing the World Trade Organisation with Understanding on Rules and Procedures Governing the Settlement of Disputes and Trade Policy Review Mechanism (Marrakesh, 15 April 1994; TS 57 (1996); Cm 3277); and the Final Act embodying the Results of the Uruguay Round of Multilateral Trade Negotiations (Marrakesh, 15 April 1994; TS 55 (1996); Cm 3283). Both Treaties entered into force on 1 January 1995.

2   Agreement establishing the World Trade Organisation with Understanding on Rules and Procedures Governing the Settlement of Disputes and Trade Policy Review Mechanism (Marrakesh, 15 April 1994; TS 57 (1996); Cm 3277) art III(1); and see note 1.

3   General Agreement on Trade in Services with Annexes (Marrakesh, 15 April 1994; TS 58 (1996); Cm 3276). The Treaty entered into force on 1 January 1995.

4   See the Annex on Telecommunications in the General Agreement on Trade in Services with Annexes (Marrakesh, 15 April 1994; TS 58 (1996); Cm 3276).

5   Fourth Protocol to the General Agreement on Trade in Services, Decision on Commitments in Basic Telecommunications, adopted by the Council for Trade in Services on 30 April 1996 (see 97/838 EC OJ L347, 18.12.97, p 45; 36 ILM 354, 366 (1997)). The Protocol entered into force

on 5 February 1998. The commitments are usually referred to as the WTO Basic Telecom Agreement, although they are not contained in a stand-alone agreement.

61. Internet regulatory bodies. In addition to the various non-statutory national regulatory bodies[1], a number of agencies play a governing or co-ordinating role in relation to the structure and manner of operation of the internet, such as the Internet Corporation for Assigned Names and Numbers ('ICANN')[2], the Internet Engineering Task Force ('IETF')[3] and the World Wide Web Consortium ('W3C')[4]; and the European Union Agency for Network and Information Security ('ENISA')[5].

1 See e g PARA 80.
2 ICANN was established in 1998. It is a public-private partnership, and operates under the terms of a contract with the United States' Department of Commerce. It aims to co-ordinate the stable operation of the internet's unique identifier systems. It is concerned primarily with technical issues, and most importantly with the operation of the system of internet domain names. It has no remit concerning conduct over or content on the internet. As to domain name registrations in the United Kingdom see PARA 80 note 7.
3 IETF is concerned with the architecture of the internet.
4 W3C develops interoperable technologies.
5 ENISA was established under European Parliament and Council Regulation (EC) 460/2004 (OJ L77, 13.3.2004, p 1) for the purpose of ensuring a high and effective level of network and information security within the European Union. ENISA's other objectives include providing assistance and advice to the European Commission and its member states on issues related to network and information security falling within its competencies and carrying out technical preparatory work for updating and developing European Union legislation in the field of information security. European Parliament and Council Regulation (EC) 460/2004 (OJ L77, 13.3.2004, p 1) has been repealed by the European Parliament and Council Regulation (EC) 526/2013 (OJ L165, 18.6.2013, p 41).

(2) COMMON LAW OBLIGATIONS

62. Relationship between operators and their customers. Persons engaged in telecommunications business are the agents of the persons handing in signed messages for transmission, for the purpose of making a contract, with the necessary formalities, when required, as to signature[1]. However, they are only agents for the transmission of a message in the terms in which the message is delivered to them by the sender[2]. For any omission, delay or negligence in the duty of transmitting or delivering messages they are liable to the sender[3], with whom there is privity of contract, but not to the person to whom it is sent, with whom there is none[4]. They are not common carriers, even if carriers at all of the messages transmitted[5].

1 *Godwin v Francis* (1870) LR 5 CP 295; *McBlain v Cross* (1871) 25 LT 804. In both cases the message, as handed to the telegraph clerk for transmission, was duly signed by the sender.
2 *Henkel v Pape* (1870) LR 6 Exch 7; *Ross v Long* (1899) 40 NSR 174; *Hamilton v Clancy* [1914] 2 IR 514. See also CONTRACT vol 22 (2012) PARA 278.
3 For the measure of damages see *Sanders v Stuart* (1876) 1 CPD 326, where a telegraph company negligently omitted to send a telegram in cipher, and it was held that the plaintiff was not entitled to recover for loss of commission on the order to which the telegram related, but only nominal damages. A telegraph company could by notice contract itself out of liability for mistakes in unrepeated telegrams: *MacAndrew v Electric Telegraph Co* (1855) 17 CB 3, where the company advised that important telegrams should be repeated and charged at a higher rate.
4 *Playford v United Kingdom Electric Telegraph Co* (1869) LR 4 QB 706; *Dickson v Reuter's Telegram Co* (1877) 3 CPD 1, CA.
5 See *Dickson v Reuter's Telegram Co* (1877) 3 CPD 1, CA. Cf the Post Office Act 1969 s 7(4) (repealed): see POSTAL SERVICES vol 85 (2012) PARA 252 et seq. See also CARRIAGE AND CARRIERS vol 7 (2015) PARA 3 et seq.

63. Legal effects of telecommunications. The legal effects of telecommunications are considered elsewhere in this work in respect of the acceptance of an offer by telephone or telex[1], the formation of a contract by telegram[2], defamation by telegram[3] or broadcasting[4], the serving of claim forms and other documents by electronic means[5] and the stopping of a cheque by teletransmission[6].

1 See CONTRACT vol 22 (2012) PARA 283.
2 See CONTRACT vol 22 (2012) PARA 277.
3 See DEFAMATION vol 32 (2012) PARAS 565, 618.
4 As to publication in permanent form by broadcasting see DEFAMATION vol 32 (2012) PARA 576; as to privileged reports see DEFAMATION vol 32 (2012) PARA 627 et seq; and as to slander of title etc see DEFAMATION vol 32 (2012) PARA 778.
5 See CIVIL PROCEDURE vol 11 (2009) PARA 139.
6 See FINANCIAL SERVICES AND INSTITUTIONS vol 49 (2008) PARA 847.

64. Telecommunication apparatus as the subject of demise. An agreement for the supply of a telephone service to a house may be so framed as to create a relationship analogous to that of landlord and tenant between the parties in respect of the wires and other apparatus placed in the house[1].

1 *Keith Prowse & Co v National Telephone Co* [1894] 2 Ch 147; *National Telephone Co v Griffen* [1906] 2 IR 115. There are no express statutory provisions exempting telecommunication apparatus from distress (cf electricity fittings: see ENERGY AND CLIMATE CHANGE vol 43 (2011) PARA 591).

65. Rating of telecommunication apparatus. A company or a person (including a telecommunications operator) who has the exclusive occupation of telecommunication apparatus is liable to pay rates in respect of it[1]; but occupation is not exclusive where it is subject to control and regulation by others[2]. An easement or wayleave over land for telegraphic or telephonic posts or works is a rateable occupation of that land[3].

With a view to securing the central rating en bloc of certain hereditaments the Secretary of State has made regulations designating a number of corporate bodies and has prescribed in relation to them a group of relevant non-domestic hereditaments, including telecommunications hereditaments[4].

1 *Electric Telegraph Co v Salford Overseers* (1855) 11 Exch 181, a case in respect of telegraph wires and posts which would now fall within the definition of 'electronic communications apparatus' in the electronic communications code: see PARA 168 note 6. See also LOCAL GOVERNMENT FINANCE vol 70 (2012) PARA 65.

2 See *Paris and New York Telegraph Co v Penzance Union* (1884) 12 QBD 552, DC.
3 *Lancashire Telephone Co v Manchester Overseers* (1884) 14 QBD 267, CA; and see LOCAL GOVERNMENT FINANCE vol 70 (2012) PARA 76.

4 See the Central Rating List (England) Regulations 2005, SI 2005/551 (in relation to England); the Central Rating List (Wales) Regulations 2005, SI 2005/422 (in relation to Wales); and LOCAL GOVERNMENT FINANCE vol 70 (2012) PARA 177.

66. Telecommunications and taxation. Where the cables of a submarine telegraph company communicate with telegraphic lines in the United Kingdom belonging to a public telecommunications operator, which collects the total charges in the United Kingdom, and, after deducting what is due to it, hands over the balance to the submarine telegraph company, that company is, to that extent, carrying on business in the United Kingdom, and was liable to tax on the balance of profits earned in the United Kingdom[1].

Amounts that may in accordance with generally accepted accounting practice be taken into account in determining profit or loss for accounting purposes in respect of:

(1)   expenditure on the acquisition of a wireless telegraphy licence[2], an indefeasible right to use a telecommunications system or a right derived, directly or indirectly, from such a licence or right; or

(2)   receipts from the disposal of such a licence or right, are treated as items of a revenue nature for tax purposes, provided they are so taken into account in any relevant statutory accounts of the taxpayer[3].

There must also be taken into account for tax purposes as an item of a revenue nature any amount in respect of the revaluation of any such right that, in accordance with normal accounting practice, falls to be taken into account for accounting purposes[4].

Special provision is made as to the place of supply for value added tax purposes in connection with the provision of telecommunication services[5].

1   *Erichsen v Last* (1881) 8 QBD 414, CA; and see INCOME TAXATION vol 58 (2014) PARA 97. As to the meaning of 'United Kingdom' see PARA 14 note 7.
2   Ie a licence granted under the Wireless Telegraphy Act 2006 s 8 in accordance with regulations made under s 14 (bidding for licences). See BROADCASTING vol 4 (2011) PARA 514 et seq.
3   See the Income Tax (Trading and Other Income) Act 2005 ss 146, 147; and INCOME TAXATION vol 58 (2014) PARA 276.
4   See the Income Tax (Trading and Other Income) Act 2005 s 148; and INCOME TAXATION vol 58 (2014) PARA 276.
5   See the Value Added Tax Act 1994 s 7A, Sch 4A paras 8, 15; and VALUE ADDED TAX.

67.   Telecommunications undertakers and the common law. As the telecommunications undertaker enjoys no special position at common law[1], it is not practicable to provide a service without special statutory powers. Thus, in the case of electronic communications apparatus placed in or over a street, statutory provisions were introduced to provide immunity from claims of interference with the rights of members of the public and of the highway authority[2], and of owners of property adjoining the highway in relation to the highway[3]. It was also necessary to reconcile the rights of the telecommunications undertaker with those of other public utility undertakers in relation to the highway[4]. Similarly, at common law, electronic communications apparatus may only be placed on private property with the consent of persons having rights in the land, and statutory provision is made to prevent such persons from arbitrarily withholding or withdrawing their consent[5]. Subject to any statutory provisions, the undertaker's rights and liabilities under the common law and, where submarine cables are concerned, under Admiralty law, are preserved[6].

1   *R v United Kingdom Electric Telegraph Co Ltd* (1862) 31 LJMC 166.
2   See eg the Telecommunications Act 1984 Sch 2 para 9 (which contains power to install and maintain electronic communications apparatus in streets); PARA 174; and HIGHWAYS, STREETS AND BRIDGES vol 55 (2012) PARA 302. As to statutory authority as a defence to nuisance see NUISANCE vol 78 (2010) PARA 192.
3   See eg the Telecommunications Act 1984 Sch 2 para 19 (which contains power to lop trees overhanging a street which obstruct electronic communications apparatus along that street); PARA 178; and HIGHWAYS, STREETS AND BRIDGES vol 55 (2012) PARA 382.
4   See eg the Telecommunications Act 1984 Sch 2 para 23; PARA 191; and HIGHWAYS, STREETS AND BRIDGES vol 55 (2012) PARA 302.
5   See the Telecommunications Act 1984 Sch 2 para 5; and PARA 171. Written agreement is also required under Sch 2 para 2: see PARA 163.
6   In *National Telephone Co v Baker* [1893] 2 Ch 186, the rule in *Rylands v Fletcher* (1868) LR 3 HL 330 (see NUISANCE vol 78 (2010) PARA 148 et seq) was held to apply in relation to injury to telephone circuits by electrical energy discharged by undertakers operating tramways, although

the undertakers were protected from liability by the terms of their statutory powers. See also *Eastern and South African Telegraph Co Ltd v Cape Town Tramways Companies Ltd* [1902] AC 381, PC. The owners of submarine cables were held entitled, in respect of injury to their cables by anchors, to common law relief in *Submarine Telegraph Co v Dickson* (1864) 15 CBNS 759, and to Admiralty relief in *The Clara Killam* (1870) LR 3 A & E 161.

(3) LEGISLATION FOR TELECOMMUNICATIONS

68. European Union law and the telecommunications sector. Since 1987[1], there has been a substantial amount of regulatory activity in the telecommunications sector at a European Union level[2]. Over one hundred different directives, decisions, regulations, recommendations and resolutions, relating to every aspect of the industry, have been officially adopted since 1986[3]. For the United Kingdom, these regulatory initiatives have not always required a legislative response, since some of the issues had already been addressed by the regime established under the Telecommunications Act 1984.

The European Commission's[4] involvement in the telecommunications market has primarily been founded in two different aspects of European law: the application of European competition law to the industry[5], and the establishment of an internal market for telecommunications[6].

The EC Communications Directives[7] are implemented in the United Kingdom both by regulations and by the Communications Act 2003[8].

1   See the European Commission Green Paper on the Development of the Common Market for Telecommunications Services and Equipment, COM(87) 290 final of June 30, 1987.
2   Many of the provisions extend to encompass the European Economic Area (ie the European Union member states and Norway, Iceland and Liechtenstein) under the Agreement on the European Economic Area (Oporto, 2 May 1992; Cm 2073 (OJ L1, 3.1.94, p 3)) as adjusted by the Protocol (Brussels, 17 March 1993; Cm 2183 (OJ L1, 3.1.94, p 572)) (the 'EEA Agreement'). As to the EEA Agreement see COMPETITION vol 18 (2009) PARA 36.
3   A compilation of all telecommunications related texts can be obtained from: European Commission, DG XIII/A/1, BU31 2/07, Rue de la Loi 200, B-1049 Brussels, Belgium.
4   As to the European Commission see EUROPEAN UNION vol 47A (2014) PARAS 48, 49.
5   See the Treaty on the Functioning of the European Union (Rome, 25 March 1957; TS 1 (1973); Cmnd 5179) ('TFEU') arts 101, 102, 106. The Treaty was formerly known as the Treaty Establishing the European Community; it has been renamed and its provisions renumbered: see PARA 17 note 17. See also eg Commission Directive (EC) 2002/77 (OJ L249, 17.9.2002, p 21) on competition in the markets for electronic communications networks and services; and Commission Directive (EC) 2008/63 (OJ L162, 21.6.2008, p 20) on competition in the markets in telecommunications terminal equipment.
6   See the EU Treaty art 114 (as renamed and renumbered: see note 5).
7   Ie European Parliament and Council Directive (EC) 2002/19 (OJ L108, 24.4.2002, p 7) on access to, and interconnection of, electronic communications networks and associated facilities (amended by European Parliament and Council Directive (EC) 2009/140 (OJ L337, 18.12.2009, p 37) (corrected in OJ L241, 10.9.2013, p 8)); European Parliament and Council Directive (EC) 2002/20 (OJ L108, 24.4.2002, p 21) on the authorisation of electronic communications networks and services (amended by European Parliament and Council Directive (EC) 2009/140 (OJ L337, 18.12.2009, p 37) (corrected in OJ L241, 10.9.2013, p 8)); European Parliament and Council Directive (EC) 2002/21 (OJ L108, 24.4.2002, p 33) on a common regulatory framework for electronic communications networks and services (amended by European Parliament and Council Regulation (EC) 717/2007 (OJ L171, 29.6.2007, p 32)); European Parliament and Council Regulation (EC) 544/2009 (OJ L167, 29.6.2009, p 12); and European Parliament and Council Directive (EC) 2009/140 (OJ L337, 18.12.2009, p 37 (corrected in OJ L241, 10.9.2013, p 8)); European Parliament and Council Directive (EC) 2002/22 (OJ L108, 24.4.2002, p 51) on universal service and users' rights relating to electronic communications networks and services (amended by European Parliament and Council Directive (EC) 2009/136 (OJ L337, 18.12.2009, p 11) (corrected in OJ L241, 10.9.2013, p 9); and Council Directive (EC) 2002/58 (OJ L201, 31.7.2002, p 37) concerning the processing of personal data and the protection of privacy in the electronic communications sector (amended by European Parliament

and Council Directive (EC) 2006/24 (OJ L105, 13.4.2006, p 54); and by European Parliament and Council Directive (EC) 2009/136 (OJ L337, 18.12.2009, p 11)), replacing Council Directive (EC) 97/66 (OJ L24, 30.1.98, p 1). See also Commission Regulation (EU) 611/2013 (OJ L173, 26.6.2013, p 2) on the measures applicable to the notification of personal data breaches under European Parliament and Council Directive (EC) 2002/58; European Parliament and Council Directive (EU) 2014/61 (OJ L155, 23.5.2014, p 1) on measures to reduce the cost of deploying high-speed electronic communications networks. Member states must adopt and publish the laws, regulations and administrative provisions necessary to comply with European Parliament and Council Directive (EU) 2014/61 on measures to reduce the cost of deploying high-speed electronic communications networks by 1 January 2016 and must apply those measures from 1 July 2016: see art 13. The European Parliament and Council Regulation (EC) 717/2007 (OJ L171, 29.6.2007, p 32) is now replaced by European Parliament and Council Regulation (EC) 531/2012 (OJ L172, 30.6.2012, p 10) on roaming on public mobile telephone networks within the Union. See also PARA 1.

8   As to the implementing regulations see e g the Electronic Communications (Universal Service) Regulations 2003, SI 2003/33 (amended by SI 2003/330); and the Electronic Communications (Market Analysis) Regulations 2003, SI 2003/330 (amended by SI 2011/1043). See also the Mobile Roaming (European Communities) Regulations 2007, SI 2007/1933 (amended by SI 2009/1591, SI 2012/1809, SI 2009/1591, SI 2012/1809, SI 2013/822, SI 2014/2715), which implemented European Parliament and Council Regulation (EC) 717/2007 (OJ L171, 29.6.2007, p 32) on roaming on public mobile telephone networks within the European Union. The European Parliament and Council Regulation (EC) 717/2007 (OJ L171, 29.6.2007, p 32) is now replaced by European Parliament and Council Regulation (EC) 531/2012 (OJ L172, 30.6.2012, p 10) on roaming on public mobile telephone networks within the Union. See also Commission Implementing Regulation (EU) 1203/2012 (OJ L347, 15.12.2012, p 1) on the separate sale of regulated retail roaming services within the European Union (with application from 1 July 2014 to 30 June 2022). Council Directive (EC) 2002/58 (OJ L201, 31.7.2002, p 37) is implemented by the Privacy and Electronic Communications (EC Directive) Regulations 2003, SI 2003/2426: see PARA 228 et seq. See also PARA 1.

69.   The Telecommunications Act 1984.   Prior to the enactment of the Communications Act 2003[1], the main statute relating to telecommunications and other electronic communications was the Telecommunications Act 1984[2]. Telecommunications Act 1984 extends to Scotland, and to Northern Ireland[3]. Any specified provisions of the Telecommunications Act 1984 may, by Order in Council, be extended to the Isle of Man[4] or any of the Channel Islands[5] with specified   exceptions,   adaptations   and   modifications[6].   However,   the Telecommunications   Act   1984   has   been   substantially   repealed   by   the Communications Act 2003[7] and the Wireless Telegraphy Act 2006[8], and many of the remaining provisions have been amended by the 2003 Act[9].

Among the matters governed by the Telecommunications Act 1984 were the appointment[10] and functions[11] of the Director General of Telecommunications, the abolition of the exclusive privilege of British Telecommunications of running telecommunication systems[12], the general duties of the Secretary of State and the Director General of Telecommunications[13], the transfer of the undertaking of British   Telecommunications[14]   to   a   successor   company   nominated   by   the Secretary of State[15] and the dissolution of British Telecommunications[16].

Provisions of the Telecommunications Act 1984 that continued to have effect until their repeal by the Wireless Telegraphy Act 2006 included those relating to the amendment and enforcement of the Wireless Telegraphy Acts[17] and the approval[18]   and   marking[19]   of   wireless   telegraphy   apparatus[20].   The Telecommunications Act 1984 abolished the advisory committee on interference with wireless telegraphy[21].

In addition, the Telecommunications Act 1984 provides for the giving of directions by the Secretary of State in the interests of national security or relations with the government of a country or territory outside the United Kingdom[22]; the use of certain conduits for telecommunication purposes[23]; and restrictions on the disclosure of information which has been obtained under or by virtue of the provisions of the Telecommunications Act 1984 and which relates to the private affairs of any individual or to any particular business[24].

1   As to the Communications Act 2003 see PARA 70.
2   Ie the Telecommunications Act 1984 (see s 110(1)). The provisions of the Telegraph Acts 1863 to 1962 which formerly regulated these matters have, with minor exceptions, been repealed by successive statutes. The remaining provisions are the Telegraph Act 1863 s 1; the Telegraph Act 1868 s 1; and the Telegraph Act 1870 ss 1, 3. As to the Telegraph Acts 1863 to 1962 see PARA 46 note 2.
3   Telecommunications Act 1984 s 110(6).
4   As to the provisions of the Telecommunications Act 1984 that have been extended to the Isle of Man see the Telecommunications Act 1984 (Isle of Man) Order 1984, SI 1984/861, art 2, Schedule Pt I (subject to the exceptions, adaptations and modifications set out in Schedule Pt II).
5   As to the provisions of the Telecommunications Act 1984 that have been extended to Guernsey see the Wireless Telegraphy (Guernsey) Order 1994, SI 1994/1064, art 3(1) (substituted by SI 2006/3325) (subject to the exceptions, adaptations and modifications in the Wireless Telegraphy (Guernsey) Order 1994, SI 1994/1064, Schedule Pt I (amended by SI 2006/3325)). As to the provisions of the Telecommunications Act 1984 that were extended to Jersey see the Wireless Telegraphy (Jersey) Order 2003, SI 2003/3196, art 3(1) (subject to the exceptions, adaptations and modifications in Schedule Pt I), but that order has been revoked.
6   Telecommunications Act 1984 s 108.
7   See the Communications Act 2003 s 406(7), Sch 19.
8   See the Wireless Telegraphy Act 2006 s 125(1), Sch 9 Pt 1. The Telecommunications Act 1984 Pt VI (ss 75–92) (repealed) is consolidated in part in the Wireless Telegraphy Act 2006.
9   See the Communications Act 2003 ss 106(2), 406(1), Sch 3, Sch 17.
10   See the Telecommunications Act 1984 s 1, Sch 1 (prospectively repealed); and PARA 14 note 2.
11   Functions have now been transferred to OFCOM: see PARA 14.
12   See the Telecommunications Act 1984 s 2 (repealed); and PARA 49. As to the meaning of 'telecommunication system' see PARA 52.
13   See the Telecommunications Act 1984 s 3 (repealed). As to the Secretary of State see PARA 76 note 1.
14   As to British Telecommunications see PARA 51 et seq.
15   See the Telecommunications Act 1984 ss 60–68, 70–73 (largely repealed); and PARA 51.
16   See the Telecommunications Act 1984 s 69 (repealed); and PARA 51.
17   See the Telecommunications Act 1984 ss 74–83 (repealed).
18   See the Telecommunications Act 1984 s 84 (repealed).
19   See the Telecommunications Act 1984 s 85 (repealed).
20   As to the meaning of 'wireless telegraphy apparatus' see BROADCASTING vol 4 (2011) PARA 510 note 1.
21   Telecommunications Act 1984 s 89 (repealed). That committee was established under the Wireless Telegraphy Act 1949 s 9(1)(a) (repealed). It was abolished on 16 July 1984, and the provisions of the Wireless Telegraphy Act 1949 relating to the committee ceased to have effect as from that date by virtue of the Telecommunications Act 1984 s 89; and the Telecommunications Act 1984 (Appointed Day) (No 2) Order 1984, SI 1984/876, art 2, Sch 1.
22   See the Telecommunications Act 1984 s 94; and PARA 77. As to the meaning of 'United Kingdom' see PARA 14 note 7.
23   See the Telecommunications Act 1984 s 98; and PARAS 180–181.
24   See the Telecommunications Act 1984 s 101; and PARA 42.

70. The Communications Act 2003. The Communications Act 2003 repeals most of the provisions of the Telecommunications Act 1984, and amends some of those that remain in force[1].

The Communications Act 2003 extends to Northern Ireland[2] and Her Majesty may by Order in Council extend the provisions of the Act, with such modifications as appear to Her Majesty in Council to be appropriate, to any of the Channel Islands or to the Isle of Man[3], but this does not authorise the extension to any place of a provision of the Communications Act 2003 so far as it gives effect to an amendment of an enactment that is not itself capable of being extended there in exercise of a power conferred on Her Majesty in Council[4]. The extended power applicable in relation to orders made by the Secretary of State[5] applies to the power to make an Order in Council under these provisions as it applies to any power of the Secretary of State to make an order under the Communications Act 2003, but as if references to the Secretary of State were references to Her Majesty in Council[6]. Specific provisions of the Communications Act 2003 have been extended to Guernsey, Jersey and the Isle of Man[7].

The Communications Act 2003 makes provision with respect to the functions of OFCOM[8], including the regulation of electronic communications networks and services[9].

1   See PARA 69.
2   See the Communications Act 2003 s 411(5).
3   See the Communications Act 2003 s 411(6).
4   See the Communications Act 2003 s 411(7).
5   Ie the Communications Act 2003 s 402(3): see PARA 74 text to notes 11–13. As to the Secretary of State see PARA 76 note 1.
6   Communications Act 2003 s 411(8).
7   See the Communications (Bailiwick of Guernsey) Order 2003, SI 2003/3195 (amended by SI 2004/715; SI 2004/1116; SI 2005/856; SI 2006/3325; SI 2012/2688); the Communications (Bailiwick of Guernsey) Order 2004, SI 2004/307; the Communications (Bailiwick of Guernsey) (No 2) Order 2004, SI 2004/715; the Communications (Bailiwick of Guernsey) (No 3) Order 2004, SI 2004/1116; the Communications (Jersey) Order 2003, SI 2003/3197 (amended by SI 2004/308; SI 2004/716; SI 2004/1114; SI 2005/855; and SI 2006/3324); the Broadcasting and Communications (Jersey) Order 2004, SI 2004/308 (amended by SI 2006/3324); the Broadcasting and Communications (Jersey) (No 2) Order 2004, SI 2004/716; the Broadcasting and Communications (Jersey) (No 3) Order 2004, SI 2004/1114; the Communications (Isle of Man) Order 2003, SI 2003/3198 (amended by SI 2004/309; SI 2004/718; SI 2004/1115; SI 2007/278; and SI 2011/1503); the Broadcasting and Communications (Isle of Man) Order 2004, SI 2004/309 (amended by SI 2007/278); the Broadcasting and Communications (Isle of Man) (No 2) Order 2004, SI 2004/718; and the Broadcasting and Communications (Isle of Man) (No 3) Order 2004, SI 2004/1115.

    Specific provisions of the Wireless Telegraphy Act 2006 have been extended to Jersey, Guernsey and the Isle of Man: see the Wireless Telegraphy (Jersey) Order 2006, SI 2006/3324; the Wireless Telegraphy (Guernsey) Order 2006, SI 2006/3325, and the Wireless Telegraphy (Isle of Man) Order 2007, SI 2007/278.

8   As to the meaning of 'OFCOM' see PARA 14 note 1; and as to OFCOM see PARA 2 et seq.
9   See the Communications Act 2003; and PARA 81 et seq. As to the meanings of 'electronic communications network' and 'electronic communications service' see PARA 53.

71.   The Wireless Telegraphy Act 2006. The Wireless Telegraphy Act 2006 repeals the provisions of the Telecommunications Act 1984[1] relating to wireless telegraphy, the Wireless Telegraphy Acts 1949 and 1967, the Marine etc Broadcasting (Offences) Act 1967 and related enactments, and consolidates them with minor amendments[2].

1   Ie the Telecommunications Act 1984 Pt VI (ss 75–92).
2   See BROADCASTING.

72.   Digital Economy Act 2010. The Digital Economy Act 2010 amends the Communications Act 2003 by imposing a new duty on OFCOM to prepare reports on the United Kingdom communications infrastructure[1]. The Digital Economy Act 2010 also makes provisions relating to online infringement of copyright, powers in relation to internet domain registries[2], the regulation of television services and radio services[3] and the regulation of the use of the electromagnetic spectrum[4].

1   See the Communications Act 2003 ss 134A, 134B; and PARA 150.

2 As to online infringement of copyright and powers in relation to internet domain registries see PARAS 134, 135; and INFORMATION TECHNOLOGY LAW vol 57 (2012) PARA 508 et seq.
3 See the Communications Act 2003 ss 198A–198D, 271A; and see BROADCASTING vol 4 (2011) PARA 638 et seq.
4 As to regulation of the use of the electromagnetic spectrum see BROADCASTING vol 4 (2011) PARA 520 et seq.

73. Application of enactments to territorial sea and other waters. Her Majesty may by Order in Council provide for an area of the territorial sea[1] to be treated, for the purposes of any provision to which these provisions[2] apply, as if it were situated in such part of the United Kingdom as may be specified in the Order, and for jurisdiction with respect to questions arising in relation to the territorial sea under any such provision to be conferred on courts in a part of the United Kingdom so specified[3]. These provisions apply to:

(1) provision made by or under Part 2 of the Communications Act 2003[4];
(2) any provision of the enactments relating to the management of the radio spectrum[5] that is not contained in Part 2 or the Wireless Telegraphy Act 2006[6]; and
(3) any provision of Chapter 1 of Part 5 of the Communications Act 2003[7] so far as it relates to a matter as respects which provision falling within head (1) or head (2) above is made or a matter as respects which the Wireless Telegraphy Act 2006 makes provision[8].

An Order in Council under the Petroleum Act 1998 or the Energy Act 2004[9] as to the application of civil law to offshore installations[10] may make provision for treating an installation with respect to which provision is made under the relevant provision of the Petroleum Act 1998 or the Energy Act 2004[11] and which is outside the territorial sea but in waters to which the relevant provision of Petroleum Act 1998 or the Energy Act 2004[12] applies, and waters within 500 metres of the installation, as if for the purposes of provisions mentioned in heads (1) to (3) above they were situated in such part of the United Kingdom as is specified in the Order[13].

The extended power applicable in relation to orders made by the Secretary of State[14] applies to the power to make an Order in Council under these provisions as it applies to any power of the Secretary of State to make an order under the Communications Act 2003, but as if references to the Secretary of State were references to Her Majesty in Council[15].

A statutory instrument containing an Order in Council under these provisions is subject to annulment in pursuance of a resolution of either House of Parliament[16].

1 'Territorial sea' means the territorial sea adjacent to the United Kingdom: Communications Act 2003 s 410(7). As to the territorial sea see WATER AND WATERWAYS vol 100 (2009) PARA 31. As to the meaning of 'United Kingdom' see PARA 14 note 7.
2 Ie the Communications Act 2003 s 410: see text and notes 1–16.
3 Communications Act 2003 s 410(2). The jurisdiction conferred on a court by an Order in Council under s 410 is in addition to any jurisdiction exercisable apart from that provision by that or any other court: s 410(4).
4 Communications Act 2003 s 410(1)(a). The provisions referred to in head (1) in the text is the Communications Act 2003 Pt 2 (ss 32–197).
5 As to the meaning of 'enactments relating to the management of the radio spectrum' see PARA 17 note 4.
6 Communications Act 2003 s 410(1)(b) (amended by the Wireless Telegraphy Act 2006 Sch 7 para 35).
7 Ie the Communications Act 2003 Pt 5 Ch 1 (ss 369–372): see PARA 38.
8 Communications Act 2003 s 410(1)(c) (amended by the Wireless Telegraphy Act 2006 Sch 7 para 35).

9 Ie under the Petroleum Act 1998 s 11 or under the Energy Act 2004 s 87: see ENERGY AND CLIMATE CHANGE vol 42 (2011) PARA 164; ENERGY AND CLIMATE CHANGE vol 44 (2011) PARA 1080.

10 'Installation' includes any floating structure or device maintained on a station by whatever means, and installations in transit: Communications Act 2003 s 410(7).

11 See note 9.

12 See note 9.

13 Communications Act 2003 s 410(3) (amended by the Energy Act 2004 s 87(5)).

14 Ie the Communications Act 2003 s 402(3): see PARA 74 text to note 11–13. As to the Secretary of State see PARA 76 note 1.

15 Communications Act 2003 s 410(5).

16 Communications Act 2003 s 410(6). At the date at which this volume states the law, no such order has been made.

74. Orders or regulations made under the Telecommunications Act 1984 and Communications Act 2003. Every power conferred by the Communications Act 2003 including the power to appoint a manager in respect of the property and affairs of the internet domain registry[1] on the Secretary of State[2] to make orders or regulations (other than in relation to the compulsory acquisition of land by the provider of an electronic communications network[3] in whose case the electronic communications code[4] applies and the entry on land by persons nominated by such a provider[5]) is a power exercisable by statutory instrument[6]. A statutory instrument containing an order or regulations made in exercise of any such power, other than:

(1)   an order for the abolition or cessation of a pre-commencement regulator[7] or a commencement order[8]; or

(2)   any order that is required, by any provision of the Communications Act 2003, to be laid before Parliament and approved in draft[9],

is subject to annulment in pursuance of a resolution of either House of Parliament[10].

Every power of the Secretary of State to make an order or regulations under the Communications Act 2003, other than a commencement order or an order as to the abolition or cessation of a pre-commencement regulator, or an order made in exercise of the power of compulsory acquisition mentioned above, includes power:

(a)   to make different provision for different cases (including different provision in respect of different areas)[11];

(b)   to make provision subject to such exemptions and exceptions as the Secretary of State thinks fit[12]; and

(c)   to make such incidental, supplemental, consequential and transitional provision as the Secretary of State thinks fit[13].

Any power of the Secretary of State to make an order under the Telecommunications Act 1984 is exercisable by statutory instrument, which is generally[14] subject to annulment in pursuance of a resolution of either House of Parliament[15]. Any such order may make different provision with respect to different cases or descriptions of case[16]. Similar provisions apply to the powers of the Secretary of State to make orders or regulations under the Communications Act 2003[17].

OFCOM[18] also has powers to make orders and regulations, and the procedure for regulations and orders made by OFCOM under the Communications Act 2003[19] applies as well to its powers to make orders under the Telecommunications Act 1984[20].

1 Ie the Communications Act 2003 s 124P: see INFORMATION TECHNOLOGY LAW vol 57 (2012) PARA 510.

2　As to the Secretary of State see PARA 76 note 1.
3　As to the meaning of 'electronic communications network' see PARA 53.
4　As to the meaning of 'electronic communications code' see PARA 155 note 1.
5　Ie the powers conferred by the Communications Act 2003 s 118, Sch 4: see PARA 164.
6　Communications Act 2003 s 402(1) (amended by the Digital Economy Act 2010 s 20(3)).
7　Ie under the Communications Act 2003 s 31: see PARA 14. As to the meaning of 'pre-commencement regulator' see PARA 14 note 2.
8　Communications Act 2003 s 402(2)(a). The reference to a commencement order is an order under the Communications Act 2003 s 411.
9　Communications Act 2003 s 402(2)(c).
10　Communications Act 2003 s 402(2) (amended by the Wireless Telegraphy Act 2006 s 125(1), Sch 9 Pt 1).
11　Communications Act 2003 s 402(3)(a). In exercise of the powers conferred on him under s 402(3), the Secretary of State has made the Television Multiplex Services (Reservation of Digital Capacity) Order 2008, SI 2008/1420; and the Local Digital Television Programme Services Order 2012, SI 2012/292.
12　Communications Act 2003 s 402(3)(b).
13　Communications Act 2003 s 402(3)(c). In exercise of the powers conferred on him under s 402(3), the Secretary of State has made the Communications (Bailiwick of Guernsey) (Amendment) Order 2012, SI 2012/2688.
14　Ie except in the case of an order under the Telecommunications Act 1984 s 110(5): see s 104(1) (amended by the Communications Act 2003 s 406(7), Sch 19).
15　Telecommunications Act 1984 s 104(1).
16　Telecommunications Act 1984 s 104(2).
17　See the Communications Act 2003 s 402; and text and notes 1–13.
18　As to the meaning of 'OFCOM' see PARA 14 note 1; and as to OFCOM see PARA 2 et seq.
19　See the Communications Act 2003 s 403; and PARA 39.
20　Telecommunications Act 1984 s 104(1A) (added by the Communications Act 2003 s 406(1), Sch 17 para 73).

75.　Other legislation relating to telecommunications. There is special legislation relating to wireless telegraphy[1] and to submarine cables[2]. The Broadcasting Acts 1990 and 1996 make provision with respect to television and radio broadcasting, although not all broadcasting transmission platforms are licensed under those Acts[3]. Particular provision is made in relation to air navigation services[4]. There is also legislation dealing with the protection of telecommunication apparatus[5], such apparatus on a highway which is stopped up or diverted[6] or on a right of way which is extinguished[7], and such apparatus in streets[8]. There is statutory provision for the authorisation and facilitation of electronic communications[9].

The installation or alteration of microwave antennae by an electronic communications code operator[10] is subject to control under the planning legislation[11].

1　As to wireless telegraphy see the Wireless Telegraphy Act 2006; and BROADCASTING vol 4 (2011) PARA 514 et seq. As to spectrum use see BROADCASTING vol 4 (2011) PARA 537 et seq.
2　As to submarine cables see PARA 48.
3　Some, eg Virgin Media, are solely subject to the regime governing the provision of electronic communication services. As to broadcasting see BROADCASTING vol 4 (2011) PARA 504 et seq.
4　See the European Parliament and Council Regulation (EC) 550/2004 (OJ L96, 31.3.2004, p 10) on the provision of air navigation services in the single European sky (amended by European Parliament and Council Regulation (EC) 1070/2009 (OJ L300, 14.11.2009, p 34)); Commission Implementing Regulation (EU) 1035/2011 (OJ L271, 18.10.2011, p 23) laying down common requirements for the provision of air navigation services (amended by Commission Implementing Regulation (EU) 923/2012 (OJ L281, 13.10.2012, p 1); and Commission Implementing Regulation (EU) 448/2014 (OJ L132, 3.5.2015, p 53)); the Air Navigation (Single European Sky) (Penalties) Order 2009, SI 2009/1735 (amended by SI 2013/2874); the Transport Act 2000 Pt I Ch III (ss 66–72); and AIR LAW vol 2 (2008) PARAS 28, 55 et seq.
5　See PARA 193.
6　See the Town and Country Planning Act 1990 ss 256, 260; and PARAS 194–195.

7 See the New Towns Act 1981 s 24; and PARA 195.
8 See the New Roads and Street Works Act 1991; and HIGHWAYS, STREETS AND BRIDGES vol 55 (2012) PARA 36.
9 See the Electronic Communications Act 2000; and CIVIL PROCEDURE vol 11 (2009) PARA 948.
10 As to the meaning of 'electronic communications code operator' see PARA 179 note 4.
11 This includes apparatus such as masts for mobile telephone networks: see the Town and Country Planning General Development Order 1995, SI 1995/418, Sch 2 Pts 24, 25; and PLANNING vol 81 (2010) PARA 531 et seq.

(4) REGULATORY AUTHORITIES OTHER THAN OFCOM

(i) The Secretary of State

76. Functions of the Secretary of State. The Secretary of State[1] has various duties and functions relating to telecommunications[2]. These include responsibilities relating to the appointment of members of OFCOM[3], as well as consultation with OFCOM, giving approvals and directions, and generally overseeing the functions of OFCOM[4]. The Secretary of State also has powers in relation to promptness standards[5], the obtaining of information[6], and the guaranteeing of borrowing by OFCOM[7]. The Secretary of State has power to make orders and regulations[8], including orders for the commencement of provisions of the Communications Act 2003[9] and orders effecting consequential amendments[10], pre-consolidation amendments[11] and modifications necessary as a consequence of the implementation of European Directives[12].

There are a few functions remaining to the Secretary of State under the Telecommunications Act 1984, principally:

(1) the power to give directions in the interests of national security[13];
(2) the power to make orders[14];
(3) the power to modify, repeal or amend certain enactments and instruments[15].

The Secretary of State was responsible for the appointment of the Director General of Telecommunications[16].

1 In any enactment, 'Secretary of State' means one of Her Majesty's principal Secretaries of State: see the Interpretation Act 1978 s 5, Sch 1. This title relates to matters within the responsibilities of both the Secretary of State for Business, Innovation and Skills and the Secretary of State for Culture, Media and Sport. As to the office of Secretary of State see CONSTITUTIONAL AND ADMINISTRATIVE LAW vol 20 (2014) PARA 153.
2 As to the Secretary of State's annual report on his functions see PARA 78.
3 See the Office of Communications Act 2002; and PARA 2 et seq. As to OFCOM see PARA 2 et seq.
4 See the Communications Act 2003; and PARA 14 et seq.
5 Ie under the Communications Act 2003 s 9: see PARA 21.
6 Ie under the Communications Act 2003 s 24: see PARA 34.
7 Ie under the Communications Act 2003 s 29: see PARA 37.
8 As to the making of orders or regulations by the Secretary of State see PARA 74.
9 See the Communications Act 2003 s 411.
10 See the Communications Act 2003 s 406. See e g the Communications Act 2003 (Amendment of the Medicines (Monitoring of Advertising) Regulations 1994) Order 2003, SI 2003/3093; the Communications Act 2003 (Consequential Amendments No 2) Order 2003, SI 2003/3182; and the Communications Act 2003 (Consequential Amendments) Order 2004, SI 2004/945.
11 See the Communications Act 2003 s 407. Where:
    (1) enactments relating to broadcasting;
    (2) enactments referring to enactments falling within head (1); or
    (3) enactments relating to connected matters,
    are to be repealed and re-enacted, the Secretary of State may make an order modifying the enactments mentioned in heads (1)–(2) so as to facilitate the consolidation of those enactments or any of them: see s 407 (amended by the Wireless Telegraphy Act 2006 s 125(1), Sch 9 Pt 1).

For the purposes of the Communications Act 2003 s 407, 'enactments relating to broadcasting' means the Broadcasting Act 1990; the Broadcasting Act 1996, the Communications Act 2003 Pt 3 (ss 198–362) and the other provisions of the Communications Act 2003 so far as relating to the Broadcasting Act 1990, the Broadcasting Act 1996 or the Communications Act 2003 Pt 3: ss 405(1), 407(5).

12 See the Communications Act 2003 s 409.
13 See the Telecommunications Act 1984 s 94(1); and PARA 77.
14 See the Telecommunications Act 1984 s 104; and PARA 74.
15 See the Telecommunications Act 1984 s 109.
16 See the Telecommunications Act 1984 s 1(1) (prospectively repealed); and PARA 14 note 2.

77. Directions in the national interest. After consultation with OFCOM[1] and providers of public electronic communications networks[2], the Secretary of State[3] may give to them such directions of a general character as appear to the Secretary of State to be necessary in the interests of national security or relations with the government of a country or territory outside the United Kingdom[4]; and if it appears to him to be so necessary, he may, after such consultation, give to them a direction requiring them, according to the circumstances, to do or not to do a specified thing[5]. The Secretary of State must not give a direction in either instance above unless he believes that the conduct required by the direction is proportionate to what is sought to be achieved by that conduct[6].

A person to whom any of these directions is given must give effect to it notwithstanding any other duty imposed on him by or under Part 1 or Chapter 1 of Part 2 of the Communications Act 2003[7] and, in the case of a direction to a provider of a public electronic communications network, notwithstanding that it relates to him in a capacity other than as the provider of such a network[8]. A person must not disclose, or be required by virtue of any direction or otherwise to disclose, anything done by virtue of these provisions if the Secretary of State has notified him that he is of the opinion that disclosure is against the interests of national security or external relations or the commercial interests of some other person[9].

With Treasury approval, the Secretary of State may make grants to providers of public electronic communications networks to defray or contribute towards losses they may sustain by complying with any such directions[10].

1 As to the meaning of 'OFCOM' see PARA 14 note 1; and as to OFCOM see PARA 2 et seq.
2 Telecommunications Act 1984 s 94(8) (amended by the Communications Act 2003 s 406(1), Sch 17 para 70(1), (7)). As to the meaning of 'public electronic communications network' see PARA 98 note 6.
3 As to the Secretary of State see PARA 76 note 1.
4 Telecommunications Act 1984 s 94(1) (amended by the Communications Act 2003 Sch 17 para 70(2)). As to the meaning of 'United Kingdom' see PARA 14 note 7. The Secretary of State must lay before each House of Parliament a copy of every direction given under the Telecommunications Act 1984 s 94 unless he is of opinion that disclosure of the direction is against the interests of national security or external relations or the commercial interests of any person: s 94(4). The power under s 94 to give directions includes power to give a direction if it appears to the Secretary of State requisite or expedient to do so in order:
   (1)   to discharge or facilitate the discharge of an obligation binding on the United Kingdom government by virtue of it being a member of an international organisation or a party to an international agreement (s 106(4)(a));
   (2)   to attain or facilitate the attainment of any other objects the attainment of which is in his opinion requisite or expedient in view of that government being such a member or party (s 106(4)(b)); or
   (3)   to enable that government to become such a member or party (s 106(4)(c)).
5 Telecommunications Act 1984 s 94(2) (amended by the Communications Act 2003 Sch 17 para 70(3)).
6 Telecommunications Act 1984 s 94(2A) (added by the Communications Act 2003 Sch 17 para 70(4)). See also note 4.

7   Ie the Communications Act 2003 Pt 1 (ss 1–31) or Pt 2 Ch 1 (ss 32–151).
8   Telecommunications Act 1984 s 94(3) (amended by the Communications Act 2003 Sch 17
    para 70(5)).
9   Telecommunications Act 1984 s 94(5).
10 Telecommunications Act 1984 s 94(6) (amended by the Communications Act 2003 Sch 17
    para 70(6)). The grants come from money provided by Parliament: Telecommunications
    Act 1984 s 94(7). As to the Treasury see CONSTITUTIONAL AND ADMINISTRATIVE LAW vol 20
    (2014) PARAS 262–265.

78.   Annual report on the Secretary of State's functions.   The Secretary of
State[1] must prepare and lay before Parliament regular reports on the carrying out
by him of certain functions[2]. This requirement applies to the Secretary of State's
functions under the following enactments:

(1)   the Communications Act 2003[3];

(2)   the Office of Communications Act 2002[4];

(3)   the enactments relating to the management of the radio spectrum[5] so far
      as not comprised in the Communications Act 2003[6];

(4)   the Broadcasting Act 1990[7];

(5)   the Broadcasting Act 1996[8].

The first report under these provisions had to relate to the period beginning
with 19 March 2002[9] and ending with the period of 12 months which began
with the first date to be appointed[10] for the purposes of the transfer of functions
to OFCOM[11]. Every subsequent report must relate to the period of 12 months
beginning with the end of the period to which the previous report related[12]. The
obligation to prepare and lay a report before Parliament is an obligation to do
that as soon as reasonably practicable after the end of the period to which the
report relates[13].

1   See PARA 76 note 1.
2   Communications Act 2003 s 390(1).
3   Communications Act 2003 s 390(2)(a). Where a report for the purposes of s 390 relates to a
    period the whole or a part of which falls before the time when the whole of the Communications
    Act 2003 is in force, the functions referred to in s 390(2) are to be taken as excluding all
    functions under the specified enactments that cease to be functions of the Secretary of State
    when the whole of the Communications Act 2003 is in force: s 390(6).
4   Communications Act 2003 s 390(2)(b). See note 3.
5   As to the meaning of 'enactments relating to the management of the radio spectrum' see PARA 17
    note 4.
6   Communications Act 2003 s 390(2)(c). See note 3.
7   Communications Act 2003 s 390(2)(d). See note 3.
8   Communications Act 2003 s 390(2)(e). See note 3.
9   Ie the date of the passing of the Office of Communications Act 2002.
10 Ie for the purposes of the Communications Act 2003 s 2: see PARA 14.
11 Communications Act 2003 s 390(3).
12 Communications Act 2003 s 390(4).
13 Communications Act 2003 s 390(5).

79.   Expenses incurred by the Secretary of State.   There is to be paid out of
money provided by Parliament any expenditure incurred by the Secretary of
State[1] for or in connection with the carrying out of any of his functions under the
Communications Act 2003 and any increase attributable to the Communications
Act 2003 in the sums which are payable out of money so provided under any
other Act[2]. Similarly, there is to be paid out of money provided by Parliament
any administrative expenses incurred by the Secretary of State in consequence of
the provisions of the Telecommunications Act 1984 and any increase attributable
to Telecommunications Act 1984 in the sums so payable under any other Act[3].

1   As to the Secretary of State see PARA 76 note 1.
2   Communications Act 2003 s 399.
3   Telecommunications Act 1984 s 105.

(ii) Other Regulators

80.   Non-statutory regulators and mediators.   In addition to OFCOM[1] and the
Secretary of State[2], there are various other bodies with some regulatory functions
in relation to communications. These include the Ombudsman Services[3], the
Communications and Internet Services Adjudication Scheme ('CISAS')[4] and
PhonepayPlus, formerly the Independent Committee for the Supervision of
Standards of Telephone Information Services ('ICSTIS')[5]. Certain organisations,
such as the Internet Watch Foundation('IWF')[6] and the Family Online Safety
Institute (formerly the Internet Content Rating Association ('ICRA'))[7], are
particularly concerned with the protection of children. The authoritative
database of United Kingdom domain name registrations is managed by
Nominet[8].

The Office of the Telecommunications Adjudicator ('OTA') was established by
OFCOM and the telecommunications industry, and subsequently OTA2 was
established as a follow-on to the OTA to ensure that communications providers
cooperate and that a competitive environment exists in the telecommunications
sector[9].

1   As to OFCOM see PARA 2 et seq.
2   As to the Secretary of State see PARA 76 note 1.
3   As to the Ombudsman Services see PARA 99 note 18.
4   CISAS provides an independent dispute resolution service for communications providers and
    their customers.
5   PhonepayPlus (formerly ICSTIS) regulates all phone-paid services (ie premium rate goods and
    services which can be bought by charging the cost to a telephone bill or pre-pay account) in the
    United Kingdom. It imposes standards for the promotion, content and operation of premium
    rate services through a Code of Practice, and it has the power to investigate complaints from
    consumers and to fine companies and bar access to services. See *Independent Committee for the
    Supervision of Standards of Telephone Information Services v Hornan* [2007] EWHC 2307
    (Admin), [2007] All ER (D) 114 (Sep) (power of committee to sue for monetary debt service
    providers in liquidation); and *Phonepayplus Ltd v Ashraf* [2014] EWHC 4303 (Ch), [2014] All
    ER (D) 247 (Dec) (recovery of fines imposed under code of practice). See also *R (on the
    application of Ordanduu) v Phonepayplus Ltd* [2015] EWHC 50 (Admin), 2015] All ER (D)
    108 (Jan) (judicial review of actions taken after emergency procedure was invoked against
    premium rate service provider).
6   The IWF aims to combat child abuse images on the internet. It operates a hotline to enable the
    public to report instances of potential abuse, and alerts service providers to criminal material
    found on their servers. It is self-regulatory, with no statutory basis.
7   In order to protect children from potentially harmful material on the internet, the Family Online
    Safety Institute has developed a labelling system which enables the blocking of access to certain
    websites. The institute is self-regulatory, with no statutory basis.
8   Nominet is the United Kingdom domain name registry. It provides advice on registering and
    maintaining a domain name, and operates a dispute resolution service to assist in resolving
    disputes relating to domain names. It is a private, non-for-profit company which has not been
    granted any regulatory functions.
9   The OTA2 primarily deals with major or strategic issues affecting the rollout and performance
    of Openreach products as defined in the OTA2 Memorandum of Understanding: see the OTA2
    website, which at the date this volume states the law is available at www.offta.org.uk.

(5) REGULATION OF ELECTRONIC COMMUNICATIONS NETWORKS AND SERVICES

(i) Notifications

81. Notification by providers. OFCOM[1] is given power to require that a person must not:

(1)   provide a designated electronic communications network[2];

(2)   provide a designated electronic communications service[3]; or

(3)   make available a designated associated facility[4],

unless, before beginning to provide it or to make it available, he has given a notification to OFCOM of his intention to provide that network or service, or to make that facility available[5].

Before:

(a)   providing or making available the notified network, service or facility with any significant differences; or

(b)   ceasing to provide it or to make it available,

a person who has given a notification[6] must give a further notification to OFCOM of the differences or (as the case may be) of his intention to cease to provide the network or service or to make the facility available[7].

A notification for the purposes of these provisions must be sent to OFCOM in such manner as OFCOM may require and must contain all such information as OFCOM may require[8].

The only information OFCOM may require a notification to contain is:

(i)   a declaration of the relevant proposal of the person giving the notification[9];

(ii)   the time when it is intended that effect should be given to the relevant proposal[10];

(iii)   particulars identifying the person giving the notification[11];

(iv)   particulars identifying one or more persons with addresses in the United Kingdom[12] who, for the purposes of matters relating to the notified network, service or facility, are authorised to accept service at an address in the United Kingdom on behalf of the person giving the notification[13];

(v)   particulars identifying one or more persons who may be contacted if there is an emergency that is caused by or affects the provision of the notified network, service or facility[14];

(vi)   addresses and other particulars necessary for effecting service on or contacting each of the persons mentioned in heads (iii) to (v) above[15].

There are penalties for contravention of the provisions described above[16].

There are procedural requirements imposed on OFCOM regarding the making or withdrawal of a designation[17]. Where OFCOM has reasonable grounds to believe that a person has contravened his obligations[18] it may notify that person and allow him a specified period of time in which to make representations to OFCOM and to comply with his obligations[19].

Where a person (the 'notified provider') has been given a notification[20], OFCOM has allowed the notified provider an opportunity of making representations about the notified determination and the period allowed for the making of the representations has expired[21], OFCOM may:

(A) give the notified provider a decision (a 'confirmation decision')[22] confirming the imposition of requirements in accordance with the notification[23]; or

(B) inform the notified provider that they are satisfied with the notified provider's representations and that no further action will be taken[24].

OFCOM may not give a confirmation decision to the notified provider unless, after considering any representations, they are satisfied that the notified provider has, in one or more of the respects notified, been in contravention[25] of his obligations[26]. It is the duty of a person to whom a confirmation decision has been given to comply with any requirement imposed by it[27].

A penalty imposed by a confirmation decision must be paid to OFCOM and if not paid within the period specified by them, is to be recoverable by them accordingly[28].

1 As to the meaning of 'OFCOM' see PARA 14 note 1; and as to OFCOM see PARA 2 et seq. OFCOM has not, however, implemented the notification provisions under the Communications Act 2003 s 33 or designated any services for which notification is required.

2 Communications Act 2003 s 33(1)(a). As to the meaning of 'electronic communications network' see PARA 53.

3 Communications Act 2003 s 33(1)(b). As to the meaning of 'electronic communications service' see PARA 53.

4 Communications Act 2003 s 33(1)(c). As to the meaning of 'associated facility' see PARA 53.

5 Communications Act 2003 s 33(1). An electronic communications network, electronic communications service or associated facility is designated for the purposes of s 33 if it is of a description of networks, services or facilities that is for the time being designated by OFCOM as a description of networks, services or facilities for which notification under s 33 is required: s 33(2). See note 1.

Where a description of electronic communications network, electronic communications service or associated facility is designated for the purposes of s 33 at a time when a network, service or facility of that description is already being provided or made available by a person:

(1) that person's obligation under s 33 to give a notification before beginning to provide or make available that network, service or facility will have effect as an obligation to give a notification within such period after the coming into force of the designation as may be specified in the notice in which the designation is contained (s 33(11)(a)); and

(2) that notification is to be one stating that that person is already providing the network or service, or making the facility available (rather than that it is his intention to do so) (s 33(11)(b)).

Section 33(11) has effect subject to any transitional provision which is contained in the notification setting out the designation and treats a person as having given the notification required by s 33(11): s 33(12).

6 Ie for the purposes of the Communications Act 2003 s 33(1).

7 Communications Act 2003 s 33(3). See further note 9.

8 Communications Act 2003 s 33(4). See further note 9.

9 Communications Act 2003 s 33(5)(a). The declaration of the relevant proposal that may be required under s 33(5) is whichever of the following is appropriate in the case of the person giving the notification:

(1) a declaration of his proposal to provide the network or service described in the notification or to make available the facility so described (s 33(6)(a));

(2) a declaration of his proposal to make the modifications that are so described of the network, service or facility specified in the notification (s 33(6)(b)); or

(3) a declaration of his proposal to cease to provide the network or service so specified or to cease to make available the facility so specified (s 33(6)(c)).

The reference in s 33(3) (see the text and note 7) to providing or making available a notified network, service or facility with significant differences is a reference to continuing to provide it, or to make it available, after a change in whatever falling within heads (i)–(vi) in the text was last notified to OFCOM under s 33: s 33(9).

10 Communications Act 2003 s 33(5)(b). See note 9.

11 Communications Act 2003 s 33(5)(c). See note 9.

12 As to the meaning of 'United Kingdom' see PARA 14 note 7.

13   Communications Act 2003 s 33(5)(d). References in the Communications Act 2003 s 33 to accepting service at an address are references:

(1)   to accepting service of documents or process at that address; or

(2)   otherwise to receiving notifications at that address,

and the reference in s 33(7) to effecting service at an address is to be construed accordingly: s 33(10).

Requirements imposed under s 33(4) (see the text and note 8) are not to require a notification by a person to contain particulars falling within head (iv) in the text in a case in which:

(a)   that person is resident in a member state or has a place of business in a member state (s 33(7)(a));

(b)   the notification contains a statement under s 33(8) (s 33(7)(b));

(c)   the notification sets out an address in a member state at which service will be accepted by the person who, in accordance with that statement, is authorised to accept it (s 33(7)(c)); and

(d)   OFCOM is satisfied that adequate arrangements exist for effecting service on that person at that address (s 33(7)(d)).

The statement mentioned above is one which:

(i)   declares that the person authorised, for the purposes of matters relating to the notified network, service or facilities, to accept service on behalf of the person giving the notification is that person himself (s 33(8)(a)); or

(ii)   identifies another person who is resident in a member state, or has a place of business in such state, as the person so authorised (s 33(8)(b)).

See note 9.

14   Communications Act 2003 s 33(5)(e). See note 9.

15   Communications Act 2003 s 33(5)(f). See note 9.

16   Ie penalties for contravention of the Communications Act 2003 s 33: see s 35A; and PARA 82.

17   Before making or withdrawing a designation for the purposes of the Communications Act 2003 s 33 or imposing or modifying a requirement under s 34(4), OFCOM must consult such of the persons who, in its opinion, are likely to be affected by it as it thinks fit: s 34(1). Before making or withdrawing a designation for the purposes of s 33 OFCOM must also consult the Secretary of State: s 34(2). The way in which a designation for the purposes of s 33 or a requirement under s 33(4) is to be made or imposed or may be withdrawn or modified, is by a notice published in such manner as OFCOM considers appropriate for bringing the designation, requirement, withdrawal or modification to the attention of the persons who, in its opinion, are likely to be affected by it: s 34(3). A designation for the purposes of s 33 may be framed by reference to any such description of networks, services or facilities, or such other factors, as OFCOM thinks fit: s 34(4). Requirements imposed under s 33(4) may make different provision for different cases: s 34(5). As to the Secretary of State see PARA 76 note 1.

18   Ie under the Communications Act 2003 s 33.

19   See the Communications Act 2003 s 35. Where OFCOM determines that there are reasonable grounds for believing that a person has contravened s 33, it may give him a notification under s 35: s 35(1). A notification under s 35 is one which:

(1)   sets out the determination made by OFCOM (s 35(2)(a));

(2)   specifies the contravention in respect of which the determination has been made (Communications Act 2003 s 35(2)(b) (s 35(2)(b)–(e) substituted by SI 2011/1210));

(3)   specifies the period during which the person notified has an opportunity to make representations (Communications Act 2003 s 35(2)(c) (as so substituted));

(4)   specifies information to be provided by the person to OFCOM (s 35(2)(d) (as so substituted)); and

(5)   specifies any penalty which OFCOM is minded to impose in accordance with s 35A (see PARA 82) (s 35(2)(e) (as so substituted)).

A notification under s 35 may be given in respect of more than one contravention of s 33 and, if it is given in respect of a continuing contravention, may be given in respect of any period during which the contravention has continued: s 35(8). Where a notification under s 35 has been given to a person in respect of a contravention of s 33, OFCOM may give a further notification in respect of the same contravention if, and only if:

(a)   the subsequent notification is in respect of so much of a period during which the contravention in question was continuing as falls after a period to which the earlier notification relates (s 35(9)(a)); or

(b)   the earlier notification has been withdrawn without a penalty having been imposed by reference to the notified contravention: s 35(9).

20   Ie under the Communications Act 2003 s 35.

21 Communications Act 2003 s 36(1).

22 A confirmation decision:
  (1)   must be given to the person without delay (Communications Act 2003 s 36(4)(a) (s 36(2)–(4) substituted by SI 2011/1210));
  (2)   must include reasons for the decision (Communications Act 2003 s 36(4)(b) (as so substituted));
  (3)   may require immediate action by the person to comply with requirements imposed by virtue of s 35(2)(d), or may specify a period within which the person must comply with those requirements (s 36(4)(c) (as so substituted)); and
  (4)   may require the person to pay:
    (a)   the penalty specified in the notification under s 35 (s 36(4)(d)(i) (as so substituted)); or
    (b)   such lesser penalty as OFCOM considers appropriate in the light of the person's representations or steps taken by the person to comply with the condition or remedy the consequences of the contravention (s 36(4)(d)(ii) (as so substituted)), and
  may specify the period within which the penalty is to be paid: s 36(4) (as so substituted).

23 Communications Act 2003 s 36(2)(a) (as substituted: see note 22). The notification referred to in head (a) in the text is a notification under s 35 (see note 19): s 36(2)(a).

    For the purposes of Pt 2 Ch 1 (ss 32–151), where there is a contravention of an obligation that requires a person to do anything within a particular period or before a particular time, that contravention will be taken to continue after the end of that period, or after that time, until that thing is done: s 151(6). References in Pt 2 Ch 1 to remedying the consequences of a contravention include references to paying an amount to a person by way of compensation for loss or damage suffered by that person or in respect of annoyance, inconvenience or anxiety to which he has been put: s 151(7).

24 Communications Act 2003 s 36(2)(b) (as substituted: see note 22). See note 23.

25 'Contravention' includes a failure to comply; and cognate expressions are to be construed accordingly: Communications Act 2003 s 405(1).

26 Communications Act 2003 s 36(3) (as substituted: see note 22). The reference in the text to obligations is a reference to those under the Communications Act 2003 s 33.

27 Communications Act 2003 s 36(5) (amended by SI 2011/1210). The duty is enforceable in civil proceedings by OFCOM either for an injunction or for any other appropriate remedy or relief: Communications Act 2003 s 36(6).

28 Communications Act 2003 s 36(7) (added by SI 2011/1210).

82. Penalties for contravention of notification provisions.

The following provisions apply where a person is given a notification[1] which specifies a proposed penalty[2].

Where the notification relates to more than one contravention, a separate penalty may be specified in respect of each contravention[3]. Where the notification relates to a continuing contravention, no more than one penalty may be specified in respect of the period of contravention specified in the notification[4]. In relation to a continuing contravention, a penalty may be specified in respect of each day on which the contravention continues after:

(1)   the giving of a confirmation decision[5] which requires immediate action[6]; or

(2)   the expiry of any period specified in the confirmation decision for complying with a requirement so specified[7].

1 Ie under the Communications Act 2003 s 35: see PARA 81.

2 Communications Act 2003 s 35A(1) (s 35A added by SI 2011/1210). The amount of any other penalty (ie other than as mentioned in the Communications Act 2003 s 35A(4): see text and notes 6, 7) specified in a notification under s 35 is to be such amount not exceeding £10,000 as OFCOM determine to be appropriate, and proportionate to the contravention in respect of which it is imposed: s 35A(6) (as so added). The Secretary of State may by order amend s 35A so as to substitute a different maximum penalty for the maximum penalty for the time being specified in s 35A(6): s 35A(7) (as so added). No order is to be made containing provision

authorised by s 35A(7) unless a draft of the order has been laid before Parliament and approved by a resolution of each House: s 35A(8) (as so added). At the date at which this volume states the law, no such order has been made.

3   Communications Act 2003 s 35A(2) (as added: see note 2). As to the meaning of 'contravention' see PARA 81 note 25.

4   Communications Act 2003 s 35A(3) (as added: see note 2).

5   Ie under the Communications Act 2003 s 36(4)(c).

6   Communications Act 2003 s 35A(4)(a) (as added: see note 2). The amount of a penalty under s 35A(4) is to be such amount not exceeding £100 per day as OFCOM determine to be appropriate and proportionate to the contravention in respect of which it is imposed: s 35A(5) (as so added).

7   Communications Act 2003 s 35A(4)(b) (as added: see note 2). See note 6.

(ii) Fixing of Charges

83. Fixing of charges. A person who, at any time in a charging year[1], is a person to whom these provisions[2] apply[3] must:

(1)   in respect of the network, service or facility provided or made available by him[4];

(2)   in respect of the application to him of a universal service condition[5];

(3)   in respect of the application to him of an SMP apparatus condition[6]; or

(4)   in respect of the application of the electronic communications code[7] in his case[8],

pay to OFCOM the administrative charge (if any) that is fixed by it for the case that is applicable to him[9].

OFCOM must not fix the administrative charge for a charging year unless at the time the charge is fixed there is in force a statement by OFCOM of the principles that it is proposing to apply in fixing charges under these provisions for that year, and the charge is fixed in accordance with those charging principles[10]. Those principles must be such as appear to OFCOM to be likely to secure, on the basis of such estimates of the likely costs as it is practicable for it to make:

(a)   that, on a year by year basis, the aggregate amount of the charges payable to OFCOM is sufficient to meet, but does not exceed, the annual cost to OFCOM of carrying out certain functions[11];

(b)   that the cost of carrying out those functions is met by the imposition of charges that are objectively justifiable and proportionate to the matters in respect of which they are imposed[12];

(c)   that the relationship between meeting the cost of carrying out those functions and the amounts of the charges is transparent[13];

(d)   that the charges fixed for persons who are liable to charges by reason only of being persons to whom SMP apparatus conditions apply are referable only to things done in, or in connection with, the setting, modification or enforcement of SMP apparatus conditions or the carrying out of certain functions[14]; and

(e)   that the charges fixed for persons who are liable to charges[15] are referable only to costs incurred in, or in connection with, the carrying out of certain functions[16].

OFCOM's power to fix charges for a particular case includes:

(i)   power to provide that the charges in that case are to be equal to the amounts produced by a computation made in the manner, and by reference to the factors, specified by it[17];

(ii)   power to provide for different charges to be imposed in that case on different descriptions of persons[18]; and

(iii)   power to provide for particular descriptions of persons[19] to be excluded from the liability to pay charges in that case[20].

As soon as reasonably practicable after the end of each charging year, OFCOM must publish a statement setting out, in respect of that year:

(A)   the aggregate amounts of the administrative charges for that year that have been received by OFCOM[21];

(B)   the aggregate amount of the administrative charges for that year that remain outstanding and are likely to be paid or recovered[22]; and

(C)   the cost to OFCOM of carrying out certain functions[23].

OFCOM's power to fix a charge is to be exercisable only by the publication or giving of such notification as it considers appropriate for bringing the charge to the attention of the persons who, in its opinion, are likely to be affected by it, and includes power, by setting it out in that notification, to fix the time at which the charge is to become due to OFCOM[24]. A charge fixed[25] for a charging year[26] may be fixed in terms providing for a deduction from the charge on a proportionate basis to be made for a part of the year during which the network, service or facility in respect of which it is fixed is not provided or made available by the person otherwise liable to the charge, the universal service condition in respect of which it is fixed does not apply in that person's case; the SMP apparatus condition in respect of which it is fixed does not apply in that person's case or the electronic communications code does not apply in that person's case[27]. Such a charge may also be fixed so that it is referable, in whole or in part, to the provision or making available of a network, service or facility during a part of the year falling before the fixing of the charge, to the application of a universal service condition to a person for a part of the year so falling, to a person's being a person to whom an SMP apparatus condition applies for a part of the year so falling or to the application of the electronic communications code in a person's case during a part of the year so falling[28].

A charge may be fixed so as to be referable to a time before it is fixed to the extent only that both the imposition of the charge and the amount of the charge are required by, and consistent with, the statement of charging principles[29] in force at the beginning of the charging year[30]. Before making or revising a statement of charging principles, OFCOM must consult such of the persons who, in OFCOM's opinion, are likely to be affected by those principles as it thinks fit[31].

1   For the purposes of the Communications Act 2003 s 38, 'charging year' means:
     (1)   the period beginning with the commencement of s 38 (ie 25 July 2003: see the Communications Act 2003 (Commencement No 1) Order 2003, SI 2003/1900 (amended by SI 2003/3142)) and ending with the next 31 March (Communications Act 2003 s 38(12)(a)); or
     (2)   any subsequent period of 12 months beginning with 1 April (Communications Act 2003 s 38(12)(b)).

2   Ie the Communications Act 2003 s 38.

3   The Communications Act 2003 s 38 applies to a person at a time if, at that time, he is:
     (1)   providing an electronic communications network of a description which is, at that time, designated for the purposes of s 38 (s 38(2)(a));
     (2)   providing an electronic communications service of a description which is, at that time, so designated (s 38(2)(b));
     (3)   making available an associated facility of a description which is, at that time, so designated (s 38(2)(c));
     (4)   a person who without being a communications provider is designated in accordance with regulations under s 66 (see PARA 102) (s 38(2)(d));
     (5)   a supplier of apparatus to whom an SMP apparatus condition applies (s 38(2)(e)); or
     (6)   a person in whose case the electronic communications code applies by virtue of a

direction given under s 106 (see PARA 155) otherwise than for the purposes of the provision by him of an electronic communications network of a designated description (s 38(2)(f)).

As to the meanings of 'electronic communications network', 'electronic communications service', and 'associated facility' see PARA 53. As to the meanings of 'SMP condition', 'SMP services condition' and 'SMP apparatus condition' see PARA 87 note 8.

4   Communications Act 2003 s 38(1)(a).

5   Communications Act 2003 s 38(1)(b). The reference to a universal service condition is a reference relating to matters mentioned in the Communications Act 2003 s 66(3) (see PARA 102). As to the meaning of 'universal service condition' see PARA 87 note 5.

6   Communications Act 2003 s 38(1)(c).

7   As to the meaning of 'electronic communications code' see PARA 155 note 1.

8   Communications Act 2003 s 38(1)(d).

9   Communications Act 2003 s 38(1). As to the meaning of 'OFCOM' see PARA 14 note 1; and as to OFCOM see PARA 2 et seq.

10 Communications Act 2003 s 38(3).

11 Communications Act 2003 s 38(4)(a). The functions referred to in the text are the functions mentioned in the Communications Act 2003 s 38(5). Those functions are:

   (1)   the relevant Chapter 1 functions (s 38(5)(a));

   (2)   the carrying out for a Chapter 1 purpose of any research by OFCOM or the Consumer Panel into any of the matters mentioned in s 14(1)(c)–(f) (see PARA 26) (s 38(5)(b));

   (3)   the publication under s 26 (see PARA 34) of any information or advice that it appears to OFCOM to be appropriate to make available to the persons mentioned in s 26(2)(a)–(c) (see PARA 34 heads (1)–(3)) (s 38(5)(c)); and

   (4)   the function of taking any steps that OFCOM considers it necessary to take:

      (a)   in preparation for the carrying out of any of the functions mentioned in heads (1)–(3) (s 38(5)(d)(i)); or

      (b)   for the purpose of facilitating the carrying out of those functions or otherwise in connection with carrying them out (s 38(5)(d)(ii)).

The relevant Chapter 1 functions are:

   (i)   OFCOM's functions under ss 33–37, 44 (see PARAS 81, 86) (s 38(6)(a));

   (ii)   the setting, modification and enforcement of conditions under s 45 (see PARA 87) (s 38(6)(b));

   (iii)   the supervision, as respects the requirements of ss 33–37 and of any such conditions, of communications providers and of persons who make associated facilities available (s 38(6)(c));

   (iv)   the monitoring of compliance with those requirements and with any such conditions (s 38(6)(d));

   (v)   the functions conferred on OFCOM by or under s 55 (see PARA 99) (s 38(6)(e));

   (vi)   its functions under ss 106–119 (see PARAS 155–165) (s 38(6)(g));

   (vii)   its functions under ss 185–191 (see PARA 217 et seq) (s 38(6)(h));

   (viii)   securing international co-operation in relation to the regulation of electronic communications networks, electronic communications services and associated facilities (s 38(6)(i));

   (ix)   securing the harmonisation and standardisation of the regulation of electronic communications networks, electronic communications services and associated facilities (s 38(6)(j));

   (x)   market analysis and any monitoring of the controls operating in the markets for electronic communications networks, electronic communications services and associated facilities (s 38(6)(k));

   (xi)   OFCOM's functions under ss 38–43 (see PARA 84, 85) (s 38(6)(l)).

A purpose is a Chapter 1 purpose for the purposes of head (2) if it is the purpose of ascertaining the effectiveness of one or more of the following:

   (A)   the regulation of the provision of electronic communications networks or electronic communications services (s 38(7)(a));

   (B)   the regulation of the making available of associated facilities (s 38(7)(b));

   (C)   the mechanisms in place for the handling, by communications providers and by persons making such facilities available, of complaints made to them by consumers in markets for such services or facilities (s 38(7)(c));

   (D)   the mechanisms in place for resolving disputes between such consumers and communications providers or persons who make such facilities available (s 38(7)(d)).

References in the Communications Act 2003 to consumers in a market for a service include, where the service is a postal service, addressees: s 405(5A) (added by the Postal Services Act 2011 Sch 12 para 68). As to the Consumer Panel see PARAS 28–29.

12 Communications Act 2003 s 38(4)(b).
13 Communications Act 2003 s 38(4)(c).
14 Communications Act 2003 s 38(4)(d). The functions referred to in head (d) in the text are those functions mentioned in the Communications Act 2003 s 38(6)(l) (see note 11 head (xi)): s 38(4)(d).
15 Ie by reason only of being persons falling within the Communications Act 2003 s 38(2)(f) (see note 3 head (6)).
16 Communications Act 2003 s 38(4)(e). The functions referred to in head (e) in the text are the functions mentioned in the Communications Act 2003 s 38(6)(g) and s 38(6)(l) (see note 11 heads (vi), (xi)): s 38(4)(e).
17 Communications Act 2003 s 38(8)(a).
18 Communications Act 2003 s 38(8)(b).
19 Ie persons falling within the Communications Act 2003 s 38(2)(d)–(f) (see note 3 heads (4)–(6)).
20 Communications Act 2003 s 38(8)(c).
21 Communications Act 2003 s 38(9)(a). Any deficit or surplus shown (after applying this provision for all previous years) by a statement under s 38(9) must be carried forward and taken into account in determining what is required to satisfy the requirement imposed by virtue of s 38(4)(a) (see head (a) in the text) in relation to the following year: s 38(10).
    Section 34 (see PARA 81) applies in relation to the making and withdrawal of a designation for the purposes of s 38 as it applies to the making and withdrawal of a designation for the purposes of s 33 (see PARA 81): s 38(11).
22 Communications Act 2003 s 38(9)(b). See note 21.
23 Communications Act 2003 s 38(9)(c). The functions referred to in head (C) in the text are the functions mentioned in the Communications Act 2003 s 38(5): s 38(9)(c). See note 21.
24 Communications Act 2003 s 39(1).
25 Ie under the Communications Act 2003 s 38.
26 In the Communications Act 2003 s 39 'charging year' has the same meaning as in s 38: s 39(8).
27 Communications Act 2003 s 39(2).
28 Communications Act 2003 s 39(3).
29 References to a statement of charging principles are references to a statement by OFCOM of the principles that it is proposing to apply in fixing charges under the Communications Act 2003 s 38 for a charging year: s 39(7).
30 Communications Act 2003 s 39(4).
31 Communications Act 2003 s 39(5). The way in which a statement of charging principles must be made or may be revised is by the publication of the statement or revised statement in such manner as OFCOM considers appropriate for bringing it to the attention of the persons who, in its opinion, are likely to be affected by it: s 39(6).

84.   Non-payment of charges. OFCOM[1] is not entitled to bring proceedings for the recovery from a person of an administrative charge fixed for any year[2] unless it has given that person a notification[3] with respect to the amount it is seeking to recover[4]. Where OFCOM determines that there are reasonable grounds for believing that a person is in contravention (whether in respect of the whole or a part of a charge) of a requirement to pay such an administrative charge, it may give him a notification under these provisions[5].

Such a notification is one which sets out the determination made by OFCOM and specifies the period during which the person notified has an opportunity of making representations about the notified determination[6].

A notification under these provisions:

(1)   may be given in respect of contraventions of more than one requirement to pay an administrative charge[7]; and

(2)   if it is given in respect of a continuing contravention, may be given in respect of any period during which the contravention has continued[8].

Where a notification has been given to a person in respect of an amount outstanding, OFCOM may give a further notification in respect of the whole or a part of that amount if, and only if:

(a)   the subsequent notification is in respect of so much of a period during which that amount was outstanding as falls after a period to which the earlier notification relates[9]; or

(b)   the earlier notification has been withdrawn without a penalty having been imposed in respect of the matters notified[10].

Where:

(i)   a person (the 'notified charge payer') has been given a notification[11];

(ii)   OFCOM has allowed the notified charge payer an opportunity of making representations about the notified determination[12]; and

(iii)   the period allowed for the making of the representations has expired[13], OFCOM may impose a penalty on the notified charge payer if he has, in one or more of the respects notified, been in contravention of a requirement to pay an administrative charge[14].

The amount of a penalty imposed is to be such amount, not exceeding twice the amount of the charge fixed for the relevant year[15], as OFCOM determines to be appropriate; and it must be proportionate to the contravention in respect of which it is imposed[16]. Where OFCOM imposes a penalty on a person, it must without delay notify that person of that decision and of its reasons for that decision; and, in that notification, it must fix a reasonable period after it is given as the period within which the penalty is to be paid[17]. A penalty imposed under these provisions must be paid to OFCOM and, if not paid within the period fixed by OFCOM, is to be recoverable by it accordingly[18].

Provision is made in relation to the suspension of service provision in cases of non-payment of administrative charges[19].

1   As to the meaning of 'OFCOM' see PARA 14 note 1; and as to OFCOM see PARA 2 et seq.
2   Ie under the Communications Act 2003 s 38: see PARA 83.
3   Ie under the Communications Act 2003 s 40.
4   Communications Act 2003 s 40(1).
5   Communications Act 2003 s 40(2).
6   Communications Act 2003 s 40(3) (amended by SI 2011/1210).
7   Communications Act 2003 s 40(9)(a).
8   Communications Act 2003 s 40(9)(b).
9   Communications Act 2003 s 40(10)(a).
10   Communications Act 2003 s 40(10)(b).
11   Communications Act 2003 s 41(1)(a). The reference to notification in head (i) in the text is a notification under the Communications Act 2003 s 40.
12   Communications Act 2003 s 41(1)(b).
13   Communications Act 2003 s 41(1)(c).
14   Communications Act 2003 s 41(2) (amended by SI 2011/1210). The reference to administrative charge in the text is a charge fixed under the Communications Act 2003 s 38: see PARA 83.
      Where a notification under s 40 relates to more than one contravention, a separate penalty may be imposed in respect of each contravention: s 41(3). Where such a notification relates to a continuing contravention, no more than one penalty may be imposed in respect of the period of contravention specified in the notification: s 41(4).
15   In the Communications Act 2003 s 41, the 'relevant year', in relation to a contravention of a requirement to pay the whole or a part of the administrative charge fixed for any year, means that year: s 41(9).
16   Communications Act 2003 s 41(5). In making that determination, OFCOM must have regard to any representations made to it by the notified charge payer and any steps taken by him towards paying the amounts that he was notified under s 40 were outstanding: s 41(6).
17   Communications Act 2003 s 41(7) (amended by SI 2011/1210).
18   Communications Act 2003 s 41(8). The provisions of s 41 do not affect OFCOM's power, apart from those provisions, to bring proceedings (whether before or after the imposition of a penalty under s 41) for the recovery of the whole or part of an amount due to it under s 38(1) (see PARA 83): s 41(10).
19   See PARA 85.

85. Suspension of service provision for non-payment of charges. OFCOM[1] may give a direction[2] to a person who is a communications provider[3] or who makes associated facilities[4] available (the 'contravening provider') if it is satisfied:

(1) that he is or has been in serious or repeated contravention[5] of requirements to pay administrative charges fixed for any year[6] (whether in respect of the whole or a part of the charges)[7];

(2) that the contraventions are not contraventions relating only to charges in respect of the application to the contravening provider of SMP apparatus conditions[8];

(3) that, in the case of a single serious contravention, a notification has been given to the contravening provider[9] and the period for making representations[10] has expired[11];

(4) that, in the case of a repeated contravention, the bringing of proceedings for the recovery of the amounts outstanding has failed to secure complete compliance by the contravening provider with the requirements to pay the charges fixed in his case, or has no reasonable prospect of securing such compliance[12];

(5) that, in the case of a repeated contravention, an attempt, by the imposition of penalties[13], to secure such compliance has failed[14]; and

(6) that the giving of the direction is appropriate and proportionate to the contravention in respect of which it is given[15].

Such a direction is:

(a) a direction that the entitlement of the contravening provider to provide electronic communications networks[16] or electronic communications services[17], or to make associated facilities available, is suspended (either generally or in relation to particular networks, services or facilities)[18]; or

(b) a direction that that entitlement is restricted in the respects set out in the direction[19].

A direction must specify the networks, services and facilities to which it relates and, except so far as it otherwise provides, takes effect for an indefinite period beginning with the time at which it is notified to the person to whom it is given[20]. A direction, in providing for the effect of a suspension or restriction to be postponed may provide for it to take effect only at a time determined by or in accordance with the terms of the direction and, in connection with the suspension or restriction contained in the direction or with the postponement of its effect, may impose such conditions on the contravening provider as appears to OFCOM to be appropriate for the purpose of protecting that provider's customers[21]. Those conditions may include a condition requiring the making of payments by way of compensation for loss or damage suffered by the contravening provider's customers as a result of the direction or in respect of annoyance, inconvenience or anxiety to which they have been put in consequence of the direction[22]. OFCOM is not to give a direction unless it has:

(i) notified the contravening provider of the proposed direction and of the conditions (if any) which it is proposing to impose by that direction[23];

(ii) provided him with an opportunity of making representations about the proposals and of proposing steps for remedying the situation[24]; and

(iii) considered every representation and proposal made to it during the period allowed by it[25] for the contravening provider to take advantage of that opportunity[26].

If OFCOM considers it appropriate to do so (whether or not in consequence of any representations or proposals made to it), it may revoke a direction, or modify its conditions:

(A)   with effect from such time as it may direct[27];

(B)   subject to compliance with such requirements as it may specify[28]; and

(C)   to such extent and in relation to such networks, services or facilities, or parts of a network, service or facility, as it may determine[29].

A person is guilty of an offence if he provides an electronic communications network or electronic communications service, or makes available any associated facility while his entitlement to do so is suspended by a direction[30] or in contravention of a restriction contained in such a direction[31].

The duty of a person to comply with a condition of a direction[32] is a duty owed to every person who may be affected by a contravention of the condition[33]. Where such a duty is owed to a person, a breach of the duty that causes that person to sustain loss or damage[34], and an act which, by inducing a breach of the duty or interfering with its performance, causes that person to sustain loss or damage and is done wholly or partly for achieving that result[35], is actionable at the suit or instance of that person[36].

1   As to the meaning of 'OFCOM' see PARA 14 note 1; and as to OFCOM see PARA 2 et seq.

2   Ie under the Communications Act 2003 s 42.

3   As to the meaning of 'communications provider' see PARA 17 note 23.

4   As to the meaning of 'associated facility' see PARA 53.

5   For the purposes of the Communications Act 2003 s 42 there are repeated contraventions by a person of requirements to pay administrative charges to the extent that:

     (1)   in the case of a previous notification given to that person under s 40, OFCOM has determined for the purposes of s 41(2) (see PARA 84) that such a contravention did occur (s 42(9)(a)); and

     (2)   in the period of 24 months following the day of the making of that determination, one or more further notifications have been given to that person in respect of the same or different failures to pay administrative charges (s 42(9)(b) (amended by SI 2011/1210)).

6   Ie under the Communications Act 2003 s 38: see PARA 83.

7   Communications Act 2003 s 42(1)(a) (amended by SI 2011/1210).

8   Communications Act 2003 s 42(1)(b). As to the meaning of 'SMP apparatus condition' see PARA 87 note 8.

9   Ie under the Communications Act 2003 s 40: see PARA 96.

10   Ie under the Communications Act 2003 s 40: see PARA 96.

11   Communications Act 2003 s 42(1)(ba) (added by SI 2011/1210).

12   Communications Act 2003 s 42(1)(c) (amended by SI 2011/1210).

13   Ie under the Communications Act 2003 s 41: see PARA 84.

14   Communications Act 2003 s 42(1)(d) (amended by SI 2011/1210).

15   Communications Act 2003 s 42(1)(e) (substituted by SI 2011/1210).

16   As to the meaning of 'electronic communications network' see PARA 53.

17   Communications Act 2003 s 42(2)(a).

18   As to the meaning of 'electronic communications service' see PARA 53.

19   Communications Act 2003 s 42(2)(b).

20   Communications Act 2003 s 42(3).

21   Communications Act 2003 s 42(4).

22   Communications Act 2003 s 42(5).

23   Communications Act 2003 s 42(6)(a).

24   Communications Act 2003 s 42(6)(b).

25   Communications Act 2003 s 42(6)(c).

26   That period is such reasonable period as OFCOM may specify, beginning with the day of the giving of the notification: Communications Act 2003 s 42(7) (substituted by SI 2011/1210).

27   Communications Act 2003 s 42(8)(a).

28   Communications Act 2003 s 42(8)(b).

29   Communications Act 2003 s 42(8)(c).

30   Ie under the Communications Act 2003 s 42.

31   Communications Act 2003 s 43(1). A person guilty of such an offence is liable:

(1)   on summary conviction, to a fine not exceeding the statutory maximum (s 43(2)(a));

(2)   on conviction on indictment, to a fine (s 43(2)(b)).

As to the statutory maximum see SENTENCING AND DISPOSITION OF OFFENDERS vol 92 (2010) PARA 140.

32 Ie under the Communications Act 2003 s 42.

33 Communications Act 2003 s 43(3).

34 Communications Act 2003 s 43(4)(a).

35 Communications Act 2003 s 43(4)(b).

36 Communications Act 2003 s 43(4). In proceedings brought against a person by virtue of s 43(4)(a) (see text to note 21) it is a defence for that person to show that he took all reasonable steps and exercised all due diligence to avoid contravening the condition in question: s 43(5). Sections 96A–99 (see PARAS 117–120) apply in relation to a contravention of conditions imposed by a direction under s 42 as they apply in relation to a contravention of conditions set under s 45 (see PARA 87): s 43(6) (amended by SI 2011/1210).

(iii) Register of Providers required to Notify or Pay Charges

86.   Duty of OFCOM to keep publicly accessible register.   It is the duty of OFCOM[1] to establish and maintain a register[2], in which OFCOM must record:

(1)   every designation by it[3];

(2)   every withdrawal by it of such a designation[4];

(3)   every notification given to it[5]; and

(4)   every notification treated as given to it by a transitional provision[6].

Information recorded in the register must be so recorded in such manner as OFCOM considers appropriate[7]. It is the duty of OFCOM to publish a notification setting out:

(a)   the times at which the register is for the time being available for public inspection[8]; and

(b)   the fees that must be paid for, or in connection with, an inspection of the register[9].

OFCOM must make the register available for public inspection during such hours, and on payment of such fees, as are set out in the notification[10] for the time being in force[11].

1 As to the meaning of 'OFCOM' see PARA 14 note 1; and as to OFCOM see PARA 2 et seq.

2 Ie a register for the purposes of the Communications Act 2003 s 33 (see PARA 81): s 44(1).

3 Communications Act 2003 s 44(2)(a). The reference in head (1) in the text to designation is a reference to designation for the purposes of the Communications Act 2003 s 33 (see PARA 81) or s 38 (see PARA 83).

4 Communications Act 2003 s 44(2)(b).

5 Communications Act 2003 s 44(2)(c). The reference in head (3) in the text to notification is a reference to notification under the Communications Act 2003 s 33: see PARA 81.

6 Communications Act 2003 s 44(2)(d). The reference in head (4) in the text to transitional provisions is a reference to transitional provisions made under s 33(12) (see PARA 81 note 5).

7 Communications Act 2003 s 44(3).

8 Communications Act 2003 s 44(4)(a). The publication of a notification under s 44(4) must be in such manner as OFCOM considers appropriate for bringing it to the attention of the persons who, in its opinion, are likely to be affected by it: s 44(5).

9 Communications Act 2003 s 44(4)(b). See note 8.

10 Ie under the Communications Act 2003 s 44(4): see text and notes 8, 9.

11 Communications Act 2003 s 44(6).

(iv) Conditions of Entitlement to Provide Network or Service

A. SETTING AND APPLICATION OF CONDITIONS

87. Power of OFCOM to set conditions of entitlement to provide network or service. OFCOM[1] has the power to set conditions under the following provisions[2] binding the persons to whom they are applied[3]. A condition set by OFCOM under these provisions must be either:

(1) a general condition[4]; or

(2) a condition of one of the following descriptions:
   (a) a universal service condition[5];
   (b) an access-related condition[6];
   (c) a privileged supplier condition[7];
   (d) a significant market power condition (an 'SMP condition')[8].

OFCOM's power to set a condition making provision authorised or required by Chapter 1 of Part 2 of the Communications Act 2003[9] includes each of the following:

(i) power to impose a requirement on the person or persons to whom the condition is applied to comply with such directions with respect to the matters to which the condition relates as may be given from time to time by OFCOM or by another person specified in the condition[10];

(ii) power to impose an obligation with respect to those matters that is framed by reference to, or is conditional upon, the giving of a consent or of an approval, or on the making of a recommendation, by OFCOM or by another person so specified[11];

(iii) power, for the purposes of provision made by virtue of either of the preceding heads, to confer a discretion exercisable from time to time by OFCOM or by another person specified in the condition or determined in accordance with provision contained in it[12];

(iv) power[13] to set different conditions for different cases (including different conditions in relation to different parts of the United Kingdom)[14]; and

(v) power to revoke or modify the conditions for the time being in force[15].

1 As to the meaning of 'OFCOM' see PARA 14 note 1; and as to OFCOM see PARA 2 et seq.
2 Ie the Communications Act 2003 s 45.
3 Ie in accordance with the Communications Act 2003 s 46 (see PARA 88): s 45(1).
4 Communications Act 2003 s 45(2)(a). A 'general condition' is a condition which contains only provisions authorised or required by one or more of the Communications Act 2003 s 51, s 52, s 57, s 58 or s 64 (see PARAS 98–100; and BROADCASTING vol 4 (2011) PARA 719): ss 45(3), 151(1).
5 Communications Act 2003 s 45(2)(b)(i). A 'universal service condition' is a condition which contains only provisions authorised or required by the Communications Act 2003 s 67 (see PARA 102): ss 45(4), 151(1).
6 Communications Act 2003 s 45(2)(b)(ii). An 'access-related condition' is a condition which contains only provisions authorised by the Communications Act 2003 s 73 (see PARA 104): ss 45(5), 151(1).
7 Communications Act 2003 s 45(2)(b)(iii). A 'privileged supplier condition' is a condition which contains only the provision required by s 77 (see PARA 105): ss 45(6), 151(1).
8 Communications Act 2003 s 45(2)(b)(iv). An 'SMP condition' is either an SMP services condition or an SMP apparatus condition: ss 45(7), 151(1). An 'SMP services condition' is a condition which contains only provisions which:
   (1) are authorised or required by one or more of ss 87–91 (see PARA 111 et seq) (s 45(8)(a) (s 45(8) amended by SI 2011/1210)); or
   (2) in the case of a condition applying to a person falling within the Communications

Act 2003 s 46(8)(b) (see PARA 88), correspond to provision authorised or required by one or more of ss 87–89A (s 45(8)(b) (as so amended)).

An 'SMP apparatus condition' is a condition containing only provisions authorised by s 93 (see PARA 114): s 45(9). As to SMP conditions see further PARA 106 et seq.

9   Ie the Communications Act 2003 Pt 2 Ch 1 (ss 32–151).

10 Communications Act 2003 s 45(10)(a). The directions that may be authorised by virtue of s 45(10) do not include directions withdrawing, suspending or restricting a person's entitlement: (1) to provide, in whole or in part, any electronic communications network or electronic communications service; or (2) to make available, in whole or in part, any associated facilities: s 45(11). As to the meanings of 'electronic communications network', 'electronic communications service' and 'associated facilities' see PARA 53.

11 Communications Act 2003 s 45(10)(b). See note 10.

12 Communications Act 2003 s 45(10)(c). See note 10.

13 Ie subject to the Communications Act 2003 s 51(3): see PARA 98.

14 Communications Act 2003 s 45(10)(d). As to the meaning of 'United Kingdom' see PARA 14 note 7. See note 10.

15 Communications Act 2003 s 45(10)(e). See note 10.

88. Persons to whom conditions may apply.   A condition[1] is not to be applied to a person except in accordance with the following provisions[2]. A general condition[3] may be applied:

(1)   to every person providing an electronic communications network[4] or electronic communications service[5]; or

(2)   to every person providing such a network or service of a particular description specified in the condition[6].

A universal service condition[7], access-related condition[8], privileged supplier condition[9] or SMP condition[10] may be applied to a particular person specified in the condition[11].

1   Ie set under the Communications Act 2003 s 45: see PARA 87.

2   Communications Act 2003 s 46(1). The provisions referred to in the text are the Communications Act 2003 s 46: s 46(1).

3   As to the meaning of 'general condition' see PARA 87 note 4. As to general conditions see further PARA 98 et seq.

4   As to the meaning of 'electronic communications network' see PARA 53.

5   Communications Act 2003 s 46(2)(a). As to the meaning of 'electronic communications service' see PARA 53.

6   Communications Act 2003 s 46(2)(b).

7   As to the meaning of 'universal service condition' see PARA 87 note 5. The particular person to whom a universal service condition is applied:

(1)   except in the case of a condition relating to matters mentioned in the Communications Act 2003 s 66(3), must be a communications provider designated in accordance with regulations under s 66 (see PARA 102) (s 46(5)(a)); and

(2)   in that excepted case, must be a communications provider so designated or a person who is not such a provider but who is so designated for the purposes only of conditions relating to those matters (s 46(5)(b)).

As to universal service conditions see further PARA 102.

8   As to the meaning of 'access-related condition' see PARA 87 note 6. The particular person to whom an access-related condition is applied:

(1)   in the case of a condition falling within the Communications Act 2003 s 74(1) (see PARA 104), may be any person whatever (s 46(6)(a)); and

(2)   in any other case, must be a person who provides an electronic communications network or makes associated facilities available (s 46(6)(b)).

As to the meaning of 'associated facility' see PARA 53. As to access-related conditions see further PARA 104.

9   As to the meaning of 'privileged supplier condition' see PARA 87 note 7. A privileged supplier condition may also be applied generally:

(1)   to every person to whom such a condition is required to apply under the Communications Act 2003 s 77 (see PARA 105) (s 46(4)(a)); or

(2)   to every such person who is of a particular description specified in the condition (s 46(4)(b)).

As to privileged supplier conditions see further PARA 105.

10 As to the meaning of 'SMP condition' see PARA 87 text and note 8. As to SMP conditions see further PARA 106 et seq.

The particular person to whom an SMP services condition is applied must:

(1)   be a communications provider or a person who makes associated facilities available (Communications Act 2003 s 46(7)(a)); and

(2)   fall within s 46(8) (s 46(7)(b)).

A person falls within s 46(8) if:

(a)   he is a person whom OFCOM has determined to be a person having significant market power in a specific market for electronic communications networks, electronic communications services or associated facilities (a 'services market') (s 46(8)(a)); or

(b)   it appears to OFCOM that he is a person on whom it is necessary, for the purpose of securing compliance with an international obligation of the United Kingdom, to impose a condition containing provision that corresponds to provision which, in the case of a person falling within head (a), must be made (or may be made) under any of ss 87–89A (see PARAS 111, 112) (s 46(8)(b) (amended by SI 2011/1210)).

As to the meaning of 'international obligation of the United Kingdom' see PARA 33 note 7. As to the meaning of 'United Kingdom' see PARA 14 note 7. 'Significant market power' is to be construed in accordance with the Communications Act 2003 s 78 (see PARA 106): s 151(1). As to the meaning of 'SMP services condition' see PARA 87 note 8. As to SMP services conditions see further PARA 111.

The particular person to whom an SMP apparatus condition is applied must be:

(i)   a person who supplies electronic communications apparatus (s 46(9)(a)); and

(ii)   a person whom OFCOM has determined to be a person having significant market power in a specific market for electronic communications apparatus (an 'apparatus market') (s 46(9)(b)).

'Electronic communications apparatus':

(A)   in relation to SMP apparatus conditions and in s 141 (see PARA 143), means apparatus that is designed or adapted for a use which consists of or includes the sending or receiving of communications or other signals (within the meaning of s 32: see PARA 53 note 7) that are transmitted by means of an electronic communications network; and

(B)   in all other contexts, has the same meaning as in the electronic communications code: s 151(1).

As to the meaning of 'electronic communications code' see PARA 155 note 1. As to the meaning of 'SMP apparatus condition' see PARA 87 note 8. As to SMP apparatus conditions see further PARA 114.

11 Communications Act 2003 s 46(3).

89. Test for setting or modifying conditions.

89.   Test for setting or modifying conditions.   OFCOM[1] must not, in exercise or performance of any power or duty under Chapter 1 of Part 2 of the Communications Act 2003[2]:

(1)   set a condition[3]; or

(2)   modify a condition[4],

unless it is satisfied that the condition or (as the case may be) the modification satisfies the test[5] that the condition or modification is:

(a)   objectively justifiable in relation to the networks, services, facilities, apparatus or directories to which it relates[6];

(b)   not such as to discriminate unduly against particular persons or against a particular description of persons[7];

(c)   proportionate to what the condition or modification is intended to achieve[8]; and

(d)   in relation to what it is intended to achieve, transparent[9].

1   As to the meaning of 'OFCOM' see PARA 14 note 1; and as to OFCOM see PARA 2 et seq.
2   Ie the Communications Act 2003 Pt 2 Ch 1 (ss 32–151).
3   Communications Act 2003 s 47(1)(a). The setting of a condition referred to in head (1) is a condition set under s 45 (see PARA 87): s 47(1)(a).
4   Communications Act 2003 s 47(1)(a).
5   Ie the test in the Communications Act 2003 s 47(2): s 47(1).

6 Communications Act 2003 s 47(2)(a). Head (a) in the text does not apply in relation to the setting of a general condition: s 47(2)(a), 47(3) (added by SI 2011/1210).
7 Communications Act 2003 s 47(2)(b).
8 Communications Act 2003 s 47(2)(c).
9 Communications Act 2003 s 47(2)(d).

90. Procedure for setting, modifying and revoking conditions. Subject to specified provisions of the Communications Act 2003[1]:

(1)   the way in which conditions are to be set or modified[2] is by the publication of a notification setting out the conditions or modifications[3]; and

(2)   the way in which such a condition is to be revoked is by the publication of a notification stating that the condition is revoked[4].

Where the provisions for domestic consultations for these conditions[5] apply, OFCOM[6] must comply with the applicable requirements of those provisions and provisions for EU consultations[7] before:

(a)   setting conditions[8]; or

(b)   modifying or revoking a condition so set[9].

Where the provisions for domestic consultations[10] for these conditions do not apply to the setting, modification or revocation of conditions[11]:

(i)   the conditions, or their modification or revocation, must be temporary[12]; and

(ii)   the notification[13] must state the period for which the conditions, or their modification or revocation, are to have effect[14].

The publication of a notification[15] must be in such manner as appears to OFCOM to be appropriate for bringing the contents of the notification[16]:

(A)   in the case of a notification setting general conditions, to the attention of such persons as OFCOM considers appropriate[17]; and

(B)   in any other case, to the attention of the persons who, in OFCOM's opinion, are likely to be affected by the contents of the notification[18].

Provision is made with respect to the delivery of copies of notifications[19].

1 Ie the Communications Act 2003 ss 49–151.
2 Ie under the Communications Act 2003 s 45: see PARA 87.
3 Communications Act 2003 s 48(1)(a). Nothing in ss 49–151 imposing a duty on OFCOM to set or modify a condition is to be taken as dispensing with any of the requirements of ss 48, 48A, 48B (see PARAS 91, 92): s 48(7).
4 Communications Act 2003 s 48(1)(b).
5 Ie the Communications Act 2003 s 48A: see PARA 91.
6 As to the meaning of 'OFCOM' see PARA 14 note 1; and as to OFCOM see PARA 2 et seq.
7 Ie the Communications Act 2003 s 48B; see PARA 92.
8 Communications Act 2003 s 48(2)(a) (s 48(2) substituted by SI 2011/1210). The setting of conditions referred to in the text is that under the Communications Act 2003 s 45: see PARA 87. In the case of a proposal by OFCOM with respect to an SMP condition, the applicable requirements of ss 79–86 (see PARAS 106–110) must also be complied with: s 48(4) (amended by SI 2011/1210). As to the meaning of 'SMP condition' see PARA 87 text and note 8. As to SMP conditions see further PARA 106 et seq.
9 Communications Act 2003 s 48(2)(b) (as substituted: see note 8).
10 Ie the Communications Act 2003 s 48A: see PARA 91.
11 Ie because of the Communications Act 2003 s 48A(2): see PARA 91.
12 Communications Act 2003 s 48(2A)(a) (ss 48(2A), (2B), 48B added by SI 2011/1210). Where OFCOM propose to extend or make permanent any such temporary conditions, modification or revocation:
    (1)   The Communications Act 2003 s 48A (PARA 91) and s 48B(1) (PARA 92) do not apply in relation to the proposal (s 48(2B)(a) (as so added)); and
    (2)   the provisions of s 48B(2)–(9) (PARA 92) apply in relation to the proposal so that the requirement for OFCOM to send a copy of the proposal, and of a statement setting out

the reasons for it, applies without reference to first making any appropriate modifications (s 48(2B)(b), 48B(2) (as so added)).
13　Ie published under the Communications Act 2003 s 48(1).
14　Communications Act 2003 s 48(2A)(b) (as added: see note 12).
15　Ie under the Communications Act 2003 s 48 or s 48A (see PARA 91).
16　Communications Act 2003 s 48(6) (amended by SI 2011/1210).
17　Communications Act 2003 s 48(6)(a).
18　Communications Act 2003 s 48(6)(b).
19　See the Communications Act 2003 s 48C; and PARA 96.

91.　Domestic consultation where there is a proposal for setting, modifying and revoking conditions.　Subject to certain exceptions[1], where OFCOM[2] propose to set, modify or revoke:

(1)　SMP apparatus conditions[3]; or

(2)　any other conditions[4] where what is proposed would, in OFCOM's opinion, have a significant impact on a market for any of the services, facilities, apparatus or directories in relation to which they have functions under Chapter 1 of Part 2 of the Communications Act 2003[5],

OFCOM must publish a notification stating that they are proposing to set, modify or revoke the conditions that are specified in the notification, setting out the effect of those conditions, modifications or revocations, giving their reasons for making the proposal and specifying the period[6] within which representations may be made to OFCOM about their proposal[7].

OFCOM must consider every representation about the proposal made to them during the period specified in the notification and have regard to every international obligation of the United Kingdom (if any) which has been notified to them for these purposes by the Secretary of State[8].

These provisions[9] do not apply where the proposal is of EU significance[10] and in OFCOM's opinion there are exceptional circumstances; and there is an urgent need to act in order to safeguard competition and to protect the interests of consumers[11]. Where the proposal is not of EU significance, OFCOM may then give effect to it, with any modifications that appear to OFCOM to be appropriate[12].

1　See the Communications Act 2003 s 48A(2); and text and note 11.
2　As to the meaning of 'OFCOM' see PARA 14 note 1; and as to OFCOM see PARA 2 et seq.
3　Communications Act 2003 s 48A(1)(a) (s 48A added by SI 2011/1210). As to the meaning of 'SMP apparatus condition' see PARA 87 note 8. As to SMP apparatus conditions see further PARA 114.
4　Ie set under the Communications Act 2003 s 45: see PARA 87.
5　Communications Act 2003 s 48A(1)(b) (as added: see note 3). As to the functions referred to in the text see Pt 2 Ch 1 (ss 32–151).
6　That period must end no less than one month after the day of the publication of the notification: Communications Act 2003 s 48A(4) (as added: see note 3). But where OFCOM are satisfied that there are exceptional circumstances justifying the use of a shorter period, the period specified as the period for making representations may be whatever shorter period OFCOM consider reasonable in those circumstances: s 48A(5) (as so added).
7　Communications Act 2003 s 48A(3) (as added: see note 3).
8　Communications Act 2003 s 48A(6) (as added: see note 3).
9　Ie the Communications Act 2003 s 48A.
10　In relation to a proposal:
　　(1)　to set, modify or revoke a condition under the Communications Act 2003 s 45 (s 150A(1)(a) (s 150A added by SI 2011/1210));
　　(2)　to give a direction, approval or consent for the purposes of such a condition (Communications Act 2003 s 150A(1)(b) (as so added));
　　(3)　to modify or withdraw such a direction, approval or consent (s 150A(1)(c) (as so added));

(4)   to identify a market for the purposes of making or reviewing a market power determination (s 150A(1)(d) (as so added)); or

(5)   to make or review a market power determination (s 150A(1)(e) (as so added)),

the proposal is of EU significance for the purposes of Pt 2 Ch 1 (ss 32–151) if:

(a)   European Parliament and Council Directive (EC) 2002/21 (OJ L108, 24.4.2002, p 33) on a common regulatory framework for electronic communications networks and services (the 'Framework Directive') (see PARA 97 note 21), art 7(3) applies, or would apply but for art 7(9), in relation to it (Communications Act 2003 s 150A(2)(a) (as so added));

(b)   (in a case within head (1), (2) or (3)) the condition is an access-related condition falling within s 73(2) or an SMP services condition (s 150A(2)(b) (as so added));

(c)   (in a case within head (4) or (5)) the market in question is a services market (s 150A(2)(c) (as so added)); and

(d)   in OFCOM's opinion it would affect trade between member states (s 150A(2)(d) (as so added)).

As to the meaning of 'access-related condition' see PARA 87 note 6. As to the meaning of 'SMP apparatus condition' see PARA 87 note 8.

11   Communications Act 2003 s 48A(2) (as added: see note 3).

12   Communications Act 2003 s 48A(7) (as added: see note 3).

92.   EU consultation where there is a proposal for setting, modifying and revoking conditions.   Where, after considering every representation and having regard to every international obligation of the United Kingdom[1] in relation to a proposal of EU significance[2], OFCOM[3] wishes to proceed with the proposal, after making any modifications of the proposal that appear to OFCOM to be appropriate, OFCOM must send a copy of the proposal, and of a statement setting out the reasons for it, to the European Commission[4], BEREC[5] and the regulatory authorities in every other member state[6].

If at the end of the period of one month[7] no notification has been given to OFCOM by the Commission[8], OFCOM may give effect to the proposal, with any modifications that appear to OFCOM to be appropriate[9]. Before giving effect to the proposal[10], OFCOM must consider any comments made by the Commission, BEREC and any regulatory authority in any other member State[11].

Where such a notification is given by the Commission to OFCOM during that period:

(1)   during the period of three months beginning with the notification, OFCOM must co-operate with the Commission and BEREC to identify the most appropriate and effective measure[12];

(2)   OFCOM may give effect to the proposal, with any modifications that appear to them to be appropriate, within one month (or such longer period as may be allowed[13]) of the Commission:

(a)   issuing a recommendation to amend or withdraw the proposal[14]; or

(b)   taking a decision to lift its reservations[15];

(3)   in a case in which OFCOM give effect to the proposal despite a recommendation of the Commission to amend or withdraw the proposal, OFCOM must send to the Commission a copy of a reasoned justification for their decision[16];

(4)   if at the end of the period of one month[17] the Commission has neither issued a recommendation nor lifted its reservations[18], OFCOM may give effect to the proposal, with any modifications that appear to them to be appropriate[19].

1   Ie after complying with the Communications Act 2003 s 48A(6). As to the meaning of 'United Kingdom' see PARA 14 note 7.

2   As to the meaning of 'EU significance' see PARA 91 note 10.

3   As to the meaning of 'OFCOM' see PARA 14 note 1; and as to OFCOM see PARA 2 et seq.
4   As to the European Commission see EUROPEAN UNION vol 47A (2014) PARAS 48, 49.
5   As to BEREC see PARA 58.
6   Communications Act 2003 s 48B(1), (2) (s 48B added by SI 2011/1210). References in Pt 2 Ch 1 (ss 32–151) to the regulatory authorities of member states are references to such of the authorities of the member states as have been notified to the European Commission as the regulatory authorities of those states for the purposes of the Framework Directive: s 151(1), (5).
7   Ie referred to in the European Parliament and Council Directive (EC) 2002/21 (OJ L108, 24.4.2002, p 33) on a common regulatory framework for electronic communications networks and services ('the Framework Directive') (see PARA 97 note 21), art 7(3).
8   Ie under the Framework Directive art 7a(1).
9   Communications Act 2003 s 48B(3) (as added: see note 6).
10   Ie under the Communications Act 2003 s 48B(3).
11   Communications Act 2003 s 48B(4) (as added: see note 6).
12   Communications Act 2003 s 48B(5), (6) (as added: see note 6).
13   Ie under the Framework Directive art 7a(6).
14   Communications Act 2003 s 48B(5), (7)(a) (as added: see note 6). The recommendation referred to in the text is issued under the Framework Directive art 7a(5)(a).
15   Communications Act 2003 s 48B(5), (7)(b) (as added: see note 6). The decision taken to lift its reservation is in accordance with the Framework Directive art 7a(5)(b).
16   Communications Act 2003 s 48B(5), (8) (as added: see note 6).
17   Ie referred to in the Framework Directive art 7a(5).
18   Ie in accordance with the Framework Directive art 7a(5).
19   Communications Act 2003 s 48B(5), (9) (as added: see note 6).

93.   Directions and approvals for the purposes of a condition of entitlement.
Where:
(1)   a condition[1] has effect by reference to directions, approvals or consents given by a person (whether OFCOM[2] itself or another)[3]; and
(2)   that person ('the responsible person'[4]) is proposing to give a direction, approval or consent that affects the operation of that condition, or to modify or withdraw a direction, approval or consent so as to affect the condition's operation[5],
the responsible person must not give, modify or withdraw the direction, approval or consent unless he is satisfied that to do so is:
(a)   objectively justifiable in relation to the networks, services, facilities, apparatus or directories to which it relates[6];
(b)   not such as to discriminate unduly against particular persons or against a particular description of persons[7];
(c)   proportionate to what it is intended to achieve[8]; and
(d)   in relation to what it is intended to achieve, transparent[9].
Where the provisions relating to domestic consultations for directions, approvals and consents[10] apply, the applicable requirements for those provisions and the provisions relating to EU consultations for directions, approvals and consents[11] must be complied with before the direction, approval or consent is given, modified or withdrawn[12].
Where the provisions relating to domestic consultations for directions, approvals and consents[13] do not apply[14]:
(i)   the direction, approval or consent given, or its modification or withdrawal, must be temporary[15]; and
(ii)   the instrument that gives, modifies or withdraws the direction, approval or consent must state the period for which it is to have effect[16].
Where the responsible person is a person other than OFCOM, that person must refer to OFCOM such of the following questions as are relevant in the case in question:
(A)   whether OFCOM is of the opinion that what is proposed would have a

significant impact on a market for any of the services, facilities, apparatus or directories in relation to which it has functions under Chapter 1 of Part 2 of the Communications Act 2003[17];

(B)   whether OFCOM is of the opinion that there are exceptional circumstances and there is an urgent need to act in order to safeguard competition and to protect the interests of consumers[18]; and

(C)   whether the proposal is of EU significance[19].

OFCOM must immediately determine any question so referred to them[20].

Provision is made with respect to the delivery of copies of notifications in respect of these directions etc[21].

1   Ie set by OFCOM under the Communications Act 2003 s 45: see PARA 87.
2   As to the meaning of 'OFCOM' see PARA 14 note 1; and as to OFCOM see PARA 2 et seq.
3   Communications Act 2003 s 49(1)(a).
4   Ie referred to as such in the Communications Act 2003 ss 49, 49A–49C (see PARAS 94, 95, 97): s 49(1)(b) (amended by SI 2011/1210). Where the responsible person is a person other than OFCOM, that person must in giving, modifying or withdrawing the direction be under the same duty as OFCOM to act in accordance with the six European Union (EU) requirements set out in the Communications Act 2003 s 4 (see PARA 17): s 49(3) (amended by SI 2011/1210).
5   Communications Act 2003 s 49(1)(b).
6   Communications Act 2003 s 49(2)(a). Head (a) in the text does not apply in relation to a direction, approval or consent affecting a general condition: s 49(2)(a), (2A) (s 49(2) amended and s 49(2A) added by SI 2011/1210).
7   Communications Act 2003 s 49(2)(b).
8   Communications Act 2003 s 49(2)(c).
9   Communications Act 2003 s 49(2)(d).
10   Ie the Communications Act 2003 s 49A: see PARA 94.
11   Ie the Communications Act 2003 s 49B: see PARA 95.
12   Communications Act 2003 s 49(4) (substituted by SI 2011/1210).
13   Ie the Communications Act 2003 s 49A: see PARA 94.
14   Ie because of the Communications Act 2003 s 49A(2): see PARA 94.
15   Communications Act 2003 s 49(4A)(a) (ss 49(4A)–(4D), 49B added by SI 2011/1210). Where it is proposed to extend or make permanent any such temporary direction, approval or consent, or modification or withdrawal:
     (1)   the Communications Act 2003 ss 49A and 49B(1) do not apply in relation to the proposal (s 49(4B)(a) (as so added)); and
     (2)   the provisions of s 49B(2)–(10) (see PARA 95) apply in relation to the proposal so that the requirement for the responsible person to send a copy of the proposal, and of a statement setting out the reasons for it, applies without reference to first making any appropriate modifications (see ss 49(4B)(b), 49B(2) (as so added)).
16   Communications Act 2003 s 49(4A)(b) (as added: see note 15).
17   Communications Act 2003 s 49(4C)(a) (as added: see note 15). The opinion referred to head (a) in the text is the opinion mentioned in s 49A(1)(b) (see PARA 94): s 49(4C)(a) (as so added).
18   Communications Act 2003 s 49(4C)(b) (as added: see note 15). The opinion referred to head (b) in the text is the opinion mentioned in s 49A(2): s 49(4C)(b) (as so added).
19   Communications Act 2003 s 49(4C)(c) (as added: see note 15). As to the meaning of 'EU significance' see PARA 91 note 10.
20   Communications Act 2003 s 49(4D) (as added: see note 15).
21   See the Communications Act 2003 s 49C; and PARA 97.

94. Domestic consultation for directions, approvals and consents. Subject to certain exceptions[1], where the responsible person[2] is proposing to give, modify or withdraw a direction, approval or consent for the purposes of:

(1)   an SMP apparatus condition[3]; or

(2)   any other condition[4] where what is proposed would, in OFCOM's opinion, have a significant impact on a market for any of the services, facilities, apparatus or directories in relation to which they have functions under Chapter 1 of Part 2 of the Communications Act 2003[5],

the responsible person must publish a notification:

(a)   stating that there is a proposal to give, modify or withdraw the direction, approval or consent[6];

(b)   identifying the responsible person[7];

(c)   setting out the direction, approval or consent to which the proposal relates[8];

(d)   setting out the effect of the direction, approval or consent or of its proposed modification or withdrawal[9];

(e)   giving reasons for the making of the proposal[10]; and

(f)   specifying the period[11] within which representations may be made about the proposal to the responsible person[12].

The responsible person must:

(i)   consider every representation about the proposal made to that person during the period specified in the notification[13]; and

(ii)   have regard to every international obligation of the United Kingdom (if any) which has been notified to OFCOM for these purposes by the Secretary of State[14].

Where the proposal is not of EU significance[15], the responsible person may then give effect to the proposal, with any modifications that appear to that person to be appropriate[16]. The publication of a notification under these provisions must be in such manner as appears to the responsible person to be appropriate for bringing the contents of the notification to the attention of such persons as that person considers appropriate[17].

These provisions[18] do not apply where the proposal is of EU significance and in OFCOM's opinion there are exceptional circumstances and there is an urgent need to act in order to safeguard competition and to protect the interests of consumers[19].

1   See the Communications Act 2003 s 49A(2); and text and note 19.

2   As to the meaning of 'responsible person' see PARA 93 note 4.

3   Communications Act 2003 s 49A(1)(a) (s 49A added by SI 2011/1210). As to the meaning of 'SMP apparatus condition' see PARA 87 note 8. As to SMP apparatus conditions see further PARA 114.

4   Ie set under the Communications Act 2003 s 45: see PARA 87.

5   Communications Act 2003 s 49A(1)(b) (as added: see note 3). As to the meaning of 'OFCOM' see PARA 14 note 1; and as to OFCOM see PARA 2 et seq.

6   Communications Act 2003 s 49A(3)(a) (as added: see note 3).

7   Communications Act 2003 s 49A(3)(b) (as added: see note 3).

8   Communications Act 2003 s 49A(3)(c) (as added: see note 3).

9   Communications Act 2003 s 49A(3)(d) (as added: see note 3).

10 Communications Act 2003 s 49A(3)(e) (as added: see note 3).

11 That period must be one ending not less than one month after the day of the publication of the notification but where the responsible person is satisfied that there are exceptional circumstances justifying the use of a shorter period, the period specified as the period for making representations may be whatever shorter period that person considers reasonable in those circumstances: Communications Act 2003 s 49A(4), (5) (as added: see note 3).

12 Communications Act 2003 s 49A(3)(f) (as added: see note 3).

13 Communications Act 2003 s 49A(6)(a) (as added: see note 3).

14 Communications Act 2003 s 49A(6)(b) (as added: see note 3). As to the meaning of 'United Kingdom' see PARA 14 note 7. As to the Secretary of State see PARA 76 note 1.

15 As to the meaning of 'EU significance' see PARA 91 note 10.

16 Communications Act 2003 s 49A(7) (as added: see note 3).

17 Communications Act 2003 s 49A(8) (as added: see note 3).

18 Ie the Communications Act 2003 s 49A.

19 Communications Act 2003 s 49A(2) (as added: see note 3).

95. EU consultation for directions, approvals and consents. Where, after considering every representation and having regard to every international obligation of the United Kingdom[1] in relation to a proposal of EU significance[2], the responsible person[3] wishes to proceed with the proposal[4], after the responsible person has made any modifications of the proposal that appear to the person to be appropriate, the person must send a copy of the proposal, and of a statement setting out the reasons for it, to the European Commission, BEREC and the regulatory authorities in every other member state[5].

If at the end of the period of one month[6] no notification has been given to the responsible person by the Commission[7], the responsible person may give effect to the proposal, with any amendments that appear to the responsible person to be appropriate[8]. Before giving effect to such a proposal[9], the responsible person must consider any comments made by the Commission, BEREC and any regulatory authority in any other member state[10].

Where such a notification is given by the Commission to the responsible person during that period[11]:

(1)   during the period of three months beginning with the notification, the responsible person must co-operate with the Commission and BEREC to identify the most appropriate and effective measure[12];

(2)   the responsible person may give effect to the proposal, with any modifications that appear to that person to be appropriate, within one month (or such longer period as may be allowed[13]) of the Commission:

    (a)   issuing a recommendation to amend or withdraw the proposal[14]; or

    (b)   taking a decision to lift its reservations[15];

(3)   in a case in which the responsible person is a person other than OFCOM and the Commission has recommended that the proposal be amended or withdrawn, the responsible person may give effect to the proposal only with the agreement of OFCOM[16];

(4)   in a case in which the responsible person gives effect to the proposal despite a recommendation of the Commission to amend or withdraw it, the responsible person must send to the Commission a copy of the responsible person's reasoned justification for the decision[17].

(5)   if at the end of the period of one month[18] the Commission has neither issued a recommendation nor lifted its reservations[19], the responsible person may give effect to the proposal, with any modifications that appear to that person to be appropriate[20].

1   Ie after complying with the Communications Act 2003 s 49A(6): see PARA 94. As to the meaning of 'United Kingdom' see PARA 14 note 7.
2   As to the meaning of 'EU significance' see PARA 91 note 10.
3   As to the meaning of 'the responsible person' see PARA 93 note 4.
4   Communications Act 2003 s 49B(1) (s 49B added by SI 2011/1210).
5   Communications Act 2003 s 49B(2) (as added: see note 4). As to the regulatory authorities of member states see PARA 92 note 6. As to BEREC see PARA 58.
6   Ie referred to in European Parliament and Council Directive (EC) 2002/21 (OJ L108, 24.4.2002, p 33) on a common regulatory framework for electronic communications networks and services ('the Framework Directive') (see PARA 97 note 21), art 7(3).
7   Ie under the Framework Directive art 7a(1).
8   Communications Act 2003 s 49B(3) (as added: see note 4).
9   Ie under the Communications Act 2003 s 49B(3).
10 Communications Act 2003 s 49B(4) (as added: see note 4).
11 Communications Act 2003 s 49B(5) (as added: see note 4).
12 Communications Act 2003 s 49B(6) (as added: see note 4).
13 Ie under the Framework Directive art 7a(6).
14 Communications Act 2003 s 49B(7)(a) (as added: see note 4). The text refers to a recommendation in accordance with the Framework Directive art 7a(5)(a).

15 Communications Act 2003 s 49B(7)(b) (as added: see note 4). The text refers to a decision to lift reservations in accordance with the Framework Directive art 7a(5)(b).
16 Communications Act 2003 s 49B(8) (as added: see note 4).
17 Communications Act 2003 s 49B(9) (as added: see note 4).
18 Ie referred to in the Framework Directive art 7a(5).
19 Ie in accordance with the Framework Directive art 7a(5).
20 Communications Act 2003 s 49B(10) (as added: see note 4).

96. Delivery of copies of notifications in respect of conditions. OFCOM[1] must send to the Secretary of State[2] a copy of every notification published[3]. OFCOM must send to the European Commission[4] a copy of every notification published[5] with respect to:

(1) a universal service condition[6];
(2) an access-related condition[7];
(3) an SMP services condition[8].

OFCOM must send to BEREC[9] a copy of every notification published[10] with respect to a proposal of EU significance[11]. Where a notification published[12] relates to a proposal to which the provisions relating to domestic consultation[13] did not apply because in OFCOM's opinion there were exceptional circumstances and there was an urgent need to act in order to safeguard competition and to protect the interests of consumers[14], OFCOM must send a copy of a statement setting out the reasons for the proposal and for the urgent need to act to the Commission, BEREC and the regulatory authorities in every other member state[15].

1 As to the meaning of 'OFCOM' see PARA 14 note 1; and as to OFCOM see PARA 2 et seq.
2 As to the Secretary of State see PARA 76 note 1.
3 Communications Act 2003 s 48C(1) (s 48C added by SI 2011/1210). References to every notification published in the text are to every notification published under the Communications Act 2003 s 48(1) (see PARA 90) or s 48A(3) (see PARA 91): s 48C(1) (as so added).
4 As to the European Commission see EUROPEAN UNION vol 47A (2014) PARAS 48, 49.
5 Ie under the Communications Act 2003 s 48(1): see PARA 90.
6 Communications Act 2003 s 48C(2)(a) (as added: see note 3). As to the meaning of 'universal service condition' see PARA 87 note 5.
7 Communications Act 2003 s 48C(2)(b) (as added: see note 3). The access-related condition referred to in the text is one falling under s 73(2) (see PARA 104): s 48C(2)(b) (as so added). As to the meaning of 'access-related condition' see PARA 87 note 6.
8 Communications Act 2003 s 48C(2)(c) (as added: see note 3). As to the meaning of 'SMP services condition' see PARA 87 note 8.
9 As to BEREC see PARA 58.
10 Ie under the Communications Act 2003 s 48(1).
11 Communications Act 2003 s 48C(3) (as added: see note 3). As to the meaning of 'EU significance' see PARA 91 note 10.
12 Ie under the Communications Act 2003 s 48(1).
13 Ie the Communications Act 2003 s 48A: see PARA 91.
14 Ie because of the Communications Act 2003 s 48A(2).
15 Communications Act 2003 s 48C(4) (as added: see note 3). As to the regulatory authorities of member states see PARA 92 note 6.

97. Delivery of copies of notifications in respect of directions, approvals and consents. The responsible person[1] must send to the Secretary of State[2]:

(1) a copy of every notification published[3];
(2) a copy of every direction, approval or consent given for the purposes of a condition set[4]; and
(3) a copy of every instrument modifying or withdrawing such a direction, approval or consent[5].

The responsible person must send to the European Commission[6]:

(a)   a copy of every direction, approval or consent given for the purposes of a universal service condition, an access-related condition[7] or an SMP services condition[8]; and

(b)   a copy of every instrument modifying or withdrawing such a direction, approval or consent[9].

The responsible person must send to BEREC[10]:

(i)   a copy of every direction, approval or consent given for the purposes of a condition[11] where the proposal to give the direction, approval or consent was a proposal of EU significance[12];

(ii)   a copy of every instrument modifying or withdrawing a direction, approval or consent given for the purposes of a condition set[13] where the proposal to modify or withdraw the direction, approval or consent was a proposal of EU significance[14].

In a case in which the responsible person is a person other than OFCOM[15], the responsible person must send to OFCOM:

(A)   a copy of every notification published[16];

(B)   a copy of every direction, approval or consent given for the purposes of a condition set[17];

(C)   a copy of every instrument modifying or withdrawing such a direction, approval or consent[18];

(D)   a copy of every proposal and statement setting out reasons after the responsible person had made any modifications of the proposal that appear to be appropriate[19];

(E)   a copy of any comments about such a proposal made by the Commission, BEREC or any regulatory authority in any other member state[20];

(F)   a copy of every notification given to the responsible person by the Commission[21];

(G)   a copy of every recommendation made in respect of the proposal by the Commission[22].

Where because the proposal is of EU significance and in OFCOM's opinion, there are exceptional circumstances; and there is an urgent need to act in order to safeguard competition and to protect the interests of consumers[23], the provisions relating to domestic consultation for directions, approvals and consents[24] did not apply in relation to a proposal to give a direction, approval or consent for the purposes of a condition, or to modify or withdraw such a direction, approval or consent, the responsible person must send a copy of a statement setting out the reasons for the proposal and for the urgent need to act to the Commission, BEREC and the regulatory authorities in every other member state[25].

1   As to the meaning of 'responsible person' see PARA 93 note 4. In a case in which the responsible person is a person other than OFCOM, references to OFCOM in the Communications Act 2003 s 395(4), (5), (6A) are to be read as references to the responsible person in relation to copies of directions, approvals, consents, instruments and statements to which s 49C(2), (3), (5) apply: s 49C(6) (s 49C added by SI 2011/1210).

2   As to the Secretary of State see PARA 76 note 1.

3   Communications Act 2003 s 49C(1)(a) (as added: see note 1). The reference to notification published in head (1) in the text is to notification published under the Communications Act 2003 s 49A(3) (see PARA 94): s 49C(1) (as so added).

4   Communications Act 2003 s 49C(1)(b) (as added: see note 1). The reference to the setting of a condition in head (2) in the text is a condition set under s 45 (see PARA 87): s 49C(1)(b) (as so added).

5   Communications Act 2003 s 49C(1)(c) (as added: see note 1).

6   As to the 'European Commission' see EUROPEAN UNION vol 47A (2014) PARAS 48, 49.

7   Ie falling within the Communications Act 2003 s 73(2): see PARA 104. As to the meaning of 'access-related condition' see PARA 87 note 6.
8   Communications Act 2003 s 49C(2)(a) (as added: see note 1). As to the meaning of 'SMP services condition' see PARA 87 note 8.
9   Communications Act 2003 s 49C(2)(b) (as added: see note 1).
10 As to BEREC see PARA 58.
11 Ie set under the Communications Act 2003 s 45: see PARA 87.
12 Communications Act 2003 s 49C(3)(a) (as added: see note 1). As to the meaning of 'EU significance' see PARA 91 note 10.
13 Ie under the Communications Act 2003 s 45: see PARA 87.
14 Communications Act 2003 s 49C(3)(b) (as added: see note 1).
15 As to the meaning of 'OFCOM' see PARA 14 note 1; and as to OFCOM see PARA 2 et seq.
16 Communications Act 2003 s 49C(4)(a) (as added: see note 1). The reference in head (A) in the text to notification published in the text is to notification published under the Communications Act 2003 s 49A(3) (see PARA 94): s 49C(4)(a) (as so added).
17 Communications Act 2003 s 49C(4)(b) (as added: see note 3). The reference to the setting of a condition is a condition set under s 45 (see PARA 87): s 49C(4)(b) (as so added).
18 Communications Act 2003 s 49C(4)(c) (as added: see note 1).
19 Communications Act 2003 s 49C(4)(d) (as added: see note 1). References in head (D) to a proposal and statement are to those which s 49B(2) apply: s 49C(4)(d) (as so added).
20 Communications Act 2003 s 49C(4)(e) (as added: see note 1). As to the regulatory authorities of member states see PARA 92 note 6.
21 Communications Act 2003 s 49C(4)(f) (as added: see note 1). The reference in head (F) in the text to notification given is to notification under the Framework Directive art 7a. For the purposes of Pt 2 Ch 1 (ss 32–151), the 'Framework Directive' means European Parliament and Council Directive (EC) 2002/21 (OJ L108, 24.4.2002, p 33) on a common regulatory framework for electronic communications networks and services (amended by the European Parliament and Council Directive (EC) 2009/140 (OJ L337, 18.12.2009, p 37): Communications Act 2003 s 151(1).
22 Communications Act 2003 s 49C(4)(g) (as added: see note 1). The reference in head (G) in the text to a recommendation made is to a recommendation under the Framework Directive art 7a(5)(a).
23 Ie because of the Communications Act 2003 s 49A(2).
24 Ie the Communications Act 2003 s 49A.
25 Communications Act 2003s 49C(5) (as added: see note 1). As to the regulatory authorities of member states see PARA 92 note 6.

B. TYPES OF CONDITIONS

(A) General Conditions

98. Matters to which general conditions may relate. Subject to certain provisions[1], the only conditions that may be set as general conditions[2] are conditions falling within one or more of the following heads:
(1)   conditions making such provision as OFCOM considers appropriate for protecting the interests of the end-users of public electronic communications services[3];
(2)   conditions making such provision as OFCOM considers appropriate for securing service interoperability[4] and for securing, or otherwise relating to, network access[5];
(3)   conditions making such provision as OFCOM considers appropriate for securing the proper and effective functioning of public electronic communications networks[6];
(4)   conditions for giving effect to determinations or regulations[7];
(5)   conditions requiring the provision, availability and use, in the event of a disaster[8], of electronic communications networks, electronic communications services and associated facilities[9];
(6)   conditions making such provision as OFCOM considers appropriate for

securing the protection of public health by the prevention or avoidance
of the exposure of individuals to electro-magnetic fields created in
connection with the operation of electronic communications
networks[10];

(7)   conditions requiring compliance with relevant international standards[11].

1   Ie the Communications Act 2003 ss 52–64: see PARA 99 et seq.
2   Ie by OFCOM under the Communications Act 2003 s 45: see PARA 87. As to general conditions
    see further PARAS 99–100. As to the meaning of 'OFCOM' see PARA 14 note 1; and as to
    OFCOM see PARA 2 et seq.
3   Communications Act 2003 s 51(1)(a). 'Public electronic communications service' means any
    electronic communications service that is provided so as to be available for use by members of
    the public: s 151(1). As to the meaning of 'electronic communications service' see PARA 53. For
    the purposes of s 151, a service is made available to members of the public if members of the
    public are customers, in respect of that service, of the provider of that service: s 151(9).
        The power under head (1) in the text to set conditions for protecting the interests of the
    end-users of public electronic communications services includes power to set conditions for that
    purpose which:
    (1)   relate to the supply, provision or making available of goods, services or facilities in
            association with the provision of public electronic communications services (s 51(2)(a)
            (amended by SI 2011/1210));
    (2)   give effect to European Union (EU) obligations to provide protection for such end-users
            in relation to the supply, provision or making available of those goods, services or
            facilities (Communications Act 2003 s 51(2)(b) (amended by SI 2011/1210));
    (3)   specify requirements in relation to the provision of services to disabled end-users
            (Communications Act 2003 s 51(2)(c) (s 51(2)(c)–(h) added by SI 2011/1210));
    (4)   require the provision, free of charge, of specified information, or information of a
            specified kind, to end-users (Communications Act 2003 s 51(2)(d) (as so added));
    (5)   in order to prevent the degradation of service and the hindering or slowing down of
            traffic over networks, impose minimum requirements in relation to the quality of public
            electronic communications networks (s 51(2)(e) (as so added));
    (6)   require a communications provider, in specified circumstances, to block access to
            telephone numbers or services in order to prevent fraud or misuse, and enable them to
            withhold fees payable to another communications provider in those circumstances
            (s 51(2)(f) (as so added));
    (7)   impose a limit on the duration of a contract between an end-user and a
            communications provider (s 51(2)(g) (as so added)); and
    (8)   ensure that conditions and procedures for the termination of a contract do not act as a
            disincentive to an end-user changing communications provider (s 51(2)(h) (as so
            added)).
        'End-user', in relation to a public electronic communications service, means:
    (a)   a person who, otherwise than as a communications provider, is a customer of the
            provider of that service;
    (b)   a person who makes use of the service otherwise than as a communications provider; or
    (c)   a person who may be authorised, by a person falling within head (a), so to make use of
            the service: s 151(1).
        Where OFCOM propose to set a general condition of a kind specified in head (5) above,
    they must notify the European Commission and BEREC and take due account of comments and
    recommendations made by the Commission: s 51(2A) (added by SI 2011/1210). As to the
    European Commission see EUROPEAN UNION vol 47A (2014) PARAS 48, 49. As to BEREC see
    PARA 58.
        The power to set general conditions in relation to a description of electronic communications
    network or electronic communications service does not include power:
    (i)   to set conditions that are made applicable according to the identity of the provider of a
            network or service; or
    (ii)   to set conditions that differ according to the identity of the provider of the networks or
            services to which they relate: Communications Act 2003 s 51(3).
4   'Service interoperability' means interoperability between different electronic communications
    services: Communications Act 2003 s 151(1).
5   Communications Act 2003 s 51(1)(b). For the purposes of the Communications Act 2003
    Pt 2 Ch 1 (ss 32–151), references to network access are references to:
    (1)   interconnection of public electronic communications networks; or

(2)   any services, facilities or arrangements which are not comprised in interconnection but
       are services, facilities or arrangements by means of which a person making available
       associated facilities is able, for the purposes of the provision of an electronic
       communications service (whether by him or by another), to make use of anything
       mentioned in s 151(4),

and references to providing network access include references to providing any such services,
making available any such facilities or entering into any such arrangements: s 151(1), (3).

The things referred to in head (2) are:

(a)   any electronic communications network or electronic communications service provided
       by another communications provider (s 151(4)(a));
(b)   any apparatus comprised in such a network or used for the purposes of such a network
       or service (s 151(4)(b));
(c)   any electronic communications apparatus (s 151(4)(ba) (added by SI 2011/1210));
(d)   any facilities made available by another that are associated facilities by reference to any
       network or service (whether one provided by that provider or by another)
       (Communications Act 2003 s 151(4)(c));
(e)   any other services or facilities which are provided or made available by another person
       and are capable of being used for the provision of an electronic communications service
       (s 151(4)(d)).

For the purposes of Pt 2 Ch 1, references to interconnection are references to the linking
(whether directly or indirectly by physical or logical means, or by a combination of physical and
logical means) of one public electronic communications network to another for the purpose of
enabling the persons using one of them to be able to communicate with users of the other one or
to make use of services provided by means of the other one (whether by the provider of that
network or by another person): s 151(1), (2).

The power to set general conditions falling within head (2) in the text does not include
power to set conditions containing provision which under s 73 (see PARA 110) or any of
ss 87–91 (see PARA 115) must be or may be included, in a case in which it appears to OFCOM
to be appropriate to do so, in an access-related condition or SMP condition: s 51(4) (amended
by SI 2011/1210). As to the meaning of 'access-related condition' see PARA 87 note 6. As to
access-related conditions see further PARA 104. As to the meaning of 'SMP condition' see PARA
87 text and note 8. As to SMP conditions see further PARA 106 et seq.

6   Communications Act 2003 s 51(1)(c). 'Public electronic communications network' means an
    electronic communications network provided wholly or mainly for the purpose of making
    electronic communications services available to members of the public: s 151(1). The conditions
    falling within head (3) in the text include conditions making such provision as OFCOM
    considers appropriate for the purpose, in accordance with EU obligations, of preventing or
    restricting electro-magnetic interference:
    (1)   with the provision of an electronic communications network or electronic
           communications service (s 51(5)(a) (s 51(5) amended by SI 2011/1210)); or
    (2)   with, or with the receipt of, anything conveyed or provided by means of such a network
           or service (Communications Act 2003 s 51(5)(b) (as so amended)).
    For the purposes of s 51, 'electro-magnetic interference' means interference by means of the
    emission or reflection of electro-magnetic energy in the course of, or in connection with, the
    provision any electronic communications network or electronic communications service: s 51(6).

7   Communications Act 2003 s 51(1)(d). The reference in head (4) in the text to determinations or
    regulations are those made under s 71 (see PARA 102): Communications Act 2003 s 51(1)(d).

8   For the purposes of the Communications Act 2003 s 51, 'disaster' includes any major incident
    having a significant effect on the general public; and for this purpose a major incident includes
    any incident of contamination involving radioactive substances or other toxic materials: s 51(7).

9   Communications Act 2003 s 51(1)(e) (amended by SI 2011/1210).

10 Communications Act 2003 s 51(1)(f).

11 Communications Act 2003 s 51(1)(g). 'Relevant international standards' means:
    (1)   any standards or specifications from time to time drawn up and published in
           accordance with European Parliament and Council Directive (EC) 2002/21 (OJ L108,
           24.4.2002, p 33) on a common regulatory framework for electronic communications
           networks and services ('the Framework Directive') (see PARA 97 note 21), art 17;
    (2)   the standards and specifications from time to time adopted by the European Committee
           for Standardisation, the European Committee for Electrotechnical Standardisation or
           the European Telecommunications Standards Institute; and
    (3)   the international standards and recommendations from time to time adopted by the

International Telecommunication Union, the International Organisation for Standardisation or the International Electrotechnical Committee: Communications Act 2003 s 151(1).

99. General conditions: customer interests. It is the duty of OFCOM[1] to set such general conditions (if any) as it considers appropriate for securing that:

(1) public communications providers[2]; or

(2) such descriptions of them as OFCOM considers appropriate, establish and maintain procedures, standards and policies with respect to the following matters[3]:

  (a) the handling of complaints made to public communications providers by any of their domestic and small business customers, where the complaint relates to contractual conditions, or to the performance of a contract for the supply of an electronic communications network or service[4];

  (b) the resolution of disputes between such providers and any of their domestic and small business customers where the complaint relates to contractual conditions, or to the performance of a contract for the supply of an electronic communications network or service[5];

  (c) the provision of remedies and redress in respect of matters that form the subject matter of such complaints or disputes[6];

  (d) the payment of compensation to a person in respect of delay in porting a number to another public communications provider, or abuse of the process for porting a number[7];

  (e) the information about service standards and about the rights of domestic and small business customers that is to be made available to those customers by public communications providers[8];

  (f) any other matter appearing to OFCOM to be necessary for securing effective protection for the domestic and small business customers of such providers[9].

It is the duty of OFCOM, in setting conditions[10], to secure so far as it considers appropriate:

(i) that the procedures established and maintained for the handling of complaints and the resolution of disputes are easy to use, transparent, non-discriminatory and effective[11];

(ii) that domestic and small business customers have the right to use those procedures free of charge[12]; and

(iii) that where public communications providers are in contravention of conditions[13], the providers follow such procedures as may be required by the general conditions[14].

OFCOM may make orders in the absence of conditions set[15] in certain circumstances[16]. Provision is also made setting out the procedures and criteria for approval by OFCOM of codes of practice for dealing with customer complaints[17] and of dispute procedures[18].

1 As to the meaning of 'OFCOM' see PARA 14 note 1; and as to OFCOM see PARA 2 et seq.

2 Communications Act 2003 s 52(1)(a). 'Public communications provider' means:

  (1) a provider of a public electronic communications network;

  (2) a provider of a public electronic communications service; or

  (3) a person who makes available facilities that are associated facilities by reference to a public electronic communications network or a public electronic communications service: s 151(1).

As to the meaning of 'public electronic communications network' see PARA 98 note 6. As to the meaning of 'public electronic communications service' see PARA 98 note 3. As to the meaning of 'associated facilities' see PARA 53.

Subject to s 55 (which provides for the making of orders by OFCOM in the absence of conditions under s 52: see note 16), OFCOM's duties under s 52(1), (3) (see the text to note 8) so far as relating to procedures for the handling of complaints are to be performed, to such extent as it considers appropriate, by the setting of general conditions requiring public communications providers to establish and maintain procedures that conform with a code of practice which is applicable to the providers to whom the conditions apply and for the time being approved by OFCOM for these purposes: s 52(4). Subject to s 55, OFCOM's duties under s 52(1), (3) so far as relating to procedures for resolving disputes are to be performed, to such extent as it considers appropriate, by the setting of general conditions requiring public communications providers to establish and maintain procedures for resolving disputes and to secure that those procedures are, and continue to be, approved by OFCOM: s 52(5).

3   Communications Act 2003 s 52(1)(b). See note 2.
4   Communications Act 2003 s 52(2)(a) (amended by SI 2011/1210). For the purposes of the Communications Act 2003 s 52, 'domestic and small business customer', in relation to a public communications provider, means a customer of that provider who is neither himself a communications provider nor a person who is such a customer in respect of an undertaking carried on by him for which more than ten individuals work (whether as employees or volunteers or otherwise): s 52(6).
5   Communications Act 2003 s 52(2)(b) (amended by SI 2011/1210).
6   Communications Act 2003 s 52(2)(c).
7   Communications Act 2003 s 52(2)(ca) (added by SI 2011/1210).
8   Communications Act 2003 s 52(2)(d).
9   Communications Act 2003 s 52(2)(e).
10   Ie in accordance with the Communications Act 2003 s 52(1): see the text to note 1–3.
11   Communications Act 2003 s 52(3)(a) (amended by SI 2011/1210).
12   Communications Act 2003 s 52(3)(b).
13   Ie set in accordance with the Communications Act 2003 s 52(1), (2): see text and notes 1–9.
14   Communications Act 2003 s 52(3)(c). See further note 2.
15   Ie under the Communications Act 2003 s 52.
16   See the Communications Act 2003 s 55. OFCOM may make an order under s 55 if, at any time, it considers in relation to any one or more public communications providers:
    (1)   that it is not practicable, or at least not appropriate, for OFCOM's duties under s 52(1), (3) to be performed in a particular respect by the setting of general conditions (s 55(1)(a)); and
    (2)   that it is necessary to make the order for the purpose:
        (a)   of securing the necessary protection for the customers of that provider or of those providers (s 55(1)(b)(i)); or
        (b)   of securing compliance with a European Union (EU) obligation (s 55(1)(b)(ii) (amended by SI 2011/1043)).
An order under the Communications Act 2003 s 55 may make such of the following provisions as OFCOM thinks fit:
    (i)   provision imposing requirements with respect to the complaints and disputes mentioned in s 52(2) (s 55(2)(a));
    (ii)   provision for the enforcement of those requirements (s 55(2)(b));
    (iii)   provision making other arrangements for the purposes of those requirements (s 55(2)(c)).
The power to make provision by an order under s 55 includes, in particular:
    (A)   power to establish a body corporate with the capacity to make its own rules and to establish its own procedures (s 55(3)(a));
    (B)   power to determine the jurisdiction of a body established by such an order or, for the purposes of the order, of any other person (s 55(3)(b));
    (C)   power to confer jurisdiction with respect to any matter on OFCOM itself (s 55(3)(c));
    (D)   power to provide for a person on whom jurisdiction is conferred by the arrangements to make awards of compensation, to direct the reimbursement of costs or expenses, or to do both (s 55(3)(d));
    (E)   power to provide for such a person to enforce, or to participate in the enforcement of, any awards or directions made under such an order (s 55(3)(e)); and
    (F)   power to make such other provision as OFCOM thinks fit for the enforcement of such awards and directions (s 55(3)(f)).

An order under s 55 may require such public communications providers as may be determined by or under the order to make payments to OFCOM in respect of expenditure incurred by OFCOM in connection with the establishment and maintenance, in accordance with such an order, of a body corporate or of a procedure or the making of any other arrangements for the purposes of the requirements of such an order: s 55(4). The consent of the Secretary of State is required for the making by OFCOM of an order under s 55: s 55(5). Section 403 (see PARA 39) applies to the power of OFCOM to make an order under s 55: s 55(6). A statutory instrument containing an order made by OFCOM under s 55 is subject to annulment in pursuance of a resolution of either House of Parliament: s 55(7). At the date at which this volume states the law, no such order has been made.

17 See the Communications Act 2003 s 53. Where a code of practice is submitted to OFCOM for approval, it must approve that code if and only if, in its opinion, it makes all such provision as OFCOM considers necessary in relation to the matters dealt with in the code for the protection of the domestic and small business customers of the public communications providers to whom the code applies: s 53(1). It is the duty of OFCOM to keep under review the codes of practice for the time being approved by it: s 53(2). OFCOM may at any time, by a notification given or published in such manner as it considers appropriate:
(1) approve modifications that have been made to an approved code (s 53(3)(a));
(2) withdraw its approval from a code (s 53(3)(b)); or
(3) give notice that the withdrawal of its approval will take effect from such time as may be specified in the notification unless such modifications of the code as are specified in the notification are made before that time (s 53(3)(b)).
In considering whether to approve a code of practice or whether or in what manner to exercise its powers under s 53(2) and (3), OFCOM must have regard to the following matters:
(a) the need to secure that customers are able readily to comprehend the procedures that are provided for by an approved code of practice (s 53(4), (5)(a));
(b) the need to secure that there is consistency between the different codes for the time being approved by OFCOM (s 53(4), (5)(b)); and
(c) the need to secure that the number of different codes so approved is kept to a minimum (s 53(4), (5)(c)).
For these purposes, 'approval' means approval for the purposes of s 52(4) (see note 3) and 'approve' and 'approved' are to be construed accordingly; and 'domestic and small business customer' has the same meaning as in s 52 (see note 4): s 53(6).

18 See the Communications Act 2003 s 54. Before giving its approval to any dispute procedures, OFCOM must consult the Secretary of State: s 54(1). OFCOM is not to approve dispute procedures unless it is satisfied that the arrangements under which the procedures have effect:
(1) are administered by person who is for practical purposes independent (so far as decisions in relation to disputes are concerned) of both OFCOM and the communications providers to whom the arrangements apply (s 54(2)(a));
(2) give effect to procedures that are easy to use, transparent, non-discriminatory and effective (s 54(2)(b) (amended by SI 2011/1210));
(3) give, in the case of every communications provider to whom the arrangements apply, a right to each of his domestic and small business customers to use the procedures free of charge (Communications Act 2003 s 54(2)(c));
(4) ensure that all information necessary for giving effect to the procedures is obtained (s 54(2)(d));
(5) ensure that disputes are effectively investigated (s 54(2)(e));
(6) include provision conferring power to make awards of appropriate compensation (s 54(2)(f)); and
(7) are such as to enable awards of compensation to be properly enforced (s 54(2)(g)).
OFCOM may approve dispute procedures subject to such conditions (including conditions as to the provision of information to OFCOM) as it may think fit: s 54(3). It is the duty of OFCOM to keep under review the dispute procedures for the time being approved by it: s 54(4). OFCOM may at any time, by a notification given or published in such manner as it considers appropriate modify the conditions of its approval of any dispute procedures or withdraw such an approval or give notice that the modification of those conditions, or the withdrawal of such an approval, will take effect from such time as may be specified in the notification unless the procedures (or the arrangements under which they have effect) are modified before that time in the manner required by the notification: s 54(5). In considering whether to approve dispute procedures or whether or in what manner to exercise its powers under s 54(3)–(5), OFCOM must have regard to the following matters:
(a) the need to secure that customers are able readily to comprehend dispute procedures (s 54(6), (7)(a));

(b)   the need to secure that there is consistency between the different procedures for the time being approved by OFCOM (s 54(6), (7)(b)); and

(c)   the need to secure that the number of different sets of procedures so approved is kept to a minimum (s 54(6), (7)(c)).

For these purposes, 'approval' means approval for the purposes of s 52(5) (see note 2) and 'approve' and 'approved' are to be construed accordingly; 'dispute procedures' means any such procedures as may fall to be approved for the purposes of s 52(5); and 'domestic and small business customer' has the same meaning as in s 52 (see note 4): s 54(8).

Ombudsman Services (formerly known as the Office of the Telecommunications Ombudsman ('OTELO')) operates an OFCOM-approved dispute resolution scheme, as does CISAS (Communications & Internet Services Adjudication Scheme). They are not regulators but dispute resolution bodies governed by contractual agreement with the member providers. See PARA 80.

100.   General conditions: telephone numbers.   It is the duty of OFCOM[1] to publish a document (to be known as the 'National Telephone Numbering Plan') setting out:

(1)   the numbers[2] that it has determined to be available for allocation[3] by it as telephone numbers[4];

(2)   such restrictions as it considers appropriate on the adoption[5] of numbers available for allocation in accordance with the Plan[6];

(3)   such requirements as they consider appropriate, for the purpose of protecting consumers, in relation to the tariff principles and maximum prices applicable to numbers so adopted or available for allocation[7]; and

(3)   such restrictions as it considers appropriate on the other uses to which numbers available for allocation in accordance with the Plan may be put[8].

It is OFCOM's duty:

(a)   from time to time to review the National Telephone Numbering Plan[9]; and

(b)   to make any revision of the Plan that it thinks fit in consequence of such a review[10].

OFCOM must also keep such day-to-day records as it considers appropriate of the telephone numbers allocated by it in accordance with the National Telephone Numbering Plan[11]. The publication of the National Telephone Numbering Plan, or of a revision of it, must be in such manner as appears to OFCOM to be appropriate for bringing the contents of the Plan, or of the revised Plan, to the attention of such persons as OFCOM considers appropriate[12]. The Secretary of State may by order exclude such numbers as may be described in the order from the numbers that are to be treated as telephone numbers[13].

When OFCOM allocate telephone numbers in accordance with the National Telephone Numbering Plan, they must specify whether an allocation may be transferred from one person to another, and may set out the conditions under which the allocation may be transferred[14]. If OFCOM allocate telephone numbers for a limited period of time, the limitation must be objectively justifiable in relation to the services to which it relates, taking account of the need to allow for an appropriate period of investment amortisation[15].

OFCOM may set general conditions to ensure that telephone users are able to communicate with every normal telephone number[16]. General conditions may include conditions which:

(i)   prohibit the adoption of telephone numbers by a communications provider except in cases where the numbers have been allocated by OFCOM to a person[17];

(ii)   impose tariff principles and maximum prices for the purpose of protecting consumers in relation to the provision of an electronic communications service by means of telephone numbers adopted or available for use[18];

(iii)   regulate the use by a communications provider, for the purpose of providing an electronic communications network or electronic communications service, of telephone numbers not allocated to that provider[19];

(iv)   impose restrictions on the adoption of telephone numbers by a communications provider, and on other practices by communications providers in relation to telephone numbers allocated to them[20];

(v)   impose requirements on a communications provider in connection with the adoption by him of telephone numbers[21];

(vi)   require an allocation of particular telephone numbers to be transferred from one communications provider to another in the circumstances provided for in the conditions[22];

(vii)   impose such requirements and restrictions on a communications provider from whom an allocation is required to be transferred as may be provided for, in relation to the transfer, in the conditions[23];

(viii) require payments of such amounts as may be determined by OFCOM to be made to it by a person in respect of the allocation to him of telephone numbers[24];

(ix)   require payments of such amounts as may be determined by OFCOM to be made to it by a person in respect of transfers of allocations from one person to another[25]; and

(x)   require communications providers to secure compliance with such rules relating to the use of telephone numbers by their customers as OFCOM may set out in general conditions or determine in accordance with provision made by the general conditions[26].

General conditions may also:

(A)   provide for the procedure to be followed on the making of applications to OFCOM for the allocation of telephone numbers[27];

(B)   provide for the information that must accompany such applications and for the handling of such applications[28];

(C)   provide a procedure for telephone numbers to be reserved pending the making and disposal of an application for their allocation[29];

(D)   provide for the procedure to be followed on the making of applications for telephone numbers to be reserved, and for the handling of such applications[30];

(E)   regulate the procedures to be followed, the system to be applied and the charges to be imposed for the purposes of, or in connection with, the adoption by a communications provider of telephone numbers allocated to that provider[31];

(F)   regulate the procedures to be followed, the system to be applied and the charges to be imposed for the purposes of, or in connection with, the transfer of an allocation from one person to another[32].

General conditions may make modifications from time to time of, or of the method of determining, the amounts of periodic payments falling to be made[33] and make different provision in relation to different descriptions of communications provider and different descriptions of telephone number[34].

OFCOM may set conditions that apply to persons other than communications providers and relate to the allocation of telephone numbers to such persons, the transfer of allocations to and from such persons and the use of telephone numbers by such persons[35].

Provision is made with respect to the modification of documents referred to in numbering conditions[36], the withdrawal of telephone number allocations[37] and numbering reorganisations[38].

It is the duty of OFCOM, in the carrying out of the above functions[39], to secure that what appears to it to be the best use is made of the numbers[40] that are appropriate for use as telephone numbers, and to encourage efficiency and innovation for that purpose[41]. It is also the duty of OFCOM, in carrying out those functions, to secure that there is no undue discrimination by communications providers against other communications providers in relation to the adoption of telephone numbers for purposes connected with the use by one communications provider, or his customers, of an electronic communications network or electronic communications service provided by another[42].

1   As to the meaning of 'OFCOM' see PARA 14 note 1; and as to OFCOM see PARA 2 et seq.

2   For the purposes of the Communications Act 2003 s 56, 'number' includes data of any description: s 56(10).

3   References in the Communications Act 2003 s 56 to the allocation of a number are references to its allocation for the purposes of general conditions under s 58 (see the text and note 17–34) or in accordance with conditions under s 59 (see the text and note 35): s 56(9). See also note 4.

4   Communications Act 2003 s 56(1)(a). For the purposes of Pt 2 Ch 1 (ss 32–151), references to a telephone number are (subject to s 56(7): see the text and note 13) references to any number that is used (whether or not in connection with telephony) for any one or more of the following purposes:

     (1)   identifying the destination for, or recipient of, an electronic communication (ss 56(5)(a), 151(1));

     (2)   identifying the origin, or sender, of an electronic communication (ss 56(5)(b), 151(1));

     (3)   identifying the route for an electronic communication (ss 56(5)(c), 151(1));

     (4)   identifying the source from which an electronic communication or electronic communications service may be obtained or accessed (ss 56(5)(d), 151(1));

     (5)   selecting the service that is to be obtained or accessed, or required elements or characteristics of that service (ss 56(5)(e), 151(1)); or

     (6)   identifying the communications provider by means of whose network or service an electronic communication is to be transmitted, or treated as transmitted (ss 56(5)(f), 151(1)).

For the purposes of s 56, 'electronic communication' means a communication for transmission by means of an electronic communications network: s 56(10). As to the meaning of 'electronic communications network' see PARA 53.

5   For the purposes of the Communications Act 2003 Pt 2 Ch 1, references to the adoption of a telephone number by a communications provider are references to his doing any of the following in relation to a number allocated (whether or not to that provider) by OFCOM:

     (1)   allocating or transferring that number to a particular customer or piece of apparatus (Communications Act 2003 s 56(6)(a));

     (2)   using that number for identifying a service or route used by that provider or by any of his customers (s 56(6)(b));

     (3)   using that number for identifying a communication as one to be transmitted by that provider (s 56(6)(c));

     (4)   designating that number for use in selecting a service or the required elements or characteristics of a service (s 56(6)(d));

     (5)   authorising the use of that number by others for any of the purposes mentioned in s 56(5) (see note 4) (s 56(6)(e)).

'Allocation' and 'adoption', in relation to telephone numbers, and cognate expressions, are to be construed in accordance with s 56: s 151(1).

6   Communications Act 2003 s 56(1)(b).

7　Communications Act 2003 s 56(1)(ba) (added by SI 2011/1210).

8　Communications Act 2003 s 56(1)(c).

9　Communications Act 2003 s 56(2)(a). This duty must be performed in compliance with the requirements, so far as applicable, of s 60 (see the text and note 36): s 56(2).

10　Communications Act 2003 s 56(2)(b). See note 9.

11　Communications Act 2003 s 56(3).

12　Communications Act 2003 s 56(4).

13　Communications Act 2003 s 56(7). This is for the purposes of Pt 2 Ch 1: s 56(7). No order is to be made containing provision authorised by s 56(7) unless a draft of the order has been laid before Parliament and approved by a resolution of each House: s 56(8). As to the order that has been made see the Telephone Number Exclusion (Domain Names and Internet Addresses) Order 2003, SI 2003/3281. As to the Secretary of State see PARA 76 note 1. As to the power of the Secretary of State to make orders under the Communications Act 2003 see s 402; and PARA 74.

14　Communications Act 2003 s 56A(1) (added by SI 2011/1210).

15　Communications Act 2003 s 56A(2) (added by SI 2011/1210).

16　See the Communications Act 2003 s 57. General conditions may impose such requirements as OFCOM considers appropriate for securing that every end-user of a public electronic communications service is able, by means of that service to make calls or otherwise transmit electronic communications to every normal telephone number and to receive every call or other electronic communication that is made or transmitted to him using such a service from apparatus identified by a normal telephone number: s 57(1). 'Normal telephone number' means a telephone number which has been made available, in accordance with the National Telephone Numbering Plan, as a number to be used for the purpose of identifying the destination for, or the recipient of, electronic communications and is for the time being a number adopted by a communications provider to be used for such a purpose or a number in use for such a purpose by a person other than a communications provider to whom it has been allocated in accordance with conditions under s 59 (see the text and note 35): s 57(2). For the purposes of s 57, 'electronic communication' has the same meaning as in s 56 (see note 4): s 57(3).

17　Communications Act 2003 s 58(1)(a).

18　Communications Act 2003 s 58(1)(aa) (added by SI 2011/1210).

19　Communications Act 2003 s 58(1)(b).

20　Communications Act 2003 s 58(1)(c).

21　Communications Act 2003 s 58(1)(d). The conditions that may be set under head (v) in the text include conditions imposing requirements with respect to the provision of information for purposes connected with the compilation of directories and the provision of directory inquiry facilities: s 58(3).

22　Communications Act 2003 s 58(1)(e).

23　Communications Act 2003 s 58(1)(f).

24　Communications Act 2003 s 58(1)(g). General conditions providing for payments to be made to OFCOM in respect of anything mentioned in head (viii) or head (ix) in the text:

    (1)　must set out the principles according to which the amounts of the payments are to be determined (s 58(6)(a));

    (2)　may provide for the payments to consist of a lump sum in respect of a particular allocation or transfer or of sums payable periodically while an allocation remains in force, or of both (s 58(6)(b));

    (3)　may provide for the amounts to be determined by reference to any indication according to which the allocation has been made as mentioned in s 58(5), or any other factors (including the costs incurred by OFCOM in connection with the carrying out of its functions by virtue of s 56 (see the text and notes 1–13) and s 58) as OFCOM thinks fit (s 58(6)(c)).

Payments that are required to be made to OFCOM in respect of anything mentioned in head (viii) or head (ix) in the text must be paid to it as soon as they become due in accordance with the conditions imposing the obligation to pay; and, if not so paid, are recoverable by OFCOM accordingly: s 58(9).

25　Communications Act 2003 s 58(1)(h). See note 24.

26　Communications Act 2003 s 58(1)(i).

27　Communications Act 2003 s 58(2)(a). The procedure to be followed on the making of an application for the allocation of numbers that are available for allocation in accordance with the National Telephone Numbering Plan must require OFCOM's determination of the application to be made:

(1)   in the case of an application made in response to an invitation in accordance with s 58(5), before the end of six weeks after the day on which the application is received (s 58(4)(a)); and

(2)   in any other case, before the end of three weeks after that day (s 58(4)(b)).

Where OFCOM is proposing to allocate any telephone numbers, it may invite persons to indicate the payments each would be willing to make to OFCOM if allocated the numbers, and make the allocation according to the amounts indicated: see s 58(5).

28   Communications Act 2003 s 58(2)(b).
29   Communications Act 2003 s 58(2)(c).
30   Communications Act 2003 s 58(2)(d).
31   Communications Act 2003 s 58(2)(e).
32   Communications Act 2003 s 58(2)(f).
33   Ie by virtue of by virtue of conditions containing provisions authorised by the Communications Act 2003 s 58.
34   Communications Act 2003 s 58(7). However, nothing in s 58(7) authorises the modification, after it has been fixed, of the amount of a periodic payment fixed in accordance with arrangements made in relation to numbers allocated as mentioned in s 58(5): s 58(8).
35   See the Communications Act 2003 s 59(1). The conditions that may be set include conditions imposing obligations corresponding to any of the obligations that may be imposed on communications providers by general conditions making provision for, or in connection with:

(1)   the allocation of telephone numbers (s 59(2)(a));
(2)   the transfer of allocations (s 59(2)(b)); or
(3)   the use of telephone numbers (s 59(2)(c)).

Section 45(10) (see PARA 87 text and notes 9–15) applies to OFCOM's power to set a condition under s 59 as it applies to its power to set a condition under s 45: s 59(3). Sections 47–49 (see PARAS 89–93) apply in relation to the setting of conditions under s 59 and the modification and revocation of such conditions and the giving, modification or withdrawal of any direction, approval or consent for the purposes of a condition under s 59, as they apply in the case of general conditions and in the case of directions, approvals and consents given for the purposes of general conditions: s 59(4). It is the duty of a person who is not a communications provider but applies for the allocation of a telephone number, or is allocated such a number, to comply with any conditions set under s 59: s 59(5). That duty is enforceable in civil proceedings by OFCOM for an injunction or for any other appropriate remedy or relief, but this does not apply in the case of a person against whom the obligations contained in the condition in question are enforceable (by virtue of his having become a communications provider) as obligations imposed by general conditions: s 59(6), (7).

36   See the Communications Act 2003 s 60. 'Numbering conditions' means:

(1)   general conditions the making of which is authorised by s 57 or s 58;
(2)   conditions set under s 59: s 60(7).

Where numbering conditions for the time being have effect by reference to provisions, as they have effect from time to time, of the National Telephone Numbering Plan or another document published by OFCOM, OFCOM must not revise or otherwise modify the relevant provisions unless it is satisfied that the revision or modification is:

(a)   objectively justifiable in relation to the matters to which it relates;
(b)   not such as to discriminate unduly against particular persons or against a particular description of persons;
(c)   proportionate to what the modification is intended to achieve; and
(d)   in relation to what it is intended to achieve, transparent: s 60(1), (2).

'Relevant provisions', in relation to the Plan or document, means the provisions of the Plan or document by reference to which (as they have effect from time to time) the numbering conditions in question have effect: s 60(7). Before revising or otherwise modifying the relevant provisions, OFCOM must publish a notification:

(i)   stating that it is proposing to do so (s 60(3)(a));
(ii)   specifying the Plan or other document that it is proposing to revise or modify (s 60(3)(b));
(iii) setting out the effect of its proposed revisions or modifications (s 60(3)(c));
(iv)   giving its reasons for making the proposal (s 60(3)(d)); and
(v)   specifying the period within which representations may be made to OFCOM about its proposal (s 60(3)(e)).

That period must be one ending not less than one month after the day of the publication of the notification: s 60(4). The publication of a notification must be in such manner as appears to OFCOM to be appropriate for bringing the contents of the notification to the attention of such persons as OFCOM considers appropriate: s 60(6). OFCOM may give effect, with or without modifications, to a proposal with respect to which it has published a notification under s 60(3) only if it has considered every representation about the proposal that is made to it within the period specified in the notification and it has had regard to every international obligation of the United Kingdom (if any) which has been notified to it for these purposes by the Secretary of State: s 60(5). As to the meaning of 'international obligation of the United Kingdom' see PARA 33 note 7.

37 See the Communications Act 2003 s 61; and PARA 101.
38 See the Communications Act 2003 s 62; and PARA 101.
39 Ie its functions under the Communications Act 2003 ss 56–62: see the text and notes 1–38. See also PARA 101.
40 For the purposes of the Communications Act 2003 s 63, 'number' has the same meaning as in s 56 (see note 2): s 63(3).
41 Communications Act 2003 s 63(1).
42 Communications Act 2003 s 63(2).

101. Withdrawal of telephone number allocations and numbering reorganisations. Where OFCOM[1] has allocated[2] telephone numbers[3] for the purposes of any numbering conditions[4], it may withdraw that allocation if, and only if, the case is one in which the withdrawal of an allocation is authorised by the following provisions[5]. The withdrawal of an allocation is authorised[6] if:

(1) consent to the withdrawal is given by the person[7] to whom the numbers are for the time being allocated[8];

(2) the withdrawal is made for the purposes of a transfer of the allocation required by numbering conditions[9];

(3) the withdrawal is made for the purposes of a numbering reorganisation applicable to a particular series of telephone numbers[10];

(4) the withdrawal is made in circumstances specified in the numbering conditions and for the purpose of securing that what appears to OFCOM to be the best and most efficient use is made of the numbers and other data that are appropriate for use as telephone numbers[11];

(5) the allocated numbers are numbers that have not been adopted during such period after their allocation as may be specified in the numbering conditions[12]; or

(6) the allocated numbers are comprised in a series of numbers which have not to a significant extent been adopted or used during such period as may be so specified[13].

The withdrawal of an allocation is also authorised where:

(a) there have been serious or repeated contraventions[14], by the person to whom the allocation is for the time being allocated, of the numbering conditions[15]; and

(b) it appears to OFCOM that the taking of other steps in respect of the contraventions is likely to prove ineffective for securing future compliance[16].

The withdrawal of an allocation is also authorised where:

(i) the person to whom the allocation is for the time being allocated is not a communications provider[17]; and

(ii) it appears to OFCOM that contraventions by that person of numbering conditions makes the withdrawal of the allocation appropriate[18].

Where OFCOM is proposing to withdraw an allocation in exercise of the power under head (5) or (6) above[19], it must:

(A) give a notification[20] of its proposal[21];

(B) consider any representations made to it about the proposal within the period of one month following the day on which the notification is given[22]; and

(C)   ensure that the withdrawal (if OFCOM decides to proceed with it after considering those representations) does not take effect until the end of the three months beginning with the end of the period mentioned in head (B)[23].

The following provisions[24] apply to the withdrawal of an allocation for the purposes of a numbering reorganisation that is applicable to a particular series of telephone numbers[25]. The allocation is to be withdrawn only if the reorganisation, so far as it relates to numbers of any description, is not such as to discriminate unduly against particular communications providers, against particular users of the allocated numbers or against a particular description of such providers or users[26]. The allocation must not be withdrawn if the reorganisation fails to provide for withdrawn allocations to be replaced by allocations of telephone numbers so nearly resembling the numbers to which the withdrawal relates as the purpose of the reorganisation allows[27]. Where a replacement allocation is made for the purposes of the re-organisation, no payment is to be made to OFCOM in respect of the making of the replacement allocation but specified provisions apply[28].

1   As to the meaning of 'OFCOM' see PARA 14 note 1; and as to OFCOM see PARA 2 et seq.
2   As to the meaning of 'allocated' see PARA 100 note 3.
3   As to the meaning of 'telephone number' see PARA 100 note 4.
4   In the Communications Act 2003 s 61, 'numbering conditions' means:
     (1)   general conditions the making of which is authorised by s 58 (see PARA 100) (s 61(9)(a)); or
     (2)   conditions set under s 59 (see PARA 100) (s 61(9)(b)).
5   Communications Act 2003 s 61(1).
6   Subject to the Communications Act 2003 s 62: see text and notes 25–28.
7   As to the meaning of 'person' see PARA 14 note 2.
8   Communications Act 2003 s 61(2)(a).
9   Communications Act 2003 s 61(2)(b).
10   Communications Act 2003 s 61(2)(c).
11   Communications Act 2003 s 61(2)(d). OFCOM's power to set conditions specifying circumstances for the purposes of head (4) in the text, and its power to withdraw an allocation in the specified circumstances, are each exercisable only in a manner that does not discriminate unduly:
     (1)   against particular communications providers (s 61(5)(a));
     (2)   against particular users of the allocated numbers (s 61(5)(b)); or
     (3)   against a particular description of such providers or users (s 61(5)(c));
     and the purposes for which those powers may be exercised do not include the carrying out of a numbering reorganisation of the sort mentioned in head (3) in the text: s 61(5).
     As to the meaning of 'communications provider' see PARA 17 note 23.
12   Communications Act 2003 s 61(2)(e).
13   Communications Act 2003 s 61(2)(f).
14   For the purposes of the Communications Act 2003 s 61 there are repeated contraventions by a person of numbering conditions to the extent that:
     (1)   in the case of a previous notification of a contravention given to that person under s 96A, OFCOM have given a confirmation decision to that person under s 96C(2) in respect of the contravention (s 61(8)(a) (s 61(8) substituted by SI 2011/1210)); and
     (2)   in the period of 24 months following the giving of that confirmation decision, one or more further confirmation decisions have been given to the person in respect of contraventions of numbering conditions (Communications Act 2003 s 61(8)(b) (as so substituted)).
15   Communications Act 2003 s 61(3)(a) (amended by SI 2011/1210).
16   Communications Act 2003 s 61(3)(b).
17   Communications Act 2003 s 61(4)(a).
18   Communications Act 2003 s 61(4)(b).
19   Ie the power conferred by virtue of the Communications Act 2003 s 61(2)(e) or (f).
20   A notification for the purposes of the Communications Act 2003 s 61(6) must be given in such manner as OFCOM considers appropriate for bringing it to the attention of:

    (1)   the person to whom the numbers to which the proposed withdrawal relates are for the time being allocated (s 61(7)(a));

    (2)   every person appearing to OFCOM to be a person to whom communications are or may be transmitted using one of those numbers for identifying the destination or route (s 61(7)(b));

    (3)   every person who uses one or more of those numbers for obtaining access to services or for communication (s 61(7)(c)); and

    (4)   every other person who, in OFCOM's opinion, is likely to be affected by the proposal (s 61(7)(d)).

21 Communications Act 2003 s 61(6)(a).
22 Communications Act 2003 s 61(6)(b).
23 Communications Act 2003 s 61(6)(c).
24 Ie the Communications Act 2003 s 62.
25 Communications Act 2003 s 62(1).
26 Communications Act 2003 s 62(2).
27 Communications Act 2003 s 62(3).
28 Communications Act 2003 s 62(4). The specified provision that applies is the Communications Act 2003 s 62(5): s 62(4)(b). Where s 62(5) applies:

    (1)   a provision for the making of periodic payments in respect of the withdrawn allocation is to be treated, to the extent that OFCOM determine that it should, as a provision requiring the making of periodic payments in respect of the replacement allocation (s 62(5)(a)); and

    (2)   OFCOM may, if they think fit, make such repayments or adjustments of a provision for payment as appear to them to be appropriate in consequence of differences between the numbers to which the withdrawn allocation relates and the numbers to which the replacement allocation relates (s 62(5)(b)).

(B) Universal Service Conditions

102. Universal service conditions. The Secretary of State must by order (the 'universal service order')[1] set out the extent to which the things listed below[2] must, for the purpose of securing compliance with European Union (EU) obligations for the time being in force, be provided, made available or supplied throughout the United Kingdom[3]. Those things are:

    (1)   electronic communications networks[4] and electronic communications services[5];

    (2)   facilities capable of being made available as part of or in connection with an electronic communications service[6];

    (3)   particular methods of billing for electronic communications services or of accepting payment for them[7];

    (4)   directories capable of being used in connection with the use of an electronic communications network or electronic communications service[8]; and

    (5)   directory inquiry facilities capable of being used for purposes connected with the use of such a network or service[9].

The universal service order may contain guidance about matters relating to the pricing of things that the order says must be provided, made available or supplied[10]. Before making or varying the universal service order, the Secretary of State must consult OFCOM and such other persons as he considers appropriate[11]. The Secretary of State must also take due account of the desirability of not favouring one form of electronic communications network, electronic communications service or associated facility, or one means of providing or making available such a network, service or facility, over another, before making or varying the universal service order[12].

OFCOM may by regulations make provision for the designation of the persons to whom universal service conditions are to be applicable[13]. Those regulations are not to authorise the designation of a person other than a communications provider[14]. OFCOM may from time to time review the designations for the time being in force in accordance with regulations under these provisions[15]; and on such a review, consider what (if any) universal service conditions should continue to apply to each of the designated persons[16]. The procedure to be followed in the case of every such review must be the procedure provided for in regulations made by OFCOM[17]. Regulations made by OFCOM must provide for a person's designation as a person to whom universal service conditions are to be applicable to cease to have effect where, in any such case as may be described in the regulations, the universal service conditions applied to him are all revoked[18]. Regulations made by OFCOM under these provisions providing a procedure for the designation of persons, or for the conduct of a review[19], must not provide for any procedure other than one appearing to OFCOM to be efficient, objective and transparent, and not to involve, or to tend to give rise to, any undue discrimination against any person or description of persons[20]. Where OFCOM designates a person in accordance with regulations under these provisions or a designation of a person in accordance with any such regulations ceases to have effect, OFCOM must give a notification of that designation, or of that fact, to the European Commission[21].

OFCOM may set any such universal service conditions as it considers appropriate for securing compliance with the obligations set out in the universal service order[22]. OFCOM may also set universal service conditions which apply to a designated universal service provider who proposes to make a disposal to another person of a substantial part or all of the designated universal service provider's local access network assets but this does not apply where the disposal is made by a company to a connected company[23]. Universal service conditions applied to a person must include a condition requiring him to publish information about his performance in complying with the universal service conditions that apply to him[24]. Universal service conditions may impose an obligation on a person to whom they apply to do one or both of the following, if required to do so by OFCOM:

(a)   to make facilities available for enabling information published in pursuance of a condition applied to that person[25] to be independently audited[26];

(b)   to meet the costs of any independent auditing of that information[27] that is required by OFCOM[28].

Universal service conditions may impose performance targets on designated universal service providers[29] with respect to any of the matters in relation to which obligations may be imposed by such conditions[30]. In setting a universal service condition, OFCOM must have regard to any guidance about matters relating to pricing that is contained in the universal service order[31].

OFCOM is required to keep under review universal tariffs and to monitor changes to those tariffs[32]. OFCOM may from time to time review the extent (if any) of the financial burden for a particular designated universal service provider of complying in relation to any matter with any one or more of the universal service conditions applied to him[33]. Where OFCOM has concluded[34] that complying in relation to any matter with universal service conditions imposes a financial burden on a particular designated universal service provider and has published that conclusion[35], OFCOM must determine, in the case of the designated universal service provider, whether it considers it would be unfair for that provider to bear, or to continue to bear, the whole or any part of the burden[36].

1 'Universal service order' means the order for the time being in force under the Communications Act 2003 s 65: s 151(1). As to the Secretary of State see PARA 76 note 1.

2 Ie the things falling within the Communications Act 2003 s 65(2): see heads (1)–(5) in the text.

3 Communications Act 2003 s 65(1) (amended by SI 2011/1043). As to the order that has been made see the Electronic Communications (Universal Service) Order 2003, SI 2003/1904 (amended by SI 2003/2426; and SI 2011/1209). As to the power of the Secretary of State to make orders under the Communications Act 2003 see s 402; and PARA 74. As to the meaning of 'United Kingdom' see PARA 14 note 7.

4 As to the meaning of 'electronic communications network' see PARA 53.

5 Communications Act 2003 s 65(2)(a). As to the meaning of 'electronic communications service' see PARA 53.

6 Communications Act 2003 s 65(2)(b).

7 Communications Act 2003 s 65(2)(c).

8 Communications Act 2003 s 65(2)(d). Where universal service conditions require a designated universal service provider to supply a directory capable of being used in connection with the use of an electronic communications network or electronic communications service or to make available directory inquiry facilities capable of being used for purposes connected with use of such a network or service, the universal service conditions applied to the provider must include the conditions that OFCOM considers appropriate for securing that the provider does not unduly discriminate against a source of relevant information:

   (1) in the compiling of the directory or the answering of directory inquiries (s 69(1), (2)(a)); or

   (2) in the treatment in the directory, or for the purposes of the facilities, of any relevant information from that source (s 69(1), (2)(b)).

   For these purposes, references to relevant information are references to information provided for inclusion in the directory or for use in the answering of directory inquiries and references to a source of relevant information are references to a communications provider or designated universal service provider who provides relevant information: s 69(3). As to the meaning of 'designated universal service provider' see note 29. As to the meaning of 'communications provider' see PARA 17 note 23.

9 Communications Act 2003 s 65(2)(e). See note 8.

10 Communications Act 2003 s 65(3).

11 Communications Act 2003 s 65(4). As to the meaning of 'OFCOM' see PARA 14 note 1; and as to OFCOM see PARA 2 et seq. As to the meaning of 'person' see PARA 14 note 2.

12 Communications Act 2003 s 65(5) (added by SI 2011/1210).

13 Communications Act 2003 s 66(1). At the date at which this volume states the law, no such order has been made. Section 403 (see PARA 39) applies to the power of OFCOM to make regulations under s 66: s 66(10).

14 Communications Act 2003 s 66(2). The regulations may provide for a person other than a communications provider to be designated for the purposes only of conditions relating to the supply of directories capable of being used in connection with the use of an electronic communications network or electronic communications service and the making available of directory inquiry facilities capable of being used for purposes connected with the use of such a network or service: s 66(3).

15 Ie under the Communications Act 2003 s 66.

16 Communications Act 2003 s 66(4).

17 Communications Act 2003 s 66(5).

18 Communications Act 2003 s 66(6).

19 Ie under the Communications Act 2003 s 66(4): see the text and notes 15–16.

20 Communications Act 2003 s 66(7).

21 Communications Act 2003 s 66(8). A notification under s 66 must identify the person who has been designated, or the person whose designation has ceased to have effect: s 66(9). As to the European Commission see EUROPEAN UNION vol 47A (2014) PARAS 48, 49.

22 Communications Act 2003 s 67(1).

23 Communications Act 2003 s 67(1A), (1B) (added by SI 2011/1210). As to the meaning of 'connected company' see the Corporation Tax Act 2010 s 1122(2); and INCOME TAXATION vol 59 (2014) PARA 1775.

24 Communications Act 2003 s 67(2). A condition set in accordance with s 67(2) must contain provision which:

    (1)   requires information published in accordance with it to be updated from time to time and published again (s 67(3)(a));

    (2)   requires information so published to satisfy the requirements that OFCOM considers appropriate for securing that it is adequate (s 67(3)(b)); and

    (3)   requires information so published to be framed by reference to the quality of service parameters, definitions and measurement methods for the time being set out in Annex III to the Universal Service Directive (Communications Act 2003 s 67(3)(c)).

'Universal Service Directive' means European Parliament and Council Directive (EC) 2002/22 (OJ L108, 24.4.2002, p 51) on universal service and users' rights relating to electronic communications networks and services (as amended by European Parliament and Council Directive (EC) 2009/136 (OJ L337, 18.12.2009, p 11): Communications Act 2003 s 151(1). A condition set in accordance with s 67(2) may impose requirements as to the times at which information published in accordance with it is to be published and the manner in which that information is to be published: s 67(4).

25 Ie under the Communications Act 2003 s 67(2): see the text and note 24.

26 Communications Act 2003 s 67(5)(a).

27 The reference in the Communications Act 2003 in s 67(5) to the independent auditing of information is a reference to its being audited by a qualified auditor for accuracy and for its usefulness in the making of comparisons with information published by other designated universal service providers: s 67(6). 'Qualified auditor' means a person who is eligible for appointment as a statutory auditor under the Companies Act 2006 Pt 42 (ss 1209–1264) (see COMPANIES vol 15 (2009) PARA 958), and if the appointment to carry out such auditing as is mentioned in the Communications Act 2003 s 67(5) were an appointment as a statutory auditor, would not be prohibited from acting by the Companies Act 2006 s 1214 (independence requirement: see COMPANIES vol 15 (2009) PARA 971): Communications Act 2003 s 67(9) (substituted by SI 2008/948).

28 Communications Act 2003 s 67(5)(b).

29 'Designated universal service provider' means a person who is for the time being designated in accordance with regulations under the Communications Act 2003 s 66 as a person to whom universal service conditions are applicable: s 151(1).

30 Communications Act 2003 s 67(7).

31 Communications Act 2003 s 67(8).

32 See the Communications Act 2003 s 68 (amended by SI 2011/1210).

33 See the Communications Act 2003 s 70(1). Where regulations under s 66 require the financial burden of so complying to be taken into account in determining whom to designate and the regulations provide for a particular method of calculating that burden to be used for the purposes of that determination, that must be the method of calculation applied on a review under s 70: s 70(2). Where s 70(2) does not apply, the financial burden of so complying is to be taken to be the amount calculated by OFCOM to be the net cost of compliance after allowing for market benefits accruing to the designated universal service provider from his designation and the application to him of universal service conditions: s 70(3). After carrying out a review under s 70 OFCOM must either cause the calculations made by it on the review to be audited by a person who appears to it to be independent of designated universal service providers or itself carry out an audit of those calculations: s 70(4). OFCOM must ensure, in the case of every audit carried out under s 70(4), that a report on the audit is prepared and, if not prepared by OFCOM, is provided to it: s 70(5). OFCOM is under a duty to publish its conclusions on the review and a summary of the report of the audit which was carried out as respects the calculations made for the purposes of that review: s 70(6). The publication of anything under s 70(6) must be a publication in such manner as OFCOM considers appropriate for bringing it to the attention of the persons who, in its opinion, are likely to be affected by it: s 70(7).

34 Ie on a review under the Communications Act 2003 s 70: see the text and note 33.

35 In accordance with the Communications Act 2003 s 70: see the text and note 33.

36 Communications Act 2003 s 71(1), (2). If OFCOM determines that it would be unfair for the designated universal service provider to bear, or to continue to bear, the whole or a part of the burden and an application for a determination under s 71(3) is made to OFCOM by that provider, OFCOM may determine that contributions are to be made by communications providers to whom general conditions are applicable for meeting that burden: s 71(3). The making of any of the following must be in accordance with regulations made by OFCOM:

    (1)   a determination by OFCOM of the extent of the financial burden that exists for the designated universal service provider of complying in relation to any matter with universal service conditions (s 71(4)(a));

(2) an application for a determination made to OFCOM by the provider for the purposes of s 71(3)(b) (s 71(4)(b));

(3) a determination by OFCOM of whether it is or would be unfair for the designated universal service provider to bear, or to continue to bear, the burden of complying in relation to any matter with universal service conditions (s 71(4)(c));

(4) a determination of the extent (if any) to which that is or would be unfair (s 71(4)(d)).

The assessment, collection and distribution of contributions under s 71(3) is not to be carried out except in accordance with a mechanism provided for in a scheme contained in regulations made by OFCOM: s 71(5). It is the duty of OFCOM to exercise its power to make regulations under s 71 in the manner which it considers will secure that the assessment, collection and distribution of contributions under s 71(3) is carried out:

(a) in an objective and transparent manner (s 71(6)(a));

(b) in a manner that does not involve, or tend to give rise to, any undue discrimination against particular communications providers or particular designated universal service providers, or against a particular description of them (s 71(6)(b)); and

(c) in a manner that avoids, or (if that is impracticable) at least minimises, any distortion of competition or of customer demand (s 71(6)(c)).

Regulations made by OFCOM under s 71 may provide for a scheme containing the provision mentioned in s 71(5), and for any fund set up for the purposes of such a scheme, to be administered either by OFCOM or by such other person as may be specified in the regulations: s 71(7). A person other than OFCOM is not to be specified in such regulations as the administrator of such a scheme or fund unless he is a person who OFCOM is satisfied is independent of both the persons who are designated universal service providers and communications providers to whom general conditions are applicable: s 71(8). Section 403 (see PARA 39) applies to the powers of OFCOM to make regulations under s 71: s 71(9).

Where regulations that provide for the sharing of the financial burden of providing universal services are in place under s 71, OFCOM must prepare and publish an annual report: see s 72.

103. Tariffs for universal services. It is the duty of OFCOM[1] to keep under review universal service tariffs[2] and to monitor changes to those tariffs[3]. Universal service conditions may require one or more of the following:

(1) the use of a common tariff, or of common tariffs, in relation to anything[4] which must be provided, made available or supplied[5];

(2) the use, in such cases as may be specified or described in the conditions, of such special tariffs in relation to anything so mentioned as may be so specified or described[6];

(3) the fixing of tariffs used in accordance with the conditions by the use of such methods, and by reference to such methods of computing costs, as may be so specified or described[7].

Universal service conditions must secure that the terms on which a person is provided with anything[8] required by the universal service order do not require him to pay for an unnecessary additional service[9] or to pay, in respect of anything required by the order, any amount that is attributable to the provision to him of such a service[10].

It is the duty of OFCOM, in setting a universal service condition about universal service tariffs, to have regard to anything ascertained by it in the performance of its duty[11] to keep under review and monitor changes to universal service tariffs[12].

1 As to the meaning of 'OFCOM' see PARA 14 note 1; and as to OFCOM see PARA 2 et seq.

2 References to a universal service tariff are references to any of the tariffs used by designated universal service providers or, where there is no designated universal service provider, by other persons, in relation to the things for the time being required by the universal service order: Communications Act 2003 s 68(6) (amended by SI 2011/1210). 'Tariff' includes a pricing structure: Communications Act 2003 s 68(8). As to the universal service order and the universal service conditions see PARA 102. As to the meaning of 'designated universal service provider' see PARA 102 note 29.

3 Communications Act 2003 s 68(1).

4   Ie anything mentioned in the Communications Act 2003 s 65(2): see PARA 102 heads (1)–(5).
5   Communications Act 2003 s 68(2)(a).
6   Communications Act 2003 s 68(2)(b).
7   Communications Act 2003 s 68(2)(c).
8   References in the Communications Act 2003 s 68 to providing a person with anything include references to making it available or supplying it to him: s 68(7). As to the meaning of 'person' see PARA 14 note 2.
9   The references, in relation to a person, to an unnecessary additional service are references to anything the provision of which he has to accept by reason of his being provided, at his request, with something required by the order (the 'requested service') and is not necessary for the purpose of providing him with the requested service: Communications Act 2003 s 68(4).
10   Communications Act 2003 s 68(3).
11   Ie under the Communications Act 2003 s 68(1).
12   Communications Act 2003 s 68(5).

(C) Access-related Conditions

104. Access-related conditions. The only conditions that OFCOM[1] may set[2] as access-related conditions[3] are those authorised by the following provisions[4]. Access-related conditions may include conditions relating to the provision of such network access[5] and service interoperability[6] as appears to OFCOM appropriate for the purpose of securing efficiency, sustainable competition, efficient investment and innovation and the greatest possible benefit for the end-users of public electronic communications services[7].

Access-related conditions may include conditions appearing to OFCOM to be appropriate for securing that persons to whom the electronic communications code[8] applies participate, in arrangements for sharing the use of electronic communications apparatus[9] and apportioning and making contributions towards costs incurred in relation to shared electronic communications apparatus[10].

In the case of conditions[11] which have been set by OFCOM in relation to a particular person (the 'system provider')[12], OFCOM must not give effect to a proposal to modify or revoke any of the conditions unless:

(1)   it has carried out an analysis for the purpose of determining[13] whether that person is or remains a person on whom SMP services conditions are capable of being imposed[14];

(2)   it has determined in consequence of that analysis that he is not[15]; and

(3)   it is satisfied that the modification or revocation will not have an adverse effect on any or all of the following matters[16]:

    (a)   the accessibility to any persons of services that are for the time being included in the list of must-carry services[17];

    (b)   the prospects for effective competition in the market for programme services provided by being broadcast or otherwise transmitted in digital form[18]; and

    (c)   the prospects for effective competition in the markets for conditional access systems[19] and other associated facilities[20].

OFCOM may make available to such persons as it considers appropriate information about electronic communications apparatus that in OFCOM's opinion is suitable for shared use and it may impose such restrictions as it considers appropriate on the use and further disclosure of information so made available[21].

1   As to the meaning of 'OFCOM' see PARA 14 note 1; and as to OFCOM see PARA 2 et seq.
2   Ie under the Communications Act 2003 s 45: see PARA 87.
3   As to the meaning of 'access-related condition' see PARA 87 note 6.

4   Ie by the Communications Act 2003 s 73: s 73(1).
5   As to the meaning of 'network access' see PARA 98 note 5.
6   As to the meaning of 'service interoperability' see PARA 98 note 4.
7   Communications Act 2003 s 73(2) (amended by SI 2011/1210). As to the meaning of 'public
    electronic communications service' see PARA 98 note 3. As to the meaning of 'person' see PARA
    14 note 2.
        The conditions that may be set by virtue of the Communications Act 2003 s 73(2) include
    conditions which, for the purpose of securing end-to-end connectivity for the end-users of public
    electronic communications services provided by means of a series of electronic communications
    networks impose obligations on a person controlling network access to any of those networks
    and require the interconnection of the networks: s 74(1). 'End-to-end connectivity' means the
    facility:
    (1)   for different end-users of the same public electronic communications service to be able
           to communicate with each other; and
    (2)   for the end-users of different such services to be able, each using the service of which he
           is the end-user, to communicate with each other: s 74(3).
        As to the meaning of 'interconnection' see PARA 98 note 5. The conditions that may be set by
    virtue of s 73(2) also include:
    (a)   conditions which impose such obligations on a person controlling network access to
           customers as OFCOM consider necessary for the purpose of securing service
           interoperability (s 74(1A) (added by SI 2011/1210).
    (b)   such conditions imposing obligations on a person providing facilities for the use of
           application programme interfaces or electronic programme guides as OFCOM
           considers to be necessary for securing:
           (i)   that persons are able to have access to such programme services provided in
                  digital form as OFCOM may determine (Communications Act 2003 s 74(2)(a));
                  and
           (ii)   that the facility for using those interfaces or guides is provided on terms which
                  are fair and reasonable and do not involve, or tend to give rise to, any undue
                  discrimination against any person or description of persons (s 74(2)(b)).
    'Application programme interface' means a facility for allowing software to make use, in
    connection with any of the matters mentioned in s 74(4), of facilities contained in other
    software; and 'electronic programme guide' means a facility by means of which a person has
    access to any service which consists of the listing or promotion, or both the listing and the
    promotion, of some or all of the programmes included in any one or more programme services,
    and a facility for obtaining access, in whole or in part, to the programme service or services
    listed or promoted in the guide: s 74(3). The matters referred to above are:
    (A)   allowing a person to have access to programme services (s 74(4)(a));
    (B)   allowing a person, other than a communications provider or a person who makes
           associated facilities available, to make use of an electronic communications network by
           means of which a programme service is broadcast or otherwise transmitted (s 74(4)(b));
    (C)   allowing a person to become the end-user of a description of public electronic
           communications service (s 74(4)(c)).
    Section 74 is not to be construed as restricting the provision that may be made under s 73(2):
    s 74(5).
8   As to the meaning of 'electronic communications code' see PARA 155 note 1.
9   As to the meaning of 'electronic communications apparatus' see PARA 88 note 10.
10 Communications Act 2003 s 73(3) (amended by SI 2011/1210). The power to set access-related
    conditions falling within the Communications Act 2003 s 73(3) is to be exercised for the
    purpose of encouraging efficient investment in infrastructure and promoting innovation:
    s 73(3A) (added by SI 2011/1210). Access-related conditions may include conditions containing
    any provision required by the Communications Act 2003 s 75(2): s 73(5).
        It is the duty of OFCOM to ensure:
    (1)   that access-related conditions are applied to every person who provides a conditional
           access system in relation to a protected programme service (s 75(2)(a)); and
    (2)   that those conditions make all such provision as is required by the provision contained
           from time to time in Part I of Annex I to the Access Directive (conditions relating to
           access to digital programme services) (Communications Act 2003 s 75(2)(b)).
        'Conditional access system' means any system, facility, arrangements or technical measure
    under or by means of which access to programme services requires:
    (a)   a subscription to the service or to a service that includes that service; or
    (b)   an authorisation to view it, or to listen to it, on a particular occasion,

and 'protected programme service' means a programme service the programmes included in which cannot be viewed or listened to in an intelligible form except by the use of a conditional access system: s 75(3).

'Access Directive' means European Parliament and Council Directive (EC) 2002/19 (OJ L108, 24.4.2002, p 7) on access to, and interconnection of, electronic communications networks and associated facilities (amended by European Parliament and Council Directive (EC) 2009/140 (OJ L337, 18.12.2009, p 37): Communications Act 2003 s 151(1).

11 Ie conditions falling within the Communications Act 2003 s 75(2).
12 Communications Act 2003 s 76(1).
13 Ie in accordance with the Communications Act 2003 Pt 2 Ch 1 (ss 32–151).
14 Communications Act 2003 s 76(2)(a).
15 Communications Act 2003 s 76(2)(b).
16 Communications Act 2003 s 76(2)(c).
17 Communications Act 2003 s 76(3)(a). The list of must-carry services referred to in the text are those in the Communications Act 2003 s 64: see BROADCASTING vol 4 (2011) PARA 719.
18 Communications Act 2003 s 76(3)(b).
19 'Conditional access system' has the same meaning as in the Communications Act 2003 s 75: s 76(4).
20 Communications Act 2003 s 76(3)(c).
21 Communications Act 2003 s 76A (added by SI 2011/1210).

(D) *Privileged Supplier Conditions*

105.   Privileged supplier conditions.   It is the duty of OFCOM[1] to secure that privileged supplier conditions[2] containing all such provision[3] as it considers appropriate are applied to every public communications provider[4] to whom the following provisions[5] apply[6]. The provision that may be contained in a condition set[7] as a privileged supplier condition is any provision that OFCOM considers appropriate for any one or more of the following purposes:

(1)   requiring the provider to whom it applies to keep separate accounts in relation to his public electronic communications network[8] or public electronic communications service[9] and other matters[10];

(2)   requiring that provider to submit the accounts of the different parts of his undertaking, and any financial report relating to a part of that undertaking, to a qualified auditor[11] for auditing[12];

(3)   requiring the accounts of the different parts of his undertaking to be published[13];

(4)   securing, by means other than the keeping of separate accounts, the structural separation of the different parts of his undertaking[14].

OFCOM is not required to apply a condition to a person where it is satisfied that that person has an annual turnover in relation to all his communications activities that is less than £50 million[15].

1   As to the meaning of 'OFCOM' see PARA 14 note 1; and as to OFCOM see PARA 2 et seq.
2   As to the meaning of 'privileged supplier condition' see PARA 87 note 7.
3   Ie all such provision falling within the Communications Act 2003 s 77(3): see the text to notes 7–14.
4   As to the meaning of 'public communications provider' see PARA 99 note 2.
5   Ie the Communications Act 2003 s 77.
6   Communications Act 2003 s 77(1). Section 77 applies to every public communications provider who enjoys special or exclusive rights in relation to the provision of any non-communications services and is not such a provider in respect only of associated facilities: s 77(2). 'Special or exclusive rights' has the same meaning as in the Treaty on the Functioning of the European Union (Rome, 25 March 1957; TS 1 (1973); Cmnd 5179) ('TFEU') art 106: Communications Act 2003 s 77(9). The Treaty was formerly known as the Treaty Establishing the European Community; it has been renamed and its provisions renumbered: see PARA 17 note 17. 'Non-communications services', in relation to a person, means services other than those

consisting in, or connected with, the provision by him of an electronic communications network or an electronic communications service: Communications Act 2003 s 77(9).

7 Ie under the Communications Act 2003 s 45: see PARA 87.
8 As to the meaning of 'public electronic communications network' see PARA 98 note 6.
9 As to the meaning of 'public electronic communications service' see PARA 98 note 3.
10 Communications Act 2003 s 77(3)(a).
11 'Qualified auditor' means a person who is eligible for appointment as a statutory auditor under the Companies Act 2006 Pt 42 (ss 1209–1264) (see COMPANIES vol 15 (2009) PARA 958) and if the appointment to carry out such auditing as is mentioned in the Communications Act 2003 s 77(3)(b) were an appointment as a statutory auditor, would not be prohibited from acting by the Companies Act 2006 1214 (independence requirement): Communications Act 2003 s 77(9) (definition substituted by SI 2008/948).
12 Communications Act 2003 s 77(3)(b).
13 Communications Act 2003 s 77(3)(c).
14 Communications Act 2003 s 77(3)(d).
15 Communications Act 2003 s 77(4). As to the meaning of 'person' see PARA 14 note 2. Where in a case falling within s 77(4) OFCOM is not required to apply a privileged supplier condition to a person, it may apply such a condition to him if it thinks fit: s 77(5). The reference in s 77(4) to a person's communications activities is a reference to any activities of his that consist in, or are connected with, either or both of the following:
    (1) the provision of any one or more electronic communications networks (s 77(6)(a));
    (2) the provision of any one or more electronic communications services (s 77(6)(b)).
    The making, for the purposes of s 77(4), of a determination of the period in respect of which a person's annual turnover in relation to any activities is computed and a determination of the amount in euros of that turnover for any period, must be in accordance with such rules as OFCOM considers to be reasonable: s 77(7). OFCOM must publish any rules made by it for the purposes of s 77(7) in such manner as it considers appropriate for bringing them to the attention of the persons who, in its opinion, are likely to be affected by them: s 77(8). At the date at which this volume states the law, no such rules have been published.

(E) SMP Conditions

106. Procedure for making market power determination. For the purposes of Chapter 1 of Part 2 of the Communications Act 2003[1] a person is to be taken to have significant market power in relation to a market if he enjoys a position which amounts to or is equivalent to dominance of the market[2]. A person is to be taken to enjoy a position of dominance of a market if he is one of a number of persons who enjoy such a position in combination with each other[3]. A person or combination of persons may also be taken to enjoy a position of dominance of a market by reason wholly or partly of his or their position in a closely related market if the links between the two markets allow the market power held in the closely related market to be used in a way that influences the other market so as to strengthen the position in the other market of that person or combination of persons[4].

Before making a market power determination[5], OFCOM[6] must:
(1) identify (by reference, in particular, to area and locality) the markets which in its opinion are the ones which in the circumstances of the United Kingdom are the markets in relation to which it is appropriate to consider whether to make the determination[7]; and
(2) carry out an analysis of the identified markets[8].

In identifying or analysing any services market for these purposes, OFCOM must take due account of all applicable guidelines and recommendations which have been issued or made by the European Commission in pursuance of the provisions of a European Union (EU) instrument and which relate to market identification and analysis[9]. In considering whether to make or revise a market power determination in relation to a services market, OFCOM must take due account of all applicable guidelines and recommendations which have been issued or made by the European Commission in pursuance of the provisions of an EU instrument and which relate to market analysis or the determination of what constitutes significant market power[10]. The way in which a market is to be identified for these purposes[11], or a market power determination is to be made, is by the publication of a notification containing the identification or determination[12]. The publication of such a notification must be in such manner as appears to OFCOM to be appropriate for bringing the contents of the notification to the attention of the persons who, in OFCOM's opinion, are likely to be affected by the matters notified[13].

Where the provisions relating to domestic consultation for market identifications and market power determinations[14] apply, OFCOM must comply with the applicable requirements for those provisions and the provisions relating to EU consultations for market identifications and market power determinations[15] before:

(a) identifying a market for the purposes of making a market power determination[16]; or

(b) making a market power determination[17].

Where the provisions relating to domestic consultation for market identifications and market power determinations[18] do not apply[19], any identification of a market or market power determination must be temporary and the notification published[20] containing the identification or determination must state the period for which the identification or determination is to have effect[21].

1 Ie the Communications Act 2003 Pt 2 Ch 1 (ss 32–151).
2 Communications Act 2003 s 78(1). As to the meaning of 'person' see PARA 14 note 2. References in s 78 to dominance of a market must be construed in accordance with any applicable provisions of European Parliament and Council Directive (EC) 2002/21 (OJ L108, 24.4.2002, p 33) on a common regulatory framework for electronic communications networks and services ('the Framework Directive') (see PARA 97 note 21), art 14: Communications Act 2003 s 78(2).
3 Communications Act 2003 s 78(3). The matters that must be taken into account in determining whether a combination of persons enjoys a position of dominance of a services market include, in particular, the matters set out in Annex II to the Framework Directive: Communications Act 2003 s 78(5). 'Services market', in relation to a market power determination or market identification, is to be construed in accordance with s 46(8)(a) (see PARA 88 note 10): s 151(1).
4 Communications Act 2003 s 78(4).
5 'Market power determination' means:
      (1) a determination, for the purposes of provisions of the Communications Act 2003 Pt 2 Ch 1, that a person has significant market power in an identified services market or an identified apparatus market; or
      (2) a confirmation for such purposes of a market power determination reviewed on a further analysis under s 84 or s 85 (see PARA 110): s 151(1).
    'Apparatus market', in relation to a market power determination, is to be construed in accordance with s 46(9)(b) (see PARA 88 note 10): s 151(1).
6 As to the meaning of 'OFCOM' see PARA 14 note 1; and as to OFCOM see PARA 2 et seq.
7 Communications Act 2003 s 79(1)(a).
8 Communications Act 2003 s 79(1)(b). As to the meaning of 'United Kingdom' see PARA 14 note 7.
9 Communications Act 2003 s 79(2) (s 79(2), (3), (7) amended by SI 2011/1043). References in the Communications Act 2003 s 79 to guidelines and recommendations issued by the European Commission and to a European Union (EU) instrument include references to guidelines and recommendations issued, and an EU instrument made, after the commencement of s 79 (ie 25 July 2003: see the Communications Act 2003 (Commencement No 1) Order 2003, SI 2003/1900 (amended by SI 2003/3142)): Communications Act 2003 s 79(7) (as so amended). It has been held that guidelines and recommendations issued by the European Commission do not have binding effect, and therefore cannot be challenged under the Treaty on the Functioning of the European Union (Rome, 25 March 1957; TS 1 (1973); Cmnd 5179) art 230: see Case T-109/06 *Vodafone Espana SA v EC Commission* [2007] ECR II-5151, [2008] 4 CMLR 1378,

CFI; Case T-295/06 *Base NV v EC Commission* (22 February 2008) (OJ C107, 26.04. 2008, p 26), CFI. The Treaty was formerly known as the Treaty Establishing the European Community; it has been renamed and its provisions renumbered: see PARA 17 note 17. As to the European Commission see EUROPEAN UNION vol 47A (2014) PARAS 48, 49.

10 Communications Act 2003 s 79(3) (as amended: see note 9).

11 Ie for the purposes of the Communications Act 2003 s 79.

12 Communications Act 2003 s 79(4). Notifications for these purposes:

    (1)   may be given separately (s 79(5)(a));

    (2)   may be contained in a single notification relating to both the identification of a market and the making of a market determination in relation to that market (s 79(5)(b)); or

    (3)   may be contained in a single notification under s 48(1) (see PARA 90) with respect to the setting or modification of an SMP condition and either:

        (a)   the making of the market power determination by reference to which OFCOM sets or modifies that condition (s 79(5)(c)(i)); or

        (b)   the making of that market power determination and the identification of the market in relation to which that determination is made (s 79(5)(c)(ii)).

As to the meaning of 'SMP condition' see PARA 87 note 8.

OFCOM must send a copy of every notification published under s 79(4) or s 80A(3) (see PARA 107) to the Secretary of State: s 81(1) (s 81 substituted by SI 2011/1210). OFCOM must send to the European Commission a copy of every notification published under the Communications Act 2003 s 79(4) with respect to a market power determination in relation to a services market: s 81(2) (as so substituted). OFCOM must send to BEREC a copy of every notification published under s 79(4) where the proposal to identify the market or make a market power determination was a proposal of EU significance: s 81(3) (as so substituted). Where a notification published under s 79(4) relates to a proposal to which s 80A did not apply because of s 80A(2), OFCOM must send a copy of a statement setting out the reasons for the proposal and for the urgent need to act to the Commission, BEREC and the regulatory authorities in every other member state: s 81(4) (as so substituted). As to the regulatory authorities of member states see PARA 92 note 6. As to the Secretary of State see PARA 76 note 1.

13 Communications Act 2003 s 79(6).

14 Ie the Communications Act 2003 s 80A: see PARA 107.

15 Ie the Communications Act 2003 s 80B: see PARA 108.

16 Communications Act 2003 s 80(1)(a) (s 80(1) substituted by, and s 80(1A), (1B) added by, SI 2011/1210). The power of OFCOM to identify a market or make a market power determination is subject to the Communications Act 2003 s 83 (see PARA 109): s 80(7) (amended by SI 2011/1210).

17 Communications Act 2003 s 80(1)(b) (as substituted: see note 16).

18 Ie the Communications Act 2003 s 80A: see PARA 107.

19 Is because of the Communications Act 2003 s 80A(2).

20 Ie under the Communications Act 2003 s 79(4): see text and notes 12.

21 Communications Act 2003 s 80(1A) (as added: see note 16). Where OFCOM proposes to extend or make permanent any such temporary identification or determination:

    (1)   s 80A (see PARA 107) and s 80B(1) (see PARA 108) do not apply in relation to the proposal (s 80(1B)(a) (as so added)); and

    (2)   the provisions of s 80B(2)–(8) (see PARA 108) apply in relation to the proposal as if OFCOM had to send a copy of the proposal, and of a statement setting out the reasons for it, to the European Commission, BEREC and the regulatory authorities in every other member state (ss 80(1B)(b), 80B(2) (as so added)).

107. Domestic consultation for market identifications and market power determinations. Subject to certain exceptions[1], where:

    (1)   OFCOM[2] proposes to identify a market for the purposes of making a market power determination or to make a market power determination[3]; and

    (2)   (in the case of a services market) the proposed identification or determination is in OFCOM's opinion likely to result in the setting, modification or revocation of SMP services conditions that will have a significant impact on the market[4],

OFCOM must publish a notification of what it is proposing to do[5].

    For these purposes, notifications:

(a)   may be given separately[6];
(b)   may be contained in a single notification relating to both the identification of a market and the making of a market power determination in relation to that market[7]; or
(c)   may be contained in a single notification[8] with respect to the setting or modification of an SMP condition and either:
    (i)   the making of the market power determination by reference to which OFCOM are proposing to set or modify that condition[9]; or
    (ii) the making of that market power determination and the identification of the market in relation to which they are proposing to make that determination[10].

A notification[11] relating to a proposal to identify a market or to make a market power determination must:

(A)   state that OFCOM are proposing to identify that market or to make that market power determination[12];
(B)   set out the effect of the proposal[13];
(C)   give their reasons for making the proposal[14]; and
(D)   specify the period[15] within which representations may be made to OFCOM about their proposal[16].

The publication of a notification[17] must be in such manner as appears to OFCOM to be appropriate for bringing the contents of the notification to the attention of the persons who, in OFCOM's opinion, are likely to be affected by the matters notified[18].

OFCOM must consider every representation about the proposal made to them during the period specified in the notification and have regard to every international obligation of the United Kingdom (if any) which has been notified to them for these purposes by the Secretary of State[19].

Where the proposal is not of EU significance[20], OFCOM may then give effect to it, with any modifications that appear to OFCOM to be appropriate[21].

The above provisions[22] do not apply where the proposal is of EU significance and in OFCOM's opinion there are exceptional circumstances and there is an urgent need to act in order to safeguard competition and to protect the interests of consumers[23].

1   See the Communications Act 2003 s 80A(2); and text and note 23.
2   As to the meaning of 'OFCOM' see PARA 14 note 1; and as to OFCOM see PARA 2 et seq.
3   Communications Act 2003 s 80A(1)(a) (s 80A added by SI 2011/1210).
4   Communications Act 2003 s 80A(1)(b) (as added: see note 3).
5   Communications Act 2003 s 80A(3) (as added: see note 3). OFCOM must send to the Secretary of State a copy of every notification published under s 80A(3): s 81(1) (s 81 substituted by SI 2011/1210).
6   Communications Act 2003 s 80A(4)(a) (as added: see note 3).
7   Communications Act 2003 s 80A(4)(b) (as added: see note 3).
8   Ie under the Communications Act 2003 s 48A(3): see PARA 91.
9   Communications Act 2003 s 80A(4)(c)(i) (as added: see note 3).
10 Communications Act 2003 s 80A(4)(c)(ii) (as added: see note 3).
11 Ie under the Communications Act 2003 s 80A.
12 Communications Act 2003 s 80A(5)(a) (as added: see note 3).
13 Communications Act 2003 s 80A(5)(b) (as added: see note 3).
14 Communications Act 2003 s 80A(5)(c) (as added: see note 3).
15 That period must be a period of not less than one month after the day of the publication of the notification but where OFCOM are satisfied that there are exceptional circumstances justifying the use of a shorter period, the period specified as the period for making representations may be whatever shorter period OFCOM considers reasonable in those circumstances: s 80A(6), (7) (as added: see note 3).
16 Communications Act 2003 s 80A(5)(d) (as added: see note 3).

17 Communications Act 2003 s 80A(9) (as added: see note 3). As to the meaning of 'United Kingdom' see PARA 14 note 7. As to the Secretary of State see PARA 76 note 1.
18 Ie under the Communications Act 2003 s 80A.
19 Communications Act 2003 s 80A(8) (as added: see note 3).
20 As to the meaning of 'EU significance' see PARA 91 note 10.
21 Communications Act 2003 s 80A(10) (as added: see note 3).
22 Ie the Communications Act 2003 s 80A.
23 Communications Act 2003 s 80A(2) (as added: see note 3).

108. EU consultation for market identifications and market power determinations. Where, after considering every representation and having regard to every international obligation of the United Kingdom[1] in relation to a proposal of EU significance[2] OFCOM[3] wishes to proceed with the proposal[4], after making any modifications of the proposal that appear to OFCOM to be appropriate, OFCOM must send a copy of the proposal, and of a statement setting out the reasons for it, to the European Commission, BEREC and the regulatory authorities in every other member state[5].

If at the end of the period of one month[6] no indication has been given to OFCOM by the Commission[7], OFCOM may give effect to the proposal, with any modifications that appear to them to be appropriate[8]. Before giving effect to the proposal[9], OFCOM must consider any comments made by the Commission, BEREC and any regulatory authority in any other member state[10]. Where such an indication is given by the Commission to OFCOM during that period the following apply[11]:

(1) if the Commission requires[12] OFCOM to withdraw the proposal, OFCOM must amend or withdraw the proposal within six months of the date of the Commission's decision[13];

(2) OFCOM may give effect to the proposal, with any modifications that appear to them to be appropriate:

(a) if the Commission takes a decision to lift its reservations[14]; or

(b) if at the end of the period of two months[15] the Commission has neither required OFCOM to withdraw the proposal[16] nor lifted its reservations[17].

1 Ie after complying with the Communications Act 2003 s 80A(9): see PARA 107. As to the meaning of 'United Kingdom' see PARA 14 note 7.
2 As to the meaning of 'EU significance' see PARA 91 note 10.
3 As to the meaning of 'OFCOM' see PARA 14 note 1; and as to OFCOM see PARA 2 et seq.
4 Communications Act 2003 s 80B(1) (s 80B added by SI 2011/1210).
5 Communications Act 2003 s 80B(2) (as added: see note 4). As to the regulatory authorities of member states see PARA 92 note 6.
6 Ie referred to in the European Parliament and Council Directive (EC) 2002/21 (OJ L108, 24.4.2002, p 33) on a common regulatory framework for electronic communications networks and services ('the Framework Directive') (see PARA 97 note 21), art 7(3).
7 Ie under the Framework Directive art 7(4).
8 Communications Act 2003 s 80B(3) (as added: see note 4).
9 Ie under the Communications Act 2003 s 80B(3).
10 Communications Act 2003 s 80B(4) (as added: see note 4).
11 Communications Act 2003 s 80B(5) (as added: see note 4).
12 Ie under the Framework Directive art 7(5)(a).
13 Communications Act 2003 s 80B(6) (as added: see note 4). Where a proposal is amended under head (1) in the text, s 80 applies in relation to the amended proposal as if it were a new proposal: s 80B(7) (as so added).
14 Communications Act 2003 s 80B(8)(a) (as added: see note 4). The reference in head (a) in the text to the Commission's decision to lift its reservations is one in accordance with the Framework Directive art 7(5)(b).
15 Ie referred to in the Framework Directive art 7(4).
16 Ie under the Framework Directive art 7(5)(a).

17 Communications Act 2003 s 80B(8)(b) (as added: see note 4). The reference in head (b) in the
    text to the Commission's decision to lift its reservations is one in accordance with the
    Framework Directive art 7(5)(b).

109. Special rules for transnational markets. Special provisions apply where a
services market[1] is for the time being identified by a decision of the European
Commission[2] as a transnational market[3]. Where the market area[4] includes the
whole or a part of the United Kingdom[5], OFCOM[6] must enter into and maintain
arrangements with the other relevant regulatory authorities[7] about the extent to
which the agreement of all the relevant regulatory authorities is required for the
doing of any of the things mentioned below and the procedures to be followed
for securing that agreement where it is required[8].
   Those things are:
   (1)   the identification of the whole or a part of the market as a market in
         relation to which it is appropriate to determine whether a person has
         significant market power[9];
   (2)   the making of such a determination in relation to the whole or a part of
         the market[10];
   (3)   the setting of a condition the setting of which requires such a
         determination to have been made[11];
   (4)   the modification or revocation of such a condition[12].
OFCOM must not do any of those things except in accordance with
arrangements maintained under them[13]. The arrangements may include
arrangements requiring OFCOM, when doing any of those things, to comply
with:
   (a)   a decision made by one or more other regulatory authorities[14]; or
   (b)   a decision made by a person appointed under the arrangements to act
         on behalf of some or all of the relevant regulatory authorities[15].

1   As to the meaning of 'services market' see PARA 106 note 3.
2   Ie under European Parliament and Council Directive (EC) 2002/21 (OJ L108, 24.4.2002, p 33)
    on a common regulatory framework for electronic communications networks and services ('the
    Framework Directive') (see PARA 97 note 21), art 15(4). As to the European Commission see
    EUROPEAN UNION vol 47A (2014) PARAS 48, 49.
3   Communications Act 2003 s 83(1).
4   In the Communications Act 2003 s 83, 'market area', in relation to a services market identified
    by the European Commission as a transnational market, means the area identified by that
    Commission as the area for which the market operates: s 83(6).
5   As to the meaning of 'United Kingdom' see PARA 14 note 7.
6   As to the meaning of 'OFCOM' see PARA 14 note 1; and as to OFCOM see PARA 2 et seq.
7   In the Communications Act 2003 s 83, 'relevant regulatory authorities', in relation to a services
    market identified by the European Commission as a transnational market, means the regulatory
    authorities for each member state the whole or a part of which is comprised in the market area:
    s 83(6). As to the regulatory authorities of member states see PARA 92 note 6.
8   Communications Act 2003 s 83(2).
9   Communications Act 2003 s 83(3)(a). As to the meaning of 'significant market power' see PARAS
    88 note 10, 106.
10 Communications Act 2003 s 83(3)(b).
11 Communications Act 2003 s 83(3)(c).
12 Communications Act 2003 s 83(3)(d).
13 Communications Act 2003 s 83(4).
14 Communications Act 2003 s 83(5)(a).
15 Communications Act 2003 s 83(5)(b).

110. Review of market power determinations and SMP conditions. Where
OFCOM[1] has identified and analysed a services market[2] for the purposes of

making a market power determination[3], OFCOM may, and when required[4] must, carry out further analyses of the identified market for one or both of the following purposes[5]:

(1) reviewing market power determinations made on the basis of an earlier analysis[6];

(2) deciding whether to make proposals for the modification of SMP conditions[7] set by reference to a market power determination made on such a basis[8].

Where on, or in consequence of, a further analysis[9], OFCOM determines that a person to whom any SMP conditions apply is no longer a person with significant market power in that market, it must revoke every SMP services condition applied to that person by reference to the market power determination made on the basis of the earlier analysis[10].

Where OFCOM has identified and analysed an apparatus market for the purposes of making a market power determination, OFCOM must, at such intervals as it considers appropriate, carry out further analyses of the identified market for one or both of the following purposes[11]:

(a) reviewing market power determinations made on the basis of an earlier analysis[12];

(b) deciding whether to make proposals for the modification of SMP conditions set by reference to any such market power determination[13].

Where on, or in consequence of, a further analysis[14], OFCOM determines that a person to whom any SMP conditions apply is no longer a person with significant market power in that market, it must revoke every SMP apparatus condition[15] applied to that person by reference to the market power determination made on the basis of the earlier analysis[16].

OFCOM must not set an SMP services condition[17] by a notification which does not also make the market power determination by reference to which the condition is set unless:

(i) the condition is set by reference to a market power determination which has been reviewed[18] and, in consequence of that review, is confirmed in the notification setting the condition[19]; or

(ii) the condition is set by reference to a market power determination made in relation to a market in which OFCOM is satisfied there has been no material change[20] since the determination was made[21].

OFCOM must not modify or revoke SMP services conditions applying to a person except in the following cases[22]. The first case is where, for the purpose of determining whether to make the modification or revocation, OFCOM has carried out a further analysis[23] of the market in question, and reviewed the market power determination for the time being in force in that person's case[24]. The second case is where OFCOM is satisfied that there has not in the case of an unmodified condition, since the condition was set or in any other case, since the condition was last modified, been a material change in the market identified or otherwise used for the purposes of the market power determination by reference to which the condition was set or last modified[25].

OFCOM must not modify SMP apparatus conditions applying to a person except where, for the purpose of determining whether to make the modification or revocation, it has carried out a further analysis[26] of the market in question, and reviewed the market power determination for the time being in force in that person's case[27].

In the exercise by OFCOM of its powers to identify and analyse services markets, to make and review market power determinations in respect of such markets and to set, modify and revoke SMP services conditions by reference to such determinations[28]:

(A)   where[29] the European Commission[30] has adopted a revised recommendation identifying a services market not previously notified to the Commission, OFCOM must ensure that within the specified period[31] it has carried out any identification and analysis of markets that is necessary in consequence of the recommendation and sent the Commission copies of any resulting proposals with respect to market identification, market power determinations and SMP services conditions[32];

(B)   where, following the identification and analysis of a services market, OFCOM have made a market power determination after 25 May 2011, in relation to it, it must ensure that within the specified period[33] it has carried out a further analysis of the market and reviewed the identification and determination made on the basis of the earlier analysis and sent the Commission copies of any resulting proposals with respect to market identification, market power determinations and SMP services conditions[34];

(C)   where it appears to OFCOM that it is unlikely to be able to comply with the requirements of heads (A) or (B) within the specified period, it may request assistance from BEREC[35].

1   As to the meaning of 'OFCOM' see PARA 14 note 1; and as to OFCOM see PARA 2 et seq.
2   See PARA 106.
3   As to the meaning of 'market power determination' see PARA 106 note 5.
4   Ie by the Communications Act 2003 s 84A: see text and notes 28–35.
5   Communications Act 2003 s 84(1), (2) (s 84(2) amended by SI 2011/1210). Before carrying out a further analysis under the Communications Act 2003 s 84(2), OFCOM may review any of its decisions identifying the markets which it was appropriate to consider for the purpose of carrying out an earlier analysis: s 84(5). Where, on such a review, OFCOM concludes that the appropriate markets have changed it must identify the markets it now considers to be the appropriate ones and those markets are the identified markets for the purposes of the further analysis: s 84(6).
       Sections 79–83 (see PARAS 106–109) apply:
       (1)   in relation to the identification of a services market for the purposes of reviewing a market power determination under s 84, as they apply in relation to the identification of such a market for the purpose of making a market determination (s 84(7)(a)); and
       (2)   in relation to the review of such a determination, as they apply in relation to the making of such a determination (s 84(7)(b)).
6   Communications Act 2003 s 84(2)(a).
7   As to the meaning of 'SMP condition' see PARA 87 text and note 8.
8   Communications Act 2003 s 84(2)(b).
9   Ie under the Communications Act 2003 s 84: see the text and notes 1–10.
10   Communications Act 2003 s 84(4). As to the meaning of 'SMP services condition' see PARA 87 note 8. As to the meaning of 'person' see PARA 14 note 2.
11   Communications Act 2003 s 85(1), (2). Before carrying out any further analysis under s 85(2), OFCOM may review any of its decisions identifying the markets which it was appropriate to consider for the purpose of carrying out any earlier analysis: s 85(4). Where on such a review OFCOM concludes that the appropriate markets have changed it must identify the markets it now considers to be the appropriate ones and those markets are the identified markets for the purposes of the further analysis: s 85(5). Where on such a review OFCOM concludes that there is no person at all with significant market power in relation to the identified market it must so inform the Secretary of State and the Secretary of State may by order remove or restrict OFCOM's power under Pt 2 Ch 1 (ss 32–151) to set SMP apparatus conditions by reference to that market: s 85(6). As to the Secretary of State see PARA 76 note 1. As to the power of the Secretary of State to make orders under the Communications Act 2003 see s 402; and PARA 74.

Sections 79, 80, 80A and 81(1) (see PARAS 106, 107) apply:

(1)   in relation to the identification of an apparatus market for the purposes of reviewing a market power determination under s 85, as they apply in relation to the identification of such a market for the purpose of making a market determination (s 85(7)(a) (s 85(7) amended by SI 2011/1210)); and

(2)   in relation to the review of such a determination, as they apply in relation to the making of such a determination (s 85(7)(b) (as so amended)).

12 Communications Act 2003 s 85(2)(a).

13 Communications Act 2003 s 85(2)(b).

14 Ie under the Communications Act 2003 s 85: see the text and notes 11–16.

15 As to the meaning of 'SMP apparatus condition' see PARA 87 note 8.

16 Communications Act 2003 s 85(3).

17 As to the meaning of 'SMP services condition' see PARA 87 note 8.

18 Ie under the Communications Act 2003 s 84: see the text and notes 1–10.

19 Communications Act 2003 s 86(1)(a).

20 A change is a material change for the purposes of the Communications Act 2003 s 86(1) or s 86(4) if it is one that is material to the setting of the condition in question or the modification or revocation in question: s 86(6).

21 Communications Act 2003 s 86(1)(b).

22 Communications Act 2003 s 86(2). The cases referred to in the text are those falling within the Communications Act 2003 s 86(3) (see the text and note 24) or s 86(4) (see the text and note 25): s 86(2).

23 Ie under the Communications Act 2003 s 84: see the text and notes 1–10.

24 Communications Act 2003 s 86(3).

25 Communications Act 2003 s 86(4). See note 22.

26 Ie under the Communications Act 2003 s 85: see the text and notes 11–15.

27 Communications Act 2003 s 86(5).

28 Communications Act 2003 s 84A(1) (s 84A added by SI 2011/1210).

29 Ie under European Parliament and Council Directive (EC) 2002/21 (OJ L108, 24.4.2002, p 33) on a common regulatory framework for electronic communications networks and services ('the Framework Directive') (see PARA 97 note 21), art 15(1).

30 As to the European Commission see EUROPEAN UNION vol 47A (2014) PARAS 48, 49.

31 For these purposes, 'the specified period' means the period of 2 years from the adoption of the recommendation: Communications Act 2003 s 84A(7)(a) (as added: see note 28).

32 Communications Act 2003 s 84A(2) (as added: see note 28).

33 For these purposes, 'the specified period' means the period of 3 years from the publication under the Communications Act 2003 s 79(4) (see PARA 106) of the notification of the market power determination made on the basis of the earlier analysis, subject to any extension of that period under the Framework Directive art 16(6)(a): Communications Act 2003 s 84A(7)(b) (as added: see note 28).

34 Communications Act 2003 s 84A(3), (4) (as added: see note 28).

35 Communications Act 2003 s 84A(5) (as added: see note 28). The request for assistance referred to in the text is a request under the Framework Directive art 16(7). Where OFCOM requests such assistance:

(1)   it must inform the Commission of the request (Communications Act 2003 s 84A(6)(a) (as so added));

(2)   heads (a)and (b) in the text applies in the case in question as if the requirement to act within the specified period was remove (see s 84A(6)(b) (as so added)); and

(3)   within six months of the assistance being provided it must send copies of any resulting proposals to the Commission (s 84A(6)(c) (as so added)).

As to BEREC see PARA 58.

111.   SMP services conditions: subject matter. Where OFCOM[1] has made a determination that a person to whom the following provisions apply[2] (the 'dominant provider') has significant market power[3] in an identified services market[4], it must:

(1)   set such SMP conditions[5] authorised by these provisions as it considers appropriate to apply to that person in respect of the relevant network[6] or relevant facilities[7]; and

(2)   apply those conditions to that person[8].

These provisions authorise SMP conditions requiring the dominant provider to give such entitlements as OFCOM may from time to time direct as respects the provision of network access[9] to the relevant network, the use of the relevant network and the availability of the relevant facilities[10].

The conditions[11] may include provision for securing fairness and reasonableness in the way in which requests for network access are made and responded to, and for securing that the obligations contained in the conditions are complied with within the periods and at the times required by or under the conditions[12].

The authorised SMP conditions also include one or more of the following:

(a) a condition which is of a technical or operational nature and appears to OFCOM to be appropriate for securing the proper operation of an electronic communications network in compliance with a condition[13] requiring the dominant provider to give such entitlements as OFCOM may from time to time direct as respects the provision of network access to the relevant network, the use of the relevant network and the availability of the relevant facilities[14];

(b) a condition requiring the dominant provider not to discriminate unduly against particular persons, or against a particular description of persons, in relation to matters connected with network access to the relevant network or with the availability of the relevant facilities[15];

(c) a condition requiring the dominant provider to publish, in such manner as OFCOM may from time to time direct, all such information as OFCOM may direct for the purpose of securing transparency in relation to such matters[16];

(d) a condition requiring the dominant provider to publish, in such manner as OFCOM may from time to time direct, the terms and conditions on which he is willing to enter into an access contract[17];

(e) a condition requiring the terms and conditions on which the dominant provider is willing to enter into an access contract to include such terms and conditions as may be specified or described in the condition[18];

(f) a condition requiring the dominant provider to make such modifications as OFCOM may direct of any offer by that provider which sets out the terms and conditions on which he is willing to enter into an access contract[19].

(g) conditions requiring the dominant provider to maintain a separation for accounting purposes between such different matters relating to network access to the relevant network, or to the availability of the relevant facilities, as OFCOM may from time to time direct[20];

(h) conditions imposing on the dominant provider[21]:

(i) such price controls as OFCOM may direct in relation to matters connected with the provision of network access to the relevant network, or with the availability of the relevant facilities[22];

(ii) such rules as it may make in relation to those matters about the recovery of costs and cost orientation[23];

(iii) such rules as it may make for those purposes about the use of cost accounting systems[24]; and

(iv) obligations to adjust prices in accordance with such directions given by OFCOM as it may consider appropriate[25].

1   As to the meaning of 'OFCOM' see PARA 14 note 1; and as to OFCOM see PARA 2 et seq.
2   The Communications Act 2003 s 87 applies to a person who provides a public electronic communications network and a person who makes available facilities that are associated

facilities by reference to such a network: s 87(2). As to the meaning of 'person' see PARA 14 note 2. As to the meaning of 'public electronic communications network' see PARA 98 note 6.

3   See PARA 106.

4   As to the meaning of 'services market' see PARA 88 note 10.

5   As to the meaning of 'SMP condition' see PARA 87 text and note 8.

6   'Relevant network', in relation to such a person, means the public electronic communications network provided by him: Communications Act 2003 s 87(12).

7   Communications Act 2003 s 87(1)(a). 'Relevant facilities', in relation to a person to whom s 87 applies, means the associated facilities made available by that person in relation to a public electronic communications network: s 87(12).

8   Communications Act 2003 s 87(1)(b).

9   As to the meaning of 'network access' see PARA 98 note 5.

10   Communications Act 2003 s 87(3). In determining what conditions authorised by s 87(3) to set in a particular case, OFCOM must take into account, in particular, the following factors:

   (1)   the technical and economic viability (including the viability of other network access products, whether provided by the dominant provider or another person), having regard to the state of market development, of installing and using facilities that would make the proposed network access unnecessary (s 87(4)(a) (amended by SI 2011/1210));

   (2)   the feasibility of the provision of the proposed network access (Communications Act 2003 s 87(4)(b));

   (3)   the investment made by the person initially providing or making available the network or other facility in respect of which an entitlement to network access is proposed (taking account of any public investment made) (s 87(4)(c) (amended by SI 2011/1210));

   (4)   the need to secure effective competition (including, where it appears to OFCOM to be appropriate, economically efficient infrastructure based competition) in the long term (Communications Act 2003 s 87(4)(d) (amended by SI 2011/1210));

   (5)   any rights to intellectual property that are relevant to the proposal (s 87(4)(e)); and

   (6)   the desirability of securing that electronic communications services are provided that are available throughout the member states (s 87(4)(f)).

11   Ie the conditions authorised by the Communications Act 2003 s 87(3).

12   Communications Act 2003 s 87(5).

13   Ie in compliance with a condition under the Communications Act 2003 s 87(3): see text and note 10.

14   Communications Act 2003 s 87(5A) (s 87(5A)–(5C) added by SI 2011/1210). A condition falling within the Communications Act 2003 s 87(5A) may provide that compliance with the condition is not required unless a person on whom an entitlement is or may be conferred in pursuance of a requirement imposed by a condition under s 87(3) fulfils such technical or operational requirements as may be specified by OFCOM: s 87(5B) (as so added). It is the duty of OFCOM, when setting a condition falling within s 87(5A), to ensure that it contains all such provision as they consider appropriate for the purpose of taking account of the relevant international standards: s 87(5C) (as so added).

15   Communications Act 2003 s 87(6)(a).

16   Communications Act 2003 s 87(6)(b).

17   Communications Act 2003 s 87(6)(c). 'Access contract' means a contract for the provision by a person to whom s 87 applies to another person of network access to the relevant network or a contract under which the relevant facilities are made available by a person to whom s 87 applies to another person: s 87(12).

18   Communications Act 2003 s 87(6)(d).

19   Communications Act 2003 s 87(6)(e).

20   Communications Act 2003 s 87(7). The SMP conditions authorised by s 87(7) include conditions imposing requirements about the accounting methods to be used in maintaining the separation: s 87(8).

21   Ie subject to the Communications Act 2003 s 88: see note 22.

22   Communications Act 2003 s 87(9)(a). The SMP conditions authorised by s 87(9) include conditions requiring the application of presumptions in the fixing and determination of costs and charges for the purposes of the price controls, rules and obligations imposed by virtue of s 87(9): s 87(10).

   OFCOM is not to set an SMP condition falling within s 87(9) except where:

   (1)   it appears to OFCOM from the market analysis carried out for the purpose of setting that condition that there is a relevant risk of adverse effects arising from price distortion (s 88(1)(a)); and

    (2)   it also appears to OFCOM that the setting of the condition is appropriate for the purposes of promoting efficiency, promoting sustainable competition and conferring the greatest possible benefits on the end-users of public electronic communications services (s 88(1)(b)).

In setting an SMP condition falling within s 87(9) OFCOM must take account of the extent of the investment in the matters to which the condition relates of the person to whom it is to apply: s 88(2). For these purposes there is a relevant risk of adverse effects arising from price distortion if the dominant provider might so fix and maintain some or all of his prices at an excessively high level or so impose a price squeeze, as to have adverse consequences for end-users of public electronic communications services: s 88(3). 'Dominant provider' has the same meaning as in s 87: s 88(5). In considering the matters mentioned in head (2) OFCOM may have regard to the prices at which services are available in comparable competitive markets and determine what it considers to represent efficiency by using such cost accounting methods as it thinks fit: s 88(4).

23 Communications Act 2003 s 87(9)(b).

24 Communications Act 2003 s 87(9)(c). Where OFCOM sets a condition authorised by s 87 which imposes rules on the dominant provider about the use of cost accounting systems, it is its duty also to set, and to apply to him, an SMP condition which imposes on him an obligation:
    (1)   to make arrangements for a description to be made available to the public of the cost accounting system used in pursuance of that condition (s 87(11)(a)); and
    (2)   to include in that description details of:
        (a)   the main categories under which costs are brought into account for the purposes of that system (s 87(11)(b)(i)); and
        (b)   the rules applied for the purposes of that system with respect to the allocation of costs (s 87(11)(b)(ii)).

25 Communications Act 2003 s 87(9)(d).

112. Conditions as to network access and carrier selection. Where:

    (1)   OFCOM[1] has made a determination that a person (the 'dominant provider') has significant market power[2] in an identified services market[3];

    (2)   that person is the provider of an electronic communications network[4] or a person who makes associated facilities[5] available[6]; and

    (3)   OFCOM considers that there are exceptional circumstances making it appropriate for conditions with respect to the provision of network access[7] to be applied to the dominant provider in addition to those that are required to be or may be applied to him apart from these provisions[8],

OFCOM may set the additional SMP conditions[9] and apply them to the dominant provider if it has submitted the additional conditions to the European Commission[10] for approval and the Commission has approved the imposition on the dominant provider of the obligations contained in those conditions[11].

Where head (1) applies[12] and:

    (a)   the dominant provider is the provider of a public electronic communications network[13] or a person who makes available facilities that are associated facilities by reference to such a network[14];

    (b)   it appears to OFCOM that the setting of conditions applying to the dominant provider[15] has failed to address competition problems identified by OFCOM in carrying out a market analysis for the purpose of setting or modifying those conditions[16]; and

    (c)   OFCOM has identified important and persisting competition problems or market failures in relation to the provision of network access[17],

OFCOM may set an SMP services condition ('functional separation condition'[18]) requiring the dominant provider to transfer activities relating to the provision of network access to an independently operating business entity which is a part of the dominant provider[19].

Where OFCOM propose to apply a functional separation condition to a person, they must submit their proposal, including the draft functional separation condition, to the European Commission[20]. OFCOM may set the functional separation condition and apply it to a person if the Commission has approved the imposition on the person of the obligations contained in the condition, and OFCOM have considered the impact that the obligations contained in the condition and approved by the Commission are likely to have on SMP services conditions set in relation to the services markets which, in OFCOM's opinion, will be affected by the proposed condition[21].

Where head (1) applies[22] and:

(i)   the dominant provider is the provider of a public electronic communications network or a person who makes associated facilities available[23]; and

(ii)   the dominant provider decides to transfer a substantial part or all of the dominant provider's local access network assets to an independently operating business entity (which may be a part of the dominant provider or another person) for the purpose of using the assets to provide products or services to the dominant provider and to other persons on the same timescales, terms and conditions, including those relating to price and service levels and by means of the same systems and processes[24],

the dominant provider must notify OFCOM of the decision to transfer the assets, any changes to its intentions and the taking effect of the transfer[25].

1   As to the meaning of 'OFCOM' see PARA 14 note 1; and as to OFCOM see PARA 2 et seq.
2   As to significant market power see PARA 106. As to the meaning of 'person' see PARA 14 note 2.
3   Communications Act 2003 s 89(1)(a). As to the meaning of 'services market' see PARA 88 note 10.
4   As to the meaning of 'electronic communications network' see PARA 53.
5   As to the meaning of 'associated facilities' see PARA 53.
6   Communications Act 2003 s 89(1)(b).
7   As to the meaning of 'network access' see PARA 98 note 5.
8   Communications Act 2003 s 89(1)(c).
9   As to the meaning of 'SMP condition' see PARA 87 text and note 8.
10 As to the European Commission see EUROPEAN UNION vol 47A (2014) PARAS 48, 49.
11 Communications Act 2003 s 89(2).
12 Communications Act 2003 s 89A(1)(a) (ss 89A–89C added by SI 2011/1210).
13 As to the meaning of 'public electronic communications network' see PARA 98 note 6.
14 Communications Act 2003 s 89A(1)(b) (as added: see note 12).
15 Ie under the Communications Act 2003 s 87 and, where OFCOM think it appropriate, s 88).
16 Communications Act 2003 s 89A(1)(c) (as added: see note 12).
17 Communications Act 2003 s 89A(1)(d) (as added: see note 12).
18 Ie referred to in the Communications Act 2003 s 89A, 89B as such.
19 Communications Act 2003 s 89A(2) (as added: see note 12). Where a functional separation condition is imposed on the dominant provider, the products or services specified in the condition must be given to the dominant provider and to other persons on the same timescales, terms and conditions, including those relating to price and service levels, and by means of the same systems and processes: s 89A(3) (as so added).
    A functional separation condition must, where relevant, specify:
    (1)   the precise nature and level of separation, specifying in particular the legal status of the entity to which activities are transferred (s 89A(4)(a) (as so added));
    (2)   an identification of the assets of that entity and the products or services to be supplied by it (s 89A(4)(b) (as so added));
    (3)   the governance arrangements (including incentive structures) to ensure the independence of the staff employed in that entity (s 89A(4)(c) (as so added));
    (4)   rules for ensuring compliance with the obligations imposed by the condition (s 89A(4)(d) (as so added));
    (5)   rules for ensuring transparency of operational procedures, in particular towards

persons, other than the dominant provider, who in OFCOM's opinion are likely to be affected by the condition (s 89A(4)(e) (as so added)); and

(6) a monitoring programme to ensure compliance, including a requirement for the publication of an annual report (s 89A(4)(f) (as so added)).

20 Communications Act 2003 s 89B(1) (as added: see note 12). The proposal must set out:

(1) evidence justifying the conclusions mentioned in head (b) and (c) in the text (s 89B(2)(a) (as so added));

(2) a reasoned assessment that there is little or no prospect of effective and sustainable infrastructure based competition within a reasonable time frame (s 89B(2)(b) (as so added));

(3) an analysis of the expected impact of the condition on OFCOM, the person on whom the condition is to be imposed, the staff of the entity to which activities are to be transferred, the electronic communications sector as a whole, incentives to invest in the electronic communications sector, particularly with regard to the need to ensure social and territorial cohesion, competition in the services market affected by the condition and other persons who in OFCOM's opinion are likely to be affected by the condition, including, in particular, consumers (s 89B(2)(c) (as so added)); and

(4) an analysis of the reasons why a functional separation condition would be the most effective means of addressing important and persisting competition problems or market failures identified by OFCOM (s 89B(2)(d) (as so added)).

A proposal for a functional separation condition is to be submitted to the European Commission under s 89B before OFCOM carry out a consultation under s 48A (see PARA 91) in relation to the condition: s 89B(4) (as so added).

21 Communications Act 2003 s 89B(3) (as added: see note 12).

22 Communications Act 2003 s 89C(1)(a) (as added: see note 12).

23 Communications Act 2003 s 89C(1)(b) (as added: see note 12).

24 Communications Act 2003 s 89C(1)(c), (2) (as added: see note 12).

25 Communications Act 2003 s 89C(3) (as added: see note 12). Where OFCOM receive a notification under s 89C, it must, as soon as reasonably practicable, consider the impact that the transfer is likely to have on SMP services conditions set in relation to the services markets which, in OFCOM's opinion, will be affected by the proposed transfer: s 89C(4) (as so added).

113. Conditions as to regulation of services for end users and leased lines.
Where:

(1) OFCOM[1] has made a determination that a person (the 'dominant provider') has significant market power[2] in an identified services market[3] (the 'relevant market')[4];

(2) the relevant market is one for the end-users of public electronic communications services[5] that are available in that market[6]; and

(3) it appears to OFCOM that the test set out below is satisfied in the case of that provider[7],

it must set, and apply to that provider, such SMP conditions[8] authorised by these provisions as it considers appropriate[9].

That test is that OFCOM is unable, by the setting of access-related conditions[10] and SMP conditions[11], to perform, or fully to perform, its duties for the purpose of fulfilling European Union (EU) obligations[12] in relation to the market situation in the relevant market[13]. Where OFCOM sets a condition which is authorised by these provisions and imposes regulatory control on tariffs or other matters to which costs are relevant, it must also set, and apply to the dominant provider, an SMP condition which requires him, to the extent that OFCOM consider it appropriate:

(a) to use such cost accounting systems as may be determined by it[14];

(b) to have the use of those systems audited annually by a qualified auditor[15]; and

(c) to publish an annual statement about compliance by the dominant provider with the obligations imposed by virtue of head (a)[16].

1   As to the meaning of 'OFCOM' see PARA 14 note 1; and as to OFCOM see PARA 2 et seq.

2   As to significant market power see PARA 106. As to the meaning of 'person' see PARA 14 note 2.
3   As to the meaning of 'services market' see PARA 88 note 10.
4   Communications Act 2003 s 91(1)(a).
5   As to the meaning of 'public electronic communications service' see PARA 98 note 3.
6   Communications Act 2003 s 91(1)(b).
7   Communications Act 2003 s 91(1)(c).
8   As to the meaning of 'SMP condition' see PARA 87 text and note 8.
9   Communications Act 2003 s 91(1).
10   As to the meaning of 'access-related condition' see PARA 87 note 6.
11   Ie SMP conditions authorised or required by the Communications Act 2003 ss 87–89: see PARAS 111–112. As to the meaning of 'SMP condition' see PARA 87 text and note 8. The SMP conditions authorised by s 91 are conditions imposing on the dominant provider such regulatory controls as OFCOM may from time to time direct in relation to the provision by that provider of any public electronic communications service to the end-users of that service: s 91(5).
12   Ie its duties under the Communications Act 2003 s 4: see PARA 17.
13   Communications Act 2003 s 91(2), (3) (s 91(3) amended by SI 2011/1210). The reference to the market situation in the relevant market is a reference to the situation revealed by such market analyses of that market as may have been carried out for the purposes of the Communications Act 2003 Pt 2 Ch 1 (ss 32–151): s 91(4).
14   Communications Act 2003 s 91(6)(a).
15   Communications Act 2003 s 91(6)(b). For these purposes, 'qualified auditor' means a person who:
    (1)   is eligible for appointment as a statutory auditor under the Companies Act 2006 Pt 42 (ss 1209–1264) (see COMPANIES vol 15 (2009) PARA 958) (Communications Act 2003 s 91(8)(a) (s 91(8) substituted by SI 2008/948)); and
    (2)   if the appointment to carry out such auditing as is mentioned in head (b) in the text were an appointment as a statutory auditor, would not be prohibited from acting by the Companies Act 2006 s 1214 (independence requirement: see COMPANIES vol 15 (2009) PARA 971) (s 91(8)(b) (as so substituted)).
16   Communications Act 2003 s 91(6)(c).

114. SMP apparatus conditions: subject matter. Where OFCOM[1] has made a determination that a person (the 'dominant supplier') has significant market power in an identified apparatus market[2], it may:

    (1)   set such SMP conditions[3] authorised by these provisions as it considers appropriate to apply to that person in respect of the supply of electronic communications apparatus[4]; and

    (2)   apply those conditions to that person[5].

These provisions authorise the setting of SMP conditions of each of the following descriptions:

    (a)   conditions requiring the dominant supplier to maintain such a separation for accounting purposes between matters relating to the supply of electronic communications apparatus and other matters as may be described in the conditions[6];

    (b)   conditions imposing requirements about the accounting methods to be used in maintaining the separation[7]; and

    (c)   conditions imposing such rules as OFCOM may make, for the purpose of securing the maintenance of the separation, about the use of cost accounting systems[8].

These provisions also authorise the setting of SMP conditions imposing price controls in relation to the hiring of telephones which are hardwired to an electronic communications network[9]. Conditions set under these provisions must not make provision in relation to the supply of electronic communications apparatus unless the apparatus is of a description of apparatus as respects the supply of which the dominant supplier has been found to have significant market power[10].

1   As to the meaning of 'OFCOM' see PARA 14 note 1; and as to OFCOM see PARA 2 et seq.
2   As to significant market power see PARA 106. As to the meaning of 'person' see PARA 14 note 2. As to the meaning of 'apparatus market' see PARA 88 note 10.
3   As to the meaning of 'SMP condition' see PARA 87 text and note 8.
4   Communications Act 2003 s 93(1)(a). As to the meaning of 'electronic communications apparatus' see PARA 88 note 10.
5   Communications Act 2003 s 93(1)(b).
6   Communications Act 2003 s 93(2)(a).
7   Communications Act 2003 s 93(2)(b).
8   Communications Act 2003 s 93(2)(c).
9   Communications Act 2003 s 93(3). For the purposes of s 93, a telephone is hardwired to an electronic communications network where, in order for it to be used with that network it has to be physically attached to apparatus comprised in the network and the attachment has to be effected by a process that requires the use of a tool: s 93(5). As to the meaning of 'electronic communications network' see PARA 53.
10 Communications Act 2003 s 93(4).

C. ENFORCEMENT OF CONDITIONS

115.   Notification of contravention of SMP apparatus conditions. Where OFCOM[1] determines that there are reasonable grounds for believing that a person[2] is contravening, or has contravened, an SMP apparatus condition[3], it may give that person a notification under the following provisions[4]. A notification under these provisions is one which:

(1)   sets out the determination made by OFCOM[5];
(2)   specifies the condition and contravention in respect of which that determination has been made[6]; and
(3)   specifies the period during which the person notified has an opportunity of:
    (a)   making representations about the matters notified[7];
    (b)   complying with notified conditions of which he remains in contravention[8]; and
    (c)   remedying the consequences of notified contraventions[9].

The period for doing those things is the period of one month beginning with the day after the one on which the notification was given[10].

A notification under these provisions:

(i)   may be given in respect of more than one contravention[11]; and
(ii)   if it is given in respect of a continuing contravention, may be given in respect of any period during which the contravention has continued[12].

Where a notification has been given to a person in respect of a contravention of a condition, OFCOM may give a further notification in respect of the same contravention of that condition if, and only if:

(A)   the contravention is one occurring after the time of the giving of the earlier notification[13];
(B)   the contravention is a continuing contravention and the subsequent notification is in respect of so much of a period as falls after a period to which the earlier notification relates[14]; or
(C)   the earlier notification has been withdrawn without a penalty having been imposed in respect of the notified contravention[15].

Before giving a notification under these provisions, OFCOM must consider whether it would be more appropriate to proceed under the Competition Act 1998 and if considers that it would be more appropriate to proceed under the Competition Act 1998, it must not give such a notification[16].

1   As to the meaning of 'OFCOM' see PARA 14 note 1; and as to OFCOM see PARA 2 et seq.

2 As to the meaning of 'person' see PARA 14 note 2.
3 As to the meaning of 'SMP apparatus condition' see PARA 87 note 8.
4 Communications Act 2003 s 94(1) (amended by SI 2011/1210).
5 Communications Act 2003 s 94(2)(a).
6 Communications Act 2003 s 94(2)(b).
7 Communications Act 2003 s 94(2)(c), (3)(a).
8 Communications Act 2003 s 94(2)(c), (3)(b).
9 Communications Act 2003 s 94(2)(c), (3)(c).
10 Communications Act 2003 s 94(4). Section 94(4) is subject to s 94(5)–(7)and s 98(3) (repealed):
   s 94(4). OFCOM may, if it thinks fit, allow a longer period for doing those things either:
   (1) by specifying a longer period in the notification (s 94(5)(a)); or
   (2) by subsequently, on one or more occasions, extending the specified period (s 94(5)(b)).
   The person notified will have a shorter period for doing those things if a shorter period is
   agreed between OFCOM and the person notified: s 94(6). The person notified will also have a
   shorter period if:
   (a) OFCOM has reasonable grounds for believing that the contravention is a repeated
        contravention (s 94(7)(a));
   (b) it has determined that, in those circumstances, a shorter period would be appropriate
        (s 94(7)(b)); and
   (c) the shorter period has been specified in the notification (s 94(7)(c)).
   For the purposes of s 94, a contravention is a repeated contravention, in relation to a
   notification with respect to that contravention, if:
   (i)   a previous notification under s 94 has been given in respect of the same contravention
         or in respect of another contravention of the same condition (s 94(11)(a)); and
   (ii) the subsequent notification is given no more than 12 months after the day of the
         making by OFCOM of a determination for the purposes of s 95(2) or s 96(2) (see PARAS
         116, 119) that the contravention to which the previous notification related did occur
         (s 94(11)(b)).
11 Communications Act 2003 s 94(8)(a).
12 Communications Act 2003 s 94(8)(b).
13 Communications Act 2003 s 94(9)(a).
14 Communications Act 2003 s 94(9)(b).
15 Communications Act 2003 s 94(9)(c).
16 Communications Act 2003 s 94(10), (10A) (s 94(10) substituted; s 94(10A), (10B) added by the
   Enterprise and Regulatory Reform Act 2013 Sch 14 para 17). In a case where OFCOM decides
   that it would be more appropriate to proceed under the Competition Act 1998, it must publish
   a statement to that effect in such manner as it considers appropriate for bringing the decision to
   the attention of persons whom it considers are likely to be affected by it: Communications
   Act 2003 s 94(10B) (as so added).

116. Enforcement notification for contravention of SMP apparatus conditions. Where:

(1) a person (the 'notified provider') has been given a notification of a
     contravention of an SMP apparatus condition[1];

(2) OFCOM has allowed the notified provider an opportunity of making
     representations about the matters notified[2]; and

(3) the period allowed for the making of the representations has expired[3],

OFCOM may give the notified provider an enforcement notification[4] if it is
satisfied:

(a) that he has, in one or more of the respects notified, been in
     contravention of a condition specified in the notification[5]; and

(b) that he has not, during the period allowed, taken all such steps as
     OFCOM considers appropriate:
     (i)   for complying with that condition[6]; and
     (ii) for remedying the consequences of the notified contravention of
           that condition[7].

A decision of OFCOM to give an enforcement notification to a person:

(A)   must be notified by it to that person, together with the reasons for the decision, no later than one week after the day on which it is taken[8]; and

(B)   must fix a reasonable period for the taking of the steps required by the notification[9].

It is the duty of a person to whom an enforcement notification has been given to comply with it[10].

1   Communications Act 2003 s 95(1)(a). The notification referred to in the text is one by OFCOM under the Communications Act 2003 s 94: see PARA 115. As to the meaning of 'OFCOM' see PARA 14 note 1; and as to OFCOM see PARA 2 et seq. As to the meaning of 'person' see PARA 14 note 2. As to the meaning of 'SMP apparatus condition' see PARA 87 note 8.
2   Communications Act 2003 s 95(1)(b).
3   Communications Act 2003 s 95(1)(c).
4   An enforcement notification is a notification which imposes one or both of the following requirements on the notified provider:
     (1)   a requirement to take such steps for complying with the notified condition as may be specified in the notification (Communications Act 2003 s 95(3)(a));
     (2)   a requirement to take such steps for remedying the consequences of the notified contravention as may be so specified (s 95(3)(b)).
5   Communications Act 2003 s 95(2)(a). The notification referred to in the text is one by OFCOM under s 94: see PARA 115.
6   Communications Act 2003 s 95(2)(b)(i).
7   Communications Act 2003 s 95(2)(b)(ii).
8   Communications Act 2003 s 95(4)(a).
9   Communications Act 2003 s 95(4)(b).
10   Communications Act 2003 s 95(5). That duty is enforceable in civil proceedings by OFCOM for an injunction or for any other appropriate remedy or relief: s 95(6).

117. Notification of contravention of conditions other than SMP apparatus conditions. Where OFCOM[1] determines that there are reasonable grounds for believing that a person[2] is contravening, or has contravened, a condition (other than an SMP apparatus condition)[3], it may give that person a notification under the following provisions[4]. A notification under these provisions is one which:

(1)   sets out the determination made by OFCOM[5];

(2)   specifies the condition and contravention in respect of which that determination has been made[6];

(3)   specifies the period during which the person notified has an opportunity to make representations[7];

(4)   specifies the steps that OFCOM thinks should be taken by the person in order to:
     (a)   comply with the condition[8];
     (b)   remedy the consequences of the contravention[9];

(5)   specifies any penalty which OFCOM is minded to impose[10];

(6)   where the contravention is serious, specifies any direction which OFCOM is minded to give[11]; and

(7)   where the contravention relates to a condition set[12], specifies any direction which OFCOM is minded to give[13].

A notification under these provisions may be given in respect of more than one contravention and if it is given in respect of a continuing contravention, may be given in respect of any period during which the contravention has continued[14].

Where a notification has been given to a person in respect of a contravention of a condition, OFCOM may give a further notification in respect of the same contravention of that condition if, and only if:

(i)   the contravention is one occurring after the time of the giving of the earlier notification[15];

(ii)   the contravention is a continuing contravention and the subsequent notification is in respect of so much of a period as falls after a period to which the earlier notification relates[16]; or

(iii)   the earlier notification has been withdrawn without a penalty having been imposed in respect of the notified contravention[17].

Before giving a notification under these provisions, OFCOM must consider whether it would be more appropriate to proceed under the Competition Act 1998 and, if considers that it would be more appropriate to proceed under the Competition Act 1998, it must not give such a notification[18].

1   As to the meaning of 'OFCOM' see PARA 14 note 1; and as to OFCOM see PARA 2 et seq.
2   As to the meaning of 'person' see PARA 14 note 2.
3   Ie set under the Communications Act 2003 s 45. As to the meaning of 'SMP apparatus condition' see PARA 87 note 8.
4   Communications Act 2003 s 96A(1) (s 96A added by SI 2011/1210).
5   Communications Act 2003 s 96A(2)(a) (as added: see note 4).
6   Communications Act 2003 s 96A(2)(b) (as added: see note 4).
7   Communications Act 2003 s 96A(2)(c) (as added: see note 4).
8   Communications Act 2003 s 96A(2)(d)(i) (as added: see note 4).
9   Communications Act 2003 s 96A(2)(d)(ii) (as added: see note 4).
10   Communications Act 2003 s 96A(2)(e) (as added: see note 4). The penalties referred to in the text are those OFCOM is minded to impose under s 96B: see PARA 119.
11   Communications Act 2003 s 96A(2)(f) (as added: see note 4). The directions referred to in the text are those OFCOM is minded to give under s 100: see PARA 121.
12   Ie under the Communications Act 2003 ss 87–91: see PARA 111 et seq.
13   Communications Act 2003 s 96A(2)(f) (as added: see note 4). The directions referred to in the text are those OFCOM is minded to give under s 100A: see PARA 122.
14   Communications Act 2003 s 96A(3) (as added: see note 4).
15   Communications Act 2003 s 96A(4)(a) (as added: see note 4).
16   Communications Act 2003 s 96A(4)(b) (as added: see note 4).
17   Communications Act 2003 s 96A(4)(c) (as added: see note 4).
18   Communications Act 2003 s 96A(5), (6) (s 96A as added; s 96A(5)–(7) substituted by the Enterprise and Regulatory Reform Act 2013 Sch 14 para 18). In a case where OFCOM decides that it would be more appropriate to proceed under the Competition Act 1998, it must publish a statement to that effect in such manner as it considers appropriate for bringing the decision to the attention of persons whom it considers are likely to be affected by it: Communications Act 2003 s 96A(7) (as so added and substituted).

118.   Enforcement of notification of contravention of conditions other than SMP apparatus conditions. Where:

(1)   a person has been given a notification of a contravention of a condition other than an SMP apparatus condition[1];

(2)   OFCOM has allowed the person an opportunity to make representations about the matters notified[2]; and

(3)   the period allowed for the making of representations has expired[3],

OFCOM may:

(a)   give the person a decision (a 'confirmation decision') confirming the imposition of requirements on the person, or the giving of a direction to the person, or both, in accordance with the notification[4]; or

(b)   inform the person that it is satisfied with the person's representations and that no further action will be taken[5].

OFCOM may not give a confirmation decision to a person unless, after considering any representations, it is satisfied that the person has, in one or more of the respects notified, been in contravention of a condition specified in the notification[6].

A confirmation decision:

(i)   must be given to the person without delay[7];

(ii)   must include reasons for the decision[8];

(iii)   may require immediate action by the person to comply with specified requirements[9], or may specify a period within which the person must comply with those requirements[10]; and

(iv)   may require the person to pay the penalty specified in the notification[11], or such lesser penalty as OFCOM considers appropriate in the light of the person's representations or steps taken by the person to comply with the condition or remedy the consequences of the contravention, and may specify the period within which the penalty is to be paid[12].

It is the duty of the person to comply with any requirement imposed by a confirmation decision[13].

1   Communications Act 2003 s 96C(1)(a) (s 96A added by SI 2011/1210). The notification referred to in the text is one by OFCOM under the Communications Act 2003 s 96A: see PARA 117. As to the meaning of 'OFCOM' see PARA 14 note 1; and as to OFCOM see PARA 2 et seq. As to the meaning of 'person' see PARA 14 note 2. As to the meaning of 'SMP apparatus condition' see PARA 87 note 8.

2   Communications Act 2003 s 96C(1)(b) (as added: see note 1).

3   Communications Act 2003 s 96C(1)(c) (as added: see note 1).

4   Communications Act 2003 s 96C(2)(a) (as added: see note 1). The notification referred to in the text is one by OFCOM under s 96A: see PARA 117.

5   Communications Act 2003 s 96C(2)(b) (as added: see note 1).

6   Communications Act 2003 s 96C(3) (as added: see note 1). The notification referred to in the text is one by OFCOM under s 96A: see PARA 117.

7   Communications Act 2003 s 96C(4)(a) (as added: see note 1).

8   Communications Act 2003 s 96C(4)(b) (as added: see note 1).

9   Ie of a kind mentioned in Communications Act 2003 s 96A(2)(d): see PARA 117.

10   Communications Act 2003 s 96C(4)(c) (as added: see note 1).

11   Ie under the Communications Act 2003 s 96A: see PARA 117.

12   Communications Act 2003 s 96C(4)(d) (as added: see note 1). A penalty imposed by a confirmation decision must be paid to OFCOM and if not paid within the period specified by them, is to be recoverable by them accordingly: s 96C(7) (as so added).

13   Communications Act 2003 s 96C(5) (as added: see note 1). That duty is enforceable in civil proceedings by OFCOM for an injunction or for any other appropriate remedy or relief: s 96C(6).

119. Penalties for contravention of conditions. Where[1]:

(1)   a person (the 'notified provider') has been given a notification of a contravention of an SMP apparatus condition[2];

(2)   OFCOM[3] has allowed the notified provider an opportunity of making representations about the matters notified[4]; and

(3)   the period allowed for the making of the representations has expired[5],

OFCOM may impose a penalty on the notified provider if he:

(a)   has, in one or more of the respects notified, been in contravention of a condition specified in the notification[6]; and

(b)   has not, during the period allowed[7], taken the steps OFCOM considers appropriate for complying with the notified condition and for remedying the consequences of the notified contravention of that condition[8].

Where a notification relates to more than one contravention, a separate penalty may be imposed in respect of each contravention[9]. Where such a notification relates to a continuing contravention, no more than one penalty may be imposed in respect of the period of contravention specified in the notification[10]. OFCOM may also impose a penalty on the notified provider if he has contravened, or is contravening, a requirement of an enforcement notification[11] in respect of the notified contravention[12].

Where OFCOM imposes a penalty on a person under the provisions described above, it must within one week of making its decision to impose the penalty, notify that person of that decision and of OFCOM's reasons for that decision and in that notification, fix a reasonable period after it is given as the period within which the penalty is to be paid[13]. A penalty imposed under these provisions must be paid to OFCOM; and, if not paid within the fixed period, is recoverable by OFCOM accordingly[14].

Where a person is given a notification of a contravention of a condition other than an SMP apparatus condition[15] which specifies a proposed penalty, the following applies[16]:

(i) where the notification relates to more than one contravention, a separate penalty may be specified in respect of each contravention[17];

(ii) where the notification relates to a continuing contravention, no more than one penalty may be specified in respect of the period of contravention specified in the notification[18];

(iii) in relation to a continuing contravention, a penalty may be specified in respect of each day on which the contravention continues after:

(A) the giving of a confirmation decision[19] which requires immediate action[20]; or

(B) the expiry of any period specified in the confirmation decision for complying with a requirement so specified[21].

The amount of a penalty imposed under these provisions[22] is to be such amount not exceeding 10 per cent of the turnover[23] of the person's relevant business[24] for the relevant period[25] as OFCOM determines to be appropriate; and it must be proportionate to the contravention in respect of which it is imposed[26]. In making a determination in relation to a penalty imposed where a person has been given a notification of a contravention of an SMP apparatus condition[27], OFCOM must have regard to any representations made to it by the person, any steps taken by him towards complying with the conditions contraventions of which have been notified to him[28], and any steps taken by him for remedying the consequences of those contraventions[29].

1   The Communications Act 2003 s 96 applies in addition to the Communications Act 2003 s 95 (see PARA 116) where the circumstances in heads (1)–(3) in the text exist.

2   Communications Act 2003 s 96(1)(a). The notification referred to in the text is one by OFCOM under the Communications Act 2003 s 94: see PARA 115. As to the meaning of 'person' see PARA 14 note 2. As to the meaning of 'SMP apparatus condition' see PARA 87 note 8.

3   As to the meaning of 'OFCOM' see PARA 14 note 1; and as to OFCOM see PARA 2 et seq.

4   Communications Act 2003 s 96(1)(b).

5   Communications Act 2003 s 96(1)(c).

6   Communications Act 2003 s 96(2)(a). The notification referred to in the text is one by OFCOM under s 94: see PARA 115.

7   Ie the period allowed under the Communications Act 2003 s 94: see PARA 115.

8   Communications Act 2003 s 96(2)(b).

9   Communications Act 2003 s 96(3).

10 Communications Act 2003 s 96(4).

11 Ie given under the Communications Act 2003 s 95: see PARA 116.

12 Communications Act 2003 s 96(5).

13 Communications Act 2003 s 96(6).

14 Communications Act 2003 s 96(7).

15 Ie under the Communications Act 2003 s 96A: see PARA 117.

16 Communications Act 2003 s 96B(1) (s 96B added by SI 2011/1210).

17 Communications Act 2003 s 96B(2) (as added: see note 16).

18 Communications Act 2003 s 96B(3) (as added: see note 16).

19 Ie under the Communications Act 2003 s 96C(4)(c): see PARA 118.

20 Communications Act 2003 s 96B(4)(a) (as added: see note 16). The amount of a penalty under s 96C(4) is to be such amount not exceeding £20,000 per day as OFCOM determines to be appropriate and proportionate to the contravention in respect of which it is imposed: s 96B(5) (as so added).

21 Communications Act 2003 s 96B(4)(b) (as added: see note 16). See note 20.

22 Ie under the Communications Act 2003 s 96 (see PARA 119) or notified under s 96A (see PARA 117) (other than a penalty falling within s 96B(4) (see text and notes 20, 21)).

23 For the purposes of the Communications Act 2003 s 97, the turnover of a person's relevant business for a period is to be calculated in accordance with such rules as may be set out by order made by the Secretary of State, and provision may also be made by such an order for determining what is to be treated as the network, service, facility or business by reference to which the calculation of that turnover falls to be made: see s 97(3), (4). See the Electronic Communications (Networks and Services) (Penalties) (Rules for Calculation of Turnover) Order 2003, SI 2003/2712. As to the Secretary of State see PARA 76 note 1.

24 'Relevant business' means (subject to the provisions of an order under the Communications Act 2003 s 97(3) (see note 23) and to s 97(6), (7)) so much of any business carried on by the person as consists in any one or more of the following:
    (1)   the provision of an electronic communications network;
    (2)   the provision of an electronic communications service;
    (3)   the making available of associated facilities;
    (4)   the supply of directories for use in connection with the use of such a network or service;
    (5)   the making available of directory inquiry facilities for use for purposes connected with the use of such a network or service;
    (6)   any business not falling within any of heads (1)–(5) which is carried on in association with any business in respect of which any access-related condition is applied to the person carrying it on: s 97(5) (definition amended by SI 2011/1210).
As to the meaning of 'electronic communications network' see PARA 53. As to the meaning of 'access-related condition' see PARA 87 note 6. As to access-related conditions see further PARA 104. In the case of a contravention of an SMP apparatus condition, the relevant business is so much of any business carried on by the person in respect of whose contravention the penalty is imposed as consists in the supply of electronic communications apparatus: Communications Act 2003 s 97(6). So much of any business of a person on whom the penalty is imposed as falls within head (6) is to be disregarded for the purposes of s 97 except in relation to a contravention of an access-related condition imposed in respect of that business or a contravention of an enforcement notification given under s 95 (see PARA 116) or a confirmation decision under s 96C (see PARA 118) relating to such a condition: s 97(7) (amended by SI 2011/1210). As to the meaning of 'electronic communications apparatus' see PARA 88 note 10. As to the meaning of 'SMP apparatus condition' see PARA 87 note 8. As to SMP apparatus conditions see further PARA 114.

25 'Relevant period, in relation to a contravention by a person of a condition set under the Communications Act 2003 s 45 (see PARA 87), means:
    (1)   except in a case falling within head (2) or head (3), the period of one year ending with 31 March next before the time when notification of the contravention was given under s 94 (see PARA 115) or 96A (see PARA 117);
    (2)   in the case of a person who at that time has been carrying on that business for a period of less than a year, the period, ending with that time, during which he has been carrying it on; and
    (3)   in the case of a person who at that time has ceased to carry on that business, the period of one year ending with the time when he ceased to carry it on: s 97(5) (definition amended by SI 2011/1210).

26 Communications Act 2003 s 97(1) (amended by SI 2011/1210).

27 Ie in relation to a penalty imposed under the Communications Act 2003 s 96: see text and notes 1–14.

28 Ie under the Communications Act 2003 s 94: see PARA 115.

29 Communications Act 2003 s 97(2) (amended by SI 2011/1210).

120. Power to deal with urgent cases: contravention of condition. Where OFCOM[1] determines:
    (1)   that it is entitled to give a notification of a contravention of a condition

other than an SMP apparatus condition[2] with respect to a contravention by a person (the 'contravening provider') of a condition set by OFCOM[3];

(2) that there are reasonable grounds for suspecting that the case is an urgent case[4]; and

(3) that the urgency of the case makes it appropriate for OFCOM to take action[5],

OFCOM has power to give to the contravening provider:

(a) a direction that his entitlement to provide electronic communications networks[6] or electronic communications services[7], or to make associated facilities[8] available, is suspended (either generally or in relation to particular networks, services or facilities)[9]; or

(b) a direction that that entitlement is restricted in the respects set out in the direction[10].

As soon as reasonably practicable after giving a direction, OFCOM must give the person to whom it is given:

(i) an opportunity of making representations to it about the grounds on which the direction was given and its effect[11]; and

(ii) an opportunity of proposing steps to remedy the situation[12].

As soon as practicable after the period allowed by OFCOM for making those representations has ended and in any event within three months beginning with the day on which the direction[13] was given, it must determine whether the contravention providing the grounds for the giving of the direction did occur and whether the circumstances made it an urgent case justifying the giving of the direction[14]. If OFCOM decides that the contravention did occur and that the direction was justified, it may confirm the direction[15]. If not, it must exercise its power to revoke it[16]. As soon as reasonably practicable after determining whether to confirm the direction, OFCOM must notify the person to whom it was given of its decision[17]. Conditions included in a direction[18] have effect only if the direction is confirmed[19].

A person is guilty of an offence if he provides an electronic communications network or electronic communications service, or makes available any associated facility, while his entitlement to do so is suspended by a direction[20] or in contravention of a restriction contained in such a direction[21].

1 As to the meaning of 'OFCOM' see PARA 14 note 1; and as to OFCOM see PARA 2 et seq.
2 Ie under the Communications Act 2003 s 96A see PARA 117. As to the meaning of 'SMP apparatus condition' see PARA 87 note 8.
3 Communications Act 2003 s 98(1)(a) (amended by SI 2011/1210). The reference in the text to a condition is to a condition set under the Communications Act 2003 s 45: see PARA 87. As to the meaning of 'person' see PARA 14 note 2.
4 Communications Act 2003 s 98(1)(b). A case is an urgent case for the purposes of s 98 if the contravention has resulted in, or creates an immediate risk of:
   (1) a serious threat to the safety of the public, to public health or to national security (s 98(2)(a));
   (2) serious economic or operational problems for persons (other than the contravening provider) who are communications providers or persons who make associated facilities available (s 98(2)(b)); or
   (3) serious economic or operational problems for persons who make use of electronic communications networks, electronic communications services or associated facilities (s 98(2)(c)).
5 Communications Act 2003 s 98(1)(c).
6 As to the meaning of 'electronic communications network' see PARA 53.
7 As to the meaning of 'electronic communications service' see PARA 53.
8 As to the meaning of 'associated facilities' see PARA 53.

9   Communications Act 2003 s 98(4)(a) (s 98(4) amended by SI 2011/1210). A direction must specify the networks, services and facilities to which it relates and except so far as it otherwise provides, takes effect for an indefinite period beginning with the time at which it is notified to the person to whom it is given: Communications Act 2003 s 98(5). A direction,

 (1)   in providing for the effect of a suspension or restriction to be postponed, may provide for it to take effect only at a time determined by or in accordance with the terms of the direction (s 98(6)(a)); and

 (2)   in connection with the suspension or restriction contained in the direction or with the postponement of its effect, may impose such conditions on the contravening provider as appear to OFCOM to be appropriate for the purpose of protecting his customers (s 98(6)(b)).

Those conditions may include a condition requiring the making of payments:

 (a)   by way of compensation for loss or damage suffered by the contravening provider's customers as a result of the direction (s 98(7)(a)); or

 (b)   in respect of annoyance, inconvenience or anxiety to which they have been put in consequence of the direction (s 98(7)(b)).

As to the procedure for directions see PARA 124.

 OFCOM has power to revoke a direction:

 (i)   with effect from such time as it may direct (s 98(8)(a));

 (ii)   subject to compliance with such requirements as it may specify (s 98(8)(b)); and

 (iii) to such extent and in relation to such networks, services or facilities, or parts of a network, service or facility, as it may determine (s 98(8)(c)).

10 Communications Act 2003 s 98(4)(b) (as amended: see note 9). See note 9.
11 Communications Act 2003 s 99(1)(a).
12 Communications Act 2003 s 99(1)(b).
13 Ie under the Communications Act 2003 s 98(4): see text and notes 9–10.
14 Communications Act 2003 s 99(2) (amended by SI 2011/1210). The period of three months mentioned in the Communications Act 2003 s 99(2) may be extended by up to three months if OFCOM require additional time to consider representations received or decide that it is necessary to obtain additional information from the person in order to make a determination under s 99(2): s 99(2A) (added by SI 2011/1210).
15 Communications Act 2003 s 99(3).
16 Communications Act 2003 s 99(4).
17 Communications Act 2003 s 99(5).
18 Ie by virtue of the Communications Act 2003 s 98(7): see note 9.
19 Communications Act 2003 s 99(6).
20 Ie under the Communications Act 2003 s 98(4).
21 Communications Act 2003 s 103(1) (amended by SI 2011/1210). A person guilty of an offence under the Communications Act 2003 s 103 is liable:

 (1)   on summary conviction, to a fine not exceeding the statutory maximum (s 103(3)(a));

 (2)   on conviction on indictment, to a fine (s 103(3)(b)).

As to the statutory maximum see SENTENCING AND DISPOSITION OF OFFENDERS vol 92 (2010) PARA 140. Sections 96A–99 (see PARAS 117–120) apply in relation to a contravention of conditions imposed by a direction under s 98 as they apply in relation to a contravention of conditions set under s 45 (see PARA 87), other than SMP apparatus conditions: s 103(4) (substituted by SI 2011/1210). As to civil liability see PARA 125.

121.   Suspending service provision for contraventions of conditions other than SMP apparatus conditions.   OFCOM[1] may give a direction to a person[2] where:

 (1)   either of the following heads is satisfied in relation to the person[3]:

 (a)   the person is in serious contravention of a condition[4], other than SMP apparatus conditions[5] and the proposed direction has been notified to the person[6] and confirmed by a confirmation decision[7]; or

 (b)   the person has repeatedly contravened a condition[8], other than SMP apparatus conditions; and an attempt, by the imposition of penalties or the giving of notifications[9] and confirmation decisions[10], or both, to secure compliance with the contravened conditions has failed[11]; and

(2)   the giving of a direction is appropriate and proportionate to the contravention in respect of which it is imposed[12].

A direction under these provisions is:

(i)   a direction that the entitlement of the person to provide electronic communications networks[13] or electronic communications services[14], or to make associated facilities[15] available, is suspended (either generally or in relation to particular networks, services or facilities)[16]; or

(ii)   a direction that that entitlement is restricted in the respects set out in the direction[17].

A direction must specify the networks, services and facilities to which it relates; and, except so far as it otherwise provides, it takes effect for an indefinite period beginning with the time at which it is notified to the person to whom it is given[18]. A direction in providing for the effect of a suspension or restriction to be postponed, may provide for it to take effect only at a time determined by or in accordance with the terms of the direction[19]. A direction in connection with the suspension or restriction contained in the direction or with the postponement of its effect, may impose such conditions on the person as appear to OFCOM to be appropriate for the purpose of protecting that provider's customers[20]. If OFCOM considers it appropriate to do so (whether or not in consequence of representations or proposals made to it), it may revoke a direction under these provisions or modify its conditions:

(A)   with effect from such time as it may direct[21];

(B)   subject to compliance with such requirements as it may specify[22]; and

(C)   to such extent and in relation to such networks, services or facilities, or parts of a network, service or facility, as it may determine[23].

A person is guilty of an offence if he provides an electronic communications network or electronic communications service, or makes available any associated facility, while his entitlement to do so is suspended by a direction[24] or in contravention of a restriction contained in such a direction[25].

1   As to the meaning of 'OFCOM' see PARA 14 note 1; and as to OFCOM see PARA 2 et seq.

2   As to the meaning of 'person' see PARA 14 note 2.

3   Communications Act 2003 s 100(1)(a) (s 100(1) substituted by SI 2011/1210).

4   Ie a condition set under the Communications Act 2003 s 45: see PARA 87.

5   As to the meaning of 'SMP apparatus condition' see PARA 87 note 8.

6   Ie under the Communications Act 2003 s 96A: see PARA 117.

7   Communications Act 2003 s 100(1A) (s 100(1A)–(1D) added by SI 2011/1210). The reference in the text to a confirmation decision is a confirmation decision under the Communications Act 2003 s 96C (see PARA 118): s 100(1)(b) (as so substituted). Where the condition in head (1)(a) in the text is satisfied, a direction under s 100 is given where OFCOM give a confirmation decision under s 96C to the person in respect of a direction proposed in a notification under s 96A: s 100(1C) (as so added).

8   Ie a condition set under the Communications Act 2003 s 45: see PARA 87. For the purposes of s 100, there are repeated contraventions by a person of conditions set under s 45 to the extent that:

    (1)   in the case of a previous notification of a contravention given to that person under s 96A, OFCOM has given a confirmation decision to that person under s 96C(2) in respect of the contravention (s 100(7)(a) (s 100(7)(a), (b) substituted by SI 2011/1210));

    (2)   in the period of 24 months following the giving of that confirmation decision, one or more further confirmation decisions have been given to the person in respect of contraventions of a condition under the Communications Act 2003 s 45 (s 100(7)(b) (as so substituted)); and

    (3)   the previous confirmation decision and the subsequent ones all relate to contraventions of the same condition (whether the same contravention or different contraventions) (s 100(7)(c) (amended by SI 2011/1210)).

9   Ie under the Communications Act 2003 s 96A: see PARA 117.

10   Ie under the Communications Act 2003 s 96C: see PARA 118.

11 Communications Act 2003 s 100(1B) (as added: see note 6). Where the condition in head (1)(b) is satisfied, a direction under s 100 is to be given in accordance with the procedure set out in s 102: s 100(1D) (as so added).

12 Communications Act 2003 s 100(1)(b) (as substituted: see note 11).

13 As to the meaning of 'electronic communications networks' see PARA 53.

14 As to the meaning of 'electronic communications services' see PARA 53.

15 As to the meaning of 'associated facilities' see PARA 53.

16 Communications Act 2003 s 100(2)(a) (amended by SI 2011/1210).

17 Communications Act 2003 s 100(2)(b).

18 Communications Act 2003 s 100(3).

19 Communications Act 2003 s 100(4)(a).

20 Communications Act 2003 s 100(4)(b) (amended by SI 2011/1210). The conditions may include a condition requiring the making of payments:
  (1)   by way of compensation for loss or damage suffered by the person's customers as a result of the direction (Communications Act 2003 s 100(5)(a) (amended by SI 2011/1210)); or
  (2)   in respect of annoyance, inconvenience or anxiety to which they have been put in consequence of the direction (Communications Act 2003 s 100(5)(b)).

21 Communications Act 2003 s 100(6)(a).

22 Communications Act 2003 s 100(6)(b).

23 Communications Act 2003 s 100(6)(c).

24 Ie under the Communications Act 2003 s 100.

25 Communications Act 2003 s 103(1) (amended by SI 2011/1210). A person guilty of an offence under the Communications Act 2003 s 103 is liable:
  (1)   on summary conviction, to a fine not exceeding the statutory maximum (s 103(3)(a));
  (2)   on conviction on indictment, to a fine (s 103(3)(b)).
As to the statutory maximum see SENTENCING AND DISPOSITION OF OFFENDERS vol 92 (2010) PARA 140. Sections 96A–99 (see PARAS 117–120) apply in relation to a contravention of conditions imposed by a direction under s 100 as they apply in relation to a contravention of conditions set under s 45 (see PARA 87), other than SMP apparatus conditions: s 103(4) (substituted by SI 2011/1210). As to civil liability see PARA 125.

122.   Suspending service provision for contraventions of SMP services conditions.   OFCOM[1] may give a direction to a person who provides a public electronic communications network[2], or a person who makes available facilities that are associated facilities[3] by reference to such a network, if OFCOM are satisfied that:

(1)   the person is or has been in contravention of conditions[4]; and

(2)   the provision of an electronic communications service[5] by the person on that public electronic communications network could result in significant harm to competition[6].

A direction is given where OFCOM give a confirmation decision[7] to the person in respect of a direction proposed in a notification[8]. A direction under these provisions is:

(a)   a direction that the entitlement of the person to provide an electronic communications service over the public electronic communications network to which the contravened condition relates is suspended (either generally or in relation to particular services)[9]; or

(b)   a direction that the person may not begin to provide an electronic communications service over the public electronic communications network to which the contravened provision relates[10].

A direction must specify the electronic communications services to which it relates and takes effect for an indefinite period beginning with the time at which a confirmation decision relating to the direction is given to the person[11]. A direction may provide for a suspension or prohibition to take effect only at a time determined by or in accordance with the terms of the direction[12]. A direction in connection with a suspension or prohibition contained in the direction or with the postponement of its effect, may impose such conditions on the person to whom it is given as appear to OFCOM to be appropriate for the purpose of protecting that person's customers[13].

If OFCOM considers it appropriate to do so (whether or not in consequence of representations or proposals made to them), it may revoke a direction under these provisions or modify its conditions:

(i)   with effect from such time as they may direct[14];

(ii)   subject to compliance with such requirements as they may specify[15]; and

(iii) to such extent and in relation to such services, or parts of a service, as they may determine[16].

A person is guilty of an offence if he provides an electronic communications network or electronic communications service, or makes available any associated facility, while his entitlement to do so is suspended by a direction[17] or in contravention of a restriction contained in such a direction[18].

1   As to the meaning of 'OFCOM' see PARA 14 note 1; and as to OFCOM see PARA 2 et seq.
2   As to the meaning of 'public electronic communications network' see PARA 98 note 6.
3   As to the meaning of 'associated facilities' see PARA 53.
4   Communications Act 2003 s 100A(1)(a) (s 100A added by SI 2011/1210). The reference in the text to conditions are those under the Communications Act 2003 s 87–91 (see PARA 111 et seq): s 100A(1)(a) (as so added).
5   As to the meaning of 'electronic communications service' see PARA 53.
6   Communications Act 2003 s 100A(1)(b) (as added: see note 4).
7   Ie under the Communications Act 2003 s 96C: see PARA 118.
8   Communications Act 2003 s 100A(2) (as added: see note 4). The notification referred to in the text is a notification under s 96A (see PARA 117): s 100A(2) (as so added).
9   Communications Act 2003 s 100A(3)(a) (as added: see note 4).
10 Communications Act 2003 s 100A(3)(b) (as added: see note 4).
11 Communications Act 2003 s 100A(4) (as added: see note 4). The reference to a confirmation decision is one given under s 96C (see PARA 118): s 100A(4)(b) (as so added).
12 Communications Act 2003 s 100A(5)(a) (as added: see note 4).
13 Communications Act 2003 s 100A(5)(b) (as added: see note 4). Those conditions may include a condition requiring the making of payments:
    (1)   by way of compensation for loss or damage suffered by the person's customers as a result of the direction (s 100A(6)(a) (as so added)); or
    (2)   in respect of annoyance, inconvenience or anxiety to which they have been put in consequence of the direction (s 100A(6)(b) (as so added)).
14 Communications Act 2003 s 100A(7)(a) (as added: see note 4).
15 Communications Act 2003 s 100A(7)(b) (as added: see note 4).
16 Communications Act 2003 s 100A(7)(c) (as added: see note 4).
17 Ie under the Communications Act 2003 s 100A.
18 Communications Act 2003 s 103(1) (amended by SI 2011/1210). A person guilty of an offence under the Communications Act 2003 s 103 is liable:
    (1)   on summary conviction, to a fine not exceeding the statutory maximum (s 103(3)(a));
    (2)   on conviction on indictment, to a fine (s 103(3)(b)).
    As to the statutory maximum see SENTENCING AND DISPOSITION OF OFFENDERS vol 92 (2010) PARA 140. Sections 96A–99 (see PARAS 117–120) apply in relation to a contravention of conditions imposed by a direction under s 100A as they apply in relation to a contravention of conditions set under s 45 (see PARA 87), other than SMP apparatus conditions: s 103(4) (substituted by SI 2011/1210). As to civil liability see PARA 125.

123.   Suspending apparatus supply for contraventions of conditions. OFCOM[1] may give a direction to a person who supplies electronic communications apparatus[2] (the 'contravening supplier') if it is satisfied:

(1)   that he is or has been in serious and repeated contravention of any SMP apparatus conditions[3];

(2)   that an attempt, by the imposition of penalties or the giving of

enforcement notifications[4] or both, to secure compliance with the contravened conditions has failed[5]; and

(3) that the giving of the direction is appropriate and proportionate to the seriousness (when repeated as they have been) of the contraventions[6].

Such a direction is a direction to the contravening supplier to cease to act as a supplier of electronic communications apparatus (either generally or in relation to apparatus of a particular description), or a direction imposing such restrictions as may be set out in the direction on the supply by that supplier of electronic communications apparatus (either generally or in relation to apparatus of a particular description)[7].

A direction takes effect, except so far as it otherwise provides, for an indefinite period beginning with the time at which it is notified to the person to whom it is given[8]. A direction under these provisions:

(a) may provide for a prohibition or restriction to take effect only at a time determined by or in accordance with the terms of the direction[9]; and

(b) in connection with a prohibition or restriction contained in the direction or with the postponement of its effect, may impose such conditions on the contravening supplier as appear to OFCOM to be appropriate for the purpose of protecting that supplier's customers[10].

If OFCOM considers it appropriate to do so (whether or not in consequence of representations or proposals made to it), it may at any time revoke a direction or modify its conditions:

(i) with effect from such time as it may direct[11];

(ii) subject to compliance with such requirements as it may specify[12]; and

(iii) to such extent and in relation to such apparatus or descriptions of apparatus as it may determine[13].

A person is guilty of an offence if he supplies electronic communications apparatus while prohibited from doing so by a direction[14] or in contravention of a restriction contained in such a direction[15].

1   As to the meaning of 'OFCOM' see PARA 14 note 1; and as to OFCOM see PARA 2 et seq.
2   As to the meaning of 'electronic communications apparatus' see PARA 88 note 10. As to the meaning of 'person' see PARA 14 note 2.
3   Communications Act 2003 s 101(1)(a). As to the meaning of 'SMP apparatus condition' see PARA 87 note 8. For the purposes of the Communications Act 2003 s 101, there are repeated contraventions by a person of SMP apparatus conditions to the extent that:
    (1) in the case of a previous notification given to that person under s 94 (see PARA 115), OFCOM has determined for the purposes of s 95(2) or s 96(2) (see PARAS 116, 119) that such a contravention did occur (s 101(7)(a));
    (2) in the period of 12 months following the day of the making of that determination, one or more further notifications have been given to that person in respect of contraventions of an SMP apparatus condition (s 101(7)(b)); and
    (3) the previous notification and the subsequent ones all relate to contraventions of the same condition (whether the same contravention or different contraventions) (s 101(7)(c)).
4   Ie under the Communications Act 2003 s 95: see PARA 116.
5   Communications Act 2003 s 101(1)(b).
6   Communications Act 2003 s 101(1)(c). As to the procedure for directions see PARA 124.
7   Communications Act 2003 s 101(2).
8   Communications Act 2003 s 101(3).
9   Communications Act 2003 s 101(4)(a).
10 Communications Act 2003 s 101(4)(b). The conditions may include a condition requiring the making of payments:
    (1) by way of compensation for loss or damage suffered by the contravening supplier's customers as a result of the direction (s 101(5)(a)); or
    (2) in respect of annoyance, inconvenience or anxiety to which they have been put in consequence of the direction (s 101(5)(b)).

11 Communications Act 2003 s 101(6)(a).
12 Communications Act 2003 s 101(6)(b).
13 Communications Act 2003 s 101(6)(c).
14 Ie under the Communications Act 2003 s 101.
15 Communications Act 2003 s 103(2). A person guilty of an offence under s 103 is liable:
    (1)   on summary conviction, to a fine not exceeding the statutory maximum (s 103(3)(a));
    (2)   on conviction on indictment, to a fine (s 103(3)(b)).
  As to the statutory maximum see SENTENCING AND DISPOSITION OF OFFENDERS vol 92 (2010)
PARA 140. Sections 94–96 (see PARAS 115, 116, 119) and ss 97–99 (see PARAS 119, 120) apply in
relation to a contravention of conditions imposed by a direction under s 101 as they apply in
relation to a contravention of SMP apparatus conditions: s 103(5) (added by SI 2011/1210).

124. Procedure for directions. Except:

(1)   in an urgent case[1]; or

(2)   in a case where a person is in serious contravention of a condition[2], other than SMP apparatus conditions[3] and the proposed direction has been notified to the person[4] and confirmed by a confirmation decision[5],

OFCOM is not to give a direction suspending service provision[6] or apparatus supply[7] unless it has:

(a)   notified the contravening provider[8] or contravening supplier[9] of the proposed direction and of the conditions (if any) which it is proposing to impose by that direction[10];

(b)   provided him with an opportunity of making representations about the proposals and of proposing steps for remedying the situation[11]; and

(c)   considered every representation and proposal made to it during the period allowed by it for the contravening provider or the contravening supplier to take advantage of that opportunity[12].

That period must be:

(i)   in relation to a direction suspending service provision[13], such reasonable period as OFCOM may determine[14];

(ii)   in relation to a direction suspending apparatus supply[15], a period not less than one month after the day of the giving of the notification[16].

As soon as practicable after giving a direction in an urgent case, OFCOM must provide the contravening provider or contravening supplier with an opportunity of making representations about the effect of the direction and of any of its conditions and proposing steps for remedying the situation[17].

In relation to a direction suspending service provision[18] in an urgent case, as soon as practicable after the period allowed by OFCOM for making those representations has ended (and in any event within three months beginning with the day on which the direction was given), it must determine:

(A)   whether the contravention providing the grounds for the giving of the direction did occur[19]; and

(B)   whether the circumstances made it an urgent case justifying the giving of the direction[20].

1 A case is an urgent case for the purposes of the Communications Act 2003 s 102 if OFCOM:
    (1)   considers that it would be inappropriate, because the contraventions in question fall within s 102(5), to allow time, before giving a direction under s 100 or 101 (see PARAS 121, 123) for the making and consideration of representations (s 102(4)(a)); and
    (2)   decides for that reason to act in accordance with s 102(3) (see the text and note 17), instead of s 102(1) (s 102(4)(b)).
  The contraventions fall within s 102(5) if they have resulted in, or create an immediate risk of:
    (a)   a serious threat to the safety of the public, to public health or to national security (s 102(5)(a));
    (b)   serious economic or operational problems for persons (apart from the contravening

provider or contravening supplier) who are communications providers or persons who make associated facilities available (s 102(5)(b)); or

   (c)   serious economic or operational problems for persons who make use of electronic communications networks, electronic communications services or associated facilities (s 102(5)(c)).

As to the meaning of 'OFCOM' see PARA 14 note 1; and as to OFCOM see PARA 2 et seq. As to the meaning of 'communications provider' see PARA 17 note 23. As to the meaning of 'associated facilities' see PARA 53. As to the meanings of 'electronic communications network' and 'electronic communications service' see PARA 53.

2 Ie a condition set under the Communications Act 2003 s 45.

3 As to the meaning of 'SMP apparatus condition' see PARA 87 note 8.

4 Ie under the Communications Act 2003 s 96A.

5 Ie a case where the Communications Act 2003 s 100(1A) (see PARA 121) is satisfied: s 102(1) (amended by SI 2011/1210). The confirmation decision referred to in the text is one given under the Communications Act 2003 s 96C (see PARA 118): S 102(1) (as so amended).

6 Ie under the Communications Act 2003 s 100: see PARA 121.

7 Ie under the Communications Act 2003 s 101: see PARA 123.

8 'Contravening provider' means a person who is a communications provider or makes associated facilities available: Communications Act 2003 s 102(6) (definition substituted by SI 2011/1210).

9 'Contravening supplier' has the same meaning as in the Communications Act 2003 s 101 (see PARA 123): s 102(6).

10 Communications Act 2003 s 102(1)(a).

11 Communications Act 2003 s 102(1)(b).

12 Communications Act 2003 s 102(1)(c).

13 Ie under the Communications Act 2003 s 100: see PARA 121.

14 Communications Act 2003 s 102(2)(a) (s 102(2) substituted by SI 2011/1210).

15 Ie under the Communications Act 2003 s 101: see PARA 123.

16 Communications Act 2003 s 102(2)(b) (as substituted: see note 14).

17 Communications Act 2003 s 102(3).

18 Ie under the Communications Act 2003 s 100: see PARA 121.

19 Communications Act 2003 s 102(3A)(a) (s 102(3A), (3B) added by SI 2011/1210). The period of three months mentioned in the Communications Act 2003 s 102(3A) may be extended by up to three months if OFCOM:

   (1)   requires additional time to consider representations received (s 102(3B)(a) (as so added)); or

   (2)   decides that it is necessary to obtain additional information from the person in order to make a determination under s 102(3A) (s 102(3B)(b) (as so added)).

20 Communications Act 2003 s 102(3A)(b) (s 102(3A), (3B) added by SI 2011/1210). See note 19.

125. Civil liability for breach of conditions or confirmation decision.

The obligation of a person to comply with:

   (1)   the conditions[1] which apply to him[2];

   (2)   requirements imposed on him by an enforcement notification[3];

   (3)   requirements imposed on the person by a notification[4] and a confirmation decision[5]; and

   (4)   the conditions imposed by a direction[6],

is a duty owed to every person who may be affected by a contravention of the condition or requirement[7].

Where a duty is owed by virtue of these provisions[8] to a person:

   (a)   a breach of the duty that causes that person to sustain loss or damage[9]; and

   (b)   an act which by inducing a breach of the duty or interfering with its performance, causes that person to sustain loss or damage and is done wholly or partly for achieving that result[10],

is actionable at the suit or instance of that person[11].

1 Ie the conditions set under the Communications Act 2003 s 45: see PARA 87. As to the meaning of 'person' see PARA 14 note 2.

2   Communications Act 2003 s 104(1)(a). The consent of OFCOM is required for the bringing of proceedings by virtue of head (1) in the text: s 104(4). Where OFCOM gives a consent for the purposes of s 104(4) subject to conditions relating to the conduct of the proceedings, the proceedings are not to be carried on by that person except in compliance with those conditions: s 104(5). As to the meaning of 'OFCOM' see PARA 14 note 1; and as to OFCOM see PARA 2 et seq.

3   Communications Act 2003 s 104(1)(b). The reference in the text to an enforcement notification is an enforcement notification under s 95: see PARA 116.

4   Ie under the Communications Act 2003 s 96A: see PARA 117.

5   Communications Act 2003 s 104(1)(ba) (added by SI 2011/1210). The reference to a confirmation decision is a confirmation decision under the Communications Act 2003 s 96C (see PARA 118): s 104(1)(ba) (as so added).

6   Communications Act 2003 s 104(1)(c) (amended by SI 2011/1210). The directions referred to in the text are those imposed under the Communications Act 2003 s 98 (see PARA 122) or s 100 (see PARA 121) or s 100A (see PARA 122): s 104(1)(c) (as so amended).

7   Communications Act 2003 s 104(1).

8   Ie the Communications Act 2003 s 104.

9   Communications Act 2003 s 104(2)(a). In proceedings brought against a person by virtue of head (a) in the text, it is a defence for that person to show that he took all reasonable steps and exercised all due diligence to avoid contravening the condition or requirement in question: s 104(3). See also note 2.

10 Communications Act 2003 s 104(2)(b).

11 Communications Act 2003 s 104(2).

(v) Security of Public Electronic Communications Networks and Services

126. Notification of breach of security and enforcement of obligations in relation to protecting security. Network providers[1] and service providers[2] must take technical and organisational measures appropriately to manage risks to the security of public electronic communications networks and public electronic communications services[3]. A network provider must also take all appropriate steps to protect, so far as possible, the availability of the provider's public electronic communications network[4].

A network provider must notify OFCOM[5] of a breach of security which has a significant impact on the operation of a public electronic communications network and of a reduction in the availability of a public electronic communications network which has a significant impact on the network[6]. A service provider must notify OFCOM of a breach of security which has a significant impact on the operation of a public electronic communications service[7]. If OFCOM receives a notification[8], it must, where it thinks it appropriate, notify the regulatory authorities in other member states and the European Network and Information Security Agency ('ENISA')[9]. OFCOM may also inform the public of a notification or require the network provider or service provider to inform the public, if OFCOM thinks that it is in the public interest to do so[10]. OFCOM must prepare an annual report summarising notifications received by it during the year, and any action taken in response to a notification and must sent a copy of the annual report to the European Commission and to ENISA[11].

OFCOM may carry out, or arrange for another person to carry out, an audit of the measures[12] taken by a network provider or a service provider[13]. A network provider or a service provider must co-operate with such an audit and pay the costs of the audit[14].

The obligation of a person to comply with the above requirements[15] is a duty owed to every person who may be affected by a contravention of a requirement[16].

The amount of a penalty imposed[17] is to be such amount not exceeding £2 million as OFCOM determines to be appropriate and proportionate to the contravention in respect of which it is imposed[18].

1 For these purposes, 'network provider' means a provider of a public electronic communications network: Communications Act 2003 s 105A(5) (s 105A–105D added by SI 2011/1210). As to the meaning of 'public electronic communications network' see PARA 98 note 6.
2 For these purposes, 'service provider' means a provider of a public electronic communications service: Communications Act 2003 s 105A(5) (as added: see note 1). As to the meaning of 'public electronic communications service' see PARA 98 note 3.
3 Communications Act 2003 s 105A(1) (as added: see note 1). Measures under s 105A(1) must, in particular, include measures to prevent or minimise the impact of security incidents on end-users: s 105A(2) (as so added). Measures under s 105A(1) taken by a network provider must also include measures to prevent or minimise the impact of security incidents on interconnection of public electronic communications networks: s 105A(3) (as so added).
4 Communications Act 2003 s 105A(4) (as added: see note 1).
5 As to the meaning of 'OFCOM' see PARA 14 note 1; and as to OFCOM see PARA 2 et seq.
6 Communications Act 2003 s 105B(1) (as added: see note 1).
7 Communications Act 2003 s 105B(2) (as added: see note 1).
8 Ie under the Communications Act 2003 s 105B.
9 Communications Act 2003 s 105B(3) (as added: see note 1).
10 Communications Act 2003 s 105B(4) (as added: see note 1).
11 Communications Act 2003 s 105B(5), (6) (as added: see note 1).
12 Ie under the Communications Act 2003 s 105A.
13 Communications Act 2003 s 105C(1) (as added: see note 1).
14 Communications Act 2003 s 105C(2) (as added: see note 1).
15 Ie the Communications Act 2003 s 105A–105C.
16 Communications Act 2003 s 105D(2) (as added: see note 1). Section 104 (civil liability for breach of conditions or confirmation decision: see PARA 125) applies in relation to that duty as it applies in relation to the duty set out in s 104(1): s 105D(2)(a) (as so added). Section 104(4) (need for consent of OFCOM to bring proceedings) applies in relation to proceedings brought by virtue of s 105D as it applies in relation to proceedings by virtue of s 104(1)(a): s 105D(2)(b) (as so added).
   Sections 96A–96C (see PARAS 117–119), 98–100 (see PARAS 120, 121), 102 (see PARA 124), 103 (see PARA 123) apply in relation to a contravention of a requirement under ss 105A to 105C as they apply in relation to a contravention of a condition set under s 45 (see PARA 87), other than an SMP apparatus condition: s 105D(1) (as so added). As to the meaning of 'SMP apparatus condition' see PARA 87 note 8.
17 Ie under the Communications Act 2003 ss 96A–96C, as applied by s 105D.
18 Communications Act 2003 s 105D(3) (as added: see note 1).

(vi) Regulation of Premium Rate Services

127. Conditions regulating premium rate services. OFCOM[1] has the power, for the purpose of regulating the provision, content, promotion and marketing of premium rate services[2], to set conditions[3] that bind the persons to whom they are applied[4]. Such conditions may be applied either:

(1) generally to every person who provides a premium rate service[5]; or
(2) to every person who is of a specified description of such persons, or who provides a specified description of such services[6].

The only provision that may be made by conditions under this power is provision requiring the person to whom the condition applies to comply, to the extent required by the condition, with:

(a) directions given in accordance with an approved code[7] by the enforcement authority[8] and for the purpose of enforcing its provisions[9]; and
(b) if there is no such code, the provisions of the order for the time being in force[10].

The power to set a condition[11] includes power to modify or revoke the conditions for the time being in force under these provisions[12].

There are procedures for setting, modifying, revoking[13] and enforcing these conditions[14]. OFCOM may give a direction to the contravening provider to secure the suspension of the provision of premium rate services provided[15].

1   As to the meaning of 'OFCOM' see PARA 14 note 1; and as to OFCOM see PARA 2 et seq.

2   A service is a 'premium rate service' for the purposes of the Communications Act 2003 Pt 2 Ch 1 (ss 32–151) if:

    (1)   it is a service falling within s 120(8) (ss 120(7)(a), 151(1));

    (2)   there is a charge for the provision of the service (ss 120(7)(b), 151(1));

    (3)   the charge is required to be paid to a person providing an electronic communications service by means of which the service in question is provided (ss 120(7)(c), 151(1)); and

    (4)   that charge is imposed in the form of a charge made by that person for the use of the electronic communications service (ss 120(7)(d), 151(1)).

    A service falls within s 120(8) if its provision consists in:

    (a)   the provision of the contents of communications transmitted by means of an electronic communications network (s 120(8)(a)); or

    (b)   allowing the user of an electronic communications service to make use, by the making of a transmission by means of that service, of a facility made available to the users of the electronic communications service (s 120(8)(b)).

    References in s 120 to a facility include, in particular, references to:

    (i)   a facility for making a payment for goods or services (s 120(14)(a));

    (ii)   a facility for entering a competition or claiming a prize (s 120(14)(b)); and

    (iii)   a facility for registering a vote or recording a preference (s 120(14)(c)).

3   Ie under the Communications Act 2003 s 120.

4   Communications Act 2003 s 120(1). As to the meaning of 'person' see PARA 14 note 2.

5   Communications Act 2003 s 120(2)(a). For the purposes of Pt 2 Ch 1, a person provides a premium rate service (the 'relevant service') if:

    (1)   he provides the contents of the relevant service (s 120(9)(a));

    (2)   he exercises editorial control over the contents of the relevant service (s 120(9)(b));

    (3)   he is a person who packages together the contents of the relevant service for the purpose of facilitating its provision (s 120(9)(c));

    (4)   he makes available a facility comprised in the relevant service; or

    (5)   he falls within s 120(10), (11) or (12) (s 120(9)(d)).

    A person falls within s 120(10) if:

    (a)   he is the provider of an electronic communications service used for the provision of the relevant service (s 120(10)(a)); and

    (b)   under arrangements made with a person who is a provider of the relevant service falling within heads (1)–(4), he is entitled to retain some or all of the charges received by him in respect of the provision of the relevant service or of the use of his electronic communications service for the purposes of the relevant service (s 120(10)(b)).

    A person falls within s 120(11) if:

    (i)   he is the provider of an electronic communications network used for the provision of the relevant service (s 120(11)(a)); and

    (ii)   an agreement relating to the use of the network for the provision of that service subsists between the provider of the network and a person who is a provider of the relevant service falling within heads (1)–(4) (s 120(11)(b)).

    A person falls within s 120(12) if:

    (A)   he is the provider of an electronic communications network used for the provision of the relevant service (s 120(12)(a)); and

    (B)   the use of that network for the provision of premium rate services, or of services that include or may include premium rate services, is authorised by an agreement subsisting between that person and either an intermediary service provider or a person who is a provider of the relevant service by virtue of s 120(10) or (11) (s 120(12)(b)).

For the purposes of s 120, 'intermediary service provider' means a person who provides an electronic communications service used for the provision of the relevant service or an electronic communications network so used and is a party to an agreement with a provider of the relevant service falling within heads (1)–(4), or another intermediary service provider, which relates to the use of that electronic communications service or network for the provision of premium rate services, or of services that include or may include premium rate services: s 120(15). Where one or more persons are employed or engaged under the direction of another to do any of the things mentioned in heads (1)–(4), only that other person is a provider of the relevant service for the purposes of Pt 2 Ch 1: s 120(13).

6   Communications Act 2003 s 120(2)(b).

7   'Approved code' means a code for the time being approved under the Communications Act 2003 s 121 (see PARA 128): s 120(15).

8   'Enforcement authority', in relation to such a code, means the person who under the code has the function of enforcing it: Communications Act 2003 s 120(15).

9   Communications Act 2003 s 120(3)(a). See *Phonepayplus Ltd v Ashraf* [2014] EWHC 4303 (Ch), [2014] All ER (D) 247 (Dec) (OFCOM lawfully delegated to Phonepayplus all powers of enforcement of the code).

10   Communications Act 2003 s 120(3)(b). The reference to the provisions of the order being in force is to an order under s 122 (see PARA 129): s 120(3).

11   Ie under the Communications Act 2003 s 120.

12   Communications Act 2003 s 120(4). Section 47(see PARA 89) applies to the setting, modification and revocation of a condition under s 120 as it applies to the setting, modification and revocation of a condition under s 45 (see PARA 87): s 120(5) (amended by SI 2011/1210).

13   The way in which conditions are to be set or modified under the Communications Act 2003 s 120 (see text and notes 1–12) or revoked is by the publication of a notification setting out the conditions or modifications or as the case may be, stating the condition is revoked: see the Communications Act 2003 s 120A(1), (2) (s 120A added by SI 2011/1210). Before setting such conditions, or modifying or revoking a condition so set, OFCOM must publish a notification:

(1)   stating that it is proposing to set, modify or revoke the conditions that are specified in the notification (Communications Act 2003 s 120A(3)(a) (as so added));

(2)   setting out the effect of those conditions, modifications or revocations (s 120A(3)(b) (as so added));

(3)   giving its reasons for making the proposal (s 120A(3)(c) (as so added)); and

(4)   specifying the period within which representations may be made to OFCOM about their proposal (s 120A(3)(d) (as so added)).

The period referred to in head (4) must end no less than one month after the day of the publication of the notification but where OFCOM are satisfied that there are exceptional circumstances justifying the use of a shorter period, the period specified as the period for making representations may be whatever shorter period OFCOM consider reasonable in those circumstances: s 120A(3), (4) (as so added). Please note that the Electronic Communications and Wireless Telegraphy Regulations 2011, SI 2011/1210 added two provisions as the Communications Act 2003 s 120A(3). OFCOM may give effect to the proposal, with any modifications that appear to OFCOM to be appropriate, after considering every representation about the proposal made to them during the period specified in the notification and having regard to every international obligation of the United Kingdom (if any) which has been notified to them for these purposes by the Secretary of State: s 120A(5) (as so added). The publication of a notification under s 120A must be in such manner as appears to OFCOM to be appropriate for bringing the contents of the notification to the attention of the persons who, in OFCOM's opinion, are likely to be affected by its contents and OFCOM must send a copy of every notification published to the Secretary of State: s 120A(6), (7).

14   The Communications Act 2003 ss 94–96 (see PARAS 115, 116, 119) apply in relation to a contravention of conditions set under s 120 as they apply in relation to a contravention of a condition set under s 45 (see PARA 87): s 123(1). The amount of the penalty imposed under s 96 as applied by s 123 is to be such amount not exceeding £250,000 as OFCOM determines to be appropriate and proportionate to the contravention in respect of which it is imposed: s 123(2) (amended by SI 2005/3469). In making that determination OFCOM must have regard to:

(1)   any representations made to it by the notified provider (Communications Act 2003 s 123(3)(a));

(2)   any steps taken by him towards complying with the conditions contraventions of which have been notified to him under s 94 (as applied) (s 123(3)(b)); and

(3)   any steps taken by him for remedying the consequences of those contraventions (s 123(3)(c)).

The Secretary of State may by order amend s 123 so as to substitute a different maximum penalty for the maximum penalty for the time being specified in s 123(2): s 123(4). No order is to be made containing provision authorised by s 123(4) unless a draft of the order has been laid before Parliament and approved by a resolution of each House: s 123(5). As to regulations made under s 123(4) see the Communications Act 2003 (Maximum Penalty and Disclosure of Information) Order 2005, SI 2005/3469.

15 OFCOM may give a direction to a person who is a communications provider (the 'contravening provider') if it is satisfied:

(1)   that he is or has been in serious and repeated contravention of conditions set under the Communications Act 2003 s 120 (see text and notes 1–12) (s 124(1)(a));

(2)   that an attempt, by the imposition of penalties or the giving of enforcement notifications under s 95 (as applied by s 123: see note 14) or both, to secure compliance with the contravened conditions has failed (s 124(1)(b));

(3)   that the giving of the direction is appropriate and proportionate to the seriousness (when repeated as they have been) of the contraventions (s 124(1)(c)); and

(4)   that the giving of the direction is required for reasons of public policy (s 124(1)(d)).

For the purposes of s 124 there are repeated contraventions by a person of conditions set under s 120 to the extent that:

(a)   in the case of a previous notification given to that person under s 94 (as applied by s 123: see note 14), OFCOM has determined for the purposes of s 95(2) or 96(2) (as so applied) that such a contravention did occur (s 124(9)(a)); and

(b)   in the period of 12 months following the day of the making of that determination, one or more further notifications have been given to that person in respect of contraventions of a condition set under s 120 (s 124(9)(b)).

For the purposes of s 120 the seriousness of repeated contraventions of conditions set under s 120 has to be determined by reference to the seriousness of the contraventions of the approved code or order by reference to which the conditions have effect: s 124(10).

OFCOM may also give a direction to a person who is a communications provider (the 'contravening provider') if it is satisfied:

(i)   that he is, or has been, in contravention of conditions set under s 120 in respect of a premium rate service (s 124(2)(a));

(ii)   that the circumstances of the contravention make it appropriate for OFCOM to suspend or restrict the provision of premium rate services provided by the contravening provider without the conditions set out in s 124(1) being satisfied (s 124(2)(b)); and

(iii) that in those circumstances the giving of the direction is urgently required for reasons of public policy (s 124(2)(c)).

A direction under s 124 is either a direction to the contravening provider to secure the suspension of the provision of premium rate services provided by him or a direction requiring him to secure compliance with restrictions, set out in the direction, on the provision of such services: s 124(3). Such a direction must specify the services to which it relates and, except so far as it otherwise provides, takes effect for an indefinite period beginning with the time at which it is notified to the person to whom it is given: s 124(4). A direction, in providing for the effect of a suspension or restriction to be postponed, may provide for it to take effect only at a time determined by or in accordance with the terms of the direction; and in connection with the suspension or restriction contained in the direction or with the postponement of its effect, may impose such conditions on the contravening provider as appear to OFCOM to be appropriate for the purpose of protecting that provider's customers: s 124(5). Those conditions may include a condition requiring the making of payments by way of compensation for loss or damage suffered by the contravening provider's customers as a result of the direction or in respect of annoyance, inconvenience or anxiety to which they have been put in consequence of the direction: s 124(6).

If OFCOM considers it appropriate to do so (whether or not in consequence of representations or proposals made to it), it may revoke a direction or modify its conditions:

(A)   with effect from such time as it may direct (s 124(7)(a));

(B)   subject to compliance with such requirements as it may specify (s 124(7)(b)); and

(C)   to such extent and in relation to such services as it may determine (s 124(7)(c)).

Sections 102 and 103 (procedure and enforcement: see PARAS 122, 123, 124) apply in the case of a direction under s 124 as they apply in the case of a direction under s 100 (see PARA 122), but as if references in s 103(1) to an electronic communications network or electronic communications service were references to a premium rate service: s 124(8).

128.   Approval of code for premium rate services.

If it appears to OFCOM[1]:

(1)   that a code has been made by any person for regulating the provision and contents of premium rate services[2], and the facilities made available in the provision of such services[3];

(2)   that the code contains provision for regulating, to such extent (if any) as

OFCOM thinks fit, the arrangements made by the providers[4] of premium rate services for promoting and marketing those services[5]; and

(3) that it would be appropriate for it to approve that code[6],

it may approve that code for those purposes[7].

OFCOM is not to approve a code unless it is satisfied:

(a) that there is a person who, under the code, has the function of administering and enforcing it[8];

(b) that that person is sufficiently independent of the providers of premium rate services[9];

(c) that adequate arrangements are in force for funding the activities of that person in relation to the code[10];

(d) that the provisions of the code are objectively justifiable in relation to the services to which it relates[11];

(e) that those provisions are not such as to discriminate unduly against particular persons or against a particular description of persons[12];

(f) that those provisions are proportionate to what they are intended to achieve[13]; and

(g) that, in relation to what those provisions are intended to achieve, they are transparent[14].

OFCOM is not to approve so much of a code as imposes an obligation as respects a premium rate service on a person who is a provider of the service[15] (the 'relevant provider') unless it is satisfied that the obligation:

(i) arises only if there is no one who is a provider of the service[16] against whom it is practicable to take action[17];

(ii) arises only after a notice identifying the service and setting out respects in which requirements of the code have been contravened in relation to it has been given to the relevant provider by the person responsible for enforcing the code[18]; and

(iii) is confined to an obligation to secure that electronic communications networks[19] provided by the relevant provider are not used for making the service available to persons who are in the United Kingdom[20].

The provision that may be contained in a code and approved under these provisions includes, in particular, provision about the pricing of premium rate services and provision for the enforcement of the code[21]. The provision for the enforcement of a code that may be approved includes:

(A) provision for the payment, to a person specified in the code, of a penalty not exceeding the maximum penalty for the time being specified[22];

(B) provision requiring a provider of a premium rate service to secure that the provision of the service is suspended or otherwise ceases or is restricted in any respect[23];

(C) provision for the imposition on a person, in respect of a contravention of the code, of a temporary or permanent prohibition or restriction on his working in connection with the provision of premium rate services or, in the case of a body corporate, on its providing such services or on its carrying on other activities in connection with their provision[24].

OFCOM may at any time[25] approve modifications that have been made to an approved code, or withdraw its approval from an approved code[26]. Where OFCOM gives or withdraws an approval, it must give notification of its approval or of the withdrawal of the approval[27].

1   As to the meaning of 'OFCOM' see PARA 14 note 1; and as to OFCOM see PARA 2 et seq.

2   As to the meaning of 'premium rate service' see PARA 127 note 2. As to the meaning of 'person' see PARA 14 note 2. As to the position where no code has been made see PARA 129.
3   Communications Act 2003 s 121(1)(a).
4   'Provider', in relation to a premium rate service, is to be construed in accordance with the Communications Act 2003 s 120(9)–(12) (see PARA 127); and cognate expressions are to be construed accordingly: s 151(1).
5   Communications Act 2003 s 121(1)(b).
6   Ie for the purposes of the Communications Act 2003 s 120: see PARA 127.
7   Communications Act 2003 s 121(1)(c).
8   Communications Act 2003 s 121(2)(a).
9   Communications Act 2003 s 121(2)(b).
10 Communications Act 2003 s 121(2)(c).
11 Communications Act 2003 s 121(2)(d). See also *R (on the application of Ordanduu GmbH) v Phonepayplus Ltd* [2015] EWHC 50 (Admin), [2015] All ER (D) 108 (Jan) (lawfulness of emergency procedure invoked against premium rate service provider).
12 Communications Act 2003 s 121(2)(e).
13 Communications Act 2003 s 121(2)(f).
14 Communications Act 2003 s 121(2)(g).
15 Ie by virtue only of the Communications Act 2003 s 120(12): see PARA 127 note 5.
16 Ie otherwise than by virtue of the Communications Act 2003 s 120(12).
17 Communications Act 2003 s 121(3)(a).
18 Communications Act 2003 s 121(3)(b).
19 As to the meaning of 'electronic communications network' see PARA 53.
20 Communications Act 2003 s 121(3)(c). As to the meaning of 'United Kingdom' see PARA 14 note 7.
21 Communications Act 2003 s 121(4).
22 Communications Act 2003 s 121(5)(a). The maximum penalty referred to in the text is that specified by the Communications Act 2003 s 123(2): see PARA 127.
23 Communications Act 2003 s 121(5)(b).
24 Communications Act 2003 s 121(5)(c).
25 Ie for the purposes of the Communications Act 2003 s 120: see PARA 127.
26 Communications Act 2003 s 121(6).
27 Communications Act 2003 s 121(7). The notification must be published in such manner as OFCOM considers appropriate for bringing it to the attention of the persons who, in OFCOM's opinion, are likely to be affected by the approval or withdrawal: s 121(8).

129.   Orders by OFCOM in the absence of a code. OFCOM[1] may make an order if, at any time, it considers that there is no code in force relating to premium rate services[2] to which it thinks it would be appropriate to give, or to continue to give, its approval[3]. Such an order may make such of the following provisions as OFCOM thinks fit:

(1)   provision imposing requirements with respect to the provision and contents of premium rate services, and with respect to the facilities made available in the provision of such services (including provision about pricing)[4];

(2)   provision imposing requirements with respect to the arrangements made by the providers of premium rate services for the promotion and marketing of those services[5];

(3)   provision for the enforcement of requirements imposed by virtue of head (1) or head (2) above[6];

(4)   provision making other arrangements for the purposes of those requirements[7].

The power to make such an order includes, in particular:

(a)   power to establish a body corporate with the capacity to make its own rules and to establish its own procedures[8];

(b)   power to determine the jurisdiction of a body established by such an order or, for the purposes of the order, of any other person[9];

(c) power to confer jurisdiction with respect to any matter on OFCOM itself[10];

(d) power to provide for a person on whom jurisdiction is conferred by the arrangements to make awards of compensation, to direct the reimbursement of costs or expenses, or to do both[11];

(e) power to provide for such a person to enforce, or to participate in the enforcement of, any awards or directions made under such an order[12];

(f) power to make provision[13] for the enforcement of the provisions of the order[14]; and

(g) power to make such other provision as OFCOM thinks fit for the enforcement of such awards and directions[15].

An order may require such providers of premium rate services as may be determined by or under the order to make payments to OFCOM in respect of expenditure incurred by OFCOM in connection with:

(i) the establishment and maintenance, in accordance with such an order, of any body corporate or procedure[16]; or

(ii) the making of other arrangements for the purposes of the requirements of such an order[17].

An order is not to impose an obligation as respects a premium rate service on a person who is a provider of the service[18] (the 'relevant provider') unless the obligation:

(A) arises only if there is no one who is a provider of the service[19] against whom it is practicable to take action[20];

(B) arises only after a notice identifying the service and setting out respects in which requirements of the order have been contravened in relation to it has been given to the relevant provider by OFCOM[21]; and

(C) is confined to an obligation to secure that electronic communications networks provided by the relevant provider are not used for making the service available to persons who are in the United Kingdom[22].

The consent of the Secretary of State is required for the making by OFCOM of an order under these provisions[23].

1 As to the meaning of 'OFCOM' see PARA 14 note 1; and as to OFCOM see PARA 2 et seq.
2 As to the meaning of 'premium rate service' see PARA 127 note 2.
3 Communications Act 2003 s 122(1). The reference in the text to approval is to an approval under s 121 (see PARA 128): s 122(1). Section 403 (see PARA 39) applies to the power of OFCOM to make an order under s 122: s 122(7). A statutory instrument containing an order made by OFCOM under s 122 is subject to annulment in pursuance of a resolution of either House of Parliament: s 122(8). At the date at which this volume states the law, no such order has been made.
4 Communications Act 2003 s 122(2)(a).
5 Communications Act 2003 s 122(2)(b).
6 Communications Act 2003 s 122(2)(c).
7 Communications Act 2003 s 122(2)(d).
8 Communications Act 2003 s 122(3)(a).
9 Communications Act 2003 s 122(3)(b).
10 Communications Act 2003 s 122(3)(c).
11 Communications Act 2003 s 122(3)(d).
12 Communications Act 2003 s 122(3)(e).
13 The provision referred to in the text is one falling within the Communications Act 2003 s 121(5)(c): see PARA 128 head (C) in the text.
14 Communications Act 2003 s 122(3)(f).
15 Communications Act 2003 s 122(3)(g).
16 Communications Act 2003 s 122(4)(a).
17 Communications Act 2003 s 122(4)(b).

18 Ie by virtue only of the Communications Act 2003 s 120(12): see PARA 127 note 5. As to the meaning of 'person' see PARA 14 note 2.
19 Ie otherwise than by virtue of the Communications Act 2003 s 120(12).
20 Communications Act 2003 s 122(5)(a).
21 Communications Act 2003 s 122(5)(b).
22 Communications Act 2003 s 122(5)(c). As to the meaning of 'United Kingdom' see PARA 14 note 7.
23 Communications Act 2003 s 122(6). As to the Secretary of State see PARA 76 note 1.

(vii) Persistent Misuse of Network Services

130. Notification of misuse of networks and services. Where OFCOM[1] determines that there are reasonable grounds for believing that a person has persistently misused an electronic communications network or electronic communications services[2], it may give that person a notification[3] which:

(1) sets out the determination made by OFCOM[4];
(2) specifies the use that OFCOM considers constitutes persistent misuse[5]; and
(3) specifies the period during which the person notified has an opportunity of making representations about the matters notified[6].

That period must not be less than seven days in an urgent case, and not less than one month in any other case[7].

1 As to the meaning of 'OFCOM' see PARA 14 note 1; and as to OFCOM see PARA 2 et seq.
2 As to the meanings of 'electronic communications network' and 'electronic communications services' see PARA 53. As to the meaning of 'person' see PARA 14 note 2. For the purposes of the Communications Act 2003 Pt 2 Ch 1 (ss 32–151), a person misuses an electronic communications network or electronic communications service if:
    (1) the effect or likely effect of his use of the network or service is to cause another person unnecessarily to suffer annoyance, inconvenience or anxiety (s 128(5)(a)); or
    (2) he uses the network or service to engage in conduct the effect or likely effect of which is to cause another person unnecessarily to suffer annoyance, inconvenience or anxiety (s 128(5)(b)).
  For the purposes of Pt 2 Ch 1, the cases in which a person is to be treated as persistently misusing a network or service include any case in which his misuse is repeated on a sufficient number of occasions for it to be clear that the misuse represents:
    (a) a pattern of behaviour or practice (s 128(6)(a)); or
    (b) recklessness as to whether persons suffer annoyance, inconvenience or anxiety (s 128(6)(b)).
  For the purpose of determining whether misuse on a number of different occasions constitutes persistent misuse for the purposes of Pt 2 Ch 1, each of the following is immaterial:
    (i) that the misuse was in relation to a network on some occasions and in relation to a service on others (s 128(7)(a));
    (ii) that different networks or services were involved on different occasions (s 128(7)(b)); and
    (iii) that the persons who were or were likely to suffer annoyance, inconvenience or anxiety were different on different occasions (s 128(7)(c)).
  If he considers that appropriate alternative means of dealing with it exists, the Secretary of State may by order provide that a use of a description specified in the order is not to be treated for the purposes of Pt 2 Ch 1 as a misuse of an electronic communications network or electronic communications service: s 128(8). At the date at which this volume states the law, no such order has been made. For the purposes of Pt 2 Ch 1, 'misuse', in relation to an electronic communications network or electronic communications service, is to be construed in accordance with s 128(5), (8); and cognate expressions are to be construed accordingly: s 151(1). As to the Secretary of State see PARA 76 note 1. As to the power of the Secretary of State to make orders under the Communications Act 2003 see s 402; and PARA 74. See also Ofcom and the Information Commissioner's Office's Joint Action Plan on tackling nuisance calls and messages (December 2014) which at the date at which this volume states the law is on the OFCOM website.
3 Ie under the Communications Act 2003 s 128: s 128(1).

4   Communications Act 2003 s 128(2)(a).
5   Communications Act 2003 s 128(2)(b).
6   Communications Act 2003 s 128(2)(c). As to enforcement notifications and penalties see PARAS 131–132.
7   Communications Act 2003 s 128(3). A case is an urgent case for the purposes of s 128(3) if OFCOM considers that the misuse in question is continuing and that the harm it causes makes it necessary for it to be stopped as soon as possible: s 128(4).

131.   Enforcement notifications for stopping persistent misuse.   The following provisions apply where:

(1)   a person (the 'notified misuser') has been given a notification[1];

(2)   OFCOM[2] has allowed the notified misuser an opportunity of making representations about the matters notified[3]; and

(3)   the period allowed for the making of the representations has expired[4].

OFCOM may give the notified misuser an enforcement notification[5] if it is satisfied:

(a)   that he has, in one or more of the notified respects, persistently[6] misused an electronic communications network[7] or electronic communications service[8]; and

(b)   that he has not, since the giving of the notification, taken all such steps as OFCOM considers appropriate for securing that his misuse is brought to an end and is not repeated and remedying the consequences of the notified misuse[9].

A decision of OFCOM to give an enforcement notification to a person must fix a reasonable period for the taking of the steps required by the notification[10].

It is the duty of a person to whom an enforcement notification has been given to comply with it[11].

1   Communications Act 2003 s 129(1)(a). The notification referred to in the text is a notification under s 128: see PARA 130. As to the meaning of 'person' see PARA 14 note 2. See also Ofcom and the Information Commissioner's Office's Joint Action Plan on tackling nuisance calls and messages (December 2014) which at the date at which this volume states the law is on the OFCOM website.
2   As to the meaning of 'OFCOM' see PARA 14 note 1; and as to OFCOM see PARA 2 et seq.
3   Communications Act 2003 s 129(1)(b).
4   Communications Act 2003 s 129(1)(c).
5   An enforcement notification is a notification which imposes a requirement on the notified misuser to take all such steps for:
     (1)   securing that his misuse is brought to an end and is not repeated (s 129(3)(a)); and
     (2)   remedying the consequences of the notified misuse, as may be specified in the notification (s 129(3)(b)).
     As to the meaning of 'misuse' see PARA 130 note 2. References in s 129 to remedying the consequences of misuse include references to paying an amount to a person:
     (a)   by way of compensation for loss or damage suffered by that person (s 129(7)(a)); or
     (b)   in respect of annoyance, inconvenience or anxiety to which he has been put (s 129(7)(b)).
6   'Persistent' and 'persistently', in relation to misuse of an electronic communications network or electronic communications service, are to be construed in accordance with the Communications Act 2003 s 128(6), (7) (see PARA 130 note 2): s 151(1).
7   As to the meaning of 'electronic communications network' see PARA 53.
8   Communications Act 2003 s 129(2)(a). As to the meaning of 'electronic communications service' see PARA 53.
9   Communications Act 2003 s 129(2)(b).
10   Communications Act 2003 s 129(4).
11   Communications Act 2003 s 129(5). The duty is enforceable in civil proceedings by OFCOM for an injunction or for any other appropriate remedy or relief: s 129(6).

132.   Penalties for persistent misuse.   The following provisions apply[1] where:

(1) a person (the 'notified misuser') has been given a notification[2];

(2) OFCOM[3] has allowed the notified misuser an opportunity of making representations about the matters notified[4]; and

(3) the period allowed for the making of the representations has expired[5].

OFCOM may impose a penalty on the notified misuser if he has, in one or more of the notified respects, persistently misused an electronic communications network[6] or electronic communications service[7]. OFCOM may also impose a penalty on the notified misuser if he has contravened a requirement of an enforcement notification given in respect of the notified misuse[8].

The amount of a penalty imposed is to be such amount not exceeding £2,000,000 as OFCOM determines to be appropriate and proportionate to the misuse in respect of which it is imposed[9]. In making that determination, OFCOM must have regard to:

(a) any representations made to it by the notified misuser[10];

(b) any steps taken by him for securing that his misuse is brought to an end and is not repeated[11]; and

(c) any steps taken by him for remedying the consequences of the notified misuse[12].

Where OFCOM imposes a penalty on a person under these provisions, it must:

(i) notify the person penalised[13]; and

(ii) in that notification, fix a reasonable period after it is given as the period within which the penalty is to be paid[14].

Such a penalty must be paid to OFCOM; and, if not paid within the fixed period, is recoverable by it accordingly[15].

1 Ie in addition to the Communications Act 2003 s 129: see PARA 131.

2 Communications Act 2003 s 130(1)(a). The notification referred to in the text is a notification under s 128: see PARA 130. As to the meaning of 'person' see PARA 14 note 2. See also Ofcom and the Information Commissioner's Office's Joint Action Plan on tackling nuisance calls and messages (December 2014) which at the date at which this volume states the law is on the OFCOM website.

3 As to the meaning of 'OFCOM' see PARA 14 note 1; and as to OFCOM see PARA 2 et seq.

4 Communications Act 2003 s 130(1)(b).

5 Communications Act 2003 s 130(1)(c).

6 As to the meaning of 'electronic communications network' see PARA 53.

7 Communications Act 2003 s 130(2). As to the meaning of 'electronic communications service' see PARA 53.

8 Communications Act 2003 s 130(3).

9 Communications Act 2003 s 130(4) (amended by SI 2010/2291). The Secretary of State may by order amend the Communications Act 2003 s 130 so as to substitute a different maximum penalty for the maximum penalty for the time being specified in s 130(4): s 130(9). No order is to be made containing provision authorised by s 130(9) unless a draft of the order has been laid before Parliament and approved by a resolution of each House: s 130(10). In exercise of this power the Secretary of State has made the Communications Act 2003 (Maximum Penalty for Persistent Misuse of Network or Service) Order 2010, SI 2010/2291. As to the Secretary of State see PARA 76 note 1. As to the power of the Secretary of State to make orders under the Communications Act 2003 see s 402; and PARA 74.

10 Communications Act 2003 s 130(5)(a).

11 Communications Act 2003 s 130(5)(b).

12 Communications Act 2003 s 130(5)(c).

13 Communications Act 2003 s 130(6)(a).

14 Communications Act 2003 s 130(6)(b).

15 Communications Act 2003 s 130(7). It is possible for a person both to be liable for an offence under ss 125–127 (see PARAS 207–208) and to have a penalty imposed on him under s 130 in respect of the same conduct: s 130(8).

133. Statement of policy on persistent misuse. It is the duty of OFCOM[1] to prepare and publish a statement of its general policy with respect to the exercise of its powers relating to persistent misuse[2]. OFCOM may from time to time revise that statement as it thinks fit[3]. Where OFCOM makes or revises its statement of policy, it must publish that statement or (as the case may be) the revised statement in such manner as it considers appropriate for bringing it to the attention of the persons who, in its opinion, are likely to be affected by it[4]. It is the duty of OFCOM, in exercising its powers[5], to have regard to the statement for the time being in force[6].

1 As to the meaning of 'OFCOM' see PARA 14 note 1; and as to OFCOM see PARA 2 et seq.
2 Communications Act 2003 s 131(1). The powers referred to in the text are those under the Communications Act 2003 ss 128–130 (see PARAS 130–132): s 131(1). See also Ofcom and the Information Commissioner's Office's Joint Action Plan on tackling nuisance calls and messages (December 2014) which at the date at which this volume states the law is on the OFCOM website.
3 Communications Act 2003 s 131(2).
4 Communications Act 2003 s 131(3).
5 Ie the powers conferred by the Communications Act 2003 ss 128–130: see PARAS 130–132.
6 Communications Act 2003 s 131(4).

(viii) Online Infringement of Copyright

134. Obligations in relation to online infringement of copyright. A copyright owner[1] may make a copyright infringement report[2] to the internet service provider[3] who provided the internet access service if it appears to the owner that a subscriber[4] to an internet access service has infringed the owner's copyright by means of the service or has allowed another person to use the service and that person has infringed the owner's copyright[5]. This and the obligation to provide copyright infringement lists[6] to copyright owners are initial obligations[7] for which OFCOM[8] may by order approve codes made to regulate those obligations[9]. OFCOM must prepare progress reports about the infringement of copyright by subscribers for the Secretary of State[10]. The Secretary of State may direct OFCOM to assess whether a technical obligation[11] should be imposed which obliges a provider to limit internet access to the subscriber to reduce or prevent infringement[12].

1 As to the meaning of 'copyright owner' see INFORMATION TECHNOLOGY LAW vol 57 (2012) PARA 526 note 1.
2 As to the meaning of 'copyright infringement report' see INFORMATION TECHNOLOGY LAW vol 57 (2012) PARA 526 note 5.
3 As to the meaning of 'internet service provider' see INFORMATION TECHNOLOGY LAW vol 57 (2012) PARA 526 note 6.
4 As to the meaning of 'subscriber' see INFORMATION TECHNOLOGY LAW vol 57 (2012) PARA 526 note 2.
5 See the Communications Act 2003 s 124A; and INFORMATION TECHNOLOGY LAW vol 57 (2012) PARA 526.
6 See the Communications Act 2003 s 124B; and INFORMATION TECHNOLOGY LAW vol 57 (2012) PARA 527. As to the meaning of 'copyright infringement list' see the Communications Act 2003 s 124A; INFORMATION TECHNOLOGY LAW vol 57 (2012) PARA 527.
7 As to the meaning of 'initial obligations' see INFORMATION TECHNOLOGY LAW vol 57 (2012) PARA 527.
8 As to the meaning of 'OFCOM' see PARA 14 note 1; and as to OFCOM see PARA 2 et seq.
9 See the Communications Act 2003 ss 124C-124E, 124M; and INFORMATION TECHNOLOGY LAW vol 57 (2012) PARA 528, 530. As to subscriber appeals see s 124K; and see INFORMATION TECHNOLOGY LAW vol 57 (2012) PARA 529. As to enforcement of obligations see s 124L; and INFORMATION TECHNOLOGY LAW vol 57 (2012) PARA 526.

10 See the Communications Act 2003 s 124F; and INFORMATION TECHNOLOGY LAW vol 57 (2012) PARA 531.
11 As to the meaning of 'technical obligation' see INFORMATION TECHNOLOGY LAW vol 57 (2012) PARA 532.
12 See the Communications Act 2003 ss 124G–124J; and INFORMATION TECHNOLOGY LAW vol 57 (2012) PARA 532–535. As to subscriber appeals see s 124K; and INFORMATION TECHNOLOGY LAW vol 57 (2012) PARA 536. As to enforcement of obligations see s 124L; and INFORMATION TECHNOLOGY LAW vol 57 (2012) PARA 526.

(ix) Internet Domain Registries

135. Powers in relation to internet domain registries. As from a day to be appointed[1], where the Secretary of State[2] is satisfied that a serious relevant failure[3] in relation to a qualifying internet domain registry[4] is taking place or has taken place and wishes to appoint a manager in respect of the property and affairs of the internet domain registry to remedy the failure[5] or apply to the High Court or a county court for an order to alter the registry's constitution[6], the Secretary of State must notify the internet domain registry, specifying the failure and a period during which the registry has the opportunity to make representations to the Secretary of State[7].

1 The Communications Act 2003 ss 124O–124R are added, as from a day to be appointed by the Digital Economy Act 2010 ss 19–21. At the date at which this volume states the law no such day had been appointed.
2 As to the Secretary of State see PARA 76 note 1.
3 There is a relevant failure if the registry, or any of its registrars or end-users, engages in prescribed practices that are unfair or involve the misuse of internet domain names or the arrangements made by the registry for dealing with complaints in connection with internet domain names do not comply with prescribed requirements: see the Communications Act 2003 s 120O; and INFORMATION TECHNOLOGY LAW vol 57 (2012) PARA 508. The relevant failure is serious if it has adversely affected or is likely adversely to affect the reputation or availability of electronic communications networks or electronic communications services provided in the United Kingdom or a part of the United Kingdom or the interests of consumers or members of the public in the United Kingdom or a part of the United Kingdom: see the Communications Act 2003 s 120O; and INFORMATION TECHNOLOGY LAW vol 57 (2012) PARA 508. As to the meaning of 'registrars' or 'end-users' see INFORMATION TECHNOLOGY LAW vol 57 (2012) PARA 508. See note 1.
4 As to the meaning of 'qualifying internet domain registry' see INFORMATION TECHNOLOGY LAW vol 57 (2012) PARA 508. See note 1.
5 See the Communications Act 2003 ss 124P, 124Q; and see INFORMATION TECHNOLOGY LAW vol 57 (2012) PARA 509–511. See note 1.
6 See the Communications Act 2003 s 124R; and see INFORMATION TECHNOLOGY LAW vol 57 (2012) PARA 512. See note 1.
7 See the Communications Act 2003 s 124O; and see INFORMATION TECHNOLOGY LAW vol 57 (2012) PARA 508. See note 1.

(x) Information Provisions

136. Power to require information. OFCOM[1] may require certain persons[2] to provide it with all such information as it considers necessary for the purpose of carrying out its functions under Chapter 1 of Part 2[3] of the Communications Act 2003[4]. Those persons are:
  (1) a communications provider[5];
  (2) a person who has been a communications provider[6];
  (3) a person who makes, or has made, any associated facilities[7] available to others[8];
  (4) a person, other than a communications provider, to whom a universal service condition[9] applies or has applied[10];

(5)   a person who supplies electronic communications apparatus[11];

(6)   a person not falling within heads (1) to (5) above who appears to OFCOM to have information required by it for the purpose of carrying out its functions under Chapter 1 of Part 2 of the Communications Act 2003[12].

The information that may be required by OFCOM includes, in particular, information that it requires for any one or more of the following purposes:

(a)   ascertaining whether a contravention of a condition or other requirement set or imposed by or under Chapter 1 of Part 2 of the Communications Act 2003 has occurred or is occurring[13];

(b)   ascertaining or verifying the administrative charges payable by a person to OFCOM[14];

(c)   ascertaining whether a provision of a condition of entitlement to provide a network or service[15] which is for the time being in force continues to be effective for the purpose for which it was made[16];

(d)   ascertaining or verifying amounts payable by virtue of a condition for giving effect to a determination or regulation made for the sharing of the burden of universal service obligations[17];

(e)   making a designation in accordance with regulations for the designation of universal service providers[18];

(f)   carrying out a review of compliance costs[19];

(g)   identifying markets and carrying out market analyses in accordance with, or for the purposes of, any provision of Chapter 1 of Part 2 of the Communications Act 2003[20];

(h)   considering a matter in exercise of that duty[21];

(i)   preparing a progress report about the infringement of copyright by subscribers to internet access services[22];

(j)   carrying out an assessment, taking steps to prepare for obligations or providing a report[23];

(k)   preparing a report on electronic communications networks matters and electronic communications services matters[24];

(l)   preparing a report on internet domain names[25];

(m)   assessing the security of a public electronic communications network or a public electronic communications service[26];

(n)   assessing the availability of a public electronic communications network[27];

(o)   identifying electronic communications apparatus that is suitable for shared use[28];

(p)   statistical purposes connected with the carrying out of any of OFCOM's functions under Chapter 1 of Part 2 of the Communications Act 2003[29].

The descriptions of information that a person may be required to provide[30] include, in particular information concerning future developments of an electronic communications network or electronic communications service that could have an impact on the wholesale services made available by the person to competitors and if a market power determination made in relation to a wholesale market is in force in the person's case, accounting data relating to any retail market associated with the wholesale market[31].

A person required to provide information under these provisions must provide it in such manner and within such reasonable period as may be specified by OFCOM[32].

OFCOM may require a communications provider, or a person who makes associated facilities available to others, to provide OFCOM with all such information as it considers necessary for the purpose of the carrying out, with a view to publication, and in the interest of the end-users of public electronic communications services, of comparative overviews of the quality and prices of such services[33]. OFCOM may also require a communications provider, or a person who makes associated facilities available to others, to provide it, for use for such statistical purposes as it thinks fit, with information relating to any electronic communications network[34], electronic communications service or associated facilities[35]. A person required to provide such information must provide it in such manner and within such reasonable period as may be specified by OFCOM[36].

1 As to the meaning of 'OFCOM' see PARA 14 note 1; and as to OFCOM see PARA 2 et seq.
2 Ie persons falling within the Communications Act 2003 s 135(2): see heads (1)–(6) in the text. As to the meaning of 'person' see PARA 14 note 2.
3 Ie the Communications Act 2003 Pt 2 Ch 1 (ss 32–151), relating to networks, services and the radio spectrum: see s 135.
4 Communications Act 2003 s 135(1). The powers in s 135 are subject to the limitations in s 137 (see PARA 137): s 135(5).
5 Communications Act 2003 s 135(2)(a). As to the meaning of 'communications provider' see PARA 17 note 23.
6 Communications Act 2003 s 135(2)(b).
7 As to the meaning of 'associated facilities' see PARA 53.
8 Communications Act 2003 s 135(2)(c).
9 As to the meaning of 'universal service condition' see PARA 87 note 5.
10 Communications Act 2003 s 135(2)(d).
11 Communications Act 2003 s 135(2)(e). As to the meaning of 'electronic communications apparatus' see PARA 99 note 10.
12 Communications Act 2003 s 135(2)(f).
13 Communications Act 2003 s 135(3)(a).
14 Communications Act 2003 s 135(3)(b). The reference to the administrative charges in the text is a reference to charges under s 38: see PARA 83. As to the meaning of 'person' see PARA 14 note 2.
15 Ie set under the Communications Act 2003 s 45: see PARA 87.
16 Communications Act 2003 s 135(3)(c).
17 Communications Act 2003 s 135(3)(d). The condition referred to in the text is one falling within s 51(1)(d): see PARA 98.
18 Communications Act 2003 s 135(3)(e). The regulations referred to in the text are those made under the Communications Act 2003 s 66: see PARA 102.
19 Communications Act 2003 s 135(3)(f). The review referred to in the text is a review under s 66 or s 70: see PARA 102.
20 Communications Act 2003 s 135(3)(g).
21 Communications Act 2003 s 135(3)(i).
22 Communications Act 2003 s 135(3)(ia) (s 135(3)(ia), (ib) added by the Digital Economy Act 2010 s 16). The progress report referred to in the text is one required under the Communications Act 2003 s 124F (see PARA 134; and INFORMATION TECHNOLOGY LAW vol 57 (2012) PARA 531): s 135(3)(ia) (as so added).
23 Communications Act 2003 s 135(3)(ib) (as added: see note 22) The reference in the text to carrying out an assessment, taking steps or providing a report is to assessment, preparation and provision of a report under s 124G (see PARA 134; and INFORMATION TECHNOLOGY LAW vol 57 (2012) PARA 532–535): s 135(3)(ib) (as so added).
24 Communications Act 2003 s 135(3)(ic) (s 135(3)(ic), (id) added by the Digital Economy Act 2010 s 1). The report referred to in the text is one required under the Communications Act 2003 s 134A (see PARA 150): s 135(3)(ic) (as so added).
25 Communications Act 2003 s 135(3)(id) (as added: see note 24). The report referred to in the text is one required under s 134C (see INFORMATION TECHNOLOGY LAW vol 57 (2012) PARA 506): s 135(3)(id) (as so added).
26 Communications Act 2003 s 135(3)(ie) (s 135(3)(ie)–(ig) added by SI 2011/1210).
27 Communications Act 2003 s 135(3)(if) (as added: see note 26).
28 Communications Act 2003 s 135(3)(ig) (as added: see note 26).

29 Communications Act 2003 s 135(3)(j).
30 Ie under the Communications Act 2003 s 135(1).
31 Communications Act 2003 s 135(3A) (added by SI 2011/1210).
32 Communications Act 2003 s 135(4). As to contravention of the notification provisions see PARA 138 et seq.
33 Communications Act 2003 s 136(1), (2). The powers in s 136 are subject to the limitations in s 137 (see PARA 137): s 136(5). As to the meaning of 'public electronic communications service' see PARA 98 note 3.
34 As to the meaning of 'electronic communications network' see PARA 53.
35 Communications Act 2003 s 136(3).
36 Communications Act 2003 s 136(4).

137. Restrictions on imposing information requirements. The purposes for which, and manner in which, information may be required by OFCOM[1] are limited by the following provisions[2].

OFCOM is not to require the provision of information for the purpose of ascertaining whether a contravention of a general condition[3] has occurred, or is occurring, unless:

(1) the requirement is imposed for the purpose of investigating a matter about which OFCOM has received a complaint[4];

(2) the requirement is imposed for the purposes of an investigation that OFCOM has decided to carry out into whether or not the general condition in question has been complied with[5];

(3) the condition in question is one which OFCOM has reason to suspect is one that has been or is being contravened[6];

(4) the condition in question is one[7] for giving effect to a determination or regulation made for the sharing of the burden of universal service obligations[8]; or

(5) the condition in question is one relating to the effective and efficient use of telephone numbers[9].

OFCOM is not to require the provision of information[10] except:

(a) by a demand for the information that describes the required information and sets out OFCOM's reasons for requiring it[11]; and

(b) where the making of a demand for the information is proportionate to the use to which the information is to be put in the carrying out of OFCOM's functions[12].

OFCOM is not to require the provision of information for a purpose assessing the security of a public electronic communications network or a public electronic communications service[13] or assessing the availability of a public electronic communications network[14] unless:

(i) the requirement is imposed for the purpose of investigating a matter about which OFCOM have received a complaint[15];

(ii) the requirement is imposed for the purposes of an investigation that OFCOM have decided to carry out into whether or not an obligation[16] has been complied with[17]; or

(iii) OFCOM have reason to suspect that an obligation[18] has been or is being contravened[19].

The reasons for requiring information for statistical purposes must set out the statistical purposes for which the information is required[20].

A demand for information required by OFCOM must be contained in a notice served on the person from whom the information is required[21]. However, in the case of information required by OFCOM for the purpose of ascertaining who is liable to administrative charges[22], the demand may:

(A)   be made by being published in such manner as OFCOM considers appropriate for bringing it to the attention of the persons who are described in the demand as the persons from whom the information is required[23]; and

(B)   take the form of a general demand for a person so described to provide information when specified conditions relevant to his liability to such charges are satisfied in his case[24].

1   Ie under the Communications Act 2003 ss 135, 136: see PARA 136. As to the meaning of 'OFCOM' see PARA 14 note 1; and as to OFCOM see PARA 2 et seq.
2   Communications Act 2003 s 137(1).
3   As to the meaning of 'general condition' see PARA 87 note 4. As to general conditions see further PARA 98 et seq.
4   Communications Act 2003 s 137(2)(a).
5   Communications Act 2003 s 137(2)(b).
6   Communications Act 2003 s 137(2)(c) (amended by SI 2011/1210).
7   Ie a condition falling within the Communications Act 2003 s 51(1)(d): see PARA 98.
8   Communications Act 2003 s 137(2)(d).
9   Communications Act 2003 s 137(2)(e) (amended by SI 2011/1210).
10 Ie under the Communications Act 2003 s 135 or s 136: see PARA 136.
11 Communications Act 2003 s 137(3)(a).
12 Communications Act 2003 s 137(3)(b).
13 Ie specified in the Communications Act 2003 s 135(3)(ie): see PARA 136.
14 Ie specified in the Communications Act 2003 s 135(3)(if): see PARA 136.
15 Communications Act 2003 s 137(2A)(a) (s 137(2A) added by SI 2011/1210).
16 Ie under the Communications Act 2003 s 105A: see PARA 126.
17 Communications Act 2003 s 137(2A)(b) (as added: see note 15).
18 Ie under the Communications Act 2003 s 105A: see PARA 126.
19 Communications Act 2003 s 137(2A)(c) (as added: see note 15).
20 Communications Act 2003 s 137(4).
21 Communications Act 2003 s 137(5). As to service of notices see PARA 44 et seq.
22 Ie under the Communications Act 2003 s 38: see PARA 83.
23 Communications Act 2003 s 137(6)(a).
24 Communications Act 2003 s 137(6)(b).

138. Notification of contravention of information requirements. Where OFCOM[1] determines that there are reasonable grounds for believing that a person[2] is contravening, or has contravened, a requirement to provide information[3], it may give that person a notification[4] which:

(1)   sets out the determination made by OFCOM[5];

(2)   specifies the requirement and contravention in respect of which that determination has been made[6];

(3)   specifies the period during which the person notified has an opportunity to make representations[7];

(4)   specifies the information to be provided by the person to OFCOM in order to comply with requirements[8];

(5)   specifies any penalty which OFCOM is minded to impose[9]; and

(6)   where the contravention is serious, specifies any direction which OFCOM is minded to give[10].

A notification may be given in respect of more than one contravention and, if it is given in respect of a continuing contravention, may be given in respect of any period during which the contravention has continued[11]. Where a notification has been given to a person in respect of a contravention of a requirement, OFCOM may give a further notification in respect of the same contravention of that requirement if, and only if:

(a)   the contravention is one occurring after the time of the giving of the earlier notification[12];

(b)   the contravention is a continuing contravention and the subsequent notification is in respect of so much of a period as falls after a period to which the earlier notification relates[13]; or

(c)   the earlier notification has been withdrawn without a penalty having been imposed in respect of the notified contravention[14].

OFCOM may not give a person a notification under these provisions in respect of a contravention of a requirement[15] of information for identifying electronic communications apparatus that is suitable for shared use if the information required was previously provided by the person to OFCOM within the period of six months ending with the day on which the requirement was imposed[16].

1   As to the meaning of 'OFCOM' see PARA 14 note 1; and as to OFCOM see PARA 2 et seq.
2   As to the meaning of 'person' see PARA 14 note 2.
3   Ie a requirement imposed under the Communications Act 2003 ss 135, 136: see PARA 136.
4   Communications Act 2003 s 138(1).
5   Communications Act 2003 s 138(2)(a).
6   Communications Act 2003 s 138(2)(b) (amended by SI 2011/1210).
7   Communications Act 2003 s 138(2)(c) (substituted by SI 2011/1210).
8   Communications Act 2003 s 138(2)(d) (s 138(2)(d)–(f) added by SI 2011/1210). The requirements referred to in the text are those under the Communications Act 2003 s 135 or s 136: see PARA 136.
9   Communications Act 2003 s 138(2)(e) (as added: see note 8). The penalty referred to in the text is one imposed in accordance with s 139: see PARA 140.
10 Communications Act 2003 s 138(2)(f) (as added: see note 8). The directions referred to in the text is one given under s 140: see PARA 142.
11 Communications Act 2003 s 138(8).
12 Communications Act 2003 s 138(9)(a).
13 Communications Act 2003 s 138(9)(b).
14 Communications Act 2003 s 138(9)(c). As to penalties for contravention see PARA 140.
15 Ie imposed under the Communications Act 2003 s 135(3)(ig): see PARA 136.
16 Communications Act 2003 s 138(9A) (added by SI 2011/1210).

139.   Enforcement of notification of contravention of information requirements. Where:

(1)   a person has been given a notification of contravention of information requirements[1];

(2)   OFCOM[2] has allowed the person an opportunity to make representations about the matters notified[3]; and

(3)   the period allowed for the making of representations has expired[4],

OFCOM may:

(a)   give the person a decision (a 'confirmation decision') confirming the imposition of requirements on the person, or the giving of a direction to the person, or both, in accordance with the notification[5]; or

(b)   inform the person that it is satisfied with the person's representations and that no further action will be taken[6].

OFCOM may not give a confirmation decision to a person unless, after considering any representations, it is satisfied that the person has, in one or more of the respects notified, been in contravention of a requirement[7].

A confirmation decision:

(i)   must be given to the person without delay[8];

(ii)   must include reasons for the decision[9];

(iii) may require immediate action by the person to comply with a requirement[10] or may specify a period within which the person must comply with the requirement[11]; and

(iv)　may require the person to pay:

(A)　the penalty specified in the notification[12], or

(B)　such lesser penalty as OFCOM considers appropriate in the light of the person's representations or steps taken by the person to comply with the condition or remedy the consequences of the contravention[13],

and may specify the period within which the penalty is to be paid[14].

A penalty imposed by a confirmation decision must be paid to OFCOM and if not paid within the period specified by it, is to be recoverable by it accordingly[15].

It is the duty of the person to comply with any requirement imposed by a confirmation decision[16]. Such a duty is enforceable in civil proceedings by OFCOM for an injunction or for any other appropriate remedy or relief[17].

1　Communications Act 2003 s 139A(1)(a) (s 139A added by SI 2011/1210). The notification referred to in the text is a notification under the Communications Act 2003 s 138: see PARA 138.
2　As to the meaning of 'OFCOM' see PARA 14 note 1; and as to OFCOM see PARA 2 et seq.
3　Communications Act 2003 s 139A(1)(b) (as added: see note 1).
4　Communications Act 2003 s 139A(1)(c) (as added: see note 1).
5　Communications Act 2003 s 139A(2)(a) (as added: see note 1). The notification referred to in the text is a notification under s 138: see PARA 138.
6　Communications Act 2003 s 139A(2)(b) (as added: see note 1).
7　Communications Act 2003 s 139A(3) (as added: see note 1). The requirement referred to in the text is one notified under s 138: see PARA 138.
8　Communications Act 2003 s 139A(4)(a) (as added: see note 1).
9　Communications Act 2003 s 139A(4)(b) (as added: see note 1).
10　Ie notified under the Communications Act 2003 s 138(2)(d): see PARA 138.
11　Communications Act 2003 s 139A(4)(c) (as added: see note 1).
12　Communications Act 2003 s 139A(4)(d)(i) (as added: see note 1). The penalty referred to in the text is one specified in the notification under s 138: see PARA 138.
13　Communications Act 2003 s 139A(4)(d)(ii) (as added: see note 1).
14　Communications Act 2003 s 139A(4)(d) (as added: see note 1).
15　Communications Act 2003 s 139A(7) (as added: see note 1).
16　Communications Act 2003 s 139A(5) (as added: see note 1).
17　Communications Act 2003 s 139A(6) (as added: see note 1).

140.　Penalties for contravention of information requirements. Where a person[1] is given a notification of a contravention of the information requirements[2] which specifies a proposed penalty[3], OFCOM[4] may specify a penalty if no proceedings for an offence[5] have been brought against the notified person in respect of the contravention[6].

Where a notification relates to more than one contravention, a separate penalty may be specified in respect of each contravention[7]. Where such a notification relates to a continuing contravention, no more than one penalty may be specified in respect of the period of contravention specified in the notification[8]. In relation to a continuing contravention, a penalty may be specified in respect of each day on which the contravention continues after the giving of a confirmation decision[9] which requires immediate action or the expiry of any period specified in the confirmation decision for complying with a requirement so specified but the amount of penalty is to be such[10].

In relation to a continuing contravention, the amount of a penalty is to be such amount as OFCOM determines to be appropriate and proportionate to the contravention in respect of which it is imposed, not exceeding £500 per day[11]. The amount of any other penalty imposed under these provisions is to be such amount not exceeding £2,000,000 as OFCOM determines to be both appropriate and proportionate to the contravention in respect of which it is imposed[12].

1   As to the meaning of 'person' see PARA 14 note 2.
2   Ie under the Communications Act 2003 s 138: see PARA 138.
3   Communications Act 2003 s 139(1) (substituted by SI 2011/1210).
4   As to the meaning of 'OFCOM' see PARA 14 note 1; and as to OFCOM see PARA 2 et seq.
5   Ie under the Communications Act 2003 s 144: see PARA 146.
6   Communications Act 2003 s 139(2) (s 139(2)–(4), (5) amended by SI 2011/1210).
7   Communications Act 2003 s 139(3) (as amended: see note 6).
8   Communications Act 2003 s 139(4) (as amended: see note 6).
9   Ie under the Communications Act 2003 s 139A(4)(c): see PARA 139.
10   Communications Act 2003 s 139(4A) (s 139(4A), (4B) added by SI 2011/1210).
11   Communications Act 2003 s 139(4B) (as added: see note 10).
12   Communications Act 2003 s 139(5) (amended by SI 2011/1210). The Secretary of State may by order amend the Communications Act 2003 s 139 so as to substitute a different maximum penalty for the maximum penalty for the time being specified in s 139(5): s 139(9). No order is to be made containing provision authorised by s 139(9) unless a draft of the order has been laid before Parliament and approved by a resolution of each House: s 139(10). In exercise of this power the Secretary of State has made the Communications Act 2003 (Maximum Penalty for Contravention of Information Requirements) Order 2011, SI 2011/1773. As to the Secretary of State see PARA 76 note 1. As to the power of the Secretary of State to make orders under the Communications Act 2003 see s 402; and PARA 74.

141. Power to deal with urgent cases: contravention of information requirements. The following provisions apply where OFCOM[1] determines:

(1)   that it is entitled to give a notification[2] with respect to a contravention by a person ('P') of a requirement to provide information[3];

(2)   that there are reasonable grounds for suspecting that the case is an urgent case[4]; and

(3)   that the urgency of the case makes it appropriate for OFCOM to take action under these provisions[5].

A case is an urgent case for these purposes if the contravention has resulted in, or creates an immediate risk of:

(a)   a serious threat to the safety of the public, to public health or to national security[6];

(b)   serious economic or operational problems for persons (other than P) who are communications providers or persons who make associated facilities available[7]; or

(c)   serious economic or operational problems for persons who make use of electronic communications networks, electronic communications services or associated facilities[8].

OFCOM may give P a direction:

(i)   that the entitlement of P to provide electronic communications networks or electronic communications services, or to make associated facilities available, is suspended (either generally or in relation to particular networks, services or facilities)[9]; or

(ii)   that that entitlement is restricted in the respects set out in the direction[10].

As soon as reasonably practicable after giving a direction[11], OFCOM must give the person to whom it is given an opportunity to make representations to it about the grounds on which it was given and its effect and an opportunity to propose steps to remedy the situation[12]. As soon as practicable after the period allowed by OFCOM for making those representations has ended (and in any event within three months beginning with the day on which the direction was given), it must determine whether the contravention providing the grounds for the giving of the direction did occur and whether the circumstances made it an urgent case justifying the giving of the direction[13]. If OFCOM requires additional time to consider representations received or decides that it is necessary to obtain additional information from the person in order to make a determination[14], the period of three months[15] may be extended by up to three months[16].

If OFCOM decides that the contravention did occur and that the direction was justified, it may confirm the direction[17]. If not, it must exercise its power to revoke it[18]. As soon as reasonably practicable after deciding whether to confirm the direction, OFCOM must notify the person to whom it was given of its decision[19].

1   As to the meaning of 'OFCOM' see PARA 14 note 1; and as to OFCOM see PARA 2 et seq.
2   Ie under the Communications Act 2003 s 138: see PARA 138.
3   Communications Act 2003 s 139B(1)(a) (s 139B, 139C added by SI 2011/1210). The requirement to provide information referred to in the text is one imposed under the Communications Act 2003 s 135 or s 136 (see PARA 136): s 139B(1)(a) (as so added).
4   Communications Act 2003 s 139B(1)(b) (as added: see note 3).
5   Communications Act 2003 s 139B(1)(c) (as added: see note 3).
6   Communications Act 2003 s 139B(2)(a) (as added: see note 3).
7   Communications Act 2003 s 139B(2)(b) (as added: see note 3).
8   Communications Act 2003 s 139B(2)(c) (as added: see note 3).
9   Communications Act 2003 s 139B(3)(a) (as added: see note 3). The provisions of s 140(3)–(6) (see PARA 142) apply in relation to a direction under s 139B(3) as they apply in relation to a direction under s 140: s 139B(4) (as so added).
10 Communications Act 2003 s 139B(3)(b) (as added: see note 3).
11 Ie under the Communications Act 2003 s 139B(3).
12 Communications Act 2003 s 139C(1) (as added: see note 3).
13 Communications Act 2003 s 139C(2) (as added: see note 3).
14 Ie under the Communications Act 2003 s 139C(2).
15 Ie mentioned in the Communications Act 2003 s 139C(2).
16 Communications Act 2003 s 139C(3) (as added: see note 3).
17 Communications Act 2003 s 139C(4) (as added: see note 3).
18 Communications Act 2003 s 139C(5) (as added: see note 3).
19 Communications Act 2003 s 139C(6) (as added: see note 3).

142.   Suspending service provision for information contraventions.   OFCOM[1] may give a direction to a person who is a communications provider[2] or who makes associated facilities[3] available (the 'contravening provider') if it is satisfied:

(1)   that he is or has been in serious or repeated contravention of requirements to provide information to enable OFCOM to carry out its Chapter 1 functions or for related purposes[4];

(2)   that the requirements are not requirements imposed for purposes connected with the carrying out of OFCOM's functions in relation to SMP apparatus conditions[5];

(3)   in the case of a repeated contravention, that an attempt, by the imposition of penalties or the giving of notifications[6] and confirmation decisions[7], or both, or the bringing of proceedings for an offence[8], to secure compliance with the contravened requirements has failed[9]; and

(4)   that the giving of the direction is appropriate and proportionate to the contravention in respect of which it is given[10].

Such a direction may be:

(a)   a direction that the entitlement of the contravening provider to provide electronic communications networks[11] or electronic communications services[12], or to make associated facilities available, is suspended (either generally or in relation to particular networks, services or facilities)[13]; or

(b)   a direction that that entitlement is restricted in the respects set out in the direction[14].

A direction must specify the networks, services and facilities to which it relates; and, except so far as it otherwise provides, it takes effect for an indefinite period beginning with the time at which it is notified to the person to whom it is given[15]. A direction:

(i)   in providing for the effect of a suspension or restriction to be postponed, may provide for it to take effect only at a time determined by or in accordance with the terms of the direction[16]; and

(ii)   in connection with the suspension or restriction contained in the direction or with the postponement of its effect, may impose such conditions on the contravening provider as appear to OFCOM to be appropriate for the purpose of protecting that provider's customers[17].

Those conditions may include a condition requiring the making of payments by way of compensation for loss or damage suffered by the contravening provider's customers as a result of the direction, or in respect of annoyance, inconvenience or anxiety to which they have been put in consequence of the direction[18].

If OFCOM considers it appropriate to do so (whether or not in consequence of any representations or proposals made to it), it may revoke a direction or modify its conditions:

(A)   with effect from such time as it may direct[19];

(B)   subject to compliance with such requirements as it may specify[20]; and

(C)   to such extent and in relation to such networks, services or facilities, or parts of a network, service or facility, as it may determine[21].

1   As to the meaning of 'OFCOM' see PARA 14 note 1; and as to OFCOM see PARA 2 et seq.
2   As to the meaning of 'communications provider' see PARA 17 note 23. As to the meaning of 'person' see PARA 14 note 2.
3   As to the meaning of 'associated facilities' see PARA 53.
4   Communications Act 2003 s 140(1)(a) (amended by SI 2011/1210). The requirements referred to in the text are those imposed under the Communications Act 2003 s 135, s 136, or either of them: see PARA 136. 'Chapter 1 functions' are functions under Pt 2 Ch 1 (ss 32–151). For the purposes of s 140, there are repeated contraventions by a person of requirements imposed under s 135, s 136, or either of them, to the extent that:
    (1)   in the case of a previous notification of a contravention given to that person under s 138 (see PARA 138), OFCOM has given a confirmation decision to that person under s 139A(2) (see PARA 139) in respect of the contravention (s 140(7)(a) (s 140(7)(a), (b) substituted by SI 2011/1210)); and
    (2)   in the period of 24 months following the giving of that confirmation decision, one or more further confirmation decisions have been given to that person in respect of contraventions of numbering conditions (Communications Act 2003 s 140(7)(b) (as so substituted)),
    and for these purposes it is immaterial whether the confirmation decisions related to the same contravention or to different contraventions of the same or different requirements or of requirements under different provisions: s 140(7).
5   Communications Act 2003 s 140(1)(b). As to the meaning of 'SMP apparatus condition' see PARA 87 note 8.
6   Ie under the Communications Act 2003 s 138: see PARA 138.
7   Ie under the Communications Act 2003 s 139A: see PARA 139.
8   Ie under the Communications Act 2003 s 144: see PARA 146.
9   Communications Act 2003 s 140(1)(c) (substituted by SI 2011/1210).
10 Communications Act 2003 s 140(1)(d) (substituted by SI 2011/1210). As to the procedure see PARA 144.

11 As to the meaning of 'electronic communications network' see PARA 53.
12 As to the meaning of 'electronic communications services' see PARA 53.
13 Communications Act 2003 s 140(2)(a).
14 Communications Act 2003 s 140(2)(b).
15 Communications Act 2003 s 140(3).
16 Communications Act 2003 s 140(4)(a).
17 Communications Act 2003 s 140(4)(b).
18 Communications Act 2003 s 140(5).
19 Communications Act 2003 s 140(6)(a).
20 Communications Act 2003 s 140(6)(a).
21 Communications Act 2003 s 140(6)(c).

143. Suspending apparatus supply for information contraventions. OFCOM[1] may give a direction to a person[2] who supplies electronic communications apparatus[3] (the 'contravening supplier') if it is satisfied:

(1)   that he is or has been in serious and repeated contravention of requirements to provide information for the purposes of OFCOM's Chapter 1 functions[4];

(2)   that an attempt, by the imposition of penalties[5] or the bringing of proceedings for an offence[6], to secure compliance with the contravened requirements has failed[7]; and

(3)   that the giving of the direction is appropriate and proportionate to the seriousness (when repeated as they have been) of the contraventions[8].

Such a direction may be:

(a)   a direction to the contravening supplier to cease to act as a supplier of electronic communications apparatus (either generally or in relation to apparatus of a particular description)[9]; or

(b)   a direction imposing such restrictions as may be set out in the direction on the supply by that supplier of electronic communications apparatus (either generally or in relation to apparatus of a particular description)[10].

A direction takes effect, except so far as it otherwise provides, for an indefinite period beginning with the time at which it is notified to the person to whom it is given[11]. A direction:

(i)   may provide for a prohibition or restriction to take effect only at a time determined by or in accordance with the terms of the direction[12]; and

(ii)   in connection with a prohibition or restriction contained in the direction or with the postponement of its effect, may impose such conditions on the contravening supplier as appear to OFCOM to be appropriate for the purpose of protecting that supplier's customers[13].

Those conditions may include a condition requiring the making of payments by way of compensation for loss or damage suffered by the contravening supplier's customers as a result of the direction, or in respect of annoyance, inconvenience or anxiety to which they have been put in consequence of the direction[14].

If OFCOM considers it appropriate to do so (whether or not in consequence of representations or proposals made to it), it may revoke a direction or modify its conditions:

(A)   with effect from such time as it may direct[15];

(B)   subject to compliance with such requirements as it may specify[16]; and

(C)   to such extent and in relation to such apparatus or descriptions of apparatus as it may determine[17].

1   As to the meaning of 'OFCOM' see PARA 14 note 1; and as to OFCOM see PARA 2 et seq.

2   As to the meaning of 'person' see PARA 14 note 2.
3   As to the meaning of 'electronic communications apparatus' see PARA 88 note 10.
4   Communications Act 2003 s 141(1)(a). The requirements referred to in the text are those imposed under s 135: see PARA 136. For the purposes of s 141, contraventions by a person of requirements imposed under s 135 are repeated contraventions if:
    (1)   in the case of a previous notification given to that person under s 138 (see PARA 138), OFCOM has determined for the purposes of s 139(2) (see PARA 140) that such a contravention did occur (s 141(7)(a)); and
    (2)   in the period of 12 months following the day of the making of that determination, one or more further notifications have been given to that person in respect of contraventions of such requirements (s 141(7)(b)),
   and for these purposes it is immaterial whether the notifications related to the same contravention or to different contraventions of the same or different requirements: s 141(7).
5   Ie under the Communications Act 2003 s 139: see PARA 140.
6   Ie under the Communications Act 2003 s 144: see PARA 146.
7   Communications Act 2003 s 141(1)(b).
8   Communications Act 2003 s 141(1)(c). As to the procedure see PARA 144.
9   Communications Act 2003 s 141(2)(a).
10   Communications Act 2003 s 141(2)(b).
11   Communications Act 2003 s 141(3).
12   Communications Act 2003 s 141(4)(a).
13   Communications Act 2003 s 141(4)(b).
14   Communications Act 2003 s 141(5).
15   Communications Act 2003 s 141(6)(a).
16   Communications Act 2003 s 141(6)(b).
17   Communications Act 2003 s 141(6)(c).

144.   Procedure for directions. Except in an urgent case[1] or a case where a proposed direction has been notified to a person[2] OFCOM[3] is not to give a direction suspending service provision or apparatus supply[4] unless it has:
    (1)   notified the contravening provider[5] or contravening supplier[6] of the proposed direction and of the conditions (if any) which it is proposing to impose by that direction[7];
    (2)   provided him with an opportunity of making representations about the proposals and of proposing steps for remedying the situation[8]; and
    (3)   considered every representation and proposal made to it during the period allowed by it for the contravening provider or the contravening supplier to take advantage of that opportunity[9].
That period must be:
    (a)   in relation to a direction suspending service[10], such reasonable period as OFCOM may determine[11];
    (b)   in relation to a direction suspending apparatus supply[12], a period ending not less than one month after the day of the giving of the notification[13].
As soon as practicable after giving a direction in an urgent case, OFCOM must provide the contravening provider or contravening supplier with an opportunity of making representations about the effect of the direction and of any of its conditions and proposing steps for remedying the situation[14].

In relation to a direction suspending service in an urgent case, as soon as practicable after the period allowed by OFCOM for making those representations has ended (and in any event within three months beginning with the day on which the direction was given), it must determine whether the contravention providing the grounds for the giving of the direction did occur and whether the circumstances made it an urgent case justifying the giving of the direction[15]. The period of three months[16] may be extended by up to three months if OFCOM:
    (i)   require additional time to consider representations received[17]; or

    (ii)   decide that it is necessary to obtain additional information from the person in order to make a determination[18].

1   A case is an urgent case for the purposes of the Communications Act 2003 s 142 if OFCOM:

    (1)   considers that it would be inappropriate, because the contraventions in question fall within s 142(5), to allow time, before giving a direction under s 140 (see PARA 142) or s 141 (see PARA 143), for the making and consideration of representations (s 142(4)(a)); and

    (2)   decides for that reason to act in accordance with s 142(3) (see the text to note 14) instead of s 142(1) (see the text to notes 2–9) (s 142(4)(b)).

    The contraventions fall within s 142(5) if they have resulted in, or create an immediate risk of:

    (a)   a serious threat to the safety of the public, to public health or to national security (s 142(5)(a));

    (b)   serious economic or operational problems for persons (apart from the contravening provider or contravening supplier) who are communications providers or persons who make associated facilities available (s 142(5)(b)); or

    (c)   serious economic or operational problems for persons who make use of electronic communications networks, electronic communications services or associated facilities (s 142(5)(c)).

2   Ie in the Communications Act 2003 s 138(2)(f): see PARA 138.
3   As to the meaning of 'OFCOM' see PARA 14 note 1; and as to OFCOM see PARA 2 et seq.
4   Ie under the Communications Act 2003 s 140 or s 141: see PARAS 142–143.
5   'Contravening provider' has the same meaning as in the Communications Act 2003 s 140 (see PARA 142): s 142(6).
6   'Contravening supplier' has the same meaning as in the Communications Act 2003 s 141 (see PARA 143): s 142(6).
7   Communications Act 2003 s 142(1)(a).
8   Communications Act 2003 s 142(1)(b).
9   Communications Act 2003 s 142(1)(c).
10   Ie under the Communications Act 2003 s 140: see PARA 142.
11   Communications Act 2003 s 142(2A)(a) (s 142(2A) added by SI 2011/1210).
12   Ie under the Communications Act 2003 s 141: see PARA 143.
13   Communications Act 2003 s 142(2A)(b) (as added: see note 11).
14   Communications Act 2003 s 142(3).
15   Communications Act 2003 s 142(3A) (s 142(3A), (3B) added by SI 2011/1210).
16   Ie mentioned in the Communications Act 2003 s 142(3A).
17   Communications Act 2003 s 142(3B)(a) (as added: see note 15).
18   Communications Act 2003 s 142(3B)(b) (as added: see note 15).The determination referred to in the text is a determination under s 142(3A): s 142(3B)(b) (as so added).

145. Enforcement of directions. A person[1] is guilty of an offence if he provides an electronic communications network[2] or electronic communications service[3], or makes available any associated facility[4], while his entitlement to do so is suspended by a direction by OFCOM[5], or in contravention of a restriction contained in such a direction[6].

A person is guilty of an offence if he supplies electronic communications apparatus[7] while prohibited from doing so by a direction by OFCOM[8], or in contravention of a restriction contained in such a direction[9].

A person guilty of an offence under these provisions is liable:

    (1)   on summary conviction, to a fine not exceeding the statutory maximum[10];

    (2)   on conviction on indictment, to a fine[11].

1   As to the meaning of 'person' see PARA 14 note 2.
2   As to the meaning of 'electronic communications network' see PARA 53.
3   As to the meaning of 'electronic communications service' see PARA 53.
4   As to the meaning of 'associated facilities' see PARA 53.
5   Ie under the Communications Act 2003 s 140: see PARA 142. As to the meaning of 'OFCOM' see PARA 14 note 1; and as to OFCOM see PARA 2 et seq.

6   Communications Act 2003 s 143(1).
7   As to the meaning of 'electronic communications apparatus' see PARA 88 note 10.
8   Ie under the Communications Act 2003 s 141: see PARA 140.
9   Communications Act 2003 s 143(2).
10 Communications Act 2003 s 143(3)(a). As to the statutory maximum see SENTENCING AND DISPOSITION OF OFFENDERS vol 92 (2010) PARA 140.
11 Communications Act 2003 s 143(3)(b). Sections 96A–99 (see PARAS 117–120) apply in relation to a contravention of conditions imposed by a direction under s 139B or s 140 as they apply in relation to a contravention of conditions set under s 45 (see PARA 87), other than SMP apparatus conditions: s 143(4) (substituted by SI 2011/1210). The Communications Act 2003 ss 94–96 and 97 to 99 apply in relation to a contravention of conditions imposed by a direction under s 141 as they apply in relation to a contravention of SMP apparatus conditions: s 143(5) (added by SI 2011/1210). As to the meaning of 'SMP apparatus condition' see PARA 87 note 8.

146.   Offences in connection with information requirements.   A person[1] who fails to provide information in accordance with a requirement of OFCOM[2] is guilty of an offence and is liable, on summary conviction, to a fine not exceeding the statutory maximum[3] and, on conviction on indictment, to a fine[4]. In proceedings against a person for such an offence, it is a defence for that person to show:

(1)   that it was not reasonably practicable for him to comply with the requirement within the period specified by OFCOM[5]; but

(2)   that he has taken all reasonable steps to provide the required information after the end of that period[6].

Proceedings for such an offence may be brought in respect of a contravention by a person of a requirement imposed on him[7] only if:

(a)   OFCOM has given the person a notification[8] in respect of that contravention[9];

(b)   the notification required the person to provide information, a confirmation decision has been given[10] in respect of that requirement and the period allowed under that decision has expired without the required information having been provided[11]; and

(c)   OFCOM has not imposed a financial penalty[12] in respect of that contravention[13].

A person is guilty of an offence if, in pursuance of any requirement to provide information[14], he provides any information that is false in any material particular and, at the time he provides it, he either knows it to be false or is reckless as to whether or not it is false[15]. A person guilty of such an offence is liable, on summary conviction, to a fine not exceeding the statutory maximum and, on conviction on indictment, to imprisonment for a term not exceeding two years or to a fine, or to both[16].

1   As to the meaning of 'person' see PARA 14 note 2.
2   Ie under the Communications Act 2003 s 135 or s 136: see PARA 136. As to the meaning of 'OFCOM' see PARA 14 note 1; and as to OFCOM see PARA 2 et seq.
3   As to the statutory maximum see SENTENCING AND DISPOSITION OF OFFENDERS vol 92 (2010) PARA 140.
4   Communications Act 2003 s 144(1).
5   Communications Act 2003 s 144(2)(a).
6   Communications Act 2003 s 144(2)(b).
7   Ie under the Communications Act 2003 s 135 or 136: see PARA 136.
8   Ie under the Communications Act 2003 s 138: see PARA 138.
9   Communications Act 2003 s 144(5)(a).
10 Ie under the Communications Act 2003 s 139A: see PARA 139.
11 Communications Act 2003 s 144(5)(b) (substituted by SI 2011/1210).
12 Ie under the Communications Act 2003 s 139: see PARA 140.
13 Communications Act 2003 s 144(5)(c).

14 Ie under the Communications Act 2003 s 135 or s 136: see PARA 135.
15 Communications Act 2003 s 144(3).
16 Communications Act 2003 s 144(4).

147. Statement of policy on information gathering. It is the duty of OFCOM[1] to prepare and publish a statement of its general policy with respect to the exercise of its powers to require the provision of information[2] and the uses to which it is proposing to put information obtained under those powers[3]. OFCOM may from time to time revise that statement as it thinks fit[4]. Where OFCOM makes or revises its statement of policy, it must publish that statement or (as the case may be) the revised statement in such manner as it considers appropriate for bringing it to the attention of the persons who, in its opinion, are likely to be affected by it[5]. It is the duty of OFCOM, in exercising the powers conferred on it in relation to the provision of information[6], to have regard to the statement for the time being in force[7].

1 As to the meaning of 'OFCOM' see PARA 14 note 1; and as to OFCOM see PARA 2 et seq.
2 Ie under the Communications Act 2003 ss 135, 136: see PARA 136.
3 Communications Act 2003 s 145(1). As to the policy statement on information gathering at the date this volume states the law, see the OFCOM website.
4 Communications Act 2003 s 145(2).
5 Communications Act 2003 s 145(3).
6 Ie by the Communications Act 2003 ss 135–144: see PARAS 136–146.
7 Communications Act 2003 s 145(4).

148. Provision of information by OFCOM. OFCOM[1] must comply with a request made by a person[2] under these provisions[3]:

(1) to notify the person whether or not a notification of his intention to provide a network or service is required to be submitted by him[4];

(2) to notify the person whether a notification submitted by him for that purpose satisfies the requirements of Chapter 1 of Part 2 of the Communications Act 2003[5];

(3) to provide the person with such information about his rights as may be necessary for the purpose of facilitating the negotiation by him of his right to network access[6]; or

(4) to provide the person with such information as it considers necessary to enable him to apply for a direction[7] applying the electronic communications code to be made in his case[8].

Such a request must be made in such manner as OFCOM may require[9].

OFCOM is not required to comply with a request under these provisions if (without having been asked to do so) it has already given that person the notification or information for which he is asking[10].

Any notification or information which must be given or provided by OFCOM must be given or provided before the end of the period of one week beginning with the day on which the request for the notification or information was made to OFCOM[11].

1 As to the meaning of 'OFCOM' see PARA 14 note 1; and as to OFCOM see PARA 2 et seq.
2 As to the meaning of 'person' see PARA 14 note 2.
3 Ie the Communications Act 2003 s 146.
4 Communications Act 2003 s 146(1)(a). The notification referred to in the text is that under s 33: see PARA 81.
5 Communications Act 2003 s 146(1)(b).
6 Communications Act 2003 s 146(1)(c). As to the meaning of 'network access' see PARA 98 note 5.
7 Ie under the Communications Act 2003 s 106: see PARA 155.

8   Communications Act 2003 s 146(1)(d).
9   Communications Act 2003 s 146(2).
10   Communications Act 2003 s 146(3).
11   Communications Act 2003 s 146(4).

149. Using information published by communications provider. Any person[1] has a right to use, free of charge, information published by a communications provider[2] if the use is to sell or make available an interactive guide or other technique for evaluating the cost of alternative usage patterns in relation to electronic communications services[3].

1   As to the meaning of 'person' see PARA 14 note 2.
2   As to the meaning of 'communications provider' see PARA 17 note 23.
3   Communications Act 2003 s 146A(1), (2) (added by SI 2011/1210). As to the meaning of 'electronic communications services' see PARA 53.

(xi) Reports

150. Reports on infrastructure. OFCOM[1] must prepare reports in accordance with the following[2] and each report must deal with specified electronic communications networks matters[3] and electronic communications services matters[4]:

(1)   the first report must relate to the position on a day specified in the report which falls within the period of 12 months from 8 June 2010[5] and be sent to the Secretary of State by OFCOM not more than two months after the specified day[6];

(2)   a further report must be prepared for each relevant period and be sent to the Secretary of State by OFCOM as soon as practicable after the end of the relevant period[7].

The period referred to in head (2) is the period of three years beginning with the day specified in the first report and each subsequent period of three years beginning with the end of the previous period[8]. In a report[9], OFCOM is required to include only information about, and analysis of, such networks, services and providers as it considers appropriate[10].

The specified electronic communications networks matters are:

(a)   the different types of electronic communications network provided in the United Kingdom ('UK networks')[11];

(b)   the geographic coverage of the different UK networks[12];

(c)   the proportion of the population covered by the different UK networks[13];

(d)   the extent to which UK networks share infrastructure[14];

(e)   the capacity of the different UK networks[15];

(f)   the extent to which the providers of the different UK networks allow other communications providers to use their networks to provide services[16];

(g)   the amount of time for which the different UK networks are and are not available, including the steps that have been or are to be taken to maintain or improve the level of availability[17];

(h)   the preparations made by providers of UK networks for responding to an emergency[18], including preparations for restoring normal operation of UK networks disrupted by the emergency[19]; and

(i)   the standard of the different UK networks in comparison with electronic communications networks provided in a range of other countries, having regard, in particular, to their coverage and capacity[20].

The specified electronic communications services matters are:

(i) the use of the electromagnetic spectrum for wireless telegraphy in the United Kingdom[21];

(ii) the different types of electronic communications service provided in the United Kingdom ('UK services')[22];

(iii) the geographic coverage of the different UK services[23];

(iv) the proportion of the population covered by the different UK services[24];

(v) the amount of time for which the different UK services are and are not available, including the steps that have been or are to be taken to maintain or improve the level of availability[25];

(vi) the preparations made by providers of UK services for responding to an emergency, including preparations for restoring normal operation of UK services disrupted by the emergency[26]; and

(vii) the standard of the different UK services in comparison with electronic communications services provided in a range of other countries[27].

The preparations referred to in heads (h) and (vi) include the steps taken to assess the risks of different types of emergency occurring, the steps taken to reduce or remove those risks and the testing of proposed responses to different types of emergency[28].

Where there is a significant change[29] in connection with a matter listed in heads (a)–(i) or (i)–(vii) and OFCOM considers that the change should be brought to the attention of the Secretary of State, OFCOM must prepare a report on the change and send it to the Secretary of State as soon as practicable[30].

OFCOM must publish every report as soon as practicable after it sends it to the Secretary of State and in such manner as it considers appropriate for bringing it to the attention of persons who, in its opinion, is likely to have an interest in it[31]. OFCOM may exclude information from a report when it is published if it considers that it is information that it could refuse to disclose in response to a request under the Freedom of Information Act 2000[32].

1 As to the meaning of 'OFCOM' see PARA 14 note 1; and as to OFCOM see PARA 2 et seq.
2 Ie the Communications Act 2003 s 134A(2) and (3): see text and notes 5–7.
3 See the Communications Act 2003 s 134A(1)(a) (ss 134A, 134B added by the Digital Economy Act 2010 s 1). The specified electronic communications networks matters are those listed in the Communications Act 2003 s 134B(1): see the text and notes 11–20. OFCOM must prepare a report on specified matters relating to internet domain names if requested to do so by the Secretary of State: see s 134C; and INFORMATION TECHNOLOGY LAW vol 57 (2012) PARA 506.
4 See the Communications Act 2003 s 134A(1)(b) (as added: see note 3). The specified electronic communications services matters are those listed in s 134B(2): see the text and notes 21–27.
5 Ie the day on which the Communications Act 2003 s 134A came into force: Communications Act 2003 s 134A(2)(a) (as added: see note 3).
6 Communications Act 2003 s 134A(2)(b) (as added: see note 3). As to the Secretary of State see PARA 76 note 1.
7 Communications Act 2003 s 134A(3) (as added: see note 3).
8 Communications Act 2003 s 134A(4) (as added: see note 3).
9 Ie under the Communications Act 2003 s 134A: see text and notes 1–8.
10 Communications Act 2003 s 134B(4) (as added: see note 3).
11 Communications Act 2003 s 134B(1)(a) (as added: see note 3). As to the meaning of 'United Kingdom' see PARA 14 note 7.
12 Communications Act 2003 s 134B(1)(b) (as added: see note 3).
13 Communications Act 2003 s 134B(1)(c) (as added: see note 3).
14 Communications Act 2003 s 134B(1)(d) (as added: see note 3).
15 Communications Act 2003 s 134B(1)(e) (as added: see note 3).
16 Communications Act 2003 s 134B(1)(f) (as added: see note 3).

17 Communications Act 2003 s 134B(1)(g) (as added: see note 3).
18 For the purposes of the Communications Act 2003 s 134B, 'emergency' means an event or situation that seriously disrupts a UK network or UK service: s 134B(5) (as added: see note 3).
19 Communications Act 2003 s 134B(1)(h) (as added: see note 3).
20 Communications Act 2003 s 134B(1)(i) (as added: see note 3).
21 Communications Act 2003 s 134B(2)(a) (as added: see note 3).
22 Communications Act 2003 s 134B(2)(b) (as added: see note 3).
23 Communications Act 2003 s 134B(2)(c) (as added: see note 3).
24 Communications Act 2003 s 134B(2)(d) (as added: see note 3).
25 Communications Act 2003 s 134B(2)(e) (as added: see note 3).
26 Communications Act 2003 s 134B(2)(f) (as added: see note 3).
27 Communications Act 2003 s 134B(2)(g (as added: see note 3).
28 Communications Act 2003 s 134B(3) (as added: see note 3).
29 A change is significant, for the purposes of the Communications Act 2003 s 134B(5), if OFCOM considers that it has, or is likely to have, a significant adverse impact on:
    (1)   persons carrying on business in the United Kingdom or a part of the United Kingdom (s 134A(6)(a) (as added: see note 3)); or
    (2)   the general public in the United Kingdom or a part of the United Kingdom (s 134A(6)(b) (as so added)).
30 Communications Act 2003 s 134A(5) (as added: see note 3).
31 Communications Act 2003 s 134A(7) (as added: see note 3). As to OFCOM's latest reports on infrastructure at the date this volume states the law, see the OFCOM website.
32 Communications Act 2003 s 134A(8) (as added: see note 3).

(xii) Emergencies

151. Powers to deal with emergencies. If the Secretary of State[1] has reasonable grounds for believing that it is necessary to do so:
    (1)   to protect the public from any threat to public safety or public health[2]; or
    (2)   in the interests of national security[3],
he may, by a direction to OFCOM[4], require it to give a direction[5] to a person (the 'relevant provider') who provides an electronic communications network[6] or electronic communications service[7] or who makes associated facilities[8] available[9]. Such a direction may be:
    (a)   a direction that the entitlement of the relevant provider to provide electronic communications networks or electronic communications services, or to make associated facilities available, is suspended (either generally or in relation to particular networks, services or facilities)[10]; or
    (b)   a direction that that entitlement is restricted in the respects set out in the direction[11].
Such a direction must specify the networks, services and facilities to which it relates and, except so far as it otherwise provides, it takes effect for an indefinite period beginning with the time at which it is notified to the person to whom it is given[12]. Such a direction in providing for the effect of a suspension or restriction to be postponed, may provide for it to take effect only at a time determined by or in accordance with the terms of the direction[13]. Such a direction, in connection with the suspension or restriction contained in the direction or with the postponement of its effect, may impose such conditions on the relevant provider as appear to OFCOM to be appropriate for the purpose of protecting that provider's customers[14].

Where OFCOM gives a direction[15] to a person, it must, as soon as practicable after doing so, provide that person with an opportunity of making representations about the effect of the direction, and proposing steps for remedying the situation[16].

If OFCOM considers it appropriate to do so[17], it may, without revoking it, at any time modify the terms of a direction[18] in such manner as it considers appropriate[19].

If the Secretary of State considers it appropriate to do so, he may, by a direction to OFCOM, require it to revoke a direction[20].

Where OFCOM modifies or revokes a direction it has given, it may do so:

(i) with effect from such time as it may direct[21];

(ii) subject to compliance with such requirements as it may specify[22]; and

(iii) to such extent and in relation to such networks, services or facilities, or parts of a network, service or facility, as it may determine[23].

A person is guilty of an offence if he provides an electronic communications network or electronic communications service, or makes available any associated facility while his entitlement to do so is suspended by a direction[24] or in contravention of a restriction contained in such a direction[25]. The duty of a person to comply with a condition of a direction is a duty owed to every person who may be affected by a contravention of the condition[26]. Where a duty is owed by virtue of this provision to a person:

(A) a breach of the duty that causes that person to sustain loss or damage[27]; and

(B) an act which, by inducing a breach of the duty or interfering with its performance, causes that person to sustain loss or damage and is done wholly or partly for achieving that result[28],

is actionable at the suit or instance of that person[29]. In proceedings brought against a person by virtue of head (A) above it is a defence for that person to show that he took all reasonable steps and exercised all due diligence to avoid contravening the condition in question[30].

1 As to the Secretary of State see PARA 76 note 1.
2 Communications Act 2003 s 132(1)(a).
3 Communications Act 2003 s 132(1)(b).
4 As to the meaning of 'OFCOM' see PARA 14 note 1; and as to OFCOM see PARA 2 et seq.
5 Ie under the Communications Act 2003 s 132(3).
6 As to the meaning of 'electronic communications network' see PARA 53.
7 As to the meaning of 'electronic communications service' see PARA 53.
8 As to the meaning of 'associated facilities' see PARA 53.
9 Communications Act 2003 s 132(1). OFCOM must comply with a requirement of the Secretary of State under s 132(1) by giving to the relevant provider such direction under s 132(3) (see the text and note 10, 11) as it considers necessary for the purpose of complying with the Secretary of State's direction: s 132(2).
10 Communications Act 2003 s 132(3)(a).
11 Communications Act 2003 s 132(3)(b).
12 Communications Act 2003 s 132(4).
13 Communications Act 2003 s 132(5)(a).
14 Communications Act 2003 s 132(5)(b). Those conditions may include a condition requiring the making of payments:
(1) by way of compensation for loss or damage suffered by the relevant provider's customers as a result of the direction (s 132(6)(a)); or
(2) in respect of annoyance, inconvenience or anxiety to which they have been put in consequence of the direction (s 132(6)(b)).
15 Ie under the Communications Act 2003 s 132(3): see the text and note 10, 11.
16 Communications Act 2003 s 132(7).
17 Ie whether in consequence of any representations or proposals made to it under the Communications Act 2003 s 132(3) or otherwise.
18 Ie under the Communications Act 2003 s 132(3): see the text and note 10, 11.
19 Communications Act 2003 s 132(8).

20 Communications Act 2003 s 132(9). The direction referred to in the text is a direction under the Communications Act 2003 s 132(3) (see the text and note 10, 11). It is the duty of OFCOM to comply with:
    (1)   a requirement under s 132(9) to revoke a direction (s 132(11)(a)); and
    (2)   a requirement contained in that direction as to how it should exercise its powers under s 132(10) (see text and notes 21–23) in the case of the required revocation (s 132(11)(b)).
21 Communications Act 2003 s 132(10)(a). See further note 20.
22 Communications Act 2003 s 132(10)(b). See further note 20.
23 Communications Act 2003 s 132(10)(c). See further note 20.
24 Ie under the Communications Act 2003 s 132.
25 Communications Act 2003 s 133(1). A person guilty of such an offence is liable:
    (1)   on summary conviction, to a fine not exceeding the statutory maximum (s 133(2)(a));
    (2)   on conviction on indictment, to a fine (s 133(2)(b)).
As to the statutory maximum see SENTENCING AND DISPOSITION OF OFFENDERS vol 92 (2010) PARA 140. Sections 96A–99 (see PARAS 117–120) apply in relation to a contravention of conditions imposed by a direction under s 132 as they apply in relation to a contravention of conditions set under s 45 (see PARA 87), other than SMP apparatus conditions: s 133(6) (amended by SI 2011/1210). As to the meaning of 'SMP apparatus condition' see PARA 87 note 8.
26 Communications Act 2003 s 133(3).
27 Communications Act 2003 s 133(4)(a).
28 Communications Act 2003 s 133(4)(b).
29 Communications Act 2003 s 133(4).
30 Communications Act 2003 s 133(5).

(xiii) Leases and Licences

152. Restrictions in leases and licences. The following provisions[1] apply where provision contained in a lease[2], licence or other agreement relating to premises has the effect of imposing on the occupier a prohibition or restriction under which his choice of:

(1)   the person from whom he obtains electronic communications services[3], or particular electronic communications services[4]; or

(2)   the person through whom he arranges to be provided with electronic communications services, or particular electronic communications services[5],

is confined to a person with an interest in the premises, to a person selected by a person with such an interest, or to persons who are one or the other[6].

The provisions also apply where:

(a)   provision contained in a lease for a year or more has the effect of imposing any other prohibition or restriction on the lessee with respect to an electronic communications matter[7]; or

(b)   provision contained in an agreement relating to premises to which a lease for a year or more applies has the effect of imposing a prohibition or restriction on the lessee with respect to such a matter[8].

A provision falling within head (1) or head (2) above[9] will have effect:

(i)   as if the prohibition or restriction applied only where the lessor, licensor or other party to the agreement has not given his consent to a departure from the requirements imposed by the prohibition or restriction[10]; and

(ii)   as if the lessor, licensor or other party were required not to withhold that consent unreasonably[11].

A provision falling within head (a) or head (b) above[12] will have effect:

(A)   in relation to things done inside a building occupied by the lessee under the lease[13]; or

(B)   for purposes connected with the provision to the lessee of an electronic communications service[14],

as if the prohibition or restriction applied only where the lessor has not given his consent in relation to the matter in question and as if the lessor were required not to withhold that consent unreasonably[15].

Where a provision[16] imposes a requirement on a lessor, licensor or party to an agreement not unreasonably to withhold his consent in relation to an electronic communications matter or in relation to the obtaining by the occupier of premises of an electronic communications service from or through a particular person, the question whether the consent is unreasonably withheld has to be determined having regard to all the circumstances and to the principle that no person should unreasonably be denied access to an electronic communications network or to electronic communications services[17].

OFCOM may by order provide for these provisions not to apply in certain cases[18]. These provisions apply to provisions contained in leases, licences or agreements granted or entered into before 25 July 2003[19] to the extent only that provision to that effect is contained in an order made by OFCOM[20].

1   Ie the Communications Act 2003 s 134. Section 134 is not to be construed as affecting the operation of the Electronic Communications Code, 1984, para 2(3)(lessees etc bound by rights granted under code by owners): Communications Act 2003 s 134(10). As to the code see PARA 155 note 1; and 166 et seq.

2   'Lease' includes a leasehold tenancy (whether in the nature of a head lease, sub-lease or underlease) and an agreement to grant such a tenancy; and 'lessor' and 'lessee' are to be construed accordingly: Communications Act 2003 s 134(8).

3   As to the meaning of 'electronic communications services' see PARA 53.

4   Communications Act 2003 s 134(1)(a).

5   Communications Act 2003 s 134(1)(b).

6   Communications Act 2003 s 134(1).

7   Communications Act 2003 s 134(2)(a). References in the Communications Act 2003 s 134 to electronic communications matters are references to:

    (1)   the provision of an electronic communications network or electronic communications service (s 134(7)(a));

    (2)   the connection of electronic communications apparatus to a relevant electronic communications network or of any such network to another (s 134(7)(b)); and

    (3)   the installation, maintenance, adjustment, repair, alteration or use for purposes connected with the provision of such a network or service of electronic communications apparatus (s 134(7)(c)).

   'Relevant electronic communications network' means:

    (a)   a public electronic communications network that is specified for the purposes of s 134 in an order made by the Secretary of State; or

    (b)   an electronic communications network that is, or is to be, connected (directly or indirectly) to such a network: s 134(8).

   At the date at which this volume states the law, no such order has been made.

   As to the meaning of 'electronic communications network' see PARA 53. As to the meaning of 'public electronic communications network' see PARA 98 note 6. 'Alteration' has the same meaning as in the electronic communications code (see PARA 168 note 5): s 134(8). As to the meaning of 'electronic communications code' see PARA 155 note 1. As to the Secretary of State see PARA 76 note 1. As to the power of the Secretary of State to make orders under the Communications Act 2003 see s 402; and PARA 74.

8   Communications Act 2003 s 134(2)(b).

9   Ie a provision falling within the Communications Act 2003 s 134(1): see the text to notes 1–6.

10 Communications Act 2003 s 134(3)(a).

11 Communications Act 2003 s 134(3)(b).

12 Ie a provision falling within the Communications Act 2003 s 134(2)(a) or (b): see the text to notes 7–8.

13 Communications Act 2003 s 134(4)(a).

14 Communications Act 2003 s 134(4)(b).

15 Communications Act 2003 s 134(4).

16 Ie a provision falling within the Communications Act 2003 s 134(1) (see the text to notes 1–6) or s 134(2) (see the text to notes 7–8).
17 Communications Act 2003 s 134(5).
18 Communications Act 2003 s 134(6). As to the meaning of 'OFCOM' see PARA 14 note 1; and as to OFCOM see PARA 2 et seq. The consent of the Secretary of State is required for the making by OFCOM of an order under s 134: s 134(11). Section 403 (see PARA 39) applies to the powers of OFCOM to make orders under s 134: s 134(12). A statutory instrument containing an order made by OFCOM under s 134 is subject to annulment in pursuance of a resolution of either House of Parliament: s 134(13). At the date at which this volume states the law, no such order has been made.
19 Ie before the commencement of the Communications Act 2003 s 134. As to commencement see the Communications Act 2003 (Commencement No 1) Order 2003, SI 2003/1900 (amended by SI 2003/3142).
20 Communications Act 2003 s 134(9).

(xiv) Local Authority Powers in relation to Network and Services

153. Powers of local authorities in connection with networks. A local authority[1] may borrow money for the purpose of providing a public electronic communications network[2] or public electronic communications service[3]. A local authority may:

(1) provide a public electronic communications network part of which is outside its area[4]; and

(2) provide a public electronic communications service even if some of the persons to whom it provides the service are outside its area[5].

1 For the purposes of the Communications Act 2003 s 148, 'local authority' means:
    (1) in relation to England, a London borough council or a district council (s 148(3)(a));
    (2) in relation to Wales, a county council or a county borough council (s 148(3)(b)).
    As to counties and districts in England, and their councils, see LOCAL GOVERNMENT vol 69 (2009) PARA 24 et seq; as to counties and county boroughs in Wales, and their councils, see LOCAL GOVERNMENT vol 69 (2009) PARA 37 et seq; as to London boroughs, and their councils, see LONDON GOVERNMENT vol 71 (2013) PARA 15.
2 As to the meaning of 'public electronic communications network' see PARA 98 note 6.
3 Communications Act 2003 s 148(1)(a).
4 Communications Act 2003 s 148(1)(b). As to the meaning of 'public electronic communications service' see PARA 98 note 3.
5 Communications Act 2003 s 148(2).

(xv) Sale of Duchy of Lancaster Land

154. Sale of Duchy of Lancaster land in connection with network. The Chancellor and Council of the Duchy of Lancaster[1] may, if they think fit, agree with a person who provides a public electronic communications network[2] for the sale, and they may absolutely make sale, for such sum of money as appears to them sufficient consideration for the same, of any land which:

(1) belongs to Her Majesty in right of the Duchy of Lancaster[3]; and

(2) is land which that person seeks to acquire for, or in connection with, the provision of his network[4].

1 As to the Duchy of Lancaster see CROWN AND CROWN PROCEEDINGS vol 29 (2014) PARA 214 et seq.
2 As to the meaning of 'public electronic communications network' see PARA 98 note 6; definition applied by the Communications Act 2003 s 397(2).
3 Communications Act 2003 s 397(1)(a).
4 Communications Act 2003 s 397(1)(b).

(6) THE ELECTRONIC COMMUNICATIONS CODE

(i) Adaptation of the Telecommunications Code by the Electronic Communications Code

155. Application of electronic communications code. The electronic communications code[1] is to have effect:

(1) in the case of a person to whom it is applied by a direction given by OFCOM[2]; and

(2) in the case of the Secretary of State[3] or any Northern Ireland department where the Secretary of State or that department is providing or proposing to provide an electronic communications network[4].

The only purposes for which the electronic communications code may be applied in a person's case by a direction under these provisions[5] are:

(a) the purposes of the provision by him of an electronic communications network[6]; or

(b) the purposes of the provision by him of a system of conduits[7] which he is making available, or proposing to make available, for use by providers of electronic communications networks for the purposes of the provision by them of their networks[8].

A direction applying the electronic communications code in any person's case may provide for that code to have effect in his case[9]:

(i) in relation only to such places or localities as may be specified or described in the direction[10];

(ii) for the purposes only of the provision of such electronic communications network, or part of an electronic communications network, as may be so specified or described[11]; or

(iii) for the purposes only of the provision of such conduit system, or part of a conduit system, as may be so specified or described[12].

1 For the purposes of the Communications Act 2003 Pt 2 Ch 1 (ss 32–151), 'electronic communications code' means the code set out in the Telecommunications Act 1984 Sch 2 (where it is called the 'telecommunications code') (see PARA 166): Communications Act 2003 ss 106(1), 151(1). Schedule 3 (which amends the Telecommunications Act 1984 Sch 2 for the purpose of translating the telecommunications code into a code applicable in the context of the regulatory regime established by the Communications Act 2003) has effect: s 106(2). In February 2013, the Law Commission made recommendations to the government on reforming the electronic communications code. A consultation took place on the draft revised electronic communications code particularly on such issues as the definition of land, how consideration is to be determined, upgrading and sharing apparatus and contracting out of the revised code. At the date at which this volume states the law, any feedback received from the consultation is being analysed.

2 Communications Act 2003 s 106(3)(a). As to the meaning of 'OFCOM' see PARA 14 note 1; and as to OFCOM see PARA 2 et seq. As to the meaning of 'person' see PARA 14 note 2. As to the procedure for directions see PARA 156. As to directions under s 106 at the date at which this volume states the law see the OFCOM website.

3 As to the Secretary of State see PARA 76 note 1.

4 Communications Act 2003 s 106(3)(b). As to the meaning of 'electronic communications network' see PARA 53.

5 Ie the Communications Act 2003 s 106.

6 Communications Act 2003 s 106(4)(a).

7 For the purposes of the Communications Act 2003 s 106, 'conduit' includes a tunnel, subway, tube or pipe: s 106(7).

8 Communications Act 2003 s 106(4)(b).

9 Communications Act 2003 s 106(5). The Secretary of State may by order provide for the electronic communications code to have effect for all purposes with a different amount substituted for the amount for the time being specified in para 16(3) of the code (minimum

compensation): Communications Act 2003 s 106(6). At the date at which this volume states the law, no such order has been made. As to the power of the Secretary of State to make orders under the Communications Act 2003 see s 402; and PARA 74.
10 Communications Act 2003 s 106(5)(a).
11 Communications Act 2003 s 106(5)(b).
12 Communications Act 2003 s 106(5)(c).

156. Procedure for directions applying electronic communications code.
OFCOM[1] is not to give a direction applying the electronic communications code[2] in any person's case except on an application made for the purpose by that person[3]. If OFCOM publishes a notification setting out its requirements with respect to:

(1) the content of an application for a direction applying the electronic communications code[4]; and

(2) the manner in which such an application is to be made[5],

such an application must be made in accordance with the requirements for the time being in force[6].

In considering whether to apply the electronic communications code in any person's case, OFCOM must have regard, in particular, to each of the following matters[7]:

(a) the benefit to the public of the electronic communications network or conduit system by reference to which the code is to be applied to that person[8];

(b) the practicability of the provision of that network or system without the application of the code[9];

(c) the need to encourage the sharing of the use of electronic communications apparatus[10];

(d) whether the person in whose case it is proposed to apply the code will be able to meet liabilities arising as a consequence of the application of the code in his case and any conduct of his in relation to the matters with which the code deals[11].

Before giving a direction applying the electronic communications code, OFCOM must:

(i) publish[12] a notification of its proposal to give the direction[13]; and

(ii) consider any representations about that proposal that are made to it within the period specified in the notification[14].

A notification for the purposes of head (i) must contain the following:

(A) a statement of OFCOM's proposal[15];

(B) a statement of its reasons for that proposal[16];

(C) a statement of the period within which representations may be made to it about the proposal[17].

The period specified as the period within which representations may be made must end no less than one month after the day of the publication of the notification[18].

1 As to the meaning of 'OFCOM' see PARA 14 note 1; and as to OFCOM see PARA 2 et seq.
2 As to such directions see PARA 155. As to the meaning of 'electronic communications code' see PARA 155 note 1.
3 Communications Act 2003 s 107(1). As to the meaning of 'person' see PARA 14 note 2. The Electronic Communications and Wireless Telegraphy Regulations 2011, SI 2011/1210, reg 3 makes provision about the time within which an application under the Communications Act 2003 s 107(1) must be determined: s 107(1A) (added by SI 2011/1210). Where:
    (1) a person authorised to provide public electronic communications networks applies to a competent authority for the granting of rights to install facilities on, over or under public or private property for the purposes of such a network;

(2)   a person authorised to provide electronic communications networks other than to the public applies to a competent authority for the granting of rights to install facilities on, over or under public property for the purposes of such a network; or

(3)   a person applies to OFCOM for a direction applying the electronic communications code in the person's case;

except in cases of expropriation, the competent authority must make its decision within six months of receiving the completed application: Electronic Communications and Wireless Telegraphy Regulations 2011, SI 2011/1210, reg 3.

4   Communications Act 2003 s 107(2)(a). As to notifications under s 107(2) at the date at which this volume states the law see the OFCOM website.

5   Communications Act 2003 s 107(2)(b).

6   Communications Act 2003 s 107(2). OFCOM may from time to time review the requirements for the time being in force for the purposes of s 107(2) and on any such review, modify them in such manner as it thinks fit by giving a notification of the revised requirements: s 107(3). A modification may not be made under s 107(3) unless the modification is objectively justifiable and proportionate to what it is intended to achieve: s 107(3A) (s 107(3A)–(3C) added by SI 2011/1210). Before making such a modification, OFCOM must publish a notification of the proposed modification which contains a statement of the proposal, a statement of its reasons for the proposal, and a statement of the period within which representations may be made to it about the proposal: Communications Act 2003 s 107(3B) (as so added). The period specified must end no less than one month after the day of the publication of the notification: s 107(3C) (as so added).

7   Communications Act 2003 s 107(4). For the purposes of s 3(6), (7) (see PARA 16 text and note 36) OFCOM's duty under s 107(4) ranks equally with its duties under s 3: s 107(5).

8   Communications Act 2003 s 107(4)(a).

9   Communications Act 2003 s 107(4)(b).

10   Communications Act 2003 s 107(4)(c).

11   Communications Act 2003 s 107(4)(d).

12   The publication by OFCOM of a notification for any of the purposes of the Communications Act 2003 s 107 must be a publication in such manner as OFCOM considers appropriate for bringing the notification to the attention of the persons who, in its opinion, are likely to be affected by it: s 107(10).

13   Communications Act 2003 s 107(6)(a). As to notifications under s 107(6) at the date at which this volume states the law see the OFCOM website.

14   Communications Act 2003 s 107(6)(b).

15   Communications Act 2003 s 107(7)(a). The statement of OFCOM's proposal must: (1) contain a statement that it proposes to apply the code in the case of the person in question; (2) set out any proposals of its to impose terms under s 106(5) (see PARA 155 text and note 9–12); but this is subject to s 113(7) (see PARA 161 text to notes 22–23) and s 115(5) (see PARA 161 note 38): s 107(8).

16   Communications Act 2003 s 107(7)(b).

17   Communications Act 2003 s 107(7)(c).

18   Communications Act 2003 s 107(9).

157. Register of persons in whose case electronic communications code applies.

It is the duty of OFCOM[1] to establish and maintain a register of persons in whose case the electronic communications code[2] applies by virtue of a direction given by OFCOM[3]. OFCOM must record in the register every direction given[4]. Information recorded in the register must be recorded in such manner as OFCOM considers appropriate[5]. It is the duty of OFCOM to publish a notification setting out[6]:

(1)   the times at which the register is for the time being available for public inspection[7]; and

(2)   the fees that must be paid for, or in connection with, an inspection of the register[8].

OFCOM must make the register available for public inspection during such hours, and on payment of such fees, as are set out in the notification for the time being in force[9].

1   As to the meaning of 'OFCOM' see PARA 14 note 1; and as to OFCOM see PARA 2 et seq.

2   As to the meaning of 'electronic communications code' see PARA 155 note 1.
3   Communications Act 2003 s 108(1). The code referred to in the text is one that applies by virtue of a direction under s 106 (see PARA 155): s 108(1).
4   Communications Act 2003 s 108(2). The direction referred to in the text is one given under s 106 (see PARA 155): s 108(2).
5   Communications Act 2003 s 108(3).
6   Communications Act 2003 s 108(4). The publication of a notification under s 108(4) must be a publication in such manner as OFCOM considers appropriate for bringing it to the attention of the persons who, in its opinion, are likely to be affected by it: s 108(5). As to notifications under s 108(4) at the date at which this volume states the law see the OFCOM website.
7   Communications Act 2003 s 108(4)(a).
8   Communications Act 2003 s 108(4)(b).
9   Communications Act 2003 s 108(5). The notification referred to in the text is one being in force under s 108(4) (see the text and notes 6–8): s 108(6).

158. Restrictions and conditions. Where the electronic communications code[1] is applied in any person's case by a direction given by OFCOM[2], that code is to have effect in that person's case subject to such restrictions and conditions as may be contained in regulations made by the Secretary of State[3]. In exercising this power to make regulations[4], it is the duty of the Secretary of State to have regard to each of the following:

(1)   the duties imposed on OFCOM[5];
(2)   the need to protect the environment and, in particular, to conserve the natural beauty and amenity of the countryside[6];
(3)   the need to promote economic growth in the United Kingdom[7];
(4)   the need to ensure that highways are not damaged or obstructed, and traffic not interfered with, to any greater extent than is reasonably necessary[8];
(5)   the need to encourage the sharing of the use of electronic communications apparatus[9];
(6)   the need to ensure that restrictions and conditions are objectively justifiable and proportionate to what they are intended to achieve[10];
(7)   the need to secure that a person in whose case the code is applied will be able to meet liabilities arising as a consequence of the application of the code in his case and any conduct of his in relation to the matters with which the code deals[11].

The power of the Secretary of State to provide by regulations for the restrictions and conditions subject to which the electronic communications code has effect includes power to provide for restrictions and conditions which are framed by reference to any one or more of the following:

(a)   the making of a determination in accordance with the regulations by a person specified in the regulations[12];
(b)   the giving of an approval or consent by a person so specified[13]; or
(c)   the opinion of any person[14].

Before making any regulations, the Secretary of State must consult OFCOM and such other persons as he considers appropriate[15].

Where OFCOM determines that there are reasonable grounds for believing that a person in whose case the electronic communications code applies is contravening, or has contravened, a requirement imposed by virtue of any restrictions or conditions[16], it may give him a notification[17]. A notification is one which:

(i)   sets out the determination made by OFCOM[18];
(ii)   specifies the requirement and the contravention in respect of which that determination has been made[19];

(iii)   specifies the period during which the person notified has an opportunity to make representations[20];

(iv)   specifies the steps that OFCOM thinks should be taken by the person in order to comply with the requirement and remedy the consequences of the contravention[21];

(v)   specifies any penalty which OFCOM is minded to impose[22];

(vi)   where the contravention is serious, specifies any direction which OFCOM is minded to give[23].

1   As to the meaning of 'electronic communications code' see PARA 155 note 1.
2   As to the meaning of 'OFCOM' see PARA 14 note 1; and as to OFCOM see PARA 2 et seq.
3   Communications Act 2003 s 109(1). As to the regulations made see the Electronic Communications Code (Conditions and Restrictions) Regulations 2003, SI 2003/2553 (amended by SI 2009/584; SI 2013/755; and SI 2013/1403). As to the Secretary of State see PARA 76 note 1. As to the power of the Secretary of State to make regulations under the Communications Act 2003 see s 402; and PARA 74.
4   Ie under the Communications Act 2003 s 109.
5   Communications Act 2003 s 109(2)(a). The duties referred to in the text are those imposed by the Communications Act 2003 ss 3, 4: see PARAS 16–17.
6   Communications Act 2003 s 109(2)(b). If the Secretary of State has complied with head (2) in connection with any particular exercise before 6 April 2018 of the power to make regulations under s 109 and the regulations in question are expressed to cease to have effect (other than for transitional purposes) before that date, the Secretary of State is to be treated as also having complied with any duty imposed in connection with that exercise of that power by any of the following:
    (1)   National Parks and Access to the Countryside Act 1949 s 11A(2) (see OPEN SPACES AND COUNTRYSIDE vol 78 (2010) PARA 641) (Communications Act 2003 s 109(2A), (2B) (added by the Growth and Infrastructure Act 2013 s 9));
    (2)   Countryside and Rights of Way Act 2000 s 85(1) (see OPEN SPACES AND COUNTRYSIDE vol 78 (2010) PARA 659) (Communications Act 2003 s 109(2A), (2B) (as so added));
    (3)   Norfolk and Suffolk Broads Act 1988 s 17A(1) (Communications Act 2003 s 109(2A), (2B) (as so added)).
7   Communications Act 2003 s 109(2)(ba) (added by the Growth and Infrastructure Act 2013 s 9).
8   Communications Act 2003 s 109(2)(c).
9   Communications Act 2003 s 109(2)(d). As to the meaning of 'electronic communications apparatus' see PARA 88 note 10.
10 Communications Act 2003 s 109(2)(da) (added by SI 2011/1210).
11 Communications Act 2003 s 109(2)(e).
12 Communications Act 2003 s 109(3)(a).
13 Communications Act 2003 s 109(3)(b).
14 Communications Act 2003 s 109(3)(c).
15 Communications Act 2003 s 109(4).
16 Ie under the Communications Act 2003 s 109: see the text and notes 1–15.
17 Communications Act 2003 s 110(1). The notification referred to in the text is a notification under s 110. A notification under s 110 may be given in respect of more than one contravention and, if it is given in respect of a continuing contravention, may be given in respect of any period during which the contravention has continued: s 110(8). Where a notification has been given to a person in respect of a contravention of a requirement, OFCOM may give a further notification in respect of the same contravention of that requirement if, and only if:
    (1)   the contravention is one occurring after the time of the giving of the earlier notification (s 110(9)(a));
    (2)   the contravention is a continuing contravention and the subsequent notification is in respect of so much of a period as falls after a period to which the earlier notification relates (s 110(9)(b)); or
    (3)   the earlier notification has been withdrawn without a penalty having been imposed in respect of the notified contravention (s 110(9)(c)).
18 Communications Act 2003 s 110(2)(a).
19 Communications Act 2003 s 110(2)(b) (amended by SI 2011/1210).
20 Communications Act 2003 s 110(2)(c) (substituted by SI 2011/1210).
21 Communications Act 2003 s 110(2)(d) (added by SI 2011/1210).

22 Communications Act 2003 s 110(2)(e) (added by SI 2011/1210). The penalty referred to in the text is one imposed in accordance with the Communications Act 2003 s 110A (see PARA 160): s 110(2)(e) (as so added).

23 Communications Act 2003 s 110(2)(f) (added by SI 2011/1210). The direction referred to in the text is one given under the Communications Act 2003 s 113(4) (see PARA 161): s 110(2)(f) (as so added).

159. Confirmation decision for contravention of electronic communications code restrictions. Where:

   (1)   a person (the 'notified provider') has been given a notification[1];

   (2)   OFCOM has allowed the notified provider an opportunity of making representations about the matters notified[2]; and

   (3)   the period allowed for the making of the representations has expired[3],

OFCOM may:

   (a)   give the notified provider a decision (a 'confirmation decision') confirming the imposition of requirements on the notified provider, or the giving of a direction to the notified provider, or both, in accordance with the notification[4]; or

   (b)   notify the notified provider that they are satisfied with the representations and that no further action will be taken[5].

OFCOM may not give a confirmation decision to the notified provider unless, after considering any representations, it is satisfied that the notified provider has, in one or more of the respects notified, been in contravention of a requirement specified in the notification[6].

A confirmation decision:

   (i)   must be given to the person without delay[7];

   (ii)   must include reasons for the decision[8];

   (iii)   may require immediate action by the person to comply with specified requirements[9], or may specify a period within which the person must comply with those requirements[10]; and

   (iv)   may require the person to pay:

      (A)   the penalty specified in the notification[11]; or

      (B)   such lesser penalty as OFCOM consider appropriate in the light of the person's representations or steps taken by the person to comply with the condition or remedy the consequences of the contravention[12], and

may specify the period within which the penalty is to be paid[13].

It is the duty of a person to whom a confirmation decision has been given to comply with any requirement imposed by it[14]. A penalty imposed by a confirmation decision must be paid to OFCOM and if not paid within the period specified by them, is to be recoverable by them accordingly[15].

1   Communications Act 2003 s 111(1)(a). The notification referred to in the text is a notification under s 110: s 111(1)(a).

2   Communications Act 2003 s 111(1)(b).

3   Communications Act 2003 s 111(1)(c).

4   Communications Act 2003 s 111(2)(a) (s 111(2)–(4) substituted by SI 2011/1210). The notification referred to in the text is a notification under the Communications Act 2003 s 110 (see PARA 158): s 111(2)(a) (as so substituted).

5   Communications Act 2003 s 111(2)(b) (as substituted: see note 4).

6   Communications Act 2003 s 111(3) (as substituted: see note 4). The notification referred to in the text is a notification under s 110 (see PARA 158): s 111(3) (as so substituted).

7   Communications Act 2003 s 111(4)(a) (as substituted: see note 4).

8   Communications Act 2003 s 111(4)(b) (as substituted: see note 4).

9   Ie of a kind mentioned in the Communications Act 2003 s 110(2)(d): see PARA 158.

10 Communications Act 2003 s 111(4)(c) (as substituted: see note 4).
11 Communications Act 2003 s 111(4)(d)(i) (as substituted: see note 4). The reference to the penalty specified in the notification is under s 110(2)(e): s 111(4)(d)(i) (as so substituted).
12 Communications Act 2003 s 111(4)(d)(ii) (as substituted: see note 4).
13 Communications Act 2003 s 111(4)(d).
14 Communications Act 2003 s 111(5) (amended by SI 2011/1210). That duty is enforceable in civil proceedings by OFCOM for an injunction or for any other appropriate remedy or relief: Communications Act 2003 s 111(6).
15 Communications Act 2003 s 111(7) (added by SI 2011/1210).

160. Penalties for contravention of electronic communications code restrictions. The following provisions[1] apply where a person is given a notification[2] which specifies a proposed penalty[3]. Where the notification relates to more than one contravention, a separate penalty may be specified in respect of each contravention[4]. Where the notification relates to a continuing contravention, no more than one penalty may be specified in respect of the period of contravention specified in the notification[5]. In relation to a continuing contravention, a penalty may be specified in respect of each day on which the contravention continues after the giving of a confirmation decision[6] which requires immediate action or the expiry of any period specified in the confirmation decision for complying with a requirement so specified[7].

In relation to a continuing contravention, the amount of a penalty[8] is to be such amount not exceeding £100 per day as OFCOM[9] determines to be appropriate and proportionate to the contravention in respect of which it is imposed[10]. The amount of any other penalty specified in a notification[11] is to be such amount not exceeding £10,000 as OFCOM determine to be appropriate and proportionate to the contravention in respect of which it is imposed[12].

1 Ie the Communications Act 2003 s 110A: see the text and notes 2–12.
2 Ie under the Communications Act 2003 s 110: see PARA 158.
3 Communications Act 2003 s 110A(1) (s 110A added by SI 2011/1210).
4 Communications Act 2003 s 110A(2) (as added: see note 3).
5 Communications Act 2003 s 110A(3) (as added: see note 3).
6 Ie under the Communications Act 2003 s 111(4)(c).
7 Communications Act 2003 s 110A(4) (as added: see note 3).
8 As to the meaning of 'OFCOM' see PARA 14 note 1; and as to OFCOM see PARA 2 et seq.
9 Ie under the Communications Act 2003 s 110A(4).
10 Communications Act 2003 s 110A(5) (as added: see note 3).
11 Ie under the Communications Act 2003 s 110.
12 Communications Act 2003 s 110A(6) (as added: see note 3). The Secretary of State may by order amend s 110A so as to substitute a different maximum penalty for the maximum penalty for the time being specified in s 110A(6): s 110A(7) (as so added). No order is to be made containing provision authorised by s 110A(7) unless a draft of the order has been laid before Parliament and approved by a resolution of each House: s 110A(8) (as so added). At the date at which this volume states the law, no such order had been made. As to the Secretary of State see PARA 76 note 1. As to the power of the Secretary of State to make orders under the Communications Act 2003 see s 402; and PARA 74.

161. Suspension, modification and revocation of application of electronic communications code. OFCOM[1] may suspend the application of the electronic communications code[2] in any person's case if it is satisfied:

(1) that he is or has been in serious or repeated contravention of requirements to pay administrative charges[3] (whether in respect of the whole or a part of the charges)[4];

(2) that, in the case of a single serious contravention, a notification has been given to the contravening provider[5] and the period for making representations[6] has expired[7];

(3)   that, in the case of a repeated contravention, the bringing of proceedings for the recovery of the amounts outstanding has failed to secure complete compliance by the contravening provider with the requirements to pay the charges fixed in his case, or has no reasonable prospect of securing such compliance[8];

(4)   that, in the case of a repeated contravention, an attempt, by the imposition of penalties[9], to secure such compliance has failed[10]; and

(5)   that the suspension of the application of the code is appropriate and proportionate to the contraventions[11].

OFCOM may also, if the electronic communications code has been applied by a direction[12] in any person's case, suspend to the specified extent[13] the application in that person's case of the electronic communications code if:

(a)   OFCOM gives a direction[14] for the suspension or restriction of that person's entitlement to provide an electronic communications network[15], or a part of such a network[16]; or

(b)   that person is a person in whose case there have been repeated[17] or serious contraventions of requirements imposed by virtue of any restrictions or conditions[18] subject to which the code applies[19].

A suspension of the application of the code in any person's case must be by a further direction given to that person[20] by OFCOM[21]. The statement required[22] to be included, in the case of a direction for the purposes of these provisions, in the statement of OFCOM's proposal is a statement of its proposal to suspend the application of the code[23]. A suspension of the application of the electronic communications code in any person's case:

(i)   ceases to have effect if the suspension is under head (a) above[24] and the network suspension or restriction[25] ceases to have effect[26]; but

(ii)   subject to that continues in force until such time (if any) as it is withdrawn by OFCOM[27].

Where the application of the electronic communications code is suspended in a person's case, he is not, while it is so suspended, entitled to exercise any right conferred on him by or by virtue of the code[28]. However, the suspension, in a person's case, of the application of the electronic communications code does not, except so far as otherwise provided by a transitional scheme[29]:

(A)   affect (as between the original parties to it) any agreement entered into for the purposes of the code or any agreement having effect in accordance with it[30];

(B)   affect anything done under the code before the suspension of its application[31]; or

(C)   require the removal of, or prohibit the use of, any apparatus lawfully installed on, in or over any premises before that suspension[32].

OFCOM may at any time modify the terms on which[33] the code is applied in a person's case[34]. OFCOM may revoke a direction applying the electronic communications code in a person's case if an application for the revocation has been made by that person[35]. If at any time it appears to OFCOM that a person in whose case the electronic communications code has been applied is not the provider of an electronic communications network or conduit system for the purposes of which the code applies, OFCOM may revoke the direction applying the code in his case[36]. A modification or revocation is made by a further direction[37] to the person in whose case the electronic communications code has been applied by the direction being modified or revoked[38]. A modification[39] may not be made unless the modification is objectively justifiable and proportionate to what it is intended to achieve[40].

OFCOM may put in place a transitional scheme in cases where the code has ceased to apply to a provider by reason of the code being either suspended, revoked or modified in relation to that provider[41].

1   As to the meaning of 'OFCOM' see PARA 14 note 1; and as to OFCOM see PARA 2 et seq.
2   As to the meaning of 'electronic communications code' see PARA 155 note 1.
3   Ie charges fixed under the Communications Act 2003 s 38: see PARA 83. As to the meaning of 'repeated contravention' see s 42(9), applied by s 113(12); and PARA 85 note 5.
4   Communications Act 2003 s 113(1)(a) (amended by SI 2011/1210).
5   Ie under the Communications Act 2003 s 40: see PARA 84.
6   Ie under the Communications Act 2003 s 40: see PARA 84.
7   Communications Act 2003 s 113(1)(aa) (added by SI 2011/1210).
8   Communications Act 2003 s 113(1)(b) (amended by SI 2011/1210).
9   Ie under the Communications Act 2003 s 41: see PARA 84.
10 Communications Act 2003 s 113(1)(c) (amended by SI 2011/1210).
11 Communications Act 2003 s 113(1)(d) (substituted by SI 2011/1210). As to the procedure for directions see PARA 162.
12 Ie under the Communications Act 2003 s 106: see PARA 155.
13 Ie to the extent specified in the Communications Act 2003 s 113(3) (see note 16) or s 113(5) (see note 19).
14 Ie under the Communications Act 2003 s 42 (suspending service provision for non-payment: see PARA 85), s 100 (suspending service provision for contraventions of conditions: see PARA 121) (including s 100 applied by s 105D (enforcement of obligations in relation to security of public electronic communications networks and services: see PARA 126)), s 132 (suspension or restriction of a provider's entitlement on grounds of public safety or health or national security: see PARA 151) or s 140 (suspending service provision for information contraventions: see PARA 142).
15 As to the meaning of 'electronic communications network' see PARA 53.
16 See the Communications Act 2003 s 113(2) (amended by SI 2011/1210). The extent, in any person's case, of a suspension under the Communications Act 2003 s 113(2) must not go beyond the application of the code for the purposes of so much of an electronic communications network as that person is prohibited from providing by virtue of the suspension or restriction of his entitlement to provide such a network, or part of a network: s 113(3).
17 For these purposes, there are repeated contraventions by a person of conditions or restrictions under the Communications Act 2003 s 109 if:
     (1)   in the case of a previous notification given to the person under s 110, OFCOM have given a confirmation decision to the person under s 111(2) (see PARA 159) (s 113(13)(a) (s 113(13) added by SI 2011/1210));
     (2)   in the period of 24 months following the giving of that confirmation decision, one or more further confirmation decisions have been given to the person in respect of contraventions of a condition or restriction under the Communications Act 2003 s 109 (see PARA 158) (s 113(13)(b) (as so added)); and
     (3)   the previous confirmation decision and the subsequent ones all relate to contraventions of the same condition or restriction (whether the same contravention or different contraventions (s 113(13)(c) (as so added)).
18 Ie under the Communications Act 2003 s 109: see PARA 158.
19 See the Communications Act 2003 s 113(4) (amended by SI 2011/1210). The extent, in any person's case, of a suspension under the Communications Act 2003 s 113(4) must not go beyond the following applications of the code in his case:
     (1)   its application for the purposes of electronic communications networks, or parts of such a network, which are not yet in existence at the time of the suspension (s 113(5)(a));
     (2)   its application for the purposes of conduit systems, or parts of such systems, which are not yet in existence or not yet used for the purposes of electronic communications networks (s 113(5)(b)); and
     (3)   its application for other purposes in circumstances in which the provision of an electronic communications network, or part of such a network, would not have to cease if its application for those purposes were suspended (s 113(5)(c)).
     As to the meaning of 'conduit system' see PARA 168 note 4.

20 Ie under the Communications Act 2003 s 106: see PARA 155.
21 Communications Act 2003 s 113(6).
22 Ie by the Communications Act 2003 s 107(8): see PARA 156 note 15.
23 Communications Act 2003 s 113(7).
24 Ie the suspension is under the Communications Act 2003 s 113(2).
25 The reference to the network suspension or restriction, in relation to a suspension of the
   application of the electronic communications code, is a reference to the suspension or restriction
   of an entitlement to provide an electronic communications network, or part of such a network,
   which is the suspension or restriction by reference to which the application of the code was
   suspended under the Communications Act 2003 s 113(2): s 113(9).
26 Communications Act 2003 s 113(8)(a).
27 Communications Act 2003 s 113(8)(b).
28 Communications Act 2003 s 113(10).
29 Ie a scheme contained in an order under the Communications Act 2003 s 117: see note 41.
30 Communications Act 2003 s 113(11)(a).
31 Communications Act 2003 s 113(11)(b).
32 Communications Act 2003 s 113(11)(c).
33 Ie by virtue of the Communications Act 2003 s 106(5): see PARA 155.
34 Communications Act 2003 s 115(1).
35 Communications Act 2003 s 115(2).
36 Communications Act 2003 s 115(3).
37 Ie under the Communications Act 2003 s 106: see PARA 155.
38 Communications Act 2003 s 115(4). The matters required by s 107(8) (see PARA 156 note 15) to
   be included, in the case of a direction for the purposes of s 115, in the statement of OFCOM's
   proposal are whichever of the following is applicable:
   (1)   a statement of the proposal to modify terms imposed under s 106(5) (see PARA 155)
          (s 115(5)(a));
   (2)   a statement of the proposal to revoke the direction applying the code (s 115(5)(b)).
39 Ie under the Communications Act 2003 s 115.
40 Communications Act 2003 s 115(4A) (added by SI 2011/1210).
41 See the Communications Act 2003 s 117.
   Where it appears to OFCOM:
   (1)   that the electronic communications code has ceased or is to cease to apply, to any
          extent, in the case of any person (the 'former operator') (s 117(1)(a));
   (2)   that it has ceased or will cease so to apply for either of the following reasons:
          (a)   the suspension under s 113 of the application of the code in the former operator's
                 case (s 117(1)(b), (2)(a));
          (b)   the revocation or modification under s 115 of the direction applying the code in
                 his case (s 117(1)(b), (2)(b)) and
   (3)   that it is appropriate for transitional provision to be made in connection with it ceasing
          to apply in the case of the former operator (s 117(1)(c)),
   it may by order make a scheme containing any such transitional provision as it thinks fit in that
   case: s 117(1).
   A scheme contained in an order under s 117 may, in particular:
   (i)   impose any one or more of the following obligations on the former operator:
          (A)   an obligation to remove anything installed in pursuance of any right conferred by
                 or in accordance with the code (s 117(3)(a), (4)(a));
          (B)   an obligation to restore land to its condition before anything was done in
                 pursuance of any such right (s 117(3)(a), (4)(b)); or
          (C)   an obligation to pay the expenses of any such removal or restoration (s 117(3)(a),
                 (4)(c));
   (ii)   provide for those obligations to be enforceable in such manner (otherwise than by
          criminal penalties) and by such persons as may be specified in the scheme (s 117(3)(b));
   (iii) authorise the retention of apparatus on any land pending its subsequent use for the
          purposes of an electronic communications network, electronic communications service
          or conduit system to be provided by any person (s 117(3)(c));
   (iv)   provide for the transfer to such persons as may be specified in, or determined in
          accordance with, the scheme of any rights or liabilities arising out of any agreement or
          other obligation entered into or incurred in pursuance of the code by the former
          operator (s 117(3)(d));
   (v)   provide, for the purposes of any provision contained in the scheme by virtue of any of

heads (i)–(iv), for such questions arising under the scheme as are specified in the scheme, or are of a description so specified, to be referred to, and determined by, OFCOM (s 117(3)(e)).

Sections 110, 111(see PARAS 158, 159), 112 (now repealed) apply in relation to the requirements imposed by virtue of a scheme contained in an order under s 117 as they apply in relation to a requirement imposed by virtue of restrictions or conditions under s 109: s 117(5). Section 403 (see PARA 39) applies to the power of OFCOM to make an order under s 117: s 117(6).

162. Procedure for directions suspending electronic communications code.

Except in an urgent case[1] or a case of a single serious contravention, OFCOM[2] is not to give a direction[3] suspending the application of the electronic communications code[4] in the case of any person (the 'operator') unless it has[5]:

(1) notified the operator of the proposed suspension and of the steps (if any) that it is proposing to take to make a transitional scheme[6];

(2) provided him with an opportunity of making representations about the proposals and of proposing steps for remedying the situation that has given rise to the proposed suspension[7]; and

(3) considered every representation and proposal made to it during the period allowed by it for the operator to take advantage of that opportunity[8].

That period is such reasonable period as OFCOM may specify, beginning with the day on which the notification is given[9].

As soon as practicable after giving a direction[10] in an urgent case, OFCOM must provide the operator with an opportunity of:

(a) making representations about the effect of the direction and of any steps taken in relation to the making of a transitional scheme in connection with the suspension[11]; and

(b) proposing steps for remedying the situation that has given rise to the situation[12].

As soon as practicable after the period allowed by OFCOM for making those representations has ended (and in any event within three months beginning with the day on which the direction was given), it must determine:

(i) whether the contravention providing the grounds for the giving of the direction did occur[13]; and

(ii) whether the circumstances made it an urgent case justifying the giving of the direction[14].

The period of three months referred to above[15] may be extended by up to three months if OFCOM:

(A) require additional time to consider representations received[16]; or

(B) decide that it is necessary to obtain additional information from the person in order to make a determination[17].

If OFCOM decides that the contravention did occur and that the direction was justified, it may confirm the direction[18]. If not, it must revoke it[19].

1 A case is an urgent case for the purposes of the Communications Act 2003 s 114 if OFCOM:
    (1) considers that it would be inappropriate, because the circumstances appearing to OFCOM to require the suspension fall within s 114(5), to allow time, before giving a direction under s 113, for the making and consideration of representations (s 114(4)(a)); and
    (2) decides for that reason to act in accordance with s 114(3), instead of s 114(1) (s 114(4)(b)).
    Circumstances fall within s 114(5) if they have resulted in, or create an immediate risk of:
    (a) a serious threat to the safety of the public, to public health or to national security (s 114(5)(a));

(b)　serious economic or operational problems for persons (apart from the operator) who are communications providers or persons who make associated facilities available (s 114(5)(b)); or

(c)　serious economic or operational problems for persons who make use of electronic communications networks, electronic communications services or associated facilities (s 114(5)(c)).

As to the meanings of 'associated facilities', 'electronic communications network' and 'electronic communications service' see PARA 53.

2　As to the meaning of 'OFCOM' see PARA 14 note 1; and as to OFCOM see PARA 2 et seq.
3　Ie under the Communications Act 2003 s 113(4): see PARA 161 text and note 19.
4　As to the meaning of 'electronic communications code' see PARA 155 note 1.
5　Communications Act 2003 s 114(1) (amended by SI 2011/1210).
6　Communications Act 2003 s 114(1)(a). The reference in the text to a transitional scheme is a reference to a scheme under s 117: see PARA 161 note 41.
7　Communications Act 2003 s 114(1)(b).
8　Communications Act 2003 s 114(1)(c).
9　Communications Act 2003 s 114(2) (substituted by SI 2011/1210).
10　Ie under the Communications Act 2003 s 113: see PARA 116.
11　Communications Act 2003 s 114(3)(a).
12　Communications Act 2003 s 114(3)(b).
13　Communications Act 2003 s 114(3A)(a) (s 114(3A)–(3D) added by SI 2011/1210).
14　Communications Act 2003 s 114(3A)(b) (s 114(3A)–(3D) added by SI 2011/1210).
15　Ie mentioned in the Communications Act 2003 s 114(3A).
16　Communications Act 2003 s 114(3B)(a) (as added: see note 13).
17　Communications Act 2003 s 114(3B)(b) (as added: see note 13). The text refers to making a determination under s 114(3A).
18　Communications Act 2003 s 114(3C) (as added: see note 13).
19　Communications Act 2003 s 114(3D) (as added: see note 13).

163.　Notification of cessation by person to whom electronic communications code applies.　The following provisions[1] apply where, by virtue of a direction[2], the electronic communications code[3] applies in any person's case for the purposes of the provision by him of an electronic communications network[4] or a system of conduits[5]. If that person ceases to provide that network or conduit system, he must notify OFCOM of that fact[6]. A notification under these provisions[7] must be given within such period and in such manner as may be required by OFCOM[8]. OFCOM may impose a penalty on a person who fails to comply with a requirement imposed by or under these provisions[9]. The amount of a penalty imposed on a person under these provisions is to be such amount not exceeding £1,000 as OFCOM may determine to be both appropriate and proportionate to the matter in respect of which it is imposed[10].

Where OFCOM imposes a penalty on a person under these provisions, it must:

(1)　within one week of making its decision to impose the penalty, notify that person of that decision and of its reasons for that decision[11]; and

(2)　in that notification, fix a reasonable period after it is given as the period within which the penalty is to be paid[12].

A penalty imposed under these provisions must be paid to OFCOM; and if not paid within the fixed period, is recoverable by OFCOM accordingly[13].

1　Ie the Communications Act 2003 s 116.
2　Ie under the Communications Act 2003 s 106: see PARA 155.
3　As to the meaning of 'electronic communications code' see PARA 155 note 1.
4　Ie which is not of a description designated for the purposes of the Communications Act 2003 s 33: see PARA 81. As to the meaning of 'electronic communications network' see PARA 53.
5　Communications Act 2003 s 116(1). The text refers to such a system of conduits as is mentioned in s 106(4)(b) (see PARA 151 head (b)): s 116(1).

6   Communications Act 2003 s 116(2). As to the meaning of 'OFCOM' see PARA 14 note 1; and as
    to OFCOM see PARA 2 et seq.
7   Ie the Communications Act 2003 s 116.
8   Communications Act 2003 s 116(3).
9   Communications Act 2003 s 116(4).
10 Communications Act 2003 s 116(5). The Secretary of State may by order amend s 116 so as to
    substitute a different maximum penalty for the maximum penalty for the time being specified in
    s 116(5): s 116(8). No order is to be made containing provision authorised by s 116(8) unless a
    draft of the order has been laid before Parliament and approved by a resolution of each House:
    s 116(9). At the date at which this volume states the law, no such order had been made. As to
    the Secretary of State see PARA 76 note 1. As to the power of the Secretary of State to make
    orders under the Communications Act 2003 see s 402; and PARA 74.
11 Communications Act 2003 s 116(6)(a).
12 Communications Act 2003 s 116(6)(b).
13 Communications Act 2003 s 116(7).

164.   Compulsory acquisition of land.   Provision is made for compulsory
acquisition of land by the provider of an electronic communications network[1] in
whose case the electronic communications code[2] applies, and for entry on land
by persons nominated by such a provider[3].

The Secretary of State[4] may authorise a code operator[5] to purchase
compulsorily any land in England or Wales which is required by the operator for,
or in connection with, the establishment or running of the operator's network[6] or
as to which it can reasonably be foreseen that it will be so required[7]. No order is
to be made authorising such a compulsory purchase by a code operator except
with OFCOM's consent[8]. This power to purchase land compulsorily includes
power to acquire an easement or other right over land by the creation of a new
right[9]. The Acquisition of Land Act 1981 is to apply to any compulsory purchase
under these provisions as if the code operator were a local authority within the
meaning of that Act[10]. Specified provisions of the Town and Country Planning
Act 1990[11] have effect in relation to land acquired compulsorily by a code
operator under these provisions as they have effect in relation to land acquired
compulsorily by statutory undertakers[12]. Where a code operator has acquired
land under these provisions, he must not dispose of that land, or of an interest or
right in or over it, except with OFCOM's consent[13].

A person nominated by a code operator, and duly authorised in writing by the
Secretary of State, may, at any reasonable time, enter upon and survey land in
England or Wales for the purpose of ascertaining whether the land would be
suitable for use by the code operator for, or in connection with, the establishment
or running of the operator's network[14]. This does not apply, however, in relation
to land covered by buildings or used as a garden or pleasure ground[15]. Where, in
exercise of this power, any damage is caused to land or to chattels, the code
operator must either make good the damage or pay compensation in respect of
the damage to every person interested in the land or chattels[16]. Where, in
consequence of an exercise of the power conferred by these provisions, a person
is disturbed in his enjoyment of land or chattels, the code operator must pay that
person compensation in respect of the disturbance[17]. The determination of any
dispute as to compensation is to be in accordance with the Town and Country
Planning Act 1990[18].

For the purpose of the acquisition by agreement by a code operator of land in
England or Wales, the provisions of Part I of the Compulsory Purchase Act 1965
(so far as applicable)[19], apply as they apply for the purposes of that Act[20].

1   As to the meaning of 'electronic communications network' see PARA 53.
2   As to the meaning of 'electronic communications code' see PARA 151 note 1.

3   See the Communications Act 2003 s 118, Sch 4.
4   As to the Secretary of State see PARA 76 note 1. In exercising his powers under the
    Communications Act 2003 Sch 4, it is the duty of the Secretary of State to have regard, in
    particular, to each of the following:
    (1)   the duties imposed on OFCOM by ss 3, 4 (see PARAS 16–17) (Sch 4 para 2(a));
    (2)   the need to protect the environment and, in particular, to conserve the natural beauty
          and amenity of the countryside (Sch 4 para 2(b));
    (3)   the need to ensure that highways are not damaged or obstructed, and traffic not
          interfered with, to any greater extent than is reasonably necessary (Sch 4 para 2(c)); and
    (4)   the need to encourage the sharing of the use of electronic communications apparatus
          (Sch 4 para 2(d)).
    As to the meaning of 'OFCOM' see PARA 14 note 1; and as to OFCOM see PARA 2 et seq. As to
    the meaning of 'electronic communications apparatus' see PARA 88 note 10.
5   'Code operator' means a provider of an electronic communications network in whose case the
    electronic communications code is applied by a direction under the Communications Act 2003
    s 106 (see PARA 155): Sch 4 para 1.
6   'Operator's network', in relation to a code operator, means so much of the electronic
    communications network provided by the operator as is not excluded from the application of
    the electronic communications code under the Communications Act 2003 s 106(5) (see PARA
    155): Sch 4 para 1.
7   Communications Act 2003 Sch 4 para 3(1).
8   Communications Act 2003 Sch 4 para 3(2).
9   Communications Act 2003 Sch 4 para 3(3).
10 Communications Act 2003 Sch 4 para 3(4). As to the Acquisition of Land Act 1981 see
    COMPULSORY ACQUISITION OF LAND vol 18 (2009) PARA 501 et seq.
11 Ie the Town and Country Planning Act 1990 ss 238–240 (use and development of consecrated
    land and burial ground); s 241 (use and development of land for open spaces); and ss 271–274
    (extinguishment of rights of way, and rights as to apparatus, of statutory undertakers):
    Communications Act 2003 Sch 4 para 3(6). See CREMATION AND BURIAL vol 24 (2010) PARAS
    1350, 1352; PLANNING vol 83 (2010) PARAS 1133–1135, 1140, 1196–1199.
12 Communications Act 2003 Sch 4 para 3(5).
13 Communications Act 2003 Sch 4 para 3(7).
14 Communications Act 2003 Sch 4 para 6(1). The Town and Country Planning Act 1990
    ss 324(8), 325(1)–(5), (8), (9) (supplementary provisions relating to powers of entry) have effect
    in relation to this power as they have effect in relation to the powers conferred by s 324 and
    subject to the modifications set out below: Communications Act 2003 Sch 4 para 6(3). Those
    modifications are:
    (1)   in the Town and Country Planning Act 1990 s 324(8) (power to search and bore for the
          purpose of ascertaining the nature of the subsoil or the presence of minerals) the
          reference to the presence of minerals is omitted (Communications Act 2003 Sch 4
          para 6(4)(a)); and
    (2)   in the Town and Country Planning Act 1990 s 325(1) (24 hours' notice to be given of
          an intended entry upon occupied land) 28 days' notice is to be given instead of 24
          hours' notice (Communications Act 2003 Sch 4 para 6(4)(b)).
    See PLANNING vol 81 (2010) PARA 65.
15 Communications Act 2003 Sch 4 para 6(2).
16 Communications Act 2003 Sch 4 para 6(5).
17 Communications Act 2003 Sch 4 para 6(6).
18 The Town and Country Planning Act 1990 s 118 (determination of disputes as to compensation)
    applies to any question of disputed compensation under the Communications Act 2003 Sch 14
    para 6 as it applies to such questions under the Town and Country Planning Act 1990 Pt IV
    (ss 107–118): Communications Act 2003 Sch 4 para 6(7). See PLANNING vol 83 (2010) PARA
    1109.
19 Ie the Compulsory Purchase Act 1965 ss 1–32, other than ss 4–8 (time limits, notices to treat
    etc) and s 31 (ecclesiastical property). See COMPULSORY ACQUISITION OF LAND.
20 Communications Act 2003 Sch 4 para 9(1).

165.   Power to give assistance in relation to certain proceedings. The
following provisions[1] apply where any actual or prospective party to certain
proceedings[2] (other than the operator, within the meaning of the electronic
communications code[3]) applies to OFCOM[4] for assistance under these

provisions in relation to those proceedings[5]. OFCOM may grant the application if, on any one or more of the following grounds, it thinks fit to do so:

(1)   on the ground that the case raises a question of principle[6];

(2)   on the ground that it is unreasonable, having regard to the complexity of the case or to any other matter, to expect the applicant to deal with the case without assistance under these provisions[7];

(3)   by reason of any other special consideration[8].

Assistance by OFCOM under these provisions may include:

(a)   giving advice or arranging for the giving of advice by a solicitor or counsel[9];

(b)   procuring or attempting to procure the settlement of the matter in dispute[10];

(c)   arranging for the giving of any assistance usually given by a solicitor or counsel:

    (i)   in the steps preliminary or incidental to proceedings[11]; or

    (ii)   in arriving at, or giving effect to, a compromise to avoid proceedings or to bring them to an end[12];

(d)   arranging for representation by a solicitor or counsel[13];

(e)   arranging for the giving of any other assistance by a solicitor or counsel[14];

(f)   any other form of assistance which OFCOM considers appropriate[15].

In so far as expenses are incurred by OFCOM in providing the applicant with assistance under these provisions, the recovery of those expenses (as taxed or assessed in such manner as may be prescribed by rules of court) will constitute a first charge for the benefit of OFCOM:

(A)   on any costs or expenses which (whether by virtue of a judgment or order of a court, or an agreement or otherwise) are payable to the applicant by any other person in respect of the matter in connection with which the assistance is given[16]; and

(B)   so far as relates to costs or expenses, on the applicant's rights under a compromise or settlement arrived at in connection with that matter to avoid proceedings, or to bring them to an end[17].

1   Ie the Communications Act 2003 s 119.

2   Ie any proceedings falling within the Communications Act 2003 s 119(2). The proceedings falling within s 119(2) are any actual or prospective proceedings in which there falls to be determined any question arising under, or in connection with:

    (1)   the electronic communications code as applied in any person's case by a direction under s 106 (see PARA 155) (s 119(2)(a)); or

    (2)   any restriction or condition subject to which that code applies (s 119(2)(b)).

3   As to the meaning of 'electronic communications code' see PARA 155 note 1.

4   As to the meaning of 'OFCOM' see PARA 14 note 1; and as to OFCOM see PARA 2 et seq.

5   Communications Act 2003 s 119(1).

6   Communications Act 2003 s 119(3)(a).

7   Communications Act 2003 s 119(3)(b).

8   Communications Act 2003 s 119(3)(c).

9   Communications Act 2003 s 119(4)(a).

10 Communications Act 2003 s 119(4)(b).

11 Communications Act 2003 s 119(4)(c)(i).

12 Communications Act 2003 s 119(4)(c)(ii).

13 Communications Act 2003 s 119(4)(d). Nothing in head (d) in the text is to be taken to affect the law and practice regulating the descriptions of persons who may appear in, conduct or defend any proceedings, or who may address the court in any proceedings: s 119(5).

14 Communications Act 2003 s 119(4)(e).

15 Communications Act 2003 s 119(4)(f).

16 Communications Act 2003 s 119(6)(a). A charge conferred by s 119(6) is subject to any charge imposed by the Legal Aid, Sentencing and Punishment of Offenders Act 2012 s 25 and any provision made by or under the Legal Aid, Sentencing and Punishment of Offenders Act 2012 Pt 1 (ss 1–43) for the payment of any sum to the Lord Chancellor (see LEGAL AID vol 65 (2015) PARA 155): see the Communications Act 2003 s 119(7) (amended by the Legal Aid, Sentencing and Punishment of Offenders Act 2012 Sch 5 para 61).

17 Communications Act 2003 s 119(6)(b). See note 16.

(ii) Application and Provisions of the Electronic Communications Code

A. APPLICATION OF THE CODE TO EXISTING ARRANGEMENTS

166. Effect of the code on existing arrangements. Neither the electronic communications code (formerly the telecommunications code)[1], nor the repeal by the Telecommunications Act 1984 of any provision of the Telegraph Acts 1863 to 1916[2] (which contain provisions confirming or continuing in force certain agreements), prejudices any rights or liabilities[3] which may arise at any time under any agreement which was entered into before the code came into force[4] and which relates to the installation, maintenance, adjustment, repair, alteration[5] or inspection of any electronic communications apparatus[6] or to keeping any such apparatus installed on, under or over any land[7].

Except as otherwise provided[8], the code does not authorise the contravention of any provision made by or under any enactment passed before the Telecommunications Act 1984[9], and, with certain exceptions[10], the provisions of the code are without prejudice to any rights or liabilities arising under any agreement to which the operator is a party[11].

1 See PARA 155 note 1. See also PARA 52 note 9.
2 As to these Acts see PARA 46 note 2.
3 This includes any rights or liabilities transferred by virtue of the Telecommunications Act 1984 s 60 (repealed) (vesting of property of British Telecommunications in the successor company: see PARA 51): Sch 2 para 28(6).
4 As to the coming into force of the code see PARA 168 note 15.
5 As to the meaning of 'alteration' see PARA 168 note 5.
6 As to the meaning of 'electronic communications apparatus' in the electronic communications code see PARA 168 note 6.
7 Telecommunications Act 1984 Sch 2 para 28(6) (amended by the Communications Act 2003 s 106(2), Sch 3 paras 1, 5(a)).
8 Ie by the Telecommunications Act 1984 Sch 4.
9 Telecommunications Act 1984 Sch 2 para 27(1) (amended by the Communications Act 2003 s 406(7), Sch 19).
10 Ie except the Telecommunications Act 1984 Sch 2 para 8(5) (see PARA 173), Sch 2 para 21 (see PARA 184) and Sch 2 para 27(1) (see note 9): Sch 2 para 27(2).
11 Telecommunications Act 1984 Sch 2 para 27(2).

167. Effect of agreements concerning sharing of apparatus. Where:

(1) the electronic communications code[1] has been applied[2] in a person's case[3];

(2) the code expressly or impliedly imposes a limitation on the use to which electronic communications apparatus[4] installed by that person may be put or on the purposes for which it may be used[5]; and

(3) that person is a party to a relevant agreement or becomes a party to an agreement which (after he has become a party to it) is a relevant agreement[6],

the limitation is not to preclude either the doing of anything in relation to that apparatus, or its use for particular purposes, to the extent that the doing of that thing, or the use of the apparatus for those purposes, is in pursuance of the agreement[7].

An agreement is a 'relevant agreement' if it is an agreement in relation to electronic communications apparatus which:

(a) relates to the sharing by different parties to the agreement of the use of that apparatus; and

(b) is an agreement that satisfies the following requirements[8]:

    (i) every party to the agreement is a person in whose case the code applies by virtue of a direction under the Communications Act 2003[9]; or

    (ii) one or more of the parties to the agreement is a person in whose case the code so applies and every other party to the agreement is a qualifying person[10].

A person is a qualifying person for this purpose if he is either:

(A) a person who provides an electronic communications network[11] without being a person in whose case the code applies[12]; or

(B) a designated[13] provider of an electronic communications service[14] consisting in the distribution of a programme service[15] by means of an electronic communications network[16].

These provisions are not to be construed, in relation to a person who is entitled or authorised by or under a relevant agreement to share the use of apparatus installed by another party to the agreement, as affecting any consent requirement[17] imposed (whether by a statutory provision[18] or otherwise) on that person[19].

1   As to the meaning of 'electronic communications code' see PARA 155 note 1.

2   Ie by a direction under the Communications Act 2003 s 106: see PARA 155.

3   Telecommunications Act 1984 Sch 2 para 29(1)(a) (Sch 2 para 29 added by the Communications Act 2003 Sch 3 para 11).

4   As to the meaning of 'electronic communications apparatus' see PARA 168 note 6.

5   Telecommunications Act 1984 Sch 2 para 29(1)(b) (as added: see note 3).

6   Telecommunications Act 1984 Sch 2 para 29(1)(c) (as added: see note 3).

7   Telecommunications Act 1984 Sch 2 para 29(2) (as added: see note 3).

8   Telecommunications Act 1984 Sch 2 para 29(4) (as added: see note 3).

9   Telecommunications Act 1984 Sch 2 para 29(5)(a). The direction referred to in the text is a direction under the Communications Act 2003 s 106: see PARA 155.

10 Telecommunications Act 1984 Sch 2 para 29(5)(b) (as added: see note 3).

11 As to the meaning of 'electronic communications network' see PARA 53.

12 Telecommunications Act 1984 Sch 2 para 29(6)(a).

13 'Designated' means designated by an order made by the Secretary of State: Telecommunications Act 1984 Sch 2 para 29(7) (as added: see note 3). As to the Secretary of State see PARA 76 note 1. At the date at which this volume states the law, no such order has been made.

14 As to the meaning of 'electronic communications service' see PARA 53.

15 'Programme service' has the same meaning as in the Broadcasting Act 1990 (see BROADCASTING vol 4 (2011) PARA 507 note 11): Telecommunications Act 1984 Sch 2 para 29(7) (as added: see note 4).

16 Telecommunications Act 1984 Sch 2 para 29(6)(b) (as added: see note 3).

17 'Consent requirement', in relation to a person, means a requirement for him to obtain consent or permission to or in connection with:

    (1) the installation by him of apparatus; or

    (2) the doing by him of any other thing in relation to apparatus the use of which he is entitled or authorised to share: Telecommunications Act 1984 Sch 2 para 29(4) (as added: see note 3).

18 'Statutory provision' means a provision of an enactment or of an instrument having effect under an enactment: Telecommunications Act 1984 Sch 2 para 29(4) (as added: see note 3).
19 Telecommunications Act 1984 Sch 2 para 29(3) (as added: see note 3).

B. THE PROVISIONS OF THE CODE

(A) Agreement to Carry Out Works

168. Right to execute works. The written[1] agreement of the occupier[2] for the time being of any land is required for conferring on the operator[3] a right for the statutory purposes[4]:

(1) to execute any works on that land for or in connection with the installation, maintenance, adjustment, repair or alteration[5] of electronic communications apparatus[6];

(2) to keep electronic communications apparatus installed on, under or over that land[7];

(3) to enter that land to inspect any apparatus kept installed, whether on, under or over that land or elsewhere, for the purposes of the operator's network[8].

A right falling within heads (1) to (3) above[9] is not exercisable except in accordance with the terms, whether as to payment or otherwise, subject to which it is conferred, and accordingly every person[10] for the time being bound by such a right[11] has the benefit of those terms[12]. Such a right is not subject to the provisions of any enactment requiring the registration of interests in, charges on or other obligations affecting land[13].

Any consent given, or deemed to have been given, for the purposes of any provision of the Telegraph Acts 1863 to 1916[14] before the code came into force[15] has effect as an agreement given for the purposes of the code[16].

The ownership of any property is not affected by the fact that it is installed on or under, or affixed to, any land by any person in exercise of a right conferred by or in accordance with the code[17].

Anything done by the operator in exercise of a right conferred in relation to any land by agreement[18] is deemed to be done in exercise of a statutory power except as against[19]:

(a) a person who, being the owner of the freehold estate in that land or a lessee[20] of the land, is not for the time being bound by the right[21]; or

(b) a person having the benefit of any covenant or agreement which has been entered into as respects the land under any enactment and which, by virtue of that enactment, binds or will bind persons deriving title or otherwise claiming under the covenantor or, as the case may be, a person who was a party to the agreement[22].

1 'Writing' includes typing, printing, lithography, photography and other modes of representing or reproducing words in a visible form; and expressions referring to writing are to be construed accordingly: Interpretation Act 1978 s 5, Sch 1.
2 For the purposes of the Telecommunications Act 1984 Sch 2 paras 2, 3, 4, references to the occupier of any land have effect:
    (1) in relation to any footpath, bridleway or restricted byway that crosses and forms part of any agricultural land or any land which is being brought into use for agriculture, as references to the occupier of that land (Sch 2 para 2(8)(a)(i) (amended by SI 2006/1177));
    (2) in relation to any street, not being such a footpath, bridleway or restricted byway, as references to the street managers within the meaning of the New Roads and Street Works Act 1991 Pt III (ss 48–106) (see HIGHWAYS, STREETS AND BRIDGES vol 55 (2012)

PARA 409) (see the Telecommunications Act 1984 Sch 2 para 2(8)(a)(ii) (amended by the New Roads and Street Works Act 1991 Sch 8 para 114; and SI 2006/1177));

(3)   in relation to any land, not being a street which is unoccupied, as references to the person, if any, who for the time being exercises powers of management or control over the land or, if there is no such person, to every person whose interest in the land would be prejudicially affected by the exercise of the right in question (Telecommunications Act 1984 Sch 2 para 2(8)(a)(iii) (amended by the New Roads and Street Works Act 1991 Sch 8 para 114)).

'Bridleway' and 'footpath' have the same meanings as in the Highways Act 1980 (see HIGHWAYS, STREETS AND BRIDGES vol 55 (2012) PARA 68); 'restricted byway' has the same meaning as in the Countryside and Rights of Way Act 2000 Pt II (ss 47–72) (see HIGHWAYS, STREETS AND BRIDGES vol 55 (2012) PARA 611); 'agricultural' has the same meaning as in the Highways Act 1980 (see HIGHWAYS, STREETS AND BRIDGES vol 55 (2012) PARA 236); and 'street' has the same meaning as in the New Roads and Street Works Act 1991 Pt III (see HIGHWAYS, STREETS AND BRIDGES vol 55 (2012) PARA 9): Telecommunications Act 1984 Sch 2 para 1(1) (amended by the New Roads and Street Works Act 1991 Sch 8 para 113(2)(d); SI 1995/3210 (NI 19); and SI 2006/1177). In relation to any land which, other than in connection with a street on that land, is divided horizontally into different parcels, references to a place over or under the land have effect in relation to each parcel as not including references to any place in a different parcel: Telecommunications Act 1984 Sch 2 para 1(3).

3   'Operator' means:

(1)   where the code (see PARA 151 note 1) is applied in any person's case by a direction under the Communications Act 2003 s 106 (see PARA 151), that person (Telecommunications Act 1984 Sch 2 para 1(1) (definition substituted by the Communications Act 2003 s 106(2), Sch 3 paras 1, 3(1)); and

(2)   where it applies by virtue of s 106(3)(b) (see PARA 151 head (2)), the Secretary of State (Telecommunications Act 1984 Sch 2 para 1(1) (definition as so substituted)). As to the Secretary of State see PARA 76 note 1.

4   'Statutory purposes' means the purposes of the provision of the operator's network: Telecommunications Act 1984 Sch 2 para 1(1) (amended by the Communications Act 2003 Sch 3 para 3(2)(b)). 'Operator's network' means:

(1)   in relation to an operator falling within head (1) of the definition of 'operator' (see note 3 head (1)), so much of any electronic communications network or conduit system provided by that operator as is not excluded from the application of the code under the Communications Act 2003 s 106(5) (see PARA 155); and

(2)   in relation to an operator falling within head (2) of that definition (see note 3 head (2)), the electronic communications network which the Secretary of State is providing or proposing to provide: Telecommunications Act 1984 Sch 2 para 1(1) (definition substituted by the Communications Act 2003 Sch 3 para 3(1)).

As to the meaning of 'electronic communications network' see PARA 53. 'Conduit system' means a system of conduits provided so as to be available for use by providers of electronic communications networks for the purposes of the provision by them of their networks; and 'conduit' includes a tunnel, subway, tube or pipe: Telecommunications Act 1984 Sch 2 para 1(1) (definitions added by the Communications Act 2003 Sch 3 para 2(1)).

5   References to the alteration of any apparatus include references to the moving, removal or replacement of the apparatus: Telecommunications Act 1984 Sch 2 para 1(1), (2).

6   Telecommunications Act 1984 Sch 2 para 2(1)(a) (amended by the Communications Act 2003 Sch 3 para 5(a)). 'Electronic communications apparatus' means:

(1)   any apparatus (within the meaning of the Communications Act 2003: see PARA 16 note 4) which is designed or adapted for use in connection with the provision of an electronic communications network;

(2)   any apparatus (within the meaning of the Communications Act 2003) that is designed or adapted for a use which consists of or includes the sending or receiving of communications or other signals that are transmitted by means of an electronic communications network;

(3)   any line;

(4)   any conduit, structure, pole or other thing in, on, by or from which any electronic communications apparatus is or may be installed, supported, carried or suspended,

and references to the installation of electronic communications apparatus are to be construed accordingly: Telecommunications Act 1984 Sch 2 para 1(1) (definition added by the Communications Act 2003 Sch 3 para 2(2)).

References to electronic communications apparatus installed on, under or over any land include references to electronic communications apparatus so installed before the code came into force (see note 15): Telecommunications Act 1984 Sch 2 para 28(1) (amended by the Communications Act 2003 Sch 3 para 5(a)). Without prejudice to the provisions of the code, where the operator has a right conferred by or in accordance with the code for the statutory purposes to keep electronic communications apparatus installed on, under or over any land, he is not entitled to keep that apparatus so installed if, at a time when the apparatus is not, or is no longer, used for the purposes of the operator's network, there is no reasonable likelihood that it will be so used: Telecommunications Act 1984 Sch 2 para 22 (amended by the Communications Act 2003 Sch 3 para 5(a), (d)).

Except for the purposes of the Telecommunications Act 1984 Sch 2 para 21 (see PARA 189), and without prejudice to Sch 2 para 6(3) (see PARA 171 note 17), and Sch 2 para 7(3) (see PARA 172), any electronic communications apparatus kept installed on, under or over any land is deemed, as against any person who was at any time entitled to require but was not entitled to enforce its removal (ie by virtue of Sch 2 para 21: see PARA 189), to have been lawfully so kept at that time: Sch 2 para 21(9) (amended by the Communications Act 2003 Sch 3 para 5(a)).

Any development (eg the installation, alteration or replacement in, on, over or under land of any electronic communications apparatus) in pursuance of a right conferred on an operator under the Telecommunications Act 1984 Sch 2 is permitted, subject to certain limitations: see the Town and Country Planning General Development Order 1995, SI 1995/418, Sch 2 Pts 24, 25; and PLANNING vol 81 (2010) PARA 531 et seq.

7　Telecommunications Act 1984 Sch 2 para 2(1)(b) (amended by the Communications Act 2003 Sch 3 para 5(a)).

8　Telecommunications Act 1984 Sch 2 para 2(1)(c) (amended by the Communications Act 2003 Sch 3 para 5(d)). Subject to the provisions of the Telecommunications Act 1984 Sch 2 para 9(2) and Sch 2 para 11(2), Sch 2 para 2 does not require any person to give his agreement to the exercise of any right conferred by any of Sch 2 paras 9–12 (see PARAS 174–176, 182): Sch 2 para 2(9).

9　Ie under the Telecommunications Act 1984 Sch 2 para 2(1).

10　As to the meaning of 'person' see PARA 14 note 2.

11　As to the persons bound by the right see PARA 164.

12　Telecommunications Act 1984 Sch 2 para 2(5).

13　Telecommunications Act 1984 Sch 2 para 2(7).

14　As to these Acts see PARA 46 note 2. Consents were required under the Telegraph Act 1863 s 9 (works under streets or public roads), ss 12, 13 (works above streets), s 21 (works interfering with access to private land), s 22 (works within a certain distance of dwelling houses), s 32 (works affecting railway and canal undertakings), s 35 (works on the seashore), and the Telegraph (Construction) Act 1908 s 3 (public recreation grounds) (all repealed). However, the system of control of telegraph works contained in the Telegraph Acts 1863 to 1916 has been completely superseded by the code contained in the Telecommunications Act 1984 Sch 2.

15　References in the Telecommunications Act 1984 Sch 2 para 28 to the coming into force of the code have effect as references to the time at which the code comes into force in relation to the operator: Sch 2 para 28(12). The code came into force generally on 5 August 1984: see the Telecommunications Act 1984 (Appointed Day) (No 2) Order 1984, SI 1984/876, art 4, Sch 2.

16　Telecommunications Act 1984 Sch 2 para 28(3)(a). As to the effect of notices given and applications made under the former Telegraph Acts after the coming into force of the code see PARA 192.

17　Telecommunications Act 1984 Sch 2 para 27(4).

18　Ie in accordance with the Telecommunications Act 1984 Sch 2 para 2 or Sch 2 para 3.

19　Telecommunications Act 1984 Sch 2 para 4(1).

20　'Lease' includes any leasehold tenancy, whether in the nature of a head lease, sub-lease or underlease, and any agreement to grant such a tenancy, but not a mortgage by demise or sub-demise; and 'lessee' is to be construed accordingly: Telecommunications Act 1984 Sch 2 para 2(8)(b).

21　Telecommunications Act 1984 Sch 2 para 4(1)(a).

22　Telecommunications Act 1984 Sch 2 para 4(1)(b).

169. Persons bound by the agreement. A person[1] who is the owner of the freehold estate in any land or is a lessee[2] of any land is not bound by a right to execute works[3] conferred by the occupier[4] of that land unless:

(1)　he conferred the right himself as occupier of the land[5];

(2)　he has agreed in writing to be bound by the right[6];

(3)　he is for the time being treated[7] as having so agreed[8]; or

(4)   he is otherwise bound[9].

Where a person owning an interest in land agrees in writing[10] that his interest should be bound by such a right, that right, except so far as the contrary intention appears, binds the owner from time to time of that interest and also[11]:

(a)   the owner from time to time of any other interest in the land, being an interest created after the right is conferred and not having priority over the interest to which the agreement relates[12]; and

(b)   any other person who is at any time in occupation of the land and whose right to occupation of the land derives, by contract or otherwise, from a person who at the time the right to occupation was granted was bound by virtue of this provision[13].

A variation of such a right or of the terms on which it is exercisable is capable of binding persons who are not parties to the variation in the same way[14] as such a right is capable of binding persons who are not parties to the conferring of the right[15].

Any consent given or deemed to have been given for the purposes of any provision of the Telegraph Acts 1863 to 1916[16] before the code came into force[17] has effect, to any extent that is necessary for ensuring that the same persons are bound under the code as were bound by the consent, as if it were an agreement to confer a right or, as the case may require, to bind any interest in land of the person who gave, or is deemed to have given, the consent[18].

1   As to the meaning of 'person' see PARA 14 note 2.
2   As to the meaning of 'lessee' see PARA 168 note 20.
3   Ie a right conferred by the Telecommunications Act 1984 Sch 2 para 2(1): see PARA 168.
4   As to the meaning of 'occupier' see PARA 168 note 2.
5   Telecommunications Act 1984 Sch 2 para 2(2)(a).
6   Telecommunications Act 1984 Sch 2 para 2(2)(b).
7   Ie treated as having so agreed by virtue of the Telecommunications Act 1984 Sch 2 para 2(3). If a right falling within Sch 2 para 2(1) has been conferred by the occupier of any land for purposes connected with the provision, to the occupier from time to time of that land, of any electronic communications services (see PARA 53), and:
     (1)   the person conferring the right is also the owner of the freehold estate in that land or is a lessee of the land under a lease for a term of a year or more (Sch 2 para 2(3)(a)); or
     (2)   in a case not falling within head (1), a person owning the freehold estate in the land or a lessee of the land under a lease for a term of a year or more has agreed in writing that his interest in the land should be bound by the right (Sch 2 para 2(3)(b)),
     then, subject to Sch 2 para 2(4) (see the text and notes 10–13), that right, as well as binding the person who conferred it, has effect, at any time when the person who conferred it or a person bound by it under Sch 2 para 2(2)(b) (see the text and note 6) or Sch 2 para 2(4) is the occupier of the land, as if every person for the time being owning an interest in that land had agreed in writing to the right being conferred for those purposes and, subject to its being exercised solely for those purposes, to be bound by it: Sch 2 para 2(3) (amended by the Communications Act 2003 s 106(2), Sch 3 paras 1, 5(b)).
8   Telecommunications Act 1984 Sch 2 para 2(2)(c).
9   Telecommunications Act 1984 Sch 2 para 2(2)(d). The reference to being bound in the text is by virtue of Sch 2 para 2(4): see the text and notes 10–13.
10   Ie whether when agreeing to the right as occupier or for the purposes of the Telecommunications Act 1984 Sch 2 para 2(3)(b), or otherwise. As to the meaning of 'writing' see PARA 163 note 1.
11   Telecommunications Act 1984 Sch 2 para 2(4).
12   Telecommunications Act 1984 Sch 2 para 2(4)(a).
13   Telecommunications Act 1984 Sch 2 para 2(4)(b).
14   Ie in the same way as under the Telecommunications Act 1984 Sch 2 para 2(2)–(4): see the text and notes 5–13.
15   Telecommunications Act 1984 Sch 2 para 2(6).
16   As to these Acts see PARA 46 note 2. As to such consent see PARA 168 note 14.
17   As to the date when the code (see PARA 155 note 1) came into force see PARA 168 note 15.

18 Telecommunications Act 1984 Sch 2 para 28(3)(b). Where, by virtue of Sch 2 para 28(3), any person is bound by any right, that right is not exercisable except on the same terms and subject to the same conditions as the right which, by virtue of the giving of the consent, was exercisable before the code came into force; and where under any enactment repealed by the Telecommunications Act 1984 those terms or conditions included a requirement for the payment of compensation or required the determination of any matter by any court or person, the amount of the compensation or, as the case may be, that matter must be determined after the coming into force of the code in like manner as if the Telecommunications Act 1984 had not been passed: Sch 2 para 28(4).

170. Agreement required for obstructing access. A right[1] to execute any works on any land, to keep electronic communications apparatus[2] installed on, under or over any land or to enter any land is not exercisable so as to interfere with or obstruct any means of entering or leaving any other land[3] unless the occupier[4] for the time being of the other land conferred, or is otherwise bound by, a right to interfere with or obstruct that means of entering or leaving the other land[5]. The written[6] agreement of the occupier for the time being of the other land is required for conferring any right for these purposes on the operator[7].

Nothing in these provisions[8] requires the person who is the occupier of, or who owns any interest in, any land which is a street[9] or to which the provisions relating to tidal waters[10] apply, to agree to the exercise of any right on any other land[11].

1 Ie a right conferred in accordance with the Telecommunications Act 1984 Sch 2 para 2(1) (see PARA 168), or under Sch 2 para 9, 10 or 11 (see PARAS 174–176).
2 As to the meaning of 'electronic communications apparatus' see PARA 168 note 6.
3 'Means of entering or leaving any land' includes any means of entering or leaving the land provided for use in emergencies: Telecommunications Act 1984 Sch 2 para 3(3).
4 As to the meaning of 'occupier' see PARA 168 note 2.
5 Telecommunications Act 1984 Sch 2 para 3(1) (amended by the Communications Act 2003 s 106(2), Sch 3 paras 1, 5(a)). The Telecommunications Act 1984 Sch 2 para 2(2), (4)–(7) (see PARAS 168–169) applies in relation to a right falling within Sch 2 para 3(1) as it applies in relation to a right falling within Sch 2 para 2(1) (see PARA 168): Sch 2 para 3(4).
6 As to the meaning of 'writing' see PARA 168 note 1.
7 Telecommunications Act 1984 Sch 2 para 3(2). As to the meaning of 'operator' see PARA 168 note 3. Subject to certain exceptions, anything done by the operator in accordance with Sch 2 para 3 is deemed to be done in exercise of a statutory power: see Sch 2 para 4(1); and PARA 168.
8 Ie the Telecommunications Act 1984 Sch 2 para 3.
9 As to the meaning of 'street' see PARA 163 note 2.
10 Ie the Telecommunications Act 1984 Sch 2 para 11: see PARA 176.
11 Telecommunications Act 1984 Sch 2 para 3(5) (amended by the Roads (Scotland) Act 1984 s 156(1), Sch 9 para 92(1), (4)(f)).

171. Power to dispense with agreement. Where the operator[1] requires any person[2] to agree[3] that any right should be conferred on the operator, or that any right should bind that person or any interest in land, the operator may give a notice[4] to him of the right and of the agreement that he requires[5]. Where the period of 28 days beginning with the giving of the notice has expired without the giving of the required agreement, the operator may apply to the court[6] for an order conferring the proposed right, or providing for it to bind any person or any interest in land, and in either case dispensing with the need for the agreement[7] of the person to whom the notice was given[8].

The court must make an order upon such application only if it is satisfied that any prejudice caused by the order:

(1) is capable of being adequately compensated for by money[9]; or

(2) is outweighed by the benefit accruing from the order to persons whose

access to an electronic communications network or to electronic communications services[10] will be secured by the order[11].

In determining the extent of the prejudice and the weight of the benefit, the court must have regard to all the circumstances and to the principle that no person should unreasonably be denied access to an electronic communications network or to electronic communications services[12].

An order in respect of a proposed right may direct that the right is to have effect with such modifications, be exercisable on such terms and be subject to such conditions as may be specified in it[13].

Where the operator gives notice to any person, and:

(a)   that notice requires that person's agreement in respect of a right which is to be exercisable, in whole or in part, in relation to electronic communications apparatus[14] already kept installed on, under or over the land in question[15]; and

(b)   that person is entitled to require the removal of that apparatus but is not entitled[16] to enforce its removal[17],

then, on the operator's application, the court may confer on the operator such temporary rights as appear to it reasonably necessary for securing that, pending the determination of any proceedings[18], the service provided by the operator's network[19] is maintained and the apparatus properly adjusted and kept in repair[20].

1   As to the meaning of 'operator' see PARA 168 note 3.
2   As to the meaning of 'person' see PARA 14 note 2.
3   Ie to agree for the purposes of the Telecommunications Act 1984 Sch 2 para 2 or Sch 2 para 3: see PARAS 163–165.
4   As to the giving of notices under the electronic communications code see PARA 187. As to the meaning of 'electronic communications code' see PARA 151 note 1.
5   Telecommunications Act 1984 Sch 2 para 5(1).
6   'Court' means, without prejudice to any right of appeal, in relation to England and Wales, the county court: Telecommunications Act 1984 Sch 2 para 1(1). For the purposes of proceedings under Sch 2 para 5 in a county court in England and Wales, the County Courts Act 1984 s 63(1) (relating to assessors: see CIVIL PROCEDURE vol 12 (2009) PARA 1133) has effect as if the words 'on the application of any party' were omitted; and where an assessor is summoned by virtue of this provision he may, if so directed by the judge, inspect the land to which the proceedings relate without the judge and report on the land to the judge in writing, and the judge may take the report into account in determining whether to make an order under this provision and what order to make: Telecommunications Act 1984 Sch 2 para 5(6).
7   Where an order under the Telecommunications Act 1984 Sch 2 para 5 for the purpose of conferring any right or making provision for a right to bind any person or any interest in land dispenses with the need for the agreement of any person, the order has the same effect and incidents as the agreement of the person the need for whose agreement is dispensed with and accordingly is capable of variation or release by a subsequent agreement: Sch 2 para 5(7).
8   Telecommunications Act 1984 Sch 2 para 5(2).
9   Telecommunications Act 1984 Sch 2 para 5(3)(a). See also note 11.
10 As to the meanings of 'electronic communications network' and 'electronic communications services' see PARA 53.
11 Telecommunications Act 1984 Sch 2 para 5(3)(b) (amended by the Communications Act 2003 s 106(2), Sch 3 paras 1, 5(c)). Under similar provisions in the Telegraph (Construction) Act 1916 s 1 (repealed), the court was not to give its consent unless the refusal was contrary to the public interest. In *Cartwright v Post Office* [1969] 2 QB 62, [1969] 1 All ER 421, CA, it was held that failure to give consent to placing a telegraph line across private land was contrary to public interest where the line was for the benefit of two farmhouses in a remote and exposed area. The following principles can also be deduced from cases under the earlier legislation:
   (1)   in exercising its discretion the court will consider the character of the district, the feeling of the locality, the amount of existing or probable future traffic, and the relative danger, inconvenience and expense involved in the conflicting proposals (*Wandsworth District Local Board v Postmaster-General* (1884) 4 Ry & Can Tr Cas 301; *Re*

Postmaster-General and Watford UDC (1908) 72 JP 184; *Re Postmaster-General and Woolwich Borough Council* (1908) 72 JP 186; *Croydon Corpn v Postmaster-General* (1910) 74 JP 424; *Re Postmaster-General and Tottenham UDC* (1910) 74 JP 434; *Postmaster-General v Darlington Corpn* (1914) 15 Ry & Can Tr Cas 333);

(2)   unsightliness is not in itself a sufficient ground of objection to poles (*Re Postmaster-General and Tottenham UDC* (1910) 74 JP 434), but it might be so if there were a street of which it really could be said that it was a thing of beauty (*Postmaster-General v Southgate Corpn* (1935) 79 Sol Jo 181).

12 Telecommunications Act 1984 Sch 2 para 5(3) (amended by the Communications Act 2003 Sch 3 para 5(c)). As to the power of potential subscribers to require the operator to give notice under these provisions see the Telecommunications Act 1984 Sch 2 para 8; and PARA 168.

13 Telecommunications Act 1984 Sch 2 para 5(4). The terms and conditions are to include such terms and conditions as appear to the court appropriate for ensuring that the least possible loss and damage is caused by the exercise of the right in respect of which the order is made to persons who occupy, own interests in, or are from time to time on the land in question: Sch 2 para 5(5). As to financial conditions see Sch 2 para 7; and PARA 172.

Under similar repealed legislation it was held that if the convenient user or enjoyment of private land is interfered with by the placing of a telegraphic line on it, or if the land has any special advantages which the placing of the line will or may reasonably be expected to injure, the court may have regard to those circumstances in considering what terms to impose: see *Postmaster-General v Brooks* [1922] 2 KB 176.

14 As to the meaning of 'electronic communications apparatus' see PARA 163 note 6.

15 Telecommunications Act 1984 Sch 2 para 6(1)(a) (amended by the Communications Act 2003 Sch 3 para 5(a)).

16 Ie by virtue of the Telecommunications Act 1984 Sch 2 para 21: see PARA 189.

17 Telecommunications Act 1984 Sch 2 para 6(1)(b). In any case where it is shown that a person with an interest in the land was entitled to require the removal of the apparatus immediately after it was installed, the court, in determining whether the apparatus should continue to be kept installed on, under or over the land, must disregard the fact that the apparatus has already been installed there: Sch 2 para 6(3).

18 Ie proceedings under the Telecommunications Act 1984 Sch 2 para 5 (see PARA 171) or Sch 2 para 21 (see PARA 189).

19 As to the meaning of 'operator's network' see PARA 168 note 4.

20 Telecommunications Act 1984 Sch 2 para 6(2) (amended by the Communications Act 2003 Sch 3 para 5(d)).

172. Financial terms where agreement is dispensed with. Where an order has been made[1] dispensing with the need for a person's[2] agreement, the terms and conditions[3] in the order must include[4]:

(1)   such terms with respect to the payment of consideration in respect of the giving of the agreement, or the exercise of the rights to which the order relates, as it appears to the court[5] would have been fair and reasonable if the agreement had been given willingly and subject to the other provisions of the order[6]; and

(2)   such terms as appear to the court appropriate for ensuring that that person and persons from time to time bound[7] by the rights to which the order relates are adequately compensated, whether by the payment of such consideration or otherwise, for any loss or damage sustained by them in consequence of the exercise of those rights[8].

In determining what terms should be specified in such an order for requiring an amount to be paid to any person in respect of the provisions of the order conferring any right or providing for any right to bind any person or any interest in land, or in respect of the exercise of any right to which the order relates, the court must take into account the prejudicial effect, if any, of the order or, as the case may be, of the exercise of the right on that person's enjoyment of, or on any interest of his in, land other than the land in relation to which the right is conferred[9].

In a case where such an order is made in consequence of an application made in connection with proceedings concerning the removal of apparatus[10], the court, in determining what terms should be specified in the order for requiring an amount to be paid to any person, must take into account, to such extent as it thinks fit, any period during which that person was entitled to require the removal of any electronic communications apparatus[11] from the land in question, but was not entitled[12] to enforce its removal; but where the court takes any such period into account it may also take into account any compensation[13] paid[14].

Where the amount of any sum required to be paid by virtue of terms specified in any such order has been determined, the court may, if it thinks fit, require the whole or any part of any such sum to be paid into court; and pending the determination of the amount of any such sum, it may order the payment into court of such amount on account as it thinks fit[15].

1 Ie under the Telecommunications Act 1984 Sch 2 para 5(4): see PARA 171.
2 As to the meaning of 'person' see PARA 14 note 2.
3 Ie the terms and conditions specified by virtue of the Telecommunications Act 1984 Sch 2 para 5(4): see PARA 171.
4 Telecommunications Act 1984 Sch 2 para 7(1).
5 As to the meaning of 'court' see PARA 171 note 6.
6 Telecommunications Act 1984 Sch 2 para 7(1)(a). See *Mercury Telecommunications Ltd v London and India Dock Investments Ltd* (1995) 69 P & CR 135, where the court held that 'fair and reasonable' should be determined by reference to comparable transactions; and that compulsory purchase principles are not applicable to the Telecommunications Act 1984 Sch 2 para 7(1)(a). As to the requirement of agreement to execute certain works see PARAS 168–170.
7 Ie bound by virtue of the Telecommunications Act 1984 Sch 2 para 2(4): see PARA 164.
8 Telecommunications Act 1984 Sch 2 para 7(1)(b). The terms specified may provide for the making of payments from time to time to such persons as may be determined under those terms (Sch 2 para 7(4)(a)); and for questions arising in consequence of those terms, whether as to the amount of any loss or damage caused by the exercise of a right or otherwise, to be referred to arbitration or to be determined in such other manner as may be specified in the order (Sch 2 para 7(4)(b)).
   Under similar repealed legislation it was held that the body or person having control of a street or public road could not impose on the then Postmaster General as a condition of consent to the construction of a telegraph line in or on the street or road a payment of money which had no relation to actual damage but was in the nature of compensation for use and occupation, such a condition being inconsistent with the true character and capacity of the person having control of the public roads: *Postmaster-General v Edinburgh Corpn* (1897) 10 Ry & Can Tr Cas 247; *Postmaster-General v Hutchings* [1916] 1 KB 774. The same considerations did not apply in the case of the owner of a private road not subject to public rights: *Postmaster-General v Brooks* [1922] 2 KB 176.
9 Telecommunications Act 1984 Sch 2 para 7(2).
10 Ie proceedings under the Telecommunications Act 1984 Sch 2 para 21: see PARA 189.
11 As to the meaning of 'electronic communications apparatus' see PARA 168 note 6.
12 Ie by virtue of the Telecommunications Act 1984 Sch 2 para 21: see PARA 189.
13 Ie compensation paid under the Telecommunications Act 1984 Sch 2 para 4(4): see PARA 185.
14 Telecommunications Act 1984 Sch 2 para 7(3) (amended by the Communications Act 2003 s 106(2), Sch 3 paras 1, 5(a)).
15 Telecommunications Act 1984 Sch 2 para 7(5). Where the terms specified in any order require the payment of any sum to a person who cannot be found or ascertained, that sum is to be paid into court: Sch 2 para 7(6).

173. Notices and applications by potential subscribers. Where:

(1)   it is reasonably necessary for the agreement[1] of any person[2] to the conferring of any right, or to any right binding any person or any

interest in land, to be obtained by the operator[3] before another person, called the 'potential subscriber', may be afforded access to the operator's network[4]; and

(2) the operator has not given a notice[5] or, if he has given a notice, has not made an application[6] in respect of that right[7],

the potential subscriber may at any time give a notice to the operator requiring him to give a notice or make an application in respect of that right[8].

At any time after such a notice has been given to the operator, he may apply to the court[9] to have the notice set aside on the ground that the conditions in heads (1) and (2) above are not satisfied or on the ground that, even if the agreement were obtained, the operator would not afford the potential subscriber access to the operator's network and could not be required to afford him access to that network[10].

Subject to any order of the court made in or pending such proceedings begun by the operator, if at any time after the expiration of the 28-day period beginning with the giving of the notice to the operator, he has not complied with the notice, the potential subscriber may himself, on the operator's behalf, give the required notice and, if necessary, make an application[11] or, as the case may be, make the required application[12].

On the application of the potential subscriber, the court may give such directions as it thinks fit[13]:

(a) with respect to the separate participation of the operator in the proceedings to which the application gives rise[14]; and

(b) requiring the operator to provide information to the court[15].

1 As to the necessity for agreement to execute certain works see PARAS 163–165.
2 As to the meaning of 'person' see PARA 14 note 2.
3 As to the meaning of 'operator' see PARA 163 note 3.
4 Telecommunications Act 1984 Sch 2 para 8(1)(a) (amended by the Communications Act 2003 s 106(2), Sch 3 paras 1, 5(a)). As to the meaning of 'operator's network' see PARA 168 note 4.
5 As to the giving of notices under the electronic communications code see PARA 192.
6 Ie an application under the Telecommunications Act 1984 Sch 2 para 5 dispensing with the need for agreement: see PARA 171.
7 Telecommunications Act 1984 Sch 2 para 8(1)(b).
8 Telecommunications Act 1984 Sch 2 para 8(1). A covenant, condition or agreement which would have the effect of preventing or restricting the taking by any person as a potential subscriber of any step under Sch 2 para 8 is void to the extent that it would have that effect: Sch 2 para 8(5).
9 As to the meaning of 'court' see PARA 171 note 6.
10 Telecommunications Act 1984 Sch 2 para 8(2) (amended by the Communications Act 2003 Sch 3 paras 1, 5(a)).
11 Ie an application under the Telecommunications Act 1984 Sch 2 para 5: see PARA 171.
12 Telecommunications Act 1984 Sch 2 para 8(3). Nothing in Sch 2 para 5 is to be construed as requiring the operator to reimburse the potential subscriber for any costs incurred by him in or in connection with the taking of any step under Sch 2 para 8 on the operator's behalf: Sch 2 para 8(6).
13 Telecommunications Act 1984 Sch 2 para 8(4).
14 Telecommunications Act 1984 Sch 2 para 8(4)(a).
15 Telecommunications Act 1984 Sch 2 para 8(4)(b).

(B) Rights, Powers and Duties of Operators

174. Street works. Subject to certain provisions[1], the operator[2] has, for the statutory purposes[3], the right to do any of the following[4]:

(1) install electronic communications apparatus[5], or keep such apparatus installed, under, over, in, on, along or across a street[6];

(2)   inspect, maintain, adjust, repair or alter[7] any electronic communications apparatus so installed[8]; and

(3)   execute any works requisite for or incidental to the purposes of any works falling within head (1) or head (2) above including for those purposes the following kinds of works[9]:
    (a)   breaking up or opening a street[10];
    (b)   tunnelling or boring under a street[11]; and
    (c)   breaking up or opening a sewer, drain or tunnel[12].

However, these rights are not exercisable in a street which is not a maintainable highway[13], without either the agreement of the occupier of the land[14] or an order of the court[15] dispensing with the need for that agreement[16].

1   Ie subject to the Telecommunications Act 1984 Sch 2 para 3 (see PARA 170); 10–28 (see PARA 175 et seq): Sch 2 para 9(2) (amended by the Communications Act 2003 s 406(7), Sch 19).
2   As to the meaning of 'operator' see PARA 168 note 3.
3   As to the meaning of 'statutory purposes' see PARA 168 note 4.
4   Telecommunications Act 1984 Sch 2 para 9(1).
5   As to the meaning of 'electronic communications apparatus' see PARA 163 note 6.
6   Telecommunications Act 1984 Sch 2 para 9(1)(a) (amended by the New Roads and Street Works Act 1991 s 168(1), (2), Sch 8 para 115, Sch 9; and the Communications Act 2003 s 106(2), Sch 3 paras 1, 5(a)). As to the meaning of 'street' see PARA 168 note 2.
7   As to the meaning of 'alter' see PARA 168 note 5.
8   Telecommunications Act 1984 Sch 2 para 9(1)(b) (amended by the Communications Act 2003 Sch 3 para 5(a)).
9   Telecommunications Act 1984 Sch 2 para 9(1)(c).
10 Telecommunications Act 1984 Sch 2 para 9(1)(c)(i) (amended by the New Roads and Street Works Act 1991 Sch 8 para 115).
11 Telecommunications Act 1984 Sch 2 para 9(1)(c)(ii) (amended by the New Roads and Street Works Act 1991 Sch 8 para 115).
12 Telecommunications Act 1984 Sch 2 para 9(1)(c)(iii).
13 'Maintainable highway' in England and Wales means a maintainable highway within the meaning the New Roads and Street Works Act 1991 Pt III (ss 48–106) (see HIGHWAYS, STREETS AND BRIDGES vol 55 (2012) PARA 411 et seq), other than one which is a footpath, bridleway or restricted byway that crosses and forms part of any agricultural land or any land which is being brought into use for agriculture: Telecommunications Act 1984 Sch 2 para 1(1) (amended by the New Road and Street Works Act 1991 Sch 8 para 113(2)(a); and by SI 2006/1177). As to the meanings of 'bridleway', 'footpath', 'restricted byway' and 'agriculture' see PARA 168 note 2.
14 Ie the agreement required by Telecommunications Act 1984 Sch 2 para 2: see PARA 163.
15 Ie an order under the Telecommunications Act 1984 Sch 2 para 5: see PARA 166.
16 Telecommunications Act 1984 Sch 2 para 9(2) (amended by the New Roads and Street Works Act 1991 Sch 8 para 115). As to restrictions on the use of certain conduits see PARA 181.

175.   Power to fly lines.   Subject to certain provisions[1], where any electronic communications apparatus[2] is kept installed on or over any land for the purposes of the operator's network[3], the operator[4] has, for the statutory purposes[5], the right to install and keep installed lines[6] which[7]:

(1)   pass over other land adjacent to or in the vicinity of the land on or over which that apparatus is so kept[8];

(2)   are connected to that apparatus[9]; and

(3)   are not at any point in the course of passing over the other land less than three metres above the ground or within two metres of any building over which they pass[10].

However, the right does not include authorisation to install or keep on or over any land:
    (a)   any electronic communications apparatus used to support, carry or suspend a line installed in pursuance of that right[11]; or

(b)   any line which by reason of its position interferes with the carrying on of any business[12] carried on that land[13].

1   Ie subject to the Telecommunications Act 1984 Sch 2 paras 3, 10(2), 11–28 (see PARA 176 et seq): Sch 2 para 10(1).
2   As to the meaning of 'electronic communications apparatus' see PARA 168 note 6.
3   As to the meaning of 'operator's network' see PARA 168 note 4.
4   As to the meaning of 'operator' see PARA 168 note 3.
5   As to the meaning of 'statutory purposes' see PARA 168 note 4.
6   'Line' means any wire, cable, tube, pipe or similar thing (including its casing or coating) which is designed or adapted for use in connection with the provision of any electronic communications network or electronic communications service: Telecommunications Act 1984 Sch 2 para 1(1) (definition substituted by the Communications Act 2003 s 106(2), Sch 3 paras 1, 2(3)).
7   Telecommunications Act 1984 Sch 2 para 10(1) (amended by the Communications Act 2003 Sch 3 para 5(a)).
8   Telecommunications Act 1984 Sch 2 para 10(1)(a).
9   Telecommunications Act 1984 Sch 2 para 10(1)(b).
10   Telecommunications Act 1984 Sch 2 para 10(1)(c).
11   Telecommunications Act 1984 Sch 2 para 10(2)(a) (amended by the Communications Act 2003 Sch 3 para 5(a)).
12   'Business' includes a trade, profession or employment and includes any activity carried on by a body of persons (whether corporate or unincorporate): Telecommunications Act 1984 Sch 2 para 10(3) (added by the Communications Act 2003 Sch 3 para 6).
13   Telecommunications Act 1984 Sch 2 para 10(2)(b) (amended by the Communications Act 2003 s 406(7), Sch 19).

176. Works in tidal waters. Subject to certain provisions[1], the operator[2] has the right for the statutory purposes[3]:

(1)   to execute any works, including placing any buoy or sea mark, on any tidal water or lands[4] for or in connection with the installation, maintenance, adjustment, repair or alteration[5] of electronic communications apparatus[6];

(2)   to keep electronic communications apparatus installed on, under or over tidal water or lands[7]; and

(3)   to enter any tidal water or lands to inspect any electronic communications apparatus so installed[8].

1   Ie subject to the Telecommunications Act 1984 Sch 2 paras 3, 11(2)–28: Sch 2 para 11(1). No rights are exercisable by any person by virtue of the electronic communications code in relation to any land comprised in the tunnel system and lying in or under the bed of the sea: Channel Tunnel Act 1987 s 32 (substituted by the Communications Act 2003 s 406(1), Sch 17 para 84).
2   As to the meaning of 'operator' see PARA 168 note 3.
3   As to the meaning of 'statutory purposes' see PARA 168 note 4.
4   'Tidal water or lands' includes any estuary or branch of the sea, the shore below mean high water springs and the bed of any tidal water: Telecommunications Act 1984 Sch 2 para 11(11). As to tidal waters see WATER AND WATERWAYS vol 100 (2009) PARA 71 et seq.
5   As to the meaning of 'alteration' see PARA 168 note 5.
6   Telecommunications Act 1984 Sch 2 para 11(1)(a) (amended by the Communications Act 2003 s 106(2), Sch 3 paras 1, 5(a)). See also note 8. As to the meaning of 'electronic communications apparatus' see PARA 168 note 6.
7   Telecommunications Act 1984 Sch 2 para 11(1)(b) (as amended: see note 6). See also note 8.
8   Telecommunications Act 1984 Sch 2 para 11(1)(c) (as amended: see note 6). A right conferred by Sch 2 para 11 is not to be exercised in relation to any land in which a Crown interest subsists unless agreement to the exercise of the right in relation to that land has been given in respect of that interest: Sch 2 para 11(2). Agreement required by the electronic communications code to be given in respect of any Crown interest subsisting in any land must be given by the appropriate authority (Sch 2 para 26(3)), that is to say:
    (1)   in the case of land belonging to Her Majesty in right of the Crown, the Crown Estate Commissioners or, as the case may require, the government department having the management of the land in question (Sch 2 para 26(3)(a));

(2)   in the case of land belonging to Her Majesty in right of the Duchy of Lancaster, the Chancellor of that Duchy (Sch 2 para 26(3)(b));

(3)   in the case of land belonging to the Duchy of Cornwall, such person as the Duke of Cornwall, or the possessor for the time being of the Duchy, appoints (Sch 2 para 26(3)(c));

As to the Crown Estate Commissioners see CROWN AND CROWN PROCEEDINGS vol 29 (2014) PARA 194 et seq. As to the Chancellor of the Duchy of Lancaster see CROWN AND CROWN PROCEEDINGS vol 29 (2014) PARA 219; and as to the Duchy of Lancaster see CROWN AND CROWN PROCEEDINGS vol 29 (2014) PARA 214 et seq. As to the Duchy of Cornwall see CROWN AND CROWN PROCEEDINGS vol 29 (2014) PARA 232 et seq.

Any question arising as to what authority is the appropriate authority in relation to any land must be referred to the Treasury, whose decision is final: Sch 2 para 26(3). As to the Treasury see CONSTITUTIONAL AND ADMINISTRATIVE LAW vol 20 (2014) PARAS 262–265.

177. Notices on overhead apparatus. Where, for the purposes of the operator's network[1], the operator[2] has installed any electronic communications apparatus[3] the whole or part of which is at a height of three metres or more above the ground, the operator must, before the expiration of the period of three days beginning with the completion of the installation, in a secure and durable manner affix a notice[4]:

(1)   to every major item of apparatus installed[5]; or

(2)   if no major item of apparatus is installed, to the nearest major item of electronic communications apparatus to which the apparatus that is installed is directly or indirectly connected[6].

The notice must be affixed in a position where it is reasonably legible, and must give the name of the operator and an address in the United Kingdom[7] at which any notice of objection[8] to the overhead apparatus may be given in respect of the apparatus in question[9].

If the operator contravenes these requirements he is guilty of an offence[10], but in any proceedings for the offence it is a defence for the person charged to prove that he took all reasonable steps and exercised all due diligence to avoid committing the offence[11].

1   As to the meaning of 'operator's network' see PARA 168 note 4.

2   As to the meaning of 'operator' see PARA 168 note 3.

3   As to the meaning of 'electronic communications apparatus' see PARA 168 note 6.

4   Telecommunications Act 1984 Sch 2 para 18(1) (amended by the Communications Act 2003 s 106(2), Sch 3 paras 1, 5(a), (d)).

5   Telecommunications Act 1984 Sch 2 para 18(1)(a).

6   Telecommunications Act 1984 Sch 2 para 18(1)(b) (amended by the Communications Act 2003 Sch 3 para 5(a)).

7   As to the meaning of 'United Kingdom' see PARA 14 note 7.

8   Ie a notice of objection under the Telecommunications Act 1984 Sch 2 para 17: see PARA 187.

9   Telecommunications Act 1984 Sch 2 para 18(2). A person giving such a notice at that address in respect of that apparatus is deemed to have been furnished with that address for the purposes of Sch 2 para 24(2A)(a) (see PARA 192 note 6): Sch 2 para 18(2) (amended by the Communications Act 2003 s 406(1), Sch 17 para 75). As to the requirement of legibility see *Lloyd Jones v T Mobile (UK) Ltd* [2003] EWCA Civ 1162, [2003] 3 EGLR 55, [2003] All ER (D) 561 (Jul).

10   Telecommunications Act 1984 Sch 2 para 18(3). The offence is punishable on summary conviction by a fine not exceeding level 2 on the standard scale: Sch 2 para 18(3). However, Sch 2 para 18(3) does not apply where the electronic communications code has effect by virtue of the Communications Act 2003 s 106(3)(b) (ie where the Secretary of State is running a communications network: see PARA 155 head (2)): Telecommunications Act 1984 Sch 2 para 26(4) (amended by the Communications Act 2003 Sch 3 para 10).

As to the standard scale see SENTENCING AND DISPOSITION OF OFFENDERS vol 92 (2010) PARA 142.

11   Telecommunications Act 1984 Sch 2 para 18(4).

178.   Tree lopping. Where any tree overhangs any street[1] and, in doing so, either:

(1)   obstructs or interferes with the working of any electronic communications apparatus[2] used for the purposes of the operator's network[3]; or

(2)   will obstruct or interfere with the working of any electronic communications apparatus which is about to be installed for those purposes[4],

the operator[5] may, by notice[6] to the occupier of the land on which the tree is growing, require the tree to be lopped so as to prevent the obstruction or interference[7].

If, within the period of 28 days beginning with the giving of this notice, the occupier of the land gives the operator a counter-notice objecting to the lopping, the notice has effect only if confirmed by a court order[8].

If at any time a notice given by the operator has not been complied with and either a period of 28 days beginning with the giving of the notice has expired without a counter-notice having been given, or a court order confirming the notice has come into force, the operator may himself cause the tree to be lopped[9].

Where:

(a)   a notice is complied with, either without a counter-notice having been given or after the notice has been confirmed; or

(b)   the operator exercises the power to lop the tree himself,

the court, on an application made by a person who has sustained loss or damage in consequence of the lopping of the tree or who has incurred expenses in complying with the notice, must order the operator to pay him such compensation in respect of the loss, damage or expenses as it thinks fit[10].

1   As to the meaning of 'street' see PARA 168 note 2.
2   As to the meaning of 'electronic communications apparatus' see PARA 168 note 6.
3   Telecommunications Act 1984 Sch 2 para 19(1)(a) (amended by the Communications Act 2003 s 106(2), Sch 3 paras 1, 5(a), (d)). As to the meaning of 'operator's network' see PARA 168 note 4.
4   Telecommunications Act 1984 Sch 2 para 19(1)(b) (amended by the Communications Act 2003 Sch 3 para 5(a)).
5   As to the meaning of 'operator' see PARA 168 note 3.
6   As to notices under the electronic communications code see PARA 192.
7   Telecommunications Act 1984 Sch 2 para 19(1).
8   Telecommunications Act 1984 Sch 2 para 19(2). As to the meaning of 'court' see PARA 171 note 6.
9   Telecommunications Act 1984 Sch 2 para 19(3). Where the operator lops a tree in exercise of this power, he must do so in a husband-like manner and in such a way as to cause the minimum damage to the tree: Sch 2 para 19(4). Power to lop authorises the cutting of the lateral branches of a tree, but not of the top: *Unwin v Hanson* [1891] 2 QB 115, CA.
10   Telecommunications Act 1984 Sch 2 para 19(5).

179.   Compensation for obstructed access. Where a shelter or other accommodation is provided by a local authority[1] in a position obstructing access to any electronic communications apparatus[2] kept installed for the purposes of an electronic communications code network[3] and the operator[4] of that network notifies the local authority that he requires to obtain access to the apparatus, the authority, unless it temporarily removes the shelter or accommodation for the purpose of affording such access or so much of it as is necessary for that purpose, is liable to repay to the operator so much of the expenses reasonably incurred by him in obtaining such access as is attributable to the situation of the shelter or accommodation[5]. These provisions[6] also apply where a parish council or meeting provides[7] public seats, shelters or other things which obstruct such access[8], and where a parking place for bicycles and motor cycles is provided[9] by a parish or community council[10].

1   Ie under the Local Government (Miscellaneous Provisions) Act 1953 s 4: see HIGHWAYS, STREETS AND BRIDGES vol 55 (2012) PARA 569. For these purposes, 'local authority' means the council of a county, borough or district and the Common Council of the City of London: s 18(1). As to counties, boroughs and districts in England, and their councils, see LOCAL GOVERNMENT vol 69 (2009) PARA 24 et seq; as to counties and county boroughs in Wales, and their councils, see LOCAL GOVERNMENT vol 69 (2009) PARA 37 et seq; as to London boroughs, and their councils, see LONDON GOVERNMENT vol 71 (2013) PARA 15;as to the Common Council of the City of London see LONDON GOVERNMENT vol 71 (2013) PARA 34 et seq.
2   As to the meaning of 'electronic communications apparatus' see PARA 168 note 6; definition applied by the Telecommunications Act 1984 s 109(1), Sch 4 para 1(1).
3   'Electronic communications code network' means:
    (1)   so much of an electronic communications network or conduit system provided by an electronic communications code operator (see note 4) as is not excluded from the application of the electronic communications code (see PARA 155 note 1) by a direction under the Communications Act 2003 s 106 (see PARA 155); and
    (2)   an electronic communications network which the Secretary of State is providing or proposing to provide (see PARA 155): see s 406(1), Sch 17 para 1(1).
    As to the meaning of 'electronic communications network' see PARA 53. As to the meaning of 'conduit system' see PARA 168 note 4. As to the Secretary of State see PARA 76 note 1.
4   For these purposes, 'operator', in relation to an electronic communications code network, means:
    (1)   the electronic communications code operator providing that network; or
    (2)   the Secretary of State, to the extent that he is providing or proposing to provide that network: see the Communications Act 2003 Sch 17 para 1(1).
    'Electronic communications code operator' means a person in whose case the electronic communications code is applied by a direction under s 106 (see PARA 155): Sch 17 para 1(1).
5   Local Government (Miscellaneous Provisions) Act 1953 s 6(1) (amended by the Telecommunications Act 1984 Sch 4 para 31; and the Communications Act 2003 Sch 17 para 22). Any dispute as to the amount payable by a local authority must be determined in accordance with the Public Health Act 1936 s 278(2) (see ENVIRONMENTAL QUALITY AND PUBLIC HEALTH): Local Government (Miscellaneous Provisions) Act 1953 s 6(3).
6   Ie the Local Government (Miscellaneous Provisions) Act 1953 s 6.
7   Ie under the Parish Councils Act 1957 Pt I (ss 1–7): see HIGHWAYS, STREETS AND BRIDGES vol 55 (2012) PARA 399.
8   See the Parish Councils Act 1957 s 5(4); and HIGHWAYS, STREETS AND BRIDGES vol 55 (2012) PARAS 552, 571.
9   Ie under the Road Traffic Regulation Act 1984 s 57(1): see ROAD TRAFFIC vol 89 (2011) PARA 601.
10 See the Road Traffic Regulation Act 1984 s 58(4); and ROAD TRAFFIC vol 89 (2011) PARA 602. As to parish councils see LOCAL GOVERNMENT vol 69 (2009) PARA 27 et seq; and as to community councils see LOCAL GOVERNMENT vol 69 (2009) PARA 41 et seq.

(C) Use of Conduits for Telecommunication Purposes

180. Meaning of 'relevant conduit'. 'Conduit' includes a tunnel or subway[1], and 'relevant conduit' means[2]:

(1)   any conduit which, whether or not it is itself an electric line[3], is maintained by an electricity authority[4] for the purpose of enclosing, surrounding or supporting such a line, including, where the conduit is connected to any box, chamber or other structure (including a building) maintained by an electricity authority for purposes connected with the conveyance, transmission or distribution of electricity, that box, chamber or structure[5]; or

(2)   a water main[6] or any other conduit maintained by a water authority[7] for the purpose of conveying water from one place to another[8]; or

(3)　　a public sewer[9]; or

Reference to the authority with control of a relevant conduit means[10]:

(a)　　in relation to a conduit or structure within head (1) or head (2) above, the authority by which it is maintained[11];

(b)　　in relation to a public sewer, subject to certain provisions[12], the person[13] in whom it is vested[14].

1　Telecommunications Act 1984 s 98(9).
2　Telecommunications Act 1984 s 98(6).
3　'Electric line' has the same meaning as in the Electricity Act 1989: Telecommunications Act 1984 s 98(9) (definition amended by the Electricity Act 1989 s 112(1), Sch 16 para 29(1), (2)). See also ENERGY AND CLIMATE CHANGE vol 43 (2011) PARA 507. As to the meaning of 'Great Britain' see PARA 14 note 7.
4　'Electricity authority' means a person authorised by a licence under the Electricity Act 1989 Pt I (ss 1–64) to supply or participate in the transmission of electricity: Telecommunications Act 1984 s 98(9) (definition amended by the Electricity Act 1989 Sch 16 para 29(1), (2); the Energy Act 2004 s 143(1), Sch 19 para 2; and SI 1992/231). As to the supply of electricity see ENERGY AND CLIMATE CHANGE vol 43 (2011) PARA 524 et seq. As to the meaning of 'person' see PARA 14 note 2.
5　Telecommunications Act 1984 s 98(6)(a).
6　'Water main' in England and Wales means a water main or resource main within the meaning of the Water Industry Act 1991 (see WATER AND WATERWAYS vol 100 (2009) PARAS 138 note 11, 179 note 4): Telecommunications Act 1984 s 98(9) (definition amended by the Water Act 1989 s 190(1), Sch 25 para 68; and the Water Consolidation (Consequential Provisions) Act 1991 s 2(1), Sch 1 para 38(1)). As to the meaning of 'England' and 'Wales' see PARA 14 note 7.
7　'Water authority' in England and Wales means the Environment Agency, the Natural Resources Body for Wales or a water undertaker: Telecommunications Act 1984 s 98(9) (definition amended by the Water Act 1989 s 190(1), Sch 25 para 68; SI 2013/755 and by virtue of SI 1996/593). As to the Environment Agency see ENVIRONMENTAL QUALITY AND PUBLIC HEALTH vol 45 (2010) PARA 68 et seq. As to the Natural Resources Body for Wales see FORESTRY vol 52 (2014) PARA 38. As to water undertakers see WATER AND WATERWAYS vol 100 (2009) PARA 134 et seq.
8　Telecommunications Act 1984 s 98(6)(b).
9　Telecommunications Act 1984 s 98(6)(c). 'Public sewer' in England and Wales has the same meaning as in the Public Health Act 1936 (see ENVIRONMENTAL QUALITY AND PUBLIC HEALTH vol 45 (2010) PARA 289): Telecommunications Act 1984 s 98(9) (amended by SI 2006/3336).
10　Telecommunications Act 1984 s 98(7).
11　Telecommunications Act 1984 s 98(7)(a).
12　Ie subject to the Telecommunications Act 1984 s 98(8): see note 15.
13　See note 4.
14　Telecommunications Act 1984 s 98(7)(b) (amended by the Water Act 1989 Sch 25 para 68). However, where the functions of an authority with control of a public sewer are discharged on its behalf by another person in pursuance of any enactment, and the other person is authorised by the authority with control of the sewer to act on its behalf for the purposes of the matters referred to in the Telecommunications Act 1984 s 98(1) (see PARA 181), s 98 has effect in relation to that sewer as if any reference to the authority with control of the sewer included, to such extent as may be necessary for the other person so to act, references to the other person: s 98(8) (amended by the Water Act 1989 Sch 25 para 68).

181.　Use of relevant conduits. The functions of an authority with control of a relevant conduit[1] include the power[2]:

(1)　　to carry out, or to authorise another person[3] to carry out, any works in relation to that conduit for or in connection with the installation, maintenance, adjustment, repair or alteration[4] of electronic communications apparatus[5];

(2)　　to keep such apparatus installed in that conduit or to authorise any other person to keep such apparatus so installed[6];

(3)　　to authorise any person to enter that conduit to inspect such apparatus kept installed there[7];

(4)　to enter into agreements, on such terms (including terms as to the payments to be made to the authority) as it thinks fit, in connection with the doing of anything authorised by or under these provisions[8]; and

(5)　to carry on an ancillary business consisting in the making and carrying out of such agreements[9].

Where the doing by an authority with control of a public sewer[10] of anything authorised by these provisions[11] would otherwise constitute a contravention of any obligation imposed (whether by virtue of any conveyance or agreement or otherwise) on the authority, the doing of that thing does not constitute such a contravention to the extent that it consists in, or in authorising, the carrying out of works or inspections, or keeping of apparatus, wholly inside a public sewer[12].

Without prejudice to these general powers[13], the Secretary of State[14] may by order[15] provide for any local Act under or in accordance with which any conduits (whether or not relevant conduits) are kept installed in streets[16] to be amended in such manner as appears to him requisite or expedient for securing[17]:

(a)　that there is power for those conduits to be used for the purposes of any electronic communications network or of any electronic communications service[18];

(b)　that the terms, including terms as to payment, on which those conduits are used for those purposes are reasonable[19]; and

(c)　that the use of those conduits for those purposes is not unreasonably inhibited, whether directly or indirectly, by reason of the terms of any consent, licence or agreement which has been given, granted or made in relation to any of those conduits for the purposes of that Act[20].

Nothing in the electronic communications code[21] conferring rights on operators[22] authorises the doing of anything inside a relevant conduit without the agreement of the authority with control of that conduit[23]. The agreement of the authority with control of a public sewer is sufficient in all cases to confer a right[24] on an operator where the right is to be exercised wholly inside that sewer[25].

1　As to the authority with control of a relevant conduit see PARA 175. As to the meanings of 'relevant conduit' and 'conduit' see PARA 175.

2　Telecommunications Act 1984 s 98(1). Where any enactment or subordinate legislation within the meaning of the Interpretation Act 1978 (see STATUTES AND LEGISLATIVE PROCESS vol 96 (2012) PARA 609) expressly or impliedly imposes any limitation on the use to which a relevant conduit may be put, that limitation does not have effect so as to prohibit the doing of anything authorised by or under the Telecommunications Act 1984 s 98: s 98(2). Subject to the provisions of s 98(2) and s 98(3) (see the text and notes 10–12), s 98(1) is without prejudice to the rights of any person with an interest in land on, under or over which a relevant conduit is situated: s 98(4).

3　As to the meaning of 'person' see PARA 14 note 2.

4　As to the meaning of 'alteration' see PARA 168 note 5; definition applied by the Telecommunications Act 1984 s 98(9).

5　Telecommunications Act 1984 s 98(1)(a) (s 98(1) amended by the Communications Act 2003 s 406(1), Sch 17 para 71(1), (2)). As to the meaning of 'electronic communications apparatus' see PARA 168 note 6; definition applied by the Telecommunications Act 1984 s 98(9).

6　Telecommunications Act 1984 s 98(1)(b) (as amended: see note 5).

7　Telecommunications Act 1984 s 98(1)(c) (as amended: see note 5).

8　Telecommunications Act 1984 s 98(1)(d).

9　Telecommunications Act 1984 s 98(1)(e).

10　As to the authority with control of a public sewer see the Telecommunications Act 1984 s 98(8); and PARA 180 note 14. As to the meaning of 'public sewer' see PARA 180 note 9.

11　Ie authorised by the Telecommunications Act 1984 s 98.

12　Telecommunications Act 1984 s 98(3).

13 Ie without prejudice to the Telecommunications Act 1984 s 98(1)–(4).
14 As to the Secretary of State see PARA 76 note 1.
15 As to orders under the Telecommunications Act 1984 see PARA 69.
16 As to the meaning of 'street' see PARA 168 note 2; definition applied by the Telecommunications Act 1984 s 98(9).
17 Telecommunications Act 1984 s 98(5). At the date at which this volume states the law, no such order has been made.
18 Telecommunications Act 1984 s 98(5)(a) (amended by the Communications Act 2003 Sch 17 para 71(3)).
19 Telecommunications Act 1984 s 98(5)(b).
20 Telecommunications Act 1984 s 98(5)(c).
21 As to the meaning of 'electronic communications code' see PARA 155 note 1.
22 Ie the Telecommunications Act 1984 Sch 2 paras 2–14: see PARAS 168 et seq, 182 et seq.
23 Telecommunications Act 1984 Sch 2 para 15(1).
24 Ie a right under the Telecommunications Act 1984 Sch 2 paras 2–14.
25 Telecommunications Act 1984 Sch 2 para 15(2).

(D) Rights to Cross Railways, Canals and Tramways

182. Right to cross relevant land. For the statutory purposes[1], the operator[2] has the right[3], in order to cross any relevant land[4] with a line[5], to install and keep the line and other electronic communications apparatus[6] on, under or over that land[7], and:

(1) to execute any works on that land for or in connection with the installation, maintenance, adjustment, repair or alteration[8] of that line or the other electronic communications apparatus[9]; and

(2) to enter on that land to inspect the line or the other apparatus[10].

Electronic communications apparatus must not be installed in pursuance of this right in any position on the relevant land in which it interferes with traffic on the railway, canal or tramway on that land[11].

The operator must not execute any works on any land in pursuance of this right unless he has given the person with control of the land[12] 28 days' notice of his intention to do so[13], or the works are emergency works[14]. If at any time before the notice expires the person with control of the land gives the operator notice of objection to the works, the operator is entitled to execute those works only[15]:

(a) if, within the period of 28 days beginning with the giving of the notice of objection, neither the operator nor that person has given notice to the other requiring him to agree to an arbitrator to whom the objection may be referred[16]; or

(b) in accordance with an award made on such a reference[17]; or

(c) to the extent that the works have at any time become emergency works[18].

If the operator exercises any power to execute emergency works on any land, he must, as soon as reasonably practicable after commencing them, give the person with control of the land a notice identifying the works and containing[19]:

(i) a statement of the reason why the works are emergency works[20]; and

(ii) either the matters required in the usual notice[21], or a reference to an earlier notice with respect to those works[22].

If within a 28-day period of the giving of such a notice, the person to whom it was given gives a notice to the operator requiring him to pay compensation, the operator is liable to pay him compensation in respect of loss or damage sustained in consequence of the carrying out of the emergency works[23]. In default of agreement, any question as to the amount of that compensation must be referred to arbitration[24].

If the operator commences the execution of any works in contravention of any of these provisions he is guilty of an offence[25].

1   As to the meaning of 'statutory purposes' see PARA 168 note 4.
2   As to the meaning of 'operator' see PARA 168 note 3.
3   Ie has the right subject to the Telecommunications Act 1984 Sch 2 paras 12(2)–28: Sch 2 para 12(1).
4   For these purposes, 'relevant land' means land which is used wholly or mainly either as a railway, canal or tramway or in connection with a railway, canal or tramway on that land; and a reference to the person with control of any such land is a reference to the person carrying on the railway, canal or tramway undertaking in question: Telecommunications Act 1984 Sch 2 para 12(10). 'Railway' includes a light railway: Sch 2 para 1(1).
5   As to the meaning of 'line' see PARA 175 note 6.
6   As to the meaning of 'electronic communications apparatus' see PARA 168 note 6.
7   Telecommunications Act 1984 Sch 2 para 12(1) (amended by the Communications Act 2003 s 106(2), Sch 3 paras 1, 5(a)). See *Bridgewater Canal Co Ltd v GEO Networks Ltd* [2010] EWCA Civ 1348, [2011] 1 WLR 1487, [2011] 1 P&CR 381. A line installed in pursuance of this right need not cross the relevant land in question by a direct route or by the shortest route from the point at which the line enters that land, but it must not cross that land by any route which, in the horizontal plane, exceeds that shortest route by more than 400 metres: Telecommunications Act 1984 Sch 2 para 12(2). Any line or other apparatus lawfully installed before the code came into force which if the code had come into force could have been installed under Sch 2 para 12 is (subject to Sch 2 para 28(6): see PARA 161) to be treated for the purposes of the code as if it had been so installed: Sch 2 para 28(2). As to the code see PARA 155 note 1. As to the coming into force of the code see PARA 168 note 15.
8   As to meaning of 'alteration' see PARA 163 note 5.
9   Telecommunications Act 1984 Sch 2 para 12(1)(a) (amended by the Communications Act 2003 Sch 3 para 5(a)).
10 Telecommunications Act 1984 Sch 2 para 12(1)(b).
11 Telecommunications Act 1984 Sch 2 para 12(3) (amended by the Communications Act 2003 Sch 3 para 5(a)). As to the right to require alteration when apparatus interferes with the undertaking see PARA 184.
12 As to the person with control of the land see note 4.
13 Telecommunications Act 1984 Sch 2 para 12(4)(a). Such a notice must contain a plan and section of the proposed works or (in lieu of a plan and section) any description of the proposed works, whether or not in the form of a diagram, which the person with control of the land has agreed to accept for these purposes: Sch 2 para 12(5). As to notices under the electronic communications code generally see PARA 192.
14 Telecommunications Act 1984 Sch 2 para 12(4)(b). 'Emergency works' in relation to the operator or a relevant undertaker for the purposes of Sch 2 para 23, means works the execution of which at the time it is proposed to execute them is requisite in order to put an end to, or prevent, the arising of circumstances then existing or imminent which are likely to cause:
    (1)   danger to persons or property,
    (2)   the interruption of any service provided by the operator's network or, as the case may be, interference with the exercise of any functions conferred or imposed on the undertaker by or under any enactment; or
    (3)   substantial loss to the operator or, as the case may be, the undertaker,
    and such other works as in all the circumstances it is reasonable to execute with those works: Sch 2 para 1(1) (amended by the Communications Act 2003 Sch 3 para 3(2)(a)). As to the meaning of 'operator's network' see PARA 168 note 4.
15 Telecommunications Act 1984 Sch 2 para 12(6).
16 Telecommunications Act 1984 Sch 2 para 12(6)(a). Reference to an arbitrator is made under Sch 2 para 13: see PARA 183.
17 Telecommunications Act 1984 Sch 2 para 12(6)(b).
18 Telecommunications Act 1984 Sch 2 para 12(6)(c).
19 Telecommunications Act 1984 Sch 2 para 12(7).
20 Telecommunications Act 1984 Sch 2 para 12(7)(a).
21 Ie the matters required under a notice under the Telecommunications Act 1984 Sch 2 para 12(4): see note 13.
22 Telecommunications Act 1984 Sch 2 para 12(7)(b).
23 Telecommunications Act 1984 Sch 2 para 12(8).
24 Telecommunications Act 1984 Sch 2 para 12(8). As to arbitration see PARA 183.

25 Telecommunications Act 1984 Sch 2 para 12(9). The offence is punishable on summary conviction by a fine not exceeding level 3 on the standard scale: Sch 2 para 12(9). As to the standard scale see SENTENCING AND DISPOSITION OF OFFENDERS vol 92 (2010) PARA 142. However, Sch 2 para 12(9) does not apply where the electronic communications code has effect by virtue of the Communications Act 2003 s 106(3)(b) (ie where the Secretary of State is running an electronic communications network: see PARA 155): Telecommunications Act 1984 Sch 2 para 26(4) (amended by the Communications Act 2003 Sch 3 para 10).

183. Reference to arbitration. Any question or objection which is referred to arbitration in accordance with the provisions relating to the crossing of relevant land[1] is to be referred to the arbitration of a single arbitrator appointed by agreement between the parties concerned or, in default of agreement, by the President of the Institution of Civil Engineers[2]. The arbitrator has the power[3]:

(1) to require the operator[4] to submit to the arbitrator a plan and section in such form as the arbitrator thinks requisite for the purposes of the arbitration[5];

(2) to require the observations on any such plan or section of the person[6] who objects to the works to be submitted to the arbitrator in such form as he thinks requisite for those purposes[7];

(3) to direct the operator or that person to furnish him with such information and to comply with such other requirements as he thinks requisite for those purposes[8];

(4) to make an award requiring modifications to the proposed works and specifying the terms on which and the conditions subject to which the works may be executed[9]; and

(5) to award such sum as he may determine in respect of one or both of the following matters:

(a) compensation to the person who objects to the works, in respect of loss[10] or damage sustained by that person in consequence of the carrying out of the works[11]; and

(b) consideration payable to that person for the right to carry out the works[12].

Where a question as to compensation in respect of emergency works is referred to arbitration[13], the arbitrator:

(i) has the power to direct the operator or the person who requires the payment of compensation to furnish him with such information and to comply with such other requirements as he thinks requisite for the purposes of the arbitration[14]; and

(ii) may award to the person requiring the payment of compensation such sum, if any, as he may determine in respect of the loss[15] or damage sustained by that person in consequence of the carrying out of the emergency works in question[16].

In determining what award to make on a reference[17], the arbitrator must have regard to all the circumstances and to the principle that no person should unreasonably be denied access to an electronic communications network or to electronic communications services[18].

1 Ie the Telecommunications Act 1984 Sch 2 para 12: see PARA 182.
2 Telecommunications Act 1984 Sch 2 para 13(1).
3 Telecommunications Act 1984 Sch 2 para 13(2).
4 As to the meaning of 'operator' see PARA 168 note 3.
5 Telecommunications Act 1984 Sch 2 para 13(2)(a). The arbitrator may treat compliance with any requirement made in pursuance of Sch 2 para 13(2)(a)–(c) or Sch 2 para 13(3)(a) (see the text and note 14) as a condition of his making an award: Sch 2 para 13(4).

6   As to the meaning of 'person' see PARA 14 note 2.
7   Telecommunications Act 1984 Sch 2 para 13(2)(b). See also note 5.
8   Telecommunications Act 1984 Sch 2 para 13(2)(c). See also note 5.
9   Telecommunications Act 1984 Sch 2 para 13(2)(d).
10 In relation to a person carrying on a railway, canal or tramway undertaking, references to loss include references to any increase in the expenses of carrying on that undertaking: Telecommunications Act 1984 Sch 2 para 13(6)(a).
11 Telecommunications Act 1984 Sch 2 para 13(2)(e)(i).
12 Telecommunications Act 1984 Sch 2 para 13(2)(e)(ii). See *Bridgewater Canal Co Ltd v GEO Networks Ltd* [2010] EWCA Civ 1348, [2011] 1 WLR 1487, [2011] 1 P&CR 381. The consideration must be determined on the basis of what would have been fair and reasonable if the objector had given his authority willingly for the works to be executed on the same terms and subject to the same conditions, if any, as are contained in the award: Sch 2 para 13(6)(b).
13 As to the meaning of 'emergency works' PARA 182 note 14.
14 Telecommunications Act 1984 Sch 2 para 13(3)(a). See also note 5.
15 As to loss see note 10.
16 Telecommunications Act 1984 Sch 2 para 13(3)(b).
17 Ie under the Telecommunications Act 1984 Sch 2 para 13.
18 Telecommunications Act 1984 Sch 2 para 13(5) (amended by the Communications Act 2003 s 106(2), Sch 3 paras 1, 5(c)). As to the meanings of 'electronic communications network' and 'electronic communications services' see PARA 53.

184. Alteration of apparatus on relevant land. The person with control[1] of any relevant land[2] may, on the ground that any electronic communications apparatus[3] kept installed on, under or over that land for the purposes of the operator's network[4] interferes, or is likely to interfere, with the carrying on of the railway[5], canal or tramway undertaking carried on by that person, or anything done or to be done for the purposes of that undertaking, give notice[6] to the operator[7] requiring him to alter[8] that apparatus[9]. The operator must within a reasonable time and to the reasonable satisfaction of the person giving the notice comply with the notice unless before the expiration of the 28-day period beginning with the giving of the notice he gives a counter-notice to the person with control of the land in question specifying the respects in which he is not prepared to comply with the original notice[10].

Where a counter-notice has been given, the operator is not required to comply with the original notice, but the person with control of the relevant land may apply to the court[11] for an order requiring the alteration of any electronic communications apparatus to which the notice relates[12]. The court must not make an order unless it is satisfied that the order is necessary on one of the grounds specified above[13]; and, in determining whether to make such an order, the court must have regard to all the circumstances and to the principle that no person should unreasonably be denied access to an electronic communications network or to electronic communications services[14].

1   As to the person with control of relevant land see PARA 182 note 4; definition applied by the Telecommunications Act 1984 Sch 2 para 14(6).
2   As to the meaning of 'relevant land' see PARA 182 note 4; definition applied by the Telecommunications Act 1984 Sch 2 para 14(6).
3   As to the meaning of 'electronic communications apparatus' see PARA 168 note 6.
4   As to the meaning of 'operator's network' see PARA 168 note 4.
5   As to the meaning of 'railway' see PARA 182 note 4.
6   As to notices under the electronic communications code see PARA 192.
7   As to the meaning of 'operator' see PARA 168 note 3.
8   As to the meaning of 'alter' see PARA 168 note 5.
9   Telecommunications Act 1984 Sch 2 para 14(1) (amended by the Communications Act 2003 s 106(2), Sch 3 paras 1, 5(d)). As to the power to require alteration of apparatus on land other than relevant land see PARA 188.
10 Telecommunications Act 1984 Sch 2 para 14(2).

11 As to the meaning of 'court' see PARA 171 note 6.
12 Telecommunications Act 1984 Sch 2 para 14(3) (amended by the Communications Act 2003 Sch 3 para 5(d)).
13 Ie one of the grounds specified in the Telecommunications Act 1984 Sch 2 para 14(1): see the text and note 9.
14 Telecommunications Act 1984 Sch 2 para 14(4) (amended by the Communications Act 2003 Sch 3 para 5(c)). An order under the Telecommunications Act 1984 Sch 2 para 14 may take such form and be on such terms as the court thinks fit; and it may impose such conditions and may contain such directions to the operator or the person with control of the land in question as the court thinks necessary for resolving any difference between the operator and that person and for protecting their respective interests: Sch 2 para 14(5). As to the meanings of 'electronic communications network' and 'electronic communications services' see PARA 53.

(E) Rights of Persons affected by Works

185. Compensation for depreciation. Where, upon a right in relation to any land being conferred or varied in accordance with an agreement[1], there is a depreciation in the value of any relevant interest[2] in the land and that depreciation is attributable to the fact that the restrictions on removal of apparatus[3] will apply to the removal from the land (when the owner for the time being of that interest becomes the occupier of the land) of any electronic communications apparatus[4] installed in pursuance of that right, the operator[5] must pay compensation to the person[6] who, at the time the right is conferred or, as the case may be, varied, is the owner of that relevant interest[7].

The amount of that compensation must be equal, subject to payment of legal expenses[8], to the amount of the depreciation[9]. Any question as to a person's entitlement to compensation or as to the amount of any compensation must, in default of agreement, be referred to and determined by the appropriate tribunal[10].

A claim for compensation must be made by giving the operator notice[11] of the claim, specifying particulars of:

(1) the land in respect of which the claim is made[12];

(2) the claimant's interest in the land and, so far as known to the claimant, any other interests in the land[13];

(3) the right or variation in respect of which the claim is made[14]; and

(4) the amount of the compensation claimed[15].

The claim may be made at any time before the claimant becomes the occupier of the land in question, or at any time in the three-year period beginning with that time[16].

Without prejudice to the powers of the appropriate tribunal in respect of the costs of any proceedings before it, where compensation is payable there is also payable, by the operator to the claimant, any reasonable valuation or legal expenses incurred by the claimant for the purposes of the preparation and prosecution of his claim for that compensation[17].

1 Ie in accordance with the Telecommunications Act 1984 Sch 2 para 2: see PARA 168.
2 'Relevant interest' in relation to land subject to a right conferred or varied in accordance with the Telecommunications Act 1984 Sch 2 para 2 means any interest in respect of which the following two conditions are satisfied at the time the right is conferred or varied:
    (1) the owner of the interest is not the occupier of the land but may become the occupier of the land by virtue of that interest (Sch 2 para 4(5)(a)); and
    (2) the owner of the interest becomes bound by the right or variation by virtue only of Sch 2 para 2(3) (see PARA 169) (Sch 2 para 4(5)(b)).
  See *Finsbury Business Centre Ltd v Mercury Communications Ltd* [1994] RVR 108, where the Lands Tribunal held that a person cannot have a 'relevant interest' if he is the present occupier

and if he himself confers a right on an operator to install electronic communications apparatus. See also *Alexander v United Artists plc* [1994] RVR 7.

3 Ie by virtue of the Telecommunications Act 1984 Sch 2 para 21: see PARA 189.

4 As to the meaning of 'electronic communications apparatus' see PARA 168 note 6.

5 As to the meaning of 'operator' see PARA 168 note 3.

6 As to the meaning of 'person' see PARA 14 note 2.

7 Telecommunications Act 1984 Sch 2 para 4(4) (amended by the Communications Act 2003 s 106(2), Sch 3 paras 1, 5(a)). A person is not entitled to compensation under any provision of the electronic communications code if he is entitled to compensation in respect of the same matter under any enactment repealed by the Telecommunications Act 1984 (ie by virtue of Sch 2 para 28(4): see PARA 169 note 18): Sch 2 para 28(5).

8 Ie by virtue of the Telecommunications Act 1984 Sch 2 para 4(9): see the text and note 17.

9 Telecommunications Act 1984 Sch 2 para 4(4).

10 Telecommunications Act 1984 Sch 2 para 4(6) (amended by SI 2009/1307). 'Appropriate tribunal' means, in the application of the Telecommunications Act 1984 to England and Wales, the Upper Tribunal; Sch 2 para 4(10A) (added by SI 2009/1307). As to the Upper Tribunal see COMPULSORY ACQUISITION OF LAND vol 18 (2009) PARA 720 et seq; and COURTS AND TRIBUNALS vol 24 (2010) PARA 883 et seq. The Land Compensation Act 1961 s 4 (costs: see COMPULSORY ACQUISITION OF LAND vol 18 (2009) PARAS 716–717) applies, with the necessary modifications, in relation to any such determination: Telecommunications Act 1984 Sch 2 para 4(6) (as so amended). For the purposes of assessing any compensation under Sch 2 para 4(4) (see the text and note 9), the provisions of the Land Compensation Act 1961 s 5 rr (2), (3), (4) (see COMPULSORY ACQUISITION OF LAND vol 18 (2009) PARAS 754, 760, 789) have effect, subject to the necessary modifications, as they have effect for the purposes of assessing compensation for the compulsory acquisition of any interest in land: Telecommunications Act 1984 Sch 2 para 4(8). The provisions of the Land Compensation Act 1973 s 10(1)–(3) (compensation in respect of mortgages, trusts of land and settled land: see COMPULSORY ACQUISITION OF LAND vol 18 (2009) PARA 898) apply in relation to compensation under the Telecommunications Act 1984 Sch 2 para 4(4) as they apply in relation to compensation under the Land Compensation Act 1973 Pt I (ss 1–19): Telecommunications Act 1984 Sch 2 para 4(10) (amended by the Trusts of Land and Appointment of Trustees Act 1996 s 25(1), Sch 3 para 22).

11 As to notices under the electronic communications code see PARA 192.

12 Telecommunications Act 1984 Sch 2 para 4(7)(a).

13 Telecommunications Act 1984 Sch 2 para 4(7)(b).

14 Telecommunications Act 1984 Sch 2 para 4(7)(c).

15 Telecommunications Act 1984 Sch 2 para 4(7)(d).

16 Telecommunications Act 1984 Sch 2 para 4(7). As to the effect on a compensation claim of the giving of a notice of objection to overhead apparatus see PARA 187 note 8.

17 Telecommunications Act 1984 Sch 2 para 4(9) (amended by SI 2009/1307).

186. Compensation for injurious affection. Where a right conferred by or in accordance with certain provisions of the electronic communications code[1] is exercised, compensation is payable by the operator[2] under the provisions of the Compulsory Purchase Act 1965 relating to compensation for injurious affection to neighbouring land[3] as if those provisions had effect in relation to injury caused by the exercise of such a right as they have effect in relation to injury caused by the execution of works on land that has been compulsorily purchased[4]. Compensation is not payable on any such claim for compensation unless the amount of the compensation exceeds £50[5].

Except as provided by the code, the operator is not liable to compensate any person for, or to be subject to any other liability in respect of, any loss or damage caused by the lawful exercise of any right conferred by or in accordance with the code[6].

1 Ie under the Telecommunications Act 1984 Sch 2 paras 2–15: see PARA 168 et seq.

2 As to the meaning of 'operator' see PARA 163 note 3.

3 Ie the Compulsory Purchase Act 1965 s 10: see COMPULSORY ACQUISITION OF LAND vol 18 (2009) PARA 718.

4 Telecommunications Act 1984 Sch 2 para 16(1). This does not confer any entitlement to compensation on any person in respect of the exercise of a right conferred in accordance with

Sch 2 para 2 or Sch 2 para 3 (see PARAS 168–170) if that person conferred the right or is bound by it by virtue of Sch 2 para 2(2)(b) or (d); but, apart from this, the entitlement of any person to compensation is to be determined irrespective of his ownership of any interest in the land where the right is exercised: Sch 2 para 16(2). As to the effect on a claim for compensation of the giving of a notice of objection to overhead apparatus see PARA 187 note 8. See also Sch 2 para 28(5); and PARA 185 note 7.

5   Telecommunications Act 1984 Sch 2 para 16(3). Under previous repealed legislation, it was held reasonable, when compensation was directed to be made by the former Postmaster General, to order the payment of an annual sum and not of a lump sum: *Postmaster-General v Brooks* [1922] 2 KB 176. It was also held that the body or person having control of a street or public road could not impose on the Postmaster General as a condition of consent to the construction of a telegraphic line in or on the street or road a payment of a sum of money which had no relation to actual damage, but was in the nature of compensation for use and occupation: *Postmaster-General v Edinburgh Corpn* (1897) 10 Ry & Can Tr Cas 247; *Postmaster-General v Hutchings* [1916] 1 KB 774.

6   Telecommunications Act 1984 Sch 2 para 27(3).

187.   Objections to overhead apparatus.   Where the operator[1] has completed the installation for the purposes of the operator's network[2] of any electronic communications apparatus[3] the whole or part of which is at a height of three metres or more above the ground[4], then, at any time before the expiration of a three-month period beginning with the completion of the installation of the apparatus, a person[5] who is the occupier of or owns an interest in[6]:

(1)   any land over or on which the apparatus has been installed[7]; or

(2)   any land the enjoyment of which, or any interest in which, is, because of its nearness to the land on or over which the apparatus has been installed, capable of being prejudiced by the apparatus[8],

may give the operator notice of objection in respect of that apparatus[9].

At any time after the expiration of a two-month period beginning with the giving of a notice of objection but before the expiration of a four-month period beginning with the giving of that notice, the person who gave the notice may apply to the court[10] to have the objection upheld[11], and, subject to one exception[12], the court must uphold the objection if the apparatus appears materially to prejudice the applicant's enjoyment of or interest in the land in right of which the objection is made and the court is not satisfied that the only possible alterations of the apparatus will[13]:

(a)   substantially increase the cost or diminish the quality of the service provided by the operator's network to persons who have, or may in future have, access to it[14];

(b)   involve the operator in substantial additional expenditure, disregarding any expenditure occasioned solely by the fact that any proposed alteration was not adopted originally or, as the case may be, that the apparatus has been unnecessarily installed[15]; or

(c)   give to any person a case at least as good as the applicant has to have an objection under these provisions upheld[16].

The court must not uphold the objection if the applicant is bound by a right of the operator[17] to install the apparatus conferred by agreement and it appears to the court unreasonable, having regard to the fact that the applicant is so bound and the circumstances in which he became so bound, for the applicant to have given notice of objection[18].

If it upholds the objection, the court may by order:

(i)   direct the alteration of the apparatus to which the objection relates[19];

(ii) authorise the installation (instead of the apparatus to which the objection relates), in a manner and position specified in the order, of any apparatus so specified[20];

(iii) direct that no objection may be made in respect of any apparatus the installation of which is authorised by the court[21].

The court must not make any order directing the alteration of any apparatus or authorising the installation of any apparatus unless it is satisfied either[22]:

(A) that the operator has all such rights as it appears to the court appropriate that he should have for the purpose of making the alteration or, as the case may be, installing the apparatus[23]; or

(B) that he would have all those rights if the court, on an application for such an order[24], dispensed with the need for the agreement of any person[25], and that it would be appropriate for the court to dispense with the need for that agreement[26].

Accordingly, for the purposes of dispensing with the need for the agreement of any person to the alteration or installation of any apparatus, the court has the same powers as it would have if an application had been duly made[27] for an order dispensing with the need for that person's agreement[28].

1   As to the meaning of 'operator' see PARA 168 note 3.
2   As to the meaning of 'operator's network' see PARA 168 note 4.
3   As to the meaning of 'electronic communications apparatus' see PARA 168 note 6.
4   Telecommunications Act 1984 Sch 2 para 17(1) (amended by the Communications Act 2003 s 106(2), Sch 3 paras 1, 5(a), (d)).
5   As to the meaning of 'person' see PARA 14 note 2.
6   Telecommunications Act 1984 Sch 2 para 17(2).
7   Telecommunications Act 1984 Sch 2 para 17(2)(a).
8   Telecommunications Act 1984 Sch 2 para 17(2)(b). No notice of objection may be given in respect of any apparatus if the apparatus replaces any electronic communications apparatus which is not substantially different from the new apparatus, and is not in a significantly different position: Sch 2 para 17(3) (amended by the Communications Act 2003 Sch 3 para 5(a)). As to notices under the electronic communications code generally see PARA 192. As to the obligation to affix a notice containing the operator's name and address to overhead apparatus see PARA 177. Where a person has both given a notice under Sch 2 para 17 and applied for compensation (see PARAS 185–186), the court may give such direction as it thinks fit for ensuring that no compensation is paid until any proceedings under the Communications Act 2003 Sch 2 para 17 have been disposed of; and, if the court makes an order under Sch 2 para 17, it may provide in that order for some or all of the compensation otherwise payable to that person not to be so payable, or, if the case so requires, for some or all of any compensation paid to that person to be repaid to the operator: Sch 2 para 17(4).
9   Telecommunications Act 1984 Sch 2 para 17(2).
10 As to the meaning of 'court' see PARA 171 note 6.
11 Telecommunications Act 1984 Sch 2 para 17(5).
12 Ie subject to the Telecommunications Act 1984 Sch 2 para 17(7): see the text and note 18.
13 Telecommunications Act 1984 Sch 2 para 17(6).
14 Telecommunications Act 1984 Sch 2 para 17(6)(a) (amended by the Communications Act 2003 Sch 3 para 5(a)). In considering the matters in heads (a)–(c) in the text, the court must have regard to all the circumstances and to the principle that no person should unreasonably be denied access to an electronic communications network or to electronic communications services: Communications Act 2003 Sch 2 para 17(8) (amended by the Communications Act 2003 Sch 3 para 5(c)). As to the meanings of 'electronic communications network' and 'electronic communications services' see PARA 53.
15 Telecommunications Act 1984 Sch 2 para 17(6)(b). See also note 14.
16 Telecommunications Act 1984 Sch 2 para 17(6)(c). For the purposes of head (c) in the text and Sch 2 para 17(10), the court has power on an application under the Telecommunications Act 1984 Sch 2 para 17 to give the applicant directions for bringing the application to the notice of such other interested persons as it thinks fit: Sch 2 para 17(11). See also note 14.
17 Ie falling within the Telecommunications Act 1984 Sch 2 para 2 or Sch 2 para 3(1): see PARAS 168–170.

18 Telecommunications Act 1984 Sch 2 para 17(7).
19 Telecommunications Act 1984 Sch 2 para 17(9)(a).
20 Telecommunications Act 1984 Sch 2 para 17(9)(b).
21 Telecommunications Act 1984 Sch 2 para 17(9)(c).
22 Telecommunications Act 1984 Sch 2 para 17(10).
23 Telecommunications Act 1984 Sch 2 para 17(10)(a). See also note 26.
24 Ie on an application under the Telecommunications Act 1984 Sch 2 para 5: see PARA 166.
25 Telecommunications Act 1984 Sch 2 para 17(10)(b)(i). See also note 26.
26 Telecommunications Act 1984 Sch 2 para 17(10)(b)(ii). For these purposes, the court has the power to give the applicant directions for bringing the application to the notice of such other interested persons as it thinks fit: Sch 2 para 17(11).
27 Ie under the Telecommunications Act 1984 Sch 2 para 5: see PARA 171.
28 Telecommunications Act 1984 Sch 2 para 17(10).

188. Alteration of apparatus. Where any electronic communications apparatus[1] is kept installed on, under or over any land for the purposes of the operator's network[2], a person[3] with an interest in that land or adjacent land may, notwithstanding the terms of any agreement binding that person, by notice[4] given to the operator[5] require the alteration of the apparatus on the ground that the alteration is necessary to enable that person to carry out a proposed improvement[6] of the land in which he has an interest[7]. Where such a notice is given, the operator must comply with it unless he gives a counter-notice within a 28-day period beginning with the giving of the notice[8]. Where a counter-notice has been given to any person, the operator need only make the required alteration if, on an application by that person, the court[9] makes an order requiring the alteration to be made[10].

The court must only make such an order if, having regard to all the circumstances and to the principle that no person should unreasonably be denied access to an electronic communications network or to electronic communications services[11], it is satisfied[12] that the alteration is necessary for the stated purpose[13], and that the alteration will not substantially interfere with any service which is or is likely to be provided using the operator's network[14]. The court must not make such an order unless it is satisfied either:

(1) that the operator has all such rights as it appears to the court appropriate that he should have for the purpose of making the alteration[15]; or

(2) that:

(a) he would have all those rights if the court, on an application for such an order[16], dispensed with the need for the agreement of any person[17]; and

(b) it would be appropriate for the court to dispense with the need for that agreement[18].

Unless the court otherwise thinks fit, an order made under these provisions on the application of any person must require that person to reimburse the operator in respect of any expenses which the operator incurs in or in connection with the execution of any works in compliance with the order[19].

1 As to the meaning of 'electronic communications apparatus' see PARA 168 note 6.
2 As to the meaning of 'operator's network' see PARA 168 note 4.
3 As to the meaning of 'person' see PARA 14 note 2.
4 As to notices under the electronic communications code see PARA 192.
5 As to the meaning of 'operator' see PARA 168 note 3.
6 For these purposes, 'improvement' includes development and change of use: Telecommunications Act 1984 Sch 2 para 20(9).

7   Telecommunications Act 1984 Sch 2 para 20(1) (amended by the Communications Act 2003
    s 106(2), Sch 3 paras 1, 5(a), (d)). As to the alteration of apparatus on relevant land see PARA
    179.
8   Telecommunications Act 1984 Sch 2 para 20(2).
9   As to the meaning of 'court' see PARA 171 note 6.
10 Telecommunications Act 1984 Sch 2 para 20(3). The order may provide for the alteration to be
    carried out with such modifications, on such terms and subject to such conditions as the court
    thinks fit, but the court must not include any such modifications, terms or conditions in its order
    without the consent of the applicant; and if such consent is not given, the court may refuse to
    make the order: Sch 2 para 20(7).
11 As to the meanings of 'electronic communications network' and 'electronic communications
    services' see PARA 53.
12 Telecommunications Act 1984 Sch 2 para 20(4) (amended by the Communications Act 2003
    Sch 3 para 5(c)).
13 Telecommunications Act 1984 Sch 2 para 20(4)(a).
14 Telecommunications Act 1984 Sch 2 para 20(4)(b) (amended by the Communications Act 2003
    Sch 3 paras 5(d), 7).
15 Telecommunications Act 1984 Sch 2 para 20(5)(a). See also note 18.
16 Ie on an application under the Telecommunications Act 1984 Sch 2 para 5: see PARA 171.
17 Telecommunications Act 1984 Sch 2 para 20(5)(b)(i). See also note 18.
18 Telecommunications Act 1984 Sch 2 para 20(5)(b)(ii). Accordingly, for the purposes of
    dispensing with the need for the agreement of any person to the alteration of any apparatus, the
    court has the same powers as it would have if an application had been duly made under Sch 2
    para 5 (see PARA 171) for an order dispensing with the need for that person's agreement: Sch 2
    para 20(5). For these purposes, the court has the power to give directions to the applicant for
    bringing the application to the notice of such other interested persons as it thinks fit: Sch 2
    para 20(6).
19 Telecommunications Act 1984 Sch 2 para 20(8).

189. Removal of apparatus. Where a right has been conferred in relation to
land in accordance with an agreement[1] and anything has been done in exercise of
that right, any person[2], being the occupier of the land[3], the owner of the freehold
estate in the land or a lessee[4] of the land, who is not for the time being bound by
the right[5] has the right to require the operator[6] to restore the land to its
condition before that thing was done[7]. To the extent that the performance of any
such duty involves the removal of any electronic communications apparatus[8]
from any land, it is enforceable only subject to the following restrictions[9].

The person entitled to require the removal of any of the operator's electronic
communications apparatus[10] must give a notice[11] to the operator requiring its
removal[12]. If the operator does not give that person a counter-notice within a
28-day period beginning with the giving of the notice, that person is entitled to
enforce the removal of the apparatus[13]. The counter-notice must do one or both
of the following things:

(1)   state that the person receiving it is not entitled to require the removal of
      the apparatus[14];
(2)   specify the steps which the operator proposes to take for the purpose of
      securing a right as against that person to keep the apparatus on the
      land[15].

Where a counter-notice is given to any person[16], that person may only enforce
the removal of the apparatus in pursuance of an order of the court[17]. Where the
counter-notice specifies steps which the operator is proposing to take to secure a
right to keep the apparatus on the land, the court must not make an order unless
it is satisfied:

(a)   that the operator is not intending to take those steps or is being
      unreasonably dilatory in the taking of those steps[18]; or
(b)   that the taking of those steps has not secured, or will not secure, for the

operator as against that person any right to keep the apparatus installed on, under or over the land or, as the case may be, to reinstall it if it is removed[19].

Where any person is entitled to enforce the removal of any apparatus under these provisions[20], that person may, without prejudice to any other method available to him for enforcing the removal of that apparatus, apply to the court for authority to remove it himself[21]; and on such an application the court may, if it thinks fit, give that authority[22].

These provisions apply[23] in a slightly amended form where the relevant person is entitled to require the alteration of electronic communications apparatus in consequence of the stopping up, closure, change or diversion of any street or the extinguishment or alteration of any public right of way[24].

1   Ie an agreement under the Telecommunications Act 1984 Sch 2 para 2 or Sch 2 para 3: see PARAS 168–170.
2   As to the meaning of 'person' see PARA 14 note 2.
3   As to the meaning of 'occupier of land' see PARA 168 note 2.
4   As to the meaning of 'lessee' see PARA 168 note 20.
5   As to the persons who are bound by the right see PARA 169.
6   As to the meaning of 'operator' see PARA 168 note 3.
7   Telecommunications Act 1984 Sch 2 para 4(2).
8   As to the meaning of 'electronic communications apparatus' see PARA 168 note 6.
9   Telecommunications Act 1984 Sch 2 para 4(3) (amended by the Communications Act 2003 s 106(2), Sch 3 paras 1, 5(a)). The restrictions referred to in the text are those in the Telecommunications Act 1984 Sch 2 para 21: see the text and notes 10–24. These restrictions also apply where any person is for the time being entitled to require the removal of any of the operator's electronic communications apparatus, whether under any enactment or because that apparatus is kept on, under or over that land otherwise than in pursuance of a right binding that person, or for any other reason: see Sch 2 para 21(1) (amended by the Communications Act 2003 Sch 3 para 5(a)).
10 Reference to the operator's electronic communications apparatus includes electronic communications apparatus which, whether or not vested in the operator, is being used, is to be used or has been used for the purposes of the operator's network: Telecommunications Act 1984 Sch 2 para 21(11) (amended by the Communications Act 2003 Sch 3 para 5(a), (d)). As to the meaning of 'operator's network' see PARA 168 note 4.
11 As to the giving of notices under the electronic communications code see PARA 192.
12 Telecommunications Act 1984 Sch 2 para 21(2) (amended by the Communications Act 2003 Sch 3 para 5(a)).
13 Telecommunications Act 1984 Sch 2 para 21(3). However, a person is not entitled to enforce the removal of any apparatus on the ground only that he is entitled to give a notice under Sch 2 para 11 (tidal waters: see PARA 176), Sch 2 para 14 (alteration of apparatus crossing a linear obstacle: see PARA 179), Sch 2 para 17 (objections to overhead apparatus: see PARA 182), or Sch 2 para 20 (alteration of apparatus: see PARA 188); and Sch 2 para 21 is without prejudice to Sch 2 para 23 (undertaker's works: see PARAS 190–191) and to the power to enforce an order of the court under Sch 2 para 11, Sch 2 para 14, Sch 2 para 17 or Sch 2 para 20: Sch 2 para 21(12).
14 Telecommunications Act 1984 Sch 2 para 21(4)(a).
15 Telecommunications Act 1984 Sch 2 para 21(4)(b). The steps may include any steps which the operator could take for the purpose of enabling him, if the apparatus is removed, to reinstall the apparatus; and the fact that by reason of Sch 2 para 21(6)–(12) any proposed reinstallation is only hypothetical does not prevent the operator from taking those steps or any court or person from exercising any function in consequence of those steps having been taken: Sch 2 para 21(5).
16 Ie given to any person under the Telecommunications Act 1984 Sch 2 para 21(3): see the text and note 13.
17 Telecommunications Act 1984 Sch 2 para 21(6). As to the meaning of 'court' see PARA 171 note 6.
18 Telecommunications Act 1984 Sch 2 para 21(6)(a).
19 Telecommunications Act 1984 Sch 2 para 21(6)(b).
20 Ie whether by virtue of the Telecommunications Act 1984 Sch 2 para 21(3) (see the text and note 13), or under a court order under Sch 2 para 21(6) (see the text and notes 16–19).

21 Telecommunications Act 1984 Sch 2 para 21(7). Where any apparatus is removed by any person under an authority given by the court, any expenses incurred by him in or in connection with the removal of the apparatus are recoverable by him from the operator in any court of competent jurisdiction; and in so giving an authority to any person the court may also authorise him, in accordance with the directions of the court, to sell any apparatus removed under the authority and to retain the whole or a part of the proceeds of sale on account of those expenses: Sch 2 para 21(8).

22 Telecommunications Act 1984 Sch 2 para 21(7). In giving an authority to any person the court may also authorise him, in accordance with its directions, to sell any apparatus removed under the authority and to retain the whole or a part of the proceeds of sale on account of his expenses: Sch 2 para 21(8).

23 Ie where the Telecommunications Act 1984 Sch 2 para 21 is applied either in pursuance of an enactment amended by Sch 4 or otherwise. For an example of where Sch 2 para 21 is applied see the Highways Act 1980 s 334; and HIGHWAYS, STREETS AND BRIDGES vol 55 (2012) PARAS 35–37.

24 See the Telecommunications Act 1984 Sch 2 para 21(10) (amended by the Communications Act 2003 Sch 3 para 5(a)). In such a case:
   (1) the removal of the apparatus constitutes compliance with a requirement to make any other alteration (Telecommunications Act 1984 Sch 2 para 21(10)(a));
   (2) a counter-notice under Sch 2 para 21(3) (see the text and note 13) may state in addition to, or instead of, any of the matters mentioned in Sch 2 para 21(4) (see heads (1) and (2) in the text), that the operator requires the relevant person to reimburse him in respect of any expenses which he incurs in or in connection with the making of any alteration in compliance with the requirements of the relevant person (Sch 2 para 21(10)(b));
   (3) an order made under Sch 2 para 21 on an application by the relevant person in respect of a counter-notice containing such a statement must, unless the court otherwise thinks fit, require the relevant person to reimburse the operator in respect of any expenses which he so incurs (Sch 2 para 21(10)(c)); and
   (4) Sch 2 para 21(8) (see notes 21–22) does not apply (Sch 2 para 21(10)(d)).

(F) Undertaker's Works

190. Meanings of 'relevant undertaker' and 'undertaker's works'. 'Relevant undertaker' means:
   (1) any person[1] (including a local authority) authorised by any public general or local Act or by any order or scheme made under or confirmed by any Act to carry on any railway, tramway, road transport, water transport, canal, inland navigation, dock, harbour, pier or lighthouse undertaking[2]; or
   (2) any person (apart from the operator[3]) to whom the electronic communications code[4] is applied by a direction under the Communications Act 2003[5]; and
   (3) any person to whom these provisions[6] are applied by any Act amended by or under or passed after the Telecommunications Act 1984[7].
'Undertaker's works' means:
   (a) in relation to a relevant undertaker falling within head (1) above, any works which that undertaker is authorised to execute for the purposes of, or in connection with, his carrying on of the undertaking there mentioned[8];
   (b) in relation to a relevant undertaker falling within head (2) above, any works which that undertaker is authorised to execute by or in accordance with any provision of the electronic communications code[9];
   (c) in relation to a relevant undertaker falling within head (3) above, the works for the purposes of which these provisions[10] are applied to that undertaker[11].

1 As to the meaning of 'person' see PARA 14 note 2.

2   Telecommunications Act 1984 Sch 2 para 23(10)(a) (amended by the Water Act 1989 s 190(1), Sch 25 para 68(3), Sch 27 Pt I; the Electricity Act 1989 s 112(4), Sch 18). As to railway undertakings see RAILWAYS AND TRAMWAYS vol 86 (2013) PARA 108; as to road transport undertakings see ROAD TRAFFIC vol 90 (2011) PARA 1086.

3   As to the meaning of 'operator' see PARA 168 note 3.

4   As to the meaning of 'electronic communications code' see PARA 155 note 1.

5   Telecommunications Act 1984 Sch 2 para 23(10)(b) (amended by the Communications Act 2003 s 106(2), Sch 3 paras 1, 8). The direction referred to in the text is a direction under the Communications Act 2003 s 106: see PARA 155.

6   Ie the Telecommunications Act 1984 Sch 2 para 23.

7   Telecommunications Act 1984 Sch 2 para 23(10)(c).
      For an example of an Act amended by the Telecommunications Act 1984 s 109(1), Sch 4 so as to apply Sch 2 para 23 to particular undertakers see the Highways Act 1980 s 177(12) (substituted by the Telecommunications Act 1984 Sch 4 para 76(10); and amended by the Communications Act 2003 s 406(1), Sch 17 para 56) and the Highways Act 1980 s 334(8) (substituted by the Telecommunications Act 1984 Sch 4 para 76(14); and amended by the Communications Act 2003 Sch 17 para 56); and HIGHWAYS, STREETS AND BRIDGES vol 55 (2012) PARAS 35–37. The application of the Telecommunications Act 1984 Sch 2 para 23 by virtue of head (3) in the text to any person for the purposes of any works is without prejudice to its application by virtue of head (1) in the text to that person for the purposes of any other works: Sch 2 para 23(11).

8   Telecommunications Act 1984 Sch 2 para 23(10)(a).

9   Telecommunications Act 1984 Sch 2 para 23(10)(b).

10 Ie the Telecommunications Act 1984 Sch 2 para 23.

11 Telecommunications Act 1984 Sch 2 para 23(10)(c). The application of Sch 2 para 23 by virtue of head (c) in the text to any person for the purposes of any works is without prejudice to its application by virtue of head (a) in the text to that person for the purposes of any other works: Sch 2 para 23(11).

191. Execution of undertaker's works.

Where a relevant undertaker[1] is proposing to execute any undertaker's works[2] which involve or are likely to involve a temporary or permanent alteration of any electronic communications apparatus[3] kept installed on, under or over any land for the purposes of the operator's network[4], the relevant undertaker must, not less than ten days before the works are commenced, give the operator[5] a notice[6] specifying the nature of the undertaker's works, the alteration or likely alteration involved and the time and place at which the works will be commenced[7]. However, this does not apply in relation to any emergency works[8] of which the relevant undertaker gives the operator notice as soon as practicable after commencing the works[9].

Where a notice has been given by a relevant undertaker to the operator, the operator may, within the ten-day period beginning with the giving of the notice, give the relevant undertaker a counter-notice which may state either[10]:

(1)   that the operator intends himself to make any alteration made necessary or expedient by the proposed undertaker's works[11]; or

(2)   that he requires the undertaker in making any such alteration to do so under the supervision and to the satisfaction of the operator[12].

Where no counter-notice is given or the operator, having given a counter-notice, fails within a reasonable time to make any alteration made necessary or expedient by the proposed undertaker's works or, as the case may be, unreasonably fails to provide the required supervision, the relevant undertaker may himself execute works for the purpose of making the alteration or, as the case may be, may execute such works without the supervision of the operator, but in either case the undertaker must execute the works to the satisfaction of the operator[13].

If the relevant undertaker or any of his agents executes any works without the required notice having been given[14], or unreasonably fails to comply with any reasonable requirement of the operator[15], he is guilty of an offence[16].

1　As to the meaning of 'relevant undertaker' see PARA 190.
2　As to the meaning of 'undertaker's works' see PARA 190.
3　As to the meaning of 'electronic communications apparatus' see PARA 168 note 6.
4　Telecommunications Act 1984 Sch 2 para 23(1) (amended by the Communications Act 2003 s 106(2), Sch 3 paras 1, 5(a), (d)). As to the meaning of 'operator's network' see PARA 168 note 4.
5　As to the meaning of 'operator' see PARA 168 note 3.
6　As to notices under the electronic communications code see PARA 192.
7　Telecommunications Act 1984 Sch 2 para 23(2).
8　As to the meaning of 'emergency works' in relation to an undertaker under the Telecommunications Act 1984 Sch 2 para 23 see PARA 182 note 14.
9　Telecommunications Act 1984 Sch 2 para 23(3).
10　Telecommunications Act 1984 Sch 2 para 23(4).
11　Telecommunications Act 1984 Sch 2 para 23(4)(a). Where a counter-notice states that the operator intends himself to make any alteration, the operator, subject to Sch 2 para 23(7) (see the text and note 13), has the right, instead of the relevant undertaker, to execute any works for the purpose of making that alteration; and any expenses incurred by the operator in or in connection with the execution of those works and the amount of any loss or damage sustained by him in consequence of the alteration is recoverable by him from the undertaker in any court of competent jurisdiction: Sch 2 para 23(5).
12　Telecommunications Act 1984 Sch 2 para 23(4)(b). Where a counter-notice states that any alteration is to be made under the supervision and to the satisfaction of the operator, the relevant undertaker must not make the alteration except as required by the notice or under Sch 2 para 23(7) (see the text and note 13) and any expenses incurred by the operator in or in connection with the provision of that supervision and the amount of any loss or damage sustained by him in consequence of the alteration is recoverable by him from the undertaker in any court of competent jurisdiction: Sch 2 para 23(6).
13　Telecommunications Act 1984 Sch 2 para 23(7).
14　Telecommunications Act 1984 Sch 2 para 23(8)(a).
15　Telecommunications Act 1984 Sch 2 para 23(8)(b).
16　Telecommunications Act 1984 Sch 2 para 23(8). A person guilty of an offence is liable on summary conviction to a fine which:
　　(1)　if the service provided by the operator's network is interrupted by the works or failure, must not exceed level 4 on the standard scale (Sch 2 para 23(8)(i) (amended by the Communications Act 2003 Sch 3 para 5(d))); and
　　(2)　if that service is not so interrupted, must not exceed level 3 on the standard scale (Telecommunications Act 1984 Sch 2 para 23(8)(ii)).
As to the standard scale see SENTENCING AND DISPOSITION OF OFFENDERS vol 92 (2010) PARA 142.

(G) Notices

192. Notices under the code. Any notice required to be given by the operator[1] to any person[2] for the purposes of any provision of the electronic communications code[3] must be in a form approved by OFCOM[4] as adequate for indicating to that person the effect of the notice and of so much of the code as is relevant to the notice and to the steps that may be taken by that person under the code in respect of that notice[5].

Any notice so required to be given to any person is not to be sent to him by post unless it is sent by a registered post service or by recorded delivery[6].

If it is not practicable, for the purposes of giving any notice under the code, after reasonable inquiries to ascertain the name and address of the person who is for the purposes of any provision of the code the occupier[7] of any land, or of the owner of any interest in any land, a notice may be given by addressing it to a person by the description of 'occupier' of the land (describing it), or, as the case may be, 'owner' of the interest (describing both the interest and the land), and by delivering it to some person on the land or, if there is no person on the land to whom it can be delivered, by affixing it, or a copy of it, to some conspicuous object on the land[8].

Any person who before the coming into force of the code[9] has:

(1)   given a notice, called the 'Telegraph Acts notice', under or for the purposes of any provision of the Telegraph Acts 1863 to 1916[10] to any person[11]; or

(2)   made any application under or for the purposes of any such provision (including, in particular, an application for any matter to be referred to any court or person)[12],

may give a notice to the person to whom the Telegraph Acts notice was given or, as the case may be, to every person who is or may be a party to the proceedings resulting from the application, stating that a specified step required to be taken under or for the purposes of the code, being a step equivalent to the giving of the Telegraph Acts notice or the making of the application, and any steps required to be so taken before the taking of that step, should be treated as having been so taken[13].

Where a Telegraph Acts notice has been given to any person, he may apply to the court[14] for an order setting aside the notice on the ground that it is unreasonable in all the circumstances to treat the giving of that notice or the making of the application in question as equivalent to the taking of the specified steps; but, unless the court sets aside the notice, the steps specified in the notice are to be treated as having been taken and any proceedings already commenced must be continued accordingly[15].

1   As to the meaning of 'operator' see PARA 168 note 3.
2   As to the meaning of 'person' see PARA 14 note 2.
3   As to the meaning of 'electronic communications code' see PARA 155 note 1.
4   As to the meaning of 'OFCOM' see PARA 14 note 1; and as to OFCOM see PARA 2 et seq. In any proceedings under the code, a certificate issued by OFCOM and stating that a particular form has been approved by it is conclusive evidence of the matter certified: Telecommunications Act 1984 Sch 2 para 24(6) (amended by the Communications Act 2003 s 106(2), Sch 3 paras 1, 9(3)).
5   Telecommunications Act 1984 Sch 2 para 24(1) (amended by the Communications Act 2003 Sch 3 para 9(1)).
6   Telecommunications Act 1984 Sch 2 para 24(2) (substituted by the Communications Act 2003 Sch 3 para 9(2)). For the purposes, in the case of such a notice, of the Communications Act 2003 s 394 (see PARA 44) and the application of the Interpretation Act 1978 s 7 in relation to that provision, the proper address of a person is:
     (1)   if the person to whom the notice is to be given has furnished the person giving the notice with an address for service under the electronic communications code, that address (Telecommunications Act 1984 Sch 2 para 24(2A)(a) (Sch 2 para 24(2A) added by the Communications Act 2003 Sch 3 para 9(2)); and
     (2)   only if he has not, the address given by the Communications Act 2003 s 394 (see PARA 44) (Telecommunications Act 1984 Sch 2 para 24(2A)(b) (as so added)).
     As to the case where a notice containing an address has been affixed to overhead apparatus see PARA 177 note 9.
7   As to the meaning of 'occupier' see PARA 163 note 2.
8   Telecommunications Act 1984 Sch 2 para 24(5).
9   As to the coming into force of the electronic communications code see PARA 163 note 15.
10   As to the Telegraph Acts 1863 to 1916 see PARA 53 note 1.
11   Telecommunications Act 1984 Sch 2 para 28(7)(a).
12   Telecommunications Act 1984 Sch 2 para 28(7)(b).
13   Telecommunications Act 1984 Sch 2 para 28(7). Such a notice may be given with respect to an application notwithstanding that proceedings resulting from the application have been commenced: Sch 2 para 28(8).

14 As to the meaning of 'court' see PARA 171 note 6.
15 Telecommunications Act 1984 Sch 2 para 28(9).

(H) Protection of Apparatus

193. Apparatus affected by electrical works. A licence holder[1] may execute works[2] notwithstanding that they involve a temporary or permanent alteration of any electronic communications apparatus[3] used for the purpose of an electronic communications code network[4] operated by a person[5] to whom the electronic communications code applies[6].

A licence holder who installs or alters, or changes the mode of operation of, any electric line[7] or electrical plant[8] is under a duty to take reasonable precautions for securing that the operation of the line or plant does not interfere with the operation of any electronic communications apparatus which is under the control of a person to whom the electronic communications code applies and which is not unusually sensitive to interference with its operation[9]. However, in the case of any electronic communications apparatus which is subsequently installed or altered or whose mode of operation is subsequently changed, this duty does not apply in relation to any momentary interference[10] with its operation or, where it is installed in unreasonably close proximity to the electric line or plant, any other interference with its operation[11].

The provisions described above are to be read as also applying in the converse case of a person to whom the electronic communications code applies who installs or alters, or changes the mode of operation of, any electronic communications apparatus[12].

Any dispute arising between the parties must be referred to arbitration; and, in default of agreement between the parties, the arbitrator must be appointed by the President of the Chartered Institute of Arbitrators[13].

1   As to the meaning of 'licence holder' for these purposes see the Electricity Act 1989 ss 3(7), 64(1); and ENERGY AND CLIMATE CHANGE vol 43 (2011) PARAS 507, 715.
2   Ie works in pursuance of the Electricity Act 1989 s 10(1), Sch 4 paras 1, 2: see ENERGY AND CLIMATE CHANGE vol 43 (2011) PARA 718.
3   As to the meaning of 'electronic communications apparatus' see PARA 168 note 6.
4   As to the meaning of 'electronic communications code network' see PARA 179 note 3.
5   As to the meaning of 'person' see PARA 14 note 2.
6   Electricity Act 1989 Sch 4 para 3(1)(d) (amended by the Communications Act 2003 s 406(1), Sch 17 para 99). See also ENERGY AND CLIMATE CHANGE vol 43 (2011) PARA 719. As to the meaning of 'electronic communications code' see PARA 155 note 1. Where a licence holder is proposing to execute works involving a temporary or permanent alteration of any electronic communications apparatus, the provisions of the Telecommunications Act 1984 Sch 2 para 23(1) apply: see the Electricity Act 1989 s 112(1), Sch 16 para 1(6); and ENERGY AND CLIMATE CHANGE vol 43 (2011) PARA 719.
7   As to the meaning of 'electric line' see the Electricity Act 1989 s 64(1); and ENERGY AND CLIMATE CHANGE vol 43 (2011) PARA 507.
8   As to the meaning of 'electrical plant' see the Electricity Act 1989 s 64(1); and ENERGY AND CLIMATE CHANGE vol 43 (2011) PARA 507.
9   Electricity Act 1989 Sch 4 para 5(1) (amended by the Communications Act 2003 Sch 17 para 99). See also ENERGY AND CLIMATE CHANGE vol 43 (2011) PARA 720.
10 As to the meaning of 'momentary interference' for these purposes see the Electricity Act 1989 Sch 4 para 5(5); and ENERGY AND CLIMATE CHANGE vol 43 (2011) PARA 720.
11 Electricity Act 1989 Sch 4 para 5(2). See also ENERGY AND CLIMATE CHANGE vol 43 (2011) PARA 720.
12 Electricity Act 1989 Sch 4 para 5(3) (amended by the Communications Act 2003 Sch 17 para 99). See also ENERGY AND CLIMATE CHANGE vol 43 (2011) PARA 720. In such a case, the provisions have effect as if:
    (1)   any reference to a licence holder were a reference to that person (Electricity Act 1989 Sch 4 para 5(3)(a));

(2) any reference to an electric line or electrical plant were a reference to such apparatus (Sch 4 para 5(3)(b)); and

(3) any reference to such apparatus under the control of the person to whom the code applies were a reference to the line or plant under the control of the licence holder (Sch 4 para 5(3)(c)).

13 Electricity Act 1989 Sch 4 para 5(4). See also ENERGY AND CLIMATE CHANGE vol 43 (2011) PARA 720. The provisions of the Arbitration Act 1996 Pt I (ss 1–84) apply subject to the adaptations and exclusions specified in ss 95–98: see s 94; and ARBITRATION vol 2 (2008) PARA 1201 et seq.

194. Apparatus on highways stopped up or diverted. Where, in pursuance of an order[1], a highway[2] is stopped up or diverted or, as the case may be, any right to use vehicles on that highway is extinguished[3], and immediately before the date on which the order came into force there was under, in, on, over, along or across the highway any electronic communications apparatus[4] kept installed for the purposes of an electronic communications code network[5], the operator[6] of that network has the same powers in respect of the apparatus as if the order had not come into force[7]. But any person entitled to land over which the highway subsisted is entitled to require the alteration[8] of the apparatus[9]. Where any such order provides for the improvement of a highway for which the Secretary of State[10] is not the highway authority[11] and immediately before the date on which the order came into force there was under, in, on, over, along or across the highway any electronic communications apparatus kept installed for the purposes of an electronic communications code network[12], the local highway authority[13] is entitled to require the alteration of the apparatus[14].

1 Ie an order under the Town and Country Planning Act 1990 s 247, 248 or 249: see HIGHWAYS, STREETS AND BRIDGES vol 55 (2012) PARA 821 et seq.

2 'Highway' has the same meaning as in the Highways Act 1980 (see s 328(1), (2); and HIGHWAYS, STREETS AND BRIDGES vol 55 (2012) PARA 7): Town and Country Planning Act 1990 s 336(1).

3 Town and Country Planning Act 1990 s 256(1)(a).

4 As to the meaning of 'electronic communications apparatus' see PARA 168 note 6.

5 Town and Country Planning Act 1990 s 256(1)(b) (amended by the Communications Act 2003 s 406(1), Sch 17 para 103). As to the meaning of 'electronic communications code network' see PARA 179 note 3.

6 As to the meaning of 'operator' see PARA 179 note 4.

7 Town and Country Planning Act 1990 s 256(1) (amended by the Communications Act 2003 Sch 17 para 103). See also HIGHWAYS, STREETS AND BRIDGES vol 55 (2012) PARA 826.

8 As to the meaning of 'alteration' see PARA 168 note 5; definition applied by the Town and Country Planning Act 1990 s 256(5).

9 Town and Country Planning Act 1990 s 256(2). See also HIGHWAYS, STREETS AND BRIDGES vol 55 (2012) PARA 826. The Telecommunications Act 1984 Sch 2 para 21 (see PARA 189) applies to any entitlement under the Town and Country Planning Act 1990 s 256 to require the alteration, moving or replacement of any electronic communications apparatus as it applies to an entitlement to require the removal of such apparatus: s 256(6).

10 As to the Secretary of State for these purposes see HIGHWAYS, STREETS AND BRIDGES vol 55 (2012) PARA 52 et seq. See also PARA 76 note 1.

11 Town and Country Planning Act 1990 s 256(3)(a) (amended by the New Roads and Street Works Act 1991 s 168(1), Sch 8 para 126).

12 Town and Country Planning Act 1990 s 256(3)(b) (amended by the Communications Act 2003 Sch 17 para 103).

13 As to local highway authorities see HIGHWAYS, STREETS AND BRIDGES vol 55 (2012) PARA 59 et seq.

14 Town and Country Planning Act 1990 s 256(3). However, s 256(3) does not have effect so far as it relates to the alteration of any such apparatus for the purposes of major highway works, major bridge works or major transport works within the meaning of the New Roads and Street Works Act 1991 Pt III (ss 48–106): Town and Country Planning Act 1990 s 256(4) (amended by the New Roads and Street Works Act 1991 Sch 8 para 126). See also HIGHWAYS, STREETS AND BRIDGES vol 55 (2012) PARA 826.

195. Apparatus on extinguished rights of way. Where an order extinguishing a public right of way is made by a local authority[1] or on the application of a local authority[2], or any order is made by a competent authority[3] which authorises the stopping up or diversion of a footpath, bridleway or restricted byway[4], and at the time of the publication of the notice of the order[5] any electronic communications apparatus[6] was kept installed for the purposes of an electronic communications code network[7] under, in, on, over, along or across the land over which the right of way subsisted[8], then, notwithstanding the making of the order, the power of the operator of the electronic communications code network to remove the apparatus is exercisable at any time not later than the end of the period of three months from the date on which the right of way is extinguished or authorised to be stopped up or diverted, and is exercisable in respect of the whole or any part of the apparatus after the end of that period if before the end of that period the operator has given notice to the authority of its intention to remove the apparatus or that part of it, as the case may be[9]. The operator may, by notice given in that behalf to the authority not later than the end of the three-month period, abandon the apparatus or any part of it[10]; and the operator is in any case deemed at the end of that period to have abandoned any part of the apparatus which he has then neither removed nor given notice of his intention to remove[11].

1 Ie an order under the Town and Country Planning Act 1990 s 258(1): see HIGHWAYS, STREETS AND BRIDGES vol 55 (2012) PARA 825. As soon as practicable after the making of an order under s 258(1) extinguishing a public right of way in circumstances in which s 260(1) (see the text to note 8) applies in relation to the operator of any electronic communications code network, the person who made the order must give notice to the operator of the making of the order: s 260(8) (amended by the Communications Act 2003 s 406(1), Sch 17 para 103). As to the meaning of 'local authority' see the Town and Country Planning Act 1990 s 336(1); and PLANNING vol 81 (2010) PARA 3. The provisions of s 256(5), (6) (see PARA 189; and HIGHWAYS, STREETS AND BRIDGES vol 55 (2012) PARA 826) apply for the purposes of s 260: s 260(9).
2 Ie under the Town and Country Planning Act 1990 s 251(1): see HIGHWAYS, STREETS AND BRIDGES vol 55 (2012) PARA 825. Section 260(8) also applies: see note 1.
3 As to the meaning of 'competent authority' see the Town and Country Planning Act 1990 s 257(4) (definition applied by s 260(2)); and HIGHWAYS, STREETS AND BRIDGES vol 55 (2012) PARA 826. For the purposes of s 260(3)–(7), references to the authority are references to the authority which made the order, or, as the case may be, on whose application it was made: s 260(2). 'Development' has the meaning assigned to it by s 55 (see PLANNING vol 81 (2010) PARA 292): s 336(1). As to local planning authorities see s 1; and PLANNING vol 81 (2010) PARAS 2, 43 et seq.
4 Ie under the Town and Country Planning Act 1990 s 257: see HIGHWAYS, STREETS AND BRIDGES vol 55 (2012) PARA 669. Section 260(8) also applies: see note 1. 'Footpath' and 'bridleway' have the same meanings as in the Highways Act 1980 s 329 (see HIGHWAYS, STREETS AND BRIDGES vol 55 (2012) PARA 68), and 'restricted byway' has the same meaning as in the Countryside and Rights of Way Act 2000 Pt II (ss 47–72) (see HIGHWAYS, STREETS AND BRIDGES vol 55 (2012) PARA 611): Town and Country Planning Act 1990 s 336(1) (amended by SI 2006/1177).
5 Ie the notice required by the Town and Country Planning Act 1990 s 252(1) or Sch 14 para 1: see HIGHWAYS, STREETS AND BRIDGES vol 55 (2012) PARA 828.
6 As to the meaning of 'electronic communications apparatus' see PARA 168 note 6.
7 As to the meaning of 'electronic communications code network' see PARA 179 note 3.
8 Town and Country Planning Act 1990 s 260(1) (amended by SI 2006/1177). See also note 1.
9 Town and Country Planning Act 1990 s 260(3) (amended by the Communications Act 2003 Sch 17 para 103). See also note 1. As to the expense of providing a new line see note 10. Similar provisions as to telegraphic lines apply where an order is made extinguishing a public right of way on the application of a development corporation or local highway authority under the New Towns Act 1981: see s 24; and PLANNING vol 83 (2010) PARA 1545.
10 Town and Country Planning Act 1990 s 260(4). The operator is entitled to recover from the authority the expense of providing, in substitution for the apparatus and any other electronic communications apparatus connected with it which is rendered useless in consequence of the removal or abandonment of the former apparatus, any electronic communications apparatus in

such other place as the operator may require: s 260(6) (amended by the Communications Act 2003 Sch 17 para 103). Where under the Town and Country Planning Act 1990 s 260 the operator has abandoned the whole or any part of any electronic communications apparatus, that apparatus or part vests in the authority, and is deemed, with its abandonment, to cease to be kept installed for the purposes of the electronic communications code network: s 260(7) (amended by the Communications Act 2003 Sch 17 para 103). See also note 1.

11 Town and Country Planning Act 1990 s 260(5); and see note 10. See also note 1.

196. Apparatus affected by work relating to the Channel Tunnel and Rail Link. The Channel Tunnel Act 1987 and the Channel Tunnel Rail Link Act 1996 make provision regarding apparatus that may be affected by the works relating to the Channel Tunnel and the associated Channel Tunnel Rail Link.

Any electrical works or equipment constructed, erected, laid, maintained, worked or used, must be so constructed, erected or laid and so maintained, worked or used, and certain railway works[1] must be worked, so that any electricity conveyed by, used in, or in connection with, any such works or equipment, and the working of the railway, does not cause unavoidable interference[2] with any electronic communications apparatus[3] installed for the purposes of an electronic communications code network[4] or the service provided by such a network[5].

Where the appropriate authority[6] stops up and discontinues the whole or any part of any highway[7], and the land which ceases to be a highway contains electronic communications apparatus, the following provisions are to apply[8]:

(1) the authority must, as soon as practicable, serve notice on any operator of an electronic communications code network[9] which has notified the authority of its interest in the highway[10];

(2) the rights of the operator of the network for the purposes of which the apparatus is used to remove the affected apparatus are exercisable, notwithstanding the stopping up, but not following the expiration of a period of 28 days from the date of service of a notice[11], unless the operator has given notice to the appropriate authority, before the expiration of the notice period, of his intention to remove the apparatus[12];

(3) the operator may by notice given to the appropriate authority abandon the apparatus or any part of it[13];

(4) the operator is entitled to recover from the appropriate authority the expense of providing, in substitution of the apparatus and any apparatus connected with it and rendered useless in consequence of the removal or abandonment, apparatus in such other place as the operator may require[14].

If any damage to the apparatus or interruption to the service provided by the electronic communications code network is caused by reason or consequence of the construction of any work, or by subsidence resulting from the work, the appropriate authority must bear and pay the cost reasonably incurred by the operator of the network to make good the damage or restore the service[15] and must:

(a) pay reasonable compensation to the operator for the losses sustained[16]; and

(b) indemnify the operator against claims, demands, proceedings, costs, damages and expenses made against, recovered from or incurred by the operator[17],

by reason or in consequence of any such damage or interruption[18].

Provision is made for the determination of differences between the appropriate authority and any operator[19].

1 Ie the Channel Tunnel Act 1987 s 5, Sch 1 Pt I Works Nos 3–5.

2 Ie whether by induction or not: Channel Tunnel Act 1987 s 45, Sch 7 Pt X para 2(1).

3 As to the meaning of 'electronic communications apparatus' see PARA 168 note 6.

4 As to the meaning of 'electronic communications code network' see PARA 179 note 3.

5 Channel Tunnel Act 1987 Sch 7 Pt X para 2(1) (Sch 7 Pt X para 2 amended by the Communications Act 2003 s 406(1), Sch 17 para 86). This provision does not apply to any electronic communications apparatus kept or installed for the purposes of an electronic communications code network and installed in any part of the railway: Channel Tunnel Act 1987 Sch 7 Pt X para 2(2) (as so amended). Unless otherwise agreed in writing between the appropriate authority (see note 6) and an operator of an electronic communications code network, Sch 7 Pt X has effect for the protection of that operator: Sch 7 Pt X para 1(1) (amended by the Communications Act 2003 Sch 17 para 86).

6 For these purposes, 'appropriate authority' means:
   (1)   in relation to the acquisition of land required for the Concessionaires' scheduled works and other works in connection with those works, or for any purpose of the Channel Tunnel Act 1987 Pt IV (ss 35–36), the Secretary of State;
   (2)   in relation to any other matter concerning the Concessionaires' scheduled works or such other works, the Concessionaires;
   (3)   in relation to the Kent County Council's scheduled works and other works in connection with those works, that Council; and
   (4)   in relation to the Railways Board's scheduled works and other works in connection with those works, the Railways Board: s 49.

   The 'Concessionaires' means the person or persons who, under the Concession, have for the time being the function of constructing and operating or (as the case may be) of operating the tunnel system: s 1(8). The 'Concession' referred to above is between Her Majesty's Government in the United Kingdom and the Government of the French Republic on the one hand and private Concessionaires on the other hand which, in accordance with the Treaty, art 1, regulates, together with that Treaty, the construction and operation of the Channel fixed link referred to in art 1: Channel Tunnel Act 1987 s 1(1)(b). The 'Treaty' means the Treaty between United Kingdom of Great Britain and Northern Ireland and the French Republic concerning the Construction and Operation by Private Concessionaires of a Channel Fixed Link, signed at Canterbury on 12 February 1986, together with its supplementary protocols and arrangements: Channel Tunnel Act 1987 s 1(1)(a).

7 Ie under powers granted by the Channel Tunnel Act 1987 s 6, Sch 2 para 16. The powers granted by Sch 2 para 15 (underpinning of buildings) must, as far as reasonably practicable, be exercised so as not to obstruct or render less convenient the access to any apparatus kept installed for the purposes of an electronic communications code network: Sch 7 Pt X para 4 (amended by the Communications Act 2003 Sch 17 para 86). The powers granted by the Channel Tunnel Act 1987 Sch 2 para 22 (temporary interference with highways) do not affect the rights of the operator of any electronic communications code network to maintain, inspect, repair, renew or remove apparatus or open or break up that highway for those purposes: Sch 7 Pt X para 5 (amended by the Communications Act 2003 Sch 17 para 86). See also the Channel Tunnel Rail Link Act 1996 s 52, Sch 15 Pt IV para 4(1) (Sch 15 Pt IV para 4 amended by the Communications Act 2003 Sch 17 para 139).

8 Channel Tunnel Act 1987 Sch 7 Pt X para 3(1) (Sch 7 Pt X para 3 amended by the Communications Act 2003 Sch 17 para 86).

9 As to the meaning of 'electronic communications code network' see PARA 179 note 3.

10 Channel Tunnel Act 1987 Sch 7 Pt X para 3(6) (as amended: see note 8). See also the Channel Tunnel Rail Link Act 1996 Sch 15 Pt IV para 4(2) (as amended: see note 7).

11 See the Channel Tunnel Act 1987 Sch 7 Pt X para 3(6).

12 Channel Tunnel Act 1987 Sch 7 Pt X para 3(2) (as amended: see note 8).

13 Channel Tunnel Act 1987 Sch 7 Pt X para 3(3) (as amended: see note 8). The operator is deemed to have abandoned it upon the expiration of the 28 day notice period, unless the operator has served notice of an intention to remove it: Sch 7 Pt X para 3(3). Where the operator abandons the apparatus, it vests in the appropriate authority; and the apparatus is deemed with its abandonment to cease to be kept installed for the purposes of an electronic communications code network: Sch 7 Pt X para 3(5) (as so amended). See also the Channel Tunnel Rail Link Act 1996 Sch 15 Pt IV para 4(3) (as amended: see note 7).

14 Channel Tunnel Act 1987 Sch 7 Pt X para 3(4) (as amended: see note 8). See also the Channel Tunnel Rail Link Act 1996 Sch 15 Pt IV para 4(4)–(8) (as amended: see note 7).

15 Channel Tunnel Act 1987 Sch 7 Pt X para 6(1) (Sch 7 Pt X para 6 amended by the Communications Act 2003 Sch 17 para 86). See also the Channel Tunnel Rail Link Act 1996 Sch 15 Pt IV para 5(1), (2) (Sch 15 Pt IV para 5 amended by the Communications Act 2003 Sch 17 para 139).

16 Channel Tunnel Act 1987 Sch 7 Pt X para 6(1)(a). See also the Channel Tunnel Rail Link Act 1996 Sch 15 Pt IV para 5(1)(a) (as amended: see note 15).

17 Channel Tunnel Act 1987 Sch 7 Pt X para 6(1)(b). See also the Channel Tunnel Rail Link Act 1996 Sch 15 Pt IV para 5(1)(b) (as amended: see note 15).

18 Channel Tunnel Act 1987 Sch 7 Pt X para 6(1). Nothing in Sch 7 Pt X para 6(1) imposes liability on the appropriate authority with respect to damage or interruption which is attributable to the act, neglect or default of the operator of the network, its officers, servants, contractors or agents: Sch 7 Pt X para 6(2) (as amended: see note 15). See also the Channel Tunnel Rail Link Act 1996 Sch 15 Pt IV para 5(3) (as amended: see note 15). The operator must give the appropriate authority reasonable notice of any claim or demand; and no settlement or compromise is to be made without the prior consent of that appropriate authority: Channel Tunnel Act 1987 Sch 7 Pt X para 6(3). See also the Channel Tunnel Rail Link Act 1996 Sch 15 Pt IV para 5(4) (as amended: see note 15).

19 Channel Tunnel Act 1987 Sch 7 Pt X para 7 (Sch 7 Pt X para 7 amended by the Communications Act 2003 Sch 17 para 86). See also the Channel Tunnel Rail Link Act 1996 Sch 15 Pt IV para 6.

(7) APPROVAL OF COMMUNICATIONS APPARATUS

197. Apparatus to which requirements apply. All apparatus[1] must conform with the requirements contained in the Radio Equipment and Telecommunications Terminal Equipment Regulations 2000[2], with the following exceptions[3]. The regulations do not apply to apparatus exclusively used for the purposes of public security, defence, state security (including the economic well-being of the state) or the activities of the state in the area of criminal law[4], nor to the following equipment[5]:

(1)   radio equipment used by radio amateurs[6] unless that equipment is available commercially[7];

(2)   marine equipment[8];

(3)   cabling and wiring[9];

(4)   receive only radio equipment intended to be used solely for the reception of sound and television broadcasting services[10];

(5)   products, appliances and components related to civil aviation[11];

(6)   air-traffic management equipment and systems[12].

1   'Apparatus' means any equipment that is either radio equipment or telecommunications terminal equipment or both: Radio Equipment and Telecommunications Terminal Equipment Regulations 2000, SI 2000/730, reg 2(1). 'Radio equipment' means a product, or a relevant component thereof, capable of communication by means of the emission and/or reception of radio waves utilising the spectrum allocated to terrestrial/space radio communication; 'radio waves' means electromagnetic waves of frequencies from 9 kHz to 3,000 GHz propagated in space without artificial guide; and 'telecommunications terminal equipment' means a product enabling communication, or a relevant component thereof, which is intended to be connected directly or indirectly by any means whatsoever to interfaces of public telecommunications networks: reg 2(1). 'Interface' means either or both of:
      (1)   a network termination point which is a physical connection point at which a user is provided with access to public telecommunications networks; and
      (2)   an air interface specifying the radio path between radio equipment, and their technical specifications: reg 2(1).
   'Public telecommunications networks' means telecommunications networks used wholly or partly for the provision of publicly available telecommunications services: reg 2(1).
      As to the approval of wireless telegraphy apparatus under the Wireless Telegraphy Act 2006 see BROADCASTING vol 4 (2011) PARAS 534–536.

2   Ie the Radio Equipment and Telecommunications Terminal Equipment Regulations 2000, SI 2000/730. The regulations came into force on 8 April 2000 (see reg 1(1)) and implement

European Parliament and Council Directive (EC) 1999/5 (OJ L91, 7.4.1999, p 10) on radio equipment and telecommunications terminal equipment and the mutual recognition of their conformity. As from 13 June 2016, Council Directive (EC) 1999/5 (OJ L91, 7.4.99, p 10) is replaced by European Parliament and Council Directive (EU) 2014/53 (OJ L153, 22.5.2014, p 62) on the harmonisation of the laws of the member states relating to the making available on the market of radio equipment: see art 50.

3 Radio Equipment and Telecommunications Terminal Equipment Regulations 2000, SI 2000/730, reg 3(1).

Where apparatus incorporates, as an integral part or as an accessory, a medical device or an active implantable medical device, the apparatus is to be governed by the regulations without prejudice to the application of Council Directive (EC) 93/42 (OJ L169, 12.7.93, p 1) concerning medical devices, or Council Directive (EC) 90/385 (OJ L189, 20.7.90, p 17) on the approximation of the laws of the member states relating to active implantable medical devices, or the Medical Devices Regulations 1994, SI 1994/3017, or the Active Implantable Medical Devices Regulations 1992, SI 1992/3146 (both revoked: see now the Medical Devices Regulations 2002, SI 2002/618 (see MEDICAL PRODUCTS AND DRUGS vol 75 (2013) PARA 472 et seq): Radio Equipment and Telecommunications Terminal Equipment Regulations 2000, SI 2000/730, reg 3(2) (amended by SI 2003/1903).

'Active implantable medical device' has the meaning in Council Directive (EC) 90/385 (OJ L189, 20.7.90, p 17) art 1; and 'medical device' has the meaning in Council Directive (EC) 93/42 (OJ L169, 12.7.93, p 1) art 1: Radio Equipment and Telecommunications Terminal Equipment Regulations 2000, SI 2000/730, reg 2(1).

Where apparatus constitutes a component or a separate technical unit of a vehicle, the apparatus is to be governed by the regulations without prejudice to the application of Council Directive (EC) 72/245 (OJ L152, 5.7.72, p 15) (now repealed: see the European Parliament and Council Regulation (EC) 661/2009 (OJ L200, 31.7.2009, p 1) concerning type-approval requirements for the general safety of motor vehicles, their trailers and systems, components and separate technical units intended therefor); Council Directive (EC) 92/61 (OJ L225, 10.8.92, p 72) (now repealed: see now the European Parliament and Council Directive (EC) 2002/24 (OJ L 124, 9.5.2002, p 1) relating to the type-approval of two or three-wheel motor vehicles); the Motor Vehicles (Type Approval) Regulations 1980, SI 1980/1182, or the Motorcycle (EC Type Approval) Regulations 1995, SI 1995/1513 (revoked: see now the Motor Cycles Etc (EC Type Approval) Regulations 1999, SI 1999/2920 (see ROAD TRAFFIC vol 89 (2011) PARA 503): Radio Equipment and Telecommunications Terminal Equipment Regulations 2000, SI 2000/730, reg 3(3) (amended by SI 2003/1903). 'Component or a separate technical unit of a vehicle' has the meaning in Council Directive (EC) 92/61 (OJ L225, 10.8.92, p 72) (repealed), art 2: Radio Equipment and Telecommunications Terminal Equipment Regulations 2000, SI 2000/730, reg 2(1).

4 Radio Equipment and Telecommunications Terminal Equipment Regulations 2000, SI 2000/730, reg 3(4).

5 Ie equipment listed in the Radio Equipment and Telecommunications Terminal Equipment Regulations 2000, SI 2000/730, Sch 1, which reproduces European Parliament and Council Directive (EC) 1999/5 (OJ L91, 7.4.1999, p 10) Annex 1: Radio Equipment and Telecommunications Terminal Equipment Regulations 2000, SI 2000/730, reg 3(5). See note 2.

6 Ie within the International Telecommunication Union (ITU) radio regulations art 1 definition 53.

7 Radio Equipment and Telecommunications Terminal Equipment Regulations 2000, SI 2000/730, Sch 1 para 1. Kits of components to be assembled by radio amateurs and commercial equipment modified by and for the use of radio amateurs are not regarded as commercially available equipment: Sch 1 para 1.

8 Radio Equipment and Telecommunications Terminal Equipment Regulations 2000, SI 2000/730, Sch 1 para 1. The reference to marine equipment in the text is to equipment falling within the scope of Council Directive (EC) 96/98 (OJ L46, 17.2.97, p 25) on marine equipment (replaced by European Parliament and Council Directive (EU) 2014/90 (OJ L257, 28.8.2014, p 146) on marine equipment as from 18 September 2016): Radio Equipment and Telecommunications Terminal Equipment Regulations 2000, SI 2000/730, Sch 1 para 2.

9 Radio Equipment and Telecommunications Terminal Equipment Regulations 2000, SI 2000/730, Sch 1 para 3.

10 Radio Equipment and Telecommunications Terminal Equipment Regulations 2000, SI 2000/730, Sch 1 para 4.

11 Radio Equipment and Telecommunications Terminal Equipment Regulations 2000, SI 2000/730, Sch 1 para 5. The reference to products, appliances and components relating to civil aviation are to those within the meaning of Council Regulation (EC) 3922/91 of

16 December 1991 (OJ L373, 21.12.91, p 4) on the harmonisation of technical requirements and administrative procedure in the field of civil aviation, art 2: Radio Equipment and Telecommunications Terminal Equipment Regulations 2000, SI 2000/730, Sch 1 para 5.

12 Radio Equipment and Telecommunications Terminal Equipment Regulations 2000, SI 2000/730, Sch 1 para 6. The reference to air-traffic management equipment and systems are to those within the meaning of Council Directive (EC) 93/65 (OJ L187, 29.7.93, p 52) on the definition and use of compatible technical specifications for the procurement of air-traffic management equipment and systems, art 1: Radio Equipment and Telecommunications Terminal Equipment Regulations 2000, SI 2000/730, Sch 1 para 6.

198.   Essential standards.   Apparatus[1] when properly installed and maintained and used for its intended purpose must satisfy the essential requirements set out below[2].

The following essential requirements apply to all apparatus[3]:

(1)   the protection of the health and safety of the user and any other person, including the objectives with respect to safety requirements contained in the Directive[4] relating to low voltage (but as if there were no voltage limit)[5];

(2)   the protection requirements with respect to electromagnetic compatibility contained in the Directive[6] relating to electromagnetic compatibility[7].

In addition, radio equipment[8] must be so constructed that it effectively uses the spectrum allocated to terrestrial/space radio communication and orbital resources so as to avoid harmful interference[9].

When a measure has been adopted[10] and published in the Official Journal of the European Union determining that apparatus must be so constructed that[11]:

(a)   it interworks via networks with other apparatus and that it can be connected to interfaces[12] of the appropriate type throughout the EU[13]; or

(b)   it does not harm the network or its functioning nor misuse network resources, thereby causing an unacceptable degradation of service[14]; or

(c)   it incorporates safeguards to ensure that the personal data and privacy of the user and of the subscriber are protected[15]; or

(d)   it supports certain features ensuring avoidance of fraud[16]; or

(e)   it supports certain features ensuring access to emergency services[17] or

(f)   it supports certain features in order to facilitate its use by users with a disability[18],

apparatus within the scope of that measure must meet the requirements of that measure from the date specified in that measure[19].

1   As to the meaning of 'apparatus' see PARA 197 note 1.

2   Radio Equipment and Telecommunications Terminal Equipment Regulations 2000, SI 2000/730, reg 4(1).

3   Radio Equipment and Telecommunications Terminal Equipment Regulations 2000, SI 2000/730, reg 4(2).

4   Ie Council Directive (EC) 73/23 (OJ L77, 26.03.73, p 29) on the harmonisation of the laws of member states relating to electrical equipment designed for use within certain voltage limits (repealed: see now European Parliament and Council Directive (EC) 2006/95 (OJ L374, 27.12.2006, p 10) on the harmonisation of the laws of member states relating to electrical equipment designed for use within certain voltage limits).

5   Radio Equipment and Telecommunications Terminal Equipment Regulations 2000, SI 2000/730, reg 4(2)(a).

6   Ie the protection requirements in Council Directive (EC) 89/336 (OJ L139, 23.5.89, p 19) on the approximation of the laws of the member states relating to electromagnetic compatibility (repealed: see now European Parliament and Council Directive (EC) 2004/108 (OJ L390, 31.12.2004, p 24).

7   Radio Equipment and Telecommunications Terminal Equipment Regulations 2000, SI 2000/730, reg 4(2)(b).
8   As to the meaning of 'radio equipment' see PARA 197 note 1.
9   Radio Equipment and Telecommunications Terminal Equipment Regulations 2000, SI 2000/730, reg 4(3). 'Harmful interference' means interference which endangers the functioning of a radio navigation service or of other safety services or which otherwise seriously degrades, obstructs or repeatedly interrupts a radio communications service operating in accordance with the applicable European Union (EU) or national regulations: reg 2(1) (amended by virtue of the European Union (Amendment) Act 2008 s 3(6)).
10 Ie by the Commission pursuant to European Parliament and Council Directive (EC) 1999/5 (OJ L91, 7.4.1999, p 10) arts 3.3, 6.2, 15. As from 13 June 2016, Council Directive (EC) 1999/5 (OJ L91, 7.4.99, p 10) is replaced by European Parliament and Council Directive (EU) 2014/53 (OJ L153, 22.5.2014, p 62) on the harmonisation of the laws of the member states relating to the making available on the market of radio equipment: see art 50. 'Commission' means the Commission of the European Union: Radio Equipment and Telecommunications Terminal Equipment Regulations 2000, SI 2000/730, reg 2(1) (amended by SI 2011/1043). As to the Commission see European Union vol 47A (2014) PARA 48 et seq.
11 Radio Equipment and Telecommunications Terminal Equipment Regulations 2000, SI 2000/730, reg 4(4) (amended by SI 2011/1043).
12 As to the meaning of 'interface' see PARA 197 note 1.
13 Radio Equipment and Telecommunications Terminal Equipment Regulations 2000, SI 2000/730, reg 4(4)(a) (amended by SI 2011/1043). Except for the references to the European Union in the definition of 'Commission' (see note 10) and in relation to the Official Journal, a reference to the European Union includes a reference to the EEA; and for this purpose the 'EEA' means the European Economic Area ((ie the European Union member states and Norway, Iceland and Liechtenstein) under the Agreement on the European Economic Area (Oporto, 2 May 1992; Cm 2073 (OJ L1, 3.1.94, p 3)) as adjusted by the Protocol (Brussels, 17 March 1993; Cm 2183 (OJ L1, 3.1.94, p 572)) (the 'EEA Agreement')): Radio Equipment and Telecommunications Terminal Equipment Regulations 2000, SI 2000/730, reg 2(4) (added by SI 2003/1903; and amended by SI 2011/1043). As to the EEA Agreement see COMPETITION vol 18 (2009) PARA 36.
14 Radio Equipment and Telecommunications Terminal Equipment Regulations 2000, SI 2000/730, reg 4(4)(b).
15 Radio Equipment and Telecommunications Terminal Equipment Regulations 2000, SI 2000/730, reg 4(4)(c).
16 Radio Equipment and Telecommunications Terminal Equipment Regulations 2000, SI 2000/730, reg 4(4)(d).
17 Radio Equipment and Telecommunications Terminal Equipment Regulations 2000, SI 2000/730, reg 4(4)(e).
18 Radio Equipment and Telecommunications Terminal Equipment Regulations 2000, SI 2000/730, reg 4(4)(f).
19 Radio Equipment and Telecommunications Terminal Equipment Regulations 2000, SI 2000/730, reg 4(4).

199.   Duty relating to the placing on the market and putting into service of apparatus.   Subject to exceptions[1], no person may place on the market or put into service any apparatus[2] unless the following requirements[3] and (in the case of radio equipment[4]) certain additional requirements[5] have been complied with in relation to it[6].

The requirements in respect of any apparatus are that:

(1)   it satisfies the essential requirements[7]; and without prejudice to other means of complying for the purpose of satisfying those requirements, where a harmonised standard[8] covers one or more of the relevant essential requirements, any apparatus or part thereof constructed in accordance with that harmonised standard or part thereof is to be presumed to comply with that or, as the case may be, those essential requirements[9];

(2)   the information accompanying the apparatus has been provided as required[10];

(3)　　the appropriate conformity assessment procedures in respect of the apparatus have been carried out[11];

(4)　　the requirements as to the CE and other marking[12] have been complied with[13]; and

(5)　　a declaration of conformity has been drawn up in respect of it[14] by the manufacturer of the apparatus or other responsible person[15].

This does not prohibit the putting into service of apparatus in relation to which the requirements set out in heads (2) to (5) above have not been complied with[16].

In respect of radio equipment using frequency bands whose use is not harmonised throughout the European Union (EU) it is also a requirement that notification of intention to place it on the market must have been given[17].

For the purposes of the above requirements[18], apparatus is not to be regarded as being placed on the market where that apparatus:

(a)　　is intended to be exported to a country outside the EU[19]; or

(b)　　is imported into the EU for re-export to a country outside the EU[20]; or

(c)　　is transferred from the manufacturer in a third country to his authorised representative established within the EU who is responsible on behalf of the manufacturer for ensuring compliance with the specified Directive[21]; or

(d)　　is transferred to a manufacturer for further processing (for example, to modify the product or to integrate it into another product, or to put his own name on the product)[22],

save that this exemption does not apply if the CE marking, or any inscription liable to be confused with it, is affixed to the apparatus[23].

No offence under the Telecommunications Act 1984 or the Wireless Telegraphy Acts, nor any offence of incitement to commit such an offence, is committed by reason only that apparatus which does not comply with these provisions is displayed at a trade fair, exhibition or demonstration if a notice is displayed in relation to the apparatus to the effect that it does not satisfy the provisions of the Radio Equipment and Telecommunications Terminal Equipment Regulations 2000 and that it may not be placed on the market or put into service until those provisions are satisfied by a responsible person[24]. This exemption does not apply, however, in any case in which radio equipment is switched on and thereby causes harmful interference[25] or endangers public health[26].

The Secretary of State[27] and OFCOM[28] must so exercise their respective functions under Part VI of the Telecommunications Act 1984[29] and the Wireless Telegraphy Acts that the putting into service of radio equipment which complies with the Radio Equipment and Telecommunications Terminal Equipment Regulations 2000 is restricted only for reasons related to the effective and appropriate use of the radio spectrum, avoidance or harmful interference of public health[30].

Notwithstanding these provisions, apparatus could be placed on the market before 8 April 2001, and apparatus so placed on the market could be put into service, if (in either case) it was in accordance with the provisions previously in force[31].

1　See the Radio Equipment and Telecommunications Terminal Equipment Regulations 2000, SI 2000/730, regs 5(4), 6–8; the text and notes 14, 16–26; and PARA 201.
2　As to the meaning of 'apparatus' see PARA 197 note 1.
3　Ie the Radio Equipment and Telecommunications Terminal Equipment Regulations 2000, SI 2000/730, reg 5(2) (see heads (1)–(5) in the text).
4　As to the meaning of 'radio equipment' see PARA 197 note 1.

5   Ie the requirements of the Radio Equipment and Telecommunications Terminal Equipment
     Regulations 2000, SI 2000/730, reg 5(3): see the text to note 17.
6   Radio Equipment and Telecommunications Terminal Equipment Regulations 2000,
     SI 2000/730, reg 5(1) (amended by SI 2003/1903). Failure to comply with this provision is an
     offence: see PARA 215.
7   Ie set out in the Radio Equipment and Telecommunications Terminal Equipment
     Regulations 2000, SI 2000/730, reg 4: see PARA 198.
8   'Harmonised standard' means a technical specification adopted by a recognised standards body
     under a mandate from the Commission in conformity with the procedures laid down in Council
     Directive (EC) 98/34 (OJ L204, 21.7.98, p 37) for the purpose of establishing a European
     requirement, compliance with which is not compulsory: Radio Equipment and
     Telecommunications Terminal Equipment Regulations 2000, SI 2000/730, reg 2(1). As to the
     meaning of 'Commission' see PARA 198 note 10.
9   Radio Equipment and Telecommunications Terminal Equipment Regulations 2000,
     SI 2000/730, reg 5(2)(a).
10   Radio Equipment and Telecommunications Terminal Equipment Regulations 2000,
     SI 2000/730, reg 5(2)(b). The reference in the text to the information provided is information
     provided in accordance with the Radio Equipment and Telecommunications Terminal
     Equipment Regulations 2000, SI 2000/730, reg 11: see PARA 200.
11   Radio Equipment and Telecommunications Terminal Equipment Regulations 2000,
     SI 2000/730, reg 5(2)(c). The conformity assessment procedures referred to in the text is one in
     accordance with reg 9. For these purposes, the appropriate conformity assessment procedure for
     apparatus must, subject to reg 9(2), be chosen from the procedures set out in Schs 2, 3, 4 and 5
     as follows:
     (1)   for telecommunications terminal equipment which does not make use of the spectrum
            allocated to terrestrial/space radio communications and for the receiving parts of radio
            equipment, the conformity assessment procedures which may be chosen from are those
            laid down in Schs 2, 4 and 5 (reg 9(1)(a));
     (2)   where radio equipment is not within the scope of head (1) and the manufacturer has
            fully applied harmonised standards, the conformity assessment procedures which may
            be chosen from are those laid down in Schs 3, 4 and 5 (reg 9(1)(b));
     (3)   where radio equipment is not within the scope of head (1) and the manufacturer has
            not applied harmonised standards or has applied them only in part, the conformity
            assessment procedures which may be chosen from are those laid down in Schs 4 and 5
            (reg 9(1)(c)).
     As an alternative to the procedures set out in reg 9(1), compliance of the apparatus with the
     essential requirements identified in:
     (a)   reg 4(2)(a) (see PARA 198 head (1)) may be demonstrated by using the procedures
            specified in Council Directive (EC) 73/23 (OJ L77, 26.3.73, p 29) (Radio Equipment
            and Telecommunications Terminal Equipment Regulations 2000, SI 2000/730,
            reg 9(2)(a)), and
     (b)   the Radio Equipment and Telecommunications Terminal Equipment Regulations 2000,
            SI 2000/730, reg 4(2)(b) (see PARA 198 head (2)) may be demonstrated by using the
            procedures specified in Council Directive (EC) 89/336 (OJ L139, 23.5.89, p 19)
            art 10(1), (2) (Radio Equipment and Telecommunications Terminal Equipment
            Regulations 2000, SI 2000/730, reg 9(2)(b)),
     where apparatus is within the scope of either of those Directives: Radio Equipment and
     Telecommunications Terminal Equipment Regulations 2000, SI 2000/730, reg 9(2).
     Any technical documentation or other information in relation to apparatus required to be
     retained under the conformity assessment procedure used must be retained by the person
     specified in that respect in that conformity assessment procedure for the appropriate period
     specified in that procedure: reg 9(3). Failure to comply with this provision is an offence: see
     PARA 215.
12   Ie the requirements of the Radio Equipment and Telecommunications Terminal Equipment
     Regulations 2000, SI 2000/730, reg 10 and Sch 7: see PARA 197. 'CE marking' has the meaning
     given in reg 10 (see PARA 202 note 1): reg 2(1).
13   Radio Equipment and Telecommunications Terminal Equipment Regulations 2000,
     SI 2000/730, reg 5(2)(d) (amended by SI 2003/1903).
14   Ie in accordance with the Radio Equipment and Telecommunications Terminal Equipment
     Regulations 2000, SI 2000/730, Sch 2, 3, 4 or 5.
15   Radio Equipment and Telecommunications Terminal Equipment Regulations 2000,
     SI 2000/730, reg 5(2)(e). 'Responsible person' means the manufacturer of apparatus or his
     authorised representative within the European Union (EU), or any other person who places the

apparatus on the market: Radio Equipment and Telecommunications Terminal Equipment Regulations 2000, SI 2000/730, reg 2(1) (definition amended by SI 2011/1043). As to references to the European Union see PARA 198 note 13.

16 Radio Equipment and Telecommunications Terminal Equipment Regulations 2000, SI 2000/730, reg 5(4) (added by SI 2003/1903).

17 Radio Equipment and Telecommunications Terminal Equipment Regulations 2000, SI 2000/730, reg 5(3) (amended by SI 2011/1043). The notification referred to in the text must be one in accordance with the Radio Equipment and Telecommunications Terminal Equipment Regulations 2000, SI 2000/730, reg 12: reg 5(3).

18 Ie the Radio Equipment and Telecommunications Terminal Equipment Regulations 2000, SI 2000/730, reg 5.

19 Radio Equipment and Telecommunications Terminal Equipment Regulations 2000, SI 2000/730, reg 6(1)(a) (amended by SI 2011/1043).

20 Radio Equipment and Telecommunications Terminal Equipment Regulations 2000, SI 2000/730, reg 6(1)(b) (amended by SI 2011/1043).

21 Radio Equipment and Telecommunications Terminal Equipment Regulations 2000, SI 2000/730, reg 6(1)(c) (amended by SI 2011/1043). 'Directive' means Council Directive (EC) 1999/5 (OJ L91, 7.4.1999, p 10) on radio equipment and telecommunications terminal equipment and the mutual recognition of their conformity: Radio Equipment and Telecommunications Terminal Equipment Regulations 2000, SI 2000/730, reg 2(1). As from 13 June 2016, Council Directive (EC) 1999/5 (OJ L91, 7.4.99, p 10) is replaced by European Parliament and Council Directive (EU) 2014/53 (OJ L153, 22.5.2014, p 62) on the harmonisation of the laws of the member states relating to the making available on the market of radio equipment: see art 50.

22 Radio Equipment and Telecommunications Terminal Equipment Regulations 2000, SI 2000/730, reg 6(1)(d).

23 Radio Equipment and Telecommunications Terminal Equipment Regulations 2000, SI 2000/730, reg 6(1).

24 Radio Equipment and Telecommunications Terminal Equipment Regulations 2000, SI 2000/730, reg 6(2) (substituted by SI 2003/1903).

25 As to the meaning of 'harmful interference' see PARA 198 note 9.

26 Radio Equipment and Telecommunications Terminal Equipment Regulations 2000, SI 2000/730, reg 6(3) (added by SI 2003/1903).

27 As to the Secretary of State see PARA 76 note 1.

28 'OFCOM' means the Office of Communications established under the Office of Communications Act 2002: Radio Equipment and Telecommunications Terminal Equipment Regulations 2000, SI 2000/730, reg 2(1) (definition added by SI 2003/3144). As to OFCOM see PARA 2 et seq.

29 Ie the Telecommunications Act 1984 Pt VI (ss 75–92) (repealed: see now the Wireless Telegraphy Act 2006).

30 Radio Equipment and Telecommunications Terminal Equipment Regulations 2000, SI 2000/730, reg 6(4) (added by SI 2003/1903; and amended by SI 2003/3144).

31 Radio Equipment and Telecommunications Terminal Equipment Regulations 2000, SI 2000/730, reg 8. The provisions referred to in the text are Council Directive (EC) 98/13 (OJ L74, 12.3.98, p 1) (repealed), the Telecommunication Terminal Equipment Regulations 1992, SI 1992/2423 (revoked), or the Telecommunications Act 1984 s 22 (repealed) or s 84 (repealed): Radio Equipment and Telecommunications Terminal Equipment Regulations 2000, SI 2000/730, reg 8.

200. Information accompanying apparatus. There must be prominently displayed on, or accompany the apparatus[1], information for the user as follows[2]:

(1) in the case of all apparatus:

    (a) its intended use[3]; and

    (b) a declaration of its conformity to the applicable essential requirements[4];

(2) in the case of radio equipment[5], sufficient information on the packaging and the instructions for use to identify the member states[6] or the geographical area within the member states where it is intended to be used; and marking on the apparatus[7] must be used when appropriate to

alert the user that restrictions or requirements for authorisation of the use of the radio equipment apply in certain member states[8];

(3) in the case of telecommunications terminal equipment[9], sufficient information to identify the interfaces[10] of public telecommunications networks[11] to which the equipment is intended to be connected[12].

1 As to the meaning of 'apparatus' see PARA 197 note 1.

2 Radio Equipment and Telecommunications Terminal Equipment Regulations 2000, SI 2000/730, reg 11.

3 Radio Equipment and Telecommunications Terminal Equipment Regulations 2000, SI 2000/730, reg 11(a).

4 Radio Equipment and Telecommunications Terminal Equipment Regulations 2000, SI 2000/730, reg 11(a). As to the essential requirements see the Radio Equipment and Telecommunications Terminal Equipment Regulations 2000, SI 2000/730, reg 4; and PARA 198.

5 As to the meaning of 'radio equipment' see PARA 197 note 1.

6 For these purposes, a reference to a member state includes a reference to an EEA state; an 'EEA state' means a state which is a contracting party to the EEA Agreement; and the 'EEA Agreement' means the Agreement on the European Economic Area signed at (Oporto, 2 May 1992; Cm 2073 (OJ L1, 3.1.94, p 3)) as adjusted by the Protocol (Brussels, 17 March 1993; Cm 2183 (OJ L1, 3.1.94, p 572)): Radio Equipment and Telecommunications Terminal Equipment Regulations 2000, SI 2000/730, reg 2(4) (added by SI 2003/1903; and amended by SI 2011/1043). As to the EEA Agreement see COMPETITION vol 18 (2009) PARA 36.

7 Ie as provided for in the Radio Equipment and Telecommunications Terminal Equipment Regulations 2000, SI 2000/730, Sch 7 para 5: see PARA 202.

8 Radio Equipment and Telecommunications Terminal Equipment Regulations 2000, SI 2000/730, reg 11(b).

9 As to the meaning of 'telecommunications terminal equipment' see PARA 197 note 1.

10 As to the meaning of 'interface' see PARA 197 note 1.

11 As to the meaning of 'public telecommunications networks' see PARA 197 note 1.

12 Radio Equipment and Telecommunications Terminal Equipment Regulations 2000, SI 2000/730, reg 11(c).

201. The right to connect. Operators of public telecommunications networks[1]:

(1) must connect or permit the connection, at an interface[2], of any telecommunications terminal equipment[3] which meets the essential standards[4] or is equipment which was placed on the market before 8 April 2001 and complied with the provisions then applicable[5];

(2) must not discontinue such connection lawfully made of any such equipment[6].

No apparatus is required under these provisions or otherwise to be, or to be permitted to be, connected or kept connected if that apparatus:

(a) met the requirements of the essential standards at the time when the connection was made but no longer does so[7];

(b) was placed on the market before 8 April 2001 and complied with the provisions then applicable[8] at the time when the connection was made but no longer does so[9];

(c) causes serious damage to a network or harmful radio interference[10] or harm to the network or its functioning (and the operator may refuse connection of that apparatus, disconnect that apparatus or withdraw that apparatus from service provided the operator at the earliest practical opportunity informs the Secretary of State[11] and OFCOM[12] of its action)[13]; or

(d) is, in case of emergency, required to be disconnected to protect the network (provided that the user may be offered, without delay and without costs, an alternative solution and that the operator immediately informs the Secretary of State and OFCOM)[14].

In any case in which a public telecommunications operator:

(i)   refuses connection of apparatus declared to be compliant with the provisions of the specified Directive[15]; or

(ii)   disconnects such apparatus[16]; or

(iii) withdraws it from service[17],

the Secretary of State and OFCOM may, if they are of the opinion that the apparatus would not cause serious damage to a network or harmful interference or harm to the network or its functioning, require the operator to provide connection, reconnect the apparatus or restore it to service (as the case may be)[18].

1   As to the meaning of 'public telecommunications network' see PARA 197 note 1.
2   As to the meaning of 'interface' see PARA 197 note 1.
3   As to the meaning of 'telecommunications terminal equipment' see PARA 197 note 1.
4   Ie the requirements of the Radio Equipment and Telecommunications Terminal Equipment Regulations 2000, SI 2000/730, reg 4: see PARA 198.
5   Radio Equipment and Telecommunications Terminal Equipment Regulations 2000, SI 2000/730, reg 7(1)(a) (reg 7 substituted by SI 2003/1903). The provisions referred to in the text are Council Directive (EC) 98/13 (OJ L74, 12.3.98, p 1) (repealed), the Telecommunication Terminal Equipment Regulations 1992, SI 1992/2423 (revoked), or the Telecommunications Act 1984 s 22 (repealed) or s 84 (repealed).
6   Radio Equipment and Telecommunications Terminal Equipment Regulations 2000, SI 2000/730, reg 7(1)(b) (as substituted: see note 5).
7   Radio Equipment and Telecommunications Terminal Equipment Regulations 2000, SI 2000/730, reg 7(2)(a) (as substituted: see note 5).
8   See note 5.
9   Radio Equipment and Telecommunications Terminal Equipment Regulations 2000, SI 2000/730, reg 7(2)(b) (as substituted: see note 5).
10 As to the meaning of 'harmful interference' see PARA 198 note 9.
11 As to the Secretary of State see PARA 76 note 1.
12 As to the meaning of 'OFCOM' see PARA 199 note 28, and as to OFCOM see PARA 2 et seq.
13 Radio Equipment and Telecommunications Terminal Equipment Regulations 2000, SI 2000/730, reg 7(2)(c) (reg 7(2) as substituted (see note 5); reg 7(2)(c), (d) amended by SI 2003/3144).
14 Radio Equipment and Telecommunications Terminal Equipment Regulations 2000, SI 2000/730, reg 7(2)(d) (as substituted and amended: see note 13).
15 Radio Equipment and Telecommunications Terminal Equipment Regulations 2000, SI 2000/730, reg 7(3)(a). 'Directive' means Council Directive (EC) 1999/5 (OJ L91, 7.4.1999, p 10) on radio equipment and telecommunications terminal equipment and the mutual recognition of their conformity: Radio Equipment and Telecommunications Terminal Equipment Regulations 2000, SI 2000/730, reg 2(1). As from 13 June 2016, Council Directive (EC) 1999/5 (OJ L91, 7.4.99, p 10) is replaced by European Parliament and Council Directive (EU) 2014/53 (OJ L153, 22.5.2014, p 62) on the harmonisation of the laws of the member states relating to the making available on the market of radio equipment: see art 50.
16 Radio Equipment and Telecommunications Terminal Equipment Regulations 2000, SI 2000/730, reg 7(3)(b).
17 Radio Equipment and Telecommunications Terminal Equipment Regulations 2000, SI 2000/730, reg 7(3)(c).
18 Radio Equipment and Telecommunications Terminal Equipment Regulations 2000, SI 2000/730, reg 7(3) (amended by SI 2003/3144).

202.   CE marking. The CE marking[1] must be accompanied by:

(1)   the identification number of all notified bodies[2] used where the conformity assessment procedure is carried out in accordance with specified procedures[3]; and

(2)   in the case of radio equipment[4], the equipment class[5] identifier where one has been assigned[6].

There must be marked on the apparatus[7]:

(a)   the name of the responsible person[8];

(b)   the type identification of the apparatus[9]; and

(c)   the batch or serial number assigned to the apparatus by the manufacturer[10].

Where apparatus is subject to other Directives concerning other aspects and which also provide for the affixing of the CE marking, the markings must indicate that the apparatus in question is also presumed to conform to the provisions of those other Directives[11]. However, should one or more of those Directives allow the manufacturer, during a transitional period, to choose which arrangements to apply, the CE marking must indicate conformity to the provisions only of those Directives applied by the manufacturer[12]. In this case, the particulars of those Directives, as published in the Official Journal, must be given in the documents, notices or instructions required by those Directives and accompanying such products[13].

The affixing of markings on apparatus which are likely to mislead third parties as to the meaning or form of the CE marking is prohibited[14], but subject to this any other marking may be affixed to apparatus provided that the visibility and legibility of the CE marking is not thereby reduced[15].

1   'CE marking' means a marking in the form set out in European Parliament and Council Directive (EC) 1999/5 (OJ L91, 7.4.99, p 10) Annex VII para 1, as set out in the Radio Equipment and Telecommunications Terminal Equipment Regulations 2000, SI 2000/730, Sch 7: reg 10(1). As from 13 June 2016, Council Directive (EC) 1999/5 (OJ L91, 7.4.99, p 10) is replaced by European Parliament and Council Directive (EU) 2014/53 (OJ L153, 22.5.2014, p 62) on the harmonisation of the laws of the member states relating to the making available on the market of radio equipment: see art 50. As to the form the CE marking has to take see the Radio Equipment and Telecommunications Terminal Equipment Regulations 2000, SI 2000/730, Sch 7 paras 1–5.

2   For the purposes of the Radio Equipment and Telecommunications Terminal Equipment Regulations 2000, SI 2000/730, a notified body is a body which has been:

    (1)   appointed as a notified body by the Secretary of State pursuant to reg 15 (see PARA 205) (reg 14(a));

    (2)   appointed by a member state other than the United Kingdom and notified to the Commission and the other member states pursuant to art 11 of the Directive (Radio Equipment and Telecommunications Terminal Equipment Regulations 2000, SI 2000/730, reg 14(b));

    (3)   recognised for the purpose of carrying out those functions by inclusion in a mutual recognition agreement relating to the Directive or a similar agreement which has been concluded between the European Union and a state other than an EEA state (Radio Equipment and Telecommunications Terminal Equipment Regulations 2000, SI 2000/730, reg 14(c) (added by SI 2003/1903).

    As to the Secretary of State see PARA 76 note 1. As to the meanings of 'member state' and 'EEA state' see PARA 200 note 6. As to the meaning of 'Commission' see PARA 198 note 10. 'Directive' means Council Directive (EC) 1999/5 (OJ L91, 7.4.1999, p 10) on radio equipment and telecommunications terminal equipment and the mutual recognition of their conformity: Radio Equipment and Telecommunications Terminal Equipment Regulations 2000, SI 2000/730, reg 2(1). As from 13 June 2016, Council Directive (EC) 1999/5 (OJ L91, 7.4.99, p 10) is replaced by European Parliament and Council Directive (EU) 2014/53 (OJ L153, 22.5.2014, p 62) on the harmonisation of the laws of the member states relating to the making available on the market of radio equipment: see art 50. As to the meaning of 'United Kingdom' see PARA 14 note 7.

3   Radio Equipment and Telecommunications Terminal Equipment Regulations 2000, SI 2000/730, reg 10(2)(a). The conformity assessment procedures referred to in the text are those in accordance with the Radio Equipment and Telecommunications Terminal Equipment Regulations 2000, SI 2000/730, Sch 3, 4 or 5.

4   As to the meaning of 'radio equipment' see PARA 197 note 1.

5   'Equipment class' means a class identifying particular types of apparatus (see note 6) which under the Directive are considered similar and those interfaces for which the apparatus is

designed; apparatus may belong to more than one equipment class: Radio Equipment and Telecommunications Terminal Equipment Regulations 2000, SI 2000/730, reg 2(1). As to the meaning of 'interface' see PARA 197 note 1.

6   Radio Equipment and Telecommunications Terminal Equipment Regulations 2000, SI 2000/730, reg 10(2)(b).

7   As to the meaning of 'apparatus' see PARA 197 note 1.

8   Radio Equipment and Telecommunications Terminal Equipment Regulations 2000, SI 2000/730, reg 10(3)(a) (substituted by SI 2003/1903).

9   Radio Equipment and Telecommunications Terminal Equipment Regulations 2000, SI 2000/730, reg 10(3)(b) (as substituted: see note 8).

10   Radio Equipment and Telecommunications Terminal Equipment Regulations 2000, SI 2000/730, reg 10(3)(c) (as substituted: see note 8).

11   Radio Equipment and Telecommunications Terminal Equipment Regulations 2000, SI 2000/730, reg 10(4).

12   Radio Equipment and Telecommunications Terminal Equipment Regulations 2000, SI 2000/730, reg 10(4).

13   Radio Equipment and Telecommunications Terminal Equipment Regulations 2000, SI 2000/730, reg 10(4).

14   Radio Equipment and Telecommunications Terminal Equipment Regulations 2000, SI 2000/730, reg 10(6).

15   Radio Equipment and Telecommunications Terminal Equipment Regulations 2000, SI 2000/730, reg 10(5).

203. Notice before placing radio equipment on the market. The responsible person[1] must, not less than four weeks before the date it is intended to place on the market in the United Kingdom[2] radio equipment[3] using frequency bands whose use is not harmonised throughout the European Union (EU)[4], give notice in writing to OFCOM[5] which contains[6]:

(1)   such information as is required by OFCOM about the radio characteristics of the equipment, in particular its frequency bands, channel spacing, type of modulation and RF power[7]; and

(2)   where appropriate, the identification number of all the notified bodies[8] used[9].

Such notice is effective in respect of all items of equipment, whether placed on the market at the same time or at different times, which are in all material respects identical to each other[10].

1   As to the meaning of 'responsible person' see PARA 199 note 15.

2   As to the meaning of 'United Kingdom' see PARA 14 note 7.

3   As to the meaning of 'radio equipment' see PARA 197 note 1.

4   As to references to the European Union see PARA 198 note 13.

5   As to the meaning of 'OFCOM' see PARA 199 note 28, and as to OFCOM see PARA 2 et seq.

6   Radio Equipment and Telecommunications Terminal Equipment Regulations 2000, SI 2000/730, reg 12(1) (amended by SI 2003/3144; and SI 2011/1043).

7   Radio Equipment and Telecommunications Terminal Equipment Regulations 2000, SI 2000/730, reg 12(1)(a) (amended by SI 2003/3144).

8   As to the meaning of 'notified body' see PARA 202 note 2.

9   Radio Equipment and Telecommunications Terminal Equipment Regulations 2000, SI 2000/730, reg 12(1)(b). Failure to comply with this provision is an offence: see PARA 210.

10   Radio Equipment and Telecommunications Terminal Equipment Regulations 2000, SI 2000/730, reg 12(2).

204. Publication of and access to information. Each public telecommunications network[1] operator must, in relation to all interfaces[2] in use by the operator at the time these provisions come into force[3], notify such interfaces to OFCOM[4] and publish within 90 days of such coming into force, in an accurate and adequate manner, the technical specifications of the interfaces in accordance with the provisions described below[5]. Before services are provided through any interface which is not published as described above, the public telecommunications network operator must:

(1) notify such interface to OFCOM[6]; and

(2) publish the technical specification of the interface in an accurate and adequate manner and in accordance with the provisions described below[7].

Where any interface to which these provisions apply is modified by the public telecommunications network operator:

(a) he must notify such modification to OFCOM and publish such modification in an accurate and adequate manner and in accordance with the provisions described below[8]; and

(b) the modification must include any change in the description of any interface which may affect the maintenance of effective interoperability of services by means of the interface[9].

Where any interface to which these provisions apply is withdrawn, the public telecommunications network operator must notify such withdrawal to OFCOM and publish such withdrawal in accordance with the provisions described below[10].

The requirements as to publication are[11] that:

(i) the interface specification published must:

(A) be in sufficient detail to permit the design of telecommunications terminal equipment[12] capable of utilising all services provided through the corresponding interface[13];

(B) detail any changes in existing interfaces[14]; and

(C) include, inter alia, all the information necessary to allow manufacturers to carry out, at their choice, the relevant tests for the essential requirements applicable to the telecommunications terminal equipment[15]; and

(ii) the interface specification must be made readily available by the public telecommunications network operator[16].

If, following any representation made to it, OFCOM concludes that any interface specification contains insufficient information for these purposes, OFCOM may direct the public telecommunications network operator to amend the interface specification in order to remedy the defect and to publish the amended interface specification in accordance with the provisions described above[17].

Nothing in these provisions requires the public telecommunications network operator to publish or send to OFCOM information which it has already published or sent to the Director General of Telecommunications[18].

1 As to the meaning of 'public telecommunications network' see PARA 197 note 1.

2 As to the meaning of 'interface' see PARA 197 note 1.

3 Ie 25 July 2003: see the Radio Equipment and Telecommunications Terminal Equipment (Amendment) Regulations 2003, SI 2003/1903.

4 As to the meaning of 'OFCOM' see PARA 199 note 28, and as to OFCOM see PARA 2 et seq.

5 Radio Equipment and Telecommunications Terminal Equipment Regulations 2000, SI 2000/730, reg 13(1) (reg 13 substituted by SI 2003/1903; Radio Equipment and Telecommunications Terminal Equipment Regulations 2000, SI 2000/730, reg 13(1), (2)(a), (3)(a), (4) amended by SI 2003/3144).

6 Radio Equipment and Telecommunications Terminal Equipment Regulations 2000, SI 2000/730, reg 13(2)(a) (as substituted and amended: see note 5).

7 Radio Equipment and Telecommunications Terminal Equipment Regulations 2000, SI 2000/730, reg 13(2)(b) (as substituted: see note 5).

8 Radio Equipment and Telecommunications Terminal Equipment Regulations 2000, SI 2000/730, reg 13(3)(a) (as substituted and amended: see note 5).
9 Radio Equipment and Telecommunications Terminal Equipment Regulations 2000, SI 2000/730, reg 13(3)(b) (as substituted: see note 5).
10 Radio Equipment and Telecommunications Terminal Equipment Regulations 2000, SI 2000/730, reg 13(4) (as substituted and amended: see note 5).
11 Radio Equipment and Telecommunications Terminal Equipment Regulations 2000, SI 2000/730, reg 13(5) (as substituted: see note 5).
12 As to the meaning of 'telecommunications terminal equipment' see PARA 197 note 1.
13 Radio Equipment and Telecommunications Terminal Equipment Regulations 2000, SI 2000/730, reg 13(5)(a)(i) (as substituted: see note 5).
14 Radio Equipment and Telecommunications Terminal Equipment Regulations 2000, SI 2000/730, reg 13(5)(a)(ii) (as substituted: see note 5).
15 Radio Equipment and Telecommunications Terminal Equipment Regulations 2000, SI 2000/730, reg 13(5)(a)(iii) (as substituted: see note 5).
16 Radio Equipment and Telecommunications Terminal Equipment Regulations 2000, SI 2000/730, reg 13(5)(b) (as substituted: see note 5).
17 Radio Equipment and Telecommunications Terminal Equipment Regulations 2000, SI 2000/730, reg 13(6) (reg 13 as substituted (see note 5); reg 13(6) further substituted by SI 2003/3144).
18 Radio Equipment and Telecommunications Terminal Equipment Regulations 2000, SI 2000/730, regs 2(1), 13(7) (reg 13(7) as substituted (see note 5); and amended by SI 2003/3144). As to the Director General of Telecommunications see the Telecommunications Act 1984 s 1 (prospectively repealed); and PARA 14 note 2.

205. Notified bodies appointed by the Secretary of State. The Secretary of State[1], applying the specified criteria[2] and such other criteria as he thinks fit, may from time to time appoint such persons as he thinks fit to be notified bodies[3]. An appointment:

(1) may relate to such descriptions of apparatus[4] as the Secretary of State may from time to time determine[5];

(2) may be made subject to such conditions as the Secretary of State may from time to time determine, and such conditions may include conditions which are to apply upon or following termination of the appointment[6];

(3) must, without prejudice to the generality of head (2) above and subject as mentioned below[7], require the appointed body to carry out the procedures and specific tasks for which it has been appointed, including (where so provided as part of those procedures) surveillance to ensure that the responsible person[8] duly fulfils the obligations arising out of the relevant conformity assessment procedure[9];

(4) must be terminated upon 90 days' notice in writing given to the Secretary of State by the notified body[10]; and

(5) may be terminated if it appears to the Secretary of State that any of the conditions of the appointment are not complied with[11].

Subject to heads (4) and (5) above, an appointment under these provisions may be for the time being or for such period as may be specified in the appointment[12]. If for any reason the appointment of a notified body is terminated under these provisions, the Secretary of State may:

(a) give such directions (either to the body the subject of the termination or to another notified body) for the purpose of making such arrangements for the determination of outstanding applications as he considers appropriate[13]; and

(b) without prejudice to the generality of the foregoing, authorise another notified body to take over its functions in respect of such cases as he may specify[14].

A notified body appointed by the Secretary of State may charge such fees in connection with, or incidental to, the performance of its functions as it may determine; but such fees must not exceed the sum of the following:

(i) the costs incurred or to be incurred by the notified body in performing the relevant function[15]; and

(ii) an amount on account of profit which is reasonable in the circumstances having regard to the character and extent of the work done or to be done by the body on behalf of the applicant and the commercial rate normally charged on account of profit for that work or similar work[16].

A notified body may require the payment of fees or a reasonable estimate thereof in advance of carrying out the work requested by the applicant[17].

1 As to the Secretary of State see PARA 76 note 1.
2 See the Radio Equipment and Telecommunications Terminal Equipment Regulations 2000, SI 2000/730, Sch 6.
3 Radio Equipment and Telecommunications Terminal Equipment Regulations 2000, SI 2000/730, reg 15(1). As to the meaning of 'notified body' see PARA 202 note 2.
4 As to the meaning of 'apparatus' see PARA 197 note 1.
5 Radio Equipment and Telecommunications Terminal Equipment Regulations 2000, SI 2000/730, reg 15(2)(a).
6 Radio Equipment and Telecommunications Terminal Equipment Regulations 2000, SI 2000/730, reg 15(2)(b).
7 Ie subject to the Radio Equipment and Telecommunications Terminal Equipment Regulations 2000, SI 2000/730, reg 15(4) (see note 9).
8 As to the meaning of 'responsible person' see PARA 199 note 15.
9 Radio Equipment and Telecommunications Terminal Equipment Regulations 2000, SI 2000/730, reg 15(2)(c). As to the conformity assessment procedure see PARA 199 note 11. A notified body appointed by the Secretary of State is not required to carry out the functions referred to in reg 15(2)(c) if:
   (1) the documents submitted to it in relation to carrying out such functions are not in English or another language acceptable to that body (reg 15(4)(a)); or
   (2) the responsible person has not submitted with his application the amount of the fee which the body requires to be submitted with the application pursuant to reg 16 (see the text to notes 15–17) (reg 15(4)(b)).
10 Radio Equipment and Telecommunications Terminal Equipment Regulations 2000, SI 2000/730, reg 15(2)(d).
11 Radio Equipment and Telecommunications Terminal Equipment Regulations 2000, SI 2000/730, reg 15(2)(e).
12 Radio Equipment and Telecommunications Terminal Equipment Regulations 2000, SI 2000/730, reg 15(3).
13 Radio Equipment and Telecommunications Terminal Equipment Regulations 2000, SI 2000/730, reg 15(5)(a).
14 Radio Equipment and Telecommunications Terminal Equipment Regulations 2000, SI 2000/730, reg 15(5)(b).
15 Radio Equipment and Telecommunications Terminal Equipment Regulations 2000, SI 2000/730, reg 16(1)(a).
16 Radio Equipment and Telecommunications Terminal Equipment Regulations 2000, SI 2000/730, reg 16(1)(b).
17 Radio Equipment and Telecommunications Terminal Equipment Regulations 2000, SI 2000/730, reg 16(2).

206. Enforcement provisions for non compliance of the Radio Equipment and Telecommunications Terminal Equipment Regulations 2000. Detailed enforcement provisions are provided by the Radio Equipment and Telecommunications Terminal Equipment Regulations 2000[1].

Except in the case of apparatus[2] which, in the opinion of an enforcement authority[3], is liable to endanger the safety of persons and (where appropriate) of property, where an enforcement authority has reasonable grounds for suspecting that the CE marking[4] has been affixed to apparatus in relation to which any provision of the regulations has not been complied with, it may serve notice in writing on:

(1)   the manufacturer of the apparatus or his authorised representative established within the European Union (EU)[5]; or

(2)   in a case where neither the manufacturer of the apparatus nor his authorised representative established within the EU has placed the apparatus on the market, the person who places it on the market in the United Kingdom[6],

and no other action pursuant to the regulations may be taken in respect of apparatus until such notice has been given and the person to whom it is given has failed to comply with its requirements[7]. Notwithstanding this, however, for the purpose of ascertaining whether or not the CE marking has been correctly affixed, action may be taken pursuant to the powers of search and seizure[8].

A notice which is given under these provisions must:

(a)   state that the enforcement authority suspects that the CE marking has not been correctly affixed to the apparatus[9];

(b)   specify the respect in which it is so suspected and give particulars thereof[10];

(c)   require the person to whom the notice is given:

(i)   to secure that any apparatus to which the notice relates conforms as regards the provisions concerning the correct affixation of the CE marking within such period as may be specified in the notice[11]; or

(ii)   to provide evidence within that period, to the satisfaction of the enforcement authority, that the CE marking has been correctly affixed[12]; and

(d)   warn that person that if the non-conformity continues after, or if satisfactory evidence has not been provided within, the period specified in the notice, further action may be taken under the regulations in respect of that apparatus or apparatus of the same type placed on the market by that person[13].

Provisions of the Communications Act 2003[14] apply for the purposes of enforcement of the provisions in the regulations relating to the right to connect[15] and to publication of and access to information[16].

An enforcement authority must, where action has been taken by it to prohibit or restrict the supply or taking into service (whether under the regulations or otherwise) of any relevant apparatus, forthwith inform the Secretary of State of the action taken, and the reasons for it, with a view to this information being passed by him to the Commission[17].

1   See the Radio Equipment and Telecommunications Terminal Equipment Regulations 2000, SI 2000/730, reg 18(1), Sch 9 (reg 18(1) amended by SI 2003/1903; and the Radio Equipment and Telecommunications Terminal Equipment Regulations 2000, SI 2000/730, Sch 9 substituted by SI 2003/3144). These provisions are subject to the Radio Equipment and Telecommunications Terminal Equipment Regulations 2000, SI 2000/730, reg 18(2) (see text and notes 5–7) and reg 18(5) (see text and notes 14–16).

2   As to the meaning of 'apparatus' see PARA 197 note 1.

3   'Enforcement authority' has the meaning given in the Radio Equipment and Telecommunications Terminal Equipment Regulations 2000, SI 2000/730, Sch 9 paras 1, 2: reg 2(1). It is the duty of the following authorities to enforce the regulations in Great Britain:

(1)   OFCOM, in so far as action taken to enforce a regulation relates to the protection and management of the radio spectrum (Sch 9 para 1(a) (as substituted: see note 1)); and

(2)   a local weights and measures authority within its area (Sch 9 para 1(b)) (as so substituted).

The Secretary of State may also enforce the regulations: Sch 9 para 2 (as so substituted). 'Local weights and measures authority' has the meaning given by the Weights and Measures Act 1985 s 69 (see WEIGHTS AND MEASURES vol 99 (2012) PARA 519): Radio Equipment and Telecommunications Terminal Equipment Regulations 2000, SI 2000/730, Sch 9 para 3 (as so substituted). As to the meaning of 'OFCOM' see PARA 199 note 28, and as to OFCOM see PARA 2 et seq. As to the Secretary of State see PARA 76 note 1. As to the meaning of 'Great Britain' see PARA 14 note 7.

Where an enforcement authority has reasonable grounds for suspecting that any regulation has been contravened in relation to any apparatus, the authority may serve a suspension notice: see the Radio Equipment and Telecommunications Terminal Equipment Regulations 2000, SI 2000/730, Sch 9 paras 5, 6. For the purpose of ascertaining whether any regulation has been contravened in relation to any apparatus, an enforcement authority or an officer of the authority has power to make any purchase of such apparatus, inspect any apparatus and enter any premises other than premises occupied only as a person's residence and seize and detain any apparatus or records required as evidence in proceedings for an offence in respect of the contravention: see Sch 9 paras 7–10, 12, 13. An enforcement authority may apply for an order for the forfeiture of any apparatus on the grounds that there has been a contravention: see Sch 9 para 21. As to provisions relating to recovery of expenses of enforcement and disclosure of information obtained in relation to imported apparatus by the Commissioners for Her Majesty's Revenue and Customs: see Sch 9 paras 14, 15. As to the Commissioners for Her Majesty's Revenue and Customs see INCOME TAXATION vol 58 (2014) PARA 33. As to provisions relating to the service of documents, savings for certain privileges and commencement of proceedings see Sch 9 paras 16–18.

4   As to the CE marking see PARA 202.

5   Radio Equipment and Telecommunications Terminal Equipment Regulations 2000, SI 2000/730, reg 18(2)(a) (reg 18(2)(a), (b) amended by SI 2011/1043). As to references to the European Union see PARA 198 note 13.

6   Radio Equipment and Telecommunications Terminal Equipment Regulations 2000, SI 2000/730, reg 18(2)(b) (as amended: see note 5).

7   Radio Equipment and Telecommunications Terminal Equipment Regulations 2000, SI 2000/730, reg 18(2).

8   Radio Equipment and Telecommunications Terminal Equipment Regulations 2000, SI 2000/730, reg 18(3) (amended by SI 2003/3144). The text refers to powers of search and seizure under the Radio Equipment and Telecommunications Terminal Equipment Regulations 2000, SI 2000/730, Sch 9 para 8 (see note 3): reg 18(3) (as so amended).

9   Radio Equipment and Telecommunications Terminal Equipment Regulations 2000, SI 2000/730, reg 18(4)(a).

10   Radio Equipment and Telecommunications Terminal Equipment Regulations 2000, SI 2000/730, reg 18(4)(b).

11   Radio Equipment and Telecommunications Terminal Equipment Regulations 2000, SI 2000/730, reg 18(4)(c)(i).

12   Radio Equipment and Telecommunications Terminal Equipment Regulations 2000, SI 2000/730, reg 18(4)(c)(ii).

13   Radio Equipment and Telecommunications Terminal Equipment Regulations 2000, SI 2000/730, reg 18(4)(d).

14   Ie the Communications Act 2003 ss 94–97, 98(1)–(3), which apply for the purposes of the enforcement of the Radio Equipment and Telecommunications Terminal Equipment Regulations 2000, SI 2000/730, regs 7, 13, as if the requirements in those regulations were conditions set under the Communications Act 2003 s 45. See PARA 115 et seq.

15   Ie the Radio Equipment and Telecommunications Terminal Equipment Regulations 2000, SI 2000/730, reg 7: see PARA 201.

16   Radio Equipment and Telecommunications Terminal Equipment Regulations 2000, SI 2000/730, reg 18(5) (amended by SI 2003/1903; and SI 2003/3144). The reference in the text is to publication and access to information under the Radio Equipment and Telecommunications Terminal Equipment Regulations 2000, SI 2000/730, reg 13 (see PARA 204).

17   Radio Equipment and Telecommunications Terminal Equipment Regulations 2000, SI 2000/730, reg 18A (added by SI 2003/3144). As to the meaning of 'Commission' see PARA 198 note 10.

(8) OFFENCES

(i) Offences relating to Networks and Services

207.   Dishonestly obtaining electronic communications services.   A person who:

(1)   dishonestly obtains an electronic communications service[1]; and

(2)   does so with intent to avoid payment of a charge applicable to the provision of that service[2],

is guilty of an offence[3].

A person guilty of such an offence is liable:

(a)   on summary conviction, to imprisonment for a term not exceeding six months or to a fine not exceeding the statutory maximum[4], or to both[5];

(b)   on conviction on indictment, to imprisonment for a term not exceeding five years or to a fine, or to both[6].

A person is guilty of an offence if he has in his possession or under his control anything that may be used for obtaining an electronic communications service, or in connection with obtaining such a service[7], and he intends:

(i)   to use the thing to obtain an electronic communications service dishonestly[8];

(ii)   to use the thing for a purpose connected with the dishonest obtaining of such a service[9];

(iii)   dishonestly to allow the thing to be used to obtain such a service[10]; or

(iv)   to allow the thing to be used for a purpose connected with the dishonest obtaining of such a service[11].

A person is guilty of an offence if he supplies or offers to supply anything which may be used for the purpose of obtaining an electronic communications service, or for a purpose connected with the obtaining of such a service, and he knows or believes that the intentions in relation to that thing of the person to whom it is supplied or offered fall within heads (i)–(iv) above[12].

A person guilty of an offence under these provisions[13] is liable:

(A)   on summary conviction, to imprisonment for a term not exceeding six months or to a fine not exceeding the statutory maximum, or to both[14]; and

(B)   on conviction on indictment, to imprisonment for a term not exceeding five years or to a fine, or to both[15].

1   Communications Act 2003 s 125(1)(a). As to the meaning of 'electronic communications service' see PARA 53.
2   Communications Act 2003 s 125(1)(b).
3   Communications Act 2003 s 125(1). It is not an offence under s 125 to obtain a service mentioned in the Copyright, Designs and Patents Act 1988 s 297(1) (dishonestly obtaining a broadcasting service provided from a place in the United Kingdom: see COPYRIGHT vol 23 (2013) PARA 1038): Communications Act 2003 s 125(2) (amended by SI 2003/2498).
4   As to the statutory maximum see SENTENCING AND DISPOSITION OF OFFENDERS vol 92 (2010) PARA 140.
5   Communications Act 2003 s 125(3)(a).
6   Communications Act 2003 s 125(3)(b).
7   Communications Act 2003 s 126(1).
8   Communications Act 2003 s 126(3)(a). An intention does not fall within s 126(3) if it relates exclusively to the obtaining of a service mentioned in the Copyright, Designs and Patents Act 1988 s 297(1): Communications Act 2003 s 126(4).
    For the purposes of s 126, references, in the case of a thing used for recording data, to the use of that thing include references to the use of data recorded by it: s 126(6).
9   Communications Act 2003 s 126(3)(b). See note 8.

10 Communications Act 2003 s 126(3)(c). See note 8.
11 Communications Act 2003 s 126(3)(d). See note 8.
12 Communications Act 2003 s 126(2).
13 Ie the Communications Act 2003 s 126.
14 Communications Act 2003 s 126(5)(a).
15 Communications Act 2003 s 126(5)(b).

208.   Improper use of public electronic communications network. A person is guilty of an offence if he:

(1)   sends, by means of a public electronic communications network[1], a message or other matter that is grossly offensive[2] or of an indecent, obscene or menacing character[3]; or

(2)   causes any such message or matter to be so sent[4].

A person is guilty of an offence if, for the purpose of causing annoyance, inconvenience or needless anxiety to another, he:

(a)   sends, by means of a public electronic communications network, a message that he knows to be false[5];

(b)   causes such a message to be sent[6]; or

(c)   persistently makes use of a public electronic communications network[7].

A person guilty of an offence under these provisions is liable, on summary conviction, to imprisonment for a term not exceeding six months[8] or to a fine not exceeding level 5 on the standard scale[9], or to both[10].

1 As to the meaning of 'public electronic communications network' see PARA 98 note 6.

2 It is for the justices to determine as a question of fact whether a message is grossly offensive for these purposes, applying the standards of an open and just multi-racial society (ie via the application of reasonably enlightened, but not perfectionist, contemporary standards); and the words must be judged in the context of the message and all relevant circumstances: *DPP v Collins* [2006] UKHL 40, [2006] 4 All ER 602, [2006] 1 WLR 2223. Whether a message falls into the category of grossly offensive depends on whether it is couched in terms liable to cause gross offence to those to whom it relates: *DPP v Collins*. For an offence to be committed the defendant has to intend his words to be grossly offensive to those to whom they relate, or be aware that they might be taken to be so: *DPP v Collins*.

3 Communications Act 2003 s 127(1)(a). The offence is complete when the message is sent; and an offence is committed when a message which would be found by a reasonable person to be grossly offensive is sent, regardless of whether a person hears the message: *DPP v Collins* [2006] UKHL 40, [2006] 4 All ER 602, [2006] 1 WLR 2223. See *Chambers v DPP* [2012] EWHC 2157 (Admin), [2013] 1 All ER 149, DC (ostensibly threatening message not of menacing character when considered in proper context). As to the criminal liability of company directors, managers, secretaries, etc see the Communications Act 2003 s 404; and PARA 216. As to threatening telephone calls see CRIMINAL LAW vol 25 (2010) PARA 115; and as to harassment by telephone calls see CRIMINAL LAW vol 25 (2010) PARA 163.

    The provisions of s 127(1), (2) do not apply to anything done in the course of providing a programme service (within the meaning of the Broadcasting Act 1990: see BROADCASTING vol 4 (2011) PARA 507 note 11): Communications Act 2003 s 127(4).

4 Communications Act 2003 s 127(1)(b). See note 3.

5 Communications Act 2003 s 127(2)(a). As to bomb hoaxes see CRIMINAL LAW vol 26 (2010) PARA 791. An offence committed under s 127(2) is a penalty offence for the purposes of the Criminal Justice and Police Act 2001 Pt 1 Ch 1 (ss 1–11) (on the spot penalties for disorderly behaviour): see s 1; and CRIMINAL LAW vol 26 (2010) PARA 541. Until a day to be appointed, it is also an offence in respect of which a sexual offences prevention order may be made: see the Sexual Offences Act 2003 ss 104–113 (prospectively repealed by the Anti-Social Behaviour, Crime and Policing Act 2014 s 185); and SENTENCING AND DISPOSITION OF OFFENDERS vol 92 (2010) PARAS 360–367, 600–603. See note 3.

6 Communications Act 2003 s 127(2)(b). See notes 3, 5.

7 Communications Act 2003 s 127(2)(c). See notes 3, 5.

8 As from a day to be appointed this maximum term of imprisonment is increased to a maximum term of 51 weeks (see the Criminal Justice Act 2003 s 281(4), (5), (7) (not yet in force)),

although this does not affect the penalty for any offence committed before that day (s 281(6)(b) (not yet in force)). At the date at which this volume states the law no such day had been appointed.

9   As to the standard scale see SENTENCING AND DISPOSITION OF OFFENDERS vol 92 (2010) PARA 142.
10   Communications Act 2003 s 127(3).

209.   Summary proceedings under the Telecommunications Act 1984.

Proceedings for any offence under the Telecommunications Act 1984 which is punishable on summary conviction may be commenced at any time within 12 months after the commission of the offence[1]. This does not apply, however, for the purposes of an offence under any provision of the Enterprise Act 2002 as applied by the Telecommunications Act 1984[2].

1   Telecommunications Act 1984 s 103(1) (renumbered by the Enterprise Act 2002 s 278(1), Sch 25 para 13(1), (10)(a)).
2   The provisions of the Enterprise Act 2002 referred to above is as applied by virtue of the Telecommunications Act 1984 s 13B (repealed): s 103(2) (added by the Enterprise Act 2002 Sch 25 para 13(1), (10)(b)).

(ii) Interception of Communications

210.   Unlawful interception of communications.

It is an offence for a person[1] intentionally and without lawful authority[2] to intercept, at any place in the United Kingdom[3], any communication[4] in the course of its transmission by means of a public telecommunication system[5]. It is also an offence for a person intentionally and without lawful authority[6], and otherwise than in circumstances in which his conduct is excluded from criminal liability[7], to intercept, at any place in the United Kingdom, any communication in the course of its transmission by means of a private telecommunication system[8].

Any interception of a communication which is carried out at any place in the United Kingdom by, or with the express or implied consent of, a person having the right to control the operation or the use of a private telecommunication system is actionable at the suit or instance of the sender or recipient, or intended recipient, of the communication if it is without lawful authority and is either[9]:

(1)   an interception of that communication in the course of its transmission by means of that private system[10]; or

(2)   an interception of that communication in the course of its transmission, by means of a public telecommunication system, to or from apparatus[11] comprised in that private telecommunication system[12].

Where the United Kingdom is a party to an international agreement which:

(a)   relates to the provision of mutual assistance in connection with, or in the form of, the interception of communications[13];

(b)   requires the issue of a warrant, order or equivalent instrument in cases in which assistance is given[14]; and

(c)   is designated for these purposes by an order made by the Secretary of State[15],

it is the duty of the Secretary of State to secure that no request for assistance in accordance with the agreement is made on behalf of a person in the United Kingdom to the competent authorities of a country or territory outside the United Kingdom except with lawful authority[16].

A person who is guilty of an offence[17] is liable, on conviction on indictment, to imprisonment for a term not exceeding two years or to a fine, or to both; and, on summary conviction, to a fine not exceeding the statutory maximum[18].

No proceedings for an offence may be instituted in England and Wales, except by or with the consent of the Director of Public Prosecutions[19].

The Interception of Communications Commissioner[20] may serve a monetary penalty notice on a person if the Commissioner:

(i) considers that the person:

    (A) has without lawful authority intercepted, at any place in the United Kingdom, any communication in the course of its transmission by means of a public telecommunication system[21];

    (B) was not, at the time of the interception, making an attempt to act in accordance with an interception warrant which might, in the opinion of the Commissioner, explain the interception concerned[22], and

(ii) does not consider that the person has committed an offence[23].

1 'Person' includes any organisation and any association or combination of persons: Regulation of Investigatory Powers Act 2000 s 81(1).

2 Conduct has lawful authority if, and only if:

    (1) it is authorised by or under the Regulation of Investigatory Powers Act 2000 s 3 or s 4 (s 1(5)(a));

    (2) it takes place in accordance with a warrant under s 5 (an 'interception warrant') (s 1(5)(b)); or

    (3) it is in exercise, in relation to any stored communication, of any statutory power that is exercised (apart from s 1) for the purpose of obtaining information or of taking possession of any document or other property (s 1(5)(c)).

Conduct, whether or not prohibited by s 1, which has lawful authority for the purposes of s 1 by virtue of head (1) or head (2) is to be taken to be lawful for all other purposes: s 1(5). 'Document' includes a map, plan, design, drawing, picture or other image: s 81(1). 'Statutory', in relation to any power or duty, means conferred or imposed by or under any enactment or subordinate legislation: s 81(1). 'Enactment' includes an enactment passed after 28 July 2000: s 81(1). As to lawful authority see further POLICE AND INVESTIGATORY POWERS vol 84A (2013) PARA 657 et seq. See *R (on the application of NTL Group Ltd) v Ipswich Crown Court* [2002] EWHC 1585 (Admin), [2003] QB 131, [2003] 1 Cr App Rep 225, which considered the Regulation of Investigatory Powers Act 2000 s 1(5)(c) (head (3) above).

    Interception of a communication by a person may be lawful if the communication is one which, is both a communication sent by a person who has consented to the interception and a communication the intended recipient of which has so consented: see s 3; and POLICE AND INVESTIGATORY POWERS vol 84A (2013) PARA 658. Interception may also be authorised under s 4 in specified circumstances: see POLICE AND INVESTIGATORY POWERS vol 84A (2013) PARA 659.

3 As to the meaning of 'United Kingdom' see PARA 14 note 7. As to when the interception of a communication takes place in the United Kingdom see the Regulation of Investigatory Powers Act 2000 s 2(4); and POLICE AND INVESTIGATORY POWERS vol 84A (2013) PARA 657.

4 As to the meaning of 'communication' for these purposes see the Regulation of Investigatory Powers Act 2000 s 81(1); and POLICE AND INVESTIGATORY POWERS vol 84A (2013) PARA 656. References to the interception of a communication do not include references to the interception of any communication broadcast for general reception: s 2(3).

5 Regulation of Investigatory Powers Act 2000 s 1(1). As to the meaning of 'public telecommunication system' for these purposes see s 2(1); and POLICE AND INVESTIGATORY POWERS vol 84A (2013) PARA 656. A telephone conversation tape recorded by one of the parties to the conversation but not made available to a third party is not an interception: *R v Hardy* [2002] EWCA Crim 3012, [2003] 1 Cr App Rep 494. As to offences of interception and disclosure of messages under the Wireless Telegraphy Act 2006 see BROADCASTING vol 4 (2011) PARA 576.

6 Regulation of Investigatory Powers Act 2000 s 1(2)(a).

7 Ie excluded by the Regulation of Investigatory Powers Act 2000 s 1(6): s 1(2)(b). The circumstances in which a person makes an interception of a communication in the course of its transmission by means of a private telecommunication system are such that his conduct is excluded from criminal liability under s 2(2) if he is a person with a right to control the operation or the use of the system, or he has the express or implied consent of such a person to make the interception: s 1(6). In s 1(6) 'control' does not mean merely the unrestricted physical

ability to use and operate the system, but the power to authorise and forbid others' use of it: *R v Stanford* [2006] EWCA Crim 258, [2006] 1 WLR 1554, [2006] 2 Cr App Rep 91.

8   Regulation of Investigatory Powers Act 2000 s 1(2)(b). As to the meaning of 'private telecommunication system' for these purposes see s 2(1); and POLICE AND INVESTIGATORY POWERS vol 84A (2013) PARA 656 note 14.

9   Regulation of Investigatory Powers Act 2000 s 1(3).

10   Regulation of Investigatory Powers Act 2000 s 1(3)(a).

11   For these purposes, 'apparatus' includes any equipment, machinery or device and any wire or cable: Regulation of Investigatory Powers Act 2000 s 81(1).

12   Regulation of Investigatory Powers Act 2000 s 1(3)(b).

13   Regulation of Investigatory Powers Act 2000 s 1(4)(a).

14   Regulation of Investigatory Powers Act 2000 s 1(4)(b).

15   Regulation of Investigatory Powers Act 2000 s 1(4)(c). The Convention on Mutual Assistance in Criminal Matters between the Member States of the European Union (Brussels, 29 May 2000; Misc 7 (2001); Cmd 5229) is hereby designated for the purposes of the Regulation of Investigatory Powers Act 2000 s 1(4): see the Regulation of Investigatory Powers (Designation of an International Agreement) Order 2004, SI 2004/158, art 2.

16   Regulation of Investigatory Powers Act 2000 s 1(4).

17   Ie under the Regulation of Investigatory Powers Act 2000 s 1(1) (see the text and notes 1–5) or s 1(2) (see the text and notes 6–7).

18   Regulation of Investigatory Powers Act 2000 s 1(7). As to the statutory maximum see SENTENCING AND DISPOSITION OF OFFENDERS vol 92 (2010) PARA 140.

19   Regulation of Investigatory Powers Act 2000 s 1(8). As to the Director of Public Prosecutions see CRIMINAL PROCEDURE vol 27 (2010) PARAS 23, 33 et seq.

20   As to the Interception of Communications Commissioner see POLICE AND INVESTIGATORY POWERS vol 84A (2013) PARA 645 et seq.

21   Regulation of Investigatory Powers Act 2000 s 1(1A)(a)(i) (s 1(1A), (1B) added by SI 2011/1340). See further the Regulation of Investigatory Powers Act 2000 Sch A1; and POLICE AND INVESTIGATORY POWERS vol 84A (2013) PARA 661 et seq.

22   Regulation of Investigatory Powers Act 2000 s 1(1A)(a)(ii) (as added: see note 21).

23   Regulation of Investigatory Powers Act 2000 s 1(1A)(b). The offence referred to in the text is one committed under s 1(1): see text and notes 1–5.

(iii) Re-programming of Mobile Telephones

211. Offences in relation to the re-programming of mobile telephones. A person commits an offence if he:

(1)   changes a unique device identifier[1];

(2)   interferes with the operation of a unique device identifier[2];

(3)   offers or agrees to change, or interfere with the operation of, a unique device identifier[3]; or

(4)   offers or agrees to arrange for another person to change, or interfere with the operation of, a unique device identifier[4],

except where he is the manufacturer of the device, or he does such an act with the written consent of the manufacturer of the device[5].

A person commits an offence if he:

(a)   has in his custody or under his control anything which may be used for the purpose of changing or interfering with the operation of a unique device identifier, and he intends to use the thing unlawfully for that purpose, or to allow it to be used unlawfully for that purpose[6];

(b)   supplies anything which may be used for the purpose of changing or interfering with the operation of a unique device identifier, and he knows or believes that the person to whom the thing is supplied intends to use it unlawfully for that purpose, or to allow it to be used unlawfully for that purpose[7];

(c)   offers to supply anything which may be used for the purpose of changing or interfering with the operation of a unique device identifier, and knows or believes that the person to whom the thing is offered intends if it is supplied to him to use it unlawfully for that purpose, or to allow it to be used unlawfully for that purpose[8].

1   Mobile Telephones (Re-programming) Act 2002 s 1(1)(a) (amended by the Violent Crime Reduction Act 2006 s 62). 'Unique device identifier' means an electronic equipment identifier which is unique to a mobile wireless communications device: Mobile Telephones (Re-programming) Act 2002 ss 1(2), 2(4).
2   Mobile Telephones (Re-programming) Act 2002 s 1(1)(b).
3   Mobile Telephones (Re-programming) Act 2002 s 1(1)(c) (s 1(1)(c), (d) added by the Violent Crime Reduction Act 2006 s 62).
4   Mobile Telephones (Re-programming) Act 2002 s 1(1)(d) (as added: see note 3).
5   Mobile Telephones (Re-programming) Act 2002 s 1(3). A person guilty of an offence under the Mobile Telephones (Re-programming) Act 2002 s 1 is liable:
    (1)   on summary conviction, to imprisonment for a term not exceeding six months or to a fine not exceeding the statutory maximum, or to both (s 1(4)(a)); or
    (2)   on conviction on indictment, to imprisonment for a term not exceeding five years or to a fine, or to both (s 1(4)(b)).
    As to the statutory maximum see SENTENCING AND DISPOSITION OF OFFENDERS vol 92 (2010) PARA 140.
6   Mobile Telephones (Re-programming) Act 2002 s 2(1). A thing is used by a person unlawfully for a purpose if in using it for that purpose a person commits an offence under s 1 (see the text and notes 1–5): s 2(5).
    A person guilty of an offence under s 2 is liable:
    (1)   on summary conviction, to imprisonment for a term not exceeding six months or to a fine not exceeding the statutory maximum, or to both (s 2(6)(a)); or
    (2)   on conviction on indictment, to imprisonment for a term not exceeding five years or to a fine, or to both (s 2(6)(b)).
7   Mobile Telephones (Re-programming) Act 2002 s 2(2). As to the penalty for such an offence see note 6.
8   Mobile Telephones (Re-programming) Act 2002 s 2(3). As to the penalty for such an offence see note 6.

(iv) Submarine Telegraphs

212. Offences relating to submarine cables. The Submarine Telegraph Act 1885 gave effect to the Convention for the Protection of Submarine Cables of 1884[1]. It is concerned with the protection of submarine cables from the operation of vessels other than those repairing or laying the cables, and with the protection of other vessels from the operations of the owners of the cables[2]. The Submarine Telegraph Act 1885 extends (so far as such extension is consistent with the tenor of the Act) to the whole of Her Majesty's dominions, and to all places within the jurisdiction of the Admiral of England and to all places within Her Majesty's jurisdiction[3].

A person must not unlawfully and wilfully, or by culpable negligence, break or injure any submarine cable under the high seas in such manner as might interrupt or obstruct in whole or in part telegraphic or telephonic communication, or any pipe-line[4] or high-voltage power cable under the high seas[5]; and any person who does so or attempts to do so commits an offence[6]. However, it is a defence for a person to show:

(1)   that he acted with the object of preserving the life or limb of himself or any other person, or of protecting the vessel to which he belongs or any other vessel, and that he took all reasonable precautions to avoid injury to a cable or pipe-line[7]; or

(2)   that in the bona fide attempt to repair one such cable or pipe-line injury has been done to another or it has been broken[8].

The owner of a cable who, on laying or repairing his own cable, breaks or injures another cable must bear the cost of repairing the breakage or injury[9].

Where an offence under the Submarine Telegraph Act 1885 has been committed by means of a vessel[10] or any boat belonging to a vessel, the master[11] of the vessel is deemed to have been in charge of and navigating such vessel or boat, and is liable to be punished accordingly, until some other person is shown to have been in charge of and navigating it[12].

The provisions of the Submarine Telegraph Act 1885 are in addition to and not in derogation of any other common law or statutory provision, or the law of a British possession, for the protection of submarine cables, and nothing in those provisions prevents a person being liable under any such statutory provision or law or otherwise to any criminal proceedings other than are provided for by that legislation, so that no person is to be punished twice for the same offence; and nothing in that legislation, nor in any proceedings with respect to any matter, is to exempt a person from any liability in any action or suit with reference to the same matter so that no person is to be required to pay compensation twice in respect of the same injury[13].

The provisions of the merchant shipping legislation relating to legal proceedings[14] are applied by the Submarine Telegraph Act 1885, and the offences may be tried and fines recovered accordingly[15].

Owners of ships or vessels who can prove that they have lost an anchor, a net or other fishing gear in order to avoid injuring a submarine cable or pipe-line are entitled to compensation[16] from the owner of the cable[17].

1   Submarine Telegraph Act 1885 s 2. The English text of the Convention for the Protection of Submarine Cables (Paris, 14 March 1884; 75 BFSP 356; C 5910) is set out in the Submarine Telegraph Act 1885 s 2, Schedule. The Convention for the Protection of Submarine Cables (Paris, 14 March 1884; 75 BFSP 356; C 5910) applies outside territorial waters to all legally established submarine cables landed on the territories, colonies or possessions of one or more of the high contracting parties: art 1. As to the development of submarine cables see PARA 48.

2   See the Submarine Telegraph Act 1885 s 3; and the Convention for the Protection of Submarine Cables (Paris, 14 March 1884; 75 BFSP 356; C 5910) arts 2, 4–7.

3   Submarine Telegraph Act 1885 s 11. As to Her Majesty's dominions see COMMONWEALTH vol 13 (2009) PARA 707. As to certain colonial possessions at the date of the Convention for the Protection of Submarine Cables (Paris, 14 March 1884; 75 BFSP 356; C 5910) which were excepted from its provisions unless they gave notice of accession see the additional article to the Convention.

4   Ie including a pipe-line under the territorial sea adjacent to the United Kingdom: Continental Shelf Act 1964 s 8(1A) (added by the Petroleum Act 1998 Sch 4 para 2(4); amended by the Energy Act 2004 s 103(1)(b); and the Marine and Coastal Access Act 2009 Sch 4 para 1). As to the meaning of 'United Kingdom' see PARA 14 note 7. As to the territorial sea see WATER AND WATERWAYS vol 100 (2009) PARA 31.

5   Submarine Telegraph Act 1885 s 3(1); Continental Shelf Act 1964 s 8(1) (amended by the Energy Act 2004 ss 103(1)(a), 197(9), Sch 23 Pt 1). See also the Convention for the Protection of Submarine Cables (Paris, 14 March 1884; 75 BFSP 356; C 5910) art 2, which by virtue of the Submarine Telegraph Act 1885 s 2 has the force of law (see the text to note 1).

6   Submarine Telegraph Act 1885 s 3(2). Any person guilty of such an offence is liable on conviction summarily or on indictment:
    (1)   if he acted wilfully, to imprisonment for a term not exceeding five years or a fine, or both (s 3(2)(a) amended by virtue of the Criminal Justice Act 1948 s 1(1), (2); the Criminal Law Act 1977 s 32(1); and the Magistrates' Courts Act 1980 ss 17(1), 32(2), Sch 1 para 11));
    (2)   if he acted by culpable negligence, to imprisonment for a term not exceeding three months or a fine (not exceeding the prescribed sum if tried summarily), or both (Submarine Telegraph Act 1885 s 3(2)(b) (as so amended)).
    As to the prescribed sum see SENTENCING AND DISPOSITION OF OFFENDERS vol 92 (2010) PARA 141.

Any person who within or (being a Commonwealth citizen) without Her Majesty's dominions in any manner procures, counsels, aids, abets or is accessory to an offence under the Submarine Telegraph Act 1885 s 3 is guilty and punishable as if he were a principal: s 3(5) (amended by the British Nationality Act 1981 s 52(6), Sch 7).

7 Submarine Telegraph Act 1885 s 3(3); Continental Shelf Act 1964 s 8(1).

8 Submarine Telegraph Act 1885 s 3(4); Continental Shelf Act 1964 s 8(1). This defence does not, however, apply so as to exempt a person from any liability under the Submarine Telegraph Act 1885 or otherwise to pay the cost of repairing the breakage or injury: s 3(4).

9 Convention for the Protection of Submarine Cables (Paris, 14 March 1884; 75 BFSP 356; C 5910) art 4. This is expressed to be without prejudice to the application, if need be, of art 2 (see note 5).

10 'Vessel' means every description of vessel used in navigation in whatever way it is propelled; and any reference to a vessel includes a reference to a boat belonging to such vessel: Submarine Telegraph Act 1885 s 12.

11 'Master' includes every person having command or charge of a vessel: Submarine Telegraph Act 1885 s 12.

12 Submarine Telegraph Act 1885 s 9.

13 Submarine Telegraph Act 1885 s 10.

14 Ie the Merchant Shipping Act 1995 Pt XII (ss 274–291): see SHIPPING AND MARITIME LAW vol 94 (2008) PARA 1100 et seq.

15 Submarine Telegraph Act 1885 s 7 (amended by the Merchant Shipping Act 1995 s 314(2), Sch 13 para 7(b)).

16 The amount of compensation is not necessarily limited to the bare cost of the equipment lost; it is compensation for the sacrifice of the equipment but not to pay further the damages resulting from the sacrifice: see *Agincourt Steamship Co Ltd v Eastern Extension, Australasia and China Telegraph Co Ltd* [1907] 2 KB 305, CA.

17 Convention for the Protection of Submarine Cables (Paris, 14 March 1884; 75 BFSP 356; C 5910) art 7; Continental Shelf Act 1964 s 8(1). In order to establish a claim to such compensation in respect of a submarine cable, a statement, supported by the evidence of the crew, should wherever possible be drawn up immediately after the occurrence; and the master must, within 24 hours after his return to or next putting into port, make a declaration to the proper authorities, which must communicate the information to the consular authorities of the country to which the owner of the cable belongs: Convention for the Protection of Submarine Cables (Paris, 14 March 1884; 75 BFSP 356; C 5910) art 7. Such a statement is admissible in any proceedings as prima facie evidence of the facts or matters stated in it: Submarine Telegraph Act 1885 s 8(1). See also PARA 214 note 6.

213. Prevention of collisions at sea. Vessels[1] engaged in laying or repairing submarine cables must complete such operations as quickly as possible and must conform to agreed regulations as to signals, with a view to preventing collisions at sea. When a ship engaged in repairing a cable exhibits such signals other vessels must:

(1) withdraw to or keep beyond a distance of a nautical mile from the ship so as not to interfere with its operations, and keep fishing gear and nets at the same distance[2];

(2) keep beyond a distance of a quarter of a nautical mile from buoys showing the position of a cable which is being laid or is out of order or broken, and keep fishing gear and nets at the same distance[3].

Safety regulations under the Merchant Shipping Act 1995[4] have been extended to authorise regulations for carrying into effect certain articles of the Convention for the Protection of Submarine Cables[5] and any contravention of such regulations may be punished accordingly; and, as regards sea fishing vessels, enforcement of the regulations is under the sea fisheries legislation[6].

1 As to the meaning of 'vessel' see PARA 212 note 10.

2 Convention for the Protection of Submarine Cables (Paris, 14 March 1884; 75 BFSP 356; C 5910) art 5, which, however, permits fishing vessels 24 hours in which to obey such signals. The Convention is set out in the Submarine Telegraph Act 1885 s 2, Schedule: see PARA 212 note 1.

3   Convention for the Protection of Submarine Cables (Paris, 14 March 1884; 75 BFSP 356; C 5910) art 6.
4   Ie made under the Merchant Shipping Act 1995 s 85: see SHIPPING AND MARITIME LAW vol 94 (2008) PARA 591.
5   Convention for the Protection of Submarine Cables (Paris, 14 March 1884; 75 BFSP 356; C 5910) arts 5, 6.
6   Submarine Telegraph Act 1885 s 5(1) (amended by the Merchant Shipping Act 1995 s 314(2), Sch 13 para 7(a)). As to sea fishing vessels see the Sea Fisheries Act 1968 s 8(6); and FISHERIES AND AQUACULTURE vol 51 (2013) PARA 278.

214. Enforcement of Convention for the Protection of Submarine Cables. Offences against the Convention for the Protection of Submarine Cables[1] may be verified by all means of proof allowed by the legislation of the country of the court[2]. When the officers commanding the warships of, or ships specially commissioned by, one of the high contracting parties[3] have reason to believe that an offence against the Convention has been committed by a vessel other than a warship, they may demand from the captain or master the production of the vessel's official documents proving its nationality, and must indorse on them the fact that they have been exhibited[4]. Regardless of the nationality of the vessel, those officers may then prepare formal statements of the facts in the form and language used in the country to which the officer making them belongs, and they may be considered, in the country in which they are adduced, as evidence in accordance with the laws of that country[5]. Such a statement is admissible in any proceedings, civil or criminal, as prima facie evidence of the facts and matters stated in it[6].

1   Ie the Convention for the Protection of Submarine Cables (Paris, 14 March 1884; 75 BFSP 356; C 5910). The Convention is set out in the Submarine Telegraph Act 1885 s 2, Schedule: see PARA 212 note 1.
2   Convention for the Protection of Submarine Cables (Paris, 14 March 1884; 75 BFSP 356; C 5910) art 10. The tribunals competent to take cognisance of infractions of the Convention are those of the country to which the vessel on board which the offence was committed belongs: art 8. Prosecutions for infractions provided against by arts 2, 5, 6 are to be instituted by the state of that country, or in its name: art 9.
3   See PARA 212 note 1.
4   Convention for the Protection of Submarine Cables (Paris, 14 March 1884; 75 BFSP 356; C 5910) art 10. Authority to exercise these powers is given by the Submarine Telegraph Act 1885 s 6(1). If any person obstructs such an officer in the exercise or performance of these powers or refuses or neglects to comply with his lawful demand or direction, he is liable on summary conviction to a fine not exceeding level 3 on the standard scale or imprisonment for a term not exceeding two months: s 6(2) (amended by the Criminal Justice Act 1982 ss 38(1), (6), (8), 46(1), (3), (4)). As to the standard scale see SENTENCING AND DISPOSITION OF OFFENDERS vol 92 (2010) PARA 142.
5   Convention for the Protection of Submarine Cables (Paris, 14 March 1884; 75 BFSP 356; C 5910) art 10. The accused and witnesses are entitled to add in their own language any explanations they consider useful and the declarations are to be signed: art 10.
6   Submarine Telegraph Act 1885 s 8(1). If evidence contained in such a statement (or one drawn up under the Convention for the Protection of Submarine Cables (Paris, 14 March 1884; 75 BFSP 356; C 5910) art 7: see PARA 212) was taken on oath in the presence of the person charged in the evidence and that person had an opportunity of cross-examination or reply, the officer drawing up the statement may certify those facts: Submarine Telegraph Act 1885 s 8(2). Any such document purporting to be signed by an officer authorised to act under the for the Protection of Submarine Cables (Paris, 14 March 1884; 75 BFSP 356; C 5910) is admissible in evidence without proof of his signature, and if purporting to be signed by someone else is deemed to have been so signed until the contrary is proved: Submarine Telegraph Act 1885 s 8(3).

(v) Offences relating to Telecommunications Apparatus

215. Offences and proceedings under the Radio Equipment and Telecommunications Terminal Equipment Regulations 2000. Any person[1] who:

(1)   contravenes or fails to comply with the requirements of the general duty relating to the placing on the market and putting into service of apparatus[2], or with the requirement to give notice before doing so[3]; or

(2)   fails to supply or retain a copy of the appropriate documentation under the conformity assessment procedure[4] as required[5],

is guilty of an offence[6].

However, no offence is committed merely by reason of failure to comply with the requirement to give notice before placing apparatus on the market[7] in respect of equipment which uses frequency bands the use of which by that equipment is consistent with the United Kingdom Plan for Frequency Authorisation[8].

In proceedings against any person for certain offences under the Radio Equipment and Telecommunications Terminal Equipment Regulations 2000[9], it is a defence for that person to show that he took all reasonable steps and exercised all due diligence to avoid committing the offence[10]. Where in proceedings against any person, the defence provided above involves an allegation that the commission of the offence was due:

(a)   to the act or default of another[11]; or

(b)   to reliance on information given by another[12],

that person is not, without the leave of the court, entitled to rely on the defence unless, not less than seven clear days before the hearing of the proceedings, he has served a notice on the person bringing the proceedings[13].

Such a notice must give such information identifying or assisting in the identification of the person who committed the act or default or gave the information as is in the possession of the person serving the notice at the time he serves it[14]. A person is not entitled to rely on the defence provided above by reason of his reliance on information supplied by another, unless he shows that it was reasonable in all the circumstances for him to have relied on the information, having regard in particular to the steps which he took, and those which might reasonably have been taken, for the purpose of verifying the information, and to whether he had any reason to disbelieve the information[15].

Where the commission by any person of a specified offence[16] is due to the act or default committed by some other person in the course of any business of his, the other person is guilty of the offence and may be proceeded against and punished whether or not proceedings are taken against the first-mentioned person[17].

Where a body corporate is guilty of an offence[18] in respect of any act or default which is shown to have been committed with the consent or connivance of, or to be attributable to any neglect on the part of, any director, manager, secretary or other similar officer of the body corporate or any person who was purporting to act in any such capacity he, as well as the body corporate, is guilty of that offence and is liable to be proceeded against and punished accordingly[19].

1   As to the meaning of 'person' see PARA 14 note 2.

2   Ie under the Radio Equipment and Telecommunications Terminal Equipment Regulations 2000, SI 2000/730, reg 5(1): see PARA 199. As to the meaning of 'apparatus' see PARA 197 note 1. As to those regulations generally see PARA 197 et seq.

3   Radio Equipment and Telecommunications Terminal Equipment Regulations 2000, SI 2000/730, reg 19(1)(a) (reg 19(1) renumbered; reg 19(1)(a) amended by SI 2003/1903). The reference in the text to the requirement to give notice is a requirement under the Radio Equipment and Telecommunications Terminal Equipment Regulations 2000, SI 2000/730, reg 12 (see PARA 203): reg 19(1)(a) (as renumbered). A person guilty of an offence under reg 19(1)(a) is liable on summary conviction to imprisonment for a term not exceeding three months or to a fine not exceeding level 5 on the standard scale, or to both: see reg 20(1). As to the standard scale see SENTENCING AND DISPOSITION OF OFFENDERS vol 92 (2010) PARA 142.

4   Ie as required by the Radio Equipment and Telecommunications Terminal Equipment Regulations 2000, SI 2000/730, reg 9(3): see PARA 199 note 11.
5   Radio Equipment and Telecommunications Terminal Equipment Regulations 2000, SI 2000/730, reg 19(1)(b) (as renumbered and amended: see note 3). A person guilty of an offence under reg 19(1)(b) is liable on summary conviction to a fine not exceeding level 5 on the standard scale: see reg 20(2).
6   Radio Equipment and Telecommunications Terminal Equipment Regulations 2000, SI 2000/730, reg 19(1) (as renumbered: see note 3).
7   Ie under the Radio Equipment and Telecommunications Terminal Equipment Regulations 2000, SI 2000/730, reg 12: see PARA 203.
8   Radio Equipment and Telecommunications Terminal Equipment Regulations 2000, SI 2000/730, reg 19(2) (added by SI 2003/1903). The Plan is published under the Communications Act 2003 s 153: see BROADCASTING vol 4 (2011) PARA 538.
9   Ie under the Radio Equipment and Telecommunications Terminal Equipment Regulations 2000, SI 2000/730, reg 19(1) (see the text and notes 1–6) or Sch 9 para 11(1) (obstruction of authorised officer).
10 Radio Equipment and Telecommunications Terminal Equipment Regulations 2000, SI 2000/730, reg 21(1) (amended by SI 2003/3144).
11 Radio Equipment and Telecommunications Terminal Equipment Regulations 2000, SI 2000/730, reg 21(2)(a).
12 Radio Equipment and Telecommunications Terminal Equipment Regulations 2000, SI 2000/730, reg 21(2)(b).
13 Radio Equipment and Telecommunications Terminal Equipment Regulations 2000, SI 2000/730, reg 21(2).
14 Radio Equipment and Telecommunications Terminal Equipment Regulations 2000, SI 2000/730, reg 21(3).
15 Radio Equipment and Telecommunications Terminal Equipment Regulations 2000, SI 2000/730, reg 21(4).
16 Ie under the Radio Equipment and Telecommunications Terminal Equipment Regulations 2000, SI 2000/730, reg 19(1) (see the text and notes 1–6) or Sch 9 para 11(1) (obstruction of authorised officer).
17 Radio Equipment and Telecommunications Terminal Equipment Regulations 2000, SI 2000/730, reg 22(1) (amended by SI 2003/3144).
18 Ie under the Radio Equipment and Telecommunications Terminal Equipment Regulations 2000, SI 2000/730 including where the body corporate is guilty by virtue of reg 22(1) (see the text and notes 16–17).
19 Radio Equipment and Telecommunications Terminal Equipment Regulations 2000, SI 2000/730, reg 22(2). Where the affairs of a body corporate are managed by its members, reg 22(2) applies in relation to the acts and defaults of a member in connection with his functions of management as if he were a director of the body corporate: reg 22(3).

(vi) Criminal Liability of Directors, etc

216. Criminal liability of company directors, managers, secretaries, etc.
Where an offence under any enactment of the Communications Act 2003, the Telecommunications Act 1984 or Part 3 of the Postal Services At 2011[1], is committed by a body corporate and is proved to have been committed with the consent or connivance of, or to be attributable to any neglect on the part of, a director[2], manager, secretary or other similar officer of the body corporate, or a person who was purporting to act in any such capacity, he (as well as the body corporate) is guilty of that offence and is liable to be proceeded against and punished accordingly[3].

Similarly, where an offence under the Wireless Telegraphy Act 2006 is committed by a body corporate and is proved to have been committed with the consent or connivance of, or to be attributable to any neglect on the part of a director[4], manager, secretary or other similar officer of the body corporate, or a person who was purporting to act in any such capacity, he (as well as the body corporate) is guilty of that offence and is liable to be proceeded against and punished accordingly[5].

1 See the Communications Act 2003 s 404(4) (amended by the Wireless Telegraphy Act 2006 Sch 9 Pt 1; the Enterprise and Regulatory Reform Act 2013 Sch 21 para 2; and the Postal Services Act 2011 Sch 12 para 67).
2 'Director', in relation to a body corporate whose affairs are managed by its members, means a member of the body corporate: Communications Act 2003 s 404(3).
3 Communications Act 2003 s 404(1).
4 'Director', in relation to a body corporate whose affairs are managed by its members, means a member of the body corporate: Wireless Telegraphy Act 2006 s 110(3).
5 Wireless Telegraphy Act 2006 s 110(1).

(9) DISPUTES AND APPEALS

217. Reference of disputes to OFCOM. The following provisions[1] apply in the case of a dispute relating to the provision of network access[2] if it is:

(1) a dispute between different communications providers[3];
(2) a dispute between a communications provider and a person who makes associated facilities[4] available[5];
(3) a dispute between different persons making such facilities available[6];
(4) a dispute between a communications provider and a person who is identified, or is a member of a class identified, in a condition imposed[7] on the communications provider[8]; or
(5) a dispute relating to entitlements to network access that the communications provider is required to provide to that person by or under that condition[9].

The provisions also apply in the case of any other dispute if:

(a) it relates to rights or obligations[10] conferred or imposed by or under a condition set[11], or any of the enactments relating to the management of the radio spectrum[12];
(b) it is a dispute between different communications providers[13]; and
(c) it is not an excluded dispute[14].

Any one or more of the parties to the dispute may refer it to OFCOM[15]. A reference made under these provisions is to be made in such manner as OFCOM may require[16].

OFCOM may invite any one or more of the parties to a dispute falling within heads (1) to (3)[17] to refer the dispute[18] to OFCOM[19].

1 Ie the Communications Act 2003 s 185.
2 'Network access' has the same meaning in the Communications Act 2003 Pt 2 Ch 3 (ss 185–197) as in Pt 2 Ch 1 (ss 32–151) (see PARA 98 note 5): s 197(1). For the purposes of s 185, the disputes that relate to the provision of network access include disputes as to the terms or conditions on which it is or may be provided in a particular case: s 185(8)(a).
3 Communications Act 2003 s 185(1)(a). As to the meaning of 'communications provider' see PARA 17 note 23.
4 As to the meaning of 'associated facilities' see PARA 53.
5 Communications Act 2003 s 185(1)(b).
6 Communications Act 2003 s 185(1)(c).
7 Ie under the Communications Act 2003 s 45: see PARA 87.
8 Communications Act 2003 s 185(1A)(a) (s 185(1A) added by SI 2011/1210).
9 Communications Act 2003 s 185(1A)(b) (as added: see note 8).
10 For the purposes of the Communications Act 2003 s 185, the disputes that relate to an obligation include disputes as to the terms or conditions on which any transaction is to be entered into for the purpose of complying with that obligation: s 185(8)(b).
11 Ie under the Communications Act 2003 s 45: see PARA 87.
12 Communications Act 2003 s 185(2)(a) (amended by SI 2011/1210). As to the meaning of 'enactments relating to the management of the radio spectrum' see PARA 17 note 4.
13 Communications Act 2003 s 185(2)(b).

14 Communications Act 2003 s 185(2)(c). A dispute is an excluded dispute for the purposes of s 185(2) if it is about obligations imposed on a communications provider by SMP apparatus conditions: s 185(7) (amended by SI 2011/1210). As to the meaning of 'SMP apparatus condition' see PARA 87 note 8.
15 Communications Act 2003 s 185(3). As to the meaning of 'OFCOM' see PARA 14 note 1; and as to OFCOM see PARA 2 et seq.
16 Communications Act 2003 s 185(4). The way in which a requirement under s 185(4) is to be imposed, or may be withdrawn or modified, is by a notice published in such manner as OFCOM considers appropriate for bringing the requirement, withdrawal or modification to the attention of the persons who, in its opinion, are likely to be affected by it: s 185(5). Requirements imposed under s 185(4) may make different provision for different cases: s 185(6).
17 Ie the Communications Act 2003 s 185(1): see text and notes 1–6.
18 Ie under the Communications Act 2003 s 185(3): see text and note 15.
19 Communications Act 2003 s 185A (added by SI 2011/1210).

218.   Action by OFCOM on dispute reference. The following provisions[1] apply where a dispute is referred to OFCOM[2]. OFCOM must decide whether or not it is appropriate for it to handle the dispute[3].

In relation to a dispute relating to the provision of network access that is a dispute between different communications providers, a dispute between a communications provider and a person who makes associated facilities available or a dispute between different persons making such facilities available[4], OFCOM may in particular take into account its priorities and available resources in considering whether it is appropriate for it to handle the dispute[5].

In relation to:

(1)   a dispute relating to the provision of network access that is between a communications provider and a person who is identified, or is a member of a class identified, in a condition imposed on the communications provider; or a dispute relating to entitlements to network access that the communications provider is required to provide to that person by or under that condition[6]; or

(2)   any other dispute between different communications providers that relates to rights or obligations conferred or imposed by or under a condition set, or any of the enactments relating to the management of the radio spectrum and is not an excluded dispute[7];

unless it considers:

(a)   that there are alternative means available for resolving the dispute[8];

(b)   that a resolution of the dispute by those means would be consistent with the European Union (EU) requirements[9]; and

(c)   that a prompt and satisfactory resolution of the dispute is likely if those alternative means are used for resolving it, its decision must be a decision that it is appropriate for it to handle the dispute[10].

As soon as reasonably practicable after OFCOM has decided:

(i)   that it is appropriate for it to handle the dispute[11]; or

(ii)   that it is not[12],

it must inform each of the parties to the dispute of its decision and of its reasons for it[13].

The notification must state the date of the decision[14]. In relation to a dispute falling within heads (1) or (2)[15], where OFCOM decides that it is not appropriate for it to handle the dispute; but the dispute is not resolved by other means before the end of the four months after the day of OFCOM's decision, the dispute may be referred back to OFCOM by one or more of the parties to the dispute[16].

1   Ie the Communications Act 2003 s 186.
2   Communications Act 2003 s 186(1). The reference in the text to a dispute is a dispute referred to OFCOM under and in accordance with the Communications Act 2003 s 185 (see PARA 212): s 186(1). As to the meaning of 'OFCOM' see PARA 14 note 1; and as to OFCOM see PARA 2 et seq.
3   Communications Act 2003 s 186(2).
4   Ie a dispute falling within s 185(1): see PARA 217.
5   Communications Act 2003 s 186(2A) (added by SI 2011/1210).
6   Ie a dispute falling within s 185(1A): see PARA 217.
7   Ie a dispute falling within s 185(2): see PARA 217.
8   Communications Act 2003 s 186(3)(a) (s 186(3) amended SI 2011/1210).
9   Communications Act 2003 s 186(3)(b) (as amended: see note 8). The reference in the text to EU requirements are to the requirements set out in the Communications Act 2003 s 4: see PARA 17.
10   Communications Act 2003 s 186(3).
11   Communications Act 2003 s 186(4)(a).
12   Communications Act 2003 s 186(4)(b).
13   Communications Act 2003 s 186(4).
14   Communications Act 2003 s 186(5).
15   Ie a dispute falling within s 185(1A) or s 185(2): see PARA 217.
16   Communications Act 2003 s 186(6) (amended by SI 2011/1210).

219.   Legal proceedings about referred disputes.   Where a dispute is referred or referred back to OFCOM[1], the reference is not to prevent:

(1)   the person making it[2];

(2)   another party to the dispute[3];

(3)   OFCOM[4]; or

(4)   any other person[5],

from bringing, or continuing, any legal proceedings[6] with respect to any of the matters under dispute[7].

Nor is the reference or reference back to OFCOM[8] of a dispute to prevent OFCOM from:

(a)   giving a notification in respect of something that it has reasonable grounds for believing to be a contravention of any obligation imposed by or under any enactment[9];

(b)   exercising any of its other powers under any enactment in relation to a contravention of such an obligation[10]; or

(c)   taking any other step in preparation for or with a view to doing anything mentioned in head (a) or head (b) above[11].

If, in any legal proceedings with respect to a matter to which a dispute relates, the court orders the handling of the dispute by OFCOM to be stayed:

(i)   OFCOM is required to make a determination for resolving the dispute only if the stay is lifted or expires[12]; and

(ii)   the period during which the stay is in force must be disregarded in determining the period within which OFCOM is required to make such a determination[13].

1   Ie under the Communications Act 2003 Pt 2 Ch 3 (ss 185–197): see PARA 217 et seq. As to the meaning of 'OFCOM' see PARA 14 note 1; and as to OFCOM see PARA 2 et seq.
2   Communications Act 2003 s 187(1)(a).
3   Communications Act 2003 s 187(1)(b).
4   Communications Act 2003 s 187(1)(c).
5   Communications Act 2003 s 187(1)(d).
6   For the purposes of the Communications Act 2003 s 187, 'legal proceedings' means civil or criminal proceedings in or before a court: s 187(5).
7   Communications Act 2003 s 187(1). Section 187(1) is subject to s 190(8) (see PARA 217) and to any agreement to the contrary binding the parties to the dispute: s 187(4).
8   Ie under the Communications Act 2003 Pt 2 Ch 3.

9   Communications Act 2003 s 187(2)(a).
10 Communications Act 2003 s 187(2)(b).
11 Communications Act 2003 s 187(2)(c).
12 Communications Act 2003 s 187(3)(a).
13 Communications Act 2003 s 187(3)(b).

220.   Procedure for resolving disputes. The following provisions[1] apply where:

(1)   OFCOM has decided[2] that it is appropriate for it to handle a dispute[3]; or

(2)   a dispute is referred back to OFCOM[4].

OFCOM must:

(a)   consider the dispute[5]; and

(b)   make a determination for resolving it[6].

The procedure for the consideration and determination of the dispute is to be the procedure that OFCOM considers appropriate[7]. In the case of a dispute referred back to OFCOM[8], that procedure may involve allowing the continuation of a procedure that has already been begun for resolving the dispute by alternative means[9].

Except in exceptional circumstances[10], OFCOM must make its determination no more than four months after the following day, namely:

(i)   in a case falling within head (1) above, the day of the decision by OFCOM that it is appropriate for it to handle the dispute[11]; and

(ii)   in a case falling within head (2) above, the day on which the dispute is referred back to it[12].

Where it is practicable for OFCOM to make its determination before the end of the four month period, it must make it as soon in that period as practicable[13]. OFCOM must:

(A)   send a copy of its determination, together with a full statement of its reasons for it, to every party to the dispute[14]; and

(B)   publish so much of its determination as (having regard, in particular, to the need to preserve commercial confidentiality) it considers it appropriate to publish[15].

The publication of information under these provisions must be in such manner as OFCOM considers appropriate for bringing it to the attention, to the extent that OFCOM considers appropriate, of members of the public[16].

1   Ie the Communications Act 2003 s 188.
2   Ie under the Communications Act 2003 s 186(2): see PARA 218. As to the meaning of 'OFCOM' see PARA 14 note 1; and as to OFCOM see PARA 2 et seq.
3   Communications Act 2003 s 188(1)(a).
4   Ie under the Communications Act 2003 s 186(6) (see PARA 218): s 188(1).
5   Communications Act 2003 s 188(2)(a).
6   Communications Act 2003 s 188(2)(b).
7   Communications Act 2003 s 188(3).
8   Ie under the Communications Act 2003 s 186(6): see PARA 218.
9   Communications Act 2003 s 188(4).
10 And subject to the Communications Act 2003 s 187(3): see PARA 219.
11 Communications Act 2003 s 188(5)(a).
12 Communications Act 2003 s 188(5)(b).
13 Communications Act 2003 s 188(6).
14 Communications Act 2003 s 188(7)(a).
15 Communications Act 2003 s 188(7)(b).
16 Communications Act 2003 s 188(8).

221.   Disputes involving other member states.   The following provisions[1] apply where it appears to OFCOM[2] that a dispute referred or referred back to it under Chapter 3 of Part 2 of the Communications Act 2003[3] relates partly to a matter falling within the jurisdiction of the regulatory authorities of another member state[4]. A dispute relates to matters falling within the jurisdiction of the regulatory authorities of another member state to the extent that:

(1)   it relates to the carrying on of activities by one or both of the parties to the dispute in more than one member state or to activities carried on by different parties to the dispute in different member states[5]; and

(2)   the activities to which the dispute relates, so far as they are carried on in another member state, are carried on in the member state for which those authorities are the regulatory authorities[6].

Before taking any steps under Chapter 3 of Part 2 of the Communications Act 2003 in relation to the reference or the dispute, OFCOM:

(a)   must co-ordinate their efforts with the other regulatory authorities within whose jurisdiction the matter falls[7];

(b)   may consult BEREC[8] in order to bring about a consistent resolution of the dispute[9]; and

(c)   may request BEREC to adopt an opinion as to the action to be taken to resolve the dispute[10].

It is the duty of OFCOM to secure that steps taken in relation to the reference or dispute (whether taken by it or by the other regulatory authorities) are, so far as practicable, agreed between OFCOM and those authorities[11]. Where an opinion is received from BEREC in relation to the reference or dispute, it is the duty of OFCOM to secure that steps taken in relation to the reference or dispute take account of the opinion (whether the opinion was requested by OFCOM or by the other regulatory authorities)[12].

1   Ie the Communications Act 2003 s 189.
2   As to the meaning of 'OFCOM' see PARA 14 note 1; and as to OFCOM see PARA 2 et seq.
3   Ie the Communications Act 2003 Pt 2 Ch 3 (ss 185–197) other than a dispute falling within s 185(1).
4   Communications Act 2003 s 189(1). References in Pt 2 Ch 3, in relation to a dispute, to the regulatory authorities of other member states are references to such of the authorities of the other member states as have been notified under the European Parliament and Council Directive (EC) 2002/21 (OJ L108, 24.4.2002, p 33) on a common regulatory framework for electronic communications networks and services ('the Framework Directive') to the European Commission as the regulatory authorities of those states for the purposes of the matters to which the dispute relates: Communications Act 2003 s 197(2). As to the European Commission see EUROPEAN UNION vol 47A (2014) PARAS 48, 49. For the purposes of s 197, 'the Framework Directive' has the same meaning as in the Communications Act 2003 Pt 2 Ch 1 (see PARA 97 note 21): s 197(3). 'Other member state' means a member state other than the United Kingdom: s 405(1). As to the meaning of 'United Kingdom' see PARA 14 note 7.
5   Communications Act 2003 s 189(2)(a). For the purposes of s 189(2), the activities that are carried on in a member state include anything done by means of an electronic communications network, or part of such a network, which is situated in that member state: s 189(3).
6   Communications Act 2003 s 189(2)(b). See note 5.
7   Communications Act 2003 s 189(4)(a) (s 189(4) amended by SI 2011/1210).
8   As to BEREC see PARA 58.
9   Communications Act 2003 s 189(4)(b) (as amended: see note 7).
10 Communications Act 2003 s 189(4)(c) (as amended: see note 7).
11 Communications Act 2003 s 189(5). Accordingly, s 188 (see PARA 220) is to have effect in relation to the reference as if the period for making a determination which is specified in s 188(5) were such period (if any) as may be agreed between OFCOM and the other regulatory authorities within whose jurisdiction the matter falls: s 189(6). OFCOM must:
    (1)   ensure, so far as practicable, that a period agreed under s 189(6) is long enough for

BEREC to provide an opinion, if one has been requested by OFCOM or by the other regulatory authorities (s 189(7)(a) (s 189(7), (8) added by SI 2011/1210)); and

(2)   agree to any necessary extension of the period if an opinion is requested from BEREC (by OFCOM or by the other regulatory authorities) after the period has been agreed (Communications Act 2003 s 189(7)(b) (as so added)).

Section 189(7) does not apply if the dispute in question has resulted in, or creates an immediate risk of:

(a)   a serious threat to the safety of the public, to public health or to national security (s 189(8)(a) (as so added));

(b)   serious economic or operational problems for persons who are communications providers or persons who make associated facilities available (s 189(8)(b) (as so added)); or

(c)   serious economic or operational problems for persons who make use of electronic communications networks, electronic communications services or associated facilities, or for other users of the radio spectrum (s 189(8)(c) (as so added)).

12 Communications Act 2003 s 189(5A) (added by SI 2011/1210).

222.   Resolution of referred disputes. Where OFCOM[1] makes a determination for resolving a dispute referred to it under Chapter 3 of Part 2 of the Communications Act 2003[2], its only powers are those conferred by the following provisions[3]. Its main power (except in the case of a dispute relating to rights and obligations conferred or imposed by or under the enactments relating to the management of the radio spectrum[4]) is to do one or more of the following:

(1)   to make a declaration setting out the rights and obligations of the parties to the dispute[5];

(2)   to give a direction fixing the terms or conditions of transactions between the parties to the dispute[6];

(3)   to give a direction imposing an obligation, enforceable by the parties to the dispute, to enter into a transaction between themselves on the terms and conditions fixed by OFCOM[7]; and

(4)   for the purpose of giving effect to a determination by OFCOM of the proper amount of a charge in respect of which amounts have been paid by one of the parties of the dispute to the other, to give a direction, enforceable by the party to whom the sums are to be paid, requiring the payment of sums by way of adjustment of an underpayment or overpayment[8].

Its main power in the excepted case is to make a declaration setting out the rights and obligations of the parties to the dispute[9].

In relation to a dispute relating to the provision of network access that is a dispute between different communications providers, a dispute between a communications provider and a person who makes associated facilities available or a dispute between different persons making such facilities available[10], OFCOM must exercise its powers[11] in the way that seems to them most appropriate for the purpose of securing efficiency, sustainable competition, efficient investment and innovation and the greatest possible benefit for the end-users of public electronic communications services[12].

Nothing in these provisions prevents OFCOM from exercising the following powers in consequence of its consideration under Chapter 3 of Part 2 of the Communications Act 2003 of any dispute:

(a)   its powers under Chapter 1 of Part 2 of the Communications Act 2003[13] to set, modify or revoke general conditions, universal service conditions, access related conditions, privileged supplier conditions or SMP conditions[14];

(b)   its powers to vary, modify or revoke wireless telegraphy licences or grants of recognised spectrum access[15];

(c)   its power under the Wireless Telegraphy Act 2006 to make, amend or revoke regulations[16].

In the case of a dispute referred back to OFCOM[17]:

(i)   OFCOM may, in making its determination, take account of decisions already made by others in the course of an attempt to resolve the dispute by alternative means[18]; and

(ii)   the determination made by OFCOM may include provision ratifying decisions so made[19].

Where OFCOM makes a determination for resolving a dispute, it may require a party to the dispute:

(A)   to make payments to another party to the dispute in respect of costs and expenses incurred by that other party in consequence of the reference of the dispute to OFCOM, or in connection with it[20]; and

(B)   to make payments to OFCOM in respect of costs and expenses incurred by it in dealing with the dispute[21].

A determination made by OFCOM for resolving a dispute referred or referred back to it under Chapter 3 of Part 2 of the Communications Act 2003 binds all the parties to the dispute[22].

1   As to the meaning of 'OFCOM' see PARA 14 note 1; and as to OFCOM see PARA 2 et seq.
2   Ie the Communications Act 2003 Pt 2 Ch 3 (ss 185–197).
3   Communications Act 2003 s 190(1). The powers referred to in the text are those conferred by s 190: s 190(1).
4   As to the meaning of 'enactments relating to the management of the radio spectrum' see PARA 17 note 4.
5   Communications Act 2003 s 190(2)(a).
6   Communications Act 2003 s 190(2)(b).
7   Communications Act 2003 s 190(2)(c).
8   Communications Act 2003 s 190(2)(d).
9   Communications Act 2003 s 190(3).
10   Ie a dispute falling within the Communications Act 2003 s 185(1).
11   Ie under the Communications Act 2003 s 190(2): see text and notes 1–8.
12   Communications Act 2003 s 190(2A) (added by SI 2011/1210).
13   Ie the Communications Act 2003 Pt 2 Ch 1 (ss 32–151). See PARA 87 et seq.
14   Communications Act 2003 s 190(4)(a). As to the meaning of 'general condition' see PARA 87 note 4. As to the meaning of 'universal service condition' see PARA 87 note 5. As to the meaning of 'access-related condition' see PARA 87 note 6. As to the meaning of 'privileged supplier condition' see PARA 87 note 7. As to the meaning of 'SMP condition' see PARA 87 text and note 8.
15   Communications Act 2003 s 190(4)(b). See BROADCASTING vol 4 (2011) PARA 517. As to the meaning of 'wireless telegraphy licence' see BROADCASTING vol 4 (2011) PARA 510 note 12. As to recognised spectrum access see BROADCASTING vol 4 (2011) PARA 544.
16   Communications Act 2003 s 190(4)(c). The reference in the text to OFCOM's power to make, amend or revoke regulations is a power under the Wireless Telegraphy Act 2006 s 8 (see BROADCASTING vol 4 (2011) PARA 514 et seq) or s 45 (see BROADCASTING vol 4 (2011) PARA 519): Communications Act 2003 s 190(4)(c) (amended by the Wireless Telegraphy Act 2006 s 123, Sch 7 paras 25, 27).
17   Ie under the Communications Act 2003 s 186(6): see PARA 213.
18   Communications Act 2003 s 190(5)(a).
19   Communications Act 2003 s 190(5)(b).
20   Communications Act 2003 s 190(6)(a). OFCOM may not, under head (A) in the text, require a party to the dispute to make payments to another party unless OFCOM has considered:
    (1)   the conduct of the party before and after the reference to OFCOM (including, in particular, whether any attempt has been made to resolve the dispute) (s 190(6A)(a) (s 190(6A), (6B) added by SI 2011/1210)); and
    (2)   whether OFCOM has made a decision in the party's favour in respect of the whole or a part of the dispute (Communications Act 2003 s 190(6A)(b) (as so added)).

21 Communications Act 2003 s 190(6)(b). OFCOM may not, under head (B) in the text, require payments to be made to it by a party to the dispute unless:
    (1)   the dispute relates to the rights and obligations of the parties to the dispute under the enactments relating to the management of the radio spectrum (s 190(6B)(a) (as added: see note 20); or
    (2)   it has considered the matters referred to s 190(6A)(a) and (b) (see heads (1) and (2) in note 20) (s 190(6B)(b) (as so added)).
22 Communications Act 2003 s 190(8). Section 190(8) is subject to s 192 (see PARA 224): s 190(9).

223. OFCOM's power to require information in connection with dispute.
Where a dispute has been referred or referred back to OFCOM[1] under Chapter 3 of Part 2 of the Communications Act 2003[2], it may require any person[3] to provide it with all such information as it may require for the purpose of[4]:

(1)   deciding whether it is appropriate for it to handle the dispute[5];

(2)   determining whether it is necessary for it to consult the regulatory authorities of another member state[6]; or

(3)   considering the dispute and making a determination for resolving it[7].

A person required to provide information under these provisions must provide it in such manner and within such reasonable period as may be specified by OFCOM[8].

1 As to the meaning of 'OFCOM' see PARA 14 note 1; and as to OFCOM see PARA 2 et seq.
2 Ie the Communications Act 2003 Pt 2 Ch 3 (ss 185–197).
3 Ie any person to whom the Communications Act 2003 s 191(2) applies. Section 191(2) applies to:
    (1)   a party to the dispute (s 191(2)(a)); and
    (2)   a person who is not a party to the dispute but who appears to OFCOM to have information that is relevant to the matters mentioned in heads (1)–(3) in the text (s 191(2)(b)).
4 Communications Act 2003 s 191(1). Sections 138–144 (see PARA 137) apply for the enforcement of a requirement under s 191 as they apply for the enforcement of requirements under s 135 or s 136 (see PARA 136): s 191(5).
5 Communications Act 2003 s 191(1)(a).
6 Communications Act 2003 s 191(1)(b).
7 Communications Act 2003 s 191(1)(c).
8 Communications Act 2003 s 191(3). In fixing the period within which information is to be provided in accordance with a requirement under s 191, OFCOM must have regard, in particular, to:
    (1)   its obligation to make a determination for resolving the dispute within the period specified in s 188 (see PARA 220) (s 191(4)(a));
    (2)   the nature of the dispute (s 191(4)(b)); and
    (3)   the information that is required (s 191(4)(c)).
  See also note 3.

224. Appeals against decisions by OFCOM, Secretary of State and others.
A person affected by a decision to which the following provisions[1] apply[2] may appeal against it to the Competition Appeal Tribunal[3]. The means of making an appeal is by sending the Tribunal a notice of appeal in accordance with Tribunal rules[4]. The notice of appeal must be sent within the period specified, in relation to the decision appealed against, in those rules[5]. The notice of appeal must set out:

(1)   the provision under which the decision appealed against was taken[6]; and

(2)   the grounds of appeal[7].

The grounds of appeal must be set out in sufficient detail to indicate:

(a)   to what extent (if any) the appellant contends that the decision appealed against was based on an error of fact or was wrong in law or both[8]; and

(b) to what extent (if any) the appellant is appealing against the exercise of a discretion by OFCOM, by the Secretary of State, by the Competition and Markets Authority or by another person[9].

1 Ie the Communications Act 2003 s 192.

2 The Communications Act 2003 s 192 applies to the following decisions:
(1) a decision by OFCOM under the Communications Act 2003 Pt 2 (ss 32–197) or any of the Wireless Telegraphy Act 2006 Pts 1–3 that is not a decision specified in the Communications Act 2003 Sch 8 (s 192(1)(a) (amended by the Wireless Telegraphy Act 2006 s 123 Sch 7 paras 25, 28));
(2) a decision (whether by OFCOM or another) to which effect is given by a direction, approval or consent given for the purposes of a provision of a condition set under the Communications Act 2003 s 45 (see PARA 87) (s 192(1)(b));
(3) a decision to which effect is given by the modification or withdrawal of such a direction, approval or consent (s 192(1)(c));
(4) a decision by the Secretary of State to which effect is given by one of the following:
    (a) a specific direction under s 5 (see PARA 18) that is not about the making of a decision specified in Sch 8 (s 192(1)(d)(i));
    (b) a restriction or condition set by regulations under s 109 (see PARA 158) (s 192(1)(d)(ii));
    (c) an order under s 124P (see PARA 135 and INFORMATION TECHNOLOGY LAW vol 57 (2012) PARA 509–511) (s 192(1)(d)(iia) (added by the Digital Economy Act 2010 s 20));
    (d) a direction to OFCOM under the Communications Act 2003 s 132 (see PARA 151) (s 192(1)(d)(iii));
    (e) a specific direction under the Wireless Telegraphy Act 2006 s 5 (see BROADCASTING vol 4 (2011) PARA 542) that is not about the making of a decision specified in the Communications Act 2003 Sch 8 (s 192(1)(d)(iv) (amended by the Wireless Telegraphy Act 2006 s 123, Sch 7 paras 25, 28)).
(5) a decision by the Competition and Markets Authority to which effect is given by an order made under the Communications Act 2003 s 193A (see PARA 225) (s 192(1)(e) (added by the Enterprise and Regulatory Reform Act 2013 Sch 15 para 43)).
As to the Secretary of State see PARA 76 note 1. As to the meaning of 'OFCOM' see PARA 14 note 1; and as to OFCOM see PARA 2 et seq. As to the Competition and Markets Authority see COMPETITION vol 18 (2009) PARA 23A.
   Decisions which are not subject to appeal include decisions to institute, bring or carry on any criminal or civil proceedings; decisions (other than one under the Communications Act 2003 s 119 (see PARA 165) to take preliminary steps for the purpose of enabling any such proceedings to be instituted and in the Communications Act 2003; decisions relating to the making or revision of a statement under s 38 (see PARA 83), s 131 (see PARA 133), and s 145 (see PARA 147); decisions required to be published in a notification under s 44(4) (see PARA 86) and s 108(4) (see PARA 157); decisions given effect to by an order under s 55 (see PARA 99), s 122 (see PARA 129) and s 134(6) (see PARA 152); decisions given effect to by regulations under s 66 (see PARA 102) and s 71 (see PARA 102), decisions relating to ss 124A–124N (see PARA 134; and INFORMATION TECHNOLOGY LAW vol 57 (2012) PARA 526 et seq) or to anything done under them: see Sch 8 (amended by the Digital Economy Act 2010 s 16; and the Wireless Telegraphy Act 2006 Sch 7 para 36).
   For the purposes of the Communications Act 2003 s 192 and Sch 8, references to a decision under an enactment:
    (i) include references to a decision that is given effect to by the exercise or performance of a power or duty conferred or imposed by or under an enactment (s 192(7)(a)); but
    (ii) include references to a failure to make a decision, and to a failure to exercise a power or to perform a duty, only where the failure constitutes a failure to grant an application or to comply with any other form of request to make the decision, to exercise the power or to perform the duty (s 192(7)(b)),
and references in ss 193–196 (see PARAS 225–227) to a decision appealed against are to be construed accordingly: s 192(7). For the purposes of ss 192–196, a decision to which effect is given by the exercise or performance of a power or duty conferred or imposed by or under an enactment must be treated, except where provision is made for the making of that decision at a different time, as made at the time when the power is exercised or the duty performed: s 192(8).

3 Communications Act 2003 ss 192(2), 197(1). As to the Competition Appeal Tribunal see COMPETITION vol 18 (2009) PARAS 13–17. See *T-Mobile (UK) Ltd v Office of Communications*

[2008] EWCA Civ 1373, [2009] 1 WLR 1565, [2008] All ER (D) 131 (Dec). See also *British Telecommunications plc v Office of Communications (Ethernet Determinations)* [2014] CAT 14, [2014] All ER (D) 31 (Nov) (Competition Appeal Tribunal considered appeals against a determination issued by OFCOM after complaints from five communications providers that BT was in breach of a condition in respect of overcharging).

4   Communications Act 2003 s 192(3). 'Tribunal rules' means rules made under the Enterprise Act 2002 s 15 (see COMPETITION vol 18 (2009) PARA 16): Communications Act 2003 s 197(1).

5   Communications Act 2003 s 192(4).

6   Communications Act 2003 s 192(5)(a).

7   Communications Act 2003 s 192(5)(b).

8   Communications Act 2003 s 192(6)(a). The Communications Act 2003 s 192(6) does not limit an appeal against a factual finding to scrutinising the finding on the material that OFCOM has considered; fresh evidence may be admitted if it is in the interests of justice to do so: *British Telecommunications plc v Office of Communications (Hutchinson 3G UK Ltd intervening)* [2011] EWCA Civ 245, [2011] 4 All ER 372.

9   Communications Act 2003 s 192(6)(b) (amended by the Enterprise and Regulatory Reform Act 2013 Sch 15 para 43).

225. Price control references. Tribunal rules[1] must provide in relation to appeals[2] relating to price control[3] that the price control matters arising in that appeal, to the extent that they are matters of a description specified in the rules, must be referred by the Competition Appeal Tribunal to the Competition and Markets Authority ('CMA') for determination[4].

Where a price control matter is referred in accordance with Tribunal rules to the CMA for determination, the determination of the matter is to be carried out on behalf of the CMA by a group constituted for the purpose by the chair of the CMA[5] and is to be performed[6]:

(1)   in accordance with the provision made by the rules[7];

(2)   in accordance with directions given to the CMA by the Tribunal in exercise of powers conferred by the rules[8]; and

(3)   subject to the rules and any such directions, using such procedure as the CMA considers appropriate[9].

The provision that may be made by Tribunal rules about the determination of a price control matter referred to the CMA in accordance with the rules includes provision about the period within which that matter is to be determined by the CMA[10]. Where the CMA determines a price control matter in accordance with Tribunal rules, it must notify the Tribunal of the determination it has made[11]. The notification must be given as soon as practicable after the making of the notified determination[12]. Where a price control matter arising in an appeal is required to be referred to the CMA, the Tribunal, in deciding the appeal on the merits[13], must decide that matter in accordance with the determination of the CMA[14].

Where a determination is made on a price control matter referred[15], the CMA may make an order in respect of the costs incurred by it in connection with the reference (a 'costs order')[16]. A costs order may require the payment to the CMA of some or all of those costs by such parties to the appeal which gave rise to the reference, other than OFCOM, as the CMA considers appropriate[17]. A costs order must:

(a)   set out the total costs incurred by the CMA in connection with the reference[18]; and

(b)   specify the proportion of those costs to be paid by each party to the appeal in respect of whom the order is made[19].

In deciding on the proportion of costs to be paid by a party to the appeal the CMA must, in particular, consider:

(i)   the extent to which the determination on the reference upholds OFCOM's decision in relation to the price control matter in question[20];

(ii)   the extent to which the costs were attributable to the involvement in the appeal of the party[21]; and

(iii) the conduct of the party[22].

A costs order:

(A)   must be made as soon as reasonably practicable after the making of the determination on the reference[23]; but

(B)   does not take effect unless the Tribunal, in deciding the appeal which gave rise to the reference, decides the price control matter which is the subject of the reference in accordance with the determination of the CMA[24].

1   As to the meaning of 'Tribunal rules' see PARA 224 note 4.
2   Ie under the Communications Act 2003 s 192(2): see PARA 224.
3   For the purposes of the Communications Act 2003 s 193, an appeal relates to price control if the matters to which the appeal relates are or include price control matters: s 193(9). For the purposes of s 193, 'price control matter' means a matter relating to the imposition of any form of price control by an SMP condition the setting of which is authorised by s 87(9) (see PARA 111); s 91 (see PARA 113); or s 93(3) (see PARA 114): s 193(10) (amended by the Enterprise and Regulatory Reform Act 2013 Sch 15 para 44). As to the meaning of 'SMP condition' see PARA 87 text and note 8.
4   Communications Act 2003 s 193(1) (s 193(1)–(4), (6)–(8), amended by the Enterprise and Regulatory Reform Act 2013 Sch 6 para 98). As to the Competition Appeal Tribunal see COMPETITION vol 18 (2009) PARAS 13–17. As to the Competition and Markets Authority see COMPETITION vol 18 (2009) PARA 23A.
    The Enterprise Act 2002 s 117 (offences of supplying false or misleading information: see COMPETITION vol 18 (2009) PARA 266) has effect in relation to information supplied to the Competition Commission in connection with its functions under the Communications Act 2003 s 193 as it has effect in relation to information supplied to it in connection with its functions under the Enterprise Act 2002 Pt 3 (ss 22–130): Communications Act 2003 s 193(8) (as so amended). As to the Competition Commission see COMPETITION vol 18 (2009) PARA 9 et seq.
5   Ie under the Enterprise and Regulatory Reform Act 2013 Sch 4: see COMPETITION vol 18 (2009) PARA 23A.
6   Communications Act 2003 s 193(2) (as amended: see note 4).
7   Communications Act 2003 s 193(2)(a).
8   Communications Act 2003 s 193(2)(b) (as amended: see note 4).
9   Communications Act 2003 s 193(2)(c) (as amended: see note 4).
10 Communications Act 2003 s 193(3) (as amended: see note 4).
11 Communications Act 2003 s 193(4) (as amended: see note 4).
12 Communications Act 2003 s 193(5).
13 Ie under the Communications Act 2003 s 195 (see PARA 226).
14 Communications Act 2003 s 193(6) (as amended: see note 4). See *British Telecommunications plc v Competition Commission* [2013] EWCA Civ 154, [2013] All ER (D) 46 (Mar). The Communications Act 2003 s 193(6) does not apply to the extent that the Tribunal decides, applying the principles applicable on an application for judicial review, that the determination of the CMA is a determination that would fall to be set aside on such an application: s 193(7) (as so amended).
15 Ie by virtue of the Communications Act 2003 s 193.
16 Communications Act 2003 s 193A(1) (s 193A added by the Enterprise and Regulatory Reform Act 2013 s 54). The functions of the CMA under the Communications Act 2003 s 193A, other than those under s 193A(9), (10) (see note 17), are to be carried out on behalf of the CMA by the group constituted by the chair of the CMA in relation to the reference in question: s 193A(11) (as so added).
17 Communications Act 2003 s 193A(2) (as added: see note 16). An amount payable to the CMA by virtue of an order made under s 193A is recoverable summarily as a civil debt (but this does not affect any other method of recovery): s 193A(9) (as so added). The CMA must pay any sums it receives by virtue of s 193A into the Consolidated Fund: s 193A(10) (as so added). As to the Consolidated Fund see CONSTITUTIONAL AND ADMINISTRATIVE LAW vol 20 (2014) PARA 480 et seq; PARLIAMENT vol 78 (2010) PARAS 1028–1031.

18 Communications Act 2003 s 193A(3)(a) (as added: see note 16).
19 Communications Act 2003 s 193A(3)(b) (as added: see note 16).
20 Communications Act 2003 s 193A(4)(a) (as added: see note 16).
21 Communications Act 2003 s 193A(4)(b) (as added: see note 16).
22 Communications Act 2003 s 193A(4)(c) (as added: see note 16).
23 Communications Act 2003 s 193A(5)(a) (as added: see note 16).
24 Communications Act 2003 s 193A(5)(b) (as added: see note 16). In a case where the Tribunal decides the price control matter in question otherwise than as mentioned in head (B) in the text, the CMA may make an order under s 193A(6) in respect of the costs incurred by it in connection with the reference: s 193A(6) (as so added). Communications Act 2003 s 193A(2)–(4) apply in relation to an order under s 193A(6) as they apply in relation to an order under s 193A(1); but for that purpose the reference in s 193A(4)(a) to the determination on the reference is to be read as a reference to the decision of the Tribunal mentioned in s 193A(6): s 193A(7) (as so added). An order under s 193A(6) must be made as soon as reasonably practicable after the decision of the Tribunal mentioned in s 193A(6): s 193A(8) (as so added).

226. Decisions of Competition Appeal Tribunal. The Competition Appeal Tribunal[1] must dispose of an appeal[2] in accordance with the following provisions[3]. The Tribunal must decide the appeal on the merits and by reference to the grounds of appeal set out in the notice of appeal[4]. The Tribunal's decision must include a decision as to what (if any) is the appropriate action for the decision-maker[5] to take in relation to the subject-matter of the decision under appeal[6]. The Tribunal must then remit the decision under appeal to the decision-maker with such directions (if any) as the Tribunal considers appropriate for giving effect to its decision[7]. The Tribunal must not direct the decision-maker to take any action which he would not otherwise have power to take in relation to the decision under appeal[8]. In the case of an appeal against a decision given effect to by a restriction or condition set by regulations[9], the Tribunal must take only such steps for disposing of the appeal as it considers are not detrimental to good administration[10].

1 As to the Competition Appeal Tribunal see COMPETITION vol 18 (2009) PARAS 13–17.
2 Ie an appeal under the Communications Act 2003 s 192(2): see PARA 224.
3 Communications Act 2003 s 195(1). The provision referred to in the text is s 195: s 195(1). In its application to a decision of the Tribunal under s 195, the Enterprise Act 2002 Sch 4 para 1(2)(b) (exclusion of commercial information from documents recording Tribunal decisions: see COMPETITION vol 18 (2009) PARA 15) is to have effect as if for the reference to the undertaking to which commercial information relates there were substituted a reference to any person to whom it relates: Communications Act 2003 s 195(8).
4 Communications Act 2003 s 195(2).
5 For the purposes of the Communications Act 2003 s 195, 'decision-maker' means:
  (1) OFCOM, the Secretary of State or the CMA, according to who took the decision appealed against (s 195(9)(a) (s 195(9)(a), (b)(i) amended by the Enterprise and Regulatory Reform Act 2013 Sch 15 para 45)); or
  (2) in the case of an appeal against:
    (a) a direction, approval or consent given by a person other than OFCOM, the Secretary of State or the CMA (Communications Act 2003 s 195(9)(b)(i) (as so amended)); or
    (b) the modification or withdrawal by such a person of such a direction, approval or consent (s 195(9)(b)(ii)),
    that other person: s 195(9).
  As to the Secretary of State see PARA 76 note 1. As to the meaning of 'OFCOM' see PARA 14 note 1; and as to OFCOM see PARA 2 et seq.
6 Communications Act 2003 s 195(3).
7 Communications Act 2003 s 195(4). It is the duty of the decision-maker to comply with every direction given under s 195(4): s 195(6).
8 Communications Act 2003 s 195(5). See *Vodafone Ltd v British Telecommunications plc* [2010] EWCA Civ 391, [2010] 3 All ER 1028 (tribunal could not give retrospective directions).
9 Ie under the Communications Act 2003 s 109: see PARA 158.
10 Communications Act 2003 s 195(7).

227. Appeals from Competition Appeal Tribunal. A decision of the Competition Appeal Tribunal[1] on an appeal[2] may itself be appealed[3]. An appeal under these provisions:

(1) lies to the Court of Appeal[4]; and

(2) must relate only to a point of law arising from the decision of the Tribunal[5].

An appeal under these provisions may be brought by:

(a) a party to the proceedings before the Tribunal[6]; or

(b) any other person who has a sufficient interest in the matter[7].

An appeal under these provisions requires the permission of the Tribunal or of the court to which it is to be made[8].

1 As to the Competition Appeal Tribunal see COMPETITION vol 18 (2009) PARAS 13–17.
2 Ie on an appeal under the Communications Act 2003 s 192(2): see PARA 224.
3 Communications Act 2003 s 196(1). For the purposes of s 196, references to a decision of the Tribunal include references to a direction given by it under s 195(4) (see PARA 226): s 196(5).
4 Communications Act 2003 s 196(2)(a).
5 Communications Act 2003 s 196(2)(b).
6 Communications Act 2003 s 196(3)(a).
7 Communications Act 2003 s 196(3)(b).
8 Communications Act 2003 s 196(4).

(10) DATA PROTECTION AND SECURITY OBLIGATIONS

228. Security of public electronic communications services. A provider of a public electronic communications service[1] (the 'service provider') must take appropriate[2] technical and organisational measures to safeguard the security of that service[3]. If necessary, those measures may be taken by the service provider in conjunction with the provider of the electronic communications network[4] by means of which the service is provided, and that network provider must comply with any reasonable requests made by the service provider for these purposes[5].

The measures must at least:

(1) ensure that personal data can be accessed only by authorised personnel for legally authorised purposes[6];

(2) protect personal data stored or transmitted against accidental or unlawful destruction, accidental loss or alteration, and unauthorised or unlawful storage, processing, access or disclosure[7]; and

(3) ensure the implementation of a security policy with respect to the processing of personal data[8].

Where, notwithstanding the taking of such measures, there remains a significant risk to the security of the public electronic communications service, the service provider must inform the subscribers[9] concerned of:

(a) the nature of that risk[10];

(b) any appropriate measures that the subscriber may take to safeguard against that risk[11]; and

(c) the likely costs to the subscriber involved in the taking of such measures[12].

Information provided for this purpose must be provided to the subscriber free of any charge other than the cost to the subscriber of receiving or collecting the information[13].

The Information Commissioner may audit the measures taken by a provider of a public electronic communications service to safeguard the security of that service[14].

1 For these purposes, 'public electronic communications service' has the meaning given in the Communications Act 2003 s 151 (see PARA 98 note 3): Privacy and Electronic Communications (EC Directive) Regulations 2003, SI 2003/2426, reg 2(1).

2 For the purposes of the Privacy and Electronic Communications (EC Directive) Regulations 2003, SI 2003/2426, reg 5(1), a measure is only to be taken to be appropriate if, having regard to the state of technological developments, and the cost of implementing it, it is proportionate to the risks against which it would safeguard: reg 5(4).

3 Privacy and Electronic Communications (EC Directive) Regulations 2003, SI 2003/2426, reg 5(1). This is subject to reg 5(2) (see the text to notes 4–5). The Regulations came into force on 11 December 2003 (see reg 1) and implement in part European Parliament and Council Directive (EC) 2002/58 (OJ L201, 31.7.2002, p 37) of 12 July 2002 concerning the processing of personal data and the protection of privacy in the electronic communications sector (arts 2, 4, 5(3), 6–13, 15, 16). The Secretary of State must carry out a review of the implementation in the United Kingdom of the Directive, set out the conclusions of the review in a report and publish the report before the end of a specified review period: see the Privacy and Electronic Communications (EC Directive) Regulations 2003, SI 2003/2426, reg 37 (added by SI 2011/1208). 'Review period' means the period of five years beginning with 26 May 2011 and each successive period of five years: see the Privacy and Electronic Communications (EC Directive) Regulations 2003, SI 2003/2426, reg 37(4), (5) (as so added).

Nothing in the Privacy and Electronic Communications (EC Directive) Regulations 2003, SI 2003/2426, relieves a person of his obligations under the Data Protection Act 1998 in relation to the processing of personal data: Privacy and Electronic Communications (EC Directive) Regulations 2003, SI 2003/2426, reg 4. As to those obligations see CONFIDENCE AND INFORMATIONAL PRIVACY vol 19 (2011) PARA 174. As to the requirement imposed on the providers of public electronic communications services or networks to retain certain categories of data, see the Data Retention Regulations 2014, SI 2014/2042; and PARA 240.

4 For these purposes, 'electronic communications network' has the meaning given by the Communications Act 2003 s 32 (see PARA 53): Privacy and Electronic Communications (EC Directive) Regulations 2003, SI 2003/2426, reg 2(1).

5 Privacy and Electronic Communications (EC Directive) Regulations 2003, SI 2003/2426, reg 5(2).

6 Privacy and Electronic Communications (EC Directive) Regulations 2003, SI 2003/2426, reg 5(1A)(a) (added by SI 2011/1208).

7 Privacy and Electronic Communications (EC Directive) Regulations 2003, SI 2003/2426, reg 5(1A)(b) (added by SI 2011/1208).

8 Privacy and Electronic Communications (EC Directive) Regulations 2003, SI 2003/2426, reg 5(1A)(c) (added by SI 2011/1208).

9 'Subscriber' means a person who is a party to a contract with a provider of public electronic communications services for the supply of such services: Privacy and Electronic Communications (EC Directive) Regulations 2003, SI 2003/2426, reg 2(1).

10 Privacy and Electronic Communications (EC Directive) Regulations 2003, SI 2003/2426, reg 5(3)(a).

11 Privacy and Electronic Communications (EC Directive) Regulations 2003, SI 2003/2426, reg 5(3)(b).

12 Privacy and Electronic Communications (EC Directive) Regulations 2003, SI 2003/2426, reg 5(3)(c).

13 Privacy and Electronic Communications (EC Directive) Regulations 2003, SI 2003/2426, reg 5(5).

14 Privacy and Electronic Communications (EC Directive) Regulations 2003, SI 2003/2426, reg 5(6) (added by SI 2011/1208). As to the Information Commissioner see CONFIDENCE AND INFORMATIONAL PRIVACY vol 19 (2011) PARA 109 et seq.

229. Confidentiality of communications. A person[1] must not store or gain access to information stored, in the terminal equipment of a subscriber[2] or user[3] unless the following requirements are met[4].

Those requirements are that the subscriber or user of that terminal equipment:

(1) is provided with clear and comprehensive information about the purposes of the storage of, or access to, that information[5]; and

(2) has given his or her consent[6].

Where an electronic communications network is used by the same person to store or access information in the terminal equipment of a subscriber or user on more than one occasion, it is sufficient for these purposes[7] that the requirements in heads (1) and (2) are met in respect of the initial use[8].

The requirements in heads (1) and (2) do not apply to the technical storage of, or access to, information:

(a) for the sole purpose of carrying out the transmission of a communication over an electronic communications network[9]; or

(b) where such storage or access is strictly necessary for the provision of an information society service[10] requested by the subscriber or user[11].

1 As to the meaning of 'person' see PARA 14 note 2.
2 As to the meaning of 'subscriber' see PARA 228 note 9.
3 'User' means any individual using a public electronic communications service: Privacy and Electronic Communications (EC Directive) Regulations 2003, SI 2003/2426, reg 2(1). 'Individual' means a living individual; and includes an unincorporated body of such individuals: reg 2(1).
4 Privacy and Electronic Communications (EC Directive) Regulations 2003, SI 2003/2426, reg 6(1) (amended by SI 2011/1208). This is subject to the Privacy and Electronic Communications (EC Directive) Regulations 2003, SI 2003/2426, reg 6(4) (see the text to notes 9–11).
5 Privacy and Electronic Communications (EC Directive) Regulations 2003, SI 2003/2426, reg 6(2)(a).
6 Privacy and Electronic Communications (EC Directive) Regulations 2003, SI 2003/2426, reg 6(2)(b) (substituted by SI 2011/1208). For these purposes, consent may be signified by a subscriber who amends or sets controls on the internet browser which the subscriber uses or by using another application or programme to signify consent: Privacy and Electronic Communications (EC Directive) Regulations 2003, SI 2003/2426, reg 6(3A) (added by SI 2011/1208).
7 Ie the Privacy and Electronic Communications (EC Directive) Regulations 2003, SI 2003/2426, reg 6.
8 Privacy and Electronic Communications (EC Directive) Regulations 2003, SI 2003/2426, reg 6(3).
9 Privacy and Electronic Communications (EC Directive) Regulations 2003, SI 2003/2426, reg 6(4)(a) (amended by SI 2011/1208).
10 For these purposes, 'information society service' has the meaning given in the Electronic Commerce (EC Directive) Regulations 2002, SI 2002/2013, reg 2(1) (see COPYRIGHT vol 23 (2013) PARA 964): Privacy and Electronic Communications (EC Directive) Regulations 2003, SI 2003/2426, reg 2(1).
11 Privacy and Electronic Communications (EC Directive) Regulations 2003, SI 2003/2426, reg 6(4)(b).

230. Personal data breach. If a personal data breach[1] occurs, the service provider[2] must, without undue delay, notify that breach to the Information Commissioner[3] and such notification[4] must contain at least a description of:

(1) the nature of the breach[5];

(2) the consequences of the breach[6]; and

(3) the measures taken or proposed to be taken by the provider to address the breach[7].

If a personal data breach is likely to adversely affect the personal data or privacy of a subscriber[8] or user[9], the service provider must also, without undue delay, notify that breach to the subscriber or user concerned[10] but is not required if the service provider has demonstrated, to the satisfaction of the Information Commissioner that:

(a) it has implemented appropriate technological protection measures which render the data unintelligible to any person who is not authorised to access it[11]; and

(b) that those measures were applied to the data concerned in that breach[12].

Such notification[13] must contain at least:

(i)   a description of the nature of the breach[14];
(ii)   information about contact points within the service provider's organisation from which more information may be obtained[15]; and
(iii)   recommendations of measures to allow the subscriber to mitigate the possible adverse impacts of the breach[16].

If the service provider has not notified the subscriber or user[17], the Information Commissioner may, having considered the likely adverse effects of the breach, require it to do so[18]. The Information Commissioner may also audit the compliance of service providers[19].

Service providers must maintain an inventory[20] of personal data breaches comprising the facts surrounding the breach, the effects of that breach and remedial action taken which must be sufficient to enable the Information Commissioner to verify compliance with the Privacy and Electronic Communications (EC Directive) Regulations 2003[21].

If a service provider fails to comply with the notification requirements[22], the Information Commissioner may issue a fixed monetary penalty notice in respect of that failure[23] The amount of a fixed monetary penalty[24] is £1,000[25]. Before serving such a notice, the Information Commissioner must serve the service provider with a notice of intent[26]. The Information Commissioner may not serve a fixed monetary penalty notice until the time within which representations may be made has expired[27]. A service provider on whom a fixed monetary penalty is served may appeal to the Tribunal[28] against the issue of the fixed monetary penalty notice[29]. The penalty is recoverable:

(A)   if a county court so orders, as if it were payable under an order of that court[30];
(B)   if the High Court so orders, as if it were payable under an order of that court[31].

1   'Personal data breach' means a breach of security leading to the accidental or unlawful destruction, loss, alteration, unauthorised disclosure of, or access to, personal data transmitted, stored or otherwise processed in connection with the provision of a public electronic communications service: Privacy and Electronic Communications (EC Directive) Regulations 2003, SI 2003/2426, reg 2(1)(a) (definition added by SI 2011/1208).
2   As to the meaning of 'service provider' see PARA 228; definition applied by the Privacy and Electronic Communications (EC Directive) Regulations 2003, SI 2003/2426, reg 5A(1) (as added: see note 3).
3   Privacy and Electronic Communications (EC Directive) Regulations 2003, SI 2003/2426, reg 5A(2) (reg 5A–5C added by SI 2011/1208). As to the Information Commissioner see CONFIDENCE AND INFORMATIONAL PRIVACY vol 19 (2011) PARA 109 et seq.
4   Ie referred to in the Privacy and Electronic Communications (EC Directive) Regulations 2003, SI 2003/2426, reg 5A(2).
5   Privacy and Electronic Communications (EC Directive) Regulations 2003, SI 2003/2426, reg 5A(4)(a) (as added: see note 3).
6   Privacy and Electronic Communications (EC Directive) Regulations 2003, SI 2003/2426, reg 5A(4)(b) (as added: see note 3).
7   Privacy and Electronic Communications (EC Directive) Regulations 2003, SI 2003/2426, reg 5A(4)(c) (as added: see note 3).
8   As to the meaning of 'subscriber' see PARA 228 note 9.
9   As to the meaning of 'user' see PARA 229 note 3.
10 Privacy and Electronic Communications (EC Directive) Regulations 2003, SI 2003/2426, reg 5A(3) (as added: see note 3).
11 Privacy and Electronic Communications (EC Directive) Regulations 2003, SI 2003/2426, reg 5A(6)(a) (as added: see note 3).
12 Privacy and Electronic Communications (EC Directive) Regulations 2003, SI 2003/2426, reg 5A(6)(b) (as added: see note 3).
13 Ie the Privacy and Electronic Communications (EC Directive) Regulations 2003, SI 2003/2426, reg 5A(3).

14 Privacy and Electronic Communications (EC Directive) Regulations 2003, SI 2003/2426, reg 5A(5)(a) (as added: see note 3).

15 Privacy and Electronic Communications (EC Directive) Regulations 2003, SI 2003/2426, reg 5A(5)(b) (as added: see note 3).

16 Privacy and Electronic Communications (EC Directive) Regulations 2003, SI 2003/2426, reg 5A(5)(c) (as added: see note 3).

17 Ie in compliance with the Privacy and Electronic Communications (EC Directive) Regulations 2003, SI 2003/2426, reg 5A(3).

18 Privacy and Electronic Communications (EC Directive) Regulations 2003, SI 2003/2426, reg 5A(7) (as added: see note 3).

19 Privacy and Electronic Communications (EC Directive) Regulations 2003, SI 2003/2426, reg 5B (as added: see note 3). The reference in the text to the compliance of service providers is compliance with the provisions of reg 5A (see text and notes 1–18).

20 The inventory must only include information necessary for this purpose: Privacy and Electronic Communications (EC Directive) Regulations 2003, SI 2003/2426, reg 5A(8).

21 Privacy and Electronic Communications (EC Directive) Regulations 2003, SI 2003/2426, reg 5A(8) (as added: see note 3).

22 Ie of the Privacy and Electronic Communications (EC Directive) Regulations 2003, SI 2003/2426, reg 5A.

23 Privacy and Electronic Communications (EC Directive) Regulations 2003, SI 2003/2426, reg 5C(1) (as added: see note 3). The fixed monetary penalty notice must state:

    (1)   the name and address of the service provider (reg 5C(7)(a) (as so added));

    (2)   details of the notice of intent served on the service provider (reg 5C(7)(b) (as so added));

    (3)   whether there have been any written representations (reg 5C(7)(c) (as so added));

    (4)   details of any early payment discounts (reg 5C(7)(d) (as so added));

    (5)   the grounds on which the Information Commissioner imposes the fixed monetary penalty (reg 5C(7)(e) (as so added));

    (6)   the date by which the fixed monetary penalty is to be paid (reg 5C(7)(f) (as so added)); and

    (7)   details of, including the time limit for, the service provider's right of appeal against the imposition of the fixed monetary penalty (reg 5C(7)(h) (as so added)).

24 Ie under the Privacy and Electronic Communications (EC Directive) Regulations 2003, SI 2003/2426, reg 5C.

25 Privacy and Electronic Communications (EC Directive) Regulations 2003, SI 2003/2426, reg 5C(2) (as added: see note 3). A service provider may discharge liability for the fixed monetary penalty if he pays to the Information Commissioner the amount of £800 within 21 days of receipt of the notice of intent: reg 5C(6) (as so added). Any sum received by the Information Commissioner by virtue of this regulation must be paid into the Consolidated Fund: reg 5C(9) (as so added). As to the Consolidated Fund see CONSTITUTIONAL AND ADMINISTRATIVE LAW vol 20 (2014) PARA 480 et seq; PARLIAMENT vol 78 (2010) PARA 1028 et seq.

26 Privacy and Electronic Communications (EC Directive) Regulations 2003, SI 2003/2426, reg 5C(3) (reg 5C as added: see note 3). The notice of intent must:

    (1)   state the name and address of the service provider (reg 5C(4)(a) (as so added));

    (2)   state the nature of the breach (reg 5C(4)(b) (as so added));

    (3)   indicate the amount of the fixed monetary penalty (reg 5C(4)(c) (as so added));

    (4)   include a statement informing the service provider of the opportunity to discharge liability for the fixed monetary penalty (reg 5C(4)(d) (as so added));

    (5)   indicate the date on which the Information Commissioner proposes to serve the fixed monetary penalty notice (reg 5C(4)(e) (as so added)); and

    (6)   inform the service provider that he may make written representations in relation to the proposal to serve a fixed monetary penalty notice within the period of 21 days from the service of the notice of intent (reg 5C(4)(f) (as so added)).

27 Privacy and Electronic Communications (EC Directive) Regulations 2003, SI 2003/2426, reg 5C(6) (as added: see note 3).

28 Ie the Upper Tribunal, in any case where it is determined by or under Tribunal Procedure Rules that the Upper Tribunal is to hear the appeal; or the First-tier Tribunal, in any other case: Data Protection Act 1998 s 70(1); Privacy and Electronic Communications (EC Directive) Regulations 2003, SI 2003/2426, reg 2(2). As to the Upper Tribunal and First-tier Tribunal see COURTS AND TRIBUNALS vol 24 (2010) PARA 883 et seq.

29 Privacy and Electronic Communications (EC Directive) Regulations 2003, SI 2003/2426, reg 5C(8) (as added: see note 3).

30 Privacy and Electronic Communications (EC Directive) Regulations 2003, SI 2003/2426, reg 5C(10)(a) (as added: see note 3).

31 Privacy and Electronic Communications (EC Directive) Regulations 2003, SI 2003/2426, reg 5C(10)(b) (as added: see note 3).

231. Restrictions on the processing of certain traffic data. Traffic data[1] relating to subscribers[2] or users[3] which is processed and stored by a public communications provider[4] must, when no longer required for the purpose of the transmission of a communication, be:

(1)   erased[5];

(2)   in the case of an individual[6], modified so that it ceases to constitute personal data of that subscriber or user[7]; or

(3)   in the case of a corporate subscriber[8], modified so that it ceases to be data that would be personal data if that subscriber was an individual[9].

Traffic data held by a public communications provider for purposes connected with the payment of charges by a subscriber or in respect of interconnection payments may, however, be processed and stored by that provider until the end of the period during which legal proceedings may be brought in respect of payments due or alleged to be due or, where such proceedings are brought within that period, the time when those proceedings are finally determined[10]. Traffic data relating to a subscriber or user may also be processed and stored by a provider of a public electronic communications service if:

(a)   such processing and storage are for the purpose of marketing electronic communications services[11], or for the provision of value added services[12] to that subscriber or user[13]; and

(b)   the subscriber or user to whom the traffic data relates has previously notified the provider that he consents to such processing or storage[14]; and

(c)   such processing and storage are undertaken only for the duration necessary for the purposes specified in head (a) above[15].

Where a user or subscriber has given his consent to the processing or storage of data, he is able to withdraw it at any time[16].

Processing of traffic data in accordance with these provisions may not be undertaken by a public communications provider unless the subscriber or user to whom the data relates has been provided with information regarding the types of traffic data which are to be processed and the duration of such processing and, in the case of processing for the purpose of marketing electronic communications services or for the provision of value added services[17], he has been provided with that information before his consent has been obtained[18].

Processing of traffic data in accordance with these provisions is restricted to what is required for the purposes of one or more of the activities listed below and must be carried out only by the public communications provider or by a person acting under his authority[19]. Those activities are activities relating to:

(i)   the management of billing or traffic[20];

(ii)   customer inquiries[21];

(iii)   the prevention or detection of fraud[22];

(iv)   the marketing of electronic communications services[23]; or

(v)   the provision of a value added service[24].

Nothing in the Privacy and Electronic Communications (EC Directive) Regulations 2003 is to prevent the furnishing of traffic data to a person who is a competent authority for the purposes of any provision relating to the settling of disputes (by way of legal proceedings or otherwise) which is contained in, or made by virtue of, any enactment[25].

A relevant public communications provider[26] may, for the purpose of providing an emergency alert service[27] or for the purpose of testing an emergency alert service as the case may be, disregard certain restrictions on the processing of traffic data relating to users or subscribers[28] if the certain conditions are met[29].

1 'Traffic data' means any data processed for the purpose of the conveyance of a communication on an electronic communications network or for the billing in respect of that communication; and includes data relating to the routing, duration or time of a communication: Privacy and Electronic Communications (EC Directive) Regulations 2003, SI 2003/2426, reg 2(1). As to the meaning of 'electronic communications network' see PARA 228 note 4.

2 As to the meaning of 'subscriber' see PARA 228 note 9.

3 As to the meaning of 'user' see PARA 229 note 3.

4 'Public communications provider' means a provider of a public electronic communications network or a public electronic communications service: Privacy and Electronic Communications (EC Directive) Regulations 2003, SI 2003/2426, reg 2(1). For these purposes, 'public electronic communications network' has the meaning given in the Communications Act 2003 s 151 (see PARA 98 note 5): Privacy and Electronic Communications (EC Directive) Regulations 2003, SI 2003/2426, reg 2(1). As to the meaning of 'public electronic communications service' see PARA 228 note 1.

5 Privacy and Electronic Communications (EC Directive) Regulations 2003, SI 2003/2426, reg 7(1)(a). This is subject to reg 7(2), (3) (see the text to notes 10–15).

6 As to the meaning of 'individual' see PARA 229 note 3.

7 Privacy and Electronic Communications (EC Directive) Regulations 2003, SI 2003/2426, reg 7(1)(b). See note 5.

8 'Corporate subscriber' means a subscriber who is:
    (1)   a company within the meaning of the Companies Act 2006 (see COMPANIES vol 14 (2009) PARA 24);
    (2)   a company incorporated in pursuance of a Royal Charter or letters patent (see COMPANIES vol 14 (2009) PARA 3);
    (3)   a corporation sole; or
    (4)   any other body corporate or entity which is a legal person distinct from its members: Privacy and Electronic Communications (EC Directive) Regulations 2003, SI 2003/2426, reg 2(1) (amended by virtue of the Companies Act 2006 s 1297(5)).

9 Privacy and Electronic Communications (EC Directive) Regulations 2003, SI 2003/2426, reg 7(1)(c). See note 5.

10 Privacy and Electronic Communications (EC Directive) Regulations 2003, SI 2003/2426, reg 7(2), (5). Legal proceedings are not taken to be finally determined:
    (1)   until the conclusion of the ordinary period during which an appeal may be brought by either party (excluding any possibility of an extension of that period, whether by order of a court or otherwise), if no appeal is brought within that period (reg 7(6)(a)); or
    (2)   if an appeal is brought, until the conclusion of that appeal (reg 7(6)(b)).
    References in reg 7(6) to an appeal include references to an application for permission to appeal: reg 7(7).

11 For these purposes, 'electronic communications service' has the meaning given by the Communications Act 2003 s 32 (see PARA 53): Privacy and Electronic Communications (EC Directive) Regulations 2003, SI 2003/2426, reg 2(1).

12 'Value added service' means any service which requires the processing of traffic data or location data beyond that which is necessary for the transmission of a communication or the billing in respect of that communication: Privacy and Electronic Communications (EC Directive) Regulations 2003, SI 2003/2426, reg 2(1). 'Bill' includes an invoice, account, statement or other document of similar character; and 'billing' is to be construed accordingly: reg 2(1).

13 Privacy and Electronic Communications (EC Directive) Regulations 2003, SI 2003/2426, reg 7(3)(a).

14 Privacy and Electronic Communications (EC Directive) Regulations 2003, SI 2003/2426, reg 7(3)(b) (amended by SI 2011/1208).

15 Privacy and Electronic Communications (EC Directive) Regulations 2003, SI 2003/2426, reg 7(3)(c).

16 Privacy and Electronic Communications (EC Directive) Regulations 2003, SI 2003/2426, reg 7(4).

17 Ie in accordance with the Privacy and Electronic Communications (EC Directive) Regulations 2003, SI 2003/2426, reg 7(3): see the text and notes 13–15.

18 Privacy and Electronic Communications (EC Directive) Regulations 2003, SI 2003/2426, reg 8(1).

19 Privacy and Electronic Communications (EC Directive) Regulations 2003, SI 2003/2426, reg 8(2).

20 Privacy and Electronic Communications (EC Directive) Regulations 2003, SI 2003/2426, reg 8(3)(a).

21 Privacy and Electronic Communications (EC Directive) Regulations 2003, SI 2003/2426, reg 8(3)(b).

22 Privacy and Electronic Communications (EC Directive) Regulations 2003, SI 2003/2426, reg 8(3)(c).

23 Privacy and Electronic Communications (EC Directive) Regulations 2003, SI 2003/2426, reg 8(3)(d).

24 Privacy and Electronic Communications (EC Directive) Regulations 2003, SI 2003/2426, reg 8(3)(e).

25 Privacy and Electronic Communications (EC Directive) Regulations 2003, SI 2003/2426, reg 8(4). 'Enactment' includes an enactment comprised in, or in an instrument made under, an Act of the Scottish Parliament: reg 2(1).

26 For these purposes, 'relevant public communications provider' means a person who:
   (1)   provides a public electronic communications network (Privacy and Electronic Communications (EC Directive) Regulations 2003, SI 2003/2426, reg 16A(8)(c)(i) (reg 16A added by SI 2015/355)).
   (2)   provides cellular mobile electronic communications services (Privacy and Electronic Communications (EC Directive) Regulations 2003, SI 2003/2426, reg 16A(8)(c)(ii) (as so added)); and
   (3)   holds a wireless telegraphy licence granted under the Wireless Telegraphy Act 2006 s 8 (see BROADCASTING vol 4 (2011) PARA 514 et seq) (Privacy and Electronic Communications (EC Directive) Regulations 2003, SI 2003/2426, reg 16A(8)(c)(iii) (as so added)).

27 'Emergency alert service' means a service comprising one or more communications to mobile telecommunications devices over a public electronic communications network to warn, advise or inform users or subscribers in relation to an aspect or effect of an emergency which may affect or have affected them by reason of their location: Privacy and Electronic Communications (EC Directive) Regulations 2003, SI 2003/2426, reg 16A(8)(a) (as added: see note 26).

28 Ie the restrictions on the processing of traffic data under the Privacy and Electronic Communications (EC Directive) Regulations 2003, SI 2003/2426, reg 7(1) (see text and notes 1–9) and reg 8(2) (see text and note 19): reg 16A(2)(a) (as added: see note 26).

29 Privacy and Electronic Communications (EC Directive) Regulations 2003, SI 2003/2426, reg 16A(1), (4) (as added: see note 26).
   For the purpose of providing an emergency alert service, the specified conditions that have to be met are:
   (1)   the relevant public communications provider is notified by a relevant public authority that an emergency within the meaning of the Civil Contingencies Act 2004 s 1(1) (see ARMED CONFLICT AND EMERGENCY vol 3 (2011) PARA 151) has occurred, is occurring or is about to occur and it is expedient to use an emergency alert service (Privacy and Electronic Communications (EC Directive) Regulations 2003, SI 2003/2426, reg 16A(3)(a) (as added: see note 26));
   (2)   the relevant public communications provider is directed by the relevant public authority to convey a specified communication over a specified time period to users or subscribers of the relevant public communications provider's public electronic communications network whom the provider considers are in one or more specified places in the United Kingdom which is or may be affected by the emergency or have been in a specified place affected by the emergency since the emergency occurred but are no longer in the place (reg 16A(3)(b) (as so added)); and
   (3)   the relevant public communications provider complies with that direction (reg 16A(3)(c) (as so added)).
   For the purpose of testing an emergency alert service, the specified conditions that have to be met are:
   (a)   the relevant public communications provider is notified by a Minister of the Crown that, in the Minister's opinion, it is necessary to test an emergency alert service for the

purpose of ensuring that the service is maintained in good working order and is an effective means of communicating with users and subscribers in an emergency (reg 16A(5)(a) (as so added));

(b)   the Minister gives directions as to how the test is to be conducted (reg 16A(5)(b) (as so added)); and

(c)   the relevant public communications provider complies with the directions in head (b) (reg 16A(5)(c) (as so added)).

Traffic data which relate to users or subscribers of a public electronic communications network and are processed in accordance with this regulation must, within 7 days of the expiry of the time period specified by the relevant public authority pursuant to head (2) or, as the case may be, within 48 hours of receipt of the Minister's directions pursuant to head (b), be:

(i)   erased (reg 16A(6)(a) (as so added)); or

(ii)   in the case of an individual, modified so that they cease to constitute personal data of that user or subscriber; or in the case of a corporate subscriber, modified so that they cease to be data that would be personal data if that user or subscriber was an individual (reg 16A(6)(b) (as so added)).

The processing of traffic data or location data in accordance with this regulation shall be carried out only by the relevant public communications provider or by a person acting under the relevant public communications provider's authority (reg 16A(7) (as so added)).

'Relevant public authority' means:

(A)   a Minister of the Crown (reg 16A(8)(b)(i) (as so added));

(B)   the Welsh Ministers (reg 16A(8)(b)(iii) (as so added));

(C)   a chief officer of police within the meaning of the Police Act 1996 s 101(1) (see POLICE AND INVESTIGATORY POWERS vol 84 (2013) PARA 5) (Privacy and Electronic Communications (EC Directive) Regulations 2003, SI 2003/2426, reg 16A(8)(b)(v) (as so added));

(D)   the chief constable of the British Transport Police Force (reg 16A(8)(b)(viii) (as so added));

(E)   the Environment Agency (reg 16A(8)(ix) (as so added));

(F)   the Natural Resources Body for Wales (reg 16A(8)(xi) (as so added)).

232. Itemised billing and line identification. At the request of a subscriber[1], a provider of a public electronic communications service[2] must provide that subscriber with bills[3] that are not itemised[4].

OFCOM[5] has a duty, when exercising its functions under Chapter 1 of Part 2 of the Communications Act 2003[6], to have regard to the need to reconcile the rights of subscribers receiving itemised bills with the rights to privacy of calling users[7] and called subscribers, including the need for sufficient alternative privacy-enhancing methods of communications or payments to be available to such users and subscribers[8].

Where a facility enabling the presentation of calling line[9] identification is available, the provider of a public electronic communications service must provide users originating a call by means of that service with a simple means to prevent presentation of the identity of the calling line on the connected line as respects that call[10]. The provider of a public electronic communications service must provide subscribers to the service, as respects the line and all calls originating from that line, with a simple means of preventing presentation of the identity of that subscriber's line on any connected line[11]. These measures must be provided free of charge[12].

In relation to incoming calls, where a facility enabling the presentation of calling line identification is available, the provider of a public electronic communications service must provide the called subscriber[13] with a simple means to prevent, free of charge for reasonable use of the facility, presentation of the identity of the calling line on the connected line[14]. Where a facility enabling the presentation of calling line identification prior to the call being established is available, the provider of a public electronic communications service must provide the called subscriber with a simple means of rejecting incoming calls where the presentation of the calling line identification has been prevented by the calling user or subscriber[15]. Where a facility enabling the presentation of connected line identification is available, the provider of a public electronic communications service must provide the called subscriber with a simple means to prevent, without charge, presentation of the identity of the connected line on any calling line[16].

Where a provider of a public electronic communications service provides facilities for calling or connected line identification, he must provide information to the public regarding the availability of such facilities, including information regarding the options to be made available for the purposes of prevention of calling or connected line identification[17]. For these purposes, a communications provider[18] must comply with any reasonable requests made by the provider of the public electronic communications service by means of which facilities for calling or connected line identification are provided[19].

A communications provider may override anything done to prevent the presentation of the identity of a calling line where:

(1) a subscriber has requested the tracing of malicious or nuisance calls received on his line[20]; and

(2) the provider is satisfied that such action is necessary and expedient for the purposes of tracing such calls[21].

Any term of a contract for the provision of public electronic communications services which relates to such prevention will have effect subject to the provisions above as to the tracing of malicious or nuisance calls[22]. Nothing in the Privacy and Electronic Communications (EC Directive) Regulations 2003 is to prevent a communications provider, for the purposes of any action relating to the tracing of malicious or nuisance calls, from storing and making available to a person with a legitimate interest data containing the identity of a calling subscriber which was obtained while malicious or nuisance calls were being traced at the request of a subscriber[23].

In order to facilitate responses to emergency calls[24], all such calls are excluded from the requirements as to withholding caller identification on outgoing calls[25], and no person is entitled to prevent the presentation on the connected line of the identity of the calling line[26].

1   As to the meaning of 'subscriber' see PARA 223 note 6.
2   As to the meaning of 'public electronic communications service' see PARA 223 note 1.
3   As to the meaning of 'bill' see PARA 224 note 10.
4   Privacy and Electronic Communications (EC Directive) Regulations 2003, SI 2003/2426, reg 9(1).
5   'OFCOM' means the Office of Communications as established by the Office of Communications Act 2002 s 1: Privacy and Electronic Communications (EC Directive) Regulations 2003, SI 2003/2426, reg 2(1). As to OFCOM see PARA 2 et seq.
6   Ie the Communications Act 2003 Pt 2 Ch 1 (ss 32–151).
7   As to the meaning of 'user' see PARA 229 note 3.
8   Privacy and Electronic Communications (EC Directive) Regulations 2003, SI 2003/2426, reg 9(2).
9   Any reference in the Privacy and Electronic Communications (EC Directive) Regulations 2003, SI 2003/2426, to a line is to be construed as including a reference to anything that performs the function of a line; and 'connected', in relation to a line, is to be construed accordingly: reg 2(4).
10 Privacy and Electronic Communications (EC Directive) Regulations 2003, SI 2003/2426, reg 10(1), (2). This is subject to regs 15, 16: see the text to notes 20–26.
11 Privacy and Electronic Communications (EC Directive) Regulations 2003, SI 2003/2426, reg 10(3).
12 Privacy and Electronic Communications (EC Directive) Regulations 2003, SI 2003/2426, reg 10(4).

13	For the purposes of the Privacy and Electronic Communications (EC Directive) Regulations 2003, SI 2003/2426, reg 11, 'called subscriber' means the subscriber receiving a call by means of the service in question whose line is the called line (whether or not it is also the connected line): reg 11(5).

14	Privacy and Electronic Communications (EC Directive) Regulations 2003, SI 2003/2426, reg 11(1), (2).

15	Privacy and Electronic Communications (EC Directive) Regulations 2003, SI 2003/2426, reg 11(3).

16	Privacy and Electronic Communications (EC Directive) Regulations 2003, SI 2003/2426, reg 11(4).

17	Privacy and Electronic Communications (EC Directive) Regulations 2003, SI 2003/2426, reg 12.

18	For these purposes, 'communications provider' has the meaning given by the Communications Act 2003 s 405 (see PARA 17 note 20): Privacy and Electronic Communications (EC Directive) Regulations 2003, SI 2003/2426, reg 2(1).

19	Privacy and Electronic Communications (EC Directive) Regulations 2003, SI 2003/2426, reg 13.

20	Privacy and Electronic Communications (EC Directive) Regulations 2003, SI 2003/2426, reg 15(1)(a).

21	Privacy and Electronic Communications (EC Directive) Regulations 2003, SI 2003/2426, reg 15(1)(b).

22	Privacy and Electronic Communications (EC Directive) Regulations 2003, SI 2003/2426, reg 15(2).

23	Privacy and Electronic Communications (EC Directive) Regulations 2003, SI 2003/2426, reg 15(3).

24	For the purposes of the Privacy and Electronic Communications (EC Directive) Regulations 2003, SI 2003/2426, reg 16, 'emergency calls' means calls to either the national emergency call number 999 or the single European emergency call number 112: reg 16(1).

25	Ie the requirements of the Privacy and Electronic Communications (EC Directive) Regulations 2003, SI 2003/2426, reg 10: see the text to notes 9–12.

26	Privacy and Electronic Communications (EC Directive) Regulations 2003, SI 2003/2426, reg 16(2), (a), (b). The restriction on the processing of location data under reg 14(2) (see PARA 233) is to be disregarded: reg 16(2)(c).

233. Restrictions on the processing of location data. The following provisions do not apply to the processing of traffic data[1].

Location data[2] relating to a user[3] or subscriber[4] of a public electronic communications network[5] or a public electronic communications service[6] may only be processed:

(1)	where that user or subscriber cannot be identified from such data[7]; or

(2)	where necessary for the provision of a value added service[8], with the consent of that user or subscriber[9].

Prior to obtaining the consent of the user or subscriber under head (2) above, the public communications provider in question must provide the following information to the user or subscriber to whom the data relates:

(a)	the types of location data that will be processed[10];

(b)	the purposes and duration of the processing of that data[11]; and

(c)	whether the data will be transmitted to a third party for the purpose of providing the value added service[12].

A user or subscriber who has given his consent to the processing of data must be able to withdraw such consent at any time; and, in respect of each connection to the public electronic communications network in question or each transmission of a communication, must be given the opportunity to withdraw such consent, using a simple means and free of charge[13].

Processing of location data in accordance with these provisions must only be carried out by:

(i)	the public communications provider in question[14];

(ii)	the third party providing the value added service in question[15]; or

(iii)   a person acting under the authority of a person falling within head (i) or head (ii)[16].

Where the processing is carried out for the purposes of the provision of a value added service, it must be restricted to what is necessary for those purposes[17].

A relevant public communications provider[18] may, for the purpose of providing an emergency alert service[19] or for the purpose of testing an emergency alert service as the case may be, disregard certain restrictions on the processing of location data relating to users or subscribers[20] if the certain conditions are met[21].

1   Privacy and Electronic Communications (EC Directive) Regulations 2003, SI 2003/2426, reg 14(1). As to the meaning of 'traffic data' see PARA 231 note 1.
2   'Location data' means any data processed in an electronic communications network or by an electronic communications service indicating the geographical position of the terminal equipment of a user of a public electronic communications service, including data relating to:
    (1)   the latitude, longitude or altitude of the terminal equipment;
    (2)   the direction of travel of the user; or
    (3)   the time the location information was recorded: Privacy and Electronic Communications (EC Directive) Regulations 2003, SI 2003/2426, reg 2(1) (definition amended by SI 2011/1208).
    As to the meaning of 'electronic communications network' see PARA 228 note 4.
3   As to the meaning of 'user' see PARA 229 note 3.
4   As to the meaning of 'subscriber' see PARA 228 note 9.
5   As to the meaning of 'public electronic communications network' see PARA 231 note 4.
6   As to the meaning of 'public electronic communications service' see PARA 228 note 1.
7   Privacy and Electronic Communications (EC Directive) Regulations 2003, SI 2003/2426, reg 14(2)(a).
8   As to the meaning of 'value added service' see PARA 231 note 12.
9   Privacy and Electronic Communications (EC Directive) Regulations 2003, SI 2003/2426, reg 14(2)(b). In order to facilitate responses to emergency calls (see PARA 232 note 24), the restriction on the processing of location data under reg 14(2) is to be disregarded in respect of such calls: reg 16(2)(c).
10 Privacy and Electronic Communications (EC Directive) Regulations 2003, SI 2003/2426, reg 14(3)(a).
11 Privacy and Electronic Communications (EC Directive) Regulations 2003, SI 2003/2426, reg 14(3)(b).
12 Privacy and Electronic Communications (EC Directive) Regulations 2003, SI 2003/2426, reg 14(3)(c).
13 Privacy and Electronic Communications (EC Directive) Regulations 2003, SI 2003/2426, reg 14(4).
14 Privacy and Electronic Communications (EC Directive) Regulations 2003, SI 2003/2426, reg 14(5)(a)(i).
15 Privacy and Electronic Communications (EC Directive) Regulations 2003, SI 2003/2426, reg 14(5)(a)(ii).
16 Privacy and Electronic Communications (EC Directive) Regulations 2003, SI 2003/2426, reg 14(5)(a)(iii).
17 Privacy and Electronic Communications (EC Directive) Regulations 2003, SI 2003/2426, reg 14(5)(b).
18 As to the meaning of 'relevant public communications provider' see PARA 231 note 26.
19 As to the meaning of 'emergency alert service' see PARA 231 note 27.
20 Ie the restrictions on the processing of location data under the Privacy and Electronic Communications (EC Directive) Regulations 2003, SI 2003/2426, reg 14(2) (see text and notes 2–9) and 14(5) (see text and note 14–17): reg 16A(2)(b) (reg 16A added by SI 2015/355).
21 Privacy and Electronic Communications (EC Directive) Regulations 2003, SI 2003/2426, reg 16A(1), (4) (as added: see note 20).
    For the purpose of providing an emergency alert service, the specified conditions that have to be met are:
    (1)   the relevant public communications provider is notified by a relevant public authority that an emergency within the meaning of the Civil Contingencies Act 2004 s 1(1) (see ARMED CONFLICT AND EMERGENCY vol 3 (2011) PARA 151) has occurred, is occurring

or is about to occur and it is expedient to use an emergency alert service (Privacy and Electronic Communications (EC Directive) Regulations 2003, SI 2003/2426, reg 16A(3)(a) (as so added)).

(2) the relevant public communications provider is directed by the relevant public authority to convey a specified communication over a specified time period to users or subscribers of the relevant public communications provider's public electronic communications network whom the provider considers are in one or more specified places in the United Kingdom which is or may be affected by the emergency or have been in a specified place affected by the emergency since the emergency occurred but are no longer in the place (reg 16A(3)(b) (as so added)); and

(3) the relevant public communications provider complies with that direction (reg 16A(3)(c) (as so added)).

For the purpose of testing an emergency alert service, the specified conditions that have to be met are:

(a) the relevant public communications provider is notified by a Minister of the Crown that, in the Minister's opinion, it is necessary to test an emergency alert service for the purpose of ensuring that the service is maintained in good working order and is an effective means of communicating with users and subscribers in an emergency (reg 16A(5)(a) (as so added));

(b) the Minister gives directions as to how the test is to be conducted (reg 16A(5)(b) (as so added)); and

(c) the relevant public communications provider complies with the directions in head (b) (reg 16A(5)(c) (as so added)).

Location data which relate to users or subscribers of a public electronic communications network and are processed in accordance with this regulation must, within 7 days of the expiry of the time period specified by the relevant public authority pursuant to head (2) or, as the case may be, within 48 hours of receipt of the Minister's directions pursuant to head (b), be:

(i) erased (reg 16A(6)(a) (as so added)); or

(ii) in the case of an individual, modified so that they cease to constitute personal data of that user or subscriber; or in the case of a corporate subscriber, modified so that they cease to be data that would be personal data if that user or subscriber was an individual (reg 16A(6)(b) (as so added)).

The processing of traffic data or location data in accordance with this regulation is to be carried out only by the relevant public communications provider or by a person acting under P's authority (reg 16A(7) (as so added)).

As to the meaning of 'relevant public authority' see PARA 231 note 29.

234. Termination of automatic call forwarding. Where calls[1] originally directed to another line[2] are being automatically forwarded to a subscriber's line as a result of action taken by a third party, and the subscriber[3] requests his provider of electronic communications services[4] (the 'subscriber's provider') to stop the forwarding of those calls, the subscriber's provider must ensure, free of charge, that the forwarding is stopped without any avoidable delay[5]. For this purpose, every other communications provider[6] must comply with any reasonable requests made by the subscriber's provider to assist in the prevention of that forwarding[7].

1 'Call' means a connection established by means of a telephone service available to the public allowing two-way communication in real time; and 'communication' means any information exchanged or conveyed between a finite number of parties by means of a public electronic communications service, but does not include information conveyed as part of a programme service, except to the extent that such information can be related to the identifiable subscriber or user receiving the information: Privacy and Electronic Communications (EC Directive) Regulations 2003, SI 2003/2426, reg 2(1). As to the meaning of 'user' see PARA 229 note 3.

2 As to the meaning of 'line' see PARA 232 note 9.

3 As to the meaning of 'subscriber' see PARA 228 note 9.

4 As to the meaning of 'electronic communications service' see PARA 231 note 11.

5 Privacy and Electronic Communications (EC Directive) Regulations 2003, SI 2003/2426, reg 17(1).

6 As to the meaning of 'communications provider' see PARA 232 note 18.

7   Privacy and Electronic Communications (EC Directive) Regulations 2003, SI 2003/2426, reg 17(2).

235. Directories of subscribers. The following provisions[1] apply in relation to a directory of subscribers[2], whether in printed or electronic form, which is made available to members of the public or a section of the public, including by means of a directory inquiry service[3].

The personal data[4] of an individual[5] subscriber must not be included in a directory unless that subscriber has, free of charge, been informed by the collector of the personal data of the purposes of the directory in which his personal data is to be included, and has been given the opportunity to determine whether such of his personal data as is considered relevant by the producer of the directory should be included in the directory[6].

Where personal data of an individual subscriber is to be included in a directory with facilities which enable users of that directory to obtain access to that data solely on the basis of a telephone number[7], the information to be provided as to the purpose of the directory must include information about those facilities, and the express consent of the subscriber to the inclusion of his data in a directory with such facilities must be obtained[8].

Data relating to a corporate subscriber[9] must not be included in a directory where that subscriber has advised the producer of the directory that it does not want its data to be included in that directory[10].

Where the data of an individual subscriber has been included in a directory, that subscriber must, without charge, be able to verify, correct or withdraw that data at any time[11]. Where a request has been made under this provision for data to be withdrawn from or corrected in a directory, that request is to be treated as having no application in relation to an edition of a directory that was produced before the producer of the directory received the request[12].

1   Ie the Privacy and Electronic Communications (EC Directive) Regulations 2003, SI 2003/2426, reg 18.
2   As to the meaning of 'subscriber' see PARA 228 note 9.
3   Privacy and Electronic Communications (EC Directive) Regulations 2003, SI 2003/2426, reg 18(1).
4   Expressions used in the Privacy and Electronic Communications (EC Directive) Regulations 2003, SI 2003/2426, that are not defined in reg 2(1) and are defined in the Data Protection Act 1998 have the same meaning as in that Act: Privacy and Electronic Communications (EC Directive) Regulations 2003, SI 2003/2426, reg 2(2). As to the meaning of 'personal data' see CONFIDENCE AND INFORMATIONAL PRIVACY vol 19 (2011) PARA 97.
5   As to the meaning of 'individual' see PARA 229 note 3.
6   Privacy and Electronic Communications (EC Directive) Regulations 2003, SI 2003/2426, reg 18(2).
7   For the purposes of the Privacy and Electronic Communications (EC Directive) Regulations 2003, SI 2003/2426, reg 18, 'telephone number' has the same meaning as in the Communications Act 2003 s 56(5) (see PARA 100 note 4), but does not include any number which is used as an internet domain name, an internet address or an address or identifier incorporating either an internet domain name or an internet address, including an electronic mail address: Privacy and Electronic Communications (EC Directive) Regulations 2003, SI 2003/2426, reg 18(8).
8   Privacy and Electronic Communications (EC Directive) Regulations 2003, SI 2003/2426, reg 18(3).
9   As to the meaning of 'corporate subscriber' see PARA 231 note 8.
10 Privacy and Electronic Communications (EC Directive) Regulations 2003, SI 2003/2426, reg 18(4).
11 Privacy and Electronic Communications (EC Directive) Regulations 2003, SI 2003/2426, reg 18(5).

12 Privacy and Electronic Communications (EC Directive) Regulations 2003, SI 2003/2426, reg 18(6). For the purposes of reg 18(6), an edition of a directory which is revised after it was first produced is to be treated as a new edition: reg 18(7).

236. Use of telecommunication services for direct marketing. A person[1] must not use or instigate the use of a public electronic communications service[2], and a subscriber[3] must not permit his line[4] to be used, for the purposes of making unsolicited calls[5] for direct marketing purposes, where the called line is that of a subscriber who has previously notified the caller that such calls should not for the time being be made on that line, or the number allocated to a subscriber in respect of the called line is one listed in the register[6] kept for the purpose[7].

A person must neither transmit, nor instigate the transmission of, communications comprising recorded matter for direct marketing purposes by means of an automated calling[8] or communications system, unless the called line is that of a subscriber who has previously notified the caller that for the time being he consents to such communications being sent by, or at the instigation of, the caller on that line[9]. A subscriber must not permit his line to be used in contravention of this provision[10].

A person must neither transmit, nor instigate the transmission of, unsolicited communications for direct marketing purposes by means of a facsimile machine[11], where the called line is that of:

(1) an individual[12] subscriber, except where the individual subscriber has previously notified the caller that he consents for the time being to such communications being sent by, or at the instigation of, the caller[13];

(2) a corporate subscriber[14] who has previously notified the caller that such communications should not be sent on that line[15]; or

(3) a subscriber, and the number allocated to that line is listed in the register[16] kept for the purpose[17].

Where a public electronic communications service is used for the transmission of a communication for direct marketing purposes, the person using or instigating the use of the service must ensure that the following information is provided with that communication[18]:

(a) in relation to a communication by an automated calling system[19] or a facsimile machine[20]:
  (i) the name of the person[21]; and
  (ii) either the address of the person or a telephone number on which he can be reached free of charge[22];

(b) in relation to a communication by unsolicited telephone call[23]:
  (i) the name of the person[24]; and
  (ii) if the recipient of the call so requests, either the address of the person or a telephone number on which he can be reached free of charge[25].

1 As to the meaning of 'person' see PARA 14 note 2.
2 As to the meaning of 'public electronic communications service' see PARA 228 note 1.
3 As to the meaning of 'subscriber' see PARA 228 note 9.
4 As to the meaning of 'line' see PARA 232 note 9.
5 As to the meaning of 'call' see PARA 234 note 1. As to the meaning of 'user' see PARA 229 note 3.
6 As to the register see the Privacy and Electronic Communications (EC Directive) Regulations 2003, SI 2003/2426, reg 26 (amended by SI 2004/1039).
7 Privacy and Electronic Communications (EC Directive) Regulations 2003, SI 2003/2426, reg 21(1), (2). See also Ofcom and the Information Commissioner's Office's Joint Action Plan on tackling nuisance calls and messages (December 2014) which at the date at which this volume states the law is on the OFCOM website.
8 An automated calling system is a system which is capable of:

(1)   automatically initiating a sequence of calls to more than one destination in accordance with instructions stored in that system (Privacy and Electronic Communications (EC Directive) Regulations 2003, SI 2003/2426, reg 19(4)(a)); and

(2)   transmitting sounds which are not live speech for reception by persons at some or all of the destinations so called (reg 19(4)(b)).

9   Privacy and Electronic Communications (EC Directive) Regulations 2003, SI 2003/2426, reg 19(1), (2) (reg 19(1) amended by SI 2011/1208).

10   Privacy and Electronic Communications (EC Directive) Regulations 2003, SI 2003/2426, reg 19(3).

11   Privacy and Electronic Communications (EC Directive) Regulations 2003, SI 2003/2426, reg 20(1). The provisions of reg 20 are without prejudice to the provisions of reg 19: reg 20(7).

12   As to the meaning of 'individual' see PARA 229 note 3.

13   Privacy and Electronic Communications (EC Directive) Regulations 2003, SI 2003/2426, reg 20(1)(a), (2).

14   As to the meaning of 'corporate subscriber' see PARA 231 note 8.

15   Privacy and Electronic Communications (EC Directive) Regulations 2003, SI 2003/2426, reg 20(1)(b).

16   As to the register see the Privacy and Electronic Communications (EC Directive) Regulations 2003, SI 2003/2426, reg 25.

17   Privacy and Electronic Communications (EC Directive) Regulations 2003, SI 2003/2426, reg 20(1)(c). A person is not to be held to have contravened this provision where the number allocated to the called line has been listed on the register for less than 28 days preceding that on which the communication is made: reg 20(4). Where a subscriber, who has caused a number allocated to a line of his to be listed in the register kept under reg 25, has notified a caller that he does not, for the time being, object to such communications being sent on that line by that caller, such communications may be sent by that caller on that line, notwithstanding that the number allocated to that line is listed in the register: reg 20(5). Where a subscriber has given a caller such notification in relation to a line of his, the subscriber is free to withdraw that notification at any time; and where such notification is withdrawn, the caller must not send such communications on that line: reg 20(6).

18   Privacy and Electronic Communications (EC Directive) Regulations 2003, SI 2003/2426, reg 24(1).

19   Ie communications to which the Privacy and Electronic Communications (EC Directive) Regulations 2003, SI 2003/2426, reg 19 applies: see text and notes 8–10.

20   Ie communications to which the Privacy and Electronic Communications (EC Directive) Regulations 2003, SI 2003/2426, reg 20 applies: see text and notes 11–17.

21   Privacy and Electronic Communications (EC Directive) Regulations 2003, SI 2003/2426, reg 24(1)(a), (2)(a).

22   Privacy and Electronic Communications (EC Directive) Regulations 2003, SI 2003/2426, reg 24(1)(a), (2)(b).

23   Ie communications to which the Privacy and Electronic Communications (EC Directive) Regulations 2003, SI 2003/2426, reg 21 applies.

24   Privacy and Electronic Communications (EC Directive) Regulations 2003, SI 2003/2426, reg 24(1)(b), (2)(a).

25   Privacy and Electronic Communications (EC Directive) Regulations 2003, SI 2003/2426, reg 24(1)(b), (2)(b).

237.   Use of electronic mail for direct marketing purposes.   The following provisions apply to the transmission of unsolicited communications by means of electronic mail[1] to individual subscribers[2].

Except in the circumstances referred to below[3], a person[4] may neither transmit, nor instigate the transmission of, unsolicited communications for the purposes of direct marketing by means of electronic mail unless the recipient of the electronic mail has previously notified the sender that he consents for the time being to such communications being sent by, or at the instigation of, the sender[5]. A subscriber must not permit his line[6] to be used in contravention of this requirement[7].

A person may, however, send or instigate the sending of electronic mail for the purposes of direct marketing where:

(1)   that person has obtained the contact details of the recipient of that

electronic mail in the course of the sale or negotiations for the sale of a product or service to that recipient[8];

(2)   the direct marketing is in respect of that person's similar products and services only[9]; and

(3)   the recipient has been given a simple means of refusing (free of charge except for the costs of the transmission of the refusal) the use of his contact details for the purposes of such direct marketing, at the time that the details were initially collected, and, where he did not initially refuse the use of the details, at the time of each subsequent communication[10].

A person must neither transmit, nor instigate the transmission of, a communication for the purposes of direct marketing by means of electronic mail:

(a)   where the identity of the person on whose behalf the communication has been sent has been disguised or concealed[11];

(b)   where a valid address to which the recipient of the communication may send a request that such communications cease has not been provided[12];

(c)   where that electronic mail would contravene regulations relating to commercial communications[13]; or

(d)   where that electronic mail encourages recipients to visit websites which contravene regulations relating to commercial communications[14].

1   'Electronic mail' means any text, voice, sound or image message sent over a public electronic communications network which can be stored in the network or in the recipient's terminal equipment until it is collected by the recipient; and includes messages sent using a short message service: Privacy and Electronic Communications (EC Directive) Regulations 2003, SI 2003/2426, reg 2(1). As to the meaning of 'public electronic communications network' see PARA 231 note 4.

2   Privacy and Electronic Communications (EC Directive) Regulations 2003, SI 2003/2426, reg 22(1). As to the meaning of 'individual' see PARA 229 note 3. As to the meaning of 'subscriber' see PARA 228 note 9.

3   See the text and notes 8–10.

4   As to the meaning of 'person' see PARA 14 note 2.

5   Privacy and Electronic Communications (EC Directive) Regulations 2003, SI 2003/2426, reg 22(2). See *Microsoft Corpn v McDonald t/a Bizads* [2006] EWHC 3410 (Ch), [2007] Bus LR 548, [2006] All ER (D) 153 (Dec).

6   As to the meaning of 'line' see PARA 232 note 9.

7   Privacy and Electronic Communications (EC Directive) Regulations 2003, SI 2003/2426, reg 22(4).

8   Privacy and Electronic Communications (EC Directive) Regulations 2003, SI 2003/2426, reg 22(3)(a).

9   Privacy and Electronic Communications (EC Directive) Regulations 2003, SI 2003/2426, reg 22(3)(b).

10   Privacy and Electronic Communications (EC Directive) Regulations 2003, SI 2003/2426, reg 22(3)(c).

11   Privacy and Electronic Communications (EC Directive) Regulations 2003, SI 2003/2426, reg 23(a) (amended by SI 2011/1208).

12   Privacy and Electronic Communications (EC Directive) Regulations 2003, SI 2003/2426, reg 23(b).

13   Privacy and Electronic Communications (EC Directive) Regulations 2003, SI 2003/2426, reg 23(c) (reg 23(c), (d) added by SI 2011/1208). The regulations referred to in the text are those under the Electronic Commerce (EC Directive) Regulations 2002, SI 2002/2013, reg 7 (see INFORMATION TECHNOLOGY LAW vol 57 (2012) PARA 592).

14   Privacy and Electronic Communications (EC Directive) Regulations 2003, SI 2003/2426, reg 23(d) (as added: see note 13). As to regulations referred to in the text see note 13.

238. Enforcement provisions. To the extent that any term in a contract between a subscriber[1] to and the provider of a public electronic communications service[2] or such a provider and the provider of an electronic communications network[3] would be inconsistent with a requirement of the Privacy and Electronic Communications (EC Directive) Regulations 2003, that term is void[4].

A person[5] who suffers damage by reason of any contravention of the Privacy and Electronic Communications (EC Directive) Regulations 2003 by any other person is entitled to bring proceedings for compensation from that other person for that damage[6]. In such proceedings, it is a defence for the other person to prove that he had taken such care as in all the circumstances was reasonably required to comply with the relevant requirement[7].

The enforcement provisions of the Data Protection Act 1998[8] may also be invoked[9].

Where it is alleged that there has been a contravention of any of the requirements, either OFCOM[10] or a person aggrieved by the alleged contravention may request the Information Commissioner[11] to exercise his enforcement functions[12] in respect of that contravention, but those functions are exercisable by the Commissioner whether or not he has been so requested[13].

The Information Commissioner may require a communications provider ('A')[14] to provide information to the Information Commissioner by serving on the provider a notice ('a third party information notice')[15]. The third party information notice may require A to release information held by A about another person's use of an electronic communications network or an electronic communications service where the Information Commissioner believes that the information requested is relevant information[16]. The notice must set out:

(1)   the information requested[17];

(2)   the form in which the information must be provided[18];

(3)   the time limit[19] within which the information must be provided[20]; and

(4)   information about the rights of appeal conferred by the Privacy and Electronic Communications (EC Directive) Regulations 2003[21].

A person is not required[22] to disclose any information in respect of:

(a)   any communication between a professional legal adviser and the adviser's client in connection with the giving of legal advice with respect to the client's obligations, liabilities or rights under the Privacy and Electronic Communications (EC Directive) Regulations 2003[23]; or

(b)   any communication between a professional legal adviser and the adviser's client, or between such an adviser or the adviser's client and any other person, made in connection with or in contemplation of proceedings under or arising out of these Privacy and Electronic Communications (EC Directive) Regulations 2003 (including proceedings before the Tribunal) and for the purposes of such proceedings[24].

A communications provider on whom a third party information notice has been served may appeal to the Tribunal[25] against the notice[26].

1   As to the meaning of 'subscriber' see PARA 228 note 9.
2   As to the meaning of 'public electronic communications service' see PARA 228 note 1.
3   As to the meaning of 'electronic communications network' see PARA 228 note 4.
4   Privacy and Electronic Communications (EC Directive) Regulations 2003, SI 2003/2426, reg 27.
5   As to the meaning of 'person' see PARA 14 note 2.
6   Privacy and Electronic Communications (EC Directive) Regulations 2003, SI 2003/2426, reg 30(1). The provisions of reg 30 are without prejudice to those of reg 31 (see the text to notes 8–12): reg 30(3).
7   Privacy and Electronic Communications (EC Directive) Regulations 2003, SI 2003/2426, reg 30(2).
8   Ie the provisions of the Data Protection Act 1998 Pt V (ss 40–50), ss 55A–55E, Sch 6, Sch 9 (see CONFIDENCE AND INFORMATIONAL PRIVACY vol 19 (2011) PARA 152 et seq), which are extended

for the purposes of the Privacy and Electronic Communications (EC Directive) Regulations 2003, SI 2003/2426, and, for those purposes, have effect subject to the modifications set out in Sch 1: see reg 31(1), Sch 1 (amended by SI 2011/1208).

9 See the Privacy and Electronic Communications (EC Directive) Regulations 2003, SI 2003/2426, reg 31. The provisions of reg 31 are without prejudice to those of reg 30 (see the text to notes 6–7): reg 31(3). See further regs 32–33, Sch 1.

10 As to the meaning of 'OFCOM' see PARA 232 note 5, and as to OFCOM see PARA 2 et seq.

11 Ie the Information Commissioner appointed under the Data Protection Act 1998 s 6 (see CONFIDENCE AND INFORMATIONAL PRIVACY vol 19 (2011) PARA 109): Privacy and Electronic Communications (EC Directive) Regulations 2003, SI 2003/2426, reg 2(1).

12 'Enforcement functions' means the functions of the Information Commissioner under the provisions referred to in the Privacy and Electronic Communications (EC Directive) Regulations 2003, SI 2003/2426, reg 31(1) as extended by reg 31(1) (see note 8) and the functions set out in regs 31A, 31B (see text and notes 14–26): reg 31(2) (amended by SI 2011/1208).

13 Privacy and Electronic Communications (EC Directive) Regulations 2003, SI 2003/2426, reg 32. OFCOM must comply with any reasonable request made by the Commissioner, in connection with his enforcement functions, for advice on technical and similar matters relating to electronic communications: reg 33.

14 As to the meaning of 'communications provider' see PARA 232 note 18.

15 Privacy and Electronic Communications (EC Directive) Regulations 2003, SI 2003/2426, reg 31A(1) (regs 31A, 31B added by SI 2011/1208).

16 Privacy and Electronic Communications (EC Directive) Regulations 2003, SI 2003/2426, reg 31A(2) (as added: see note 15). Relevant information is information which the Information Commissioner considers is necessary to investigate the compliance of any person with the Privacy and Electronic Communications (EC Directive) Regulations 2003, SI 2003/2426: reg 31A(3) (as so added).

17 Privacy and Electronic Communications (EC Directive) Regulations 2003, SI 2003/2426, reg 31A(4)(a) (as added: see note 15).

18 Privacy and Electronic Communications (EC Directive) Regulations 2003, SI 2003/2426, reg 31A(4)(b) (as added: see note 15).

19 The time limit referred to head (3) does not expire before the end of the period in which an appeal may be brought. If an appeal is brought, the information requested need not be provided pending the determination or withdrawal of the appeal: Privacy and Electronic Communications (EC Directive) Regulations 2003, SI 2003/2426, reg 31A(5) (as added: see note 15). In an urgent case, the Commissioner may include in the notice a statement that the case is urgent and a statement of his reasons for reaching that conclusion, in which case reg 31A(5) will not apply: reg 31A(6) (as so added). Where reg 31A(6) applies, the communications provider has a minimum of 7 days (beginning on the day on which the notice is served) to provide the information requested: reg 31A(7) (as so added).

20 Privacy and Electronic Communications (EC Directive) Regulations 2003, SI 2003/2426, reg 31A(4)(c) (as added: see note 15).

21 Privacy and Electronic Communications (EC Directive) Regulations 2003, SI 2003/2426, reg 31A(4)(d) (as added: see note 15).

22 Ie by virtue of the Privacy and Electronic Communications (EC Directive) Regulations 2003, SI 2003/2426, reg 31A.

23 Privacy and Electronic Communications (EC Directive) Regulations 2003, SI 2003/2426, reg 31A(8)(a) (as added: see note 15).

24 Privacy and Electronic Communications (EC Directive) Regulations 2003, SI 2003/2426, reg 31A(8)(b) (as added: see note 15).

25 Ie the Upper Tribunal, in any case where it is determined by or under Tribunal Procedure Rules that the Upper Tribunal is to hear the appeal; or the First-tier Tribunal, in any other case: Data Protection Act 1998 s 70(1); Privacy and Electronic Communications (EC Directive) Regulations 2003, SI 2003/2426, reg 2(2). As to the Upper Tribunal and First-tier Tribunal see COURTS AND TRIBUNALS vol 24 (2010) PARA 883 et seq.

26 Privacy and Electronic Communications (EC Directive) Regulations 2003, SI 2003/2426, reg 31B(1) (as added: see note 15). Appeals are to be determined in accordance with the Data Protection Act 1998 s 49, Sch 6 as modified by the Privacy and Electronic Communications (EC Directive) Regulations 2003, SI 2003/2426, Sch 1: reg 31B(2) (as so added).

239. National security and legal requirements. Nothing in the Privacy and Electronic Communications (EC Directive) Regulations 2003 requires a communications provider[1] to do, or refrain from doing, anything (including the processing of data) if exemption from the requirement in question is required for the purpose of safeguarding national security[2].

A certificate signed by a Minister of the Crown certifying that exemption from any requirement of the Privacy and Electronic Communications (EC Directive) Regulations 2003 is or at any time was required for the purpose of safeguarding national security is conclusive evidence of that fact[3]. Such a certificate may identify the circumstances in which it applies by means of a general description and may be expressed to have prospective effect[4].

Any person[5] directly affected by the issuing of such a certificate may appeal to the Tribunal[6] against the issuing of the certificate[7]. If, on an appeal, the Tribunal finds that, applying the principles applied by a court on an application for judicial review, the Minister did not have reasonable grounds for issuing the certificate, the Tribunal may allow the appeal and quash the certificate[8].

Where, in any proceedings under or by virtue of the Privacy and Electronic Communications (EC Directive) Regulations 2003, it is claimed by a communications provider that a certificate of a minister which identifies the circumstances in which it applies by means of a general description applies in the circumstances in question, any other party to the proceedings may appeal to the Tribunal on the ground that the certificate does not apply in those circumstances and, subject to any determination that the certificate does not so apply[9], the certificate will be conclusively presumed so to apply[10].

Specific provisions of the Data Protection Act 1998 apply for these purposes[11].

Nothing in the Privacy and Electronic Communications (EC Directive) Regulations 2003 requires a communications provider to do, or refrain from doing, anything (including the processing of data):

(1)   if compliance with the requirement in question:
        (a)   would be inconsistent with any requirement imposed by or under an enactment[12] or by a court order[13]; or
        (b)   would be likely to prejudice the prevention or detection of crime or the apprehension or prosecution of offenders[14]; or

(2)   if exemption from the requirement in question:
        (a)   is required for the purposes of, or in connection with, any legal proceedings (including prospective legal proceedings)[15];
        (b)   is necessary for the purposes of obtaining legal advice[16]; or
        (c)   is otherwise necessary for the purposes of establishing, exercising or defending legal rights[17].

Where the above provisions apply[18] apply, communications providers must establish and maintain internal procedures for responding to requests for access to users' personal data[19]. Communications providers must on demand provide the Information Commissioner[20] with information about:

(i)   those procedures[21];
(ii)   the number of requests received[22];
(iii)   the legal justification for the request[23]; and
(iv)   the communications provider's response[24].

1   As to the meaning of 'communications provider' see PARA 232 note 18.
2   Privacy and Electronic Communications (EC Directive) Regulations 2003, SI 2003/2426, reg 28(1).
3   Privacy and Electronic Communications (EC Directive) Regulations 2003, SI 2003/2426, reg 28(2).

4 Privacy and Electronic Communications (EC Directive) Regulations 2003, SI 2003/2426, reg 28(3).

5 As to the meaning of 'person' see PARA 14 note 2.

6 Ie the Upper Tribunal, in any case where it is determined by or under Tribunal Procedure Rules that the Upper Tribunal is to hear the appeal or the First-tier Tribunal, in any other case: Privacy and Electronic Communications (EC Directive) Regulations 2003, SI 2003/2426, reg 28(8)(a) (substituted by SI 2010/22). As to the Upper Tribunal and First-tier Tribunal see COURTS AND TRIBUNALS vol 24 (2010) PARA 874 et seq.

7 Privacy and Electronic Communications (EC Directive) Regulations 2003, SI 2003/2426, reg 28(4).

8 Privacy and Electronic Communications (EC Directive) Regulations 2003, SI 2003/2426, reg 28(5). As to judicial review see JUDICIAL REVIEW.

9 Ie under the Privacy and Electronic Communications (EC Directive) Regulations 2003, SI 2003/2426, reg 28(7). On any appeal under reg 28(6), the Tribunal may determine that the certificate does not apply: see reg 28(7).

10 Privacy and Electronic Communications (EC Directive) Regulations 2003, SI 2003/2426, reg 28(6).

11 See the Privacy and Electronic Communications (EC Directive) Regulations 2003, SI 2003/2426, reg 28(8)(b)–(d). The provisions applied are those of the Data Protection Act 1998 s 28(8), (9), (10), (12); s 58 (with modifications); s 67(1), (2), (5)(f); Sch 6. See further CONFIDENCE AND INFORMATIONAL PRIVACY vol 19 (2011) PARAS 95, 117, 139, 168–170.

12 As to the meaning of 'enactment' see PARA 231 note 25.

13 Privacy and Electronic Communications (EC Directive) Regulations 2003, SI 2003/2426, reg 29(1)(a)(i).

14 Privacy and Electronic Communications (EC Directive) Regulations 2003, SI 2003/2426, reg 29(1)(a)(ii).

15 Privacy and Electronic Communications (EC Directive) Regulations 2003, SI 2003/2426, reg 29(1)(b)(i).

16 Privacy and Electronic Communications (EC Directive) Regulations 2003, SI 2003/2426, reg 29(1)(b)(ii).

17 Privacy and Electronic Communications (EC Directive) Regulations 2003, SI 2003/2426, reg 29(1)(b)(iii).

18 Ie the Privacy and Electronic Communications (EC Directive) Regulations 2003, SI 2003/2426, regs 28, 29.

19 Privacy and Electronic Communications (EC Directive) Regulations 2003, SI 2003/2426, reg 29A(1) (reg 29A added by SI 2011/1208).

20 As to the Information Commissioner see CONFIDENCE AND INFORMATIONAL PRIVACY vol 19 (2011) PARA 109.

21 Privacy and Electronic Communications (EC Directive) Regulations 2003, SI 2003/2426, reg 29A(2)(a) (as added: see note 19).

22 Privacy and Electronic Communications (EC Directive) Regulations 2003, SI 2003/2426, reg 29A(2)(b) (as added: see note 19).

23 Privacy and Electronic Communications (EC Directive) Regulations 2003, SI 2003/2426, reg 29A(2)(c) (as added: see note 19).

24 Privacy and Electronic Communications (EC Directive) Regulations 2003, SI 2003/2426, reg 29A(2)(d) (as added: see note 19).

240–300. Requirements as to retention of communications data. Until 31 December 2016[1], the Secretary of State[2] may by notice (a 'retention notice') require a public telecommunications operator to retain relevant communications data[3] if the Secretary of State considers that the requirement is necessary and proportionate for one or more of the specified purposes falling within the Regulation of Investigatory Powers Act 2000[4]. The relevant communications data[5] referred to in the text are those relating to fixed network telephony[6], mobile telephony[7] and internet access, internet email or internet telephony[8].

A public telecommunications operator who retains communications data by virtue of the above provision[9] must:

(1) secure that the data is of the same integrity and subject to at least the same security and protection as the data on any system from which it is derived[10];

(2)   secure, by appropriate technical and organisational measures, that the data can be accessed only by specially authorised personnel[11]; and

(3)   protect, by appropriate technical and organisational measures, the data against accidental or unlawful destruction, accidental loss or alteration, or unauthorised or unlawful retention, processing, access or disclosure[12].

A public telecommunications operator who retains communications data[13] by virtue of the above provisions must destroy the data if the retention of the data ceases to be authorised by virtue of that provision and is not otherwise authorised by law[14]. It is sufficient for the operator to make arrangements for the deletion of the data to take place at such monthly or shorter intervals as appear to the operator to be practicable[15].

As from a day to be appointed, a public telecommunications operator who retains relevant communications data by virtue of the above provisions must not disclose the data except:

(a)   in accordance with:

    (i)   the specified provisions of the Regulation of Investigatory Powers Act 2000[16]; or

    (ii)   a court order or other judicial authorisation or warrant[17]; or

(b)   as provided by regulations[18].

It is the duty of a public telecommunications operator on whom a requirement or restriction is imposed by:

(A)   a retention notice[19];

(B)   head (a) or head (b) above[20];

(C)   heads (1) to (3) above[21] or provisions relating to disclosure of retained data[22],

to comply with the requirement or restriction concerned[23].

The Secretary of State may reimburse any expenses incurred by a public telecommunications operator in complying with these provisions[24].

The Information Commissioner[25] must audit compliance with requirements or restrictions imposed[26] by this Part in relation to the integrity, security or destruction of data retained[27].

A telecommunications provider who retains communications data by virtue of a specified code of practice[28] must not disclose the data except in accordance with heads (a)(i) or (ii) above[29].

Specific provisions of the Regulation of Investigatory Powers Act 2000 apply for these purposes[30].

1   The Data Retention and Investigatory Powers Act 2014 ss 1–7 are repealed on 31 December 2016: s 8(3).

2   As to the Secretary of State see PARA 76 note 1.

3   See note 5.

4   See the Data Retention and Investigatory Powers Act 2014 s 1; and POLICE AND INVESTIGATORY POWERS vol 84A (2013) PARA 678A. The specified purposes referred to in the text are those purposes falling within the Regulation of Investigatory Powers Act 2000 s 22(2)(a)–(h) (purposes for which communications data may be obtained): see POLICE AND INVESTIGATORY POWERS vol 84A (2013) PARA 680. As to retention notices see the Data Retention Regulations 2014, SI 2014/2042, regs 4–6, 11. See also Joined Cases C-293/12 and C-594/12 *Digital Rights Ireland Ltd v Minister for Communications, Marine and Natural Resources; Re Landesregierung* [2015] QB 127, [2014] 2 All ER (Comm) 1, ECJ; and CONFIDENCE AND INFORMATIONAL PRIVACY vol 19 (2011) PARA 174. See also the Retention of Communications Data Draft Code of Practice (March 2015) which at the date at which this volume states the law is on the Government website.

5   The Data Retention Regulations 2014, SI 2014/2042, Schedule specifies the communications data that is of the kind mentioned in the Data Retention (EC Directive) Regulations 2009,

SI 2009/859, Schedule: reg 3. The Data Retention Regulations 2014, SI 2014/2042 was made under the Data Retention and Investigatory Powers Act 2014 s 1. The Data Retention (EC Directive) Regulations 2009, SI 2009/859 were revoked by the Data Retention Regulations 2014, SI 2014/2042. As to transitional provisions see reg 14.

6   Ie specified in the Data Retention Regulations 2014, SI 2014/2042, Schedule Pt 1 (paras 1–4). The data so specified are:
    (1)   data necessary to trace and identify the source of a communication, ie
        (a)   the calling telephone number; and
        (b)   the name and address of the subscriber or registered user of any such telephone (Schedule para 1);
    (2)   data necessary to identify the destination of a communication, ie
        (a)   the telephone number dialled and, in cases involving supplementary services such as call forwarding or call transfer, any telephone number to which the call is forwarded or transferred; and
        (b)   the name and address of the subscriber or registered user of any such telephone (Schedule para 2);
    (3)   data necessary to identify the date, time and duration of a communication, ie the date and time of the start and end of the call (Schedule para 3); and
    (4)   data necessary to identify the type of communication, ie the telephone service used (Schedule para 4).
'Telephone service' means calls (including voice, voicemail and conference and data calls), supplementary services (including call forwarding and call transfer) and messaging and multi-media services (including short message services, enhanced media services and multi-media services): reg 2(f).

7   Ie specified in the Data Retention Regulations 2014, SI 2014/2042, Schedule Pt 2 (paras 5–10). The data so specified are:
    (1)   data necessary to trace and identify the source of a communication, ie:
        (a)   the calling telephone number; and
        (b)   the name and address of the subscriber or registered user of any such telephone (Schedule para 5);
    (2)   data necessary to identify the destination of a communication, ie:
        (a)   the telephone number dialled and, in cases involving supplementary services such as call forwarding or call transfer, any telephone number to which the call is forwarded or transferred; and
        (b)   the name and address of the subscriber or registered user of any such telephone (Schedule para 6);
    (3)   data necessary to identify the date, time and duration of a communication, ie the date and time of the start and end of the call (Schedule para 7);
    (4)   data necessary to identify the type of communication, ie the telephone service used (Schedule para 8);
    (5)   data necessary to identify users' communication equipment (or what purports to be their equipment), ie:
        (a)   the International Mobile Subscriber Identity ('IMSI') and the International Mobile Equipment Identity ('IMEI') of the telephone from which a telephone call is made;
        (b)   the IMSI and the IMEI of the telephone dialled;
        (c)   in the case of pre-paid anonymous services, the date and time of the initial activation of the service and the cell ID from which the service was activated (Schedule para 9); and
    (6)   data necessary to identify the location of mobile communication equipment, ie:
        (a)   the cell ID at the start of the communication; and
        (b)   data identifying the geographic location of cells by reference to their cell ID (Schedule para 10).
'Cell ID' means the identity or location of the cell from which a mobile telephony call started or in which it finished: reg 2.

8   Ie specified in the Data Retention Regulations 2014, SI 2014/2042, Schedule Pt 3 (paras 11–15). The data so specified are:
    (1)   data necessary to trace and identify the source of a communication, ie:
        (a)   the user ID allocated;
        (b)   the user ID and telephone number allocated to the communication entering the public telephone network; and

(c)   the name and address of the subscriber or registered user to whom an Internet Protocol ('IP') address, user ID or telephone number was allocated at the time of the communication (Schedule para 11);

(2)   data necessary to identify the destination of a communication, ie:

(a)   in the case of internet telephony, the user ID or telephone number of the intended recipient of the call;

(b)   in the case of internet e-mail or internet telephony, the name and address of the subscriber or registered user and the user ID of the intended recipient of the communication (Schedule para 12);

(3)   data necessary to identify the date, time and duration of a communication, ie

(a)   in the case of internet access, the date and time of the log-in to and log-off from the internet access service, based on a specified time zone, the IP address, whether dynamic or static, allocated by the internet access service provider to the communication; and the user ID of the subscriber or registered user of the internet access service; and

(b)   in the case of internet e-mail or internet telephony, the date and time of the log-in to and log-off from the internet e-mail or internet telephony service, based on a specified time zone (Schedule para 13);

(4)   data necessary to identify the type of communication, ie in the case of internet e-mail or internet telephony, the internet service used (Schedule para 14); and

(5)   data necessary to identify users' communication equipment (or what purports to be their equipment), ie:

(a)   in the case of dial-up access, the calling telephone number; and

(b)   in any other case, the digital subscriber line ('DSL') or other end point of the originator of the communication (Schedule para 15).

'User ID' means a unique identifier allocated to persons when they subscribe to or register with an internet access service or internet communications service: reg 2.

9   Ie the Data Retention and Investigatory Powers Act 2014 s 1.

10   Data Retention Regulations 2014, SI 2014/2042, reg 7(1)(a).

11   Data Retention Regulations 2014, SI 2014/2042, reg 7(1)(b).

12   Data Retention Regulations 2014, SI 2014/2042, reg 7(1)(c).

13   Ie the Data Retention and Investigatory Powers Act 2014 s 1.

14   Data Retention Regulations 2014, SI 2014/2042, reg 7(2). The requirement in reg 7(2) to destroy the data is a requirement to delete the data in such a way as to make access to the data impossible: reg 7(3).

15   Data Retention Regulations 2014, SI 2014/2042, reg 7(4).

16   Data Retention and Investigatory Powers Act 2014 s 1(6)(a)(i).The provisions referred to in the text are the Regulation of Investigatory Powers Act 2000 Pt 1 Ch 2 (ss 21–25) (acquisition and disclosure of communications data).

17   Data Retention and Investigatory Powers Act 2014 s 1(6)(a)(ii).

18   Data Retention and Investigatory Powers Act 2014 s 1(6)(b). A public telecommunications operator must put in place adequate security systems (including technical and organisational measures) governing access to communications data retained by virtue of s 1 in order to protect against any disclosure of a kind which does not fall within heads (a) or (b) in the text: Data Retention Regulations 2014, SI 2014/2042, reg 8(1). A public telecommunications operator who retains communications data by virtue of the Data Retention and Investigatory Powers Act 2014 s 1 must retain the data in such a way that it can be transmitted without undue delay in response to requests: reg 8(2).

19   Data Retention Regulations 2014, SI 2014/2042, reg 12(1)(a).

20   Data Retention Regulations 2014, SI 2014/2042, reg 12(1)(b). The requirement or restriction referred to in the text is a requirement or restriction imposed by the Data Retention and Investigatory Powers Act 2014 s 1(6).

21   Ie the Data Retention Regulations 2014, SI 2014/2042, reg 7.

22   Data Retention Regulations 2014, SI 2014/2042, reg 12(1)(c). The requirement or restriction referred to in the text is a requirement or restriction imposed by the Data Retention Regulations 2014, SI 2014/2042, reg 8.

23   Data Retention Regulations 2014, SI 2014/2042, reg 12(1). Such a duty is enforceable by civil proceedings by the Secretary of State for an injunction or for any other appropriate relief: reg 12(2).

24   See the Data Retention Regulations 2014, SI 2014/2042, reg 13. The provisions referred to in the text are the Data Retention and Investigatory Powers Act 2014 s 1(1)–(6) and the Data Retention Regulations 2014, SI 2014/2042, Pt 2 (regs 2–14).

25 As to the Information Commissioner see CONFIDENCE AND INFORMATIONAL PRIVACY vol 19 (2011) PARA 109 et seq.
26 Ie the Data Retention Regulations 2014, SI 2014/2042, Pt 2 (regs 2–14).
27 Data Retention Regulations 2014, SI 2014/2042, reg 9. The reference in the text to data retained is to data retained under the Data Retention and Investigatory Powers Act 2014 s 1.
28 Ie under the Anti-terrorism, Crime and Security Act 2001 s 102: see POLICE AND INVESTIGATORY POWERS vol 84A (2013) PARA 678.
29 See the Data Retention Regulations 2014, SI 2014/2042, reg 15.
30 See the Data Retention Regulations 2014, SI 2014/2042, reg 10. The provisions applied are those of the Regulation of Investigatory Powers Act 2000 ss 71(2) (with modifications), 71(11), 72(4) (with modifications). See further POLICE AND INVESTIGATORY POWERS vol 84A (2013) PARA 654.

TIME

1. THE DIVISIONS OF TIME

(1) THE YEAR

(i) The Calendar Year

301. The calendar. The origins of the English calendar are found in the almanac attached to the Book of Common Prayer[1]. The almanac was part of the common law[2] and was recognised by statute in 1662[3]. However, various factors[4] required the revision of that calendar, and the first full year under the English calendar as it exists today was 1753[5].

1   See ECCLESIASTICAL LAW vol 34 (2011) PARA 730 et seq.
2   *R v Dyer* (1703) 6 Mod Rep 41; *Brough v Perkins* (1703) 2 Ld Raym 992; *Tutton v Darke, Nixon v Freeman* (1860) 5 H & N 647. Judicial notice is taken of the day on which a feast mentioned in the almanac falls: *R v Dyer* (1703) 6 Mod Rep 41; *Brough v Perkins* (1703) 2 Ld Raym 992.
3   See the Act of Uniformity 1662 (repealed).
4   See PARA 302.
5   See the Calendar (New Style) Act 1750; the Calendar Act 1751; and PARA 302. The Calendar (New Style) Act 1750 was repealed by 22 Vict c 2 (1859) s 1, Schedule (repealed), in so far as it required the keeping and observance of certain days.

302. Length and divisions of the year. The calendar year begins on 1 January[1] and the common year consists of 365 days. The year is divided into 12 unequal parts, called 'calendar months'. In common years the month of February contains 28 days; in a leap year that month contains 29 days, and thus the total number of days in that year is increased to 366. Leap years occur once in every four years, the years so designated being those of which the number when divided by four is an integer, subject, however, to this exception, that the centennial year is a leap year only when it is a multiple of 400[2].

In any period of a year in which the month of February has 29 days there must be 366 days; and any child born on 29 February or on any previous day in a year in which February has 29 days must live 366 days to complete his anniversary[3].

The ecclesiastical year still begins on 25 March[4], but all feast days, whether movable or fixed, are dated according to the new style[5]. The legal year was formerly divided into four terms: Michaelmas, Hilary, Easter and Trinity[6].

1   See the Calendar (New Style) Act 1750 and the Calendar Act 1751, by which three changes were introduced. From the beginning of the year 1752 the year was made to begin on 1 January instead of 25 March; the system of intercalation was altered by the introduction of the exception mentioned in the text to note 2; and 11 days were suppressed, the day which would have been 3 September 1752 being made 14 September. As to the necessity for these changes see the explanation in note 2.
2   Calendar (New Style) Act 1750 s 2. The necessity for the changes in the calendar introduced by the Calendar (New Style) Act 1750 and the Calendar Act 1751 (see PARA 301 note 3) arose in the following way. Before 1582 the year was regulated throughout Christendom by the Julian Calendar. The problem being to adjust the civil year, consisting of so many complete days, to the solar year, consisting of the same number of days and something less than six hours in addition, and to preserve the same interval between the beginning of the year and the equinox, the system of intercalating a day in which the extra hours should be absorbed was devised. In every fourth year according to the Julian Calendar a day was interposed between the twenty-fourth and twenty-fifth days of February. The sixth day before the calends of March was made to consist of two days: '*id biduum pro uno die habetur*'. This system of intercalation was in eventually discovered to be erroneous. It had the effect of making the year unduly long, so that, whereas in the year when the calendar was introduced the spring equinox fell on 25 March, and in the year

325, the date of the Council of Nicaea, on 21 March, by the year 1582 it had come to fall on 11 March. To restore the equinox to the position in the year which it occupied in the year 325, to rectify the error and to provide against its recurrence in the future, it was ordained by Pope Gregory XIII that ten days should be suppressed, and that the number of intercalations in every 400 years should be reduced by three. The Gregorian Calendar was adopted in every country in Christendom, including Scotland, but excepting England and the countries in which the Orthodox or Greek Church was recognised. The consequence was that during the seventeenth century and the first half of the eighteenth there was a lack of harmony between the system prevailing in England and that prevailing in the greater part of Europe. From the date when the Gregorian Calendar was introduced there was a difference of ten days between an English and a continental almanac, and that difference was increased to eleven days when the eighteenth century began. In order to assimilate the English calendar to the calendar recognised throughout Europe the Calendar (New Style) Act 1750 was passed. The English calendar is therefore now the same as the Gregorian Calendar.

As to months generally see PARAS 307–311.

3 See the Calendar (New Style) Act 1750. See also *R v Worminghall Inhabitants* (1817) 6 M & S 350, where service beginning on 13 October in the year before a leap year and ending on 11 October of the next succeeding year was held not to be a service for one year, although it had lasted for 365 days. According to the Roman theory regarding the intercalated day (see note 2), the anniversary of the birthday of a child born in a leap year on 24 or 25 February would in a common year fall on 24 February, and so St Matthias' Day is, in the Church of Rome, still kept in a leap year on 25 February, not as in common years on 24 February. The calendar in this respect was altered on the revision of the Prayer Book in 1662. The Statute De Anno et Die Bissextili (40 Hen 3 (1256)), in which the Roman theory of intercalation was adopted, was repealed by the Civil Procedure Acts Repeal Act 1879 (repealed). The Calendar (New Style) Act 1750 was amended to exclude the Table of Lessons by the Statute Law (Repeals) Act 1971 s 1, Schedule Pt II.

4 See *R v Swyer* (1830) 10 B & C 486.

5 Calendar (New Style) Act 1750 s 3. Cf the Calendar Act 1751 s 2. However, in the calendar year next but one after the commencement of the Easter Act 1928, and in all subsequent years, the dates of Easter and of the movable feasts dependent on those dates will be governed by that Act, and the Calendar (New Style) Act 1750 s 3, and the Calendar Act 1751 s 2, will be amended accordingly: see the Easter Act 1928 s 1 (not yet in force). Easter Day is to be the first Sunday after the second Saturday in April: see s 1. The Easter Act 1928 is to commence on a day to be fixed by Order in Council (s 2(2) (not yet in force)) and may be extended to certain parts of the British dominions (see s 2(3) (not yet in force), Schedule; South Africa Act 1962 s 2(3), Sch 5; Zimbabwe Act 1979 s 6(3), Sch 3). At the date at which this volume states the law no such Order in Council has been made under this power, although a private member's Bill was unsuccessfully presented in 1999, attempting to bring the Easter Act 1928 into force: see the Easter Act 1928 (Commencement) Bill 1999, HL Bill 24.

The day for the swearing and admission of the Lord Mayor of London in the Guildhall changed from 8 November to the Friday preceding the second Saturday in November: see the Michaelmas Term Act 1750 s 11 (repealed); the Calendar Act 1751 s 4; the Supreme Court of Judicature (Consolidation) Act 1925 ss 223, 226, Sch 6 (repealed); the City of London (Various Powers) Act 1959 ss 5(2), 20 (repealed); and cf LONDON GOVERNMENT vol 71 (2013) PARA 27.

6 For the terms and sittings of the courts see CIVIL PROCEDURE vol 11 (2009) PARA 64.

(ii) Other Usages of the Term 'Year'

303. Statutory definitions of 'year'. The term 'year', besides denoting the solar year of the calendar, may also mean any like period of time running from a date arbitrarily fixed by statute, contract[1] or otherwise.

'Financial year', when used in any Act of Parliament passed after 1889, with reference to the Consolidated Fund or the National Loans Fund[2], or money provided by Parliament, or to the Exchequer, or to taxes or finance, means, unless the contrary intention appears, the 12 calendar months ending on 31 March[3]. It is with reference to the year so computed that the public accounts are made up, the budget is prepared and the supplies are voted[4].

For financial years beginning before April 2015, the accounts of local and other authorities which are subject to audit had to be made up yearly to 31 March or to such other date as the Secretary of State[5] might direct[6].

For the purposes of assessment to income tax in England the year is defined as running from 6 April to the following 5 April[7].

For social security purposes 'benefit year' is accorded a special meaning[8].

1   The meaning of 'year' in a covenant providing for payments on 1 May in each year for eight years from 5 May was considered in *IRC v Hobhouse* [1956] 3 All ER 594, [1956] 1 WLR 1393. As to the exclusion of the ordinary meaning of a word when used in a written instrument see DEEDS AND OTHER INSTRUMENTS vol 32 (2012) PARA 364 et seq. As to the meaning of 'year' in contracts see PARA 304.

2   As to the Consolidated Fund see CONSTITUTIONAL AND ADMINISTRATIVE LAW vol 20 (2014) PARA 480 et seq; PARLIAMENT vol 78 (2010) PARA 1028–1031; and as to the National Loans Fund see CONSTITUTIONAL AND ADMINISTRATIVE LAW vol 20 (2014) PARA 500 et seq; FINANCIAL SERVICES AND INSTITUTIONS vol 49 (2008) PARA 1334.

3   See the Interpretation Act 1978 ss 5, 22(1), Sch 1, Sch 2 para 4(1)(a) (s 22(1) amended by the Legislative and Regulatory Reform Act 2006 s 25(2); Interpretation Act 1978 Sch 2 para 4(1)(a) amended by the Family Law Reform Act 1987 s 33, Sch 2 para 74, Sch 3 para 1, Sch 4); and PARLIAMENT vol 78 (2010) PARAS 1035; STATUTES AND LEGISLATIVE PROCESS vol 96 (2012) PARA 1212. As to the issue of Treasury bills in any financial year see CONSTITUTIONAL AND ADMINISTRATIVE LAW vol 20 (2014) PARA 504; FINANCIAL SERVICES AND INSTITUTIONS vol 49 (2008) PARAS 1389–1390. The definition of 'financial year' was extended to the financial year when used with reference to the National Loans Fund by the National Loans Act 1968 s 1(6) (repealed): see now the Interpretation Act 1978 Sch 1. 'Financial year' is similarly defined (ie as the 12 months ending with 31 March) in the Coal Industry Act 1994 s 65 for the purposes of the Coal Authority (see MINES, MINERALS AND QUARRIES vol 76 (2013) PARA 58). For the method of determining the financial year of a company see the Companies Act 2006 ss 390–392; and COMPANIES vol 15 (2009) PARAS 711–713.

4   The date fixed by the National Loans Act 1968 s 21(1) (amended by the Finance Act 2003 s 212(1), (2)) as the date up to which the annual finance accounts should be made is 31 March. The history of the financial year before that time is as follows. From the earliest recorded times the yearly accounts of public receipt and expenditure were made up to Michaelmas. The financial year ended on 29 September until 1752 when, in consequence of the change of style, 10 October was substituted, the other quarter days being 5 January, 5 April and 5 July. Just before the end of the eighteenth century a change was introduced with a view to establishing a uniform system with regard to the several branches of revenue and expenditure. It was then arranged that the year should end with 5 January, and the first annual accounts on that system were for the year which ended on 5 January 1804. That was the date fixed by 42 Geo 3 c 70 (Public Accounts) (1801–2) s 4 (repealed). In 1832 another change was made, for, whereas previously the budget had been made up for the year ending 5 January, Lord Althorp presented his budget for the year ending 5 April 1833, and at the same time supplies were taken up to 31 March 1833. There were thus three different terminations to the financial year, 5 April, 31 March and 5 January, which, being fixed by statute for the purpose of the financial accounts, could not be altered without legislation. The Public Revenue and Consolidated Fund Charges Act 1854 was accordingly enacted to fix the date at 31 March: see Parliamentary Papers on Public Income and Expenditure, printed by order of the House of Commons, 29 July 1869, Pt II, App 13 at 326 et seq. The Public Revenue and Consolidated Fund Charges Act 1854 s 2 is now replaced by the National Loans Act 1968 s 21. As to the date of commencement of the year for the purposes of assessment to income tax see the text to note 7. As to the granting of supply see PARLIAMENT vol 78 (2010) PARA 1043 et seq.

5   'Secretary of State' means one of Her Majesty's Principal Secretaries of State: see the Interpretation Act 1978 s 5, Sch 1. Accordingly, many modern statutes refer simply to the 'Secretary of State' without reference to a particular department or ministry. As to the office of Secretary of State see CONSTITUTIONAL AND ADMINISTRATIVE LAW vol 20 (2014) PARA 153.

6   See the Audit Commission Act 1998 s 2, Sch 2 paras 1, 2 (repealed): and LOCAL GOVERNMENT vol 69 (2009) PARA 757. The Audit Commission Act 1998 was repealed on 1 April 2015 by the Local Audit and Accountability Act 2014 s 1(2) (see the Local Audit and Accountability Act 2014 (Commencement No 7, Transitional Provisions and Savings) Order 2015, SI 2015/841, art 3 (a)). Despite that repeal, however, the Audit Commission Act 1998 Pt 2 (ss 2–32) continues to have effect for and in relation to accounts and statements of accounts, and the audit of accounts to which s 2 (required audit of accounts) applies, for a financial year

beginning before 1 April 2015: see the Local Audit and Accountability Act 2014 (Commencement No 7, Transitional Provisions and Savings) Order 2015, SI 2015/841, art 5. As to the authorities to which the Audit Commission Act 1998 s 2 applies see LOCAL GOVERNMENT vol 69 (2009) PARA 757. Further transitional provisions apply to the Audit Commission Act 1998 s 2(1)(b) (with modifications) for a transitional period beginning with 1 April 2015 and ending with 31 March 2017: see the Local Audit and Accountability Act 2014 (Commencement No 7, Transitional Provisions and Savings) Order 2015, SI 2015/841, arts 2, 6; and LOCAL GOVERNMENT vol 69 (2009) PARA 757.

7 See the Income Tax Act 2007 s 4(3), (5); and INCOME TAXATION vol 58 (2014) PARA 2. As to the meaning of 'England' see PARA 318 note 2.

8 See the Social Security Contributions and Benefits Act 1992 s 21(6); and WELFARE BENEFITS AND STATE PENSIONS vol 104 (2014) PARA 410.

304. Meaning of 'year' and 'leap year' in contracts. By the terms of a contract any date may be fixed for the beginning of a year, and, in the absence of any express definition of the term, it may appear from the contract that a period beginning or not beginning on 1 January, as the case may be, was intended[1]. Similarly the words 'leap year' in a contract may mean calendar year or any period of 12 months not necessarily commencing on 1 January but including a leap day, according to the circumstances[2].

1 The word 'year' in a covenant may well mean in one context the calendar year, even though in another context in the same instrument a period of years runs from another date: see eg *IRC v Hobhouse* [1956] 3 All ER 594, [1956] 1 WLR 1393. Contracts of hiring were frequently made from a quarter day to the corresponding day of the next year. A hiring from one Whit Sunday to the next (although Whit Sunday is a movable feast and so the period may be less than 365 days) is deemed to be a hiring for a year (*R v Newstead Inhabitants* (1770) Burr SC 669), but a hiring from Monday after Michaelmas, which fell on a Saturday, until next Michaelmas Day was held not to be a hiring for a year (*R v Standon Massey Inhabitants* (1809) 10 East 576).

2 *Director of Savings v Woolf* (1997) Times, 9 July (construction of prospectus for pensioner's guaranteed income bond).

305. Meaning of 'in any one year'. The expressions 'in any one year' or 'in each year' may refer to the calendar year[1] or to any period of 12 calendar months, according to the context in which the expression is used[2].

The term 'in any one year' may even be used to denote a season or part of a year[3].

1 As to the calendar year see PARAS 301–302.

2 *Shankland v Airdrieonians Football and Athletic Society* 1956 SLT (Sh Ct) 69. See also *Cathcart v Hardy* (1814) 2 M & S 534, where the absence of a spiritual person from his benefice for more than a certain time in one year meant, for the purpose of 43 Geo 3 c 84 (Benefices) (1802–3) (repealed), absence for more than that time during the 12 calendar months preceding the suit; *Bartlett v Kirwood* (1853) 2 E & B 771 (Pluralities Act 1838 s 120, defining a year as the period commencing on 1 January and ending on 31 December); cf ECCLESIASTICAL LAW vol 34 (2011) PARA 458. However, where a director was to receive a certain sum by way of remuneration 'in each year' (*Salton v New Beeston Cycle Co* [1899] 1 Ch 775), or where, under the companies legislation, a general meeting was to be held once at least in every year, it was held that a calendar year was contemplated (*Gibson v Barton* (1875) LR 10 QB 329, DC). As to the annual general meetings of companies see COMPANIES vol 14 (2009) PARA 630. A bequest to servants of a year's wages is prima facie taken to be intended for servants who have been hired at yearly wages, but the nature of the gift may explain for whom it is intended: *Re Ravensworth, Ravensworth v Tindale* [1905] 2 Ch 1, CA. See also *Blackwell v Pennant* (1852) 9 Hare 551; and WILLS AND INTESTACY vol 102 (2010) PARAS 366–367.

3 See *Grant v Maddox* (1846) 15 M & W 737 (see LICENSING AND GAMBLING vol 67 (2008) PARA 238); *R v Swyer* (1830) 10 B & C 486, where the three years mentioned in a charter were held to mean the three terms during which three successive mayors might hold office. See also CUSTOM AND USAGE vol 32 (2012) PARA 70; DEEDS AND OTHER INSTRUMENTS.

(2) DIVISIONS SHORTER THAN A YEAR

(i) Quarters and Quarter Days

306.   Division of the year into quarters.   For some purposes[1], and especially in the relations of landlord and tenant, the year is divided into four quarters, the four usual quarter days being the four feast days, Lady Day (25 March), Midsummer Day (24 June), Michaelmas Day (29 September) and Christmas Day (25 December)[2].

The half-quarter days are 2 February, 9 May, 11 August and 11 November (Martinmas).

1   Ie corresponding to the terms and sittings of the courts: see CIVIL PROCEDURE vol 11 (2009) PARA 64.
2   As to the commencement, duration and determination of tenancies see generally LANDLORD AND TENANT vol 62 (2012) PARAS 1 et seq, 198 et seq; and AGRICULTURAL LAND vol 1 (2008) PARAS 352–354 (commencement of an agricultural tenancy according to custom).

(ii) Months

307.   Variant meanings of 'month'.   'Month' is used in several senses. It may mean one of the 12 unequal parts into which the calendar year is divided; it may mean the period which, beginning on any day of a calendar month other than the first, ends on the day next before the corresponding day of the next month; or it may denote a lunar month, that is to say a period consisting of 28 days[1].

1   As to the meaning of 'months' in a charterparty see CUSTOM AND USAGE vol 32 (2012) PARA 70; and as to the meaning of 'months' for the purpose of income tax liability see INCOME TAXATION. A six months' tenancy might mean a tenancy for 168 days or a tenancy for half a year or 182 days: *Catesby's Case* (1607) 6 Co Rep 61b. As to the period of notice to determine a tenancy from year to year see LANDLORD AND TENANT vol 62 (2012) PARA 216 et seq. As to the meaning of 'month' in statutes before and after 1850 see PARAS 308, 309; and as to the meaning of 'month' in instruments pre-1926 and after 1925 see PARAS 308, 310. As to a calendar month running from an arbitrary date see PARA 311.
    Where 'month' occurs in any judgment, order, direction or other document, it means calendar month: see CIVIL PROCEDURE vol 11 (2009) PARA 90.

308.   Meaning of 'month' in pre-1850 statutes and pre-1926 instruments.   As a general rule, and in the absence of anything to indicate an intention to the contrary, where the term 'month'[1] is used in a contract made and coming into operation before 1926, or in a statute enacted before 1851, it is taken to mean a lunar month[2]. The question whether it was intended to use the word in another sense must be decided according to the ordinary rules of construction; it may be shown that in a particular place, business or trade the word has acquired a secondary meaning[3].

1   As to the variant meanings of 'month' see PARA 307. As to the meaning of 'month' in instruments pre-1926 and after 1925 see PARAS 308, 310. As to a calendar month running from an arbitrary date see PARA 311.
2   *Lacon v Hooper* (1795) 6 Term Rep 224; *Re Humphreys, ex p Humphreys* (1833) Mont & B 413; *Helsham-Jones v Hennen & Co* (1914) 84 LJ Ch 569; *P Phipps & Co (Northampton and Towcester Breweries) Ltd v Rogers* [1925] 1 KB 14, CA. See also *Morrell v Studd and Millington* [1913] 2 Ch 648. As to contracts after 1925, and statutes after 1850 see PARAS 309–310. In the absence of evidence showing a contrary intention, a stipulation for so many months' notice of determination of a tenancy meant so many lunar months' notice: *Rogers v Kingston-upon-Hull Dock Co* (1864) 11 LT 42; *P Phipps & Co (Northampton and Towcester Breweries) Ltd v Rogers* [1925] 1 KB 14, CA. In *R v Chawton Inhabitants* (1841) 1 QB 247, the lease being given for six months and so on from six months until either party should give six

calendar months' notice, it was held that the context showed that the lease was intended to be for calendar months. In *Lang v Gale* (1813) 1 M & S 111, it appeared from the conditions of sale that calendar months were intended. Calendar months were taken to be intended in *Biddulph v St John and Keeffe* (1805) 2 Sch & Lef 521; *Dowling v Foxall* (1809) 1 Ball & B 193; *Hipwell v Knight* (1835) 1 Y & C Ex 401; and *Erith Engineering Co Ltd v Sanford Riley Stoker Co and Babcock and Wilcox Ltd* (1920) 37 RPC 217, CA (notice to determine licence to use patent). However, the general rule in favour of lunar months was upheld in *Tullet v Linfield* (1764) 3 Burr 1455 ('a month to plead'); *Crooke v M'Tavish* (1828) 1 Bing 307 (construction of statute); *Simpson v Margitson* (1847) 11 QB 23 (action by agent for commission claimed in respect of sale of land); *Walcot v Botfield* (1854) 2 Eq Rep 758 (provision in a will for residence for six months); and *Hutton v Brown* (1881) 45 LT 343 (hire of chattels at a weekly rate for 26 months). See also DEEDS AND OTHER INSTRUMENTS vol 32 (2012) PARA 374.

3 *Bruner v Moore* [1904] 1 Ch 305; *Helsham-Jones v Hennen & Co* (1914) 84 LJ Ch 569; *P Phipps & Co (Northampton and Towcester Breweries) Ltd v Rogers* [1925] 1 KB 14, CA. Cf CUSTOM AND USAGE vol 32 (2012) PARA 65 et seq; DEEDS AND OTHER INSTRUMENTS vol 32 (2012) PARA 374.

309. Meaning of 'month' in statutes after 1850. In the construction of statutes passed after 1850, unless the contrary intention appears, 'month' means calendar month[1].

1 Interpretation Act 1978 ss 5, 22(1), Sch 1, Sch 2 para 4(1)(a) (s 22(1) amended by the Legislative and Regulatory Reform Act 2006 s 25(2); Interpretation Act 1978 Sch 2 para 4(1)(a) amended by the Family Law Reform Act 1987 s 33, Sch 2 para 74, Sch 3 para 1, Sch 4). See also STATUTES AND LEGISLATIVE PROCESS vol 96 (2012) PARA 1218. The year 1850 is named because in that year a similar enactment, 13 & 14 Vict c 21 (Interpretation of Acts) (1850) (repealed), generally known as Lord Brougham's Act, was passed. See also ECCLESIASTICAL LAW vol 34 (2011) PARA 1 et seq. Before the passing of the Interpretation Act 1889 (repealed), provision had already been made in several statutes with regard to the construction of the word 'month' in those statutes: see e g the Bills of Exchange Act 1882 s 14(4), where 'month' in a bill of exchange is defined to mean a calendar month; and FINANCIAL SERVICES AND INSTITUTIONS vol 49 (2008) PARAS 1434, 1439. In any sentence of imprisonment, 'month' means calendar month unless the contrary is expressed: Prison Act 1952 s 24(1). This does not apply, however, in relation to a person detained in England and Wales in pursuance of a sentence of the International Criminal Court: see the International Criminal Court Act 2001 s 42(6), Sch 7 paras 1, 2(1)(a); and SENTENCING AND DISPOSITION OF OFFENDERS vol 92 (2010) PARA 763. See also *A-G (Slavin) v Halpin* [1951] IR 196. As to the meanings of 'England' and 'Wales' see PARA 318 note 2.

 As to the variant meanings of 'month' see PARA 307. As to the meaning of 'month' in instruments pre-1926 and after 1925 see PARAS 308, 310. As to a calendar month running from an arbitrary date see PARA 311.

310. Meaning of 'month' in instruments after 1925. In all deeds, contracts, wills, orders and other instruments executed, made or coming into operation after 31 December 1925, unless the context otherwise requires, 'month' means calendar month[1]. In mortgage transactions a month has always been taken to mean a calendar month[2]; and according to the custom in the City of London a month in a mercantile transaction has always been deemed to be a calendar month[3].

In ecclesiastical matters the computation has to be made according to the calendar, and thus six months' notice has always been taken to mean six calendar months[4].

1 Law of Property Act 1925 s 61(a). See DEEDS AND OTHER INSTRUMENTS vol 32 (2012) PARA 371. Where 'month' occurs in any judgment, order, direction or other document under the Civil Procedure Rules, time is computed by calendar months: see CPR 2.10. This follows the former RSC Ord 3 r 1: see *Re A Debtor (No 266 of 1940), ex p Judgment Creditors v Judgment Debtor* [1940] Ch 470, [1940] 2 All ER 303, CA; and CIVIL PROCEDURE vol 11 (2009) PARA 90. See also *Re Figgis, Roberts v McLaren* [1969] 1 Ch 123, [1968] 1 All ER 999.

 As to the Civil Procedure Rules (CPR) see CIVIL PROCEDURE. As to the extent to which cases decided under RSC or CCR may be cited in relation to CPR see CIVIL PROCEDURE vol 11 (2009) PARA 33.

As to the variant meanings of 'month' see PARA 307. As to the meaning of 'month' in statutes before and after 1850 see PARAS 308, 309. As to a calendar month running from an arbitrary date see PARA 311.

2 *Schiller v Petersen & Co* [1924] 1 Ch 394, CA. See MORTGAGE vol 77 (2010) PARA 729.

3 *Turner v Barlow* (1863) 3 F & F 946, where the contract related to work to be done by the defendant as an engraver, and it was held that the transaction was not a mercantile one, and that accordingly the general rule applied. The exception does not extend to commercial documents elsewhere than in the City: *Bruner v Moore* [1904] 1 Ch 305. In *Webb v Fairmaner* (1838) 3 M & W 473, commented on in *Simpson v Margitson* (1847) 11 QB 23, it was apparently assumed that calendar months were intended: see *Re An Indenture etc, Sir Herbert Marshall & Sons Ltd v John Brinsmead & Sons Ltd* (1912) 106 LT 460; CUSTOM AND USAGE vol 32 (2012) PARAS 68, 70; DEEDS AND OTHER INSTRUMENTS vol 32 (2012) PARA 374.

4 *Catesby's Case* (1607) 6 Co Rep 61b. See also *Franco v Alvares* (1746) 3 Atk 342; *Bluck v Rackham* (1846) 5 Moo PCC 305. This computation is that with which the Church is supposed to be most familiar: see *Cathcart v Hardy* (1814) 2 M & S 534; and PARA 305 note 2. Cf ECCLESIASTICAL LAW vol 34 (2011) PARA 1 et seq.

311. Calendar month running from arbitrary date. When the period prescribed is a calendar month running from any arbitrary date the period expires upon the day in the succeeding month corresponding to the date upon which the period starts, save that, if the period starts at the end of a calendar month which contains more days than the next succeeding month, the period expires at the end of that succeeding month[1].

If a period of one calendar month includes the last day of February there must be 29 or 28 days, according to whether the year is or is not a leap year[2].

1 A period of a month which begins on 28 January, or any later day in that month, must in the ordinary year terminate on 28 February. Such a period can never extend into a third month: see *Migotti v Colvill* (1879) 4 CPD 233, CA, where it was held that a sentence of imprisonment for one calendar month pronounced on 31 October ends on 30 November, and a bill of exchange dated 29 January and payable in one calendar month is, apart from days of grace, payable on 28 February, or, in a leap year, on 29 February. Cf *CA Stewart & Co v Phs Van Ommeren (London) Ltd* [1918] 2 KB 560, CA, where a stipulation for payment for the hire of a ship in a charterparty 'per calendar month' was held to refer to the ensuing calendar month and not to the next 30 or 31 days on which the ship should in fact be on hire. When a calendar month's notice of action is required and is given on 28 April, action may be commenced on 29 May: *Freeman v Read* (1863) 4 B & S 174. This was cited with approval in *Dodds v Walker* [1981] 2 All ER 609 at 610–611, [1981] 1 WLR 1027 at 1029, HL, per Lord Diplock. Where an application for a new tenancy was to be made 'not less than two months' after the giving of the landlord's notice, an application made on 23 May was held to have been made exactly two calendar months, no more and no less, after the giving of notice on 23 March, applying the corresponding date rule: *EJ Riley Investments Ltd v Eurostile Holdings Ltd* [1985] 3 All ER 181, [1985] 1 WLR 1139, CA (applying *Dodds v Walker* [1981] 2 All ER 609, [1981] 1 WLR 1027, HL). The corresponding date rule has also been applied by the European Court of Justice: see Case 152/85 *Misset v EC Council* [1987] ECR 223, (1987) Times, 23 March, ECJ. Where the period expires on the last day of a month containing fewer days than that in which the period began, no account is to be taken of anomalies arising by comparison with periods commencing on adjacent days: *University of Cambridge v Murray* [1993] ICR 460, EAT. See also FINANCIAL SERVICES AND INSTITUTIONS vol 49 (2008) PARA 1439. See also the Prison Act 1952 s 24(1); and PARA 309.

As to the variant meanings of 'month' see PARA 307. As to the meaning of 'month' in statutes before and after 1850 see PARAS 308, 309; and as to the meaning of 'month' in instruments pre-1926 and after 1925 see PARAS 308, 310.

2 See *R v Worminghall Inhabitants* (1817) 6 M & S 350. See also note 1; and PARA 302 note 3.

(iii) Weeks, Days and Hours

312. Meaning of 'week'. A week is strictly the time between midnight on Saturday and the same hour on the next succeeding Saturday, but the term is also applied to any period of seven successive days[1]. There is no equivalent, when calculating periods of weeks, of the corresponding date rule used in construing periods of months[2].

1   See eg the definitions of 'week' in the Employment Rights Act 1996 s 235(1) (see EMPLOYMENT vol 39 (2014) PARA 126) and in the Social Security Contributions and Benefits Act 1992 ss 30C(7), 122, 137 (s 30C prospectively repealed by the Welfare Reform Act 2007 ss 28(1), 67, Sch 3, para 9(1), (5), Sch 8. At the date at which this volume states the law, no such day had been appointed). As to the meanings of 'week' and 'benefit week' for social security purposes see WELFARE BENEFITS AND STATE PENSIONS vol 104 (2014) PARAS 157, 158, 299; and as to the meaning of 'weeks' in a contract for the engagement of an actress see CUSTOM AND USAGE vol 32 (2012) PARA 70. As to the meaning of 'successive weeks' see *City of Aberdeen v Watt* (1901) 3 F (Ct of Sess) 787; and HIGHWAYS, STREETS AND BRIDGES vol 55 (2012) PARA 154.

2   *Okolo v Secretary of State for the Environment* [1997] 4 All ER 242, CA (for the purposes of the Acquisition of Land Act 1981 s 23(4), six weeks means 42 days). As to the corresponding date rule see PARA 311.

313.   Meaning of 'day' and 'night'. The term 'day' is, like the terms 'year' and 'month', used in more senses than one[1]. A day is strictly the period of time which begins with one midnight and ends with the next. It may also denote any period of twenty-four hours[2], or the period of time between sunrise and sunset[3]. A 'business day' is defined as any day except Saturday, Sunday, a bank holiday, Good Friday or Christmas Day[4].

The term 'night' is also defined differently for different purposes[5].

1   See *Hoye (Inspector of Taxes) v Forsdyke* [1981] 1 WLR 1442, 55 TC 281 (where it was held that the meaning of 'day' depends wholly on the context, and that in the Finance Act 1977 s 31, Sch 7 para 2 (repealed: see now the Income Tax (Earnings and Pensions) Act 2003 s 378; and INCOME TAXATION vol 58 (2014) PARA 874) the statutory context indicated it meant a calendar day of 24 hours, not a working day). As to the meaning of 'lay days', 'running days', 'working days' and 'weather working days' see *Nielsen v Wait* (1885) 16 QBD 67, CA; *Alvion Steamship Corpn Panama v Galban Lobo Trading Co SA of Havana* [1955] 1 QB 430, [1954] 3 All ER 324 (affd [1955] 1 QB 430, [1955] 1 All ER 457, CA); and CARRIAGE AND CARRIERS vol 7 (2015) PARAS 285, 289. See also CUSTOM AND USAGE vol 32 (2012) PARA 70. As to fractions of a day see PARA 345.

2   *Mercantile Marine Insurance Co v Titherington* (1864) 5 B & S 765; *Cornfoot v Royal Exchange Assurance Corpn* [1904] 1 KB 40, CA. Cf INSURANCE vol 60 (2011) PARAS 307–308. See also *Yeoman v R* [1904] 2 KB 429, CA (charterparty); *Alvion Steamship Corpn Panama v Galban Lobo Trading Co SA of Havana* [1955] 1 QB 430, [1955] 1 All ER 457, CA; and CARRIAGE AND CARRIERS vol 7 (2015) PARA 289. In *Lancashire and Yorkshire Rly Co v Swann* [1916] 1 KB 263, where a railway advice note provided for payment of demurrage if the goods were not unloaded and removed within 48 hours of the dispatch of the notice and stated that the times for unloading were up to 1 pm on Saturday and up to 6 pm on other weekdays, it was held that in calculating the period of 48 hours the whole of each day except Sunday was to be counted, so that the defendant, who began unloading on a Saturday, the day after the dispatch of the notice, and finished on a Tuesday, was liable to pay one day's demurrage. As to the meaning of 'day of incapacity for work' see WELFARE BENEFITS AND STATE PENSIONS vol 104 (2014) PARA 465. As to the meaning of 'clear days' see PARA 335.

3   See *Tutton v Darke, Nixon v Freeman* (1860) 5 H & N 647 (for the purpose of distress the day ends with sunset, and any distraint of goods after sunset and before sunrise is illegal). Note that the common law right to distrain for arrears of rent has been abolished by the Tribunals, Courts and Enforcement Act 2007 s 71: see LANDLORD AND TENANT vol 62 (2012) PARA 288. By the South Metropolitan Gaslight and Coke Company's Act 1869 (repealed), 'day' was defined as 24 hours running from 9 am: see *LCC v South Metropolitan Gas Co* [1904] 1 Ch 76, CA, where the word in issue was 'daily'.

4   See CPR 6.2(b); and CIVIL PROCEDURE vol 11 (2009) PARA 151. As to bank holidays see PARA 321.

5   Eg for the purposes of the Shops Act 1950 s 31 (repealed) (employment of young persons at night), 'night' covered the period from 10 pm until 6 am. As to the meaning of 'night' in connection with poaching see ANIMALS vol 2 (2008) PARA 791.

314. Meaning of 'hour'. 'Hour' may mean any one of the 24 parts of a day or any period of 60 minutes[1]. 'Hours' may be used loosely as meaning a period of time, as in the phrase 'hours of darkness'[2].

1   See PARA 345 text and note 6.
2   In certain road traffic regulations 'hours of darkness' is defined as the time between half-an-hour after sunset and half-an-hour before sunrise: see e g the Road Vehicles Lighting Regulations 1989, SI 1989/1796, reg 3(2), Table; and ROAD TRAFFIC vol 89 (2011) PARA 197.

(3) THE LEGAL TIME

315. Local time. Apart from statute[1] or special convention, the hour of the day must be ascertained by reference to the sun in a particular place. At a given moment, therefore, the solar time is different in different places. The hour at which a court is fixed to sit means prima facie the hour at the locality where the particular court is to sit, and not Greenwich mean time[2]. However, Greenwich mean time is now applied by statute and has been in use throughout the United Kingdom since 1884[3].

1   For the purposes of statute, expressions of time are taken to refer to Greenwich mean time: see PARA 316.
2   *Curtis v March* (1858) 3 H & N 866, where failure to appear in court in Dorchester, when the judge took his seat at 10 am (according to Greenwich mean time) constituted no default, since according to the local time it was some minutes short of 10 am. As to Greenwich mean time see PARA 316.
3   See PARA 316.

316. Greenwich mean time. For the purpose of statutes, subordinate legislation, deeds or other legal instruments, it is provided by statute that, unless the contrary is expressed (and subject to the provisions regarding British summer time[1]), expressions of time are to be taken to refer to Greenwich mean time[2] and not to local time[3]. Regard must be had to this rule in applying legislation in which certain hours of the day are specified within which acts may or may not be done[4]. It is understood that where an event is provided for in an instrument such as a policy of insurance, the hour or day of that event must be fixed with reference to Greenwich mean time, and not local time. However, the statutory rule should not be applied in a case where the instrument was executed or the event was expected to happen or did happen in a foreign country[5].

It has been held that 'sunset' in certain enactments is not such an expression of time as previously mentioned[6], but refers to local time[7].

1   Ie subject to the Summer Time Act 1972 s 3: see PARA 318. As to statutes and subordinate legislation generally see STATUTES AND LEGISLATIVE PROCESS. As to deeds and other legal instruments generally see DEEDS AND OTHER INSTRUMENTS.
2   Greenwich mean time ('GMT') was established in 1884 at the International Meridian Conference, Washington DC. GMT is the solar time at the prime meridian passing through the Royal Observatory at Greenwich (longitude 0°) between 01:00 GMT on the last Sunday in October and 01:00 GMT on the last Sunday in March.
3   See the Interpretation Act 1978 ss 9, 23(3), Sch 2 paras 1, 6; and CIVIL PROCEDURE vol 11 (2009) PARA 784. However, see also *R v Logan* [1957] 2 QB 589, [1957] 2 All ER 688, C-MAC, where it was held that a statute said to commence on 1 January came into force on the day which was 1 January in the particular place where the Act had to be applied.
4   See e g the requirement that a meeting of creditors in the winding-up of a company by the court must be called between 10.00 and 16.00 hours on a business day: Insolvency Rules 1986 SI 1986/1925, r 4.60(3); and COMPANY AND PARTNERSHIP INSOLVENCY vol 16 (2011) PARA 609.
5   See *R v Logan* [1957] 2 QB 589, [1957] 2 All ER 688, C-MAC.
6   See PARA 313.

7   *Gordon v Cann* (1899) 80 LT 20, DC, where the obligation imposed by what is now the Road
    Vehicle Lighting Regulations 1989, SI 1989/1796, reg 25 (see ROAD TRAFFIC vol 89 (2011) PARA
    197), to light a carriage used on the road half-an-hour after sunset was in question, and it was
    held that regard must be had to the actual hour of sunset at the particular place; *MacKinnon v
    Nicolson* 1916 JC 6, where 'sunset' and 'sunrise' in the Salmon Fisheries (Scotland) Act 1862
    s 27 (repealed), which made it an offence to fish for salmon between those times in certain
    circumstances, were held in Scotland to mean the times at which the sun sets and rises at the
    locus of the alleged offence. See also the Night Poaching Act 1828 s 12; and ANIMALS vol 2
    (2008) PARA 791.

317.   British summer time.   The period of summer time ('British summer
time'[1]) is a period prescribed by statute[2], and is the period beginning at one
o'clock, Greenwich mean time, in the morning of the last Sunday in March and
ending at one o'clock, Greenwich mean time, in the morning of the last Sunday
in October[3].

1   'British summer time' was first introduced as a daylight saving measure in 1916 and was defined
    as one hour in advance of Greenwich mean time (see PARA 316), applicable during a particular
    period in the year, by the Summer Time Act 1916 (repealed). Subsequent Summer Time Acts
    amended this period (see the text and note 2).
2   See the Summer Time Act 1972 s 1 (amended by SI 2002/262). This Act consolidated the
    Summer Time Acts 1922 to 1947 (repealed). Council Directive (EC) 97/44 (OJ L206, 1.8.97,
    p 62) and the Summer Time Order 1997, SI 1997/2982 (lapsed) (made under the Summer Time
    Act 1972 s 2 (repealed)), provided for the summer time arrangements for the years 1998, 1999,
    2000 and 2001. The Summer Time Act 1922 (repealed), originally a temporary measure, was
    made permanent by the Summer Time Act 1925 s 1(1) (repealed). As to the territorial
    application of the Summer Time Act 1972 see PARA 318.
3   Summer Time Act 1972 s 1(2) (substituted by SI 2002/262). At the beginning of summer time
    clocks are put forward one hour, and at the end of summer time they are put back one hour. As
    to Greenwich mean time see PARA 316. As to the reckoning of time during summer time see
    PARA 318.

318.   Reckoning of time during summer time.   During the period of summer
time[1], the time for general purposes in Great Britain[2] is one hour in advance of
Greenwich mean time[3].

Wherever any reference to a point of time occurs in any enactment, Order in
Council, order, regulation, rule, byelaw, deed, notice or other document
whatsoever, the time referred to is, during the period of summer time, deemed to
be the time fixed for general purposes under the Summer Time Act 1972[4].
However, nothing in the Summer Time Act 1972 affects the use of Greenwich
mean time for the purposes of astronomy, meteorology or navigation, or affects
the construction of any document mentioning or referring to a point of time in
connection with any of those purposes[5].

1   As to British summer time see PARA 317.
2   'Great Britain' means England, Wales and Scotland: see the Union with Scotland Act 1706,
    preamble art 1; the Interpretation Act 1978 s 22(1), Sch 2 para 5(a); and CONSTITUTIONAL AND
    ADMINISTRATIVE LAW vol 20 (2014) PARA 3. 'England' means, subject to any alteration of
    boundaries under the Local Government Act 1972 Pt IV (ss 53–78), the area consisting of the
    counties established by s 1 (see LOCAL GOVERNMENT vol 69 (2009) PARAS 5, 24, 27), Greater
    London and the Isles of Scilly: Interpretation Act 1978 s 5, Sch 1. 'Wales' means the combined
    area of the counties which were created by the Local Government Act 1972 s 20 (see LOCAL
    GOVERNMENT vol 69 (2009) PARAS 5, 37, 41), but subject to any alteration made under s 73
    (consequential alteration of boundary following alteration of watercourse) (see LOCAL
    GOVERNMENT vol 69 (2009) PARA 90): Interpretation Act 1978 Sch 1 (definition substituted by
    the Local Government (Wales) Act 1994 s 1(3), Sch 2 para 9). The Summer Time Act 1972,
    however, applies also to Northern Ireland, the Channel Islands and the Isle of Man: see ss 4(1),
    5(1).
3   See the Summer Time Act 1972 s 1(1) (amended by SI 2002/262). As to Greenwich mean time
    see PARA 316.

4 Summer Time Act 1972 s 3(1) (amended by SI 2002/262). A print-out from a Lion Intoximeter device recording results of a breath test for excess alcohol was not admissible for failure to comply with the Summer Time Act 1972 ss 1, 3 even though timed according to Greenwich mean time when British summer time was in effect at the time of the offence: *Parker v DPP* [1993] RTR 283, 157 JP 218. For the purposes of the Police and Criminal Evidence Act 1984 s 69 (repealed in relation to England and Wales by the Youth Justice and Criminal Evidence Act 1999 ss 60, 67(3), Sch 6), errors in the time or date of such print-outs caused by the Intoximeter device recording Greenwich mean time during British summer time which do not affect any material aspect of the document produced do not render the document inadmissible as evidence: *DPP v McKeown* [1997] 1 All ER 737, [1997] 1 WLR 295, HL; *DPP v Horswill* (2 July 1997, unreported).

   See further STATUTES AND LEGISLATIVE PROCESS; DEEDS AND OTHER INSTRUMENTS.

5 Summer Time Act 1972 s 3(2).

319. Timing of things done electronically. Where the Communications Act 2003[1] authorises the giving or sending of a notification or other document by its delivery to a particular person (the 'recipient') and the notification or other document is transmitted to the recipient by means of an electronic communications network[2] or by other means but in a form that nevertheless requires the use of apparatus by the recipient to render it intelligible, and the statutory requirements[3] are complied with, the transmission has effect for the purposes of specified enactments[4] as a delivery of the notification or other document to the recipient[5]. The Secretary of State[6] may by order make provision specifying, for the purposes of the specified enactments, the manner of determining the times at which things done under those enactments by means of electronic communications networks are done[7], and an order may also make provision about the manner of proving in any legal proceedings the times at which things done under those enactments by means of electronic communications networks are done[8]. An order may provide for such presumptions to apply (whether conclusive or not) as the Secretary of State considers appropriate[9].

   Under the Electronic Communications Act 2000, the appropriate minister[10] may by order made by statutory instrument modify the provisions of any enactment or subordinate legislation, or any scheme, licence, authorisation or approval issued, granted or given by or under any enactment or subordinate legislation, in such manner as he may think fit for the purpose of authorising or facilitating the use of electronic communications[11] or electronic storage (instead of other forms of communication or storage) for specified purposes[12]. Such an order may contain, inter alia, provision, in relation to cases in which the use of electronic communications or electronic storage is so authorised, for the determination of the time at which, or date on which, a thing done using any such communication or storage was done, or as to the manner in which they may be proved in legal proceedings[13].

1 Ie the Communications Act 2003 s 394: see TELECOMMUNICATIONS vol 97 (2015) PARA 44.
2 As to the meaning of 'electronic communications network' see TELECOMMUNICATIONS vol 97 (2015) PARA 53.
3 Ie the requirements imposed by or under the Communications Act 2003 s 395: see TELECOMMUNICATIONS vol 97 (2015) PARA 45.
4 Ie the enactments specified in the Communications Act 2003 s 394(2) (amended by the Wireless Telegraphy Act 2006 s 125(1), Sch 9 Pt 1; and the Postal Services Act 2011 Sch 12 Pt 2 paras 56, 65 (a), (b)), namely:
   (1)   the Communications Act 2003;
   (2)   the Office of Communications Act 2002;
   (3)   the Telecommunications Act 1984 Sch 2;
   (4)   the Broadcasting Act 1990;

(5)   the Broadcasting Act 1996; and

(6)   the Postal Services Act 2011 Pt 3 (ss 27–67).

5   See the Communications Act 2003 s 395(1), (2); and TELECOMMUNICATIONS vol 97 (2015) PARA 45.

6   As to the Secretary of State for these purposes see TELECOMMUNICATIONS vol 97 (2015) PARA 76 note 1.

7   See the Communications Act 2003 s 396(1); and TELECOMMUNICATIONS vol 97 (2015) PARA 45.

8   See the Communications Act 2003 s 396(3); and TELECOMMUNICATIONS vol 97 (2015) PARA 45. At the date at which this volume states the law, no order had been made under s 396.

9   See the Communications Act 2003 s 396(4); and TELECOMMUNICATIONS vol 97 (2015) PARA 45.

10   As to the appropriate minister see the Electronic Communications Act 2000 ss 9, 10; and CIVIL PROCEDURE vol 11 (2009) PARA 947.

11   'Electronic communication' means a communication transmitted (whether from one person to another, from one device to another or from a person to a device or vice versa), by means of an electronic communications network, or by other means but while in an electronic form: Electronic Communications Act 2000 s 15(1) (amended by the Communications Act 2003 s 406(1), Sch 17 para 158).

12   The purposes specified are:

(1)   the doing of anything which under any such provisions is required to be or may be done or evidenced in writing or otherwise using a document, notice or instrument (Electronic Communications Act 2000 s 8(2)(a));

(2)   the doing of anything which under any such provisions is required to be or may be done by post or other specified means of delivery (s 8(2)(b));

(3)   the doing of anything which under any such provisions is required to be or may be authorised by a person's signature or seal, or is required to be delivered as a deed or witnessed (s 8(2)(c));

(4)   the making of any statement or declaration which under any such provisions is required to be made under oath or to be contained in a statutory declaration (s 8(2)(d));

(5)   the keeping, maintenance or preservation, for the purposes or in pursuance of any such provisions, of any account, record, notice, instrument or other document (s 8(2)(e));

(6)   the provision, production or publication under any such provisions of any information or other matter (s 8(2)(f));

(7)   the making of any payment that is required to be or may be made under any such provisions (s 8(2)(g)).

13   See the Electronic Communications Act 2000 s 8(4)(g), (5)(b); and CIVIL PROCEDURE vol 11 (2009) PARA 947. As to orders which have been made under this power see CIVIL PROCEDURE vol 11 (2009) PARA 947.

(4) GENERAL HOLIDAYS AND SUNDAYS

(i) Holidays

320.   Meaning of 'holidays'. The term 'holidays' used in the larger sense covers:

(1)   the common law holidays, namely (in England and Wales[1]) Good Friday and Christmas Day;

(2)   the statutory holidays, which include those established by the Banking and Financial Dealings Act 1971[2], and those made by statutes and rules relating to legal procedure[3]; and

(3)   holidays made by proclamation[4].

The Treasury may by order suspend financial dealings on specified days without such days being declared bank holidays[5].

1   Common law and statutory holidays are not uniform throughout Great Britain: see the Banking and Financial Dealings Act 1971 s 1(1), Sch 1; and PARA 321. As to the meanings of 'England' and 'Wales' see PARA 318 note 2.

2   See PARA 321.

3   Eg the Senior Courts Act 1981 s 71 (rules of court may make provision for regulating the
    vacations to be observed by the High Court): see CIVIL PROCEDURE vol 11 (2009) PARA 65.
4   Eg New Year's Day: see PARA 321.
5   See the Banking and Financial Dealings Act 1971 s 2; and PARA 321. As to the Treasury see
    CONSTITUTIONAL AND ADMINISTRATIVE LAW vol 20 (2014) PARAS 262–265.

321.   Bank holidays.   The following days must be kept in England and Wales
as closed holidays in all banks:

(1)   Easter Monday;
(2)   the last Monday in May;
(3)   the last Monday in August;
(4)   26 December, provided that day is not a Sunday; and
(5)   27 December in a year in which 25 or 26 December is a Sunday[1].

If, however, in any year it is inexpedient that one of these days should be a
bank holiday, another day may be substituted by royal proclamation[2]. By the
same means a special day may be proclaimed a bank holiday either throughout
the United Kingdom[3] or in any place or locality in the United Kingdom[4]. Since
1974, New Year's Day (or, as appropriate, 2 or 3 January) has each year been
declared a bank holiday in England, Wales and Northern Ireland by
proclamation in the London Gazette; and since 1978 the first Monday in May
has been declared a bank holiday by royal proclamation.

1   Banking and Financial Dealings Act 1971 s 1(1), Sch 1 para 1. Bank holidays in Scotland are
    New Year's Day (if it is not a Sunday or, if it is a Sunday, 3 January); 2 January (if it is not a
    Sunday or, if it is a Sunday, 3 January); Good Friday; the first Monday in May; the first Monday
    in August; 30 November, if it is not a Saturday or Sunday or, if it is a Saturday or Sunday, the
    first Monday following that day; and Christmas Day (if it is not a Sunday or, if it is a Sunday,
    26 December): Sch 1 para 2 (amended by the St Andrew's Day Bank Holiday (Scotland)
    Act 2007 s 1). Bank holidays in Northern Ireland are 17 March (if it is not a Sunday or, if it is
    a Sunday, 18 March); Easter Monday; the last Monday in May; the last Monday in August;
    26 December (if it is not a Sunday); and 27 December (in a year in which 25 or 26 December is
    a Sunday): Banking and Financial Dealings Act 1971 Sch 1 para 3. As to the meanings of
    'England' and 'Wales' see PARA 318 note 2.
       As to service of process on a bank holiday see PARA 322.
2   See the Banking and Financial Dealings Act 1971 s 1(2). As to royal proclamations generally see
    CONSTITUTIONAL AND ADMINISTRATIVE LAW vol 20 (2014) PARA 590.
3   'United Kingdom' means Great Britain and Northern Ireland: Interpretation Act 1978 s 5, Sch 1.
    As to the meaning of 'Great Britain' see PARA 318 note 2. Neither the Channel Islands nor the
    Isle of Man is within the United Kingdom. See further CONSTITUTIONAL AND ADMINISTRATIVE
    LAW vol 20 (2014) PARA 3. See also STATUTES AND LEGISLATIVE PROCESS vol 96 (2012) PARA
    1208.
4   Banking and Financial Dealings Act 1971 s 1(3).

322.   Service of process on a bank holiday.   If a document (other than a claim
form) is served at any time on a bank holiday[1], it will be treated as having been
served on the next business day[2].

1   As to bank holidays see PARA 321.
2   See CPR 6.26; CPR PD6A—*Service within the United Kingdom* paras 10.6, 10.7; and CIVIL
    PROCEDURE vol 11 (2009) PARA 151. See also PARAS 327, 329. As to the meaning of 'business
    day' see CPR 6.2(b); PARA 313; and CIVIL PROCEDURE vol 11 (2009) PARA 151.

323.   Statutory provisions regarding holidays other than bank holidays.   The
rest days and leave of members of police forces are determined by the Secretary
of State[1].

Agricultural workers in England who were employed, and continue to work,
under a contract of employment made before 1 October 2013 are entitled to any
such holidays[2] as are referred to in that contract[3].

1 See the Police Regulations 2003, SI 2003/527, regs 26, 33; and POLICE AND INVESTIGATORY POWERS vol 84 (2013) PARAS 192–193. As to the Secretary of State see PARA 303 note 5.

2 Ie established by provisions as to holidays made by order by the Agricultural Wages Board under the Agricultural Wages Act 1948 s 3 (repealed): see AGRICULTURAL PRODUCTION AND MARKETING vol 1 (2008) PARA 1236. The Agricultural Wages Board was abolished by the Enterprise and Regulatory Reform Act 2013: see AGRICULTURAL PRODUCTION AND MARKETING vol 1 (2008) PARA 1243.

3 See the Agricultural Wages (England and Wales) Order 2012 (revoked but saved for certain purposes by the Enterprise and Regulatory Reform Act 2013 (Commencement No 1, Transitional Provisions and Savings) Order 2013, SI 2013/1455, art 4); and AGRICULTURAL PRODUCTION AND MARKETING vol 1 (2008) PARA 1236. Agricultural workers in England employed after 1 October 2013 are subject to general statutory provisions regarding holidays: see EMPLOYMENT vol 39 (2014) PARA 291 et seq.

The provisions of the Agricultural Wages (England and Wales) Order 2012 have effect in relation to agricultural workers in Wales on and from 1 October 2013 until such time as the Welsh Ministers make an agricultural wages order under the Agricultural Sector (Wales) Act 2014: see s 12. At the date at which this volume states the law no such order had been made.

As to the meanings of 'England' and 'Wales' see PARA 318 note 2.

(ii) Sundays

324. Sundays at common law and judicial acts. The common law does not generally prohibit the doing on a Sunday of any act which is otherwise lawful nor render void any such act so done[1].

Sunday is, however, a non-juridical day[2], that is a day on which no judicial act[3] ought to be done[4]. In a case of emergency, however, an interim injunction[5], being an act in exercise of the equitable jurisdiction[6] originally of the Lord Chancellor, can be granted validly on a Sunday[7].

1 *Drury v Defontaine* (1808) 1 Taunt 131; *Begbie v Levi* (1830) 1 Cr & J 180; *Rawlins v West Derby Overseers* (1846) 2 CB 72; *Child v Edwards* [1909] 2 KB 753.

2 Non-juridical days are sometimes referred to as 'dies non juridicus'.

3 It has been held in Canada that the prohibition applies only to judicial acts by a judge or judicial officer and does not extend to acts by administrative tribunals even when required to act judicially: *A-G for Canada v Hirsch* (1960) 24 DLR (2d) 93.

4 See *Mackalley's Case* (1611) 9 Co Rep 65a and 66b, where it was held that an inquisition was bad on its appearing that the inquest was held on a Sunday; *Asmole v Goodwin* (1699) 2 Salk 624; and *Hoyle v Lord Cornwallis* (1720) 1 Stra 387, where the execution of a writ of inquiry on a Sunday was held to be void. The holding of an inquest on a Sunday is prohibited by the Coroners Rules 1984, SI 1984/552, r 18: see CORONERS vol 24 (2010) PARAS 128, 206. A claim form dated on a Sunday is a nullity, and the court takes notice of the fact that it was dated on that day: *Hanson v Shackelton* (1835) 4 Dowl 48 (citing the following passage from 3 Shepherd's Abridgement 181: 'If any part of the proceedings in a suit of law be entered and recorded to be done on Sunday, it makes the whole void'). See also *Taylor v Phillips* (1802) 3 East 155. As to the extent, if any, to which cases decided under RSC or CCR may be cited in relation to CPR see PARA 310 note 1. As to service of process, and arrest on a Sunday see PARA 327. The taking of sureties and commitment to prison in default are judicial acts which cannot be done on a Sunday: *Taylor v Phillips* (1802) 3 East 155; *R v Ramsay* (1867) 16 WR 191. See also, however, *Secretary of State for Employment v Associated Society of Locomotive Engineers and Firemen (No 2)* [1972] 2 QB 455, [1972] 2 All ER 949, CA, where the Court of Appeal sat on a Sunday to hear an appeal against a decision of the National Industrial Relations Court granting a ballot order under the emergency procedures of the Industrial Relations Act 1971 (repealed). Ministerial acts, however, may be lawfully done on a Sunday (*Mackalley's Case* (1611) 9 Co Rep 65a and 66b). A bill of exchange is not invalid merely because it is dated on a Sunday: see FINANCIAL SERVICES AND INSTITUTIONS vol 49 (2008) PARA 1415.

5 As to interim injunctions generally see CIVIL PROCEDURE vol 11 (2009) PARA 316 et seq.

6 As to the equitable nature of injunctions see EQUITABLE JURISDICTION vol 47 (2014) PARA 76.

7 *Re N (infants)* [1967] Ch 512, [1967] 1 All ER 161, where Stamp J held that an injunction is an exception to the general common law rule that a judicial act cannot be done on a Sunday. As to the effect of a period expiring on a Sunday see PARA 340.

325. Particular acts prohibited on Sundays and other days. Acts which are by statute prohibited on Sundays[1], and in some instances (indicated by the addition in parentheses of the days concerned) also on other specified days, include the following:

(1)   killing or taking game (Christmas Day)[2];

(2)   subject to exceptions, opening a large shop for the service of retail customers[3] (alternatively, the Jewish Sabbath)[4];

(3)   holding coroner's inquests[5].

1   As to Sunday trading generally see the Sunday Trading Act 1994; and TRADE AND INDUSTRY vol 97 (2015) PARA 1005 et seq. See also PARA 326.

2   As to killing or taking game on Christmas Day see ANIMALS vol 2 (2008) PARA 803. As to the meaning of 'game' see ANIMALS vol 2 (2008) PARA 717. There are also close seasons during which the taking and killing of game is prohibited: see ANIMALS vol 2 (2008) PARAS 804, 806.

3   See the Sunday Trading Act 1994 s 1(1), Sch 1 (Sch 1 amended by the Licensing Act 2003 s 198(1), Sch 6 para 110; the Christmas Day (Trading) Act 2004 s 4(1), (2); SI 2004/470; and SI 2006/2407). See also *Bury Metropolitan Borough Council v Law and Cowburn* (1983) 147 JP 540, DC, where taking customers' names was held not to be serving customers. As to Sunday trading generally see PARA 326.

4   Sunday Trading Act 1994 s 1(1), Sch 2 Pt II. See also *R v London Committee of Deputies of British Jews, ex p Helmcourt Ltd* (1981) Times, 16 July, CA (sincerity of conscientious objection to trading on Saturday); *Barking and Dagenham London Borough Council v Essexplan* (1982) 81 LGR 408; and TRADE AND INDUSTRY vol 97 (2015) PARA 1009.

5   See CORONERS vol 24 (2010) PARAS 128, 206.

326. Sunday trading. The law governing trading in large shops and working on Sundays is contained principally in the Sunday Trading Act 1994 and the Employment Rights Act 1996, which together reformed the legislation and make provision as to the rights of shopworkers in relation to Sunday trading[1]. The general rule is that a large shop[2] may not open on Sunday for the serving of retail customers unless it is occupied by persons observing the Jewish Sabbath[3]. However, a large shop may open for any continuous period of six hours on a Sunday (not being Easter Day) beginning no earlier than 10 am and ending no later than 6 pm[4]. This does not apply where the Sunday is Christmas Day as the opening of large shops on Christmas Day is prohibited by the Christmas Day (Trading) Act 2004[5].

When a large shop is open on Sunday for the serving of retail customers, it must display a notice, inside and outside the shop, specifying the Sunday opening hours[6].

A local authority can restrict loading and unloading at large shops on Sunday mornings[7].

A retailer's lease or agreement entered into prior to the commencement of the provisions of the Sunday Trading Act 1994 may not be construed to require a shop to open on a Sunday[8].

Shop workers are protected against dismissal, redundancy or other detriment if they refuse to work on Sunday[9]. A shop worker also has the right to give notice of objection to working on a Sunday[10] and a shop owner has an obligation to explain a shop worker's rights in a written statement[11].

Contravention of the Sunday trading restrictions constitutes an offence[12].

The law relating to Sunday trading is covered in detail elsewhere in this work[13].

1   See TRADE AND INDUSTRY vol 97 (2015) PARA 1005 et seq. See also EMPLOYMENT vol 39 (2014) PARAS 320–324; EMPLOYMENT vol 40 (2014) PARA 615; EMPLOYMENT vol 41 (2014) PARA 787.

2   As to the meaning of 'large shop' see TRADE AND INDUSTRY vol 97 (2015) PARA 1005 note 3. Certain categories of shop are exempted from the general restriction on Sunday trading,

including registered pharmacies, shops in railway stations and farm shops: see the Sunday Trading Act 1994 Sch 1 paras 2(1), (2)(a), 3; and TRADE AND INDUSTRY vol 97 (2015) PARAS 1005, 1007.

3 See the Sunday Trading Act 1994 s 1(1), Sch 1 para 2(1), (2)(b), Sch 2 Pt II para 8(1); and TRADE AND INDUSTRY vol 97 (2015) PARAS 1005, 1009.

4 See the Sunday Trading Act 1994 s 1(1), Sch 1 para 2(2)(a), (3), (4) (Sch 1 para 2(3) substituted by SI 2004/470; Sunday Trading Act 1994 Sch 1 para 2(4) amended by the Christmas Day (Trading) Act 2004 s 4(1), (2)(a)); and TRADE AND INDUSTRY vol 97 (2015) PARA 1007.

5 See the Sunday Trading Act 1994 s 1(1), Sch 1 para 2(5) (added by the Christmas Day (Trading) Act 2004 s 4(2)(b)); and TRADE AND INDUSTRY vol 97 (2015) PARA 1006.

6 See the Sunday Trading Act 1994 Sch 1 para 6 (amended by SI 2004/470); and TRADE AND INDUSTRY vol 97 (2015) PARA 1008.

7 See the Sunday Trading Act 1994 s 2, Sch 3 (Sch 3 amended by the Christmas Day (Trading) Act 2004 s 4(3); and by SI 2004/470); and TRADE AND INDUSTRY vol 97 (2015) PARA 1010.

8 See the Sunday Trading Act 1994 s 3; and TRADE AND INDUSTRY vol 97 (2015) PARA 1011.

9 See the Employment Rights Act 1996 ss 45, 101(1)–(3), 105(1), (4), 108(3)(h), 109(3)(h); and EMPLOYMENT vol 39 (2014) PARA 320.

10 See the Employment Rights Act 1996 s 40; and EMPLOYMENT vol 39 (2014) PARAS 323–324.

11 See the Employment Rights Act 1996 s 42; and EMPLOYMENT vol 39 (2014) PARAS 324, 326.

12 See the Sunday Trading Act 1994 Sch 1 para 7; and TRADE AND INDUSTRY vol 97 (2015) PARAS 1005, 1008.

13 See the Sunday Trading Act 1994; and TRADE AND INDUSTRY vol 97 (2015) PARA 1005 et seq. See also the Employment Rights Act 1996; and EMPLOYMENT vol 39 (2014) PARAS 320–324; EMPLOYMENT vol 40 (2014) PARA 615; EMPLOYMENT vol 41 (2014) PARA 787.

327. Service of process on a Sunday. If a document in civil proceedings (other than a claim form[1]) is served at any time on a Sunday, it will be treated as having been served on the next business day[2]. The issue or execution of a warrant by a magistrates' court on a Sunday is valid[3]. The service of a notice not concerned with a judicial proceeding is not ordinarily rendered void by its being effected on a Sunday[4].

1 A writ dated on a Sunday was held to be a nullity: see *Hanson v Shackelton* (1835) 4 Dowl 48; and PARA 324 note 3.

2 See CPR 6.26; CPR PD6A—*Service within the United Kingdom* para 10; and CIVIL PROCEDURE vol 11 (2009) PARA 151. See also PARA 329. As to the meaning of 'business day' see CPR 6.2(b); PARA 313; and CIVIL PROCEDURE vol 11 (2009) PARA 151.

3 See *Magee v Morris* [1954] 2 All ER 276, [1954] 1 WLR 806, DC (execution of search warrant on a Sunday). Note, however, the procedural requirements where a warrant is issued when a court office is closed: see the Criminal Procedure Rules, SI 2014/1610, r 18.7; and CRIMINAL PROCEDURE vol 27 (2010) PARA 136. Service of process on Sunday was formerly forbidden by the Sunday Observance Act 1677 s 6, but subsequently permitted in respect of search and arrest warrants by the Magistrates' Courts Act 1952 s 102(3). The Sunday Observance Act 1677 s 6 was repealed by the Statute Law (Repeals) Act 1969 s 1, Schedule Pt IV, and consequently the Magistrates' Courts Act 1952 s 102(3), was repealed as unnecessary by the Criminal Law Act 1977 s 65(5), Sch 13.

4 *R v Leominster Inhabitants* (1862) 2 B & S 391 (notice of removal of a pauper); *Sangster v Noy* (1867) 16 LT 157 (notice of intention to quit by tenant). See also the cases cited in PARA 324 note 1.

328. Declaration of 'non-business day' by suspension of financial dealings.
The Treasury[1] has power to declare any day a non-business day[2]. If it appears to the Treasury necessary or expedient to do so in the national interest, then, by order laid before Parliament, it may give with respect to a day specified in the order, subject to any exceptions for which provision may be made by the order, all or any of the following directions[3]:

(1) a direction that no person carrying on the business of a banker may, without Treasury permission, effect on that day in the course of that business any transaction or any transaction of a specified kind[4];

(2)   a direction that no person on that day may without Treasury permission deal in any foreign currency[5] or foreign currency of a specified kind[6];

(3)   a direction that no person may on that day deal in any gold[7] or gold of a specified kind without Treasury permission[8];

(4)   a direction that no person may on that day deal in silver bullion without Treasury permission[9];

(5)   a direction that no member of any commodity exchange[10] or, as the case may be, a specified commodity exchange, may on that day, without Treasury permission, deal in futures in any commodity, or specified futures in any commodity[11];

(6)   a direction that no member of a stock exchange in the United Kingdom may on that day effect any transaction on that exchange[12];

(7)   a direction that no building society[13] may on that day effect in the course of its business any transaction or a transaction of a specified kind without Treasury permission[14].

An obligation on a person to do a thing on a day on which he is prevented from doing it, or is unable to do it, by reason of any such order is deemed to be complied with if he does it as soon as practicable afterwards[15]. A person who knowingly or recklessly contravenes a direction under these provisions[16] is guilty of an offence[17].

1   As to the functions of the Treasury see CONSTITUTIONAL AND ADMINISTRATIVE LAW vol 20 (2014) PARA 262.
2   As to the meaning of 'business day' see PARA 313.
3   Banking and Financial Dealings Act 1971 s 2(1): see FINANCIAL SERVICES AND INSTITUTIONS vol 49 (2008) PARA 832. As to the making of orders generally see STATUTES AND LEGISLATIVE PROCESS vol 96 (2012) PARA 1030 et seq.
4   Banking and Financial Dealings Act 1971 s 2(1)(a). This provision does not, however, authorise the giving of directions to a person carrying on the business of a savings bank in respect of that business: s 2(2) (amended by SI 2001/1149).
5   'Foreign currency' means any currency other than sterling and any units of account defined by reference to more than one currency (whether or not including sterling): Banking and Financial Dealings Act 1971 s 2(6) (definition added by the Finance Act 1987 s 69).
6   Banking and Financial Dealings Act 1971 s 2(1)(b) (amended by the Finance Act 1981 s 136(2), Sch 19).
7   'Gold' includes gold coin, gold bullion and gold wafers: Banking and Financial Dealings Act 1971 s 2(6) (definition added by the Finance Act 1987 s 69).
8   Banking and Financial Dealings Act 1971 s 2(1)(c) (amended by the Finance Act 1981 Sch 19; and the Finance Act 1987 s 69).
9   Banking and Financial Dealings Act 1971 s 2(1)(d).
10   'Commodity exchange' means an association established in the United Kingdom for the purpose of facilitating dealings by its members in a commodity: Banking and Financial Dealings Act 1971 s 2(6). As to the meaning of 'United Kingdom' see PARA 321 note 3.
11   Banking and Financial Dealings Act 1971 s 2(1)(e).
12   Banking and Financial Dealings Act 1971 s 2(1)(g).
13   'Building society' means a building society within the meaning of the Building Societies Act 1986: Banking and Financial Dealings Act 1971 s 2(6) (definition added by the Building Societies Act 1986 s 120(1), Sch 18 Pt I para 8).
14   Banking and Financial Dealings Act 1971 s 2(1)(h) (added by the Building Societies Act 1986 Sch 18 Pt I para 8).
15   Banking and Financial Dealings Act 1971 s 2(3): see FINANCIAL SERVICES AND INSTITUTIONS vol 49 (2008) PARA 832.
16   Ie the provisions of the Banking and Financial Dealings Act 1971 s 2(1).
17   Banking and Financial Dealings Act 1971 s 2(4). Such a person is liable on summary conviction to a fine of an amount not exceeding the prescribed sum (s 2(4)(a) (amended by the Magistrates Court Act 1980 s 32(2))) or on conviction on indictment to imprisonment for a term not exceeding two years or a fine or both (Banking and Financial Dealings Act 1971 s 2(4)(b)). As to the prescribed sum see SENTENCING AND DISPOSITION OF OFFENDERS vol 92 (2010) PARA 141.

Where an offence under the Banking and Financial Dealings Act 1971 s 2 which has been committed by a body corporate is proved to have been committed with the consent or connivance of, or to be attributable to any neglect on the part of, a director, manager, secretary or other similar officer of the body corporate, or any person purporting to act in any such capacity, that person is also guilty of the offence and is liable to be proceeded against: s 2(5). Where the affairs of a body corporate are managed by its members the same criminal liability applies in relation to the acts and defaults of a member in connection with his functions of management as if he were a director of the body corporate: s 2(5).

2. COMPUTATION OF TIME

(1) CALCULATION OF A PRESCRIBED PERIOD OF TIME

329. Days included or excluded in the running of time from or to a given date. Where a law or contract prescribes a period of time running from a given day or event to another day or event, and the question arises whether the computation is to be made inclusively or exclusively of the first-mentioned or of the last-mentioned day, regard must be had to the context and to the purposes for which the computation has to be made[1]. Where there is room for doubt, the enactment or instrument ought to be construed so as to give effect to, and not defeat, the intention of Parliament or of the parties, as the case may be[2]. Expressions such as 'from such a day' or 'until such a day' are equivocal, since they do not make it clear whether the inclusion or the exclusion of the day named may be intended[3]. As a general rule, however, the effect of defining a period in such a manner is to exclude the first day and to include the last day[4].

1   As to the construction of statutes generally see STATUTES AND LEGISLATIVE PROCESS vol 96 (2012) PARA 1078 et seq. As to the construction of contracts generally see DEEDS AND OTHER INSTRUMENTS vol 32 (2012) PARA 364 et seq; and as to the commencement of interests or benefits under an instrument see PARA 330. For the purpose of computing any period of time in proceedings to which the CPR apply, any document (other than a claim form) served after 4.30 pm on any business day or at any time on a Saturday, Sunday or bank holiday is to be treated as having been served on the next business day: see CPR 6.26; CPR PD6A—*Service within the United Kingdom*; PARA 327; and CIVIL PROCEDURE vol 11 (2009) PARA 151. As to the meaning of 'business day' see PARA 313.

2   *Pugh v Duke of Leeds* (1777) 2 Cowp 714; *Lester v Garland* (1808) 15 Ves 248; *Re North, ex p Hasluck* [1895] 2 QB 264, CA; *Ladyman v Wirral Estates Ltd* [1968] 2 All ER 197. As to the duration of contracts of employment see EMPLOYMENT vol 41 (2014) PARA 723. As to time in respect of the right to bring a claim see LIMITATION PERIODS vol 68 (2008) PARA 920 et seq.

3   *R v Stevens and Agnew* (1804) 5 East 244; *Lester v Garland* (1808) 15 Ves 248 (approved in *Re North, ex p Hasluck* [1895] 2 QB 264, CA); *Dakins v Wagner* (1835) 3 Dowl 535; *Wilkinson v Gaston* (1846) 9 QB 137.

4   *Pugh v Duke of Leeds* (1777) 2 Cowp 714; *Lester v Garland* (1808) 15 Ves 248; *Kerr v Jeston* (1842) 1 Dowl NS 538; *Russell v Ledsam* (1845) 14 M & W 574 (affd sub nom *Ledsam v Russell* (1847) 16 M & W 633, Ex Ch; (1848) 1 HL Cas 687); *Robinson v Waddington* (1849) 13 QB 753, where the day upon which a notice is served or an act is done was held to be excluded in computing the time for certain statutory appeals; *Backhouse v Mellor* (1859) 28 LJ Ex 141; *Isaacs v Royal Insurance Co Ltd* (1870) LR 5 Exch 296; *Re Hanson, ex p Forster* (1887) 56 LT 573, DC; *South Staffordshire Tramways Co v Sickness and Accident Assurance Association* [1891] 1 QB 402, CA; *Re Maud, ex p Townend* (1891) 8 Morr 144, DC; *Radcliffe v Bartholomew* [1892] 1 QB 161, DC, where the statutory time for laying a complaint was held to exclude the day on which the offence was committed; *Sickness and Accident Assurance Association v General Accident Assurance Corpn* (1892) 19 R (Ct of Sess) 977; *Sheffield Corpn v Sheffield Electric Light Co* [1898] 1 Ch 203; *Goldsmiths' Co v West Metropolitan Rly Co* [1904] 1 KB 1, CA (approving *Russell v Ledsam* (1845) 14 M & W 574, but distinguished in *Hare v Gocher* [1962] 2 QB 641, [1962] 2 All ER 763, DC); *Queen Anne's Bounty v Tithe Redemption Commission (No 2)* [1939] Ch 155, [1938] 4 All ER 368, CA; *Cartwright v MacCormack (Trafalgar Insurance Co Ltd, third party)* [1963] 1 All ER 11, [1963] 1 WLR 18, CA; *Trow v Ind Coope (West Midlands) Ltd* [1967] 2 QB 899, [1967] 2 All ER 900, CA, where, in a lease for a period 'beginning with the date of ...', the first day was included (followed in *Hammond v Haigh Castle & Co Ltd* [1973] 2 All ER 289, [1973] ICR 148, NIRC (dismissal from employment); and *Re Lympne Investments Ltd* [1972] 2 All ER 385, [1972] 1 WLR 523); *Re Figgis, Roberts v McLaren* [1969] 1 Ch 123, [1968] 1 All ER 999 (devise to wife if she should be living at the expiration of a period of three months from the testator's death); *Warr v Warr* [1975] Fam 25, [1975] 1 All ER 85 (divorce: two-year separation period); *Dodds v Walker* [1981] 2 All ER 609, [1981] 1 WLR 1027, HL (termination of business tenancy); *IRC v Trustees of Sir John Aird's Settlement* [1984] Ch 382, [1983] 3 All ER 481, CA (appointments of capital to beneficiaries of discretionary trust contingent upon their surviving

for the period of one day the designated person, with the day of the contingent event excluded). Both days must be included if the word 'inclusive' is added: *Sickness and Accident Assurance Association v General Accident Assurance Corpn* (1892) 19 R (Ct of Sess) 977. As to 'clear days' see PARA 335.

For cases dealing with the period for bringing a claim for unfair dismissal see *Camden and Islington Community Services NHS Trust v Kennedy* [1996] IRLR 381, EAT; *Biggs v Somerset County Council* [1996] 2 All ER 734, [1996] IRLR 203, CA; *Hassan v Odeon Cinemas Ltd* [1998] ICR 127; *Widdicombe v Longcombe Software Ltd* [1998] ICR 710.

330. Date of commencement of interest or benefit. Where by any instrument some interest or benefit is secured for a certain time, as in a lease for years or letters patent availing for a certain period, and the date of the commencement of the term is expressed in the instrument, the term commences from midnight at the end of that day[1]. Where the date of the commencement of the term is not expressed, the rule is that prima facie the day of the date of the instrument[2] (being the date on which the instrument was delivered or issued, or, in the case of a deed, the day on which the deed was delivered[3]), is included in the term[4].

However, it may appear from the context that the anniversary of the initial day, and not the initial day itself, was intended to be included[5]. An indication to this effect in a lease is afforded by a provision that rent is to be paid on the usual quarter days, since it is presumed that rent is intended to be paid during the continuance of the term[6].

1   *Meggeson v Groves* [1917] 1 Ch 158, where a tenancy for a term of years from 25 March was held to commence at midnight on 25/26 March. See also *Rains v Ogle* [1921] 1 KB 576; and *WH Brakspear & Sons Ltd v Barton* [1924] 2 KB 88, cases in which premises were agreed to be let from 25 March 1920, and rent was held to have been increased since 25 March 1920, within the meaning of the Increase of Rent and Mortgage Interest (Restrictions) Act 1920 s 1 (repealed); *Cartwright v MacCormack (Trafalgar Insurance Co Ltd, Third Party)* [1963] 1 All ER 11, [1963] 1 WLR 18, CA, where a motor insurance cover note was held to cover the period from midnight on the day of issue until midnight on the day of expiry.

2   'The day of the date hereof' and 'the date hereof' mean the same thing: *Pugh v Duke of Leeds* (1777) 2 Cowp 714; *Watson v Pears* (1809) 2 Camp 294; *Williams v Nash* (1859) 28 Beav 93. Note, however, that where it can be proven that the instrument was delivered or issued on a different day, the presumption in the rule referred to in the text is disregarded: see DEEDS AND OTHER INSTRUMENTS vol 32 (2012) PARA 393.

3   As to the delivery of deeds see DEEDS AND OTHER INSTRUMENTS vol 32 (2012) PARA 231. As to the construction of instruments generally see DEEDS AND OTHER INSTRUMENTS.

4   *Clayton's Case* (1585) 5 Co Rep 1a, where in regard to a lease dated 26 May to have and to hold for three years from henceforth, the deed not being delivered until 20 June, it was held that, as this day was included in the term, so 19 June of the third year was the last day of the term; see also *English v Cliff* [1914] 2 Ch 376, where a term prescribed by a settlement dated 13 May 1892 was held to commence from midnight on 12 May. However, see *Cornish v Cawsy* (1648) Aleyn 75. As to the construction of instruments executed on a day subsequent to that named in the instrument see also *Pugh v Duke of Leeds* (1777) 2 Cowp 714, where the deed was delivered on the date named in it, and would have been void, as not being a lease in possession, unless construed as taking effect on the day of its date; *Doe d Cox v Day* (1809) 10 East 427; *Steele v Mart* (1825) 4 B & C 272; *Wilkinson v Gaston* (1846) 9 QB 137 at 142; *Browne v Burton* (1847) 5 Dow & L 289. In *Pugh v Duke of Leeds* (1777) 2 Cowp 714, *Doe d Cox v Day* (1809) 10 East 427, and *Russell v Ledsam* (1845) 14 M & W 574 (affd sub nom *Ledsam v Russell* on other grounds (1847) 16 M & W 633, Ex Ch; (1848) 1 HL Cas 687), where the efficacy of renewed letters patent depending on the date when prior letters came into force was in question, the decision was based on the principle that the courts strive to uphold transactions if this is possible ('ut res magis valeat quam pereat'): see LANDLORD AND TENANT vol 62 (2012) PARA 236.

5   Eg insurance policies: see INSURANCE vol 60 (2011) PARA 167 et seq. See *Pugh v Duke of Leeds* (1777) 2 Cowp 714 per Lord Mansfield CJ.

6   *Ackland v Lutley* (1839) 9 Ad & El 879; *Sandill v Franklin* (1875) LR 10 CP 377, where, by agreement dated 20 December 1872, property was let for a year and so on from year to year at an annual rent, the first payment to be made on 25 March 1873, and it was held that the term

began on 26 December. As to a lease dated on a day subsequent to that on which the term actually began see *Simner v Watney* (1911) 28 TLR 162, CA; *Ladyman v Wirral Estates Ltd* [1968] 2 All ER 197; and LANDLORD AND TENANT vol 62 (2012) PARA 259. As to division of the year into quarters, and quarter days, see PARA 306.

331.   Tenancy period terminable by notice.   Where a tenancy is terminable by notice, the day to be specified in the notice to quit[1] given by a landlord must depend on the method of computation[2] adopted. The last day of a tenancy will therefore be determined as either the day before the anniversary, or the anniversary, of the day from which the tenancy from year to year runs, according to whether or not that day is included or excluded in the year[3].

1   See LANDLORD AND TENANT vol 62 (2012) PARA 213.
2   As to the method of computation see LANDLORD AND TENANT vol 62 (2012) PARAS 216–220, 235–239.
3   *Sidebotham v Holland* [1895] 1 QB 378, CA, where a notice to quit on 19 May, being the day on which the tenancy began, was held good; *Ladyman v Wirral Estates Ltd* [1968] 2 All ER 197, where the tenancy ran from 1 May, and notice to quit on 30 April was held good; *Mannai Investment Co Ltd v Eagle Star Life Assurance Co Ltd* [1997] AC 749, [1997] 3 All ER 352, HL. See LANDLORD AND TENANT vol 62 (2012) PARA 236.

332.   Duration of protection order.   The benefit of a protection order expressed to be given until a day for which a meeting of creditors is convened must clearly be intended to cover that day[1].

1   *Backhouse v Mellor* (1859) 28 LJ Ex 141. Cf *Ammerman v Digges* (1861) 12 ICLR App I, where, in a letter of licence from creditors to a debtor 'for and during a year from the date thereof', it was held that the day of the date should be excluded in calculating the year.

333.   Period of accumulations.   The period of 21 years from the death of the settlor or testator which constitutes the second of the statutory periods for which a direction for accumulation may validly be made[1] includes the whole of the anniversary of the date of death[2].

1   See the Law of Property Act 1925 s 164(1)(b) (repealed); and PERPETUITIES AND ACCUMULATIONS vol 80 (2013) PARA 131. Note that the statutory restrictions imposed by the Law of Property Act 1925 s 164 on the periods of time for accumulations have been abolished (see the Perpetuities and Accumulations Act 2009 ss 13, 21, Schedule) but continue to apply to wills or instruments executed before 6 April 2010 (see s 15(1); Perpetuities and Accumulations Act 2009 (Commencement) Order 2010, SI 2010/37): see PERPETUITIES AND ACCUMULATIONS vol 80 (2013) PARAS 131, 142.
2   *Gorst v Lowndes* (1841) 11 Sim 434. See also PERPETUITIES AND ACCUMULATIONS vol 80 (2013) PARA 141.

(2) PERIOD ON EXPIRATION OF WHICH AN ACT MAY BE DONE

334.   Exclusion of day of expiration.   When it is prescribed that an act may not be done before the expiration of a fixed period, the person for whose benefit that delay is prescribed has the benefit of the entire period. The period is therefore computed to exclude the day from which it runs as well as the day on which it expires[1], and the act may not be done before midnight of that day[2].

The Criminal Procedure Rules provide that notice of appeal from the magistrates' court to the Crown Court must be served not more than 21 days after:

(1)   sentence or the date sentence is deferred to (whichever is earlier), if the appeal is against conviction or against a finding of guilt[3];

(2)   sentence, if the appeal is against sentence[4]; or

(3)   the order or failure to make an order about which the appellant wants to appeal, in any other case[5].

1   *Blunt v Heslop* (1838) 8 Ad & El 577. See also *R v Long* [1960] 1 QB 681, [1959] 3 All ER 559, CCA; cf *Rightside Properties Ltd v Gray* [1975] Ch 72, [1974] 2 All ER 1169 (notice to complete purchase of land). However, see also *Schnabel v Allard* [1967] 1 QB 627, [1966] 3 All ER 816, CA (notice to quit: first day included, last day excluded). In *Browne v Black* [1912] 1 KB 316, CA, decided on a statute which provided that no attorney should commence an action for costs until after the expiration of one month or more after he had delivered his bill or sent it by post, it was held that both days must be excluded, the expression 'or more' being equivalent to 'at least': see LEGAL PROFESSIONS vol 66 (2015) PARA 728. In *Re Hector Whaling Ltd* [1936] Ch 208 provision for not less than 21 days' notice of a special resolution in what is now the Companies Act 2006 s 307(2), was held to mean 21 clear days exclusive of the day of service of the notice and the day of the meeting: see COMPANIES vol 14 (2009) PARA 632. However, in *Re Starkey, ex p Farquhar* (1826) Mont & M 7, it was held that in counting the two months between the day on which a mortgage was executed and that on which a commission in bankruptcy issued, the day of execution should be included. See also *R v Shropshire Justices* (1838) 8 Ad & El 173; *Mitchell v Foster* (1840) 12 Ad & El 472; *Young v Higgon* (1840) 6 M & W 49. In these cases the intending plaintiff had to give notice of action so many days at least before commencing his action, and it was held that the days on which notice was given and proceedings taken must both be excluded (overruling *R v Adderley* (1780) 2 Doug KB 463 and *Castle v Burditt* (1790) 3 Term Rep 623). See further *Roberts v Stacey* (1810) 13 East 21; *Zouch v Empsey* (1821) 4 B & Ald 522 (requirement of 14 days' notice at least to creditors before motion to discharge debtor); *Chambers v Smith* (1843) 12 M & W 2, where 'not less than 15 days' was held to mean 15 clear days; *Freeman v Read* (1863) 4 B & S 174 (Limitation of Actions and Costs Act 1842 s 4, requiring one calendar month's notice before action (cited with approval by Lord Diplock in *Dodds v Walker* [1981] 2 All ER 609 at 610–611, [1981] 1 WLR 1027 at 1029, HL)); *Re Railway Sleepers Supply Co* (1885) 29 ChD 204 (following *Young v Higgon* (1840) 6 M & W 49); *E J Riley Investments Ltd v Eurostile Holdings Ltd* [1985] 3 All ER 181, [1985] 1 WLR 1139, CA (applying *Dodds v Walker* [1981] 2 All ER 609, [1981] 1 WLR 1027, HL) where the last day was included so that two calendar months exactly was held to be 'not less than two months'. See also, in relation to time limits on applications in tenancy renewals, LANDLORD AND TENANT vol 63 (2012) PARA 837.
    As to expressions showing an intention to exclude days see PARA 335.

2   *Page v More* (1850) 15 QB 684. For instance, when seven days' notice to quit is required in order to determine a tenancy, a notice given on Monday (although given before noon) requiring the tenant to quit on the next Monday at noon is not good: *Weston v Fidler* (1903) 47 Sol Jo 567, DC. See also *Lawford v Davies* (1878) 4 PD 61, where 21 days' residence required by statute before marriage was held not to be satisfied by residence from early on the morning of 1 July until noon on 21 July; *Sullivan v Sheehan* (1916) 50 ILT 41, where it was held that a summons for possession served on the day of the expiry of a notice to quit was premature; *Carapanayoti & Co Ltd v Comptoir Commercial Andre & Cie SA* [1972] 1 Lloyd's Rep 139, CA, where the port of destination had to be declared not later than 21 days before the commencement of the shipping period, and it was held that the day of commencement was to be excluded in making the calculation; *Manorlike Ltd v Le Vitas Travel Agency and Consultancy Services Ltd* [1986] 1 All ER 573, [1986] 1 EGLR 79, where notice to quit 'within a period of three months' was valid notice, since 'within' was capable of meaning 'during' or 'before or at the expiry of' that period and therefore included midnight on the last day of the period, so that the notice gave the tenant the full three months' notice to which it was entitled. As to the determination of weekly, monthly or other periodic tenancies see LANDLORD AND TENANT vol 62 (2012) PARA 234.

3   See the Criminal Procedure Rules 2014, SI 2014/1610, r 63.2(2)(b)(i); and CRIMINAL PROCEDURE vol 28 (2010) PARA 701. The time-limit mentioned in the text has been held to exclude the day of decision but to include the twenty-first day: *Goldsmiths' Co v West Metropolitan Rly Co* [1904] 1 KB 1, CA; *Stewart v Chapman* [1951] 2 KB 792, 35 Cr App Rep 102, DC. As to appeals against conviction or sentence see the Magistrates' Courts Act 1980 s 108; and CRIMINAL PROCEDURE vol 28 (2010) PARA 695.

4   See the Criminal Procedure Rules 2014, SI 2014/1610, r 63.2(2)(b)(ii); and CRIMINAL PROCEDURE vol 28 (2010) PARA 701.

5   See the Criminal Procedure Rules 2014, SI 2014/1610, r 63.2(2)(b)(iii); and CRIMINAL PROCEDURE vol 28 (2010) PARA 701.

335. Expressions showing intention to exclude days. In many statutes[1], statutory rules[2] and byelaws[3] the intention to exclude the first and last days of a period[4], and therefore to give the person affected a clear interval of time between the two, is put beyond all doubt by the insertion of words such as 'clear days'[5] or so many days 'at least'[6].

1   See eg:
    (1)   the Bills of Exchange Act 1882 s 14(2), with reference to bills payable at a fixed period after date or sight (see FINANCIAL SERVICES AND INSTITUTIONS vol 49 (2008) PARA 1434 et seq);
    (2)   the Companies Act 2006 s 307(1), (2) (notice of general meeting of company) (see PARA 334 note 1; and COMPANIES vol 14 (2009) PARA 632); and
    (3)   the Protection from Eviction Act 1977 s 5(1)(b) (notice to quit to be not less than four weeks before the date it takes effect) (see note 5; and LANDLORD AND TENANT vol 62 (2012) PARA 234).
2   CPR 2.8 provides explicit rules for the computation of any period of time for doing any act specified by the CPR, a practice direction or a judgment or order of the court: see CIVIL PROCEDURE vol 11 (2009) PARA 88; and note 5. As to the application of the CPR see PARA 310 note 1.
3   As to byelaws made by local authorities see LOCAL GOVERNMENT vol 69 (2009) PARA 553 et seq; LONDON GOVERNMENT vol 71 (2013) PARAS 60, 314.
4   Ie the day from which a period runs and the day on which it expires: see PARA 334.
5   A period of time for doing any act specified by the CPR, a practice direction or judgment or order of the court expressed as a number of days must be computed as a number of clear days: CPR 2.8(1), (2). 'Clear days' means that the day on which the period begins and, if the end of the period is defined by reference to an event, the day on which the event occurs, are not included in the computation: CPR 2.8(3). See further CIVIL PROCEDURE vol 11 (2009) PARA 88.
6   *R v Herefordshire Justices* (1820) 3 B & Ald 581, where ten clear days' notice of appeal to the sessions was required; *Zouch v Empsey* (1821) 4 B & Ald 522 ('at least'); *Re Prangley* (1836) 4 Ad & El 781; *R v Shropshire Justices* (1838) 8 Ad & El 173 ('at least'); *Young v Higgon* (1840) 6 M & W 49 ('at least'); *Chambers v Smith* (1843) 12 M & W 2, where 'not less than 15 days' was held to mean 15 clear days (followed in *R v Turner* [1910] 1 KB 346, CCA); *R v Middlesex Justices* (1845) 3 Dow & L 109; *R v Aberdare Canal Co* (1850) 14 QB 854; *Watson v Eales* (1857) 23 Beav 294, where both days were excluded in computing 'ten clear days' between the date of a notice to pay calls and the date of the forfeiture of shares on default; *Re Railway Sleepers Supply Co* (1885) 29 ChD 204, where, in an interval of 'not less than 14 days' between the passing and confirming of a resolution, the day of the meeting at which the resolution was passed and the day of the confirmatory meeting were both excluded; *Sneath v Valley Gold Ltd* [1893] 1 Ch 477, CA, where for the purpose of a requirement of 'at least 14 days' notice' the day of notice of a company meeting and the day of the meeting were both excluded; *R v Long* [1960] 1 QB 681, [1959] 3 All ER 559, CCA, where 'at least three days' in the Criminal Justice Act 1948 s 23(1) (repealed) was held to mean three clear days; *Schnabel v Allard* [1967] 1 QB 627, [1966] 3 All ER 816, CA, where it was held (overruling *Thompson v Stimpson* [1961] 1 QB 195, [1960] 3 All ER 500, DC) that in the context of a notice to quit between a landlord and a tenant 'not less than four weeks' meant a period of four weeks, including the first and excluding the last day; *Rightside Properties Ltd v Gray* [1975] Ch 72, [1974] 2 All ER 1169, where it was held that a condition requiring 'at least 21 days' notice' meant 21 days exclusive of the day of service and the day of expiry of the notice. See also the cases cited in PARA 334 note 1.

(3) PERIOD WITHIN WHICH AN ACT MUST BE DONE

336. Exclusion of first day. The general rule in cases in which a period is fixed within which a person must act or take the consequences is that the day of the act or event from which the period runs should not be counted against him[1].

This general rule applies irrespective of whether the limitation of time is imposed by the act of a party or by statute[2]. Thus, where a period is fixed within which a criminal prosecution or a civil claim may be commenced, the day on which the offence is committed or the cause of action arises is excluded in the computation[3]. In the same way, where a statute provides that something may only be done within a certain period from the passing of the Act, the day on which the Act was passed is excluded[4]; and many other instances may be cited[5]. In particular, where an act is required by the Civil Procedure Rules, a practice direction or by any judgment or order of the court to be done within a specified period, the day on which the period begins is not included in computing the number of days[6]. Further, the rule excluding the day from which the period runs has been applied in construing the statutory provision by which the fact that goods seized by the sheriff are allowed to remain in his hands for 21 days constitutes an act of bankruptcy on the part of the owner, the date of the seizure being omitted in the computation[7].

The court has no power to extend a period of time limited by statute for doing an act unless the statute so provides[8].

1   *Lester v Garland* (1808) 15 Ves 248 (cited with approval by Lord Diplock in *Dodds v Walker* [1981] 2 All ER 609 at 610, [1981] 1 WLR 1027 at 1029, HL; and see also *Pritam Kaur v S Russell & Sons Ltd* [1973] QB 336, [1973] 1 All ER 617, CA); *Pellew v Wonford Inhabitants* (1829) 9 B & C 134 (followed in *R v West Riding of Yorkshire Justices* (1833) 4 B & Ad 685); *Blunt v Heslop* (1838) 8 Ad & El 577 (cf PARA 334 note 1); *Webb v Fairmaner* (1838) 3 M & W 473; *Cartwright v MacCormack (Trafalgar Insurance Co Ltd, Third Party)* [1963] 1 All ER 11, [1963] 1 WLR 18, CA. See also, however, *Trow v Ind Coope (West Midlands) Ltd* [1967] 2 QB 899, [1967] 2 All ER 900, CA (approving *Hare v Gocher* [1962] 2 QB 641, [1962] 2 All ER 763, DC) (period 'beginning with the date of': first day included in calculating period); *Hammond v Haigh Castle & Co Ltd* [1973] 2 All ER 289, [1973] ICR 148, NIRC, where the four-week period for making a complaint of unfair dismissal was held to include the day of termination of the contract; *Pruden v Cunard Ellerman Ltd* [1993] IRLR 317, EAT. See further *Swainston v Hetton Victory Club Ltd* [1983] 1 All ER 1179, [1983] ICR 341, CA (whether complaint of unfair dismissal 'presented' within three-month period); and *Trafford Metropolitan Borough Council v Total Fitness UK Ltd* [2002] EWCA Civ 1513, [2003] 2 P & CR 8 (general rule did not apply where landlord gave more notice than necessary and specified termination date of lease). Cf CIVIL PROCEDURE vol 11 (2009) PARA 88 et seq; and see note 2. Cf also the Export Control Order 2008, SI 2008/3231, art 2(3), by which any reference in that order to time after an event is a reference to a period of that length of time beginning on the day of that event.

2   The principle is of general application to statutes, whether they deal with civil or criminal matters: *Marren v Dawson Bentley & Co Ltd* [1961] 2 QB 135 at 143, [1961] 2 All ER 270 at 274 per Havers J.

3   See *Marren v Dawson Bentley & Co Ltd* [1961] 2 QB 135, [1961] 2 All ER 270 per Havers J. See also *Hardy v Ryle* (1829) 9 B & C 603 (overruling *Clarke v Davey* (1820) 4 Moore CP 465); *Radcliffe v Bartholomew* [1892] 1 QB 161, DC. Cf *Gelmini v Moriggia* [1913] 2 KB 549. In calculating the period for service of a notice of intended prosecution under what is now the Road Traffic Offenders Act 1988 s 1(1)(c) (see ROAD TRAFFIC vol 90 (2011) PARA 785), the date of the commission of the offence is excluded: *Stewart v Chapman* [1951] 2 KB 792, [1951] 2 All ER 613, DC. See, however, *Trow v Ind Coope (West Midlands) Ltd* [1967] 2 QB 899, [1967] 2 All ER 900, CA (statute); and *Hammond v Haigh Castle & Co Ltd* [1973] 2 All ER 289, [1973] ICR 148, NIRC (statute), which, it is submitted, are exceptions to the general rule, for which see also *Pritam Kaur v S Russell & Sons Ltd* [1973] QB 336, [1973] 1 All ER 617, CA; *Tanglecroft Ltd v Hemdale Group Ltd* [1975] 3 All ER 599, [1975] 1 WLR 1544, CA; and *Dodds v Walker* [1981] 2 All ER 609, [1981] 1 WLR 1027, HL. See also CRIMINAL PROCEDURE vol 28 (2010) PARA 701; LIMITATION PERIODS vol 68 (2008) PARA 920.

4   *Goldsmiths' Co v West Metropolitan Rly Co* [1904] 1 KB 1, CA (exercise of power of compulsory acquisition of land within three years from the passing of an Act). See also *Tiverton and North Devon Rly Co v Loosemore* (1884) 9 App Cas 480, HL (followed in *Great Western Rly Co v Midland Rly Co* [1908] 2 Ch 644, CA; affd sub nom *Midland Rly Co v Great Western Rly Co* [1909] AC 445, HL), where, notwithstanding a similar limit of time imposed by statute for the exercise of statutory powers in the construction of a railway, the company was held entitled, on acquiring a right to the land, to construct the railway under its common law powers after the expiration of the period so limited; *Truss v Olivier* (1924) 40 TLR 588, DC (proceedings to be taken within six months from the passing of an Act). As to the time within which proceedings must be taken see further LIMITATION PERIODS vol 68 (2008) PARA 901 et seq.

5   *Ex p Fallon* (1793) 5 Term Rep 283 (enrolment of annuity); *Watson v Pears* (1809) 2 Camp 294; *Williams v Burgess* (1840) 12 Ad & El 635 (filing of warrant of attorney within 21 days after execution); *Re Higham and Jessop* (1840) 9 Dowl 203 (award to be made within two calendar months after appointment of umpire); *Gibson v Muskett* (1842) 3 Scott NR 427; *Williams v Nash* (1859) 28 Beav 93 (payment of stamp duty on letters patent within three years; as to the time for such payments now see PATENTS AND REGISTERED DESIGNS vol 79 (2014) PARA 314 et seq). See also the Insolvency Act 1986 Pts VIII–XI (ss 252–385) (see BANKRUPTCY AND INDIVIDUAL INSOLVENCY vol 5 (2013) PARA 782). As to the time within which proceedings must be taken see ss 240, 341, 387; CIVIL PROCEDURE; LIMITATION PERIODS vol 68 (2008) PARA 901 et seq.

6   See CPR 2.8(1), (2), (3); and CIVIL PROCEDURE vol 11 (2009) PARA 88. As to application of the CPR see PARA 310 note 1.

7   *Re North, ex p Hasluck* [1895] 2 QB 264, CA.

8   *Kerridge v Lamdin* [1951] 1 KB 478, [1950] 2 All ER 1110, CA. See also *Donegal Tweed Co Ltd v Stephenson* (1929) 98 LJKB 657, DC. Cf CIVIL PROCEDURE.

337. Last day of period. Subject to certain exceptions[1], the general rule is that, when an act may be done or a benefit enjoyed during a certain period, the act may be done or the benefit enjoyed up to the last moment of the last day of that period[2]. Hence, a notice required to be given within so many days from or before a given date must be at the latest given on the last of such days[3].

However, where an act is required by the Civil Procedure Rules, a practice direction, or by any judgment or order of the court to be done within a specified period and the end of the period is defined by reference to an event, the day on which that event occurs is not included in computing the number of days[4].

Where the court gives a judgment, order or direction which imposes a time limit for doing any act in proceedings to which the Civil Procedure Rules apply, the last date for compliance must, wherever practicable, be expressed as a calendar date and include the time of day by which the act must be done[5]. Where the date by which an act must be done is inserted in any document to which the Civil Procedure Rules apply, the date must, wherever practicable, be expressed as a calendar date[6].

1   See PARA 338 et seq.

2   *Startup v Macdonald* (1843) 6 Man & G 593; *Afovos Shipping Co SA v Pagnan, The Afovos* [1983] 1 All ER 449, [1983] 1 WLR 195, HL, where the time limit for payment under a charterparty expired at midnight, and notice to exercise the option of withdrawal was sent before midnight but after the normal banking hours, and it was held that the notice was premature and invalid.

3   *Steedman v Hakim* (1888) 22 QBD 16, CA; *Chambon v Heighwey* (1890) 54 JP 520, DC; *Elliott v Popular Playhouse Ltd* (1909) Times, 1 April. For an example of the amendment of a writ on the last day of a limitation period see *Seabridge v H Cox & Sons (Plant Hire) Ltd* [1968] 2 QB 46, [1968] 1 All ER 570, CA (though see also *Ketteman v Hansel Properties Ltd* [1987] AC 189, [1988] 1 All ER 38, HL, overruling *Seabridge v H Cox & Sons (Plant Hire) Ltd* [1968] 2 QB 46, [1968] 1 All ER 570, CA, on the basis that under RSC Ord 15 r 8(4)(a) (see now CPR 19.3; CPR PD19A—*Addition and Substitution of Parties*; and CIVIL PROCEDURE vol 11 (2009) PARA 211) a defendant is not added as a party to an action until the amended writ has been served on him although the relevant amendment to the writ takes place on its being stamped). As to the extent, if any, to which cases decided under RSC or CCR may be cited in relation to CPR see PARA 310 note 1.

4   See CPR 2.8(1), (2), (3)(b); and CIVIL PROCEDURE vol 11 (2009) PARA 88.

5   See CPR 2.9(1); and CIVIL PROCEDURE vol 11 (2009) PARA 89.

6   See CPR 2.9(2); and CIVIL PROCEDURE vol 11 (2009) PARA 89.

338. Period for performance fixed by contract or will. Where a period is fixed by contract within which work is to be done or goods delivered, the day from which the period is made to run is generally excluded, and therefore the corresponding day at the end of the period is included[1]. Similarly, where a testator has by his will imposed on a person who is to take a benefit under it the performance of some condition within a limited time, the day of the testator's death is not included in the computation[2].

1   *Webb v Fairmaner* (1838) 3 M & W 473 (sale of goods on 5 October to be paid for in two months; writ issued on 5 December held to be premature). See also SALE OF GOODS AND SUPPLY OF SERVICES vol 91 (2012) PARA 69. As to time in relation to contracts generally see CONTRACT vol 22 (2012) PARA 546 et seq. As to insurance policies see INSURANCE vol 60 (2011) PARA 167 et seq.

2   *Lester v Garland* (1808) 15 Ves 248; *Miller v Wheatley* (1891) 28 LR Ir 144, where a devise was made to a person with a condition of defeasance on his failing to assume the testator's name within one year of his death and the name was assumed on the anniversary of that date; *Re Figgis, Roberts v McLaren* [1969] 1 Ch 123, [1968] 1 All ER 999 (devise to wife if she should be living at the expiration of a period of three months from testator's death). A condition requiring a decision to be taken within a reasonable time is not void for uncertainty: *Re Burton's Settlements, Scott v National Provincial Bank Ltd* [1955] Ch 82, [1954] 3 All ER 193. As to the time for payment of legacies generally see WILLS AND INTESTACY vol 103 (2010) PARA 1055 et seq.

339.   Former 'year and a day' rule.   The 'year and a day' rule, which stipulated that for the crime of murder to be committed death had to occur within a year and a day of the hurt being done, has been abolished for all purposes[1].

1   See the Law Reform (Year and a Day Rule) Act 1996 s 1; and CRIMINAL LAW vol 25 (2010) PARA 92. In computing that period of a year and a day, the day on which the hurt was done was to be included. Cases in which the year and a day rule prevailed are mentioned in *Sir Henry Constable's Case* (1601) 5 Co Rep 106a at 107b. See also 1 Hawk PC 162.

   Note, however, the continued application of the 'year and a day' rule to acts or omissions causing death which occurred before 17 June 1996: see the Law Reform (Year and a Day Rule) Act 1996 s 3(2); and CRIMINAL LAW vol 25 (2010) PARA 92.

340.   Period expiring on Sunday or holiday.   The fact that the last day of a prescribed period is a Sunday[1], or other non-juridical day[2], does not as a general rule give the person who is called upon to act an extra day; it is no excuse for his omission to do the act on some prior day[3].

This general rule does not, however, hold good where the effect of it would be to render performance of the act impossible. This would be the case if the whole of the prescribed period consisted of holidays, in which case the act may lawfully be done on the next possible day[4].

Again, the general rule does not hold good where the act has to be done, not by the party only, but by the court or by the party in conjunction with the court. In such cases, when the last day limited for the performance of it happens to be a day when the court or its office is closed, the act may be done on the next practicable day[5].

1   As to acts prohibited on a Sunday see PARA 324 et seq. As to the calculation of a prescribed period see PARAS 329–333.
2   Ie a day on which no judicial act ought to be done: see PARA 324.
3   *Mesure v Britten* (1796) 2 Hy Bl 617; *R v Middlesex Justices* (1843) 7 Jur 396; *Rawlins v West Derby Overseers* (1846) 2 CB 72; *Rowberry v Morgan* (1854) 9 Exch 730; *Peacock v R* (1858) 4 CBNS 264; *Ex p Simpkin* (1859) 2 E & E 392; *Déchène v Montreal City* [1894] AC 640, PC. In all these cases the period limited for the doing of an act by one of the parties to a legal proceeding expired on a Sunday or other non-juridical day, and it was held that the doing of the act could not be postponed until the next day: cf PARA 341. See also *McNiven v Glasgow Corpn* 1920 SC 584, where the time limited for commencing an action against a public authority expired on a Sunday, and a writ served on the following day was held to be out of time. In *Child v Edwards* [1909] 2 KB 753 it was held that distress levied on a Monday in respect of rent which fell due on the preceding Sunday was lawfully levied (note, however, that the common law right to distrain for arrears of rent has been abolished by the Tribunals, Courts and

Enforcement Act 2007 s 71: see LANDLORD AND TENANT vol 62 (2012) PARA 288). In *Mardorf Peach & Co Ltd v Attica Sea Carriers Corpn of Liberia* [1977] AC 850, [1977] 1 All ER 545, HL, the position where the due date for punctual payment under a charterparty falls on a day when banks are closed was considered: see further LANDLORD AND TENANT vol 62 (2012) PARA 259. Sunday is reckonable as one of the 14 days within which an application to justices to state a case must be made: see MAGISTRATES vol 71 (2013) PARA 706.

4   *Mayer v Harding* (1867) LR 2 QB 410, where a case stated had to be lodged in the Queen's Bench within three days after it was received from the magistrates, it was received on Good Friday, and it was validly lodged on the following Wednesday when the court office next opened. See also *Waterton v Baker* (1868) LR 3 QB 173; and MAGISTRATES vol 71 (2013) PARA 710.

5   *Morris v Barrett* (1859) 7 CBNS 139; *Hughes v Griffiths* (1862) 13 CBNS 324. See also PARA 341. In *Mumford v Hitchcocks* (1863) 14 CBNS 361, it was held that the appearance to a writ was the combined act of the party and the court, and that therefore, if the court were closed on the last day of the limited period, appearance might be entered on the next day. Where a limitation period expires on a non-juridical day, it has been held that a writ issued on the next day when the court offices are open is not statute-barred: *Pritam Kaur v S Russell & Sons Ltd* [1973] QB 336, [1973] 1 All ER 617, CA (considering *Hodgson v Armstrong* [1967] 2 QB 299, [1967] 1 All ER 307, CA); *The Clifford Maersk* [1982] 3 All ER 905, [1982] 1 WLR 1292 (applying *Pritam Kaur v S Russell & Sons Ltd* [1973] QB 336, [1973] 1 All ER 617, CA). See also *Re Philipp and Lion* [1994] 1 BCLC 739, [1994] BCC 261 (applying *Pritam Kaur v S Russell & Sons Ltd* [1973] QB 336, [1973] 1 All ER 617, CA) (court offices closed on final day for making application for disqualification of company director; time extended to the next day the court office was open); and see further *Nottingham City Council v Calverton Parish Council* [2015] EWHC 503 (Admin), [2015] All ER (D) 44 (Mar). Cf *Swainston v Hetton Victory Club Ltd* [1983] 1 All ER 1179, [1983] ICR 341, CA, where the time limit for a complaint to a tribunal expired at midnight on a Sunday; the tribunal offices were closed, but a street letter box was available throughout the weekend for communications; and a complaint not presented until Monday was out of time since it could have been presented on Sunday (distinguishing *Pritam Kaur v S Russell & Sons Ltd* [1973] QB 336, [1973] 1 All ER 617, CA; and following the dictum of Sir John Donaldson P in *Hammond v Haigh Castle & Co Ltd* [1973] 2 All ER 289 at 291, [1973] ICR 148 at 151, NICR; and *Post Office v Moore* [1981] ICR 623, EAT). As to the extent, if any, to which cases decided under RSC or CCR may be cited in relation to CPR see PARA 310 note 1. As to the expiry of time when the court offices are closed see CIVIL PROCEDURE vol 11 (2009) PARA 88 et seq; and cf COURTS AND TRIBUNALS.

341.   Special provisions as to the period within which an act must be done.
Various Acts of Parliament and statutory rules make provision for cases in which the day or the last day on which an act may be done falls on a Sunday or other holiday and for the exclusion of such days in the computation of prescribed periods[1].

When a meeting of a vestry[2], corporation (whether ecclesiastical or civil), or a public company for the transaction of secular business is required by any Act, charter, grant, constitution, deed, testament, law, prescription or usage to be held on any Sunday, the meeting must take place on the preceding Saturday or the next succeeding Monday[3].

Where the day or the last day on which anything is required or permitted by or under the Local Government Act 1972 to be done is a Sunday, Christmas Day, Good Friday, bank holiday[4] or a day appointed for public thanksgiving or mourning, the requirement or permission is deemed to relate to the first day thereafter which is not one of those days[5].

Where the last day of the time of payment as fixed by a bill is a non-business day, the bill is due and payable on the succeeding business day[6].

When the time prescribed by the Civil Procedure Rules, a practice direction, or by any judgment or order of the court for doing any act at the court office ends on a day on which that office is closed the act is in time if done on the next day on which that office is open[7].

When a term of imprisonment or of detention in a young offender institution, a secure college, a secure training centre or a remand centre[8] expires on a Sunday, Christmas Day or Good Friday or a bank holiday (and, in the case of a person serving a term of more than five days, a Saturday), the prisoner or detainee is to be discharged on the day next preceding[9].

Where by a special Act power was given to test gas 'daily' it was held to include power to test on Sundays[10].

1   As to computation under rules of court see PARA 343. No person must be compelled to make any payment or do any act on a bank holiday which he could not be compelled to make or do on Christmas Day or Good Friday; the obligation to make the payment or do the act applies to the day following the bank holiday: Banking and Financial Dealings Act 1971 s 1(4).

2   Vestries have now been rendered virtually obsolete: see ECCLESIASTICAL LAW vol 34 (2011) PARA 299.

3   Sunday Observance Act 1833 s 1 (amended by the Statute Law Repeals (No 2) Act 1890). The Sunday Observance Act 1833 was repealed as to boroughs by the Municipal Corporations Act 1882 s 5. As to boroughs see LOCAL GOVERNMENT vol 69 (2009) PARA 25. As to ecclesiastical corporations see ECCLESIASTICAL LAW vol 34 (2011) PARA 1013. As to civil corporations see CORPORATIONS vol 24 (2010) PARA 305. As to public companies see COMPANIES vol 14 (2009) PARA 73 et seq.

4   As to bank holidays see PARA 321.

5   Local Government Act 1972 s 243(1). See also LOCAL GOVERNMENT vol 69 (2009) PARA 128. Similar provision is made in respect of elections by the Representation of the People Act 1983 s 119(1)(a), (2) (s 119(2) substituted by the Representation of the People Act 1985 s 19(4); and amended by the Electoral Administration Act 2006 ss 20, 74(2), Sch 1 Pt 4 paras 49, 51(1), Sch 2; Fixed-term Parliaments Act 2011 Schedule, para 9) (cf PARA 344; and ELECTIONS AND REFERENDUMS vol 37 (2013) PARA 230); in relation to individual and corporate insolvency by the Insolvency Act 1986 Pts VIII–XI (ss 252–385) (see BANKRUPTCY AND INDIVIDUAL INSOLVENCY vol 5 (2013) PARA 782); and in relation to acts under the Municipal Corporations Act 1882 (see s 230); the specified days, however, not including bank holidays and days appointed for mourning, but extending to the Monday and Tuesday in Easter week and days appointed for public fast or humiliation. See also *Re Counter's Petition, Buckingham v Counter* [1938] 2 KB 90, [1938] 1 All ER 186, CA.

6   See the Bills of Exchange Act 1882 s 14(1); and FINANCIAL SERVICES AND INSTITUTIONS vol 49 (2008) PARA 1437. See also PARA 328.

7   CPR 2.8(5); and see CIVIL PROCEDURE vol 11 (2009) PARA 88. The rule (formerly contained in RSC Ord 3 r 4) does not affect the operation of what is now the Limitation Act 1980 (*Morris v Richards* (1881) 45 LT 210; *Gelmini v Moriggia* [1913] 2 KB 549); nor does it apply to acts not affected by the offices being closed (*Re Lambert, ex p Saffery* (1877) 5 ChD 365, CA; *Chambon v Heighwey* (1890) 54 JP 520, DC). When the last day for moving the court under rules of court was a Sunday, it was held that notice of motion ought to have been given for the following day: *Taylor v Jones* (1875) 34 LT 131. As to the extent, if any, to which cases decided under RSC or CCR may be cited in relation to CPR see PARA 310 note 1. By virtue of the Insolvency Rules 1986, SI 1986/1925, r 12.9 (substituted by SI 1999/1022) (see BANKRUPTCY AND INDIVIDUAL INSOLVENCY vol 5 (2013) PARA 782; COMPANY AND PARTNERSHIP INSOLVENCY vol 17 (2011) PARA 1014), the provisions of CPR 2.8, 3.1(2)(a) are applied to anything required or authorised to be done by the Insolvency Rules.

8   As to custodial institutions see PRISONS AND PRISONERS vol 85 (2012) PARA 480 et seq.

9   Criminal Justice Act 1961 s 23(3) (amended by the Criminal Justice Act 1982 s 77, Sch 14 para 10; Legal Aid, Sentencing and Punishment of Offenders Act 2012 Sch 10 para 2); Criminal Justice Act 1961 s 23(4) (amended by the Criminal Justice Act 1988 s 123, Sch 8 para 1; Criminal Justice and Public Order Act 1994 s 168(2), Sch 10 para 11; Criminal Justice and Courts Act 2015 Sch 9 paras 5, 6). As from a day to be appointed, these provisions will not apply to remand centres: see the Criminal Justice Act 1961 s 23(4) (prospectively amended by the Criminal Justice and Court Services Act 2000 s 74, Sch 7 Pt II para 33). At the date at which this title states the law, no such day had been appointed.

10 See the Gaslight and Coke and other Gas Companies Acts Amendment Act 1880 s 7 (repealed); *LCC v South Metropolitan Gas Co* [1904] 1 Ch 76, CA, a case on the interpretation of the Act. As a result of that decision the law was subsequently modified by the London Gas Act 1905 ss 5(5), 10 (repealed). As to the testing of gas see now ENERGY AND CLIMATE CHANGE vol 43 (2011) PARA 349.

(4) COMPUTATION OF PERIOD WHEN HOLIDAYS INTERVENE

342. Period when holidays intervene: general rule of computation. Where a period is fixed within which some act must be done, Sundays and holidays in general count like other days[1], and it makes no difference that the last day of the period falls on a Sunday[2].

In a charterparty in which it is stipulated that a thing is to be done in so many days, prima facie consecutive days are intended, and holidays or non-working days are not excluded unless there is a port custom[3] or something in the context to show that working days only were to be included[4].

1   *Wheeler v Green* (1839) 7 Dowl 194; *Pennell v Churchwardens of Uxbridge* (1862) 8 Jur NS 99; *Re Gilbert, ex p Viney* (1877) 4 ChD 794, CA; *Aspinall v Sutton* [1894] 2 QB 349; *Blackwell v Blackwell* (1920) 89 LJP 143 (period limited for complying with decree for restitution of conjugal rights); *Benton v Sanderson Kayser Ltd* [1989] ICR 136, [1989] IRLR 19, CA (four week period prescribed by the Employment Protection (Consolidation) Act 1978 s 84(4) (repealed) (see now the Employment Rights Act 1996 s 138(3); and EMPLOYMENT vol 41 (2014) PARA 865) means four calendar weeks not four working weeks); *Stainer v Secretary of State for the Environment and Shepway District Council* (1992) 65 P & CR 310, [1994] JPL 44 (Christmas and bank holidays to be included in the calculation of the six week time limit for challenging a decision of the Secretary of State contained in the Town and Country Planning Act 1990 s 288 (see PLANNING vol 82 (2010) PARAS 842–843)). Cf *Niemann v Moss* (1860) 6 Jur NS 775, where by the terms of the charterparty holidays were to be excluded and it was held that nevertheless Sundays were to be included. As to the exceptions to the general rule see PARA 343 et seq.

    As to Sundays and holidays in general see PARAS 320–328.

2   As to when the period expires on a Sunday or holiday see PARA 340.

3   As to port customs see CUSTOM AND USAGE vol 32 (2012) PARA 92.

4   See *Nielsen v Wait* (1885) 16 QBD 67, CA; *Alvion Steamship Corpn Panama v Galban Lobo Trading Co SA of Havana* [1955] 1 QB 430, [1955] 1 All ER 457, CA; CUSTOM AND USAGE vol 32 (2012) PARAS 92–93. See also CARRIAGE AND CARRIERS vol 7 (2015) PARA 289.

343. Computation under rules of court etc. Where any period specified by the Civil Procedure Rules, a practice direction or by any judgment or order of the court for doing any act, being a period of five days or less, includes a Saturday, Sunday or bank holiday[1], Christmas Day or Good Friday, that day does not count in the computation of time[2].

1   As to bank holidays see PARA 321.

2   CPR 2.8(4) (see CIVIL PROCEDURE vol 11 (2009) PARA 88). See also *Re Yeoland Consols Ltd* (1888) 58 LT 108 (time for filing affidavit supporting winding-up petition); *Brammall v Mutual Industrial Corpn* (1915) 84 LJ Ch 474 (time prescribed by rules to elapse between service of notice of motion and day named for hearing); *Re Display Multiples Ltd* [1967] 1 All ER 685, [1967] 1 WLR 571 (advertisement of winding up petition); *Tanglecroft Ltd v Hemdale Group Ltd* [1975] 3 All ER 599, [1975] 1 WLR 1544, CA (order that judgment be not drawn up for seven days); *Adan v Brent London Borough Council* (1999) 32 HLR 848, CA (time limit, which expired on day county court office was closed, extended until next day office was open). See also CPR 2.8(5); CIVIL PROCEDURE vol 11 (2009) PARA 88; and PARA 341. By virtue of the Insolvency Rules 1986, SI 1986/1925, r 12.9 (substituted by SI 1999/1022) (see BANKRUPTCY AND INDIVIDUAL INSOLVENCY vol 5 (2013) PARA 782; COMPANY AND PARTNERSHIP INSOLVENCY vol 17 (2011) PARA 1014), CPR 2.8, 3.1(2)(a) (see CIVIL PROCEDURE vol 11 (2009) PARAS 88, 249) are applied to anything required or authorised to be done by the Insolvency Rules. As to the CPR generally, and as to the extent, if any, to which cases decided under RSC or CCR may be cited in relation to the CPR, see PARA 310 note 1.

344. Computation for purposes of elections. In computing any period of not more than seven days for the purposes of the legislation relating to election campaigns and legal proceedings concerning elections[1], Saturday, Sunday,

Christmas Eve, Christmas Day, Good Friday, a bank holiday[2] and any day appointed for public thanksgiving or mourning are to be disregarded[3].

1 Ie for the purposes of the Representation of the People Act 1983 Pt II (ss 67–119) and Pt III (ss 120–186) (see ELECTIONS AND REFERENDUMS vol 37 (2013) PARA 231 et seq; ELECTIONS AND REFERENDUMS vol 38A (2013) PARA 761 et seq).

2 'Bank holiday' in relation to any election means a day which is a bank holiday (as provided for by the Banking and Financial Dealings Act 1971 s 1, Sch 1) (see PARA 321) in the part of the United Kingdom in which the constituency or electoral area is situated: Representation of the People Act 1983 s 119(3) (substituted by the Representation of the People Act 1985 s 19(4)) (see ELECTIONS AND REFERENDUMS vol 37 (2013) PARA 230).

3 Representation of the People Act 1983 s 119(1)(b), (2) (s 119(2) substituted by the Representation of the People Act 1985 s 19(4); and amended by the Electoral Administration Act 2006 ss 20, 74(2), Sch 1 Pt 4 paras 49, 51(1), Sch 2; and the Fixed-term Parliaments Act 2011 Schedule paras 6, 9) (see ELECTIONS AND REFERENDUMS vol 37 (2013) PARA 230). Note, however, that where a bank holiday or day appointed for public thanksgiving or mourning was not appointed as such before the dissolution of Parliament under the Fixed-term Parliaments Act 2011 s 3(1), that day will not be disregarded in computing the period: Representation of the People Act 1983 s 119(1)(b), (2), Sch 1 para 2 (s 119(2) as amended).

   As to the computation of time for the purposes of legal proceedings concerning elections see the Representation of the People Act 1983 s 186; and ELECTIONS AND REFERENDUMS vol 38A (2013) PARA 768.

(5) FRACTIONS OF A DAY

345. Computing fractions of a day: the general rule. In computing a period of time counted in years or months, fractions of a day are generally disregarded, so that the period is regarded as complete even though it is short to the extent of a fraction of a day[1].

Where the day of the date of an instrument of lease is included in the term it is immaterial that the tenant's enjoyment cannot begin with the beginning of that day[2]. Similarly, in calculating a person's age the day of his birth counts as a whole day. Formerly at common law a person attained a specified age on the day next before the anniversary of his birthday[3], but in respect of anniversaries falling on a date after 1 January 1970, the time at which a person attains a particular age expressed in years is the commencement of the relevant anniversary of the date of his birth[4].

In contracts where payment has to be made at a certain rate per day a part of a day counts as a whole day, unless it appears from the context that the contrary was intended[5]. Where it is stipulated that money is to be paid at a given hour, the whole period between that hour and the next hour is intended; the hour is considered as the 24th aliquot part of the day[6].

1 *Pugh v Duke of Leeds* (1777) 2 Cowp 714 at 720 per Lord Mansfield CJ (cited in *Re Railway Sleepers Supply Co* (1885) 29 ChD 204 at 205); *Lester v Garland* (1808) 15 Ves 248; *Cartwright v MacCormack (Trafalgar Insurance Co Ltd, third party)* [1963] 1 All ER 11, [1963] 1 WLR 18, CA; *Trow v Ind Coope (West Midlands) Ltd* [1967] 2 QB 899, [1967] 2 All ER 900, CA; *Re Figgis, Roberts v McLaren* [1969] 1 Ch 123, [1968] 1 All ER 999. See also *Re Seaford, Seaford v Seifert* [1968] P 53, [1968] 1 All ER 482, CA (cited and applied in *Re Palmer (deceased) (a debtor)* [1994] Ch 316, [1994] 3 All ER 835, CA); *Warr v Warr* [1975] Fam 25, [1975] 1 All ER 85. This paragraph was cited with approval in *R v Crown Court at Middlesex Guildhall, ex p Okoli* [2000] Crim LR 921, DC.

2 *Clayton's Case* (1585) 5 Co Rep 1a; *R v St Mary, Warwick, Inhabitants* (1853) 1 E & B 816, where an occupation which began on 29 September and ceased before midnight on the ensuing 30 September was held, for the purpose of a settlement, to be an occupation for a year. See also *Bedding v McCarthy* (1993) 27 HLR 103, [1994] 2 EGLR 40, CA, (tenancy agreements deal with years, months, weeks and sometimes days, but not with hours). As to the calculation of

days making a quarter of a year see PARA 306; and cf LANDLORD AND TENANT vol 62 (2012) PARA 219. As to the computation of period of a lease generally see LANDLORD AND TENANT vol 62 (2012) PARAS 216–220, 235–239.

3   *Fitzhugh v Dennington* (1704) 2 Ld Raym 1094; *Roe d Wrangham v Hersey* (1771) 3 Wils 274, where a will made on 31 January by a person who was born on 1 February 21 years before was held valid; *Toder v Sansam* (1775) 1 Bro Parl Cas 468, HL; *Grant v Grant* (1840) 4 Y & C Ex 256; *Re Shurey, Savory v Shurey* [1918] 1 Ch 263. A gift to a person on attaining his 25th year means that he is to take the property on his 24th birthday: see CHILDREN AND YOUNG PERSONS vol 9 (2012) PARAS 1–2.

4   Family Law Reform Act 1969 s 9(1): see CHILDREN AND YOUNG PERSONS vol 9 (2012) PARA 2. This provision applies only where the relevant anniversary falls on a date after 1 January 1970 and, in relation to any enactment, deed, will or other instrument, has effect subject to any provision in it: s 9(2). Section 9 abrogated the old common law rule stated in *Re Shurey, Savory v Shurey* [1918] 1 Ch 263.

5   *Commercial Steamship Co v Boulton* (1875) LR 10 QB 346, Ex Ch. Cf *Cornfoot v Royal Exchange Assurance Corpn* [1904] 1 KB 40, CA; *Yeoman v R* [1904] 2 KB 429, CA, where the intention of the parties as indicated by the charterparty was that regard should be had to hours. See CARRIAGE AND CARRIERS vol 7 (2015) PARA 289; cf CONTRACT vol 22 (2012) PARA 500 et seq; SALE OF GOODS AND SUPPLY OF SERVICES vol 91 (2012) PARAS 69, 166.

6   *Knox v Simmons* (1793) 4 Bro CC 433; *Anon* (1844) 1 Coll 273; *Bernard v Norton* (1864) 10 LT 183.

346. Priorities as between events happening on the same day. The general rule that fractions of a day are to be disregarded[1] does not apply where the object of a statute would be defeated unless the precise hour of an occurrence were noted[2], or where conflicting claims depend on the question which of two events was first in order of time, for in such cases the particular hour when the events occurred may become material. So, for example, rival claimants may have been born, or execution may have been issued and the judgment debtor may have died[3] or committed an act of bankruptcy[4], on the same day. In such cases the rights of the parties have to be determined by the ascertainment of the particular moments of the day at which the several events happened[5]. The same principle has been applied where two writs in the same matter were issued against the same defendant on the same day, for the issuing of the original writ was held to be an act of the party and not a judicial act, and therefore the doctrine according to which it is assumed that a judicial act is dated from the earliest moment of the day on which it is done had no application[6].

If on one and the same day an award is made and signed and a rule nisi obtained calling upon the arbitrator to show cause why a case for the opinion of the court should not be stated, it becomes necessary to discuss the question which of the two events occurred first, for the court has no jurisdiction to grant the rule nisi if previously the award has been signed[7].

If on the same day a debt becomes payable and the creditor dies intestate, and there is a doubt which event occurred first it will be presumed that the death took place before the debt should have been paid, so that the Limitation Act 1980[8] will not begin to run until letters of administration are taken out[9].

Where two or more persons die in circumstances rendering it uncertain which of them survived the other or others, a statutory presumption as to the order in which the deaths occurred arises for purposes affecting the title to property[10].

1   As to this rule see PARA 345.

2   *Combe v Pitt* (1763) 3 Burr 1423; *Chick v Smith* (1840) 8 Dowl 337; *Campbell v Strangeways* (1877) 3 CPD 105 (moment from which a dog licence began to run).

3   *Chick v Smith* (1840) 8 Dowl 337 (followed in *Wright v Mills* (1859) 4 H & N 488; and *Campbell v Strangeways* (1877) 3 CPD 105 at 106, where *Combe v Pitt* (1763) 3 Burr 1423 at

1434 per Lord Mansfield CJ was cited). See also *Roe d Wrangham v Hersey* (1771) 3 Wils 274. As to the priority of writs for the purpose of execution see CIVIL PROCEDURE vol 12 (2009) PARA 1297.

4 *Ex p D'Obree, ex p le Mesurier* (1803) 8 Ves 82 (followed in *Wydown's Case* (1807) 14 Ves 80; and *Ex p Dufrene* (1812) 1 Ves & B 51); *Franklin v Lord Brownlow* (1808) 14 Ves 550; *Sadler v Leigh* (1815) 4 Camp 195; *Thomas v Desanges* (1819) 2 B & Ald 586; *Godson v Sanctuary* (1832) 4 B & Ad 255; *Re Newton, ex p Bignold* (1836) 3 Mont & A 9; *Pewtress v Annan* (1841) 9 Dowl 828.

5 Similarly, a difference of five minutes in the registration of two deeds relating to the same land in the Middlesex Registry might have determined a question of priorities: see *Re North, ex p Hasluck* [1895] 2 QB 264 at 273, CA, per Rigby J. See also *Re Seaford, Seaford v Seifert* [1968] P 53, [1968] 1 All ER 482, CA; *Eaglehill Ltd v J Needham Builders Ltd* [1973] AC 992, [1972] 3 All ER 895, HL (notice of dishonour of bill of exchange arriving on same day as bill presented for payment); *Re Palmer (deceased) (a debtor)* [1994] Ch 316, [1994] 3 All ER 835, CA.

6 *Pugh v Robinson* (1786) 1 Term Rep 116; *Clarke v Bradlaugh* (1881) 8 QBD 63, CA; *Warne v Lawrence* (1886) 54 LT 371. As to the presumption applicable to judicial acts see PARA 347.

7 *Tabernacle Permanent Building Society v Knight* [1892] AC 298, HL.

8 See the Limitation Act 1980 ss 2, 5; and LIMITATION PERIODS vol 68 (2008) PARA 952 et seq.

9 *Atkinson v Bradford Third Equitable Benefit Building Society* (1890) 25 QBD 377, CA. Cf LIMITATION PERIODS vol 68 (2008) PARA 923.

10 See WILLS AND INTESTACY vol 103 (2010) PARA 746.

(6) SPECIAL RULES AFFECTING EXECUTIVE AND JUDICIAL ACTS

347. The Crown and judicial acts. An exceptional rule prevails in regard to acts done on behalf of the Crown and judicial acts. When the title of the Crown[1] and of a subject accrue on the same day, the title of the Crown prevails[2]. In the case of judicial acts, it is a general, but perhaps not a universal, rule that the act is taken to date from the earliest moment of the day on which it is done[3]. The fact, therefore, that at some earlier hour on the same day something has been done or has happened which if it had been done or had happened on the previous day would have nullified the act is immaterial[4].

1 Eg land passing to the Crown by escheat where it is disclaimed by a trustee in bankruptcy: see CROWN AND CROWN PROCEEDINGS vol 29 (2014) PARA 147. As to Crown property see further CROWN AND CROWN PROCEEDINGS vol 29 (2014) PARAS 69, 114 et seq.

2 *R v Giles* (1820) 8 Price 293 at 334, referring to *R v Crump and Hanbury* (1670), cited in Park at 126.

3 *Clarke v Bradlaugh* (1881) 8 QBD 63 at 66, CA, where Lord Coleridge CJ refused to recognise the rule as universal, referring to *Pie v Coke* (1616) Hob 128. See also *Re Warren, ex p Wheeler v Trustee in Bankruptcy* [1938] Ch 725, [1938] 2 All ER 331, DC (priority of judicial act over earlier non-judicial act on same day); *Re Seaford, Seaford v Seifert* [1968] P 53, [1968] 1 All ER 482, CA (spouse dying before decree absolute purported to be made; doctrine of relation back not applicable); *Re Palmer (deceased) (a debtor)* [1994] Ch 316, [1994] 3 All ER 835, CA (rule could not operate to cause a statutory instrument modifying primary legislation to be applied so as to make an insolvency administration order take effect during the lifetime of the deceased person). As to the precise moment at which statutes, statutory instruments and byelaws come into operation see STATUTES AND LEGISLATIVE PROCESS vol 96 (2012) PARA 684 et seq.

4 *Lord Porchester v Petrie* (1783) 3 Doug KB 261; *Edwards v R* (1854) 9 Exch 628.

348. Date of judgment or order. A judgment or order of the court must bear the date on which it is given or made[1], and it takes effect from the day when it is given or made, or such later date as the court may specify[2].

1 See CPR 40.2(2)(a); and CIVIL PROCEDURE vol 12 (2009) PARA 1137. As to the CPR see PARA 310 note 1.

2   CPR 40.7(1). However, as to a judgment on failure to acknowledge service entered against a
    state see CPR 40.10; and CIVIL PROCEDURE vol 12 (2009) PARA 1142. A party against whom a
    judgment or order has been made may apply, on the ground of matters which have occurred
    since the date of the judgment or order, for a stay of execution: see CPR 40.8A; and CIVIL
    PROCEDURE vol 12 (2009) PARA 1142. At common law a judgment related back to the first day
    of the term, and it was said that the priority of one of two judgments signed on the same day
    could not be averred: *Lord Porchester v Petrie* (1783) 3 Doug KB 261; *Pugh v Robinson* (1786)
    1 Term Rep 116. As to the extent, if any, to which cases decided under RSC or CCR may be
    cited in relation to CPR see PARA 310 note 1.

(7) CONSTRUCTION OF EXPRESSIONS LIMITING TIME

349.   Meaning of 'a reasonable time'.   Where anything is limited to be done
within a 'reasonable time' or at a 'reasonable hour', the question what is a
reasonable time or reasonable hour must necessarily depend on the
circumstances, and is therefore a question of fact[1]. If a contract is silent as to
time for performance of an act, the law implies that it is to be done within a
reasonable time, and what period is reasonable is a question of fact[2].

1   *Pitt v Shew* (1821) 4 B & Ald 208 (where a reasonable time was allowed to a landlord to
    appraise and sell distrained goods); *Burton v Griffiths* (1843) 11 M & W 817; *Charnock v
    Liverpool Corpn* [1968] 3 All ER 473, [1968] 1 WLR 1498, CA (reasonable time for repair of
    car). As respects contracts for the sale of goods it has been expressly enacted that the question of
    what is a reasonable time or a reasonable hour is a question of fact: see the Sale of Goods
    Act 1979 ss 29(5), 59; and SALE OF GOODS AND SUPPLY OF SERVICES vol 91 (2012) PARAS 118,
    166. As to what constitutes a reasonable time in reference to particular transactions see
    eg CARRIAGE AND CARRIERS vol 7 (2015) PARAS 543 et seq, 671 et seq; CONTRACT vol 22
    (2012) PARA 500 et seq; FINANCIAL SERVICES AND INSTITUTIONS vol 49 (2008) PARA 1460;
    INSURANCE vol 60 (2011) PARA 300. See also *Bescol (Electric) Ltd v Merlin Mouldings Ltd*
    (1952) 69 RPC 297 (where an undertaking not to do something 'in future' was construed as an
    undertaking for a limited time); and COMPETITION vol 18 (2009) PARA 403.
2   *Hick v Raymond and Reid* [1893] AC 22, HL. The length requisite for reasonable notice may,
    however, involve questions partly of fact and partly of law: see *Tindal v Brown* (1786) 1 Term
    Rep 167 at 168 per Lord Mansfield CJ, and at 169 per Ashurst J.

**350.   Meaning of 'good reason' for extending the period within which an
application for judicial review must be made.**   A claim form for judicial review
must be filed promptly and in any event not later than three months after the
grounds to make the claim first arose[1]. The court can extend or abridge time but
will only exercise this power where it is satisfied there are very good reasons for
doing so[2]. The time may not be extended by agreement between the parties[3]. The
following have been held[4] to be 'good reason' for extending time: time taken by
a local planning authority to obtain counsel's opinion about whether to bring
proceedings for failure to comply with an enforcement notice[5]; time taken to
obtain legal aid[6]; the pursuit of alternative remedies[7]; the importance of the point
of law at issue[8]; and other reasons based on 'public policy'[9]. The following have
been held not to be 'good reason' for extending time: delay on the part of the
applicant's non-legal professional adviser[10]; time spent corresponding with the
court about alternative remedies[11]; and time taken pursuing political redress[12].

1   See CPR 54.5(1); and CPR PD54A—*Judicial Review* paras 5.6, 5.7. Note, however, that
    CPR 54.5(1) does not apply to certain planning decisions or decisions made under the Public
    Contracts Regulations 2006, SI 2006/5: see CPR 54.5(5), (6); and JUDICIAL REVIEW vol 61
    (2010) PARA 658. As to the Public Contracts Regulations 2006 see CONSTITUTIONAL AND
    ADMINISTRATIVE LAW vol 20 (2014) PARA 528 et seq. As to judicial review of planning decisions
    see PLANNING vol 82 (2010) PARA 846.
        Provisions of the Limitation Act 1980 do not apply to applications for judicial review: see
    LIMITATION PERIODS vol 68 (2008) PARA 918.

2 See Administrative Court Notes for Guidance on Applying for Judicial Review Section 5.6.
3 See CPR 54.5(2); and JUDICIAL REVIEW vol 61 (2010) PARA 658.
4 As to the extent, if any, to which cases decided under RSC or CCR may be cited in relation to CPR see PARA 310 note 1.
5 *R v Chichester Justices, ex p Chichester District Council* (1990) 60 P & CR 342.
6 *R v Stratford-on-Avon District Council, ex p Jackson* [1985] 3 All ER 769, [1985] 1 WLR 1319, CA.
7 *R v Rochdale Metropolitan Borough Council, ex p Cromer Ring Mill Ltd* [1982] 3 All ER 761.
8 *R v Secretary of State for the Home Office, ex p Ruddock* [1987] 2 All ER 518, [1987] 1 WLR 1482; *R v Isle of Wight County Council, ex p O'Keefe* (1989) 59 P & CR 283; *R v Ministry of Agriculture, Fisheries and Food, ex p Dairy Trade Federation Ltd* [1995] COD 3.
9 *R v Secretary of State for Transport, ex p Presvac Engineering Ltd* (1992) 4 Admin LR 121.
10 *R v Tavistock General Comr, ex p Worth* [1985] STC 564, 59 TC 116.
11 *R v Lincoln Crown Court, ex p Jones* [1990] COD 15.
12 *R v London Borough of Bexley, ex p Barnehurst Golf Club Ltd* [1992] COD 382 (organising a lobby of Parliament).

351. Meaning of 'undue delay'. The High Court may refuse to grant leave to apply for judicial review, or refuse any leave sought on the application, if it considers that there has been undue delay in making the application, and if it considers that the granting of the relief sought would be likely to cause substantial hardship to any person, or substantially prejudice the rights of any person, or be detrimental to good administration[1].

'Undue delay' arises whenever an application for judicial review is not made promptly and in any event within three months from the date when grounds for the application first arose[2]. When considering whether an application is made promptly, the court will take into account all the facts and circumstances including whether the applicant received prior warning of the decision complained of[3], and the length of time between the taking of the decision and its communication to the applicant[4]. Time starts running when the grounds for application objectively first arose, whether or not that was known to the applicant[5]. In the case of an application for a quashing order in respect of any judgment, order or conviction, the date when grounds for the application first arose will be taken to be the date of that judgment, order or conviction[6]. It is not clear whether time runs from the making or the coming into force of subordinate legislation[7]. Time runs from the time when a public duty was first owed[8].

1 See the Senior Courts Act 1981 s 31(6); and JUDICIAL REVIEW vol 61 (2010) PARA 602.
2 *R v Stratford-on-Avon District Council, ex p Jackson* [1985] 3 All ER 769, [1985] 1 WLR 1319, CA; *R v Dairy Produce Quota Tribunal for England and Wales, ex p Caswell* [1990] 2 AC 738, [1990] 2 All ER 434, HL. As to time limits applicable to applications for judicial review see PARA 350; and JUDICIAL REVIEW vol 61 (2010) PARA 658.
3 *R v Secretary of State for Transport, ex p Presvac Engineering Ltd* (1992) 4 Admin LR 121.
4 *R v Redbridge Justices, ex p Gurmit Ram* [1992] QB 384, [1992] 1 All ER 652.
5 *R v Secretary of State for Foreign Affairs, ex p World Development Movement* [1995] 1 All ER 611, [1995] 1 WLR 386. See also *R v Secretary of State for Trade and Industry, ex p Greenpeace Ltd* [1998] Env LR 415, [1998] COD 59 (grounds of the application might arise earlier than the decision impugned where there was an earlier act or decision that could have been challenged).
6 CPR PD54A—*Judicial Review* para 4.1.
7 Cf *R v HM Treasury, ex p Smedley* [1985] QB 657, [1985] 1 All ER 589, CA; and *R v HM Customs and Excise Comr, ex p Eurotunnel plc* [1995] COD 291, (1995) Independent, 23 February.
8 *R v Herefordshire County Council, ex p Cheung* (1986) Times, 4 April.

352. Meanings of 'immediately' and 'forthwith'. There appears to be no material difference between the terms 'immediately'[1] and 'forthwith'[2]. A provision to the effect that a thing must be done 'forthwith' or 'immediately' means that it must be done as soon as possible[3] in the circumstances, the nature of the act to be done being taken into account[4].

1   For cases where immediate payment of money has been held to mean payment within a reasonable time after demand see *Brighty v Norton* (1862) 3 B & S 305; *Toms v Wilson* (1863) 4 B & S 442, Ex Ch; *Re Burghardt, ex p Trevor* (1875) 1 ChD 297; *Moore v Shelley* (1883) 8 App Cas 285, PC; *Bank of Baroda v Panessar* [1987] Ch 335, [1986] 3 All ER 751 (applying *Brighty v Norton* (1862) 3 B & S 305). In *Pybus v Mitford* (1672) 2 Lev 75 at 77, it was said that, although 'immediately' in strictness excludes all mean time, yet to make good the deeds and intents of the parties it should be construed to mean such convenient time as is requisite for doing the thing. See *Burgess v Boetefeur* (1844) 7 Man & G 481.

2   *R v Worcester Justices* (1839) 7 Dowl 789; *Hancock v Somes* (1859) 1 E & E 795; *Roberts v Brett* (1865) 20 CBNS 148, HL; *Re Sullivan, ex p Sullivan* (1866) 36 LJ Bcy 1; *Re Sillence, ex p Sillence* (1877) 7 ChD 238; *R v Berkshire Justices* (1879) 4 QBD 469 at 471; *Re Southam, ex p Lamb* (1881) 19 ChD 169, CA; *Keith, Prowse & Co v National Telephone Co* [1894] 2 Ch 147. See also *Ex p Lowe* (1846) 3 Dow & L 737; *R v Aston* (1850) 19 LJMC 236. In *Thompson v Gibson* (1841) 8 M & W 281 and *Grace v Clinch* (1843) 4 QB 606, the same expression was used; cf *Roberts v Brett* (1865) 11 HL Cas 337. In *Costar v Hetherington* (1859) 1 E & E 802, the direction that justices on dismissing a complaint should forthwith give a certificate was held to mean forthwith on demand, and not forthwith on the dismissal. For cases of contract see *Simpson v Henderson* (1829) Mood & M 300 (contract to take cargo on board a vessel forthwith); *Doe d Pittman v Sutton* (1841) 9 C & P 706 (covenant to put premises in repair forthwith); *Staunton v Wood* (1851) 16 QB 638, where on a contract for the delivery of goods forthwith and for payment in 14 days it was held that delivery should be made within 14 days; *Roberts v Brett* (1865) 11 HL Cas 337. In *Hillingdon London Borough Council v Cutler* [1968] 1 QB 124, [1967] 2 All ER 361, CA, a demolition order was required to be made 'forthwith', and it was held that it could be made 'at any reasonable time thereafter'. In *R v Secretary of State for Social Services, ex p Child Poverty Action Group* [1990] 2 QB 540, [1989] 1 All ER 1047, CA, it was held that 'forthwith' in the Social Security Act 1975 s 98(1) (repealed) meant 'as soon as reasonably possible'.

3   'As soon as possible' in a manufacturing contract means within a reasonable time, regard being had to the manufacturer's ability to produce the goods and the orders he already has in hand: *Attwood v Emery* (1856) 1 CBNS 110. See also CONTRACT vol 22 (2012) PARA 501. As to the time for delivery of goods see SALE OF GOODS AND SUPPLY OF SERVICES vol 91 (2012) PARAS 166–167, 299. For the purposes of what is now the Prison Rules 1999, SI 1999/728, r 53(1) (disciplinary charges to be laid against prisoners 'as soon as possible'), it was held that the circumstances of the particular case are to be taken into account, and that the authorities are allowed time to carry out a preliminary investigation: *R v Board of Visitors of Dartmoor Prison, ex p Smith* [1987] QB 106, [1986] 2 All ER 651, CA. See also PRISONS AND PRISONERS vol 85 (2012) PARA 574. As to the meaning of 'instantly' see *R v Brownlow* (1839) 11 Ad & El 119 at 127, where the word was held to mean not at the time, but instantly after. As to the meanings of 'with all possible dispatch', 'with all reasonable speed' and 'immediately' in connection with charterparty cases see CARRIAGE AND CARRIERS vol 7 (2015) PARA 245 et seq.

4   *R v Price, ex p Heard* (1854) 8 Moo PCC 203; *Re Southam, ex p Lamb* (1881) 19 ChD 169 at 173, CA (citing *Hyde v Watts* (1843) 12 M & W 254, where the effecting of an insurance was the act to be done); *Re Lyon, ex p Lyon* (1882) 45 LT 768; *Re Darbyshire, ex p Hill* (1883) 53 LJ Ch 247; *Lowe v Fox* (1885) 15 QBD 667, CA (affd (1887) 12 App Cas 206, HL); *Re Muscovitch, ex p Muscovitch, Bankrupts v Official Receiver* [1938] 4 All ER 570 (affd [1939] Ch 694, [1939] 1 All ER 135, CA); *Sameen v Abeyewickrema* [1963] AC 597, [1963] 3 All ER 382, PC.

353.   Meanings of 'directly', 'peremptory' and 'on' or 'upon'.   'Directly' means speedily, or at least as soon as practicable[1].

The term 'peremptory' is used in regard to judicial proceedings[2]. For example a peremptory order (now often called an 'unless order')[3] is an order by which a person is required to do something within a fixed time or suffer the consequences[4].

'On' or 'upon' may mean simultaneously with the act to which it relates or within a reasonable time after it, according to the circumstances[5].

1   *Duncan v Topham* (1849) 8 CB 225; *Minister of Agriculture v Kelly* [1953] NI 151. 'Directly' cannot mean 'within a reasonable time': *Duncan v Topham* (1849) 8 CB 225. Cf CONTRACT vol 22 (2012) PARA 501. As to the meaning of 'reasonable time' see PARA 349.

2   Eg a peremptory plea (as distinguished from a plea in abatement). Pleas in abatement were abolished by the Supreme Court of Judicature Act 1875 Schedule, Order XIX, Rule 13.

3   As to peremptory or unless orders generally see CIVIL PROCEDURE vol 11 (2009) PARA 41. As to peremptory orders made under the Arbitration Act 1996 see ARBITRATION vol 2 (2008) PARAS 1250, 1252. As to peremptory orders to pay bills of exchange see FINANCIAL SERVICES AND INSTITUTIONS vol 49 (2008) PARA 1423.

4   *Beazley v Bailey* (1846) 16 M & W 58. The fact that an order is peremptory does not prevent alteration of it on special circumstances being shown: *Falck v Axthelm* (1889) 24 QBD 174, CA.

5   *R v Arkwright* (1848) 12 QB 960; *Robertson v Robertson and Favagrossa* (1883) 8 PD 94, CA, per Jessel MR; *Scott v Scott* [1921] P 107, CA. See also *Mackinnon v Peate* [1936] 2 All ER 240, DC, where 'registered on or after' was construed to mean registered for the first time on or after; *Dagger v Shepherd* [1946] KB 215, [1946] 1 All ER 133, CA, where a notice to quit 'on or before' was not invalid for uncertainty; *A-G's Reference (No 2 of 1994)* [1995] 2 All ER 1000, [1994] 1 WLR 1579 (meaning of 'on taking the sample' and meaning of 'there and then' in the Water Act 1989 s 148(1)(b) (repealed)).

354–400.   Meaning of 'within so many days'.

The requirement that a notice is to be given within so many days of a certain day does not mean that it must be given at least so many days before that day[1], nor is a notice which is required to be given on a certain day invalid because it is given before that day[2].

1   *Elliott v Popular Playhouse Ltd* (1909) Times, 1 April, where it was held that a notice required to be given 'within seven days prior to' a certain day is not required to be given at least seven days before that day. See also *Stewart v Chapman* [1951] 2 KB 792, [1951] 2 All ER 613, DC; and *Rightside Properties Ltd v Gray* [1975] Ch 72, [1974] 2 All ER 1169.
    As to the meaning of 'day' see PARA 313.

2   *Elliott v Popular Playhouse Ltd* (1909) Times, 1 April.

TORT

1. THE GENERAL LAW OF TORT

(1) NATURE AND DEFINITION OF TORT

401. Rights of action in tort. Rights of action in tort[1] may be defined as civil rights of action which are available for the recovery of unliquidated damages[2] by persons[3] who have sustained injury or loss from acts or omissions of others in breach of duty or contravention of right[4] imposed or conferred by law[5], rather than by agreement[6]. The nature of tort is further illuminated by way of its distinction from other legal categories. The principal distinctions to be drawn are between torts and crimes[7] and between torts and other civil wrongs[8].

1 The English word 'tort' derives from the Latin 'tortum', meaning twisted, crooked or wrong. There have been many attempts to define a tort. The nineteenth century legal scholar, Sir Frederick Pollock, expressed it as: 'An act which causes harm to a determinate person, whether intentionally or not, not being a breach of a duty arising out of a personal relation or contract, and which is either contrary to law or an omission of a specific legal duty, or a violation of an absolute right'. Another often-cited definition comes from Sir John Salmond, this being: 'A tort is a civil wrong for which the remedy is a common law action for unliquidated damages and which is not exclusively the breach of a contract or the breach of a trust or other merely equitable obligation'.

2 Other remedies (eg injunctions, orders for restitution or recovery of possession and declarations) are also available in appropriate cases, but the right to unliquidated damages is the only remedy which is common to all rights of action arising from tortious conduct. As to unliquidated damages see DAMAGES vol 29 (2014) PARA 311.

3 'Person' in this context includes every person recognised by the law as being capable of owing a duty to some other person and of committing a breach of the duty. It includes not only individuals and bodies corporate, but all persons associated together in such a way or for such a purpose as will create the duty. As to special rules applicable to particular persons see PARA 418 et seq.

4 It is a well established legal principle that violation of a legal right committed knowingly creates a cause of action: see *Best v Samuel Fox & Co Ltd* [1952] AC 716 at 729, [1952] 2 All ER 394 at 397, HL, per Lord Goddard CJ (citing *Lumley v Gye* (1853) 2 E & B 216; *Rogers v Rajendro Dutt* (1860) 13 Moo PCC 209; *Quinn v Leathem* [1901] AC 495, HL).

5 The principal reference made here by the use of the words 'by law' is to the common law. The civil action for breach of statutory duty is a common law action (see further PARA 500 et seq), but statute may also confer a right of civil action analogous to a common law right of action in tort (see eg the Consumer Protection Act 1987 Pt I (ss 1–9); and CONSUMER PROTECTION vol 21 (2011) PARA 642 et seq).

6 Although the description 'by agreement' primarily refers here to contract, it is intended also to cover rights of action arising from bailment (see BAILMENT AND PLEDGE). It is clear that a right of action for breach of contract and a right of action for tort are distinct rights.

7 See further PARA 403.

8 See further PARA 404.

402. The structure of the law of tort. The structure of the modern law of tort reflects its historical origins in the old system of the forms of action. Tort law today is divided into distinct domains, for example trespass, nuisance and negligence, which correspond with particular forms of action in the old law. Some jurists have consequently preferred to consider this branch of the law as a body of only loosely connected principles establishing specific liabilities (a law of torts)[1] rather than a coherent set of liability rules deriving from a general principle that it is tortious to injure another person without legal justification (a law of tort)[2]. However, whichever of these alternative analyses is preferred, it seems indisputable that from time to time in the past the common law has recognised new duties and liabilities and has the capacity to do so in the future[3], although a cause of action must be found either in principle or on authority[4].

1 This view was taken by eg Sir John Salmond: see *Salmond and Heuston on the Law of Torts* (21st Edn, 1996) pp 15–18.
2 This view was taken by eg Sir Percy Winfield: see Winfield *Province of the Law of Tort* (1931) Ch 3.
3 See eg *Ashby v White* (1703) 2 Ld Raym 938 (right to vote); *Campbell v MGN Ltd* [2004] UKHL 22, [2004] 2 AC 457, [2004] 2 All ER 995 (private information). The development of the law in this area may be affected by the Human Rights Act 1998: see PARA 810; and RIGHTS AND FREEDOMS vol 88A (2013) PARA 14 et seq.
    For instances where the common law has rejected new liabilities see PARA 412 et seq.
4 See *Best v Samuel Fox & Co Ltd* [1952] AC 716 at 730, [1952] 2 All ER 394 at 397, HL, per Lord Goddard.

403. Distinction between tort and crime. A crime is an unlawful act or default which is an offence against the public, and renders the person who is guilty of the act or default liable to legal punishment[1]. The same act or omission may be both a crime and a tort, for the duty giving rise to a potential claim for damages against the tortfeasor may co-exist with a duty imposed for the benefit of the public, a breach of which gives rise to a criminal offence[2]. Where a person is convicted of a criminal offence, the court of criminal jurisdiction may make an order requiring the offender to pay compensation for any personal injury, loss or damage resulting from that offence or any other offence which is taken into consideration by the court in determining sentence[3]. A person who has sustained personal injury directly attributable to a crime of violence, an offence of trespass on a railway, or the apprehension or attempted apprehension of an offender or suspected offender, the prevention or attempted prevention of an offence, or the giving of help to any constable who is engaged in any such activity may also claim a payment of compensation from the Criminal Injuries Compensation Authority[4].

1 See CRIMINAL LAW vol 25 (2010) PARAS 1–2.
2 Certain acts of trespass, for example, are actionable in tort and are also crimes (see PARA 525 et seq); so are public nuisances (see NUISANCE vol 78 (2010) PARAS 174, 187 et seq); and defamatory libels (see DEFAMATION vol 32 (2012) PARA 505). The Criminal Law Act 1967 s 1 repealed the former rule that, if the act were also a felony, no action could be brought until the defendant had been prosecuted for felony.
3 As to compensation orders see the Powers of Criminal Courts (Sentencing) Act 2000 s 130; and SENTENCING AND DISPOSITION OF OFFENDERS vol 92 (2010) PARA 375 et seq. See also PARA 474.
4 See the Criminal Injuries Compensation Act 1995; Criminal Injuries Compensation Authority *The Criminal Injuries Compensation Scheme* (2008); and CRIMINAL PROCEDURE vol 28 (2010) PARA 905 et seq.

404. Distinction between tort and other private law categories. The same circumstances may give rise to concurrent claims in tort and for other private law wrongs, including breach of contract[1] and unjust enrichment[2].

Remedies in contract and tort may exist concurrently and arise on the same facts[3]. A claimant may rely on the more advantageous remedy unless the remedy in tort is so inconsistent with the contract that it must be taken to be limited or excluded[4]. Damages in tort are assessed on the assumption that the tort was not committed; damages in contract are assessed on the assumption that the contract would be performed[5].

Where facts are such as to give a person a right of action in tort or a right of action in restitution for money had and received, he may elect to pursue the remedy in restitution, but judgment and satisfaction in respect of the restitutionary claim bars the right to sue in tort[6].

1 See CONTRACT vol 22 (2012) PARAS 208–209.
2 See RESTITUTION vol 88 (2012) PARA 560.

3   See *Henderson v Merrett Syndicates Ltd* [1995] 2 AC 145 at 193, [1994] 3 All ER 506 at
     532, HL, per Lord Goff (disapproving contrary dicta in *Tai Hing Cotton Mill Ltd v Liu Chong
     Hing Bank Ltd* [1986] AC 80 at 107, [1985] 2 All ER 947 at 957, PC).
4   *Henderson v Merrett Syndicates Ltd* [1995] 2 AC 145 at 194, [1994] 3 All ER 506 at
     532–533, HL, per Lord Goff.
5   As to the assessment of damages for tort see DAMAGES vol 29 (2014) PARA 408 et seq. As to the
     assessment of damages for breach of contract see DAMAGES vol 29 (2014) PARA 499 et seq.
     Certain principles in relation to damages are common to both tort and contract see DAMAGES
     vol 29 (2014) PARA 339 et seq.
6   *United Australia Ltd v Barclays Bank Ltd* [1941] AC 1, [1940] 4 All ER 20, HL. See further
     PARA 472.

405.   The concept of 'fault' in tort law.   Liability in tort is normally premised
on the fault of the defendant or someone for whom the defendant is responsible[1].
Fault may consist in negligence, which is the failure to exercise that care which
the circumstances demand[2], or the intentional infliction of injury (including
injury without actual damage)[3]. Torts involving the intentional infliction of
injury may involve a more extensive or more onerous liability than torts of mere
negligence[4].

The unlawfulness of conduct does not necessarily entail fault in English law,
though unlawfulness is an element of some tortious liabilities[5].

Strict and absolute liability (that is liability without fault) is rare in the
modern law[6].

1   Eg through vicarious liability: see PARAS 512, 786 et seq.
2   See PARA 497.
3   See PARA 491.
4   See PARA 491.
5   See PARA 498 et seq.
6   As to strict and absolute liability see PARAS 523–524.

(2) HYBRID OR AMBIGUOUS FORMS OF CIVIL LIABILITY

**406.   Identification of wrong as a tort or as another category of breach of
obligation.**   Certain civil wrongs are hard to ascribe exclusively to the law of tort
as opposed to some other class of obligation[1]. Some of them may give rise to
concurrent rights of action, being remediable by a claim in tort or for breach of
some other obligation, at the claimant's election[2]. Others may not generate a
tortious liability at all and may best be regarded as sui generis[3].

1   As to the interrelation of claims in tort and for breach of contract see PARA 404; and CONTRACT
     vol 22 (2012) PARA 209. As to the nature of liability for breach of statutory duty see PARAS
     500–503.
2   Eg the breach of a bailee's duty of care: see PARA 407; and BAILMENT AND PLEDGE vol 4 (2011)
     PARA 146.
3   Eg the liability of the innkeeper for the safety of guests' property: see PARA 411; and LICENSING
     AND GAMBLING vol 67 (2008) PARA 197 et seq.

407.   Breach of bailment obligations.   Bailment[1] is a transaction sui generis[2]. It
is commonly, but not invariably, created by contract[3]. The principal common law
duties of a bailee are to take reasonable care of the goods and to refrain from
converting them[4]. Neither of these duties is peculiar to bailment[5] and both can
normally be enforced in tort against a bailee[6]. Some obligations of a bailee are,
however, incapable of being categorised as tortious or contractual in nature[7]. A
claim against a bailee can therefore (according to circumstances) be brought in
contract, tort or bailment[8]. In particular circumstances, a claim may also lie
against a bailee in restitution[9].

1 See generally BAILMENT AND PLEDGE.
2 *Building and Civil Engineering Holidays Scheme Management Ltd v Post Office* [1966] 1 QB 247 at 261, [1965] 1 All ER 163 at 167, CA, per Lord Denning MR; *Yearworth v North Bristol NHS Trust* [2009] EWCA Civ 37 at [48], [2010] QB 1 at [48], [2009] 2 All ER 986 at [48] per Lord Judge CJ. See also BAILMENT AND PLEDGE vol 4 (2011) PARA 101.
3 Eg bailment by way of carriage: see CARRIAGE AND CARRIERS vol 7 (2015) PARA 56 et seq.
4 *Morris v CW Martin & Sons Ltd* [1966] 1 QB 716 at 738, [1965] 2 All ER 725 at 738, CA, per Salmon LJ. As to conversion by bailees see BAILMENT AND PLEDGE vol 4 (2011) PARA 232 et seq. As to conversion of goods see further PARA 604 et seq.
5 A person can convert another's goods without being in possession of them: see e g PARA 609 et seq. A duty of care can plainly be owed towards the goods of another person where the person owing the duty is not a bailee: see generally NEGLIGENCE. But some facets of the bailee's duty of care (eg the duty to guard against theft, or against the deliberate wrongs of third parties generally) are substantially peculiar to bailment and to certain other narrow categories of relation and are not a facet of the general law of tort: see *P Perl (Exporters) Ltd v Camden London Borough Council* [1984] QB 342, [1983] 3 All ER 161, CA; *Maloco v Littlewoods Ltd* [1987] AC 241, sub nom *Smith v Littlewoods Organisation Ltd* [1987] 1 All ER 710, HL.
6 A claim against a bailee for breach of the duty of care is a claim in tort for the purposes of what are now the Limitation Act 1980 (see LIMITATION PERIODS vol 68 (2008) PARA 979 et seq) (*Chesworth v Farrar* [1967] 1 QB 407, [1966] 2 All ER 107), the County Courts Act 1984 (see COURTS AND TRIBUNALS) (*Turner v Stallibrass* [1898] 1 QB 56, CA) and the Postal Services Act 2000 s 90 (exclusion of liability) (see POSTAL SERVICES vol 85 (2012) PARA 276) (*American Express Co v British Airways Board* [1983] 1 All ER 557, [1983] 1 WLR 701).
7 Eg the strict liability of the bailee for loss or damage resulting from his unlawful departure from the terms of the bailment (see BAILMENT AND PLEDGE vol 4 (2011) PARA 124) which can be visited not only on a contractual bailee but also on the unrewarded bailee under a gratuitous bailment: see *Mitchell v Ealing London Borough Council* [1979] QB 1, [1978] 2 All ER 779.
8 *Sutcliffe v Chief Constable of West Yorkshire* [1996] RTR 86 at 90, 159 JP 770 at 774, CA, per Otton LJ.
9 See DAMAGES vol 29 (2014) PARA 567 et seq. See generally BAILMENT AND PLEDGE vol 4 (2011) PARA 233.

408. Breach of agent's warranty of authority. Claims against an agent for breach of warranty of authority[1] have been variously classed in the past as claims in tort[2], quasi-tort[3], and quasi-contract[4], or even as sui generis[5], distinct from both contract and tort. The preponderance of case-law authority, however, treats them as contractual[6]. In appropriate circumstances, a claim may also be sustainable against the agent in tort for negligent misstatement[7].

1 See PARAS 431, 793; and AGENCY vol 1 (2008) PARA 161; DAMAGES vol 29 (2014) PARA 577 et seq.
2 *West London Commercial Bank Ltd v Kitson* (1884) 13 QBD 360, CA, considered by Mocatta J in *V/O Rasnoimport v Guthrie & Co Ltd* [1966] 1 Lloyd's Rep 1 at 12–13; *Hawke's Bay Milk Corpn Ltd v Watson* [1974] 1 NZLR 236.
3 Holdsworth *History of English Law* (3rd Edn, 1923) vol 8 p 89.
4 *Lomax v Dankel* (1981) 29 SASR 68, SA SC; Winfield *Province of the Law of Tort* (1931) p 178.
5 See *Farley Health Products Ltd v Babylon Trading Co* (1987) Times, 29 July.
6 *Collen v Wright* (1857) 8 E & B 647 at 657–658 per Willes J; *Dickson v Reuter's Telegram Co Ltd* (1877) 3 CPD 1 at 5, CA, per Bramwell LJ; *Yonge v Toynbee* [1910] 1 KB 215 at 228, CA, per Buckley LJ; *Allan and Anderson Ltd v AH Basse Rederi A/S, The Piraeus* [1974] 2 Lloyd's Rep 266, CA; *SEB Trygg Liv Holding AB v Manches* [2005] EWCA Civ 1237 at [60], [2006] 1 All ER 437 at [60], [2006] 1 WLR 2276 at [60] per Buxton LJ; *OBG Ltd v Allan* [2007] UKHL 21 at [93], [2008] 1 AC 1 at [93], [2007] 4 All ER 545 at [93] per Lord Hoffmann.
7 See PARA 496; and NEGLIGENCE vol 78 (2010) PARA 14. See also MISREPRESENTATION vol 76 (2013) PARA 797 et seq.

409. Misrepresentation. Claims against a person who makes a misrepresentation[1] may lie in tort for deceit[2] or for negligent misstatement[3]. A misrepresentation which induces the making of a contract may become a term of that contract and give rise to a claim for breach of contract[4]. Alternatively a misrepresentation may be the subject of a collateral contract[5]. The liability imposed by statute for certain non-fraudulent misrepresentations[6] has been characterised as a liability sui generis, sounding neither in contract nor in tort[7], but affords an equivalent measure of damages to that recoverable in tort for deceit[8].

1 As to misrepresentation see PARA 492 et seq; and MISREPRESENTATION vol 76 (2013) PARA 701 et seq.
2 See PARA 494; and MISREPRESENTATION vol 76 (2013) PARA 754 et seq.
3 See PARA 496; and MISREPRESENTATION vol 76 (2013) PARAS 762, 797 et seq; NEGLIGENCE vol 78 (2010) PARA 14.
4 See MISREPRESENTATION vol 76 (2013) PARA 816. See also CONTRACT.
5 As to collateral contracts see CONTRACT vol 22 (2012) PARA 332.
6 See the Misrepresentation Act 1967 s 2(1), (2); and PARA 495; MISREPRESENTATION vol 76 (2013) PARAS 800, 810, 832; but c f PARA 417 (damages based on contractual measure for innocent misrepresentation). See also DAMAGES vol 29 (2014) PARA 426 et seq.
7 *Farley Health Products Ltd v Babylon Trading Co* (1987) Times, 29 July, obiter per Lawson J.
8 *Royscot Trust Ltd v Rogerson* [1991] 2 QB 297, [1991] 3 All ER 294, CA. In *Smith New Court (Securities) Ltd v Citibank NA* [1997] AC 254 at 282–283, sub nom *Smith New Court Securities Ltd v Scrimgeour Vickers (Asset Management) Ltd* [1996] 4 All ER 769 at 793, HL, Lord Steyn noted that there had been trenchant academic criticism of *Royscot Trust Ltd v Rogerson* but declined to express a concluded view on its correctness. See also *Smith New Court (Securities) Ltd v Citibank NA* [1997] AC 254 at 267, sub nom *Smith New Court Securities Ltd v Scrimgeour Vickers (Asset Management) Ltd* [1996] 4 All ER 769 at 779, HL, per Lord Browne-Wilkinson. See further MISREPRESENTATION vol 76 (2013) PARA 810; DAMAGES vol 29 (2014) PARA 428.

410. Common carriers. Common carriers[1] traditionally occupy one of the trades of common calling[2], and owe special obligations not arising under the general law of tort. The common carrier owes an obligation not to refuse to carry goods of a kind which he holds himself out to carry, provided his operations extend to the proposed destination and the consignor is willing and able to pay a reasonable charge for carriage[3]. Common carriers are bailees of goods entrusted to them[4] but their liability differs from that of ordinary bailees, such as private carriers[5]. Subject to various restrictions and defences[6], the common carrier is strictly answerable at common law for loss or damage occurring to the consignor's goods[7]. While it appears that the common carrier's liability in respect of goods, at least, does not depend on contract[8], some authorities favour a contractual analysis[9]. Other authorities treat the common carrier's liability as one sounding in tort[10]. It has been held preferable to conclude that the liability of the common carrier, similarly to that of the innkeeper at common law[11], is founded on status and custom of the realm[12] rather than on contract, tort or bailment[13].

1 As to common carriers see generally CARRIAGE AND CARRIERS.
2 Ie a carrier carries on his business as public employment (Chitty and Temple (1857) pp 14–15) and undertakes to carry for hire the goods of all persons indifferently: see CARRIAGE AND CARRIERS. See also PARA 411.
3 See CARRIAGE AND CARRIERS vol 7 (2015) PARAS 7–8.
4 Ie because they are voluntarily in possession of goods which belong to another: see BAILMENT AND PLEDGE vol 4 (2011) PARA 101.
5 As to private carriers see generally CARRIAGE AND CARRIERS vol 7 (2015) PARA 56 et seq.
6 See CARRIAGE AND CARRIERS vol 7 (2015) PARAS 7–37.
7 See CARRIAGE AND CARRIERS vol 7 (2015) PARA 16.
8 *London and North Western Rly Co v Richard Hudson & Sons Ltd* [1920] AC 324, HL; *Eastman Chemical International AG v NMT Trading Ltd and Eagle Transport Ltd* [1972] 2 Lloyd's Rep 25. See also CARRIAGE AND CARRIERS vol 7 (2015) PARA 16.

9   See e g *Fleming v Manchester, Sheffield and Lincolnshire Rly Co* (1878) 4 QBD 81 at 83 per Bramwell LJ. See also Palmer *Bailment* (3rd Edn, 2009) para 27–029 note 212.
10 See eg *Pozzi v Shipton* (1838) 8 Ad & El 963 per Patteson J; *Marshall v York, Newcastle and Berwick Rly Co* (1851) 11 CB 655 at 663–664 per Williams J; but cf Palmer *Bailment* (3rd Edn, 2009) para 27–029 note 212.
11 *Readhead v Midland Rly Co* (1869) LR 4 QB 379 at 382, Ex Ch; *Clarke v West Ham Corpn* [1909] 2 KB 858 at 879, CA. As to innkeepers see PARA 411; and LICENSING AND GAMBLING vol 67 (2008) PARA 183 et seq.
12 *Compania Maritima San Basilio SA v Oceanus Mutual Underwriting Association (Bermuda) Ltd, The Eurysthenes* [1977] QB 49 at 67, [1976] 3 All ER 243 at 251, CA, per Lord Denning MR; and see CARRIAGE AND CARRIERS vol 7 (2015) PARA 3; CUSTOM AND USAGE vol 32 (2012) PARA 1 et seq.
13 It is an open question whether a claim against a common carrier for loss of or damage to goods counts as a claim in tort for the purposes of the Torts (Interference with Goods) Act 1977 s 1 (see PARA 603) and lies in conversion under the statutory form of that tort created by s 2(2) (see PARA 612).

411.   Innkeepers.   The innkeeper[1] occupies one of the trades of common calling[2] and owes an obligation to receive travellers who present themselves as willing to pay a reasonable charge for accommodation[3]. Subject to various restrictions and defences[4], he is strictly answerable at common law for loss or damage[5] occurring to the goods of guests when those goods are within the hospitium of the inn[6]. His liability for goods does not depend on bailment[7] (because the goods for which he is answerable may not be within his possession)[8] or on contract[9]. It is founded on status and custom of the realm and does not come under any other head of law[10]. The liability of innkeepers is now substantially modified by statute[11].

1   See generally LICENSING AND GAMBLING vol 67 (2008) PARA 183 et seq.
2   Ie an innkeeper offers a service in respect of a public need and is bound by the common law or custom to provide shelter and sustenance to all travellers. See LICENSING AND GAMBLING vol 67 (2008) PARA 186. Common carriers are also engaged in common calling: see PARA 410.
3   See LICENSING AND GAMBLING vol 67 (2008) PARA 186.
4   See LICENSING AND GAMBLING vol 67 (2008) PARAS 187–194, 198–204.
5   *Day v Bather* (1863) 2 H & C 14. But some authorities hold that the strict common law liability does not extend to damage but only loss of the goods: *Winkworth v Raven* [1931] 1 KB 652; *Williams v Owen* [1956] 1 All ER 104, [1955] 1 WLR 1293.
6   See LICENSING AND GAMBLING vol 67 (2008) PARAS 197–198.
7   *Robins & Co v Gray* [1895] 2 QB 501 at 503–504, CA, per Lord Esher MR; and see LICENSING AND GAMBLING vol 67 (2008) PARA 197.
8   See generally BAILMENT AND PLEDGE.
9   See LICENSING AND GAMBLING vol 67 (2008) PARA 197. At common law, the innkeeper cannot contract out of the liability imposed on him by custom of the realm: *Williams v Linnitt* [1951] 1 KB 565 at 585, [1951] 1 All ER 278 at 290, CA, per Denning LJ. But see the Hotel Proprietors Act 1956 s 2(3).
10 *Robins & Co v Gray* [1895] 2 QB 501 at 503–504, CA, per Lord Esher MR; and see LICENSING AND GAMBLING vol 67 (2008) PARA 197.
11 See the Hotel Proprietors Act 1956; and LICENSING AND GAMBLING vol 67 (2008) PARA 186 et seq.

(3) THE CONJUNCTION OF DAMAGE AND INJURY IN TORT

(i) Damnum absque Injuria

412.   Damage without infringement of legal right (damnum absque injuria).
The world is full of harm for which the law furnishes no remedy[1]. A person may sustain loss or damage and yet possess no remedy in tort, because his legal rights

have not been infringed in any way which the law regards as unjustifiable, so that he has suffered no legal wrong[2]. This doctrine is embodied in the Latin phrase 'damnum absque injuria'[3].

1 *D v East Berkshire Community Health NHS Trust* [2005] UKHL 23 at [100], [2005] 2 AC 373 at [100], [2005] 2 All ER 443 at [100] per Lord Rodger.
2 'You must have in our law injury as well as damage. The act of the defendant, if lawful, may still cause a great deal of damage to the plaintiff': *Day v Brownrigg* (1878) 10 ChD 294 at 304, CA, per Jessel MR. See also *Mayor of Bradford v Pickles* [1895] AC 587 at 601, HL, per Lord Macnaghten; *Clark v London General Omnibus Co Ltd* [1906] 2 KB 648 at 663, CA, per Sir Gorell Barnes P; *Hammerton v Earl of Dysart* [1916] 1 AC 57 at 84, HL, per Lord Parker of Waddington.
      An important category of damnum absque injuria is pure economic loss caused by negligent act: see eg *Weller & Co v Foot and Mouth Disease Research Institute* [1966] 1 QB 569, [1965] 3 All ER 560; *Spartan Steel and Alloys Ltd v Martin & Co (Contractors) Ltd* [1973] QB 27, [1972] 3 All ER 557, CA; *Murphy v Brentwood District Council* [1991] 1 AC 398, [1990] 2 All ER 908, HL. Economic loss caused by negligent misrepresentation is recoverable where responsibility has been assumed: see *Hedley Byrne & Co Ltd v Heller & Partners Ltd* [1964] AC 465, [1963] 2 All ER 575, HL; and MISREPRESENTATION. Loss caused by perjury (*Hargreaves v Bretherton* [1959] 1 QB 45, [1958] 3 All ER 122) or by contempt of court is also damnum absque injuria (*Chapman v Honig* [1963] 2 QB 502, [1963] 2 All ER 513, CA).
3 See eg *Hay (or Bourhill) v Young* [1943] AC 92 at 106, [1942] 2 All ER 396 at 404, HL, per Lord Wright; *Crofter Hand Woven Harris Tweed Co Ltd v Veitch* [1942] AC 435 at 442, [1942] 1 All ER 142, HL, per Viscount Simon LC; *Hunter v Canary Wharf Ltd* [1997] AC 655 at 699, [1997] 2 All ER 426 at 445, HL, per Lord Lloyd. The phrase 'damnum sine injuria' is also found: see eg *Watkins v Secretary of State for the Home Department* [2006] UKHL 17 at [53], [2006] 2 AC 395 at [53], [2006] 2 All ER 353 at [53] per Lord Rodger.

413.   User of land. Subject to the planning legislation, an owner or occupier of land may use it for any purpose for which it might be used in the ordinary course of the enjoyment of land; and, even though in so doing he may inflict injury upon his neighbour, the neighbour has no actionable cause of complaint[1]. For example, without incurring liability, he may win the underlying minerals in the ordinary way, even if water is thereby allowed to percolate into an adjoining mine[2]; he may abstract underground water flowing in no defined channel, and so stop the flow of his neighbour's spring[3] or cause the surface of the neighbour's land to subside[4]; he may grow poisonous yew trees on his land[5] so long as they do not overhang the fences[6], although animals which stray in may be poisoned, or although third persons may remove the clippings and deposit them elsewhere[7]; he may erect a high wall or disfiguring buildings, and thus deprive his neighbour's house of its outlook[8] or amenities[9]; he may cut off light[10] or air[11] from an adjoining house and even 'let it down'[12] by excavations on his own land, provided the neighbour has no legal right to light, air or support[13]; and he may interfere with his neighbour's privacy by opening a new window providing a view over next-door's garden[14].

1 *Rylands v Fletcher* (1868) LR 3 HL 330 at 338 per Lord Cairns; *Wilson v Waddell* (1876) 2 App Cas 95 at 99, HL, per Lord Blackburn; *West Cumberland Iron and Steel Co v Kenyon* (1879) 11 ChD 782 at 786–787, CA, per James LJ; *Whalley v Lancashire and Yorkshire Rly Co* (1884) 13 QBD 131 at 135–136, CA, per Brett LJ; *Southwark London Borough Council v Tanner; Baxter v Camden London Borough Council (No 2)* [2001] 1 AC 1, [1999] 4 All ER 449, HL. As to planning legislation see PLANNING.
2 *Smith v Kenrick* (1849) 7 CB 515; *Baird v Williamson* (1863) 15 CBNS 376; *Wilson v Waddell* (1876) 2 App Cas 95, HL. See MINES, MINERALS AND QUARRIES vol 76 (2013) PARA 271.
3 *Chasemore v Richards* (1859) 7 HL Cas 349; *Mayor of Bradford v Pickles* [1895] AC 587, HL. See WATER AND WATERWAYS vol 100 (2009) PARAS 97, 106.
4 *Popplewell v Hodkinson* (1869) LR 4 Exch 248; *Stephens v Anglian Water Authority* [1987] 3 All ER 379, [1987] 1 WLR 1381, CA.
5 *Ponting v Noakes* [1894] 2 QB 281. See FORESTRY vol 52 (2014) PARA 60.

6   *Crowhurst v Amersham Burial Board* (1878) 4 ExD 5. See also *Smith v Giddy* [1904] 2 KB 448. A tenant who takes a lease of land overhung at the date of the lease by yew trees growing on land retained by his landlord has no right of action against the landlord if his cattle are poisoned: *Cheater v Cater* [1918] 1 KB 247, CA.
7   *Wilson v Newberry* (1871) LR 7 QB 31.
8   *Aldred's Case* (1610) 9 Co Rep 57b at 58b per Wray CJ. See also REAL PROPERTY AND REGISTRATION vol 87 (2012) PARAS 1013–1014. However, a claim will lie if the outlook or amenities are interfered with by an act that amounts to a public nuisance resulting in special damage to the person whose outlook or amenities are injured: *Campbell v Paddington Corpn* [1911] 1 KB 869, DC. See also NUISANCE vol 78 (2010) PARA 128.
9   *Hunter v Canary Wharf Ltd* [1997] AC 655, [1997] 2 All ER 426, HL (television reception).
10 *Levet v Gas Light and Coke Co* [1919] 1 Ch 24.
11 *Webb v Bird* (1863) 13 CBNS 841. See also *Chastey v Ackland* [1895] 2 Ch 389, CA (on appeal [1897] AC 155, HL); and REAL PROPERTY AND REGISTRATION vol 87 (2012) PARAS 1040–1042.
12 *Wyatt v Harrison* (1832) 3 B & Ad 871; *Partridge v Scott* (1838) 3 M & W 220; *Birmingham Corpn v Allen* (1877) 6 ChD 284, CA. Possibly in this case he must not dig negligently: see *Dodd v Holme* (1834) 1 Ad & El 493. See also *Southwark and Vauxhall Water Co v Wandsworth Board of Works* [1898] 2 Ch 603, CA. See BOUNDARIES vol 4 (2011) PARA 374.
13 As to rights or easements of light, air or support see REAL PROPERTY AND REGISTRATION vol 87 (2012) PARAS 971 et seq, 1013 et seq, 1040 et seq.
14 *Tapling v Jones* (1865) 11 HL Cas 290 at 305 per Lord Westbury LC. See also *Browne v Flower* [1911] 1 Ch 219.

414.   Trade rivalry.   Injury or loss occasioned to a person's trade, calling or profession by the interference of others is not actionable at common law, even though the interference is concerted[1], if the means used to inflict the loss are not unlawful and the real purpose is not to injure another, but to forward or defend the trade or occupation of the person or persons who work the injury[2]. Thus the following are cases of damnum absque injuria: damage resulting from the setting up of a rival school to entice away the claimant's scholars[3]; persuading an employer not to renew the claimant's employment[4]; and the underselling of a rival trader to get a monopoly of a trade[5]. The prevention, restriction or distortion of competition or the abuse of a dominant position within the common market may, however, result in a liability in damages for breach of the EU Treaty[6].

1   As to the tort of conspiracy see PARA 712 et seq.
2   *Sorrell v Smith* [1925] AC 700, HL; *Crofter Hand Woven Harris Tweed Co Ltd v Veitch* [1942] AC 435, [1942] 1 All ER 142, HL.
3   *Gloucester Grammar School Case* (1410) YB 11 Hen 4, fo 47, pl 21. Cf *Sweeney v Coote* [1907] AC 221, HL.
4   *Allen v Flood* [1898] AC 1, HL.
5   *Mogul Steamship Co Ltd v McGregor, Gow & Co* [1892] AC 25, HL; *Ajello v Worsley* [1898] 1 Ch 274; *Imperial Tobacco Co of India Ltd v Bonnan* [1924] AC 755, PC.
6   See the Treaty on the Functioning of the European Union (Rome, 25 March 1957; TS 1 (1973); Cmnd 5179) ('TFEU') arts 101, 102. The Treaty was formerly known as the Treaty Establishing the European Community. As to the renaming and renumbering of the Treaty see EUROPEAN UNION vol 47A (2014) PARA 6.
    See Case C–453/99 *Courage Ltd v Crehan* [2002] QB 507, [2001] ECR I-6297, ECJ. As to monopolies generally see COMPETITION vol 18 (2009) PARA 361 et seq.

415.   Use of a name, likeness or identity.   The annoyance or inconvenience resulting from the assumption of another's name[1], likeness[2] or voice[3], or the name of his residence[4], is not actionable unless the use amounts to passing off[5], infringement of a trade mark[6] or a breach of contract[7], confidence[8] or copyright[9], or is defamatory[10] or otherwise infringes his legal rights[11].

1   *Du Boulay v Du Boulay* (1869) LR 2 PC 430 at 441–442 per Lord Chelmsford; *Dockrell v Dougall* (1899) 80 LT 556, CA (use of doctor's name in an advertisement). Cf *Earl Cowley v*

Countess Cowley [1901] AC 450, HL, refusing injunction to prevent divorced woman's use of title she acquired as wife of her former husband but was no longer entitled to use.
2   *Corelli v Wall* (1906) 22 TLR 532 (postcards).
3   *Sim v HJ Heinz & Co Ltd* [1959] 1 All ER 547, [1959] 1 WLR 313, CA.
4   *Day v Brownrigg* (1878) 10 ChD 294, CA (private residence); *Street v Union Bank of Spain and England* (1885) 30 ChD 156 (telegraphic address).
5   See eg *Irvine v Talksport Ltd* [2003] EWCA Civ 423, [2003] 2 All ER 881, [2003] 1 WLR 1576, where it was held that the use of the claimant's image in the defendant's advertising indicated that he had endorsed its radio station. As to passing-off actions see PARA 699; and TRADE MARKS AND TRADE NAMES vol 97A (2014) PARA 398 et seq.
6   As to trade marks see TRADE MARKS AND TRADE NAMES vol 97A (2014) PARA 1 et seq.
7   See eg *Pollard v Photographic Co* (1888) 40 ChD 345 (image taken by commercial photographer); and COPYRIGHT vol 23 (2013) PARA 612. See also CONTRACT.
8   See eg *Pollard v Photographic Co* (1888) 40 ChD 345; and CONFIDENCE AND INFORMATIONAL PRIVACY vol 19 (2011) PARA 1 et seq. See also PARA 700; and COPYRIGHT vol 23 (2013) PARA 614.
9   As to infringement of copyright in general see COPYRIGHT vol 23 (2013) PARA 858 et seq.
10 *Tolley v JS Fry & Sons Ltd* [1931] AC 333, HL (caricature of an amateur golfer used as an advertisement of goods held to be capable of amounting to a libel). See DEFAMATION vol 32 (2012) PARAS 511–512.
11 See eg the Copyright, Designs and Patents Act 1988 s 85 (amended by SI 1995/3297; and SI 2003/2498), which provides that, subject to various exceptions, a person who for private and domestic purposes commissions the taking of a photograph or the making of a film, where copyright subsists in the resulting work, has the right not to have (inter alia) copies of the work issued to the public, or the work exhibited or shown in public. See COPYRIGHT vol 23 (2013) PARA 1023.

(ii) Damage and Causation in Tort

416.   Injuria sine damno. The cause of action in certain torts may be complete without proof of actual damage or loss[1], and in such cases the infringement of right alone is the tort. Nominal damages are recoverable[2] or, in suitable instances, an injunction may be granted[3]; but, if damages for particular loss are sought, causal connection between the tort and the alleged loss must be shown in the usual case[4].

1   Eg trespass to the person, trespass to goods (eg by seizure or removal) and trespass to land (see PARA 525 et seq); libel and slanders actionable per se (see DEFAMATION vol 32 (2012) PARA 501 et seq). Cf *Watkins v Secretary of State for the Home Department* [2006] UKHL 17, [2006] 2 AC 395, [2006] 2 All ER 353, ruling that damage remains an element of the tort of misfeasance in public office and that liability does not arise for invasion of a constitutional right per se.
2   *Armstrong v Sheppard and Short Ltd* [1959] 2 QB 384, [1959] 2 All ER 651, CA. As to nominal damages see DAMAGES vol 29 (2014) PARAS 319–320, 420.
3   *Woollerton & Wilson Ltd v Richard Costain Ltd* [1970] 1 All ER 483, [1970] 1 WLR 411; *Patel v WH Smith (Eziot) Ltd* [1987] 2 All ER 569, [1987] 1 WLR 853, CA.
4   See DAMAGES vol 29 (2014) PARA 364 et seq. As to trespass to goods see PARA 685 et seq. As to causation see PARA 417. For exceptions see PARA 417.

417.   Causation: claimant to prove on balance of probabilities. A claimant on whom the burden of proving damage lies discharges the burden if he shows that, on a balance of probabilities, the tortious conduct caused or materially contributed to the injury or damage[1]. Exceptionally, it is enough that the tortious conduct materially contributed to the risk of the injury or damage occurring, provided the risks are all of the same or similar types[2]. In such cases the defendant's liability is proportional to the risk for which he was responsible[3] (unless statute provides otherwise[4]). The exceptional liability for materially contributing to risk does not arise if the defendant merely adds a different and dissimilar risk to risks to which the claimant is already exposed[5]. Even if causation is established by these principles, liability will not arise in respect of harm that is too remote. In negligence and nuisance and under the rule in *Rylands v Fletcher*[6] only such damages are recoverable as are the reasonably foreseeable consequences of the tortious act[7]. In deceit[8], cases of knowingly wrongful conversion[9], and negligent statutory misrepresentation under the Misrepresentation Act 1967[10] the defendant is responsible for all direct consequences, and this may apply to all intentional torts[11]. Innocent misrepresentation attracts the contractual measure of damages[12].

1   *Bonnington Castings Ltd v Wardlaw* [1956] AC 613, [1956] 1 All ER 615, HL; *Bailey v Ministry of Defence* [2008] EWCA Civ 883, [2009] 1 WLR 1052, (2008) 103 BMLR 134.
2   *McGhee v National Coal Board* [1972] 3 All ER 1008, [1973] 1 WLR 1, HL; *Fairchild v Glenhaven Funeral Services Ltd* [2002] UKHL 22, [2003] 1 AC 32, [2002] 3 All ER 305.
3   *Barker v Corus UK Ltd* [2006] UKHL 20, [2006] 2 AC 572, [2006] 3 All ER 785.
4   See eg the Compensation Act 2006 s 3 (mesothelioma); and HEALTH AND SAFETY AT WORK vol 53 (2014) PARA 602.
5   *Wilsher v Essex Area Health Authority* [1988] AC 1074, [1988] 1 All ER 871, HL.
6   See *Rylands v Fletcher* (1868) LR 3 HL 330; PARA 596; and NUISANCE vol 78 (2010) PARA 148 et seq. As to negligence see generally NEGLIGENCE; and as to nuisance see generally NUISANCE.
7   See DAMAGES vol 29 (2014) PARAS 409–411.
8   *Doyle v Olby (Ironmongers) Ltd* [1969] 2 QB 158, [1969] 2 All ER 119 CA; *East v Maurer* [1991] 2 All ER 733, [1991] 1 WLR 461, CA; *Smith Kline & French Laboratories v Long* [1988] 3 All ER 887, [1989] 1 WLR 1, CA; *Smith New Court Securities Ltd v Citibank NA* [1997] AC 254, sub nom *Smith New Court Securities Ltd v Scrimgeour Vickers (Asset Management) Ltd* [1996] 4 All ER 769, HL. See also MISREPRESENTATION vol 76 (2013) PARA 788 et seq.
9   *Kuwait Airways Corpn v Iraqi Airways Co (Nos 4 and 5)* [2002] UKHL 19 at [103]–[104], [2002] 2 AC 883 at [103]–[104], [2002] 3 All ER 209 at [103]–[104] per Lord Nicholls, suggesting a different approach based on foreseeability where the defendant acts in good faith.
10 *Royscot Trust Ltd v Rogerson* [1991] 2 QB 297, [1991] 3 All ER 294, CA. See PARA 495; and MISREPRESENTATION vol 76 (2013) PARA 800.
11 *Smith New Court Securities Ltd v Citibank NA* [1997] AC 254 at 279–280, sub nom *Smith New Court Securities Ltd v Scrimgeour Vickers (Asset Management) Ltd* [1996] 4 All ER 769 at 789, HL, per Lord Steyn.
12 *William Sindall plc v Cambridgeshire County Council* [1994] 3 All ER 932, [1994] 1 WLR 1016, CA, per curiam. As to the contractual measure of damages see DAMAGES vol 29 (2014) PARA 499 et seq.

(4) SPECIFIC PARTIES IN ACTIONS IN TORT

418. The Crown. In general, by virtue of the Crown Proceedings Act 1947[1], the Crown is subject to liability in tort in respect of Her Majesty's government in the United Kingdom or the Scottish Administration[2] to the same extent as a private person of full age and capacity for:

  (1)   torts committed by Crown servants or agents[3];

  (2)   any breach of the common law duties of an employer to his servants or agents[4];

  (3)   any breach of the common law duties attaching to the ownership, occupation, possession or control of property[5]; and

  (4)   any failure to comply with a statutory duty binding both upon the Crown and upon persons other than the Crown and its officers[6].

1   See the Crown Proceedings Act 1947 s 2(1); and CONSTITUTIONAL AND ADMINISTRATIVE LAW vol 20 (2014) PARA 191. As to the limitations on proceedings against the Crown see CONSTITUTIONAL AND ADMINISTRATIVE LAW vol 20 (2014) PARA 191; CROWN AND CROWN PROCEEDINGS vol 29 (2014) PARA 85 et seq. It remains the case at common law that the Crown can do no wrong: *Chagos Islanders v Attorney General* [2004] EWCA Civ 997, (2004) Times, 21 September, [2004] All ER (D) 85 (Aug).

2   See the Crown Proceedings Act 1947 s 40(2)(b) (amended by the Scotland Act 1998 s 125, Sch 8
    para 7(3)(a)), considered in *Trawnik v Lennox* [1985] 2 All ER 368, [1985] 1 WLR 532, CA.
3   See the Crown Proceedings Act 1947 s 2(1)(a).
4   See the Crown Proceedings Act 1947 s 2(1)(b).
5   See the Crown Proceedings Act 1947 s 2(1)(c).
6   See the Crown Proceedings Act 1947 s 2(2); and CONSTITUTIONAL AND ADMINISTRATIVE LAW
    vol 20 (2014) PARA 191; CROWN AND CROWN PROCEEDINGS vol 29 (2014) PARA 85 et seq.

419.   Public bodies and public officers.   Unless the contrary is provided by
legislation, a public body[1] which is not a servant or agent of the Crown has the
same duties and is subject to the same liabilities as the general law would impose
on a private person doing the same things[2]. Its liability may be personal (that is,
for its own acts or omissions) or vicarious (that is, for torts committed by its
servants and agents in the scope of their employment or authority)[3]. Whether for
these purposes the holder of a public office is a servant under a contract of
employment with the body which appointed him depends on the precise nature
of the relationship in the individual case[4]. Under the Human Rights Act 1998, it
is unlawful for a 'public authority' to act in a way which is incompatible with a
right guaranteed by the Convention for the Protection of Human Rights and
Fundamental Freedoms[5] which has been incorporated into domestic law by
virtue of the same Act, and the authority may be liable to damages in
proceedings brought by the victim of an unlawful act if such award is necessary
to afford just satisfaction to the person in whose favour it is made[6].

1   The meaning of 'public body' varies according to the context: see CONSTITUTIONAL AND
    ADMINISTRATIVE LAW vol 20 (2014) PARA 601.
2   *Mersey Docks and Harbour Board Trustees v Gibbs* (1866) LR 1 HL 93. See CONSTITUTIONAL
    AND ADMINISTRATIVE LAW vol 20 (2014) PARAS 647–648.
3   See eg *X (minors) v Bedfordshire County Council* [1995] 2 AC 633, [1995] 3 All ER 353, HL,
    where the House of Lords gave separate consideration to claims based on a direct duty of care
    (personal liability) and claims based on duties of care owed by their servants and agents
    (vicarious liability). As to the vicarious liability of employers in general see PARA 767 et seq. As
    to public officers and public authorities see further PARAS 807–810.
4   See CONSTITUTIONAL AND ADMINISTRATIVE LAW vol 20 (2014) PARA 607 et seq.
5   See the Convention for the Protection of Human Rights and Fundamental Freedoms (Rome,
    4 November 1950; TS 71 (1953); Cmd 8969); PARA 810; and RIGHTS AND FREEDOMS vol 88A
    (2013) PARAS 23 et seq, 88.
6   See the Human Rights Act 1998 s 6(1); and PARA 810.

420.   Foreign monarchs and states.   A monarch or other head of state enjoys
state immunity in his public capacity and diplomatic privilege, the latter
extending to members of his family forming part of his household and his private
servants[1]. A claim will not generally lie against a foreign state unless it submits to
the jurisdiction[2]. There is no exception for actions in respect of torture[3]. State
immunity extends not only to the state itself but also to the government of that
state and any department of that government[4]. It does not extend to an entity
which is distinct from the executive organs of the government of the state and
capable of suing or being sued unless the proceedings relate to anything done by
it in the exercise of sovereign authority and the circumstances are such that a
state would have been so immune[5]. The exercise of sovereign authority here
refers to acts which are of their own character governmental acts: it is not
enough that the entity acted on the directions of the state because such an act
need not possess the character of a governmental act[6]. Statutory exceptions from
the immunity include actions in respect of death, personal injury or damage to or
loss of property caused by an act or omission in the United Kingdom, actions in
respect of the state's commercial transactions and contracts which fall to be

performed in the United Kingdom, and actions in respect of the state's ownership, possession, or use of immovable property in the United Kingdom, such as occupiers' liability[7], but this liability does not extend to buildings used for the official purposes of a diplomatic mission[8]. The above-stated principles of state immunity do not apply to proceedings relating to anything done by or in relation to the armed forces of a state while present in the United Kingdom[9]. The question of immunity in such a case is addressed as a matter of common law and turns on a distinction between sovereign and non-sovereign activities[10].

1   See the State Immunity Act 1978 ss 14, 20; the Diplomatic Privileges Act 1964 s 2, Sch 1 arts 1, 31; and INTERNATIONAL RELATIONS LAW vol 61 (2010) PARA 244 et seq.
2   See the State Immunity Act 1978 ss 1, 2; and INTERNATIONAL RELATIONS LAW vol 61 (2010) PARA 244. As to submission to the jurisdiction see INTERNATIONAL RELATIONS LAW vol 61 (2010) PARA 246.
3   *Jones v Ministry of the Interior of the Kingdom of Saudi Arabia* [2006] UKHL 26, [2007] 1 AC 270, [2007] 1 All ER 113.
4   See the State Immunity Act 1978 s 14(1); and INTERNATIONAL RELATIONS LAW vol 61 (2010) PARA 245.
5   See the State Immunity Act 1978 s 14(1), (2); and INTERNATIONAL RELATIONS LAW vol 61 (2010) PARA 245.
6   See *Kuwait Airways Corpn v Iraqi Airways Co* [1995] 3 All ER 694, [1995] 1 WLR 1147, HL, where the defendant's seizure of the claimant's aircraft was a governmental act, and hence attracted the immunity, but its subsequent retention and use of the aircraft pursuant to national legislation were not governmental acts and fell outside the immunity.
7   See the State Immunity Act 1978 ss 2–10; and INTERNATIONAL RELATIONS LAW vol 61 (2010) PARA 244 et seq.
8   See the State Immunity Act 1978 s 16(1)(b); and INTERNATIONAL RELATIONS LAW vol 61 (2010) PARAS 250, 259.
9   See the State Immunity Act 1978 s 16(2); and INTERNATIONAL RELATIONS LAW vol 61 (2010) PARA 259. This exception is capable of extending to acts done by the civilian component of a state's armed forces: *Holland v Lampen-Wolfe* [2000] 3 All ER 833, [2000] 1 WLR 1573, HL (education).
10 See eg *Littrell v United States of America (No 2)* [1994] 4 All ER 203, [1995] 1 WLR 82, CA (no action for personal injuries in respect of treatment at a US military hospital); *Holland v Lampen-Wolfe* [2000] 3 All ER 833, [2000] 1 WLR 1573, HL (immunity for publication of libel). See also ARMED FORCES.

421.   Diplomats. Heads of a mission, the members of their staff having diplomatic rank and the members of their households are immune from civil jurisdiction in respect of their torts, except in the case of an action relating to any professional or commercial activity exercised outside their official functions or an action relating to succession in which they are involved as executor, administrator, heir or legatee as a private person[1]. Members of the administrative and technical staff of a mission, and their households, and members of the mission's service staff, are similarly immune in respect of acts performed in the course of their duties[2].

1   See the Diplomatic Privileges Act 1964 s 2, Sch 1 arts 1, 31, 37(1); and INTERNATIONAL RELATIONS LAW vol 61 (2010) PARAS 274, 279.
2   See the Diplomatic Privileges Act 1964 Sch 1 art 37(2), (3); and INTERNATIONAL RELATIONS LAW vol 61 (2010) PARAS 280–281. As to the immunities of international organisations and consular officials see INTERNATIONAL RELATIONS LAW vol 61 (2010) PARAS 265 et seq, 307 et seq.

422.   European Union. The European Union is liable for damage caused by its institutions or its servants in the performance of their duties in accordance with the general principles common to the laws of the member states[1]. Jurisdiction is vested in the Court of Justice of the European Union[2].

1 Treaty on the Functioning of the European Union (Rome, 25 March 1957; TS 1 (1973); Cmnd 5179) ('TFEU') art 340; and EUROPEAN UNION vol 47A (2014) PARAS 38, 144 et seq. The Treaty was formerly known as the Treaty Establishing the European Community. As to the renaming and renumbering of the Treaty see EUROPEAN UNION vol 47A (2014) PARA 6.
2 See TFEU art 268; and EUROPEAN UNION vol 47A (2014) PARAS 65, 144. As to the Court of Justice of the European Union see EUROPEAN UNION vol 47A (2014) PARA 51 et seq.

423. Local authorities. In principle, a local authority is subject to the same liabilities as a private person in the same circumstances[1]. It may be liable both for its own tortious acts or omissions (personal liability) and for torts committed by its servants and agents in the scope of their employment or authority (vicarious liability)[2]. A local authority may also be liable as a 'public authority' under the Human Rights Act 1998[3]. However, no claim will lie against a local authority for doing that which the legislature has directed to be done or where the legislature has expressly or impliedly authorised the infringement of private rights[4]. If the legislature authorises the authority to act in a particular sphere, but leaves it to the authority's discretion whether and, if so, how to act, it is presumed that the legislature intended the discretion to be exercised carefully so as to avoid the infringement of private rights, and the authority may be liable for unnecessary damage caused by its carelessness or the carelessness of its servants and agents in the scope of their employment or authority[5].

1 *Foreman v Mayor of Canterbury* (1871) LR 6 QB 214. See further PARAS 807–810.
2 See e g *X (minors) v Bedfordshire County Council* [1995] 2 AC 633, [1995] 3 All ER 353, HL. As to local authorities generally see LOCAL GOVERNMENT vol 69 (2009) PARA 22 et seq.
3 See PARA 419.
4 *Metropolitan Asylum District Managers v Hill* (1881) 6 App Cas 193 at 208, HL, per Lord Blackburn, and at 213 per Lord Watson; *Edgington v Swindon Corpn* [1939] 1 KB 86, [1938] 4 All ER 57; *Smeaton v Ilford Corpn* [1954] Ch 450, [1954] 1 All ER 923. See also PARA 809.
5 *Metropolitan Asylum District Managers v Hill* (1881) 6 App Cas 193 at 213, HL, per Lord Watson; *Manchester Corpn v Farnworth* [1930] AC 171, HL; *Tate & Lyle Industries Ltd v GLC* [1983] 2 AC 509, [1983] 1 All ER 1159, HL; *X (minors) v Bedfordshire County Council* [1995] 2 AC 633 at 728, [1995] 3 All ER 353 at 362, HL, per Lord Jauncey.

424. Highway authorities. A person who suffers injuries caused by the defective state of a highway may have a cause of action against the relevant highway authority in negligence[1], in public nuisance[2], or for breach of statutory duty[3]. The highway authority's duty to maintain the highway[4] is a duty to ensure it is safe for the relevant traffic[5]. The duty is generally limited to a duty to repair and keep in repair[6], and does not allow liability for the failure to erect traffic signs[7] or paint warning marks on the road at a dangerous point[8], but it is now expressly provided that the highway authority has the duty to ensure, so far as is reasonably practicable, that safe passage along a highway is not endangered by snow or ice[9].

The highway authority's general statutory duties to promote road safety do not themselves give rise to private rights of action in the event of breach or generate a common law duty of care, and the same applies a fortiori to its associated statutory powers[10]. In an action against a highway authority in respect of damage resulting from its failure to maintain a highway maintainable at the public expense, it is a defence (without prejudice to any other defence or the application of the law relating to contributory negligence) to prove that the authority had taken such care as in all the circumstances was reasonably required to secure that the part of the highway to which the action relates was not dangerous for traffic[11]. For the purposes of such a defence, however, it is not relevant to prove that the authority had arranged for a competent person to carry out or supervise the maintenance of that part of the highway unless it is also proved that the authority had given him proper instructions with regard to the maintenance of the highway and that he had carried them out[12].

1   See e g *Bird v Pearce* [1979] RTR 369, CA. See further PARA 809; and NEGLIGENCE vol 78 (2010) PARA 51 et seq. But the highway authority's common law liability is only for dangers it has introduced, or for dangers introduced by a third party that it has unreasonably failed to abate, and not for its mere failure to improve the highway's safety: *Stovin v Wise (Norfolk County Council, third party)* [1996] AC 923, [1996] 3 All ER 801, HL; *Gorringe v Calderdale Borough Council* [2004] UKHL 15, [2004] 2 All ER 326, [2004] 1 WLR 1057.
2   See e g *Skilton v Epsom and Ewell UDC* [1937] 1 KB 112, [1936] 2 All ER 50, CA; *Macfarlane v Gwalter* [1959] 2 QB 332, [1958] 1 All ER 181, CA. See further PARA 809; and NUISANCE vol 78 (2010) PARA 187.
3   See e g *Roe v Sheffield City Council* [2003] EWCA Civ 1, [2004] QB 653, [2003] LGR 389. See further PARAS 500 et seq, 809.
4   See the Highways Act 1980 s 41; and HIGHWAYS, STREETS AND BRIDGES vol 55 (2012) PARA 274.
5   *Littler v Liverpool Corpn* [1968] 2 All ER 343n, CA; *Rider v Rider* [1973] QB 505, [1973] 1 All ER 294, CA; *Mills v Barnsley Metropolitan Borough Council* [1992] PIQR P291, CA; *Jones v Rhondda Cynon Taff CBC* [2008] EWCA Civ 1497, [2009] RTR 151.
6   *Goodes v East Sussex County Council* [2000] 3 All ER 603, [2000] 1 WLR 1356, HL.
7   *Lavis v Kent County Council* [1992] PIQR P351, CA.
8   *Gorringe v Calderdale Metropolitan Borough Council* [2004] UKHL 15, [2004] 2 All ER 326, [2004] 1 WLR 1057.
9   See the Highways Act 1980 s 41(1A) (added by the Railways and Transport Safety Act 2003 s 111) (HIGHWAYS, STREETS AND BRIDGES vol 55 (2012) PARA 274) effectively reversing *Goodes v East Sussex County Council* [2000] 3 All ER 603, [2000] 1 WLR 1356, HL, on this precise issue.
10 *Gorringe v Calderdale Metropolitan Borough Council* [2004] UKHL 15, [2004] 2 All ER 326, [2004] 1 WLR 1057 (where the House of Lords was considering the now-repealed Highways Act 1980 s 39, but its reasoning is of general application).
11 See the Highways Act 1980 s 58(1); PARA 516; and HIGHWAYS, STREETS AND BRIDGES vol 55 (2012) PARA 309. For the matters to which the court must have particular regard for the purposes of the defence see s 58(2); PARA 516; and HIGHWAYS, STREETS AND BRIDGES vol 55 (2012) PARA 309. See *Griffiths v Liverpool Corpn* [1967] 1 QB 374, [1966] 2 All ER 1015, CA (considering the equivalent defence in earlier legislation); *Cross v Kirklees Metropolitan Borough Council* [1998] 1 All ER 564, CA; *Jones v Rhondda Cynon Taff County Borough Council* [2008] EWCA Civ 1497, [2009] RTR 151.
12 See the Highways Act 1980 s 58(2); PARA 516; and HIGHWAYS, STREETS AND BRIDGES vol 55 (2012) PARA 309.
    Under the Human Rights Act 1998, it is unlawful for public bodies, including highway authorities, to act in a way incompatible with the Convention for the Protection of Human Rights and Fundamental Freedoms (Rome, 4 November 1950; TS 71 (1953); Cmd 8969) (commonly referred to as the 'European Convention on Human Rights'): see PARA 810; and RIGHTS AND FREEDOMS vol 88A (2013) PARAS 23 et seq, 88.

425.   Postal operators.   OFCOM[1] may impose a consumer protection condition requiring postal operators to assume specified liability in respect of specified loss of or damage to specified postal packets[2]. A postal operator may accept a limited liability for loss of or damage to postal packets so far as the loss or damage is due to any wrongful act of, or any neglect or default by, their officer, servant, employee, agent or sub-contractor while performing or purporting to perform in that capacity his functions in relation to the receipt, conveyance, delivery or other dealing with the packet[3]. Otherwise, neither a universal service provider (or a postal operator) nor any of its officers, servants, employees, agents or sub-contractors is liable in tort[4] for anything done or omitted to be done in relation to any postal packet in the course of transmission by post or for any omission to carry out arrangements for the collection of anything to be conveyed by post[5]. Such liability is also excluded in respect of any person engaged in or about the conveyance of postal packets, or such person's officer, servant, employee, agent or sub-contractor[6].

1   Ie the Office of Communications: see TELECOMMUNICATIONS vol 97 (2015) PARA 2 et seq.
2   See the Postal Services Act 2011 s 51(1), (2); and POSTAL SERVICES.
3   See the Postal Services Act 2000 ss 91, 92 (both amended by the Postal Services Act 2011 s 91(1), (2), Sch 12 paras 1, 26); and POSTAL SERVICES vol 85 (2012) PARAS 276–277. For analysis of the extent of liability for this statutory tort see *Building and Civil Engineering Holidays Scheme Management Ltd v Post Office* [1966] 1 QB 247, [1965] 1 All ER 163, CA (decided under earlier legislation).
4   'Tort' here includes liability in bailment: see *American Express Co v British Airways Board* [1983] 1 All ER 557, [1983] 1 WLR 701; and PARA 407.
5   See the Postal Services Act 2000 s 90(A1), (A2), (1), (2) (s 90(1A), (1B) added and s 90(1), (2) amended by the Postal Services Act 2011 s 91(1), (2), Sch 12 paras 1, 25); and POSTAL SERVICES vol 85 (2012) PARA 276. Thus the addressee of a letter on the envelope of which the Post Office stamped 'Remember that Road Accidents are Caused by People Like You' could not recover damages in libel: *Boakes v Postmaster-General* (1962) Times, 27 October, CA. It should be noted that a claimant cannot evade the bar by suing in contract because acceptance of a letter for transmission by post does not give rise to a contractual relationship: *Triefus & Co Ltd v Post Office* [1957] 2 QB 352, [1957] 2 All ER 387, CA (theft of packets by Post Office employee).
6   See the Postal Services Act 2000 s 90(3) (amended by the Postal Services Act 2011 s 91(1), (2), Sch 12 paras 1, 25); and POSTAL SERVICES vol 85 (2012) PARA 276.

426.   Corporations. A corporation is liable vicariously when its employee commits a tort in the course of his employment[1]. A corporation is also liable for a tort authorised or committed by the directing mind of the corporation, for that will be a tort by the corporation itself[2]. A corporation is not exempted from liability on the grounds that its tortious conduct, or tortious conduct that it authorised, was ultra vires[3]. Where an employee of a corporation commits an act which is ultra vires and not in the course of his employment, the corporation is not liable[4].

A corporation can sue for any tort in the same way as an individual, except that some torts such as assault and false imprisonment, by their nature, cannot be committed against a corporation[5].

A corporation is not a 'person' entitled to sue for unlawful harassment for the purposes of the Protection from Harassment Act 1997[6]. It has yet to be resolved whether bodies corporate enjoy a right to privacy at common law or under the Convention for the Protection of Human Rights and Fundamental Freedoms (1950)[7].

1   See COMPANIES vol 14 (2009) PARA 296; CORPORATIONS vol 24 (2010) PARA 477 et seq. As to vicarious liability of employers see PARA 767 et seq.
2   *Lennard's Carrying Co Ltd v Asiatic Petroleum Co Ltd* [1915] AC 705, HL. The person who represents the corporation's directing mind need not have a concurrent personal liability: *Williams v Natural Life Health Foods* [1998] 2 All ER 577, [1998] 1 WLR 830, HL (director not assuming personal responsibility in respect of his statements on behalf of the company).
3   *Campbell v Paddington Corpn* [1911] 1 KB 869, DC. The validity of an act done by a company may not be called into question on the ground of lack of capacity by reason of anything in the company's constitution: see the Companies Act 2006 s 39; and COMPANIES vol 14 (2009) PARA 265.
4   *Poulton v London and South Western Rly Co* (1867) LR 2 QB 534.
5   See COMPANIES vol 14 (2009) PARA 300; CORPORATIONS vol 24 (2010) PARA 481.
6   *Daiichi Pharmaceuticals UK Ltd v Stop Huntingdon Animal Cruelty* [2003] EWHC 2337 (QB), [2004] 1 WLR 1503, [2005] 1 BCLC 27.
7   See the Convention for the Protection of Human Rights and Fundamental Freedoms (Rome, 4 November 1950; TS 71 (1953); Cmd 8969) (commonly called the 'European Convention on Human Rights'); the Human Rights Act 1998; PARA 810; and RIGHTS AND FREEDOMS vol 88A (2013) PARAS 88, 317 et seq. Cf *R v Broadcasting Standards Commission, ex p British*

Broadcasting Corpn [2001] QB 885, [2000] 3 All ER 989, CA (where the Court of Appeal accepted that a corporation had a right to privacy for the purposes of the Broadcasting Act 1996 ss 110, 111).

427. Trade unions. A trade union is not a body corporate but it is capable of suing and being sued in its own name[1].

A trade union is liable in tort for its own acts and for acts done on its behalf[2] except that by statute it is given a limited immunity in respect of tortious acts in contemplation or furtherance of a trade dispute[3]. Further, a trade union may be liable for the tort of inducing breach or threatening to interfere with the performance of a contract only if the act was authorised or endorsed by specified persons[4] and has not been repudiated by the executive, president or general secretary as soon as reasonably practicable after coming to the knowledge of any of them[5].

Various limitations apply to the amount of damages which may be awarded against a trade union in any proceedings in tort except in respect of personal injury as a result of negligence, nuisance or breach of duty, breach of duty in connection with the ownership, occupation, possession, control or use of property, or product liability under Part I of the Consumer Protection Act 1987[6].

A trade union does not have sufficient legal personality to enable it to sue in defamation[7].

1 See the Trade Union and Labour Relations (Consolidation) Act 1992 s 10(1); and EMPLOYMENT vol 41 (2014) PARA 897. This provision does not apply to a 'special register body': see s 117(1), (2), (3)(a)(i); and EMPLOYMENT vol 41 (2014) PARA 899.

2 See the Trade Union and Labour Relations (Consolidation) Act 1992 ss 10, 12(1), (2), 117(3); and EMPLOYMENT vol 41 (2014) PARA 897 et seq.

3 See the Trade Union and Labour Relations (Consolidation) Act 1992 s 219; and EMPLOYMENT vol 41A (2014) PARA 1363. The immunity does not apply to picketing unless it amounts to lawful peaceful picketing: see the Trade Union and Labour Relations (Consolidation) Act 1992 ss 219(3), 220; and EMPLOYMENT vol 41A (2014) PARA 1385. An act is not protected if it is action to enforce trade union membership, or action taken because of dismissal for taking unofficial action, or secondary action which is not lawful picketing, or if it amounts to pressure to impose a union recognition requirement: see ss 222–225; and EMPLOYMENT vol 41A (2014) PARAS 1365–1368. On the requirement of a ballot before industrial action by a trade union see ss 226–234; and EMPLOYMENT vol 41A (2014) PARA 1370 et seq.

4 See the Trade Union and Labour Relations (Consolidation) Act 1992 s 20; and EMPLOYMENT vol 41A (2014) PARA 1388. As to interference with the performance of a contract see PARA 703 et seq.

5 See the Trade Union and Labour Relations (Consolidation) Act 1992 s 21; and EMPLOYMENT vol 41A (2014) PARA 1389.

6 Ie the Consumer Protection Act 1987 Pt I (ss 1–9). See the Trade Union and Labour Relations (Consolidation) Act 1992 s 22; and EMPLOYMENT vol 41A (2014) PARA 1390.

7 *Electrical, Electronic, Telecommunication and Plumbing Union v Times Newspapers Ltd* [1980] QB 585, [1980] 1 All ER 1097.

428. Unincorporated associations. Unincorporated associations, such as members' clubs, cannot generally sue or be sued in the association's name[1]; but a member or members having the same interest in a claim as other members may sue or be sued as representatives of the latter[2]. No special rules determine whether a cause of action in tort subsists against the members of an unincorporated association. Mere common membership of a club does not give rise to a duty of care[3] but neither does it give rise to an immunity available to one member in a claim brought by another, so, if according to ordinary principles there is vicarious liability for the tort of an employee of the association, or if someone has been ordered to commit an act constituting a tort, or if there is a breach of the duties of an employer to an employee, or breach of any other duty of care, a cause of action would be established[4].

1 However, cf eg trade unions (see PARA 427; and EMPLOYMENT vol 41 (2014) PARA 897) and friendly societies (see FINANCIAL SERVICES AND INSTITUTIONS vol 50 (2008) PARA 2290 et seq).
2 See CPR 19.6; and CIVIL PROCEDURE vol 11 (2009) PARA 229; CLUBS vol 13 (2009) PARA 279. See also *Mercantile Marine Service Association v Toms* [1916] 2 KB 243, CA (libel claimants lacking common interest); *Campbell v Thompson* [1953] 1 QB 445, [1953] 1 All ER 831 (common interest of defendants in personal injury case); *Winder v Ward* (1957) Times, 26 February, CA (members of hunt lacking common interest in trespass). Cf *Prudential Assurance Co v Newman Industries Ltd* [1981] Ch 229, [1979] 3 All ER 507 (representative action brought by minority shareholder in company). Damages can be awarded in respect of property in which the members have a common interest: *EMI Records Ltd v Riley* [1981] 2 All ER 838, [1981] 1 WLR 923.
3 *Robertson v Ridley* [1989] 2 All ER 474, [1989] 1 WLR 872, CA. As to the duty of care see NEGLIGENCE vol 78 (2010) PARA 2 et seq.
4 *Prole v Allen* [1950] 1 All ER 476; *Owen v Northampton Borough Council* (1992) 156 LGR 23, CA; *Grice v Stourport Tennis, Hockey and Squash Club* [1997] CLY 3859, CA. See also CLUBS vol 13 (2009) PARA 231. As to vicarious liability for the tort of an employee see PARA 767 et seq.

429. Employer and employee. Where an employer expressly authorises his employee to do a particular act which is in itself a tort, or which necessarily results in a tort, the employer is liable to a claim in tort at the suit of the person injured[1]. His liability is equally clear where he ratifies a tort committed by his employee without his authority[2]. An employer is also liable whenever his employee commits a tort in the course of his employment[3]. An employee who commits a tort is liable in damages to the person injured, and his liability is not affected by the existence of a contract of employment, or, where he commits a tort in the course of his employment, by the existence of the corresponding liability of his employer for the same tort[4].

An employer has no right to recover damages against the wrongdoer in respect of the loss of services which he sustains when his employee is injured[5].

1 See PARA 778. As to employers' vicarious liability see PARA 767 et seq. As to liability of employers generally see PARA 759 et seq.
2 See PARA 779.
3 See PARA 780 et seq.
4 See PARA 770.
5 See PARA 804. No person is liable in tort under the law of England and Wales on the ground only of having deprived another of the services of his menial servant: Administration of Justice Act 1982 s 2(c)(i).

430. Independent contractors. If the person employed to do particular work is not an employee[1] but is an independent contractor the employer is not as a rule liable for any tort committed by him in the course of his employment, and any person injured thereby must look to the independent contractor for compensation[2].

1 As to the liability of employers for torts committed by employees see PARA 767 et seq.
2 See PARA 777. For the exceptional circumstances where an employer of an independent contractor is liable for the torts of the independent contractor see PARAS 777, 799.

431. Principal and agent. Where a principal gives his agent express authority to do a particular act which is tortious or which necessarily results in a tort the principal is liable to third persons for any damage caused thereby[1]. Where the principal has not expressly authorised the tort, he may be liable for a tort committed by his agent while acting within the scope of his implied authority[2]. Where the tort by the agent falls entirely outside the scope of his authority the principal is not liable[3].

1 See AGENCY vol 1 (2008) PARA 150. See also PARA 778.
2 See AGENCY vol 1 (2008) PARA 151. See also PARA 779.
3 See AGENCY vol 1 (2008) PARA 151. See also PARAS 780–785.

432. Partnerships. A partnership and each of its partners are jointly and severally liable to any person not himself a partner for torts committed by any partner either while acting in the ordinary course of the business of the firm, or with the authority of his co-partners[1].

1 See the Partnership Act 1890 ss 10, 12; and PARTNERSHIP vol 79 (2014) PARA 69. See also *Hamlyn v John Houston & Co* [1903] 1 KB 81, CA; *Mercantile Credit Co Ltd v Garrod* [1962] 3 All ER 1103; *Flynn v Robin Thompson & Partners* [2000] All ER (D) 329, CA; *Dubai Aluminium Co Ltd v Salaam (Livingstone, third parties)* [2002] UKHL 48, [2003] 2 AC 366, [2003] 1 All ER 97; *JJ Coughlan Ltd v Ruparelia* [2003] EWCA Civ 1057, [2003] 37 LS Gaz R 34, [2004] PNLR 4. Each partner may also have a personal liability in tort which is distinct from this liability: *Meekins v Henson* [1964] 1 QB 472, [1962] 1 All ER 899.

433. Husband and wife; civil partners. The liability in tort of a married woman to persons other than her husband is the same as that of other persons[1]. A husband is liable for the torts of his wife only where the liability arises according to those principles of the law of torts which make one person answerable in tort for the acts of another[2]. In the law of England and Wales, marriage has the same effect in relation to same sex couples as it has in relation to opposite sex couples[3].

Each of the parties to a marriage has the like right of action in tort against the other as if they were not married[4]. Where such an action is brought during the subsistence of the marriage the court may stay the proceedings if it appears either that no substantial benefit will accrue to either party from the continuation of the proceedings[5] or that the question or questions in issue could be more conveniently disposed of under provisions of the Married Women's Property Act 1882 relating to the determination of questions between husband and wife as to the title to or possession of property[6].

Each of the parties to a civil partnership also has ordinary rights of action in tort against the other[7]. If an action in tort is brought by one civil partner against the other during the subsistence of the civil partnership, the court may stay the proceedings if it appears either that no substantial benefit would accrue to either civil partner from the continuation of the proceedings[8], or that the question or questions in issue could more conveniently be disposed of on a property dispute application under the Civil Partnership Act 2004[9].

1 See the Law Reform (Married Women and Tortfeasors) Act 1935 s 1; and MATRIMONIAL AND CIVIL PARTNERSHIP LAW vol 72 (2015) PARA 252. In existing England and Wales legislation a reference to marriage is to be read as including a reference to marriage of a same sex couple: Marriage (Same Sex Couples) Act 2013 Sch 3 para 1(1)(a). A reference to a married couple is to be read as including a reference to a married same sex couple (Sch 3 para 1(1)(b)) and a reference to a person who is married is to be read as including a reference to a person who is married to a person of the same sex (Sch 3 para 1(1)(c)). See MATRIMONIAL AND CIVIL PARTNERSHIP LAW vol 72 (2015) PARA 2.
2 See the Law Reform (Married Women and Tortfeasors) Act 1935 s 3; and MATRIMONIAL AND CIVIL PARTNERSHIP LAW vol 72 (2015) PARA 252.
3 See the Marriage (Same Sex Couples) Act 2013 s 11(1); and MATRIMONIAL AND CIVIL PARTNERSHIP LAW vol 72 (2015) PARA 2.

4 See the Law Reform (Husband and Wife) Act 1962 s 1(1); and MATRIMONIAL AND CIVIL PARTNERSHIP LAW vol 72 (2015) PARA 258.
5 See the Law Reform (Husband and Wife) Act 1962 s 1(2)(a); and MATRIMONIAL AND CIVIL PARTNERSHIP LAW vol 72 (2015) PARA 258.
6 See the Law Reform (Husband and Wife) Act 1962 s 1(2)(b); and MATRIMONIAL AND CIVIL PARTNERSHIP LAW vol 72 (2015) PARA 258. The provisions referred to in the text are those of the Married Women's Property Act 1882 s 17: see MATRIMONIAL AND CIVIL PARTNERSHIP LAW vol 72 (2015) PARA 269.
7 See MATRIMONIAL AND CIVIL PARTNERSHIP LAW vol 72 (2015) PARA 258.
8 Civil Partnership Act 2004 s 69(1), (2)(a): see MATRIMONIAL AND CIVIL PARTNERSHIP LAW vol 72 (2015) PARA 258.
9 Civil Partnership Act 2004 s 69(2)(b). As to property disputes (ie disputes relating to the determination of title to or possession of property) under s 66 see MATRIMONIAL AND CIVIL PARTNERSHIP LAW vol 72 (2015) PARA 269. Without prejudice to s 69(2)(b), the court may in such an action exercise any power which could be exercised on an application under s 66, or give such directions as it thinks fit for the disposal under s 66 of any question arising in the proceedings: s 69(3).

434. Mentally disordered persons. Mentally disordered persons are liable to the same extent as persons generally, provided that they have that state of mind which is required for liability in the particular tort[1]. A defendant will not be excused merely because he would be entitled in criminal proceedings arising out of the same facts to a defence of insanity[2]. However, if the defendant's conduct is, because of his mental disorder, involuntary and purely automatic, he is not liable in tort[3].

A person who, by reason of mental disorder[4] or otherwise, lacks capacity to conduct proceedings, must have a litigation friend to conduct proceedings on his behalf[5].

No one can be liable for a person's compulsory admission to hospital or any other act purporting to be done in pursuance of the Mental Health Act 1983 unless the act was done in bad faith or without reasonable care[6]. No civil proceedings may be brought in respect of any such act without the leave of the High Court[7].

1 *Morriss v Marsden* [1952] 1 All ER 925.
2 *Morriss v Marsden* [1952] 1 All ER 925 (assault and battery; defendant knowing the nature and quality of his acts but unaware that was he was doing was wrong).
3 *Morriss v Marsden* [1952] 1 All ER 925 at 927. In an action in negligence the standard of care may be varied to reflect the defendant's mental disability even if his conduct is not fully involuntary: *Mansfield v Weetabix Ltd* [1998] 1 WLR 1263, [1998] RTR 390, CA (overruling *Roberts v Ramsbottom* [1980] 1 All ER 7, [1980] 1 WLR 823 on this point).
4 'Mental disorder' means any disorder or disability of the mind; and 'mentally disordered' is to be construed accordingly: see the Mental Health Act 1983 s 1(2) (amended by the Mental Health Act 2007 s 1(1), (2)); and MENTAL HEALTH AND CAPACITY vol 75 (2013) PARA 761.
5 See CPR Pt 21; and CIVIL PROCEDURE vol 11 (2009) PARA 222. Lack of capacity is assessed under the Mental Capacity Act 2005: see MENTAL HEALTH AND CAPACITY.
6 See the Mental Health Act 1983 s 139(1); and MENTAL HEALTH AND CAPACITY vol 75 (2013) PARA 759.
7 See the Mental Health Act 1983 s 139(2); and MENTAL HEALTH AND CAPACITY vol 75 (2013) PARA 759.

435. General liability of children for tort. Minority as such is not a defence in the law of tort. If a child is of tender years it is a question of fact whether he had the capacity or particular state of mind required for the tort for which it is sought to make him liable[1]. A child of an age at which he is capable of distinguishing between right and wrong is liable for the consequences of his own wrongful conduct[2] unless the action is directly founded upon a contract on which he cannot be sued[3].

Accordingly, a child can be sued for the return of money which he has stolen or obtained by fraud[4], for trespass[5], for damage done by a dangerous animal kept by him[6], for wrongful retention of the claimant's goods[7], for defamation[8], for fraudulently passing off spurious goods as being of the claimant's manufacture[9], for representing his business as being connected with the claimant's business[10], or for negligence[11].

A child is in the same position as any other claimant suing in tort, except that he must sue by his litigation friend[12].

1 See CHILDREN AND YOUNG PERSONS vol 9 (2012) PARA 26; Bac Abr, *Infancy and Age (A), (H)*. In Canada it has been held that a child aged five years is too young to be found guilty of negligence: *Walmsley v Humenick* [1954] 2 DLR 232.
2 *Watts v Creswell* (1714) 9 Vin Abr 415. See also CHILDREN AND YOUNG PERSONS vol 9 (2012) PARAS 23, 26.
3 See PARA 436.
4 *Bristow v Eastman* (1794) 1 Esp 172; *Re Seager, Seeley v Briggs* (1889) 60 LT 665; *Cowern v Nield* [1912] 2 KB 419 at 423–424, DC.
5 Bac Abr, *Infancy and Age (H)*; *Burnard v Haggis* (1863) 14 CB NS 45 (trespass to goods). Cf *Gorely v Codd* [1966] 3 All ER 891, [1967] 1 WLR 19; *Wilson v Pringle* [1987] QB 237, [1986] 2 All ER 440 (both trespass to the person).
6 Cf *North v Wood* [1914] 1 KB 629 (action against father rejected because daughter was old enough to have sole responsibility for the animal).
7 *Mills v Graham* (1804) 1 Bos & PNR 140; *Ballet v Mingay* [1943] KB 281, [1943] 1 All ER 143, CA (both detinue). See BAILMENT AND PLEDGE vol 4 (2011) PARA 185. Actions in detinue have been abolished, and defaulting bailees may now be sued in conversion: see the Torts (Interference with Goods) Act 1977 s 2; and PARAS 602, 612.
8 *Hodsman v Grissel* (1608) Noy 129. As to defamation see DEFAMATION vol 32 (2012) PARA 501 et seq.
9 *Chubbs v Griffiths* (1865) 35 Beav 127.
10 *Woolf v Woolf* [1899] 1 Ch 343.
11 *Gorely v Codd* [1966] 3 All ER 891, [1967] 1 WLR 19. Cf *Donaldson v McNiven* [1952] 2 All ER 691 (action against the father). On the standard of care owed by a minor see *Mullin v Richards* [1998] 1 All ER 920, [1998] 1 WLR 1305, CA.
12 See CPR Pt 21; and CIVIL PROCEDURE vol 11 (2009) PARA 222.

436. Liability of children for tort founded on contract. A child is not liable for a tort which is founded on a contract on which he cannot be sued[1], as in the case of the warranty of goods[2], or for a fraudulent misrepresentation as to his age which induces a party to contract with him[3]. However, even where there is such a contract, the claim in tort may proceed provided it can be framed without reliance on the contract as the basis of the claim[4].

1 *Jennings v Rundall* (1799) 8 Term Rep 335; *Cowern v Nield* [1912] 2 KB 419, DC; *R Leslie Ltd v Sheill* [1914] 3 KB 607, CA. In considering the range of contracts on which children can be sued see the Minors' Contracts Act 1987; and CHILDREN AND YOUNG PERSONS vol 9 (2012) PARA 12 et seq; CONTRACT vol 22 (2012) PARA 613. As to torts founded on contract on which a child cannot be sued see CHILDREN AND YOUNG PERSONS vol 9 (2012) PARA 27. As to the general liability of children for their torts see PARA 435.
2 *Howlett v Haswell* (1814) 4 Camp 118 (horse).
3 *Cowern v Nield* [1912] 2 KB 419, DC; *R Leslie Ltd v Sheill* [1914] 3 KB 607, CA. The child may, however, be under an equitable obligation to restore money or property obtained by fraud, or its proceeds, and, under the Minors' Contracts Act 1987 s 3(1), the court at its discretion may order a person party to any contract that is unenforceable because of his minority to transfer to the other party any property he acquired under the contract, or any property representing it: see CHILDREN AND YOUNG PERSONS vol 9 (2012) PARAS 23–24. Since this statutory power is discretionary a claimant may elect to claim against the minor in restitution, which is available as of right and expressly saved by s 3(2).
4 *Bristow v Eastman* (1794) 1 Esp 172; *Burnard v Haggis* (1863) 14 CB NS 45; *Ballett v Mingay* [1943] KB 281, [1943] 1 All ER 143, CA.

437. Liability of parents and other persons. A parent is not liable without more for a tort committed by his child[1], but may be liable for his child's torts if vicarious liability can be established independently, if he has previously authorised or subsequently ratified the child's act[2], or if he has failed to exercise proper supervision of the child[3]. Thus where a child causes an injury to others the parent or any other person in charge of the child[4] may be liable if the parent or other person has control of a dangerous thing which causes the injury[5] or is negligent, either in permitting the child to use a thing which is dangerous in itself or known to be dangerous or capable of causing danger to others[6] or in not exercising proper control and supervision of the child[7].

Irrespective of any pre-existing relationship with the child, a person who leaves a source of danger which causes injury or damage through the child's reasonably foreseeable and preventable intervention is prima facie liable for the loss[8].

A parent may be liable in tort to and be sued by his child[9]. The parent's right of reasonable punishment acts as a defence against liability in battery unless actual bodily harm is caused[10]. There is no equivalent right for teachers in the child's school[11].

A parent owes a duty of care to his child whilst the child is under his responsibility, and may be liable for failing to guard against and prevent the child suffering injury[12]. However, there is an area of parental discretion in which the courts should not intrude[13]. A duty of care to the child may also be assumed by others who take responsibility for him[14]. Liability may also arise on the part of strangers who negligently expose the child to a danger, even where there would be no danger to an adult[15].

Whether a child is guilty of contributory negligence is judged with reference to the child's age[16].

1 See CHILDREN AND YOUNG PERSONS vol 9 (2012) PARA 28.

2 *Moon v Towers* (1860) 8 CBNS 611.

3 See CHILDREN AND YOUNG PERSONS vol 9 (2012) PARA 28.

4 Eg a school: *Carmarthenshire County Council v Lewis* [1955] AC 549, [1955] 1 All ER 565, HL. As to the liability of school authorities and teachers in relation to injuries caused by children under their care see generally *Gow v Glasgow Education Authority* 1922 SC 260, Ct of Sess; *Langham v Wellingborough School* (1932) 101 LJKB 513; *Rawsthorne v Ottley* [1937] 3 All ER 902 (boys tipped up coke lorry delivering to school); *Ricketts v Erith Borough Council* [1943] 2 All ER 629; *Clark v Monmouthshire County Council* (1954) 118 JP 244, 52 LGR 246, CA (children playing with knife). In respect of objects fired or thrown at other children see *Jackson v LCC and Chappell* (1912) 28 TLR 359, CA; *Rich v LCC* [1953] 2 All ER 376, [1953] 1 WLR 895, CA. The standard of a reasonably careful parent may not aptly be applied to a master in respect of horseplay in a large school: see *Beaumont v Surrey County Council* (1968) 66 LGR 580, 112 Sol Jo 704. See also EDUCATION vol 36 (2011) PARAS 1009–1010.

5 *North v Wood* [1914] 1 KB 629 (dog known by father to be savage; daughter of sufficient age to exercise control over dog: father not responsible for damage done by dog). As to liability for injuries caused by animals in the possession of persons under 16 see now the Animals Act 1971 ss 2, 6(3); and ANIMALS vol 2 (2008) PARAS 747–748.

6 *Dixon v Bell* (1816) 5 M & S 198 (loaded gun); *Brown v Fulton* (1881) 9 R 36, Ct of Sess (horse); *Bebee v Sales* (1916) 32 TLR 413 (air gun); *Thomas v Bishop* [1976] CLY 1872 (guns). Ordinary toys are not a danger for which special precautions have to be taken: see *Chilvers v LCC* (1916) 32 TLR 363; *Wray v Essex County Council* [1936] 3 All ER 97, CA (oilcan spout injured boy).

7 *Williams v Eady* (1893) 10 TLR 41, CA (phosphorus available to youths); but see *Crouch v Essex County Council* (1966) 64 LGR 240 (warning may discharge the duty). Cf *Gorley v Codd* [1966] 3 All ER 891, [1967] 1 WLR 19; *Donaldson v McNiven* [1952] 2 All ER 691, CA (no failure of supervision), distinguished in *Newton v Edgerley* [1959] 3 All ER 337, [1959] 1 WLR 1031.

8   *Martin v Stanborough* (1924) 41 TLR 1, CA (removing chocks for wheel of car on hill); *Haynes v Harwood* [1935] 1 KB 146, CA (unattended horse bolted, perhaps after stone was thrown); *Shiffman v Grand Priory in the British Realm of the Venerable Order of the Hospital of St John of Jerusalem* [1936] 1 All ER 557, sub nom *Shiftman v Order of the Hospital of St John* 80 Sol Jo 346 (releasing guy ropes of flagpole); *Wells v Metropolitan Water Board* [1937] 4 All ER 639, 54 TLR 104 (tampering with valve box). Cf *Prince v Gregory* [1959] 1 All ER 133, [1959] 1 WLR 177, CA (lime mortar left in street; no liability).

9   *Roberts v Roberts* (1657) Hard 96 (injunction against felling timber); *Ash v Lady Ash* (1696) Comb 357 (trespass to the person); *Young v Rankin* 1934 SC 499, Ct of Sess (car accident). As to limitation see LIMITATION PERIODS vol 68 (2008) PARA 952 et seq.

10 See the Children Act 2004 s 58(3), (4); and CHILDREN AND YOUNG PERSONS vol 9 (2012) PARA 635; CRIMINAL LAW vol 25 (2010) PARA 173. See also *Murray v Moutrie* (1834) 6 Car & P 471 at 473 per Tindal CJ.

11 See the Education Act 1996 s 548; PARA 538; and EDUCATION vol 35 (2011) PARA 627.

12 *S v Walsall Metropolitan Borough Council* [1985] 3 All ER 294, [1985] 1 WLR 1150, CA; *Barrett v Enfield London Borough Council* [2001] 2 AC 550, [1999] 3 All ER 193, HL (local authority undertaking child's upbringing; arguable duty of care). Cf *Eastham v Eastham* [1982] CLY 2141; *Surtees v Kingston-upon-Thames Borough Council* [1991] 2 FLR 559, CA (no parental liability on the facts).

13 *Barrett v Enfield London Borough Council* [1998] QB 367 at 377, [1997] 3 All ER 171 at 178, CA, per Lord Woolf MR (and on appeal [2001] 2 AC 550 at 587, [1999] 3 All ER 193 at 226, HL, per Lord Hutton). See also *Porter v Barking and Dagenham London Borough Council* (1990) Times, 9 April (care should not stifle independence).

14 For the liability of school authorities and teachers for injuries suffered in the course of organised activities see *Gibbs v Barking Corpn* [1936] 1 All ER 115, CA (vaulting in gym); *Fryer v Salford Corpn* [1937] 1 All ER 617 (cooker); *Gillmore v LCC* [1938] 4 All ER 331 (polished floor of gym); *Ralph v LCC* (1947) 63 TLR 546 (game of touch); *Wright v Cheshire County Council* [1952] 2 All ER 789, CA (vaulting in gym); *Butt v Inner London Education Authority* (1968) 66 LGR 379 (machinery); *Affutu-Nartey v Clark* (1984) Times, 9 February (master tackling boy in game of rugby); *Woodland v Essex County Council* [2013] UKSC 66, [2014] AC 537, [2014] 1 All ER 482. Cf *Smoldon v Whitworth and Nolan* [1997] PIQR P133, CA (rugby referee). A school need not insure pupils against injuries whilst playing sport: see *Van Oppen v Clerk to the Bedford Charity Trustees* [1989] 3 All ER 389, [1990] 1 WLR 235, CA.

For the liability of school authorities and teachers for injuries from the state of the premises see *Ching v Surrey County Council* [1910] 1 KB 736 (playground); *Morris v Caernarvon County Council* [1910] 1 KB 840, CA (door); *Woodward v Hastings Corpn* [1945] KB 174, [1944] 2 All ER 565, CA (uncleared snow); *Reffell v Surrey County Council* [1964] 1 All ER 743, [1964] 1 WLR 358 (glass door); *Ward v Hertfordshire County Council* [1970] 1 All ER 535, [1970] 1 WLR 356, CA (playground).

The school should ensure the reasonable safety of premises to which it takes pupils on school trips (*Brown v Nelson* (1971) 69 LGR 20: no liability on the facts) and of the transport it provides to and from the school (*Shrimpton v Hertfordshire County Council* (1911) 104 LT 145, HL). The extent of the school's duty of supervision, if any, while the pupils are off the premises depends on the facts: see *Camkin v Bishop* [1941] 2 All ER 713, CA. On the school's duty to prevent the bullying of its pupils see *Bradford-Smart v West Sussex County Council* [2002] EWCA Civ 7, [2002] LGR 489, [2002] 1 FCR 425 (no liability on the facts).

The duty of care may also be owed to a child by a hospital: see *Gravestock v Lewisham Group Hospital Management Committee* (1955) Times, 27 May (hospital).

15 See eg *Yachuk v Oliver Blais Co Ltd* [1949] AC 386, [1949] 2 All ER 150, PC (nine-year-old sold petrol; burn injuries).

16 *Gough v Thorne* [1966] 3 All ER 398, [1966] 1 WLR 1387, CA. Contributory negligence has been found against very young children: see eg *McKinnell v White* 1971 SLT 61 (5-year-old); *Donovan v Landy's Ltd* [1963] IR 441 (6-year-old); *Morales v Eccleston* [1991] RTR 151, CA (75% contributory negligence by 11-year-old). Cases where there has been held not to be contributory negligence by children include: *Gough v Thorne* [1966] 3 All ER 398, [1966] 1 WLR 1387, CA (13-year-old); *Lynch v Nurdin* (1841) 1 QB 29 (7-year-old); *Gardner v Grace* (1858) 1 F & F 359 (3-year-old); *Lay v Midland Rly Co* (1875) 34 LT 30 (4-year-old); *Harrold v Watney* [1898] 2 QB 320, CA (4-year-old). See also *Culkin v McFie & Sons Ltd* [1939] 3 All ER 613 (7-year-old); *Jones v Lawrence* [1969] 3 All ER 267 (7-year-old). See also *Minter v D & H Contractors (Cambridge) Ltd* (1983) Times, 30 June.

438. Liability of those with a statutory duty relating to the care and welfare of children. There is a substantial body of statute law making provision for the care and welfare of children[1], and imposing duties on local authorities and others in respect of these objectives, but these duties do not generally give rise to private rights entitling an aggrieved child to sue in the tort of breach of statutory duty[2]. There may, however, be a common law duty of care, and hence a potential liability in negligence, where a child is taken into protective care[3], though the duty is owed only to the child, and (arguably) other children at risk from the child whilst in care[4], and not to the parents from whom the child is taken, because of the potential conflict of interests[5]. Whether a duty of care is owed to vulnerable children who are not in protective care is currently uncertain[6]. In other contexts in which statutory provision is made for the care and welfare of children, there may be an assumption of a duty of care towards a child, by or on behalf of the authority subject to the statutory duty, in accordance with general principles of the law of negligence[7]. Liability in the circumstances considered in this paragraph may also arise in an appropriate case under the Human Rights Act 1998[8].

1   See eg the Children and Young Persons Act 2008; and CHILDREN AND YOUNG PERSONS.

2   *X (minors) v Bedfordshire County Council* [1995] 2 AC 633, [1995] 3 All ER 353, HL. Whether such rights arise, however, is a question of statutory construction and each case therefore turns on the provisions of the relevant statute: *X v Bedfordshire County Council* [1995] 2 AC 633 at 731, [1995] 3 All ER 353 at 364, HL, per Lord Browne-Wilkinson.

3   *Barrett v Enfield London Borough Council* [2001] 2 AC 550, [1999] 3 All ER 193, HL; *D v East Berkshire Community NHS Trust* [2003] EWCA Civ 1151, [2004] QB 558, [2003] 4 All ER 796, CA; upheld without deciding this point in *D v East Berkshire Community NHS Trust* [2005] UKHL 23, [2005] 2 AC 373, [2005] 2 All ER 443.

4   *W v Essex County Council* [2001] 2 AC 592, [2000] 2 All ER 237, HL.

5   *D v East Berkshire Community NHS Trust* [2005] UKHL 23, [2005] 2 AC 373, [2005] 2 All ER 443.

6   See *X (minors) v Bedfordshire County Council* [1995] 2 AC 633, [1995] 3 All ER 353, HL, where it was held there was no duty of care, but the policy considerations which led to that conclusion were said in *D v East Berkshire Community NHS Trust* [2003] EWCA Civ 1151, [2004] QB 558, [2003] 4 All ER 796, to have shifted, warranting a finding that there was a duty of care to a child taken into care. It is not clear where this leaves the case (also considered in *X (minors) v Bedfordshire County Council* [1995] 2 AC 633, [1995] 3 All ER 353, HL) of the child not taken into care.

7   *Phelps v Hillingdon London Borough Council* [2001] 2 AC 619, [2000] 4 All ER 504, HL (assumption of responsibility to child with special educational needs).

8   See PARA 810.

439. Persons liable to a child born disabled. A child who is born alive[1] but disabled[2] has in certain circumstances a cause of action for damages in respect of his disabilities as if they were personal injuries suffered by him immediately after birth[3]. The right of action may arise if the child is born disabled as a result of an occurrence which affected either parent of the child in his or her ability to have a normal, healthy child[4], or which affected the mother during her pregnancy, or affected her or the child in the course of its birth, so that the child is born with disabilities which would not otherwise have been present[5]. No damages are recoverable in an action brought by a child alleging negligence on the part of doctors in failing to advise his or her parents that it would be advisable to terminate the pregnancy by reason of the fact that the child would be born with disabilities[6]. A person is not answerable to the child unless he was liable in tort to the parent or would, if sued in due time, have been so; and it is no answer that there could not have been such liability because the parent suffered no actionable injury, if there was a breach of legal duty which, accompanied by injury, would have given rise to the liability[7].

The mother of the child is liable if, and only if, she fails to take care for the safety of her unborn child while driving a motor vehicle[8] when she knows (or ought reasonably to know) herself to be pregnant, in which event she is to be regarded as being under the same duty to take care for the safety of the unborn child as the law imposes on her with respect to the safety of other people, and in consequence of her breach of that duty of care her child is born with disabilities[9].

A person is not liable for anything he did or omitted to do when responsible in a professional capacity for treating or advising the parent, if he took reasonable care having due regard to then received professional opinion applicable to the particular class of case; but this does not mean that he is answerable only because he departed from received opinion[10].

If in the child's action it is shown that the parent affected shared the responsibility for the child being born disabled, the damages are to be reduced to such an extent as the court thinks just and equitable having regard to the extent of the parent's responsibility[11]. In the case of an occurrence preceding the time of conception, the defendant is not answerable to the child if at that time either or both of the parents knew the risk of their child being born disabled (that is to say, the particular risk created by the occurrence); but should it be the child's father who is the defendant, this defence does not apply if he knew of the risk and the mother did not[12]. Any contract made with the parent affected which would exclude or restrict liability to the parent is equally effective in respect of liability to the child[13].

In any case where:

(1)　a child carried by a woman as the result of the placing in her of an embryo or of sperm and eggs or her artificial insemination is born disabled[14];

(2)　the disability results from an act or omission in the course of the selection, or the keeping or use outside the body, of the embryo carried by her or of the gametes used to bring about the creation of the embryo[15]; and

(3)　a person is answerable to the child in respect of the act or omission[16],

the child's disabilities are to be regarded as damage resulting from the wrongful act of that person and actionable accordingly at the suit of the child[17]. Subject to certain qualifications[18], a person is answerable to the child if he was liable in tort to one or both of the parents or would, if sued in due time, have been so[19]. It is no answer that there could not have been such liability because the parent or parents concerned suffered no actionable injury, if there was a breach of legal duty which, accompanied by injury, would have given rise to the liability[20]. A person is not answerable to the child if, at the time the embryo, or the sperm and eggs, are placed in the woman or the time of her insemination, either or both of the parents knew the risk of their child being born disabled (that is, the particular risk created by the act or omission)[21].

Where, for the purpose of instituting proceedings in relation to a child born disabled as a result of an actionable occurrence before its birth[22], it is necessary to identify a person who would or might be the parent of a child but for the statutory provisions for determining the parentage of children born as a result of artificial insemination or assisted reproduction[23], the court may, on the application of the child, make an order requiring the Human Fertilisation and Embryology Authority to disclose any information contained in the register kept by it identifying that person[24].

1 'Born' means born alive (the moment of a child's birth being when it first has a life separate from its mother) and 'birth' has a corresponding meaning: Congenital Disabilities (Civil Liability) Act 1976 s 4(2)(a).

2 For these purposes, references to a child being born disabled or with disabilities are to its being born with any deformity, disease or abnormality, including predisposition (whether or not susceptible of immediate prognosis) to physical or mental defect in the future: Congenital Disabilities (Civil Liability) Act 1976 s 4(1).

3 Congenital Disabilities (Civil Liability) Act 1976 ss 1(1), 4(3) (s 4(3) amended by the Human Fertilisation and Embryology Act 1990 s 44(2)(b)). The provisions of the Nuclear Installations Act 1965 as to liability for, and compensation in respect of, injury or damage caused by occurrences involving nuclear matter or the emission of ionising radiations (see ENERGY AND CLIMATE CHANGE vol 44 (2011) PARA 892 et seq) extend also to pre-natal injury: see the Congenital Disabilities (Civil Liability) Act 1976 ss 3, 4(6).

   The Congenital Disabilities (Civil Liability) Act 1976 applies in respect of all births after 22 July 1976 (ie the date of its passing): see s 4(5). It replaced in respect of any such birth any law in force before that date by which a person could be liable to a child in respect of disabilities with which it might be born: see s 4(5). See further *Burton v Islington Health Authority* [1993] QB 204, [1992] 3 All ER 833, CA, recognising a common law cause of action for congenital disabilities in respect of births before the passing of the 1976 Act.

   The Act provides that no damages for loss of expectation of life are recoverable unless the child lives at least 48 hours: see the Congenital Disabilities (Civil Liability) Act 1976 s 4(4) (amended by the Human Fertilisation and Embryology Act 1990 s 44(2)). However, the right to damages for loss of expectation of life has been abolished in relation to an injured person who died on or after 1 January 1983: see the Administration of Justice Act 1982 ss 1(1)(a), 73(3), (4), 76 (11). As to the survival of the right in relation to causes of action arising before that date see s 73(1).

4 Congenital Disabilities (Civil Liability) Act 1976 s 1(2)(a). In the case of an occurrence preceding the time of conception, there may be no liability if either or both of the parents knew the risk of their child being born disabled: see the text and note 12. In any case where a child carried by a woman as the result of the placing in her of an embryo or of sperm and eggs or her artificial insemination is born disabled, any reference in s 1 to a parent includes a reference to a person who would be a parent but for the Human Fertilisation and Embryology Act 1990 ss 27–29 or the Human Fertilisation and Embryology Act 2008 ss 33–47 (see CHILDREN AND YOUNG PERSONS vol 9 (2012) PARA 114 et seq): see the Congenital Disabilities (Civil Liability) Act 1976 s 4(4A) (added by the Human Fertilisation and Embryology Act 1990 s 35(4); and amended by the Human Fertilisation and Embryology Act 2008 s 56, Sch 6 Pt 1 para 15).

5 Congenital Disabilities (Civil Liability) Act 1976 s 1(2)(b).

6 *McKay v Essex Area Health Authority* [1982] QB 1166, [1982] 2 All ER 771, CA.

7 Congenital Disabilities (Civil Liability) Act 1976 s 1(3).

8 'Motor vehicle' means a mechanically propelled vehicle intended or adapted for use on roads: Congenital Disabilities (Civil Liability) Act 1976 s 4(2)(b).

9 See the Congenital Disabilities (Civil Liability) Act 1976 ss 1(1), 2.

10 Congenital Disabilities (Civil Liability) Act 1976 s 1(5).

11 Congenital Disabilities (Civil Liability) Act 1976 s 1(7).

12 Congenital Disabilities (Civil Liability) Act 1976 s 1(4). The reference to the child's father here includes, in the case of a child who has a parent by virtue of the Human Fertilisation and Embryology Act 2008 s 42 or s 43 (dealing respectively with female civil partners and agreed female parenthood conditions), a reference to the woman who is a parent by virtue of that section: Congenital Disabilities (Civil Liability) Act 1976 s 1(4A) (added by the Human Fertilisation and Embryology Act 2008 Sch 6 Pt 1 para 14).

13 See the Congenital Disabilities (Civil Liability) Act 1976 s 1(6). The effect of s 1(6) is greatly limited by the Unfair Contract Terms Act 1977 s 2(1): see CONTRACT vol 22 (2012) PARA 407 et seq; NEGLIGENCE vol 78 (2010) PARA 74.

14 Congenital Disabilities (Civil Liability) Act 1976 s 1A(1)(a) (s 1A added by the Human Fertilisation and Embryology Act 1990 s 44). References to embryos are to be construed in accordance with the Human Fertilisation and Embryology Act 1990 s 1(1) and any regulations under s 1(6) (see CHILDREN AND YOUNG PERSONS vol 9 (2012) PARA 115; MEDICAL PROFESSIONS

vol 74 (2011) PARA 166): Congenital Disabilities (Civil Liability) Act 1976 s 4(2) (amended by the Human Fertilisation and Embryology Act 1990 s 44(2)(a); and the Human Fertilisation and Embryology Act 2008 s 65, Sch 7 para 1).

15 Congenital Disabilities (Civil Liability) Act 1976 s 1A(1)(b) (as added: see note 14).

16 Congenital Disabilities (Civil Liability) Act 1976 s 1A(1)(c) (as added: see note 14).

17 Congenital Disabilities (Civil Liability) Act 1976 s 1A(1) (as added: see note 14).

18 See the Congenital Disabilities (Civil Liability) Act 1976 ss 1(5)–(7), 1A(2)–(4) (as added: see note 14).

19 Congenital Disabilities (Civil Liability) Act 1976 s 1A(2) (as added: see note 14).

20 Congenital Disabilities (Civil Liability) Act 1976 s 1A(2) (as added: see note 14).

21 Congenital Disabilities (Civil Liability) Act 1976 s 1A(3) (as added: see note 14). Section 1(5)–(7) (see the text and notes 10–13) applies for the purposes of s 1A: see s 1A(4) (as so added).

22 Ie under the Congenital Disabilities (Civil Liability) Act 1976 s 1.

23 Ie the Human Fertilisation and Embryology Act 1990 ss 27–29 and the Human Fertilisation and Embryology Act 2008 ss 33–47 (see CHILDREN AND YOUNG PERSONS vol 9 (2012) PARA 114 et seq): see the Human Fertilisation and Embryology Act 1990 s 35(1), (2A) (s 35(1) amended and s 35(2A) added by the Human Fertilisation and Embryology Act 2008 Sch 6 Pt 1 para 35).

24 See the Human Fertilisation and Embryology Act 1990 s 35(1); and CHILDREN AND YOUNG PERSONS vol 9 (2012) PARA 114 et seq. The provisions of s 34(2)–(4) (see CHILDREN AND YOUNG PERSONS vol 9 (2012) PARA 114 et seq) apply for these purposes: see s 35(3).

440. Personal representatives. On the death of any person all causes of action (other than defamation[1]) subsisting against or vested in him survive against, or for the benefit of, the estate[2]. However, the right of a person to claim damages for bereavement does not survive for the benefit of his estate on death[3]. Where a cause of action survives for the benefit of the estate of a deceased person, the damages recoverable do not include any exemplary damages or any damages for loss of income in respect of any period after the person's death[4].

These claims are brought or defended by the personal representatives of the deceased[5]. The ordinary rules for the limitation of actions govern these proceedings[6].

1 No claim for defamation lies in respect of a dead person: see DEFAMATION vol 32 (2012) PARA 506.

2 See the Law Reform (Miscellaneous Provisions) Act 1934 s 1(1) (amended by the Law Reform (Miscellaneous Provisions) Act 1970 s 7(2), Schedule; and the Administration of Justice Act 1982 s 75(1), Sch 9 Pt I). See also WILLS AND INTESTACY vol 103 (2010) PARAS 1279–1280. As to the abatement of proceedings by or against the deceased in respect of defamation see DEFAMATION vol 32 (2012) PARA 725.

3 Law Reform (Miscellaneous Provisions) Act 1934 s 1(1A) (added by the Administration of Justice Act 1982 s 4(1)). As to claims for damages for bereavement see the Fatal Accidents Act 1976 s 1A; PARA 488; and NEGLIGENCE vol 78 (2010) PARA 25 et seq. See also DAMAGES vol 29 (2014) PARA 495.

4 Law Reform (Miscellaneous Provisions) Act 1934 s 1(2)(a) (substituted by the Administration of Justice Act 1982 s 4(2)).

5 See WILLS AND INTESTACY vol 103 (2010) PARA 1273 et seq.

6 See generally LIMITATION PERIODS.

441. Bankrupts. A liability in tort may be provable as a bankruptcy debt[1]. This applies to both corporate insolvency and individual bankruptcy. Torts committed after the bankruptcy are not bankruptcy debts and it appears that the bankrupt remains liable. If a bankrupt tortfeasor is covered by liability insurance, the rights of the bankrupt against the insurer are transferred to the injured person[2]. The bankrupt may protect after-acquired property against wrongdoers until the trustee intervenes[3]. Similar provision is made for insolvent companies[4] but they should be sued before dissolution or, if they have already been dissolved, restored to the register of companies in order to secure the benefits of rights against insurers[5].

Where the claimant has a right of action in tort against the estate of a deceased person, and that estate is insolvent, he may prove in the administration of the estate for unliquidated damages[6].

Where the cause of action arises from purely personal damage to the bankrupt then the right of action remains with the bankrupt[7]. Where two separate and distinct causes of action arise from the same conduct of the defendant, resulting both in substantial damage to the bankrupt's property and in injury to the bankrupt personally, the trustee is entitled to the right of action for damage to the property, and the bankrupt retains his right to sue for the personal injury[8].

1   See the Insolvency Act 1986 s 382; and BANKRUPTCY AND INDIVIDUAL INSOLVENCY vol 5 (2013) PARA 508. A bankruptcy debt includes any debt or liability (including any liability in tort) to which the bankrupt is subject at the commencement of the bankruptcy or to which he may later become subject (including after his discharge from bankruptcy) by reason of any obligation incurred before the commencement of the bankruptcy: see s 382(1), (4); and BANKRUPTCY AND INDIVIDUAL INSOLVENCY vol 5 (2013) PARA 508. As to 'liability' see *Firma C-Trade SA v Newcastle Protection and Indemnity Association* [1991] 2 AC 1, [1990] 2 All ER 705, HL. In determining whether any liability in tort is a bankruptcy debt, the bankrupt is deemed to become subject to that liability by reason of an obligation incurred at the time when the cause of action accrued: see the Insolvency Act 1986 s 382(2); and BANKRUPTCY AND INDIVIDUAL INSOLVENCY vol 5 (2013) PARA 508.
2   See the Third Parties (Rights Against Insurers) Act 1930 s 1; and INSURANCE vol 60 (2011) PARA 651 et seq. As from a day to be appointed, the Third Parties (Rights Against Insurers) Act 1930 s 1 is repealed by the Third Parties (Rights Against Insurers) Act 2010 s 20(3), Sch 4 (not yet in force). At the date at which this volume states the law no such day had been appointed.
3   *Re Pascoe* [1944] Ch 219, [1944] 1 All ER 281, CA.
4   See the Insolvency Rules 1986, SI 1986/1925; and COMPANY AND PARTNERSHIP INSOLVENCY.
5   See *Bradley v Eagle Star Insurance Co Ltd* [1989] AC 957, [1989] 1 All ER 961, HL; and the Companies Act 2006 s 1029 et seq. A company may be restored to the register of companies at any time for the purpose of bringing proceedings against it for damages for personal injury (including damages on death) but in any other case an application to the court for restoration of a company to the register may not be made after the end of the period of six years from the date of the dissolution of the company, unless an application for administrative restoration to the register has been made in time: see the Companies Act 2006 s 1030(1), (4)–(6).
6   See the Law Reform (Miscellaneous Provisions) Act 1934 s 1(6). As to the administration of estates see WILLS AND INTESTACY vol 103 (2010) PARA 676 et seq. As to unliquidated damages see DAMAGES vol 29 (2014) PARA 311.
7   See BANKRUPTCY AND INDIVIDUAL INSOLVENCY vol 5 (2013) PARAS 448, 451.
8   See BANKRUPTCY AND INDIVIDUAL INSOLVENCY vol 5 (2013) PARA 449, which also considers the position where only one cause of action arises but there is damage both to property and to the person.

442.   Assignees. A right to sue in tort is not in general assignable[1]. A claimant may transfer to another the damages to be recovered in his claim in tort, as distinct from the cause of action itself[2]. Those rights of action in tort which pass to a trustee in bankruptcy[3] are assignable by the trustee to a third person, or even to the bankrupt[4]. Where a claimant's insurers have paid a claim made by him in respect of circumstances which afford him a cause of action in tort against another they are subrogated to the claimant's rights in respect of that tort[5].

1   *Defries v Milne* [1913] 1 Ch 98, CA.
2   *Glegg v Bromley* [1912] 3 KB 474, CA. An assignment of property may be valid even though the property cannot be recovered without litigation: *Dawson v Great Northern and City Rly Co* [1905] 1 KB 260, CA. Cf *Trendtex Trading Corpn v Crédit Suisse* [1982] AC 679, [1981]

3 All ER 520, HL (breach of contract), accepting that an assignee could support the assignment of a claim by showing a genuine commercial interest in its enforcement even in the absence of a property right.

3 See PARA 441; and see *Stein v Blake* [1996] AC 243, [1995] 2 All ER 961, HL (when one party to mutual claims became bankrupt, only the balance could be claimed).

4 *Ramsey v Hartley* [1977] 2 All ER 673, [1977] 1 WLR 686, CA (where an action based on a negligent statement was validly assigned to the bankrupt, even though it was a term of the assignment that the bankrupt could retain only 65% of the net proceeds of the action); *Weddell v JA Pearce & Major* [1988] Ch 26, [1987] 3 All ER 624.

5 *King v Victoria Insurance Co Ltd* [1896] AC 250, PC; *Compania Columbiana de Seguros v Pacific Steam Navigation Co* [1965] 1 QB 101, [1964] 1 All ER 216. See also CHOSES IN ACTION vol 13 (2009) PARA 99.

443. Trespassers. The fact that the claimant is a trespasser is not a bar to a claim that would otherwise arise[1]. However, by virtue of the occupiers' liability legislation, an occupier owes a restricted duty of care in respect of personal injuries to trespassers[2]. The occupier must be aware of the danger or have reasonable grounds to believe it exists[3], know or have reasonable grounds to believe the trespasser is in the vicinity of the danger concerned or that he may come into the vicinity of the danger[4]; and the risk must be one against which, in all the circumstances of the case, the occupier might reasonably be expected to offer some protection[5]. The duty is to take such care as is reasonable in all the circumstances of the case to see that the trespasser does not suffer injury on the premises by reason of the danger concerned[6]. A warning may suffice[7]. Acceptance of the risk will exclude liability[8] but the statute does not refer to the exclusion of liability by notice or agreement[9]. It appears that a non-occupying independent contractor would owe at least a duty of common humanity to a trespasser[10], and such a duty might also be owed to other living creatures[11].

1 *British Railways Board v Herrington* [1972] AC 877, [1972] 1 All ER 749, HL; *Revill v Newbery* [1996] QB 567, [1996] 1 All ER 291, CA.

2 See the Occupiers' Liability Act 1984 s 1(3), (4); and NEGLIGENCE vol 78 (2010) PARA 40. The Act, in addition to applying to trespassers, also applies to those using private rights of way and entering under access agreements or orders under the National Parks and Access to the Countryside Act 1949 s 60 (see OPEN SPACES AND COUNTRYSIDE vol 78 (2010) PARA 583 et seq). However, when the right conferred by the Countryside and Rights of Way Act 2000 s 2(1) is exercisable in relation to land which is access land for the purposes of Pt I (ss 1–46) (see OPEN SPACES AND COUNTRYSIDE) the owner of the land owes only a limited duty under the Occupiers' Liability Act 1984 s 1: see s 1(6A)–(6C); and NEGLIGENCE vol 78 (2010) PARA 40.

The Occupiers' Liability Act 1984 replaces the prior law in respect of personal injury: see s 1(1); and NEGLIGENCE vol 78 (2010) PARA 40. Recovery for loss or damage to property is excluded by s 1(8), and this is still covered by the duty of common humanity in *British Railways Board v Herrington* [1972] AC 877, [1972] 1 All ER 749, HL; considered in *Tutton v AD Walter Ltd* [1986] QB 61, [1985] 3 All ER 757 (bees harmed by farming sprays not used according to instructions). The Occupiers' Liability Act 1984 refers to dangers 'due to the state of the premises or to things done or omitted to be done on them' (see s 1(1)(a)), and does not apply to dangers created by the trespasser's own conduct: *Tomlinson Congleton Borough Council* [2003] UKHL 47, [2004] 1 AC 46, [2003] 3 All ER 1122. The Act is further restricted to liability as an occupier, and in *Revill v Newbery* [1996] QB 567, [1996] 1 All ER 291, CA, it was held not to apply to the negligent shooting of a burglar, this being covered by common law.

3 See the Occupiers' Liability Act 1984 s 1(3)(a); and NEGLIGENCE vol 78 (2010) PARA 40.

4 See the Occupiers' Liability Act 1984 s 1(3)(b); and NEGLIGENCE vol 78 (2010) PARA 40. The occupier will be liable if he deliberately avoids knowledge (see *Swain v Natui Ram Puri* [1996] PIQR P442, CA), but the fact that the occupier attempts to prevent entrance when he does not know that a short cut is being used does not mean that he had reason to believe within the Occupiers' Liability Act 1984 s 1(3)(b) that a trespasser would come into the vicinity of the danger (*White v St Albans City and District Council* (1990) Times, 12 March, CA). See further *Donoghue v Folkestone Properties Ltd* [2003] EWCA Civ 231, [2003] QB 1008, [2003] 3 All ER 1101.

5 See the Occupiers' Liability Act 1984 s 1(3)(c); and NEGLIGENCE vol 78 (2010) PARA 40. See further *Tomlinson Congleton Borough Council* [2003] UKHL 47, [2004] 1 AC 46, [2003] 3 All ER 1122.
6 See the Occupiers' Liability Act 1984 s 1(4); and NEGLIGENCE vol 78 (2010) PARA 40.
7 See the Occupiers' Liability Act 1984 s 1(5); and NEGLIGENCE vol 78 (2010) PARA 40. See also *Ratcliff v McConnell* [1999] 1 WLR 670, CA.
8 See the Occupiers' Liability Act 1984 s 1(6); and *Ratcliff v McConnell* [1999] 1 WLR 670, CA (dive into shallow pool).
9 If such exclusion is possible the Unfair Contract Terms Act 1977 will not apply to it since by s 1(1) that Act applies only to the Occupier's Liability Act 1957 and not the Occupier's Liability Act 1984. It might be that if the duty under the Act could be excluded, the duty of common humanity could not.
10 Before *British Railways Board v Herrington* [1972] AC 877, [1972] 1 All ER 749, HL, it had been held that the fact that a plaintiff had been a trespasser did not prevent a non-occupier owing a duty of reasonable care (see *Buckland v Guildford Gas Light and Coke Co* [1949] 1 KB 410, [1948] 2 All ER 1086), but some reservations were expressed in *British Railways Board v Herrington* [1972] AC 877 at 914, [1972] 1 All ER 749 at 772, HL, per Lord Wilberforce, at 929 and 785 per Lord Pearson, and at 942 and 797 per Lord Diplock, suggesting that occupiers and non-occupiers should be treated alike.
11 See *Tutton v AD Walter Ltd* [1986] QB 61, [1985] 3 All ER 757, cited in note 2.

444.   Convicted persons. Those convicted of crimes, whether or not they are in prison, have the same tortious rights and liabilities as others[1].

1 The provision that prohibited a convicted person from bringing any action during his imprisonment (see the Forfeiture Act 1870 s 8 (repealed)) was abolished by the Criminal Justice Act 1948 ss 70(1), 83(3), Sch 10 Pt I (repealed). As to the facilities afforded to a prisoner in connection with litigation see PRISONS AND PRISONERS vol 85 (2012) PARAS 582–583.

445.   Visiting forces. The Visiting Forces Act 1952 extends various exemptions, privileges and immunities to certain visiting forces, and empowers the Secretary of State for Defence to make arrangements by which claims in respect of acts or omissions of members of visiting forces will be satisfied by the payment by the Secretary of State out of funds provided by Parliament[1].

1 See the Visiting Forces Act 1952 ss 8(2), 9(1); and ARMED FORCES vol 3 (2011) PARAS 412, 419. The State Immunity Act 1978 Pt I (ss 1–17) does not apply to proceedings relating to anything done by or in relation to the armed forces of a state while present in the United Kingdom and, in particular, has effect subject to the Visiting Forces Act 1952: see the State Immunity Act 1978 s 16(2); *Littrel v United States of America (No 2)* [1994] 4 All ER 203, [1995] 1 WLR 82, CA (no action for personal injuries lay in respect of treatment at a US military hospital); and INTERNATIONAL RELATIONS LAW vol 61 (2010) PARA 259. See also PARA 420.

446.   Aliens. An alien[1] has rights and liabilities in tort, but an alien enemy[2], though he may be sued, cannot sue unless he is in the realm by licence of the Crown[3]. The rules relating to jurisdiction and choice of law in respect of torts committed abroad are dealt with elsewhere in this work[4].

1 See BRITISH NATIONALITY vol 4 (2011) PARA 411.
2 See ARMED CONFLICT AND EMERGENCY vol 3 (2011) PARA 195.
3 *Porter v Freudenberg, Kreglinger v S Samuel and Rosenfeld, Re Merten's Patent* [1915] 1 KB 857, CA. See further CIVIL PROCEDURE vol 11 (2009) PARA 207.
4 See PARAS 489–490; and CONFLICT OF LAWS vol 19 (2011) PARA 647 et seq.

(5) JOINT AND SEVERAL TORTFEASORS

447.   Liability of joint tortfeasors. Each of two or more joint tortfeasors is liable for the entire damage resulting from the tort[1]. The following are joint tortfeasors:

(1)   employer and employee where the employer is vicariously liable for the tort of the employee[2];

(2)   partners where they are liable for torts committed by any one of them while acting in the partnership's ordinary course of the business, or with the authority of his co-partners[3];

(3)   principal and agent where the principal is liable for the tort of the agent[4];

(4)   employer and independent contractor where the employer is liable for the tort of his independent contractor[5];

(5)   a person who instigates another to commit a tort and the person who then commits the tort[6];

(6)   persons who take concerted action to a common end and in the course of executing that joint purpose commit a tort[7].

Torts of all kinds may be joint[8].

Joint liability in tort may arise in a number of ways. The defendants may act as principal tortfeasors together, or a defendant may incur joint liability by procuring the commission of a tort by inducement, incitement or persuasion[9]. A defendant may incur vicarious joint liability for a tort committed by an agent or employee or the defendant may have assisted the principal tortfeasor in the commission of tortious acts[10]. To establish accessory liability in tort, it is not enough to show that the defendant has done acts which facilitated the principal's commission of the tort[11]. The defendant will be jointly liable with the principal if they had combined to do or secure the doing of acts which constituted a tort[12]. This requires proof of three elements:

(a)   the defendant had to have acted in a way which furthered the commission of the tort by the principal;

(b)   the defendant had to have done so in pursuance of a common design with that person; and

(c)   the defendant had to have done or have secured the doing of the acts which had constituted a tort[13].

If these requirements are satisfied, the accessory is liable for the tortious act of the principal because, by reason of the assistance, the law treats him as a party to it[14]. This does not mean that the accessory had to have joined in doing the very act that had constituted the tort[15].

1   *Ferguson v Earl of Kinnoull* (1842) 9 Cl & Fin 251, HL; *Clark v Newsam* (1847) 1 Exch 131; *London Association for Protection of Trade v Greenlands Ltd* [1916] 2 AC 15 at 31, HL, per Lord Atkinson. As only one sum may be awarded in a single proceeding for a joint tort, any award of punitive damages should reflect only the lowest figure for which any of the joint tortfeasors can be held liable, if indeed an award of punitive damages is appropriate at all: *Cassell & Co Ltd v Broome* [1972] AC 1027 at 1063, [1972] 1 All ER 801 at 817, HL, per Lord Hailsham LC, at 1090 and 840 per Lord Reid, at 1096 and 845 per Lord Morris and at 1105 and 852–853 per Viscount Dilhorne. As to contribution between tortfeasors see PARA 450 et seq.

2   See PARA 767 et seq.

3   See PARA 432.

4   See AGENCY vol 1 (2008) PARAS 150–154.

5   See PARA 799.

6   *Monsanto plc v Tilly* [1999] NLJR 1833, [1999] All ER (D) 1321, [2000] Env LR 313, CA. Directors may be joint tortfeasors with a limited company where they directed or procured the tortious act or formed the company for the express purpose of doing a wrongful act: *Rainham Chemical Works Ltd v Belvedere Fish Guano Co Ltd* [1921] 2 AC 465 at 476, HL, per Lord Buckmaster.

    Acts which merely facilitate or assist with the commission of a tort are not sufficient to give rise to liability as a joint tortfeasor: see *CBS Songs Ltd v Amstrad Consumer Electronics plc* [1988] AC 1013, [1988] 2 All ER 484, HL.

7   *The Koursk* [1924] P 140, CA; *Brooke v Bool* [1928] 2 KB 578, DC; *Scarsbrook v Mason* [1961] 3 All ER 767 (cf *S v Walsall Metropolitan Borough Council* [1985] 3 All ER 294, [1985] 1 WLR 1150, CA); and *Credit Lyonnais Bank Nederland NV (now known as Generale Bank Nederland NV) v Export Credits Guarantee Department* [1998] 1 Lloyd's Rep 19, CA; affd [2000] 1 AC 486, [1999] 1 All ER 929, HL.

8   See e g *Fish & Fish Ltd v Sea Shepherd UK* [2013] EWCA Civ 544, [2013] 3 All ER 867, [2013] 1 WLR 3700. Once a common design had been established, the question was whether the defendant who was said to be a joint tortfeasor had done something that had furthered that common design. Since it was the requirement of a common design that provided protection against indeterminate and uncertain liability, providing that the act that furthered an undoubted common design was more than de minimis, there was no further hurdle that required it to have been an essential part of or of real significance to the commission of the tort: *Fish & Fish Ltd v Sea Shepherd UK* at [58].

     For the applicability of these principles to defamation see *Gardiner v Moore* [1969] 1 QB 55, [1966] 1 All ER 365 (libel); *Chamberlain v White* (1623) Cro Jac 647 (slander); cf *Thomas v Moore* [1918] 1 KB 555, CA. See also DEFAMATION vol 32 (2012) PARA 539.

9   *CBS Songs Ltd v Amstrad Consumer Electronics plc* [1988] AC 1013 at 1058, [1988] 2 All ER 484 at 496, HL, per Lord Templeman (cited in *Sea Shepherd UK v Fish & Fish Ltd* [2015] UKSC 10 at [19]).

10   *Sea Shepherd UK v Fish & Fish Ltd* [2015] UKSC 10 at [19]–[20], [2015] 2 WLR 694 at [19]–[20].

11   *Sea Shepherd UK v Fish & Fish Ltd* [2015] UKSC 10 at [21], [2015] 2 WLR 694 at [21].

12   *Sea Shepherd UK v Fish & Fish Ltd* [2015] UKSC 10 at [21], [2015] 2 WLR 694 at [21].

13   *Sea Shepherd UK v Fish & Fish Ltd* [2015] UKSC 10 at [21], [37], [55], [2015] 2 WLR 694 at [21], [37], [55].

14   *Sea Shepherd UK v Fish & Fish Ltd* [2015] UKSC 10 at [38], [2015] 2 WLR 694 at [38].

15   *Sea Shepherd UK v Fish & Fish Ltd* [2015] UKSC 10 at [38], [2015] 2 WLR 694 at [38].

448. Several tortfeasors. If each of several persons, not acting in concert, commits a tort against another person substantially contemporaneously and causing the same or indivisible damage, each several tortfeasor is liable for the whole damage[1]. If each of several persons commits an independent tort consecutively against the same person, each is liable for the damage caused by his tortious act, assuming the damage proximately caused by each tort to be distinct[2]. Thus, if the second tortfeasor's act caused no further damage or merely duplicated damage caused by the first tort, the second tortfeasor will not be liable[3]; but, if his act aggravated the damage caused by the first tort, each tortfeasor will be liable only in respect of the part of the damage which his tort caused, assuming that it is possible to separate and quantify the aggravation of damage[4]. Where liability is premised on the material contribution of several tortfeasors to the risk of harm, rather than to the harm itself, their liability is attributed according to their relative degree of contribution to the risk[5], but an exception is made in the case of mesothelioma resulting from exposure to asbestos, where joint and several liability is stipulated by statute[6].

1   *Devonshire (Owners) v Barge Leslie (Owners)* [1912] AC 634 at 657, HL; *Bank View Mill Ltd v Nelson Corpn and Fryer & Co (Nelson) Ltd* [1942] 2 All ER 477 at 483 per Stable J (revsd on other grounds [1943] 1 KB 337, [1943] 1 All ER 299, CA); *Dingle v Associated Newspapers Ltd* [1961] 2 QB 162 at 189–190, [1961] 1 All ER 897 at 916, CA, per Devlin LJ; *Rahman v Arearose Ltd* [2001] QB 351 at [17], (2000) 62 BMLR 84 at [17], CA, per Laws LJ. As to contribution between tortfeasors see PARA 450 et seq. See also DAMAGES vol 29 (2014) PARA 368.

2   See *Dingle v Associated Newspapers Ltd* [1961] 2 QB 162 at 188–189, [1961] 1 All ER 897 at 916, CA, per Devlin LJ; *Holtby v Brigham & Cowan (Hull) Ltd* [2000] 3 All ER 421, [2000] ICR 1086, CA; *Rahman v Arearose Ltd* [2001] QB 351, (2000) 62 BMLR 84, CA.

3   *Carslogie Steamship Co Ltd v Royal Norwegian Government* [1952] AC 292 at 303, [1952] 1 All ER 20 at 25, HL (explaining *The Haversham Grange* [1905] P 307, CA); *Performance Cars Ltd v Abraham* [1962] 1 QB 33, [1961] 3 All ER 413, CA; cf *Baker v Willoughby* [1970] AC 467, [1969] 3 All ER 1528, HL (effect of second tort on first tortfeasor's liability).

4 *Holtby v Brigham & Cowan (Hull) Ltd* [2000] 3 All ER 421, [2000] ICR 1086, CA; *Rahman v Arearose Ltd* [2001] QB 351, (2000) 62 BMLR 84, CA. In the absence of evidence to apportion damage between independent tortfeasors where the damage is not indivisible, the law will, it seems, apportion the damage equally: see *Bank View Mill Ltd v Nelson Corpn and Fryer & Co (Nelson) Ltd* [1942] 2 All ER 477 at 483 per Stable J (revsd on other grounds [1943] KB 337, [1943] 1 All ER 299, CA).

5 *Barker v Corus UK Ltd* [2006] UKHL 20, [2006] 2 AC 572, [2006] 3 All ER 785.

6 See the Compensation Act 2006 s 3; and HEALTH AND SAFETY AT WORK vol 53 (2014) PARAS 602, 640.

449. Effect of judgment against, or release of, joint tortfeasor. Judgment recovered against any person liable in respect of any debt or damage is not a bar to an action, or to the continuance of an action, against any other person who is (apart from any such bar) jointly liable with him in respect of the same debt or damage[1]. However, a satisfied judgment (except in the case of a foreign judgment[2]) is a bar to a claim against other tortfeasors, whether joint or several, who are liable for the same damage[3].

A release under seal[4] or a release by way of accord and satisfaction[5] (but not a mere covenant not to sue[6]) in respect of one joint tortfeasor discharges the others, unless the claimant expressly or impliedly reserves his rights against the other tortfeasors[7], but neither form of release has the same presumptive effect in the case of several tortfeasors[8]. However, acceptance of a settlement from one tortfeasor bars continuance of proceedings against another, whether the liability is joint or several, if the entire sum agreed upon is received and it was intended to be in full satisfaction of the claim[9]. In such a case, the compromise fixes the claim as if judgment had been given, and the claimant cannot subsequently contend that the settlement figure fell short of the claim's full value and thereby justify proceedings against another tortfeasor[10].

1 Civil Liability (Contribution) Act 1978 s 3. This provision re-enacts and extends the Law Reform (Married Women and Tortfeasors) Act 1935 s 6(1)(a) (repealed), which abolished the former common law rule that judgment against one joint tortfeasor barred proceedings against the others. For the effect of the claimant's accepting payment into court by one defendant on his right to sue others jointly liable see *Townsend v Stone Toms & Partners* [1981] 2 All ER 690, [1981] 1 WLR 1153, CA. See also CPR 36.12; and CIVIL PROCEDURE vol 11 (2009) PARA 738.

2 *Kohnke v Karger* [1951] 2 KB 670, [1951] 2 All ER 179. Damages recovered under the foreign judgment will be offset against any award in this country.

3 *United Australia Ltd v Barclays Bank Ltd* [1941] AC 1, [1940] 4 All ER 20, HL.

4 See DEEDS AND OTHER INSTRUMENTS vol 32 (2012) PARA 338.

5 See CONTRACT vol 22 (2012) PARA 605 et seq.

6 See e g *Hutton v Eyre* (1815) 6 Taunt 289; *Duck v Mayeu* [1892] 2 QB 511, CA; *Apley Estates Co Ltd v De Bernales* [1947] Ch 217, [1947] 1 All ER 213, CA; and DEEDS AND OTHER INSTRUMENTS vol 32 (2012) PARAS 338, 475.

7 *Watts v Aldington* (1993) [1999] L & TR 578, CA. It is an established principle in common law that if A claimed to be the victim of a tort committed by joint tortfeasors, and if A obtained either a judgment against one or more of them, or the benefit of a settlement by which he released one or more of them, then subject to certain exceptions, A thereby released the others. One such exception would be where the agreement for the release of one (or more) joint tortfeasors contained an express or implied reservation of the claimant's right to sue the others: see *Gladman Commercial Properties v Fisher Hargreaves Proctor* [2013] EWCA Civ 1466 at [21], [24], [2013] All ER (D) 187 (Nov) at [21], [24].

8 *Duck v Mayeu* [1892] 2 QB 511, CA; *Apley Estates Co Ltd v De Bernales* [1947] Ch 217, [1947] 1 All ER 213, CA; *Cutler v McPhail* [1962] 2 QB 292, [1962] 2 All ER 474; *Gardiner v Moore* [1969] 1 QB 55, [1966] 1 All ER 365.

9 *Clark v Urquhart* [1930] AC 28, HL; *Jameson v Central Electricity Generating Board (Babcock Energy Ltd, third party)* [2000] 1 AC 455, [1999] 1 All ER 193, HL; *Heaton v AXA Equity & Law Life Assurance Society plc* [2002] UKHL 15, [2002] 2 AC 329, [2002] 2 All ER 961, HL; *Cape & Dalgleish (a firm) v Fitzgerald* [2002] UKHL 16, [2002] CP Rep 51, [2002] All ER (D) 231 (Apr).

10 *Jameson v Central Electricity Generating Board (Babcock Energy Ltd, third party)* [2000] 1 AC 455, [1999] 1 All ER 193, HL. Cf *Heaton v AXA Equity & Law Life Assurance Society plc* [2002] UKHL 15, [2002] 2 AC 329, [2002] 2 All ER 961 (compromise not intended as full satisfaction).

450. Recovery of contribution. With respect to damage which occurred after 31 December 1978[1], any person liable in respect of any damage suffered by another person may recover contribution from any other person liable in respect of the same damage (whether jointly with him or otherwise)[2]. A person is liable[3] in respect of any damage for these purposes if the person who suffered it (or anyone representing his estate or dependants[4]) is entitled to recover compensation[5] from him in respect of that damage (whatever the legal basis of his liability, whether tort, breach of contract, breach of trust or otherwise)[6]. The words 'same damage' bear their natural and ordinary meaning and no gloss on them is warranted[7]. It is not enough that the damage is substantially or materially similar[8]. Damage here is not to be equated with damages: damage suffered may be the same notwithstanding that the amount recoverable by way of damages might vary according to the cause of action which the claimant relies on[9].

This right to recover contribution supersedes any right, other than an express contractual right, to recover contribution (as distinct from indemnity) otherwise than under the above principles in corresponding circumstances[10].

1 The Civil Liability (Contribution) Act 1978 came into force on 1 January 1979: see s 10(2).
2 See the Civil Liability (Contribution) Act 1978 ss 1(1), 7(1); and DAMAGES vol 29 (2014) PARA 620 et seq. See also *Adams v Associated Newspapers Ltd* [1999] EMLR 26, CA. The Civil Liability (Contribution) Act 1978 binds the Crown: s 5.

3 See *RA Lister & Co Ltd v EG Thompson (Shipping) Ltd, The Benarty (No 2)* [1987] 3 All ER 1032, [1987] 1 WLR 1614 (liability unaffected by subsequent stay of action); *Abbey National Bank plc v Gouldman (t/a David Gouldman & Co)* [2003] EWHC 925 (Ch), [2003] 1 WLR 2042 (undertaking not to execute judgment not extinguishing liability).
4 'Dependants' has the same meaning as in the Fatal Accidents Act 1976 (see NEGLIGENCE vol 78 (2010) PARA 27): Civil Liability (Contribution) Act 1978 s 6(3).

5 References to a person's liability in respect of any damage are references to any such liability which has been or could be established in an action brought against him in England and Wales by or on behalf of the person who suffered the damage; but it is immaterial whether any issue arising in any such action was or would be determined (in accordance with the rules of private international law) by reference to the law of a country outside England and Wales: Civil Liability (Contribution) Act 1978 s 1(6). See DAMAGES vol 29 (2014) PARA 621.
    In *Royal Brompton Hospital NHS Trust v Hammond (Taylor Woodrow Construction (Holdings) Ltd, Pt 20 defendants)* [2002] UKHL 14 at [33], [2002] 2 All ER 801 at [33], [2002] 1 WLR 1397 at [33], Lord Steyn stated that a restitutionary claim could not be said to be one for 'damage suffered' and that the contrary decision in *Friends Provident Life Office v Hillier, Parker, May & Rowden (a firm) (Estates and General plc, third party)* [1997] QB 85, [1995] 4 All ER 260, CA, was incorrect. In *Charter plc v City Index Ltd (Gawler, Pt 20 defendants)* [2007] EWCA Civ 1382 at [27], [2008] Ch 313 at [27], [2008] 3 All ER 126 at [27], Carnwath LJ (with whose judgment Mummery LJ agreed) stated that Lord Steyn's words, considered as a general statement, seemed to go too far, at least where the restitutionary claim is for no more than the amount of the loss suffered by the claimant. See also the remarks of Arden LJ in the same case (at [66] et seq), and *Niru Battery Manufacturing Co v Milestone Trading Ltd (No 2)* [2004] EWCA Civ 487 at [76]–[78], [2004] 2 All ER (Comm) 289 at [76]–[78], [2004] 2 Lloyd's Rep 319 at [76]–[78] per Clarke LJ, and at [87] per Sedley LJ.
6 See the Civil Liability (Contribution) Act 1978 s 6(1); and DAMAGES vol 29 (2014) PARA 620. Under the previous Act (ie the Law Reform (Married Women and Tortfeasors) Act 1935, which remains in force for damage occurring before 1 January 1979) these contribution provisions applied only as between tortfeasors. The words 'or otherwise' in the Civil Liability (Contribution) Act 1978 s 6(1) are wide enough to include judgments, including consent

judgments, even if there was in fact no liability prior to the judgment: *BRB (Residuary) Ltd v Connex South Eastern Ltd* [2008] EWHC 1172 (QB), [2008] 1 WLR 2867, [2008] All ER (D) 338 (May).

Under the Civil Liability (Contribution) Act 1978, a person is not entitled to recover contribution or liable to make contribution by reference to any liability based on breach of any obligation assumed by him before 1 January 1979: s 7(2). Under s 7(2), a tortious duty of care which is an incident of the defendant's non-contractual relationship with the claimant is imposed by law and not assumed by him: *Lampitt v Poole Borough Council (Taylor, third party)* [1991] 2 QB 545, [1990] 2 All ER 887, CA.

7   *Royal Brompton Hospital NHS Trust v Hammond (Taylor Woodrow Construction (Holdings) Ltd, Pt 20 defendants)* [2002] UKHL 14, [2002] 2 All ER 801, [2002] 1 WLR 1397. See also *Birse Construction Ltd v Haiste Ltd* [1996] 2 All ER 1, [1996] 1 WLR 675, CA.

8   *Royal Brompton Hospital NHS Trust v Hammond (Taylor Woodrow Construction (Holdings) Ltd, Pt 20 defendants)* [2002] UKHL 14 at [27], [2002] 2 All ER 801 at [27], [2002] 1 WLR 1397 at [27] per Lord Steyn.

9   *Birse Construction Ltd v Haiste Ltd* [1996] 2 All ER 1 at 7, [1996] 1 WLR 675 at 682, CA, per Roch LJ; *Eastgate Group Ltd v Lindsey Morden Group Inc (Smith & Williamson (a firm), Pt 20 defendant)* [2001] EWCA Civ 1446, [2001] 2 All ER (Comm) 1050, [2002] 1 WLR 642; *Royal Brompton Hospital NHS Trust v Hammond (Taylor Woodrow Construction (Holdings) Ltd, Pt 20 defendants)* [2002] UKHL 14 at [6], [2002] 2 All ER 801 at [6], [2002] 1 WLR 1397 at [6] per Lord Bingham, and at [27] per Lord Steyn.

10   The right to recover contribution in accordance with the Civil Liability (Contribution) Act 1978 s 1 supersedes any right, other than an express contractual right, to recover contribution (as distinct from indemnity) otherwise than under that Act in corresponding circumstances; but nothing in the Act affects:

(1)   any express or implied contractual or other right to indemnity; or

(2)   any express contractual provision regulating or excluding contribution,

which would otherwise be enforceable (or render enforceable any agreement for indemnity or contribution which would not be enforceable apart from the 1978 Act): s 7(3). As to contractual indemnities and other contracts regulating contribution see PARA 455.

451.   Entitlement to contribution.   A person is entitled to recover contribution[1] notwithstanding that he has ceased to be liable in respect of the damage in question since the time when the damage occurred, provided that he was so liable immediately before he made or was ordered or agreed to make the payment in respect of which the contribution is sought[2]. A person who has made or agreed to make any payment in bona fide settlement or compromise of any claim made against him in respect of any damage (including a payment into court which has been accepted) is entitled to recover contribution without regard to whether or not he himself is, or ever was, liable in respect of the damage, provided, however, that he would have been liable assuming that the factual basis of the claim against him could be established[3]. Since it is necessary only for the parties to be liable for the same damage it is irrelevant whether they are jointly liable, and the legal basis for liability may differ as between the person claiming contribution and the person against whom the claim is made[4].

1   Ie under the Civil Liability (Contribution) Act 1978 s 1(1): see PARA 450; and DAMAGES vol 29 (2014) PARA 620 et seq. The statute creates an independent cause of action: *Virgo Steamship Co SA v Skaarup Shipping Corpn, The Kapetan Georgis* [1988] 1 Lloyd's Rep 352. A claim will pass to personal representatives even though liability was not established before the death: *Ronex Properties Ltd v John Laing Construction Ltd (Clarke Nicholls & Marcel (a firm), third party)* [1983] QB 398, [1982] 3 All ER 961, CA.

2   See the Civil Liability (Contribution) Act 1978 s 1(2); and DAMAGES vol 29 (2014) PARA 621. A claim for contribution must be brought within two years after the right to contribution accrued: see the Limitation Act 1980 s 10(1); and LIMITATION PERIODS vol 68 (2008) PARA 1006. The relevant date is the date of judgment or, where the case has been settled out of court, the date of the agreement to pay: see s 10(2)–(4); and LIMITATION PERIODS vol 68 (2008) PARA 1007. The period may be extended where the person seeking contribution is under a disability or is the victim of fraud, concealment or mistake: see s 10(5); and LIMITATION PERIODS vol 68 (2008) PARA 1007.

3   See the Civil Liability (Contribution) Act 1978 s 1(4); and DAMAGES vol 29 (2014) PARA 621. See *Arab Monetary Fund v Hashim (No 8)* (1993) Times, 17 June; *Dubai Aluminium Co Ltd v Salaam (Livingstone, third parties)* [2002] UKHL 48 at [69]–[70], [2003] 2 AC 366 at [69]–[70], [2003] 1 All ER 97 at [69]–[70] per Lord Hobhouse; *BRB (Residuary) Ltd v Connex South Eastern Ltd* [2008] EWHC 1172 (QB), [2008] 1 WLR 2867, [2008] All ER (D) 338 (May). A compromise fixes a claim as a judgment does, so if a claim is made against a concurrent tortfeasor there can be no inquiry as to the full value of the claim but only as to whether it was in full and final settlement: *Jameson v Central Electricity Generating Board (Babcock Energy Ltd, third party)* [2000] 1 AC 455, [1999] 1 All ER 193, HL. Under the law in force before 1 January 1979 (ie the date on which the Civil Liability (Contribution) Act 1978 came into force), contribution could not be recovered unless the person seeking it would have been liable had the plaintiff sued him to judgment: *Stott v West Yorkshire Road Car Co Ltd (Home Bakeries Ltd, third party)* [1971] 2 QB 651, [1971] 3 All ER 534, CA.

4   See the Civil Liability (Contribution) Act 1978 ss 1(1), 6(1); and *Birse Construction Ltd v Haiste Ltd (Watson, third party)* [1996] 2 All ER 1, [1996] 1 WLR 675; *K v P* [1993] Ch 140, [1993] 1 All ER 521; *Société Commerciale de Réassurance v ERAS (International) Ltd* [1992] 1 Lloyd's Rep 570 at 600, CA; *Lampitt v Poole Borough Council (Taylor, third party)* [1991] 2 QB 545 at 552, [1990] 2 All ER 887 at 890, CA, per Lord Donaldson of Lymington MR; *Friends Provident Life Office v Hillier, Parker, May & Rowden (a firm) (Estates and General plc, third party)* [1997] QB 85 at 102–103, [1995] 4 All ER 260 at 272, CA, per Auld LJ; *Royal Brompton Hospital NHS Trust v Hammond (Taylor Woodrow Construction (Holdings) Ltd, Pt 20 defendants)* [2002] UKHL 14 at [40]–[41], [2002] 2 All ER 801 at [40]–[41], [2002] 1 WLR 1397 at [40]–[41] per Lord Hope.

452. Liability to make contribution. A person is liable to make contribution[1] notwithstanding that he has ceased to be liable in respect of the damage in question since the time when the damage occurred, unless he ceased to be liable by virtue of the expiry of a period of limitation or prescription which extinguished the right on which the claim against him in respect of the damage was based[2]. A judgment given in any action brought in any part of the United Kingdom[3] by or on behalf of the person who suffered the damage[4] in question against any person from whom contribution is sought is conclusive in the proceedings for contribution as to any issue determined by that judgment in favour of the person from whom the contribution is sought[5].

1   Ie under the Civil Liability (Contribution) Act 1978 s 1(1): see PARA 450; and DAMAGES vol 29 (2014) PARA 620 et seq.

2   See the Civil Liability (Contribution) Act 1978 s 1(3); and DAMAGES vol 29 (2014) PARA 622. This reverses the decision in *George Wimpey & Co Ltd v British Overseas Airways Corpn* [1955] AC 169, [1954] 3 All ER 661, HL.

3   'United Kingdom' means Great Britain and Northern Ireland: Interpretation Act 1978 s 5, Sch 1. 'Great Britain' means England, Scotland and Wales: Union with Scotland Act 1706, preamble art I; Interpretation Act 1978 s 22(1), Sch 2 para 5(a). Neither the Isle of Man nor the Channel Islands are within the United Kingdom. See further CONSTITUTIONAL AND ADMINISTRATIVE LAW vol 20 (2014) PARA 3.

4   A claim brought by or on behalf of the person who suffered any damage includes an action brought for the benefit of his estate or dependants: see the Civil Liability (Contribution) Act 1978 s 6(2); and DAMAGES vol 29 (2014) PARA 620. As to the meaning of 'dependants' see PARA 450 note 4. Though English law is primarily applicable, s 1 also applies to claims brought by the application of foreign law by the operation of the rules of private international law, and it is irrelevant whether or not the liability was incurred in England and Wales: see *Logan v Uttlesford District Council and Hammond* [1986] NLJ Rep 541, CA; *RA Lister & Co Ltd v EG Thomson (Shipping) Ltd, The Benarty (No 2)* [1987] 3 All ER 1032 at 1038, [1987] 1 WLR 1614 at 1622; *Virgo Steamship Co SA v Skaarup Shipping Corpn, The Kapetan Georgis* [1988] 1 Lloyd's Rep 352; *Arab Monetary Fund v Hashim (No 9)* (1994) Times, 11 October.

5   See the Civil Liability (Contribution) Act 1978 s 1(5); and DAMAGES vol 29 (2014) PARA 622. Similarly, under the former law, a person who had been sued to judgment on the merits of the case and held not liable was not liable to make contribution: see *Hart v Hall and Pickles Ltd* [1969] 1 QB 405, [1968] 3 All ER 291, CA (but this would not have been so if the action had failed for want of prosecution, for that does not amount to being 'sued to judgment': *Hart v Hall and Pickles Ltd* [1969] 1 QB 405 at 411, [1968] 3 All ER 291 at 293, CA, per

Lord Denning MR). The Civil Liability (Contribution) Act 1978 s 1(5) should not be construed to bar further proceedings by way of appeal in the original action: *Moy v Pettman Smith (a firm)* [2005] UKHL 7, [2005] 1 All ER 903, [2005] 1 WLR 581 at [3]–[13] per Lord Hope, at [24] per Baroness Hale and at [66]–[69] per Lord Carswell (obiter). See also *RA Lister & Co Ltd v EG Thomson (Shipping) Ltd, The Benarty (No 2)* [1987] 3 All ER 1032 at 1039, [1987] 1 WLR 1614 at 1623 per Hobhouse J; *Nottingham Health Authority v Nottingham City Council* [1988] 1 WLR 903, CA; *Société Commerciale de Réassurance v ERAS (International) Ltd* [1992] 1 Lloyd's Rep 570. Ex turpi causa is not a defence to a claim for contribution: *K v P* [1993] Ch 140, [1993] 1 All ER 521.

453. Assessment and apportionment of contribution. In proceedings for contribution[1], the amount of the contribution recoverable from any person is such as may be found by the court to be just and equitable having regard to that person's responsibility for the damage[2]; and the court has power to exempt any person from liability to make contribution, or to direct that the contribution is to amount to a complete indemnity[3]. The court must have regard both to causation and to the relative blameworthiness of the parties[4]. There is no automatic presumption that one form of liability attracts a larger share than another even in a case where one party has been fraudulent: everything depends on the facts[5]. In assessing the contribution recoverable, the court should consider the known or likely financial consequences of any contribution order made so, where the wrongdoing has produced not only a loss to the claimant but a profit to the defendants, it is just and equitable to direct that any contributions required to allocate the cost of meeting the claim fairly among those responsible should be paid first out of their retained profits[6]. Similarly, the court should take into account the known insolvency of one of the defendants[7].

In cases of vicarious liability, where the issue of contribution arises between the employer (or principal) and another tortfeasor, the vicariously liable employer stands in his employee's shoes, and has in law the same responsibility, so his own personal innocence is irrelevant[8], though if the employee's tortious acts included acts committed both within and without the scope of his employment, or if the employer was also to some degree personally to blame, the assessment of the employer's responsibility may have to be adjusted accordingly[9]. In the ordinary course, orders for contribution payments are made severally against the persons concerned, but there is no reason in principle why the court should not make two defendants jointly and severally liable to a third so as to make provision for what is to occur in the event of insolvency[10].

Where the amount of the damages which have or might have been awarded in respect of the damage in question in any action brought in England and Wales by or on behalf of the person who suffered it[11] against the person from whom the contribution is sought was or would have been subject to any limit imposed by or under any enactment or by any agreement made before the damage occurred[12] or any reduction for contributory negligence[13], or any corresponding limit or reduction under the law of a country outside England and Wales[14], the person from whom the contribution is sought is not, by virtue of any contribution awarded, required to pay in respect of the damage a greater amount than the amount of those damages as so limited or reduced[15]. The apportionment of liability between the claimant and the defendants on grounds of contributory negligence is a separate and prior issue for determination from the issue of apportionment or contribution between the defendants[16].

The assessment of contribution does not affect or concern the claimant, and it may be sought by one of the persons concerned either on application at the close of the claimant's action without formal or separate proceedings[17] or by an additional claim[18]. An apportionment made by the trial judge will only be altered on appeal when it is clearly wrong or there has been an error in principle or a mistake of fact[19].

1   Ie under the Civil Liability (Contribution) Act 1978 s 1(1): see PARA 450; and DAMAGES vol 29 (2014) PARA 620 et seq.
2   See the Civil Liability (Contribution) Act 1978 s 2(1); and DAMAGES vol 29 (2014) PARA 624. This provision substantially re-enacts part of the Law Reform (Married Women and Tortfeasors) Act 1935 s 6(2) (repealed). For decisions under the earlier legislation see *Burnham v Boyer and Brown* [1936] 2 All ER 1165; *Croston v Vaughan* [1938] 1 KB 540, [1937] 4 All ER 249, CA; *Daniel v Rickett, Cockerell & Co Ltd and Raymond* [1938] 2 KB 322, [1938] 2 All ER 631; *Smith v Bray (Wickham, third party)* (1939) 56 TLR 200; *Rippon v Port of London Authority and Russell & Co* [1940] 1 KB 858, [1940] 1 All ER 637; *Collins v Hertfordshire County Council* [1947] KB 598, [1947] 1 All ER 633; *Weaver v Commercial Process Co Ltd* (1947) 63 TLR 466; *Bell v Holmes* [1956] 3 All ER 449, [1956] 1 WLR 1359; *Randolph v Tuck* [1962] 1 QB 175, [1961] 1 All ER 814; *Brown v Thompson* [1968] 2 All ER 708, [1968] 1 WLR 1003.
3   See the Civil Liability (Contribution) Act 1978 s 2(2); and *Diboll v City of Newcastle* [1993] PIQR P16, CA; *Adams v Associated Newspapers Ltd* [1999] EMLR 26, CA; *Cressman v Coys of Kensington (McDonald, Pt 20 defendant)* [2004] EWCA Civ 47, [2004] 1 WLR 2775, 148 Sol Jo LB 182; *Dubai Aluminium Co Ltd v Salaam (Livingstone, third parties)* [2002] UKHL 48, [2003] 2 AC 366, [2003] 1 All ER 97; *Niru Battery Manufacturing Co v Milestone Trading Ltd (No 2)* [2004] EWCA Civ 487 at [50], [73] and [78], [2004] 2 All ER (Comm) 289 at [50], [73] and [78], [2004] 2 Lloyd's Rep 319 at [50], [73] and [78] per Clarke LJ, and at [81] per Sedley LJ; *Charter plc v City Index Ltd (Gawler, Pt 20 defendants)* [2007] EWCA Civ 1382, [2008] Ch 313, [2008] 3 All ER 126. See also DAMAGES vol 29 (2014) PARA 620. A person who is only vicariously liable may be allowed a complete indemnity: *Lister v Romford Ice and Cold Storage Co Ltd* [1957] AC 555, [1957] 1 All ER 125, HL; *Nelhams v Sandwell's Maintenance Ltd and Gillespie (UK) Ltd* [1996] PIQR P52, CA. As to the employee's liability to make contribution to another liable party, in the context of the gentleman's agreement by insurers not to claim against the employee of an insured employer in respect of injury to a fellow employee, except in clear cases of collusion or wilful misconduct, see *Morris v Ford Motor Co Ltd (Cameron Industrial Services Ltd, third party) (Roberts, fourth party)* [1973] QB 792, [1973] 2 All ER 1084, CA. Cf *The Yasin* [1979] 2 Lloyd's Rep 45.
    The Civil Liability (Contribution) Act 1978 s 2(2) substantially re-enacts part of the Law Reform (Married Women and Tortfeasors) Act 1935 s 6(2) (repealed). For decisions under the earlier legislation see *Ryan v Fildes* [1938] 3 All ER 517; *Jones v Manchester Corpn* [1952] 2 QB 852, [1952] 2 All ER 125, CA; *Semtex Ltd v Gladstone* [1954] 2 All ER 206, [1954] 1 WLR 945; *Harvey v RG O'Dell Ltd* [1958] 2 QB 78, [1958] 1 All ER 657; *Thomas Saunders Partnership v Harvey* (1989) 30 ConLR 103.
4   *Miraflores (Owners) v George Livanos (Owners)* [1967] 1 AC 826 at 845, sub nom *The Miraflores (Owners) and The Abadesa (Owners)* [1967] 1 All ER 672 at 677, HL, per Lord Pearce; *Brown v Thompson* [1968] 2 All ER 708 at 709, [1968] 1 WLR 1003 at 1008, CA, per Winn LJ; *Baker v Willoughby* [1970] AC 467 at 490, [1969] 3 All ER 1528 at 1530, HL, per Lord Reid; *Madden v Quirk* [1989] 1 WLR 702 at 707, [1989] RTR 304 at 309 per Simon Brown J. In apportioning damages the court may exceptionally have regard to non-causative aspects of a defendant's conduct if there is a close connection between them and the acts or omissions giving rise to liability: *Re-Source America International Ltd v Platt Site Services Ltd (Barkin Construction Ltd, Pt 20 defendant)* [2004] EWCA Civ 665, 95 ConLR 1; *Brian Warwicker Partnership v HOK International Ltd (HOK International Ltd, Pt 20 defendant)* [2005] EWCA Civ 962, 103 ConLR 112. In apportioning damages the court cannot have regard to the possible liability of a person who is not a party before the court: *Maxfield v Llewellyn* [1961] 3 All ER 95, [1961] 1 WLR 1119, CA; *Saipem SpA and Conoco (UK) Ltd v Dredging VO2 BV and Geosite Surveys Ltd, The Volvox Hollandia (No 2)* [1993] 2 Lloyd's Rep 315.
5   *Charter plc v City Index Ltd (Gawler, Pt 20 defendants)* [2007] EWCA Civ 1382, [2008] Ch 313, [2008] 3 All ER 126; *Greene Wood & McClean (a firm) v Templeton Insurance Ltd* [2009] EWCA Civ 65 at [59], [2009] 1 WLR 2013 at [59], [2009] CP Rep 24 at [59] per Carnwath LJ.
6   *Dubai Aluminium Co Ltd v Salaam (Livingstone, third parties)* [2002] UKHL 48, [2003] 2 AC 366, [2003] 1 All ER 97.
7   *Dubai Aluminium Co Ltd v Salaam (Livingstone, third parties)* [2002] UKHL 48 at [52], [2003] 2 AC 366 at [52], [2003] 1 All ER 97 at [52] per Lord Nicholls.

8   *Dubai Aluminium Co Ltd v Salaam (Livingstone, third parties)* [2002] UKHL 48, [2003] 2 AC 366, [2003] 1 All ER 97; *Hawley v Luminar Leisure Ltd* [2006] EWCA Civ 18, [2006] Lloyd's Rep IR 307, [2006] IRLR 817.

9   *Dubai Aluminium Co Ltd v Salaam (Livingstone, third parties)* [2002] UKHL 48 at [75], [2003] 2 AC 366 at [75], [2003] 1 All ER 97 at [75] per Lord Hobhouse. Cf *Hawley v Luminar Leisure Ltd* [2006] EWCA Civ 18, [2006] Lloyd's Rep IR 307, [2006] IRLR 817 (nil contribution because negligence had negligible causative effect).

10 *Dubai Aluminium Co Ltd v Salaam (Livingstone, third parties)* [2002] UKHL 48, [2003] 2 AC 366, [2003] 1 All ER 97 (see especially at [63] per Lord Nicholls, at [78] per Lord Hobhouse, and at [167] per Lord Millett).

11 As to the meaning of 'action brought by or on behalf of the person who suffered any damage' see PARA 452 note 4.

12 See the Civil Liability (Contribution) Act 1978 s 2(3)(a); and DAMAGES vol 29 (2014) PARA 622.

13 See the Civil Liability (Contribution) Act 1978 s 2(3)(b); and DAMAGES vol 29 (2014) PARA 622. The reduction referred to is one by virtue of the Law Reform (Contributory Negligence) Act 1945 s 1 or the Fatal Accidents Act 1976 s 5: see NEGLIGENCE vol 78 (2010) PARA 25 et seq. Although contributory negligence may be ignored in the claim against one defendant because that defendant was in fraud, the amount of contribution that the other defendant may be ordered to make should not be assessed by treating the damage for which both defendants are responsible as the totality of the claimant's loss, ignoring contributory negligence, when the only reason for ignoring it is that the claim against the first defendant is in deceit: see *Nationwide Building Society v Dunlop Haywards (DHL) Ltd* [2009] EWHC 254 (Comm), [2009] 2 All ER (Comm) 715, [2010] 1 WLR 258.

14 See the Civil Liability (Contribution) Act 1978 s 2(3)(c); and DAMAGES vol 29 (2014) PARA 622.

15 See the Civil Liability (Contribution) Act 1978 s 2(3); and DAMAGES vol 29 (2014) PARA 622. This provision was necessitated by the extension of the Act to breaches of contract, in order to deal with contracts which contain either waivers of liability or limitations by virtue of a liquidated damages clause.

16 *Fitzgerald v Lane* [1989] AC 328 at 339, [1988] 2 All ER 961 at 965, HL, per Lord Ackner.

17 *Croston v Vaughan* [1938] 1 KB 540, [1937] 4 All ER 249, CA; *Bell v Holmes* [1956] 3 All ER 449, [1956] 1 WLR 1359; *T Oertli AG v EJ Bowman (London) Ltd* [1956] RPC 341. Separate proceedings may be necessary if discovery or interrogatories are required: *Clayson v Rolls Royce* [1951] 1 KB 746, [1950] 2 All ER 884, CA. The court also has power to determine the issue of contribution between defendants where the claimant's action has been settled and there are no formal third party proceedings: *Stott v West Yorkshire Road Car Co Ltd (Home Bakeries Ltd, third party)* [1971] 2 QB 651, [1971] 3 All ER 534, CA.

18 See CPR Pt 20; and CIVIL PROCEDURE vol 11 (2009) PARA 618 et seq.

19 *Ingram v United Automobile Service Ltd* [1943] KB 612, [1943] 2 All ER 71, CA; *British Fame (Owners) v Macgregor (Owners), The Macgregor* [1943] AC 197, [1943] 1 All ER 33, HL; *Brown v Thompson* [1968] 2 All ER 708, [1968] 1 WLR 1003, CA; *Diboll v City of Newcastle* [1993] PIQR P16, CA; *Parkman Consulting Engineers v Cumbrian Industrials Ltd* [2001] EWCA Civ 1621, [2002] BLR 64. If the error does not affect the result, there is no need for the appellate court to set the apportionment aside and re-examine the question for itself: *Dubai Aluminium Co Ltd v Salaam (Livingstone, third parties)* [2002] UKHL 48, [2003] 2 AC 366, [2003] 1 All ER 97.

454.   Apportionment of damages between defendants; costs at court's discretion. Where the damages assessed have been apportioned as between defendants, the costs remain entirely within the court's discretion[1]. Costs need not therefore be apportioned between the defendants in the same proportion as the damages[2]. There is some authority that a party claiming contribution may recover a contribution towards a payment made in respect of the injured party's costs[3]. If more than one action[4] is brought in respect of any damage by or on behalf of the person by whom it was suffered[5] against persons liable in respect of the damage (whether jointly or otherwise) the claimant is not entitled to costs in any of those actions, other than that in which judgment is first given, unless the court is of the opinion that there was reasonable ground for bringing the action[6].

1   See CIVIL PROCEDURE vol 12 (2009) PARA 1738.

2   *Moy v Pettman Smith (a firm) (No 2)* [2003] EWCA Civ 467, [2003] PNLR 31 (revsd on other grounds: [2005] UKHL 7, [2005] 1 All ER 903, [2005] 1 WLR 581); *Nationwide Building*

Society v Dunlop Haywards (DHL) Ltd [2009] EWHC 254 (Comm), [2009] 2 All ER (Comm) 715, [2009] 1 Lloyd's Rep 447. Cf apportionment of cases between claimant and defendant where there is a successful defence of contributory negligence: *William A Jay & Sons v JS Veevers Ltd* [1946] 1 All ER 646; *Howitt v Alexander & Sons* 1948 SC 154, Ct of Sess; *McCarthy v Raylton Productions Ltd* [1951] WN 376, CA (costs following the event). As to the situation where the claimant counterclaims see *Smith v WH Smith & Sons Ltd* [1952] 1 All ER 528, CA.

3   *Parkman Consulting Engineers v Cumbrian Industrials Ltd* [2001] EWCA Civ 1621 at [123], [2002] BLR 64 at [123] per Henry LJ; *Nationwide Building Society v Dunlop Haywards (DHL) Ltd* [2009] EWHC 254 (Comm), [2009] 2 All ER (Comm) 715, [2009] 1 Lloyd's Rep 447.

4   'Action' means an action brought in England and Wales: see the Civil Liability (Contribution) Act 1978 s 6(4). The term 'claim' is now used instead of 'action' in the Civil Procedure Rules ('CPR'): see CIVIL PROCEDURE vol 11 (2009) PARA 18.

5   As to the meaning of 'action brought by or on behalf of the person who suffered any damage' see PARA 452 note 4.

6   See the Civil Liability (Contribution) Act 1978 s 4; and DAMAGES vol 29 (2014) PARA 620. This provision replaces the Law Reform (Married Women and Tortfeasors) Act 1935 s 6(1)(b) (repealed). It differs in applying to all causes of action, and not merely to torts, and in abolishing the rule that damages in later actions cannot exceed those awarded in the first.

455.   Legality of contractual indemnity.   The statutory right to contribution[1] does not affect any express or implied contractual or other right to indemnity[2] or any express contractual provision regulating or excluding contribution[3] which would otherwise be enforceable, or render enforceable any agreement for indemnity or contribution which would not otherwise be enforceable[4]. A contractual indemnity against liability in respect of a deliberate wrongful act is unenforceable, irrespective of whether it is criminal as well as tortious[5]. A contractual indemnity against liability in respect of an unintentional tort, including one arising under a contract of insurance, may be enforced even though the tort also amounts to a criminal offence[6]. An agreement for indemnifying any person against civil liability for libel in respect of the publication of any matter is not unlawful unless at the time of publication that person knows that the matter is defamatory, and does not reasonably believe there is a good defence to any action brought upon it[7].

1   Ie under the Civil Liability (Contribution) Act 1978 s 1(1): see PARA 450; and DAMAGES vol 29 (2014) PARA 620 et seq.

2   See the Civil Liability (Contribution) Act 1978 s 7(3)(a). As to implied contractual indemnities see *Rippon v Port of London Authority and Russell & Co* [1940] 1 KB 858, [1940] 1 All ER 637; *Lexmead (Basingstoke Ltd) v Lewis* [1982] AC 225, sub nom *Lambert v Lewis* [1981] 1 All ER 1185, HL.

3   See the Civil Liability (Contribution) Act 1978 s 7(3)(b); and *Co-operative Retail Services Ltd v Taylor Young Partnership Ltd (Carillion Construction Ltd, Pt 20 defendants)* [2002] UKHL 17, [2002] 1 All ER (Comm) 918, [2002] 1 WLR 1419 (exclusion of contribution).

4   See the Civil Liability (Contribution) Act 1978 s 7(3). This substantially reproduces the Law Reform (Married Women and Tortfeasors) Act 1935 s 6(4)(c) (repealed). Indemnities and contractual provisions regulating or excluding contribution are not exclusions or restrictions of liability for the purposes of the Unfair Contract Terms Act 1977: *Thompson v T Lohan (Plant Hire) Ltd* [1987] 2 All ER 631, [1987] 1 WLR 649, CA.

5   *WH Smith & Son v Clinton and Harris* (1908) 99 LT 840. See also *Haseldine v Hosken* [1933] 1 KB 822 (intentional act done without knowledge of its unlawfulness). But an indemnity may be enforceable against a person who induces wrongdoing by fraud: *Burrows v Rhodes and Jameson* [1899] 1 QB 816.

6   *Arthur White Contractors Ltd v Tarmac Civil Engineering Ltd* [1967] 3 All ER 586, [1967] 1 WLR 1508, HL, where the House of Lords enforced the contractual indemnity even though a defendant was guilty of a criminal offence. It has long been the law that an insured motorist is entitled to indemnity under his motor insurance even in respect of an accident for which he is convicted of manslaughter: *Tinline v White Cross Insurance Association Ltd* [1921] 3 KB 327; *James v British General Insurance Co Ltd* [1927] 2 KB 311. Cf *Charlton v Fisher* [2001] EWCA

Civ 112, [2002] QB 578, [2001] 1 All ER (Comm) 769 (deliberate ramming). The indemnity may be unenforceable, though the liability results from an unintended act, if this was done in the course of deliberate violent conduct: *Gray v Barr* [1971] 2 QB 554, [1971] 2 All ER 949, CA. See also FINANCIAL SERVICES AND INSTITUTIONS vol 49 (2008) PARAS 1269–1270.

7   Defamation Act 1952 s 11; and see DEFAMATION vol 32 (2012) PARA 509.

(6) DEFENCES TO CLAIMS IN TORT

456.   Act of state as a defence to claim in tort. There is no liability in tort for acts which constitute the performance of acts of state, being the exercise of the sovereign power towards persons who owe no allegiance to the Crown or who are not friendly aliens resident, or perhaps merely present, in British territory[1].

1   See CONSTITUTIONAL AND ADMINISTRATIVE LAW vol 20 (2014) PARA 197; INTERNATIONAL RELATIONS LAW vol 61 (2010) PARAS 22–23. See also *Buron v Denman* (1848) 2 Exch 167; *Walker v Baird* [1892] AC 491, PC; *A-G v Nissan* [1970] AC 179, [1969] 1 All ER 629, HL. In the last of these cases, the House of Lords left undecided whether act of state could ever be pleaded against British subjects for acts outside the realm. In *Al Jedda v Secretary of State for Defence* [2009] EWHC 397 (QB) at [78]–[87], [2009] All ER (D) 77 (Mar) at [78]–[87], Underhill J preferred the view that it could. In British territory the defence may be available against an alien enemy (*R v Bottrill, ex p Kuechenmeister* [1947] KB 41, [1946] 2 All ER 434, CA) or perhaps against a friendly alien resident in the realm who has broken his duty of temporary allegiance, but it may be that the Crown must indicate that it has withdrawn protection (*Johnstone v Pedlar* [1921] 2 AC 262, HL).

457.   Statutory authority as a defence to claim in tort. No liability in tort can arise from acts done in pursuance, and within the scope, of statutory powers where the powers are exercised in good faith, reasonably, without negligence and for the purpose for which, and in the manner which, the statute provides[1].

1   See PARA 809; and CONSTITUTIONAL AND ADMINISTRATIVE LAW vol 20 (2014) PARA 653 et seq.

458.   Statutory defences to claims in tort. A statute may afford particular defences to liabilities it establishes itself or to tort liabilities generally. Examples are the exclusion of liability provided in relation to carriage by sea or air[1] and the exclusion of liability of a hotel proprietor, in his capacity as an innkeeper, towards a guest in relation to loss or damage to vehicles and property left in them[2].

Where in a private prosecution a person has been summarily convicted for assault or a complaint for assault against him has been heard and dismissed, release from civil proceedings for the same cause is in certain circumstances expressly conferred by statute[3].

1   See the Carriage by Air Act 1961 s 1(1), Sch 1; the Merchant Shipping Act 1995 ss 185(1), 186, Sch 7 Pt I; and CARRIAGE AND CARRIERS vol 7 (2015) PARA 121 et seq; SHIPPING AND MARITIME LAW vol 94 (2008) PARA 1042 et seq. Both statutes provide for limited liability in prescribed circumstances.
2   See the Hotel Proprietors Act 1956 s 2(2); and LICENSING AND GAMBLING vol 67 (2008) PARA 202.
3   See the Offences against the Person Act 1861 s 45; PARA 541; and CRIMINAL PROCEDURE vol 27 (2010) PARA 385. See also *Wong v Parkside Health NHS Trust* [2001] EWCA Civ 1721, [2003] 3 All ER 932.

459.   Statutory limits on liability in tort. Rights of limitation of the amount of liability conferred for the benefit of ship owners and others may be pleaded as a defence or made the subject of an action for limitation of liability[1]. There are comparable rights for the benefit of air carriers[2]. Common carriers by land have the benefit of a statutory provision for the limitation of liability in respect of loss of or injury to certain articles carried, in the absence of a declaration of value[3]. A statutory right of limitation of liability conditional on notice being exhibited is conferred in favour of hotel proprietors as innkeepers[4].

1   See SHIPPING AND MARITIME LAW vol 93 (2008) PARAS 195–197.
2   See e g CARRIAGE AND CARRIERS vol 7 (2015) PARA 155 et seq.
3   See CARRIAGE AND CARRIERS vol 7 (2015) PARA 674 et seq.
4   See the Hotel Proprietors Act 1956 s 2(3); and LICENSING AND GAMBLING vol 67 (2008) PARA 203.

460. Judicial acts and ministerial execution of decrees as defences to claims in tort. Persons exercising judicial functions in a court of justice acting within its jurisdiction are exempt from all civil liability for anything done or said by them in their judicial capacity[1]. Liability may, however, arise for judicial acts in excess of jurisdiction that are done in bad faith[2]. In general, ministerial officers acting in obedience to decrees of a court of justice are not liable for acts so done[3].

1   See CONSTITUTIONAL AND ADMINISTRATIVE LAW vol 20 (2014) PARA 607 et seq. As regards absolute privilege from liability for defamation see DEFAMATION vol 32 (2012) PARA 594 et seq. As to the liability of members of courts-martial see ARMED FORCES vol 3 (2011) PARA 634. See also *Anderson v Gorrie* [1895] 1 QB 668, CA; *Fray v Blackburn* (1863) 3 B & S 576; *Re McC (a minor)* [1985] AC 528, sub nom *McC v Mullan* [1984] 3 All ER 908, HL. For the limitation on proceedings in respect of a judicial act under the Human Rights Act 1998 see s 9; and COURTS AND TRIBUNALS vol 24 (2010) PARA 625.

2   *Re McC (a minor)* [1985] AC 528 at 540, sub nom *McC v Mullan* [1984] 3 All ER 908 at 916, HL, per Lord Bridge. No action lies against a justice of the peace (or a justices' clerk or an assistant clerk) in respect of what he does or omits to do in the execution of his duty as a justice of the peace (or as a justice's clerk or assistant clerk exercising, by virtue of an enactment, a function of a single justice of the peace) in relation to a matter within his jurisdiction: Courts Act 2003 s 31(1), (2). An action lies against a justice of the peace (or a justices' clerk or an assistant clerk) in the purported exercise of his duty (as specified above) in relation to a matter not within his jurisdiction if, but only if, he acted in bad faith: Courts Act 2003 s 32(1), (2); and see MAGISTRATES vol 71 (2013) PARA 464.
     In proceedings brought under the Human Rights Act 1998, damages may be awarded in respect of judicial acts in excess of jurisdiction that are done in good faith in order to compensate a person to the extent required by the Convention for the Protection of Human Rights and Fundamental Freedoms (Rome, 4 November 1950; TS 71 (1953); Cmd 8969) art 5.5 (compensation for arrest or detention in breach of Convention: see rights and freedoms vol 88A (2013) PARA 230): Human Rights Act 1998 s 9(3). Such awards are to be made against the Crown: s 9(4). See also *D v Home Office* [2005] EWCA Civ 38, [2006] 1 All ER 183, [2006] 1 WLR 1003 at [119] per Brooke LJ.

3   See CONSTITUTIONAL AND ADMINISTRATIVE LAW vol 20 (2014) PARA 615. As to liability for wrongful execution see CIVIL PROCEDURE; and as to the protection of the sheriff acting under a writ of execution see CIVIL PROCEDURE vol 12 (2009) PARA 1258. See also *Dews v Riley* (1851) 11 CB 434; *Demer v Cook* (1903) 88 LT 629.

461. Justification as a defence to claim in tort. In the exercise of legitimate self-redress or self-defence or the protection of property, acts may be done lawfully which otherwise would be actionable, the legitimacy of the acts providing a defence to any claim in respect of them[1]. Acts otherwise amounting to battery or false imprisonment may be justified as reasonable punishment of the actor's child, provided the punishment is not excessive and does not cause actual bodily harm[2]. Acts otherwise amounting to battery may be justified as done in the course of lawful arrest, if the force used is necessary and not more than is reasonably required[3]. So, too, a tortious act may be justified as done for the prevention of crime[4] or in time of war for the safety of the realm[5]; and an act which causes damage to property and which would otherwise be tortious may in certain circumstances be justified by reasonable necessity for preventing loss of life if the necessity did not arise from the defendant's neglect[6], or for preventing the spread of fire[7].

More specifically, justification is a defence to a defamation action, and consists in proving the truth of the allegation of which the claimant complains[8].

Certain statutes justify what would otherwise be trespass to land[9].

1   As to the remedy of self-redress see PARAS 476–477. As to self-defence and protection of property see PARAS 462–463.
2   See the Children Act 2004 s 58(3), (4); and CHILDREN AND YOUNG PERSONS vol 9 (2012) PARA 635; CRIMINAL LAW vol 25 (2010) PARA 173. See also *Murray v Moutrie* (1834) 6 Car & P 471 at 473 per Tindal CJ; *Winterburn v Brooks* (1846) 2 Car & Kir 16; cf *Anon* (circa 1695) 3 Salk 46. Corporal punishment by teachers in either state or independent schools cannot now be used as a justification for battery: see the Education Act 1996 s 548; PARAS 437, 538; and EDUCATION vol 35 (2011) PARA 627. As to reasonable punishment see RIGHTS AND FREEDOMS vol 88A (2013) PARAS 174, 633.
3   See POLICE AND INVESTIGATORY POWERS vol 84A (2013) PARA 489.
4   See *Handcock v Baker* (1800) 2 Bos & P 260, where breaking and entering the plaintiff's house and imprisoning him was justified as it was done to prevent him murdering his wife.
5   See *Maleverer v Spinke* (1537) 1 Dyer 35b at 36b.
6   *Mouse's* Case (1608) 12 Co Rep 63. As to forcible entry see PARA 589. As to abatement see PARA 477. As to retaking goods see PARA 476; and see PARA 662 et seq. As to necessity see further PARA 464.
7   See *Maleverer v Spinke* (1537) 1 Dyer 35b at 36b; *Dewey v White* (1827) Mood & M 56; and FIRE AND RESCUE SERVICES vol 51 (2013) PARA 56. Cf PARA 463.
8   See DEFAMATION vol 32 (2012) PARA 582 et seq.
9   See eg the Countryside and Rights of Way Act 2000 (see OPEN SPACES AND COUNTRYSIDE); the Police and Criminal Evidence Act 1984 (see POLICE AND INVESTIGATORY POWERS vol 84 (2013) PARA 1 et seq; POLICE AND INVESTIGATORY POWERS vol 84A (2013) PARA 432 et seq); and the Access to Neighbouring Land Act 1992 (see REAL PROPERTY AND REGISTRATION vol 87 (2012) PARA 311 et seq). See also *Grove v Eastern Gas Board* [1952] 1 KB 77, [1951] 2 All ER 1051 (forcible entry by gas board justified by statutory powers).

462.   Self-defence as a defence to claim in tort. Every person is justified is using reasonable force to defend himself and those under his care, but the force justifiable is such only as is reasonably necessary[1].

1   See PARAS 534–535; and *Cook v Beal* (1696) 1 Ld Raym 176 at 177; *Cockcroft v Smith* (1705) 2 Salk 642; *Turner (otherwise Robertson) v Metro-Goldwyn-Mayer* [1950] 1 All ER 449 at 471, HL, per Lord Oaksey (measure of force).
    A person is not entitled to use force in self-defence merely because he believes he is under threat, when in fact he is not, but it has not yet been decided whether he must actually be under attack or under threat of imminent attack, or if it is enough that he reasonably believed this to be the case: *Ashley v Chief Constable of Sussex Police* [2008] UKHL 25, [2008] 1 AC 962, [2008] 3 All ER 573.

463.   Protection of property as a defence to claim in tort. A person is justified in using force to resist a person seeking to take his goods by force or coming on his land by force[1], but no more force than is necessary or commensurate may be used and, if the entry was peaceable, a request to depart should be made before a trespasser is expelled[2]. Similarly, a person is justified in driving away from his land something that will harm it and seeks to come upon it, even if the consequence is that it goes or remains on the land of another[3]; and a person is justified in taking reasonable steps, even though it involves the use of force, to prevent interference with an incorporeal hereditament, such as a right of shooting[4]. However, the setting of traps calculated to cause grievous bodily harm is prohibited by statute[5], and tame or domestic animals may not be shot unless there is no other means of protecting the property[6]. If a private right of way is obstructed by the grantor, the grantee has a right to deviate over the grantor's land and to justify on this ground acts that otherwise would be a trespass[7].

1   *Weaver v Bush* (1798) 8 Term Rep 78. A person using force to defend property must either have possession or the right to possession: *Holmes v Bagge* (1853) 1 E & B 782 (cricket field); *Dean v Hogg* (1834) 10 Bing 345 (boat); *Roberts v Tayler* (1845) 1 CB 117. A person without possession may use force in order to exercise statutory powers: *R v Chief Constable of Devon and Cornwall, ex p Central Electricity Generating Board* [1982] QB 458, [1981] 3 All ER 826. Cf *Stroud v Bradbury* [1952] 2 All ER 76 (an inspector who sought to carry out drainage work without giving prescribed statutory notice could be lawfully resisted with a spade and pole).
2   See PARAS 588–589. Cf *Revill v Newbery* [1996] QB 567, [1996] 1 All ER 291, CA (occupier liable in negligence for shooting trespasser without warning); and NEGLIGENCE vol 78 (2010) PARA 40. But an innkeeper was not justified in wounding a man who refused to leave hostelry after a quarrel (*Moriarty v Brooks* (1834) 6 C & P 684, Ex Ch).
3   See NUISANCE vol 78 (2010) PARA 196. See also *R v Pagham, Sussex Sewers Comrs* (1828) 8 B & C 355; *Nield v London and North Western Rly Co* (1874) LR 10 Exch 4; *Greyvensteyn v Hattingh* [1911] AC 355, PC (swarm of locusts driven from boundary of land); *Maxey Drainage Board v Great Northern Rly Co* (1912) 106 LT 429 (embankment against flood water); *Gerrard v Crowe* [1921] 1 AC 395, PC; *Lagan Navigation Co v Lambeg Bleaching, Dyeing and Finishing Co Ltd* [1927] AC 226, HL; *Home Brewery Co Ltd v William Davis & Co (Leicester) Ltd* [1987] QB 339, [1987] 1 All ER 637. The principle is limited in that, while the owner is entitled to protect himself against such incursions, if the incursion has already happened or is about to happen he must not export it to his neighbour: *Arscott v Coal Authority* [2004] EWCA Civ 892, [2005] Env LR 6, [2004] All ER (D) 194 (Jul). See also *Whalley v Lancashire and Yorkshire Rly Co* (1884) 13 QBD 131, CA.
4   *Harrison v Duke of Rutland* [1893] 1 QB 142, CA (trespasser interfering with sporting rights); *Cope v Sharpe (No 2)* [1912] 1 KB 496, CA (gamekeeper setting fire to strips of heather to protect sporting rights).
5   See the Offences Against the Person Act 1861 s 31; and ANIMALS vol 2 (2008) PARA 802.
6   *Cresswell v Sirl* [1948] 1 KB 241, [1947] 2 All ER 730, CA (dog); *Hamps v Darby* [1948] 2 KB 311, [1948] 2 All ER 474, CA (homing pigeons). Cf *Deane v Clayton* (1817) 7 Taunt 489 (unlawful traps); *Tutton v AD Walter Ltd* [1986] QB 61, [1985] 3 All ER 757 (liability in negligence for spraying crop with insecticide, killing the claimants' bees). See also ANIMALS vol 2 (2008) PARAS 742, 929. As to the killing of or injury to dogs worrying livestock see now the Animals Act 1971 s 9; and ANIMALS vol 2 (2008) PARA 928.
7   *Selby v Nettlefold* (1873) 9 Ch App 111, CA. See REAL PROPERTY AND REGISTRATION vol 87 (2012) PARA 962. As to trespass to land see PARA 563 et seq.

464.   Necessity as a defence to claim in tort.   The defence of necessity is a special application of the wider defence of justification[1]. The defence of necessity is available in respect of what would otherwise be a tortious interference with persons[2] or property[3] in order to avoid greater harm. The action may be taken for either public[4] or private[5] purposes, but must not be negligent[6].

1   As to the defence of justification see PARA 461.
2   *Re F (mental patient: sterilisation)* [1990] 2 AC 1, sub nom *F v West Berkshire Health Authority (Mental Health Act Commission intervening)* [1989] 2 All ER 545, HL. A child or an unconscious or severely handicapped person may be medically treated without consent in his best interests, but a fully competent adult may not be so treated, no matter how great the risk of serious consequences unless (inter alia) the medical practitioner reasonably believes the patient lacks capacity in relation to the matter: see the Mental Capacity Act 2005 s 5; and MENTAL HEALTH AND CAPACITY vol 75 (2013) PARA 611. As to children see *Re M (child: refusal of medical treatment)* [1999] 2 FCR 577, [1999] 2 FLR 1097. As to fully competent adults see *St George's Healthcare NHS Trust v S, R v Collins, ex p S* [1999] Fam 26, [1998] 3 All ER 673, CA; *Secretary of State for the Home Department v Robb* [1995] Fam 127, [1995] 1 All ER 677 (no duty to force-feed prisoner on hunger-strike) (not following *Leigh v Gladstone* (1906) 26 TLR 139). As regards adults lacking capacity see *Re F (mental patient: sterilisation)* [1990] 2 AC 1, sub nom *F v West Berkshire Health Authority (Mental Health Act Commission intervening)* [1989] 2 All ER 545, HL; *Re T (adult: refusal of treatment)* [1993] Fam 95, sub nom *Re T (adult: refusal of medical treatment)* [1992] 4 All ER 649, CA; *Re MB (adult: medical treatment)* [1997] 2 FCR 541, [1997] 2 FLR 426, CA; *Re S (adult patient: sterilisation)* [2001] Fam 15, [2000] 2 FCR 452 (assessment of best interests). A pregnant woman's entitlement to

decide whether to undergo medical treatment is undiminished by her pregnancy, and prevails over the interests of the unborn child: *St George's Healthcare NHS Trust v S, R v Collins, ex p S* [1999] Fam 26, [1998] 3 All ER 673, CA.

3 *Mouse's Case* (1609) 12 Co Rep 63 (jettison); *Handcock v Baker* (1800) 2 Bos & P 260 (breaking and entry to prevent murder); *Dewey v White* (1827) Mood & M 56 (demolishing structure rendered dangerous by fire); *Cope v Sharpe (No 2)* [1912] 1 KB 496, CA (entering land and burning heather to create fire break); cf *Carter v Thomas* [1893] 1 QB 673 (officious interference with fire fighters; assault); *Burmah Oil Co (Burma Trading) Ltd v Lord Advocate* [1965] AC 75 at 165, [1964] 2 All ER 348 at 396, HL, per Lord Upjohn (pulling down property to prevent the spread of fire is now likely to be unreasonable: one should normally call the fire brigade). More may be done to save human life than property: *Southport Corpn v Esso Petroleum Co Ltd* [1953] 2 All ER 1204 at 1209–1210, [1953] 3 WLR 773 at 778–779 per Devlin J (affd *Esso Petroleum Co Ltd v Southport Corpn* [1956] AC 218, [1955] 3 All ER 864, HL). It is doubtful if a party whose property has been harmed may claim compensation: *Dewey v White* (1827) Mood & M 56; *Governor and Co of British Cast Plate Manufacturers v Meredith* (1794) 4 Term Rep 794 at 797 obiter per Buller J; *Southport Corpn v Esso Petroleum Co Ltd* [1953] 2 All ER 1204 at 1209, [1953] 3 WLR 773 at 778 per Devlin J. As to acts done by the Crown in defence of the realm see *The Case of the King's Prerogative in Saltpetre* (1606) 12 Co Rep 12; *A-G v De Keyser's Royal Hotel Ltd* [1920] AC 508, HL; *Burmah Oil Co (Burma Trading) Ltd v Lord Advocate* [1965] AC 75, [1964] 2 All ER 348, HL (revsd by the War Damage Act 1965 s 1(1)); *A-G v Nissan* [1970] AC 179 at 227–228, [1969] 1 All ER 629 at 651, HL, per Lord Pearce (Crown must pay for property taken in exercise of prerogative).

The defence is narrowly circumscribed and requires extreme need: *Southwark London Borough Council v Williams* [1971] Ch 734, [1971] 2 All ER 175, CA (necessity did not excuse squatting by homeless); *John Trenberth Ltd v National Westminster Bank* (1979) 39 P & CR 104 (need to repair buildings did not excuse entry without permission on adjacent land; but see now the Access to Neighbouring Land Act 1992 s 1(2) making provision for court order on application).

4 Eg defence of the realm (see *Case of the King's Prerogative in Saltpetre* (1606) 12 Co Rep 12; *A-G v De Keyser's Royal Hotel* [1920] AC 508, HL; *Burmah Oil Co (Burmah Trading) Ltd v Lord Advocate* [1965] AC 75, [1964] 2 All ER 348, HL); safety of highway (see *Dewey v White* (1827) Mood & M 56); saving life (see *Mouse's Case* (1609) 12 Co Rep 63; *Howard v Frith* (1666) 2 Keb 58; *Handcock v Baker* (1800) 2 Bos & P 260 (prevention of murder)).

5 *Cope v Sharpe (No 2)* [1912] 1 KB 496 (saving property from fire).

6 *Esso Petroleum Co Ltd v Southport Corpn* [1956] AC 218 at 235, [1955] 3 All ER 864 at 866, HL, per Earl Jowitt, and at 242 and 872 per Lord Radcliffe; *Rigby v Chief Constable of Northamptonshire* [1985] 2 All ER 985, [1985] 1 WLR 1242 (necessary to fire CS gas into building occupied by dangerous intruder but negligent to do so without available fire fighting facilities).

465. Consent as a defence to claim in tort. It is a defence that the claimant consented to acts or omissions which would otherwise have been tortious[1]. Where the claimant freely and with full knowledge exposes himself to the risk of injury or loss from another person's breach of a duty to take reasonable care this is a defence to an action for breach of that duty; the rule is expressed in the maxim volenti non fit injuria and rests on to the claimant's voluntary assumption, not merely knowledge, of the risk[2].

Delay in complaining does not of itself establish a defence of acquiescence in trespass. The other party must have been misled to his or her detriment[3].

It is not a defence to an action for nuisance that the claimant came to the nuisance[4].

1 Eg in relation to such torts as trespass to the person (see PARA 525 et seq), trespass to land (see PARA 563 et seq), wrongful interference with goods (see PARA 602 et seq), defamation (see DEFAMATION vol 32 (2012) PARA 501 et seq).

2 See NEGLIGENCE vol 78 (2010) PARA 69 et seq. For this defence in relation to breach of statutory duty see PARA 519.

3 *Jones v Stones* [1999] 1 WLR 1739, 78 P & CR 293, CA; cf *Habib Bank Ltd v Habib Bank AG Zurich* [1981] 2 All ER 650, [1981] 1 WLR 1265, CA. See also *Willmott v Barber* (1880) 15

ChD 96; *Shaw v Applegate* [1978] 1 All ER 123, [1977] 1 WLR 970, CA; *Taylors Fashions Ltd v Liverpool Victoria Trustees Co* [1982] QB 133n, [1981] 1 All ER 897, CA.
4   See NUISANCE vol 78 (2010) PARA 198.

466.   Contracting out of tortious liability.   Where parties may lawfully consent they may agree that one or more of them is not to be under liability to the other or others either in particular respects or more generally; however, freedom to contract out of liability in tort has been greatly restricted by statute[1].

1   See the Unfair Contract Terms Act 1977; the Road Traffic Act 1988 s 149; and NEGLIGENCE vol 78 (2010) PARA 74.

467.   Illegality and ex turpi causa.   The court may refuse to entertain a claim which would be in breach of public policy as expressed by the maxim ex turpi causa non oritur actio[1]. That policy is not based upon a single justification but on a group of reasons which vary in different circumstances[2]. A person participating in a criminal enterprise may be barred from recovery in respect of harm resulting directly from the illegal activity[3]. A civil court will not award damages to compensate a claimant for loss which flows from his deprivation of liberty or other punishment which the criminal courts have imposed on him in respect of a criminal act for which he was responsible[4].

1   Ie an action does not arise from a base cause. As to criminal acts in general see *Askey v Golden Wine Co Ltd* [1948] 2 All ER 35 (food safety); *Murphy v Culhane* [1977] QB 94, [1976] 3 All ER 533, CA (affray); *Meah v McCreamer (No 2)* [1986] 1 All ER 943, [1985] NLJ Rep 80 (sexual assaults); *Clunis v Camden and Islington Health Authority* [1998] QB 978, [1998] 3 All ER 180, CA (manslaughter); *Vellino v Chief Constable of Greater Manchester Police* [2001] EWCA Civ 1249, [2002] 3 All ER 78, [2002] 1 WLR 218 (injury while attempting to evade arrest); *Gray v Thames Trains Ltd* [2009] UKHL 33, [2009] 4 All ER 81, (2009) 108 BMLR 205 (manslaughter) (applied in *Griffin v UHY Hacker Young & Partners (a firm)* [2010] EWHC 146 (Ch), [2010] All ER (D) 109 (Feb)); *Stone & Rolls Ltd (in liquidation) v Moore Stephens (a firm)* [2009] UKHL 39, [2009] AC 1391, [2009] 4 All ER 431 (fraud). Cf *Revill v Newbery* [1996] QB 567, [1996] 1 All ER 291, CA. As to joint criminal ventures see the text and note 3. As to the award of damages in respect of criminal income see *Burns v Edman* [1970] 2 QB 541, [1970] 1 All ER 886 (robber's widow); cf *Hewison v Meridian Shipping Services Pte Ltd* [2002] EWCA Civ 1821, [2003] ICR 766; *Major v Ministry of Defence* [2003] EWCA Civ 1433, 147 Sol Jo LB 1206 (both obtaining employment by deception, but with different legal results). Cf *Gray v Barr* [1971] 2 QB 554, [1971] 2 All ER 949, CA (effect of illegality on insurance). As to the rights created by illegal transactions see *Tinsley v Milligan* [1994] 1 AC 340, [1993] 3 All ER 65, HL.

    The fact that the claimant is a trespasser does not bar recovery: *Westwood v Post Office* [1974] AC 1, [1973] 3 All ER 184, HL. See also the Occupiers' Liability Act 1984; and NEGLIGENCE vol 78 (2010) PARA 40.

    The maxim ex turpi causa does not apply to losses resulting from a person's suicide in consequence of the defendant's breach of a duty of care: *Kirkham v Chief Constable of the Greater Manchester Police* [1990] 2 QB 283, [1990] 3 All ER 246, CA; and see also *Reeves v Metropolitan Police Comr* [2000] 1 AC 360, [1999] 3 All ER 897, HL. Cf *Corr v IBC Vehicles Ltd* [2008] UKHL 13, [2008] 1 AC 884, [2008] 2 All ER 943 (suicide in consequence of tortiously-caused depression).

    The public conscience test adopted in some authorities (eg *Saunders v Edwards* [1987] 2 All ER 651, [1987] 1 WLR 1116 at 1127, CA) was criticised as hard to employ in *Pitts v Hunt* [1991] 1 QB 24, [1990] 3 All ER 344, CA, and stated to be of no application in determining the rights created by illegal transactions in *Tinsley v Milligan* [1994] 1 AC 340, [1993] 3 All ER 65, HL. Cf *Gray v Thames Trains Ltd* [2009] UKHL 33 at [51], [2009] 4 All ER 81 at [51], 108 BMLR 205 at [51] per Lord Hoffmann, stating that the principle against liability for losses caused by the victim's criminal conduct was justified on the ground that it is offensive to public notions of the fair distribution of resources.

    The maxim ex turpi causa bars a company's claim to recover damages for losses caused by a fraud perpetrated by the person representing its directing mind and will, at least in the case of a one-person company: *Stone & Rolls Ltd (in liquidation) v Moore Stephens (a firm)* [2009]

UKHL 39, [2009] AC 1391, [2009] 4 All ER 431 (distinguished in *Bilta (UK) Ltd (in liquidation) v Nazir* [2013] EWCA Civ 968, [2014] Ch 52, [2014] 1 All ER 168).

2 *Gray v Thames Trains Ltd* [2009] UKHL 33 at [30], [2009] 4 All ER 81 at [30], 108 BMLR 205 at [30] per Lord Hoffmann; cited with approval in *Stone & Rolls Ltd (in liquidation) v Moore Stephens (a firm)* [2009] UKHL 39 at [25], [2009] AC 1391 at [25], [2009] 4 All ER 431 at [25] per Lord Phillips.

3 *National Coal Board v England* [1954] AC 403 at 429, [1954] 1 All ER 546 at 558, HL, per Lord Asquith; *Ashton v Turner* [1981] QB 137, [1980] 3 All ER 870 (accident in getaway car); *Pitts v Hunt* [1991] 1 QB 24, [1990] 3 All ER 344, CA (encouragement of grossly dangerous motor cycling). Cf *Burrows v Rhodes* [1899] 1 QB 816 (misrepresentation that act was lawful excluded ex turpi causa); *Lane v Holloway* [1968] 1 QB 379, [1967] 3 All ER 129, CA (gross inequality of strength in a fight excluded ex turpi causa). See also *Al Hassan-Daniel v Revenue and Customs Comr* [2010] EWCA Civ 1443, [2011] QB 866, [2011] 2 All ER 31 (criminality defence did not operate under European Convention on Human Rights so as to bar a claim); *Les Laboratoires Servier v Apotex Inc* [2014] UKSC 55, [2014] 3 WLR 1257, [2015] 1 All ER 671 (availability of defence to claim on cross-undertaking in damages in patent infringement action).

4 *Askey v Golden Wine Co Ltd* [1948] 2 All ER 35; *Clunis v Camden and Islington Health Authority* [1998] QB 978, [1998] 3 All ER 180, CA; *Gray v Thames Trains Ltd* [2009] UKHL 33, [2009] 4 All ER 81, (2009) 108 BMLR 205. The decision to the contrary of Woolf J in *Meah v McCreamer* [1985] 1 All ER 367 cannot be regarded as authoritative.

468. No defence of inevitable accident to a claim in tort. Inevitable accident no longer exists as a separate defence. A person is not liable in negligence unless the claimant proves that the defendant failed to take reasonable care[1]. In trespass, too, it now seems that the claimant fails unless he proves that the defendant either intentionally or negligently committed the wrongful act[2]. Where the tort is one of strict or absolute liability, it is no defence for the defendant to prove inevitable accident[3].

1 See NEGLIGENCE vol 78 (2010) PARA 62 et seq.
2 See eg PARA 573. Even negligence may be insufficient: see PARA 525.
3 See eg NUISANCE vol 78 (2010) PARA 148.

469. Act of God. Where an injury results from natural causes which could not have been foreseen and could not have been avoided by any amount of foresight and care which could reasonably have been expected, it may be said to result from an act of God[1]. Thus in one sense it is merely a type of inevitable accident, and so relied on mainly in order to rebut an allegation of negligence[2], but its particular quality is that it affords a defence to common law torts involving strict or absolute liability[3].

1 An act of God is 'something in opposition to the act of man': *Forward v Pittard* (1785) 1 Term Rep 27 at 33 per Lord Mansfield CJ. For other examples see *Keighley's Case* (1609) 10 Co Rep 139a at 139b; *R v Leicestershire Justices* (1850) 15 QB 88 (death of another person); *Blyth v Birmingham Waterworks Co* (1856) 11 Exch 781 (extraordinary frost); *Briddon v Great Northern Rly Co* (1858) 28 LJ Ex 51 (snowfall); *Cuckson v Stones* (1858) 1 E & E 248 at 256; *Carstairs v Taylor* (1871) LR 6 Exch 217 (leak caused by rat); *Thomas v Birmingham Canal Co* (1879) 49 LJQB 851, DC; *Dixon v Metropolitan Board of Works* (1881) 7 QBD 418 at 421–422 per Lord Coleridge CJ; *Fobbing Sewers Comrs v R* (1886) 11 App Cas 449, HL; *Re Bird, Bird v Cross* (1894) 8 R 326 (onset of mental disorder). Cf *Dale v Hall* (1750) 1 Wils 281; *Oakley v Portsmouth and Ryde Steam Packet Co* (1856) 11 Exch 618 (strong tide); *Fenwick v Schmalz* (1868) LR 3 CP 313 at 316 (ordinary snowfall); *Liver Alkali Co v Johnson* (1874) LR 9 Exch 338 (fog); *Hamilton, Fraser & Co v Pandorf & Co* (1887) 12 App Cas 518, HL (rats on boat); *Greenock Corpn v Caledonian Rly Co* [1917] AC 556, HL (rain); *Cushing v Peter Walker & Son (Warrington & Burton) Ltd* [1941] 2 All ER 693 at 695 per Hallett J (gale); *Greenwood Tileries Ltd v Clapson* [1937] 1 All ER 765 at 772 per Branson J (high tide). An act of God does not rebut an allegation of negligence where it was itself the result of negligence: *Lords Bailiff-Jurats of Romney Marsh v The Corpn of the Trinity House* (1872) LR 7 Exch 247.
2 As to inevitable accident see PARA 468.

3   *Nichols v Marsland* (1876) 2 ExD 1, CA (distinguished by *Greenock Corpn v Caledonian Rly Co* [1917] AC 556, HL). See also NUISANCE vol 78 (2010) PARA 152.

(7) REMEDIES FOR TORTS

(i) Damages

470. Duty to minimise damage. There is a duty upon those who have been tortiously injured to mitigate their loss. They are under an obligation to take all reasonable steps to minimise the resulting damage and, in so far as they would have succeeded in so doing, the tortfeasor is relieved of the obligation to compensate them[1]. Where a person, acting reasonably after suffering a tortious injury, so conducts himself as undesignedly to aggravate his damage, such additional loss is recoverable from the tortfeasor[2].

1   See *Jones v Watney, Combe, Reid & Co Ltd* (1912) 28 TLR 399. The burden is on the defendant to prove that the claimant has failed to take reasonable steps to mitigate his loss: *Geest plc v Lansiquot* [2002] UKPC 48, [2003] 1 All ER 383, [2002] 1 WLR 3111 (disapproving *Selvanayagam v University of the West Indies* [1983] 1 All ER 824, [1983] 1 WLR 585, PC); *LE Jones (Insurance Brokers) Ltd v Portsmouth City Council* [2002] EWCA Civ 1723, [2003] 1 WLR 427, (2002) 87 ConLR 169. As to the duty to mitigate losses see further DAMAGES vol 29 (2014) PARAS 378–381.
2   *Wilson v United Counties Bank Ltd* [1920] AC 102 at 125, HL, per Lord Atkinson; *Wieland v Cyril Lord Carpets Ltd* [1969] 3 All ER 1006; *Pigney v Pointers Transport Services* [1957] 2 All ER 807, [1957] 1 WLR 1121; *The City of Lincoln* (1889) 15 PD 15, CA; but cf *McKew v Holland and Hannen and Cubitts (Scotland) Ltd* [1969] 3 All ER 1621, HL. As to medical treatment see *McAuley v London Transport Executive* [1957] 2 Lloyd's Rep 500, CA; *Selvanayagam v University of the West Indies* [1983] 1 All ER 824, [1983] 1 WLR 585, PC (which, it is submitted, appears wrong in placing the burden of proof of reasonableness on the plaintiff: see *Geest plc v Lansiquot* [2002] UKPC 48, [2003] 1 All ER 383, [2002] 1 WLR 3111; and note 1). See also *Roper v Johnson* (1873) LR 8 CP 167.

471. Recovery of damages and interest. The ordinary remedy for tortious injury is a claim for damages[1].

In proceedings for the recovery of damages the High Court or the County Court has a discretion to award simple interest on the damages in respect of which judgment is given or payment is made before judgment[2]. Interest is at such rate as the court thinks fit or as rules of court provide on all or any part of the damages for all or any part of the period between the date when the cause of action arose and the date of the judgment or, in the case of any sum paid before judgment, the date of the payment[3].

Where judgment is given for damages for personal injuries[4] or death which exceed £200, the High Court or the County Court is required to award interest unless it is satisfied that there are special reasons to the contrary[5].

Similar provisions require other courts of record to award interest on damages for personal injuries or death which exceed £200, but this duty and the discretion of such courts to award interest in other cases is only in respect of damages for which judgment has been given[6], not damages for which payment is made before judgment[7].

1   See DAMAGES vol 29 (2014) PARA 408 et seq.
2   See the Senior Courts Act 1981 s 35A(1) (s 35A added by the Administration of Justice Act 1982 s 15(1), Sch 1 Pt I); the County Courts Act 1984 s 69(1) (amended by the Civil Procedure Act 1997 s 10, Sch 2 para 2(2)); and DAMAGES vol 29 (2014) PARA 635. See also CIVIL PROCEDURE.
3   See the Senior Courts Act 1981 s 35A(1) (as added: see note 2); the County Courts Act 1984 s 69(1); and DAMAGES vol 29 (2014) PARA 635. See also CIVIL PROCEDURE. The Arbitration

Act 1996 gives arbitrators the power, subject to contrary agreement, to award simple or compound interest, from the date of the award or later date, until payment: see s 49(4); and ARBITRATION vol 2 (2008) PARA 1260. Interest on damages for pain, suffering and loss of amenities should be awarded from the date of the service of the claim form rather than the date when the cause of action arose: *Jefford v Gee* [1970] 2 QB 130, [1970] 1 All ER 1202, CA. Equity may also use compound interest in requiring a fiduciary to account: *Wallersteiner v Moir (No 2)* [1975] QB 373, [1975] 1 All ER 849, CA.

4 'Personal injuries' includes any disease and any impairment of a person's physical or mental condition: see the Senior Courts Act 1981 s 35A(7) (as added: see note 2); and the County Courts Act 1984 s 69(6). As to damages for personal injuries see DAMAGES vol 29 (2014) PARA 434 et seq.

5 See the Senior Courts Act 1981 s 35A(1), (2) (as added: see note 2); and the County Courts Act 1984 s 69(1), (2); and DAMAGES vol 29 (2014) PARA 635.

6 See the Law Reform (Miscellaneous Provisions) Act 1934 s 3(1), (1A) (s 3(1A) added by the Administration of Justice Act 1969 s 22). The Law Reform (Miscellaneous Provisions) Act 1934 s 3 is repealed in relation to the High Court and the County Court by the Administration of Justice Act 1982 s 15(4), (5).

7 Cf the text to note 2.

472. Election to sue for money had and received. Where a claimant has the choice of suing in tort or bringing a claim in restitution, if he elects to sue in restitution and signs judgment he cannot thereafter pursue his claim in tort[1]. The most common illustration is where the defendant wrongfully takes the claimant's goods and sells them, and the claimant, instead of suing for wrongful interference with his goods, obtains judgment in restitution for the price received by the defendant[2].

1 *United Australia Ltd v Barclays Bank Ltd* [1941] AC 1, [1940] 4 All ER 20, HL. See RESTITUTION vol 88 (2012) PARA 563. See also *Tang Man Sit v Capacious Investments Ltd* [1996] AC 514, [1996] 1 All ER 193, PC; *Island Records Ltd v Tring International plc* [1995] 3 All ER 444, [1996] 1 WLR 1256.

2 See *United Australia Ltd v Barclays Bank Ltd* [1941] AC 1, [1940] 4 All ER 20, HL. As to wrongful interference with goods see PARA 602 et seq.

473. Tort damages in light of rights under the European Convention on Human Rights. The remedy available for a tortious act may not infringe rights under the Convention for the Protection of Human Rights and Fundamental Freedoms (1950)[1]. Thus damages for a tortious act may be reduced where they have initially been set at such a high level as to threaten the principle of respect for freedom of expression guaranteed by the Convention[2].

1 Ie the Convention for the Protection of Human Rights and Fundamental Freedoms (Rome, 4 November 1950; TS 71 (1953); Cmd 8969) ('the European Convention on Human Rights'). See further PARA 810; and RIGHTS AND FREEDOMS vol 88A (2013) PARA 301 et seq.

2 *Rantzen v Mirror Group Newspapers Ltd* [1994] QB 670, [1993] 4 All ER 975, CA; *John v MGN Ltd* [1997] QB 586, [1996] 2 All ER 35, CA. See further DEFAMATION. As to the right to freedom of expression see the European Convention on Human Rights art 10(1); and RIGHTS AND FREEDOMS vol 88A (2013) PARA 398 et seq.

474. Recovery without civil proceedings. A person who has suffered loss or damage may sometimes be able to obtain compensation or recover money or property without resorting to civil proceedings, whether in tort or otherwise[1]. A court by or before which a person is convicted of an offence, instead of or in addition to dealing with him in any other way, may, on application or otherwise, make an order (a 'compensation order') requiring him to pay compensation for any personal injury, loss or damage resulting from that offence or any other offence which is taken into consideration by the court in determining sentence, or to make payments for funeral expenses or bereavement in respect of a death resulting from any such offence, other than a death due to an accident arising out of the presence of a motor vehicle on a road[2].

A person who has suffered personal injury may also be eligible for a payment under the Criminal Injuries Compensation Scheme[3]. An owner of property which has come into the possession of the police in connection with their investigation of a suspected offence, or because it has been used for purposes of crime, may apply to a magistrates' court for an order for the delivery of the property to him[4]. Where goods have been stolen, the court by or before which the offender is convicted may on the conviction order them to be restored to any person entitled to recover them from him or pay to such person a sum not exceeding the value of the stolen goods[5].

1   Indeed, the claimant may have no cause of action against the person ordered to pay compensation: *R v Chappell* (1985) 80 Cr App Rep 31, 6 Cr App Rep (S) 214, CA (where any civil claim by HM Customs and Excise in respect of VAT would have lain only against the offender's company). See also *Issa v Hackney London Borough Council* [1997] 1 All ER 999, [1997] 1 WLR 956, CA (compensation order where no other remedy for statutory nuisance).
2   See the Powers of Criminal Courts (Sentencing) Act 2000 ss 130–134; and SENTENCING AND DISPOSITION OF OFFENDERS vol 92 (2010) PARA 375 et seq. See also PARA 403.
3   See the Criminal Injuries Compensation Act 1995; and CRIMINAL PROCEDURE vol 28 (2010) PARA 905 et seq. See also PARA 403.
4   See the Police (Property) Act 1897 s 1; the Powers of Criminal Courts (Sentencing) Act 2000 ss 143–144; POLICE AND INVESTIGATORY POWERS vol 84A (2013) PARA 635; and PARA 664 et seq.
5   See the Powers of Criminal Courts (Sentencing) Act 2000 ss 148, 149; and SENTENCING AND DISPOSITION OF OFFENDERS vol 92 (2010) PARA 388.

(ii) Injunctions

475.   Availability of injunction as a remedy.   There is a discretion in the High Court or County Court to grant injunctions[1] compelling persons to do[2] or restraining them from doing[3] acts where otherwise the claimant will suffer, or continue to suffer, wrongful injury for which an award of damages will not adequately compensate him[4]. A restrictive (or prohibitory) injunction[5] may be perpetual or of an interim character[6] and may be granted where injury has already been caused and will otherwise continue, or where it has not yet been caused but is imminently threatened[7]. The court has jurisdiction to award damages either in addition to or in substitution for an injunction and even where the injury is only threatened[8].

1   As to the jurisdiction to grant injunctions see CIVIL PROCEDURE vol 11 (2009) PARA 340 et seq.
2   As to mandatory injunctions generally see CIVIL PROCEDURE vol 11 (2009) PARA 376 et seq.
3   As to restrictive injunctions generally see CIVIL PROCEDURE vol 11 (2009) PARA 356 et seq.
4   See CIVIL PROCEDURE vol 11 (2009) PARA 356.
5   Although a mandatory injunction may be granted by way of interim relief, it is less readily granted before the action is determined: CIVIL PROCEDURE vol 11 (2009) PARA 378.
6   As to interim injunctions generally see CIVIL PROCEDURE vol 11 (2009) PARA 383 et seq.
7   As to injunctions in respect of threatened injury see CIVIL PROCEDURE vol 11 (2009) PARA 384.
8   See CIVIL PROCEDURE vol 11 (2009) PARA 364 et seq. See also DAMAGES vol 29 (2014) PARA 615 et seq.

(iii) Self-redress

476.   Availability of self-redress as a remedy.   In certain cases the law recognises a right to redress for wrongs done without having recourse to the courts; rights to use force within the limits allowed for the defence of persons or of property or to take steps for the protection of property are rights of self-help, but are also of the nature of defences against wrongs in course of commission, and are discussed elsewhere[1]. There is a right of redress for trespass by encroachment on property, the occupier wronged being entitled at common law to remove the encroachment, but, other than in similar simple cases that do not justify the expense of legal proceedings, self-redress in respect of trespass to land is appropriate only in urgent cases which require an immediate remedy[2]. However, the right to retake chattels from a person who has wrongfully taken possession of them generally justifies any assault incidental to the retaking, provided no more force is used than is necessary[3]. It may also be noted that trespassing animals may be detained to secure compensation for damage done by them[4].

1 See PARAS 462–463. As to the defence of necessity see PARAS 461, 464.
2 See *Burton v Winters* [1993] 3 All ER 847 at 851–852, [1993] 1 WLR 1077 at 1081–1082, CA, per Lloyd LJ. It seems therefore no longer to be the case that, if a stranger erects by way of trespass a building on the land of another, the latter is entitled to pull it down in ejecting the intruder: *Burling v Read* (1850) 11 QB 904. As to the expulsion of trespassers see PARA 588. As to the restrictions on entry by force see PARA 589.
3 *R v Milton* (1827) Mood & M 107; *Blades v Higgs* (1865) 11 HL Cas 621. See also PARA 662.
4 See the Animals Act 1971 s 7; and ANIMALS vol 2 (2008) PARAS 758–759.

477. Abatement of nuisances. Although the remedy of abatement of a private nuisance is not one which is favoured by the law[1], a person who is damaged by a private nuisance is, in general, entitled to abate it, and for this purpose to enter after notice (except in emergency)[2] on the land of another person, provided that a breach of the peace is not caused[3]. Highway authorities have a like common law right, and by statute have other remedies[4]. The right of abatement extends to public nuisances, but some damage to the individual abating it over and above that caused to other members of the public must be shown[5].

A person entitled to the benefit of a private right of way may abate a nuisance arising from its obstruction and, in general, a dominant owner may abate interference with his easement and for that purpose may enter on the servient tenement[6].

1 See *Lagan Navigation Co v Lambeg Bleaching, Dyeing and Finishing Co Ltd* [1927] AC 226, HL; and NUISANCE vol 78 (2010) PARA 214.
2 See NUISANCE vol 78 (2010) PARA 218.
3 As to abatement see NUISANCE vol 78 (2010) PARA 214 et seq.
4 See HIGHWAYS, STREETS AND BRIDGES vol 55 (2012) PARA 343 et seq.
5 See NUISANCE vol 78 (2010) PARA 216.
6 See REAL PROPERTY AND REGISTRATION vol 87 (2012) PARAS 937–939.

(8) EXTINCTION OF LIABILITY IN TORT

(i) Limitation of Actions

478. Most tort claims to be brought within six years of cause of action. The Limitation Act 1980 provides that in general an action founded on tort may not be brought after the expiration of six years from the date on which the cause of action accrued[1]. To this there is the important exception of actions in respect of personal injuries, for which a time limit of three years is normally prescribed[2], and actions brought in defamation and malicious falsehood, for which a time limit of one year is normally prescribed[3]. Special rules also apply to tort claims in respect of successive conversions[4], conversion of goods following theft[5] and actions in respect of defective products[6].

1 See the Limitation Act 1980 s 2; and LIMITATION PERIODS vol 68 (2008) PARA 979 et seq. As to when a cause of action accrues see PARA 479. As to exceptions to the six-year limitation period see PARA 480 et seq.
2 See PARAS 481–482.
3 See the Limitation Act 1980 ss 4A, 32A; and DEFAMATION vol 32 (2012) PARAS 671, 776.
4 See the Limitation Act 1980 s 3; and LIMITATION PERIODS vol 68 (2008) PARA 987 et seq. As to conversion of goods see PARA 604 et seq.
5 See the Limitation Act 1980 s 4; and LIMITATION PERIODS vol 68 (2008) PARA 990.
6 See the Limitation Act 1980 s 11A; and LIMITATION PERIODS vol 68 (2008) PARAS 1003–1004. See also CONSUMER PROTECTION vol 21 (2011) PARA 651.

479. When a cause of action accrues. Other than in cases of personal injuries[1], the limitation period generally runs from when the cause of action accrues[2]. In respect of those torts which are actionable without proof of damage, such as trespass and libel, the cause of action accrues, and the period of limitation therefore generally runs, from the date of the tortious act[3]. Where the tort is committed only if damage is proved, for example in cases of negligence, the cause of action accrues from the date of the damage[4].

1 As to the limitation period in the case of personal injury claims see PARA 481.
2 As to the alternative limitation period for a claim in negligence relating to latent damage see PARA 480.
3 See LIMITATION PERIODS vol 68 (2008) PARAS 993–997. As to where a right of action is concealed by fraud see LIMITATION PERIODS vol 68 (2008) PARA 1220 et seq.
4 See *Pirelli General Cable Works Ltd v Oscar Faber & Partners* [1983] 2 AC 1, [1983] 1 All ER 65, HL; and LIMITATION PERIODS vol 68 (2008) PARA 980 et seq.

480. Alternative limitation period in negligence for latent damage. In a negligence action where facts relevant to the cause of action are not known at the date of its accrual, an alternative three-year limitation period[1] runs from the earliest date on which the claimant or any person in whom the cause of action was vested before him first had both the knowledge[2] required for bringing an action for damages in respect of the relevant damage and a right to bring such an action, if that period expires later than the normal six-year limitation period[3]. In negligence actions not involving personal injuries, an overriding time limit of 15 years from the date of the negligence applies[4].

1 See the Limitation Act 1980 s 14A; and LIMITATION PERIODS vol 68 (2008) PARA 982. The special time limit given in such cases is confined to actions claiming damages for negligence where the duty of care the breach of which constitutes the negligence relied on arises in tort, and does not apply to claims framed in contract: *Société Commerciale de Réassurance v ERAS (International) Ltd, Re ERAS EIL appeals* [1992] 2 All ER 82n, [1992] 1 Lloyd's Rep 570, CA.
2 'Knowledge' includes knowledge which the person might reasonably have been expected to acquire from facts observable or ascertainable by him or from facts ascertainable by him with the help of appropriate expert advice which it is reasonable for him to seek; but a person is not taken to have knowledge of a fact ascertainable only with the help of expert advice so long as he has taken all reasonable steps to obtain (and, where appropriate, to act on) that advice: Limitation Act 1980 s 14A(10) (s 14A added by the Latent Damage Act 1986 s 1). As to the knowledge necessary to start time running against a claimant see further *Haward v Fawcetts (a firm)* [2006] UKHL 9, [2006] 3 All ER 497, [2006] 1 WLR 682; and LIMITATION PERIODS vol 68 (2008) PARA 982.
3 See LIMITATION PERIODS vol 68 (2008) PARA 982.
4 See the Limitation Act 1980 s 14B (added by the Latent Damage Act 1986 s 1); and LIMITATION PERIODS vol 68 (2008) PARA 982.

481. Limitation of personal injury actions. Any action for damages for negligence, nuisance or breach of duty (including trespass to the person[1]), where the damages claimed by the claimant for the negligence, nuisance or breach of duty consist of or include damages in respect of personal injuries to the claimant or any other person, may not be brought after the expiration of a specified period[2]. The period is three years from the date on which the cause of action accrued, or the date of knowledge[3], if later, of the person injured[4]. However, where the person injured dies before the expiration of that period, the period specified as respects the cause of action surviving for the benefit of the deceased's estate is three years from the date of death or the date of the knowledge of the personal representative, whichever is the later[5].

The special time limit for actions in respect of personal injuries does not apply to any action brought for damages under the Protection from Harassment Act 1997[6].

1   *Letang v Cooper* [1965] 1 QB 232, [1964] 2 All ER 929, CA; *A v Hoare* [2008] UKHL 6, [2008] 1 AC 844, [2008] 2 All ER 1, departing from *Stubbings v Webb* [1993] AC 498, [1993] 1 All ER 322, HL.
2   See the Limitation Act 1980 s 11(1), (2); and LIMITATION PERIODS vol 68 (2008) PARA 998 et seq.
3   As to the meaning of 'date of knowledge' see the Limitation Act 1980 s 14; and LIMITATION PERIODS vol 68 (2008) PARA 999. See also *Simpson v Norwest Holst (Southern) Ltd* [1980] 2 All ER 471, [1980] 1 WLR 968; *Halford v Brookes* [1991] 3 All ER 559, [1991] 1 WLR 428, CA; *Adams v Bracknell Forest Borough Council* [2004] UKHL 29, [2005] 1 AC 76, [2004] 3 All ER 897; *A v Hoare* [2008] UKHL 6, [2008] 1 AC 844, [2008] 2 All ER 1.
4   See the Limitation Act 1980 s 11(4); and LIMITATION PERIODS vol 68 (2008) PARA 998.
5   See the Limitation Act 1980 s 11(5); and LIMITATION PERIODS vol 68 (2008) PARA 998.
6   Ie under the Protection from Harassment Act 1997 s 3 (see PARA 558): see the Limitation Act 1980 s 11(1A); and LIMITATION PERIODS vol 68 (2008) PARA 998.

482. Claims under the Fatal Accidents Act 1976. An action under the Fatal Accidents Act 1976[1] may not be brought if the death occurred when the person injured could no longer maintain an action and recover damages in respect of the injury, whether because of a time limit in the Limitation Act 1980 or in any other Act, or for any other reason[2]. The action may not be brought after the expiration of three years from the date of death, or the date of knowledge[3] of the person for whose benefit the action is brought, whichever is the later[4].

1   See PARA 488; and NEGLIGENCE vol 78 (2010) PARA 25 et seq. See also DAMAGES vol 29 (2014) PARA 489 et seq.
2   See the Limitation Act 1980 s 12(1); and LIMITATION PERIODS vol 68 (2008) PARA 1000.
3   As to the meaning of 'date of knowledge' see the Limitation Act 1980 s 14; and LIMITATION PERIODS vol 68 (2008) PARA 999.
4   See the Limitation Act 1980 s 12(2); and LIMITATION PERIODS vol 68 (2008) PARA 1000.

483. Court's power to override time limits. If it appears to the court that it would be equitable to allow an action to proceed having regard to the degree to which:

(1)   the provisions in respect of the special time limit for personal injury actions[1] or actions under the Fatal Accidents Act 1976[2] prejudice the claimant or any person whom he represents[3]; and

(2)   any decision of the court would prejudice the defendant or any person whom he represents[4],

the court may direct that those provisions are not to apply to the action or are not to apply to any specified cause of action to which the action relates[5]. This power extends to actions in respect of defective products[6] except where the damages claimed by the claimant are confined to damages for loss of or damage to property[7], but does not allow the court to exclude the overriding time limit of ten years from the time the defendant supplied the product to another (or other relevant time)[8].

1   See PARA 481.
2   See PARA 482.
3   See the Limitation Act 1980 s 33(1)(a); and LIMITATION PERIODS vol 68 (2008) PARA 1001.
4   See the Limitation Act 1980 s 33(1)(b); and LIMITATION PERIODS vol 68 (2008) PARA 1001.
5   See the Limitation Act 1980 s 33(1); and LIMITATION PERIODS vol 68 (2008) PARA 1001. For the circumstances to which the court must have regard in exercising its discretion see s 33(3), (4); and LIMITATION PERIODS vol 68 (2008) PARA 1002. The court has a broad and unfettered discretion which should not be confined to exceptional cases: *Horton v Sadler* [2006] UKHL 27, [2007] 1 AC 307, [2006] 3 All ER 1177. See also *McCafferty v Metropolitan Police District Receiver* [1977] 2 All ER 756, [1977] 1 WLR 1073, CA; *Firman v Ellis* [1978] QB 886, [1978] 2 All ER 851, CA; *Simpson v Norwest Holst Southern Ltd* [1980] 2 All ER 471, [1980] 1 WLR 968; *Thompson v Brown Construction (Ebbw Vale) Ltd* [1981] 2 All ER 296, [1981] 1 WLR 744, HL; *Halford v Brookes* [1991] 3 All ER 559, [1991] 1 WLR 428, CA; *Coad v Cornwall and Scilly Isles Health Authority* [1997] 1 WLR 189, [1997] 8 Med LR 154, CA; *Adams v Bracknell Forest Borough Council* [2004] UKHL 29, [2005] 1 AC 76, [2004] 3 All ER 897; *A v Hoare* [2008] UKHL 6, [2008] 1 AC 844, [2008] 2 All ER 1 at [52] per Lord Hoffmann, and at [84]–[89] per Lord Brown; *Cain v Francis* [2008] EWCA Civ 1451, [2009] QB 754, [2009] 2 All ER 579; *AB v Nugent Care Society* [2009] EWCA Civ 827, [2010] 1 FLR 707, [2009] Fam Law 1045.
6   Ie actions for damages by virtue of any provision of the Consumer Protection Act 1987 Pt I (ss 1–9) (see the Limitation Act 1980 s 11A (added by the Consumer Protection Act 1987 Sch 1 Pt I para 1)). Discretionary exclusion of the time limit in respect of such actions is allowed by the Limitation Act 1980 s 33(1).
7   See the Limitation Act 1980 s 33(1A)(b); and LIMITATION PERIODS vol 68 (2008) PARA 1003.
8   See the Limitation Act 1980 ss 11A(3), 33(1A)(a); and LIMITATION PERIODS vol 68 (2008) PARA 1003. As to the meaning of 'relevant time' see the Consumer Protection Act 1987 s 4(2); and LIMITATION PERIODS vol 68 (2008) PARA 1003.

(ii) Waiver and Release

484. Waiver of right to sue in tort. Waiver is the abandonment of a right, and thus is a defence against its subsequent enforcement[1]. Waiver may be by way of release by deed or accord and satisfaction[2]. The phrase 'waiver of tort' is also sometimes used to describe the claimant's election to seek restitution rather than pursuing his claim in tort: having done so, he cannot then seek damages for the tort[3]. Alternatively, where there is knowledge of the right, a waiver may be implied from conduct which is inconsistent with the continuance of the right, provided the other party is thereby induced to act to his detriment[4]. A deliberate election not to insist on full rights, although made without first obtaining full disclosure of material facts, and to come to a settlement on that basis, will be binding[5].

1   *Banning v Wright* [1972] 2 All ER 987 at 998, [1972] 1 WLR 972 at 979, HL, per Lord Hailsham LC. See also EQUITABLE JURISDICTION vol 47 (2014) PARA 250. If the cause of action is not extinguished that is not a waiver in the sense meant here.
2   See PARA 485.
3   *Brewer v Sparrow* (1827) 7 B & C 310. Cf *Rice v Reed* [1900] 1 QB 54, CA. See further PARA 472. As to restitution see further RESTITUTION. As to the measure of damages for tort see DAMAGES vol 29 (2014) PARA 408 et seq.
4   *Greenwich Healthcare NHS Trust v London and Quadrant Housing Trust* [1998] 3 All ER 437, [1998] 1 WLR 1749. Cf *Armstrong v Sheppard and Short Ltd* [1959] 2 QB 384, [1959] 2 All ER 651, CA (lack of knowledge of right). Delay in complaining does not of itself establish a defence of acquiescence in trespass: see *Jones v Stones* [1999] 1 WLR 1739, 78 P & CR 293, CA.
5   See *Law v Law* [1905] 1 Ch 140 at 158, CA, where, on a settlement of an action involving a charge of fraud, full disclosure of assets was not required by the party agreeing the settlement.

485. Release of right of action in tort. A release of a right of action may be by deed or by accord and satisfaction. A release by deed is binding even though there is no consideration[1]; but to constitute accord and satisfaction there must be satisfaction, or the promise of satisfaction, as well as the agreement or accord[2]. The scope of the release is determined according to ordinary rules applicable to the interpretation of contracts and depends on the parties' intentions[3]; whether acceptance of part-payment in respect of the claim entails a full discharge is therefore a question to be addressed on the specific facts of each case[4]. A release may be general or relate to specific claims or heads of claim[5]. A general release is an agreement containing widely drawn general words releasing all claims one party may have against the other out of the matters in dispute[6]. A party may agree to release claims or rights of which he is unaware, at least in a compromise agreement supported by valuable consideration[7], if appropriate language is used to make plain that that is his intention, but the court will be very slow to infer that he has done so in the absence of clear language[8]. A release may be vitiated by fraud[9].

In the case of joint torts, the release of one joint tortfeasor discharges the others, unless the claimant reserves his rights against the others; neither a covenant not to sue nor the release of a several tortfeasor liable for the same damage has the same effect[10]. If there are several claimants in respect of a tort affecting their part ownership of property, a release by one, or accord and satisfaction by one, will be good against all unless there is fraud[11].

1   See CONTRACT vol 22 (2012) PARAS 614–615 (releases); DEEDS AND OTHER INSTRUMENTS vol 32 (2012) PARA 475 (covenant not to sue). For an example of a case in which there was a release of a cause of action in respect of tortious acts see *Phillips v Clagett* (1843) 11 M & W 84.

2   The promise itself of one party may, in a proper case, constitute the satisfaction. As to accord and satisfaction generally see CONTRACT vol 22 (2012) PARA 605 et seq.

3   See e g *Bank of Credit and Commerce International SA (in liquidation) v Ali* [2001] UKHL 8 at [8], [2002] 1 AC 251 at [8], [2001] 1 All ER 961 at [8] per Lord Bingham, and at [22] per Lord Nicholls.

4   See *Day v McLea* (1889) 22 QBD 610, CA; *Neuchatel Asphalte Co Ltd v Barnett* [1957] 1 All ER 362, [1957] 1 WLR 356, CA; *Bell v Galynski and A Kings Loft Extensions* [1974] 2 Lloyd's Rep 13, CA; cf *D & C Builders Ltd v Rees* [1966] 2 QB 617, [1965] 3 All ER 837, CA; and CONTRACT vol 22 (2012) PARA 606.

5   *Stewart v Great Western Rly Co* (1865) 2 De GJ & Sm 319 (accord); *Hirschfeld v London, Brighton and South Coast Rly Co* (1876) 2 QBD 1, CCR (deed).

6   See e g *Roberts v Eastern Counties Rly Co* (1859) 1 F & F 460. However, acceptance of a settlement from one tortfeasor bars continuance of proceedings against another, whether the liability is joint or several, if the entire sum agreed upon is received and it was intended to be in full satisfaction of the claim: see PARA 449.

7   *Bank of Credit and Commerce International SA (in liquidation) v Ali* [2001] UKHL 8 at [22], [2002] 1 AC 251 at [22], [2001] 1 All ER 961 at [22] per Lord Nicholls. Despite the general words, such a release is ordinarily limited to those matters that were specially in the contemplation of the parties at the time: *London and South Western Rly Co v Blackmore* (1870) LR 4 HL 610 at 623 per Lord Westbury; *Bank of Credit and Commerce International SA (in liquidation) v Ali* [2001] UKHL 8 at [41]–[42], [2002] 1 AC 251 at [41]–[42], [2001] 1 All ER 961 at [41]–[42] per Lord Hoffmann (dissenting on the interpretation of the release on the facts).

8   *Salkeld v Vernon* (1798) 1 Eden 64 at 67–68 per Lord Keeper Henley.

9   *Bank of Credit and Commerce International SA (in liquidation) v Ali* [2001] UKHL 8 at [9]–[10], [2002] 1 AC 251 at [9]–[10], [2001] 1 All ER 961 at [9]–[10] per Lord Bingham.

10 See PARA 449.

11 *Wallace v Kelsall* (1840) 7 M & W 264; *Phillips v Clagett* (1843) 11 M & W 84.

(iii) Judgment

486. Judgment recovered; res judicata. If judgment[1] is recovered, the cause of action merges in the judgment, a conception which is expressed in the maxim 'transit in rem judicatam', and accordingly the claimant cannot sue again in respect of the same cause of action: he is estopped[2]. This doctrine affords no bar unless the cause of action is the same and the claimant sues in the same legal capacity in both claims[3]. A comparable estoppel (issue estoppel) arises where, even if there are two causes of action, there has been a decision on the same issue as between the same parties[4]. There is also a broader principle by which the claimant may be estopped from bringing a claim which properly belonged to earlier proceedings and with reasonable diligence might have been brought forward at that time[5].

Distinct from estoppel in principle, but analogous in result, is the rule that damages are assessed once and for all, as a consequence of which a claimant must sue once only for all his present and future losses from one cause of action and cannot bring successive claims in respect of parts of his losses[6]. However, if the continuance or repetition of a tort gives rise to fresh causes of action, new proceedings may be founded on these[7].

1   Ie a final judgment: see CIVIL PROCEDURE.
2   See generally CIVIL PROCEDURE vol 12 (2009) PARA 1190; and *Brunsden v Humphrey* (1884) 14 QBD 141 at 147–148, CA, per Bowen LJ. As to estoppel see further ESTOPPEL.
3   See CIVIL PROCEDURE vol 12 (2009) PARA 1183. For example, a claim by a person in his personal capacity, or as administrator of a deceased's estate, or as the representative of the deceased's dependants, does not preclude subsequent litigation in the other capacities: *Leggott v Great Northern Rly Co* (1876) 1 QBD 599; *Marginson v Blackburn Borough Council* [1939] 2 KB 426, [1939] 1 All ER 273, CA. See also *C (a minor) v Hackney London Borough Council* [1996] 1 All ER 973, [1996] 1 WLR 789, CA.
4   *Marginson v Blackburn Borough Council* [1939] 2 KB 426, [1939] 1 All ER 273, CA. As to issue estoppel see CIVIL PROCEDURE vol 12 (2009) PARA 1179 et seq.
5   *Henderson v Henderson* (1843) 3 Hare 100 at 115 per Wigram VC; *Talbot v Berkshire County Council* [1994] QB 290, [1993] 4 All ER 9, CA; *Wain v F Sherwood & Sons Transport Ltd* [1999] PIQR P159, (1998) Times, 16 July, CA. This principle seems to have been ignored in some cases (see *Brunsden v Humphrey* (1884) 14 QBD 141; *Darley Main Colliery Co v Mitchell* (1886) 11 App Cas 127 at 144–145, HL, per Lord Bramwell) which should therefore be treated with care.
6   See DAMAGES vol 29 (2014) PARA 335 et seq. See also *Fetter v Beale* (1701) 1 Ld Raym 339; *Brunsden v Humphrey* (1884) 14 QBD 141 at 148, CA, per Bowen LJ; *Rothwell v Chemical and Insulating Ltd* [2007] UKHL 39 at [14], [2008] AC 281 at [14], [2007] 4 All ER 1047 at [14] per Lord Hoffmann. The general rule is qualified in that provisional awards of damages and variable periodical payment orders may be made: see the Senior Courts Act 1981 s 32A; the Damages Act 1996 s 2; and the Damages (Variation of Periodical Payments) Order 2005, SI 2005/841; and DAMAGES vol 29 (2014) PARA 485. See also CIVIL PROCEDURE vol 12 (2009) PARA 1217.
7   See DAMAGES vol 29 (2014) PARA 338.

(iv) Death

487. Survival of causes of action on death. The common law rule that actions in tort do not survive for the benefit of or against the estate of a deceased person has been substantially abolished by statute[1]. On the death of any person all causes of action in tort other than defamation[2] which subsist against him now survive against his estate[3].

On the death of any person all causes of action in tort other than defamation or a claim for damages for bereavement[4] which vest in him now survive for the benefit of his estate[5].

1   As to the common law rule see *Rose v Ford* [1937] AC 826 at 841–842, [1937] 3 All ER 359 at 367–368, HL, per Lord Wright.
2   As to defamation see PARAS 559–561; and DEFAMATION vol 32 (2012) PARA 501 et seq.

3   See the Law Reform (Miscellaneous Provisions) Act 1934 s 1(1); and WILLS AND INTESTACY vol 103 (2010) PARAS 1279–1280.
4   As to claims for damages for bereavement see the Fatal Accidents Act 1976 s 1A; PARA 488; and NEGLIGENCE vol 78 (2010) PARAS 25–28. See also DAMAGES vol 29 (2014) PARA 495.
5   See the Law Reform (Miscellaneous Provisions) Act 1934 s 1(1), (1A); and WILLS AND INTESTACY vol 103 (2010) PARAS 1279–1280.

488.   Dependants' claims under the Fatal Accidents Act 1976.
Notwithstanding the death of the person injured, a person is liable to a claim for damages at the suit of a personal representative suing on behalf of particular classes of dependant under the Fatal Accidents Act 1976 if the death has been caused by any wrongful act, neglect or default which is such as would have entitled the person injured, had death not ensued, to maintain a claim and recover damages against the person liable in respect of it[1]. Damages are based on the amount of pecuniary benefit which the dependants might reasonably have been expected to enjoy had the deceased person not been killed[2]. In addition certain classes of dependant are entitled to a fixed sum in respect of damages for bereavement[3].

1   See the Fatal Accidents Act 1976 ss 1, 2; and NEGLIGENCE vol 78 (2010) PARAS 25–28. See also DAMAGES vol 29 (2014) PARA 489 et seq.
2   See NEGLIGENCE vol 78 (2010) PARA 25 et seq.
3   See the Fatal Accidents Act 1976 s 1A; and DAMAGES vol 29 (2014) PARA 495; NEGLIGENCE vol 78 (2010) PARA 25.

(9) TORTS COMMITTED ABROAD

489.   The Rome II Regulation.   Under the Rome II Regulation[1], which is directly applicable in English law, the general rule is that the law applicable to a non-contractual obligation arising out of a tort is the law of the country in which the damage occurs irrespective of the country in which the event giving rise to the damage occurred and irrespective of the country or countries in which the indirect consequences of that event occur[2]. However, where the person claimed to be liable and the person sustaining damage both have their habitual residence[3] in the same country at the time when the damage occurs, the law of that country applies[4]. Where it is clear from all the circumstances of the case that the tort or delict is manifestly more closely connected with a country other than that indicated by the above, the law of that other country applies[5]. Special provisions govern the law applicable to non-contractual obligations arising out of damage caused by a product[6], an act of unfair competition or a restriction of free competition[7], environmental damage[8], an infringement of intellectual property rights[9], and an industrial action[10]. Without prejudice to the rights of third parties, the parties may agree to submit non-contractual obligations to the law of their choice, either by an agreement entered into after the event giving rise to the damage occurred, where all the parties are pursuing a commercial activity, also by an agreement freely negotiated before the event giving rise to the damage occurred or, where all the parties are pursuing a commercial activity, also by an agreement freely negotiated before the event giving rise to the damage occurred[11]. However, where all the elements relevant to the situation at the time when the event giving rise to the damage occurs are located in a country other than the country whose law has been chosen, the choice of the parties is not to prejudice the application of provisions of the law of that other country which cannot be derogated from by agreement[12].

The law applicable to non-contractual obligations under the provisions described above governs in particular:

(1)   the basis and extent of liability, including the determination of persons who may be held liable for acts performed by them;

(2)   the grounds for exemption from liability, any limitation of liability and any division of liability;

(3)   the existence, the nature and the assessment of damage or the remedy claimed;

(4)   within the limits of powers conferred on the court by its procedural law, the measures which a court may take to prevent or terminate injury or damage or to ensure the provision of compensation;

(5)   the question whether a right to claim damages or a remedy may be transferred, including by inheritance;

(6)   persons entitled to compensation for damage sustained personally;

(7)   liability for the acts of another person; and

(8)   the manner in which an obligation may be extinguished and rules of prescription and limitation, including rules relating to the commencement, interruption and suspension of a period of prescription or limitation[13].

In assessing the conduct of the person claimed to be liable, account must be taken, as a matter of fact and in so far as is appropriate, of the rules of safety and conduct which were in force at the place and time of the event giving rise to the liability[14]. Nothing in the Rome II Regulation restricts the application of the provisions of the law of the forum in a situation where they are mandatory irrespective of the law otherwise applicable to the non-contractual obligation[15]. The person having suffered damage may bring his or her claim directly against the insurer of the person liable to provide compensation if the law applicable to the non-contractual obligation or the law applicable to the insurance contract so provides[16]. Provision is also made as to subrogation[17] and multiple liability[18].

A unilateral act intended to have legal effect and relating to a non-contractual obligation is formally valid if it satisfies the formal requirements of the law governing the non-contractual obligation in question or the law of the country in which the act is performed[19]. The law governing a non-contractual obligation under the Rome II Regulation applies to the extent that, in matters of non-contractual obligations, it contains rules which raise presumptions of law or determine the burden of proof[20]. Acts intended to have legal effect may be proved by any mode of proof recognised by the law of the forum or by any of the laws referred to above[21] under which that act is formally valid, provided that such mode of proof can be administered by the forum[22].

These provisions also apply in case of conflicts between the laws of different parts of the United Kingdom[23].

1   Ie European Parliament and Council Regulation (EC) 864/2007 (OJ L199, 31.7.2007, p 40) on the law applicable to non-contractual obligations (the 'Rome II Regulation'). See CONFLICT OF LAWS.

2   European Parliament and Council Regulation (EC) 864/2007 (OJ L199, 31.7.2007, p 40) art 4(1).

3   For the purposes of the Rome II Regulation, the habitual residence of companies and other bodies, corporate or unincorporated, is the place of central administration; and where the event giving rise to the damage occurs, or the damage arises, in the course of operation of a branch, agency or any other establishment, the place where the branch, agency or any other establishment is located is to be treated as the place of habitual residence: European Parliament and Council Regulation (EC) 864/2007 (OJ L199, 31.7.2007, p 40) art 23(1). For the purposes

of the Regulation, the habitual residence of a natural person acting in the course of his or her business activity is his or her principal place of business: art 23(2).

4 European Parliament and Council Regulation (EC) 864/2007 (OJ L199, 31.7.2007, p 40) art 4(2). The application of the law of any country specified by the Regulation means the application of the rules of law in force in that country other than its rules of private international law, ie renvoi is excluded: art 24.

5 European Parliament and Council Regulation (EC) 864/2007 (OJ L199, 31.7.2007, p 40) art 4(3). A manifestly closer connection with another country might be based in particular on a pre-existing relationship between the parties, such as a contract, that is closely connected with the tort or delict in question: art 4(3).

6 See European Parliament and Council Regulation (EC) 864/2007 (OJ L199, 31.7.2007, p 40) art 5; and CONSUMER PROTECTION.

7 See European Parliament and Council Regulation (EC) 864/2007 (OJ L199, 31.7.2007, p 40) art 6; and COMPETITION.

8 See European Parliament and Council Regulation (EC) 864/2007 (OJ L199, 31.7.2007, p 40) art 7; and ENVIRONMENTAL QUALITY AND PUBLIC HEALTH.

9 See European Parliament and Council Regulation (EC) 864/2007 (OJ L199, 31.7.2007, p 40) art 8; and COPYRIGHT; PATENTS AND REGISTERED DESIGNS; TRADE MARKS AND TRADE NAMES.

10 See European Parliament and Council Regulation (EC) 864/2007 (OJ L199, 31.7.2007, p 40) art 9; and EMPLOYMENT.

11 European Parliament and Council Regulation (EC) 864/2007 (OJ L199, 31.7.2007, p 40) art 14(1). The choice must be expressed or demonstrated with reasonable certainty by the circumstances of the case: art 14(1).

12 European Parliament and Council Regulation (EC) 864/2007 (OJ L199, 31.7.2007, p 40) art 14(2). Where all the elements relevant to the situation at the time when the event giving rise to the damage occurs are located in one or more of the member states, the parties' choice of the law applicable other than that of a member state is not to prejudice the application of provisions of European Union law, where appropriate as implemented in the member state of the forum, which cannot be derogated from by agreement: art 14(3).

13 European Parliament and Council Regulation (EC) 864/2007 (OJ L199, 31.7.2007, p 40) art 15. The Regulation departs from previous English law (see *Harding v Wealands* [2006] UKHL 32, [2007] 2 AC 1, [2006] 4 All ER 1) in treating the assessment of damage as a matter within the scope of the law applicable.

14 European Parliament and Council Regulation (EC) 864/2007 (OJ L199, 31.7.2007, p 40) art 17.

15 European Parliament and Council Regulation (EC) 864/2007 (OJ L199, 31.7.2007, p 40) art 16.

16 European Parliament and Council Regulation (EC) 864/2007 (OJ L199, 31.7.2007, p 40) art 18.

17 See European Parliament and Council Regulation (EC) 864/2007 (OJ L199, 31.7.2007, p 40) art 19.

18 See European Parliament and Council Regulation (EC) 864/2007 (OJ L199, 31.7.2007, p 40) art 20.

19 European Parliament and Council Regulation (EC) 864/2007 (OJ L199, 31.7.2007, p 40) art 21.

20 European Parliament and Council Regulation (EC) 864/2007 (OJ L199, 31.7.2007, p 40) art 22(1).

21 Ie referred to in European Parliament and Council Regulation (EC) 864/2007 (OJ L199, 31.7.2007, p 40) art 21: see the text to note 19.

22 European Parliament and Council Regulation (EC) 864/2007 (OJ L199, 31.7.2007, p 40) art 22(2).

23 European Parliament and Council Regulation (EC) 864/2007 (OJ L199, 31.7.2007, p 40) art 25; Law Applicable to Non-Contractual Obligations (England and Wales and Northern Ireland) Regulations 2008, SI 2008/2986, reg 6.

490. Where the Rome II Regulation does not apply. By statute[1], the applicable law for determining issues relating to tort[2] which do not fall to be determined under the provisions of European Union (EU) law[3] is in general the law of the country in which the events constituting the tort in question occur[4]. The statutory provisions apply irrespective of whether the relevant events occur in the forum or in some other country[5]. The general rule may be displaced where it is substantially more appropriate for the applicable law to be that of some other country connected with the tort[6]. The statutory provisions do not in any case apply to affect the determination of issues arising in any defamation claim[7], which continues to be governed by rules of the common law[8]. The jurisdiction of any court in England and Wales or Northern Ireland to entertain proceedings for trespass to or any other tort affecting immovable property extends to cases in which the property in question is situated outside that part of the United Kingdom unless the proceedings are principally concerned with a question of the title to, or the right to possession of, that property[9].

1   Ie the Private International Law (Miscellaneous Provisions) Act 1995 Pt III (ss 9–15), which came into force on 1 May 1996 (see s 16(3); and the Private International Law (Miscellaneous Provisions) Act 1995 (Commencement) Order 1996, SI 1996/995). As to the application of the Private International Law (Miscellaneous Provisions) Act 1995 Pt III to the Crown see s 15; and for transitional and saving provisions see s 14. As to private international law see further CONFLICT OF LAWS.

2   See the Private International Law (Miscellaneous Provisions) Act 1995 s 9(1), (2); and CONFLICT OF LAWS vol 19 (2011) PARA 662. The applicable law must be used for determining the issues arising in a claim, including in particular the question whether an actionable tort has occurred: see s 9(4); and CONFLICT OF LAWS vol 19 (2011) PARA 662. The applicable law to be used is to exclude any choice of law rules forming part of the law of the country or countries concerned: see s 9(5); and CONFLICT OF LAWS vol 19 (2011) PARA 662.

3   Ie the European Parliament and Council Regulation (EC) 864/2007 (OJ L199, 31.7.2007, p 40) on the law applicable to non-contractual obligations (the 'Rome II Regulation') (see PARA 489): Private International Law (Miscellaneous Provisions) Act 1995 s 15A(1) (s 15A added by SI 2008/2986). Conflicts solely between the laws of different parts of the United Kingdom fall to be determined under the above provisions of EU law for these purposes: Private International Law (Miscellaneous Provisions) Act 1995 s 15A(2) (as so added).

4   See the Private International Law (Miscellaneous Provisions) Act 1995 s 11(1); and CONFLICT OF LAWS vol 19 (2011) PARA 663. Where elements of those events occur in different countries, the applicable law under the general rule is to be taken as being:
    (1)   for a cause of action in respect of personal injury caused to an individual or death resulting from personal injury, the law of the country where the individual was when he sustained the injury (s 11(2)(a));
    (2)   for a cause of action in respect of damage to property, the law of the country where the property was when it was damaged (s 11(2)(b)); and
    (3)   in any other case, the law of the country in which the most significant element or elements of those events occurred (s 11(2)(c)).
    For these purposes, 'personal injury' includes disease or any impairment of physical or mental condition: s 11(3). See further CONFLICT OF LAWS vol 19 (2011) PARA 663.
    Rules of the common law, in so far as they:
    (a)   require actionability under both the law of the forum and the law of another country for the purpose of determining whether a tort is actionable; or
    (b)   allow (as an exception from the rules falling with head (a)) for the law of a single country to be applied for the purpose of determining the issues, or any of the issues, arising from the case in question,
    are abolished except in relation to the determination of issues arising in any defamation claim: see ss 10, 13; and CONFLICT OF LAWS vol 19 (2011) PARA 662.
    In so far as Pt III extends to any country within the United Kingdom, the 'forum' means England and Wales, Scotland or Northern Ireland, as the case may be: see s 9(7). Except where otherwise provided, the provisions of Pt III extend to England and Wales, Scotland and Northern Ireland: see s 18(3) (amended by SI 2008/2986). As to the meaning of 'United Kingdom' see PARA 452 note 3.

5   See the Private International Law (Miscellaneous Provisions) Act 1995 s 9(6); and CONFLICT OF LAWS vol 19 (2011) PARA 662.

6   See the Private International Law (Miscellaneous Provisions) Act 1995 s 12; and CONFLICT OF LAWS vol 19 (2011) PARA 664. As to the meaning of 'substantially more appropriate' see *R (on the application of Al-Jedda) v Secretary of State for Defence* [2007] UKHL 58, [2008] 1 AC 332, [2008] 3 All ER 28.

7   See the Private International Law (Miscellaneous Provisions) Act 1995 ss 9(3), 13(1); and CONFLICT OF LAWS vol 19 (2011) PARA 647. As to the meaning of 'defamation claim' for these purposes see s 13(2); and CONFLICT OF LAWS vol 19 (2011) PARA 671.

8   See the Private International Law (Miscellaneous Provisions) Act 1995 ss 10, 13; note 3; and CONFLICT OF LAWS vol 19 (2011) PARAS 662, 671. As to torts not governed by the Private International Law (Miscellaneous Provisions) Act 1995 see CONFLICT OF LAWS vol 19 (2011) PARAS 667–671.

9   Civil Jurisdiction and Judgments Act 1982 s 30(1). According to s 30(2) (amended by the Civil Jurisdiction and Judgments Act 1991 s 3, Sch 2 para 13; SI 2001/3929) (as read with the Civil Jurisdiction and Judgments Act 1982 s 1(1) (amended by SI 2001/3929; SI 2007/1655; and SI 2014/2947)) (see CONFLICT OF LAWS vol 19 (2011) PARAS 366, 688 et seq) this has effect subject to:

   (1)   the Convention on Jurisdiction and the Enforcement of Judgments in Civil and Commercial Matters (Brussels, 27 September 1968; EC 46 (1978); Cmnd 7395) (set out in the Civil Jurisdiction and Judgments Act 1982 Sch 1);

   (2)   the Convention on Jurisdiction and Enforcement of Judgments in Civil and Commercial Matters (Lugano, 16 September 1988; OJ L319, 25.11.88, p 9) (including the Protocols annexed to that Convention), which was signed by the United Kingdom on 18 September 1989 (set out in the Civil Jurisdiction and Judgments Act 1982 Sch 3C);

   (3)   European Parliament and Council Regulation (EU) 1215/2012 on jurisdiction and the recognition and enforcement of judgments in civil and commercial matters (recast) (OJ L351, 20.12.2012, p 1) as amended from time to time and as applied by virtue of the Agreement made on 19 October 2005 between the European Community and the Kingdom of Denmark on jurisdiction and the recognition and enforcement of judgments in civil and commercial matters (OJ L299, 16.11.2005, p 62; OJ L79, 21.3.2013, p 4); and

   (4)   the provisions as to allocation of jurisdiction within the United Kingdom in certain civil proceedings set out in the Civil Jurisdiction and Judgments Act 1982 Sch 4.

2. GENERAL TORTIOUS LIABILITIES

(1) INTENTIONAL INJURY

491. Intentional injury in general. There is no specific tort of causing harm intentionally or even maliciously[1]. Liability has to be brought under one of a number of more specific heads[2]. These liabilities for intentional injury receive a degree of special treatment in law.

Generally, torts of intentional injury protect against injury in a wider range of circumstances than torts of negligence, for example in respect of pure economic loss[3] and injuries to personal autonomy not involving physical harm[4].

The compensation available in respect of torts of intentional injury may also be more extensive than that available in respect of negligence. The tort of deceit[5] attracts a special measure of damages[6] which renders the defendant answerable for all losses flowing directly from the fraudulent statement, whether they were foreseeable or not[7]. A similar measure may follow from other torts which are deliberately committed[8], such as those forms of conversion which constitute an intentional and malicious interference with another's interest in goods[9].

A further distinction may be drawn as regards defences. The defendant to a claim in tort for deceit is unable to rely on the defence of contributory negligence[10], a disability which also appears to affect those who commit other deliberate torts[11], though the availability of the defence in claims for assault and battery is not settled[12].

Vicarious liability[13] may be harder to exact from a tortfeasor's employer in the case of a deliberate tort, largely because of the difficulty of holding that a malicious or dishonest act, committed without the knowledge or authority of the employer, is performed in the course of the employer's employment[14]. Liability for some deliberate torts may be attributable to the employer only where he expressly or impliedly authorised the commission of the tort, or where the employee had ostensible authority to commit it[15].

A bailee is answerable for a theft or other deliberate wrong committed or connived at by an employee who has been engaged by him only where the bailee entrusted the goods to the employee for the purpose of delegating to him some part of the bailee's duty of care[16]; it is only in such circumstances that the employee is deemed to commit the wrongful act in the course of his employment[17].

A deliberate and malicious or dishonest tort may attract an award of punitive (or 'exemplary') damages[18].

1   In general, no actions which would be legal if done with a proper motive can become illegal because they are prompted by a motive which is improper, selfish or even malicious: see *Mayor of Bradford v Pickles* [1895] AC 587, HL. Actions done in concert may, however, give rise to tortious liability if done with the predominant purpose of causing injury: see PARA 715.

2   For example, intentional interference with the person under the rule in *Wilkinson v Downton* [1897] 2 QB 57 (see PARA 557), intentionally causing loss by unlawful means (see PARA 710), malicious falsehood (see PARA 493), and malicious prosecution (see PARA 716 et seq).

3   See PARA 701 et seq.

4   Trespass to the person is actionable per se: see PARA 525.

5   As to the various states of mind which constitute deceit see *Derry v Peek* (1889) 14 App Cas 337, HL; and MISREPRESENTATION vol 76 (2013) PARA 756. As to the tort of deceit see PARA 494; and MISREPRESENTATION vol 76 (2013) PARA 788 et seq.

6   As to damages under the Misrepresentation Act 1967 s 2 see DAMAGES vol 29 (2014) PARAS 546–547; MISREPRESENTATION vol 76 (2013) PARA 810.

7   *Smith New Court Securities Ltd v Citibank NA* [1997] AC 254, sub nom *Smith New Court Securities Ltd v Scrimgeour Vickers (Asset Management) Ltd* [1996] 4 All ER 769, HL.

8   *Smith New Court Securities Ltd v Citibank NA* [1997] AC 254 at 278–280, sub nom *Smith New Court Securities Ltd v Scrimgeour Vickers (Asset Management) Ltd* [1996] 4 All ER 769 at 790, HL, per Lord Steyn.

9   As to wrongful interference with goods see PARA 602 et seq.

10 See *Standard Chartered Bank v Pakistan National Shipping Corpn (No 2)* [2002] UKHL 43, [2003] 1 AC 959, [2003] 1 All ER 173; PARA 494; and MISREPRESENTATION vol 76 (2013) PARA 760. As to contributory negligence see PARA 518; and DAMAGES vol 29 (2014) PARA 382 et seq; NEGLIGENCE vol 78 (2010) PARA 75 et seq.

11 See e g *Corporacion Nacional del Cobre de Chile v Sogemin Metals Ltd* [1997] 2 All ER 917, [1997] 1 WLR 1396 (in which it was held that the defence of contributory negligence does not apply to a conspiracy claim based on bribery). The defence of contributory negligence does not generally apply to a claim founded on conversion or intentional trespass to goods: see the Torts (Interference with Goods) Act 1977 s 11(1); and PARA 658.

12 See DAMAGES vol 29 (2014) PARA 497.

13 As to vicarious liability see generally PARA 767 et seq.

14 See *Crédit Lyonnais Bank Nederland NV (now known as Generale Bank Nederland NV) v Export Credits Guarantee Department* [2000] 1 AC 486, [1999] 1 All ER 929, HL. See also *Makanjuola v Metropolitan Police Comr* [1992] 3 All ER 617, [1989] NLJR 468 (police officer). But c f *Kuddus v Chief Constable of Leicestershire Constabulary* [2001] UKHL 29, [2002] 2 AC 122, [2001] 3 All ER 193; *Dubai Aluminium Co Ltd v Salaam (Livingstone, third parties)* [2002] UKHL 48, [2003] 2 AC 366, [2003] 1 All ER 97; *Majrowski v Guy's and St Thomas's NHS Trust* [2006] UKHL 34, [2007] 1 AC 224, [2006] 4 All ER 395. As to the liability of an employer depending on the employee having acted in the course of employment see PARA 780.

15 *Lloyd v Grace Smith & Co* [1912] AC 716, HL. See further PARAS 778–779.

16 *United Africa Co Ltd v Saka Owaode* [1955] AC 130, [1957] 3 All ER 216, PC; *Morris v CW Martin & Sons Ltd* [1966] 1 QB 716, [1965] 2 All ER 725, CA; *Transmotors Ltd v Robertson Buckley & Co Ltd* [1970] 1 Lloyd's Rep 224; *Richmond Metal Co Ltd v J Coales & Son Ltd* [1970] 1 Lloyd's Rep 423; *Port Swettenham Authority v TW Wu & Co (M) Sdn Bhd* [1979] AC 580, [1978] 3 All ER 337, PC; *Swiss Bank Corpn v Brink's-MAT Ltd* [1986] 2 Lloyd's Rep 79; *Metrotex Pty Ltd v Freight Investments Pty Ltd* [1969] VR 9, Vict SC; *Punch v Savoy's Jewellers Ltd* (1986) 26 DLR (4th) 546, Ont CA. See BAILMENT AND PLEDGE vol 4 (2011) PARA 148.

17 *Morris v CW Martin & Sons Ltd* [1966] 1 QB 716, [1965] 2 All ER 725, CA. See also *Rustenburg Platinum Mines Ltd, Johnson Matthey (Pty) Ltd and Matthey Bishop Inc v South African Airways and Pan American World Airways Inc* [1979] 1 Lloyd's Rep 19, CA; *Photo Production Ltd v Securicor (Transport) Ltd* [1980] AC 827, [1980] 1 All ER 556, HL; c f *Irving and Irving v Post Office* [1987] IRLR 289, CA.

18 As to punitive damages (often called 'exemplary damages') see DAMAGES vol 29 (2014) PARAS 325 et seq.

(2) MISREPRESENTATION

492. The torts of misrepresentation in general. Liability for misrepresentation may arise under the specific torts of malicious falsehood (which incorporates slander of title and slander of goods)[1] and deceit[2], under the statutory cause of action created by the Misrepresentation Act 1967[3], and in the tort of negligence at common law[4].

Libel and slander[5] are torts of misrepresentation in a loose sense, but it is not for the claimant to prove that the defendant has made a false representation. Instead, it is open to the defendant to exculpate himself by proving the truth of his defamatory statement[6].

1   See PARA 493; and DEFAMATION vol 32 (2012) PARAS 504, 776–779.

2   See PARA 494; and MISREPRESENTATION vol 76 (2013) PARAS 788–789.

3   See PARA 495; and MISREPRESENTATION.

4   See PARA 496; and NEGLIGENCE.

5   See PARA 559 et seq; and DEFAMATION vol 32 (2012) PARA 501 et seq.
6   See PARA 561.

493.   Misrepresentation by malicious falsehood and slander.   A claim may be brought for written or oral falsehoods which are published maliciously and are calculated in the ordinary course of things to produce, and do produce, special damage[1]. Two particular forms of this tort of injurious falsehood are slander of title[2] and slander of goods[3]. In no form of this tort is it necessary to allege or prove special damage if:

(1)   the words on which the claim is founded are calculated to cause pecuniary damage to the claimant and are published in writing or other permanent form; or

(2)   the words are calculated to cause pecuniary damage to the claimant in respect of any office, profession, calling, trade or business held or carried on by him at the time of publication[4].

1   *Ratcliffe v Evans* [1892] 2 QB 524 at 527, CA. See also *Joyce v Sengupta* [1993] 1 All ER 897, [1993] 1 WLR 337. As to malicious or injurious falsehood see DEFAMATION vol 32 (2012) PARA 776 et seq.
2   As to slander of title see DEFAMATION vol 32 (2012) PARA 778.
3   As to slander of goods see DEFAMATION vol 32 (2012) PARA 778.
4   Defamation Act 1952 s 3(1). See further DEFAMATION vol 32 (2012) PARA 785. Provided the claimant is entitled to sue for malicious falsehood, whether on proof of special damage or by reason of s 3, he may be entitled in an appropriate case to aggravated damages for injury to feelings: *Khodaparast v Shad* [2000] 1 All ER 545, [2000] 1 WLR 618, CA. As to special damages see DAMAGES vol 29 (2014) PARA 317.

494.   Misrepresentation by deceit.   On proof of the following matters a claim in tort (often called an 'action of deceit') is maintainable for damages in respect of fraudulent misrepresentation at the suit of the person to whom the representation is made[1]:

(1)   that the alleged representation consisted of something said, written or done which amounts in law to a representation[2];

(2)   that the defendant was the person who made the representation[3];

(3)   that the claimant was the person to whom the representation was made[4];

(4)   that the representation was false[5];

(5)   that the representation was a material inducement to the claimant to act on it[6];

(6)   that the claimant in fact altered his position by it[7];

(7)   that the representation was fraudulent[8]; and

(8)   that the claimant thereby suffered damage[9].

Contributory negligence cannot be raised as a defence to an action of deceit[10].

1   As to the action of deceit generally see MISREPRESENTATION vol 76 (2013) PARA 788 et seq.
2   As to what amounts to a representation see MISREPRESENTATION vol 76 (2013) PARAS 702–714.
3   As to the representor see MISREPRESENTATION vol 76 (2013) PARAS 724–732.
4   As to the representee see MISREPRESENTATION vol 76 (2013) PARAS 733–739.
5   As to falsity see MISREPRESENTATION vol 76 (2013) PARA 740 et seq.
6   As to inducement and materiality see MISREPRESENTATION vol 76 (2013) PARAS 764–776.
7   As to alteration of position see MISREPRESENTATION vol 76 (2013) PARAS 777–779.
8   As to fraudulent misrepresentation see MISREPRESENTATION vol 76 (2013) PARAS 754–760.
9   As to damage see MISREPRESENTATION vol 76 (2013) PARAS 790–792.
10   See *Alliance and Leicester Building Society v Edgestop Ltd* [1994] 2 All ER 38, [1993] 1 WLR 1462; *Nationwide Building Society v Thimbleby & Co* [1999] All ER (D) 211. See also MISREPRESENTATION vol 76 (2013) PARA 760. As to contributory negligence see PARA 518; NEGLIGENCE vol 78 (2010) PARA 75 et seq. See also DAMAGES vol 29 (2014) PARA 382 et seq.

495. Damages under the Misrepresentation Act 1967. Where a person has entered into a contract after a misrepresentation has been made to him by another party to it and as a result he suffered loss, then, if the person making the misrepresentation would be liable to damages[1] in respect of it had the misrepresentation been made fraudulently, that person may be so liable notwithstanding that the misrepresentation was not made fraudulently, unless he proves that he had reasonable ground to believe and did believe up to the time the contract was made that the facts represented were true[2].

1   As to damages for misrepresentation see DAMAGES vol 29 (2014) PARA 426 et seq.
2   See the Misrepresentation Act 1967 s 2(1); and MISREPRESENTATION vol 76 (2013) PARA 800.

496. Negligent misrepresentation. Subject to the ordinary requirements of the law of negligence, a person may owe a duty of care not to make false statements which result in physical harm to another or to his property. In certain circumstances there may also be a duty not to make false statements which cause economic loss. In order to be liable for such a false statement the defendant must generally have assumed some responsibility for the advice, opinion or information which he has tendered to the claimant, directly or indirectly, in circumstances where he knows that the advice, opinion or information will be communicated to the claimant, either specifically or as a member of an ascertainable class, and is likely to be relied upon by the claimant for the purpose for which the communication was made, provided the circumstances are such that the claimant can reasonably rely on the defendant's skill or judgment. The duty of care may arise in such a case whether the communication is in the course of the defendant's business or on some other occasion on which it is clear that the communication was intended seriously and meant to be relied upon[1].

1   See NEGLIGENCE vol 78 (2010) PARA 14; MISREPRESENTATION vol 76 (2013) PARA 797 et seq.

(3) NEGLIGENCE

497. Negligence in general. Negligence is a specific tort and in any given circumstances is the failure to exercise that care which the circumstances demand[1]. Where there is a duty to exercise care, reasonable care must be taken to avoid acts or omissions which it can be reasonably foreseen may cause harm to the claimant's interests in so far as they fall within the scope of the duty[2]. The claimant must prove that the defendant's negligence was a cause of the harm[3].

A duty of care arises more readily in respect of personal injuries and property damage than in respect of economic loss[4]. Liability in negligence generally arises only in respect of economic losses caused by personal injuries or property damage, and only exceptionally in respect of economic losses not so caused ('pure economic loss')[5].

Negligence in the sense of the failure in any given circumstances to exercise that care which the circumstances demand may also be an element of certain other torts[6].

1   See NEGLIGENCE vol 78 (2010) PARA 1. See eg *M'Alister (or Donoghue) v Stevenson* [1932] AC 562, HL.
2   As to the duty of care see NEGLIGENCE vol 78 (2010) PARA 2 et seq.
3   See NEGLIGENCE vol 78 (2010) PARA 3.
4   *Murphy v Brentwood District Council* [1991] 1 AC 398 at 487, [1990] 2 All ER 908 at 933, HL, per Lord Oliver of Aylmerton ('something more is required').
5   See NEGLIGENCE vol 78 (2010) PARA 13.

6 Eg breach of statutory duty (see PARA 510) and occupiers' liability (see NEGLIGENCE vol 78 (2010) PARAS 32, 40). As to negligence in trespass to the person see PARA 525. As to negligence in nuisance see NUISANCE vol 78 (2010) PARA 102.

(4) UNLAWFUL CONDUCT

(i) Unlawful Conduct in General

498. Injury by unlawful conduct in general. There is no general liability for causing harm by an unlawful act or omission. Causing harm by breach of a statute is actionable only if the provision in question was intended to confer private rights of action on the victim[1]. The torts of assault, battery and false imprisonment are also crimes[2], and the crime of public nuisance gives rise to tortious liability where a person suffers special damage as a result, but there is no tort of causing harm by criminal conduct[3]. Harm that is intended pursuant to a conspiracy by unlawful means is, however, actionable in tort[4]. Nor is there a general principle of tortious liability for harm or loss that is the inevitable consequence of a person's unlawful, intentional and positive acts[5]. However, an unlawful interference with the actions of a person in which the claimant has an economic interest, done with the intention to cause loss to the claimant, may give rise to liability in the tort of causing loss by unlawful means[6]. It remains to be decided whether there is a tort comprising the intentional infliction of physical harm by unlawful means, but if there is such a tort a claim for distress is not actionable upon it[7].

1 See PARA 500 et seq.
2 As to the offences of assault and battery see CRIMINAL LAW vol 25 (2010) PARAS 157–158. As to false imprisonment see CRIMINAL LAW vol 25 (2010) PARA 145.
3 See PARA 403. As to assault, battery and false imprisonment see PARA 525 et seq. As to public nuisance see PARA 499.
4 *Revenue and Customs Comrs v Total Network SL* [2008] UKHL 19, [2008] 1 AC 1174, [2008] 2 All ER 413.
5 See *Lonrho Ltd v Shell Petroleum Co Ltd* [1982] AC 173, [1981] 2 All ER 456, HL, declining to follow *Beaudesert Shire Council v Smith* (1966) 120 CLR 145, Aust HC.
6 See *OBG Ltd v Allan* [2007] UKHL 21, [2008] 1 AC 1, [2007] 4 All ER 545; and PARA 710.
7 *Mbasogo v Logo Ltd* [2006] EWCA Civ 1370, [2007] QB 846, [2007] 2 WLR 1062.

(ii) Public Nuisance

499. Public nuisance. Any person who by any act unwarranted by law or by any omission to perform a legal duty inflicts damage, injury, discomfort or inconvenience on a class[1] of Her Majesty's subjects commits an offence known as a public nuisance[2]. If an individual has suffered some special damage over and above that inflicted on the community at large, he has a right of action in tort for that nuisance[3]. In this context, in contrast with the law of private nuisance[4], the claimant need not demonstrate any possessory or proprietary interest on his part in land affected by the defendant's act[5]; he may, for example, be a mere user of the highway[6]. In further contrast with the law of private nuisance, damages may be awarded in public nuisance for personal injury and not just for interference with the use of land[7].

1 *A-G (ex rel Glamorgan County Council and Pontardawe RDC) v PYA Quarries Ltd* [1957] 2 QB 169, [1957] 1 All ER 894, CA.
2 *R v Rimmington* [2005] UKHL 63, [2006] 1 AC 459, [2006] 2 All ER 257. See also NUISANCE vol 78 (2010) PARAS 105–106. As to closure of premises associated with persistent disorder or nuisance see CRIMINAL LAW vol 26 (2010) PARA 569 et seq.

3 See NUISANCE vol 78 (2010) PARAS 108, 187. See also *Winterbottom v Lord Derby* (1867) LR 2 Exch 316 at 321–322 per Kelly CB.
4 See PARAS 594–595.
5 See e g *Tate & Lyle Industries Ltd v GLC* [1983] 2 AC 509, [1983] 1 All ER 1159, HL (no action in private nuisance, as no private rights of property in river bed; but action in public nuisance sustainable as defendants caused special loss through interference with plaintiffs' public right of navigation).
6 See e g *Holling v Yorkshire Traction Co Ltd* [1948] 2 All ER 662; *Dollman v A & S Hillman Ltd* [1941] 1 All ER 355, CA. Cf *Trevett v Lee* [1955] 1 All ER 406, [1955] 1 WLR 113, CA.
7 *Re Corby Group Litigation* [2008] EWCA Civ 463, [2009] QB 335, [2009] 4 All ER 44.

(iii) Breach of Statutory Duty

A. NATURE OF THE CAUSE OF ACTION

500. Breach of statutory duty: essentials of cause of action. Breach of statutory duty is an independent tort recognised at common law[1]. In order to succeed the claimant must establish[2] a breach of a statutory obligation[3] which, on the proper construction of the statute[4], was intended to confer private rights of action[5] upon a class of persons of whom he is one[6]; he must establish an injury or damage[7] of a kind against which the statute was designed to give protection[8]; and he must establish that the breach of statutory obligation caused, or materially contributed to, that injury or damage, or (exceptionally) to the risk of that injury or damage[9].

A defence to such a cause of action may be specially provided by statute[10]. Contributory negligence on the part of the claimant may be established by the defendant as a partial defence[11]. The maxim volenti non fit injuria, however, is not generally applicable by way of defence to a claim founded on breach by an employer of his statutory duty[12].

1 *London Passenger Transport Board v Upson* [1949] AC 155 at 168, [1949] 1 All ER 60 at 67, HL, per Lord Wright. As to the tort of breach of statutory duty see also STATUTES AND LEGISLATIVE PROCESS vol 96 (2012) PARA 759.
2 In the absence of countervailing statutory language (see e g *Nimmo v Alexander Cowan & Sons Ltd* [1968] AC 107, [1967] 3 All ER 187, HL), the onus of proving a breach of duty lies on the claimant in a claim for breach of statutory duty as it does in a claim for negligence at common law: *Bonnington Castings Ltd v Wardlaw* [1956] AC 613 at 620, 624–625, [1956] 1 All ER 615 at 618, 621, HL. See also NEGLIGENCE vol 78 (2010) PARA 62. Much of the case law in this field was developed in interpreting the Factories Act 1961, the Coal Mines Act 1911 (repealed) and the Offices, Shops and Railway Premises Act 1963. The relevant provisions of these statutes have been repealed and replaced by regulations enacted under the Health and Safety at Work etc Act 1974 in order to give effect to European Directives: see HEALTH AND SAFETY AT WORK vol 52 (2014) PARAS 306, 310 et seq. See also MINES, MINERALS AND QUARRIES vol 76 (2013) PARAS 511, 517. Breach of a duty imposed by health and safety regulations under the Health and Safety at Work etc Act 1974 is actionable except in so far as the regulations provide otherwise: s 47(2) (amended by the Employment Protection Act 1975 ss 116, 125(3), Sch 15 para 14, Sch 18); and see HEALTH AND SAFETY AT WORK vol 52 (2014) PARA 380. Though the drafting of the regulations differs from that of the statutes, general principles such as the burden of proof, the need to prove causation and the relevance of membership of a protected class remain valid for breach of statutory duty generally.
3 The violation of rights arising under primary and secondary European Union legislation may ground a claim for, or analogous to, breach of statutory duty: see *Garden Cottage Foods Ltd v Milk Marketing Board* [1984] AC 130, [1983] 2 All ER 770, HL; *R v Secretary of State for Transport, ex p Factortame Ltd (No 7)* [2001] 1 WLR 942; *Courage Ltd v Crehan (Case C-453/99)* [2002] QB 507, [2001] ECR I-6297, ECJ; *Sempra Metals Ltd v IRC* [2007] UKHL 34 at [69], [2008] 1 AC 561 at [69], [2007] 4 All ER 657 at [69] per Lord Nicholls, at [162] per Lord Walker, and at [225] per Lord Mance. The legislation in question must entail the grant of rights to individuals: see *Three Rivers District Council v Bank of England (No 3) (Summary*

Judgment) [2001] UKHL 16, [2003] 2 AC 1, [2001] 2 All ER 513; *Poole v HM Treasury* [2007] EWCA Civ 1021, [2008] 1 All ER (Comm) 1132, [2008] Lloyd's Rep IR 134.

4 *Cutler v Wandsworth Stadium Ltd* [1949] AC 398 at 407, [1949] 1 All ER 544 at 548, HL, per Viscount Simonds; *X (minors) v Bedfordshire County Council* [1995] 2 AC 633 at 731, [1995] 3 All ER 353 at 364, HL, per Lord Browne-Wilkinson. As to the construction of statutes to ascertain whether a claim may be brought see PARA 504 et seq.

5 *X (minors) v Bedfordshire County Council* [1995] 2 AC 633 at 731, [1995] 3 All ER 353 at 364, HL, per Lord Browne-Wilkinson.

6 See PARA 506.

7 *Cullen v Chief Constable of the Royal Ulster Constabulary* [2003] UKHL 39, [2004] 3 All ER 237, [2003] 1 WLR 1763 at [41]–[44] per Lord Hutton, and at [69] per Lord Millett.

8 See PARA 507. As to the measure of damages see PARA 522.

9 *Bonnington Castings Ltd v Wardlaw* [1956] AC 613, [1956] 1 All ER 615, HL (material contribution to injury or damage); *Fairchild v Glenhaven Funeral Services Ltd* [2002] UKHL 22, [2003] 1 AC 32, [2002] 3 All ER 305 (material contribution to risk). See further PARAS 514–515.

10 See PARA 516.

11 See PARA 518.

12 See PARA 519.

501. Matters for the court to take into consideration. When a court, in considering a claim that a person was negligent[1] or in breach of statutory duty[2], is determining the steps that the person was required to take to meet a standard of care, it must have regard to[3]:

(1)   whether the alleged negligence or breach of statutory duty occurred when the person was acting for the benefit of society or any of its members[4];

(2)   whether the person, in carrying out the activity in the course of which the alleged negligence or breach of statutory duty occurred, demonstrated a predominantly responsible approach towards protecting the safety or other interests of others[5]; and

(3)   whether the alleged negligence or breach of statutory duty occurred when the person was acting heroically by intervening in an emergency to assist an individual in danger[6].

1 See NEGLIGENCE.

2 As to the essentials of the cause of action for breach of statutory duty see PARA 500.

3 Social Action, Responsibility and Heroism Act 2015 ss 1, 5. The Act only applies to a claim that a person was negligent or in breach of statutory duty where the act or omission giving rise to the claim occurred on or after 13 April 2015: Social Action, Responsibility and Heroism Act 2015 (Commencement and Transitional Provision) Regulations 2015, SI 2015/808, regs 1, 2, 3.

4 Social Action, Responsibility and Heroism Act 2015 s 2.

5 Social Action, Responsibility and Heroism Act 2015 s 3.

6 Social Action, Responsibility and Heroism Act 2015 s 4.

502. Breach of statutory duty distinguished from negligence. The civil right of action for breach of statutory duty is a claim in tort arising under the common law but must be distinguished from the cause of action for negligence[1], including negligence in the exercise of a statutory power[2]. In some cases, the same injury may give rise to both types of liability[3] but this is not invariably the case. A claimant may fail to establish breach of statutory duty but establish liability in negligence, for example, because the common law duty of care goes beyond what is required by the statute[4]. Alternatively, a claimant may establish breach of statutory duty but fail to establish liability in negligence, for example, because the statute was breached without fault[5]. Naturally there are considerable similarities between the two actions where the duty imposed by statute is a duty to take care[6]. Though compliance with statutory safety regulations does not preclude liability for common law negligence[7], it may be difficult to prove negligence against a defendant who has carried out the provisions of a detailed statutory code applicable to the circumstances in question[8]. Failure to conform with the requirements of statute, on the other hand, does not necessarily constitute negligence[9], even when it may give rise to a claim for breach of statutory duty, but it may and frequently does amount to prima facie evidence of negligence[10].

1   *Caswell v Powell Duffryn Associated Collieries Ltd* [1940] AC 152 at 177–178, [1939] 3 All ER 722 at 738–739, HL, per Lord Wright; *London Passenger Transport Board v Upson* [1949] AC 155 at 168, [1949] 1 All ER 60 at 67, HL, per Lord Wright. As to the essentials of a cause of action for breach of statutory duty see PARA 500. As to breach of statutory duty and negligence see also STATUTES AND LEGISLATIVE PROCESS vol 96 (2012) PARA 760.

2   As to the negligent exercise of statutory powers see CONSTITUTIONAL AND ADMINISTRATIVE LAW vol 20 (2014) PARA 653. See also NEGLIGENCE vol 78 (2010) PARAS 17–19.

3   *National Coal Board v England* [1954] AC 403, [1954] 1 All ER 546, HL. Cf *Graham v CE Heinke & Co Ltd* [1959] 1 QB 225, [1958] 3 All ER 650, CA (claims for negligence and breach of statutory duty with payment into court; no need to specify in respect of which claim payments were made as claims were alternative not cumulative). As to payment into court see CPR Pt 36; and CIVIL PROCEDURE.

4   See eg *Franklin v Gramophone Co Ltd* [1948] 1 KB 542, [1948] 1 All ER 353, CA; *Nolan v Dental Manufacturing Co Ltd* [1958] 2 All ER 449, [1958] 1 WLR 936; *Bux v Slough Metals Ltd* [1974] 1 All ER 262, [1973] 1 WLR 1358, CA; *Killgolan v William Cooke & Co Ltd* [1956] 2 All ER 294, [1956] 1 WLR 527, CA; *Quintas v National Smelting Co Ltd* [1961] 1 All ER 630, [1961] 1 WLR 401, CA. As to the common law duty of care see NEGLIGENCE vol 78 (2010) PARA 2.

5   See eg *John Summers & Sons Ltd v Frost* [1955] AC 740, [1955] 1 All ER 870, HL; *Kelly v WRN Contracting Ltd* [1968] 1 All ER 369, [1968] 1 WLR 921; and PARA 510.

6   *Lochgelly Iron and Coal Co Ltd v M'Mullan* [1934] AC 1 at 10, HL, per Lord Atkin, at 18 per Lord Macmillan, and at 23 per Lord Wright; *East Suffolk Rivers Catchment Board v Kent* [1941] AC 74 at 88, [1940] 4 All ER 527 at 533, HL, per Lord Atkin.

7   *Franklin v Gramophone Co Ltd* [1948] 1 KB 542, [1948] 1 All ER 353, CA; *Bux v Slough Metals Ltd* [1974] 1 All ER 262, [1973] 1 WLR 1358. See also HEALTH AND SAFETY AT WORK vol 52 (2014) PARAS 376–383.

8   *England v National Coal Board* [1953] 1 QB 724 at 731–732, [1953] 1 All ER 1194 at 1198, CA, per Somervell LJ (revsd in part but not on this point sub nom *National Coal Board v England* [1954] AC 403, [1954] 1 All ER 546, HL).

9   See eg *National Coal Board v England* [1954] AC 403 at 421, [1954] 1 All ER 546, HL, per Lord Oaksey.

10 See eg *Blamires v Lancashire and Yorkshire Rly Co* (1873) LR 8 Exch 283, Ex Ch; *Cayzer, Irvine & Co v Carron Co* (1884) 9 App Cas 873 at 880, HL, per Lord Blackburn; *Phillips v Britannia Hygienic Laundry Co Ltd* [1923] 1 KB 539 at 548, DC, per McCardie J (affd [1923] 2 KB 832, CA); *Anglo-Newfoundland Development Co Ltd v Pacific Steam Navigation Co* [1924] AC 406 at 413, HL, per Lord Dunedin; *Lochgelly Iron and Coal Co Ltd v M'Mullan* [1934] AC 1 at 13, HL, per Lord Warrington; *Grealis v Opuni* [2003] EWCA Civ 177, [2004] RTR 97, [2003] All ER (D) 254 (Jan) (breach of speed limit providing evidence of negligence). The Road Traffic Act 1988 s 38(7) expressly provides that the failure on the part of any person to observe a provision of the Highway Code may in any proceedings be relied upon by any party as tending to establish or negative any liability which is in question: see further *Powell v Phillips* [1972] 3 All ER 864 at 867–868, CA, per Stephenson LJ (considering an equivalent provision in earlier legislation); and ROAD TRAFFIC vol 89 (2011) PARA 21.

503. Breach of statutory duty distinguished from special statutory remedies. The common law claim for breach of statutory duty[1], being based on a cause of action arising at common law, is to be distinguished from such claims as those to recover the penalties[2], compensation or expenses which are expressly made recoverable by certain statutes[3], and from cases in which a statute itself expressly confers a right to claim damages[4] or limits[5] or increases[6] the damages which may be recovered in respect of a particular cause of action.

1   See PARA 500 et seq.
2   See STATUTES AND LEGISLATIVE PROCESS vol 96 (2012) PARA 756.
3   Eg in legislation regarding the sale of goods or landlord and tenant matters: see DAMAGES.
4   See eg the Protection from Harassment Act 1997 s 3(1), (2) (see PARA 558); the Fatal Accidents
      Act 1976 s 1 (see DAMAGES vol 29 (2014) PARA 492; NEGLIGENCE vol 78 (2010) PARA 25 et seq.).
5   See eg CARRIAGE AND CARRIERS vol 7 (2015) PARAS 121 et seq, 155 et seq; PATENTS AND
      REGISTERED DESIGNS vol 79 (2014) PARA 547; SHIPPING AND MARITIME LAW vol 94 (2008) PARA
      1042 et seq.
6   See eg LANDLORD AND TENANT vol 63 (2012) PARAS 815–816.

B.   CONSTRUCTION OF STATUTE TO ASCERTAIN WHETHER A CLAIM FOR BREACH OF STATUTORY
DUTY MAY BE BROUGHT

504. Breach of statutory duty; matters to be considered. Whether or not an individual can bring a common law claim in respect of a breach of a duty imposed by a statute depends upon whether the intention of the statute, considered as a whole and in the circumstances in which it was made and to which it relates, was to impose a duty enforceable by an aggrieved individual[1]. No universal rule can be formulated which will answer the question whether in any given case the statute creates a private right of action[2]. In answering the question it is, however, relevant to consider whether the statute was intended to protect a limited class of persons or the public as a whole[3], whether a special statutory remedy by way of penalty or otherwise is prescribed for breach of the statute[4], whether breach of the statute was capable of causing loss or injury of a kind for which the law generally awards damages[5], the nature of the obligation imposed[6], and the statute's general aims and objectives[7]. In the case of breach of a statutory instrument or other subordinate legislation, it may be necessary to consider whether the parent enactment contemplated the creation of civil liability by the subordinate legislation[8].

1   See *Phillips v Britannia Hygienic Laundry Co Ltd* [1923] 2 KB 832 at 841–842, CA, per
      Atkin LJ; *Clarke v Brims* [1947] KB 497 at 504–505, [1947] 1 All ER 242 at 245–246 per
      Morris J; *Solomons v R Gertzenstein Ltd* [1954] 2 QB 243 at 255, [1954] 2 All ER 625 at
      631, CA, per Somervell LJ; *X (minors) v Bedfordshire County Council* [1995] 2 AC 633 at 731,
      [1995] 3 All ER 353 at 364, HL, per Lord Browne-Wilkinson. The fact that a statutory
      provision does not refer to private rights when others expressly create them indicates that the
      former provision was not intended to create them: *Norwich Union Life Insurance Society v
      Qureshi* [1999] 2 All ER (Comm) 707, [1999] CLC 1963, CA. As to the onus of proof of breach
      of duty see PARA 500 note 2. As to the rules for the interpretation and construction of statutes
      see STATUTES AND LEGISLATIVE PROCESS vol 96 (2012) PARA 1078 et seq.
2   See *X (minors) v Bedfordshire County Council* [1995] 2 AC 633 at 731, [1995] 3 All ER 353 at
      364, HL, per Lord Browne-Wilkinson. The only rule which in all circumstances is valid is that
      the answer must depend on a consideration of the whole Act and the circumstances, including
      the existing law, in which it was enacted: *Cutler v Wandsworth Stadium Ltd* [1949] AC 398 at
      407, [1949] 1 All ER 544 at 548, HL, per Lord Simonds. See also *Lonrho Ltd v Shell
      Petroleum Co Ltd (No 2)* [1982] AC 173 at 185–186, [1981] 2 All ER 456 at 461, HL, per
      Lord Diplock.
3   See PARA 506.
4   See PARA 505.
5   *Pickering v Liverpool Daily Post and Echo Newspapers plc* [1991] 2 AC 370, [1991] 1 All ER
      622, HL.
6   The absolute nature of the obligation in question may be a factor indicating that the statute was
      not intended to create private rights of action: see *Phillips v Britannia Hygienic Laundry Co Ltd*
      [1923] 2 KB 832 at 842, CA, per Atkin LJ; *Tan Chye Choo v Chong Kew Moi* [1970] 1 All ER
      266 at 272, [1970] 1 WLR 147 at 154, PC, per Lord Morris; *Todd v Adam* [2002] EWCA Civ
      509 at [29], [2002] 2 All ER (Comm) 97 at [29], [2002] 2 Lloyd's Rep 293 at [29] per
      Neuberger J. Other factors indicating that the statute was not intended to create private rights of
      action include the procedural nature of the obligation (*Calveley v Chief Constable of the
      Merseyside Police* [1989] AC 1228, [1989] 1 All ER 1025, CA) and the discretion involved in its

performance (*X (minors) v Bedfordshire County Council* [1995] 2 AC 633 at 732, [1995] 3 All ER 353 at 365, HL, per Lord Browne-Wilkinson). As to obligations imposed on local authorities see PARA 508.

7   Regulatory or welfare legislation does not normally confer private rights of action: *X (minors) v Bedfordshire County Council* [1995] 2 AC 633 at 731–732, [1995] 3 All ER 353 at 364–365, HL, per Lord Browne-Wilkinson. See also *Newman v Francis* [1953] 1 WLR 402 (recreational spaces); *Watt v Kesteven County Council* [1955] 1 QB 408, [1955] 1 All ER 473, CA (education) (but c f *Meade v Haringey London Borough Council* [1979] 2 All ER 1016, [1979] 1 WLR 637, CA); *R v Deputy Governor of Parkhurst Prison, ex p Hague* [1992] 1 AC 58, sub nom *Hague v Deputy Governor of Parkhurst Prison* [1991] 3 All ER 733, HL (regulation of prisons); *O'Rourke v Camden London Borough Council* [1998] AC 188, [1997] 3 All ER 23, HL (social policy of housing the homeless). For general statements of relevant factors see *Cutler v Wandsworth Stadium Ltd* [1949] AC 398 at 407, [1949] 1 All ER 544 at 548, HL, per Lord Simonds; *Solomons v R Gertzenstein Ltd* [1954] 2 QB 243 at 266, [1954] 2 All ER 625 at 637, CA, per Romer LJ; *Lonrho Ltd v Shell Petroleum Co Ltd (No 2)* [1982] AC 173 at 185–186, [1981] 2 All ER 456 at 461, HL, per Lord Diplock; *X (minors) v Bedfordshire County Council* [1995] 2 AC 633 at 731, [1995] 3 All ER 353 at 364, HL, per Lord Browne-Wilkinson.

8   *R v Deputy Governor of Parkhurst Prison, ex p Hague* [1992] 1 AC 58 at 170–171, sub nom *Hague v Deputy Governor of Parkhurst Prison* [1991] 3 All ER 733 at 751, HL, per Lord Jauncey.

505. Effect of provision of statutory remedy for breach of duty. In general, where an obligation is created by statute which at the same time enforces its performance in a specified manner, that performance cannot be enforced in any other manner[1]. However, this rule is subject to the ordinary rules as to the construction of statutes[2]. Where the only manner of enforcing performance for which the statute provides is by means of criminal proceedings, there are two classes of prima facie exception to the general rule[3]. The first is where the obligation was imposed for the benefit or protection of a particular class of individuals[4]. The second is where the statute creates a public right and a particular member of the public suffers particular direct and substantial damage other than and different from that which was common to the rest of the public[5].

Where the statute creates a self-contained code in which fines are only one method of enforcement for which provision is made, that is an indicator that no civil cause of action arises[6]. The availability of general public law remedies may also point in the same direction[7].

1   See *Doe d Bishop of Rochester v Bridges* (1831) 1 B & Ad 847 at 859 per Lord Tenterden CJ; *Cutler v Wandsworth Stadium Ltd* [1949] AC 398 at 407, [1949] 1 All ER 544 at 548, HL, per Lord Simonds; and STATUTES AND LEGISLATIVE PROCESS vol 96 (2012) PARA 759. For examples see *Atkinson v Newcastle and Gateshead Waterworks Co* (1877) 2 ExD 441, CA; *Vallance v Falle* (1884) 13 QBD 109, DC; *Saunders v Holborn District Board of Works* [1895] 1 QB 64, DC; *Robinson v Workington Corpn* [1897] 1 QB 619, CA; *Phillips v Britannia Hygienic Laundry Co Ltd* [1923] 2 KB 832, CA; *Square v Model Farm Dairies (Bournemouth) Ltd* [1939] 2 KB 365, [1939] 1 All ER 259, CA; *Cutler v Wandsworth Stadium Ltd* [1949] AC 398, [1949] 1 All ER 544, HL; *Biddle v Truvox Engineering Co Ltd* [1952] 1 KB 101, [1951] 2 All ER 835; *Bollinger v Costa Brava Wine Co Ltd* [1960] Ch 262, [1959] 3 All ER 800; *Richardson v Pitt-Stanley* [1995] QB 123, [1995] 1 All ER 460, CA.

   As to statutes creating a new liability without providing a remedy see eg STATUTES AND LEGISLATIVE PROCESS vol 96 (2012) PARA 761. As to the position where a statute provides a new remedy where a remedy already exists see STATUTES AND LEGISLATIVE PROCESS vol 96 (2012) PARA 762.

2   As to the rules for the interpretation of statutes see STATUTES AND LEGISLATIVE PROCESS vol 96 (2012) PARA 1078 et seq. See also STATUTES AND LEGISLATIVE PROCESS vol 96 (2012) PARA 759.

3   *Lonrho Ltd v Shell Petroleum Co Ltd (No 2)* [1982] AC 173 at 185, [1981] 2 All ER 456 at 461, HL, per Lord Diplock.

4   See PARA 506. See also *Groves v Lord Wimborne* [1898] 2 QB 402, CA; *Britannic Merthyr Coal Co v David* [1910] AC 74, HL; *Butler (or Black) v Fife Coal Co Ltd* [1912] AC 149 at 165, HL, per Lord Kinnear; *Monk v Warbey* [1935] 1 KB 75, CA; *Lonrho Ltd v Shell*

Petroleum Co Ltd (No 2) [1982] AC 173 at 185, [1981] 2 All ER 456 at 461, HL, per Lord Diplock; *Rickless v United Artists Corpn* [1988] QB 40, [1987] 1 All ER 679, CA.

5 *Ward v Hobbs* (1878) 4 App Cas 13 at 23, HL, per Earl Cairns LC; *Boyce v Paddington Borough Council* [1903] 1 Ch 109 (affd sub nom *Paddington Corpn v A-G* [1906] AC 1, HL); *Lonrho Ltd v Shell Petroleum Co Ltd (No 2)* [1982] AC 173 at 185, [1981] 2 All ER 456 at 461–462, HL, per Lord Diplock.

6 *Issa v Hackney London Borough Council* [1997] 1 All ER 999, [1997] 1 WLR 956, CA. See also *Watt v Kesteven County Council* [1955] 1 QB 408, [1955] 1 All ER 473, CA; *Clunis v Camden and Islington Health Authority* [1998] QB 978, [1998] 3 All ER 180, CA. The imposition of such a penalty does not necessarily make the breach a crime: see *A-G v Bradlaugh* (1885) 14 QBD 667 at 687, CA, per Brett MR; and CRIMINAL LAW vol 25 (2010) PARA 2. See also *X (minors) v Bedfordshire County Council* [1995] 2 AC 633, [1994] 4 All ER 602, HL.

7 *Calveley v Chief Constable of the Merseyside Police* [1989] AC 1228, [1989] 1 All ER 1025, HL (judicial review); *Olotu v Home Office* [1997] 1 All ER 385, [1997] 1 WLR 328, CA (habeas corpus and mandamus (now mandatory order)).

506. Class of persons protected by statute. An individual may sue for a breach of statutory duty[1] only if he falls within the class of persons upon whom the statute was intended to confer private rights of action. The answer to the question whether the statute confers such rights does not necessarily depend upon whether the statute was intended to protect a limited class of persons or the public as a whole[2]. Nevertheless it is of importance to determine what was the intention of the statute in this respect[3], because, if the statute on its true construction is intended to protect a particular class, it is some indication that members of that class are intended to have a right of action[4] (for example, in the case of statutes for the protection of factory workers[5], merchant seamen[6], dock labourers[7] and shipyard workers[8], or intended for the protection of the public when exposed to certain dangers[9]). On the other hand, if the statute is intended to protect the public as a whole, it will not usually be construed as giving a right of action to individual members of a particular class[10].

In any case in which a class of individuals has a common law right of action in respect of the breach of a duty imposed by a statute, a claimant to succeed must show that he is within the class of persons which is intended to be protected and to which the duty is therefore owed[11].

1 As to breach of statutory duty see PARA 500 et seq.

2 *Lonrho Ltd v Shell Petroleum Co Ltd (No 2)* [1982] AC 173 at 185–186, [1981] 2 All ER 456 at 461, HL, per Lord Diplock. See also *Monk v Warbey* [1935] 1 KB 75, CA. See further INSURANCE vol 60 (2011) PARA 707.

3 See *Butler (or Black) v Fife Coal Co Ltd* [1912] AC 149 at 165, HL, per Lord Kinnear; *Solomons v R Gertzenstein Ltd* [1954] 2 QB 243 at 265, [1954] 2 All ER 625 at 637, CA, per Romer LJ; *Lonrho Ltd v Shell Petroleum Co Ltd (No 2)* [1982] AC 173 at 185, [1981] 2 All ER 456 at 461, HL, per Lord Diplock. If a statute enforced by criminal penalties does not mention civil liability, this is an indicator that no private rights of action are conferred, but it may be countered by showing that the claimant belongs to a class protected by the statute or, if he is suing for breach of a duty to the public at large, that he suffered special damage: see *Lonrho Ltd v Shell Petroleum Co (No 2)* [1982] AC 173 at 185–186, [1981] 2 All ER 456 at 461, HL, per Lord Diplock. As to the rules for the interpretation of statutes see STATUTES AND LEGISLATIVE PROCESS vol 96 (2012) PARA 1078 et seq. As to the statutory intention and interpretation of statutes see STATUTES AND LEGISLATIVE PROCESS vol 96 (2012) PARA 1078 et seq.

4 See *Couch v Steel* (1854) 3 E & B 402; *Groves v Lord Wimborne* [1898] 2 QB 402, CA; *Butler (or Black) v Fife Coal Co Ltd* [1912] AC 149, HL; *Reffell v Surrey County Council* [1964] 1 All ER 743, [1964] 1 WLR 358; *Rickless v United Artists Corpn* [1988] QB 40, [1987] 1 All ER 679, CA.

5 See *Groves v Lord Wimborne* [1898] 2 QB 402, CA. Cf *Biddle v Truvox Engineering Co Ltd* [1952] 1 KB 101, [1951] 2 All ER 835 (purely penal provision). See also HEALTH AND SAFETY AT WORK vol 52 (2014) PARAS 380, 445 et seq. A duty which is imposed on the occupier of a factory may be owed not only to his own employees but also to other workers working in the

factory: see *Wigley v British Vinegars Ltd* [1964] AC 307, [1962] 3 All ER 161, HL. See also HEALTH AND SAFETY AT WORK vol 52 (2014) PARA 421.

6 See *Couch v Steel* (1854) 3 E & B 402.

7 See *Hawkins v Thames Stevedore Co Ltd and Union Cold Storage Co Ltd* [1936] 2 All ER 472. See HEALTH AND SAFETY AT WORK vol 53 (2014) PARAS 672, 673.

8 See *Smith v Cammell Laird & Co Ltd* [1940] AC 242, [1939] 4 All ER 381, HL.

9 Examples of provisions so intended are provisions regulating level crossings, gates or fences in connection with railways (*Williams v Great Western Rly Co* (1874) LR 9 Exch 157, as explained in *Wakelin v London and South Western Rly Co* (1886) 12 App Cas 41 at 43, HL, per Lord Halsbury LC (arguendo); *Parkinson v Garstang and Knott End Rly Co* [1910] 1 KB 615, DC; *Charman v South Eastern Rly Co* (1888) 21 QBD 524, CA; and see RAILWAYS AND TRAMWAYS vol 86 (2013) PARA 357 et seq), and provisions as to means of escape in case of fire (*Solomons v R Gertzenstein Ltd* [1954] 2 QB 243, [1954] 2 All ER 625, CA).

10 See *Clegg Parkinson & Co v Earby Gas Co* [1896] 1 QB 592 at 594 per Wills J; *Heath's Garage Ltd v Hodges* [1916] 2 KB 370, CA; *Phillips v Britannia Hygienic Laundry Co Ltd* [1923] 2 KB 832, CA; *Square v Model Farm Dairies (Bournemouth) Ltd* [1939] 2 KB 365, [1939] 1 All ER 259, CA; *London Armoury Co v Ever Ready (Great Britain) Ltd* [1941] 1 KB 742, [1941] 1 All ER 364; *Cutler v Wandsworth Stadium Ltd* [1949] AC 398, [1949] 1 All ER 544, HL; *Coote v Stone* [1971] 1 All ER 657, [1971] 1 WLR 279, CA; *Lonrho Ltd v Shell Petroleum Co Ltd (No 2)* [1982] AC 173 at 185–186, [1981] 2 All ER 456 at 461, HL, per Lord Diplock (in order to succeed, a claimant must show that he suffered particular direct and substantial damage, other than and different from that common to the public at large). But cf *Roe v Sheffield City Council* [2003] EWCA Civ 1, [2004] QB 653, [2003] LGR 389 (persons using the highway a sufficiently limited class).

11 See *Read v Croydon Corpn* [1938] 4 All ER 631; *Knapp v Railway Executive* [1949] 2 All ER 508, CA; *Hartley v Mayoh & Co* [1954] 1 QB 383, [1954] 1 All ER 375, CA; *Greenhalgh v British Railways Board* [1969] 2 QB 286, [1969] 2 All ER 114, CA; *RCA Corpn v Pollard* [1983] Ch 135 at 150, [1982] 3 All ER 771 at 780, CA.

507. Type of damage intended to be prevented by statute. For a claim for breach of statutory duty[1] to succeed, it must be shown that the injury or damage suffered by the claimant was of the kind which the statute was intended to prevent. A statute intended to protect against the occurrence of loss in a particular manner will not support a claim in respect of a loss occurring by another manner[2]. Nor will a statute intended to protect only against physical harm support a claim in respect of pure economic loss[3].

If the only damage that breach of the statute is likely to cause is damage that is not of a kind for which the law generally awards damages, that may indicate that the statute creates no private right of action[4].

1 See PARA 500 et seq.

2 See *Gorris v Scott* (1874) LR 9 Exch 125 (distinguished in *Grant v National Coal Board* [1956] AC 649, [1956] 1 All ER 682, HL); *Rodgers v National Coal Board* [1966] 3 All ER 124, [1966] 1 WLR 1559. Numerous decisions have affirmed that the statutory duty to fence dangerous machinery provides a cause of action only for injury caused by contact with the moving parts and not for injury suffered from parts or material ejected from the machine: see *Nicholls v F Austin (Leyton) Ltd* [1946] AC 493, [1946] 2 All ER 92, HL; *Carrol v Andrew Barclay & Sons Ltd* [1948] AC 477, [1948] 2 All ER 386, HL; *Close v Steel Co of Wales* [1962] AC 367, [1961] 2 All ER 953, HL. Nor is the fencing obligation intended to protect against injury caused by contact between the moving parts and a tool: see *Sparrow v Fairey Aviation Co Ltd* [1964] AC 1019, [1962] 3 All ER 706, HL; but cf *Midland and Low Moor Iron and Steel Co Ltd v Cross* [1965] AC 343, [1964] 3 All ER 752, HL. Even if there is no liability under the statute, there may be liability for common law negligence: see *Kilgollan v William Cooke & Co Ltd* [1956] 2 All ER 294, [1956] 1 WLR 527, CA.

As to the onus of proof of damage resulting from a breach of statutory duty see PARA 515. As to the measure of damages see PARA 522.

3 *Wentworth v Wiltshire County Council* [1993] QB 654, [1993] 2 All ER 256, CA. See also *Murphy v Brentwood District Council* [1991] 1 AC 398 at 490, [1990] 2 All ER 908, HL, per Lord Oliver. Cf *Merlin v British Nuclear Fuels plc* [1990] 2 QB 557, [1990] 3 All ER 711 (claim for pure economic loss under Nuclear Installations Act 1965).

4   *Pickering v Liverpool Daily Post and Echo Newspapers plc* [1991] 2 AC 370, [1991] 1 All ER 622, HL (disclosure of private information). See now CONFIDENCE AND INFORMATIONAL PRIVACY vol 19 (2011) PARA 83 et seq.

508. Liability of public authorities for breach of statutory duty. Local authorities and other bodies with statutory powers and duties are subject to the principles set out above in the same way as all persons[1], but in practice their liability is limited because many statutes under which they act are intended to pursue goals of a regulatory or welfare nature and not to give rise to private rights of action[2]. In addition, a duty may involve an element of discretion that indicates that Parliament did not intend to create such rights[3]. The failure to exercise a statutory power does not give rise to liability for breach of statutory duty and is actionable in common law negligence only in exceptional circumstances[4].

1   As to the nature of breach of statutory duty see PARA 500 et seq. As to the construction of statutes imposing duties see PARA 504 et seq. As to the interpretation of statutes see generally STATUTES AND LEGISLATIVE PROCESS vol 96 (2012) PARA 1078 et seq.

2   See *X (minors) v Bedfordshire County Council* [1995] 2 AC 633 at 731–732, [1995] 3 All ER 353 at 364, HL, per Lord Browne-Wilkinson; and PARA 504 note 7. Naturally, if on the construction of a particular statute such rights do arise, there may be liability for breach of statutory duty: see e g *Carpenter v Finsbury Borough Council* [1920] 2 KB 195. As to the liability of a highway authority for failure to repair the highway see HIGHWAYS, STREETS AND BRIDGES vol 55 (2012) PARAS 305–309.

3   See *Danns v Department of Health* [1998] PIQR P226 at P228, CA, per Leggatt LJ; and PARA 504 note 6.

4   See further PARAS 457, 809; and CONSTITUTIONAL AND ADMINISTRATIVE LAW vol 20 (2014) PARA 654. As to breach of statutory duty by public authorities see CONSTITUTIONAL AND ADMINISTRATIVE LAW vol 20 (2014) PARA 650 et seq. As to negligence generally see NEGLIGENCE.

509. Special provisions governing health and safety at work. The Health and Safety at Work etc Act 1974[1] provides for the making of regulations to replace the existing statutory provisions[2] relating to health and safety at work[3]. Breach of a duty imposed by a statutory instrument containing (whether alone or with other provision) health and safety regulations, or imposed by an existing statutory provision, is not actionable except to the extent that regulations under the Health and Safety at Work etc Act 1974[4] so provide[5].

1   See HEALTH AND SAFETY AT WORK vol 52 (2014) PARA 302 et seq. See also *Richardson v Pitt-Stanley* [1995] QB 123 at 132, [1995] 1 All ER 460 at 468, CA, per Stuart-Smith LJ (the court will more readily construe a statutory provision as providing a civil cause of action where it relates to the safety and health of a class of persons rather than where they have merely suffered economic loss).

2   As to the meaning of 'existing statutory provisions' see the Health and Safety at Work etc Act 1974 s 53(1); and HEALTH AND SAFETY AT WORK vol 52 (2014) PARA 302.

3   See the Health and Safety at Work etc Act 1974 s 15; and HEALTH AND SAFETY AT WORK vol 52 (2014) PARAS 388–389.

4   Ie regulations under the Health and Safety at Work etc Act 1974 s 47: see HEALTH AND SAFETY AT WORK vol 52 (2014) PARAS 380 et seq.

5   See the Health and Safety at Work etc Act 1974 s 47(2), (2A) (s 47(2) substituted, and s (2A) added by the Enterprise and Regulatory Reform Act 2013 s 69(3)). Regulations under the Health and Safety at Work etc Act 1974 s 47 may include provision for a defence to be available in any action for breach of the duty mentioned in s 47(2) or s 47(2A), and may include provision for any term of an agreement which purports to exclude or restrict any liability for such a breach to be void: s 47(2B) (added by the Enterprise and Regulatory Reform Act 2013 s 69(3)); see HEALTH AND SAFETY AT WORK vol 52 (2014) PARAS 380, 384.

     Civil liability for breach of statutory duty is expressly limited by the Management of Health and Safety at Work Regulations 1999, SI 1999/3242, reg 22(1) (reg 22 substituted by

SI 2013/1667) which provides that breach of a duty imposed by the following regulations will, so far as it causes damage, be actionable by a new or expectant mother:

(1)   Management of Health and Safety at Work Regulations 1999, SI 1999/3242, reg 16 (risk assessment in respect of new or expectant mothers);

(2)   reg 16A (alteration of working conditions in respect of new or expectant mothers (agency workers));

(3)   reg 17 (certificate from registered medical practitioner in respect of new or expectant mothers);

(4)   reg 17A (certificate from registered medical practitioner in respect of new or expectant mothers (agency workers)).

Any term of an agreement which purports to exclude or restrict any liability for such a breach is void: reg 22(2) (as so substituted): see HEALTH AND SAFETY AT WORK vol 52 (2014) PARA 380.

C. NATURE AND EXTENT OF STATUTORY DUTIES AND LIABILITIES

510. Absolute and qualified statutory duties. The nature of the duty imposed by a statute is a matter of the construction of the provision in question[1]. In some cases the obligation is absolute[2], that is to say, all that is necessary to prove a breach of the duty[3] is to show that the requirements of the statute have not in fact been complied with, and it is not necessary for the claimant in a claim for breach of duty to show how the failure to comply arose or that the defendant was guilty of any failure to take reasonable care to comply. Furthermore, it is not normally[4] a defence for the defendant to show that he took all reasonable precautions to secure compliance[5]. In certain instances, the duty imposed by a statute is subject to express qualification, for example, that compliance is to be ensured 'so far as is reasonably practicable' and such words must be construed in their particular statutory context[6]. In other cases, the relevant provision may be interpreted as establishing nothing more than a statutory duty of care[7].

1   *Hammond v St Pancras Vestry* (1874) LR 9 CP 316; *J and J Makin Ltd v London and North Eastern Rly Co* [1943] KB 467, [1943] 1 All ER 645, CA. As to the construction of statutes see STATUTES AND LEGISLATIVE PROCESS vol 96 (2012) PARA 1092 et seq.

2   Absolute liability is to be regarded as exceptional in English law and must be imposed in clear language: *J and J Makin Ltd v London and North Eastern Rly Co* [1943] KB 467 at 471, [1943] 1 All ER 645 at 648, CA, per Lord Greene MR; *Allison v London Underground* [2008] EWCA Civ 71 at [32], [2008] ICR 719 at [32], [2008] IRLR 440 at [32] per Smith LJ. But if on the true construction of the particular enactment the court finds that the liability is absolute, the fact that an absolute liability may appear contrary to natural justice cannot impede the court from adopting that construction: *J and J Makin Ltd v London and North Eastern Rly Co* [1943] KB 467 at 471, [1943] 1 All ER 645 at 648, CA. As to the construction of statutes determining whether or not duties imposed are absolute or qualified see STATUTES AND LEGISLATIVE PROCESS vol 96 (2012) PARA 736.

     For analysis of the terms 'absolute liability', 'no-fault liability' and 'strict liability' see *Allison v London Underground* [2008] EWCA Civ 71 at [31], [2008] ICR 719 at [31], [2008] IRLR 440 at [31] per Smith LJ. As to the justification of absolute liability see *Lewisham London Borough Council v Malcolm (Equality and Human Rights Commission intervening)* [2008] UKHL 43 at [28], [2008] 1 AC 1399 at [28], [2008] 4 All ER 525 at [28] per Lord Scott of Foscote.

     As to absolute liability contrasted to strict liability see PARA 523.

3   As to breach of statutory duty see PARA 500 et seq.

4   As to special statutory defences see PARA 516. As to other defences see PARAS 517–521.

5   See eg *Galashiels Gas Co Ltd v O'Donnell (or Millar)* [1949] AC 275, [1949] 1 All ER 319, HL; *John Summers & Sons Ltd v Frost* [1955] AC 740 at 759, [1955] 1 All ER 870 at 877, HL, per Lord Morton; *Hamilton v National Coal Board* [1960] AC 633, [1960] 1 All ER 76, HL; and the text and note 2.

6   See eg *John Summers & Sons Ltd v Frost* [1955] AC 740 at 775, [1955] 1 All ER 870 at 877, HL, where Lord Morton cited instances of duties imposed by the factories legislation which were expressly qualified. See also note 2. The imposition of a duty 'so far as is reasonably

practicable' may indicate a legislative intention to reverse the ordinary burden of proof: see *Nimmo v Alexander Cowan & Sons Ltd* [1968] AC 107, [1967] 3 All ER 187, HL.

7   See PARA 502. A court considering a claim in breach of statutory duty may, in determining whether the defendant should have taken particular steps to meet a standard of care, whether by taking precautions against a risk or otherwise, have regard to whether a requirement to take those steps might prevent a desirable activity from being undertaken at all, to a particular extent or in a particular way, or discourage persons from undertaking functions in connection with a desirable activity: Compensation Act 2006 s 1.

511.   Delegation of performance of statutory duty. Where on the true construction of a statute a personal duty is imposed on an employer to perform an act or to secure that the act is performed, the employer cannot, unless the statute permits him to do so[1], delegate his duty to an employee or other person so as to relieve himself from liability to a third person for injury suffered through a failure properly to perform the duty[2]. However, if the person who has suffered the injury is the person to whom performance of the duty was entrusted, he cannot recover against the employer if the employer proves that the injury was solely due to the employee's own fault[3], and there was no contributory fault on his part which went beyond or was independent of the fault of the employee[4].

1   See e g the Highways Act 1980 s 58(1); PARA 516; and HIGHWAYS, STREETS AND BRIDGES vol 55 (2012) PARA 309. As to the construction of statutes see STATUTES AND LEGISLATIVE PROCESS vol 96 (2012) PARA 1092 et seq.

2   *Vincent v Southern Rly Co* [1927] AC 430 at 437, HL; *Lochgelly Iron and Coal Co Ltd v M'Mullan* [1934] AC 1 at 8–9, 13, HL; *Yelland v Powell Duffryn Associated Collieries Ltd* [1941] 1 KB 154, [1941] 1 All ER 278, CA. See also HEALTH AND SAFETY AT WORK vol 52 (2014) PARA 383. This is so even though the employer is a limited company which can act only through its employees or agents: *Yelland v Powell Duffryn Associated Collieries Ltd* [1941] 1 KB 154, [1941] 1 All ER 278, CA. Such a duty is the employer's personal duty whether he performs or can perform it himself, or whether he does not or cannot perform it save by his employees or agents: *Wilsons and Clyde Coal Co Ltd v English* [1938] AC 57 at 83–84, [1937] 3 All ER 628 at 643, HL. A similar rule exists with regard to the liability of an authority for the negligent exercise of its statutory powers (see e g CONSTITUTIONAL AND ADMINISTRATIVE LAW vol 20 (2014) PARA 648; HIGHWAYS, STREETS AND BRIDGES vol 55 (2012) PARA 307) and in cases where a personal duty exists at common law (see e g PARA 799 et seq). As to the liability of a ship owner for the negligence of his agents when he is bound by statute to exercise due diligence to make a ship seaworthy see CARRIAGE AND CARRIERS vol 7 (2015) PARA 377.

3   *Smith v Baveystock & Co Ltd* [1945] 1 All ER 531, CA; *Manwaring v Billington* [1952] 2 All ER 747, CA. See also *Ginty v Belmont Building Supplies Ltd* [1959] 1 All ER 414, approved in *Ross v Associated Portland Cement Manufacturers Ltd* [1964] 2 All ER 452, [1964] 1 WLR 768 (the question is 'who was at fault?'); *Boyle v Kodak Ltd* [1969] 2 All ER 439, [1969] 1 WLR 661, HL. The employee may not be at fault if the duty delegated was beyond his competence: see *Byers v Head Wrightson & Co Ltd* [1961] 2 All ER 538, [1961] 1 WLR 961.

4   The fact that the immediate and direct cause of the injury was some wrongful act on the part of the employee is not decisive, since it may also appear that something was done or omitted by the employer which caused or contributed to the accident, e g a lack of proper supervision or instructions, the employment of insufficiently experienced men, or past acquiescence by the employer in wrong behaviour by the employee: *Ginty v Belmont Building Supplies Ltd* [1959] 1 All ER 414 at 424 per Pearson J. See also *Cakebread v Hopping Bros (Whetstone) Ltd* [1947] KB 641, [1947] 1 All ER 389, CA; *McMath v Rimmer Bros (Liverpool) Ltd* [1961] 3 All ER 1154, [1962] 1 WLR 1, CA; *Ross v Associated Portland Cement Manufacturers Ltd* [1964] 2 All ER 452, [1964] 1 WLR 768, HL; *Boyle v Kodak Ltd* [1969] 2 All ER 439, [1969] 1 WLR 661, HL. Even if not able to recover under the statute, the claimant may be able to recover at common law: *Barcock v Brighton Corpn* [1949] 1 KB 339, [1949] 1 All ER 251. See further HEALTH AND SAFETY AT WORK vol 52 (2014) PARA 383. As to contributory negligence generally see NEGLIGENCE vol 78 (2010) PARA 75 et seq.

512. Vicarious liability for breach of statutory duty. An employer may be liable vicariously for his employee's breach of statutory duty where the duty is imposed on the employee and not on the employer, unless the statute expressly or impliedly indicates otherwise[1].

1　*Majrowski v Guy's and St Thomas's NHS Trust* [2006] UKHL 34, [2007] 1 AC 224, [2006] 4 All ER 395. This decision resolved longstanding doubts on the question, which had previously been left open: see *Harrison v National Coal Board* [1951] AC 639, [1951] 1 All ER 1102, HL; *National Coal Board v England* [1954] AC 403, [1954] 1 All ER 546, HL. In Scotland, it has long been accepted that an employer may be vicariously liable in such circumstances: *Nicol v National Coal Board* (1952) 102 L Jo 357, Ct of Sess.

513. Limitation of actions for breach of statutory duty. The period of limitation for claims founded on tort[1] applies to a claim for damages for breach of statutory duty[2].

1　Ie usually six years or, in the case of personal injury claims, three years: see the Limitation Act 1980 ss 2, 11, 12; PARA 478 et seq; and LIMITATION PERIODS vol 68 (2008) PARA 979 et seq.
2　See LIMITATION PERIODS vol 68 (2008) PARA 985. Where part of the injury was suffered outside the limitation period but a material part was suffered within the period, the claimant can recover in respect of the whole of the injury (*Clarkson v Modern Foundries Ltd* [1958] 1 All ER 33, [1957] 1 WLR 1210), unless reasonably certain quantification of the two elements is possible (*Thompson v Smiths Shiprepairers (North Shields) Ltd* [1984] QB 405, [1984] 1 All ER 881). See further STATUTES AND LEGISLATIVE PROCESS vol 96 (2012) PARA 759.

D.　BREACH OF STATUTORY DUTY: CAUSATION

514. Causal connection between damages and breach of statutory duty. In general, the claimant in a claim for breach of statutory duty[1] can recover only if the damage which he has suffered was caused or materially contributed to by the breach of duty[2]. In exceptional cases, causation can be made out by proof that the defendant's breach of duty materially contributed to the risk which eventuated, or the same kind of risk as eventuated, causing the damage in question[3]. Whether sufficient causal connection between the breach and the damage is established is a matter to be determined by applying common sense to the facts of the case[4].

1　As to breach of a statutory duty see PARA 500 et seq.
2　*Bonnington Castings Ltd v Wardlaw* [1956] AC 613, [1956] 1 All ER 615, HL; *Clarke v ER Wright & Son* [1957] 3 All ER 486, [1957] 1 WLR 1191, CA. Cf where the claimant's own conduct was the exclusive cause of the accident: *Norris v William Moss & Sons Ltd* [1954] 1 All ER 324, [1954] 1 WLR 346, CA; *Ruston v Turner Bros Asbestos Co Ltd* [1959] 3 All ER 517, [1960] 1 WLR 96; *Horne v Lec Refrigeration Ltd* [1965] 2 All ER 898. As to the necessity to show that the damage was of the kind contemplated by the statute see PARA 507.
3　*Fairchild v Glenhaven Funeral Services Ltd* [2002] UKHL 22, [2003] 1 AC 32, [2002] 3 All ER 305; *Barker v Corus UK Ltd* [2006] UKHL 20, [2006] 2 AC 572, [2006] 3 All ER 785. Where causation is established on this basis, liability is proportional to the risk created by the defendant, except in the case of mesothelioma where the Compensation Act 2006 s 3 applies: see HEALTH AND SAFETY AT WORK vol 53 (2014) PARA 602.
4　*Stapley v Gypsum Mines Ltd* [1953] AC 663 at 681, [1953] 2 All ER 478 at 485, HL. See DAMAGES vol 29 (2014) PARAS 374, 393. As to the onus of proving the causal connection see PARA 515.

515. Breach of statutory duty; onus of proof of causation. In a claim for damages for breach of statutory duty[1], the onus of proving that, on a balance of probabilities[2], the breach caused or materially contributed[3] to the damage to the claimant[4], or in an appropriate case to the risk of the damage[5], lies on the claimant unless the statute expressly or by necessary implication provides otherwise[6]. The onus of proving the causal connection between the breach and the injury is not discharged by proving the breach and damage which by its nature could have resulted from the breach[7].

1 As to breach of statutory duty see PARA 500 et seq.
2 See *Corn v Weir's Glass (Hanley) Ltd* [1960] 2 All ER 300 at 306, [1960] 1 WLR 577 at 584, CA.
3 As to the measure of damages where there were causes of damage other than the breach of duty see PARA 522.
4 The onus of proving the breach of duty also lies on the claimant in the absence of countervailing statutory language: see PARA 500 note 2.
5 Ie when the liability is for material contribution to risk under the exception recognised in *Fairchild v Glenhaven Funeral Services Ltd* [2002] UKHL 22, [2003] 1 AC 32, [2002] 3 All ER 305: see PARA 514 note 3.
6 *Grand Trunk Rly Co v McAlpine* [1913] AC 838, PC; *Caswell v Powell Duffryn Associated Collieries Ltd* [1940] AC 152, [1939] 3 All ER 722, HL; *Bonnington Castings Ltd v Wardlaw* [1956] AC 613, [1956] 1 All ER 615, HL; *Corn v Weir's Glass (Hanley) Ltd* [1960] 2 All ER 300 at 306, [1960] 1 WLR 577 at 584, CA. Lord Wilberforce's contrary approach in *McGhee v National Coal Board* [1972] 3 All ER 1008 at 1012, [1973] 1 WLR 1 at 6, HL, was disapproved by the House of Lords in *Fairchild v Glenhaven Funeral Services Ltd* [2002] UKHL 22, [2003] 1 AC 32, [2002] 3 All ER 305. Where the breach of duty consists in the failure to provide safety equipment, the claimant must prove that he would have employed it if it had been provided: *Nolan v Dental Manufacturing Co Ltd* [1958] 2 All ER 449, [1958] 1 WLR 936; *McWilliams v Sir William Arrol & Co Ltd* [1962] 1 All ER 623, [1962] 1 WLR 295, HL; *Wigley v British Vinegars Ltd* [1964] AC 307, [1962] 3 All ER 161, HL.
   As to the construction and interpretation of statutes see STATUTES AND LEGISLATIVE PROCESS vol 96 (2012) PARA 1078 et seq.
7 *Bonnington Castings Ltd v Wardlaw* [1956] AC 613 at 620, [1956] 1 All ER 615 at 618, HL, per Lord Reid; *Quinn v Cameron and Roberton Ltd* [1958] AC 9 at 23, [1957] 1 All ER 760 at 764, HL, per Viscount Simonds ('post hoc, ergo propter hoc' is a fallacy). Cf *Gardiner v Motherwell Machinery and Scrap Co Ltd* [1961] 3 All ER 831n, [1961] 1 WLR 1424, HL; *McGhee v National Coal Board* [1972] 3 All ER 1008, [1973] 1 WLR 1, HL.

E. DEFENCES TO CLAIM OF BREACH OF STATUTORY DUTY

516. Statutory defences to claim of breach of statutory duty. A defence to a civil claim for breach of statutory duty[1] is in certain cases specially provided by statute. Thus it is a defence in a claim against a highway authority in respect of damage resulting from its failure to maintain a highway maintainable at the public expense to prove that the authority has taken such care as in all the circumstances was reasonably required to secure that the part of the highway to which the claim relates was not dangerous for traffic[2].

1 As to breach of statutory duty see PARA 500 et seq.
2 See the Highways Act 1980 s 58(1); and HIGHWAYS, STREETS AND BRIDGES vol 55 (2012) PARA 309. As to the liability in tort of highway authorities see PARA 424. The defence is available without prejudice to any other defence or the application of the law relating to contributory negligence: s 58(1). Matters which are in particular to be taken into account for the purposes of the defence are specified in s 58(2): see HIGHWAYS, STREETS AND BRIDGES vol 55 (2012) PARA 309. It is not relevant to prove that the authority had arranged for a competent person to carry out or supervise the maintenance of the part of the highway to which the claim relates, unless it is also proved that the authority had given him proper instructions with regard to the maintenance of the highway and that he had carried out the instructions: see s 58(2); and HIGHWAYS, STREETS AND BRIDGES vol 55 (2012) PARA 309. See also *Griffiths v Liverpool Corpn* [1967] 1 QB 374, [1966] 2 All ER 1015, CA; *Cross v Kirklees Metropolitan Borough Council* [1998] 1 All ER 564, 96 LGR 238, CA; *Jones v Rhondda Cynon Taff CBC* [2008] EWCA Civ 1497, [2009] RTR 151.

517. Claimant as author of his own misfortune. If the claimant in a claim for breach of statutory duty[1] is shown to have been the sole author of his own misfortune in the sense that the only effective cause of the injury or damage suffered by him was his own negligence, he cannot recover even though the defendant may have been guilty of a breach of statutory duty[2].

1　As to breach of statutory duty see PARA 500.
2　*Stapley v Gypsum Mines Ltd* [1953] AC 663 at 681, [1953] 2 All ER 478 at 485, HL, per Lord Reid; *Norris v William Moss & Sons Ltd* [1954] 1 All ER 324, [1954] 1 WLR 346, CA; *Rushton v Turner Bros Asbestos Co Ltd* [1959] 3 All ER 517, [1960] 1 WLR 96; *Horne v Lec Refrigeration Ltd* [1965] 2 All ER 898. As to the application of this principle in cases where the execution of a statutory duty is entrusted to the claimant see PARA 511. See also *Ginty v Belmont Building Supplies Ltd* [1959] 1 All ER 414, approved in *Ross v Associated Portland Cement Manufacturers Ltd* [1964] 2 All ER 452, [1964] 1 WLR 768, HL; *Boyle v Kodak Ltd* [1969] 2 All ER 439, [1969] 1 WLR 661, HL. As to causation see PARA 514. As to contributory negligence as a partial defence to breach of statutory duty see PARA 518.

518. Contributory negligence as a partial defence to breach of statutory duty.
Contributory negligence is a good partial defence to a claim founded on breach of statutory duty[1], even if the duty is absolute[2]. This defence is subject to the statutory provisions relating to the apportionment of liability where both parties are at fault for the damage[3], so that in a case in which both parties are to blame contributory negligence will result in the amount of damages awarded to the claimant being reduced[4].

1　As to breach of statutory duty see PARA 500 et seq.
2　See eg *Boyle v Kodak Ltd* [1969] 2 All ER 439, [1969] 1 WLR 661, HL; *Mullard v Ben Line Steamers Ltd* [1971] 2 All ER 424, [1970] 1 WLR 1414, CA. Disobedience is not necessarily contributory negligence: *Westwood v Post Office* [1974] AC 1, [1973] 3 All ER 184, HL. It is not every error of judgment, heedlessness or inadvertence with regard to personal safety that serves to establish contributory negligence: see *Caswell v Powell Duffryn Associated Collieries Ltd* [1940] AC 152 at 174, [1939] 3 All ER 722 at 736, HL, per Lord Wright. As to liabilities between employer and employee see PARA 759 et seq. See also HEALTH AND SAFETY AT WORK vol 52 (2014) PARA 382. As to the defence of contributory negligence generally see NEGLIGENCE vol 78 (2010) PARAS 75–82. See also DAMAGES vol 29 (2014) PARA 382 et seq.
3　See the Law Reform (Contributory Negligence) Act 1945 s 1(1); and DAMAGES vol 29 (2014) PARA 383; NEGLIGENCE vol 78 (2010) PARAS 75, 82. 'Fault' includes breach of statutory duty: see s 4.
4　See eg *Cakebread v Hopping Bros (Whetstone) Ltd* [1947] KB 641, [1947] 1 All ER 389, CA; *Beal v E Gomme Ltd* (1949) 65 TLR 543, CA; *Cork v Kirby Maclean Ltd* [1952] 2 All ER 402, CA; *Stapley v Gypsum Mines Ltd* [1953] AC 663, [1953] 2 All ER 478, HL; *Williams v Sykes and Harrison Ltd* [1955] 3 All ER 225, [1955] 1 WLR 1180, CA; *Hodkinson v Henry Wallwork & Co Ltd* [1955] 3 All ER 236, [1955] 1 WLR 1195, CA; *Davison v Apex Scaffolds Ltd* [1956] 1 QB 551, [1956] 1 All ER 473, CA. See also NEGLIGENCE vol 78 (2010) PARA 82.

519. Voluntary assumption of risk. The defence of 'volenti non fit injuria'[1] is available only if the defendant is not himself in breach of statutory duty[2] and is not in breach of any statutory duty vicariously through the neglect of some person who (if a fellow employee) is of superior rank to the claimant and whose commands the claimant is bound to obey or who had some special and different duty of care[3]. The defence is not available in any other circumstances[4].

1　As to the defence of volenti non fit injuria (ie that the claimant consented to acts or omissions which would otherwise have been tortious) see PARA 465; and NEGLIGENCE vol 78 (2010) PARAS 69–72.
2　As to breach of statutory duty see PARA 500 et seq.
3　*Imperial Chemical Industries Ltd v Shatwell* [1965] AC 656 at 687, [1964] 2 All ER 999, HL, per Lord Pearce. As to vicarious liability for breach of statutory duty see PARA 512.
4　*Baddeley v Earl of Granville* (1887) 19 QBD 423; *Davies v Thomas Owen & Co Ltd* [1919] 2 KB 39; *Wheeler v New Merton Board Mills Ltd* [1933] 2 KB 669, CA; *Alford v National Coal Board* [1952] 1 All ER 754 at 757, HL, per Lord Normand.

520. Intervention of a third person as a defence to breach of statutory duty.
No liability will arise where the damage suffered by the claimant was due not to
a breach of duty by the defendant but to some independent act of a third person
which the defendant could not reasonably foresee or guard against: the maxim
novus actus interveniens[1] applies[2]. Whether the maxim applies in any particular
claim depends on the construction of the particular statute imposing the duty[3].

1   Ie a subsequent extraneous event occurs after the defendant's wrongful act which breaks the
     chain of causation.

2   *Groves v Lord Wimborne* [1898] 2 QB 402 at 418, CA; *Horton v Caplin Contracts Ltd* [2002]
     EWCA Civ 1604, [2003] ICR 179. Cf *Northwestern Utilities Ltd v London Guarantee and
     Accident Co* [1936] AC 108, PC (unreasonable failure to foresee and guard against third party's
     intervention). See also DAMAGES vol 29 (2014) PARA 369; NEGLIGENCE vol 78 (2010) PARA 76.
     As to causation generally see DAMAGES vol 29 (2014) PARA 364 et seq.

3   *Cooper v Railway Executive (Southern Region)* [1953] 1 All ER 477 at 479, [1953] 1 WLR 223
     at 228 per Devlin J; *Environment Agency (formerly National Rivers Authority) v Empress
     Car Co (Abertillery) Ltd* [1999] 2 AC 22 at 31–32, sub nom *Empress Car Co (Abertillery) Ltd
     v National Rivers Authority* [1998] 1 All ER 481 at 492, HL, per Lord Hoffmann (considering
     the issue in connection with criminal liability for breach of the statute).
        As to the construction of statutes see STATUTES AND LEGISLATIVE PROCESS vol 96 (2012)
     PARA 1092 et seq.

521. Act of God as a defence to breach of statutory duty. The defence of act
of God[1] may apply to the failure to fulfil an obligation created by statute, but
whether it does apply depends on the construction of the particular statute[2]. In
the case of a statute which is to be construed as creating an absolute duty[3] or
imposing on any person liability for the damage occasioned by a particular state
of circumstances, the defence is not as a rule available[4].

1   As to the defence of act of God see PARA 469.

2   *River Wear Comrs v Adamson* (1877) 2 App Cas 743 at 750, HL, per Lord Cairns LC; *Great
     Western Rly Co v Mostyn (Owners), The Mostyn* [1928] AC 57 at 74, HL, per Viscount
     Dunedin, and at 104 per Lord Blanesburgh. As to the construction of statutes see STATUTES AND
     LEGISLATIVE PROCESS vol 96 (2012) PARA 1092 et seq.

3   See PARA 510.

4   See eg *Nitro-Phosphate and Odam's Chemical Manure Co v London and St Katharine
     Docks Co* (1878) 9 ChD 503, CA; *J and J Makin Ltd v London and North Eastern Rly Co*
     [1943] KB 467, [1943] 1 All ER 643, CA.

F. DAMAGES FOR BREACH OF STATUTORY DUTY

522. Measure of damages for breach of statutory duty. The damages
recoverable in respect of a breach of statutory duty[1] are such as are contemplated
by the statute, and this will include damages for an injury which is a foreseeable
consequence of the breach but occurs in an entirely unforeseeable way[2]. Where
the defendant's breach of duty materially contributes to the claimant's loss or
injury, and there are other contributory causes, he is liable only to the extent of
his contribution unless the loss or injury is indivisible[3].

1   As to breach of statutory duty see PARA 500 et seq.

2   *Millard v Serck Tubes Ltd* [1969] 1 All ER 598, [1969] 1 WLR 211, CA. As to reasonable
     foreseeability as a factor of remoteness of damages in torts generally see DAMAGES vol 29 (2014)
     PARA 409.

3   *Crookall v Vickers-Armstrong Ltd* [1955] 2 All ER 12, [1955] 1 WLR 659; *Holtby v Birgham
     & Cowan (Hull) Ltd* [2000] 3 All ER 421, [2000] ICR 1086, CA.

(5) STRICT AND ABSOLUTE LIABILITY

523. Strict and absolute liability in general. A number of tortious causes of action may be considered to create strict or absolute liabilities. The expression 'strict liability' is typically used where liability cannot be excused on the ground that it is not practicable or reasonably practicable to avoid the risk. 'Absolute' or 'no-fault liability' is reserved for the much smaller class of obligations which impose liability for something which the defendant could not have avoided even by the exercise of all possible care[1]. Both strict and absolute liability may arise in the tort of breach of statutory duty depending on the construction of the statutory provision in question[2]. Absolute liability arises at common law under the rule in *Rylands v Fletcher*[3]. The statutory liability for damage caused by dangerous animals may also be considered an absolute liability[4]. Other causes of action in the law of tort may be considered to have elements of strict or absolute liability, even if fault in some sense is normally required to be proved[5].

1   *Allison v London Underground* [2008] EWCA Civ 71 at [31], [2008] ICR 719 at [31], [2008] IRLR 440 at [31] per Smith LJ. As to the justification of liability in the absence of fault see *Lewisham London Borough Council v Malcolm (Equality and Human Rights Commission intervening)* [2008] UKHL 43 at [28], [2008] 1 AC 1399 at [28], [2008] 4 All ER 525 at [28] per Lord Scott.
2   See PARA 500 et seq.
3   See *Rylands v Fletcher* (1868) LR 3 HL 330; and PARA 596.
4   See PARA 524.
5   For example, in trespass to land it must be shown that the defendant's presence on the land was voluntary, but it is no defence that he reasonably considered the land to be his own: see PARA 573. Similarly, in private nuisance it is no defence that a person who unreasonably interferes with another's land took reasonable care to avoid the nuisance: *Cambridge Water Co Ltd v Eastern Counties Leather plc* [1994] 2 AC 264 at 299, [1994] 1 All ER 53 at 71, HL, per Lord Goff. But fault of some kind almost always has to be proved: *Overseas Tankship (UK) Ltd v Miller Steamship Co Pty Ltd, The Wagon Mound (No 2)* [1967] 1 AC 617 at 639, [1966] 2 All ER 709 at 716, PC, per Lord Reid. As to private nuisance generally see PARA 594 et seq; and NUISANCE.

524. Liability for damage caused by animals. In general, where any damage is caused by an animal belonging to a dangerous species[1], or in certain circumstances a dangerous animal belonging to a non-dangerous species[2], its keeper is absolutely liable for the damage[3]. Where a dog causes damage by killing or injuring livestock its keeper is strictly liable, subject to certain exceptions[4]. Liability for negligence may arise at common law in the case of all animals[5]. The person to whom livestock belongs is generally absolutely liable for damage or expense caused by their trespass on another's land[6]. In principle, liability may also arise at common law for trespass by an animal[7].

1   See the Animals Act 1971 s 2(1); and ANIMALS vol 2 (2008) PARA 747.
2   See the Animals Act 1971 s 2(2); and ANIMALS vol 2 (2008) PARA 748. See also *Cummings v Granger* [1977] QB 397, [1977] 1 All ER 104, CA; *Wallace v Newton* [1982] 2 All ER 106, [1982] 1 WLR 375; *Mirvahedy v Henley* [2003] UKHL 16, [2003] 2 AC 491, [2003] 2 All ER 401.
3   See the Animals Act 1971 s 2; and ANIMALS vol 2 (2008) PARA 747 et seq. For prescribed exceptions from liability see s 5(1)–(3); and ANIMALS vol 2 (2008) PARA 749. As to the distinction between strict and absolute liability see PARA 523.
4   See the Animals Act 1971 s 3; and ANIMALS vol 2 (2008) PARA 921. For the exceptions see s 5(1), (4); and ANIMALS vol 2 (2008) PARA 922.
5   See eg *Draper v Hodder* [1972] 2 QB 556, [1972] 2 All ER 210, CA; and ANIMALS vol 2 (2008) PARAS 750–751, 754. As to special provisions concerning the duty of care in the case of animals straying onto the highway, or from the highway onto adjoining land, see ANIMALS vol 2 (2008) PARA 754 et seq. See also *Davies v Davies* [1975] QB 172, [1974] 3 All ER 817, CA.

6   See the Animals Act 1971 s 4; and ANIMALS vol 2 (2008) PARA 755. For prescribed exceptions from liability see s 5(1), (4)–(5); and ANIMALS vol 2 (2008) PARA 755. However, it should be noted that a person is not liable for damage or expenses under s 4 where the livestock strayed from a highway and its presence there was a lawful use of the highway: s 5(5). See also ANIMALS vol 2 (2008) PARA 756.

7   See *League Against Cruel Sports Ltd v Scott* [1986] QB 240, [1985] 2 All ER 489; cf *Buckle v Holmes* [1926] 2 KB 125, CA (cat owner not liable for damage to poultry on neighbouring land); and ANIMALS vol 2 (2008) PARAS 752–757. It should be noted that the Animals Act 1971 replaces the former common law liability for cattle trespass: see s 1(1)(c). As to remedies in respect of trespassing animals see ANIMALS vol 2 (2008) PARAS 758–761.

3. TORTS TO THE PERSON

(1) TRESPASS TO THE PERSON

(i) Trespass to the Person in General

525. Types of trespass to the person. Trespass to the person may be committed by assault[1], battery[2] or false imprisonment[3]. All forms of trespass are actionable per se, that is, without proof of material damage resulting from the trespass[4].

The act complained of must be voluntary[5] and intentional[6] or reckless[7]. In the modern law, negligence is insufficient[8]. The onus of proof lies on the claimant[9]. The act must be done without the consent of the person who sues for the wrong[10].

Wrongs to the person not amounting to trespasses, and so not actionable per se, include the intentional infliction of physical harm[11] and harassment[12].

1 As to assault see PARA 528.
2 As to battery see PARA 529 et seq.
3 As to false imprisonment see PARA 543 et seq.
4 *Watkins v Secretary of State for the Home Department* [2006] UKHL 17, [2006] 2 AC 395, [2006] 2 All ER 353 at [14] per Lord Bingham.
5 *Gibbons v Pepper* (1695) 1 Ld Raym 38.
6 *Letang v Cooper* [1965] 1 QB 232 at 239–240, [1964] 2 All ER 929, CA, per Lord Denning MR. If however, A, intending to strike B, strikes C by mistake, the injury to C is regarded in law as intentional and A is liable: *James v Campbell* (1832) 5 C & P 372; *Livingstone v Ministry of Defence* [1984] NI 356; *Bici v Ministry of Defence* [2004] EWHC 786 (QB), (2004) Times, 11 June, [2004] All ER (D) 137 (Apr). As to liability for animals see PARA 524; and ANIMALS vol 2 (2008) PARAS 747 et seq, 921–922.
7 *Bici v Ministry of Defence* [2004] EWHC 786 (QB), (2004) Times, 11 June, [2004] All ER (D) 137 (Apr). Elias J stated, at [67] and [78], that only subjective recklessness would suffice: the defendant must be indifferent to a known risk.
8 In *Letang v Cooper* [1965] 1 QB 232, [1964] 2 All ER 929, CA, Lord Denning MR (with whom Danckwerts LJ agreed) held that if the act were negligent the tort of negligence, and not trespass, should be relied on; Diplock LJ considered that trespass could still be committed negligently but accepted (without deciding) that a negligent trespass might not be actionable per se: see at 244–245 and at 935–936. For practical purposes it seems therefore prudent to treat trespass to the person as a tort of intention or recklessness. Older authorities which assume that trespass to the person can be negligent should be treated with caution: see e g *Alderson v Waistell* (1844) 1 Car & Kir 358; *Holmes v Mather* (1875) LR 10 Exch 261; *Stanley v Powell* [1891] 1 QB 86; *Fowler v Lanning* [1959] 1 QB 426, [1959] 1 All ER 290.
9 *Fowler v Lanning* [1959] 1 QB 426, [1959] 1 All ER 290. The standard of proof is proportionate to the gravity of the allegation: see *Miles v Cain* (1989) Times, 15 December, CA (rape).
10 *Christopherson v Bare* (1848) 11 QB 473; *Freeman v Home Office (No 2)* [1984] QB 524, [1983] 3 All ER 589, CA. See also *Hegarty v Shine* (1878) 4 LR Ir 288, Ir CA (communication of venereal disease not actionable if caused by voluntary illicit intercourse, and consent is not vitiated by concealment of disease); *Latter v Braddell* (1881) 44 LT 369, CA (medical examination of employee, submitted to under orders of employer, without apprehension of violence, not actionable). Cf CRIMINAL LAW vol 25 (2010) PARA 125.
11 See PARA 557.
12 See PARA 558.

526. Trespass to the person; limitation of actions. Trespass is a claim for breach of duty within the meaning of the statutory provisions concerned with limitation[1] so that claims in trespass for personal injuries must generally be brought within the special three-year limitation period for personal injury claims in tort[2]. Time starts to run from the date of the trespass, or from the date of the claimant's knowledge that the injury in question was significant and attributable in whole or in part to the act or omission alleged to constitute the trespass, and of the identity of the defendant[3]. As in other actions in respect of personal injuries or death, the court has a discretion to disapply the limitation period where it considers that it would be equitable to allow an action to proceed[4].

1   See the Limitation Act 1980 s 11; and LIMITATION PERIODS vol 68 (2008) PARA 998. See also PARA 478 et seq.
2   *Letang v Cooper* [1965] 1 QB 232, [1964] 2 All ER 929, CA; *A v Hoare* [2008] UKHL 6, [2008] 1 AC 844, [2008] 2 All ER 1, departing from *Stubbings v Webb* [1993] AC 498, [1993] 1 All ER 322, HL. See further LIMITATION PERIODS vol 68 (2008) PARA 998. As to the normal limitation period for claims in tort see PARA 478 et seq.
3   See the Limitation Act 1980 ss 11(4), 14; PARA 481; and LIMITATION PERIODS vol 68 (2008) PARAS 994, 998. If it is alleged that the act or omission was that of a person other than the defendant, the claimant must also know the identity of that person and the additional facts supporting the bringing of an action against the defendant: Limitation Act 1980 s 14(1)(d); and LIMITATION PERIODS vol 68 (2008) PARA 999.
4   See the Limitation Act 1980 s 33; and LIMITATION PERIODS vol 68 (2008) PARAS 1001–1002.

527. Effect of compensation order on damages for personal injuries. The damages which may be recovered in civil proceedings for personal injuries[1], in connection with an offence of which the defendant has been convicted, may be affected by the making of a compensation order or award[2].

1   As to damages for personal injuries see DAMAGES vol 29 (2014) PARA 434 et seq.
2   As to possible deductions see DAMAGES vol 29 (2014) PARA 456 et seq.

(ii) Assault and Battery

A. ELEMENTS OF ASSAULT AND BATTERY

528. Definition of 'assault'. Assault is an intentional[1] and overt act causing another to apprehend the infliction of immediate and unlawful force[2]. The threat of violence exhibiting an intention to assault will give rise to liability only if there is also a present ability (or perhaps a perceived ability[3]) to carry the threat into execution[4]. An assault may be committed by words or gestures alone, provided they cause an apprehension of immediate and unlawful force[5]. Thus it is an assault for one person unlawfully to advance towards another in a threatening manner and with his fist clenched, with the intention of striking the other immediately[6]; or to point or brandish a weapon at another with the intention of using it[7]; or to present a firearm at another with a threat of shooting[8]; or to pursue another in a threatening manner so as to compel him to run for shelter to avoid being beaten[9]. A silent telephone call that intentionally causes fear of immediate and unlawful personal violence has also been held to constitute an assault[10].

1   See PARA 525. There appears to be no decision in which mere negligence has been held sufficient to constitute an assault.
2   *Mbasogo v Logo Ltd* [2006] EWCA Civ 1370 at [74], [2007] QB 846 at [74], [2007] 2 WLR 1062 at [74]. See also Buller's Law of Nisi Prius 15; 1 Hawk PC c 15(2) s 1, and CRIMINAL LAW vol 25 (2010) PARAS 157–159, 161–162.
3   It has been submitted that it is an assault to make a threat with an unloaded pistol, provided there is nothing to indicate that the pistol is unloaded or that the defendant does not intend to fire it: *R v St George* (1840) 9 C & P 483 at 493 per Parke B. Cf *Blake v Barnard* (1840) 9 C & P 626. See also *Osborn v Veitch* (1858) 1 F & F 317 (guns only at half-cock); and Buller's Law of Nisi Prius 15.
4   *Read v Coker* (1853) 13 CB 850; *Mbasogo v Logo Ltd* [2006] EWCA Civ 1370, [2007] QB 846, [2007] 2 WLR 1062. It is not an assault for one person merely passively to obstruct the

movements of another, as by barring his entrance into a room: *Innes v Wylie* (1844) 1 Car & Kir 257. Photographing a person against his or her will is not an assault: *Murray v Minister of Defence* [1985] 12 NIJB 12.

5 *R v Ireland* [1998] AC 147, [1997] 4 All ER 225, HL, disapproving *R v Meade and Belt* (1823) 1 Lew CC 184. Accompanying words may deprive otherwise threatening action of its effect (*Tuberville v Savage* (1669) 1 Mod Rep 3) or render otherwise ambiguous action threatening (*Read v Coker* (1853) 13 CB 850). Where words cause nervous shock they may be actionable: see *Wilkinson v Downton* [1897] 2 QB 57; and PARA 557. Words and gestures, however threatening, will not be an assault if it is clear they cannot be put into effect: *Thomas v National Union of Mineworkers (South Wales Area)* [1986] Ch 20, [1985] 2 All ER 1.

6 *Stephens v Myers* (1830) 4 C & P 349. If the offer of violence is such that the threatened blow would almost immediately have reached the person threatened, if the assailant had not been stopped, it is an assault, even though at the time the assailant was not near enough to have struck the other person: *Stephens v Myers* (1830) 4 C & P 349.

7 *Genner v Sparks* (1704) 1 Salk 79.

8 See *R v St George* (1840) 9 C & P 483; and note 3.

9 *Mortin v Shoppee* (1828) 3 C & P 373.

10 *R v Ireland* [1998] AC 147, [1997] 4 All ER 225, HL.

529. Definition of 'battery'. A battery is an act of the defendant[1] which directly and intentionally or recklessly[2] causes[3] some physical contact with the person of the claimant without his consent[4]. The term 'assault' is commonly, if strictly inaccurately, used to include battery[5].

1 As to the requirement for an act of the defendant see PARA 531.

2 *Letang v Cooper* [1965] 1 QB 232, [1964] 2 All ER 929, CA; *Bici v Ministry of Defence* [2004] EWHC 786 (QB), (2004) Times, 11 June, [2004] All ER (D) 137 (Apr). In the modern law, negligence is probably not enough: see PARA 525. If the defendant strikes a blow at one person but hits another whom he did not intend to harm, he is nonetheless liable for the battery: *Livingstone v Ministry of Defence* [1984] NI 356, CA; *Bici v Ministry of Defence* [2004] EWHC 786 (QB), (2004) Times, 11 June, [2004] All ER (D) 137 (Apr).

3 As to causation see PARA 532.

4 As to absence of consent see PARA 530.

5 As to the meaning of 'assault' see PARA 528.

530. Assault and battery; absence of consent. If the claimant has consented to the contact or has permitted it, either expressly or impliedly[1], there is no battery[2]. A participant in a sport, game or horseplay impliedly consents to the contacts which can reasonably be expected to occur in its course[3]. But the implied consent does not extend to serious foul play[4] or the use of force out of all proportion to the occasion[5]. An apparent consent may be vitiated by the defendant's fraud as to the nature of the contact[6], but not merely as to the circumstances in which it is to occur[7]. A lack of informed consent as to the risks inherent in a medical procedure does not vitiate the patient's consent to it, provided he knows its nature in broad terms, but there may be an action in negligence for breach of the duty to inform[8].

1 See eg *Latter v Braddell* (1881) 44 LT 369, CA (submission to medical examination). As to the meaning of 'battery' see PARA 529.

2 *Christopherson v Bare* (1848) 11 QB 473 at 477 per Patteson J; *Latter v Braddell* (1881) 50 LJQB 448, CA; *Freeman v Home Office (No 2)* [1984] QB 524, [1983] 3 All ER 589, CA. In a fight otherwise than in the course of a sport it is no defence to a criminal charge of assault that the other consented to the fight where actual bodily harm was intended: *A-G's Reference (No 6 of 1980)* [1981] QB 715, [1981] 2 All ER 1057, CA. In such a case, it seems that a tort action for battery will normally be barred by the maxim ex turpi causa non oritur actio (see *Matthew v Ollerton* (1693) Comb 218; *Boulter v Clark* (1747) Bull NP 16; *Murphy v Culhane* [1977] QB 94, [1976] 3 All ER 533, CA) unless the defendant resorts to excessive force out of proportion to the occasion (*Lane v Holloway* [1968] 1 QB 379, [1967] 3 All ER 129, CA).

3   *Blake v Galloway* [2004] EWCA Civ 814, [2004] 3 All ER 315, [2004] 1 WLR 2844, CA. As to liability in negligence in this context see *Condon v Basi* [1985] 2 All ER 453, [1985] 1 WLR 866, CA; *Affutu-Nartey v Clarke* (1984) Times, 9 February.

4   There may be implied consent to some conduct outside the rules that may be expected to occur in the heat of the moment: see *R v Barnes* [2004] EWCA Crim 3246, [2005] 2 All ER 113, [2005] 1 WLR 910.

5   *Lane v Holloway* [1968] 1 QB 379, [1967] 3 All ER 129, CA.

6   *Appleton v Garrett* [1996] PIQR P1 (unnecessary dental treatment). Relevant criminal cases include *R v Williams* [1923] 1 KB 340; *R v Tabassum* [2000] 2 Cr App Rep 328. A mistake as to identity may also suffice, but there was no criminal liability for assault when patients accepted treatment from a dentist not knowing that she was suspended from practice since there was only a mistake of attribute not of identity, but the court said that a civil action might lie: *R v Richardson* [1999] QB 444, [1998] 2 Cr App Rep 200, CA.

7   Failure to reveal a communicable disease prior to sexual contact is not fraud as to the nature of the act vitiating consent: see *Hegarty v Shine* (1878) 14 Cox CC 145; *R v Clarence* (1888) 22 QBD 23, CCA. See also *R v Linekar* [1995] QB 250, [1995] 3 All ER 69; *R v Richardson* [1999] QB 444, [1998] 2 Cr App Rep 200, CA.

8   *Chatterton v Gerson* [1981] QB 432, [1981] 1 All ER 257. See also MEDICAL PROFESSIONS vol 74 (2011) PARA 17.

531.   Battery must be a voluntary act of the defendant.   To constitute a battery[1] there must be a voluntary[2] and positive[3] act on the part of the defendant. There can be no battery unless there is contact with the person of the claimant, whether directly or by a weapon or projectile[4]. The touching must exceed the bounds of what is 'generally acceptable in the ordinary conduct of daily life', so pushing past someone on the street or seizing someone's hand to shake it is not a battery[5].

1   As to the meaning of 'battery' see PARA 529.

2   *Gibbons v Pepper* (1695) 2 Salk 637.

3   Merely to obstruct another is not a battery: *Innes v Wylie* (1844) 1 Car & Kir 257. Cf *Fagan v Metropolitan Police Comr* [1969] 1 QB 439, [1968] 3 All ER 442, DC (continuing act); *DPP v Santa-Bermudez* [2003] EWHC 2908 (Admin), (2004) 168 JP 373 (deception creating danger).

4   See eg *Collins v Renison* (1754) Say 138 (overturning a ladder on which a person is standing and causing him to fall); *Hopper v Reeve* (1817) 7 Taunt 698 (injuring the person of another by driving a carriage against another carriage in which he is sitting); *Forde v Skinner* (1830) 4 C & P 239 (parish officers cutting off the hair of a pauper without her consent); *Pursell v Horn* (1838) 8 Ad & El 602 (throwing water); *Dumbell v Roberts* [1944] 1 All ER 326 at 330, CA, per Scott LJ (taking fingerprints without permission); *Nash v Sheen* (1953) Times, 13 March (hairdresser liable for applying a tone-rinse to plaintiff's hair without her consent).

5   *Collins v Wilcock* [1984] 3 All ER 374 at 378, [1984] 1 WLR 1172 at 1177, DC, per Robert Goff LJ; *Re F* [1990] 2 AC 1 at 72–73, sub nom *F v West Berkshire Health Authority* [1989] 2 All ER 545 at 563–564, HL, per Lord Goff, doubting the requirement suggested in some earlier cases that the touching had to be 'hostile': see *Cole v Turner* (1704) 6 Mod Rep 149 (battery is the least touching of another in anger); *Coward v Baddeley* (1859) 4 H & N 478; *Wilson v Pringle* [1987] QB 237, [1986] 2 All ER 440, CA (schoolboy horseplay; 'hostility' not to be equated with ill-will or malevolence or an intention to injure). It is clear that liability for battery may arise for contacts that are not 'hostile' in the ordinary sense: *Re MB (An Adult: Medical Treatment)* [1997] 2 FCR 541, [1997] 2 FLR 426, CA (medical treatment). See also *Williams v Jones* (1736) Lee temp Hard 298 at 301 per Lord Hardwicke CJ; *Donnelly v Jackman* [1970] 1 All ER 987, [1970] 1 WLR 562, DC.

It is artificial to exclude liability for acceptable everyday contacts on the basis of implied consent: *Re F* [1990] 2 AC 1 at 72, sub nom *F v West Berkshire Health Authority* [1989] 2 All ER 545 at 563, HL, per Lord Goff.

532.   Battery must be caused by the defendant's unlawful act.   The unlawful act of the defendant must directly cause the contact of which the claimant complains if he is to succeed in his claim of battery[1].

1   *Dodwell v Burford* (1670) 1 Mod Rep 24. If A throws an object at B, and B to protect his person or property throws the object from him and it strikes or explodes so as to injure C, this

is a trespass to the person of C by A: *Scott v Shepherd* (1773) 2 Wm Bl 892. Striking a mother so she drops a child she is carrying is also a battery on the child: *Haystead v Chief Constable of Derbyshire* [2000] 3 All ER 890, [2000] 2 Cr App Rep 339 (criminal liability). As to the meaning of 'battery' see PARA 529. As to causation see further DAMAGES vol 29 (2014) PARA 364 et seq.

B. DEFENCES TO THE TORTS OF ASSAULT AND BATTERY

533. Use of force to effect lawful arrest or the prevention of crime. A person may use such force as is reasonable in the circumstances in the prevention of crime, or in effecting or assisting in the lawful arrest of offenders or suspected offenders or of persons unlawfully at large[1]. Therefore, as long as the force used is reasonable, there is no assault or battery[2].

1   Criminal Law Act 1967 s 3(1). The provision replaces the corresponding rules of the common law: s 3(2). See also POLICE AND INVESTIGATORY POWERS vol 84A (2013) PARA 489. What is reasonable is a question of fact: *Farrell v Secretary of State for Defence* [1980] 1 All ER 166, [1980] 1 WLR 172, HL; see also *Pollard v Chief Constable of West Yorkshire* [1999] PIQR P219, CA. As to the former common law see *Williams v Jones* (1736) Lee temp Hard 298; *Handcock v Baker* (1800) 2 Bos & P 260. As to arrest generally see POLICE AND INVESTIGATORY POWERS vol 84A (2013) PARA 485 et seq. As to the right of the police to call upon bystanders for assistance see CRIMINAL LAW vol 26 (2010) PARA 694; POLICE AND INVESTIGATORY POWERS vol 84 (2013) PARA 43.

2   As to the meaning of 'assault' see PARA 528. As to the meaning of 'battery' see PARA 529.

534. Acting in defence of person. A person who is sued for an assault or battery[1] may justify the act on the ground that it was committed in the defence of his own person and that he used no more force than was reasonably necessary[2] or at least avoided force that was grossly disproportionate[3]. A person is not entitled to use force in self-defence merely because he believes he is under threat, when in fact he is not, but it has not yet been decided whether he must actually be under attack or under threat of imminent attack, or if it is enough that he reasonably believed that he was[4].

Anyone may defend another person who is unlawfully attacked[5].

1   As to the meaning of 'assault' see PARA 528. As to the meaning of 'battery' see PARA 529.

2   This is the test at common law: see *Cook v Beal* (1697) 1 Ld Raym 176 (if A strikes B, B cannot justify drawing a sword and cutting off A's hand); *Cockroft v Smith* (1705) 11 Mod Rep 43; *Dean v Taylor* (1855) 11 Exch 68. The person threatened with attack may strike the first blow (*Chaplain of Gray's Inn Case* (1400) YB 2 Hen IV fo 8 pl 40) and may adopt a fighting posture (*Moriarty v Brooks* (1834) 6 C & P 684 at 685).

3   A test of whether the act was 'grossly disproportionate' applies to the statutory defence arising where the defendant acted only because he believed it was necessary to defend himself or another person and that the claimant was about to commit an offence, was in the course of committing an offence, or had committed an offence immediately beforehand: see the Criminal Justice Act 2003 s 329; and PARA 542.

4   *Ashley v Chief Constable of Sussex Police* [2008] UKHL 25, [2008] 1 AC 962, [2008] 3 All ER 573.

5   *Handcock v Baker* (1800) 2 Bos & P 260; *R v Duffy* [1967] 1 QB 63, [1966] 1 All ER 62, CCA.

535. Acting in defence of one's property. A person who is sued for an assault or a battery[1] may justify the act on the ground that it was committed in defending his land or chattels against a person threatening to commit or committing a trespass to the property, and that he used no more force than was reasonably necessary[2] or at least avoided force that was grossly disproportionate[3]. This defence is not limited to spontaneous acts done in response to actual violence and may extend to the use of arms with which the property owner has equipped himself in advance against an imminent apprehended attack[4]. What is reasonable in the circumstances may depend upon whether the trespasser had notice of the measures taken by the owner[5]. He may expel the trespasser by force, but if the entry was peaceable, he must first request him to leave[6]. To justify defence of property a party must either be in possession of the property (whether rightfully or not) or have a right to possession[7].

1   As to the meaning of 'assault' see PARA 528. As to the meaning of 'battery' see PARA 529.

2   This is the test at common law: see e g *Stroud v Bradbury* [1952] 2 All ER 76, DC. A defendant is not justified in overturning a ladder on which the claimant is standing, where the claimant is trespassing on the defendant's land and refuses to leave on request (*Collins v Renison* (1754) Say 138), nor in wounding the claimant while turning him out of the defendant's house (*Moriarty v Brooks* (1834) 6 C & P 684). The more violent the attack, the stronger may be the response: *R v Hussey* (1924) 18 Cr App Rep 160, CCA (gunshot fired against trespassers armed with implements). See also *Simpson v Morris* (1813) 4 Taunt 821.

3   A test of whether the act was 'grossly disproportionate' applies to the statutory defence arising where the defendant acted only because he believed it was necessary to do so to protect property and that the claimant was about to commit an offence, was in the course of committing an offence, or had committed an offence immediately beforehand: see the Criminal Justice Act 2003 s 329; and PARA 542.

4   *A-G's Reference (No 2 of 1983)* [1984] QB 456, [1984] 1 All ER 988, CA. Possession of the arms may however involve the commission of a criminal offence.

5   *Ilott v Wilkes* (1820) 3 B & Ald 304. Cf *Bird v Holbrook* (1828) 4 Bing 628. As to the duty of care owed by occupiers to trespassers see NEGLIGENCE vol 78 (2010) PARA 40.

6   *Green v Goddard* (1702) 2 Salk 641.

7   *Dean v Hogg* (1834) 10 Bing 345; *Holmes v Bagge* (1853) 1 E & B 782. Licensees with a right to occupy are in a similar position to that of a licensee with de facto possession: see *Manchester Airport plc v Dutton* [2000] QB 133, sub nom *Dutton v Manchester Airport plc* [1999] 2 All ER 675, CA.

536. Use of reasonable force to effect re-entry on land. At common law a person who is entitled to the immediate possession of land may enter on the land, and in a civil claim in tort may justify the use of so much force as is necessary to enable him to effect that entry and to expel an intruder from the land[1], provided the force used is reasonable or at least falls short of being grossly disproportionate[2].

1   This is the test at common law: *Hemmings v Stoke Poges Golf Club Ltd* [1920] 1 KB 720, CA. See also *Harvey v Brydges* (1845) 14 M & W 437 (affd (1847) 1 Exch 261, Ex Ch); *Scott v Matthew Brown & Co Ltd* (1884) 51 LT 746, [1881–85] All ER Rep 1043; *McPhail v Persons, names unknown* [1973] Ch 447, [1973] 3 All ER 393, CA.

     A right of re-entry or forfeiture in a lease on a dwelling, and (subject to exceptions) a right to recover possession of a tenancy which has come to an end, may not be enforced otherwise than by proceedings in court: see the Protection from Eviction Act 1977 ss 1, 2, 3; and CRIMINAL LAW vol 26 (2010) PARA 559 et seq; LANDLORD AND TENANT vol 63 (2012) PARA 801. It is an offence for a person who is not a displaced residential occupier or a protected intending occupier to use or threaten violence, without lawful authority, to secure entry to premises while someone is known to be present on the premises and opposed to the entry: see the Criminal Law Act 1977 ss 6, 12(3)–(5), (7), 12A; and CRIMINAL LAW vol 26 (2010) PARA 553. As to the effect of the Rent Acts in limiting recovery of possession see further LANDLORD AND TENANT vol 63 (2012) PARA 944; and c f CRIMINAL LAW vol 26 (2010) PARAS 559–561. The statutes referred to above do not, however, affect the defence to a civil claim mentioned in the text: see *Hemmings v Stoke Poges Golf Club Ltd* [1920] 1 KB 720 at 737, CA, per Bankes LJ, and at 747 per Scrutton LJ; *McPhail v Persons, names unknown* [1973] Ch 447 at 459, [1973] 3 All ER 393 at 398, CA, per Lord Denning MR.

2   A test of whether the act was 'grossly disproportionate' applies to the statutory defence arising where the defendant acted only because he believed it was necessary to do so to recover property and that the claimant was about to commit an offence, was in the course of committing an offence, or had committed an offence immediately beforehand: see the Criminal Justice Act 2003 s 329; and PARA 542.

537.   Use of reasonable force in retaking or protecting goods.   It is a defence to a claim for assault or battery[1] that reasonable force (or at least force that was not grossly disproportionate[2]) was used to retake or protect chattels which were being wrongfully withheld from the defendant[3], but it is not lawful to imprison a person to achieve this[4].

1   As to the meaning of 'assault' see PARA 528. As to the meaning of 'battery' see PARA 529.
2   A test of whether the act was 'grossly disproportionate' applies to the statutory defence arising where the defendant acted only because he believed it was necessary to do so to recover property and that the claimant was about to commit an offence, was in the course of committing an offence, or had committed an offence immediately beforehand: see the Criminal Justice Act 2003 s 329; and PARA 542.
3   *Blades v Higgs* (1861) 10 CBNS 713; affd on another point (1865) 11 HL Cas 621.
4   *Harvey v Mayne* (1872) IR 6 CL 417; cf *Sunbolf v Alford* (1838) 3 M & W 248. See also *Harrison v Duke of Rutland* [1893] 1 QB 142, CA (protecting goods from trespasser on highway), now qualified by *DPP v Jones* [1999] 2 AC 240, [1999] 2 All ER 257, HL (relaxing permissible use of highway). As to false imprisonment see PARA 543 et seq.

538.   Battery committed under parental or other authority.   Battery[1] of a child causing actual bodily harm to the child cannot be justified in any civil proceedings on the ground that it constituted reasonable punishment[2]. In other cases, an act which is otherwise an assault[3] or battery may be justified if it is done by a parent[4], teacher[5] or the master of a ship or pilot of an aeroplane[6] in pursuance of disciplinary powers conferred on him by law[7].

1   As to the meaning of 'battery' see PARA 529.
2   Children Act 2004 s 58(3). 'Actual bodily harm' has the same meaning as it has for the purposes of the Offences against the Person Act 1861 s 47 (see CRIMINAL LAW vol 25 (2010) PARA 159): Children Act 2004 s 58(4). See also PARA 437.
3   As to the meaning of 'assault' see PARA 528.
4   See *R v Derrivière* (1969) 53 Cr App Rep 637, CA (immigrant parents must conform to English standards). Cf *R v Rahman* (1985) 81 Cr App Rep 349, CA (false imprisonment). An older sibling has no right to administer punishment to a younger sibling: *R v Woods* (1921) 85 JP 272.
5   See *Ryan v Fildes* [1938] 3 All ER 517 (excessive punishment). The Education Act 1996 s 548 (see EDUCATION vol 35 (2011) PARA 627) now prohibits corporal punishment of children in both state schools and independent schools.
6   See *The Agincourt* (1824) 1 Hag Adm 271; *King v Franklin* (1858) 1 F & F 360; *Aldworth v Stewart* (1866) 4 F & F 957; *Hook v Cunard Steamship Co Ltd* [1953] 1 All ER 1021, [1953] 1 WLR 682. See the Merchant Shipping Act 1995 s 105 (master's power of arrest); PARA 551; and SHIPPING AND MARITIME LAW vol 93 (2008) PARA 447. The pilot of an aircraft may, if necessary, restrain persons whose activities may jeopardise the safety of the aircraft or its passengers, and assistance may be given by the crew and passengers: see the Civil Aviation Act 1982 s 94; and AIR LAW vol 2 (2008) PARA 641 et seq.
7   It seems unlikely, but perhaps theoretically possible, that discipline in respect of which a defence arises in a civil action for assault or battery might constitute a violation of the punished person's right not to be subject to inhuman or degrading treatment or punishment under the Convention for the Protection of Human Rights and Fundamental Freedoms (Rome, 4 November 1950; TS 71 (1953); Cmd 8969) art 3: see *A v United Kingdom* (Case 100/1997/884/1096) [1998] 3 FCR 597, 5 BHRC 137, ECtHR (violation of art 3 notwithstanding successful defence to criminal charge of battery); and RIGHTS AND FREEDOMS vol 88A (2013) PARA 158 et seq.

539.   Effect of claimant's fault on a claim for assault and battery.   Although there is authority supporting the view that damages for trespass to the person may be reduced for contributory negligence[1] where the claimant suffers damage partly as a result of his own fault and partly of an assault or battery[2] committed against him by another person[3], this is limited by the principle that contributory negligence can never be a defence for a defendant who intended to harm the claimant[4]. Indeed the Court of Appeal has held more broadly that the Law

Reform (Contributory Negligence) Act 1945 cannot, in principle, be used to reduce damages in any cases where claims are based on assault and battery[5].

1	As to contributory negligence see NEGLIGENCE vol 78 (2010) PARA 75 et seq. See also DAMAGES vol 29 (2014) PARA 382 et seq.

2	As to the meaning of 'assault' see PARA 528. As to the meaning of 'battery' see PARA 529.

3	Reductions in the damages for contributory negligence were made in *Wasson v Chief Constable of Northern Ireland* [1987] NI 420 and *Ward v Chief Constable of the Royal Ulster Constabulary* [2000] NI 543, both first-instance decisions. Further supporting dicta may also be found in *Murphy v Culhane* [1977] QB 94 at 98–99, [1976] 3 All ER 533 at 536, CA, per Lord Denning MR; *Barnes v Nayer* (1986) Times, 19 December, CA, per May LJ; *Bici v Ministry of Defence* [2004] EWHC 786 (QB) at [111], (2004) Times, 11 June at [111], [2004] All ER (D) 137 (Apr) at [111] per Elias J; *Ashley v Chief Constable of Sussex Police* [2008] UKHL 25 at [20], [2008] 1 AC 962 at [20], [2008] 3 All ER 573 at [20] per Lord Scott, and at [51] per Lord Rodger.

	In *Lane v Holloway* [1968] 1 QB 379, [1967] 3 All ER 129, CA, following *Fontin v Katapodis* (1962) 108 CLR 177, it was decided that the claimant's provocation of an attack could properly serve to reduce the level of aggravated or exemplary damages but could not be used to reduce the level of compensatory damages. As to aggravated damages see DAMAGES vol 29 (2014) PARAS 322–324. As to the compensatory nature of damages see DAMAGES vol 29 (2014) PARA 318.

	In an appropriate case, the claimant's fault taken with the surrounding circumstances may indicate that he has voluntarily assumed the risk of injury and so trigger the defence of volenti non fit injuria: see PARA 465.

4	See *Standard Chartered Bank v Pakistan National Shipping Corpn (No 2)* [2002] UKHL 43 at [45], [2003] 1 AC 959 at [45], [2003] 1 All ER 173 at [45] per Lord Rodger; and PARA 518. Note that a claimant in a personal injury claim for damages for negligence is not debarred from making any recovery by the fact that he is a trespasser and engaged in criminal activities at the time the injury is suffered: see *Revill v Newbery* [1996] QB 567, [1996] 1 All ER 291, CA (claimant held two-thirds to blame when he was injured by defendant while attempting to break in to defendant's property).

5	*Pritchard v Co-operative Group Ltd* [2011] EWCA Civ 329 at [62], [2012] QB 320 at [62], [2012] 1 All ER 205 at [62] per Aikens LJ (disapproving *Lane v Holloway* [1968] 1 QB 379, [1967] 3 All ER 129, CA, and *Murphy v Culhane* [1977] QB 94, [1976] 3 All ER 533, CA).

540.   Mental disorder no defence to claim of assault or battery.   It is no defence to assault or battery[1] that the defendant did not know that what he was doing was wrong unless it is also proved that his condition prevented him from forming the intention to make contact or cause the apprehension of contact with the person of the claimant[2].

1	As to the meaning of 'assault' see PARA 528. As to the meaning of 'battery' see PARA 529.

2	*Morriss v Marsden* [1952] 1 All ER 925. See also MENTAL HEALTH AND CAPACITY vol 75 (2013) PARA 761.

C. LEGAL REMEDIES

541.   Legal proceedings for assault and battery.   A claim may be brought without proof of damage for an assault or battery[1], and criminal proceedings may also be taken against the offender. The injured party may pursue both remedies except where summary proceedings are taken[2].

In a claim of assault or battery the claimant is entitled to recover by way of general damages compensation for any physical or mental injury which the assault has caused, and for the associated suffering or injury to feelings; these damages are determined by the circumstances of time and place and the manner of the wrong[3]. Consequential damages are recoverable if not too remote[4].

1	See PARA 525. As to the meaning of 'assault' see PARA 528. As to the meaning of 'battery' see PARA 529.

2   In summary proceedings for assault or battery, a certificate of dismissal of the charge against the defendant on its merits, or the payment of the fine or the suffering of the imprisonment awarded on conviction, will release the defendant from all further proceedings, civil or criminal, for the same cause: see the Offences Against the Person Act 1861 s 45; and CRIMINAL LAW vol 25 (2010) PARA 162. See also *Masper v Brown* (1876) 34 LT 254; *Reed v Nutt* (1890) 24 QBD 669; *Ellis v Burton* [1975] 1 All ER 395, [1975] 1 WLR 386, DC; *Wong v Parkside Health NHS Trust* [2001] EWCA Civ 1721, [2003] 3 All ER 932, CA. A conviction or dismissal of a charge against an employee, however, is no bar to a claim against the employer (*Dyer v Munday* [1895] 1 QB 742, CA; and see further PARA 784); nor is the binding over of the defendant to keep the peace, without conviction or dismissal, a bar to a claim in tort against him in respect of the same cause (*Hartley v Hindmarsh* (1866) LR 1 CP 553; *Gibbons v Harris* (1956) 106 L Jo 828). In *Hunter v Chief Constable of West Midlands Police* [1982] AC 529, [1981] 3 All ER 727, HL, it was held to be an abuse of the process of the court to initiate proceedings for the purpose of mounting a collateral attack upon a decision in previous proceedings in which the intending plaintiff had a full opportunity for argument.

3   As to damages for personal injury see DAMAGES vol 29 (2014) PARA 434 et seq. Damages for injury to feelings should be awarded as general rather than aggravated damages, except possibly in a wholly exceptional case: *Richardson v Howie* [2004] EWCA Civ 1127, [2005] PIQR Q3. As to aggravated damages see DAMAGES vol 29 (2014) PARA 322 et seq. As to the compensatory nature of damages see DAMAGES vol 29 (2014) PARAS 318, 408. There is no hard and fast rule about whether separate awards should be made for psychiatric injury and injury to feelings: if the psychiatric harm is very modest and merges with the injury to feelings, a single award covering both aspects may be more convenient, but a separate award may be warranted if the psychiatric harm is more substantial: *Martins v Choudhary* [2007] EWCA Civ 1379, [2008] 1 WLR 617 (harassment).

4   See DAMAGES vol 29 (2014) PARA 434 et seq. As to remoteness of loss see DAMAGES vol 29 (2014) PARAS 409–411.

542.   Civil proceedings for trespass to the person brought by offender. Where a person (the 'claimant') claims that another person (the 'defendant') did an act amounting to trespass to the claimant's person[1], and the claimant has been convicted in the United Kingdom of an imprisonable offence[2] committed on the same occasion as that on which the act is alleged to have been done, civil proceedings relating to the claim may be brought only with the permission of the court[3]. The court may give permission for the proceedings to be brought only if there is evidence that either:

(1)   he believed[4] that the claimant was about to commit an offence, was in the course of committing an offence, or had committed an offence immediately beforehand; and he also believed that the act was necessary to defend himself or another person, protect or recover property, prevent the commission or continuation of an offence, or apprehend, or secure the conviction, of the claimant after he had committed an offence, or was necessary to assist in achieving any of those things[5]; or

(2)   in all the circumstances, the defendant's act was grossly disproportionate[6].

If the court gives permission and the proceedings are brought, it is a defence for the defendant to prove both head (1) and head (2) above[7].

1   The reference to trespass to the person is a reference to assault, battery, or false imprisonment: Criminal Justice Act 2003 s 329(8)(a).

2   'Imprisonable offence' means an offence which, in the case of a person aged 18 or over, is punishable by imprisonment: Criminal Justice Act 2003 s 329(8)(d).

   Where a person is convicted of an offence under the Armed Forces Act 2006 s 42 (criminal conduct) and the corresponding offence under the law of England and Wales (within the meaning given by that section: see ARMED FORCES vol 3 (2011) PARA 587) is an imprisonable offence, he is to be treated for the purposes of the Criminal Justice Act 2003 s 329 as having been convicted in the United Kingdom of that corresponding offence; and in s 329(7)(a) the reference to conviction includes anything that under the Armed Forces Act 2006 s 376(1), (2) is to be treated as a conviction: Criminal Justice Act 2003 s 329(7) (substituted by the Armed Forces Act 2006 s 378(1), Sch 16 para 232).

3   Criminal Justice Act 2003 s 329(1), (2). 'Court' means the High Court or the County Court: s 329(8)(c) (amended by the Crime and Courts Act 2013 s 17(5), Sch 9 Pt 3 para 52(1)(b), (2)). A failure to get permission does not render proceedings void and can, if appropriate, be cured on application to the court, which can reflect in costs its view of the conduct of proceedings: *Adorian v Metropolitan Police Comr* [2009] EWCA Civ 18, [2009] 4 All ER 227, [2009] 1 WLR 1859, [2009] CP Rep 21.

4   References to a defendant's belief are to his honest belief, whether or not the belief was also reasonable: Criminal Justice Act 2003 s 329(8)(b).

5   Criminal Justice Act 2003 s 329(5).

6   Criminal Justice Act 2003 s 329(3).

7   Criminal Justice Act 2003 s 329(4). This is without prejudice to any other defence: s 329(6).

(iii) False Imprisonment

A. ELEMENTS AND EXAMPLES OF FALSE IMPRISONMENT

543. Restraint of person. A claim of false imprisonment lies at the suit of a person unlawfully imprisoned against the person who causes the imprisonment[1]. Any total restraint of the liberty of the person, for however short a time, by the use or threat of force or by confinement, is an imprisonment[2]. It is not necessary that the person detained is aware of the detention at the time[3]. To compel a person to remain in a given place is an imprisonment, but merely to obstruct a person attempting to pass in a particular direction or to prevent him from moving in any direction but one is not[4]. A prisoner whose liberty has been taken away by lawful authority has no residual liberty enabling him to bring a claim for false imprisonment against the prison authorities or Home Office in respect of his confinement within a particular part of the prison[5].

The gist of the claim of false imprisonment is the mere imprisonment[6]. The claimant need not prove that the imprisonment was unlawful independently of the tort or malicious, but establishes a prima facie case if he proves that he was imprisoned by the defendant; the onus then lies on the defendant of proving a justification[7].

1   See PARA 544 et seq.

2   There is an imprisonment if A, with the intention of detaining B, locks the door of a room (*Williams v Jones* (1736) Lee temp Hard 298 at 301 per Lord Hardwicke CJ), or places a sentinel at the door of a house and so prevents B from leaving the room or house (*Glynn v Houstoun* (1841) 2 Man & G 337). If a police officer tells a person charged that he must go with the officer, and the person charged submits and goes, this is an imprisonment, even though there is no touching of the person (*Horner v Battyn* (1739) Bull NP 61; *Pocock v Moore* (1825) Ry & M 321; *Chinn v Morris* (1826) 2 C & P 361; and see also *Wood v Lane* (1834) 6 C & P 774; *Grainger v Hill* (1838) 4 Bing NC 212), but if a person charged goes voluntarily with a police officer to the police station without being taken in charge, or told that he must come, this is no imprisonment (*Arrowsmith v Le Mesurier* (1806) 2 Bos & PNR 211; *Cant v Parsons* (1834) 6 C & P 504; *Peters v Stanway* (1835) 6 C & P 737; and see also *Berry v Adamson* (1827) 6 B & C 528). If C gives D in charge to a police officer, but the officer does not take D into custody, there is no imprisonment: *Simpson v Hill* (1795) 1 Esp 431; see also *Bieten v Burridge* (1811) 3 Camp 139; *George v Radford* (1828) 3 C & P 464. If a person who is charged with an offence is bailed and not committed to prison, the fact that he is in the custody of his bail and may be arrested at any time by his bail (see CRIMINAL PROCEDURE vol 27 (2010) PARA 66) does not constitute an imprisonment for which a claim will lie: *Syed Mahamad Yusuf-ud-Din v Secretary of State for India in Council* (1903) 19 TLR 496, PC.

3   *Meering v Grahame-White Aviation Co Ltd* (1919) 122 LT 44 at 53–54, CA, per Aitkin LJ; *Murray v Ministry of Defence* [1988] 2 All ER 521 at 528–529, [1988] 1 WLR 692 at 701–702, HL, per Lord Griffiths. Lord Griffiths was of the opinion that *Herring v Boyle* (1834)

1 Cr M & R 377, to apparently opposite effect, would not be decided the same way today: *Murray v Ministry of Defence* [1988] 2 All ER 521 at 528, [1988] 1 WLR 692 at 701, HL. Cf *R v Bournewood Community and Mental Health NHS Trust, ex p L* [1999] 1 AC 458, [1998] 3 All ER 289, HL.

4 *Wright v Wilson* (1699) 1 Ld Raym 739; *Bird v Jones* (1845) 7 QB 742; *Robinson v Balmain New Ferry Co Ltd* [1910] AC 295, PC.

5 *R v Deputy Governor of Parkhurst Prison, ex p Hague* [1992] 1 AC 58, sub nom *Hague v Deputy Governor of Parkhurst Prison* [1991] 3 All ER 733, HL. Loss of residual liberty may however constitute damage for the purposes of establishing liability in the tort of misfeasance in public office: *Karagozlu v Metropolitan Police Comr* [2006] EWCA Civ 1691, [2007] 2 All ER 1055, [2007] 1 WLR 1881. Cf *Racz v Home Office* [1994] 2 AC 45, [1994] 1 All ER 97, HL (the Home Office may be vicariously liable for acts of prison officers constituting misfeasance in public office). As to misfeasance in public office see PARA 808. Liability for false imprisonment may arise if the period of lawful detention is exceeded (see *R v Governor of Brockhill Prison, ex p Evans (No 2)* [2001] 2 AC 19, [2000] 4 All ER 15, HL) or if a published policy of review of executive detention is not adhered to (*R (on the application of Kambadzi) v Secretary of State for the Home Department* [2011] UKSC 23, [2011] 4 All ER 975, [2011] 1 WLR 1299).

6 *Brandt v Craddock* (1858) 27 LJ Ex 314. It is not false imprisonment to refuse to bring a miner to the surface before the proper time (*Herd v Weardale Steel, Coal and Coke Co Ltd* [1915] AC 67, HL), or to refuse to unlock the gates of a factory to allow a workman to leave before the proper time (*Burns v Johnston* [1917] 2 IR 137, Ir CA). See also *Robinson v Balmain New Ferry Co Ltd* [1910] AC 295, PC.

7 *Holroyd v Doncaster* (1826) 3 Bing 492; *Hicks v Faulkner* (1881) 8 QBD 167 at 170, DC, per Hawkins J (affd (1882) 46 LT 127, CA). In a claim of malicious prosecution, the burden lies on the claimant throughout to prove malice and the absence of reasonable and probable cause: see PARA 735. As to the defence of justification see PARA 554.

544. False imprisonment distinguished from malicious prosecution.

The imprisonment for which the claim for false imprisonment lies must be the act of the defendant or of some one for whose acts he is liable[1], or the result of his ordering, procuring, instigating or actively inciting the arrest[2]. Merely providing a police constable with information which would justify an arrest, and leaving him to exercise a discretion whether or not to effect the arrest, is insufficient to found a liability in false imprisonment[3], but if the information is false and given maliciously the giver may be regarded as the initiator of proceedings for the tort of malicious prosecution[4]. No claim for false imprisonment otherwise lies against a person who takes proceedings before a magistrate or judge in respect of an imprisonment which is caused by the orders of the magistrate or judge; the remedy, if any, of the person imprisoned in such a case, is a claim for malicious prosecution against the person who instituted the proceedings[5].

1 A principal is liable for a false imprisonment which is the act of his agent, if that act is authorised by the principal or is within the scope of the agent's employment: see PARAS 429, 431.

2 See *Davidson v Chief Constable of North Wales* [1994] 2 All ER 597, CA. If A induces B to arrest C, A is not liable for false imprisonment if B exercises an independent discretion: see PARA 545.

3 *Davidson v Chief Constable of North Wales* [1994] 2 All ER 597, CA.

4 *Martin v Watson* [1996] AC 74, [1995] 3 All ER 559, HL. As to the tort of malicious prosecution see PARA 716 et seq.

5 *Barber v Rollinson* (1833) 1 Cr & M 330; *West v Smallwood* (1838) 3 M & W 418; *Lock v Ashton* (1848) 12 QB 871; *Brown v Chapman* (1848) 6 CB 365; *Austin v Dowling* (1870) LR 5 CP 534 at 540 per Willes J. As to the distinction between false imprisonment and malicious prosecution see also PARA 717. A claim of false imprisonment does not lie against the person originating the charge in respect of a lawful remand which is the act of the magistrate: *Lock v Ashton* (1848) 12 QB 871; *Brown v Chapman* (1848) 6 CB 365. Persons exercising judicial functions in a court are not liable to proceedings for things done within their jurisdiction: see PARA 460; and CONSTITUTIONAL AND ADMINISTRATIVE LAW vol 20 (2014) PARA 607 et seq. A magistrate who remands a person charged for an unreasonable time is not liable to a claim of false imprisonment, unless he acted outside his jurisdiction and in bad faith: see the Courts

Act 2003 ss 31, 32; and MAGISTRATES vol 71 (2013) PARAS 463–464. As to the liability of persons involved in the execution of warrants see PARA 546 et seq.

545. Arrest by a private person. A private person may be liable in false imprisonment if he arrests or otherwise detains another[1]. He has certain powers of lawfully arresting others, and he is not liable in false imprisonment for a lawful arrest[2]. He must bring the person whom he has lawfully arrested before a magistrate or a police constable, not necessarily forthwith, but as soon as is reasonably possible[3]. However, if he fails to comply with this rule he is liable in a claim for false imprisonment[4].

Even though a private person does not effect the arrest himself he may be liable for an arrest made by a police constable at his instigation, if he is to be regarded as being active in promoting and causing the detention of the claimant[5]. However, the mere giving of information to a police officer, although it may lead to an arrest, does not make the giver of the information liable for the imprisonment[6].

A person arrested must be informed as soon as practicable of the reason for the arrest[7].

1　*Clubb v Wimpey & Co Ltd* [1936] 1 All ER 69; on appeal [1936] 3 All ER 148, CA.
2　See POLICE AND INVESTIGATORY POWERS vol 84A (2013) PARAS 488, 493. See also RIGHTS AND FREEDOMS vol 88A (2013) PARA 136. Anyone may use reasonable force in preventing crime, or in effecting or assisting the lawful arrest of an offender or persons unlawfully at large: see the Criminal Law Act 1967 s 3(1); and POLICE AND INVESTIGATORY POWERS vol 84A (2013) PARA 489. What is reasonable is a question of fact: *Farrell v Secretary of State for Defence* [1980] 1 All ER 166, [1980] 1 WLR 172, HL.
3　*John Lewis & Co Ltd v Tims* [1952] AC 676, [1952] 1 All ER 1203, HL.
4　*John Lewis & Co Ltd v Tims* [1952] AC 676, [1952] 1 All ER 1203, HL.
5　*Warner v Riddiford* (1858) 4 CBNS 180; *Aitken v Bedwell* (1827) Mood & M 68 (arrest by soldiers). See also *Flewster v Role* (1808) 1 Camp 187.
6　*Davidson v Chief Constable of North Wales* [1994] 2 All ER 597, CA (store detective giving information about shoplifter). See also *Gosden v Elphick* (1849) 4 Exch 445 (distinguishing *Flewster v Role* (1808) 1 Camp 187); *Danby v Beardsley* (1880) 43 LT 603. The mere signing of the charge sheet at the police station is not evidence sufficient to support a claim of false imprisonment against the person who signs it: *Grinham v Willey* (1859) 4 H & N 496; *Sewell v National Telephone Co Ltd* [1907] 1 KB 557, CA; but see *Harris v Dignum* (1859) 29 LJ Ex 23 (signing the charge sheet strong evidence of active participation in arrest); *Clubb v Wimpey & Co Ltd* [1936] 1 All ER 69 (on appeal [1936] 3 All ER 148, CA); and cf *Austin v Dowling* (1870) LR 5 CP 534. It is no defence that a person acts with no wrong motive or does not know that the arrest is unlawful: *Pike v Waldrum and Peninsular and Oriental Steam Navigation Co* [1952] 1 Lloyd's Rep 431.
7　See the Police and Criminal Evidence Act 1984 s 28; and POLICE AND INVESTIGATORY POWERS vol 84A (2013) PARA 494. As to the common law, which applies to a breach of the peace, see *Christie v Leachinsky* [1947] AC 573, [1947] 1 All ER 567, HL. Failure to inform of the reason for arrest does not render the arrest itself unlawful, and the detention is only unlawful from the time when information could have been given: *DPP v Hawkins* [1988] 3 All ER 673, [1988] 1 WLR 1166, DC. Detention becomes lawful as soon as information concerning the reason for the arrest is given: *Lewis v Chief Constable of South Wales Constabulary* [1991] 1 All ER 206, CA. As to the specificity of the information required see *Abbassy v Metropolitan Police Comr* [1990] 1 All ER 193, [1990] 1 WLR 385, CA.

546. Arrest by a police constable. A police constable has much wider powers of arrest than a private person[1]. In particular, statute authorises a constable to make an arrest with or without a warrant in prescribed circumstances[2]. If the power of arrest is conditional on the officer having reasonable grounds for suspicion of a certain matter, this depends on the information actually in the possession of the arresting officer, and it does not avail him to say that his superiors probably had other information justifying arrest of which he was unaware; the mere fact that an arresting officer has been instructed by a superior to effect the arrest is not capable of amounting to reasonable grounds for the necessary suspicion[3]. A constable is liable for false imprisonment if he unlawfully arrests or detains another in circumstances which do not amount to a valid arrest[4]. He is also liable if he makes a lawful arrest but does not comply with the conditions for continued detention[5], or if he detains the person for an unreasonable time without taking him before a magistrate[6]. A police constable acting in obedience to a warrant issued by a justice of the peace is not liable to be sued for false imprisonment unless he fails to comply with a written demand for a sight of and an opportunity to copy the warrant[7].

1   See POLICE AND INVESTIGATORY POWERS vol 84A (2013) PARA 487 et seq. As to the meaning of 'arrest' see *Murray v Ministry of Defence* [1988] 2 All ER 521, [1988] 1 WLR 692, HL (restraint of person who knew that she was being restrained amounted to arrest despite the absence of formal words); and POLICE AND INVESTIGATORY POWERS vol 84A (2013) PARA 485. Reasonable force may be used: see the Police and Criminal Evidence Act 1984 s 117; and POLICE AND INVESTIGATORY POWERS vol 84A (2013) PARA 434. What is reasonable is a question of fact: see *Farrell v Secretary of State for Defence* [1980] 1 All ER 166, [1980] 1 WLR 172, HL.

2   As to the execution of a warrant see CRIMINAL PROCEDURE vol 27 (2010) PARA 138. As to arrest without a warrant see POLICE AND INVESTIGATORY POWERS vol 84A (2013) PARA 487 et seq. As to the common law power to detain persons to prevent a breach of the peace, and the extent to which such detention may be justified under the Convention for the Protection of Human Rights and Fundamental Freedoms (Rome, 4 November 1950; TS 71 (1953); Cmd 8969) art 5, see *Austin v Metropolitan Police Comr* [2007] EWCA Civ 989, [2008] QB 660, [2008] 1 All ER 564, CA; affd [2009] UKHL 5, [2009] AC 564, [2009] 3 All ER 455; and RIGHTS AND FREEDOMS vol 88A (2013) PARA 228 et seq.

3   *O'Hara v Chief Constable of the Royal Ulster Constabulary* [1997] AC 286 at 293–294, [1997] 1 All ER 129 at 134–135, per Lord Steyn; *Raissi v Metropolitan Police Comr* [2008] EWCA Civ 1237, [2009] QB 564, [2009] 3 All ER 14. If an officer who briefs the arresting officer omits to pass on relevant material, he cannot be liable for false imprisonment by reason of wrongful arrest as he has not made the arrest, and the arresting officer will not be so liable so long as he had reasonable grounds for suspecting that the person arrested has committed an offence: *Alford v Chief Constable of Cambridgeshire Police* [2009] EWCA Civ 100, [2009] All ER (D) 232 (Feb). As to reasonable suspicion see also *Hussien v Chong Fook Kam* [1970] AC 942 at 948–949, [1969] 3 All ER 1626 at 1631, PC.

4   See *Wright v Court* (1825) 4 B & C 596; *Raissi v Metropolitan Police Comr* [2008] EWCA Civ 1237, [2009] QB 564, [2009] 3 All ER 14. As to unlawfulness in the exercise of the discretion whether or not to arrest see *Holgate-Mohammed v Duke* [1984] AC 437, [1984] 1 All ER 1054, HL. See also CRIMINAL LAW vol 25 (2010) PARA 145. As to giving the reason for arrest see PARA 545.

5   *Roberts v Chief Constable of Cheshire* [1999] 2 All ER 326, [1999] 1 WLR 662 (failure to review detention; immaterial that circumstances existed that would have justified continued detention had the review taken place).

6   See *Wright v Court* (1825) 4 B & C 596. See also CRIMINAL LAW vol 25 (2010) PARA 145. But see *Dallison v Caffery* [1965] 1 QB 348, [1964] 2 All ER 610, CA (reasonable length of detention allowed for inquiries to be made). See also *Ramsingh v A-G of Trinidad and Tobago* [2012] UKPC 16, [2012] All ER (D) 117 (Jul) (no false imprisonment where suspect detained at the police station pending medical report on alleged victim; all depended on the circumstances).

7   See the Constables Protection Act 1750 s 6; and POLICE AND INVESTIGATORY POWERS vol 84A (2013) PARA 459. The constable is not protected if he executes a lawful warrant in an unlawful way (*Horsfield v Brown* [1932] 1 KB 355; such unlawfulness may possibly arise from abuse of a discretion relating to the manner of execution: *Henderson v Chief Constable of Cleveland Police* [2001] EWCA Civ 335, [2001] 1 WLR 1103, [2001] All ER (D) 351 (Feb)) or against the wrong person (*Aaron v Alexander* (1840) 1 M & G 775, cited approvingly in *McGrath v Chief Constable of the Royal Ulster Constabulary* [2001] UKHL 39, [2001] 2 AC 731, [2001] 4 All ER 334).

547.   Liability of prison governor for false imprisonment. The governor of a prison is protected in obeying a warrant of commitment that is valid on its face and addressed to him, and is not liable to a claim for false imprisonment if he detains a person in pursuance of the warrant[1], even if in breach of the Prison Rules he places him in solitary confinement[2]. However, he is liable even if he acts in good faith and without negligence if he detains the wrong person[3], or keeps a prisoner in custody without a sufficient warrant of commitment[4] or for a longer time than is lawful[5].

It is no defence that in doing any such unlawful act the governor of a prison was obeying the order of a Secretary of State; if such orders are invalid, the Secretary of State who issued them is also liable to a claim for false imprisonment[6].

1   *Greaves v Keene* (1879) 4 ExD 73; *Henderson v Preston* (1888) 21 QBD 362, CA. No claim for breach of statutory duty in relation to the nature of confinement is available to prisoners, although there may be a claim in negligence in respect of injury to health sustained as a result of intolerable conditions: *R v Deputy Governor of Parkhurst Prison, ex p Hague* [1992] 1 AC 58, sub nom *Hague v Deputy Governor of Parkhurst Prison* [1991] 3 All ER 733, HL.

2   *R v Deputy Governor of Parkhurst Prison, ex p Hague* [1992] 1 AC 58, sub nom *Hague v Deputy Governor of Parkhurst Prison* [1991] 3 All ER 733, HL. See further PARA 543. In such a case, the prisoner's loss of residual liberty may however constitute damage for the purposes of establishing liability in the tort of misfeasance in public office: *Karagozlu v Metropolitan Police Comr* [2006] EWCA Civ 1691, [2007] 2 All ER 1055, [2007] 1 WLR 1881. As to misfeasance in public office see PARA 808. It was once considered arguable that a prisoner may have a claim for extra confinement within the prison against police officers to whose industrial action the extra confinement was attributable (see *Toumia v Evans* (1999) Times, 1 April, CA), but this has been rejected (see *Iqbal v Prison Officers Association* [2009] EWCA Civ 1312, [2010] QB 732, [2010] 2 All ER 663). See further PRISONS AND PRISONERS vol 85 (2012) PARA 417.

      Cases such as *Cobbett v Grey* (1850) 4 Exch 729 and *Osborne v Milman* (1886) 17 QBD 514 (revsd on another point (1887) 18 QBD 471, CA), which turn on the former allocation by statute of different classes of prisoners to different parts of the prison, are no longer good authority in this context: see *Arbon v Anderson* [1943] KB 252 at 254–255, [1943] 1 All ER 154 at 156 per Goddard LJ; *R v Deputy Governor of Parkhurst Prison, ex p Hague* [1992] 1 AC 58 at 119–120, sub nom *Hague v Deputy Governor of Parkhurst Prison* [1990] 3 All ER 687 at 704, CA, per Taylor LJ; *R v Deputy Governor of Parkhurst Prison, ex p Hague* [1992] 1 AC 58 at 175, sub nom *Hague v Deputy Governor of Parkhurst Prison* [1991] 3 All ER 733 at 754, HL, per Lord Jauncey. Cf unlawfully removing the prisoner to another place: *Bint v Lavender* (1825) 1 C & P 659.

3   *Aaron v Alexander* (1811) 3 Camp 35. See also PRISONS AND PRISONERS vol 85 (2012) PARA 417.

4   *Demer v Cook* (1903) 88 LT 629. See also PRISONS AND PRISONERS vol 85 (2012) PARA 417.

5   *Withers v Henley* (1614) Cro Jac 379; *Moone v Rose* (1869) LR 4 QB 486; *Mee v Cruickshank* (1902) 86 LT 708; *R v Governor of Brockhill Prison, ex p Evans (No 2)* [2001] 2 AC 19, [2000] 4 All ER 15, HL (governor liable where he calculated release date in accordance with explanation of law in previous judicial decisions subsequently overruled). Cf *Olutu v Home Office* [1997] 1 All ER 385, [1997] 1 WLR 328, CA (warrant valid on its face even though proper term of detention exceeded). The police owe a duty of care to a prisoner to report accurately to the prison authorities the date of his arrest so that the proper term may be calculated: *Clarke v Chief Constable, Northamptonshire* [1999] Prison LR 59, (1999) Times, 14 June, CA. A prisoner who is on trial is in the legal custody of the governor of the prison from which he comes to the court or from which he would have come if he had not been bailed; if a prisoner is tried and acquitted and is afterwards unlawfully detained in the precincts of the court by the warders of the prison, the governor of the prison is liable to a claim for false imprisonment, even though he was not present in court and did not direct the illegal detention and even though the warders are not his employees: *Mee v Cruickshank* (1902) 86 LT 708. See also CRIMINAL PROCEDURE vol 27 (2010) PARA 439; PRISONS AND PRISONERS vol 85 (2012) PARAS 417, 427.

6   *Cobbett v Grey* (1850) 4 Exch 729. As to the liability of the Secretary of State see *R v Deputy Governor of Parkhurst Prison, ex p Hague* [1992] 1 AC 58, sub nom *Hague v Deputy Governor of Parkhurst Prison* [1991] 3 All ER 733, HL; cf *Racz v Home Office* [1994] 2 AC 45, [1994] 1 All ER 97, HL.

548. Liability of magistrate for false imprisonment. A magistrate or other person acting in a judicial capacity is not liable for acts done within his jurisdiction[1], but he is liable to a claim for false imprisonment if he unlawfully commits a person to prison in a matter in which he has no jurisdiction if he acts in bad faith[2].

1 As to judicial privilege see CONSTITUTIONAL AND ADMINISTRATIVE LAW vol 20 (2014) PARA 607 et seq.
2 See the Courts Act 2003 ss 31, 32; and MAGISTRATES vol 71 (2013) PARAS 463, 464. See also JUDICIAL REVIEW vol 61 (2010) PARA 621.

549. Liability of ministerial officer for false imprisonment. A ministerial officer who acts under the orders of a person in a judicial capacity is not liable to a claim for false imprisonment merely because he signs an unlawful warrant issued by a person acting in a judicial capacity[1]. A solicitor is not entitled to rely on the issue of a warrant of arrest which is defective as being a judicial act if he makes that act his own, as by personally directing or taking part in the execution of the warrant[2].

1 At common law see *Dews v Riley* (1851) 11 CB 434 (clerk of county court); *Demer v Cook* (1903) 88 LT 629 (clerk of the peace); cf *Andrews v Marris* (1841) 1 QB 3 (clerk liable for improper exercise of judicial function). Under statute, no action lies against a justice's clerk in respect of what he does or omits to do in the execution of this duty in relation to a matter within his jurisdiction, and an action lies in respect of such acts or omissions in relation to a matter not within his jurisdiction only if it is proved that he acted in bad faith: see the Courts Act 2003 ss 31(2), 32(2). As to acts pursuant to judicial orders generally see CONSTITUTIONAL AND ADMINISTRATIVE LAW vol 20 (2014) PARA 615.

2 *Barker v Braham and Norwood* (1773) 2 Wm Bl 866; *Codrington v Lloyd* (1838) 8 Ad & EL 449; *Green v Elgie* (1843) 5 QB 99. Cf *Cooper v Harding* (1845) 7 QB 928; *Williams v Smith* (1863) 14 CBNS 596; and LEGAL PROFESSIONS vol 66 (2015) PARA 652. As to the distinction between false imprisonment and malicious prosecution see PARA 543.

550. Detention of a member of the armed forces. A claim for false imprisonment will not lie for the detention of a member of the naval, military or air forces of the Crown if the detention is justified by naval, military or air force law[1]. However, where the detention is illegal a claim will lie against a member of the forces responsible for the detention, even if he is acting under the order of his superiors[2].

1 See ARMED FORCES vol 3 (2011) PARA 505 et seq.
2 See ARMED FORCES vol 3 (2011) PARA 303.

551. Liability of master of a ship for false imprisonment. A claim for false imprisonment will not lie against the master of a ship for the arrest or confinement of a person on board in the proper exercise of his disciplinary powers[1].

1 See the Merchant Shipping Act 1995 s 105; and SHIPPING AND MARITIME LAW vol 93 (2008) PARA 447. See also PARA 538.

552. Detention of child by parent or schoolteacher. A parent, or a schoolteacher to whose care the parent has entrusted a child, may lawfully be able to confine a child in a reasonable manner and for sufficient reason without such detention amounting to false imprisonment[1].

1 See CHILDREN AND YOUNG PERSONS vol 9 (2012) PARA 151; EDUCATION vol 35 (2011) PARA 600. Cf *R v Rahman* (1985) 81 Cr App Rep 349, CA (criminal liability). However, the human rights of the person detained must now be considered: see the Convention for the Protection of Human Rights and Fundamental Freedoms (Rome, 4 November 1950; TS 71 (1953); Cmd 8969); PARA 810; and RIGHTS AND FREEDOMS vol 88A (2013) PARA 210 et seq.

553.   Detention of mentally disordered persons not false imprisonment. A person suffering from mental disorder may be lawfully detained in a hospital in pursuance of an application for admission for treatment or assessment, a hospital order, or a direction made under the mental health legislation[1]. Such detention therefore does not amount to false imprisonment[2].

1   See the Mental Health Act 1983 ss 2–4, 11–15, 56–58, 139(1), (2); and MENTAL HEALTH AND CAPACITY vol 75 (2013) PARA 767 et seq. Approved mental health professionals, hospital staff, police and persons authorised in writing by the hospital managers may take into custody and return to a hospital or approved place detained patients absent without leave: see s 18; and MENTAL HEALTH AND CAPACITY vol 75 (2013) PARA 918. Although such patients are unlawfully at large, police cannot enter premises to arrest them except in the course of pursuit (see the Police and Criminal Evidence Act 1984 s 17(1)(d); *D'Souza v DPP* [1992] 4 All ER 545, [1992] 1 WLR 1073, HL (the pursuit must be contemporaneous or almost contemporaneous with the entry into the premises); and POLICE AND INVESTIGATORY POWERS vol 84A (2013) PARA 463), the proper course being to apply for a warrant (ie under the Mental Health Act 1983 s 135(2): see MENTAL HEALTH AND CAPACITY vol 75 (2013) PARA 922). However, a constable may enter premises to save life or limb or prevent serious damage to property: see the Police and Criminal Evidence Act 1984 s 17(1)(e); and POLICE AND INVESTIGATORY POWERS vol 84A (2013) PARA 463. A constable who finds a mentally disordered person in a public place and in need of immediate care and control may take him to a place of safety: see the Mental Health Act 1983 s 136; and MENTAL HEALTH AND CAPACITY vol 75 (2013) PARA 923. The defences of self-defence and necessity may be available.
        The guardian of a minor under 16 may authorise his admission for assessment without full procedures where the child was not competent to consent to or reject his own treatment: *R v Kirklees Metropolitan Borough Council, ex p C* [1992] 2 FCR 321, [1992] 2 FLR 117.
2   As to false imprisonment see PARA 543 et seq.

B. DEFENCES TO THE TORT OF FALSE IMPRISONMENT

554.   Justification as defence to false imprisonment. The defendant in a claim for false imprisonment is entitled to succeed if he pleads and proves that the imprisonment was legally justified[1]. A mistaken belief that a legal power of imprisonment exists does not afford a legal justification, even if the belief is reasonable[2], but a defendant acting with lawful authority may still plead justification even if the warrant or provision under which he acts is subsequently found to have been invalid or liable to be set aside[3].

If one person arrests another without a warrant, he must normally inform the person arrested of the reason why he is arrested, that is, in substance, of the act for which he is arrested, unless the reason is apparent from the circumstances as where he is caught red-handed and his crime is patent; if the person making the arrest fails to do this, he cannot plead that the arrest was justified on a ground not disclosed to the person arrested until later[4].

1   See PARA 543 et seq. Statutory powers of arrest and detention may also be granted to other persons, eg immigration officers (see the Immigration Act 1971 ss 4(2)(d), 28A, Sch 2 paras 16–20; and IMMIGRATION AND ASYLUM vol 57 (2012) PARAS 191, 233). See also *R (on the application of Saadi) v Secretary of State for the Home Department* [2002] UKHL 41, [2002] 4 All ER 785, [2002] 1 WLR 3131, HL; *D v Home Office* [2005] EWCA Civ 38, [2006] 1 All ER 183, [2006] 1 WLR 1003 (no immunity for good faith acts).

2   *R v Governor of Brockhill Prison, ex p Evans (No 2)* [2001] 2 AC 19, [2000] 4 All ER 15, HL.

3   *Percy v Hall* [1997] QB 924, [1996] 4 All ER 523, CA (invalid byelaw); *McGrath v Chief Constable of the Royal Ulster Constabulary* [2001] UKHL 39, [2001] 2 AC 731, [2001] 4 All ER 334 (arrest warrant made out in wrong name); *Olutu v Home Office* [1997] 1 All ER 385, [1997] 1 WLR 328, CA; *Quinland v Governor of Swaleside Prison* [2002] EWCA Civ 174, [2003] QB 306, [2003] 1 All ER 1173 (both involving a calculation error in a warrant of commitment).

4   See PARA 545.

C. LEGAL REMEDIES FOR FALSE IMPRISONMENT

555. Legal remedies for the tort of false imprisonment. If a person is unlawfully imprisoned, he may use force to release himself[1]. He may also obtain his release by an application made on his behalf for a writ of habeas corpus[2].

False imprisonment is a tort actionable without proof of damage and is also an indictable offence, even if no violence is used[3]. The claimant is entitled to bring a claim for damages for the imprisonment[4].

1   *Rowe v Hawkins* (1858) 1 F & F 91. This is not so if, though the initial arrest was unlawful, the subsequent custody was lawful: *DPP v L* (1999) Times, 1 February, DC.
2   See RIGHTS AND FREEDOMS vol 88A (2013) PARA 38 et seq.
3   See CRIMINAL LAW vol 25 (2010) PARA 145. See also DAMAGES vol 29 (2014) PARA 497.
4   See PARA 556.

556. Claiming damages for false imprisonment. In a claim for false imprisonment the claimant is entitled to recover general damages for the imprisonment and any physical or mental injury which results directly from it[1]. Damages for the loss of liberty itself should reflect the length of the unlawful detention, but should be awarded on a progressively reducing scale, as the claimant is entitled to a higher rate of compensation for the initial shock of being arrested[2]. The claimant may also recover, by way of special damages[3], compensation for any consequential loss which he has incurred[4]. A separate award may be made for aggravated damages where, in view of the circumstances attending the imprisonment and/or the conduct of the defendant at the time of or before or after the imprisonment, the basic award for loss of liberty would not be sufficient compensation[5]. A false imprisonment does not merely affect a person's liberty but also his reputation, and the damage to reputation continues until it is caused to cease by an avowal that the imprisonment was false[6]. In an appropriate case, exemplary (or punitive) damages may also be awarded[7]. Provocation by the claimant may serve to negative the award of aggravated damages (but not to reduce the basic compensatory damages)[8].

Statutory compensation, calculated on the basis of principles analogous to those governing the assessment of damages for false imprisonment and other relevant civil wrongs[9], may be paid where a person has been convicted of a criminal offence and his conviction is subsequently reversed or where he is pardoned on the ground that a new or newly discovered fact shows that there has been a miscarriage of justice[10].

1   As to general damages see DAMAGES vol 29 (2014) PARA 317. False imprisonment is actionable without proof of actual damage (see PARA 555), so nominal damages at least are recoverable: see DAMAGES vol 29 (2014) PARAS 319–320, 497.
2   *Thompson v Metropolitan Police Comr* [1998] QB 498 at 515, [1997] 2 All ER 762 at 774, CA, per Lord Woolf MR, suggesting a guideline figure in straightforward cases of £500 for the first hour and £3,000 for 24 hours; these figures must be adjusted for the effects of inflation: *Thompson v Metropolitan Police Comr* [1998] QB 498 at 515 at 517, [1997] 2 All ER 762 at 776, CA.
3   As to special damages see DAMAGES vol 29 (2014) PARA 317.
4   See DAMAGES vol 29 (2014) PARA 318. In principle, it seems that an intentional wrongdoer should be liable for all the direct consequences of the wrong: see *Quinn v Leathem* [1901] AC 495 at 537, HL, per Lord Lindley; *Smith New Court Securities Ltd v Citibank NA* [1997] AC 254 at 279–280, sub nom *Smith New Court Securities Ltd v Scrimegour Vickers (Asset Management) Ltd* [1996] 4 All ER 769 at 789, HL, per Lord Steyn. All the decided cases in fact apply the test of whether the loss is a direct consequence of the trespass (see *Clark v Woods* (1848) 2 Exch 395 (money paid under illegal process to secure release from gaol); *Foxall v Barnett* (1853) 2 E & B 928 (costs of proceedings to quash coroner's inquisition); *De Mesnil v Dakin* (1867) LR 3 QB 18; *Norton v Monckton* (1895) 43 WR 350 (money paid under illegal

process to secure release from gaol); *Childs v Lewis* (1924) 40 TLR 870 (loss of directorship due to arrest on false charge)). Consequential damage was found to be too remote in *Harnett v Bond* [1925] AC 669, HL (false accusation of lunacy followed by detention for nine years); *Boyce v Bayliffe* (1807) 1 Camp 58 (cost of return travel by alternative means after imprisonment by master of ship on outward journey); *Hoey v Felton* (1861) 11 CBNS 142 (loss of prospective job). It has yet to be authoritatively determined that the concept of foreseeability established by *Overseas Tankship (UK) Ltd v Morts Dock and Engineering Co Ltd, The Wagon Mound* [1961] AC 388, [1961] 1 All ER 404, PC, has no application in false imprisonment.

5   See *Thompson v Metropolitan Police Comr* [1998] QB 498 at 516, [1997] 2 All ER 762 at 775, CA, per Lord Woolf MR; *Rowlands v Chief Constable of Merseyside Police* [2006] EWCA Civ 1773, [2007] 1 WLR 1065. Amongst older cases see *Edgell v Francis* (1840) 1 Man & G 222. As to aggravated damages see DAMAGES vol 29 (2014) PARA 322 et seq.

6   *Walter v Alltools Ltd* (1944) 61 TLR 39 at 40, (1944) 171 LT 371 at 372, CA, per Lawrence LJ; followed in *Hook v Cunard Steamship Co Ltd* [1953] 1 All ER 1021, [1953] 1 WLR 682; *Lunt v Liverpool City Justices* (5 March 1991, unreported), CA. A plea of justification may similarly serve to continue the damage to reputation so, if it is afterwards abandoned, it may properly be taken into account in estimating the damages: *Warwick v Foulkes* (1844) 12 M & W 507.

7   See *Thompson v Metropolitan Police Comr* [1998] QB 498 at 516–517, [1997] 2 All ER 762 at 775–776, CA, per Lord Woolf MR; *Rowlands v Chief Constable of Merseyside Police* [2006] EWCA Civ 1773, [2007] 1 WLR 1065. Amongst older cases see *Huckle v Money* (1763) 2 Wils 205. As to punitive damages see DAMAGES vol 29 (2014) PARA 325 et seq.

8   *Lane v Holloway* [1968] 1 QB 379, [1967] 3 All ER 129, CA.

9   *R (on the application of O'Brien) v Independent Assessor* [2004] EWCA Civ 1035, [2005] PIQR Q7.

10   See the Criminal Justice Act 1988 s 133; and CRIMINAL PROCEDURE vol 28 (2010) PARA 854.

(2) THE RULE IN WILKINSON V DOWNTON

557.   The rule in Wilkinson v Downton.   A wilful act or statement of the defendant, calculated to cause physical harm to the claimant and which in fact causes physical harm to him, is a tort[1]. This tort of wilful infringement of the right to personal safety has three elements: a conduct element, a mental element and a consequence element[2]. The conduct element requires words or conduct directed towards the claimant for which there is no justification or reasonable excuse[3]. The necessary mental element is intention to cause physical harm or severe mental or emotional distress[4]. Recklessness is not sufficient[5]. The consequence required for liability is physical harm or recognised psychiatric illness[6]. In the absence of physical harm, the consequence must be that the claimant has suffered a recognised psychiatric condition, and not merely anxiety or distress[7].

Thus a person is liable if he makes a false statement to the claimant who, as a result, suffers nervous shock and consequently physical illness[8]. A person who indirectly inflicts intentional harm on another does not commit a trespass, but there seems no reason why this tort should not apply to any type of physical harm, whether caused by an act or a statement, provided that the harm, although an indirect consequence, is calculated[9] to result from the defendant's conduct[10].

1   *Wilkinson v Downton* [1897] 2 QB 57 at 58–59 per Wright J. For an overview of the development of the tort see *OPO v MLA* [2014] EWCA Civ 1277 at [58] et seq, [2014] All ER (D) 117 (Oct) (judgment revsd by *Rhodes v OPO* [2015] UKSC 32, [2015] All ER (D) 177 (May): see the text and notes 2–6).

2   *Rhodes v OPO* [2015] UKSC 32 at [73], [2015] All ER (D) 177 (May).

3   *Rhodes v OPO* [2015] UKSC 32 at [74], [2015] All ER (D) 177 (May).

4   *Rhodes v OPO* [2015] UKSC 32 at [87], [2015] All ER (D) 177 (May). The case concerned whether a father should be permitted to publish memoirs containing details that his son might find distressing. It was held that publication of the book would not constitute the requisite conduct element of the tort of wilful infringement of the right to personal safety. Nor was there any evidence that the father had had an actual intention to cause psychiatric harm or severe

mental or emotional distress to his son. The Supreme Court refused to extend the remit of *Wilkinson v Downton* [1897] 2 QB 57, and publication was allowed.

5   *Rhodes v OPO* [2015] UKSC 32 at [87], [88] [2015] All ER (D) 177 (May).

6   *Rhodes v OPO* [2015] UKSC 32 at [88], [2015] All ER (D) 177 (May). Where a recognised psychiatric illness was the product of severe mental or emotional distress, it is sufficient that the defendant had intended to cause severe distress which had in fact resulted in recognisable illness: *Rhodes v OPO* at [83], [87].

7   See also *Wong v Parkside Health NHS Trust* [2001] EWCA Civ 1721, [2003] 3 All ER 932, CA; *Hunter v Canary Wharf Ltd* [1997] AC 655 at 707, [1997] 2 All ER 426 at 452, HL, per Lord Hoffmann; *Wainwright v Home Office* [2003] UKHL 53 at [46], [2004] 2 AC 406 at [46], [2003] 4 All ER 969 at [46] per Lord Hoffmann. Liability for anxiety or distress alone may arise under the Protection from Harassment Act 1997, but this applies only where there is a course of conduct (see PARA 558).

8   See *Wilkinson v Downton* [1897] 2 QB 57 (where the defendant falsely told the plaintiff that her husband was seriously injured in an accident, and she, believing this, suffered nervous shock resulting in physical illness); *Janvier v Sweeney* [1919] 2 KB 316, CA (where private detectives were held liable to the plaintiff for causing her nervous shock by falsely telling her that unless she procured letters for them from her mistress, they would inform the authorities that her fiancé was a traitor). It is no defence that the statement was made as a joke: *Wilkinson v Downton* [1897] 2 QB 57.

9   In *Wainwright v Home Office* [2003] UKHL 53 at [44], [2004] 2 AC 406 at [44], [2003] 4 All ER 969 at [44], Lord Hoffmann observed that Wright J in *Wilkinson v Downton* [1897] 2 QB 57 had wanted to water down the concept of intention as much as possible and had therefore devised a concept of imputed intention. In Lord Hoffmann's view, imputed intention would be insufficient if the liability were to be extended to cases of mere distress: *Wainwright v Home Office* [2003] UKHL 53 at [44], [2004] 2 AC 406 at [44], [2003] 4 All ER 969 at [44]; and see note 5. In respect of the intent required to found the tort, if the defendant wilfully did an act calculated to cause psychiatric harm, and caused that harm, intent can be imputed: *OPO v MLA* [2014] EWCA Civ 1277 at [73]. It is not enough that a person conveys bad news in a way which causes psychiatric harm to another: *OPO v MLA* at [67], [2014] All ER (D) 117 (Oct). Recklessness will not suffice: see *Rhodes v OPO* [2015] UKSC 32 at [87], [2015] All ER (D) 177 (May); and the text and notes 4–5.

10 The terms in which Wright J expressed the principle in *Wilkinson v Downton* [1897] 2 QB 57 at 58–59 (see the text and note 1) are plainly wide enough to cover such circumstances. See *Burnett v George* [1993] 1 FCR 1012, [1992] 1 FLR 525; *Khorasandjian v Bush* [1993] QB 727, [1993] 3 All ER 669, CA (overruled by *Hunter v Canary Wharf Ltd* [1997] AC 655, [1997] 2 All ER 426, HL) (both cases involving harassment by means of telephone calls calculated to do the plaintiff harm). As to harassment see now the Protection from Harassment Act 1997; PARA 558; and CRIMINAL LAW vol 25 (2010) PARA 163.

The principle in *Wilkinson v Downton* [1897] 2 QB 57 also covers excessive and unlawful means of protecting property by retributive dangers such as man traps and spring guns (*Deane v Clayton* (1817) 7 Taunt 489; *Bird v Holbrook* (1828) 4 Bing 628; and see *Ilott v Wilkes* (1820) 3 B & Ald 304), in so far as these are not covered by the Occupiers' Liability Act 1984 (see LANDLORD AND TENANT vol 62 (2012) PARA 624; NEGLIGENCE vol 78 (2010) PARA 40) and the common law duty of common humanity owed to trespassers under *Herrington v British Railways Board* [1972] AC 877, [1972] 1 All ER 749, HL (see PARA 443).

(3) HARASSMENT

558. Civil claims for harassment. A person must not pursue a course of conduct[1] which amounts to harassment of another[2] and which he knows or ought to know amounts to harassment of the other[3].

A person must not pursue a course of conduct which involves harassment of two or more persons and which he knows or ought to know involves harassment of those persons, and by which he intends to persuade any person (whether or not one of those mentioned above) either not to do something that he is entitled or required to do, or to do something that he is not under any obligation to do[4].

An actual or apprehended breach of the prohibition of conduct amounting to harassment[5] may be the subject of a claim in civil proceedings by the person who is or may be the victim of the course of conduct in question[6]; and on such a claim damages may be awarded for (among other things) any anxiety caused by, and any financial loss resulting from, the harassment[7]. Where there is an actual or apprehended breach by any person (the 'relevant person') of the prohibition of conduct involving harassment of two or more persons[8], any person who is or may be the victim of the course of conduct in question, or any person who is or may be a person whom the course of conduct is intended to persuade, may apply to the High Court or County Court for an injunction restraining the relevant person from pursuing any conduct which amounts to harassment in relation to any person or persons mentioned or described in the injunction[9].

Where the High Court or the County Court grants an injunction for the purpose of restraining the defendant from pursuing any conduct which amounts to harassment[10], the claimant may, if he considers that the defendant has done anything which he is prohibited from doing by the injunction[11], apply for the issue of a warrant for the defendant's arrest[12]. A warrant may only be issued if the application is substantiated on oath, and the judge has reasonable grounds for believing that the defendant has done anything which he is prohibited from doing by the injunction[13].

If an injunction is granted[14] and without reasonable excuse the defendant does anything which he is prohibited from doing by the injunction, he is guilty of an offence[15].

1   A 'course of conduct' must involve conduct on at least two occasions: Protection from Harassment Act 1997 s 7(1), (3) (s 7(1) amended by the Domestic Violence, Crime and Victims Act 2004 s 58(1), Sch 10 para 44; Protection from Harassment Act 1997 s 7(3) substituted by the Serious Organised Crime and Police Act 2005 s 125(1), (7)(a)). A large time gap between incidents does not mean they cannot form part of the same course of conduct: *Marinello v City of Edinburgh Council* [2011] CSIH 33, [2011] IRLR 669 (isolated incident occurred two years after other incidents). Each of a series of letters can stand as an occasion which is capable of being described as harassing and therefore capable each of contributing to a course of conduct which can arguably be said to amount to harassment: *Iqbal v Dean Manson Solicitors* [2011] EWCA Civ 123, [2011] IRLR 428. Each incident must be of sufficient gravity to constitute harassment; it is not enough that the incidents amount to harassment only by virtue of their cumulative effect: see *Conn v Sunderland City Council* [2007] EWCA Civ 1492, [2008] IRLR 324, [2007] All ER (D) 99 (Nov). See also *AVB v TDD* [2014] EWHC 1442 (QB), [2014] All ER (D) 99 (May) (conduct had not been oppressive and unacceptable).

     'Conduct' includes speech: Protection from Harassment Act 1997 s 7(4). As to the printed word see *Thomas v News Group Newspapers Ltd* [2001] EWCA Civ 1233, [2002] EMLR 78, [2001] All ER (D) 246 (Jul). 'Conduct' also includes computer-generated correspondence, because real people are responsible for programming and entering material into the computer: see *Ferguson v British Gas Trading Ltd* [2009] EWCA Civ 46, [2009] 3 All ER 304, [2010] 1 WLR 785.

2   Protection from Harassment Act 1997 s 1(1)(a). References to harassing a person include alarming the person or causing the person distress: s 7(2). 'Harassment' is not otherwise defined in the Act, but it has been held to require misconduct of such gravity as would sustain criminal liability under the Act; merely annoying, aggravating, unattractive, unreasonable or regrettable conduct is not enough but conduct which is oppressive and unacceptable will suffice. As to the offence of stalking see s 2A (added by the Protection of Freedoms Act 2012 s 111(1)); and CRIMINAL LAW vol 25 (2010) PARA 163. See *Thomas v News Group Newspapers Ltd* [2001] EWCA Civ 1233, [2002] EMLR 78, [2001] All ER (D) 246 (Jul); *Majrowski v Guy's and St Thomas' NHS Trust* [2006] UKHL 34 at [30], [2007] 1 AC 224 at [30], [2006] 4 All ER 395 at [30] per Lord Nicholls, and at [66] per Baroness Hale; *Conn v Sunderland City Council* [2007] EWCA Civ 1492, [2008] IRLR 324, [2007] All ER (D) 99 (Nov); *Ferguson v British Gas Trading Ltd* [2009] EWCA Civ 46, [2009] 3 All ER 304, [2010] 1 WLR 785.

     The Protection from Harassment Act 1997 has been construed as concerned only with harassment of an individual and not harassment of a corporate entity: see *DPP v Dziurzynski* [2002] EWHC 1380 (Admin), (2002) Times, 8 July, [2002] All ER (D) 258 (Jun); *Daiichi Pharmaceuticals UK Ltd v Stop Huntingdon Animal Cruelty* [2003] EWHC 2337 (QB), [2004] 1 WLR 1503, [2005] 1 BCLC 27. However, it has been held that a partnership can be a defendant to a civil action under the Protection from Harassment Act 1997 s 3: see *Iqbal v Dean Manson Solicitors* [2011] EWCA Civ 123, [2011] IRLR 428.

3   Protection from Harassment Act 1997 s 1(1)(b). For these purposes, the person whose course of conduct is in question ought to know that it amounts to harassment of another if a reasonable person in possession of the same information would think the course of conduct amounted to harassment of the other: s 1(2).

Section 1(1) or s 1(1A) (see text and note 4) does not apply to a course of conduct if the person who pursued it shows (s 1(3) (amended by the Serious Organised Crime and Police Act 2005 s 125(1), (2)(c))):

(1)   that it was pursued for the purpose of preventing or detecting crime (Protection from Harassment Act 1997 s 1(3)(a));

(2)   that it was pursued under any enactment or rule of law to comply with any condition or requirement imposed by any person under any enactment (s 1(3)(b));

(3)   that in the particular circumstances the pursuit of the course of conduct was reasonable (s 1(3)(c)).

Pursuing a course of conduct for the purpose of preventing or detecting crime (see head (1) above) means pursuing it for the sole purpose to prevent or detect crime. The necessary test in considering s 1(3)(a) is that of rationality on the part of the alleged harasser: *Hayes v Willoughby* [2013] UKSC 17, [2013] 2 All ER 405, [2013] 1 WLR 935 (after a certain date, the defendant's acts had not been rational and so he was not afforded the defence in the Protection from Harassment Act 1997 s 1(3)(a) for that period).

A person who pursues a course of conduct in breach of the Protection from Harassment Act 1997 s 1(1) or s 1(1A) is guilty of an offence: see s 2 (amended by the Police Reform Act 2002 s 107(2), Sch 8; and the Serious Organised Crime and Police Act 2005 s 125(1), (3)); and CRIMINAL LAW vol 25 (2010) PARA 163.

The Protection from Harassment Act 1997 is not intended to restrict rights to demonstrate and protest on matters of public interest: see *Huntingdon Life Sciences Ltd v Curtin* (1997) Times, 11 December; *DPP v Dziurzynski* [2002] EWHC 1380 (Admin) at [33], (2002) Times, 8 July at [33], [2002] All ER (D) 258 (Jun) at [33] per Rose LJ.

4   Protection from Harassment Act 1997 s 1(1A) (added by the Serious Organised Crime and Police Act 2005 s 125(1), (2)(a)). For these purposes, the person whose course of conduct is in question ought to know that it involves harassment of another if a reasonable person in possession of the same information would think the course of conduct involved harassment of the other: Protection from Harassment Act 1997 s 1(2) (amended by the Serious Organised Crime and Police Act 2005 s 125(1), (2)(b)).

5   Ie the Protection from Harassment Act 1997 s 1(1).

6   Protection from Harassment Act 1997 s 3(1). It is not a requirement of the statutory tort of harassment that the claimant be the, or even a, target of the perpetrator's conduct. The ability to bring a harassment claim extends beyond the targeted individual to those other persons who were foreseeably, and directly, harmed by the course of targeted conduct of which complaint was made, to the extent that they could properly be described as victims of it: *Levi v Bates* [2015] EWCA Civ 206, [2015] All ER (D) 139 (Mar).

7   Protection from Harassment Act 1997 s 3(2). If harassment is proven, the defendant is liable for all injury flowing from it, even if such injury is unforeseeable: *Jones v Ruth* [2011] EWCA Civ 804, [2012] 1 All ER 490, [2012] 1 WLR 1495.

The special time limit for claims in respect of personal injuries (see the Limitation Act 1980 s 11; and PARA 481) does not apply to any claim for damages brought under these provisions: s 11(1A) (added by the Protection from Harassment Act 1997 s 6).

8   Ie the Protection from Harassment Act 1997 s 1(1A).

9   Protection from Harassment Act 1997 s 3A(1), (2) (s 3A added by the Serious Organised Crime and Police Act 2005 s 125(1), (5); and amended by the Crime and Courts Act 2013 s 17(5), Sch 9 Pt 3 para 52(1)(b), (2)). See *The wife and children of Omar Othman v English National Resistance* [2013] All ER (D) 290 (Feb) (family of terrorist suspect granted continuation of injunction preventing protesters demonstrating outside their home); *Brand v Berki* [2014] EWHC 2979 (QB), [2014] All ER (D) 99 (Sep) (celebrity awarded injunction against person who had made series of false allegations against him).

10   See the Protection from Harassment Act 1997 s 3(3)(a).

11   See the Protection from Harassment Act 1997 s 3(3)(b).

12   Protection from Harassment Act 1997 s 3(3) (amended by the Crime and Courts Act 2013 Sch 9 Pt 2 para 39); Protection from Harassment Act 1997 s 3A(3) (s 3A as added: see note 9). An application may be made, where the injunction was granted by the High Court, to a judge of that court, and where the injunction was granted by the County Court, to a judge or district judge of that or any other county court: s 3(4) (amended by the Crime and Courts Act 2013

Sch 9 Pt 2 para 39), Protection from Harassment Act 1997 3A(3) (s 3A as so added). See also
CPR PD 2C—*Starting Proceedings in the County Court* para 4.
13 Protection from Harassment Act 1997 s 3(5) (amended by the Crime and Courts Act 2013 Sch 9
    Pt 2 para 39); Protection from Harassment Act 1997 s 3A(3) (s 3A as added: see note 9).
14 Ie for the purpose mentioned in the Protection from Harassment Act 1997 s 3(3)(a) (see the text
    and note 10).
15 Protection from Harassment Act 1997 s 3(6) (amended by the Crime and Courts Act 2013 Sch 9
    Pt 2 para 39); Protection from Harassment Act 1997 s 3A(3) (s 3A as added: see note 9). A
    person guilty of such an offence is liable on conviction on indictment to imprisonment for a term
    not exceeding five years, or a fine, or both, or on summary conviction to imprisonment for a
    term not exceeding six months, or a fine not exceeding the statutory maximum, or both: ss 3(9),
    3A(3) (s 3A as so added). As to the statutory maximum see SENTENCING AND DISPOSITION OF
    OFFENDERS vol 92 (2010) PARA 140.
        Where a person is convicted of an offence under s 3(6) in respect of any conduct, that
    conduct is not punishable as a contempt of court (ss 3(7), 3A(3) (s 3A as so added)), and a
    person cannot be convicted of an offence under s 3(6) in respect of any conduct which has been
    punished as a contempt of court (ss 3(8), 3A(3) (s 3A as so added)).

4. TORTS TO REPUTATION AND PRIVACY

(1) LIBEL AND SLANDER

559. Elements of libel and slander. Every person is entitled to his good name and to the esteem in which he is held by others, and has a right to claim that his reputation will not be disparaged by defamatory statements made about him to a third person without lawful justification or excuse[1]. If the defamatory statement is made in writing or some other permanent form the tort of libel[2] is committed and the law presumes damage[3]. If the defamation is oral, or in some other transient form, it constitutes the tort of slander[4], which is not actionable without proof of special damage[5] except where the statement is of a particular character.

1 The torts of libel and slander are considered in more detail elsewhere in this work: see DEFAMATION vol 32 (2012) PARA 501 et seq.
2 As to the publication of libel see DEFAMATION vol 32 (2012) PARA 560 et seq.
3 See DEFAMATION vol 32 (2012) PARA 746 et seq, 757.
4 As to the publication of slander see DEFAMATION vol 32 (2012) PARA 579 et seq.
5 See DEFAMATION vol 32 (2012) PARAS 757–759. See also DAMAGES vol 29 (2014) PARAS 317, 426.

560. What the claimant has to prove to establish claim for libel or slander. In order to establish a prima facie case in a claim for libel or slander it is necessary for the claimant to prove that the words complained of were published[1], were defamatory of him[2] and were published by the defendant in circumstances in which the defendant is responsible for the publication[3]. A statement is not defamatory unless its publication has caused or is likely to cause serious harm to the reputation of the claimant[4].

1 As to the requirement of reference to the claimant see DEFAMATION vol 32 (2012) PARAS 540–542.
2 As to defamatory statements see DEFAMATION vol 32 (2012) PARA 540 et seq.
3 As to publication of libel and slander see DEFAMATION vol 32 (2012) PARAS 560 et seq, 579 et seq.
4 See the Defamation Act 2013 s 1(1); and DEFAMATION vol 32 (2012) PARA 543. Note that harm to the reputation of a body that trades for profit is not 'serious harm' unless it has caused or is likely to cause the body serious financial loss: see s 1(2).

561. Defences to libel and slander claims. The main defences to a claim for libel or slander are:
(1) truth (meaning that the imputation conveyed by the statement complained of is substantially true)[1];
(2) honest opinion[2];
(3) reports protected by privilege[3];
(4) publication on a matter of public interest[4];
(5) the making of an offer of amends under statutory provisions[5];
(6) consent of the claimant ('leave and licence')[6];
(7) innocent dissemination[7]; and
(8) apology and payment into court[8].
It is also a defence for a website operator in respect of a statement posted on that site to show that it was not the operator who posted the statement on the website[9]. Publication of a statement in a scientific or academic journal is privileged if the statement relates to a scientific or academic matter and if, before the statement was published in the journal, an independent review of the

statement's scientific or academic merit was carried out by the editor of the journal and one or more persons with expertise in the scientific or academic matter concerned[10].

1   See the Defamation Act 2013 s 2; and DEFAMATION vol 32 (2012) PARA 582 et seq.
2   See the Defamation Act 2013 s 3; and DEFAMATION vol 32 (2012) PARA 637 et seq.
3   See the Defamation Act 2013 s 7. As to absolute privilege see DEFAMATION vol 32 (2012) PARA 594 et seq. As to qualified privilege see DEFAMATION vol 32 (2012) PARA 509 et seq.
4   See the Defamation Act 2013 s 4; and DEFAMATION vol 32 (2012) PARA 622.
5   Ie under the Defamation Act 1996 ss 2–4. As to offers of amends see DEFAMATION vol 32 (2012) PARA 663 et seq.
6   As to leave and licence see DEFAMATION vol 32 (2012) PARAS 669–670.
7   As to innocent dissemination see DEFAMATION vol 32 (2012) PARAS 660–662.
8   As to apologies and payments into court see DEFAMATION vol 32 (2012) PARA 668.
9   See the Defamation Act 2013 s 5; and DEFAMATION vol 32 (2012) PARA 660A.
10 See the Defamation Act 2013 s 6; and DEFAMATION vol 32 (2012) PARA 660A.

(2) INVASION OF PRIVACY

562.   Tort of disclosing private information without lawful authority.   There is no general tort of invasion of privacy[1]. It is, however, a tort to disclose private information concerning a natural person without lawful authority[2]. It has been held that there is no reason why misuse of private information should not be recognised as a tort for the purposes of service out of the jurisdiction, as it is a civil wrong without any equitable characteristics[3].

It should also be noted that a number of other torts may serve to protect personal privacy in particular circumstances[4]. The constant surveillance of the claimant's house, accompanied by the photographing of his every activity, may constitute a private nuisance[5] or harassment[6]. If a newspaper maliciously publishes information about a person's distant criminal past a claim in defamation may be brought[7]. It is a trespass to enter a person's home without permission[8]. If a photographer sells to the press a copy of a photograph of someone who is now an object of public interest he might be sued for infringement of copyright[9].

1   See *Wainwright v Home Office* [2003] UKHL 53, [2004] 2 AC 406, [2003] 4 All ER 969. As to the protection of the privacy of natural persons under the Convention for the Protection of Human Rights and Fundamental Freedoms (Rome, 4 November 1950; TS 71 (1953); Cmd 8969) art 8 and the Human Rights Act 1998 see PARA 810. Under other statutes, protection of privacy may extend to bodies corporate: see *R v Broadcasting Standards Commission, ex p British Broadcasting Corpn* [2001] QB 885, [2000] 3 All ER 989, CA.
2   See *Douglas v Hello! Ltd* [2001] QB 967, [2001] 2 All ER 289, CA; *A v B plc* [2002] EWCA Civ 337, [2003] QB 195, [2002] 2 All ER 545; *Campbell v MGN Ltd* [2004] UKHL 22, [2004] 2 AC 457, [2004] 2 All ER 995; *McKennitt v Ash* [2006] EWCA Civ 1714, [2008] QB 73, [2007] EMLR 113; *HRH Prince of Wales v Associated Newspapers* [2006] EWCA Civ 1776, [2008] Ch 57, [2007] 2 All ER 139. See further CONFIDENCE AND INFORMATIONAL PRIVACY.
3   *Vidal-Hall v Google Inc (The Information Commissioner intervening)* [2015] EWCA Civ 311, 165 NLJ 7648, [2015] All ER (D) 307 (Mar). See further CIVIL PROCEDURE; CONFIDENCE AND INFORMATIONAL PRIVACY.
4   See eg *Kaye v Robertson* [1991] FSR 62, (1990) Times, 21 March CA (remedy for injurious falsehood).
5   *Baron Bernstein of Leigh v Skyviews and General Ltd* [1978] QB 479 at 489, [1977] 2 All ER 902 at 909 per Griffiths J. However, a single flight over someone's land to take a photograph is not a trespass or a private nuisance or otherwise actionable: *Baron Bernstein of Leigh v Skyviews and General Ltd* [1978] QB 479 at 489, [1977] 2 All ER 902 at 909. Persistent harassment by telephone calls could amount to an actionable nuisance: *Motherwell v Motherwell* (1976) 73 DLR (3d) 62, Alta App Div; *Khorasandjian v Bush* [1993] QB 727, [1993] 3 All ER 669, CA. But note that the claim must be brought by a person with an interest

in the land affected: see NUISANCE vol 78 (2010) PARA 179. In such a case, a claim could also be brought under the Protection from Harassment Act 1997: see PARA 558.

6 Ie under the Protection from Harassment Act 1997: see PARA 558.

7 See the Rehabilitation of Offenders Act 1974 s 8; and DEFAMATION vol 32 (2012) PARAS 592, 601, 645.

8 As to trespass to land see PARA 563 et seq.

9 *Williams v Settle* [1960] 2 All ER 806, [1960] 1 WLR 1072, CA; *Nottinghamshire Healthcare NHS Trust v News Group Newspapers Ltd* [2002] EWHC 409 (Ch), [2002] RPC 962, [2002] EMLR 33. If the information in the photograph is private, there may also be a claim for wrongful disclosure of private information: see *Campbell v MGN Ltd* [2004] UKHL 22, [2004] 2 AC 457, [2004] 2 All ER 995.

5. TORTS TO LAND

(1) TRESPASS TO LAND

(i) What Constitutes Trespass to Land

563. Unlawful presence on land. A person's unlawful presence on land in the possession[1] of another is a trespass for which a claim may be brought[2], even though no actual damage is done[3]. A person trespasses upon land if he wrongfully sets foot on it, rides or drives over it[4] or takes possession of it[5], or expels the person in possession[6], or pulls down or destroys anything permanently fixed to it[7], or wrongfully takes minerals from it[8], or places or fixes anything on it[9] or in it[10], or if he erects or suffers to continue on his own land anything which invades the airspace of another[11]. He also commits a trespass to land if, having entered lawfully, he unlawfully remains after his authority to be there expires[12].

1   As to what constitutes possession in the context of trespass to land see PARAS 574–575.
2   The claimant does not have to plead trespass to land specifically in his particulars of claim: see *Drane v Evangelou* [1978] 2 All ER 437, [1978] 1 WLR 455, CA.
3   See e g *Ashby v White* (1703) 2 Ld Raym 938 at 955 per Holt CJ; *Entick v Carrington* (1765) 19 State Tr 1029 at 1066; *Armstrong v Sheppard and Short Ltd* [1959] 2 QB 384, [1959] 2 All ER 651, CA; *Mayor of London v Hall* [2010] EWCA Civ 817, [2011] 1 WLR 504, [2010] All ER (D) 171 (Jul) (see LONDON GOVERNMENT vol 71 (2013) PARA 299). See also *Sun Street Properties Ltd v Persons Unknown* [2011] EWHC 3432 (Ch), (2012) Times, 16 January, [2011] All ER (D) 72 (Dec) (lawfulness of injunction requiring persons to leave land). As to trespass on the highway see *DPP v Jones* [1999] 2 AC 240, [1999] 2 All ER 257, HL; *Harrison v Duke of Rutland* [1893] 1 QB 142, CA; *Hickman v Maisey* [1900] 1 QB 752, CA.
4   *Blundell v Catterall* (1821) 5 B & Ald 268 (crossing the seashore on foot or with bathing machine). See also *League Against Cruel Sports Ltd v Scott* [1986] QB 240, [1985] 2 All ER 489 (master of hounds liable for trespass when hounds entered prohibited land).
5   A squatter is a trespasser: *McPhail v Persons, names unknown* [1973] Ch 447 at 456, [1973] 3 All ER 393 at 396, CA, per Lord Denning MR.
6   *Murray v Hall* (1849) 7 CB 441 (expulsion of one tenant in common by another: see PARA 580; and REAL PROPERTY AND REGISTRATION vol 87 (2012) PARA 201); *Watson v Murray & Co* [1955] 2 QB 1, [1955] 1 All ER 350 (sheriff's officer executing writ of fieri facias excluding debtor from premises for purpose of holding sale there: see CIVIL PROCEDURE vol 12 (2009) PARA 1386). As to unlawful eviction by a landlord see LANDLORD AND TENANT vol 63 (2012) PARA 801 et seq.
7   *Lavender v Betts* [1942] 2 All ER 72 (landlord removing doors and windows). Cf action which does not involve a trespass, e g cutting off the gas and electricity supply: *Perera v Vandiyar* [1953] 1 All ER 1109, [1953] 1 WLR 672, CA; but see now the Protection from Eviction Act 1977 (see LANDLORD AND TENANT vol 63 (2012) PARA 801 et seq). For the measure of damages see also the Housing Act 1988 ss 27, 28; and LANDLORD AND TENANT vol 63 (2012) PARAS 802–803.
8   See MINES, MINERALS AND QUARRIES vol 76 (2013) PARA 29 et seq.
9   *Mace v Philcox* (1864) 15 CBNS 600 (placing a bathing machine on the seashore); *Leader v Moody* (1875) LR 20 Eq 145 (lessee making temporary structural alterations in a theatre); *Whitwham v Westminster Brymbo Coal and Coke Co* [1896] 2 Ch 538, CA; *Kynoch Ltd v Rowlands* [1912] 1 Ch 527, CA (tipping refuse on land); *Gregory v Piper* (1829) 9 B & C 591 (rubbish against wall); *South Wales and Liverpool Steamship Co Ltd v Nevill's Dock and Rly Co Ltd* (1913) 18 Com Cas 124 (unlawful occupation of berth by a ship in a dock); *Westripp v Baldock* [1938] 2 All ER 779 (on appeal [1939] 1 All ER 279, CA) (placing of ladders and other articles against the wall of another). As to leaving objects on land see *Konskier v B Goodman Ltd* [1928] 1 KB 421, CA; *Hudson v Nicholson* (1839) 5 M & W 437.
10 *Schweder v Worthing Gas Light and Coke Co* [1912] 1 Ch 83 (gas pipes) (further proceedings in *Schweder v Worthing Gas Light and Coke Co (No 2)* [1913] 1 Ch 118); *Bocardo SA v Star Energy UK Onshore Ltd* [2010] UKSC 35, [2011] 1 AC 380, [2010] 3 All ER 975 (oil pipeline at depths of 2,800 ft below the surface). In the latter case, the Supreme Court held that the

owner of land has possession of all the substrata below the surface in so far as the proposition can sensibly be applied (see at [26]–[27] per Lord Hope).

Exploding dynamite in a river is a trespass to the land of the riparian owner (*Marquis of Lansdowne v Kerry County Council* (1914) 48 ILT 58); so is the discharge of effluent through a sewer the construction of which is itself a trespass (*Armstrong v Sheppard and Short Ltd* [1959] 2 QB 384, [1959] 2 All ER 651, CA).

11 *Kelsen v Imperial Tobacco Co (of Great Britain and Ireland) Ltd* [1957] 2 QB 334, [1957] 2 All ER 343, where the invasion of the plaintiff's airspace by a projecting neon sign amounted to a trespass and not merely nuisance, applying *Gifford v Dent* [1926] WN 336. In *Kelsen v Imperial Tobacco Co (of Great Britain and Ireland) Ltd* above, McNair J concluded that *Pickering v Rudd* (1815) 4 Camp 219, where a board projecting over the plaintiff's land was held to be no trespass, was no longer good law. See also *Stadium Capital Holdings (No 2) Ltd v St Marylebone Property Company plc* [2010] EWCA Civ 952, [2010] All ER (D) 83 (Nov). A landowner's right in the airspace extends only to such a height as is necessary for the ordinary use and enjoyment by him of his land and structures upon it: *Baron Bernstein of Leigh v Skyviews and General Ltd* [1978] QB 479, [1977] 2 All ER 902, approving *Kelsen v Imperial Tobacco Co (of Great Britain and Ireland) Ltd* above. See also *Woollerton and Wilson Ltd v Richard Costain Ltd* [1970] 1 All ER 483, [1970] 1 WLR 411; *Anchor Brewhouse Developments Ltd v Berkley House (Docklands Developments Ltd)* [1987] 2 EGLR 173, 38 BLR 82 (intrusions by tower crane); *Laiqat v Majid* [2005] EWHC 1305 (QB), [2005] 26 EG 130 (CS), [2005] All ER (D) 231 (Jun) (intrusion by extractor fan). As to trespass by aircraft see PARA 570.

12 See *Wood v Leadbitter* (1845) 13 M & W 838; and PARAS 566, 582. A licensee must be given reasonable time to leave the land on revocation of the licence: see *Robson v Hallett* [1967] 2 QB 939, [1967] 2 All ER 407, DC.

564. Trespass and nuisance distinguished. Where there is no act of direct intrusion on another person's property, liability in trespass does not arise, although liability may arise in nuisance[1]. If an occupier of land brings onto it anything which is not naturally there, and which is likely to do damage if it escapes, he keeps it at his peril and is liable in private nuisance for all the damage which is the natural consequence of its escape[2]. However, ordinary use of land does not give rise to liability to neighbouring owners or occupiers for such mischief as it may occasion them[3].

1 As to the distinction between trespass and nuisance see *Southport Corpn v Esso Petroleum Co Ltd* [1953] 2 All ER 1204 at 1208, [1953] 3 WLR 773 at 776 per Devlin J; and NUISANCE vol 78 (2010) PARA 102. As to the elements of the tort of nuisance see NUISANCE vol 78 (2010) PARA 109 et seq. Damage is an essential element of the cause of action for nuisance (see NUISANCE vol 78 (2010) PARA 112 et seq) but not of the tort of trespass (see PARA 563).

Branches of trees or roots growing over or into another's land may give rise to a claim in nuisance, but not in trespass: *Lemmon v Webb* [1894] 3 Ch 1, CA (affd [1895] AC 1, HL); *Smith v Giddy* [1904] 2 KB 448; *Davey v Harrow Corpn* [1958] 1 QB 60, [1957] 2 All ER 305, CA; *Delaware Mansions Ltd v Westminster City Council* [2001] UKHL 55, [2002] 1 AC 321, [2001] 4 All ER 737.

As to a merely consequential, as opposed to a direct, injury (eg by allowing a structure to decay and fall on the claimant's land) see *Tenant v Goldwin* (1704) 2 Ld Raym 1089. See also *Mann v Saulnier* (1959) 19 DLR (2d) 130 (fence leaning because of decay a nuisance, not a trespass in air space). It has been held that it was trespass to allow faecal matter under the defendant's control to escape into a river in such a manner or under such conditions that it was carried, whether by the current or the wind, onto the plaintiff's land: see *Jones v Llanrwst UDC* [1911] 1 Ch 393 at 402 per Parker J. See also *Foster v Warblington UDC* [1906] 1 KB 648, CA; *Southport Corpn v Esso Petroleum Co Ltd* [1954] 2 QB 182 at 204, [1954] 2 All ER 561 at 576, CA, per Morris LJ (approving *Jones v Llanrwst UDC* [1911] 1 Ch 393); but cf *Southport Corpn v Esso Petroleum Co Ltd* [1954] 2 QB 182 at 195, [1954] 2 All ER 561 at 570, CA, per Denning LJ, holding on the facts that trespass would not lie because the damage was caused consequentially and not directly. See also the judgments in this case on appeal: *Esso Petroleum Co Ltd v Southport Corpn* [1956] AC 218 at 242, [1955] 3 All ER 864 at 872, HL, per Lord Radcliffe (distinguishing *Jones v Llanrwst UDC* [1911] 1 Ch 393), and at 244 and 873 per Lord Tucker (who inclined to agree with Denning LJ). See further *Home Brewery Co Ltd v*

William Davis & Co (Leicester) Ltd [1987] QB 339, [1987] 1 All ER 637 (doubt as to whether water forced out of osier beds by operations of defendants was trespass or nuisance; as damage was caused there was no necessity to distinguish the torts); *Miller v Jackson* [1977] QB 966, [1977] 3 All ER 338, CA (cricket balls landing in plaintiff's garden held to be a nuisance; claimant not pleading trespass).

2   See *Rylands v Fletcher* (1868) LR 3 HL 330; *Cambridge Water Co v Eastern Counties Leather plc* [1994] 2 AC 264, [1994] 1 All ER 53, HL (element of foreseeability required); *Transco plc v Stockport Metropolitan Borough Council* [2003] UKHL 61, [2004] 2 AC 1, [2004] 1 All ER 589; and NUISANCE vol 78 (2010) PARA 148 et seq.

3   See NUISANCE vol 78 (2010) PARA 118.

565.   Enforcement agent acting under the Tribunals, Courts and Enforcement Act 2007.   Where, in the process of taking control of goods and selling them to recover a sum of money[1], an enforcement agent breaches any of the procedural provisions of the Tribunals, Courts and Enforcement Act 2007[2] or acts under an enforcement power under a defective writ, warrant, liability order or other instrument[3], that breach or defect does not make the enforcement agent, or a person he is acting for, a trespasser[4]. The debtor may, however, bring proceedings for a court order for the goods to be returned to the debtor or to order the enforcement agent or a related party to pay damages in respect of loss suffered by the debtor as a result of the breach or of anything done under the defective instrument[5]. However, no damages will be awarded against an enforcement agent who acted in the reasonable belief that the instrument under which he acted was not defective[6].

1   Ie under the Commercial Rent Arrears Recovery regime: see the Taking Control of Goods Regulations 2013, SI 2013/1894; CPR PD 84—*Enforcement by Taking Control of Goods*; and CIVIL PROCEDURE vol 12 (2009) PARA 1386 et seq.

2   Tribunals, Courts and Enforcement Act 2007 Sch 12. These rules replace the common law on distress for rent: see s 65.

3   Tribunals, Courts and Enforcement Act 2007 Sch 12 para 66(1)

4   Tribunals, Courts and Enforcement Act 2007 Sch 12 para 66(2).

5   Tribunals, Courts and Enforcement Act 2007 Sch 12 para 66(3)–(9). See further CIVIL PROCEDURE vol 12 (2009) PARA 1409.

6   See the Tribunals, Courts and Enforcement Act 2007 Sch 12 para 66(8).

566.   Tenant as trespasser at determination of tenancy.   If a tenancy determines by effluxion of time or otherwise, and the former tenant remains in possession against the will of the rightful owner, the former tenant is, apart from statutory protection, a trespasser from the date of the determination of the tenancy[1]. A tenant holding over is not a trespasser until demand is made, since trespass can only be committed against the present possessor of the land[2].

1   *Coffee v McEvoy* [1912] 2 IR 290, Ir CA. As to a tenant at sufferance see LANDLORD AND TENANT vol 62 (2012) PARAS 206–207. A tenant pur autre vie holding over after the death of the cestui que vie, without consent of the person next entitled, is a trespasser: see the Cestui que Vie Act 1707 s 5; and REAL PROPERTY AND REGISTRATION vol 87 (2012) PARA 151.

2   *Hey v Moorhouse* (1839) 6 Bing NC 52. As to persons refusing to leave a ship on the termination of a licence see *Canadian Pacific Rly v Gaud* [1949] 2 KB 239, CA.

567.   Abuse of public or private right over land.   If land is subject to a public or private right of way or any similar right over land, a person who unlawfully uses the land for any purpose other than that of exercising the right to which it is subject is a trespasser, and can be sued by the person in possession of the land[1].

1   *Lade v Shepherd* (1735) 2 Stra 1004; *Northampton Corpn v Ward* (1745) 1 Wils 107; *Dovaston v Payne* (1795) 2 H Bl 257; *Cox v Glue, Cox v Saint, Cox v Mousley* (1848) 5 CB 533; *Rigg v Earl of Lonsdale* (1857) 1 H & N 923, Ex Ch; *Harrison v Duke of Rutland* [1893] 1 QB

142, CA; *Hickman v Maisey* [1900] 1 QB 752, CA (distinguished in *Randall v Tarrant* [1955] 1 All ER 600, [1955] 1 WLR 255, CA); *Staffordshire and Worcestershire Canal Navigation v Bradley* [1912] 1 Ch 91; *Iveagh v Martin* [1961] 1 QB 232 at 273, [1960] 2 All ER 668 at 683–684 per Paull J; *DPP v Jones* [1999] 2 AC 240, [1999] 2 All ER 257, HL (a peaceful non-obstructive demonstration on a road is not a trespassory assembly within the Public Order Act 1986 ss 14A, 14B(2) (see CRIMINAL LAW vol 26 (2010) PARA 536)).

In *DPP v Jones* [1999] 2 AC 240, [1999] 2 All ER 257, HL, the House of Lords ruled that the public's right of access to a public highway is not restricted to the right of passage and matters incidental or ancillary to that right, and may extend to a peaceful and non-obstructive assembly on it. Earlier cases on demonstrations and other public assemblies must now be read in that light: see e g *Ex p Lewis* (1888) 21 QBD 191; *Hubbard v Pitt* [1976] QB 142, [1975] 3 All ER 1, CA. See also HIGHWAYS, STREETS AND BRIDGES vol 55 (2012) PARA 200. The foreshore is not a public highway and the public have no general right to use it: see *Lord Fitzhardinge v Purcell* [1908] 2 Ch 139; *Iveagh v Martin* [1961] 1 QB 232 at 273, [1960] 2 All ER 668 at 683–684 per Paull J; c f *Llandudno UDC v Woods* [1899] 2 Ch 705 (injunction not granted because harm trivial); and see also FISHERIES AND AQUACULTURE vol 51 (2013) PARA 383. As to excessive user of a right of way see REAL PROPERTY AND REGISTRATION vol 87 (2012) PARA 940.

568. Trespass ab initio. If a person enters on the land of another under an authority given him by law, and, while there, abuses the authority by an act which amounts to a trespass, he becomes a trespasser ab initio, and may be sued as if his original entry were unlawful[1]. Instances of an entry under the authority of the law are the entry of a customer into a common inn, of a reversioner to see if waste has been done, or of a commoner to see his cattle[2].

To make a person a trespasser ab initio there must be a wrongful act committed; a mere nonfeasance is not enough[3].

1 *Six Carpenters' Case* (1610) 8 Co Rep 146a. A lawful entry followed by lawful seizure of some goods and unlawful seizure of others will not make the person so entering a trespasser ab initio in respect of those lawfully seized or in respect of the premises: *Canadian Pacific Wine Co v Tuley* [1921] 2 AC 417, PC; *Elias v Pasmore* [1934] 2 KB 164; *Owen and Smith (t/a Nuagin Car Service) v Reo Motors (Britain) Ltd* (1934) 151 LT 274, CA, per Maugham LJ. See also *Chic Fashions (West Wales) Ltd v Jones* [1968] 2 QB 299, [1968] 1 All ER 229, CA, in which the rule was criticised; but contra *Cinnamond v British Airports Authority* [1980] 2 All ER 368 at 373, [1980] 1 WLR 582 at 588, CA, per Lord Denning MR.

2 *Six Carpenters' Case* (1610) 8 Co Rep 146a. Where an enforcement agent acts in breach of the Tribunals, Courts and Enforcement Act 2007 Sch 12 (procedure for taking control of goods) or under an enforcement power under a defective instrument, the breach or defect does not make the enforcement agent, or the person he is acting for, a trespasser: see the Tribunals, Courts and Enforcement Act 2007 Sch 12 para 66; and PARA 565.

3 *Six Carpenters' Case* (1610) 8 Co Rep 146a; *Shorland v Govett* (1826) 5 B & C 485, where it was also said, obiter, that if a person were a trespasser ab initio that would affect the assessment of damages; *West v Nibbs* (1847) 4 CB 172; c f *Winterbourne v Morgan* (1809) 11 East 395.

569. Continuity of trespass and the effects of trespass. It may be necessary to distinguish between continuing trespass and the continuing effects of a trespass. Continuing trespass occurs when a person who is or has become a trespasser remains on the land as a trespasser[1] or when objects placed on or intruding into land by way of trespass remain unremoved[2]. In these circumstances, a new trespass is committed from day to day, successive actions may be brought[3] and the trespasser can be required to remove any trespassing material[4]. The occupier may be entitled to damages even for damage resulting from trespassory intrusion before he went into occupation[5].

Where there are continuing effects of trespass there is one act of intrusion or contact causing persisting damage but no continuing trespassory contact or intrusion. Damages must be assessed in a single action and the trespasser cannot be required to make good the harm[6].

The distinction between a continuing tort and the continuing effects of the tort may affect limitation[7].

1   _Winterbourne v Morgan_ (1809) 11 East 395 at 405 per Bayley J.
2   _Holmes v Wilson_ (1839) 10 Ad & El 503 (trespassing road buttresses not removed after being adjudged trespass); _Hudson v Nicholson_ (1839) 5 M & W 437; _Bowyer v Cook_ (1847) 4 CB 236 (tree stumps and cuttings); _Clarke v Midland Great Western Rly_ [1895] 2 IR 294, Ir CA; _Konskier v B Goodman Ltd_ [1928] 1 KB 421, CA (builders' rubbish). Damages are assessed to the judgment date unless they are awarded in lieu of an injunction, when they may take account of future harm: _Leeds Industrial Co-operative Society v Slack_ [1924] AC 851, HL.
3   _Holmes v Wilson_ (1839) 10 Ad & El 503.
4   _Holmes v Wilson_ (1839) 10 Ad & El 503.
5   By analogy with private nuisance: see _Masters v Brent London Borough Council_ [1978] QB 841, [1978] 2 All ER 664; _Delaware Mansions Ltd v Westminster City Council_ [2001] UKHL 55, [2002] 1 AC 321, [2001] 4 All ER 737.
6   _Clegg v Dearden_ (1848) 12 QB 576.
7   Analogy with other torts suggests that, in the case of continuing effects, time runs from the commission of the tort (see _Violett v Sympson_ (1857) 8 E & B 344 (maliciously opposing release from imprisonment)), but in the case of a continuing trespass time runs from day to day as long as the trespass continues (see _Massey v Johnson_ (1809) 12 East 67; _Bailey v Warden_ (1815) 4 M & S 400; _Hardy v Ryle_ (1829) 9 B & C 603 (false imprisonment); _Earl of Harrington v Derby Corpn_ [1905] 1 Ch 205 (nuisance)). See generally LIMITATION PERIODS vol 68 (2008) PARA 977 et seq.

570. Trespass by aircraft. The mere entry by an aircraft into the airspace above a person's land is not a trespass[1]. No claim may be brought in respect of trespass by aircraft by reason only of the flight of the aircraft over any property at a height above the ground which, having regard to wind, weather and all the circumstances of the case, is reasonable, or by reason of the ordinary incidents of such flight, provided the statutory conditions are complied with[2].

1   _Baron Bernstein of Leigh v Skyviews and General Ltd_ [1978] QB 479, [1977] 2 All ER 902 (aircraft pilot flying over a house to photograph it without the owner's permission).
2   See the Civil Aviation Act 1982 s 76(1); and AIR LAW vol 2 (2008) PARA 652 et seq. The Act does not merely protect the right of passage over land but applies to all flights: see _Baron Bernstein of Leigh v Skyviews and General Ltd_ [1978] QB 479 at 488–489, [1977] 2 All ER 902 at 908–909 per Griffiths J, considering the same provision in earlier legislation. However, where any material loss or damage is caused to any person or property on land or water by, or by a person in or an article or person falling from an aircraft while in flight, taking off or landing then, unless the loss or damage was contributed to by the negligence of the victim, damages in respect of the loss or damage are recoverable without proof of negligence or intention or other cause of action, as if the harm had been caused by the wilful act, neglect or default of the owner of the aircraft: see the Civil Aviation Act 1982 s 76(2); and AIR LAW vol 2 (2008) PARA 654. 'Loss or damage' includes, in relation to persons, loss of life and personal injury: s 105(1). As to taking off see _Blankley v Godley_ [1952] 1 All ER 436n.

571. Subject matter of trespass to land. The subject matter of trespass to land must be real and corporeal property, that is, land or buildings, or the vesture of land or herbage or pasture, to the exclusive possession of which the person complaining of the trespass is entitled[1]. A mere incorporeal right, such as a right of common or pasture, fishing or digging turf, or a right of way, or a right to a pew or any easement annexed to land, does not confer standing to sue for trespass to the land if such a right does not give exclusive possession[2].

1   Co Litt 4b; 2 Roll Abr 549, Trespass (H); _Burt v Moore_ (1793) 5 Term Rep 329; _Crosby v Wadsworth_ (1805) 6 East 602; _Stammers v Dixon_ (1806) 7 East 200; _Stanley v White_ (1811) 14 East 332; _Tompkinson v Russell_ (1821) 9 Price 287; _Harper v Charlesworth_ (1825) 4 B & C 574; _Cox v Glue, Cox v Saint, Cox v Mousley_ (1848) 5 CB 533; _Wellaway v Courtier_ [1918] 1 KB 200, DC; _Back v Daniels_ [1925] 1 KB 526 at 542, CA, per Scrutton LJ; _Monsanto plc v Tilly_ [2000] Env LR 313, [1999] NLJR 1833, CA. Trespass lies for an interference with an

exclusive right of cutting turf (*Wilson v Mackreth* (1766) 3 Burr 1824; *Coverdale v Charlton* (1878) 4 QBD 104, CA), or underwood (*Hoe v Taylor* (1595) 4 Cro Eliz 413), or timber (*Glenwood Lumber Co Ltd v Phillips* [1904] AC 405, PC), or for interference with a several fishery (*Holford v Bailey* (1846) 8 QB 1000 (revsd (1849) 13 QB 426, Ex Ch); *Marshall v Ulleswater Steam Navigation Co Ltd* (1863) 3 B & S 732 (affd (1865) 6 B & S 570, Ex Ch); *Crichton v Collery* (1870) 19 WR 107; *Fitzgerald v Firbank* [1897] 2 Ch 96, CA; *Nicholls v Ely Beet Sugar Factory* [1931] 2 Ch 84: see FISHERIES AND AQUACULTURE vol 51 (2013) PARA 423), or a free warren (*Lord Dacre v Tebb* (1777) 2 Wm Bl 1151; see COMMONS vol 13 (2009) PARAS 454, 464). See generally REAL PROPERTY AND REGISTRATION vol 87 (2012) PARA 325. Where trees are excepted from a lease, the lessor may enter and cut them (*Ashmead v Ranger* (1700) 1 Ld Raym 551; revsd (1702) Lords Journals, 27 April), and if the tenant cuts them the lessor may bring a claim of trespass (*Rolls v Rock* (1729) 2 Selwyn's Law of Nisi Prius (13th Edn) 1244). See also LANDLORD AND TENANT vol 62 (2012) PARA 191. A person in possession of the surface is prima facie in possession of the subsoil (*Keyse v Powell* (1853) 2 E & B 132), but possession of the surface may be in one person and possession of the subsoil in another (*Cox v Glue, Cox v Saint, Cox v Mousley* (1848) 5 CB 533). The owner of a close upon which others have a right to depasture cattle, with exclusive possession during the period of depasturage, may maintain trespass against a party who digs holes in the close, but not against one who rides over it: *Cox v Glue, Cox v Saint, Cox v Mousley* (1848) 5 CB 533. See also note 2.

2   *Wilson v Mackreth* (1766) 3 Burr 1824; *Stocks v Booth* (1786) 1 Term Rep 428 at 430; *Mainwaring v Giles* (1822) 5 B & Ald 356; *Bryan v Whistler* (1828) 8 B & C 288. A claim may be brought for the disturbance of such a right: see *Fitzpatrick v Verschoyle* [1912] 1 IR 8; *King v Brown, Durant & Co* [1913] 2 Ch 416; and REAL PROPERTY AND REGISTRATION vol 87 (2012) PARAS 657–658. A claim of trespass lies by a person who has by prescription acquired the ownership of a private chapel: see *Chapman v Jones* (1869) LR 4 Exch 273; *Duke of Norfolk v Arbuthnot* (1880) 5 CPD 390, CA. The erector of a tombstone may maintain trespass against a person who wrongfully removes it from the churchyard: *Spooner v Brewster* (1825) 3 Bing 136. See also ECCLESIASTICAL LAW vol 34 (2011) PARA 853.

572.   Proceedings for trespass in respect of land out of the jurisdiction. Any court in England and Wales or Northern Ireland has jurisdiction to entertain proceedings for trespass to land situated outside that part of the United Kingdom unless the proceedings are principally concerned with a question of title or the right to possession[1].

1   See PARA 490; and CONFLICT OF LAWS vol 19 (2011) PARA 688 et seq.

573.   Intention or negligence of the defendant. If the defendant intends to enter the land on to which he trespassed it is no defence that he mistakenly thought that it was his own land or that he had authority to be there[1]; nor is it a defence that he inadvertently crossed the boundary between the claimant's land and his own[2]. But there is no liability if his act is involuntary[3].

Liability in trespass may arise where the defendant intentionally or negligently causes or allows things under his control to enter the claimant's land[4], but not if the entry occurred without his fault[5].

1   *Conway v George Wimpey & Co Ltd* [1951] 2 KB 266 at 274, [1951] 1 All ER 363 at 366–367, CA, per Asquith LJ.

2   *Basely v Clarkson* (1681) 3 Lev 37.

3   *Smith v Stone* (1647) Sty 65 (defendant not liable where he was carried and thrown onto the plaintiff's land); *National Coal Board v JE Evans & Co (Cardiff) Ltd and Maberley Parker Ltd* [1951] 2 KB 861, [1951] 2 All ER 310, CA. Duress is not a defence: *Gilbert v Stone* (1647) Aleyn 35.

4   *Read v Edwards* (1864) 17 CB NS 245; *League Against Cruel Sports Ltd v Scott* [1986] QB 240, [1985] 2 All ER 489.

5   *Brown v Giles* (1823) 1 C & P 118. See also PARA 564 note 1.

(ii) Possession Sufficient to Support Trespass to Land

574. Form of possession sufficient to support claim for trespass. Any form of possession, so long as it is exclusive and exercised with the intention to possess[1], is sufficient to support a claim of trespass against a wrongdoer[2]. It is not necessary, in order to maintain trespass, that the claimant's possession should be lawful[3], and actual possession is good against all except those who can show a better right to possession in themselves[4]. However, a mere trespasser who goes into occupation cannot by the very act of trespass and without acquiescence give himself possession against the person whom he has ejected[5]. Such a person may eject the trespasser by force, if no more force is used than is reasonably necessary[6]. The trespasser cannot set up a jus tertii unless he claims under it[7].

1 See PARA 575.
2 It has been held that the slightest amount of possession is sufficient to entitle the person in possession, or the person who claims under those who have been or are in possession, to recover against a mere trespasser: see *Bristow v Cormican* (1878) 3 App Cas 641 at 657, HL, per Lord Hatherley. See also *Wuta-Ofei v Danquah* [1961] 3 All ER 596 at 600, [1961] 1 WLR 1238 at 1243, PC. However, mere possession is not sufficient to support a claim for trespass against the lawful owner of the land: see *Delaney v TP Smith Ltd* [1946] KB 393, [1946] 2 All ER 23, CA.
    In *Bristow v Cormican* (1878) 3 App Cas 641, HL, at 651–652, Lord Cairns LC maintained the proposition, which was not dissented from, that even in the absence of actual possession a documentary title commencing with some person rightfully in possession, or who has an admitted or proved right to be in possession, and connecting itself with the claimant in a claim of trespass would, generally speaking, and in the absence of any title in the defendant by adverse possession, be sufficient to maintain a claim of trespass. However, title need not be shown where the claimant has actual possession: see *Foster v Warblington UDC* [1906] 1 KB 648, CA. Cf *Scorell v Boxall* (1827) 1 Y & J 396.
    A licensee with a contractual right to occupy can claim possession against a trespasser if that remedy is necessary to give effect to his right (*Manchester Airport plc v Dutton* [2000] QB 133, sub nom *Dutton v Manchester Airport plc* [1999] 2 All ER 675, CA) but a licensee without rights of occupation cannot so claim (*Countryside Residential (North Thames) Ltd v T* (2000) 81 P & CR 10, CA). See also *Hounslow London Borough Council v Twickenham Garden Developments Ltd* [1971] Ch 233 at 257, [1970] 3 All ER 326 at 346 per Megarry J.
3 *Graham v Peat* (1801) 1 East 244; *Chambers v Donaldson* (1809) 11 East 65; *Asher v Whitlock* (1865) LR 1 QB 1 (approved in *Perry v Clissold* [1907] AC 73, PC).
4 *Doe d Hughes v Dyeball* (1829) Mood & M 346; *Asher v Whitlock* (1865) LR 1 QB 1; *Perry v Clissold* [1907] AC 73 at 79, PC. Cf *Delaney v TP Smith Ltd* [1946] KB 393, [1946] 2 All ER 23, CA (claim against lawful owner). The defendant to an action for trespass to land cannot set up a jus tertii unless he claims under or with the authority of the true owner, or of a person having a better right to possession than the claimant: see PARA 581. As to jus tertii where the claimant is out of possession and seeks to recover the land see *Ezekiel v Fraser* [2002] EWHC 2066 (Ch), [2002] NPC 132, not following *Doe d Carter v Barnard* (1849) 13 QB 945. As to the right to set up just tertii generally see CIVIL PROCEDURE vol 12 (2009) PARA 1626.
5 *Browne v Dawson* (1840) 12 Ad & El 624; *Stanford v Hurlstone* (1873) 9 Ch App 116.
6 *Scott v Matthew Brown & Co Ltd* (1884) 51 LT 746.
7 See PARA 581. As to the right to set up jus tertii generally see CIVIL PROCEDURE vol 12 (2009) PARA 1626.

575. What constitutes actual possession of land for the purposes of trespass. Actual possession is a question of fact[1]. It consists of two elements: the intention to possess the land and the exercise of control over it to the exclusion of other persons[2]. The extent of the control which should be exercised in order to constitute possession varies with the nature of the land; and possession means possession of that character of which the land is capable[3]. Thus a person may be in possession of minerals even though he is not in possession of the surface and has no actual occupation of the minerals[4].

1   *Bristow v Cormican* (1878) 3 App Cas 641, HL. As to acts of ownership which are evidence of possession see *Malcomson v O'Dea* (1863) 10 HL Cas 593; and CIVIL PROCEDURE vol 11 (2009) PARA 875. See also *Seddon v Smith* (1877) 36 LT 168, CA (ploughing land). Acts of ownership of one part of the land may be evidence of possession of the whole or of other parts: see *Stanley v White* (1811) 14 East 332; *Jones v Williams* (1837) 2 M & W 326; *Taylor v Parry* (1840) 1 Man & G 604; *Wild v Holt* (1842) 9 M & W 672; *Lord Advocate v Lord Blantyre* (1879) 4 App Cas 770 at 791, HL, per Lord Blackburn; *Bristow v Cormican* (1878) 3 App Cas 641, HL; *Coverdale v Charlton* (1878) 4 QBD 104 at 118, CA, per Bramwell LJ; *Clark v Elphinstone* (1880) 6 App Cas 164, PC. As to possession of land see also CONVEYANCING vol 23 (2013) PARAS 215–216; LIMITATION PERIODS vol 68 (2008) PARA 1078 et seq; REAL PROPERTY AND REGISTRATION vol 87 (2012) PARA 162; SETTLEMENTS vol 91 (2012) PARA 662. As to transfer of possession sufficient to constitute a surrender of a lease see LANDLORD AND TENANT vol 63 (2012) PARA 782. As to what amounts to possession by a mortgagee see MORTGAGE vol 77 (2010) PARA 410 et seq. As to the date of transfer of possession on a sale of land see CONVEYANCING vol 23 (2013) PARA 247. As to the right of a tenant for life of settled land to possession see SETTLEMENTS vol 91 (2012) PARA 671. As to licensees see *Manchester Airport plc v Dutton* [2000] QB 133, sub nom *Dutton v Manchester Airport plc* [1999] 2 All ER 675, CA (a licensee with a contractual right to occupy can claim possession against a trespasser if that remedy is necessary to give effect to his right); *Countryside Residential (North Thames) Ltd v T* (2000) 81 P & CR 10, CA (a licensee without rights of occupation cannot so claim). See also *Hounslow London Borough Council v Twickenham Garden Developments Ltd* [1971] Ch 233 at 257, [1970] 3 All ER 326 at 346 per Megarry J.

2   *Powell v McFarlane* (1977) 38 P & CR 452 at 470 per Slade J; *JA Pye (Oxford) Ltd v Graham* [2002] UKHL 30 at [40], [2003] 1 AC 419 at [40], [2002] 3 All ER 865 at [40] per Lord Browne-Wilkinson.

3   *Lord Advocate v Lord Lovat* (1880) 5 App Cas 273 at 288, HL, per Lord O'Hagan; *Lord Advocate v Young, North British Rly Co v Young* (1887) 12 App Cas 544 at 556, HL, per Lord Fitzgerald; *Kirby v Cowderoy* [1912] AC 599, PC; *Kynoch Ltd v Rowlands* [1912] 1 Ch 527, CA; *Hegan v Carolan* [1916] 2 IR 27; *Wuta-Ofei v Danquah* [1961] 3 All ER 596 at 600, [1961] 1 WLR 1238 at 1243, PC. Possession of an unoccupied building may be shown by holding the key or controlling entry: *Jewish Maternity Society's Trustees v Garfinkle* (1926) 95 LJKB 766. See also *Catteris v Cowper* (1812) 4 Taunt 547; *Harper v Charlesworth* (1852) 4 B & C 574; *Jones v Williams* (1837) 2 M & W 326; *Matson v Cook* (1838) 4 Bing NC 392; *Every v Smith* (1857) 26 LJ Ex 344; *Fowley Marine (Emsworth) Ltd v Gafford* [1968] 2 QB 618, [1968] 1 All ER 979, CA; *Ocean Estates v Pinder* [1969] 2 AC 19, [1969] 2 WLR 1359, PC. The possession must be exclusive: see *Powell v McFarlane* (1977) 38 P & CR 452 at 470–471 per Slade J; *JA Pye (Oxford) Ltd v Graham* [2002] UKHL 30 at [41], [2003] 1 AC 419 at [41], [2002] 3 All ER 865 at [41] per Lord Browne-Wilkinson. Even surrounding land with a fence is not sufficient if it does not achieve exclusive possession: *Marsden v Miller* (1992) 64 P & CR 239, CA. In *Coverdale v Charlton* (1878) 4 QBD 104, CA, it was held that pasturing cattle on roadside verges did not establish such possession. However, possession might have been established if the only other road users were trespassers: *Reilly v Thompson & Fagan* (1877) 11 Ir CL 238. See further the cases cited in note 4.

4   *Rich d Lord Cullen v Johnson* (1740) 2 Stra 1142; *Hodgkinson v Fletcher* (1781) 3 Doug KB 31; *Adair v Shaftoe* (circa 1790) cited in 19 Ves at 156; *Seaman v Vawdrey* (1810) 16 Ves 390; *M'Donnell v M'Kinty* (1847) 10 ILR 514; *Keyse v Powell* (1853) 2 E & B 132; *Smith v Lloyd* (1854) 9 Exch 562; *Earl of Dartmouth v Spittle* (1871) 24 LT 67; *Low Moor Co v Stanley Coal Co Ltd* (1876) 34 LT 186, CA; *Ashton v Stock* (1877) 6 ChD 719; *Elwes v Brigg Gas Co* (1886) 33 ChD 562, Ex Ch; *Thompson v Hickman* [1907] 1 Ch 550; *Glyn v Howell* [1909] 1 Ch 666. As to the property in mines and recovery of possession see MINES, MINERALS AND QUARRIES vol 76 (2013) PARAS 18 et seq, 29. As to damages for trespass in a mine and the damages thereby recoverable see MINES, MINERALS AND QUARRIES vol 76 (2013) PARAS 36, 40 et seq, 265, 270 et seq, 599.

(iii) Who may Sue for Trespass to Land

576. Person in possession as claimant in trespass to land. Trespass is an injury to a possessory right, and therefore the proper claimant in a claim of trespass to land is the person who was[1], or who is deemed to have been[2], in possession at the time of the trespass[3]. The owner has no right to sue in trespass if any other person was lawfully in possession of the land at the time of the trespass, since a mere right of property without possession is not sufficient to support the claim[4]. However, if land is vacant, the owner does have sufficient possession to sue in trespass[5]. The type of conduct necessary to evidence possession varies with the type of land, and to maintain a claim against a person who never had any title to the land the slightest amount of possession is sufficient[6]. Where possession is doubtful or equivocal, the law attaches it to the title[7].

1   A non-occupying tenant does not have such possession as will entitle him to maintain trespass: see *Thompson v Ward* [1953] 2 QB 153 at 163–164, [1953] 1 All ER 1169 at 1173–1174, CA, per Evershed MR. Cf *Brown v Draper* [1944] KB 309, [1944] 1 All ER 246, CA; and see LANDLORD AND TENANT vol 63 (2012) PARA 946 (statutory tenant losing rights by abandoning possession).

2   As to trespass by relation see PARA 577.

3   *Smith v Milles* (1786) 1 Term Rep 475; *Barton v Cordy* (1825) M'Cle & Yo 278; *Topham v Dent* (1830) 6 Bing 515; *Alexander v Bonnin* (1838) 6 Scott 611; *Brown v Notley* (1848) 3 Exch 219; *Ryan v Clark* (1849) 14 QB 65; *Turner v Cameron's Coalbrook Steam Coal Co* (1850) 5 Exch 932; *Litchfield v Ready* (1850) 5 Exch 939; *Harrison v Blackburn* (1864) 17 CBNS 678; *Stocker v Planet Building Society* (1879) 27 WR 877, CA; *Cooper v Crabtree* (1882) 20 ChD 589, CA; *Moore v Shelley* (1883) 8 App Cas 285, PC; *New Trinidad Lake Asphalt Co v A-G* [1904] AC 415 at 421, PC; *Marsden v Miller* (1992) 64 P & CR 239, CA. A tenant at sufferance can maintain a claim of trespass: see LANDLORD AND TENANT vol 62 (2012) PARA 207. As to the effect of the person in possession becoming bankrupt after a trespass see *Rose v Buckett* [1901] 2 KB 449, CA (no substantial damage done; action did not pass to trustee); and BANKRUPTCY AND INDIVIDUAL INSOLVENCY vol 5 (2013) PARAS 448–449.

4   *Wallis v Hands* [1893] 2 Ch 75. A lessor at will might bring trespass against a stranger, without first re-entering: see *Anon* (1440) YB 19 Hen 6, fo 44, pl 94; *Geary v Bearecroft* (1667) 1 Lev 202; *Harper v Charlesworth* (1825) 4 B & C 574 at 583; Bro Abr, Trespass, pl 131; 2 Roll Abr 551, Trespass (H); Com Dig, Trespass (B2). If a tenant at will commits voluntary waste, his tenancy is by that act determined and trespass can be brought against him: *Countess of Shrewsbury's Case* (1600) 5 Co Rep 13b; Co Litt 57a (note (1)), 62b; but see LANDLORD AND TENANT vol 62 (2012) PARA 580.

5   *R v St Pancras Assessment Committee* (1877) 2 QBD 581 at 588 per Lush J. However, a bare possessor who leaves without intending to return loses possession entirely: *Trustees, Executors and Agency Co Ltd v Short* (1888) 13 App Cas 793, PC.

6   *Wuta-Ofei v Danquah* [1961] 3 All ER 596 at 600, [1961] 1 WLR 1238 at 1243, PC. It is not necessary, in order to establish possession, for a claimant to take some active steps in relation to the land, such as inclosing it or cultivating it: *Wuta-Ofei v Danquah* [1961] 3 All ER 596 at 600, [1961] 1 WLR 1238 at 1243, PC. See also *Fowley Marine (Emsworth) Ltd v Gafford* [1968] 2 QB 618, [1968] 1 All ER 979, CA (foreshore).

7   *Canvey Island Comrs v Preedy* [1922] 1 Ch 179; *Jones v Chapman* (1849) 2 Exch 803 at 821 per Maule J; *Lows v Telford* (1876) 1 App Cas 414 at 426, HL. See also *Fowley Marine (Emsworth) Ltd v Gafford* [1968] 2 QB 618, [1968] 1 All ER 979, CA.

577.   Person with right to possession as claimant in trespass to land.   A person having the right to the possession of land acquires by entry[1] the lawful possession of it, and may maintain a claim of trespass against any person who, being in possession at the time of entry, wrongfully remains on the land[2].

If an owner who has a right to enter makes an entry on land, his right of possession relates back to the time at which his right of entry accrued, and he may sue for a trespass committed before his entry, the wrongdoer thus becoming a trespasser by relation[3].

The occupation of land by an employee or agent in that capacity vests the possession in the employer or principal; the employee or agent cannot sue in trespass, but the employer or principal can[4]. An occupier of lodgings can sue in trespass if he has exclusive possession[5]. A mere licensee cannot generally maintain trespass[6]. However, a licensee with a contractual right to occupy the land can claim possession against a trespasser if that is necessary to give effect to his contractual right[7].

1   The entry is effective even if made forcibly: see *Hemmings v Stoke Poges Golf Club Ltd* [1920]
     1 KB 720, CA. However, see the Protection from Eviction Act 1977; PARA 589; and LANDLORD
     AND TENANT vol 63 (2012) PARA 801 et seq. No claim for trespass to land lies at the suit of a
     tenant against a landlord for a forcible entry after the expiration of the term: *Taunton v Costar*
     (1797) 7 Term Rep 431; *Argent v Durrant* (1799) 8 Term Rep 403; *Hemmings v Stoke Poges
     Golf Club Ltd* [1920] 1 KB 720, CA. However, where (subject to exceptions) any premises are
     let as a dwelling under a tenancy which has come to an end, but the occupier continues to reside
     in the premises or part of them, it is not lawful for the owner to enforce against the occupier,
     otherwise than by proceedings in the court, his right to recover possession of the premises: see
     the Protection from Eviction Act 1977 s 3 (amended by the Housing Act 1980 s 69(1); and the
     Housing Act 1988 s 30). A landlord may be liable in damages for (amongst other things)
     unlawfully evicting the residential occupier of premises: see the Housing Act 1988 ss 27, 28; and
     LANDLORD AND TENANT vol 63 (2012) PARAS 802–803. There are further restrictions on the
     recovery of possession of premises to which the Rent Acts apply (see LANDLORD AND TENANT),
     and the contractual term of certain business premises is extended by statute (see LANDLORD AND
     TENANT vol 63 (2012) PARA 817). Where a right to possession ceases, possession is deemed to
     cease unless some act indicating an intention to retain possession is done: *Brown v Notley*
     (1848) 3 Exch 219 at 222 per Parke B; *Wuta-Ofei v Danquah* [1961] 3 All ER 596 at 599–600,
     [1961] 1 WLR 1238 at 1242–1243, PC. The slightest acts by the person having title to the land,
     or by his predecessors in title, indicating his intention to take possession may be sufficient to
     enable him to bring an action for trespass against a defendant entering upon the land without
     any title: see *Ocean Estates Ltd v Pinder* [1969] 2 AC 19 at 25, [1969] 2 WLR 1359 at 1364,
     PC.

2   *Taunton v Costar* (1797) 7 Term Rep 431; *Butcher v Butcher* (1827) 7 B & C 399; *Hey v
     Moorhouse* (1839) 6 Bing NC 52; *Jones v Chapman* (1849) 2 Exch 803 at 821, Ex Ch, per
     Maule J; *Lows v Telford* (1876) 1 App Cas 414, HL; *Hegan v Carolan* [1916] 2 IR 27.

3   *Barnett v Earl of Guildford* (1855) 11 Exch 19; *Anderson v Radcliffe* (1858) EB & E 806 (affd
     sub nom *Radcliffe v Anderson* (1860) EB & E 819); *Ocean Accident and Guarantee Corpn v
     Ilford Gas Co* [1905] 2 KB 493, CA.

4   *Bertie v Beaumont* (1812) 16 East 33; *Moore (Lessee) v Doherty* (1843) 5 ILR 449; *Mayhew v
     Suttle* (1854) 4 E & B 347, Ex Ch.

5   *Monks v Dykes* (1839) 4 M & W 567; *Lane v Dixon* (1847) 3 CB 776. See also *Lewis v
     Ponsford* (1838) 8 C & P 687 at 690 per Lord Denman CJ (a child or employee may have such
     possession of his bedroom as to permit him to sue). Cf *R v St George's Union* (1871) LR 7 QB
     90 at 97 per Cockburn J; *Allan v Liverpool Overseers, Inman v West Derby Union Assessment
     Committee and Kirkdale Overseers* (1874) LR 9 QB 180 at 191–192, DC, per Blackburn J. The
     grant of residential accommodation for a fixed or periodic term at a stated rent prima facie
     creates a tenancy, even if the stated intention of the parties is to the contrary: see *Street v
     Mountford* [1985] AC 809, [1985] 2 All ER 289, HL. A tenant who holds over after the
     termination of an ordinary tenancy and becomes a tolerated trespasser, the landlord agreeing not
     to evict, has sufficient interest to maintain an action in trespass: see *Pemberton v Southwark
     London Borough Council* [2000] 3 All ER 924, [2000] 1 WLR 1672, CA.

6   *Allan v Liverpool Overseers, Inman v West Derby Union Assessment Committee and Kirkdale
     Overseers* (1874) LR 9 QB 180. See also *Hill v Tupper* (1863) 2 H & C 121. A licensee not in
     occupation can maintain a claim in trespass so far as is necessary to vindicate his legal rights
     granted by the licence: *Vehicle Control Services Ltd v Revenue and Customs Comrs* [2013]
     EWCA Civ 186, [2013] STC 892.

7   See *Manchester Airport plc v Dutton* [2000] QB 133, sub nom *Dutton v Manchester Airport plc*
     [1999] 2 All ER 675, CA. A licensee without rights of occupation cannot so claim: *Countryside
     Residential (North Thames) Ltd v T* (2000) 81 P & CR 10, CA. See also *Hounslow London
     Borough Council v Twickenham Garden Developments Ltd* [1971] Ch 233 at 267, [1970]
     3 All ER 326 at 346 per Megarry J. As to lodgers see LANDLORD AND TENANT vol 62 (2012)
     PARA 16.

578.   Tenant as claimant in trespass to land.   If land is in the possession of a
tenant, the tenant[1] is the proper claimant to sue for trespass committed in respect
of the land[2].

1   This includes a tenant at sufferance: see *Graham v Peat* (1801) 1 East 244; and LANDLORD AND
     TENANT vol 62 (2012) PARA 207.

2   If the tenant is the person in possession see PARA 576. If the tenant is the person with the right
     to possession see PARA 577.

579. Reversioner cannot sue for trespass to land. Where the trespass is not merely of a temporary nature, but is injurious to the reversion, the reversioner, although he cannot sue in trespass[1], may sue for the injury done to his interest[2].

1   The claim by the reversioner is not a claim of trespass. In a claim of trespass to land the claimant alleges that the defendant wrongfully entered the claimant's land; whereas, in a claim by a reversioner, the claimant generally alleges that the defendant injured the claimant's reversion in land: see *Jackson v Pesked* (1813) 1 M & S 234; *Hosking v Phillips* (1848) 3 Exch 168; *Kidgill v Moor* (1850) 9 CB 364; *Metropolitan Association v Petch* (1858) 5 CBNS 504.

2   A reversioner may sue for such injuries as structural injury to a house (*Shelfer v City of London Electric Lighting Co, Meux's Brewery Co v City of London Electric Lighting Co* [1895] 1 Ch 287, CA), cutting down trees (*Cotterill v Hobby* (1825) 4 B & C 465), digging holes and spoiling the surface of land for the purpose of quarrying or mining (*Rogers v Taylor* (1857) 1 H & N 706), placing the foundation of a wall in the claimant's land (*Mayfair Property Co v Johnston* [1894] 1 Ch 508), building a house with eaves which discharged water on the claimant's land (*Tucker v Newman* (1839) 11 Ad & El 40; *Battishill v Reed* (1856) 18 CB 696), pulling down the eaves of the claimant's house and preventing the rainwater from flowing onto adjoining land (*Battishill v Reed* (1856) 18 CB 696), removing a dam placed for the purpose of diverting a stream so as to irrigate the claimant's land (*Greenslade v Halliday* (1830) 6 Bing 379), and polluting a river by pouring sewage into it (*Jones v Llanrwst UDC* [1911] 1 Ch 393 at 404 per Parker J). The reversioner has no claim if the damage is not such as will last beyond the end of the term, even if the current commercial value of the reversion is diminished: see *Rust v Victoria Graving Dock Co and London and St Katharine Dock Co* (1887) 36 ChD 113, CA (flooding of property development). As to the right of a reversioner to sue the tenant for waste injurious to the reversion see LANDLORD AND TENANT vol 62 (2012) PARAS 580–581. As to notice to landlord of adverse claims see LANDLORD AND TENANT vol 63 (2012) PARA 806. As to recovery of possession by a landlord see LANDLORD AND TENANT vol 63 (2012) PARA 808 et seq.

580. Co-owner as claimant to trespass in land. A joint tenant or a person entitled in common under a trust of land[1] can maintain a claim for trespass against his co-tenant if the co-tenant expels him from the land or destroys the subject of the co-tenancy without his consent, but not otherwise[2].

1   As to joint tenancies see REAL PROPERTY AND REGISTRATION vol 87 (2012) PARA 198 et seq. As to tenancies in common see REAL PROPERTY AND REGISTRATION vol 87 (2012) PARA 215 et seq. As to trusts of land see REAL PROPERTY AND REGISTRATION vol 87 (2012) PARA 105.

2   *Murray v Hall* (1849) 7 CB 441. See also *Wilkinson v Haygarth* (1847) 12 QB 837 (on appeal sub nom *Haygarth v Wilkinson* (1848) 12 QB 851, Ex Ch); *Cresswell v Hedges* (1862) 1 H & C 421; *Stedman v Smith* (1857) 8 E & B 1; *Watson v Gray* (1880) 14 ChD 192. Cf *Martyn v Knowllys* (1799) 8 Term Rep 145; *Cubitt v Porter* (1828) 8 B & C 257; *Jacobs v Seward* (1872) LR 5 HL 464; *Job v Potton* (1875) LR 20 Eq 84. As to the right to an account between joint tenants see REAL PROPERTY AND REGISTRATION vol 87 (2012) PARA 204. A co-tenant of a party wall may not claim trespass against his co-tenant for pulling down the wall for the purpose of rebuilding it (*Standard Bank of British South America v Stokes* (1878) 9 ChD 68; *Cubitt v Porter* (1828) 8 B & C 257) unless the defendant trespasses on the adjoining property of the claimant (*Mayfair Property Co v Johnston* [1894] 1 Ch 508) or his acts amount to an ouster from possession of the wall (*Stedman v Smith* (1857) 8 E & B 1). See BOUNDARIES vol 4 (2011) PARA 374. As to party walls generally see BOUNDARIES vol 4 (2011) PARA 364 et seq. As to what constitutes possession by co-owners for the purposes of the limitation of actions see LIMITATION PERIODS vol 68 (2008) PARA 1094.

(iv) Defences to Trespass to Land

581. Claim of right as defence to trespass to land. A defendant may plead and prove that he had a right to the possession of the land at the time of the alleged trespass, or that he acted under the authority of some person having such a right[1]; but he may not set up the title of a third person unless he claims under or by authority of such a person[2].

1   *Jones v Chapman* (1849) 2 Exch 803, Ex Ch; *Roberts v Tayler* (1845) 1 CB 117 at 126 per Cresswell J; *Ewer v Jones* (1846) 9 QB 623; *Delaney v TP Smith Ltd* [1946] KB 393, [1946] 2 All ER 23, CA. Cf *Cary v Holt* (1745) 11 East 70n; *Holmes v Newlands* (1839) 11 Ad & El 44; *Ryan v Clark* (1849) 14 QB 65.

2   *Glenwood Lumber Co v Phillips* [1904] AC 405, PC; *Nicholls v Ely Beet Sugar Factory* [1931] 2 Ch 84. Cf *Chambers v Donaldson* (1809) 11 East 65. The defendant may rely upon an authority which he in fact had, although he did not purport to rely upon it at the time of the trespass: see *Trent v Hunt* (1853) 9 Exch 14; *Phillips v Whitsed* (1860) 2 E & E 804.

582.   Leave and licence as defence to trespass to land. It is a good defence to a claim of trespass to land for the defendant to plead and prove that he entered on the land by the leave and licence of the claimant[1]. If the person in possession of land gives to another person licence to enter on the land, then, so long as the licence continues and the entry is justified by the licence, the person to whom the licence was given cannot be treated as a trespasser[2].

A person who has been let into possession of land by the person entitled to such possession has the right to occupy the land as a licensee until the licence is revoked by a competent authority, although he has no estate in the land[3]. An entry on land for the purpose of hunting or similar purposes is lawful if it is with the express or tacit consent of the person in possession of the land, but is unlawful if there is no such consent[4].

At common law, a licence to enter land which is not coupled with the grant of an interest in the land is revocable at will[5]. However, if such a licence arises by virtue of a contract between the claimant and the defendant[6] it is a matter of construction of the contract whether the licence is revocable or not[7]. In any case a licensee whose licence has been revoked has a right to a reasonable time to vacate the land after the revocation of the licence, and if the licence is to put goods on land of the licensor, the licence cannot be revoked without allowing the licensee reasonable time to remove the goods[8].

If the owner of land gives permission for the doing of an act on his land and that act is completed, then, generally speaking, he will be too late to complain of it and the owner's proprietary right will to that extent be extinguished[9].

A licence coupled with a grant of an interest in the land is not revocable[10].

In order that a licence may be a defence to a claim of trespass, the defendant must not have exceeded that which the licence allows; thus, a licence to enter a dwelling house and seize goods does not justify breaking and entering, unless a demand for the goods is first made and an intimation given of the authority under which the demand is made[11]; and a licence to enter into a house or onto land does not justify an entry except in the usual way[12]. However, where the licensee has done nothing on the premises which he was not entitled to do, his motives in entering are immaterial[13].

1   As to a licence to enter on land see LANDLORD AND TENANT vol 62 (2012) PARA 9 et seq; REAL PROPERTY AND REGISTRATION vol 87 (2012) PARA 837. Where a landlord has covenanted to do repairs a licence to enter to do the repairs is implied: see *Edmonton Corpn v WM Knowles & Son Ltd* (1961) 60 LGR 124; and LANDLORD AND TENANT vol 62 (2012) PARA 556. Where land is jointly occupied a licence given without authority by one occupier will not bind other occupiers, and an entrant under the licence will be a trespasser against those others: *Ferguson v Welsh* [1987] 3 All ER 777 at 785, [1987] 1 WLR 1553 at 1563, HL, per Lord Goff. When a householder lives in a dwelling house to which there is a garden in front and does not lock the garden gate, there is an implied licence to any member of the public, including a policeman, who has lawful reason for doing so, to proceed from the gate to the front or back door, and to inquire whether he may be admitted and to conduct his lawful business. If the licence is withdrawn he is not a trespasser during the reasonable time which he takes to leave the premises: *Robson v Hallett* [1967] 2 QB 939 at 954, [1967] 2 All ER 407 at 414, DC, per Diplock LJ. Cf *Brunner v Williams* (1975) 73 LGR 266, DC, where it was held that a weights

and measures inspector had no implied licence to enter a house garden to see whether a coal dealer was delivering coal there in breach of the Weights and Measures Act 1963 (repealed). A wife's inquiry agent has no implied licence to enter the home of her husband who is living apart from her: *Jolliffe v Willmett & Co* [1971] 1 All ER 478.

2   *Kavanagh v Gudge* (1844) 7 Man & G 316; *Knapp v London, Chatham and Dover Rly Co* (1863) 2 H & C 212. Cf *Hyde v Graham* (1862) 1 H & C 593 (locking of gate impliedly revoking licence). The plea must cover all the alleged acts of trespass: *Hayward v Grant* (1824) 1 C & P 448. A plea of leave and licence means leave and licence in fact; a licence in law must be expressly pleaded: *Moxon v Savage* (1860) 2 F & F 182. A licence is not implied by law to the purchaser of goods, although sold under an execution or distress, to enter upon the premises of the former owner and take them away, even if they have remained there with his consent: *Williams v Morris* (1841) 8 M & W 488.

3   *Littleton v M'Namara* (1875) IR 9 CL 417.

4   *Paul v Summerhayes* (1878) 4 QBD 9; and see ANIMALS vol 2 (2008) PARAS 716, 779. See also *League Against Cruel Sports v Scott* [1986] QB 240, [1985] 2 All ER 489.

5   *Wood v Leadbitter* (1845) 13 M & W 838 at 844 per Alderson B; *Thompson v Park* [1944] KB 408, [1944] 2 All ER 477, CA; *Armstrong v Sheppard and Short Ltd* [1959] 2 QB 384, [1959] 2 All ER 651, CA (licence to discharge effluent under land). Where a spouse has no proprietary rights in the spousal home, a right of occupation may arise independently of any licence from the other spouse: see *National Provincial Bank Ltd v Ainsworth* [1965] AC 1175, [1965] 2 All ER 472, HL; the Family Law Act 1996 Pt IV (ss 30–63); and MATRIMONIAL AND CIVIL PARTNERSHIP LAW vol 72 (2015) PARA 304 et seq.

6   For the position where one of the parties is an assignee of the original licensee see *Clore v Theatrical Properties Ltd and Westby & Co Ltd* [1936] 3 All ER 483, CA; *Ashburn Anstalt v WJ Arnold & Co* [1989] Ch 1, [1988] 2 All ER 147, CA.

7   See CONTRACT vol 22 (2012) PARA 548; LANDLORD AND TENANT vol 62 (2012) PARA 10. In regard to contractual licences it was said in *Hurst v Picture Theatres Ltd* [1915] 1 KB 1, CA, that since the Judicature Acts (see COURTS AND TRIBUNALS vol 24 (2010) PARA 687), *Wood v Leadbitter* (1845) 13 M & W 838 was no longer good law: see *Hurst v Picture Theatres Ltd* [1915] 1 KB 1 at 7–10, CA, per Buckley LJ. This view was approved obiter in *Winter Garden Theatre (London) Ltd v Millennium Productions Ltd* [1948] AC 173, [1947] 2 All ER 331, HL (implied power of revocation in the contract), where it was held that where a contractual licence is granted for a definite purpose and for a limited period it will be irrevocable until the purpose is achieved: *Winter Garden Theatre (London) Ltd v Millennium Productions Ltd* [1948] AC 173 at 189, [1947] 2 All ER 331 at 335–336, HL, per Viscount Simon, and at 194 and 338 per Lord Porter. Cf *Thompson v Park* [1944] KB 408, [1944] 2 All ER 477, CA (licence revoked); said to be inconsistent with later authority and no longer good law in *Verrall v Great Yarmouth Borough Council* [1981] QB 202, [1980] 1 All ER 839, CA; but it may be that the actual result was justifiable on the facts: see *Hounslow Borough Council v Twickenham Garden Developments Ltd* [1971] Ch 233 at 250, [1970] 3 All ER 326 at 339 per Megarry J.

8   See LANDLORD AND TENANT vol 62 (2012) PARA 10. See also *Robson v Hallett* [1967] 2 QB 939 at 954, [1967] 2 All ER 407 at 414, DC, per Diplock LJ; *Minister of Health v Bellotti* [1944] KB 298 at 306, [1944] 1 All ER 238 at 243–244, CA, per Lord Greene MR; *Cornish v Stubbs* (1870) LR 5 CP 334; *Mellor v Watkins* (1874) LR 9 QB 400; *Canadian Pacific Rly Co v R* [1931] AC 414, PC; *Australian Blue Metal Ltd v Hughes* [1963] AC 74, [1962] 3 All ER 335, PC. In some cases reasonable notice as well as reasonable time may be required: *Winter Garden Theatre (London) Ltd v Millennium Productions Ltd* [1948] AC 173 at 205–206, [1947] 2 All ER 331 at 344–345, HL, per Lord MacDermott. See also *Issac v Hotel de Paris Ltd* [1960] 1 All ER 348, [1960] 1 WLR 239, PC. If inadequate time is given the revocation is still valid: see *Minister of Health v Bellotti* [1944] KB 298, [1944] 1 All ER 238, CA; *Dorling v Honnor Marine Ltd* [1964] Ch 560 at 567, [1963] 2 All ER 495 at 502 per Cross J (revsd on another point [1965] Ch 1, [1964] 1 All ER 241, CA). However, damages may be recovered for any damage resulting from the lack of reasonable notice or time: *Aldin v Latimer Clarke, Muirhead & Co* [1894] 2 Ch 437.

9   *Armstrong v Sheppard and Short Ltd* [1959] 2 QB 384, [1959] 2 All ER 651, CA. This may be so even though the owner was unaware of his proprietary right at the time he gave the permission: *Armstrong v Sheppard and Short Ltd* [1959] 2 QB 384 at 401, [1959] 2 All ER 651 at 659, CA, per Lord Evershed MR. See also *Liggins v Inge* (1831) 7 Bing 682; *Feltham v Cartwright* (1839) 5 Bing NC 569; *Davies v Marshall* (1861) 10 CBNS 697.

10   See LANDLORD AND TENANT vol 62 (2012) PARA 13. A chattel interest may suffice: see *James Jones & Sons Ltd v Tankerville* [1909] 2 Ch 440 at 442 per Parker J. See also *Thomas v Sorrell* (1673) Vaugh 330 at 351; *Doe d Hanley v Wood* (1819) 2 B & Ald 724 at 738; *Vaughan v*

Hampson (1875) 33 LT 15. See further *Chandler v Kerley* [1978] 2 All ER 942, [1978] 1 WLR 693, CA; *Hardwick v Johnson* [1978] 2 All ER 935, [1978] 1 WLR 683, CA.

11 *Aikins v Brunton* (1866) 14 WR 636.

12 *Ancaster v Milling* (1823) 2 Dow & Ry KB 714.

13 *Byrne v Kinematograph Renters Society Ltd* [1958] 2 All ER 579 at 592, [1958] 1 WLR 762 at 776 per Harman J.

583. Exercise of legal right as defence to trespass to land. It is a good defence to a claim of trespass for the defendant to plead and prove that he entered on land in the exercise of a legal right, whether statutory[1] or otherwise[2]. It seems that a person may be entitled to enter on the land of another, and to do acts there which otherwise would amount to a trespass, if such entry and acts are reasonably necessary for the preservation of the property of the person entering or of the person whose land is entered, or for the preservation of life, and if the entry is made and the acts are done in a reasonable manner[3].

It is a good defence to a claim of trespass for the defendant to plead and prove that he committed the act complained of in the lawful execution of legal process[4], or in the lawful carrying out of a lawful distress[5].

The defence of justification must be specially pleaded and must cover all the acts done[6].

1 *Knapp v London, Chatham and Dover Rly Co* (1863) 2 H & C 212. As to the powers of entry of constables generally see POLICE AND INVESTIGATORY POWERS vol 84A (2013) PARA 432. Numerous statutes confer rights of entry upon private land: see eg the Atomic Energy Act 1946 s 5; and ENERGY AND CLIMATE CHANGE vol 44 (2011) PARA 912. As to access orders to allow entry onto land to allow the carrying out of works reasonably necessary for the preservation of adjoining of adjacent land, or any part of it, see the Access to Neighbouring Land Act 1992; and REAL PROPERTY AND REGISTRATION vol 87 (2012) PARA 311 et seq.

2 Eg to exercise a right to fish (*Richardson v Orford Corpn* (1793) 2 Hy Bl 182, Ex Ch; *Mannall v Fisher* (1859) 5 CBNS 856), to hunt and shoot (*Wickham v Hawker* (1840) 7 M & W 63; cf *Moore v Earl of Plymouth* (1817) 7 Taunt 614 (affd (1819) 3 B & Ald 66); *Pickering v Noyes* (1825) 4 B & C 639; *Pannell v Mill* (1846) 3 CB 625), to exercise a right of way (*Holt v Daw* (1851) 16 QB 990), to dig for minerals (*Earl of Cardigan v Armitage* (1823) 2 B & C 197; *Bassett v Mitchell* (1831) 2 B & Ad 99; *Roberts v Davey* (1833) 4 B & Ad 664; *Dand v Kingscote* (1840) 6 M & W 174; *Clayton v Corby* (1842) 2 QB 813; *Rogers v Taylor* (1857) 1 H & N 706; *Duke of Hamilton v Graham* (1871) LR 2 Sc & Div 166; cf *Smart v Morton* (1855) 5 E & B 30), to cut turf (*Fitzpatrick v Verschoyle* [1912] 1 IR 8), or under certain circumstances to abate a nuisance (*Jones v Williams* (1843) 11 M & W 176; *Turner v Ringwood Highway Board* (1870) LR 9 Eq 418; *Earl of Lonsdale v Nelson* (1823) 2 B & C 302 at 311 per Best J). See also *Phypers v Eburn* (1836) 3 Bing NC 250; *Griffin v Dighton* (1863) 5 B & S 93, Ex Ch. As to use of the highway see *Harrison v Duke of Rutland* [1893] 1 QB 142, CA; *Hickman v Maisey* [1900] 1 QB 752, CA; *Randall v Tarrant* [1955] 1 All ER 600, [1955] 1 WLR 255, CA; *DPP v Jones* [1999] 2 AC 240, [1999] 2 All ER 257, HL; and PARA 567. See also *Secretary of State for Defence v Percy* [1999] 1 All ER 732 (there is no legal right for a member of the public to enter onto private land via a public footpath for the purpose of removing an illegal byelaw notice).

3 *Cope v Sharpe (No 2)* [1912] 1 KB 496, CA (entry on land by tenant of sporting rights to prevent fire spreading). See also *Maleverer v Spinke* (1537) 1 Dyer 35b at 36b; *Howard v Frith* (1666) 2 Keb 58 (entry to preserve life); *Handcock v Baker* (1800) 2 Bos & P 260 (breaking and entering to prevent murder); cf *Kirk v Gregory* (1876) 1 ExD 55 (removal of goods for their preservation). The owner of a swarm of bees has no right to follow the bees onto the land of another: *Kearry v Pattinson* [1939] 1 KB 471, [1939] 1 All ER 65, CA. Homelessness does not constitute the sort of emergency in which the defence of necessity can be invoked: see *Southwark London Borough Council v Williams* [1971] Ch 734 at 743–744, [1971] 2 All ER 175 at 179, CA, per Lord Denning MR. See also PARA 586.

4 See eg PLANNING vol 81 (2010) PARA 65 et seq; POLICE AND INVESTIGATORY POWERS vol 84A (2013) PARA 452. See further *Semayne's Case* (1604) 5 Co Rep 91a; *Cheasley v Barnes* (1808) 10 East 73; *Shorland v Govett* (1826) 5 B & C 485; *Sowell v Champion* (1837) 6 Ad & El 407; *Pugh v Griffith* (1838) 7 Ad & El 827. Cf *Perkins v Plympton* (1831) 7 Bing 676; *Carnaby v*

Welby (1838) 8 Ad & El 872; *Jarmain v Hooper* (1843) 6 Man & G 827; *Playfair v Musgrove* (1845) 14 M & W 239; *Percival v Stamp* (1853) 9 Exch 167; *Edwards v Hodges* (1855) 15 CB 477; *Melling v Leak* (1855) 16 CB 652.

5   See *Long v Clarke* [1894] 1 QB 119 at 121, CA, per Lord Esher MR; and also LANDLORD AND TENANT vol 62 (2012) PARAS 367–368.

6   *Smith v Shirley* (1846) 3 CB 142; *Curlewis v Laurie* (1848) 12 QB 640; *Hope v Osborne* [1913] 2 Ch 349. Cf *Taylor v Cole* (1789) 3 Term Rep 292 (affd (1791) 1 Hy Bl 555); *Taylor v Smith* (1816) 7 Taunt 156. If the defendant has sufficient legal justification for the entry, it is immaterial that he claims at the time to enter for another cause: *Crowther v Ramsbottom* (1798) 7 Term Rep 654.

584.   Acquiescence as defence to trespass to land. Mere delay by the claimant in complaining of the defendant's actions is not of itself sufficient to establish the defence of acquiescence or estoppel[1]. It must further be shown that the defendant had been misled to his detriment so that it would be unconscionable for the claimant to assert his rights[2]. However, the claimant is not debarred by acquiescence from enforcing legal rights of which he was unaware at the relevant time[3].

1   As to estoppel generally see CIVIL PROCEDURE; ESTOPPEL. As to acquiescence generally see EQUITABLE JURISDICTION vol 47 (2014) PARA 252.

2   *Jones v Stones* [1999] 1 WLR 1739, 78 P & CR 293, CA; *Perlman v Rayden* [2004] EWHC 2192 (Ch), [2004] 43 EG 142 (CS), [2005] 1 P & CR DG10. See also *Willmott v Barber* (1880) 15 ChD 96; *Shaw v Applegate* [1978] 1 All ER 123, [1977] 1 WLR 970, CA; *Habib Bank Ltd v Habib Bank AG Zurich* [1981] 2 All ER 650, [1981] 1 WLR 1265, CA; *Taylors Fashions Ltd v Liverpool Victoria Trustee Co Ltd* [1982] QB 133n, [1981] 1 All ER 897, CA.

3   *Armstrong v Sheppard and Short Ltd* [1959] 2 QB 384, [1959] 2 All ER 651, CA.

585.   Defendant entitled to enter land to retake or remove goods. If a person unlawfully takes the goods of another and puts them on his own land, the owner of the goods is entitled to enter immediately on the land for the purpose of retaking his own goods, and no trespass is occasioned[1]. If a person wrongfully places his own goods on the land of another, the occupier of the land is entitled to enter the land of the owner of the goods for the purpose of depositing the goods there[2]. However, a former tenant who is no longer possessed of the premises demised cannot justify re-entering them to recover chattels left behind[3].

1   *Patrick v Colerick* (1838) 3 M & W 483; *Webb v Beavan* (1844) 6 Man & G 1055. The principle does not apply where the goods are put on land possessed by a third party, or where they are fixed to the land: see *Anthony v Haney* (1832) 8 Bing 186. See also *Wood v Manley* (1839) 11 Ad & El 34 (entry under contract for the sale of goods); *Burridge v Nicholetts* (1861) 6 H & N 383 (county court treasurer's right to possession of the accounts). Cf *Blades v Higgs* (1861) 10 CBNS 713 (retaking goods and trespass to the person).

2   *Rea v Sheward* (1837) 2 M & W 424.

3   *Wilde v Waters* (1855) 24 LJCP 193 at 195 per Maule J.

586.   Necessity as defence to trespass to land. Entry onto another person's land may be justified by the defence of necessity, provided that there was no negligence on the defendant's part creating or contributing to the necessity[1]. For the defence to be available, the danger faced by the defendant must be immediate, obvious and such that a reasonable person would conclude that there was no alternative to the act of trespass[2].

1   *Rigby v Chief Constable of Northamptonshire* [1985] 2 All ER 985, [1985] 1 WLR 1242.

2   *Monsanto plc v Tilly* [2000] Env LR 313, [1999] NLJR 1833, CA. Homelessness does not constitute the sort of emergency in which the defence of necessity can be invoked: see *Southwark London Borough Council v Williams* [1971] Ch 734 at 743–744, [1971] 2 All ER 175 at 179, CA, per Lord Denning MR.

587. Expiration of limitation period as defence to trespass to land. A claim of trespass to land is barred by lapse of the statutory period of limitation, which, except in certain specified cases, is six years from the accrual of the cause of action[1].

1 See the Limitation Act 1980 s 2; and LIMITATION PERIODS vol 68 (2008) PARA 993. As to the extension and postponement of limitation periods see LIMITATION PERIODS vol 68 (2008) PARA 1168 et seq.

(v) Remedies for Trespass to Land

588. Expulsion as remedy for trespass to land. If a trespasser peaceably enters or is on land, the person who is in, or entitled to, possession may request him to leave, and if he refuses to leave may remove him from the land, using no more force than is reasonably necessary[1]. However, if a trespasser enters with force and violence, the person in possession may remove him without a previous request to depart[2]. An owner of property is also entitled to take reasonable steps to prevent trespassers from entering his property[3]. If the force or violence used in turning out a trespasser is excessive, the person who used such force himself commits a trespass upon the person of the person removed[4]. To justify the expulsion of a trespasser, the person who uses force must be in possession or acting under the authority of the person in possession[5].

If a trespasser erects a building on the land of another, the person who is entitled to the possession of the land may pull down the building, even though the trespasser is in it[6].

The police also have statutory powers to remove trespassers on land in certain circumstances[7].

1 *Hall v Davis* (1825) 2 C & P 33; *Thomas v Marsh and Nest* (1833) 5 C & P 596; *Webster v Watts* (1847) 11 QB 311; *Shaw v Chairitie* (1850) 3 Car & Kir 21 at 25 per Lord Campbell CJ; *Jackson v Courtenay* (1857) 8 E & B 8, Ex Ch; *Scott v Matthew Brown & Co Ltd* (1884) 51 LT 746; *Hemmings v Stoke Poges Golf Club Ltd* [1920] 1 KB 720, CA. It is no part of the duty of a police constable to turn out a peaceable trespasser unless he has committed an offence: see *Wheeler v Whiting* (1840) 9 C & P 262; cf *R v Chief Constable of Devon and Cornwall, ex p Central Electricity Generating Board* [1982] QB 458, [1981] 3 All ER 826, CA (police may assist expulsion so as to prevent a breach of the peace), distinguished in *Percy v DPP* [1995] 1 WLR 1382, DC (non-violent trespass; no real risk of a breach of the peace); and see PARA 593.
2 *Weaver v Bush* (1798) 8 Term Rep 78; *Tullay v Reed* (1823) 1 C & P 6; *Polkinhorn v Wright* (1845) 8 QB 197.
3 See PARA 535.
4 *Collins v Renison* (1754) Say 138; *Gregory v Hill* (1799) 8 Term Rep 299; *Simpson v Morris* (1813) 4 Taunt 821; *Johnson v Northwood* (1817) 7 Taunt 689; *Moriarty v Brooks* (1834) 6 C & P 684, Ex Ch; *Oakes v Wood* (1837) 2 M & W 791. See also *Green v Bartram* (1830) 4 C & P 308; *Ball v Axten* (1866) 4 F & F 1019 (false imprisonment). As to trespassers being injured by animals on the land see ANIMALS vol 2 (2008) PARA 749. As to spring-guns, mantraps etc injuring trespassers see CRIMINAL LAW vol 25 (2010) PARA 141. As to injury to trespassing dogs by dog spears, traps etc see ANIMALS vol 2 (2008) PARA 783.
5 *Monks v Dykes* (1839) 4 M & W 567; *Holmes v Bagge* (1853) 1 E & B 782.
6 *Burling v Read* (1850) 11 QB 904; *Davies v Williams* (1851) 16 QB 546. It is not lawful to pull down an occupied dwelling house on one's land without prior notice to the occupier: see *Perry v Fitzhowe* (1846) 8 QB 757; *Jones v Jones* (1862) 1 H & C 1. See also the further protection in the Protection from Eviction Act 1977 ss 1–3; and CRIMINAL LAW vol 26 (2010) PARAS 559–560; LANDLORD AND TENANT vol 63 (2012) PARA 801. Cf *Jones v Foley* [1891] 1 QB 730, DC; *Lemmon v Webb* [1895] AC 1, HL (right to lop overhanging branches).
7 See the Criminal Justice and Public Order Act 1994 ss 61–62E, 63; and CRIMINAL LAW vol 26 (2010) PARAS 545–546. As to the police power to remove persons committing or participating in aggravated trespass see the Criminal Justice and Public Order Act 1994 ss 68, 69; and CRIMINAL LAW vol 26 (2010) PARA 547.

589.   Forcible entry as remedy for trespass to land.   At common law, a person entitled to the immediate possession of land may enter and, in a civil claim, may justify the use of so much force as is necessary to effect entry and to expel an intruder, provided the force used is reasonable[1]. This principle is curtailed in respect of premises let as a dwelling by the statutory restriction that, while any person is lawfully residing in the premises or part of them, a right of re-entry or forfeiture can be enforced only by proceedings in court[2].

The fact that a person (other than a displaced residential occupier or a protected intended occupier, or a person acting on behalf of such an occupier) has any interest in or right to possession or occupation of any premises does not constitute lawful authority so as to excuse him from an offence of using or threatening violence for the purpose of securing entry into any premises[3].

1   See *Hemmings v Stoke Poges Golf Club Ltd* [1920] 1 KB 720, CA; and PARA 588.
2   See the Protection from Eviction Act 1977 s 2; and LANDLORD AND TENANT vol 63 (2012) PARA 801. For the procedure relating to possession claims see LANDLORD AND TENANT vol 63 (2012) PARA 804 et seq. As to enforcement of an order made by the County Court in such proceedings see the High Court and County Courts Jurisdiction Order 1991, SI 1991/724, art 8B (added by SI 2001/2685; amended by SI 2014/821).
3   See the Criminal Law Act 1977 s 6(1), (1A), (2); and CRIMINAL LAW vol 26 (2010) PARA 553; LANDLORD AND TENANT vol 63 (2012) PARA 800.

590.   Distress damage feasant as remedy for trespass to land.   If any chattel[1] is unlawfully on the land of a person and is doing damage, the person entitled to the possession of the land may, instead of bringing a claim for trespass, distrain the chattel doing the damage[2].

1   See *Ambergate, Nottingham and Boston and Eastern Junction Rly Co v Midland Rly Co* (1853) 2 E & B 793, where the right was held to apply to an engine obstructing the railway. The common law right to seize and detain any animal by way of distress damage feasant was abolished and replaced by the Animals Act 1971 s 7: see ANIMALS vol 2 (2008) PARA 758 et seq.
2   Some damage must be shown; it need not be physical damage to the land or anything on it, but the mere costs of the distress are not sufficient: see *Arthur v Anker* [1997] QB 564, [1996] 3 All ER 783, CA (held not applicable to wheel clamping of vehicle parked on private land without authorisation).

591.   Damages for trespass to land.   In a claim of trespass, if the claimant proves the trespass he is entitled to recover nominal damages, even if he has not suffered any actual loss[1]. If the trespass has caused the claimant actual damage, he is entitled to receive such an amount as will compensate him for his loss[2]. Where the defendant has made use of the claimant's land, the claimant is entitled to receive by way of damages such a sum as should reasonably be paid for that use[3]. Where there is an oppressive, arbitrary or unconstitutional trespass by a government official or where the defendant cynically disregards the rights of the claimant in the land with the object of making a gain by his unlawful conduct, exemplary (or 'punitive') damages may be awarded[4]. If the trespass is accompanied by aggravating circumstances which do not allow an award of exemplary damages, the general damages may be increased[5].

Although damages are normally awarded only for loss that has already been suffered, in an appropriate case the court may award damages in lieu of an injunction in respect of anticipated loss which the claimant has not yet sustained[6].

1   See DAMAGES vol 29 (2014) PARA 420. As to nominal damages see DAMAGES vol 29 (2014) PARAS 314–320.
2   See DAMAGES vol 29 (2014) PARAS 420, 423–425. As to the compensatory nature of damages see DAMAGES vol 29 (2014) PARAS 318, 408.

3 See DAMAGES vol 29 (2014) PARA 421. This sum might represent, for example, what would have been a reasonable fee for the letting value of an advertising hoarding: see *Stadium Capital Holdings (No 2) Ltd v St Marylebone Property Company plc* [2010] EWCA Civ 952, [2010] All ER (D) 83 (Nov). See also *Eaton Mansions (Westminster) Ltd v Stinger Compania de Inversion SA* [2013] EWCA Civ 1308, [2014] 1 P & CR 63 (fee for the period of the trespass only).

This award may be made even though the claimant may have been unable to let the premises: *Swordheath Properties Ltd v Tabet* [1979] 1 All ER 240, [1979] 1 WLR 285, CA. See also *Inverugie Investments Ltd v Hackett* [1995] 3 All ER 841 at 845, [1995] 1 WLR 713 at 718, PC (award based on use of holiday apartments every day of the year, notwithstanding low levels of occupancy at certain times). A claim for damages proper may be appropriate where property is subject to concessionary rents and full market value would not give a proper measure of loss or gain: *Ministry of Defence v Ashman* (1993) 25 HLR 513 at 519–520, CA, per Hoffmann LJ; *Ministry of Defence v Thompson* (1993) 25 HLR 552, CA. Where there has been wrongful occupation the claimant may sue for recovery of the land together with a claim for mesne profits or claim mesne profits alone if he has re-entered or his interest has determined: *Harris v Mulkern* (1875) 1 ExD 31; *Southport Tramways Co v Gandy* [1897] 2 QB 66, CA. Despite its name, mesne profits are not confined to the defendant's actual gains but extend also to the claimant's loss: *Dunn v Large* (1783) 3 Doug KB 335.

4 *Drane v Evangelou* [1978] 2 All ER 437, [1978] 1 WLR 455, CA, applying *Rookes v Barnard* [1964] AC 1129, [1964] 1 All ER 367, HL. In *Drane v Evangelou* [1978] 2 All ER 437, [1978] 1 WLR 455, CA, a tenant was awarded exemplary damages against his landlord who evicted him. However, where the landlord had already been fined and did not make a profit from his trespass his tenant was not awarded exemplary (but only aggravated) damages: *Devonshire v Jenkins* (1979) 129 NLJ 849. See also *Branchett v Beaney* [1992] 3 All ER 910, [1992] 2 EGLR 33, CA. See further DAMAGES vol 29 (2014) PARA 328. As to exemplary or punitive damages generally see DAMAGES vol 29 (2014) PARA 325 et seq.

5 *Bisney v Swanston* (1972) 225 Estates Gazette 2299, CA; *Drane v Evangelou* [1978] 2 All ER 437, [1978] 1 WLR 455, CA. As to aggravated damages see DAMAGES vol 29 (2014) PARAS 322–324.

6 See *Jaggard v Sawyer* [1995] 2 All ER 189, [1995] 1 WLR 269, CA; and DAMAGES vol 29 (2014) PARA 314.

592. Injunction and declaration as remedy for trespass to land. The court may grant an injunction (which may be mandatory[1]) to prevent a continuance or threatened repetition of a trespass to land[2]. Where a trespass is threatened, although not committed, the court may prevent it by injunction[3]. Where the trespass is of a 'trifling' nature, or where damages are a sufficient remedy, or where the granting of an injunction would be oppressive, an injunction may be refused[4]. Where the defendant claims a right to enter upon the land in question, the court, in addition to or in substitution for damages or an injunction, may make a declaration concerning that claim[5].

1 *Kelsen v Imperial Tobacco Co (of Great Britain and Ireland) Ltd* [1957] 2 QB 334, [1957] 2 All ER 343.

2 See CIVIL PROCEDURE vol 11 (2009) PARA 442. As to the presumptive entitlement to an injunction in respect of the violation of a common law right see CIVIL PROCEDURE vol 11 (2009) PARA 357. Considerations of public welfare may justify the suspension of the injunction, but not its denial altogether: *Price's Patent Candle Co v LCC* [1908] 2 Ch 526 at 544, CA, per Cozens-Hardy MR. The injunction should not be suspended simply because no damage is suffered and the trespass will not last indefinitely: see *John Trenberth Ltd v National Westminster Bank Ltd* (1979) 39 P & CR 104, not following *Woollerton and Wilson Ltd v Richard Costain Ltd* [1970] 1 All ER 483, [1970] 1 WLR 411 (considered wrongly decided in *Jaggard v Sawyer* [1995] 2 All ER 189 at 199, [1995] 1 WLR 269 at 278, CA, per Sir Thomas Bingham MR).

3 See CIVIL PROCEDURE vol 11 (2009) PARA 442.

4 See CIVIL PROCEDURE vol 11 (2009) PARAS 442–443. See also *Armstrong v Sheppard and Short Ltd* [1959] 2 QB 384, [1959] 2 All ER 651, CA; *Llandudno UDC v Woods* [1899] 2 Ch 705; *Behrens v Richards* [1905] 2 Ch 614. In these cases an injunction was refused because the injury was trivial but in other cases an injunction was granted despite this factor: see *Patel v WH Smith (Eziot) Ltd* [1987] 2 All ER 569, [1987] 1 WLR 853, CA (vehicle parking); *Anchor Brewhouse Developments Ltd v Berkley House Docklands Development Ltd* [1987] 2 EGLR

173, 38 BLR 82 (swinging tower crane). It is submitted that a possible distinction is that the activities in the first three cases (ie drainage, religious services and access to a beach) all had elements of public interest or benefit not present in the latter two cases.

5   *Harrison v Duke of Rutland* [1893] 1 QB 142, CA; *Llandudno UDC v Woods* [1899] 2 Ch 705; *Behrens v Richards* [1905] 2 Ch 614. As to declarations see CPR 40.20; and CIVIL PROCEDURE vol 12 (2009) PARA 1145.

593.   Criminal liability in connection with trespass to land.   Though trespass to land is not in itself a criminal offence, certain specific forms of trespass[1] or trespass on specific types of property[2] are criminal or are components of more widely defined offences[3].

1   See eg:
   (1)   violence for securing entry (see the Criminal Law Act 1977 s 6; and CRIMINAL LAW vol 26 (2010) PARA 553);
   (2)   adverse occupation of residential premises (see the Criminal Law Act 1977 s 7; and CRIMINAL LAW vol 26 (2010) PARA 554);
   (3)   trespassing with a weapon of offence (see the Criminal Law Act 1977 s 8; and CRIMINAL LAW vol 26 (2010) PARA 555);
   (4)   powers to remove trespassers on land (see the Criminal Justice and Public Order Act 1994 s 61; and CRIMINAL LAW vol 26 (2010) PARA 545);
   (5)   aggravated trespass (see the Criminal Justice and Public Order Act 1994 s 68; and CRIMINAL LAW vol 26 (2010) PARA 547);
   (6)   trespassing with a firearm (see the Firearms Act 1968 s 20; and CRIMINAL LAW vol 26 (2010) PARA 635).
   As to proof of aggravated trespass see *DPP v Barnard* (1999) Times, 9 November, DC (mere trespass not sufficient).
   The police may, but are not compelled to, assist in the removal of trespassers in order to prevent a breach of the peace: see *R v Chief Constable of Devon and Cornwall, ex p Central Electricity Generating Board* [1982] QB 458, [1981] 3 All ER 826, CA, distinguished in *Percy v DPP* [1995] 3 All ER 124, [1995] 1 WLR 1382, DC (non-violent trespass; no real risk of a breach of the peace).
2   Such property types include:
   (1)   railway property (see the Railway Regulation Act 1840 s 16; the Regulation of Railways Act 1868 s 23; and RAILWAYS AND TRAMWAYS vol 86 (2013) PARA 411 et seq);
   (2)   some gardens (see the Town Gardens Protection Act 1863 s 5; and OPEN SPACES AND COUNTRYSIDE vol 78 (2010) PARA 548);
   (3)   diplomatic premises, consular premises and private residences of persons entitled to international inviolability (see the Criminal Law Act 1977 s 9; and CRIMINAL LAW vol 26 (2010) PARA 556);
   (4)   residential property (see the Criminal Law Act 1977 s 7; and CRIMINAL LAW vol 26 (2010) PARA 554).
3   Offences which may include trespass as a component include:
   (1)   burglary (see the Theft Act 1968 s 9; CRIMINAL LAW vol 25 (2010) PARA 290);
   (2)   trespassory assembly (see the Public Order Act 1986 ss 14A–14C; *DPP v Jones* [1999] 2 AC 240, [1999] 2 All ER 257, HL; and CRIMINAL LAW vol 26 (2010) PARAS 536–537);
   (3)   poaching during the day (see the Game Act 1831 ss 30, 31; and ANIMALS vol 2 (2008) PARAS 785–786);
   (4)   poaching at night (see the Night Poaching Act 1828 ss 1, 9; Night Poaching Act 1844 s 1; Criminal Law Act 1977 s 15(4)); and ANIMALS vol 2 (2008) PARAS 791–793).
   As to the general abolition of the offence of conspiracy to trespass at common law and the limited exceptions to this see the Criminal Law Act 1977 s 5; and CRIMINAL LAW vol 25 (2010) PARA 73 et seq.

(2) NUISANCE AND ASSOCIATED TORTS

594.   Private nuisance affecting land.   A nuisance which interferes with a person's use or enjoyment of his land or of some right connected with land is a private nuisance and as such an actionable tort[1]. There are three types of private nuisance:

(1)   nuisances by encroachment to another's land;

(2)   nuisance by direct physical injury to a neighbour's land; and

(3)   nuisance by interference with another's quiet enjoyment of his land[2].

In most cases the nuisance results from an activity conducted by the defendant on his land, but this is not an essential ingredient of the tort[3]; the defendant may be liable for continuing or adopting a private nuisance that was created by a trespasser on his land or natural forces[4]. In the absence of an easement[5], however, the mere presence of a building which interferes with a person's enjoyment of his land does not constitute a private nuisance[6]. The normal remedy for a private nuisance is an injunction to prevent the continuation or repetition of the nuisance, and damages in respect of loss sustained[7].

1   See NUISANCE vol 78 (2010) PARA 107 et seq. As to public nuisance, which is not specifically a tort to land, see PARA 499.

2   *Hunter v Canary Wharf Ltd* [1997] AC 655 at 695, [1997] 2 All ER 426 at 441, HL, per Lord Lloyd. See also NUISANCE vol 78 (2010) PARA 107.

3   *Hunter v Canary Wharf Ltd* [1997] AC 655 at 699, [1997] 2 All ER 426 at 445, HL, per Lord Lloyd (approving *Bank of New Zealand v Greenwood* [1984] 1 NZLR 525 at 532 per Hardie Boys J).

4   See eg *Sedleigh-Denfield v O'Callaghan* [1940] AC 880, [1940] 3 All ER 349, HL (act of trespasser); *Leakey v National Trust for Places of Historic Interest or Natural Beauty* [1980] QB 485, [1980] 1 All ER 17, CA (land movement); *Goldman v Hargrave* [1967] 1 AC 645, [1966] 2 All ER 989, PC (fire).

5   As to easements see REAL PROPERTY AND REGISTRATION vol 87 (2012) PARA 802 et seq.

6   *Hunter v Canary Wharf Ltd* [1997] AC 655, [1997] 2 All ER 426, HL (construction of building interfering with neighbouring householders' reception of television signals was not an actionable private nuisance). See NUISANCE vol 78 (2010) PARA 128.

7   See NUISANCE vol 78 (2010) PARA 230 et seq. As to damages for private nuisance see DAMAGES vol 29 (2014) PARA 425.

595.   Right to sue in private nuisance.   Private nuisance is a tort directed against a person's enjoyment of rights over land[1]. A claim for private nuisance can therefore be brought only by a person who has a right to the land affected[2]. Ordinarily the proper claimant will be the person who has actual and exclusive possession of the land, along with the right to such possession[3]: for example, a freeholder or tenant[4], or a licensee with exclusive possession[5]. Authority to be in possession is not essential, however, and a claim in private nuisance may lie at the suit of a person who has exclusive possession of land without the consent of the owner or lawful occupier[6]; there is no defence of jus tertii[7] in a claim for private nuisance[8]. A person with a reversionary interest in land can sue in private nuisance where the act or omission complained of is sufficiently enduring to damage his reversion[9].

1   *Hunter v Canary Wharf Ltd* [1997] AC 655 at 687, [1997] 2 All ER 426 at 434, HL, per Lord Goff (citing Newark 'The Boundaries of Nuisance' (1949) 65 LQR 480 at 482). See also NUISANCE vol 78 (2010) PARA 107.

2   *Hunter v Canary Wharf Ltd* [1997] AC 655, [1997] 2 All ER 426, HL. See also *Tate & Lyle Industries Ltd v GLC* [1983] 2 AC 509, [1983] 1 All ER 1159, HL; and NUISANCE vol 78 (2010) PARA 107.

3   *Hunter v Canary Wharf Ltd* [1997] AC 655 at 688, 691, [1997] All ER 426 at 435, 438, HL, per Lord Goff, at 695 and 441 per Lord Lloyd, at 703, 708 and 449, 453 per Lord Hoffmann, at 717 and 462 per Lord Cooke, and at 724 and 468 per Lord Hope.

4   *Hunter v Canary Wharf Ltd* [1997] AC 655 at 688, [1997] 2 All ER 426 at 435, HL, per Lord Goff.

5   *Newcastle-under-Lyme Corpn v Wolstanton Ltd* [1947] Ch 92 at 106–108, [1946] 2 All ER 447 at 455–456 per Evershed J; *Hunter v Canary Wharf Ltd* [1997] AC 655 at 688, [1997] All ER 426 at 435, HL, per Lord Goff, at 695 and 441 per Lord Lloyd, at 717 and 462 per Lord Cooke, and at 724 and 468 per Lord Hope.

6 *Foster v Warblington UDC* [1906] 1 KB 648, CA; *Hunter v Canary Wharf Ltd* [1997] AC 655
   at 688, 691, [1997] 2 All ER 426 at 435, 438, HL, per Lord Goff.
7 As to the defence of jus tertii see also PARA 581 (in respect of trespass to land).
8 *Hunter v Canary Wharf Ltd* [1997] AC 655 at 688, [1997] 2 All ER 426 at 435, HL, per
   Lord Goff.
9 *Hunter v Canary Wharf Ltd* [1997] AC 655 at 688, 691, [1997] 2 All ER 426 at 435, 438, HL,
   per Lord Goff, at 708 and 453 per Lord Hoffmann, at 724 and 468 per Lord Hope. Cf the
   position in relation to damage to a reversionary interest in goods: see eg PARAS 624, 633–634.

596.   The rule in Rylands v Fletcher. A person who for his own purposes
brings onto his land and collects and keeps there anything likely to do mischief if
it escapes must keep it in at his peril, and, if he fails to do so, he is prima facie
liable for the damage which is the natural consequence of its escape[1]. Liability
under this rule is a liability in private nuisance, and therefore arises only in
respect of damage to interests in land[2]. It is a strict liability in the sense that it is
no defence for the defendant to show that the thing escaped independently of any
wilful act or default on his part[3], or despite his exercise of all possible care and
precautions to prevent it[4]. Liability, however, will not arise unless damage of the
relevant type was foreseeable to the defendant if the things collected on his land
were to escape[5].
   The rule applies only to a non-natural user of the land[6]. It does not apply:
   (1)   to things naturally on the land[7];
   (2)   to things not likely to do mischief if they escape[8];
   (3)   where there is no escape from the land on which things were collected[9];
   (4)   where the escape is due to an act of God, the act of a stranger or the
         default of the claimant[10];
   (5)   where the thing which escapes is present by consent of the person
         injured[11];
   (6)   in certain cases where there is statutory authority[12].

1 *Rylands v Fletcher* (1868) LR 3 HL 330. See NUISANCE vol 78 (2010) PARA 148 et seq. For the
   purposes of the rule, it is the 'thing' that has been brought onto the land which must escape:
   Stannard (t/a Wyvern Tyres) v Gore [2012] EWCA Civ 1248, sub nom *Gore v Stannard (t/a
   Wyvern Tyres)* [2014] QB 1, [2013] 1 All ER 694 (escape of fire originating on the defendant's
   property, the ferocity of which was increased by a large stock of tyres stored there. It was held
   that the tyres were not exceptionally dangerous and that there was no exceptionally high risk of
   danger or mischief if they escaped. The case could not therefore be brought within the principles
   of *Rylands v Fletcher*); see NUISANCE vol 78 (2010) PARA 151.
2 *Cambridge Water Co Ltd v Eastern Counties Leather plc* [1994] 2 AC 264, [1994] 1 All ER
   53, HL; *Transco plc v Stockport Metropolitan Borough Council* [2003] UKHL 61, [2004]
   2 AC 1, [2004] 1 All ER 589.
3 *Rylands v Fletcher* (1868) LR 3 HL 330; *Smith v Fletcher* (1872) LR 7 Exch 305 (revsd on other
   grounds (1874) LR 9 Exch 64, Ex Ch); *Humphries v Cousins* (1877) 2 CPD 239. In the latter
   decision, the defendant was held liable even though he had no knowledge of the existence of the
   thing that escaped, but this seems inconsistent with the modern law: see *Cambridge
   Water Co Ltd v Eastern Counties Leather plc* [1994] 2 AC 264 at 301, [1994] 1 All ER 53 at
   73, HL, per Lord Goff.
4 *Cambridge Water Co Ltd v Eastern Counties Leather plc* [1994] 2 AC 264, [1994] 1 All ER
   53, HL.
5 *Cambridge Water Co Ltd v Eastern Counties Leather plc* [1994] 2 AC 264, [1994] 1 All ER
   53, HL.
6 See eg *Read v J Lyons & Co Ltd* [1947] AC 156, [1946] 2 All ER 471, HL; *Cambridge
   Water Co Ltd v Eastern Counties Leather plc* [1994] 2 AC 264, [1994] 1 All ER 53, HL
   (storage of substantial quantities of chemicals; an 'almost classic case' of non-natural user of
   land, even if on industrial premises in an industrial complex); *Transco plc v Stockport
   Metropolitan Borough Council* [2003] UKHL 61, [2004] 2 AC 1, [2004] 1 All ER 589 (piping
   of mains water supply to storage tanks was a routine function not raising any special hazard,
   and so a natural or ordinary user of land).

7 See NUISANCE vol 78 (2010) PARA 149.
8 See NUISANCE vol 78 (2010) PARA 150.
9 See NUISANCE vol 78 (2010) PARA 151.
10 See NUISANCE vol 78 (2010) PARA 152.
11 See NUISANCE vol 78 (2010) PARA 153.
12 See NUISANCE vol 78 (2010) PARA 154.

597. Liability of occupier of premises for fire. The occupier of premises is liable for damage by fire caused by his negligence, or by the negligence of an independent contractor employed by him[1]. It is doubtful that any action will lie under the Rule in *Rylands v Fletcher*[2] because the requirement is that the thing brought on to land must escape; it is not sufficient that the fire itself escapes[3]. Certainly, no claim may be brought against any person in whose house or other building, or on whose estate, any fire accidentally begins[4].

1 As to the principles applicable to liability for negligence see further NEGLIGENCE.
2 As to the rule see *Rylands v Fletcher* (1868) LR 3 HL 330; PARA 596; and NUISANCE vol 78 (2010) PARA 148 et seq. As to the application of the rule in cases concerning escape of fire, see the criteria set out in *Stannard (t/a Wyvern Tyres) v Gore* [2012] EWCA Civ 1248, sub nom *Gore v Stannard (t/a Wyvern Tyres)* [2014] QB 1, [2013] 1 All ER 694 at [22], [50], [2013] 1 All ER 694 at [22], [50] per Ward LJ. See also PARA 596; and FIRE AND RESCUE SERVICES vol 51 (2013) PARA 6; NUISANCE vol 78 (2010) PARA 151.
3 *Stannard (t/a Wyvern Tyres) v Gore* [2012] EWCA Civ 1248 at [22], [48], [50] per Ward LJ, at [59], [66] per Etherton LJ, and at [112], [145] per Lewison LJ, sub nom *Gore v Stannard (t/a Wyvern Tyres)* [2014] QB 1, [2013] 1 All ER 694. See also at [164], Lewison LJ doubting the contrary decision in *Mason v Levy Auto Parts of England Ltd* [1967] 2 QB 530, [1967] 2 All ER 62. See also FIRE AND RESCUE SERVICES vol 51 (2013) PARA 6.
4 See the Fires Prevention (Metropolis) Act 1774 s 86; and FIRE AND RESCUE SERVICES vol 51 (2013) PARA 6. The exemption in respect of fires begun accidentally does not apply to fires started accidentally but continued and not extinguished through negligence: see *Musgrove v Pandelis* [1919] 2 KB 43.

(3) DISTURBANCE OF FRANCHISES AND INCORPOREAL HEREDITAMENTS

598. Disturbance of market franchise. The owner of a market or fair has a claim in tort against anyone who unjustifiably interferes with his franchise[1]. He may recover damages, and the continuance of the disturbance may be restrained by injunction[2].

1 As to disturbance of markets see MARKETS vol 71 (2013) PARA 846 et seq.
2 See *Birmingham Corpn v Perry Bar Stadium Ltd* [1972] 1 All ER 725; *Stoke-on-Trent City Council v W & I Wass Ltd* [1988] 3 All ER 394, [1988] 1 WLR 1406, CA (proof of loss required); and CIVIL PROCEDURE vol 11 (2009) PARA 386. As to the principles governing the measure of damages for torts generally see DAMAGES vol 29 (2014) PARA 408 et seq.

599. Disturbance of ferry franchise. The owner of the exclusive right of carrying for hire goods and passengers by means of boats has a claim in tort against anyone who unjustifiably disturbs his ferry franchise[1].

1 See *Blissett v Hart* (1744) Willes 508; *Hammerton v Earl of Dysart* [1916] 1 AC 57, HL; and WATER AND WATERWAYS vol 101 (2009) PARA 848 et seq.

600. Disturbance of incorporeal hereditament. The owner of an easement, profit à prendre or other incorporeal right can sue for the disturbance of his right[1].

1 *Nicholls v Ely Beet Sugar Factory Ltd* [1936] Ch 343, CA, where it was held that if the plaintiff proved that effluent from the defendants' factory was being discharged into the river in which he

had a right of fishery he could succeed in tort without proving damage. See further REAL PROPERTY AND REGISTRATION vol 87 (2012) PARAS 1005, 1056. As to easements and profits à prendre see further REAL PROPERTY AND REGISTRATION vol 87 (2012) PARA 801 et seq.

(4) WASTE

601. Damage to land caused by waste. If a person in possession of land under a limited interest causes damage to the reversionary interest in the land, the reversioner may sue him in tort for waste[1].

1 See LANDLORD AND TENANT vol 62 (2012) PARA 577 et seq; MINES, MINERALS AND QUARRIES vol 76 (2013) PARA 373; SETTLEMENTS vol 91 (2012) PARA 887 et seq.

6. WRONGFUL INTERFERENCE WITH GOODS

(1) INTRODUCTION TO WRONGFUL INTERFERENCE WITH GOODS

602. Causes of action for wrongful interference with goods. Until 1978[1], two main causes of action lay for the protection of proprietary interests in goods. These were trover[2] (now more commonly called 'conversion'[3]) and detinue[4]. The Torts (Interference with Goods) Act 1977 abolished the former tort of detinue[5] but expanded the scope of conversion, which now lies in every case in which detinue formerly lay before it was abolished[6].

Today the law on wrongful interference encompasses the specific torts of conversion[7], trespass to goods[8], and negligence so far as it results in damage to goods or to an interest in goods[9], and any other tort so far as it results in damage to goods or to an interest in goods[10].

1 Ie the year in which the Torts (Interference with Goods) Act 1977 came into force. As to the commencement of the Torts (Interference with Goods) Act 1977 see PARA 603.

2 Trover was available in all cases where one person committed a conversion of another person's chattel. It originated as a form of trespass on the case (3 Holdsworth's History of English Law 350). 'Trover' was an old French word meaning 'to find'. It derived its name from the concept that, and was based on the fiction that, the defendant had found the goods and afterwards converted them to his use: see eg *Cooper v Chitty* (1756) 1 Burr 20; *Gordon v Harper* (1796) 7 Term Rep 9; *Burroughes v Bayne* (1860) 5 H & N 296. The fictitious allegations of loss and finding were abolished by the Common Law Procedure Act 1852, which substituted an allegation that the defendant converted to his own use or wrongfully deprived the plaintiff of the use and possession of the plaintiff's goods: see (1905) 21 LQR 43. 'Trover' was historically the name of the form of action, and 'conversion' the name of the tort; but cf the Torts (Interference with Goods) Act 1977 s 1(a) which indicates that the terms are synonymous.

3 See PARA 604 et seq.

4 Detinue lay where there was unlawful failure to deliver up goods when demanded: see *Jones v Dowle* (1841) 9 M & W 19; *Mason v Farnell* (1844) 12 M & W 674; *Clements v Flight* (1846) 16 M & W 42; *General and Finance Facilities Ltd v Cooks Cars (Romford) Ltd* [1963] 2 All ER 314, [1963] 1 WLR 644, CA; *Alicia Hosiery Ltd v Brown Shipley & Co Ltd* [1970] 1 QB 195 at 207, [1969] 2 All ER 504 at 510, per Donaldson J. It seems that detinue was originally an action chiefly used against bailees (see 3 Holdsworth's History of English Law 324). It lay when a person wrongfully detained the goods of another, or improperly parted with possession of them: see *Jones v Dowle* (1841) 9 M & W 19; *Ballett v Mingay* [1943] KB 281, [1943] 1 All ER 143, CA; *Finlayson v Taylor* (1983) 133 NLJ 720. It also lay when a bailee lost goods and could not show that the loss was without default on his part: *Reeve v Palmer* (1885) 5 CBNS 84, Ex Ch (as explained in *Wilkinson v Verity* (1871) LR 6 CP 206); *Goodman v Boycott* (1862) 2 B & S 1; *Bullen v Swan Electric Engraving Co* (1906) 22 TLR 275 at 277, per Walton J (affd (1907) 23 TLR 258, CA); *Coldman v Hill* [1919] 1 KB 443 at 455, CA, per Scrutton LJ; *Houghland v RR Low (Luxury Coaches) Ltd* [1962] 1 QB 694, [1962] 2 All ER 159, CA. It was the appropriate form of action when the return of title deeds or other specific chattels was required: see eg *Goodman v Boycott* (1862) 2 B & S 1. It did not afford a remedy when a bailee restored goods in a damaged condition (Holdsworth's History of English Law 350), nor where he misused goods without causing loss or destruction. Detinue was formerly considered an action ex contractu (*Danby v Lamb* (1861) 11 CBNS 423), but was later reckoned as an action founded on tort (see *Bryant v Herbert* (1878) 3 CPD 389, CA; *Ballett v Mingay* [1943] KB 281, [1943] 1 All ER 143, CA).

5 Torts (Interference with Goods) Act 1977 s 2(1).

6 See *Howard E Perry & Co Ltd v British Railways Board* [1980] 2 All ER 579 at 584, [1980] 1 WLR 1375 at 1380 (citing the Eighteenth Report of the Law Reform Committee (Conversion and Detinue) 1971 (Cmnd 4774) para 8); *Hillesden Securities Ltd v Ryjak Ltd* [1983] 2 All ER 184 at 187–188, [1983] 1 WLR 959 at 962–963 per Parker.

7 As to conversion see PARA 604 et seq.

8 As to trespass to goods see PARA 685 et seq.

9   As to negligence see PARA 497; and NEGLIGENCE.
10   See the Torts (Interference with Goods) Act 1977 s 1; and PARA 603.

603.   Effect of the Torts (Wrongful Interference with Goods) Act 1979. In 1978 legislation came into force amending the law concerning conversion and other torts affecting goods[1]. The Torts (Interference with Goods) Act 1977 defined 'wrongful interference', or 'wrongful interference with goods'[2], to mean:

(1)   conversion of goods (also called trover)[3];

(2)   trespass to goods[4];

(3)   negligence so far as it results in damage to goods or to an interest in goods[5];

(4)   any other tort so far as it results in damage to goods or to an interest in goods[6].

However, the Act did not replace the common law that had developed relating to the so-called 'chattel torts'; instead it introduced a common system of defences, remedies and procedures for these torts[7]. Under the Act, proceedings under Part I of the Consumer Protection Act 1987[8] in respect of any damage to goods or to an interest in goods are also included as proceedings for wrongful interference[9].

1   Torts (Interference with Goods) Act 1977, preamble. The Act partly came into force in England and Wales on 1 January 1978 (see the Torts (Interference with Goods) Act 1977 (Commencement No 1) Order 1977, SI 1977/1910) with the remainder coming into force on 1 June 1978 (see the Torts (Interference with Goods) Act 1977 (Commencement No 2) Order 1978, SI 1978/627). That part of the Act which was not already in force in Northern Ireland came into force there on 1 January 1981 (see the Torts (Interference with Goods) Act 1977 (Commencement No 3) Order 1980, SI 1980/2024).

2   'Goods' includes all chattels personal other than things in action and money: Torts (Interference with Goods) Act 1977 s 14(1).

3   Torts (Interference with Goods) Act 1977 s 1(a). As to the tort of conversion see PARA 604 et seq. As to trover see PARA 602.

4   Torts (Interference with Goods) Act 1977 s 1(b). As to trespass to goods see PARA 685 et seq.

5   Torts (Interference with Goods) Act 1977 s 1(c). As to negligence see PARA 497; and NEGLIGENCE.

6   Torts (Interference with Goods) Act 1977 s 1(d).

7   See e g PARA 655 et seq, 693.

8   Ie the Consumer Protection Act 1987 Pt I (ss 1–9) (product liability): see CONSUMER PROTECTION.

9   See the Torts (Interference with Goods) Act 1977 s 1 (amended by the Consumer Protection Act 1987 s 48, Sch 4; and SI 1987/2049).

(2) CONVERSION

(i) The Basis of Liability for Conversion

A. FEATURES OF CONVERSION

604.   Conversion: general features of the tort. The tort of conversion is broadly concerned with cases where one person has misappropriated goods belonging to another. Conversion of goods can occur in so many different circumstances that framing a precise definition of universal application is virtually impossible[1]. However, its basic features are as follows:

(1)   the defendant's conduct was inconsistent with the rights of the owner (or other person entitled to possession)[2];

(2)   the conduct was deliberate, not accidental[3]; and

(3)   the conduct was so extensive an encroachment on the rights of the owner as to exclude him from use and possession of the goods[4].

Another notable feature of conversion is that liability in the tort is strict[5]. Although the defendant's interference with the claimant's chattel, in the sense of his dealing and physical contact with it, must be deliberate, his infringement of the claimant's right need not be[6]. Indeed, there is no need to prove that the defendant was at fault at all, so complete ignorance of the existence of the claimant's right affords no general defence[7]. The classic illustration of this strict liability in operation is that of the purchaser of stolen goods. If A's car is stolen by X, who, in turn, sells the car to B, who acts in good faith, then B can be liable in conversion[8]. The reason for this is that B's dealing with the car is deliberate, not accidental, thus satisfying the criterion for liability in conversion. His good faith, which results from his lack of awareness of A's title to the chattel, is irrelevant.

1   *Kuwait Airways Corpn v Iraqi Airways Co (Nos 4 and 5)* [2002] UKHL 19 at [39], [2002] 2 AC 883 at [39], [2002] 3 All ER 209 at [39] per Lord Nicholls.

2   *Kuwait Airways Corpn v Iraqi Airways Co (Nos 4 and 5)* [2002] UKHL 19 at [39], [2002] 2 AC 883 at [39], [2002] 3 All ER 209 at [39] per Lord Nicholls. See PARA 605. The contrast is with lesser acts of interference. If these cause damage they may give rise to claims for trespass or in negligence, but they do not constitute conversion (at [39] per Lord Nicholls). As to trespass to goods see PARA 685 et seq. As to negligence see PARA 497; and NEGLIGENCE.

3   *Kuwait Airways Corpn v Iraqi Airways Co (Nos 4 and 5)* [2002] UKHL 19 at [39], [2002] 2 AC 883 at [39], [2002] 3 All ER 209 at [39] per Lord Nicholls. If A's car is carelessly damaged when another driver, B, crashes into it, then in no sense can B be said to have 'converted' A's car, as B was not deliberately dealing with it: see PARA 606.

4   *Kuwait Airways Corpn v Iraqi Airways Co (Nos 4 and 5)* [2002] UKHL 19 at [39], [2002] 2 AC 883 at [39], [2002] 3 All ER 209 at [39] per Lord Nicholls. See PARA 607. If A's car is damaged when B deliberately scratches a panel, although B will be liable in trespass to goods (see PARA 685 et seq), he will not be liable in conversion. B cannot be said to have converted the car, as he does not, in interfering with it, exclude A from the control of the car. To be liable in conversion, the defendant's interference must be far more extensive.

5   See eg *Kuwait Airways Corpn v Iraqi Airways Co (Nos 4 and 5)* [2002] UKHL 19 at [129], [2002] 2 AC 883 at [129], [2002] 3 All ER 209 at [129] per Lord Hoffmann ('The tort exists to protect proprietary or possessory rights in property; it is committed by an act inconsistent with those rights and it is a tort of strict liability').

6   See *Marfani & Co Ltd v Midland Bank Ltd* [1968] 2 All ER 573 at 577, [1968] 1 WLR 956 at 970, CA.

7   There are certain exceptions, such as cases involving the conversion of cheques and money, where good faith purchase can afford a defence: see PARA 647.

8   *Hollins v Fowler* (1875) LR 7 HL 757.

605.   Conduct must be inconsistent with a legal title. The first requirement for liability in conversion is that the defendant must have done an act in respect of a claimant's chattel which is inconsistent with the claimant's legal title[1]. Abstract acts (such as a mere oral assertion of ownership), that involve no physical contact with the claimant's chattel, are not usually considered to be inconsistent with the legal title[2].

In the majority of claims successfully litigated in conversion, the defendant is responsible for some form of physical contact with the claimant's chattel. Common examples of conversion include buying another's chattel, selling it, taking receipt of it, destroying it, transferring it for the purpose of security and so on[3]. In each case the defendant, in order to complete the wrongful act, is usually responsible for some physical dealing or contact with the chattel. In the absence of such physical contact, the courts rarely find that a conversion takes place[4].

If a claimant cannot establish a clear physical interference with his chattel, then he must show that the defendant has, by his conduct, entirely excluded the claimant from the possession and control of it. For instance, if A has title to a car, there is authority to suggest that if B surrounds the car and, whilst not making physical contact with it, prevents A from reaching it, then B may be liable in conversion[5]. Short of this high degree of control, it is unlikely that liability will be established[6].

1   *Kuwait Airways Corpn v Iraqi Airways Co (Nos 4 and 5)* [2002] UKHL 19 at [39], [2002] 2 AC 883 at [39], [2002] 3 All ER 209 at [39] per Lord Nicholls. See also Douglas, 'The Nature of Conversion' [2009] CLJ 198; Green & Randall, *The Tort of Conversion* (2009).
2   Eg if A's car is parked in London, and B, who is in Edinburgh, merely asserts that A's car 'belongs to B', then B will commit no tort. See *Edelstein v Schuler & Co* [1902] 2 KB 144 at 156, where the defendant, a broker, purported to sell shares belonging to the claimant. However, because the broker did not have physical possession of the share certificates, nor had a means of effecting their transfer, his assertion was a mere puff and did not infringe the claimant's legal title in the chattel. Denial of another's title is not sufficient: see PARA 614.
3   For common examples of conversion see PARAS 608–614.
4   See eg *Club Cruise Entertainment & Travelling Services Europe BV v Department for Transport (The Van Gogh)* [2008] EWHC 2794 (Comm), [2009] 1 All ER (Comm) 955, where the defendant, a maritime authority, improperly issued a detention notice against the claimant's ship. The court held that there was no conversion of the ship, even though the practical effect of the detention notice was that the claimant was unable to use the ship for a scheduled cruise. The claim failed because the defendant, in issuing the notice, did not physically interfere with the ship. Had the defendant physically restrained the ship, by chaining it to the dock, then there would have been liability in conversion or trespass but, in the absence of such acts, there was no liability: see at [50] per Flaux J.
      In *Kuwait Airways Corpn v Iraqi Airways Co (Nos 4 and 5)* [2002] UKHL 19, [2002] 2 AC 883, [2002] 3 All ER 209, many of the defendant's acts were abstract in nature, involving no physical interference, such as applying for insurance for the aircraft and applying for airworthiness certificates. However, other acts, such as the flying of a number of the aircraft and the re-painting them in the defendant's livery, did involve physical interference.
5   *Oakley v Lyster* [1931] 1 KB 148, CA; cf *England v Cowley* (1873) LR 8 Exch 126.
6   One case in which there was liability in conversion notwithstanding the absence of any physical interference is *Douglas Valley Finance Co Ltd v S Hughes (Hirers) Ltd* [1969] 1 QB 738, [1966] 3 All ER 214. The defendant fraudulently deprived the claimant's lorries of valuable haulage licences without physically possessing the vehicles. It was held that the defendant had committed conversion by reducing the utility of the vehicles. However, this authority is to be doubted in light of *Club Cruise Entertainment & Travelling Services Europe BV v Department for Transport (The Van Gogh)* [2008] EWHC 2794 (Comm), [2009] 1 All ER (Comm) 955.

606.   Interference with the chattel must be deliberate.   The second requirement for liability in conversion is that the defendant's interference with the claimant's chattel must be deliberate and not accidental[1]. The element of deliberateness is seen in all of the common examples of conversion as they all involve acts that are difficult to do unintentionally[2]. When a defendant takes a claimant's chattel, which is a common form of conversion, the taking is a deliberate act[3]. Similarly, when a defendant detains a claimant's chattel, another common form of conversion, the defendant must make the decision to retain the chattel. This requires a conscious choice, which can in no way be said to be accidental[4].

Where there is no deliberate act on the part of the defendant, there may however be liability in negligence[5] which establishes liability for unintentional interferences[6].

The requirement of deliberateness in conversion is not the same as the requirement for malice[7]. Although the defendant's dealing or physical contact with the claimant's chattel must be deliberate, he need not intend to infringe the claimant's rights or cause the claimant harm. Indeed he need not even be careless in respect of this possibility[8]. In many cases a defendant is entirely unaware of the claimant's existence, yet this does not prevent him being liable in conversion[9]. For instance, if a defendant, acting in good faith, buys stolen goods, he will be liable to the person from whom they were stolen despite the fact that the defendant was unaware of the existence of a better title to the goods; because the defendant, in buying the goods, deliberately takes control of them, he will be liable in conversion[10].

1   *Kuwait Airways Corpn v Iraqi Airways Co (Nos 4 and 5)* [2002] UKHL 19 at [39], [2002] 2 AC 883 at [39], [2002] 3 All ER 209 at [39] per Lord Nicholls.
2   For examples of conversion see PARAS 608–614.
3   See e g *Kuwait Airways Corpn v Iraqi Airways Co (Nos 4 and 5)* [2002] UKHL 19, [2002] 2 AC 883, [2002] 3 All ER 209 (defendant deliberately took possession of aircraft). As to taking possession see PARA 608.
4   See e g *Howard E Perry & Co v British Railways Board* [1980] 2 All ER 579, [1980] 1 WLR 1375 (detention of steel so as not to aggravate striking unions; held detention was deliberate, not accidental). As to detention of chattels see PARA 613.
5   See e g *BMW Financial Services (GB) Ltd v Bhagwanani* [2007] EWCA Civ 1230, [2007] All ER (D) 26 (Nov) where the defendant had borrowed the claimant's car with the claimant's consent, but crashed it as a result of his careless driving. The damage sustained by the car was a not deliberate, but an unintended consequence of the claimant's poor driving. The claim in conversion therefore failed.
6   See e g *Moorgate Mercantile Co Ltd v Finch and Read* [1962] 1 QB 701, [1962] 2 All ER 467, CA, where the defendant had borrowed the claimant's car, and used it to smuggle goods into the UK. The car was seized by HMRC. The loss of the car was an unintended consequence of the defendant's conduct, but the court nevertheless held that he was liable in conversion, as it adopted the fictional view that the defendant intended the seizure of the car as it was a highly likely consequence of his conduct. It is submitted that this case is now to be doubted in light of *BMW Financial Services (GB) Ltd v Bhagwanani* [2007] EWCA Civ 1230, [2007] All ER (D) 26 (Nov), and that this fictional view of intention is unnecessary, as there would be a straightforward claim in negligence.
7   Conversion carries strict liability: see PARA 604.
8   *Marfani & Co Ltd v Midland Bank Ltd* [1968] 2 All ER 573, [1968] 1 WLR 956, CA.
9   See e g *Hollins v Fowler* (1875) LR 7 HL 757, where the defendant, acting as broker, had bought and sold corn which, unknown to the defendant, belonged to the claimant. Although the defendant acted in good faith, and was entirely unaware of the existence of the claimant's title, he was still held liable in conversion.
10 *Hollins v Fowler* (1875) LR 7 HL 757.

607.   **Interference with the chattel must exclude the owner from use and possession.** The third requirement for liability in conversion is that the defendant's conduct was so extensive an encroachment on the rights of the owner as to exclude him from use and possession of the goods[1]. Because liability in conversion typically results in an order that the defendant pay the claimant the full market value of the goods[2], the defendant's interference must be of such a nature to justify an award of the full value of the chattel. Minor interferences, which do not exclude others from the chattel, do not justify such an award[3]. For instance, where a defendant deliberately scratches the panel of another's car, or punctures its tyres, the interference, although deliberate, does not exclude the person with legal title from the possession and use of the chattel, and hence does not constitute a conversion[4]. In such cases involving minor interferences, the appropriate cause of action is the tort of trespass to goods[5], not conversion.

1   *Kuwait Airways Corpn v Iraqi Airways Co (Nos 4 and 5)* [2002] UKHL 19 at [39], [2002] 2 AC 883 at [39], [2002] 3 All ER 209 at [39] per Lord Nicholls.
2   See PARA 668 et seq. See in particular PARA 669.
3   See *Fouldes v Willoughby* (1841) 8 M & W 540, where the defendant ferrymaster led the claimant's horse off the ferry and onshore in order to entice the claimant to leave as well. It was held that there was no conversion as there was no exclusion; the claimant could easily have

followed the horse onshore and taken possession again. See also *Penfolds Wines Pty Ltd v Elliott* (1946) 74 CLR 204, Aust HC. For examples of conversion see PARAS 608–614.

4   These examples were cited in *Fouldes v Willoughby* (1841) 8 M & W 540 at 549 per Alderson B. See also *Bushel v Miller* (1718) 1 Stra 128; *Kirk v Gregory* (1876) 1 Ex D 55. A modern example would be car clamping, which does not exclude one from possession, but immobilises the car: see eg *Arthur v Anker* [1997] QB 564, [1996] 3 All ER 783, CA; *Vine v Waltham Forest London Borough Council* [2000] 4 All ER 169, [2000] 1 WLR 2383, CA.

5   As to trespass to goods see PARA 685 et seq.

B. EXAMPLES OF CONVERSION

608.   Conversion by taking possession of chattel.   Possibly the most common example of a conversion is an unauthorised taking of possession of a claimant's chattel. The taking is not in itself a conversion[1]; rather, all the basic elements of conversion must be present in the taking[2]. The taking must be both deliberate[3] and to the exclusion of the claimant[4]. It is often the requirement of exclusion that causes problems for claimants. If a defendant takes possession of the claimant's chattel temporarily, or for limited purposes, then it may be that the exclusion requirement is not met[5]. In order for conversion to be established, it must be shown that the defendant, in taking possession of the chattel, excludes others from the control of the goods[6].

Another example of case where a defendant can be liable in conversion for taking the claimant's chattel is where he takes the chattel as a security. Provided that there is no legal basis for the security[7], a defendant will be liable in conversion by taking a claimant's chattel as a pledge[8] or a lien[9].

When a defendant takes possession of land upon which the claimant has a chattel situated, the defendant does not necessarily take possession of the chattel as well, thus incurring liability in conversion[10]. However, if the defendant, in taking possession of the land, forms the intention to exclude others from the chattels situated on the land, then this can amount to a conversion[11].

The requirement of taking possession does not mean that the defendant must be the first party to have taken possession from the claimant[12]. It does not matter if the defendant is the first, second or tenth person to take possession[13]; all that is required is that in taking possession the defendant must have excluded others, including the claimant, from the chattel.

1   See eg *Fouldes v Willoughby* (1841) 8 M & W 540 (defendant ferrymaster took possession of the claimant's horse by leading it ashore in order to entice the claimant to leave the ferry, but it did not amount to a conversion as there was no exclusion of the claimant: see note 5).

2   As to the general features of conversion see PARA 604.

3   As to the requirement of deliberateness see PARA 606.

4   As to the need for exclusion of the owner see PARA 607.

5   See *Fouldes v Willoughby* (1841) 8 M & W 540 (see note 1). See also *Bushel v Miller* (1718) 1 Stra 128, no conversion where the defendant moved a package, belonging to a claimant, a small distance, to allow the defendant to gain access to a locker which was blocked by the claimant's package. Although there was a taking of possession, it did not have the effect of excluding the claimant from the use and control of the package.

6   See eg *Aitken Agencies Ltd v Richardson* [1967] NZLR 65 (defendant stole the claimant's car for the purpose of joyriding; the taking had the result of excluding the claimant from the control of the chattel and hence was a conversion); *Empresa Exportadora de Azucar v Industria Azucarera Nacional SA, The Playa Larga and Marble Islands* [1983] 2 Lloyd's Rep 171. See also *White v Withers LLP* [2009] EWCA Civ 1122, [2009] 3 FCR 435, where the defendant intercepted the claimant's letters and passed them to the defendant's solicitor during a matrimonial dispute; claimant was thereby excluded from possession. Although the case was litigated in trespass, the defendant's action, in taking and detaining the letters, amounted to a conversion as well. Other examples include the taking and wearing of the claimant's pearl (*Lord Petre v Heneage* (1701) 12 Mod Rep 519). See also *Grainger v Hill* (1838) 4 Bing NC

212 where the claimant had mortgaged his ship to the defendant; before the money was due the defendant arrested and imprisoned the claimant until he gave up the register of the ship. Although the claimant had given the register to the defendant himself, because it was done under duress, the defendant was liable for his taking of possession.

7 Eg where A's goods are stolen by B, who then pledges the goods to C. C has no legal basis, as against A, to keep the goods.

8 Receipt of goods by way of pledge is conversion if the delivery of the goods is conversion: Torts (Interference with Goods) Act 1977 s 11(2). As to pledge see BAILMENT AND PLEDGE.

9 See eg *Tear v Freebody* (1858) 4 CB NS 228, where the claimant's house was improperly demolished, and the defendant took the bricks and claimed a lien over them. The defendant was liable in conversion for such a taking. As lien see further LIEN.

10 *Thorogood v Robinson* (1845) 6 QB 769, 14 LJQB 87.

11 In *Thorogood v Robinson* (1845) 6 QB 769, 14 LJQB 87, where the defendant, when lawfully taking possession of the land, had refused permission to the claimant's servants to remove certain chattels, the court held that the claimant clearly had a right to the goods, and could sue in conversion if he had made a proper demand for them by someone with appropriate authority; if such a demand had been refused by the defendant, then the defendant would have formed an intention to exclude others.

12 *International Factors Ltd v Rodriguez Ltd* [1979] QB 351 at 359, [1979] 1 All ER 17 at 21, CA, per Sir David Cairns.

13 *Kuwait Airways Corpn v Iraqi Airways Co (Nos 4 and 5)* [2002] UKHL 19, [2002] 2 AC 883, [2002] 3 All ER 209. Here, the Iraqi Army seized the claimant's aircraft, but the defendant was the Iraqi Civil Aviation Authority, an entirely separate body who subsequently took receipt of the aircraft from the army. Although they were the second wrongdoers to take possession of the aircraft, the defendants were equally liable. See also *Hollins v Fowler* (1875) LR 7 HL 757, where the defendant was a subsequent converter.

609. Conversion by destruction of chattel. A defendant may commit a conversion by destroying a chattel. If a defendant, for instance, sets the claimant's chattel on fire, breaks it up, or completely spoils it, then such things can amount to a conversion[1], as such acts involve clear physical interferences.

In order to amount to a conversion the act of destruction must be deliberate[2]. If a defendant, for example, carelessly crashes into the claimant's car, although there may be a cause of action in negligence, it will not constitute liability in conversion[3].

The interference must be of such an extent to effectively deprive the claimant of his goods[4]. If a defendant, for instance, were to merely scratch the side of the claimant's car, or puncture his tyre, then there would be no liability in conversion, as the claimant is not deprived in any way[5]. The interference must be of such a nature as to substantively deprive the claimant of the use and enjoyment of the chattel; this may be achieved by damaging or spoiling the chattel to such an extent that it is not practicable to repair it[6].

1 *Richardson v Atkinson* (1723) 1 Stra 576.

2 As to the requirement of deliberateness see PARA 606.

3 *BMW Financial Services (GB) Ltd v Bhagwanani* [2007] EWCA Civ 1230, [2007] All ER (D) 26 (Nov); cf *Moorgate Mercantile Co Ltd v Finch and Read* [1962] 1 QB 701, [1962] 2 All ER 467, CA.

4 *Fouldes v Willoughby* (1841) 8 M & W 540 at 549. As to the need for exclusion of the owner see PARA 607.

5 *Fouldes v Willoughby* (1841) 8 M & W 540 at 549 (giving the example that scratching the panel of a carriage would be a trespass rather than a conversion). As to trespass to goods see PARA 685 et seq. See also *Simmons v Lillystone* (1853) 8 Exch 431 (defendant cutting through logs of wood belonging to the claimant which had washed up on the defendant's land did not constitute a conversion as there was no substantive deprivation, merely interference).

6 When a defendant 'spoils' the claimant's chattel, as when he pours salt or water into the claimant's vat of wine, there is a conversion, as the entirety is thereby altered: *Richardson v Atkinson* (1723) 1 Stra 576. See also *Indian Oil Corpn v Greenstone Shipping SA (Panama), The Ypatianna* [1988] QB 345, [1987] 3 All ER 893.

610.   Conversion by transfer of chattel to another without owner's consent.   A defendant may commit a conversion by transferring the claimant's chattel to another person without the claimant's consent[1]. Of course, if the defendant has wrongfully taken the goods in the first place, then he will have already committed conversion[2]. However, in some cases a defendant's initial taking of possession will be lawful, such as that of a bailee who takes the claimant's goods[3]. If a bailee subsequently transfers the goods to a third party, without the claimant's consent, this transfer can constitute a conversion[4]. In such cases the conversion lies in the transfer, not the initial taking. The reason for this is that the transfer, in the sense of a physical delivery, involves an unauthorised interference with the claimant's chattel which has the effect of excluding the claimant from it[5].

The transfer may be for the purpose of creating a security interest, such as a pledge. For instance, if an employee is entrusted with a chattel for a certain purpose, and contrary to that purpose, pledges the chattel to a pawnbroker, that delivery to the pawnbroker will amount a conversion[6]. Similarly, if one entrusted with the claimant's goods, purports to sell the goods to a third party, without the claimant's consent, and delivers to the third party, this delivery can constitute a conversion[7].

It is important to note that an attempt to transfer title by sale, without anything more, cannot amount to a conversion[8]. A sale, as a purely abstract act which need not involve the physical delivery of the chattel, cannot normally amount to a conversion in itself[9]. The sale must be accompanied by some form of physical delivery in order to amount to a conversion[10]. When such a delivery takes place the purported vendor is responsible for a physical interference with the chattel and can be liable in the tort. The purported vendee can also be liable in the tort as he has taken possession of the chattel under the delivery[11].

Auctioneers who sell goods belonging to a claimant without the claimant's authority, can be liable in conversion[12]. However, if the auctioneer is unable to sell the chattel, then it is unlikely that he will be liable in conversion[13].

1   *Martindale v Smith* (1841) 1 QB 389, 10 LJQB 155 (defendant had possession of the claimant's stacks of corn, and sold them to a third party). In such cases both the transferor and transferee can be liable: *M'Combie v Davies* (1805) 6 East 538; *Glasspoole v Young* (1829) 9 B & C 696, 7 LJOS KB 305; *Metcalfe v Lumsden* (1844) 1 Car & Kir 309; *Cooper v Willommatt* (1845) 1 CB 672, 14 LJCP 219; *Mulliner v Florence* (1878) 3 QBD 484, 47 LJQB 700, CA; *Hannah v Peel* [1945] KB 509, [1945] 2 All ER 288; *Moorgate Mercantile Co Ltd v Twitchings* [1977] AC 890, [1976] 2 All ER 641, HL; *RH Willis & Son (a firm) v British Car Auctions Ltd* [1978] 2 All ER 392, [1978] 1 WLR 438, CA.
2   As to conversion by taking possession see PARA 608.
3   As to bailment see further BAILMENT AND PLEDGE.
4   See eg *Martindale v Smith* (1841) 1 QB 389, 10 LJQB 155.
5   As to the need for exclusion of the owner see PARA 607.
6   *Parker v Godin* (1728) 2 Stra 813.
7   *Consolidated Co v Curtis & Son* [1892] 1 QB 495, 61 LJQB 325.
8   *Lancashire Waggon Co v Fitzhugh* (1861) 6 H & N 502, 30 LJ Ex 231.
9   *Lancashire Waggon Co v Fitzhugh* (1861) 6 H & N 502, 30 LJ Ex 231; *Edelstein v Schuler & Co* [1902] 2 KB 144 at 156 (purported sale to a third party of the claimant's chattel by a defendant who had no control or physical proximity to the chattel, was not a conversion because there was no physical disturbance or interference with the chattel). However, where the sale falls into one of the nemo dat exceptions and does effect a transfer of title, then it would amount to a conversion.
10 *Lancashire Waggon Co v Fitzhugh* (1861) 6 H & N 502, 30 LJ Ex 231.
11 As to conversion by taking possession see PARA 608.
12 See eg *RH Willis & Son (a firm) v British Car Auctions Ltd* [1978] 2 All ER 392, [1978] 1 WLR 438, CA, where the claimant's car was taken by its hirer to the defendant auctioneers for sale

without the claimant's knowledge or consent. The auction house took possession of the car and, having sold it at the auction to a third party, delivered the car to the purchaser. It was held that this sale, being accompanied by the delivery, amounted to a conversion.

13 See *National Mercantile Bank v Rymill* (1881) 44 LT 767, CA (no conversion by the auctioneer where a rogue took the claimant's chattel and passed it to the defendant auctioneer for sale, because before the auctioneer could sell it, the rogue arranged for its sale privately). See also *Marcq v Christie Manson* [2002] EWHC 2148 (QB), [2002] 4 All ER 1005.

611. Conversion by misdelivery of chattel. Misdelivery of a chattel by a bailee can amount to a conversion[1]. If a claimant entrusts goods to a bailee with instructions to deliver to a particular person, and the bailee delivers the goods to the wrong person, then he can be liable in conversion[2]. If a bailee does deliver the goods to the wrong person, there will be no need to prove that he acted carelessly, as conversion is a tort of strict liability[3]. A bailee can protect himself from such liability through the terms of the bailment[4].

1 *Hiort v London and North Western Rly Co* (1879) 4 ExD 188, CA. (warehouseman liable in conversion when he, in good faith, allowed a fraudster, representing himself as entitled to the goods, to take the goods he was storing for the claimant). See also *Syeds v Hay* (1791) 4 Term Rep 260; *Youl v Harbottle* (1791) Peake 68 at 69; *Devereux v Barclay* (1819) 2 B & Ald 702; *Stephenson v Hart* (1828) 4 Bing 476, 6 LJOSCP 97; *Hiort v Bott* (1874) LR 9 Exch 86, 43 LJ Ex 81; *Glyn, Mills & Co v East and West India Dock Co* (1882) 7 App Cas 591, 52 LJQB 146, HL. As to bailment see further BAILMENT AND PLEDGE.

2 Although it may be thought that the more appropriate action is negligence in such cases (where one would have to prove carelessness on the part of the bailee), it should be noted that by delivering the goods to a third party, the bailee is deliberately dealing with the goods in a way which was not consented to by the claimant. As to the requirement of deliberateness see PARA 606.

3 *Motis Exports Ltd v Dampskibsselskabet AF 1912, Aktieselskab and Aktieselskabet Dampskibsselskabet Svendborg* [1999] 1 Lloyd's Rep 837 at 843, [1999] 1 All ER (Comm) 571 at 580 per Rix J. See PARA 604.

4 This was done in the case of *McKean v McIver* (1870) LR 6 Exch 36, 40 LJ Ex 30.

612. Conversion by loss of chattel by a bailee. Unlike delivery to the wrong person[1], loss of a chattel by a bailee is not a deliberate act but is purely accidental and, as such, cannot amount to conversion in the conventional sense[2]. In such cases a different rule applies. This is a form of statutory conversion introduced by the Torts (Interference with Goods) Act 1977[3], for which negligence must be proved[4].

1 See PARA 611.

2 As to the requirement of deliberateness see PARA 606.

3 This is technically referred to as a 'conversion' in the Torts (Interference with Goods) Act 1977 s 2(2) which provides that an action lies in conversion for loss or destruction of goods which a bailee has allowed to happen in breach of his duty to his bailor (that is to say it lies in a case which is not otherwise conversion, but would have been detinue before detinue was abolished). Detinue was abolished as from 1 June 1978: see s 2(1); Torts (Interference with Goods) Act (Commencement No 2) Order 1978, SI 1978/627.

4 Historically there had been two forms of bailment: one based upon a detention, the second based upon the negligent loss of a bailee. Whilst conversion completely overlapped the former kind, it was quite separate from the second, and it was not a conversion for a bailee to negligently lose a chattel. Conversion did not lie at common law against a bailee for mere negligent loss: see *Heald v Carey* (1852) 11 CB 977, 21 LJCP 97; *The Arpad* [1934] P 189 at 232, CA, per Maugham LJ. When detinue was abolished, in order to ensure that negligent loss by a bailee continued to be actionable, the Torts (Interference with Goods) Act 1977 s 2(2) extended conversion to such cases. Although this statutory form of conversion shares the same name as the common law form of the tort, it is a separate cause of action, requiring a claimant to prove a different set of facts. See further PARA 602.

613.   Conversion by detention of chattel.   A defendant who has possession of a claimant's chattel, and without lawful authority[1] prevents the claimant from retaking possession, then the defendant can be liable in conversion[2]. A typical example of this is where a defendant is lawfully in possession of the claimant's chattel[3], but subsequently refuses to hand it over when requested. This sometimes happens when, for instance, the defendant mistakenly believes that he has a valid security interest such as a pledge or lien[4]. The conversion consists not in the failure to redeliver the chattel[5], but in the refusal to allow the claimant to take it away[6].

The normal way in which a detention is proved is by a demand and refusal[7]. This involves the claimant proving that, upon demanding the return of the chattel, the claimant refused to allow the claimant to take possession[8]. Although it remains the case that a demand and refusal will be the clearest evidence of a conversion, it is not a strict requirement[9]. If a defendant has taken possession of a chattel in a way which does not incur liability (such as under a bailment for safe keeping), but subsequently makes it clear, irrespective of any demand and refusal, that he intends to exclude others from the chattel by treating it as his own, then this should suffice to establish liability in conversion[10]. Indeed, if there were a strict requirement for refusal upon demand, then the defendant could avoid liability by simply ignoring the request from the claimant.

The defendant will not incur liability in conversion if he asks for a reasonable period of time to comply with the demand from the claimant. For instance, if the goods are not in the defendant's immediate possession, but he must locate them somewhere, then he will be given time to comply[11]. Similarly, the defendant will not be liable in conversion if he asks for time to verify the claimant's title when he makes a demand for the return of the goods[12]. However, if the defendant refuses the demand simply on the basis that he honestly (but mistakenly) believes that the claimant is not entitled to them, then he will be liable in the tort[13].

1   If the defendant has a valid pledge or a lien over the chattel, then he will have lawful authority to detain the chattel. Similarly, where the defendant has a statutory power to be in possession of a chattel (eg under police powers), then he cannot incur liability for the detention: see eg *Costello v Chief Constable of Derbyshire Constabulary* [2001] EWCA Civ 381, [2001] 3 All ER 150, [2001] 1 WLR 1437 (where police had power under the Police and Criminal Evidence Act 1984 s 22 to detain the claimant's chattel for a period, they were only liable for the retention of the claimant's chattel beyond this period).

2   The basic elements of conversion (as to which see PARA 604) are all present in this case:
    (1)   there is an the interference, in that the defendant has physical possession of the chattel;
    (2)   it is deliberate, in that the detention is a conscious act; and
    (3)   there is an exclusion, as the claimant is prevented from taking his chattel.

3   Eg where the claimant has bailed goods to the defendant.

4   See eg *Brandeis Goldschmidt & Co Ltd v Western Transport Ltd* [1981] QB 864, [1982] 1 All ER 28, CA; *Howard E Perry & Co v British Railways Board* [1980] 2 All ER 579, [1980] 1 WLR 1375. See further BAILMENT AND PLEDGE; LIEN.

5   A failure to redeliver is no more than a failure to lend assistance to the claimant, which cannot attract liability in the tort.

6   *Capital Finance Co Ltd v Bray* [1964] 1 All ER 603, [1964] 1 WLR 323, CA. This is also apparent from the type of remedy that is granted in such cases: see eg *Howard E Perry & Co v British Railways Board* [1980] 2 All ER 579, [1980] 1 WLR 1375, where the claimant was granted an injunction entitling him to collect his goods, not demanding that the defendant redeliver them.

7   *Miller v Dell* [1891] 1 QB 468, 60 LJQB 404, CA; *Clayton v Le Roy* [1911] 2 KB 1031 at 1052, CA; *Barclays Mercantile Business Finance Ltd v Sibec Developments Ltd* [1993] 2 All ER 195 at 199–200, [1992] 1 WLR 1253 at 1257. The demand must be sufficiently clear: *Nixon v Sedger* (1890) 7 TLR 112, CA. The refusal must also be unambiguous: *Solomons v Dawes* (1794) 1 Esp 81; *Evans v Bell* (1847) 10 LTOS 109; *Norton v Blackie* (1864) 13 WR 80; *Jones v Hough* (1879) 5 ExD 115, CA.

8 Such detentions were historically litigated in detinue (now abolished: see PARA 602). In detinue the need for a demand and refusal was a strict one, so that if the claimant had not made such a demand for the chattel from the defendant then there could be no liability in detinue, even though there was evidence that the defendant was treating the chattel as his own and would not have given it up: *Clayton v Le Roy* [1911] 2 KB 1031, CA. There was a suggestion that this requirement applied in conversion (*General and Finance Facilities Ltd v Cooks Cars (Romford) Ltd* [1963] 2 All ER 314, [1963] 1 WLR 644, CA), but given that a mere taking possession of a chattel can, in itself, amount to a conversion (see PARA 608), it is to be doubted whether there could be a strict requirement for a demand and refusal in conversion.

9 See e g *R (on the application of Atapattu) v Secretary of State for the Home Department* [2011] EWHC 1388 (Admin), [2011] All ER (D) 20 (Jun), where the defendant made a demand for the return of his passport from the Home Office, which ignored the demand. The absence of a clear refusal did not prevent the conversion; there was other evidence that the defendant was detaining the passport. Cf *Schwarzschild v Harrods Ltd* [2008] EWHC 521 (QB), [2008] All ER (D) 299 (Mar), where the claimant made a demand for her jewellery from the defendant in 1997, which elicited no response, and again in 2001, at which point it was refused; it was held that the cause of action only arose in 2001, when there was a clear denial, even though there was evidence of a prior intention to detain.

10 See note 2.

11 *Alexander v Southey* (1821) 5 B & Ald 247.

12 *Towne v Lewis* (1849) 7 CB 608, 13 LTOS 71; *Pillot v Wilkinson* (1863) 2 H & C 72.

13 *Syeds v Hay* (1791) 4 Term Rep 260; *Verrall v Robinson* (1835) 2 Cr M & R 495; *Atkinson v Marshall* (1842) 12 LJ Ex 117 (where it was held that setting up a jus tertii, or keeping goods in order to maintain the title of a third person, is evidence of conversion); *Pillott v Wilkinson* (1864) 3 H & C 345, 34 LJ Ex 22; *Redler Grain Silos Ltd v BICC Ltd* [1982] 1 Lloyd's Rep 435, CA.

614. Denial of title alone is not a conversion. A denial of title is not of itself a conversion[1]. The reason for this is that a conversion usually requires the defendant to be responsible for some form of physical interference or dealing with the claimant's chattel in order to be liable[2]. A mere denial of title, unaccompanied by an act of physical interference, cannot amount to a conversion[3].

Where a defendant has denied the claimant's title by preventing the claimant from having access to the chattel, then this may amount to a conversion, as the denial is accompanied by some form of physical control over the chattel[4]. However, mere abstract acts, such as vague assertions of rights, unaccompanied by physical acts of control, are not sufficient for liability in the tort[5].

1 Torts (Interference with Goods) Act 1977 s 11(3).

2 See e g *Edelstein v Schuler & Co* [1902] 2 KB 144 (no conversion where a broker with no control over the claimant's chattel purported to sell it as, although there was denial of the claimant's title, there was no physical interference with the chattel). As to the elements of conversion see PARA 604. See also PARA 605.

3 *England v Cowley* (1873) LR 8 Exch 126; *Club Cruise Entertainment & Travelling Services Europe BV v Department for Transport (The Van Gogh)* [2008] EWHC 2794 (Comm), [2009] 1 All ER (Comm) 955.

4 *Oakley v Lyster* [1931] 1 KB 148, CA; *Van Oppen & Co Ltd v Tredegars Ltd* (1921) 37 TLR 504.

5 *Club Cruise Entertainment & Travelling Services Europe BV v Department for Transport (The Van Gogh)* [2008] EWHC 2794 (Comm), [2009] 1 All ER (Comm) 955; *Blue Sky One Ltd v Mahan Air* [2010] EWHC 631 (Comm), [2010] All ER (D) 02 (Jun); cf *Douglas Valley Finance Co Ltd v S Hughes (Hirers) Ltd* [1969] 1 QB 738, [1966] 3 All ER 214.

(ii) Who can Sue for Conversion

A. PROPRIETARY RIGHTS IN THE CHATTEL

615. Claimant must establish proprietary right to chattel. In order to sue in conversion[1], a claimant must establish that he holds a property right in respect of the chattel[2]. A mere contractual right relating to a chattel will not be sufficient to sue in conversion[3].

1   As to the elements of conversion see PARA 604 et seq.

2   *Addison v Round* (1836) 4 A & E 799, 7 Car & P 285; *Jarvis v Williams* [1955] 1 All ER 108, [1955] 1 WLR 71, CA; *Re Goldcorp Exchange Ltd (in receivership)* [1995] 1 AC 74, [1994] 2 All ER 806, PC; *International Factors Ltd v Rodriguez Ltd* [1979] QB 351 at 357, [1979] 1 All ER 17 at 19, CA, per Sir David Cairns; *MCC Proceeds Inc v Lehman Bros International (Europe)* [1998] 4 All ER 675 at 691, [1998] 2 BCLC 659 at 677, CA, per Mummery LJ. See also *Kahler v Midland Bank Ltd* [1950] AC 24, [1949] 2 All ER 621, HL; *Marquess of Bute v Barclays Bank Ltd* [1955] 1 QB 202 at 212, [1954] 3 All ER 365 at 369 per McNair J; cf *Iran v Barakat Galleries Ltd* [2007] EWCA Civ 1374, [2009] QB 22, [2008] 1 All ER 1177. As to the different proprietary rights in a chattel see PARA 616. See further PERSONAL PROPERTY vol 80 (2013) PARA 801 et seq. As to acquisition of ownership generally see further PERSONAL PROPERTY vol 80 (2013) PARA 816 et seq.

3   *Jarvis v Williams* [1955] 1 All ER 108, [1955] 1 WLR 71, CA; *Re Goldcorp Exchange Ltd (in receivership)* [1995] 1 AC 74, [1994] 2 All ER 806, PC. The same rule holds in respect of negligent damage to goods: *Leigh and Sillavan Ltd v Aliakmon Shipping Co Ltd (The Aliakmon)* [1986] AC 785 at 809, [1986] 2 All ER 145 at 149, HL.

616. Proprietary rights in chattels compared to such rights in land. In respect of torts which protect land, such as trespass to land and nuisance[1], because there are a number of different proprietary interests that can exist in respect of land, there are a number of different persons who can bring a claim in these torts: freeholders, lessees, the holder of an easement or profit, amongst others[2]. The position in respect of chattels is different[3], with the number of different proprietary interests being more restricted. It is not possible to create an estate in a chattel[4], or to grant a limited right of use, in the manner of an easement or restrictive covenant over a chattel[5]. The proprietary status of a lease of a chattel is currently undecided[6]. There are therefore fewer classes of litigant who can sue in conversion.

In most claims successfully litigated in conversion, the claimant is the person with the legal title to the chattel, that is, the best right one can have in respect of a chattel, roughly equivalent to freehold title to land[7]. In a small number of decided cases the person suing in conversion does not have legal title, but has been granted a security interest in a chattel, such as a pledge or lien[8]. A security interest is sufficient to sue in the tort. There is some suggestion that a lease of a chattel is a proprietary interest, entitling the holder to sue in conversion, but this is undecided[9]. Beyond legal title and security interests, therefore, there does not appear to be any other person clearly entitled to sue in the tort of conversion. If a person with legal title ('A'), contracts to grant another person ('B') a right in respect of his chattel (not being a security interest), such as a right to make some limited use of A's chattel, then this will not in itself grant B a proprietary interest in the chattel[10], and so will not give him standing to sue in conversion. However, if, as a result of being granted such a contractual right, B takes possession of the chattel, then he will acquire a relative title to the chattel, which will then entitle him to sue in conversion[11].

1   As to trespass to land see PARA 563 et seq. As to nuisance see PARAS 594–597; and NUISANCE.

2 See PARA 576 et seq.

3 As to the ownership of chattels see further PERSONAL PROPERTY vol 80 (2013) PARA 812 et seq.

4 *Re Tritton* (1889) 6 Morr 250, 5 TLR 687 (not possible to create a life estate in a painting, although you can do this through a trust); *Re Swan, Witham v Swan* [1915] 1 Ch 829, 84 LJ Ch 590.

5 *Taddy & Co v Sterious & Co* [1904] 1 Ch 354, 73 LJ Ch 191. The applicability of covenants over movables was doubted in *Barker v Stickney* [1919] 1 KB 121, 88 LJKB 315, CA. Easements and restrictive covenants apply to land only: see REAL PROPERTY AND REGISTRATION vol 87 (2012) PARAS 802 et seq, 1076 et seq.

6 *Lord Strathcona Steamship Co Ltd v Dominion Coal Co Ltd* [1926] AC 108, PC; cf *Port Line Ltd v Ben Line Steamers Ltd* [1958] 2 QB 146, [1958] 1 All ER 787; see PARA 624; and PERSONAL PROPERTY vol 80 (2013) PARA 801; REAL PROPERTY AND REGISTRATION vol 87 (2012) PARA 1079 et seq.

7 Whereas there is clear nomenclature for the 'best' right in respect of land, namely 'freehold' or 'fee simple' (see REAL PROPERTY AND REGISTRATION vol 87 (2012) PARA 66 et seq), there is no agreed term for the equivalent right in respect of chattels. The Sale of Goods Act 1979 uses the terms 'property in goods' (see s 2(1)), 'title' (see s 12) and 'ownership' (see s 35(1)(b)) interchangeably without further defining them except to say that 'property' means the general property in goods, and not merely a special property (see s 61). In this title the neutral term 'legal title' is used (cf the term 'equitable title': see PARAS 636–638). As to how the legal title in a chattel may be acquired see PARA 619 et seq.

8 See PARAS 633–634. See also BAILMENT AND PLEDGE; LIEN.

9 See PARA 624. Because a lessee of a chattel usually has possession of it, he will normally be able to establish a legal title as against a wrongdoer. It is this legal title which conversion protects, not the leasehold interest: *Burton v Hughes* (1824) 2 Bing 173, 3 LJOSCP 241. The proprietary status of a chattel lease is therefore usually irrelevant so far as conversion is concerned.

10 See eg *Taddy & Co v Sterious & Co* [1904] 1 Ch 354, 73 LJ Ch 191. The comparison with land law is that of the holder of a contractual licence: because such a right is not recognised as proprietary, it will not be able to bind a third party: *King v David Allen & Sons, Billposting Ltd* [1916] 2 AC 54, 85 LJPC 229, HL.

11 As to acquisition of legal title by taking possession see PARA 619 et seq.

617. Co-owner may sue other co-owner for conversion. If a defendant co-owner, without the authority of the other co-owner, destroys the goods, or disposes of them to a third party, or otherwise does anything equivalent to the destruction of the other's interest in the goods, he will be liable in conversion[1]. However, a co-owner may not be sued for conversion if he merely makes use of the common property in a reasonable way[2].

1 See the Torts (Interference with Goods) Act 1977 s 10(1)(a), (b); and PARA 659. The statute merely restated the position at common law: see s 10(3). For common law examples see *Fennings v Lord Grenville* (1808) 1 Taunt 241; *May v Harvey* (1811) 13 East 197; *Morgan v Marquis* (1853) 23 LJ Ex 21, 9 Exch 145; *Jacobs v Seward* (1872) LR 5 HL 464; *Baker v Barclays Bank Ltd* [1955] 2 All ER 571, [1955] 1 WLR 822. As to co-ownership of property see further PERSONAL PROPERTY vol 80 (2013) PARA 828 et seq.

2 Eg by cutting grass and making hay in the common field (*Jacobs v Seward* (1872) LR 5 HL 464), or extracting the oil and the other valuable parts of a dead whale which is owned in common (*Fennings v Lord Grenville* (1808) 1 Taunt 241).

B. LEGAL TITLE TO THE CHATTEL

(A) Establishing and Acquiring Legal Title

618. The relative nature of legal title to a chattel. The legal title to goods confers exclusive enjoyment of them[1], and has an indefinite duration[2]. This is the most important and common right that exists in relation to a chattel, and is the right held by the claimant in most successful claims in conversion[3].

The claimant's task in establishing that he holds a legal title to a chattel in order to bring a claim for conversion is made easier by the fact that title is relative, rather than absolute[4]. The law recognises that more than one title can exist in respect of any chattel[5]. When a chattel is subject to two or more titles, the priority of the titles is determined temporally, with the first in time ranking first[6]. The titles are relative in that the holder of a title has a right to exclude everyone except for those with a pre-existing title[7]. In order for a claimant to sue in conversion, he does not need to prove that he has the best or absolute right, but simply that he has a better title to the chattel than the defendant at the time of the act complained of[8]. A claimant can establish that he acquired such a right if he can prove that he took possession of the chattel prior to the defendant's interference with it[9].

However, there is a statutory defence, available in certain circumstances, that allows a defendant to plead the 'better' title of a third party[10].

1   See Austin's Jurisprudence (5th Edn) 789; and PERSONAL PROPERTY vol 80 (2013) PARA 812.
2   A right in respect of a chattel which is limited in time, such as the length of a person's life, has not been recognised: *Re Tritton* (1889) 6 Morr 250, 5 TLR 687. The status of a right in relation to a chattel for a term of years (ie a chattel lease) is undecided, with the authorities in conflict. The case of *Lord Strathcona Steamship Co v Dominion Coal Co* [1926] AC 108, 95 LJPC 71, PC suggests that it is proprietary, but *Port Line Ltd v Ben Line Steamers Ltd* [1958] 2 QB 146, [1958] 1 All ER 787 suggests that it is not. See PARA 624.
3   Examples are legion. See e g *Kuwait Airways Corpn v Iraqi Airways Co (Nos 4 and 5)* [2002] UKHL 19, [2002] 2 AC 883, [2002] 3 All ER 209.
4   See PERSONAL PROPERTY vol 80 (2013) PARAS 814–815. In *Armory v Delamirie* (1722) 1 Stra 505, the claimant, a chimney sweeper's boy, found a ring and passed it to the defendant jeweller for valuation. When the defendant refused to hand the ring back, the claimant successfully sued in conversion. Although there was likely to be a third party (the person who lost the ring) with a better legal title to the ring, the claimant only needed to establish that he had a better title to the ring than the defendant.
5   In *Armory v Delamirie* (1722) 1 Stra 505 (see note 4), there were probably at least three titles: the person who lost the ring, the chimney sweeper's boy and the jeweller.
6   In *Armory v Delamirie* (1722) 1 Stra 505 (see note 4), the title of the person who lost the ring would rank first, the chimney sweeper's boy's second, and the jeweller's third.
7   In *Armory v Delamirie* (1722) 1 Stra 505 (see note 4), the chimney sweeper's boy had a right to exclude the jeweller, but not the person with the pre-existing title, i e the loser of the ring.
8   See e g *Armory v Delamirie* (1722) 1 Stra 505.
9   As to the acquisition of the legal title by possession see PARA 620 et seq. See e g *Bridges v Hawkesworth* (1851) 21 LJQB 75, 15 Jur 1079, where the claimant found a package containing money that had been left in the defendant's shop. The dispute between the claimant and the defendant over title to the package was determined by the question of which party was the first to take possession of it (in this case, the claimant).
10   See the Torts (Interference with Goods) Act 1977 s 8(1); and PARA 656.

619.   Methods of acquiring legal title to chattel.

As conversion requires that the defendant's conduct was inconsistent with the rights of the owner (or other person entitled to possession)[1], the claimant must be able to show that he held the legal title in respect of the goods at the time of the act complained of[2]. In order to determine whether such a right existed, the law has developed a number of rules governing the acquisition of property rights in chattels. These can be divided into rules which allow a party to acquire a legal title by his own independent act[3], and those where the party derives his title from another person[4].

1   See *Kuwait Airways Corpn v Iraqi Airways Co (Nos 4 and 5)* [2002] UKHL 19, [2002] 2 AC 883, [2002] 3 All ER 209; and PARA 604.
2   See PARA 618.
3   See PARA 620 et seq. The method of acquisition is 'independent' in the sense that it does not depend (unlike derivative acquisition) upon the consent of another.
4   See PARA 627 et seq. As to the acquisition of ownership generally see further PERSONAL PROPERTY vol 80 (2013) PARA 816 et seq.

(B) Acquisition of Legal Title by Independent Act

620. Acquisition of legal title by taking possession of chattel. When a person takes possession of a chattel, he will, by this independent act, acquire a legal title to the chattel[1]. To take possession of a chattel requires one to exercise both physical and mental control over it[2].

The operation of this rule can clearly be seen in cases where the chattel is res nullius, in the sense that it is not subject to any pre-existing property rights. Where a person catches and takes possession of a wild animal, for instance, his act of taking possession creates a legal title[3].

This rule of acquisition also operates in cases where the chattel is not res nullius, but is subject to pre-existing property rights. Where a chimney sweeper's boy found a gold ring and gave it to a jeweller for valuation, the boy was able to successfully sue the jeweller in conversion when the jeweller refused to hand it back[4]. The claimant, by taking possession of the ring, had acquired a legal title to it[5]. Even though there was likely to be at least one other person with a better (that is pre-existing) property right in respect of the ring, namely the loser of it, because the claimant could show that he took possession of it prior to the defendant's wrongful interference with it, then the claimant was able to establish that he had a title to the chattel at the time of the act complained of[6].

However, in certain circumstances there is a potential statutory defence under the Torts (Interference with Goods Act) 1977[7].

1 *Armory v Delamirie* (1722) 1 Stra 505. For a more recent example see *Costello v Chief Constable of Derbyshire Constabulary* [2001] EWCA Civ 381, [2001] 3 All ER 150, [2001] 1 WLR 1437. As to the meaning of 'possession' see further PERSONAL PROPERTY vol 80 (2013) PARA 834 et seq. As to acquisition of ownership generally see further PERSONAL PROPERTY vol 80 (2013) PARA 816 et seq.

2 See eg *Young v Hichens* (1843) 6 QB 606, where the claimant, a fisherman, had almost enclosed a shoal of pilchards with his net when the defendant caused them to disperse. It was held that no title had been acquired, because although there was a clear intention to exercise control over the fish, the required physical act of control was missing.

3 See eg *Churward v Studdy* (1811) 14 East 249, where the claimant's dog caught and killed a hare while the claimant was out hunting. A farm labourer picked up the hare and gave it to his employer who refused to hand it over to the claimant. It was held that because the claimant, through his dog, was the first to possess the hare, he had acquired legal title to it, allowing him to sue the defendant in conversion.

4 *Armory v Delamirie* (1722) 1 Stra 505 (the claim was brought in 'trover', the old name for the action of conversion: see PARA 602).

5 See PARA 618.

6 *Armory v Delamirie* (1722) 1 Stra 505.

7 See the Torts (Interference with Goods) Act 1977 s 8(1); and PARA 656.

621. No need for continuing possession to acquire legal title. It is important to note that once a person has taken possession of a thing, and acquired a legal title in respect of it[1], he need not continue in possession in order to retain his legal title[2]. If a claimant, after taking possession of a thing, subsequently loses possession, either by losing the chattel or handing it to another, he will continue to hold his title, and consequently his ability to sue a defendant who wrongfully interferes with it[3]. If a claimant can demonstrate that he had taken possession of a chattel prior to the defendant's wrongful act, then he will be able to establish that he held a legal title at the time of the defendant's act; he need not prove that he was in possession at the time of the act[4].

There is, however, one well established exception to this rule which relates to wild animals. Once an animal categorised as 'wild' has been reduced to possession, the possessor will acquire title, but once he loses possession he will also lose his title[5].

1   See PARA 620.

2   See eg *Armory v Delamirie* (1722) 1 Stra 505, where the claimant voluntarily gave up possession of a ring he had found to the defendant jeweller for the purposes of valuation. He was therefore out of possession of the chattel when the defendant formed the wrongful intention to detain the ring. This did not prevent the claimant from suing for this wrongful detention.

3   See eg *Costello v Chief Constable of Derbyshire Constabulary* [2001] EWCA Civ 381, [2001] 3 All ER 150, [2001] 1 WLR 1437, where the claimant had taken possession of a stolen car and was lawfully deprived of the car by the police. By taking possession of the car the claimant acquired a legal title, and his lawful dispossession of the car by the police did not deprive him of his title. Consequently, when the police subsequently retained the car beyond the statutory time period, the claimant could maintain a claim for conversion. This is despite the fact that he had lawfully lost possession, and hence was not in possession of the chattel at the time of the defendant's wrongful interference. See also *Lotan v Cross* (1810) 2 Camp 464, where the claimant had entrusted his chaise to a friend when the defendant seized it; the claimant was able to sue notwithstanding the fact that he was not in possession at the time of the interference; *Bridges v Hawkesworth* (1851) 21 LJQB 75, 15 Jur 1079; *Parker v British Airways Board* [1982] QB 1004, [1982] 1 All ER 834, CA.

4   See Atiyah, 'A Re-examination of the Jus Tertii in Conversion' (1955) 18 MLR 97 (rebutting the academic view put forward that in such cases the defendant would be able to prove the title of a third party, under the jus tertii).

5   See *Kearry v Pattinson* [1939] 1 KB 471, [1939] 1 All ER 65, CA (swarm of bees escaping onto another man's land); and ANIMALS vol 2 (2008) PARA 711.

622.   Acquisition of legal title: the position of finder.   Where a claimant has found a chattel, his act of taking possession of the chattel will lead to the creation of a legal title[1], enabling him to sue anyone in conversion except those with a pre-existing title[2]. When the claimant takes possession he will independently acquire a new title, which, whilst not enforceable against the loser (or anyone claiming through him), can be enforced against strangers[3].

A dispute often arises between a finder of a chattel, and the occupier of the land upon which the chattel was found, as to which person was the first to possess the chattel. For example, where the claimant found a package containing money which had been left in the front part of the defendant's shop, the court held that the claimant was entitled, as against the defendant, to the possession of the package and the money it contained. The reason for this was that prior to the claimant's picking up of the package, the defendant, who was unaware that the package had been left in his shop, did not manifest sufficient physical or mental control over the package and, hence, had not taken possession of it[4]. If the occupier does have control of the land, and has manifested an intention to control things which are left upon the land, then it has been held that the occupier may thereby be said to have taken possession of things left upon the land[5].

Where the thing is found under the surface of the land, rather than on top of it, a different rule applies. In such cases the occupier of the land is said to be in possession of things buried underneath the surface of his land[6]. Should a third party dig up a chattel, therefore, then the occupier will have a pre-existing title to it[7]. This rule applies whether the finder's digging is unauthorised, and hence he is a trespasser, or whether the finder's activity was fully authorised by the occupier[8].

1 *Armory v Delamirie* (1722) 1 Stra 505; *Bridges v Hawkesworth* (1851) 21 LJQB 75, 15 Jur 1079; *Parker v British Airways Board* [1982] QB 1004, [1982] 1 All ER 834, CA. As to acquisition of ownership generally see further PERSONAL PROPERTY vol 80 (2013) PARA 816 et seq.

2 See PARAS 618, 620. See also PERSONAL PROPERTY vol 80 (2013) PARA 843.

3 *Armory v Delamirie* (1722) 1 Stra 505.

4 See *Bridges v Hawkesworth* (1851) 21 LJQB 75, 15 Jur 1079. As to the requirement of control to evidence possession of the chattel see PARA 620.

5 In *Parker v British Airways Board* [1982] QB 1004, [1982] 1 All ER 834, CA, the claimant found a gold bracelet which had been left in an airport lounge. The court held that the claimant, as finder, had taken possession of the bracelet before the occupiers of the lounge had. Although the occupiers had physical control of the premises, they had not manifested the necessary intention to control things lost upon the land.

6 *Waverley Borough Council v Fletcher* [1996] QB 334, [1995] 4 All ER 756, CA.

7 In *Waverley Borough Council v Fletcher* [1996] QB 334, [1995] 4 All ER 756, CA, a defendant metal detectorist found a gold brooch buried nine inches under the surface of the claimant's park. It was held that in such a case the legal title is acquired by the occupier of the land rather than the first party to take possession of it.

8 See *Waverley Borough Council v Fletcher* [1996] QB 334, [1995] 4 All ER 756, CA (metal detecting was prohibited in the park where a gold brooch was discovered; park owner held to have the better title to the brooch than the detectorist); *South Staffordshire Water Co v Sharman* [1896] 2 QB 44, 65 LJQB 460 (defendant found two rings while employed by the claimant to clean out a pool; pool owner held to have the better title to the rings than the cleaner).

623. Acquisition of title to stolen goods. Where a person ('A'), takes possession of stolen goods, either as the thief himself, or as transferee of the thief, he will acquire a legal title in respect of the goods[1], enabling him to sue anyone in conversion except for those with a pre-existing title[2]. So, should A in turn be dispossessed by another person ('B'), A will be able to maintain a claim against B in conversion[3] on the basis that B's actions were inconsistent with A's rights as owner[4].

1 The justification for this rule is that if thieves did not acquire title to the goods then they would be liable, in turn, to being dispossessed by a stranger with impunity: see *Jeffries v Great Western Rly Co* (1856) 5 E & B 802 at 805 per Lord Campbell CJ. See PERSONAL PROPERTY vol 80 (2013) PARAS 845–846. As to acquisition of ownership generally see further PERSONAL PROPERTY vol 80 (2013) PARA 816 et seq.

2 See PARAS 618, 620.

3 See eg *Costello v Chief Constable of Derbyshire Constabulary* [2001] EWCA Civ 381, [2001] 3 All ER 150, [2001] 1 WLR 1437, where the claimant was suspected of being in possession of a stolen car, which was then seized by the police. When the statutory period for the police to retain the car had passed, it was held that the claimant was entitled to the possession of the car and was able to sue in conversion when it was not returned. See also *Gough v Chief Constable of West Midlands Police* [2004] EWCA Civ 206, 148 Sol Jo LB 298, [2004] All ER (D) 45 (Mar); *Buckley v Gross* (1863) 3 B & S 566.

4 Ie as long as all the other elements of conversion are also present: see PARA 604 et seq.

624. Chattel leases. Where a person with legal title to a chattel ('A') leases his chattel for a term to another ('B'), the question arises of who has the title to sue a third party ('C') who wrongfully interferes with the chattel[1]. The proprietary status of a chattel lease is currently undecided.

While there is authority suggesting that a chattel lease confers a proprietary right in the lessee[2], more recent case law has taken the view that when A leases his chattel to B for a term, B only acquires a contractual right[3], which would not in itself entitle him to sue in conversion[4]. Although a lessee of a chattel may have a mere contractual right, it will be likely that he has taken possession of the chattel in pursuance of the contract. By taking possession of the chattel he will acquire, through his own independent act, a legal title to the chattel[5] enabling him to sue anyone in conversion except for those with a pre-existing title[6]. The question of the proprietary status of a chattel lease may therefore not be an issue so far as the lessee is concerned[7].

If a chattel lease is a mere contractual relationship between the lessor ('A'), and the lessee ('B'), then the lease should not affect the lessor's ability to sue a third party ('C'), who wrongfully interferes with the chattel during the lease. Although A may be out of possession at the time of the interference, a person with legal title need not retain possession of the chattel in order to sue in the chattel torts[8]. However, because A is likely to be in receipt of rent from B for the lease of the chattel for the term, C's interference with the chattel may not actually cause A substantial loss. In this situation A will only be able to recover for any damage to his 'reversionary interest'[9], which is usually the value of the chattel minus the rent that A is in receipt of[10].

Disputes between the lessor ('A') and the lessee ('B') can normally be resolved by reference to the law of contract rather than conversion: A will be under a contractual duty to refrain from taking possession for the duration of the lease, and if he does take possession he will be in breach of the contract[11]. Where A transfers his title to a third party (X) and X attempts to retake possession before the expiry of the term of the lease, the lessee's rights against X is a matter of some dispute[12]. Although there is some older authority which suggests that X will be bound by the lease if he has notice of the agreement[13], more recent cases have cast doubt upon this proposition[14].

1   As to hire of chattels see further BAILMENT AND PLEDGE vol 4 (2011) PARA 175.
2   See *Lord Strathcona Steamship Co v Dominion Coal Co* [1926] AC 108, 95 LJPC 71, PC.
3   See *Port Line Ltd v Ben Line Steamers Ltd* [1958] 2 QB 146, [1958] 1 All ER 787.
4   As to the elements of conversion see PARA 604 et seq. This is to be contrasted with the position in land law where a lessee can sue in trespass and nuisance because a lease is a clear type of property right: see PARA 578.
5   See PARA 620.
6   See PARAS 618, 620. In *Burton v Hughes* (1824) 2 Bing 173, 3 LJOSCP 241, where a lessee of a chattel brought a claim against a sheriff who had improperly seized the goods, the lessee's inability to produce the relevant deeds proving the lease was held to be irrelevant. The lessee could succeed simply on the basis that he was in possession prior to the interference.
7   A difficult case would be where A leases a chattel to B, but before B takes possession, C interferes. B could not rely on an independently acquired title in such a case (because he has not yet taken possession), but would need to rely on his interest in the lease in order to bring a claim for conversion. No such case seems to have been decided. Given, however, that the better line of authority (see *Port Line Ltd v Ben Line Steamers Ltd* [1958] 2 QB 146, [1958] 1 All ER 787) suggests that chattel leases are not proprietary, then it is unlikely that B would have title sue in such a case.
8   See PARA 621.
9   *Tancred v Allgood* (1859) 4 H & N 438, 28 LJ Ex 362; *Moukataff v British Overseas Airways Corpn Ltd* [1967] 1 Lloyd's Rep 396. If he does not plead damage to the reversionary interest, but claims to be compensated for his full legal title, then the claim is likely to fail: see *Ward v Macauley* (1791) 4 Term Rep 489; *Gordon v Harper* (1796) 7 Term Rep 9.
10   See PARA 676.
11   Such contracts are usually specifically enforceable: see *Bristol Airport plc v Powdrill* [1990] Ch 744, [1990] 2 All ER 493, CA. See further CONTRACT.
12   This question turns upon the proprietary status of a chattel lease. If, like a lease of land, a chattel lease is proprietary, then B should be able to exclude X; if it is not a property right, but a mere contractual relationship, then B does not have a contractual right against X which can prevent X from retaking possession.
13   See *De Mattos v Gibson* (1858) 4 De GF & J 276, 28 LJ Ch 165.
14   *Port Line Ltd v Ben Line Steamers Ltd* [1958] 2 QB 146, [1958] 1 All ER 787.

625. Acquisition of legal title by bailment. A bailment arises where a person with a legal title to a chattel (the 'bailor') entrusts his chattel to another person (the 'bailee')[1]. In such cases, because the bailee takes possession of the chattel, he will acquire a legal title through his own independent act, entitling him to sue in conversion[2]. This statement is wide enough to cover chattel leases, as the lessee of a chattel is also a bailee of the chattel[3]. However, the principle is much wider, and extends to any case where a bailee takes possession irrespective of whether or not he possesses under a contract for a term. For instance, it is well established that a carrier of a chattel is a bailee and, in taking possession of the chattel, will have standing to sue a third party who interferes with the chattel[4]. Similarly, where a person is in possession of a chattel as an agent for a principle, then the agent, as bailee of the goods, will have a legal title he can enforce against a third party[5]. It also seems that in certain cases an employee in possession of his employer's goods as a bailee can sue a third party[6], as can a buyer in possession of goods subject to a retention of title clause[7].

When there has been a bailment of goods, the bailor retains his ability to sue third parties who have wrongfully interfered with the chattel because a person with legal title retains title even when he is out of possession[8].

1   See BAILMENT AND PLEDGE vol 4 (2011) PARA 101.
2   See PARA 620 et seq. As to the elements of conversion see PARA 604 et seq. As to acquisition of ownership generally see further PERSONAL PROPERTY vol 80 (2013) PARA 816 et seq.
3   See BAILMENT AND PLEDGE vol 4 (2011) PARA 175. As to chattel leases see PARA 624.
4   See *The Winkfield* [1902] P 42, 71 LJP 21, CA, where the claimant, the owner of a mail ship, was in possession of a large amount of letters that it had been entrusted with as a carrier, when the ship was carelessly struck and sunk by the defendant. Although there was a third party which had legal title to the letters, because the claimant, as a bailee, had taken possession of the letters, it had acquired a legal title which enabled it to sue in the chattel torts. As to the relative nature of title see PARA 618.
5   *Morison v Gray* (1824) 2 Bing 260.
6   *Meux v Great Eastern Rly Co* [1895] 2 QB 387, 59 JP 662, CA; cf *Hopkinson v Gibson* (1805) 2 Smith 202.
7   *Indian Herbs (UK) Ltd v Hadley & Ottoway Ltd* [1999] EWCA Civ 627.
8   See PARAS 615, 618. See eg *Lotan v Cross* (1810) 2 Camp 464; *Wilson v Lombank Ltd* [1963] 1 All ER 740, [1963] 1 WLR 1294.

626.   Legal title may be independently acquired without possession.   Although taking possession is the basic means by which a person independently acquires a legal title to a chattel[1], there are other ways of acquiring the legal title.

When a person ('A') manufactures a chattel, in the sense that by his efforts he transforms a chattel from one thing into another, then by this act he will acquire a property right in the new thing[2]. In most cases this rule will produce the same outcome as the possession rule[3], as the first person to possess a new thing will be the manufacturer.

Where A's goods become mixed with B's goods to the extent that separation is factually impossible, then A and B will legally co-own the resultant mixture[4]. This rule is not dependant upon possession, as it makes no difference which of the two parties, A or B, is the first to take possession of the new mixture. A co-owner may sue the other in conversion[5].

There are rules governing the acquisition of title to offspring of animals that do not depend upon the first person to take possession of such things. For instance, if a claimant has title to a cow which calves, the claimant will acquire title to the calf even before he takes possession of it[6]. The operation of this rule varies according to the animal[7].

Where a person finds a chattel which is legally classed as treasure[8], then title will vest in the crown rather than in the finder[9].

1 See PARA 620 et seq.
2 *Clough Mill Ltd v Martin* [1984] 3 All ER 982, [1985] 1 WLR 111, CA. As to ownership by invention and creation see PERSONAL PROPERTY vol 80 (2013) PARA 822. As to acquisition of ownership generally see further PERSONAL PROPERTY vol 80 (2013) PARA 816 et seq.
3 As to acquisition of title by possession see PARA 620 et seq.
4 See *Indian Oil Corpn v Greenstone Shipping SA (Panama), The Ypatianna* [1988] QB 345, [1987] 3 All ER 893; and PERSONAL PROPERTY vol 80 (2013) PARA 824. As to co-ownership see PERSONAL PROPERTY vol 80 (2013) PARA 828 et seq.
5 See PARA 617.
6 *Tucker v Farm and General Investment Trust Ltd* [1966] 2 QB 421, [1966] 2 All ER 508, CA.
7 See ANIMALS vol 2 (2008) PARA 709.
8 Ie as defined under the Treasure Act 1996 s 1(1): see NATIONAL CULTURAL HERITAGE vol 77 (2010) PARA 1086.
9 See the Treasure Act 1996 s 4(1); and NATIONAL CULTURAL HERITAGE vol 77 (2010) PARA 1084.

(C) Derivative Acquisition of Legal Title

627. Acquisition of legal title from another person. In order to bring a claim for conversion, the claimant must show, inter alia, that the defendant's conduct was inconsistent with the claimant's legal title to the goods[1]. The claimant may be able to show that prior to the defendant's act, the claimant had acquired title to the chattel from another person. In order to do this, he will need to establish that he acquired title to the chattel through a delivery[2], deed[3] or sale[4]. If he cannot establish one of these methods, then his claim in conversion will fail unless he can show that he acquired title to the goods by some other means[5].

1 See PARAS 604–605, 615.
2 As to acquisition of title by delivery see PARA 628.
3 As to acquisition of title by deed see PARA 629.
4 As to acquisition of title by sale see PARA 630.
5 A claimant may, for example, be able to show that he has independently acquired title by taking possession (see PARA 620 et seq) or he may be a buyer in possession of a chattel which is subject to a retention of title clause (see PARA 631). As to acquisition of ownership generally see further PERSONAL PROPERTY vol 80 (2013) PARA 816 et seq.

628. Acquisition of legal title by taking delivery of chattel. One means by which a claimant may acquire legal title to a chattel from another is by a physical delivery of the chattel[1]. If a person ('A') with legal title wishes to transfer his title to another ('B'), then A can do this by allowing B to take possession of the chattel[2]. When this happens B is said to acquire title by delivery. If B can prove such a delivery prior to a wrongful interference with the chattel by a third party ('C'), then this will establish that B had a legal title at the time of the interference, which will entitle him to sue in conversion[3].

It is important to note that because delivery is a method of derivative acquisition (in that B's title derives from A's) B's title will be subject to the same defects as those found in A's title. So if A had stolen the chattel from X, then the title acquired by B will not be enforceable against X, or anyone claiming through X[4]. However, this does not affect B's ability to bring a claim against C, a third party (who is neither X nor claims through X), who interferes with the chattel. B need not establish that he has the best or absolute title in order to succeed against C, but simply that he has a title which arose at an earlier point in time to any title held by C[5].

1 *Cochrane v Moore* (1890) 25 QBD 57, 54 JP 804, CA. As to acquisition of ownership generally see further PERSONAL PROPERTY vol 80 (2013) PARA 816 et seq.
2 *Thomas v Times Book Co Ltd* [1966] 2 All ER 241, [1966] 1 WLR 911.
3 As to the requirements to sue in conversion see PARA 604 et seq. See e g *Cochrane v Moore* (1890) 25 QBD 57, 54 JP 804, CA, where A had title to a horse, and purported to make a gift

of the horse to B, but did not effect a delivery of it, choosing instead to remain in possession. When a third party ('C') seized the horse, B could not establish that he had held a legal title to the horse at the time of the seizure. However, the claim still succeeded as it was held that a trust of the horse had been created (which does not necessitate the physical delivery of the horse): see *Cochrane v Moore* at 73.

4   *Leake v Loveday* (1842) 4 Man & G 972 (defendant claimed under the title of a third party which pre-existed the claimant's title).
5   See PARA 618.

629.   Acquisition of legal title by deed.   If a person with legal title ('A') intends to transfer title to a chattel to another ('B'), he can do so by executing a valid deed[1]. If A does this then he need not transfer possession of the chattel to B in order to effect transfer of the legal title, but in this case he must take certain steps to register the deed[2].

If B can establish that title was transferred by deed prior to any wrongful interference with the chattel committed by C, then B will be able to establish that he held legal title at the time of the act complained of[3] and will therefore be able to bring a claim for conversion[4].

As with other means of derivative acquisition[5], any title acquired by B from A will be subject to the same defects in A's title.

1   The requirements for a deed are set out in the Law of Property (Miscellaneous Provisions) Act 1989 s 1(2): see DEEDS AND OTHER INSTRUMENTS vol 32 (2012) PARA 208. As to acquisition of ownership generally see further PERSONAL PROPERTY vol 80 (2013) PARA 816 et seq.
2   These requirements are set out in the Bills of Sale Act (1878) Amendment Act 1882 s 8: see FINANCIAL SERVICES AND INSTITUTIONS vol 50 (2008) PARA 1754. See also PERSONAL PROPERTY vol 80 (2013) PARA 857.
3   As to the requirements to sue in conversion see PARA 604 et seq.
4   See *Ramsay v Margrett* [1894] 2 QB 18, 63 LJQB 513, CA.
5   As to acquisition of title by delivery see PARA 628. As to acquisition of title by sale see PARA 630.

630.   Acquisition of legal title by contract of sale.   The holder of a legal title ('A') can transfer title to another ('B') by a contract of sale[1]. A contract of sale of goods is a contract by which the seller transfers or agrees to transfer the property in goods to the buyer for a money consideration, called the price[2]. When A enters such a contract with B, A's title will pass to B when the parties intend it to pass[3], which is normally at the time when the contract is made[4]. If B can prove that he entered such a contract of sale for specific goods and intended title to pass prior to C's wrongful interference with the goods, then B will be able to establish that he has title at the time of the interference[5]. B's title will be subject to any defects that were in A's title, but B need only show that it is a better title than the one claimed by C in order to bring a claim for conversion[6].

It is important to note that under a contract of sale title will pass to the buyer when the parties intend it to, which may not necessarily be the time the chattel is delivered to the buyer. Consequently, A's title may pass to B under a contract of sale before A has delivered the chattel to B. In such a case, B will be able to sue in conversion for a wrongful interference even before he has physically received the chattel. B's ability to bring such a claim even extends to wrongful acts committed by the seller, A. If A, for instance, purports to re-sell the chattel to C, and delivers it to C, then B will be able to bring a claim in conversion against A[7].

The other common case is where the seller ('A') delivers the chattel to the buyer ('B') but retains title to the chattel until B pays for it[8]. In such a case, because A retains title, he will be able to sue any party, including B, who wrongfully interferes with the chattel. A common example is where B, before paying for the chattel, purports to sell it on to C. In such a case A will have a legal title which allows him to bring a claim against B[9].

A difficulty often faced by a claimant arguing that he acquired title to a chattel prior to the defendant's wrongful interference is proving that the requirements set out in the Sale of Goods Act 1979 for a valid transfer have been met[10]. For instance, in order for title to goods to pass when there is a contract of sale, the goods must be ascertained[11]. If they cannot be ascertained, title will not pass to the buyer and hence he will not be able to bring a claim in conversion if another party wrongfully interferes with the goods[12]. However, title to unascertained goods in an identified bulk may pass, with the buyer becoming a co-owner with other purchasers from the bulk[13]. The buyer will not, however, be able to sue another co-owner of the bulk following a delivery to them[14].

1   As to the law relating to contracts of sale see further CONTRACT; SALE OF GOODS AND SUPPLY OF SERVICES. As to acquisition of ownership generally see further PERSONAL PROPERTY vol 80 (2013) PARA 816 et seq.
2   See the Sale of Goods Act 1979 s 2(1); and SALE OF GOODS AND SUPPLY OF SERVICES vol 91 (2012) PARA 1.
3   See the Sale of Goods Act 1979 s 17(1); and SALE OF GOODS AND SUPPLY OF SERVICES vol 91 (2012) PARA 110.
4   Where there is an unconditional contract for the sale of specific goods, it is presumed that the parties intend title to pass when the contract is made: see the Sale of Goods Act 1979 s 18 r 1; and SALE OF GOODS AND SUPPLY OF SERVICES vol 91 (2012) PARA 111.
5   See PARA 615.
6   See PARA 614. As to the requirements to sue in conversion see PARA 604 et seq.
7   See e g *Chinery v Viall* (1860) 5 H & N 288, 29 LJ Ex 180. The claimant (B) will also be able to sue the new buyer (C) (subject to any defence which the buyer has under the Sale of Goods Act 1979 s 24: see SALE OF GOODS AND SUPPLY OF SERVICES vol 91 (2012) PARA 155.
8   This retention of title clause is often known as a 'Romalpa clause', following *Aluminium Industrie Vaassen BV v Romalpa Aluminium Ltd* [1976] 2 All ER 552, [1976] 1 WLR 676, CA: see SALE OF GOODS AND SUPPLY OF SERVICES vol 91 (2012) PARA 108.
9   The seller (A) will also have a claim against the new buyer (C), subject to any defence the buyer will have under the Sale of Goods Act 1979 s 25 (see SALE OF GOODS AND SUPPLY OF SERVICES vol 91 (2012) PARA 156).
10 See SALE OF GOODS AND SUPPLY OF SERVICES vol 91 (2012) PARA 28 et seq.
11 See the Sale of Goods Act 1979 ss 16(1), 17(1); and SALE OF GOODS AND SUPPLY OF SERVICES vol 91 (2012) PARA 122.
12 See *Re Goldcorp Exchange Ltd (in receivership)* [1995] 1 AC 74, [1994] 2 All ER 806, PC, where a seller ('A') purported to sell gold bullion to a buyer ('B'). Because the gold was held in bulk it was therefore 'unascertained', and the requirements of a contract of sale were not satisfied. Title to the gold therefore did not pass to B and consequently, when a third party ('C') seized the gold bullion, B could not establish a legal title and his claim in conversion failed.
13 See the Sale of Goods Act 1979 s 20A; and SALE OF GOODS AND SUPPLY OF SERVICES vol 91 (2012) PARA 132. See also the common law principle established in the case of *Re Stapylton Fletcher Ltd* [1995] 1 All ER 192, [1994] 1 WLR 1181, where a wine merchant created a 'bulk' of wine crates as orders for the wine came in from his customers, and the customers consequently became co-owners of the bulk. This doctrine is wider than that in the Sale of Goods Act 1979 s 20A as the bulk was constructed as orders for wine came in (ie it was not a pre-existing identified bulk out of which undivided shares were sold).
14 See the Sale of Goods Act 1979 s 20B; and SALE OF GOODS AND SUPPLY OF SERVICES vol 91 (2012) PARA 132.

631.   Buyers in possession.   Where there is a contract for the sale of goods, the seller could, by way of a retention of title clause, retain title to the goods until he has received payment, notwithstanding the fact that he has delivered the chattel to the buyer[1]. Although the retention of title clause will prevent the buyer from acquiring a legal title from the seller, the buyer's act of taking possession will lead to the creation of a new legal title[2]. This title, arising later in time to the seller's title, will mean that the purchaser cannot use it to maintain a claim in conversion against the seller[3]. However, it will give the purchaser standing to sue a third party who takes the chattel from the purchaser's possession[4].

1   As to retention of title clauses see SALE OF GOODS AND SUPPLY OF SERVICES vol 91 (2012) PARA 108. As to acquisition of ownership generally see further PERSONAL PROPERTY vol 80 (2013) PARA 816 et seq.
2   *Indian Herbs (UK) Ltd v Hadley & Ottoway Ltd* [1999] EWCA Civ 627. As to acquisition of title by taking possession see PARA 620 et seq.
3   See PARA 618. As to the requirements to sue in conversion see PARA 604 et seq.
4   See PARA 618.

C. SECURITY INTERESTS IN THE CHATTEL

632. Possessory and non-possessory security interests. In the majority of claims successfully litigated in conversion, the claimant is the holder of a legal title in respect of the chattel[1]. Such a title is relatively easy to establish, as it only requires the claimant to show prior possession. The other type of property right that is clearly protected by conversion is that of a security interest[2]. A security interest arises when a person with a legal title ('A') grants another person ('B') a limited interest in the chattel with the purposes of securing a debt owed by A to B[3]. When a security interest is validly created, then B will have a property right that enables him to sue in conversion and, conversely, A's ability to sue in the chattel torts is restricted[4]. Security interests may be possessory[5] (which includes pledges[6] and liens[7]) or non-possessory[8] (which includes mortgages and charges[9]). In terms of conversion, different rules apply to these different forms of security interests[10].

1   See PARA 615 et seq.
2   See PARAS 632–635.
3   See BAILMENT AND PLEDGE vol 4 (2011) PARA 191.
4   As to the relative nature of title see PARA 618.
5   Ie where the interest is created by the taking of possession.
6   See PARA 633.
7   See PARA 634.
8   Ie where there is no need to take possession in order to acquire a security interest.
9   See PARA 635.
10 See *Re Cosslett (Contractors) Ltd* [1998] Ch 495, [1997] 4 All ER 115, CA; and PARA 633 et seq.

633. Pledge as a security interest enabling pledgee to sue in conversion. Pledge gives rise to a form of possessory security interest in the thing pledged[1]. A pledge arises when a person with a legal title (the 'pledgor') delivers a chattel[2] to another (the 'pledgee') for the purposes of securing a debt[3]. When this happens the pledgee acquires extensive powers, including the right to retain possession and the right to sell the chattel in the event that the pledger defaults on the debt[4]. The pledgee's interest also entitles him to sue a third party who wrongfully interferes with the chattel[5]. It is also sufficient to enable the pledgee to sue both the pledgor, and any successor in title to the pledgor[6].

When a chattel is subject to a pledge, the pledgor's ability to sue in the chattel torts is curtailed. While the pledgor is not entirely divested of his legal title[7], he will only be able to sue a third party who wrongfully interferes with the chattel if he can show that his reversionary interest has been injured by the defendant's interference[8].

1   *Re Cosslett (Contractors) Ltd* [1998] Ch 495, [1997] 4 All ER 115, CA. As to possessory and non-possessory security interests see PARA 632. As to pledge see further BAILMENT AND PLEDGE.

2 It can also arise on the delivery of documents of title to the chattel, such as bills of lading: *Sewell v Burdick* (1884) 10 App Cas 74, 54 LJQB 156, HL.

3 *Donald v Suckling* (1866) LR 1 QB 585 at 595. See BAILMENT AND PLEDGE vol 4 (2011) PARA 191; and LIEN vol 68 (2008) PARAS 810–816.

4 *Donald v Suckling* (1866) LR 1 QB 585; *Owen v Knight* (1837) 4 Bing NC 54.

5 *Swire v Leach* (1865) 18 CBNS 479, 34 LJCP 150; *Chabbra Corpn Pte Ltd v Jag Shakti (Owners), The Jag Shakti* [1986] AC 337, [1986] 1 All ER 480, PC. As to the requirements to sue in conversion see PARA 604 et seq.

6 See *Halliday v Holgate* (1868) LR 3 Exch 299, 37 LJ Ex 174, where the pledgor had become bankrupt and his interest in the chattel passed to the claimant, the trustee in bankruptcy. The court held that the pledgee was entitled, as against the claimant, to retain possession. This is important, because if a pledge was a mere contractual relationship between pledgor and pledgee, then the claimant in this case, not being privy to the contract, would not be bound by it and would be entitled to possession. The fact that the court held that the pledgee was entitled to possession means that the pledgee has more than a mere contractual right to possess, but has a property right in respect of the chattel: see PARA 615.

7 See *Franklin v Neate* (1844) 14 LJ Ex 59, 13 M & W 481 (pledgor was still able to sell his interest to a third party who, on presenting sufficient tender for the pledge, was able to sue in conversion; this would have been impossible if the pledgor had divested himself of title).

8 *Tancred v Allgood* (1859) 4 H & N 438, 28 LJ Ex 362; *Martin v Reid* (1862) 11 CBNS 730, 31 LJCP 126. The same principle applies to lien: see PARA 634.

634. Lien as a security interest enabling lienee to sue in conversion. A lien differs from a pledge in that the person with legal title, the lienor, does not deliver the chattel to the lienee for the purpose of securing a debt, but for some other reason[1]. For instance, if A delivers his car to B so that B can carry out repairs on it, then B can claim a lien over the car should A fail to pay him for the repairs[2]. A lien can be consensual (for example where A agrees in advance that B can claim a lien over the chattel should A fail to pay the debt)[3] or a lien can be arise by law[4]. This usually occurs where B has done something to improve A's goods (such as repair a car or train a horse)[5].

Like a pledgee, the lienee has the ability to sue third parties who wrongfully interfere with the chattel[6]. However, the lienee's rights are more restricted than a pledgee's, with the lienee only retaining a right so long as he is in possession of the chattel[7]. Therefore, should a lienee lose possession of a chattel prior to a third party's wrongful interference, then it is to be doubted whether the lienee would be able to sue in conversion[8].

As is the case with a pledgor, a lienor's ability to sue in conversion is curtailed. If a third party interferes with the chattel, the lienor will not be able to sue for the full value of the chattel, but only for damage to his reversionary interest[9].

1 *Re Cosslett (Contractors) Ltd* [1998] Ch 495, [1997] 4 All ER 115, CA. As to pledge as a security interest enabling pledgor to sue in conversion see PARA 633. As to the law relating to lien see further LIEN.

2 See LIEN vol 68 (2008) PARA 841.

3 See LIEN vol 68 (2008) PARAS 808, 817 et seq.

4 See LIEN vol 68 (2008) PARA 817 et seq.

5 See e g *Hatton v Car Maintenance Co Ltd* [1915] 1 Ch 621, 84 LJ Ch 847; and LIEN vol 68 (2008) PARA 843.

6 In *Lord v Price* (1874) LR 9 Exch 54, 43 LJ Ex 49, the court stated that when goods are subject to a lien, then the appropriate claimant in any claim for wrongful interference, will be the lienee rather than the lienor.

7 *Jacobs v Latour* (1828) 5 Bing 130, 6 LJOSCP 243. See LIEN vol 68 (2008) PARAS 823–826. As to possessory and non-possessory security interests see PARA 632.

8 It may be possible, according to normal principles, for a lienee to plead his prior possession and establish legal title as against the wrongdoer: see PARA 618.

9 *Lord v Price* (1874) LR 9 Exch 54, 43 LJ Ex 49. The same principle applies to pledge: see PARA 633.

635. Mortgagee's ability to sue for conversion. A person with a legal title to a chattel ('the mortgagor') can execute a bill of sale[1] transferring title to another ('the mortgagee') for the purposes of securing a debt[2]. The mortgagor can retain possession, but the bill used to execute the transfer must comply with the relevant formalities[3].

Because a mortgage involves the transfer of legal title to the mortgagee, it is clear that the mortgagee has standing to sue in the chattel torts should a third party wrongfully interfere with the chattel[4]. The mortgagor, on the other hand, has divested himself of the legal title to the chattel, thus preventing him from suing in conversion[5]. However, if the mortgagor retains possession, then he should, according to normal principles, be able to rely on his independently acquired title as against a wrongdoer[6].

Alternatively, a person with title to the goods, instead of transferring this title under a mortgage, may enter a contract with his creditor, promising the creditor the right to sell the goods in the event of default. The creditor in this case is said to have an equitable charge over the chattel. Being a purely equitable interest, however, it does not entitle the holder to sue in conversion[7].

1 The document used, a deed, must comply with the requirements set out in the Bills of Sale Act (1878) Amendment Act 1882: see DEEDS AND OTHER INSTRUMENTS vol 32 (2012) PARA 222.
2 See further MORTGAGE.
3 The bill of sale must be registered in accordance with the Bills of Sale Act (1878) Amendment Act 1882: see FINANCIAL SERVICES AND INSTITUTIONS vol 50 (2008) PARA 1754 et seq. See also FINANCIAL SERVICES AND INSTITUTIONS vol 50 (2008) PARA 1677. As to mortgages of chattels generally see MORTGAGE vol 77 (2010) PARA 231 et seq.
4 *Franklin v Neate* (1844) 14 LJ Ex 59, 13 M & W 481.
5 *Bank of New South Wales v O'Connor* (1889) 14 App Cas 273, 58 LJPC 82, PC; *Franklin v Neate* (1844) 14 LJ Ex 59, 13 M & W 481. The mortgagor has an equity of redemption and, being an equitable interest, this will probably not be sufficient to enable him to sue in the chattel torts: see PARA 636 et seq.
6 See PARA 620 et seq.
7 See PARA 636 et seq.

D. EQUITABLE TITLE TO THE CHATTEL

636. Whether equitable title to the chattel confers right to sue for conversion. In order to sue in conversion a claimant must establish that he holds a property right in respect of the chattel[1]. It is well established that a party with a better legal title to the chattel is able to bring a claim for conversion against the person who interferes with it[2]. The question that sometimes arises is whether the holder of an equitable interest in a chattel has standing to sue in conversion. In particular, there is an issue of whether the holder of an equitable interest under a trust, where the trust property is a chattel, has title to sue in conversion[3]. Other examples of persons with an equitable title in a chattel include a mortgagor of goods, who holds an equity of redemption, and a person with an equitable charge over goods[4]. Such cases would be determined on the same basis as that of a beneficiary under a trust[5].

1 See PARA 615.
2 See PARA 618 et seq.
3 See PARA 638.
4 See PARA 635.
5 See PARA 638.

637. Trustee can sue for conversion of trust property. Where there is a trust of a chattel, the trustee will have standing to sue for conversion as it is the trustee who holds the legal title to the chattel[1]. Where a third party has wrongfully interfered with the trust property, there will usually be no need for the beneficiary to attempt to bring a claim in conversion in his own name because the trustee, as holder of the legal title, will have standing to sue the wrongdoer[2]. Should the trustee decline to initiate proceedings for any reason, the beneficiary is able to bring a derivative claim, in the trustee's name[3].

The difficult case arises where, as a result of the wrongful interference, the beneficiary suffers consequential loss which is separate from the loss suffered by the trustee[4]. In such cases the beneficiary may wish to bring a claim in his own name[5].

1   *Barker v Furlong* [1891] 2 Ch 172, 60 LJ Ch 368. See PARA 615 et seq. As to the law relating to trusts generally see TRUSTS AND POWERS.
2   See PARA 615 et seq.
3   This is known as the 'Vandepitte procedure', where the trustee is joined to the proceedings: see *Vandepitte v Preferred Accident Insurance Co* [1933] AC 70, PC. See also *Performing Right Society Ltd v London Theatre of Varieties Ltd* [1924] AC 1 at 14, HL.
4   Eg where a trustee ('A') holds a car on trust for a beneficiary ('B'), and C steals the car. The costs of repairing the car are properly considered the trustee's loss, being the value of the infringed right (see PARA 668 et seq). The costs incurred by B in hiring a replacement car whilst it is being repaired are more difficult to class as the trustee's loss, as it these costs are not incurred by him. In such a case the Vandepitte procedure may offer limited recourse for B, as he would be able to recover repair costs, but not the hire replacement costs.
5   If the beneficiary had previously acquired legal title to the property by taking possession, he will be able to sue in conversion: see PARA 638. However, if had not taken possession, he has no legal title and therefore cannot maintain such an action: see PARA 638. The beneficiary may, however, have some alternative form of remedy as illustrated in *Shell UK Ltd v Total UK Ltd* [2010] EWCA Civ 180, [2011] QB 86, [2010] 3 All ER 793: see PARA 638.

638.   Whether beneficiary can sue for conversion of trust property. If a beneficiary under a trust takes possession of the trust property then he will have standing to sue in conversion[1]. The reason for this is that the beneficiary, in taking possession, will independently acquire a legal title which is enforceable as against a wrongdoer[2].

Where the beneficiary has not taken possession of the chattel under the trust, he cannot rely on an independently acquired legal title; he only has an equitable interest. Beneficiaries under a trust cannot sue in conversion unless they bring a derivative action in the name of the trustee[3].

1   See eg *Healey v Healey* [1915] 1 KB 938, 84 LJKB 1454 (beneficiary had possession of trust property (furniture) when the defendant seized it).
2   *Leigh and Sillavan Ltd v Aliakmon Shipping Co Ltd (The Aliakmon)* [1986] AC 785 at 812, [1986] 2 All ER 145 at 151, HL; *MCC Proceeds Inc v Lehman Bros* [1998] 4 All ER 675, [1998] 2 BCLC 659, CA. As to independent acquisition of legal title by taking possession see PARA 620 et seq.
3   *MCC Proceeds Inc v Lehman Bros* [1998] 4 All ER 675, [1998] 2 BCLC 659, CA. Note that an earlier Court of Appeal case suggested that a beneficiary under such a trust could sue in the chattel torts: see *International Factors Ltd v Rodriguez* [1979] QB 351, [1979] 1 All ER 17, CA. However, this case was distinguished in *MCC Proceeds Inc v Lehman Bros* which did not approve of its reasoning and noted that it was not bound by the earlier decision. One of the judges in *International Factors Ltd v Rodriguez* suggested that a contractual right was sufficient to sue in the chattel torts, but this assertion is not in line with the authorities: see PARA 615.
    The conclusion that beneficiaries cannot sue in conversion may need to be reconsidered in the light of *Shell UK Ltd v Total UK Ltd* [2010] EWCA Civ 180, [2011] QB 86, [2010] 3 All ER 793. Although the claim was in negligence, not in conversion, the approach the Court of Appeal took could theoretically be applied to conversion. As in conversion, a claimant can only sue for negligent damage to a chattel if he holds a property right in the chattel (see *Leigh and Sillavan Ltd v Aliakmon Shipping Co Ltd (The Aliakmon)* [1986] AC 785 at 812, [1986] 2 All ER 145 at 151, HL). It was suggested in *Shell UK Ltd v Total UK Ltd* that an equitable

interest, for these purposes, counts as a property right. In the case legal title to an oil refinery was held on trust for the claimants, who were beneficiaries. The defendant carelessly caused an explosion, which resulted in physical damage to the refinery. Whilst the trustee could recover for the repair costs to the plant, the main loss was that suffered by the beneficiaries whose business in supplying oil was interrupted. The court held that the beneficiaries could recover these consequential losses in the tort of negligence if they joined the trustee to the proceedings (*Shell UK Ltd v Total UK Ltd* [2010] EWCA Civ 180 at [140]–[144], [2011] QB 86 at [140]–[144], [2010] 3 All ER 793 at [140]–[144]). The basis of the decision is unclear. Given the need to join the trustee to the proceedings, it may be best understood as a derivative claim, brought in the name of the trustees (see Rushworth & Scott, 'Total Chaos?' [2010] LMCLQ 536). If so, then the case is similar to those conversion cases where beneficiaries have used the derivative action procedure to sue in their trustee's name under the Vandepitte procedure (see PARA 637). Alternatively, because the beneficiaries in the case were able to recover their own consequential losses (resulting from the interruption of the beneficiaries' business) which were not the trustee's losses, the case may be better understood as allowing a beneficiary to plead his equitable property right in the law of negligence. If this is the effect of the decision then the same principle would seem to apply in conversion cases as well (but the possible inconsistency with the outcome in *MCC Proceeds Inc v Lehman Bros* above was not considered by the Court of Appeal in *Shell UK Ltd v Total UK Ltd*). The difficulty with this interpretation is that if the beneficiary has a standing to assert that his equitable right has been infringed, then there seems to be no reason why he would need to join the trustee to the proceedings.

(iii) What can be Converted

A. CHATTELS

639. What in law is a chattel. In order to sue in conversion, the claimant must establish that he holds a property right in respect of a chattel[1]. Conversion therefore affords protection to property rights relating to chattels. A chattel is something which has a physical existence, in the sense that it can be touched[2], and is not immovable[3]. Things attached to land are considered part of the land[4] and hence cannot form the subject matter of a claim in conversion[5]. If there is an interference with things attached to land then the claimant will need to sue in trespass to land, or plead negligent damage to land[6]. However, once something has become severed from land, such as wood which has been cut or vegetables picked, then such things are separate and can form the subject matter of a claim in the chattel torts[7].

There is no closed list of the different types of chattels which can form the subject matter of a property right, and hence be protected through the chattel torts. Rather, the law occasionally takes the view that it would be inappropriate to recognise property rights in respect of a particular type of chattel. The main example of this is the human body and its parts[8]. There are also special rules relating to money[9].

1 *OBG Ltd v Allan* [2007] UKHL 21, [2008] 1 AC 1, [2007] 4 All ER 545. See PARA 615. See also *Lee v Trimcliffe Motors* [1983] CLY 3633, County Court, where it was held that conversion did not lie in respect of a car registration number, which was incapable of having a separate existence from the car itself, and over which the claimant therefore retained no right when he sold the car.

  If an asset is not a chattel, and hence is not protected by conversion, it does not automatically mean that it is not protected by law; rather, that protection must be found elsewhere. For instance, if a defendant interferes with certain intangible assets, such as contractual rights or intellectual property rights, there are remedies in various other torts which may afford protection to the claimant: see PARA 701 et seq.

2 Liability in conversion and trespass to goods focuses to a great extent on physical interference with the chattel: see PARAS 605, 687.

3 See PERSONAL PROPERTY vol 80 (2013) PARAS 805–806.

4 See LANDLORD AND TENANT vol 62 (2012) PARA 172.

5   *Greene v Cole* (1672) 2 Wms Saund 251 at 259 note (c); *Re Samuel Allen & Sons Ltd* [1907]
    1 Ch 575, 76 LJ Ch 362; *Ellis v Glover and Hobson Ltd* [1908] 1 KB 388, 77 LJKB 251, CA.
    In the past there would have been great procedural difficulties in bringing such a claim in trover
    (the old term for the cause of action in conversion: see PARA 602), as a claimant could not
    truthfully plead that land had been lost and found, as used to be required. The fictitious
    allegations of loss and finding were abolished by the Common Law Procedure Act 1852, which
    substituted an allegation that the defendant converted to his own use or wrongfully deprived the
    plaintiff of the use and possession of the plaintiff's goods: see (1905) 21 LQR 43.
6   As to trespass to land see PARA 563 et seq. As to negligence see PARA 497; and NEGLIGENCE.
7   *Dalton v Whittem* (1842) 3 QB 961, 12 LJQB 55; *London and Westminster Loan and
    Discount Co Ltd v Drake* (1859) 6 CBNS 798 at 811.
8   See PARA 640.
9   See PARA 641.

640.   The human body and its parts as chattels capable of being converted.
Whilst it is theoretically possible to hold a property right in respect of another
living person[1], such a state of affairs is deeply repugnant, amounting to slavery
and, as such, is not recognised in law. It is also the case that one cannot have
property rights in respect of their own person[2] and therefore an interference with
a person's body cannot be litigated in conversion[3].

There is also a reluctance to recognise property rights in respect of a dead
body[4]. It has frequently been stated that it is not possible to hold a property right
in respect of a corpse[5], although a deceased's executor does have a limited right
for the purposes of burial of the corpse[6].

Traditionally, the view was taken that if a body could not form the subject
matter of property rights, then parts of a body could not either[7]. This view was
subject to certain exceptions, the most well established one being the 'work and
skill' rule[8]. Under this rule, if human biomaterials were subject to work and skill,
such as a scientific method of preservation, then the material could form the
subject matter of a property right[9]. More recently it has been decided that a
sperm sample, donated before the claimant underwent radiotherapy treatment,
could form the subject matter of a property right, entitling the claimant to sue
the defendant for careless damage to the sperm[10]. The court chose not to base its
decision on the work and skill rule, but on the wider principle that sperm
samples, as physical things, could be the subject of a legal title like any other
physical thing[11]. The court expressed the view that the increasing use and value
attached to human biomaterials in the field of medical research may necessitate
the law of property to re-evaluate its traditional exclusion of human biomaterials
from its scope[12]. The case has been followed by a number of courts in
Commonwealth jurisdictions[13], mainly in respect of cases involving issues of
sperm preservation. The precise scope of the decision has not yet been tested, so
it is not yet clear if all human biomaterials can, without work and skill, form the
subject matter of a property right.

1   Such a legal state of affairs was recognised until comparatively recently in the common law
    jurisdictions, particularly in in the US. In the English case of *Pearne v Lisle* (1749) Am 75 at 76,
    Lord Hardwicke stated: 'I have no doubt but trover will lie for a Negro slave; it is as much
    property as any other thing.' Property law disputes involving slaves are occasionally cited in
    modern cases (often involving claims over animals), although they appear to be of dubious
    status: see eg the Australian case of *Grant v YYH Holdings Pty Ltd* [2012] NSWCA 360.
2   *R v Bentham* [2005] UKHL 18 at [14], [2005] 2 All ER 65 at [14], [2005] 1 WLR 1057 at [14]
    per Lord Rodger.
3   The claimant must instead sue in trespass to the person (see PARA 525 et seq) or negligent
    damage to the person (see PARA 497; and NEGLIGENCE).
4   See eg *Hayne's Case* (1614) 12 Co Rep 113, where a graverobber was prosecuted for the theft of
    a shroud that a corpse was wrapped in, rather than the corpse itself. As to property in corpses
    see CREMATION AND BURIAL vol 24 (2010) PARA 1105.

5   *Exelby v Handyside* (1749) 2 East PC 652.
6   *Dobson v North Tyneside Health Authority* [1996] 4 All ER 474 at 479, [1997] 1 WLR 596 at 600. CA. See CREMATION AND BURIAL vol 24 (2010) PARA 1103.
7   See *Dobson v North Tyneside Health Authority* [1996] 4 All ER 474, [1997] 1 WLR 596, CA, where it was held that one could have a property right in a preserved brain, but only as an exception to the general 'no-property' approach.
8   *Doodeward v Spence* (1908) 6 CLR 406, Aust HC.
9   See *eg Dobson v North Tyneside Health Authority* [1996] 4 All ER 474, [1997] 1 WLR 596, CA; *R v Kelly* [1999] QB 621, [1998] 3 All ER 741, CA; *Yearworth v North Bristol NHS Trust* [2009] EWCA Civ 37, [2010] QB 1, [2009] 2 All ER 986.
10 *Yearworth v North Bristol NHS Trust* [2009] EWCA Civ 37, [2010] QB 1, [2009] 2 All ER 986.
11 *Yearworth v North Bristol NHS Trust* [2009] EWCA Civ 37, [2010] QB 1, [2009] 2 All ER 986.
12 *Yearworth v North Bristol NHS Trust* [2009] EWCA Civ 37 at [28]–[29], [2010] QB 1 at [28]–[29], [2009] 2 All ER 986 at [28]–[29] per Lord Judge CJ.
13 See *eg Bazley v Wesley Monash IVF Pty Ltd* [2010] QSC 118; *Re Edwards* [2011] NSWSC 478; *Re Section 22 of the Human Tissue And Transplant Act 1982 (WA), ex p C* [2013] WASC 3; *JCM v ANA* 2012 BCSC 584. See also the Scottish case *Holdich v Lothian Health Board* [2013] CSOH 197, 2014 SLT 495.

641.   Money as a chattel capable of being converted.   Money, in the sense of physical coins and banknotes, can form the subject matter of a property right and is therefore protected by the tort of conversion in much the same way as any other chattel[1]. The only peculiar feature of a claim for the conversion of a bank note is the availability of a good faith purchase defence in such cases[2]. If A has title to a bank note, and B steals the bank note, and B in turn uses the bank note to pay for goods from C, then if C can show that he took the money in good faith and for value, then the money is said to 'pass into currency', destroying A's title[3]. However, this good faith purchase defence is not generally available in the chattel torts[4]. It is only applicable to money because of the important status it has as a means of currency[5].

1   See *Moffatt v Kazana* [1969] 2 QB 152, [1968] 3 All ER 271 (conversion case involving bank notes). See also *Orton v Butler* (1822) 5 B & Ald 652; *Foster v Green* (1862) 7 H & N 881. See PARA 639.
2   See *eg Lipkin Gorman (a firm) v Karpnale* [1991] 2 AC 548 at 559, HL, per Lord Templeman; and PARA 647.
3   *Hall v Dean* (1599) Cro Eliz 841; *Wookey v Pole* (1820) 4 B & Ald 1; *Miller v Race* (1758) 1 Burr 452.
4   See PARA 644.
5   See PARA 647.

642.   Documents as chattels capable of being converted.   There are a number of common documents that represent the existence of legal rights, such as cheques, share certificates, bills of sale and title deeds[1]. Such documents, having a physical existence, can be converted in much the same way as any other chattel[2]. When such documents are wrongfully interfered with, the person with title to the document often sues not just for the value of the document as a piece of paper, but for the value of the legal right it represented[3]. This is a form of consequential loss as the claimant, deprived of the document, finds it difficult to enforce his rights[4].

1   See further DEEDS AND OTHER INSTRUMENTS; FINANCIAL SERVICES AND INSTITUTIONS; MORTGAGE; REAL PROPERTY AND REGISTRATION.
2   See *eg Alsager v Close* (1842) 10 M & W 576 (cheques); *Lord v Wardle* (1837) 3 Bing NC 680 (title deeds); *BBMB Finance (Hong Kong) Ltd v Eda Holdings Ltd* [1991] 2 All ER 129, [1990] 1 WLR 409, PC (share certificates).
3   *Goggerley v Cuthbert* (1806) 2 Bos & PNR 170; *Atkins v Owen* (1836) 4 Ad & El 819; *Palmer v Jarmain* (1837) 2 M & W 282; *Alsager v Close* (1842) 10 M & W 576; *Carlon v Ireland*

(1856) 5 E & B 765; *Paine v Bevan and Bevan* (1914) 110 LT 933; *Fenton Textile Association Ltd v Thomas* (1929) 45 TLR 264.

4   The ability of a claimant to sue for the face value of the document depends upon the type of document. When a negotiable instrument is converted, the claimant will normally be entitled to the face value: *Morison v London County and Westminster Bank Ltd* [1914] 3 KB 356 at 365, CA. Other documents, which are not negotiable, but which represent debts, can result in similar outcomes: see e g *Building and Civil Engineering Holidays Scheme Management Ltd v Post Office* [1964] 2 QB 430 at 445–446.

B. INTANGIBLES

643. Contractual rights cannot be converted. The tort of conversion only protects property rights in respect of chattels[1]. To date the courts have been reluctant to extend the boundaries of the tort so as to protect intangible rights. The House of Lords has held that it is not possible to convert a contractual right, and that the tort of conversion only extends to rights relating to physical things[2].

1   See *OBG Ltd v Allan* [2007] UKHL 21, [2008] 1 AC 1, [2007] 4 All ER 545; and PARA 639. However, in the US it has been held that it was possible to convert an internet domain name: see *Kremen v Cohen* 337 F 3d 1024 (9th Cir 2003), US CA.

2   *OBG Ltd v Allan* [2007] UKHL 21, [2008] 1 AC 1, [2007] 4 All ER 545. This case involved a claim by an engineering company that was in financial difficulties against receivers who had been improperly appointed to take over the business. The defendants had interfered with the claimant's physical assets (i e the factory and plant materials) and were therefore liable in conversion and trespass to goods for this aspect of their behaviour. It was also argued that the defendants, in taking over the claimant's contractual claims against former customers and which were settled at an undervalue, had converted the claimant's contractual rights. The House of Lords rejected this argument and held that it was not possible to convert a contractual right, and that the tort of conversion only extends to rights relating to physical things (see *OBG Ltd v Allan* above (minority speeches were delivered by Lord Nicholls and Baroness Hale)). Although the defendant could be said to have reduced the value of the claimant's contractual right, this was not actionable in conversion and the claimant was instead forced to seek the protection of the economic torts (as to which see PARA 701 et seq).

The same rule applies in negligence. In *Cattle v Stockton Waterworks* (1875) LR 10 QB 453, 44 LJQB 139, the claimant had contracted to build a tunnel through a piece of land. The defendant negligently caused a flood, delaying and increasing the expenses of building the tunnel. Although the claimant's contractual right for the work was turned into a losing contract (as it now cost him more to complete the tunnel than he was being paid for the job), he had no cause of action against the defendant. This is expressed as being 'pure economic loss', but it is effectively the same principle as that seen in *OBG Ltd v Allan* [2007] UKHL 21, [2008] 1 AC 1, [2007] 4 All ER 545 (duties of non-interference do not extend to contracts).

(iv) Defences to Conversion

A. PURCHASE IN GOOD FAITH

644. No general defence of good faith purchase in claim for conversion. If A's goods are in the hands of B, and B wrongfully sells the goods to C, then in most cases C will be liable to A, even though C acted in good faith[1]. The fact that the defendant C acted in good faith, and was unaware of another's title to the chattel, will not afford him a defence to the claim[2]. This is another way of stating that liability in conversion is strict. Although good faith purchase does not provide a general defence to claims in conversion, it does provide a defence in certain limited circumstances[3].

1   See the Sale of Goods Act 1979 s 21; and SALE OF GOODS AND SUPPLY OF SERVICES vol 91 (2012) PARA 148. As to sale by a vendor in possession see PARA 645. In the example in the text C will be liable for taking possession: see PARA 620.

2 *Hollins v Fowler* (1875) LR 7 HL 757; *Marfani & Co Ltd v Midland Bank Ltd* [1968] 2 All ER 573, [1968] 1 WLR 956, CA.

3 See PARA 645 et seq.

645. Sale by a vendor in possession. Generally, where A's goods are in the hands of B, and B wrongfully sells the goods to C, C will be liable to A, even though C purchased the goods in good faith[1]. The reason for this is that the good faith sale of the chattel to C does not destroy A's pre-existing legal title[2]. However, in certain circumstances a sale by B can destroy A's title. One such example is where it is a sale by a vendor in possession[3]. If a purchaser ('A') buys goods from a vendor ('B'), but permits B to remain in possession of the goods, should B, without authorisation, re-sell the goods to a third party ('C'), then B thereby commits a conversion and will be liable to A in the tort[4]. However, if C bought the goods from A in good faith and without notice of the sale to B, then B's title to the goods is thereby destroyed, meaning that C will not be liable to any claim in conversion by A[5].

1 See the Sale of Goods Act 1979 s 21; and SALE OF GOODS AND SUPPLY OF SERVICES vol 91 (2012) PARA 148. The rule does not apply if the seller has a voidable title to the goods: see s 23; and SALE OF GOODS AND SUPPLY OF SERVICES vol 91 (2012) PARA 152. See also PARA 644.

2 *Hollins v Fowler* (1875) LR 7 HL 757; *Farquharson Bros v C King Co* [1902] AC 325, 71 LJKB 667, HL.

3 Ie under the Sale of Goods Act 1979 s 24: see the text and notes 4–5. Section 17 allows the parties to agree the date of transfer of title: see SALE OF GOODS AND SUPPLY OF SERVICES vol 91 (2012) PARA 110. The vendor may therefore transfer title despite retaining possession of the goods.

4 As to the relative nature of title see PARA 618. If the buyer has not yet paid for the goods then his damages will be reduced: *Chinery v Viall* (1860) 5 H & N 288, 29 LJ Ex 180.

5 See the Sale of Goods Act 1979 s 24; and SALE OF GOODS AND SUPPLY OF SERVICES vol 91 (2012) PARA 155.

646. Sale by a buyer in possession. Where a vendor ('A') transfers possession of goods to a purchaser of goods ('B'), but retains title to the goods[1], should B, without authorisation, resell the goods to a third party ('C'), then B thereby commits a conversion and will be liable to A in the tort. However, if C bought the goods from B in good faith and without notice of A's title, then A's title is thereby destroyed, meaning that C will not be liable in conversion to A[2].

1 Ie under a retention of title or 'Romalpa' clause: see PARA 630 note 8; and SALE OF GOODS AND SUPPLY OF SERVICES vol 91 (2012) PARA 108.

2 See the Sale of Goods Act 1979 s 25; and SALE OF GOODS AND SUPPLY OF SERVICES vol 91 (2012) PARA 156. The goods need to be sold in the 'ordinary course of business': see *Newtons of Wembley Ltd v Williams* [1964] 2 All ER 135, [1964] 1 WLR 1028. The defence under the Sale of Goods Act 1979 s 25 applies equally to cases where there is not a sale but a hire purchase agreement (see the Hire Purchase Act 1964 Pt III (ss 27–29)): s 27(5); and SALE OF GOODS AND SUPPLY OF SERVICES vol 91 (2012) PARA 156. As to hire purchase agreements see CONSUMER CREDIT vol 21 (2011) PARA 66.

647. Money. Where bank notes belonging to A wrongfully fall into B's hands, and B transfers the notes to C for consideration, and C acts in good faith, then A's title will be destroyed[1].

1 *Miller v Race* (1758) 1 Burr 452; *Wookey v Pole* (1820) 4 B & Ald 1; *Lipkin Gorman (a firm) v Karpnale* [1991] 2 AC 548 at 559, HL, per Lord Templeman. See PARA 641.

B. ESTOPPEL

648.   Estoppel as a defence to conversion.   When a person with title to a chattel ('A') entrusts possession of that chattel to a mercantile agent ('B'), then a sale of that chattel by B to C can bind A[1]. Therefore, when C buys goods from B, who is acting as a mercantile agent, A will be estopped from denying that sale[2]. A will not be able to maintain a claim in conversion against C[3].

1   See the Factors Act 1889 s 2(1); and AGENCY vol 1 (2008) PARA 148.
2   As to the law of estoppel see further ESTOPPEL.
3   There is a common law principle of estoppel which mirrors the statutory rule: see e g *Henderson & Co v Williams* [1895] 1 QB 521, 64 LJQB 308, CA. The only time that the common law rule need be invoked is when a mercantile agent is entrusted with the indicia of title, but certain requirements in the Factors Act 1889 s 2(1) (such as the need of a transfer of possession to the agent) are not met. See also *Eastern Distributors Ltd v Goldring* [1957] 2 QB 600, [1957] 2 All ER 525, CA; *Mercantile Bank of India Ltd v Central Bank of India Ltd* [1938] AC 287, [1938] 1 All ER 52, PC.

C. MINISTERIAL RECEIPT

649.   Ministerial receipt as a defence to conversion.   If a person acting as an agent receives and deals with goods on behalf of a principal, his position as agent does not provide a general defence to liability in conversion[1]. There are a number of examples of agents being held liable in the tort. For instance, if an auctioneer takes possession of goods and sells them to a third party, the auctioneer can be liable in conversion[2]. Similarly, a broker who sells goods on behalf of another can be liable in the tort[3]. However, there are certain cases where agency does provide a defence to conversion, and this is referred to as the defence of ministerial receipt[4]. There are limits to the operation of this defence[5].

1   As to acquisition of legal title by taking possession see PARA 620.
2   *Consolidated Co v Curtis & Son* [1892] 1 QB 495, 61 LJQB 325.
3   *Hollins v Fowler* (1875) LR 7 HL 757.
4   Eg, in certain contexts, warehousemen (see PARA 650), carriers (see PARA 651), auctioneers (see PARA 652) and employees (see PARA 653).
       In *Hollins v Fowler* (1875) LR 7 HL 757 at 766–767, Blackburn J stated as a general principle: '... [O]ne who deals with goods at the request of the person who has the actual custody of them, in the bona fide belief that the custodier is the true owner, or has the authority of the true owner, should be excused for what he does if the act is of such a nature as would be excused if done by the authority of the person in possession, if he was a finder of the goods, or intrusted with their custody'.
5   See PARA 654.

650.   Warehousemen and the defence of ministerial receipt.   The defence of ministerial receipt[1] can apply where a defendant stores goods on behalf of someone not entitled to the possession of the goods. If a claimant is deprived of his goods by a rogue ('X') and X then passes the goods to the defendant for the purposes of storage, the defendant's mere receipt of the goods, and keeping them for storage, will not amount to a conversion[2]. In such cases the defendant's acts are attributed to X, and the defendant is seen as being a mere 'conduit pipe' for X's wrongful conduct[3]. Further, should the defendant in such a case return the goods to X, or hold them to X's order, then the defendant will equally be protected by the defence of ministerial receipt[4].

1   As to ministerial receipt see PARA 649.
2   *Marcq v Christie Manson & Woods Ltd* [2003] EWCA Civ 731, [2004] QB 286, [2003] 3 All ER 561.

3 *Hollins v Fowler* (1875) LR 7 HL 757 at 789 per Grove J. For examples see *Greenway v Fisher* (1824) 1 C & P 190; *Re Samuel (No 2)* [1945] Ch 408, [1945] 2 All ER 437, CA.

4 *Maynegrain Pty Ltd v Campafina Bank* [1984] 1 NSWLR 258, PC.

651. Carriers and the defence of ministerial receipt. A carrier of goods is protected by the defence of ministerial receipt[1]. If a rogue entrusts the claimant's goods to the defendant carrier, with instructions to deliver the goods to a certain place, then the carrier does not thereby commit a conversion in so delivering them[2].

1 As to ministerial receipt see PARA 649. As to the law relating to carriers see generally CARRIAGE AND CARRIERS.

2 *Sheridan v New Quay Co* (1858) 4 CBNS 618, 28 LJCP 58.

652. Auctioneers and the defence of ministerial receipt. The defence of ministerial receipt[1] applies to auctioneers before they have sold another's goods[2]. If an auctioneer, for example, receives the claimant's goods from a rogue, and offers them for sale at auction, but fails to sell them and returns them to the rogue, then the auctioneer is in the same position as a warehouseman or carrier: he is protected by the defence of ministerial receipt[3]. However, should the auctioneer do more than this, and sell the goods to a third party, then he will no longer be protected by the defence[4] and may be liable in conversion[5].

1 As to ministerial receipt see PARA 649. As to the law relating to auctions see generally AUCTION.

2 *Marcq v Christie Manson & Woods Ltd* [2003] EWCA Civ 731, [2004] QB 286, [2003] 3 All ER 561.

3 *Marcq v Christie Manson & Woods Ltd* [2003] EWCA Civ 731, [2004] QB 286, [2003] 3 All ER 561. As to the position of warehousemen see PARA 650. As to the position of carriers see PARA 651.

4 *Consolidated Co v Curtis & Son* [1892] 1 QB 495, 61 LJQB 325; *National Mercantile Bank v Rymill* (1881) 44 LT 767, CA.

5 As to the elements of conversion see PARA 604.

653. Employees and the defence of ministerial receipt. Employees may be protected by the defence of ministerial receipt[1]. In one case, where the claimant's goods were stored in a warehouse belonging to an insurance company, the claimant made a demand for the goods from the defendant, an employee of the insurance company who held the key to the warehouse[2]. The court held that the defendant did not commit conversion by refusing to return the goods without an order from the insurance company, as in so doing, the defendant was acting on behalf of his employer[3]. The appropriate defendant in such a case is the employer, not the employee[4].

1 As to ministerial receipt see PARA 649.

2 *Alexander v Southey* (1821) 5 B & Ald 247.

3 *Alexander v Southey* (1821) 5 B & Ald 247. Cf *International Factors Ltd v Rodriguez Ltd* [1979] QB 351, [1979] 1 All ER 17, CA, where a company director who converted a cheque was the primary tortfeasor.

4 *Morris v CW Martin & Sons Ltd* [1966] 1 QB 716, [1965] 2 All ER 725, CA. Cf *Stephens v Elwall* (1815) 4 M & S 259 where the defendant was a clerk to a broker. He received goods belonging to the claimant and sent them to his employer, who was in the United States. The court held that the defendant could be liable for this, Lord Ellenborough saying (at 261): '... [F]or a person is guilty of a conversion who intermeddles with my property and disposes of it, and it is no answer that he acted under authority from another, who had himself no authority to dispose of it'. This appears to be inconsistent with the later cases of *Alexander v Southey* (1821) 5 B & Ald 247 and *Marcq v Christie Manson & Woods Ltd* [2003] EWCA Civ 731,

[2004] QB 286, [2003] 3 All ER 561. As the defendant in *Stephens v Elwall* was acting under the instructions of his employer, his employer, not the defendant, was the appropriate person to sue.

654. Limits of the defence of ministerial receipt. Should a defendant who is acting as an agent for a rogue ('X') exceed his authority, then he will lose the defence of ministerial receipt[1]. If a warehouseman, for instance, does more than keep the chattel on behalf of X, or deliver to the order of X, then the defendant can be liable in conversion[2]. If the defendant, for example, misdelivers to a third party, then he will be liable in the tort[3]. Further, the defence is only available if the defendant is unaware of the claimant's title and acts in good faith[4].

1   As to ministerial receipt see PARA 649. An analogous case is *Snowdon v Davis* (1808) 1 Taunt 359 where a defendant bailiff lost his defence as he seized more than was mandated by the sheriff.
2   As to the elements of conversion see PARA 604.
3   *Hiort v London and North Western Rly Co* (1879) 4 ExD 188, CA.
4   See PARAS 649–653. Had the defendant in *Alexander v Southey* (1821) 5 B & Ald 247 been aware of the claimant's title then he would have been liable in conversion (see PARA 653).

D. PLEADING THIRD PARTY'S BETTER TITLE; AVOIDING DOUBLE RECOVERY

655. Potential for multiplicity of actions in conversion. There is a possibility of a multiplicity of actions in conversion. There are two reasons for this. First, because the common law has a concept of relative title[1], there may be more than one party with a legal title to a chattel that has been converted by a defendant. In such a case the defendant may be liable to more than one person for the same act[2]. Second, because a chattel may be converted on successive occasions by different persons, a person with legal title to a chattel may be able to bring multiple claims in respect of a single chattel[3]. In such a case there is a danger of a claimant recovering more than his loss. The law therefore provides defences to prevent these outcomes[4].

1   As to the relative nature of title to chattels see PARA 618.
2   See PARA 656.
3   See PARA 657.
4   See PARAS 656–657.

656. Avoidance of double liability in conversion. It is possible for more than one person to have a legal title to a chattel[1]. For instance, if A loses his watch, and B finds it, then B will acquire a legal title to the watch[2], which is inferior to A's title, but is enforceable against others[3]. Should a third party ('C') steal the watch, then there is the potential of double liability: both A and B have a legal title and, therefore, each can bring a claim against C for the conversion of the watch.

The Torts (Interference with Goods) Act 1977 therefore provides that in proceedings to which any two or more claimants are parties, the relief must be such as to avoid double liability of the wrongdoer as between those claimants[4]. For these purposes, 'double liability' means the double liability of the wrongdoer which can arise:

(1)   where one of two or more rights of action for conversion[5] is founded on a possessory title; or

(2)   where the measure of damages in an action for conversion[6] founded on a proprietary title is or includes the entire value of the goods, although the interest is one of two or more interests in the goods[7].

While it is no defence at common law to plead the title of a third party[8], under the Torts (Interference with Goods) Act 1977, the defendant C is entitled to show that a third party (that is A in the example above) has a better title to the goods than B[9]. In order for C to invoke this defence, A will need to be identified with a view to joining him to the proceedings[10]. If the court finds C liable, then the relief ordered by the court will be such as to avoid the double liability of C[11]. If a third party with a better title is identified, but refuses to join the proceedings, then the court may make an order depriving him of any right to bring a subsequent claim against the defendant, thus preventing the defendant's double liability[12].

Where the third party with a better title ('A') cannot be identified, then the common law rules apply, meaning that a person with an inferior title ('B') can proceed with his claim against the defendant ('C')[13]. This does, however, create a danger of double liability for C: if A subsequently learns of the conversion, then he may bring a separate claim. In such a case, C will have to seek reimbursement in the form of a claim in unjust enrichment[14]. C could claim against B; or, if B has accounted over to A, then the claim in unjust enrichment will be against A.

1   See PARA 618 et seq.
2   As to the acquisition of legal title by taking possession see PARA 620.
3   See e g *Parker v British Airways Board* [1982] QB 1004, [1982] 1 All ER 834, CA. See also *Armory v Delamirie* (1722) 1 Stra 505. As to the relative nature of title to chattels see PARA 618. It may also be the case that A grants B a limited interest in the watch, such as a security interest (as to which see PARA 632 et seq).
4   Torts (Interference with Goods) Act 1977 s 7(2). On satisfaction, in whole or in part, of any claim for an amount exceeding that recoverable if s 7(2) applied, the claimant is liable to account over to the other person having a right to claim to such extent as will avoid double liability: s 7(3).
5   The Torts (Interference with Goods) Act 1977 s 7 applies to all proceedings for wrongful interference (not just conversion): see s 3(1). As to the meaning of 'wrongful interference' in the Torts (Interference with Goods) Act 1977 see PARA 603.
6   See note 5.
7   Torts (Interference with Goods) Act 1977 s 7(1).
8   See PARA 618. In the example in the text, should B sue C for the conversion of the watch, there is no common law rule which allows C to invoke the title of A: see e g *Armory v Delamirie* (1722) 1 Stra 505.
9   The defendant in an action for wrongful interference is entitled to show, in accordance with rules of court, that a third party has a better right than the plaintiff as respects all or any part of the interest claimed by the claimant, or in right of which he sues, and any rule of law (sometimes called jus tertii) to the contrary is abolished: Torts (Interference with Goods) Act 1977 s 8(1).
10 See the Torts (Interference with Goods) Act 1977 s 8(2)(b), (3); CPR 19.5A(1) which requires the claimant to disclose anyone with a better title. If he fails to do so, then a defendant may apply for a direction that a third party with a better title be made party to the proceedings: see the Torts (Interference with Goods) Act 1977 s 8(2)(c); CPR 19.5A(2), (4). See further CIVIL PROCEDURE vol 11 (2009) PARA 212.
11 See the Torts (Interference with Goods) Act 1977 s 7(2); and the text and note 4.
12 Torts (Interference with Goods) Act 1977 s 8(2)(d); CPR 19.5A(3).
13 The continuing applicability of the common law rules is evident from the number of cases applying these rules that have been decided since the enactment of the Torts (Interference with Goods) Act 1977 s 8. For instance, in both *Parker v British Airways Board* [1982] QB 1004, [1982] 1 All ER 834, CA, and *Costello v Chief Constable of Derbyshire Constabulary* [2001] EWCA Civ 381, [2001] 3 All ER 150, [2001] 1 WLR 1437, the claimant succeeded notwithstanding the fact that there was likely to be a third party with a better title. Where the statutory reform will have an effect is in cases such as *The Winkfield* [1902] P 42, 71 LJP 21, CA, where the claimant is a bailee for a known bailor who can be easily identified and joined to the proceedings.
14 Where, as the result of enforcement of a double liability, any claimant is unjustly enriched to any extent, he is liable to reimburse the wrongdoer to that extent: Torts (Interference with Goods) Act 1977 s 7(4). For example, if a converter of goods pays damages first to a finder of the

goods, and then to the true owner, the finder is unjustly enriched unless he accounts over to the true owner under s 7(3); and then the true owner is unjustly enriched and becomes liable to reimburse the converter of the goods: s 7(4). As to unjust enrichment see MISTAKE vol 77 (2010) PARA 69 et seq; RESTITUTION vol 88 (2012) PARA 401 et seq.

657.   Avoidance of double recovery in conversion.   Where a chattel belonging to a claimant is subject to successive conversions by different persons, then the claimant is able to bring separate claims against each person[1]. For instance, if A's car is stolen by B, who in turn sells it to C, then both B and C are liable to being sued by A. Should A succeed against both defendants, and each is ordered to pay the full value of the car, then there is a possibility of A recovering more than his losses. The Torts (Interference with Goods) Act 1977 introduced measures to prevent this[2].

First, there is a general power to combine proceedings: if A has brought claims against both B and C, then there is a power to combine them into a single action[3]. Second, if one of the parties is found liable and pays damages in full to the claimant, then this extinguishes the claimant's title to the chattel[4], which would extinguish any claim the claimant has against another party[5].

1   *International Factors Ltd v Rodriguez Ltd* [1979] QB 351 at 359, [1979] 1 All ER 17 at 21, CA, per Sir David Cairns.
2   The Torts (Interference with Goods) Act 1977 s 9 applies where goods are the subject of two or more claims for wrongful interference (whether or not the claims are founded on the same wrongful act, and whether or not any of the claims relates also to other goods): s 9(1). As to the meaning of 'wrongful interference' in the Torts (Interference with Goods) Act 1977 see PARA 603. Where goods are the subject of two or more claims under s 6 (allowance for improvement of the goods; see PARA 678), s 9 applies as if any claim under s 6(3) were a claim for wrongful interference: s 9(2).
3   Torts (Interference with Goods) Act 1977 s 9(3), (4) (amended by the County Courts Act 1984 s 148(1), Sch 2 Pt V para 65; and the Crime and Courts Act 2013 s 17(5), Sch 9 Pt 3 para 133(d), (e)).
4   See the Torts (Interference with Goods) Act 1977 s 5(1); and PARA 663.
5   *Cooper v Shepherd* (1846) 3 CB 266. Although the Torts (Interference with Goods) Act 1977 s 5 is silent on the issue of extinguishing claims (rather than titles), if the title is extinguished retrospectively, then it follows that there can be no cause of action for any subsequent interference. Further, if a claimant, having been paid in full by a defendant, were to subsequently pursue a further claim against another defendant, then the claimant would be unjustly enriched. As to the prevention of unjust enrichment see PARA 656.

E.   AVAILABILITY OF OTHER DEFENCES TO CONVERSION

658.   Contributory negligence no defence to conversion.   Contributory negligence is no good defence in proceedings founded on conversion[1].

1   Torts (Interference with Goods) Act 1977 s 11(1). The section also states that contributory negligence is not a defence to intentional trespass to goods: see PARA 693.
    Prior to 1 June 1978 (ie the commencement of the statutory rule: see the Torts (Interference with Goods) Act 1977 (Commencement No 2) Order 1978, SI 1978/627, art 2) there had been some doubt as to whether contributory negligence was a defence to conversion: see e g *Central Newbury Car Auctions Ltd v Unity Finance Ltd* [1957] 1 QB 371, [1956] 3 All ER 905, CA; *Ingram v Little* [1961] 1 QB 31 at 74, [1960] 3 All ER 332 at 351–352, CA, per Devlin LJ; *J Sargent (Garages) Ltd v Motor Auctions (West Bromwich) Ltd* [1977] RTR 121, CA; *Moorgate Mercantile Co Ltd v Twitchings* [1977] AC 890, [1976] 2 All ER 641, HL.

659.   Co-ownership no defence to conversion.   Co-ownership does not afford a defence to proceedings for conversion[1] where the defendant, without the authority of the other co-owner:

(1)   destroys the goods, or disposes of the goods in a way giving a good title

to the entire property in the goods, or otherwise does anything equivalent to the destruction of the other's interest in the goods; or

(2)   purports to dispose of the goods in a way which would give a good title to the entire property in the goods if he was acting with the authority of all co-owners of the goods[2].

However, a co-owner may not be sued for conversion if he merely makes use of the common property in a reasonable way[3].

1   The Torts (Interference with Goods) Act 1977 s 10(1) also applies to trespass to goods: see PARA 693.

2   Torts (Interference with Goods) Act 1977 s 10(1)(a), (b). The statute merely restated the position at common law: see s 10(3). For examples of the common law see e g *Fennings v Lord Grenville* (1808) 1 Taunt 241; *May v Harvey* (1811) 13 East 197; *Morgan v Marquis* (1853) 23 LJ Ex 21, 9 Exch 145; *Jacobs v Seward* (1872) LR 5 HL 464, HL; *Baker v Barclays Bank Ltd* [1955] 2 All ER 571, [1955] 1 WLR 822.
      The Torts (Interference with Goods) Act 1977 s 10(1) does not affect the law concerning execution or enforcement of judgments, or concerning any form of distress: s 10(2).

3   Eg by cutting grass and making hay in the common field (*Jacobs v Seward* (1872) LR 5 HL 464), or extracting the oil and the other valuable parts of a dead whale which is owned in common (*Fennings v Lord Grenville* (1808) 1 Taunt 241).

660.   Limitation of actions in conversion.   A defendant to a claim in conversion may have a defence owing to the lapse of time in between his conversion of the chattel and the claimant's issuing of proceedings. The basic rule under the Limitation Act 1980 is that both a claimant's title to a chattel[1], and his right of action against a defendant in conversion, will be destroyed six years from the time of the defendant's conversion[2]. Further, the time limit will not begin to run again should the chattel be converted subsequently, either by the original converter or a new party, within the six year limit, but will continue to run from the date of the original conversion[3].

The defence will not be available to a defendant who stole the chattel from the claimant[4], or who obtained it by blackmail or fraud[5]. However, if the chattel, following the theft, is bought by a purchaser who acts in good faith, then the time limit will begin to run from the date of that purchase[6] (although not as against the thief[7]).

1   See the Limitation Act 1980 s 3(2); and LIMITATION PERIODS vol 68 (2008) PARAS 987–988.
2   See the Limitation Act 1980 s 2; and LIMITATION PERIODS vol 68 (2008) PARA 979.
3   See the Limitation Act 1980 s 3(1); and LIMITATION PERIODS vol 68 (2008) PARA 988.
4   See the Limitation Act 1980 s 4(1); and LIMITATION PERIODS vol 68 (2008) PARA 990.
5   See the Limitation Act 1980 s 4(5)(b); and LIMITATION PERIODS vol 68 (2008) PARA 990.
6   See the Limitation Act 1980 s 4(2); and LIMITATION PERIODS vol 68 (2008) PARA 990.
7   See the Limitation Act 1980 s 4(3); and LIMITATION PERIODS vol 68 (2008) PARA 990.

661.   Bailee's power of sale and other statutory defences to conversion.   There are a number of miscellaneous statutory defences to a claim in conversion. Where a bailee is in possession of goods, and the bailor has failed to collect the goods, then in certain circumstances the bailee will have a statutory power to sell the goods[1]. The bailee has a duty to account for the proceeds of the sale[2], but has a defence to a claim in conversion[3].

A bank which, in good faith and without negligence, collects payment of cheques or other negotiable instruments in such circumstances as would give rise to a conversion of the cheque is protected by statute[4]. Other statutory provisions afford similar defences in certain circumstances to pawnbrokers[5] and those dealing with a bankrupt's property[6].

1   See the Torts (Interference with Goods) Act 1977 ss 12(3), 13, Schedule; and BAILMENT AND PLEDGE vol 4 (2011) PARA 173. The bailor must have an obligation to collect the goods, or the bailee must have a reasonable expectation to be relieved of any duty to safeguard the goods on giving notice to the bailor, but is unable to trace or communicate with the bailor: see s 12(1), (2); and BAILMENT AND PLEDGE vol 4 (2011) PARA 173.

2   See the Torts (Interference with Goods) Act 1977 s 12(5); and BAILMENT AND PLEDGE vol 4 (2011) PARA 173.

3   A sale duly made under the Torts (Interference with Goods) Act 1977 s 12 gives a good title to the purchaser as against the bailor: s 12(6).

4   See the Cheques Act 1957 s 4; and FINANCIAL SERVICES AND INSTITUTIONS vol 49 (2008) PARA 882.

5   See the Consumer Credit Act 1974 s 117; CONSUMER CREDIT vol 21 (2011) PARA 222.

6   See the Insolvency Act 1986 s 307; and BANKRUPTCY AND INDIVIDUAL INSOLVENCY vol 5 (2013) PARA 458.

(v) Remedies for Conversion

A. AVAILABILITY AND CONSEQUENCES OF REMEDIES

662. Orders for delivery of goods and awards of damages. If the claimant is able to establish a cause of action in conversion then, subject to any defences raised by the defendant[1], the next issue for the court to consider will be one of remedies. A distinction is drawn between cases where the defendant is in possession of the claimant's chattel and those where he is not.

In proceedings for conversion[2] against a person who is in possession or in control of the goods the following relief may be given, so far as appropriate[3]:

(1)   an order for delivery of the goods, and for payment of any consequential damages[4]; or

(2)   an order for delivery of the goods, but giving the defendant the alternative of paying damages by reference to the value of the goods, together in either alternative with payment of any consequential damages[5]; or

(3)   damages[6].

Relief may be given under only one of heads (1), (2) or (3)[7]. Relief under head (1) is at the discretion of the court, whilst the other two remedies may be chosen by the claimant[8].

If the defendant is in possession of the claimant's chattel, then the claimant is also entitled to use reasonable force to retake them[9].

In cases where the defendant does not have possession of the claimant's chattel[10], then the court will be limited to making an award of damages[11].

Remedies may also be available under the Consumer Credit Act 1974[12] and the court retains its jurisdiction to afford ancillary or incidental relief[13].

1   As to the possible defences to a claim for conversion see PARA 644 et seq.

2   The Torts (Interference with Goods) Act 1977 s 3 applies to all proceedings for wrongful interference (not just conversion): see s 3(1). As to the meaning of 'wrongful interference' in the Torts (Interference with Goods) Act 1977 see PARA 603.

3   Torts (Interference with Goods) Act 1977 s 3(1).

4   Torts (Interference with Goods) Act 1977 s 3(2)(a). In conversion, specific delivery had been available, before the enactment of s 3, but it took the form of an equitable order (see eg *Pusey v Pusey* (1684) 1 Vern 273). As to orders for specific delivery see PARA 664 et seq.

5   Torts (Interference with Goods) Act 1977 s 3(2)(b). Where an order is made under s 3(2)(b) the defendant may satisfy the order by returning the goods at any time before execution of judgment, but without prejudice to liability to pay any consequential damages: s 3(5).

6   Torts (Interference with Goods) Act 1977 s 3(2)(c). As to damages for conversion see PARA 668 et seq.

7   Torts (Interference with Goods) Act 1977 s 3(3)(a).

8   Torts (Interference with Goods) Act 1977 s 3(3)(b). As to the exercise of the court's discretion see PARA 665.

9   *Blades v Higgs* (1861) 25 JP 742, 10 CBNS 713; cf *Capital Finance Co Ltd v Bray* [1964] 1 All ER 603, [1964] 1 WLR 323, CA. See also *Webb v Beavan* (1844) 6 Man & G 1055; *Anthony v Haney* (1832) 8 Bing 186; *Whatford v Carty* (1960) Times, 29 October; *Austin v Dowling* (1870) LR 5 CP 534.

10   Eg where the defendant has sold the chattel to a third party, or where his conversion consisted in the destruction of the chattel.

11   See PARA 668 et seq.

12   Torts (Interference with Goods) Act 1977 s 3(8). The text refers to remedies under the Consumer Credit Act 1974 s 133: see CONSUMER CREDIT vol 21 (2011) PARA 311.

13   Torts (Interference with Goods) Act 1977 s 3(8).

663.   Extinction of claimant's title on satisfaction of claim for damages for conversion. Where damages for conversion[1] are, or would fall to be, assessed on the footing that the claimant is being compensated:

    (1)   for the whole of his interest in the goods, or

    (2)   for the whole of his interest in the goods subject to a reduction for contributory negligence,

payment of the assessed damages (under all heads), or as the case may be settlement of a claim for damages for the wrong[2] (under all heads), extinguishes the claimant's title to that interest[3].

This does not apply where damages are assessed on the footing that the claimant is being compensated for the whole of his interest in the goods, but the damages paid are limited to some lesser amount by virtue of any enactment or rule of law[4].

Where the claimant accounts over to another person (the 'third party') so as to compensate (under all heads) the third party for the whole of his interest in the goods[5], the third party's title to that interest is extinguished[6].

These provisions[7] have effect subject to any agreement varying the respective rights of the parties to the agreement, and where the claim is made in court proceedings they have effect subject to any order of the court[8].

1   This section applies to all proceedings for wrongful interference (not just conversion): see the Torts (Interference with Goods) Act 1977 s 5(1). As to the meaning of 'wrongful interference' in the Torts (Interference with Goods) Act 1977 see PARA 603.

2   This reference to the settlement of the claim includes:

    (1)   where the claim is made in court proceedings, and the defendant has paid a sum into court to meet the whole claim, the taking of that sum by the claimant (Torts (Interference with Goods) Act 1977 s 5(2)(a)); and

    (2)   where the claim is made in court proceedings, and the proceedings are settled or compromised, the payment of what is due in accordance with the settlement or compromise (s 5(2)(b)); and

    (3)   where the claim is made out of court and is settled or compromised, the payment of what is due in accordance with the settlement or compromise (s 5(2)(c)).

3   Torts (Interference with Goods) Act 1977 s 5(1).

4   Torts (Interference with Goods) Act 1977 s 5(3).

5   Ie under the Torts (Interference with Goods) Act 1977 s 7(3): see PARA 656.

6   Torts (Interference with Goods) Act 1977 s 5(4).

7   Ie the Torts (Interference with Goods) Act 1977 s 5.

8   Torts (Interference with Goods) Act 1977 s 5(5).

B. ORDER FOR SPECIFIC DELIVERY

664.   Court's power to make orders for delivery of converted chattels. Where the defendant in a conversion[1] claim is in possession of the claimant's chattel, the court may:

(1)   make an order for the delivery of the chattel together with payment of consequential losses[2]; or

(2)   make an order for the delivery of the chattel but with the alternative option of paying damages[3].

The first remedy is at the discretion of the court, whilst the other two remedies may be chosen by the claimant[4].

1   This applies to all proceedings for wrongful interference (not just conversion): see the Torts (Interference with Goods) Act 1977 s 3(1). As to the meaning of 'wrongful interference' in the Torts (Interference with Goods) Act 1977 see PARA 603.
2   See the Torts (Interference with Goods) Act 1977 s 3(2)(a); and PARA 662.
3   See the Torts (Interference with Goods) Act 1977 s 3(2)(b); and PARA 662.
4   See the Torts (Interference with Goods) Act 1977 s 3(3)(b); and PARA 662. As to the exercise of the court's discretion see PARA 665.

665.   Exercise of the court's discretion in making an order for delivery. The court's discretion to make an order for delivery will not normally be exercised in conversion cases involving ordinary articles that are replaceable[1]. The most obvious category of chattels in respect of which the court will exercise its discretion are those that are unique and cannot be replaced[2]; a painting, manuscript or a unique piece of furniture would be likely to satisfy this criterion.

Courts have also exercised their discretion in respect of goods which, although not unique, are not readily replaceable. In one case, where the court ordered the delivery of coils of steel detained by the defendant, although the steel was not unique, replacements were difficult to obtain due to an ongoing steel strike[3]. Similarly, where the defendant detained a large number of cars belonging to the claimant, although the cars had been mass-produced and where not unique, they were difficult to replace due to the manufacturer's insolvency[4].

If the court makes an order for the delivery of the chattel, it may impose various conditions on the order[5]. In particular, where damages by reference to the value of the goods would not be the whole of the value of the goods, the court may require an allowance to be made by the claimant to reflect the difference[6]. This will be relevant in cases where the claimant would be overcompensated by the return of the chattel. If the claimant, for example, had leased his chattel to the defendant under a hire purchase contract, so that damages would have been assessed by the remaining instalments due rather than by the full value of the chattel[7], then the court may order the claimant to pay the defendant a sum reflecting this as a condition for the return of the chattel. Similarly, if the defendant had improved the goods, the court may order the claimant to pay a sum to the defendant to reflect this improvement as a condition for the return of the chattel[8].

If it is shown to the satisfaction of the court that an order for delivery[9] has not been complied with, the court may revoke the order, or the relevant part of it, and make an order for payment of damages by reference to the value of the goods[10].

1   *Blue Sky One Ltd v Mahan Air* [2010] EWHC 631 (Comm), [2010] All ER (D) 02 (Jun).
2   Eg one-off works of art and family heirlooms: see e g *Pusey v Pusey* (1684) 1 Vern 273, where the court ordered the return of the 'Pusey Horn', an heirloom reputably given to the Pusey family by King Canute. See also *Garcia v De Aldama* [2002] EWHC 2087 (Ch), [2002] All ER (D) 180 (Oct) (conversion of a manuscript).
3   *Howard E Perry & Co v British Railways Board* [1980] 2 All ER 579, [1980] 1 WLR 1375.
4   *Pendragon plc v Walon Ltd* [2005] EWHC 1082 (QB), [2005] All ER (D) 59 (May). Similarly, in *Blue Sky One Ltd v Mahan Air* [2010] EWHC 631 (Comm), [2010] All ER (D) 02 (Jun), the court gave an order for specific delivery of a number of Boeing 747 aircraft that would have been difficult and time consuming to replace.

5 Torts (Interference with Goods) Act 1977 s 3(6).
6 Torts (Interference with Goods) Act 1977 s 3(6).
7 See PARA 676.
8 Torts (Interference with Goods) Act 1977 s 3(7).
9 Ie under the Torts (Interference with Goods) Act 1977 s 3(2)(a).
10 Torts (Interference with Goods) Act 1977 s 3(4).

666. Option to pay damages in lieu of delivery of converted goods. Unlike an order for delivery[1], which is a remedy at the discretion of the court[2], an order for delivery with the option of the defendant paying damages in lieu[3] is a remedy which the claimant in an action for conversion can choose[4]. If the defendant elects to pay damages instead of returning the converted chattel, then damages are assessed by reference to the value of the chattel[5]. Such an order can be made together with an order to pay consequential loss[6].

1 Ie under the Torts (Interference with Goods) Act 1977 s 3(2)(a): see PARA 662.
2 See PARA 665.
3 Ie under the Torts (Interference with Goods) Act 1977 s 3(2)(b): see PARA 662.
4 See the Torts (Interference with Goods) Act 1977 s 3(2), (3)(b); and PARA 662. This applies to all proceedings for wrongful interference (not just conversion): see s 3(1). As to the meaning of 'wrongful interference' in the Torts (Interference with Goods) Act 1977 see PARA 603.
5 See PARA 668 et seq.
6 See the Torts (Interference with Goods) Act 1977 s 3(2)(b); and PARA 662. As to consequential loss see PARAS 683–684.

667. Interlocutory orders for delivery of converted goods. The court[1] has power[2] to make an order providing for the delivery up of any goods which are or may become the subject matter of proceedings for conversion, or as to which any question may arise in proceedings[3]. Delivery must be, as the order may provide, to the claimant or to a person appointed by the court for the purpose, and may be on such terms and conditions as may be specified in the order[4].

1 Ie the High Court, the County Court or the Family Court: see the Torts (Interference with Goods) Act 1977 s 4(6), (6) (the first sub-section (6) was added by the Crime and Courts Act 2013 s 17(5), Sch 9 Pt 3 para 133(c); the second sub-section (6) of the Torts (Interference with Goods) Act 1977 s 4 was added by the Crime and Courts Act 2013 s 17(6), Sch 10 Pt 2 para 37; both came into force on 22 April 2014 (see the Crime and Courts Act 2013 (Commencement No 10 and Transitional Provision) Order 2014, SI 2014/954)).
2 The power is a discretionary one: see *Howard E Perry & Co v British Railways Board* [1980] 2 All ER 579, [1980] 1 WLR 1375 (in the absence of exceptional circumstances the court ought not to be dissuaded from making an order against a litigant merely because that litigant feared unpleasant consequences if he did what the order required him to do).
3 Torts (Interference with Goods) Act 1977 s 4(2). This section applies to all proceedings for wrongful interference (not just conversion): see s 4(1). As to the meaning of 'wrongful interference' in the Torts (Interference with Goods) Act 1977 see PARA 603. The order is made on the application of any person in accordance with rules of court: see s 4(2), (4) (amended by the Crime and Courts Act 2013 s 17(5), Sch 9 Pt 3 para 133(a)(i), (ii)).
4 Torts (Interference with Goods) Act 1977 s 4(3).

C. DAMAGES

(A) Normal Rule: the Value of the Chattel

668. Damages for conversion of goods: chattel's value as the starting point. In cases where a defendant, having converted the claimant's chattel, is in possession of it, the claimant may choose an order for damages[1] instead of pursuing an order for delivery[2]. In cases where the defendant is not in possession, an order for damages is the only available remedy[3].

The normal purpose of an award of damages in conversion is, as in other torts, to provide compensation for the claimant's loss[4]. Because conversion consists, in part, of a claimant's exclusion from his chattel[5], the normal measure of his loss is the value of his chattel[6] (plus any consequential losses)[7]. However, this is merely a starting point, and a different measure is adopted where appropriate[8].

Payment of damages in full has the effect of extinguishing the claimant's title[9].

1   Ie under the Torts (Interference with Goods) Act 1977 s 3(2)(c): see PARA 662.
2   Ie under the Torts (Interference with Goods) Act 1977 s 3(2)(a), (b): see PARA 662.
3   See PARA 662.
4   See *Albacruz (Cargo Owners) v Albazero (Owners), The Albazero* [1977] AC 774 at 841, [1976] 3 All ER 129 at 132, HL, per Lord Diplock; *BBMB Finance (Hong Kong) Ltd v Eda Holdings Ltd* [1991] 2 All ER 129, [1990] 1 WLR 409, PC; *IBL Ltd v Coussens* [1991] 2 All ER 133, CA; *Kuwait Airways Corpn v Iraqi Airways Co (Nos 4 and 5)* [2002] UKHL 19 at [67], [2002] 2 AC 883 at [67], [2002] 3 All ER 209 at [67] per Lord Nicholls. As to the compensatory nature of damages see DAMAGES vol 29 (2014) PARAS 318, 408. It is also possible for aggravated damages to be awarded under the normal principles: see DAMAGES vol 29 (2014) PARA 322 et seq.
5   See PARA 607.
6   As to the assessment of the chattel's value see PARA 669.
7   As to consequential losses see PARAS 683–684.
8   The general rule is that the measure of damages for conversion is the value of the chattel at the date of the conversion together with any consequential damage flowing from the conversion and not too remote to be recoverable in law. However, in *Glenbrook Capital LP v Hamilton (t/a Hamiltons)* [2014] EWHC 2297 (Comm), [2014] All ER (D) 119 (Jul) (a case concerning the conversion of silver) it was noted that when goods are returned after conversion, the amount by which the damages were reduced had to be the value of the goods when returned. These rules are not inflexible; any adverse factual conclusion should take account of any evidence that existed and it should be realistic (see PARA 672).
9   See the Torts (Interference with Goods) Act 1977 s 5; and PARA 663.

669. Assessing value of the chattel. Where a defendant has converted a chattel belonging to the claimant, the claimant's loss is normally measured by the value of the chattel (together with any consequential loss)[1]. When assessing the value of the chattel the starting point will be its market value[2]. This sum will normally represent the amount required to put the claimant in the position he would have been in had the conversion not occurred[3]. The amount that a claimant actually bought the chattel for, or how much he contracted to sell it for, is normally considered to be irrelevant when calculating the value of the chattel[4]. If the claimant had, for instance, recently bought the chattel for £100, but at the time of the conversion it had a market value of £50, then the court will normally make an order that the defendant pay £50 to reflect the claimant's basic loss; this sum reflects the financial advantage lost by the claimant in not being able to sell the chattel[5]. Similarly, where a claimant had contracted, prior to the defendant's conversion, to sell the chattel to a third party at a certain price, that price is also considered irrelevant when calculating the claimant's loss so far as it differs from the market value of the chattel at the time[6].

Where there is no market value for the chattel, then the court will consider other evidence of its value. In such cases a court may consider how much a claimant bought the chattel for, or had contracted to sell it[7].

In some cases the court will not asses the claimant's loss according to the value that the claimant could have sold the chattel for on the market, but by how much it would cost to replace the chattel[8]. In most cases the amount a claimant would have been able to sell the chattel for, and the replacement cost, will be the same. However, in certain cases the replacement costs will be higher, and the court will need to consider whether this higher sum, which represents the 'cost of cure', would be the more appropriate measure of damages[9]. This is likely to be the case only where the court is convinced that the claimant has a genuine intention to buy a replacement[10].

1   *Mercer v Jones* (1813) 3 Camp 477; *Reid v Fairbanks* (1853) 13 CB 692; *France v Gaudet* (1871) LR 6 QB 199 at 204; *The Arpad* [1934] P 189 at 234, CA, per Maugham LJ ('It has been held repeatedly that in trover the measure of damage generally speaking is the value of the goods'); *Solloway v McLaughlin* [1938] AC 247 at 257–259, [1937] 4 All ER 328 at 332–333, PC; *Caxton Publishing Co Ltd v Sutherland Publishing Co* [1939] AC 178 at 192, 203, [1938] 4 All ER 389 at 397, 404–405, HL, per Lord Roche; *Empresa Exportadora de Azucar v Industria Azucarera Nacional SA, The Playa Larga and Marble Islands* [1983] 2 Lloyd's Rep 171; *Chubb Cash Ltd v John Crilley & Son (a firm)* [1983] 2 All ER 294, [1983] 1 WLR 599, CA. As to trover (the old name for conversion) see PARA 602.

2   *Caxton Publishing Co Ltd v Sutherland Publishing Co* [1939] AC 178 at 192, [1938] 4 All ER 389 at 397, HL, per Lord Roche; *J & E Hall Ltd v Barclay* [1937] 3 All ER 620, CA; *Empresa Exportadora de Azucar v Industria Azucarera Nacional SA, The Playa Larga and Marble Islands* [1983] 2 Lloyd's Rep 171; *Chubb Cash Ltd v John Crilley & Son (a firm)* [1983] 2 All ER 294, [1983] 1 WLR 599, CA. The market value rule will apply in all cases where a claimant can establish that he holds a legal title. The fact that there is likely to be a third party with a pre-existing title does not affect the claimant's ability to recover the full value of the chattel: see eg *Armory v Delamirie* (1722) 1 Stra 505 (claimant entitled to the full value of the ring). See also *The Winkfield* [1902] P 42.

3   *Kuwait Airways Corpn v Iraqi Airways Co (Nos 4 and 5)* [2002] UKHL 19 at [67], [2002] 2 AC 883 at [67], [2002] 3 All ER 209 at [67].

4   *The Arpad* [1934] P 189, CA.

5   *Chubb Cash Ltd v John Crilley & Son (a firm)* [1983] 2 All ER 294, [1983] 1 WLR 599, CA.

6   *The Arpad* [1934] P 189, CA. That price may, however, be relevant when calculating consequential losses: see PARAS 683–684.

7   *France v Gaudet* (1871) LR 6 QB 199 (where there was no market for champagne that had been converted).

8   *J & E Hall Ltd v Barclay* [1937] 3 All ER 620, CA.

9   See eg *J & E Hall Ltd v Barclay* [1937] 3 All ER 620, CA, where the defendant converted the claimant's davits. They were unique and cost a great deal more to replace than to buy the closest equivalent davits.

10 See eg *J & E Hall Ltd v Barclay* [1937] 3 All ER 620, CA, where the claimants satisfied the court that they intended to rebuild the davits.

670.   Time of assessment of chattel's value.   When assessing the market value of the claimant's chattel, the standard approach is to assess the value of the chattel at the date of the conversion, not the date of judgment[1]. This is not an absolute rule, and in certain cases the court has considered it more appropriate to assess the value of the chattel at the date of judgment[2].

Where there is a rising market, so that the chattel is more valuable at the date of the judgment than at the date of the conversion, the court can award consequential loss to reflect this rise in value[3]. However, where there is a falling market, courts adopting the general approach of assessing value at the date of the conversion, have been more reluctant to make a deduction from damages to reflect the diminution in value, although there is some scope to do this[4].

1   *Caxton Publishing Co Ltd v Sutherland Publishing Co* [1939] AC 178 at 203, [1938] 4 All ER 389 at 404–405, HL, per Lord Roche; *General and Finance Facilities Ltd v Cooks Cars (Romford) Ltd* [1963] 2 All ER 314 at 319, [1963] 1 WLR 644 at 649, CA.

2   Historically, in detinue claims, the court would always assess the value at the time of the judgment (*Rosenthal v Alderton & Sons Ltd* [1946] KB 374, [1946] 1 All ER 583, CA; *Phillips v Jones* (1850) 15 QB 859 at 867–868), whereas in conversion it would be at the time of the wrong. With the abolition of detinue, the suggestion arises that it should be possible, where appropriate, to assess value in the way that it would have been assessed in detinue: see *IBL Ltd v Coussens* [1991] 2 All ER 133, CA. As to the abolition of detinue see PARA 602.

3   See PARA 671.
4   See PARA 672.

671.   Rise in chattel's value between conversion and judgment.   Where the value of the claimant's chattel increases in between the date of the conversion and the date of the judgment, a court which has assessed the value of the chattel at the date of the conversion can award the increase in value as consequential loss[1]. This consequential loss reflects the fact that the claimant, deprived of his chattel, has not benefited from the rising market value up to the date of judgment. However, it is possible for the court to refuse to award a rise in value in certain circumstances.

First, where the claimant could have prevented or reversed the effects of a conversion, he is unlikely to be awarded any rise in value of the chattel as consequential loss. In one case a defendant, who was in possession of the claimant's uncollected goods and had written to the claimant requesting that he collect the goods, eventually sold them and kept the proceeds for the claimant[2]. When the claimant eventually claimed the goods, the value had risen substantially. It was held that this rise in value was not recoverable as consequential loss, as it did not flow directly from the defendant's conversion, but the claimant's failure to pick up his goods when requested[3].

Second, if the value of the goods has risen substantially in between conversion and the judgment, but the claimant could reasonably have issued proceedings at an earlier date, then the court is unlikely to award consequential losses reflecting the full rise in value[4]. The loss in such cases is attributable to the claimant's failure to take proceedings rather than the defendant's wrongful act.

Third, where it is clear that a claimant would have sold the chattel, had it not been converted, prior to the judgment, then the rise in value will not be awarded as consequential loss[5], the reasoning being that, but for the defendant's conversion, the claimant would have suffered this loss in any case, as he would have sold the chattel before it had reached a higher value.

1   *Empresa Exportadora de Azucar v Industria Azucarera Nacional SA* [1983] 2 Lloyd's Rep 171; *BBMB Finance (Hong Kong) Ltd v Eda Holdings Ltd* [1991] 2 All ER 129 at 131, [1990] 1 WLR 409 at 412, PC (citing *Sachs v Miklos* [1948] 2 KB 23, [1948] 1 All ER 67). For older authority see *Greening v Wilkinson* (1825) 1 C & P 625, followed in *Johnson v Hook* (1883) 31 WR 812 (court may assess value of goods at date subsequent to conversion). See also *Aitken v Gardiner and Watson* [1956] OR 589, 4 DLR (2d) 119, Ont HC. As to consequential loss see PARAS 683–684.
2   *Sachs v Miklos* [1948] 2 KB 23, [1948] 1 All ER 67, CA; *IBL Ltd v Coussens* [1991] 2 All ER 133 at 139–140, CA, per Neill LJ. Cf *Empresa Exportadora de Azucar v Industria Azucarera Nacional SA, The Playa Larga and Marble Islands* [1983] 2 Lloyd's Rep 171, CA, where it was held that the claimants could not reasonably have been expected to take steps to replace the goods until some three weeks after the act of conversion.
3   *Sachs v Miklos* [1948] 2 KB 23, [1948] 1 All ER 67, CA (claimant therefore was only entitled to the sum that the defendant had sold the goods for).
4   *IBL Ltd v Coussens* [1991] 2 All ER 133 at 139–140, CA. The court may award the rise in value up to the date at which it was reasonable for the claimant to issue proceedings.
5   *IBL Ltd v Coussens* [1991] 2 All ER 133 at 139–140, CA.

672.   Fall in chattel's value between conversion and judgment.   Because the normal rule is that the value of the chattel is assessed at the date of the conversion[1], where the value of the chattel falls in between the conversion and the judgment, the claimant may stand to receive a windfall if he is awarded the value at the date of the conversion. Despite this, however, the normal practice of the courts has not been to make a reduction in the damages to reflect the drop in value[2].

There is a limited exception to this approach in cases where the defendant has converted the claimant's chattel by detaining it, but has subsequently returned it. If the value of the chattel has fallen between the conversion and the judgment, then courts have refused to award damages for the depreciation if it has not been proved that the claimant would have sold it and realised its higher value[3].

1 See PARA 670.
2 *Solloway v McLaughlin* [1938] AC 247 at 257–259, [1937] 4 All ER 328 at 332–333, PC; *BBMB Finance (Hong Kong) Ltd v Eda Holdings Ltd* [1991] 2 All ER 129, [1990] 1 WLR 409, PC.
3 *Brandeis Goldschmidt & Co Ltd v Western Transport Ltd* [1981] QB 864, [1982] 1 All ER 28, CA; *Williams v Archer* (1847) 5 CB 318; *Williams v Peel River Land and Mineral Co Ltd* (1886) 55 LT 689, CA. There is Privy Council authority which suggests that this approach could apply in all cases where there is a drop in value: see *BBMB Finance (Hong Kong) Ltd v Eda Holdings Ltd* [1991] 2 All ER 129, [1990] 1 WLR 409, PC. However, this suggestion appears inconsistent with the earlier case *Solloway v McLaughlin* [1938] AC 247, [1937] 4 All ER 328, PC. See also *Glenbrook Capital LP v Hamilton (t/a Hamiltons)* [2014] EWHC 2297 (Comm), [2014] All ER (D) 119 (Jul), where silver had been purchased by the claimant for investment and resale. Some of the silver was converted by the defendants thereby depriving the claimant of an opportunity of selling it at substantial profit at the time when the market was very high. The claimant was therefore entitled to recover damages based on the fall in value of the silver eventually delivered.

673. Measure of damages for conversion of negotiable instruments and documents. When the chattel converted is a document evincing a debt, specific rules are applied to determine the claimant's damages. In certain cases the value of the document which is evidence of a debt or other right will be equated with the value of the debt or right itself[1].

The ordinary measure of damages for the conversion of a negotiable instrument is the face value of the instrument[2]. The same rule applies to conversion of documents in the nature of negotiable instruments, or quasi-negotiable instruments, such as a bill of lading, share certificate or other document of title to goods[3].

As in all cases, the purpose of damages will be to compensate the claimant for his loss[4], and in certain cases the claimant's loss will be less than the face value of the document. If a claimant, for instance, is able to obtain payment of the debt without the converted document, then his loss is not the face value of the document[5]. In such cases the loss will be the amount representing the cost and trouble of proving the debt without production of the document[6]. Similarly, if a cheque were stopped before payment into his bank by the wrongdoer, damages for its face value would be inappropriate[7].

1 As to the conversion of documents see PARA 642.
2 *Morison v London County and Westminster Bank Ltd* [1914] 3 KB 356 at 365, HL, per Lord Reading CJ; *Lloyds Bank Ltd v EB Savory & Co* [1933] AC 201, 44 Ll L Rep 231, HL; *Marquess of Bute v Barclays Bank Ltd* [1955] 1 QB 202, [1954] 3 All ER 365; cf *Midland Bank Ltd v Eastcheap Dried Fruit Co Ltd* [1961] 2 Lloyd's Rep 251; *Building and Civil Engineering Holidays Scheme Management Ltd v Post Office* [1964] 2 QB 430 at 445–446 per Roskill J (revsd on other grounds [1966] 1 QB 247, [1965] 1 All ER 163, CA). See also *Mercer v Jones* (1813) 3 Camp 477. As to negotiable instruments see FINANCIAL SERVICES AND INSTITUTIONS vol 49 (2008) PARA 1400 et seq.
3 *BBMB Finance (Hong Kong) Ltd v Eda Holdings Ltd* [1991] 2 All ER 129, [1990] 1 WLR 409, PC; *Building and Civil Engineering Holidays Scheme Management Ltd v Post Office* [1964] 2 QB 430 at 445–446 per Roskill J (revsd on other grounds [1966] QB 247, [1965] 1 All ER 163, CA); *Ernest Scragg & Sons Ltd v Perseverance Banking and Trust Co Ltd* [1973] 2 Lloyd's Rep 101, CA; *Bavins Junior and Sims v London and South Western Bank Ltd* [1900] 1 QB 270, 69 LJQB 164, CA.
4 As to the general principles governing the recovery of damages see DAMAGES.

5   See e g *Wills v Wells* (1818) 8 Taunt 264 (claimant not entitled to the face value of an insurance policy document converted by the defendant, as claimant would still be entitled, as against the insurance company, to payment of the policy).

6   *Clegg v Baretta* (1887) 56 LT 775.

7   *International Factors Ltd v Rodriguez Ltd* [1979] QB 351 at 358, [1979] 1 All ER 17 at 20, CA, per Sir David Cairns.

(B) Awarding Less than Market Value of the Chattel

674.   Market value of the chattel as the usual starting point for damages. Because the value of the chattel usually represents a claimant's loss in a conversion case[1], the market value rule is the normal starting point for the assessment of the claimant's damages[2]. However, in certain cases the value of the chattel will not represent the claimant's loss, and some other measure of damages will be more appropriate. Examples of this are considered in the following paragraphs[3].

1   See PARA 668 et seq.

2   *Albacruz (Cargo Owners) v Albazero (Owners), The Albazero* [1977] AC 774 at 841, [1976] 3 All ER 129 at 132, HL, per Lord Diplock; *Kuwait Airways Corpn v Iraqi Airways Co (Nos 4 and 5)* [2002] UKHL 19 at [67], [2002] 2 AC 883 at [67], [2002] 3 All ER 209 at [67] per Lord Nicholls.

3   See PARA 675 (conversion by an unpaid vendor), PARA 676 (chattels subject to a lease), PARA 677 (chattels subject to a security interest), PARA 678 (allowance for improvements), PARA 679 (co-owners etc), PARA 680 (account taken of planned expenditure).

675.   Damages for conversion by an unpaid vendor. Damages representing the market value of a chattel would overcompensate the claimant where there has been a conversion by an unpaid vendor[1]. This occurs in cases where a vendor has transferred title to a chattel to a claimant under a contract of sale, but has retained possession subject to the claimant paying for the chattel[2]. If, prior to the claimant paying for the chattel, the vendor resells the chattel to a third party[3] the vendor will have committed a conversion[4]. However, as the claimant has not yet paid for the chattel, to award him the market value would be to put him in a better position than he would have been in had the vendor not converted it. In this situation the claimant will be awarded the value of the chattel minus the sum he would have had to pay for it[5].

This principle has not been extended to situations that may be thought analogous to the unpaid vendor. It does not, for instance, apply to a case where a lienor sues a lienee for the wrongful sale of his chattel[6]. In such a case, even though the lienor would have had to pay the lienee a sum of money to obtain the release of his chattel, that sum will not be deducted from the damages awarded to the lienor, meaning that he will be entitled to the full value of the chattel[7].

1   The market value of the converted chattel is the usual starting point for assessing damages: see PARAS 668 et seq, 674.

2   The Sale of Goods Act 1979 s 17 allows the parties to agree the date of transfer of title: see SALE OF GOODS AND SUPPLY OF SERVICES vol 91 (2012) PARA 110. The vendor may therefore transfer title despite retaining possession: see PARA 645.

3   The resale may destroy the claimant's title to the chattel, thus preventing the claimant from proceeding against the new purchaser: see PARA 645.

4   *Chinery v Viall* (1860) 5 H & N 288, 29 LJ Ex 180.

5   *Chinery v Viall* (1860) 5 H & N 288, 29 LJ Ex 180; *Butler v Egg Marketing Board* (1966) 114 CLR 185, [1966] ALR 1025, Aust HC.

6   *Mulliner v Florence* (1878) 3 QBD 484, 47 LJQB 700, CA. See PARA 610. As to lien generally see LIEN.

7   *Mulliner v Florence* (1878) 3 QBD 484, 47 LJQB 700, CA. The difference seems to be that in *Chinery v Viall* (1860) 5 H & N 288, 29 LJ Ex 180, the debt owed by the claimant to the

vendor related directly to the chattel, and was discharged by the vendor's conversion of the chattel; in *Mulliner v Florence* above, the debt owed to the defendant had been incurred for reasons wholly unrelated to the chattel and remained payable notwithstanding the defendant's conversion.

676. **Damages for conversion of chattels subject to a lease.** Where a claimant leases his chattel to a lessee under a hire purchase contract[1], if the chattel is converted by the lessee or a third party, then an award of damages of the full market value of the chattel[2] may overcompensate the claimant[3]. This may apply, for example, where the claimant has leased a car to the defendant under a hire purchase contract, and the defendant, having paid half of the instalments, wrongfully sells the car. If the claimant in such a case were awarded the market value of the chattel then he would be overcompensated[4], and so instead he will be awarded damages to the value of the chattel minus any instalments paid[5].

1 As to hire purchase agreements see CONSUMER CREDIT vol 21 (2011) PARA 66.
2 The market value of the converted chattel is the usual starting point for assessing damages: see PARAS 668 et seq, 674.
3 *Wickham Holdings Ltd v Brooke House Motors Ltd* [1967] 1 All ER 117, [1967] 1 WLR 295, CA.
4 Had the conversion not been committed then the claimant would have stood to receive the remaining instalments, not the full value of the chattel.
5 *Wickham Holdings Ltd v Brooke House Motors Ltd* [1967] 1 All ER 117, [1967] 1 WLR 295, CA; *Belvoir Finance Co Ltd v Stapleton* [1971] 1 QB 210, [1970] 3 All ER 664, CA.

677. **Damages for conversion of chattel subject to a security interest.** Where the claimant has mortgaged his chattel to the defendant, if the defendant wrongfully seizes the chattel[1], then he will be liable in conversion[2]. However, damages will be reduced to reflect the defendant's security interest in the chattel, measured by the outstanding debt owed to the defendant[3]. However, this rule does not apply when the mortgagor's chattel is converted by a third party[4]. Similarly, if a claimant has pledged his chattel to a defendant, and the defendant converts the chattel by wrongfully selling it, the claimant will be entitled to the value of the chattel minus the amount owing to the pledgee[5]. However, this rule does not apply to cases involving liens[6].

1 This normally happens when a mortgagee seizes the chattel before there has been a default on the debt: see eg *Brierly v Kendall* (1852) 17 QB 937, 21 LJQB 161. As to the law relating to mortgage see MORTGAGE.
2 As to the elements of conversion see PARA 604.
3 *Brierly v Kendall* (1852) 17 QB 937, 21 LJQB 161.
4 *Blue Sky One Ltd v Mahan Air* [2010] EWHC 631 (Comm), [2010] All ER (D) 02 (Jun). This can be explained in two ways. First, if a mortgagor's chattel is seized by a third party, the mortgagor remains liable to pay his debt to the mortgagee. He will therefore not be overcompensated by being awarded the full value of the chattel. Second, the mortgagor, being in possession, can rely on his legal title acquired by possession (see PARA 620 et seq) against a third party wrongdoer, and need not rely upon his equity of redemption to sue.
5 *Donald v Suckling* (1866) LR 1 QB 585. See PARA 633. As to the law relating to pledges see BAILMENT AND PLEDGE.
6 *Mulliner v Florence* (1878) 3 QBD 484, 47 LJQB 700, CA. This may be explained on the basis that a lienee, unlike a pledgee, does not have a power of sale.

678. **Damages adjusted for improvements to converted chattel.** A claimant's damages may be offset to take account of any improvements made to the converted chattel[1]. If in proceedings for conversion against a person (the 'improver') who has improved the goods, it is shown that the improver acted in the mistaken but honest belief that he had a good title to them, an allowance

must be made for the extent to which, at the time as at which the goods fall to be valued in assessing damages, the value of the goods is attributable to the improvement[2].

An allowance must also be made for a transferee of the improver, if the transferee took the improved chattel in good faith. If, in proceedings for conversion against a person ('the purchaser') who has purported to purchase the goods from the improver, or where after such a purported sale[3] the goods passed by a further purported sale on one or more occasions, on any such occasion, it is shown that the purchaser acted in good faith, the same allowance must be made as described above[4]. If in such a case[5] the person purporting to sell the goods acted in good faith, then in proceedings by the purchaser for recovery of the purchase price because of failure of consideration, or in any other proceedings founded on that failure of consideration, an allowance must, where appropriate, be made on the principle described above[6].

1   The market value of the converted chattel is the usual starting point for assessing damages: see PARAS 668 et seq, 674.
2   Torts (Interference with Goods) Act 1977 s 6(1). See *Munro v Willmott* [1949] 1 KB 295, [1948] 2 All ER 983. It appears that the burden of proving the necessary belief in his title, an improvement to the goods, and a resultant increase in the value of the goods rests upon the improver.
      In *Greenwood v Bennett* [1973] QB 195 at 202, [1972] 3 All ER 586 at 589, CA, Lord Denning suggested that the defendant could have an independent restitutionary claim against the claimant, but the Torts (Interference with Goods) Act 1977 is silent on this possibility.
3   The Torts (Interference with Goods) Act 1977 s 6 applies, with the necessary modifications, to a purported bailment or other disposition of goods as it applies to a purported sale of goods: s 6(4).
4   Torts (Interference with Goods) Act 1977 s 6(2). See the text and note 2.
5   Ie as described in the Torts (Interference with Goods) Act 1977 s 6(2).
6   Torts (Interference with Goods) Act 1977 s 6(3). For example, where a person in good faith buys a stolen car from the improver and is sued in conversion by the true owner the damages may be reduced to reflect the improvement, but if the person who bought the stolen car from the improver sues the improver for failure of consideration, and the improver acted in good faith, s 6(3) will ordinarily make a comparable reduction in the damages he recovers from the improver: see s 6(2).

679.   Damages for conversion where claimant is a co-owner of the chattel. If the claimant is a co-owner of the chattel which has been converted, then he may only recover the proportional share of the market value of the chattel[1] which reflects his interest[2].

1   The market value of the converted chattel is the usual starting point for assessing damages: see PARAS 668 et seq, 674.
2   See e g *Bloxam v Hubbard* (1804) 5 East 407.

680.   Reduction of damages for claimant's intended expenditure on the chattel. If the claimant intended to sell his chattel, and it was converted before the sale could take place, then any costs that the claimant would have incurred in effecting the sale will be deducted from the damages awarded[1]. For instance, if the claimant would have incurred costs in transferring the goods to the market, then these costs will be deducted from the value of the chattel when calculating the claimant's loss[2].

1   The market value of the converted chattel is the usual starting point for assessing damages: see PARAS 668 et seq, 674.

2 *Clarke v Nicholson* (1835) 1 Cr M & R 724; *Ewbank v Nutting* (1849) 7 CB 797; *Morgan v Powell* (1842) 3 QB 278; *Burmah Trading Corpn Ltd v Mahomed Ally Sherazee and Burmah Co Ltd* (1878) LR 5 Ind App 130, PC. See also *Reid v Fairbanks* (1853) 13 CB 692.

(C) Causation of Loss

681.   Normal rule: loss must be attributable to the defendant's conversion. If a claimant in conversion is able to establish that he has suffered a loss then he must, according to normal principles in tort law[1], establish that that loss is attributable to the defendant's conversion[2]. In most conversion cases the causal nexus between the claimant's loss and the defendant's conversion will be clear: if a defendant has, for instance, stolen a car from the claimant, then it is clear that the claimant's loss is attributable to the defendant's wrongful act. However, there are cases where, but for the defendant's conversion, the claimant would have suffered the loss in any event. The starting point in such cases is that the normal causal requirements will be applied[3], and damages may be reduced accordingly.

An example of the normal causal requirements being applied to the tort can be found in a case where the claimant had entrusted his goods to the defendant (a warehouseman) and instructed the defendant to hold the goods to the claimant's order. The defendant converted the goods when he misdelivered the goods to a rogue ('X'), who presented a forged order[4]. However, the claimant subsequently authorised the defendant to release the goods to X in any case. So although the claimant suffered a loss (as X never paid for the goods), he would have suffered this loss even if the defendant had not converted the chattel. Consequently, causation was not established and the claimant was entitled to nominal damages only[5].

Although the general principles of causation[6] apply to conversion, they are subject to an important exception in cases involving successive conversions[7].

1 See DAMAGES vol 29 (2014) PARA 364 et seq.
2 See PARA 417.
3 Lord Nicholls refers to the application of the normal rules of causation in *Kuwait Airways Corpn v Iraqi Airways Co (Nos 4 and 5)* [2002] UKHL 19 at [72]–[86], [2002] 2 AC 883 at [72]–[86], [2002] 3 All ER 209 at [72]–[86].
4 *Hiort v London and North Western Rly Co* (1879) 4 ExD 188, CA. This was a conversion by misdelivery: see PARA 611.
5 *Hiort v London and North Western Rly Co* (1879) 4 ExD 188, CA. As to nominal damages see DAMAGES vol 29 (2014) PARAS 319–320.
6 As to causation see further DAMAGES vol 29 (2014) PARA 364 et seq.
7 See PARA 682.

682.   The exception: successive conversions. If a chattel belonging to A is taken by B, who then sells it to C, then both B and C will be liable in conversion[1]. However, if A brings a claim against C, he would struggle to establish causation of loss[2]. Although A has suffered a loss (which can be measured by the value of his chattel[3]) and although C has converted the chattel, A would have suffered the loss in any event as a result of B's wrongful act[4].

Despite the fact that a subsequent converter does not normally cause the claimant's basic loss, the law permits the claimant to recover his loss against such defendants by disapplying the normal causal requirement[5]. This exception to the principles of causation, which is based on grounds of policy[6], means that successive converters, who have not caused any additional loss to a claimant, can be held liable for the basic loss suffered by the claimant.

1   See e g *Morris v Robinson* (1824) 3 B & C 196; *Brinsmead v Harrison* (1871) LR 6 CP 584 (affd (1872) LR 7 CP 547); *Hollins v Fowler* (1875) LR 7 HL 757; *Kuwait Airways Corpn v Iraqi Airways Co (Nos 4 and 5)* [2002] UKHL 19, [2002] 2 AC 883, [2002] 3 All ER 209.

2   As to the normal rule that the loss must be attributable to the defendant's conversion see PARA 681.

3   See PARA 668 et seq.

4   A may, however, have suffered additional consequential loss, such as the extra costs of searching for C and bringing a claim against him. As to consequential losses see PARAS 683–684.

5   *Kuwait Airways Corpn v Iraqi Airways Co (Nos 4 and 5)* [2002] UKHL 19 at [74], [2002] 2 AC 883 at [74], [2002] 3 All ER 209 at [74] per Lord Nicholls.

6   *Kuwait Airways Corpn v Iraqi Airways Co (Nos 4 and 5)* [2002] UKHL 19 at [74], [2002] 2 AC 883 at [74], [2002] 3 All ER 209 at [74] per Lord Nicholls. The policy here is the robust protection of property rights in chattels. Without this exception, the only person normally worth suing would be the first converter, who may be difficult to locate.

(D) Consequential Loss

683. Defendant liable for consequential losses flowing from the conversion. In addition to being entitled to the basic loss, usually measured by the market value of his chattel[1], the claimant will be entitled to any consequential losses flowing naturally and directly from the defendant's conversion[2]. There are a number of well established heads of consequential loss that have been awarded. Costs incurred by the claimant in finding a suitable replacement for his chattel have been held recoverable[3]. In cases where the defendant converts the claimant's chattel by detaining it, but subsequently returns it, then consequential losses can be awarded to reflect the deterioration in the chattel's value[4]. If the claimant has to pay storage charges to obtain the return of his chattel, then these costs may be recoverable as consequential loss[5]. If the market value of the chattel rises following the conversion then the claimant may be able to recover this as consequential loss, as he has been deprived of the benefit of a rising market[6]. Further, if the claimant, as a result of being deprived of his chattel, is prevented from earning a profit, then he may recover these losses. For instance, if a claimant is deprived of his tools, then he may recover the wages he has lost in not being able to work[7]. Similarly, if the claimant was unable to earn money by selling or hiring out the chattel, then he may be entitled to damages to reflect this loss[8].

1   See PARA 668 et seq.

2   *Re Simms* [1934] Ch 1, CA; *Hillesden Securities Ltd v Ryjack Ltd* [1983] 2 All ER 184 at 188, [1983] 1 WLR 959 at 963 per Parker J; *Empresa Exportadora de Azucar v Industria Azucarera Nacional SA, The Playa Larga and Marble Islands* [1983] 2 Lloyd's Rep 171 at 181 per Ackner LJ; c f *Chubb Cash Ltd v John Crilley & Son (a firm)* [1983] 2 All ER 294 at 299, [1983] 1 WLR 599 at 604, CA, per Bush LJ; *Saleslease Ltd v Davis* [2000] 1 All ER (Comm) 883, [1999] 1 WLR 1664, CA.

3   *Kuwait Airways Corpn v Iraqi Airways Co (Nos 4 and 5)* [2002] UKHL 19, [2002] 2 AC 883, [2002] 3 All ER 209 (claimant had to hire or purchase replacements for the aircraft which had been seized by the defendants; as these losses flowed naturally form the conversion, they were recoverable in the tort); *Davis v Oswell* (1837) 7 C & P 804 (claimant able to cover the costs of hiring replacement horses).

4   *Uzinterimpex JSC v Standard Bank plc* [2008] EWCA Civ 819, [2008] All ER (D) 196 (Jul), CA (consequential losses were not awarded in the case because of the claimant's failure to mitigate his loss: see PARA 684).

5   In *Kuwait Airways Corpn v Iraqi Airways Co (Nos 4 and 5)* [2002] UKHL 19, [2002] 2 AC 883, [2002] 3 All ER 209, the claimant had to pay the Iranian government for the storage and upkeep of some of the converted aircraft in order to obtain their return; these costs were recoverable as consequential loss.

6   See PARA 671.

7   *Bodley v Reynolds* (1846) 8 QB 779.

8 *Greer v Alstons Engineering Sales and Services Ltd* [2003] UKPC 46; *Tanks and Vessels Ltd v Devon Cider Co Ltd* [2009] EWHC 1360 (Ch), [2009] All ER (D) 16 (Jul); *Saleslease Ltd v Davis* [2000] 1 All ER (Comm) 883, [1999] 1 WLR 1664, CA. As to reasonable hiring charge (also known as market rental) see *Strand Electric and Engineering Co Ltd v Brisford Entertainments Ltd* [1952] 2 QB 246 at 254, [1952] 1 All ER 796 at 800–801, CA, a case of detinue, where Denning LJ held that a plaintiff might recover a reasonable hiring charge even though, because he would not have used the goods, he had suffered no loss. See also the similar principle enunciated in the negligence case of *Mediana (Owners) v Comet (Owners, Master and Crew), The Mediana* [1900] AC 113 at 117 per Lord Halsbury LC, HL.

684. Limitations on recovery for consequential loss. The consequential losses suffered by the claimant in a conversion case will not normally be recoverable if they were not reasonably foreseeable[1]. However, where the defendant knows he is acting wrongfully, and converts the chattel in bad faith, then there will be no need to prove reasonable foresight; the claimant need only show that the consequential loss flows naturally and directly from the wrong[2].

The claimant will not be entitled to consequential losses if he has not taken reasonable steps to mitigate such losses[3].

1 *Kuwait Airways Corpn v Iraqi Airways Co (Nos 4 and 5)* [2002] UKHL 19 at [81]–[82], [2002] 2 AC 883 at [81]–[82], [2002] 3 All ER 209 at [81]–[82]. See also *Empresa Exportadora de Azucar v Industria Azucarera Nacional SA, The Playa Larga and Marble Islands* [1983] 2 Lloyd's Rep 171 at 181 per Ackner LJ; *Hillesden Securities Ltd v Ryjak Ltd* [1983] 2 All ER 184 at 187–188, [1983] 1 WLR 959 at 962–963; *Saleslease Ltd v Davis* [2000] 1 All ER (Comm) 883, [1999] 1 WLR 1664, CA (where the extremely high hire replacement charges incurred by the claimant were not recoverable as they could not reasonably have been foreseen). As to the recovery of consequential loss see PARA 683.

2 *Kuwait Airways Corpn v Iraqi Airways Co (Nos 4 and 5)* [2002] UKHL 19 at [99] et seq, [2002] 2 AC 883 at [99] et seq, [2002] 3 All ER 209 at [99] et seq.

3 See eg *Uzinterimpex JSC v Standard Bank plc* [2008] EWCA Civ 819, [2008] All ER (D) 196 (Jul), CA, a case involving a dispute over the title to cotton. The claimant, who eventually succeeded in the action, unreasonably refused to agree to the sale of the cotton during the litigation to reduce the storage costs and prevent the cotton deteriorating. Because the claimant could easily have taken steps to mitigate these losses, he was not entitled to recover them from the defendant. As to the requirement to mitigate loss see further DAMAGES vol 29 (2014) PARAS 378–381.

(3) TRESPASS TO GOODS

(i) Basis of Liability for Trespass to Goods

685. Trespass to goods compared with conversion. Whereas conversion is typically concerned with the most serious, or 'exclusionary', interferences with another's chattel[1], trespass is associated with minor interferences[2]. For example scratching the panel of the claimant's car, or deliberately touching a painting hanging in a gallery, may not amount to a conversion, as the person with legal title is not excluded[3]. However, such interferences can amount to a trespass[4].

Trespass to goods, like conversion, is classed as a 'wrongful interference with goods' for the purpose of the Torts (Interference with Goods) Act 1977[5] and, as such, is subject to a number of the same statutory reforms discussed in relation conversion. These changes relate to the form of judgment where goods are detained[6]; interlocutory relief where goods are detained[7]; the extinction of title on satisfaction of a claim for damages[8]; allowances for improvement of the goods[9]; double liability[10]; competing rights to the goods[11]; concurrent actions[12]; and co-owners[13].

1 As to the tort of conversion see PARA 604 et seq.

2 See PARA 687.
3 See e g *Fouldes v Willoughby* (1841) 8 M & W 540; *Bushel v Miller* (1718) 1 Stra 128; *Price v Helyar* (1828) 4 Bing 597. As to the requirement for exclusion in conversion see PARA 607.
4 *Fouldes v Willoughby* (1841) 8 M & W 540. It is important to note that whilst minor interferences can be litigated in trespass, it is not a requirement that the interference be minor in order for liability in the tort. More serious interferences, which do result in the exclusion of the person with legal title, can also result in liability in the tort: see e g *White v Withers LLP* [2009] EWCA Civ 1122, [2009] 3 FCR 435 (where the claimant, who was excluded from his letters by the defendant, was able to sue in trespass). See also *Hesperides Hotels Ltd v Muftizade* [1979] AC 508, [1978] 2 All ER 1168, HL.
5 See the Torts (Interference with Goods) Act 1977 s 1(b); and PARA 603.
6 See the Torts (Interference with Goods) Act 1977 s 3; and PARAS 662–665.
7 See the Torts (Interference with Goods) Act 1977 s 4; and PARA 667.
8 See the Torts (Interference with Goods) Act 1977 s 5; and PARA 663.
9 See the Torts (Interference with Goods) Act 1977 s 6; and PARA 678.
10 See the Torts (Interference with Goods) Act 1977 s 7; and PARA 656.
11 See the Torts (Interference with Goods) Act 1977 s 8; and PARA 656.
12 See the Torts (Interference with Goods) Act 1977 s 9; and PARA 657.
13 See the Torts (Interference with Goods) Act 1977 s 10; and PARA 659.

686. Deliberate interference with another person's chattel. It is sometimes stated that trespass to goods is concerned with direct interferences with another's possession of a chattel[1]. However, as the courts take a very wide interpretation of 'possession'[2], and because legal title, without possession, seems to be sufficient to sue in trespass to goods, liability in the tort is wider than mere interferences with another's possession of a thing. Rather, liability is based upon deliberate interferences with the chattel itself[3].

1 See comments of Lord Kenyon CJ in *Ward v Macauley* (1791) 4 Term Rep 489. The notion that trespass protects the fact of possession, not one's legal title, draws a false distinction. Possession gives rise to a legal title: see PARA 620 et seq.
2 See e g *Lotan v Cross* (1810) 2 Camp 464.
3 In *Wilson v Lombank Ltd* [1963] 1 All ER 740, [1963] 1 WLR 1294, the claimant left his car with the garage for repairs, where it was seized by the defendant. It could not be said that the defendant interfered with the claimant's possession; rather it can only be said that he interfered with the car itself. As to what constitutes interference see PARAS 687–688. As to the requirement for deliberateness see PARA 689.

687. What constitutes interference with claimant's chattel. The defendant must be responsible for some physical contact with the claimant's chattel in order to be liable for trespass to goods[1]. Deliberately scratching the panel of another's car, puncturing its tyres or smashing its window, would all be examples of a trespass[2], as they each involve some form of unauthorised physical contact with another's chattel. Although physical contact often results in damage to the claimant's chattel, in the sense of physical change, it need not. Mere unauthorised physical contact, not causing damage, can be sufficient for liability in the tort[3]. For instance, if a defendant, without lawful authority, attaches a clamp to the claimant's car, then this can constitute a trespass, even though the car is not thereby damaged, but merely immobilised[4]. Merely picking up the claimant's property, and moving it to a different room in the claimant's house, is sufficient to render the defendant liable in trespass[5]. In this sense trespass is actionable per se, with such minor interferences, which do not damage the claimant's chattel, being actionable.

Although minor interferences are actionable in the tort, two factors should be noted. First, in cases involving minor interferences, damages are likely to be nominal only[6]. Second, whilst the minimal requirements for liability in the tort create the danger of excessive liability, there is a general defence in cases of reasonable touching of chattels, particularly those in the public domain, which avoids liability attaching to everyday contact with another's goods[7].

1　*Hartley v Moxham* (1842) 3 QB 701. Non-physical interference is not sufficient: see PARA 688.
2　*Fouldes v Willoughby* (1841) 8 M & W 540; *Crozier v Cundey* (1827) 6 B & C 232; *Jones v Lewis* (1836) 7 C & P 343; *Wilson v Lombank Ltd* [1963] 1 All ER 740, [1963] 1 WLR 1294; *Moore v Lambeth County Court Registrar (No 2)* [1970] 1 QB 560, [1970] 1 All ER 980, CA; *Ellis v Loftus Iron Co* (1874) LR 10 CP 10; *William Leitch & Co Ltd v Leydon* [1931] AC 90, HL.
3　This is an important rule, as it means that if a defendant does something such as touching a painting in a gallery, or an exhibit in a museum, without permission, then he can be liable in trespass (but see note 7).
4　See *Arthur v Anker* [1997] QB 564, [1996] 3 All ER 783, CA; *Vine v Waltham Forrest London Borough Council* [2000] 4 All ER 169, [2000] 1 WLR 2383, CA.
5　*Kirk v Gregory* (1876) 1 Ex D 55 (defendant moved claimant's jewellery). See also *R v IRC, ex p Rossminster Ltd* [1980] AC 952 at 1011, [1980] 1 All ER 80 at 93, HL, per Lord Diplock.
6　See eg *Kirk v Gregory* (1876) 1 Ex D 55 (claimant awarded 1 shilling as damages). As to nominal damages see further DAMAGES vol 29 (2014) PARAS 319–320.
7　In *Collins v Wilcock* [1984] 3 All ER 374 at 379, [1984] 1 WLR 1172 at 1178, DC, Goff LJ stated that there would be no trespass unless the defendant has acted beyond the 'generally acceptable standards of conduct'. Although this was a trespass to the person case, the statement appears to have been approved in the trespass to goods case *White v Withers LLP* [2009] EWCA Civ 1122 at [61], [2009] 3 FCR 435 at [61] per Ward LJ: see PARA 693.

688.　Non-physical interference not sufficient to establish trespass to goods.
Where the defendant merely impairs the claimant's ability to use his chattel, but does not cause any form of physical contact with it, then there will be no liability in trespass[1]. Locking the door to a rented room that the claimant had been staying in has been held not to amount to trespass to the claimant's items of property inside the room, as the defendant had not physically touched them[2]. Similarly, where the defendant maritime authority had wrongfully issued a detention notice on the claimant's ship, the court held that this would not amount to a conversion or trespass as it involved no physical interference with the ship but a mere impairment of use[3]. It was stated, however, that if the defendant had chained the ship to the dock, then there would be liability in trespass, as in that case there would be physical touching[4].

1　See PARA 687.
2　*Hartley v Moxham* (1842) 3 QB 701. The claim might have been successfully litigated in conversion, if the claimant had been able to show a complete exclusion from his chattel. See *Burroughes v Bayne* (1860) 5 H & N 296; *Etherton v Popplewell* (1800) 1 East 139.
3　*Club Cruise Entertainment & Travelling Services Europe BV v Department for Transport (The Van Gogh)* [2008] EWHC 2794 (Comm) at [51]–[53], [2009] 1 All ER (Comm) 955 at [51]–[53].
4　*Club Cruise Entertainment & Travelling Services Europe BV v Department for Transport (The Van Gogh)* [2008] EWHC 2794 (Comm) at [50], [2009] 1 All ER (Comm) 955 at [50].

689.　Interference with chattel must be deliberate. Where a defendant's interference with the claimant's chattel is unintended, then it will be more appropriate to sue in negligence than in trespass to goods[1]. For instance, if a defendant carelessly crashes into the claimant's car, causing damage, the appropriate action will be the tort of negligence, where the claimant will need to prove fault[2]. Trespass to goods, like conversion[3], is associated with deliberate interferences, such as where a defendant intentionally scratches the side of the claimant's car, or deliberately attaches a clamp to its wheel[4].

When the term 'deliberateness' is used in trespass, it refers to the need for some deliberate touching or physical contact with the claimant's chattel, not the harm that the claimant suffers as a result[5]. If the defendant mistakenly believes that he has a legal entitlement to touch the claimant's chattel, he will nonetheless be liable in the tort. For example, where the defendant removed a recently deceased's jewellery from one room to another for its safe keeping, but without the consent of the executors, the defendant was liable in trespass for this interference even though there was no intention to cause harm: it was sufficient that the touching had been deliberate[6]. Similarly, in a case where a defendant honestly believed that he had a legal entitlement to seize a car belonging to the claimant, his lack of fault was no defence to liability in the tort[7]. As there is no need to prove an intention to cause harm, nor that the defendant was negligent when he deliberately interfered with the chattel, trespass, like conversion, is a tort of strict liability[8].

1   Historically, if the interference was direct, then the claimant had the option of suing in trespass; but, since the case of *Williams v Holland* (1833) 10 Bing 112, negligence has become increasingly associated with unintentional but careless interferences, leaving trespass associated with intentional interferences.

2   For examples of 'negligent trespass' see *National Coal Board v J E Evans & Co (Cardiff) Ltd* [1951] 2 KB 861, [1951] 2 All ER 310, CA. See also *Everitt v Martin* [1953] NZLR 298, NZ SC; *Williams v Milotin* [1957] HCA 83, 97 CLR 465. However such cases are rare, and the current practice of litigants is to plead negligent interferences in negligence rather than trespass. Further, it has been suggested in a number of cases that where the defendant's interference with the claimant or his chattel is unintentional, then a claimant is prohibited from suing in trespass, and must sue in negligence: see e g *Fowler v Lanning* [1959] 1 QB 426, [1959] 1 All ER 290; *Letang v Cooper* [1965] 1 QB 232, [1964] 2 All ER 929, CA.

3   See PARA 606.

4   As happened in *Vine v Waltham Forest London Borough Council* [2000] 4 All ER 169, [2000] 1 WLR 2383, CA.

5   See e g *Kirk v Gregory* (1876) 1 Ex D 55. As to the requirement for deliberateness in conversion see PARA 606.

6   *Kirk v Gregory* (1876) 1 Ex D 55. See also *Colwill v Reeves* (1811) 2 Camp 575; *Moore v Lambeth County Court Registrar (No 2)* [1970] 1 QB 560 at 570, [1970] 1 All ER 980 at 984, CA, per Russell LJ.

7   *Wilson v Lombank Ltd* [1963] 1 All ER 740, [1963] 1 WLR 1294.

8   See PARA 604. Cf *Chic Fashions (West Wales) Ltd v Jones* [1968] 2 QB 299, [1968] 1 All ER 229, CA, where a different rule was applied to police officers executing a search warrant on the basis that strict liability would hinder their job, and therefore is not appropriate in such cases.

(ii) Who can Sue for Trespass to Goods

690.   Claimant in possession of the chattel. If a claimant is in possession of a chattel at the time of the defendant's interference, then he will have standing to sue in trespass to goods[1]. For example, if the claimant is in possession of a car when a defendant takes it from him, then the claimant will be able to sue in trespass for this interference[2].

The concept of possession is interpreted widely in the tort. If a bailor bails goods to a bailee, it has been held that the bailor does not lose possession and hence will be able to sue for trespass to goods should a defendant interfere with the bailee's possession[3]. If a claimant has, for instance, gratuitously loaned his chattel to a friend, he does not lose the ability to sue a defendant in trespass for an interference with the chattel during the loan[4].

1   As to whether possession of the chattel and legal title to the chattel are separate grounds for standing to sue in trespass to goods see PARA 691 note 2.

2   *Ward v Macauley* (1791) 4 Term Rep 489.

3   *Lotan v Cross* (1810) 2 Camp 464. See also *Wooderman v Baldock* (1819) 8 Taunt 676. As to the law relating to bailment see further BAILMENT AND PLEDGE.

4   See e g *Lotan v Cross* (1810) 2 Camp 464, where the claimant had lent his chaise to a friend for a day, during which the defendant interfered with it. It was held that claimant had not lost

possession, and therefore was able to sue in trespass. Similarly, in *Wilson v Lombank Ltd* [1963] 1 All ER 740, [1963] 1 WLR 1294, where the claimant had put his car into a garage for repairs, and it was taken by the defendant, it was held that the claimant had not lost possession during the time the car was at the garage.

691. Claimant with legal title to the chattel. If a claimant does not have possession at the time of the interference[1], but has a legal title to the chattel, he will normally be able to sue in trespass to goods[2]. There are several examples of this in the case law. Where a chattel was seized from a beneficiary, the trustee, although not in possession at the time of the interference, was able to sue in trespass[3]. An executor of a deceased was able to maintain a claim for trespass to goods to which he had title but had never been in possession of[4]. Where a claimant had acquired legal title to a barrel of whiskey which had washed up on a shore over which the claimant had a franchise of wreck, the claimant was able to sue the defendant in trespass for taking away the barrel even though the claimant had never taken physical control over it and was unaware of its existence[5]. The Court of Appeal has refused to strike out a claim against a defendant for trespass to certain personal letters which were sent to the claimant but intercepted before he could take possession[6]. The fact that he could not plead that his possession had been interfered with, but just his title, was not fatal to his claim[7].

Where a claimant is out of possession of his chattel because he has leased it to another, or created a security interest over it, a different rule applies[8]. The claimant in such cases will not be able to sue in trespass, but will need prove damage to his reversionary interest[9].

1 As to the situation where the claimant is in possession of the chattel at the time of interference see PARA 690.
2 *Wilson v Lombank Ltd* [1963] 1 All ER 740, [1963] 1 WLR 1294; *Ashby v Minnitt* (1838) 8 Ad & El 121; *Forman v Dawes* (1841) Car & M 127; *Pritchard v Long* (1842) 9 M & W 666; *Johnson v Diprose* [1893] 1 QB 512; cf *Brierly v Kendall* (1852) 17 QB 937, 21 LJQB 161. Although 'legal title' is conventionally treated as a separate basis from 'possession' for suing in trespass, it is to be doubted whether there is actually a distinction. When a claimant takes possession of a chattel he will acquire a legal title to it (see PARA 620 et seq). For examples of litigants suing in trespass who have acquired a legal title by taking possession see e g *Moore v Robinson* (1831) 2 B & Ad 817; *Oughton v Seppings* (1830) 1 B & Ad 241; *Carter v Johnson* (1839) 2 Mood & R 263; *Jeffries v Great Western Rly Co* (1856) 5 E & B 802.
3 *White v Morris* (1852) 11 CB 1015; *Barker v Furlong* [1891] 2 Ch 172, 60 LJ Ch 368.
4 *Tharpe v Stallwood* (1843) 5 Man & G 760.
5 *Dunwich (Bailiffs) v Sterry* (1831) 1 B & Ad 831.
6 *White v Withers LLP* [2009] EWCA Civ 1122, [2009] 3 FCR 435.
7 *White v Withers LLP* [2009] EWCA Civ 1122 at [49]–[50], [2009] 3 FCR 435 at [49]–[50] per Ward LJ.
8 As to the legal status of chattel leases and security interests (in the context of conversion) see PARAS 624, 632 et seq.
9 *Ward v Macauley* (1791) 4 Term Rep 489. As to damage to a reversionary interest (in the context of conversion) see PARAS 624, 633–634.

(iii) What can be the Subject of Trespass to Goods

692. Chattel as the subject matter of trespass to goods. Like the tort of conversion[1], trespass to goods protects rights with respect to chattels[2]. There is a suggestion that if a defendant were to wipe data from the claimant's computer, then this would amount to a trespass[3], as this does constitute a physical interference with a chattel[4].

1 As to conversion see PARA 604 et seq.

2   The standard examples of trespass to goods (eg *Fouldes v Willoughby* (1841) 8 M & W 540; *Kirk v Gregory* (1876) 1 Ex D 55) all involve physical chattels. Trespass also lies for the removal of fixtures, as these become chattels upon severance: *Pitt v Shew* (1821) 4 B & Ald 206; *Boydell v M'Michael* (1834) 1 Cr M & R 177 at 179 per Parke B; *Beck v Denbigh* (1860) 6 Jur NS 998. As to what is a chattel (in the context of conversion) see PARA 639 et seq.

3   See *Taylor v Rive Droite Music Ltd* [2005] EWCA Civ 1300, [2005] All ER (D) 72 (Nov).

4   The hard drive undergoes a physical change as the memory is wiped, as small magnets on the disk are realigned. As to physical interference see PARAS 687–688.

(iv) Defences to Trespass to Goods

693. Defences available to a claim of trespass to goods. If a defendant touches the claimant's chattel in the ordinary course of everyday life, then the defendant will be afforded a defence to a claim for trespass to goods. For instance, if a defendant were to slightly move the claimant's bicycle to get access to his own bicycle on a bike rack, then the defendant cannot be liable for trespass to goods for this deliberate touching[1].

A defendant in trespass will have a defence if he can show that the act complained of was done by the leave and licence of the claimant[2], or in the exercise of a legal right[3], or in the execution of legal process[4]. As in conversion[5], a defendant in trespass is also able to raise the title of a third party as a defence[6].

Contributory negligence is no good defence in proceedings founded on intentional trespass to goods[7]. Neither is co-ownership a defence to a claim founded on trespass to goods where the defendant without the authority of the other co-owner:

(1)   destroys the goods, or disposes of the goods in a way giving a good title to the entire property in the goods, or otherwise does anything equivalent to the destruction of the other's interest in the goods, or

(2)   purports to dispose of the goods in a way which would give a good title to the entire property in the goods if he was acting with the authority of all co-owners of the goods[8].

1   *White v Withers LLP* [2009] EWCA Civ 1122 at [61], [2009] 3 FCR 435 at [61] per Ward LJ. See also (in the context of trespass to the person) *Collins v Wilcock* [1984] 3 All ER 374 at 379, [1984] 1 WLR 1172 at 1178, DC, Goff LJ (no trespass unless the defendant has acted beyond the 'generally acceptable standards of conduct').

2   See eg *Vine v Waltham Forest London Borough Council* [2000] 4 All ER 169, [2000] 1 WLR 2383, CA, where it was accepted that if the defendant had clearly displayed a prominent sign warning that cars would be clamped, then the clamping of the claimant's car would have been legal, as the claimant could then be taken to have consented to it. See also *Arthur v Anker* [1997] QB 564, [1996] 3 All ER 783, CA.

3   Eg under statutory authority: see *De Gondouin v Lewis* (1839) 10 Ad & El 117; *Jacobsohn v Blake* (1844) 6 Man & G 919; *Chic Fashions (West Wales) Ltd v Jones* [1968] 2 QB 299, [1968] 1 All ER 229, CA. There is a statutory right to distrain animals that stray onto the claimant's land: see the Animals Act 1971 s 7; and ANIMALS vol 2 (2008) PARAS 758–759.

4   For orders executed before 6 April 2014, the primary form of protection comes from the County Courts Act 1984 s 126. For orders executed after that date, protection is afforded by the Tribunals, Courts and Enforcement Act 2007 s 62(1), Sch 12. As to execution and enforcement procedures see further CIVIL PROCEDURE vol 12 (2009) PARA 1265 et seq.

5   As to conversion see PARA 604 et seq.

6   See the Torts (Interference with Goods) Act 1977 s 8; and PARA 656.

7   Torts (Interference with Goods) Act 1977 s 11(1). This therefore does not apply to negligent trespass (as to which see PARA 689).

8   Torts (Interference with Goods) Act 1977 s 10(1). See also PARA 659.

(v) Remedies for Trespass to Goods

694. Remedies available to claimant in trespass to goods. Where the defendant in a claim for trespass to goods is in possession of the claimant's chattel, the court has the discretion to make an order for the delivery of the chattel[1]. The exercise of such discretion is governed by the same principles discussed in relation to conversion[2]. The claimant in such cases may ask, in the alternative, for an order that the defendant deliver the chattel with an option to pay damages in lieu[3], or damages[4].

Where the defendant is not in possession of the chattel, the normal remedy will be an award of damages[5].

1 See the Torts (Interference with Goods) Act 1977 s 3(2)(a); and PARA 662.
2 See PARA 662. As to conversion see PARA 604 et seq.
3 See the Torts (Interference with Goods) Act 1977 s 3(2)(b); and PARA 662.
4 See the Torts (Interference with Goods) Act 1977 s 3(2)(c); and PARAS 662, 668. As to damages for trespass to goods see PARA 695. As to damages generally see further DAMAGES.
5 See PARA 695. The claimant may also apply for an injunction to prevent the act complained of being repeated: see eg *The Tubantia* [1924] P 78.

695. Damages for trespass to goods. In a claim for trespass to goods the claimant is entitled to recover damages[1] for the resultant deprivation[2], destruction or depreciation affecting the goods. He may also, subject to the appropriate rules of remoteness of loss[3], recover damages for loss of profits or loss of use sustained by him[4]. Where the interference is minor, and does not cause any substantive loss to the claimant, he will be entitled to nominal damages only[5]. Exemplary (or punitive) damages and aggravated damages may be awarded in certain instances[6].

1 Damages are awarded on the same basis as that in conversion, namely to compensate the claimant for his loss: see PARA 668 et seq. As to the compensatory nature of damages see DAMAGES vol 29 (2014) PARAS 318, 408.
2 *Mediana (Owners) v Comet (Owners, Master and Crew), The Mediana* [1900] AC 113, HL (full value of the chattel awarded in cases of total deprivation).
3 See DAMAGES vol 29 (2014) PARA 409 et seq.
4 *Page v Rattcliff* (1832) 1 LJCP 57.
5 *Kirk v Gregory* (1876) 1 Ex D 55. As to nominal damages see DAMAGES vol 29 (2014) PARAS 319–320.
6 See *R v IRC, ex p Rossminster Ltd* [1980] AC 952 at 1000–1001, [1980] 1 All ER 80 at 85, HL, per Lord Wilberforce. See also *White v WP Brown Ltd* (1983) Times, 29 September, County Court (damages of £775 for trespass to plaintiff's handbag by store detective who snatched it in unjustified attempt to search it). As to exemplary (or punitive) damages see DAMAGES vol 29 (2014) PARA 325 et seq. As to aggravated damages see DAMAGES vol 29 (2014) PARA 322 et seq.

7. INTELLECTUAL PROPERTY TORTS

696.   Infringement of copyright.   Infringements of copyright are actionable at the suit of either the owner[1] or the exclusive licensee of the copyright[2] (or both). The normal remedy for this tort is an injunction[3], together with which the claimant may claim an account of profits[4] or an inquiry as to damages[5].

1   See the Copyright, Designs and Patents Act 1988 s 96(1); and COPYRIGHT vol 23 (2013) PARA 956 et seq.
2   See the Copyright, Designs and Patents Act 1988 s 101: and COPYRIGHT vol 23 (2013) PARA 976 et seq.
3   As to the remedy of an injunction see COPYRIGHT vol 23 (2013) PARA 959 et seq. As to injunctions generally see CIVIL PROCEDURE vol 11 (2009) PARA 331 et seq.
4   As to the remedy of an account of profits see COPYRIGHT vol 23 (2013) PARAS 966, 976.
5   As to damages see COPYRIGHT vol 23 (2013) PARAS 966, 976. As to damages generally see DAMAGES.

697.   Infringement of a patent.   The registered proprietor of a patent or his exclusive licensee may sue in tort anyone who infringes the patent[1]. The remedies available are an injunction restraining further infringement, damages or, at the claimant's option, an account of profits, the delivery up or destruction of infringing articles, and a declaration that the patent is valid and has been infringed[2].

1   As to infringement of patents generally see PATENTS AND REGISTERED DESIGNS vol 79 (2014) PARA 499 et seq. As to proceedings for infringement see PATENTS AND REGISTERED DESIGNS vol 79 (2014) PARA 520 et seq.
2   See the Patents Act 1977 s 61; and PATENTS AND REGISTERED DESIGNS vol 79 (2014) PARA 522. As to injunctions generally see CIVIL PROCEDURE vol 11 (2009) PARA 331 et seq. As to damages generally see DAMAGES.

698.   Infringement of a trade mark.   Infringement of registered trade marks is a tort actionable at the suit of the proprietor or licensee[1]. The remedies may be an injunction restraining further infringements, damages or an account of profits, and an order for the delivery up of the offending articles[2].

1   See the Trade Marks Act 1994 ss 14, 30; and TRADE MARKS AND TRADE NAMES vol 97A (2014) PARA 398 et seq.
2   As to the infringement of registered trade marks see TRADE MARKS AND TRADE NAMES vol 97A (2014) PARA 66 et seq. As to injunctions generally see CIVIL PROCEDURE vol 11 (2009) PARA 331 et seq. As to damages generally see DAMAGES.

699.   Passing off.   A person is liable in tort if, where another person's goods or services have acquired a goodwill in the market and are known by some distinguishing name, mark or other indicium, he makes a misrepresentation (whether or not intentional) leading or likely to lead the public to believe that goods or services offered by him are goods or services of the other, and the other suffers damage as a result of the erroneous belief engendered by the misrepresentation[1].

1   As to passing off generally see TRADE MARKS AND TRADE NAMES vol 97A (2014) PARA 287 et seq.

700.   Breach of confidence.   A person who has received information in confidence is not allowed to take improper advantage of it[1]. Liability for breach of confidence arises where material communicated to the defendant has the necessary quality of confidence, it was communicated or became known to him in circumstances entailing an obligation of confidence, and he makes unauthorised use of it[2], unless there exists some just cause or excuse[3]. A successful claimant may be awarded an injunction[4], and either damages for past and future losses[5] or an account of profits[6].

Though the two causes of action overlap to some extent, liability for breach of confidence is to be distinguished from liability in the tort of unauthorised disclosure of personal information[7].

1 *Seager v Copydex Ltd* [1967] 2 All ER 415 at 417, [1967] 1 WLR 923 at 931, CA, per Lord Denning MR; *A-G v Observer Ltd, A-G v Times Newspapers Ltd* [1990] 1 AC 109, sub nom *A-G v Guardian Newspapers Ltd (No 2)* [1988] 3 All ER 545, HL. The law's protection of confidence was originally a matter of equity but breach of confidence is now arguably to be regarded as a tort: see eg *McKennitt v Ash* [2006] EWCA Civ 1714 at [8], [2008] QB 73 at [8], [2007] 3 WLR 194 at [8] per Buxton LJ. Cf *Kitechnology BV v Unicor GmbH Plastmaschinen* [1995] FSR 765 at 777–778, CA, per Evans LJ (denying derivation from tort and attributing jurisdiction to equity). As to confidentiality see generally CONFIDENCE AND INFORMATIONAL PRIVACY vol 19 (2011) PARA 68 et seq.
2 See CONFIDENCE AND INFORMATIONAL PRIVACY vol 19 (2011) PARAS 1, 68 et seq.
3 See CONFIDENCE AND INFORMATIONAL PRIVACY vol 19 (2011) PARA 73 et seq.
4 See CONFIDENCE AND INFORMATIONAL PRIVACY vol 19 (2011) PARAS 84–85. As to injunctions generally see CIVIL PROCEDURE vol 11 (2009) PARA 331 et seq.
5 See CONFIDENCE AND INFORMATIONAL PRIVACY vol 19 (2011) PARA 88.
6 See CONFIDENCE AND INFORMATIONAL PRIVACY vol 19 (2011) PARA 89. As to other remedies that may be available see CONFIDENCE AND INFORMATIONAL PRIVACY vol 19 (2011) PARA 83 et seq.
7 *OBG Ltd v Allan* [2007] UKHL 21 at [118], [2008] 1 AC 1 at [118], [2007] 4 All ER 545 at [118] per Lord Hoffmann, and at [255] per Lord Nicholls. As to the tort of unauthorised disclosure of private information see PARA 562. As to the interrelationship of the two causes of action see also *HRH Prince of Wales v Associated Newspapers Ltd* [2006] EWCA Civ 1776, [2008] Ch 57, [2007] 2 All ER 139.

8. ECONOMIC TORTS

(1) TYPES OF ECONOMIC TORTS

701. Intentional wrongdoing resulting in economic loss. Economic torts is the collective name conventionally applied to the various causes of action arising in respect of intentional wrongdoing resulting in economic loss. The specific torts most normally referred to are the tort of procuring breach of contract[1], the tort of causing loss by unlawful means[2], the tort of intimidation[3] and the tort of conspiracy[4].

1 See PARA 703 et seq.
2 See PARA 710.
3 See PARA 711.
4 See PARA 712 et seq.

702. Liability for economic torts restricted by trade dispute immunities. In practice, liability for the economic torts[1] is significantly restricted by the statutory trade disputes immunities[2]. An act done by a person in contemplation or furtherance of a trade dispute is not actionable in tort on the ground only that it induces another person to break a contract or interferes or induces another person to interfere with its performance, or that it consists in his threatening that a contract (whether one to which he is a party or not) will be broken or its performance interfered with, or that he will induce another person to break a contract or interfere with its performance[3]. An agreement or combination by two or more persons to do or procure the doing of any act in contemplation or furtherance of a trade dispute is not actionable in the tort of conspiracy if the act is one which, if done without any such agreement or combination, would not be actionable in tort[4].

1 As to the economic torts see PARA 701.
2 See EMPLOYMENT vol 41A (2014) PARA 1359 et seq.
3 See the Trade Union and Labour Relations (Consolidation) Act 1992 s 219(1); and EMPLOYMENT vol 41A (2014) PARAS 1343, 1363.
4 See the Trade Union and Labour Relations (Consolidation) Act 1992 s 219(2). See also EMPLOYMENT vol 41A (2014) PARA 1363. As to trade disputes in general see EMPLOYMENT vol 41A (2014) PARA 1211 et seq.

(2) INDUCING BREACH OF CONTRACT

703. Essential elements of inducing breach of contract. Where one person intentionally[1] induces or procures[2] a second person[3] to commit a breach of contract[4] against a third person, so that the third person suffers damage[5], the first commits a wrong actionable at the suit of the third[6], unless the inducement is justifiable[7]. Merely to prevent performance of a contract, or otherwise to interfere with its performance, is not actionable in the tort of procuring breach of contract, but may give rise to liability in the distinct tort of causing loss by unlawful means[8] if the relevant requirements are satisfied[9].

1 See PARA 708.
2 See PARA 706. The tort is sometimes referred to as the tort of procuring breach of contract: see eg *DC Thomson & Co Ltd v Deakin* [1952] Ch 646 at 676–677, [1952] 2 All ER 361 at 368 per Evershed MR, and at 694 and 383 per Morris LJ; *Middlebrook Mushrooms Ltd v Transport and General Workers' Union* [1993] ICR 612 at 618, [1993] IRLR 232 at 234, CA, per Neill LJ; *JT Stratford & Son Ltd v Lindley* [1965] AC 269 at 333, [1964] 3 All ER 102 at 112, HL, per

Lord Pearce, at 338 and 115 per Lord Upjohn, and at 342 and 118 per Lord Donovan; *Boxfoldia Ltd v National Graphical Association (1982)* [1988] ICR 752, [1988] IRLR 383.

3   The person induced cannot sue: *Boulting v Association of Cinematograph, Television and Allied Technicians* [1963] 2 QB 606 at 639–640, [1963] 1 All ER 716 at 731, CA, per Upjohn LJ. An employee acting bona fide within the scope of his authority and company directors acting as a board cannot be liable for inducing the employer or company to act in breach of contract with a third party: see *Said v Butt* [1920] 3 KB 497; *DC Thomson & Co Ltd v Deakin* [1952] Ch 646 at 680–681, [1952] 2 All ER 361 at 369–370, CA, per Evershed MR; *G Scammell & Nephew Ltd v Hurley* [1929] 1 KB 419, CA. They may, however, be liable for conspiracy in an appropriate case: *De Jetley Marks v Greenwood* [1936] 1 All ER 863. As to the tort of conspiracy see PARAS 712–715.

4   See PARA 704; and CONTRACT.

5   Actual damage is the gist of the claim: *National Phonograph Co Ltd v Edison-Bell Consolidated Phonograph Co Ltd* [1908] 1 Ch 335 at 369–370, CA, per Kennedy LJ; *Sefton v Tophams Ltd* [1965] Ch 1140 at 1206, [1965] 3 All ER 1 at 21, CA, per Russell LJ, and at 1196 and 15 per Harman LJ (revsd on different grounds [1967] 1 AC 50, [1966] 1 All ER 1039, HL); *Jones Bros (Hunstanton) Ltd v Stevens* [1955] 1 QB 275 at 281–283, [1954] 3 All ER 677 at 680–681, CA, per Lord Goddard CJ. Special damage in the narrow sense of the words is not required: see *National Phonograph Co Ltd v Edison-Bell Consolidated Phonograph Co Ltd* [1908] 1 Ch 335 at 370, CA, per Kennedy LJ; *British Industrial Plastics Ltd v Ferguson* [1938] 4 All ER 504 at 511, CA, per Slesser LJ. As to special damages generally see DAMAGES vol 29 (2014) PARA 317.

6   *Lumley v Gye* (1853) 2 E & B 216; *Allen v Flood* [1898] AC 1 at 96, HL, per Lord Watson; *Read v Friendly Society of Operative Stonemasons of England, Ireland and Wales* [1902] 2 KB 732 at 738, CA, per Collins MR; *South Wales Miners' Federation v Glamorgan Coal Co Ltd* [1905] AC 239, HL; *OBG Ltd v Allan* [2007] UKHL 21 at [3], [2008] 1 AC 1 at [3], [2007] 4 All ER 545 at [3] et seq per Lord Hoffmann, and at [168] et seq per Lord Nicholls.

     The tort may be committed by inducing a second person to enter into a contract that is inconsistent with his obligations under an existing contract with a third person: see *British Motor Trade Association v Salvadori* [1949] Ch 556, [1949] 1 All ER 208; *British Motor Trade Association v Gray* 1951 SC 586, Ct of Sess; *Rickless v United Artists Corpn* [1988] QB 40, [1987] 1 All ER 679, CA.

7   As to justification see PARA 707. As to the defence that the act was done in contemplation or furtherance of a trade dispute see PARA 702; and EMPLOYMENT vol 41A (2014) PARA 1359. As to the statutory exclusion of that defence see EMPLOYMENT vol 41A (2014) PARA 1363 et seq.

8   As to causing loss by unlawful means see PARA 710.

9   *OBG Ltd v Allan* [2007] UKHL 21, [2008] 1 AC 1, [2007] 4 All ER 545, rejecting the approach of Lord Denning MR in *Torquay Hotel Co Ltd v Cousins* [1969] 2 Ch 106 at 138, [1969] 1 All ER 522 at 530, CA.

704. Requirement of a breach of contract. For there to be an inducement to breach of contract, the defendant must actually induce a breach of contract[1] or procure the violation of certain other private law obligations[2]. Procuring the breach of a secondary obligation arising by reason of the non-performance of a primary obligation under a contract will suffice[3]. It is immaterial that the breach procured is not itself actionable in damages because the contract contains a force majeure clause protecting the party in breach or some other exemption from liability[4]. But it is not tortious merely to induce another person not to enter into a contract[5] or to induce another person lawfully to terminate a contract[6]. Inducing another person to suspend contractual relations with the claimant may be lawful or unlawful depending on whether or not this is allowed by the contract[7]. But no liability arises merely for preventing or otherwise interfering with another person's performance of his contractual obligations[8].

1   There must be some evidence, even if slight, of the contract and its terms: *Middlebrook Mushrooms Ltd v Transport and General Workers' Union* [1993] ICR 612, [1993] IRLR 232, CA. See also *Daily Mirror Newspapers Ltd v Gardner* [1968] 2 QB 762 at 779–780, [1968] 2 All ER 163 at 167–168, CA, per Lord Denning MR, and at 783–784 and 169–170 per Davies LJ; *Dimbleby & Sons Ltd v National Union of Journalists* [1984] 1 All ER 751 at 757, [1984] 1 WLR 427 at 434, HL, per Lord Diplock; *Solihull Metropolitan Borough v National Union of Teachers* [1985] IRLR 211. As to breach of contract generally see CONTRACT.

2   See e g *Boulting v Association of Cinematograph, Television and Allied Technicians* [1963] 2 QB 606, [1963] 1 All ER 716, CA (inducing breach of company director's fiduciary duty); *Prudential Assurance Co Ltd v Lorenz* (1971) 11 KIR 78 (inducing breach of duty of agent); *Bent's Brewery Co Ltd v Hogan* [1945] 2 All ER 570 (inducing breach of confidence). It is not a tort to induce a breach of trust: *Metall and Rohstoff AG v Donaldson Lufkin & Jenrette Inc* [1990] 1 QB 391 at 481, [1989] 3 All ER 14 at 57–58, CA, per Slade LJ. Nor is it tortious to procure a person's unfair dismissal from employment: *Wilson v Housing Corpn* [1998] ICR 151, [1997] IRLR 346.

3   *Law Debenture Trust Corpn Ltd v Ural Caspian Oil Ltd* [1995] Ch 152, [1995] 1 All ER 157, CA.

4   *Torquay Hotel Co Ltd v Cousins* [1969] 2 Ch 106, [1969] 1 All ER 522, CA; *Merkur Island Shipping Corpn v Laughton* [1983] 2 AC 570 at 608, [1983] 2 All ER 189 at 195, HL, per Lord Diplock; *Associated British Ports v Transport and General Workers' Union* [1989] 3 All ER 796 at 806, [1989] 1 WLR 939 at 952, CA, per Neill LJ, and at 816 and 963 per Stuart-Smith LJ (revsd on other grounds [1989] 3 All ER 822, [1989] 1 WLR 939 at 970, HL). See also *Sefton v Tophams Ltd* [1965] Ch 1140, [1965] 3 All ER 1, CA; revsd [1967] 1 AC 50, [1966] 1 All ER 1039, HL.

5   *Allen v Flood* [1898] AC 1, HL; *Midland Cold Storage Ltd v Steer* [1972] Ch 630, [1972] 3 All ER 941.

6   *White v Riley* [1921] 1 Ch 1; *McManus v Bowes* [1938] 1 KB 98 at 127, [1937] 3 All ER 227 at 239, CA, per Slesser LJ; *F Bowles & Sons Ltd v Lindley* [1965] 1 Lloyd's Rep 207; *Cutsforth v Mansfield Inns Ltd* [1986] 1 All ER 577, [1986] 1 WLR 558. In the employment context, whether or not a strike notice is properly categorised as notice of termination in accordance with the terms of the employment contract depends on the meaning and effect of the words used in the contract in which they were used: *Boxfoldia Ltd v National Graphical Association (1982)* [1988] IRLR 383 at 385 per Saville J. Cf *Barretts and Baird (Wholesale) Ltd v Institution of Professional Civil Servants* [1987] IRLR 3 at 8–9 per Henry J; *Morgan v Fry* [1968] 2 QB 710 at 731, [1968] 3 All ER 452 at 460, CA, per Davies LJ and at 738–739 and 465 per Russell LJ; *Simmons v Hoover Ltd* [1977] QB 284, [1977] 1 All ER 775, EAT. Depending on the intention of the parties, individual contracts of employment may incorporate collective agreements covering strikes: *Alexander v Standard Telephones and Cables Ltd (No 2)* [1991] IRLR 286; *Lee v GEC Plessey Telecommunications* [1993] IRLR 383; c f *National Coal Board v National Union of Mineworkers* [1986] ICR 736, [1986] IRLR 439. See also the Trade Union and Labour Relations (Consolidation) Act 1992 ss 179(1), 180; and EMPLOYMENT vol 41A (2014) PARAS 1177, 1375.

      See also *Tigris International NV v China Southern Airlines Co Ltd* [2013] EWHC 2211 (Comm), [2013] All ER (D) 342 (Jul) (no breach of contract to purchase aircraft).

7   See *Rookes v Barnard* [1964] AC 1129, [1964] 1 All ER 367, HL (suspension of employee lawful); *Daily Mirror Newspapers Ltd v Gardner* [1968] 2 QB 762, [1968] 2 All ER 163, CA (suspension of supply a breach of contract).

8   *OBG Ltd v Allan* [2007] UKHL 21, [2008] 1 AC 1, [2007] 4 All ER 545, disapproving dicta in *GWK Ltd v Dunlop Rubber Co Ltd* (1926) 42 TLR 376 at 377, CA, per Lord Hewart CJ; *Torquay Hotel Co Ltd v Cousins* [1969] 2 Ch 106 at 138, [1969] 1 All ER 522 at 530, CA, per Lord Denning MR; *Merkur Island Shipping Corpn v Laughton* [1983] 2 AC 570 at 608, [1983] 2 All ER 189 at 195, HL, per Lord Diplock. Where unlawful means are employed, liability may arise in the separate tort of causing loss by unlawful means: see PARA 710.

705. Nature of the contract whose breach is induced. The precise nature of the contract whose breach is induced is immaterial[1], provided it is legally valid[2]. Liability may arise in respect of the breach of negative as well as positive contractual obligations[3], and the breach of an ongoing contractual obligation persisting after the termination of the relationship out of which it arose[4]. Conversely, liability cannot be established if the contract is unilateral and imposes no obligations on the person whose conduct was induced or procured by the defendant[5]. Nor can liability arise if the contract is void, whether because one of the parties lacks the capacity to contract[6], or because it is a gaming contract[7], or tainted with illegality[8]. Where a contract is not void but only voidable, this would appear to prevent liability for inducing its breach if the party induced was the one entitled to avoid it[9], but arguably not if it was the claimant who enjoyed the right to avoid.

1 *Lumley v Gye* (1853) 2 E & B 216; *Bowen v Hall* (1881) 6 QBD 333, CA; *Temperton v Russell* [1893] 1 QB 715, CA; *Allen v Flood* [1898] AC 1 at 126, HL, per Lord Herschell; *Quinn v Leathem* [1901] AC 495, HL; *National Phonograph Co Ltd v Edison-Bell Consolidated Phonograph Co Ltd* [1908] 1 Ch 335 at 366, CA, per Kennedy LJ. The liability applies not just to contracts of service and contracts for services but also (eg) to contracts for the conveyance of land: see eg *Smith v Morrison* [1974] 1 All ER 957, [1974] 1 WLR 659 (no liability on the facts). As to breach of contract generally see CONTRACT.

2 As to the requirements for legal validity of contracts see CONTRACT vol 22 (2012) PARA 231 et seq.

3 See eg *British Motor Trade Association v Salvadori* [1949] Ch 556, [1949] 1 All ER 208; *Rickless v United Artists Corpn* [1988] QB 40, [1987] 1 All ER 679, CA.

4 *Rickless v United Artists Corpn* [1988] QB 40 at 58, [1987] 1 All ER 679 at 698, CA, per Bingham LJ (citing the familiar example of a valid covenant against competition for 12 months after the termination of a person's employment).

5 *Dimbleby & Sons Ltd v National Union of Journalists* [1984] 1 All ER 751 at 757, [1984] 1 WLR 427 at 434, HL, per Lord Diplock.

6 *De Francesco v Barnum* (1890) 45 ChD 430. As to capacity to contract generally see CONTRACT vol 22 (2012) PARA 232.

7 *Joe Lee Ltd v Dalmeny* [1927] 1 Ch 300; *Said v Butt* [1920] 3 KB 497; *Associated British Ports v Transport and General Workers' Union* [1989] 3 All ER 796 at 816, [1989] 1 WLR 939 at 964, CA, per Stuart-Smith LJ (revsd on other grounds [1989] 3 All ER 822, [1989] 1 WLR 939 at 970, HL). As to gaming contracts generally see LICENSING AND GAMBLING vol 67 (2008) PARA 319 et seq.

8 *British Motor Trade Association v Gray* 1951 SC 586, Ct of Sess (covenants in restraint of trade); *Esso Petroleum Co Ltd v Kingswood Motors (Addlestone) Ltd* [1974] QB 142, [1973] 3 All ER 1057, DC (contravention of EU competition law). As to illegality in contracts generally see CONTRACT vol 22 (2012) PARA 424 et seq.

9 *Proform Sports Management Ltd v Proactive Sports Management Ltd* [2006] EWHC 2812 (Ch), [2007] 1 All ER 542. The contrary approach had previously been adopted in *Keane v Boycott* (1795) 2 Hy Bl 511, which was not cited to the court in *Proform Sports Management Ltd v Proactive Sports Management Ltd* [2006] EWHC 2812, [2007] 1 All ER 542. The proposed distinction between void and voidable contracts was doubted by Ferris J in *Essex Electric (Pte) Ltd v IPC Computers (UK) Ltd* [1991] FSR 690 at 709–710. As to void and voidable contracts see further CONTRACT vol 22 (2012) PARA 207.

706. Inducement to breach contract. There is an inducement if the breaking of the contract is fairly attributable to influence by way of pressure, persuasion or procuration brought to bear on the mind of the contract breaker by the defendant[1]. It is immaterial whether the inducement is direct or indirect[2], or whether it is by way of threat[3] or positive incentive[4]. The fact that an inducement to break a contract is couched as an irresistible embargo rather than in terms of seduction does not make it any the less an inducement[5]. There is no significant distinction to be made between advice and persuasion[6], nor need there be direct communication between the defendant and the contract breaker[7]. Indeed merely tacit encouragement may suffice[8].

1 *DC Thomson & Co Ltd v Deakin* [1952] Ch 646 at 686, [1952] 2 All ER 361 at 373, CA, per Sir Raymond Evershed MR, and at 693 and 378 per Jenkins LJ; *Camellia Tanker Ltd SA v International Transport Workers Federation* [1976] ICR 274, [1976] IRLR 190, CA. As to breach of contract generally see CONTRACT.

2 *OBG Ltd v Allan* [2007] UKHL 21 at [34] et seq, [2008] 1 AC 1 at [34] et seq, [2007] 4 All ER 545 at [34] et seq per Lord Hoffmann.

3 See eg *Emerald Construction Co Ltd v Lowthian* [1966] 1 All ER 1013, [1966] 1 WLR 691, CA; *Patrick Stevedores Operation Pty Ltd v International Transport Workers' Federation* [1998] 2 Lloyd's Rep 523; *Dimbleby & Sons Ltd v National Union of Journalists* [1984] 1 All ER 751, [1984] 1 WLR 427, HL.

4 See eg *South Wales Miners' Federation v Glamorgan Coal Co* [1905] AC 239, HL (offer of improved conditions of employment).

5 *JT Stratford & Son v Lindley* [1965] AC 269 at 333, [1964] 3 All ER 102 at 112, HL, per Lord Pearce.

6   *Torquay Hotel Co Ltd v Cousins* [1969] 2 Ch 106 at 147, [1969] 1 All ER 522 at 537–538, CA, per Winn LJ; *Camden Nominees Ltd v Forcey* [1940] Ch 352 at 366, sub nom *Camden Nominees Ltd v Slack* [1940] 2 All ER 1 at 11 per Simonds J; but cf *DC Thomson & Co Ltd v Deakin* [1952] Ch 646 at 686, [1952] 2 All ER 361 at 373, CA, per Sir Raymond Evershed MR.

7   See eg *Daily Mirror Newspapers Ltd v Gardner* [1968] 2 QB 762, [1968] 2 All ER 163, CA (persuasion relayed via third party).

8   See eg *Union Traffic Ltd v Transport and General Workers' Union* [1989] ICR 98 at 106, CA, per Bingham LJ (picketing); *Smithies v National Association of Operative Plasterers* [1909] 1 KB 310 (union providing strike pay to its members).

707. When inducement to breach of contract is justifiable. A person inducing a breach of contract commits no actionable wrong if his conduct is justified[1]. However, the limits of this defence have not been precisely defined, and regard must be had to the individual circumstances of each case[2]. Examples of situations in which justification may be proved are where the person inducing acts in accordance with a duty[3], or where the contract broken is one which cannot be carried out without infringing his contractual rights[4]. However, A is not justified in procuring B to breach his contract with C merely as retaliation for C's breach of his contract with A[5].

It is not a sufficient justification that the person who procured or encouraged the breach did not, in so doing, act maliciously, and had no desire to injure the claimant[6]. Nor is it sufficient that he honestly believed at the time when he procured or encouraged the breach that it was for the common interest of himself and the contract breaker that the contract breaker should breach the contract[7], while the fact that the person procuring or encouraging the breach owes the contract breaker a duty to advise him as to his position and dealings as regards the other contracting party does not excuse him from liability if the object of the advice is to procure or encourage what is illegal[8].

The inducing of a breach of contract which may lead to immorality has been held to be justified[9], but it seems that the defence will arise only if the facts are very strong[10].

1   See eg *Quinn v Leathem* [1901] AC 495 at 510, HL, per Lord Macnaghten; *South Wales Miners' Federation v Glamorgan Coal Co Ltd* [1905] AC 239, HL; *Smithies v National Association of Operative Plasterers* [1909] 1 KB 310, CA; *Camden Nominees Ltd v Forcey* [1940] Ch 352 at 366, sub nom *Camden Nominees Ltd v Slack* [1940] 2 All ER 1 at 11 per Simonds J; *Crofter Hand Woven Harris Tweed Co Ltd v Veitch* [1942] AC 435 at 442–443, [1942] 1 All ER 142 at 148, HL, per Viscount Simon LC, and at 495–496 and 175 per Lord Porter; *Edwin Hill & Partners (a firm) v First National Finance Corpn plc* [1988] 3 All ER 801, [1989] 1 WLR 225, CA. As to justification where the defendant procures the breach of contract by unlawful means see PARA 710.
     As to breach of contract generally see CONTRACT.

2   *Glamorgan Coal Co Ltd v South Wales Miners' Federation* [1903] 2 KB 545 at 573–574, CA, per Romer LJ (affd *South Wales Miners' Federation v Glamorgan Coal Co Ltd* [1905] AC 239, HL); *Crofter Hand Woven Harris Tweed Co Ltd v Veitch* [1942] AC 435 at 495–496, [1942] 1 All ER 142 at 175, HL, per Lord Porter.

3   *Brimelow v Casson* [1924] 1 Ch 302, where there was a moral duty to the defendant's members and possibly to the public. See also *De Jetley Marks v Lord Greenwood* [1936] 1 All ER 863 at 873 per Porter J; *Pritchard v Briggs* [1980] Ch 338 at 415–417, [1980] 1 All ER 294 at 326–328, CA, per Goff LJ. Cf *Timeplan Education Group v National Union of Teachers* [1997] IRLR 457 at [31], CA, per Peter Gibson LJ.

4   *Edwin Hill & Partners (a firm) v First National Finance Corpn plc* [1988] 3 All ER 801, [1989] 1 WLR 225, CA; *Meretz Investments NV v ACP Ltd* [2006] EWHC 74 (Ch), [2007] Ch 197, [2006] 3 All ER 1029 (revsd on other grounds [2007] EWCA Civ 1303, [2008] Ch 244, [2008] 2 WLR 904). See also *Smithies v National Association of Operative Plasterers* [1909] 1 KB 310 at 337, CA, per Buckley LJ; *Crofter Hand Woven Harris Tweed Co Ltd v Veitch* [1942] AC 435 at 495–496, [1942] 1 All ER 142 at 175, HL, per Lord Porter.

5   *Smithies v National Association of Operative Plasterers* [1909] 1 KB 310 at 337, 341, CA.

6 *Read v Friendly Society of Operative Stonemasons of England, Ireland and Wales* [1902] 2 KB
   88 at 96 per Darling J; *Glamorgan Coal Co v South Wales Miners' Federation* [1903] 2 KB 545
   at 574, CA, per Romer LJ (affd [1905] AC 239, HL); *Greig v Insole, World Series Cricket
   Pty Ltd v Insole* [1978] 3 All ER 449 at 485, [1978] 1 WLR 302 at 332 per Slade J; *Edwin Hill
   & Partners v First National Finance Corpn plc* [1988] 3 All ER 801, [1989] 1 WLR 225.
7 *South Wales Miners' Federation v Glamorgan Coal Co Ltd* [1905] AC 239, HL.
8 *South Wales Miners' Federation v Glamorgan Coal Co Ltd* [1905] AC 239, HL.
9 *Brimelow v Casson* [1924] 1 Ch 302; *Crofter Hand Woven Harris Tweed Co Ltd v Veitch*
   [1942] AC 435 at 495–496, [1942] 1 All ER 142 at 175, HL, per Lord Porter.
10 See *Camden Nominees Ltd v Forcey* [1940] Ch 352 at 366, sub nom *Camden Nominees Ltd v
   Slack* [1940] 2 All ER 1 at 11 per Simonds J; *Pritchard v Briggs* [1980] Ch 338 at 416, [1980]
   1 All ER 294 at 328, CA, per Goff LJ.

708. Intention to procure breach of contract. For there to be a successful
claim for inducing breach of contract, it must be shown that the defendant knew
of the existence of the contract and intended to procure its breach[1], but malice in
the sense of spite or ill-will is not required[2]; nor is it necessary to show that the
defendant intended to cause the claimant harm as a result of the breach[3]. The
defendant's actual knowledge of the contractual obligation in question is
required; constructive knowledge will not do[4]. The defendant need not have
exact knowledge of all the terms of the contract[5], but, even if he knows a
contract exists, he may escape liability if mistaken as to the scope of the
contractual obligation and unaware therefore that he is procuring its breach[6]. It
is not enough that the defendant knows he is procuring an act which, as a matter
of law or construction of the contract, is a breach, nor that he ought reasonably
to realise that it will have this effect: he must actually realise that it will have
such effect[7]. Liability does not attach to a person who acts negligently[8] or in a
'muddleheaded' manner[9]. However, it is enough to establish the tort that the
defendant consciously turned a blind eye to the existence of the contract and
induced the breach recklessly, indifferent whether it was a breach or not[10].

1 *White v Riley* [1921] 1 Ch 1 at 16, CA, per Lord Sterndale MR; *DC Thomson & Co Ltd v
   Deakin* [1952] Ch 646 at 697, [1952] 2 All ER 361 at 379, CA, per Jenkins LJ; *Rookes v
   Barnard* [1964] AC 1129 at 1212, [1964] 1 All ER 367 at 401, HL, per Lord Devlin; *Emerald
   Construction Co Ltd v Lowthian* [1966] 1 All ER 1013, [1966] 1 WLR 691, CA; *OBG Ltd v
   Allan* [2007] UKHL 21 at [39], [2008] 1 AC 1 at [39], [2007] 4 All ER 545 at [39] et seq per
   Lord Hoffmann, and at [191] et seq per Lord Nicholls; *Meretz Investments NV v ACP Ltd*
   [2007] EWCA Civ 1303, [2008] Ch 244, [2008] 2 WLR 904. As to breach of contract generally
   see CONTRACT.
2 *Allen v Flood* [1898] AC 1 at 95, HL, per Lord Watson, at 123 per Lord Herschell and at 154
   per Lord Macnaghten; *South Wales Miners' Federation v Glamorgan Coal Co Ltd* [1905] AC
   239 at 246, HL, per Lord Macnaghten; *OBG Ltd v Allan* [2007] UKHL 21 at [8], [2008] 1 AC
   1 at [8], [2007] 4 All ER 545 at [8] per Lord Hoffmann.
3 *OBG Ltd v Allan* [2007] UKHL 21 at [8], [2008] 1 AC 1 at [8], [2007] 4 All ER 545 at [8] per
   Lord Hoffmann, and at [192] per Lord Nicholls. In this respect, the tort of inducing a breach of
   contract is to be distinguished from the tort of causing loss by unlawful means: see PARA 710.
4 *Swiss Bank Corpn v Lloyds Bank Ltd* [1979] Ch 548 at 572, [1979] 2 All ER 853 at 871 per
   Browne-Wilkinson J; *OBG Ltd v Allan* [2007] UKHL 21, [2008] 1 AC 1, [2007] 4 All ER 545.
   Knowledge of past contracts is not the same as knowledge of continuing contractual relations:
   see *TimePlan Education Group Ltd v National Union of Teachers* [1997] IRLR 457, CA.
5 *JT Stratford & Son Ltd v Lindley* [1965] AC 269, [1964] 3 All ER 102, HL; *Emerald
   Construction Co Ltd v Lowthian* [1966] 1 All ER 1013, [1966] 1 WLR 691, CA; *Daily Mirror
   Newspapers Ltd v Gardner* [1968] 2 QB 762, [1968] 2 All ER 163, CA; *Greig v Insole, World
   Series Cricket Pty Ltd v Insole* [1978] 3 All ER 449, [1978] 1 WLR 302.
6 *Pritchard v Briggs* [1980] Ch 338, [1980] 1 All ER 294, CA. See also *White v Riley* [1921]
   1 Ch 1 at 26, CA, per Warrington LJ.
7 *OBG Ltd v Allan* [2007] UKHL 21 at [39], [2008] 1 AC 1 at [39], [2007] 4 All ER 545 at [39]
   per Lord Hoffmann. It is immaterial that the defendant's belief that the outcome he seeks will
   involve no breach of contract is mistaken in law: *OBG Ltd v Allan* [2007] UKHL 21 at [202],

[2008] 1 AC 1 at [202], [2007] 4 All ER 545 at [202] per Lord Nicholls. Earlier decisions taking a contrary view (see eg *Greig v Insole, World Series Cricket Pty Ltd v Insole* [1978] 3 All ER 449 at 494, [1978] 1 WLR 302 at 344 per Slade J; *Pritchard v Briggs* [1980] Ch 338 at 414–415, [1980] 1 All ER 294 at 328, CA, per Goff LJ; *Solihull Metropolitan Borough v National Union of Teachers* [1985] IRLR 211 at 213 per Warner J) must be considered impliedly disapproved. See also *Meretz Investments NV v ACP Ltd* [2007] EWCA Civ 1303, [2008] Ch 244, [2008] 2 WLR 904.

8   *OBG Ltd v Allan* [2007] UKHL 21 at [41], [2008] 1 AC 1 at [41], [2007] 4 All ER 545 at [41] per Lord Hoffmann, and at [191] per Lord Nicholls.

9   *British Industrial Plastics Ltd v Ferguson* [1940] 1 All ER 479; *Jones Bros (Hunstanton) Ltd v Stevens* [1955] 1 QB 275 at 280, [1954] 3 All ER 677 at 681–682, per Lord Goddard CJ; *OBG Ltd v Allan* [2007] UKHL 21 at [202], [2008] 1 AC 1 at [202], [2007] 4 All ER 545 at [202] per Lord Nicholls.

10 *Emerald Construction Co Ltd v Lowthian* [1966] 1 All ER 1013 at 1017, [1966] 1 WLR 691 at 701, CA, per Lord Denning MR; *Daily Mirror Newspapers Ltd v Gardner* [1968] 2 QB 762 at 781, [1968] 2 All ER 163 at 168, CA, per Lord Denning MR, and at 784 and 170 per Davies LJ; *Boxfoldia Ltd v National Graphical Association (1982)* [1988] IRLR 383 at 386 per Saville J; *OBG Ltd v Allan* [2007] UKHL 21 at [41], [2008] 1 AC 1 at [41], [2007] 4 All ER 545 at [41] per Lord Hoffmann.

709.   Remedies for inducing breach of contract.   Where a claimant is successful in his action for inducing breach of contract, he is prima facie entitled to damages for loss suffered as a result of the tort and an injunction to prevent the continuation or repetition of the tortious conduct[1]. Damages for inducing breach of contract are not necessarily calculated on the same basis as that used to calculate the damages for the actual breach, and may exceed the damages recoverable in an action for breach of contract[2]. The award of damages for inducing breach of contract is 'at large'[3]. The heads of recoverable damage include out-of-pocket expenditure[4], loss of profit[5] and, in an appropriate case, non-pecuniary loss[6].

As it is an essential part of the cause of action that the claimant should have sustained some loss[7], he cannot maintain a claim against the person inducing the breach of contract where he has already been indemnified for his loss by the contract breaker[8].

1   As to injunctions against inducing breach of contract see eg *Lumley v Gye* (1853) 2 E & B 216; *JT Stratford & Son Ltd v Lindley* [1965] AC 269, [1964] 3 All ER 102, HL; *Torquay Hotel Co Ltd v Cousins* [1969] 2 Ch 106, [1969] 1 All ER 522, CA. The court has power to grant a mandatory injunction where there is interference which is deliberate and direct, and where damages would be an inadequate remedy: see *Esso Petroleum Co Ltd v Kingswood Motors (Addlestone) Ltd* [1974] QB 142, [1973] 3 All ER 1057, DC. The claimant may in the same action join the contract breaker as a co-defendant and claim, as against him, an injunction only: see eg *De Francesco v Barnum* (1890) 45 ChD 430. As to breach of contract generally see CONTRACT.
    As to injunctions generally see CIVIL PROCEDURE vol 11 (2009) PARA 331 et seq. As to damages generally see DAMAGES.

2   *Lumley v Gye* (1853) 2 E & B 216 at 230 per Crompton J, and at 233–234 per Erle J. As the tort is one of intention it appears that all direct losses, whether foreseeable or not, may be recovered: see *Smith New Court Securities Ltd v Citibank NA* [1997] AC 254 at 279–280, sub nom *Smith New Court Securities Ltd v Scrimgeour Vickers (Asset Management) Ltd* [1996] 4 All ER 769 at 789, HL, per Lord Steyn. See also DAMAGES vol 29 (2014) PARA 411.
    Where the defendant has induced the claimant's employee to leave his employment in breach of contract and work for the defendant instead, the claimant may waive the tort and sue in restitution for the value of the employee's services: *Lightly v Clouston* (1808) 1 Taunt 112; *Foster v Stewart* (1814) 3 M & S 191.
    As to the measure of damages for breach of contract generally see DAMAGES vol 29 (2014) PARA 499 et seq.

3   *Exchange Telegraph Co Ltd v Gregory & Co Ltd* [1896] 1 QB 147 at 153, CA, per Lord Esher MR; *GWK Ltd v Dunlop Rubber Co Ltd* (1926) 42 TLR 593, CA.

4 See eg *British Motor Trade Association v Salvadori* [1949] Ch 556, [1949] 1 All ER 208 (expense of detecting the tort); *Boxfoldia Ltd v National Graphical Association (1982)* [1988] ICR 752, [1988] IRLR 383 (redundancy payments to non-striking employees who had to be laid off).

5 See eg *Exchange Telegraph Co Ltd v Gregory & Co Ltd* [1896] 1 QB 147, CA; *Goldsoll v Goldman* [1914] 2 Ch 603 (affd [1915] 1 Ch 292, CA). Damages have also been awarded for harm to commercial reputation: see *GWK v Dunlop Rubber Co* (1926) 42 TLR 376 (on appeal at (1926) 42 TLR 593, CA).

6 See *Pratt v British Medical Association* [1919] 1 KB 244; but c f *Lonrho plc v Fayed (No 5)* [1994] 1 All ER 188, [1993] 1 WLR 1489, CA.

7 *Exchange Telegraph Co Ltd v Gregory & Co Ltd* [1896] 1 QB 147, CA; *Goldsoll v Goldman* [1914] 2 Ch 603 (affd [1915] 1 Ch 292, CA); *Bents Brewery Co Ltd v Hogan* [1945] 2 All ER 570; *Jones Bros (Hunstanton) Ltd v Stevens* [1955] 1 QB 275, [1954] 3 All ER 677, CA. See also PARA 703 note 5; and DAMAGES vol 29 (2014) PARA 341.

8 *Bird v Randall* (1762) 3 Burr 1345.

(3) UNLAWFUL INTERFERENCE WITH ECONOMIC INTERESTS

(i) Unlawful Interference causing Loss

710. Causing loss by unlawful means. English law does not afford a claim in tort to every person who suffers harm or loss as the inevitable consequence of the unlawful, intentional and positive acts of another[1], but it is a tort intentionally to cause another person loss by unlawful means[2]. Liability for the use of unlawful means does not depend upon the existence of contractual relations: it is sufficient that the intended consequence of the wrongful act is damage in any form, including damage to economic expectations[3]. Means employed to injure the claimant via the agency of a third party are unlawful in the present context only if they are actionable by the third party, or would have been so actionable had the third party suffered loss, and not if they merely involve infringement of a penal or regulatory statute not intended to be actionable in private law[4]. A breach of contract constitutes unlawful means[5], so where A induces B to breach his contract with C, preventing C from performing his contract with D, D may have a claim against A for causing him loss by unlawful means[6].

The defendant may be liable even though it is not his purpose to cause loss to the claimant, and he does so only to further his own interests, but he is not liable for loss that is neither a desired end nor a means of attaining a desired end but merely a foreseeable consequence of his actions[7].

Because the defendant has ex hypothesi committed an unlawful act, it has been doubted whether a defence of justification is available[8], but there is some authority to suggest that the defence may arise in exceptional cases[9].

1 *Lonrho Ltd v Shell Petroleum Co Ltd (No 2)* [1982] AC 173, [1981] 2 All ER 456, HL; not following *Beaudesert Shire Council v Smith* (1966) 120 CLR 145, Aust HC.

2 *OBG Ltd v Allan* [2007] UKHL 21 at [6], [2008] 1 AC 1 at [6], [2007] 4 All ER 545 at [6] et seq and [45] et seq per Lord Hoffmann, and at [141] et seq per Lord Nicholls. The tort may be traced back to *Garret v Taylor* (1620) Cro Jac 567 and *Tarleton v M'Gawley* (1790) Peake 270, both cases of intimidation. As to intimidation see PARA 711. See also *Allen v Flood* [1898] AC 1 at 96, HL, per Lord Watson; *Quinn v Leathem* [1901] AC 495 at 534–535, HL, per Lord Lindley; *JT Stratford & Son Ltd v Lindley* [1965] AC 269 at 324, [1964] 3 All ER 102 at 106–107, HL, per Lord Reid, and at 328–329 and 109–110 per Viscount Radcliffe; *Hadmor Productions Ltd v Hamilton* [1983] 1 AC 191 at 228–229, [1982] 1 All ER 1042 at 1052–53, HL, per Lord Diplock; *Merkur Island Shipping Corpn v Laughton* [1983] 2 AC 570 at 606–610, [1983] 2 All ER 189 at 194–197, HL, per Lord Diplock. Mere facilitation of harm or loss is not enough: *CBS Songs Ltd v Amstrad Consumer Electronics plc* [1988] AC 1013, [1988] 2 All ER 484, HL.

3   *OBG Ltd v Allan* [2007] UKHL 21 at [8], [2008] 1 AC 1 at [8], [2007] 4 All ER 545 at [8] per Lord Hoffmann. However, at least in a three-party case, the defendant must interfere with the third party's freedom to deal with the claimant: *OBG Ltd v Allan* [2007] UKHL 21 at [51], [2008] 1 AC 1 at [51], [2007] 4 All ER 545 at [51] per Lord Hoffmann, at [270] per Lord Walker and at [320] per Lord Brown. See also *RCA Corpn v Pollard* [1983] Ch 135, [1982] 3 All ER 771, CA; *ISSAC Oren v Red Box Toy Factory* Ltd [1999] FSR 785.

4   *OBG Ltd v Allan* [2007] UKHL 21 at [49], [2008] 1 AC 1 at [49], [2007] 4 All ER 545 at [49] et seq per Lord Hoffmann, at [270] per Lord Walker, at [302] per Baroness Hale and at [320] per Lord Brown. Cf *Lonrho Ltd v Shell Petroleum Co Ltd (No 2)* [1982] AC 173, [1981] 2 All ER 456, HL. It should be noted that liability for causing loss by unlawful means is a primary liability distinct from any liability arising in the tort of breach of statutory duty. As to breach of statutory duty see PARA 500 et seq.

     For examples of unlawful means see *National Phonograph Co Ltd v Edison-Bell Consolidated Phonograph Co Ltd* [1908] 1 Ch 335, CA (deceit); *Prudential Assurance Co Ltd v Lorenz* (1971) 11 KIR 78 (breach of agency); *Bents Brewery Co Ltd v Hogan* [1945] 2 All ER 570; *Boulting v Association of Cinematograph Television and Allied Technicians* [1963] 2 QB 606, [1963] 1 All ER 716, CA (breach of director's duty); *Indata Equipment Supplies Ltd v ACL* [1998] 1 BCLC 412, [1998] FSR 248, CA (breach of confidence). Dishonest breach of trust may also constitute illegal means: *Royal Brunei Airlines Sdn Bhd v Tan* [1995] 2 AC 378, [1995] 3 All ER 97, PC.

     Crimes not giving rise to tortious liability do not constitute unlawful means: see *Hargreaves v Bretherton* [1959] 1 QB 45, [1958] 3 All ER 122 (perjury); *Chapman v Honig* [1963] 2 QB 502, [1963] 2 All ER 513, CA (criminal contempt of court). Civil contempt of court is arguably to be treated differently: *Acrow (Automation) Ltd v Rex Chainbelt Inc* [1971] 3 All ER 1175, [1971] 1 WLR 1676, CA (aiding breach of injunction).

     Restraint of trade cannot be relied upon as unlawful means: *Mogul Steamship Co Ltd v McGregor Gow & Co* [1892] AC 25, HL; *Eastham v Newcastle United Football Club Ltd* [1964] Ch 413, [1963] 3 All ER 139.

5   *Rookes v Barnard* [1964] AC 1129, [1964] 1 All ER 367, HL.

6   See eg *JT Stratford & Son Ltd v Lindley* [1965] AC 269, [1964] 3 All ER 102, HL; *Merkur Island Shipping Corpn v Laughton* [1983] 2 AC 570, [1983] 2 All ER 189, HL.

7   *OBG Ltd v Allan* [2007] UKHL 21 at [62], [2008] 1 AC 1 at [62], [2007] 4 All ER 545 at [62] per Lord Hoffmann, and at [164] et seq per Lord Nicholls.

8   *Mogul Steamship Co v McGregor, Dow & Co* (1889) 23 QBD 598 at 614, CA, per Bowen LJ (cited in *National Phonograph Co v Edison-Bell Consolidated Phonograph Co* [1908] 1 Ch 335 at 369, CA, per Kennedy LJ); *Read v Friendly Society of Operative Stonemasons of England, Ireland and Wales* [1902] 2 KB 88 at 738, per Collins MR.

9   *Rookes v Barnard* [1964] AC 1129 at 1209, [1964] 1 All ER 367 at 399–400, HL, per Lord Devlin; *Morgan v Fry* [1968] 2 QB 710 at 729, [1968] 3 All ER 452 at 459, CA, per Lord Denning MR; *Cory Lighterage Ltd v Transport and General Workers' Union* [1973] ICR 339 at 356–357, CA, per Lord Denning MR; and see PARA 711.

(ii) Intimidation

711. Intimidation in general. It is a tort to coerce another person to act in such a way as to cause loss to himself[1] or to a third party by the threat of unlawful conduct[2]. The liability so arising is a particular instance of liability for intentionally causing loss by unlawful means[3]. The elements of the tort of intimidation are the communication of a threat[4] to do something unlawful[5], the submission to that threat by the person to whom it is addressed[6], and the intention of injuring the claimant thereby[7].

The threat must be more than mere 'idle abuse'[8]. A coercive element is necessary[9]; but the mere fact that the person addressed would have acted differently if he had not been so addressed is not sufficient to show that he was acting under coercion[10]. It has long been accepted that injury caused by the threat of personal violence is actionable[11]; likewise a threat of violence to property[12]. A threat to breach one's contractual obligations also suffices[13].

The tort is actionable only on proof that the claimant has suffered damage[14]. In an appropriate case, it is possible that a defence of justification may arise[15], though this is yet to be authoritatively decided.

1 As to two-party intimidation see *Rookes v Barnard* [1964] AC 1129 at 1205, [1964] 1 All ER 367 at 397, HL, per Lord Devlin (example of trader who has been compelled to discontinue his business by means of threats of personal violence made against him by the defendant); *News Group Newspapers Ltd v Society of Graphical and Allied Trades '82 (No 2)* [1987] ICR 181, [1986] IRLR 337, CA (intimidation directed at employee who refused to participate in strike action). See also *Godwin v Uzoigwe* [1993] Fam Law 65, CA (couple who made girl work long hours without pay and social intercourse liable in tort for intimidation).

2 *Garret v Taylor* (1620) Cro Jac 567; *Tarleton v M'Gawley* (1790) Peake 270; *Rookes v Barnard* [1964] AC 1129, [1964] 1 All ER 367, HL.

3 *OBG Ltd v Allan* [2007] UKHL 21 at [6], [2008] 1 AC 1 at [6], [2007] 4 All ER 545 at [6] et seq per Lord Hoffmann.

4 As to the meaning of 'threat' see *Hodges v Webb* [1920] 2 Ch 70 at 89 per Peterson J.

5 The threat must relate to something which would be actionable by the person to whom it is addressed if carried out: see *OBG Ltd v Allan* [2007] UKHL 21 at [49], [2008] 1 AC 1 at [49], [2007] 4 All ER 545 at [49] per Lord Hoffmann; and PARA 710. An intimation that a person is going to do what he lawfully may do will not suffice: *Ware and De Freville Ltd v Motor Trade Association* [1921] 3 KB 40 at 87, CA, per Atkin LJ.

6 *Rookes v Barnard* [1964] AC 1129 at 1208, [1964] 1 All ER 367 at 399, HL, per Lord Devlin.

7 As to intention see PARA 710.

8 *News Group Newspapers Ltd v Society of Graphical and Allied Trades '82 (No 2)* [1987] ICR 181 at 204, CA, per Stuart Smith LJ.

9 *Rookes v Barnard* [1964] AC 1129 at 1207, [1964] 1 All ER 367 at 398, HL, per Lord Devlin.

10 *Hodges v Webb* [1920] 2 Ch 70 at 86 per Peterson J. As to the distinction between a threat and a mere warning of untoward consequences see *White v Riley* [1921] 1 Ch 1, CA; *Huntley v Thornton* [1957] 1 All ER 234 at 251, [1957] 1 WLR 321 at 344 per Harman J. In the case of a threatening course of conduct, an alternative cause of action may arise under the Protection from Harassment Act 1997 s 3(1): see PARA 558.

11 See eg *Keeble v Hickeringill* (1706) Holt KB 14 at 19 per Holt CJ; *Garret v Taylor* (1620) Cro Jac 567; *Tarleton v M'Gawley* (1790) Peake 270; *Rookes v Barnard* [1964] AC 1129 at 1208, [1964] 1 All ER 367 at 399, HL, per Lord Devlin; *Messenger Group Newspapers v NGA* [1984] IRLR 397 (violent picketing).

12 *Allen v Flood* [1898] AC 1 at 128, HL, per Lord Herschell.

13 *Rookes v Barnard* [1964] AC 1129, [1964] 1 All ER 367, HL. Whether a threat of vexatious litigation (apparently accepted as an alternative basis of the decision in *Garret v Taylor* (1620) Cro Jac 567) suffices may, however, be doubted in view of the general requirement of actionability.

14 As to damage see PARA 713 note 5; and DAMAGES.

15 See *Rookes v Barnard* [1964] AC 1129 at 1209, [1964] 1 All ER 367 at 399–400, HL, per Lord Devlin; *Morgan v Fry* [1968] 2 QB 710 at 729, [1968] 3 All ER 452 at 459, CA, per Lord Denning MR; *Cory Lighterage Ltd v Transport and General Workers' Union* [1973] ICR 339 at 356–357, CA, per Lord Denning MR. As to justification for causing loss by unlawful means generally see PARA 710.

(4) TORTIOUS CONSPIRACY

712. Tortious conspiracy in general. A tortious conspiracy is an unlawful combination of two or more people, intended to cause and in fact causing injury to the claimant[1]. The tort takes two forms: conspiracy to cause loss by the use of independently unlawful means[2], and conspiracy to injure by lawful means[3]. The latter constitutes an exception to the normal requirement in the economic torts of independently unlawful means, and for that reason liability is restricted by a requirement of a predominant purpose to injure which is not a requirement of conspiracy to use unlawful means[4].

If a tort is committed by several persons acting in concert, and damage is caused, the prior agreement may add nothing to the tort, and has been said to merge in it[5], for the parties will be joint tortfeasors[6]. Yet there may be good reasons in some cases for alleging a conspiracy and not (or not only) the underlying torts, for example, if the torts are committed in several different jurisdictions[7]. It is also necessary to consider conspiracy as a separate tort where the act would not have been tortious if done by one individual[8].

1 There is also the crime of conspiracy, the essence of which lies in the agreement, so that in order to establish the offence it is not necessary, as it would be to establish the tort, to prove damage: see CRIMINAL LAW vol 25 (2010) PARA 74 et seq. In a claim for damages for conspiracy, it is no objection to the making of an order for an affidavit of documents by the defendant that the documents may tend to incriminate him: *National Association of Operative Plasterers v Smithies* [1906] AC 434, HL. In certain circumstances, the offence of criminal conspiracy will be disregarded in relation to acts done in relation to a trade dispute: see EMPLOYMENT vol 41A (2014) PARA 1364.
   For a summary of historical sources see *Mogul Steamship Co Ltd v McGregor, Gow & Co* (1888) 21 QBD 544 at 550 per Lord Coleridge CJ; *Crofter Hand Woven Harris Tweed Co Ltd v Veitch* [1942] AC 435 at 443–444, [1942] 1 All ER 142 at 148, HL, per Viscount Simon LC.
2 See PARA 714.
3 See PARA 715.
4 See *Crofter Hand Woven Harris Tweed Co Ltd v Veitch* [1942] AC 435 at 462, [1942] 1 All ER 142 at 158, per Lord Wright; *Lonrho Ltd v Shell Petroleum Co Ltd (No 2)* [1982] AC 173 at 189–189, [1981] 2 All ER 456 at 464, HL, per Lord Diplock; *Revenue and Customs Comrs v Total Network SL* [2008] UKHL 19 at [66], [2008] 1 AC 1174 at [66], [2008] 2 All ER 413 at [66] per Lord Walker; cf at [56] per Lord Scott (the difference between the two forms of conspiracy is not anomalous).
5 *Ward v Lewis* [1955] 1 All ER 55, [1955] 1 WLR 9, CA. See also *Sorrell v Smith* [1925] AC 700 at 716, HL, per Lord Dunedin ('surplusage').
6 See *Pratt v British Medical Association* [1919] 1 KB 244 at 254, where it was said that all who have aided, counselled, directed or joined in the tort are joint tortfeasors.
7 *Kuwait Oil Tanker Co SAK v Al Bader* [2000] 2 All ER (Comm) 271 at 316, 319, CA, per Nourse LJ.
8 Eg the commission of the crime of cheating the revenue (see *Revenue and Customs Comrs v Total Network SL* [2008] UKHL 19, [2008] 1 AC 1174, [2008] 2 All ER 413).

713. Essential ingredients of tortious conspiracy. In order to make out a case of conspiracy the claimant must establish[1]:

(1) an agreement between two or more persons[2], which either:

    (a) where the means are lawful, is an agreement the real and predominant purpose of which is to injure the claimant[3]; or

    (b) where the means are unlawful, is an agreement an intended consequence of which is to injure the claimant[4]; and

(2) that acts done in execution of that agreement resulted in damage to the claimant[5].

1 See the classic statement of the elements of conspiracy in *Crofter Hand Woven Harris Tweed Co Ltd v Veitch* [1942] AC 435 at 440, [1942] 1 All ER 142 at 147, HL, per Viscount Simon LC (followed in *Scala Ballroom (Wolverhampton) Ltd v Ratcliffe* [1958] 3 All ER 220 at 222, [1958] 1 WLR 1057 at 1060, CA, per Hodson LJ); and see also *Lonrho Ltd v Shell Petroleum Co Ltd (No 2)* [1982] AC 173 at 188, [1981] 2 All ER 456 at 463, HL, per Lord Diplock.
2 Husband and wife may be jointly liable in the tort of conspiracy: *Midland Bank Trust Co Ltd v Green (No 3)* [1982] Ch 529, [1981] 3 All ER 744, CA. A company may sue its directors when they act improperly on its behalf to cause damage to the company by their conspiracy: *Belmont Finance Corpn Ltd v Williams Furniture Ltd* [1979] Ch 250, [1979] 1 All ER 118, CA, approved in *Stone & Rolls Ltd (in liquidation) v Moore Stephens (a firm)* [2009] UKHL 39 at [140], [2009] 4 All ER 431 at [140], [2010] 1 All ER (Comm) 125 at [140] per Lord Walker. See also *Belmont Finance Corpn Ltd v Williams Furniture Ltd (No 2)* [1980] 1 All ER 393, CA. As to representative proceedings on behalf of shareholders in an action for conspiracy against the directors of the company see *Prudential Assurance Co Ltd v Newman Industries Ltd* [1981] Ch 229, [1979] 3 All ER 507; *Prudential Assurance Co Ltd v Newman Industries Ltd (No 2)* [1982] Ch 204, [1982] 1 All ER 354, CA.

3 *Quinn v Leathem* [1901] AC 495, HL; *Crofter Hand Woven Harris Tweed Co Ltd v Veitch* [1942] AC 435, [1942] 1 All ER 142, HL. Where the primary or predominant purpose of the defendants is to further a legitimate interest but they also intend to injure the claimant it is enough to make the action tortious if they use unlawful means: *Lonrho plc v Fayed* [1992] 1 AC 448 at 463, [1991] 3 All ER 303 at 307, HL, per Lord Bridge; *Yukong Line Ltd v Rendsburg Investments Corpn of Liberia (No 2)* [1998] 4 All ER 82, [1998] 1 WLR 294.

4 *Lonrho Ltd v Shell Petroleum Co Ltd (No 2)* [1982] AC 173, [1981] 2 All ER 456, HL; *Lonrho plc v Fayed* [1992] 1 AC 448, [1991] 3 All ER 303, HL; *Meretz Investments NV v ACP Ltd* [2007] EWCA Civ 1303 at [172], [2008] Ch 244 at [172], [2008] 2 WLR 904 at [172] per Touson J. As to unlawful means see PARA 714.

5 Damage is an essential element of the cause of action: see *Crofter Hand Woven Harris Tweed Co Ltd Co v Veitch* [1942] AC 435 at 439–440, [1942] 1 All ER 142 at 146–147, HL, per Viscount Simon LC; *Lonrho Ltd v Shell Petroleum Co Ltd (No 2)* [1982] AC 173 at 188, [1981] 2 All ER 456 at 463, HL, per Lord Diplock. Where damage is not pleaded, the claim may be struck out: see eg *Ward v Lewis* [1955] 1 All ER 55, [1955] 1 WLR 9, CA. Expense of investigation has been held to suffice as damage: see *British Motor Trade Association v Salvadori* [1949] Ch 556 at 569, [1949] 1 All ER 208 at 214 per Roxburgh J. Damages for injury to reputation or injury to feelings are not recoverable in a claim for conspiracy: *Lonrho plc v Fayed (No 5)* [1994] 1 All ER 188, [1993] 1 WLR 1489, CA.

714. Conspiracy to cause loss by unlawful means. An agreement[1] to do an unlawful act is actionable in tort at the suit of someone who suffers damage[2] from it only if there was an intent to injure him, and not if it was merely foreseeable that he might be injured[3]. It need not be shown that the injury was the predominant purpose of the agreement[4]. The liability differs from the general liability for intentionally causing loss by unlawful means[5] in taking a broader view of what is unlawful for these purposes. In conspiracy, it is not necessary for the unlawful conduct to be actionable by the person at whom it was directed, and liability may therefore arise in respect of an agreement to commit a criminal offence that is intended to and does in fact cause loss to the claimant even if the offence is not one that would give rise to tortious liability in the absence of the conspiracy[6].

An agreement to break a contract[7], threaten to break a contract[8], or procure a breach of contract[9], may suffice for the tort of conspiracy. Each of the conspirators is liable for the damage caused, even if only one of their number carries out the unlawful act that injures the claimant[10].

1 See PARA 713.
2 See PARA 713.
3 *Lonrho Ltd v Shell Petroleum Co Ltd (No 2)* [1982] AC 173, [1981] 2 All ER 456, HL.
4 *Lonrho plc v Fayed* [1992] 1 AC 448, [1991] 3 All ER 303, HL; *Meretz Investments NV v ACP Ltd* [2007] EWCA Civ 1303 at [172], [2008] Ch 244 at [172] per Touson J.
5 See PARA 710.
6 *Revenue and Customs Comrs v Total Network SL* [2008] UKHL 19, [2008] 1 AC 1174, [2008] 2 All ER 413 (crime of cheating HMRC), overruling *Powell v Boladz* (1998) 39 BMLR 35 and disapproving dicta in *Yukong Line Ltd of Korea v Rendsburg Investments Corpn of Liberia, The Rialto (No 2)* [1998] 4 All ER 82 at 98–101, [1998] 1 WLR 294 at 311–314 per Toulson J, and *Michaels v Taylor Woodrow Developments Ltd* [2001] Ch 493 at [30]–[34], [2000] 4 All ER 645 at [30]–[34] per Laddie J.
7 *Camden Nominees Ltd v Forcey* [1940] Ch 352 at 365–366, sub nom *Camden Nominees Ltd v Slack* [1940] 2 All ER 1 at 11 per Simonds J; *Kuwait Oil Tanker Co SAK v Al Bader* [2000] 2 All ER (Comm) 271 at [130], CA.
8 See eg *Rookes v Barnard* [1964] AC 1129, [1964] 1 All ER 367, HL. As to the tort of intimidation see PARA 711.
9 As to the tort of inducing breach of contract see PARA 703 et seq. A cause of action for conspiracy to procure a breach of contract is not complete until the intended breach has taken place: *De Jetley Marks v Lord Greenwood* [1936] 1 All ER 863.
10 *Berryland Books v Baldwin* [2010] EWCA Civ 1440 at [46], [2010] All ER (D) 209 (Dec)

715.   Conspiracy to injure. It is a tort to cause damage in pursuance of a conspiracy of which the predominant purpose is to cause injury to another person even if no unlawful means are employed[1]. Conversely, where the primary or predominant purpose of the conspirators is to further or protect some legitimate interest of their own, but they also have the intention of injuring the claimant, it must be shown that they used unlawful means[2].

Conspiracy to injure may be committed where the conspirators act out of political or religious hatred, or from a spirit of revenge for previous real or fancied injury[3], but malice in the sense of malevolence is not an element of the cause of action[4]. An admitted desire to punish the claimant is not necessarily decisive for it is consistent with both vindictive vengeance and an intention to deter others from similarly offending[5]. Where the defendants act with mixed motives, feeling that they can kill two birds with one stone by teaching the claimant a lesson at the same time as protecting their own interests, the question is which of these purposes predominated[6]. However, a combination to forward or defend one's own interests or to further some other legitimate object is not actionable even though it involves inevitable harm to another, provided that nothing independently unlawful is done[7]. It is not for the court to determine whether the agreed conduct is reasonably calculated to advance the object of the combiners: the question is one of the defendants' honest belief[8].

1   This was conclusively decided in *Quinn v Leathem* [1901] AC 495, HL: see *Sorrell v Smith* [1925] AC 700 at 744, HL, per Lord Buckmaster. See also *Gregory v Duke of Brunswick* (1844) 6 Man & G 205, where a conspiracy to hiss an actor was held to be actionable.

2   *Lonrho plc v Fayed* [1992] 1 AC 448 at 463–468, [1991] 3 All ER 303 at 307–312, HL, per Lord Bridge. As to the meaning of 'unlawful means' in relation to conspiracy see PARA 714.

3   *Boots v Grundy* (1900) 82 LT 769 at 773 per Phillimore J, cited with approval in *Crofter Hand Woven Harris Tweed Co Ltd v Veitch* [1942] AC 435 at 493, [1942] 1 All ER 142 at 173, HL, per Lord Porter.

4   *Crofter Hand Woven Harris Tweed Co Ltd v Veitch* [1942] AC 435 at 471, [1942] 1 All ER 142 at 162, HL, per Lord Wright.

5   *Crofter Hand Woven Harris Tweed Co Ltd v Veitch* [1942] AC 435 at 475, [1942] 1 All ER 142 at 164–165, HL, per Lord Wright, following Lord Herschell in *Allen v Flood* [1898] AC 1 at 131, HL. See also *Giblan v National Amalgamated Labourers' Union* [1903] 2 KB 600.

6   *Crofter Hand Woven Harris Tweed Co Ltd v Veitch* [1942] AC 435 at 445, [1942] 1 All ER 142 at 149, HL, per Viscount Simon LC, at 478 and 166 per Lord Wright, and at 490 and 172 per Lord Porter. An example is afforded by *Trollope & Sons v London Building Trades Federation* (1895) 72 LT 342, CA, where the principal and primary motive was to injure non-union workmen and the subsidiary motive was to benefit the federation; an interlocutory injunction was granted.

7   *Mogul Steamship Co Ltd v McGregor Gow & Co* [1892] AC 25, HL; *Sorrell v Smith* [1925] AC 700 at 712, HL, per Viscount Cave LC (cited with approval in *Crofter Hand Woven Harris Tweed Co Ltd v Veitch* [1942] AC 435 at 449, [1942] 1 All ER 142 at 151, HL, per Viscount Maugham, and at 469–470 and 162 per Lord Wright). A trade union is acting with the purpose of furthering a legitimate object when it seeks to increase its membership, or to raise the wages of its members, or pursues other normal union ambitions: see *Denaby and Cadeby Main Collieries v Yorkshire Miners' Association* [1906] AC 384, HL; *Crofter Hand Woven Harris Tweed Co Ltd v Veitch* [1942] above; *JT Stratford & Son v Lindley* [1965] AC 269 at 323, [1964] 3 All ER 102 at 106, HL, per Lord Reid. See also *Thompson v British Medical Association (NSW Branch)* [1924] AC 764 at 770–771, PC (professional body's pursuit of interests of the profession). The question whether any object other than material self-interest may be treated as legitimate in this context was raised but not resolved in *Scala Ballroom (Wolverhampton) Ltd v Ratcliffe* [1958] 3 All ER 220, [1958] 1 WLR 1057.

8   *Crofter Hand Woven Harris Tweed Co Ltd v Veitch* [1942] AC 435 at 446, [1942] 1 All ER 142 at 150, HL, per Viscount Simon LC, at 469 and 161 per Lord Wright and at 481 and 167 per Lord Porter.

9. WRONGFUL USE OF PROCESS

(1) MALICIOUS PROSECUTION

(i) What Constitutes Malicious Prosecution

716. What is a malicious prosecution. A malicious prosecution is an abuse of the process of the court by wrongfully setting the law in motion on a criminal charge[1]. To be actionable as a tort the process must have been without reasonable and probable cause, must have been instituted or carried on maliciously and must have terminated in the claimant's favour[2]. The claimant must also prove damage[3].

While the common law originally recognised that malicious prosecution extended as much to civil proceedings as to criminal proceedings, in practice it has long been restricted to criminal proceedings[4]. However, it has recently been suggested by the Privy Council that this should no longer be the case, and that as the tort requires the defendant to have abused the coercive powers of the state, it should therefore apply equally to civil and criminal proceedings[5].

1 *Mohamed Amin v Jogendra Kumar Bannerjee* [1947] AC 322 at 330, PC, per Sir John Beaumont; *Martin v Watson* [1996] AC 74 at 80, [1995] 3 All ER 559 at 562, HL, per Lord Keith; *Gregory v Portsmouth City Council* [2000] 1 AC 419 at 426, [2000] 1 All ER 560 at 565, HL, per Lord Steyn. See also the statement of Crompton J in *Castrique v Behrens* (1861) 3 E & E 709 at 721, cited in *Bynoe v Bank of England* [1902] 1 KB 467 at 470–471, CA, per Collins MR, and in *Everett v Ribbands* [1952] 2 QB 198 at 220, [1952] 1 All ER 823 at 825, CA, per Somervell LJ. As to abuse of process see further CIVIL PROCEDURE vol 11 (2009) PARA 534; CRIMINAL PROCEDURE vol 27 (2010) PARA 342. As to whether malicious prosecution applies to civil proceedings as well as to criminal charges see the text and notes 4–5. As to malicious civil proceedings see PARA 748 et seq.
2 See the authorities cited in note 1. As to the elements of a claim for malicious prosecution see PARA 725 et seq.
3 *Savile v Roberts* (1698) 1 Ld Raym 374; *Gregory v Portsmouth City Council* [2000] 1 AC 419 at 426, [2000] 1 All ER 560 at 565, HL, per Lord Steyn. As to the requirement of damage in malicious prosecution see PARA 733. See, however, *Crawford Adjusters (Cayman) Ltd v Sagicor General Insurance (Cayman) Ltd* [2013] UKPC 17, [2014] AC 366, [2013] 4 All ER 8; and note 4.
4 *Crawford Adjusters (Cayman) Ltd v Sagicor General Insurance (Cayman) Ltd* [2013] UKPC 17 at [78], [2014] AC 366 at [78], [2013] 4 All ER 8 at [78]. The Privy Council in that case suggested that the early availability of an order for costs in favour of a successful defendant of civil proceedings often disabled him from proving the damage required by the tort, thereby restricting the tort to criminal proceedings only. The Privy Council went on to comment that that limitation on the scope of the tort of malicious prosecution of civil proceedings was no longer justified (at [78]) (Lords Sumption and Neuberger dissenting).
5 *Crawford Adjusters (Cayman) Ltd v Sagicor General Insurance (Cayman) Ltd* [2013] UKPC 17, [2014] AC 366, [2013] 4 All ER 8 (where it was suggested that it might be possible to limit the ambit of the tort of malicious prosecution to civil proceedings of which the basis was an allegation which might have been the subject of a criminal charge: at [78], [119]).

717. Malicious prosecution distinguished from false imprisonment. Malicious prosecution must be distinguished from false imprisonment[1] which, being a form of liability in trespass, is actionable only if the defendant directly causes the claimant's loss of liberty[2]. The intervention of independent legal authority precludes liability in false imprisonment. Where, therefore, the claimant has been judicially remanded in custody or sentenced to imprisonment following conviction for a criminal offence, on charges brought maliciously by the defendant, there may be liability for malicious prosecution but not for false imprisonment[3]. Conversely, false imprisonment may lie in respect of the claimant's wrongful arrest in connection with a criminal offence even if no prosecution is initiated. Where the defendant falsely and maliciously accuses the claimant to a police officer of having committed an offence, with the result that the officer initiates a prosecution, it is a question of fact whether the defendant, although not technically the prosecutor, is in substance the person responsible for the prosecution being brought, as may for example be the case where the facts relating to the alleged offence are solely within the defendant's knowledge[4].

A further consequence of false imprisonment being a form of liability in trespass is that, unlike malicious prosecution, it is actionable without proof of damage[5].

1 As to false imprisonment see PARA 543 et seq. See in particular PARA 544.
2 *Morgan v Hughes* (1788) 2 Term Rep 225.
3 *Lock v Ashton* (1848) 12 QB 871 (remand); *Austin v Dowling* (1870) LR 5 CP 534 at 540 per Willes J (commencement of proceedings before judicial officer bringing false imprisonment to an end).
4 *Martin v Watson* [1996] AC 74, [1995] 3 All ER 559, HL. As to whether liability for false imprisonment would arise in respect of the arrest on such facts see *Davidson v Chief Constable of North Wales* [1994] 2 All ER 597, CA (the defendant must go beyond merely laying information before the officer for him to take such action as he thought fit and must direct, procure, request or encourage the arrest).
5 As to the requirement of damage in malicious prosecution see PARA 733.

718. What is a prosecution. A prosecution exists where a criminal charge[1] is made before a judicial officer or tribunal[2], and any person who makes or is actively instrumental[3] in the making or prosecuting of the charge is deemed to prosecute it, and is called the prosecutor[4]. A person who lays before a magistrate an information stating that he suspects and has good reason to suspect another[5], or who prefers a bill of indictment[6], is engaged in a prosecution; and he may be responsible for the prosecution even though the charge made before the magistrate is an oral one[7], and even though, after making the charge before the magistrate, or even without making one[8], he is bound over to prosecute and does so[9].

1 *Rayson v South London Tramways Co* [1893] 2 QB 304, CA; *Gregory v Portsmouth City Council* [2000] 1 AC 419 at 426–427, [2000] 1 All ER 560 at 565, HL, per Lord Steyn. The tort does not extend to disciplinary proceedings even if they may be said to be quasi-criminal in nature and potentially involve serious penalties: *Gregory v Portsmouth City Council* [2000] 1 AC 419 at 430–432, [2000] 1 All ER 560 at 568–570, HL, per Lord Steyn. As to the commencement of criminal proceedings see CRIMINAL PROCEDURE vol 27 (2010) PARA 121 et seq; MAGISTRATES vol 71 (2013) PARA 521. For the purposes of a claim for malicious prosecution, the limitation period does not begin to run until the acquittal of the claimant: *Dunlop v Comrs of Customs and Excise* (1998) 142 Sol Jo LB 134, CA.
   As to malicious civil proceedings see PARAS 716, 748 et seq.
2 See *Austin v Dowling* (1870) LR 5 CP 534 at 540 per Willes J.
3 See PARA 719.
4 *Davis v Noak* (1817) 1 Stark 377; *Dubois v Keats* (1840) 11 Ad & El 329; *Fitzjohn v Mackinder* (1861) 9 CBNS 505. A prosecution is commenced when the information is laid (*R v Willace* (1797) 1 East PC 186, CCR), when the accused is brought before a magistrate (*R v Austin* (1845) 1 Car & Kir 621), or when an indictment is preferred (*R v Killminster* (1835) 7 C & P 228). An informant is unlikely to be a prosecutor in complicated criminal proceedings brought by the Serious Fraud Office: *Mahon v Rahn (No 2)* [2000] 4 All ER 41, [2000] 1 WLR 2150, CA. A witness cannot be regarded as a prosecutor if he made no deliberate attempt to mislead the police: *Hunt v AB* [2009] EWCA Civ 1092, (2009) Times, 28 October, [2009] All ER (D) 244 (Oct). See also CRIMINAL PROCEDURE vol 27 (2010) PARAS 55–56.
5 *Davis v Noak* (1817) 1 Stark 377.
6 *Payne v Porter* (1618) Cro Jac 490, where a bill of indictment was exhibited before a grand jury (grand juries have now been abolished). As to the modern procedure for preferring a bill of indictment see CRIMINAL PROCEDURE vol 27 (2010) PARAS 323–329.

7   *Clarke v Postan* (1834) 6 C & P 423.
8   *Fitzjohn v Mackinder* (1861) 9 CBNS 505, where the defendant, during the trial of an action,
    wilfully made a false allegation of perjury against the plaintiff, and was bound over by the judge
    to prosecute.
9   *Dubois v Keats* (1840) 11 Ad & El 329.

(ii) Persons Liable for Malicious Prosecution

719.   Persons liable for malicious prosecution. A person who prosecutes[1]
another may be liable as prosecutor; and so may a person who represents himself
as prosecutor, even if he did not in fact initiate the prosecution, and is present
only as a witness[2]. However, the mere fact that a witness is bound over with
another (the real prosecutor) to prosecute and give evidence will not render the
witness liable to a claim in respect of the prosecution[3].

A person who fairly states the facts to a magistrate, and makes no specific
charge against anyone, will not be responsible, in a claim for malicious
prosecution, to a person against whom the magistrate issues a warrant of arrest[4].

A person who provides information to the police in such a way as to be
actively instrumental in the making or prosecuting of a criminal charge may be
liable for malicious prosecution even if he is not technically the prosecutor[5].

1   As to what is a prosecution see PARA 718.
2   *Clements v Ohrly* (1848) 2 Car & Kir 686. See also *Osterman v Bateman* (1848) 2 Car & Kir
    728 (defendant signing indictment as witness in support of it). If during the proceedings the
    defendant heard himself described as prosecutor, without contradicting it, the jury may infer
    that he represented himself as such: *Clements v Ohrly* (1847) 2 Car & Kir 686 at 690–691 per
    Lord Denman CJ.
3   *Eagar v Dyott* (1831) 5 C & P 4. Cf *Dubois v Keats* (1840) 11 Ad & El 329; *Fitzjohn v
    Mackinder* (1861) 9 CBNS 505. See also *Hunt v AB* [2009] EWCA Civ 1092, (2009) Times,
    28 October, [2009] All ER (D) 244 (Oct); and PARA 718.
4   *Leigh v Webb* (1800) 3 Esp 165; *Cohen v Morgan* (1825) 6 Dow & Ry KB 8. See also *Milton v
    Elmore* (1830) 4 C & P 456.
5   *Martin v Watson* [1996] AC 74, [1995] 3 All ER 559, HL (relevant facts solely within
    defendant's knowledge); considered in *Hunt v AB* [2009] EWCA Civ 1092, (2009) Times,
    28 October, [2009] All ER (D) 244 (Oct). Cf *Danby v Beardsley* (1880) 43 LT 603. A hospital
    providing pathology reports for the police is not liable for malicious prosecution, as it is not the
    hospital which set the law in motion: *Evans v London Hospital Medical College* [1981]
    1 All ER 715, [1981] 1 WLR 184. An informant is unlikely to be a prosecutor in complicated
    criminal proceedings brought by the Serious Fraud Office: *Mahon v Rahn (No 2)* [2000]
    4 All ER 41, [2000] 1 WLR 2150, CA.

720.   Liability of magistrate for malicious prosecution. A magistrate who acts
as such in a prosecution has been held not to be liable to a claim for malicious
prosecution, even though he procures some of the witnesses to appear against the
person prosecuted, and though his own name is indorsed as that of a witness on
the indictment[1]. In general, a magistrate has immunity for acts within
jurisdiction but may be liable for acts done in bad faith outside his jurisdiction[2].

1   *Girlington v Pitfield* (1668) 1 Vent 47.
2   See the Courts Act 2003 ss 31–33; and MAGISTRATES vol 71 (2013) PARA 463 et seq. See also
    PARA 460. As to the liability of magistrates generally see CONSTITUTIONAL AND
    ADMINISTRATIVE LAW vol 20 (2014) PARA 607 et seq.

721.   Liability of employer for malicious prosecution by employee. An
employer is not liable for a malicious prosecution by his employee[1] unless the
prosecution was within the scope of the employee's authority, express or
implied[2]. The authority may be general, or a particular or limited authority to
act in emergency[3].

The claimant has to prove malice on the part of the employer or the employee[4].

No general authority to prosecute can be implied unless the prosecution of an offender falls within the ordinary scope of an employee's duties[5].

Where an employee's authority is limited to cases of emergency a claimant must show that the emergency existed or might reasonably have been supposed to exist[6].

1   As to the vicarious liability of employers generally see PARA 767 et seq. As to the liability of principals for torts committed by agents see AGENCY vol 1 (2008) PARAS 150–154. Irrespective of the question of his principal's liability, an agent (eg a solicitor) who acts maliciously and without reasonable and probable cause may himself be liable in a claim for malicious prosecution: *Johnson v Emerson and Sparrow* (1871) LR 6 Exch 329. See also *Stevens v Midland Counties Rly Co* (1854) 10 Exch 352 (liability of employee). See AGENCY vol 1 (2008) PARAS 191–193 (agent's liability for torts); LEGAL PROFESSIONS vol 66 (2015) PARA 652.

2   See *Michell v Williams* (1843) 11 M & W 205 at 213; *Stevens v Midland Counties Rly Co* (1854) 10 Exch 352; *Bank of New South Wales v Owston* (1879) 4 App Cas 270, PC. A prosecution by one partner in respect of the partnership property does not of itself render the other partners liable for the prosecution: *Arbuckle v Taylor* (1815) 3 Dow 160 at 178, HL, per Lord Eldon LC. A defendant is not deemed to adopt a prosecution begun by his agent without his knowledge or sanction by merely attending the magistrates' court to hear what evidence may be given: *Weston v Beeman* (1857) 27 LJ Ex 57; *Jones v Duck* (1900) Times, 16 March.

3   *Bank of New South Wales v Owston* (1879) 4 App Cas 270, PC.

4   See *Egger v Viscount Chelmsford* [1965] 1 QB 248, [1964] 3 All ER 406, CA. This decision on malice in defamation seems equally applicable to malicious prosecution. It was held that, although a principal may be liable for the malice of his agent, an innocent agent is not liable for the malice of his principal.

5   *Bank of New South Wales v Owston* (1879) 4 App Cas 270, PC. Such an authority might possibly be implied, eg in the case of the general manager of a banking company invested with general supervision and power of control, at least in the absence of his directors, or possibly in the case of a manager conducting the bank's business at a distance from the head office and the directors, but certainly not where he has the opportunity of consulting them: *Bank of New South Wales v Owston* (1879) 4 App Cas 270, PC.

6   *Bank of New South Wales v Owston* (1879) 4 App Cas 270, PC.

722. Liability of corporations and companies for malicious prosecution. A claim for damages for malicious prosecution may be brought against a corporation[1] or an incorporated company[2]. As the corporation or company is liable for a malicious prosecution as if it were an individual the ordinary principles as to the responsibility of employers acting by employees or agents apply and it is a question of fact whether an employee or agent was acting in the scope of his employment or authority[3].

1   See *Walker v South Eastern Rly Co, Smith v South Eastern Rly Co* (1870) LR 5 CP 640; *Bank of New South Wales v Owston* (1879) 4 App Cas 270 at 282, PC, where the defendant's counsel admitted liability of a corporation to such an action; *Edwards v Midland Rly Co* (1880) 6 QBD 287, where Fry J refused to follow *Stevens v Midland Counties Rly Co* (1854) 10 Exch 352; *Cornford v Carlton Bank* [1899] 1 QB 392 (affd [1900] 1 QB 22, CA, where liability to the action was admitted by the defendant's counsel). See also *Rayson v South London Tramways Co* [1893] 2 QB 304, CA.

2   *Leibo v D Buckman Ltd* [1952] 2 All ER 1057, CA.

3   *Citizen's Life Assurance Co v Brown* [1904] AC 423, PC. This case, which is a decision on malice in defamation, seems equally applicable to malicious prosecution. The malice of an employee will also be attributable, in accordance with the ordinary principles of vicarious liability, to a corporation or company sued for malicious prosecution: see further PARA 721.

(iii) Proceedings for Malicious Prosecution in Particular Courts

723. Proceedings in naval, military or air force courts. It is doubtful whether the civil courts are competent to inquire into proceedings which took place before a naval, military or air force court-martial or court of inquiry, and whether a prosecution in such a court, when within its jurisdiction, even if malicious and without reasonable and probable cause, can form the basis of a claim for malicious prosecution[1] in a court of law[2].

1 As to malicious prosecution see PARA 716 et seq.

2 In *Sutton v Johnstone* (1785) 1 Term Rep 493, on appeal at 510, 549–550, Exch Ch (affd (1787) 1 Term Rep 784, HL), Lord Mansfield and Lord Loughborough were inclined to lean against acceptance of a claim in the ordinary courts, and to reserve such matters exclusively for military tribunals, for fear that every acquittal in a court-martial would otherwise produce a civil claim, and that military discipline would otherwise decay; but it was not necessary to decide this, as reasonable and probable cause was proved. That view was followed in subsequent cases: see *Warden v Bailey* (1811) 4 Taunt 67; *Dawkins v Lord Rokeby* (1866) 4 F & F 806 at 832–833 per Willes J; *Heddon v Evans* (1919) 35 TLR 642; and (in respect of libel) *Dawkins v Lord Paulet* (1869) LR 5 QB 94; *Dawkins v Lord Rokeby* (1873) LR 8 QB 255, Ex Ch (affd (1875) LR 7 HL 744); *Grant v Secretary of State for India* (1877) 2 CPD 445; see also *R v Army Council, ex p Ravenscroft* [1917] 2 KB 504 at 508–509 per Viscount Reading CJ (in respect of mandamus); *Fraser v Hamilton* (1917) 33 TLR 431, CA (action for maliciously causing retirement). The House of Lords, however, in *Fraser v Balfour* (1918) 87 LJKB 1116, expressly stated that the House of Lords in *Sutton v Johnstone* (1787) 1 Term Rep 784 did not affirm the broad proposition advanced obiter in the Exchequer Chamber (see above) and that the question was therefore still open: see *Fraser v Balfour* (1918) 87 LJKB 1116 at 1118, HL, per Lord Finlay LC.

In *Brooks v Ministry of Defence* (1 March 2002, unreported, QBD), Garland J declined to strike out a claim for malicious prosecution relating to a military disciplinary hearing, counsel for the claimant having submitted that times have moved on as it is now possible to appeal against both conviction and sentence from courts-martial. See further ARMED FORCES vol 3 (2011) PARA 656 et seq.

724. Proceedings in foreign courts. A claim may lie in respect of malicious criminal proceedings in a foreign court subject to the same conditions as apply to such proceedings in this jurisdiction[1].

1 *Castrique v Behrens* (1861) 3 E & E 709 (following *Bank of Australasia v Nias* (1851) 16 QB 717, DC); *Taylor v Ford* (1873) 29 LT 392. As to malicious prosecution see PARA 716 et seq.

(iv) Claim for Malicious Prosecution

725. Elements of a claim for malicious prosecution. To succeed in a claim for damages for malicious prosecution[1] a claimant must prove:

(1)   the prosecution by the defendant of a criminal charge against the claimant before a tribunal into whose proceedings the criminal courts are competent to inquire[2];

(2)   that the proceedings complained of terminated in the claimant's favour[3];

(3)   that the defendant instituted or carried on the proceedings maliciously[4];

(4)   that there was an absence of reasonable and probable cause for the proceedings[5]; and

(5)   that the claimant has suffered damage[6].

1 See PARA 716 et seq.
2 As to naval, military and air force courts see PARA 723.
3 See PARA 726 et seq.
4 See PARA 728.
5 See PARAS 729–732.
6 See PARA 733.

726. Termination of previous proceedings in the claimant's favour. In a claim for damages for malicious prosecution it must be alleged and proved that the proceedings have terminated in the claimant's favour because, in the absence of proof, the court entertaining the malicious prosecution claim would be, in effect, a court of appeal from the court in which the prosecution took place[1].

The rule prevails even where the proceedings complained of have taken place abroad, provided that the foreign court had jurisdiction to entertain them and that the decision was arrived at in such circumstances as to be binding in England and Wales[2].

It is immaterial that the person convicted had no power of appealing[3].

1   *Vanderbergh v Blake* (1662) Hard 194; *Parker v Langly* (1714) 10 Mod Rep 209; *Lewis v Farrel* (1718) 1 Stra 114; *Whitworth v Hall* (1831) 2 B & Ad 695; *Castrique v Behrens* (1861) 3 E & E 709 at 721 per Crompton J; *Redway v McAndrew* (1873) LR 9 QB 74 (sufficiency of allegation of termination of proceedings); *Bynoe v Bank of England* [1902] 1 KB 467, CA. As to malicious prosecution see PARA 716 et seq. As to when proceedings terminate in the claimant's favour see PARA 727.
2   *Castrique v Behrens* (1861) 3 E & E 709; *Taylor v Ford* (1873) 29 LT 392. The principle has been applied in a malicious presentment in an ecclesiastical court: see *Fisher v Bristow* (1779) 1 Doug KB 215. As to issues of foreign jurisdiction see further CONFLICT OF LAWS. See also CIVIL PROCEDURE.
3   *Basébé v Matthews* (1867) LR 2 CP 684; *Bynoe v Bank of England* [1902] 1 KB 467, CA; *Everett v Ribbands* [1952] 2 QB 198, [1952] 1 All ER 823, CA.

727.   When proceedings terminate in the claimant's favour.   Proceedings terminate in a claimant's favour if a magistrate dismisses the charge[1], if the proceedings fail because of a defect in the indictment[2], or because they are void for want of jurisdiction[3], or are quashed because of an irregularity of procedure[4], or are discontinued on the defendant being bound over to keep the peace[5], or are abandoned[6], or there is an acquittal[7], even on one part of the indictment[8]. Where an appeal lies from a conviction and no appeal has been made by the person convicted, the proceedings have not terminated in his favour[9].

Where there has been a successful appeal from a conviction, this is a sufficient termination of the proceedings in the claimant's favour[10], but it seems that the conviction, although reversed, might be evidence on which the judge might find that there was reasonable and probable cause for the prosecution[11].

1   *Delegal v Highley* (1837) 3 Bing NC 950.
2   *Savile v Roberts* (1698) 1 Ld Raym 374; *Jones v Gwynn* (1713) 10 Mod Rep 214; *Chambers v Robinson* (1726) 2 Stra 691; *Wicks v Fentham* (1791) 4 Term Rep 247; *Pippet v Hearn* (1822) 5 B & Ald 634.
3   *Jones v Gwynn* (1713) 10 Mod Rep 214 at 220, where it was said that proceedings sufficiently terminate if they are coram non judice. See also *Atwood v Mongen* (1653) Sty 378.
4   *Herniman v Smith* [1938] AC 305, [1938] 1 All ER 1, HL.
5   *Hourihane v Metropolitan Police Comr* (1994) Independent, 18 January, CA; cf *Everett v Ribbands* [1952] 2 QB 198, [1952] 1 All ER 823, CA (proceedings determined against plaintiff).
6   *Pierce v Street* (1832) 1 LJKB 147. In Australia it has been held that the entry by the Attorney General of a nolle prosequi after an indictment had been filed is a sufficient termination: *Mann v Jacombe* (1961) 78 WN (NSW) 635, following *Gilchrist v Gardner* (1891) 12 LR (NSW) 184; but see *Goddard v Smith* (1704) 6 Mod Rep 261 (not sufficient).
7   *Morgan v Hughes* (1788) 2 Term Rep 225 at 231–232 per Buller J.
8   *Boaler v Holder* (1887) 51 JP 277, where the plaintiff had been indicted for publishing a libel knowing it to be false and was convicted of publishing it only. See also *Boaler v Holder* (1886) 54 LT 298.
9   *Mellor v Baddeley* (1834) 2 Cr & M 675, where Vaughan B stated, at 679, that failure to appeal showed acquiescence in the conviction and was evidence of reasonable and probable cause.
10   See *Mellor v Baddeley* (1834) 2 Cr & M 675. See also *Herniman v Smith* [1938] AC 305, [1938] 1 All ER 1, HL; *Berry v British Transport Commission* [1962] 1 QB 306, [1961] 3 All ER 65, CA; *Abbott v Refuge Assurance Co Ltd* [1962] 1 QB 432, [1961] 3 All ER 1074, CA; *Blaker v Weller* [1964] Crim LR 311 (in all of these cases, there had been appeals).
11   See *Reynolds v Kennedy* (1748) 1 Wils 232, as explained in *Sutton v Johnstone* (1785) 1 Term Rep 493 at 505–506 per Eyre B. In the earlier of these cases it was held that malice could not be

inferred as the original tribunal gave judgment for the defendants but in the later it was said that it would have been more correct if the court had ruled that that fact enabled it to hold that there was reasonable and probable cause. See also *Craig v Hasell* (1843) 4 QB 481. It seems clear that a conviction subsequently reversed is not conclusive evidence of reasonable and probable cause: *Herniman v Smith* [1938] AC 305, [1938] 1 All ER 1, HL.

728. Necessity for malice in fact. A claimant in a claim for damages for malicious prosecution or other abuse of legal proceedings has to prove malice in fact[1] indicating that the defendant was actuated either by spite or ill-will against the claimant, or by indirect or improper motives[2]. However, there is not malice merely because the claimant's conviction was a necessary step towards the defendant's fulfilment of some ulterior objective[3].

The claimant has the burden of proving malice[4]. In a jury trial the question of malice or no malice is for the jury not for the judge, and if there is any evidence on which the jury could find malice, the judge must leave the question to it[5]. A claimant who proves malice but not want of reasonable and probable cause still fails[6]. Malice may be inferred from want of reasonable and probable cause but lack of reasonable and probable cause is not to be inferred from malice[7].

1 As to the distinction between malice in fact and malice in law see *Bromage v Prosser* (1825) 4 B & C 247 at 255; *Shearer v Shields* [1914] AC 808 at 813–814, HL, per Viscount Haldane LC. As to malicious prosecution see PARA 716 et seq.

2 *Hicks v Faulkner* (1881) 8 QBD 167 at 175, DC. See also *Mitchell v Jenkins* (1833) 5 B & Ad 588 at 595 per Parke J; *Haddrick v Heslop and Raine* (1848) 12 QB 267 at 276 per Coleridge J (where the prosecution was for the purpose of stopping the plaintiff's mouth); *Stevens v Midland Counties Rly Co* (1854) 10 Exch 352 (where the defendant's object was to punish some one in order to deter others); *Abrath v North Eastern Rly Co* (1883) 11 QBD 440 at 455, CA, per Bowen LJ (affd (1886) 11 App Cas 247, HL); *Brown v Hawkes* [1891] 2 QB 718 at 722 per Cave J, and at 728, CA, per Bowen LJ; *Corea v Peiris* [1909] AC 549, PC; *Glinski v McIver* [1962] AC 726, [1962] 1 All ER 696, HL (alleged purpose of prosecution being to punish plaintiff for giving evidence in other proceedings could be malice). There is no claim for negligent prosecution: *Elguzouli-Daf v Metropolitan Police Comr* [1995] QB 335, [1995] 1 All ER 833, CA. See also *Thacker v Crown Prosecution Service* (1997) Times, 29 December (negligence or incompetence in bringing or continuing a prosecution cannot in themselves justify an inference of malice).

3 See *Abbott v Refuge Assurance Co Ltd* [1962] 1 QB 432, [1961] 3 All ER 1074, CA (ultimate aim of recovering property). Alderson B, in *Stevens v Midland Counties Rly Co* (1854) 10 Exch 352 at 356, may have gone too far when he said that any motive other than that of simply instituting a prosecution for the purpose of bringing a person to justice is a malicious motive.

4 *Brown v Hawkes* [1891] 2 QB 718 at 726, CA, per Lord Esher MR. For an example of the claimant failing in his claim for want of proof of malice, although he proved absence of reasonable and probable cause, see *Wershof v Metropolitan Police Comr* [1978] 3 All ER 540.

5 *Mitchell v Jenkins* (1833) 5 B & Ad 588; *Hicks v Faulkner* (1881) 8 QBD 167, DC (affd (1882) 46 LT 130, CA).

6 *Turner v Ambler* (1847) 10 QB 252; *Tempest v Snowden* [1952] 1 KB 130, [1952] 1 All ER 1, CA.

7 *Glinski v McIver* [1962] AC 726 at 744, [1962] 1 All ER 696 at 700, HL, per Viscount Simonds; *Turner v Ambler* (1847) 10 QB 252; *Johnstone v Sutton* (1786) 1 Term Rep 510, Ex Ch.

729. Existence of reasonable and probable cause for prosecution. It has been said that whether there was reasonable and probable cause for a prosecution or not is a question of fact and not law[1]. However, it is for the judge and not the jury, when there is a trial for malicious prosecution by a jury[2], to decide on the relevant facts whether there is reasonable and probable cause[3]. If the facts are disputed, it is the province of the jury to find for the judge what are the relevant facts known to the prosecutor before he made the charge[4], including the inferences to be drawn from them[5].

The question whether the defendant in a claim for malicious prosecution had an honest belief that the claimant was guilty of the charge for which the prosecution was brought is a question which may be put to the jury[6]; but there should not be added to it words which may cause the jury to consider whether there was reasonable and probable cause for that belief, as this is a question for the judge[7], and the question of the defendant's belief should not be put unless there is evidence of his lack of belief[8]. Indeed it may well be preferable in many cases to put to the jury, instead of any question about the defendant's belief, the salient disputed facts on the determination of which the judge may found his decision whether there was or was not reasonable or probable cause[9]. Although malice may be inferred from want of reasonable and probable cause, want of reasonable and probable cause is not to be inferred from malice[10].

1   *Herniman v Smith* [1938] AC 305 at 316, [1938] 1 All ER 1 at 8, HL, per Lord Atkin, following *Lister v Perryman* (1870) LR 4 HL 521 at 535 per Lord Chelmsford and at 538 per Lord Westbury. The question whether there is any evidence of want of reasonable and probable cause is a question of law: *Tempest v Snowden* [1952] 1 KB 130 at 135, [1952] 1 All ER 1 at 3, CA, per Sir Raymond Evershed MR. It has been said that the claimant must either prove that the defendant did not believe the claimant had been guilty or that a person of ordinary prudence and caution, in view of the facts which he honestly believed, would not conclude that the claimant had been guilty: see *Glinski v McIver* [1962] AC 726, [1962] 1 All ER 696, HL.

2   As to the right to trial by jury for malicious prosecution see PARA 746.

3   *Pain v Rochester and Whitfield* (1602) Cro Eliz 871; *Coxe v Wirrall* (1607) Cro Jac 193; *Johnstone v Sutton* (1786) 1 Term Rep 510 at 545, Ex Ch, per Lord Mansfield and Lord Loughborough; *Broad v Ham* (1839) 5 Bing NC 722; *Panton v Williams* (1841) 2 QB 169, Ex Ch; *Hicks v Faulkner* (1881) 8 QBD 167, DC; *Brown v Hawkes* [1891] 2 QB 718, CA; *Cox v English, Scottish and Australian Bank* [1905] AC 168 at 171, PC; *Herniman v Smith* [1938] AC 305 at 316, [1938] 1 All ER 1 at 8, HL, per Lord Atkin; *Leibo v D Buckman Ltd* [1952] 2 All ER 1057 at 1063, CA, per Denning LJ (dissenting). See also *Gibbons v Alison* (1846) 3 CB 181 (civil proceedings). The decision in *M'Donald v Rooke* (1835) 2 Bing NC 217 that the existence of reasonable and probable cause in some cases be left to the jury can no longer be regarded as authoritative. The burden of proof of want of reasonable and probable cause is on the claimant: *Cox v English, Scottish and Australian Bank* [1905] AC 168, PC. As to shifting the burden of proof see PARA 736. If on undisputed facts the judge holds that there was reasonable and probable cause there will be no case for the jury and the claimant must fail: *Blachford v Dod* (1831) 2 B & Ad 179; *Davis v Hardy* (1827) 6 B & C 225.

4   *Herniman v Smith* [1938] AC 305 at 316, [1938] 1 All ER 1 at 8–9, HL, per Lord Atkin. As to the effect of facts coming to the prosecutor's knowledge after he has commenced the prosecution see PARA 732.

5   *Taylor v Willans* (1831) 2 B & Ad 845; *Panton v Williams* (1841) 2 QB 169, Ex Ch; *Green v De Havilland* (1968) 112 Sol Jo 766.

6   *Abrath v North Eastern Rly Co* (1883) 11 QBD 440 (affd (1886) 11 App Cas 247, HL); *Herniman v Smith* [1938] AC 305 at 316, [1938] 1 All ER 1 at 8–9, HL, per Lord Atkin; *Leibo v D Buckman Ltd* [1952] 2 All ER 1057 at 1072, CA, per Hodson LJ.

7   *Herniman v Smith* [1938] AC 305 at 317, [1938] 1 All ER 1 at 9, HL, per Lord Atkin (disapproving a statement in *Hicks v Faulkner* (1881) 8 QBD 167 at 172, DC, per Hawkins J); *Tempest v Snowden* [1952] 1 KB 130, [1952] 1 All ER 1, CA.

8   *Bradshaw v Waterlow & Sons Ltd* [1915] 3 KB 527, CA; *Herniman v Smith* [1938] AC 305 at 316, [1938] 1 All ER 1 at 8, HL, per Lord Atkin; *Glinski v McIver* [1962] AC 726, [1962] 1 All ER 696, HL; *Dallison v Caffery* [1965] 1 QB 348, [1964] 2 All ER 610, CA.

9   *Leibo v D Buckman Ltd* [1952] 2 All ER 1057 at 1063–1064, CA, per Denning LJ in his dissenting judgment.

10 *Glinski v McIver* [1962] AC 726 at 744, [1962] 1 All ER 696 at 700, HL, per Viscount Simonds; *Turner v Ambler* (1847) 10 QB 252; *Johnstone v Sutton* (1786) 1 Term Rep 510, Ex Ch.

730. Meaning of 'reasonable and probable cause' for a prosecution.
Reasonable and probable cause for a prosecution has been said to be an honest belief in the guilt of the accused based on a full conviction, founded upon

reasonable grounds, of the existence of a state of circumstances which, assuming them to be true, would reasonably lead any ordinarily prudent and cautious man, placed in the position of an accuser, to the conclusion that the person charged was probably guilty of the crime imputed[1].

It has been suggested that there may be exceptions to the rule that a belief in the guilt of the accused is necessary in order to constitute reasonable and probable cause for a prosecution, for example where the prosecution feels that the case is so strong against the accused that he must prosecute, although he refuses out of fairness of mind to believe the accused guilty until the court finds him so, or where the prosecutor acts on legal advice[2] that the evidence justifies a prosecution[3].

In general, however, at least when the accused was in fact innocent[4], belief in his guilt is essential to the existence of reasonable and probable cause[5], and such belief must at the date of the prosecution be based on grounds which, or some of which[6], are reasonable[7], and arrived at after due inquiry[8].

1   *Herniman v Smith* [1938] AC 305 at 316, [1938] 1 All ER 1 at 8, HL, per Lord Atkin, approving *Hicks v Faulkner* (1881) 8 QBD 167 at 171, DC, per Hawkins J; *Glinski v McIver* [1962] AC 726, [1962] 1 All ER 696, HL. See also *Broad v Ham* (1839) 5 Bing NC 722 at 725 per Tindal CJ, who said that reasonable cause is such as would operate on the mind of a discreet man, and probable cause such as would operate on the mind of a reasonable man. As to the grounds for the prosecutor's belief in there being a reasonable and probably cause for the prosecution, see PARA 731. As to malicious prosecution see PARA 716 et seq.

2   As to the effect of taking counsel's opinion before a prosecution and acting upon it see PARA 740 note 2; and LEGAL PROFESSIONS vol 66 (2015) PARA 865. See *Glinski v McIver* [1962] AC 726 at 745, [1962] 1 All ER 696 at 701, HL, per Viscount Simonds, at 756–757 and 708 per Lord Radcliffe, and at 777 and 721 per Lord Devlin; *Abbott v Refuge Assurance Co* [1962] 1 QB 432 at 450, [1961] 3 All ER 1074 at 1084, CA, per Ormerod LJ (counsel's opinion in favour of prosecution a potent factor but not conclusive).

3   See *Tempest v Snowden* [1952] 1 KB 130 at 139, [1952] 1 All ER 1 at 5, CA, per Denning LJ. See also *Musgrove v Newell* (1836) 1 M & W 582 (see PARA 732); *Phillips v Naylor* (1859) 4 H & N 565, Ex Ch, where the prosecution acted in good faith under a mistaken view of the law; *Johnson v Emerson and Sparrow* (1871) LR 6 Exch 329 at 365 per Bramwell B; *Tims v John Lewis & Co Ltd* [1951] 2 KB 459 at 472, CA, where Lord Goddard CJ stated that the existence of reasonable and probable cause is to be determined objectively and not subjectively; *Leibo v D Buckman Ltd* [1952] 2 All ER 1057 at 1069, CA, per Jenkins LJ. It has been said that a person who, on the strength of circumstances of grave suspicion which are insufficient to convince him of the guilt of the person concerned, institutes an unsuccessful prosecution under a sense of public duty would have a defence to a claim of malicious prosecution, not because there was reasonable and probable cause, but because he could negative malice: *Shrosbery v Osmaston* (1877) 37 LT 792 at 795 per Lindley J.

4   When the jury is satisfied that the claimant, although acquitted, was in fact guilty of the charge complained of, the defendant's belief seems to be immaterial: *Heslop v Chapman* (1853) 23 LJQB 49 at 52, Ex Ch; *Leibo v D Buckman Ltd* [1952] 2 All ER 1057 at 1063–1065, CA, per Denning LJ (dissenting). Cf *Bank of New South Wales v Piper* [1897] AC 383, PC, where as the plaintiff plainly knew that he had committed the offence for which he was prosecuted, it was held unnecessary to ask the jury if the defendant had an honest belief in the plaintiff's guilt. A private citizen who gives the police an honest and reasonably accurate account of an event, and who believes and acts on the advice of a responsible police officer, has reasonable and probable cause: *Malz v Rosen* [1966] 2 All ER 10, [1966] 1 WLR 1008.

5   *Ravenga v Mackintosh* (1824) 2 B & C 693; *Broad v Ham* (1839) 5 Bing NC 722; *Hinton v Heather* (1845) 14 M & W 131; *Turner v Ambler* (1847) 10 QB 252; *Haddrick v Heslop Raine* (1848) 12 QB 267 at 274 per Lord Denman CJ; *Heslop v Chapman* (1853) 23 LJQB 49; *Williams v Banks* (1859) 1 F & F 557; *Johnson v Emerson and Sparrow* (1871) LR 6 Exch 329 at 351 per Cleasby B; *Leibo v D Buckman Ltd* [1952] 2 All ER 1057, CA; *Glinski v McIver* [1962] AC 726, [1962] 1 All ER 696, HL. See also PARA 732.

6   *Hailes v Marks* (1861) 7 H & N 56.

7   *Hicks v Faulkner* (1881) 8 QBD 167; affd (1882) 46 LT 130, CA. See also *Michell v Williams* (1843) 11 M & W 205; *Douglas v Corbett* (1856) 6 E & B 511; *Wright v Sharp* (1947) 176 LT

308; *Wershof v Metropolitan Police Comr* [1978] 3 All ER 540; *Coudrat v Revenue and Customs Comrs* [2005] EWCA Civ 616, [2005] STC 1006 (reasonable to proceed on basis of largely circumstantial evidence).

8   *Lister v Perryman* (1870) LR 4 HL 521; *Quartz Hill Consolidated Gold Mining Co v Eyre* (1883) 11 QBD 674, CA; *Abrath v North Eastern Rly Co* (1883) 11 QBD 440, CA (affd (1886) 11 App Cas 247, HL); *Brown v Hawkes* [1891] 2 QB 718, CA. As to the limit of the prosecutor's duty to test the facts see PARA 731. A question whether the defendant instituted proper inquiries before taking action should not be left to the jury unless there is evidence of his not having made proper inquiries: see *Bradshaw v Waterlow & Sons Ltd* [1915] 3 KB 527, CA, where it was also said that there could not be an absence of reasonable and probable cause when the Attorney General had granted his fiat for the prosecution and it was not shown that the facts were put before him unfairly. Similarly, the question whether the defendant honestly believed in the charge which he made ought not to be left to the jury unless there is some evidence of the absence of that belief: see PARA 729.

731. Grounds for prosecutor's belief. In establishing whether a prosecution was malicious, the presence of reasonable and probable cause for a prosecution[1] does not depend upon the actual existence, but upon a reasonable belief held in good faith in the existence, of such facts as would justify a prosecution[2]. It is not required of any prosecutor that he must have tested every possible relevant fact before he takes action; his duty is not to ascertain whether there is a defence, but whether there is reasonable and probable cause for a prosecution[3]. The belief in the existence of such facts as would justify a prosecution, or the belief in the accused's guilt, may arise out of the recollection of the prosecutor, if he has always found his memory trustworthy[4], or out of information furnished to him by others and accepted by him as true[5].

There may be reasonable and probable cause for preferring a criminal charge even though the prosecutor has before him only prima facie evidence[6], or such as might not be admissible before a jury[7], and the question will be whether the impression produced on the mind of the prosecutor by the facts before him was such as would be produced on the mind, not of a lawyer, but of a discreet and reasonable man[8].

The absence of corroboration of an accomplice's statement is not evidence of want of reasonable and probable cause[9].

Where a prosecutor had nothing before him but circumstances of mere suspicion[10], or where he knew that the acts on which the prosecution was founded were done openly and in good faith in assertion of a legal right, there is in general no reasonable and probable cause[11].

1   See PARA 730. As to malicious prosecution see PARA 716 et seq.
2   *Hicks v Faulkner* (1881) 8 QBD 167 at 173, DC. See also PARA 730. It will be assumed, until the contrary is shown, that the prosecutor, before prosecuting, was acquainted with the substance of the evidence which his witnesses afterwards gave: *Walker v South Eastern Rly Co, Smith v South Eastern Rly Co* (1870) LR 5 CP 640 at 644.
3   *Herniman v Smith* [1938] AC 305 at 319, [1938] 1 All ER 1 at 10, HL, per Lord Atkin; *Glinski v McIver* [1962] AC 726, [1962] 1 All ER 696, HL; *Dallison v Caffery* [1965] 1 QB 348, [1964] 2 All ER 610, CA.
4   *Hicks v Faulkner* (1881) 8 QBD 167 at 172–173, DC.
5   *Lister v Perryman* (1870) LR 4 HL 521 at 536 per Lord Chelmsford, and at 538 per Lord Westbury; *Hicks v Faulkner* (1881) 8 QBD 167 at 173. A prosecutor is entitled to act upon reasonable hearsay evidence (*Chatfield v Comerford* (1866) 4 F & F 1008; *Lister v Perryman* (1870) LR 4 HL 521), but the omission to sift information which appears to be suspicious may be evidence of the want of reasonable and probable cause (*Lister v Perryman* (1870) LR 4 HL 521; *Brown v Hawkes* [1891] 2 QB 718 at 728, CA, per Kay LJ).
6   *Dawson v Vansandau* (1863) 11 WR 516; *Glinski v McIver* [1962] AC 726, [1962] 1 All ER 696, HL. See also *Coudrat v Revenue and Customs Comrs* [2005] EWCA Civ 616, [2005] STC 1006 (largely circumstantial evidence).
7   *Hicks v Faulkner* (1881) 8 QBD 167, DC (affd (1882) 46 LT 130, CA).

8   *Lister v Perryman* (1870) LR 4 HL 521.
9   *Bradshaw v Waterlow & Sons Ltd* [1915] 3 KB 527, CA.
10 See e g *Clements v Ohrly* (1847) 2 Car & Kir 686 (similarity of handwriting). Cf *Marham v Pescod* (1606) Cro Jac 130 (possession of stolen goods). See also *Roberts v Orchard* (1863) 2 H & C 769 at 777, Ex Ch, per Willes J; *Leete v Hart* (1868) LR 3 CP 322 at 324 per Byles J; *Chamberlain v King* (1871) LR 6 CP 474 at 478 per Willes LJ.
11 *Huntley v Simson* (1857) 2 H & N 600 (c f *Corea v Peiris* [1909] AC 549, PC). Circumstances of suspicion against the claimant in connection with other matters, if known to the defendant at the time, afford evidence of reasonable and probable cause: *Wilkinson v Foote* (1856) 5 WR 22. See also *Brooks v Warwick* (1818) 2 Stark 389; *James v Phelps* (1840) 11 Ad & El 483; *Hinton v Heather* (1845) 14 M & W 131, where the defendant knew that he, and not the plaintiff, was in the wrong.

732. Prosecutor's knowledge at time of prosecution. The existence of reasonable and probable cause for a prosecution[1] is not sufficient unless the facts which constituted it were known to the prosecutor at the time of the prosecution[2], but, if he did know those facts, the benefit of such knowledge is not necessarily displaced by the subsequent communication of some other fact, which, although it might affect the mind of a reasonable man and may affect the prosecutor's conviction of the guilt of the accused, does not alter the facts already known to him[3]. However, if in the course of the prosecution something comes to light which shows it to be groundless, there is, it seems, no reasonable or probable cause for continuing the prosecution[4].

1   See PARA 730. As to malicious prosecution see PARA 716 et seq.
2   *Delegal v Highley* (1837) 3 Bing NC 950; *Turner v Ambler* (1847) 10 QB 252; *Heslop v Chapman* (1853) 23 LJQB 49, Ex Ch; *Johnson v Emerson and Sparrow* (1871) LR 6 Exch 329 at 351–353 per Cleasby B. If it then existed, the burden of proof would be on the claimant to show that the defendant did not know of it: *Brooks v Blain* (1869) 39 LJCP 1.
3   *Musgrove v Newell* (1836) 1 M & W 582 (discussed in *Tempest v Snowden* [1952] 1 KB 130 at 139, [1952] 1 All ER 1 at 5, CA, per Denning LJ) (representations as to good character of persons accused).
4   *Tims v John Lewis & Co Ltd* [1951] 2 KB 459 at 472, CA, per Lord Goddard CJ.

733. Damage needs to be shown for malicious prosecution claim to succeed. To support a claim for damages for malicious prosecution[1], one of three heads of damage must be shown. The damage may be:

(1)   damage to a person's fame, as where the matter of which he is accused is scandalous; or

(2)   damage done to the person, as where his life, limb or liberty is endangered; or

(3)   damage to his property, as where he is put to the expense of acquitting himself of the crime with which he is charged[2].

The claimant must show that any damage to fame suffered was a necessary and natural consequence of the charge itself, and as regards the second head of damage, that actual loss of liberty was suffered[3]. Once one of these heads of damage is proved, damages are at large and may include compensation for loss of reputation and injured feelings[4].

1   As to malicious prosecution see PARA 716 et seq.
2   *Savile v Roberts* (1698) 1 Ld Raym 374 at 378 per Holt CJ; *Berry v British Transport Commission* [1962] 1 QB 306, [1961] 3 All ER 65, CA, where the plaintiff was allowed 15 guineas costs on being acquitted on a charge of pulling a train's communication cord, but in her action for malicious prosecution was awarded the additional £64 2s legal expenses which she incurred, since there is no presumption that in criminal proceedings (unlike in civil proceedings) a successful party will be allowed costs. See also *Calix v A-G of Trinidad and Tobago* [2013] UKPC 15, [2013] 4 All ER 401, [2013] 1 WLR 3283, where the appellant's claim for damage to

reputation had to be judged on an objective basis and measured by reference to the fact that he had been previously of good character and he had been prosecuted for the very serious offence of rape.

3   *Berry v British Transport Commission* [1961] 1 QB 149, [1960] 3 All ER 322. On appeal the Court of Appeal found damage under head (3) and did not comment on the rulings of Diplock J in regard to heads (1) and (2): *Berry v British Transport Commission* [1962] 1 QB 306, [1961] 3 All ER 65, CA. It remains uncertain whether the obiter dicta in *Wiffen v Bailey and Romford UDC* [1915] 1 KB 600, CA, to the effect that it is enough if the crime is punishable by imprisonment even though the claimant has not been sentenced to imprisonment, are good law.

4   *Wershof v Metropolitan Police Comr* [1978] 3 All ER 540. A claimant's conduct may be relevant to the question of the award of exemplary (or 'punitive') damages: *Bishop v Metropolitan Police Comr* [1990] 1 LS Gaz R 30, (1989) 133 Sol Jo 1626, CA. As to exemplary or punitive damages see generally DAMAGES vol 29 (2014) PARA 325 et seq.

(v) Malicious Prosecution: Proof of Claim

734. Proof of trial and conviction or acquittal. In order to establish that there has been a malicious prosecution[1], evidence of such proceedings must be shown. Where it is necessary to prove the trial and conviction or acquittal of a person charged with an indictable offence, the record or a copy of it need not be produced, but it is sufficient to produce what purports to be a certificate by the proper officer of the court where such conviction or acquittal took place of the indictment, trial, conviction or acquittal[2]. For proof of proceedings in magistrates' courts, the register of a magistrates' court, or an extract from it certified by the designated officer as a true extract, is admissible in any legal proceedings as evidence of the proceedings of the court entered in the register[3].

1   As to malicious prosecution see PARA 716 et seq.
2   Evidence Act 1851 s 13 (amended by the Statute Law Revision Act 1892; the Access to Justice Act 1999 s 90(1), Sch 13 para 2(1), (2), (3); and the Courts Act 2003 s 109(1), Sch 8 para 34).
3   See the Magistrates' Courts Rules 1981, SI 1981/552, r 68 (amended by SI 2001/610; SI 2003/1236; SI 2005/617); and CRIMINAL PROCEDURE vol 28 (2010) PARA 618.

735. Burden of proof initially on the claimant. The burden of proof in a claim for damages for malicious prosecution[1] lies in the first instance on the claimant[2]. It is not sufficient for him to prove that he was innocent of the crime for which he was prosecuted by the defendant by proving that the prosecution terminated in his favour[3]; he must also show that the defendant acted maliciously[4] and without reasonable and probable cause[5].

1   As to malicious prosecution see PARA 716 et seq.
2   As to the burden of proof generally see CIVIL PROCEDURE vol 11 (2009) PARA 769 et seq.
3   See PARAS 726–727.
4   See PARA 728.
5   See *Cox v English, Scottish and Australian Bank* [1905] AC 168 at 170, PC, per Lord Davey, citing *Abrath v North Eastern Rly Co* (1883) 11 QBD 440 at 455, CA, per Bowen LJ (affd (1886) 11 App Cas 247, HL); *Corea v Peiris* [1909] AC 549, PC. As to the level of evidence required as to absence of reasonable and probable cause see PARA 741. As to the position where it is shown that there was no reasonable or probable cause for some of the charges, or part of the charge, preferred against the claimant see PARA 742. As to the meaning of 'reasonable and probable cause' see PARA 730.

736. Absence of reasonable and probable cause for prosecution; shifting the burden of proof. In a claim for malicious prosecution[1], if want of reasonable care on the part of the defendant is relied upon, that, as an element in the absence of reasonable and probable cause[2], must be proved by the claimant[3]; and so if facts existed which, if known to the defendant, would have constituted reasonable and probable cause, the burden of showing that they were not known to him would lie on the claimant[4]. The burden of proof, in the sense of the burden of adducing evidence, is not stationary; when the claimant has given such evidence as, if not answered, will entitle him to a verdict, the burden of proof is shifted to the defendant[5].

1 As to malicious prosecution see PARA 716 et seq.

2 See PARAS 729–730.

3 *Abrath v North Eastern Rly Co* (1883) 11 QBD 440, CA; affd (1886) 11 App Cas 247, HL. It was there said that the want of reasonable care on the part of the prosecutor to inform himself of the true state of the case was a 'fundamental fact' in the determination of the question of reasonable and probable cause, as distinguished from mere evidence of it: see *Abrath v North Eastern Rly Co* at 450–451, CA, per Brett MR, and at 460 per Bowen LJ. Lord Bramwell, however, doubted this in (1886) 11 App Cas 247 at 254. Orders to provide further information as to the grounds which the defendant had for instituting the prosecution are not generally made (see *Maass v Gas Light and Coke Co* [1911] 2 KB 543, CA), but this may need re-consideration in light of legal developments (see *Gibbs v Rea* [1998] AC 786 at 794, [1998] 3 WLR 72 at 77, PC). It is settled practice that the claimant is not entitled to particulars of reasonable and probable cause when the defence merely denies want of reasonable and probable cause: *Roberts v Owen* (1890) 6 TLR 172, DC; *Weinberger v Inglis* [1918] 1 Ch 133); *Stapeley v Annetts* [1969] 3 All ER 1541, [1970] 1 WLR 20, CA, where Lord Denning (at 1542 and 23) said that the contrary statement in *Alman v Oppert* [1901] 2 KB 576 at 578, CA, per Collins LJ was an error. It is only where the defendant puts forward a positive allegation of reasonable and probable cause that he should be required to give particulars of it: *Stapeley v Annetts* [1969] 3 All ER 1541 at 1542, [1970] 1 WLR 20 at 22, CA, per Lord Denning MR. As to the procedure for obtaining further information see CPR Pt 18; and CIVIL PROCEDURE.

4 *Brooks v Blain* (1869) 39 LJCP 1.

5 *Abrath v North Eastern Rly Co* (1883) 11 QBD 440 at 456, CA, per Bowen LJ.

737. Inference of malice from want of reasonable and probable cause in bringing prosecution. In a claim for malicious prosecution, those facts which constitute the want of reasonable and probable cause may also supply evidence of malice[1]. However, if there is no other evidence of malice than what in the judge's opinion[2] establishes a want of reasonable and probable cause, any jury, upon the question of malice, is not bound by that opinion, but may determine for itself whether there was such a want of reasonable and probable cause as to amount to malice[3]. If the defendant, in prosecuting the claimant, honestly believed in his guilt, the jury should not infer malice if the only evidence of it is the absence of reasonable and probable cause[4].

1 *Parrott v Fishwick* (1772) 9 East 362n; *Johnstone v Sutton* (1786) 1 Term Rep 510 at 545, Ex Ch; *Mitchell v Jenkins* (1833) 5 B & Ad 588; *Quartz Hill Consolidated Gold Mining Co v Eyre* (1883) 11 QBD 674 at 687, CA per Brett MR, and at 694 per Bowen LJ; *Mills v Kelvin and James White Ltd* 1913 SC 521; *Meering v Grahame-White Aviation Co Ltd* (1919) 122 LT 44 at 49, CA, per Warrington LJ. As to malice see further PARAS 728, 738 et seq. As to want of reasonable and probable cause see PARAS 729–730.

2 For the principle that it is for the judge to decide whether there is reasonable and probable cause see PARA 729.

3 *Quartz Hill Consolidated Gold Mining Co v Eyre* (1883) 11 QBD 674 at 687, CA, per Brett MR, approving *Hicks v Faulkner* (1881) 8 QBD 167 at 174–175, DC.

4 *Brown v Hawkes* [1891] 2 QB 718, CA; *Meering v Grahame-White Aviation Co Ltd* (1919) 122 LT 44 at 55, CA, per Atkin LJ. See also *Stewart v Beaumont* (1866) 4 F & F 1034. As to trial by jury for malicious prosecution see PARA 746.

738. Further instances in which malice in bringing a prosecution may be inferred. Where the defendant's alleged justification for bringing a prosecution shows a gross ignorance of law, malice may be inferred by the jury[1].

The advertising of the indictment by the defendant is evidence of malice[2], and so is improper conduct on his part in substantiating it[3]. The fact that the defendant has on a previous occasion made a charge against the claimant would also seem to be evidence of malice[4].

Where the prosecutor knows that the accused is innocent there is, of course, clear evidence of malice, and the fact that he was bound on his recognisances to prosecute will be no answer to an action[5].

1 *Brooks v Warwick* (1818) 2 Stark 389. Cf *Snow v Allen* (1816) 1 Stark 502, where the defendant was advised by his solicitor on the authority of a reported case that he was acting rightly. As to trial by jury for malicious prosecution see PARA 746. As to the requirement of malice see also PARAS 728, 737.
2 *Chambers v Robinson* (1726) 2 Stra 691.
3 *Heath v Heape* (1856) 1 H & N 478.
4 Cf the analogous rule in defamation: *Barrett v Long* (1851) 3 HL Cas 395.
5 *Dubois v Keats* (1840) 11 Ad & El 329; *Fitzjohn v Mackinder* (1861) 9 CBNS 505.

739. Where malice is not implied. In a claim for malicious prosecution[1], the mere fact that the claimant was acquitted for want of prosecution does not prove malice on the part of the defendant[2]. Where the motives of the defendant are mixed, the claimant will fail unless he establishes that the dominant purpose is something other than the vindication of the law[3].

1 As to malicious prosecution see PARA 716 et seq.
2 *Purcell v Macnamara* (1808) 9 East 361. See also *Sykes v Dunbar* (1799) 1 Camp 201n. As to the requirement of malice see PARAS 728, 737 et seq.
3 *Abbott v Refuge Assurance Co Ltd* [1962] 1 QB 432, [1961] 3 All ER 1074, CA.

740. Proof of defendant's motive for bringing prosecution. The defendant in a claim for damages for malicious prosecution[1] may give evidence of all the facts that were before his mind at the time of the prosecution, whether for the purpose of negativing malice or of establishing reasonable and probable cause[2].

1 As to malicious prosecution see PARA 716 et seq.
2 *Thomas v Russell* (1854) 9 Exch 764 at 765 per Pollock CB. See also *Abrath v North Eastern Rly Co* (1883) 11 QBD 440, CA; affd (1886) 11 App Cas 247, HL. The fact that the defendant relied on the opinion of counsel may afford a defence, but only if the opinion was founded on a fair statement of the facts, and was acted on in good faith: *Hewlett v Cruchley* (1813) 5 Taunt 277; *Ravenga v Mackintosh* (1824) 2 B & C 693; *Abbott v Refuge Assurance Co Ltd* [1962] 1 QB 432 at 455–456, [1961] 3 All ER 1074 at 1087–1088, CA, per Upjohn LJ; *Glinski v McIver* [1962] AC 726 at 745, [1962] 1 All ER 696 at 701, HL, per Viscount Simonds, at 756–757 and 708 per Lord Radcliffe, and at 777 and 721 per Lord Devlin; *Malz v Rosen* [1966] 2 All ER 10, [1966] 1 WLR 1008. The same approach applies in respect of reliance on the advice of a police officer: *Riches v DPP* [1973] 2 All ER 935, [1973] 1 WLR 1019, CA. See also *Reynolds v Metropolitan Police Comr* [1985] QB 881, [1984] 3 All ER 649, CA (advice of Director of Public Prosecutions).
   As to the requirement of malice see PARAS 728, 737 et seq. As to reasonable and probable cause see PARAS 729–730.

741. Only slight evidence of absence of reasonable and probable cause is necessary. In proving the absence of reasonable and probable cause in a claim for damages for malicious prosecution[1] the claimant has to prove a negative, and, in general, need only give slight evidence of that[2].

However, absence of reasonable and probable cause cannot be inferred from the most express malice[3]. The mere innocence of the claimant is not prima facie proof of its absence[4], and the fact that no indictment was preferred[5], or that the defendant did not give evidence at the trial although he was present in court[6], does not prove it.

1   As to malicious prosecution see PARA 716 et seq. As to reasonable and probable cause see PARAS
    729–730.
2   *Cotton v James* (1830) 1 B & Ad 128 at 133 per Lord Tenterden CJ; *Taylor v Willans* (1831) 2
    B & Ad 845 at 857 per Lord Tenterden CJ. Cf *Fish v Scott* (1792) Peake 135. A jury, if any (see
    PARA 746), should not be asked whether the defendant had an honest belief in the guilt of the
    claimant unless there is evidence of want of reasonable and probable cause: *Trebeck v Croudace*
    [1918] 1 KB 158, [1916–1917] All ER Rep 441, CA (the issue is omitted from the report in
    [1918] 1 KB 158). See also PARA 729. It would seem that the burden of proof is on the claimant
    to put in the depositions: see *Lea v Charrington* (1889) 5 TLR 218 at 219 (on appeal 23 QBD
    45, DC; affd 23 QBD 272, CA). The defendant cannot rely on the depositions of the witnesses
    in his favour, but must call the witnesses: *Jackson v Bull and Alison* (1838) 2 Mood & R 176.
3   *Anon* (1703) 6 Mod Rep 73; *Johnstone v Sutton* (1786) 1 Term Rep 510 at 545, Ex Ch;
    Incledon v Berry (1805) 1 Camp 203n; *Turner v Ambler* (1847) 10 QB 252; *Glinski v McIver*
    [1962] AC 726 at 744, [1962] 1 All ER 696 at 700, HL, per Viscount Simonds. As to the
    requirement of malice see PARAS 728, 737 et seq.
4   See PARA 735. The proof of innocence may, however, involve with it other circumstances, eg that
    the prosecutor knew that his evidence was false, which would show that there was no
    reasonable and probable cause: *Abrath v North Eastern Rly Co* (1883) 11 QBD 440 at
    462, CA, per Bowen LJ. See also Buller's Law of Nisi Prius (5th Edn) 14.
5   *Wallis v Alpine* (1805) 1 Camp 204n.
6   *Taylor v Willans* (1831) 2 B & Ad 845. See also *Incledon v Berry* (1805) 1 Camp 203n; *Purcell
    v Macnamara* (1808) 9 East 361. From this fact, however, a want of reasonable and probable
    cause may be inferred: *Taylor v Willans* (1831) 2 B & Ad 845 at 857 per Lord Tenterden CJ. See
    also *Shufflebottom v Allday* (1857) 5 WR 315.

**742.   Proof of absence of reasonable and probable cause on some charges
only.**   If the claimant in a claim for damages for malicious prosecution[1] was
indicted on more than one charge, it is sufficient for him to show that there was
no reasonable and probable cause[2] for some of the charges in the indictment,
although there may have been cause for others[3]. If the indictment contained only
one charge, it is in general sufficient for the claimant to show that there was no
reasonable and probable cause for part of the charge[4].

1   As to malicious prosecution see PARA 716 et seq.
2   As to reasonable and probable cause see PARAS 729–730.
3   *Reed v Taylor* (1812) 4 Taunt 616; *Ellis v Abrahams* (1846) 8 QB 709. See also *R v Prosser*
    (circa 1770), cited in 1 Term Rep at 533; *Delisser v Towne* (1841) 1 QB 333; *Boaler v Holder*
    (1886) 54 LT 298; *Boaler v Holder* (1887) 51 JP 277.
4   *Palmer v Birmingham Manufacturing Co* (1902) 18 TLR 552 (charge of larceny of several
    articles; absence of reasonable and probable cause as to some of articles); *Leibo v
    D Buckman Ltd* [1952] 2 All ER 1057, CA (charge of stealing £35, later reduced to £27 3s;
    evidence on which jury entitled to hold that prosecutor had no honest belief in plaintiff's guilt as
    regards any part of money alleged to have been stolen; even assuming that prosecutor had
    reasonable and probable cause for preferring charge in respect of one sum of £7 1s, plaintiff
    entitled to judgment). It has been suggested that in such a case the question might resolve itself
    into one of degree, and that, if the theft of 20s was charged and reasonable and probable cause
    was shown as regards 19s, the prosecutor, if sued for malicious prosecution, might be entitled to
    succeed, even if in making the charge he acted maliciously, while if reasonable and probable
    cause was shown as to 1s only, he would not be so entitled: see *Leibo v D Buckman Ltd* [1952]
    2 All ER 1057 at 1071, CA, per Jenkins LJ.

743.   Defendant's disbelief in the claimant's guilt.   If the facts before the
defendant when prosecuting prima facie amounted to reasonable and probable
cause, but the defendant did not actually believe the claimant to be guilty and he
was not so in fact, it seems that in general the want of such belief is conclusive
evidence of the want of reasonable and probable cause[1]. However, there may be
exceptions to the rule that a belief in the guilt of the claimant is essential to the
existence of reasonable and probable cause[2]. The claimant must prove the

absence of such a belief if he alleges that it was absent[3]. The question whether such a belief existed ought not to be left to any jury unless there is some evidence that it was absent[4].

1   *Broad v Ham* (1839) 5 Bing NC 722. See the cases cited in PARA 730 note 5; and note 3. As to malicious prosecution see PARA 716 et seq. As to reasonable and probable cause see PARAS 729–730.
2   See PARA 730.
3   *Turner v Ambler* (1847) 10 QB 252. See also *Delegal v Highley* (1837) 3 Bing NC 950; *Lister v Perryman* (1870) LR 4 HL 521. As to the sufficiency of grounds of belief see PARA 731. As to the use of orders for further information see PARA 736 note 3; and CIVIL PROCEDURE.
4   See PARA 729. As to trial by jury for cases of malicious prosecution see PARA 746.

744. Matters not amounting to evidence in proceedings for malicious prosecution. The fact that the jury took time to consider its verdict before acquitting an accused person is no proof of reasonable and probable cause for bringing the prosecution[1].

Neither the observations of the judge at the trial of the indictment[2], nor the observations of the magistrate in dismissing a charge, or of a jury in acquitting[3], can be used by the claimant as evidence[4].

On the issue of reasonable and probable cause evidence is probably not admissible at all to prove the claimant's bad character[5].

1   *Willans v Taylor* (1829) 3 Moo & P 350 at 365 per Park J, not following *Smith v Macdonald* (1799) 3 Esp 7. As to malicious prosecution see PARA 716 et seq. As to reasonable and probable cause see PARAS 729–730. As to trial by jury for malicious prosecution see PARA 746.
2   *Barker v Angell* (1841) 2 Mood & R 371, not following *Warne v Terry* (1836) unreported per Littledale J, there cited.
3   *Hibberd v Charles* (1860) 2 F & F 126.
4   *Wetzlar v Zachariah* (1867) 16 LT 432. Cf *Richards v Turner* (1840) Car & M 414. On principle, such observations would appear to be equally inadmissible for the defendant. Indeed, the reasons given by Mellor J in *Wetzlar v Zachariah* (1867) 16 LT 432 (inability of the prisoner to reply), apply rather to evidence against the claimant than for him: see *Brown v Foster* (1857) 1 H & N 736, where the plaintiff's counsel at the magistrates' court was called by the defendant at the trial as to the possible alteration by the plaintiff, during a remand, of a book produced in evidence.
5   See CIVIL PROCEDURE vol 11 (2009) PARA 801.

745. Matters to be pleaded by the claimant bringing proceedings for malicious prosecution. A claimant bringing proceedings for malicious prosecution[1] must expressly state in his particulars of claim[2]:

(1)   the previous proceedings instituted by the defendant of which he complains[3];

(2)   that in so far as they were capable of doing so they terminated in his favour[4];

(3)   that there was no reasonable and probable cause for the defendant instituting or carrying on those proceedings[5];

(4)   that the defendant was actuated by malice[6]; and

(5)   that he has suffered damage[7].

1   As to malicious prosecution see PARA 716 et seq.
2   As to particulars of claim see CIVIL PROCEDURE vol 11 (2009) PARA 123.
3   See PARA 718.
4   *Basébé v Matthews* (1867) LR 2 CP 684; *Redway v McAndrew* (1873) LR 9 QB 74; *Metropolitan Bank Ltd v Pooley* (1885) 10 App Cas 210 at 216, HL, per Lord Selbourne LC, and at 228 per Lord Fitzgerald. See also PARAS 726–727.
5   As to reasonable and probable cause see PARAS 729–730.
6   As to the requirement for malice see PARAS 728, 737 et seq.

7 See PARA 733. As to pleading damage see DAMAGES vol 29 (2014) PARA 627. See also CIVIL PROCEDURE.

(vi) Trial by Jury for Malicious Prosecution

746. Right to trial by jury for malicious prosecution proceedings. On the application of any party to an action in respect of malicious prosecution[1] to be tried in the Queen's Bench Division, the action must be tried with a jury[2] unless the court is of opinion that the trial requires any prolonged examination of documents or accounts or any scientific[3] or local investigation which cannot conveniently be made with a jury or unless the court is of opinion that the trial will involve 'section 6 proceedings'[4].

This does not affect the court's power to order different questions of fact in an action to be tried by different modes of trial[5].

1 Senior Courts Act 1981 s 69(1)(b) (amended by the Defamation Act 2013 s 11(1)). As to malicious prosecution see PARA 716 et seq. The application for trial by jury must be made within 28 days of service of the defence: see the Senior Courts Act 1981 s 69(2); CPR 26.11(1); and CIVIL PROCEDURE vol 12 (2009) PARA 1132. See also *Gregory v Metropolitan Police Comr* [2014] EWHC 3922 (QB), [2015] 1 All ER 1029, [2014] All ER (D) 292 (Nov).
  The right to trial by jury under the Senior Courts Act 1981 s 69(1) is restricted to malicious prosecution in criminal matters and there is no right to jury trial in respect of the malicious presentation of a petition in bankruptcy: *Woodward v IRC* (2002) 73 TC 516. The court has a discretion to order a jury trial in such a case: Senior Courts Act 1981 s 69(3).
2 As to the right to trial by jury generally see CIVIL PROCEDURE vol 12 (2009) PARA 1132.
3 Scientific investigation includes a medical investigation: *Darragh v Chief Constable of Thames Valley Police* [1998] 43 LS Gaz R 32, (1998) Times, 20 October, CA.
4 Senior Courts Act 1981 s 69(1) (amended by the Justice and Security Act 2013 s 19(1), Sch 2 Pt 2 para 8(1), (2)). 'Section 6 proceedings' are proceedings in which a closed material application may be made to the court under the Justice and Security Act 2013 s 6: see ss 6, 8(1), 14; and CIVIL PROCEDURE.
5 See the Senior Courts Act 1981 s 69(4).

(2) MALICIOUS PROCUREMENT OF ISSUE OF SEARCH WARRANT

747. When a claim lies for malicious procurement of a search warrant. A claim[1] lies where a person falsely and maliciously[2] and without reasonable and probable cause[3] procures the issue of a search warrant to the damage of another person[4]. However, where a person fairly and honestly lays the facts on which he relies and on which he bases his suspicions before a magistrate who then orders the issue of a search warrant, he is not liable for the exercise of the magistrate's discretion[5].

1 The claim is analogous to malicious prosecution (as to which see PARA 716 et seq). See *Reynolds v Metropolitan Police Comr* [1985] QB 881, [1984] 3 All ER 649, CA; *Gibbs v Rea* [1998] AC 786, [1998] 3 WLR 72, PC.
2 'Malice' in this tort means spite, ill-will, improper motive or intentional abuse of the process of the court: see *Gibbs v Rea* [1998] AC 786 at 797, [1998] 3 WLR 72, PC. An application in the first instance for separate search warrants against two different persons in respect of one thing suspected to be stolen does not necessarily show malice: *Utting v Berney* (1888) 5 TLR 39. As to malice see also PARAS 728, 737 et seq.
  Incompetence or negligence on the part of the police will not entitle a person to bring a claim for damages on these grounds: *Keegan v Chief Constable of Merseyside Police* [2003] EWCA Civ 936, [2003] 1 WLR 2187. Cf the view taken by the European Court of Human Rights: Application 28867/03 *Keegan v United Kingdom* (2006) 44 EHRR 716, [2006] All ER (D) 235 (Jul), ECtHR (breaking into home, mistakenly believing suspect lived there, infringed the

Convention for the Protection of Human Rights and Fundamental Freedoms (Rome, 4 November 1950; TS 71 (1953); Cmd 8969) arts 8 and 13).

3   As to want of reasonable and probable cause (in the context of malicious prosecution) see PARA 729 et seq.

4   See *Cooper v Booth* (1785) 3 Esp 135 at 144 (cited in argument sub nom *Boot v Cooper* in *Johnstone v Sutton* (1786) 1 Term Rep 510 at 535, Ex Ch); *Elsee v Smith* (1822) 1 Dow & Ry KB 97; *Hensworth v Fowkes* (1833) 4 B & Ad 449; *Wyatt v White* (1860) 5 H & N 371. See also *Everett v Ribbands* [1952] 2 QB 198 at 205, [1952] 1 All ER 832 at 826, CA, per Denning LJ; *Reynolds v Metropolitan Police Comr* [1985] QB 881, [1984] 3 All ER 649, CA.
An essential of the claim for malicious prosecution is that the proceedings maliciously instituted by the defendant must have terminated in the claimant's favour (see PARA 726). This is not a requirement of a claim for malicious procurement of the issue of a search warrant because the application for a search warrant, being granted on information without notice, is incapable of terminating in the claimant's favour (see the cases cited above). As to warrants to search for stolen goods see the Theft Act 1968 s 26; and CRIMINAL LAW vol 25 (2010) PARA 302.

5   *Hope v Evered* (1886) 17 QBD 338 at 340, DC, per Lord Coleridge CJ; *Lea v Charrington* (1889) 23 QBD 45, DC (on appeal 23 QBD 272, CA). See also *Leigh v Webb* (1800) 3 Esp 165; *Elsee v Smith* (1822) 1 Dow & Ry KB 97. There is no tort of maliciously refusing bail: see *Gizzonio v Chief Constable of Derbyshire* (1998) Times, 28 April, CA.

(3) MALICIOUS CIVIL PROCEEDINGS

748.   Malicious civil proceedings generally.   The tort of malicious proceedings is not at present generally available in respect of civil proceedings, and has only been admitted in a civil context in a few special cases of abuse of legal process[1]. These include malicious institution of bankruptcy or winding-up proceedings[2], malicious arrest or detention[3], malicious execution against property[4], and malicious arrest of a ship[5]. Excluding the last of these, a common feature of these situations is the initial abuse of legal process with arguably immediate and perhaps irreversible damage to the reputation of the victim[6]. Liability for abuse of process is considered to be a distinct tort by some authorities[7], but it has also been said that it too closely resembles liability for malicious proceedings to be treated separately[8].

The proceedings referred to in this context are proceedings in due form of law; if the proceedings complained of were wholly void or illegal a claim of trespass will lie for an interference with person or property under cover of them, and malice need not be alleged or proved[9].

The tort of malicious proceedings does not extend to disciplinary proceedings[10].

1   *Gregory v Portsmouth City Council* [2000] 1 AC 419 at 428, [2000] 1 All ER 560 at 565, HL, per Lord Steyn. See also *Metall und Rohstoff v Donaldson Lufkin & Jenrette Inc* [1990] 1 QB 391 at 471, [1989] 3 All ER 14 at 51–52, CA, per Slade LJ. In *Gregory v Portsmouth City Council* [2000] 1 AC 419 at 432–433, [2000] 1 All ER 560 at 570–571, HL, Lord Steyn doubted the desirability of extending the tort of malicious proceedings to civil legal proceedings generally. However, the Privy Council has since suggested that malicious prosecution should indeed apply equally to civil as to criminal proceedings: see *Crawford Adjusters (Cayman) Ltd v Sagicor General Insurance (Cayman) Ltd* [2013] UKPC 17, [2014] AC 366, [2013] 4 All ER 8 (Lords Sumption and Neuberger dissenting); and PARA 716. As to claims for malicious prosecution see PARA 716 et seq.
2   See PARA 751.
3   See PARAS 752–753.
4   See PARA 754.
5   See PARA 755.

6   *Gregory v Portsmouth City Council* [2000] 1 AC 419 at 427, [2000] 1 All ER 560 at 566, HL, per Lord Steyn. In the case of malicious arrest of a ship, the loss is merely financial: *Gregory v Portsmouth City Council* [2000] 1 AC 419 at 427, [2000] 1 All ER 560 at 566, HL. As to the

requirement that damage be proved see *Savile v Roberts* (1698) 1 Ld Raym 374 at 378 per Holt CJ; *Barker v Braham and Norwood* (1773) 3 Wils 368; *Bates v Pilling* (1826) 6 B & C 38; *Clissold v Cratchley* [1910] 2 KB 244, CA.

7   See PARA 757.

8   *Gregory v Portsmouth City Council* [2000] 1 AC 419 at 427, [2000] 1 All ER 560 at 565, HL, per Lord Steyn.

9   *Barker v Braham and Norwood* (1773) 3 Wils 368; *Bates v Pilling* (1826) 6 B & C 38; *Clissold v Cratchley* [1910] 2 KB 244, CA.

10 *Gregory v Portsmouth City Council* [2000] 1 AC 419, [2000] 1 All ER 560, HL.

749. Preliminary steps prior to issue of process. It is not an abuse of process for a solicitor to send a letter threatening legal proceedings before process has been issued and when to do so was legitimate for asserting the rights of his client[1].

1   *Pitman Training Ltd v Nominet UK* [1997] FSR 797 at 809–811, [1998] ITCLR 11 at 21–23 per Sir Richard Scott V-C. Cf *Grainger v Hill* (1838) 4 Bing NC 212, (proceedings effectively begun). A landlord who maliciously served a notice to quit on a tenant in circumstances which amounted to contempt of court committed no tort: *Chapman v Honig* [1963] 2 QB 502, [1963] 2 All ER 513, CA.

750. Proof of damage necessary to bring claim of malicious civil proceedings. The rule that proof of damage (unless damage is implied by law) is essential to a cause of action[1] applies to those actions based on malicious civil proceedings which are maintainable[2]. Broadly, the bringing of an ordinary civil claim, although brought maliciously and without reasonable and probable cause, will not support a claim by the person sued against the claimant for maliciously bringing the first action[3]. The reason given is that the claim cannot cause legal damage either to reputation, person or property[4]. As regards the first head of damage (reputation), damage is not a necessary consequence of civil claims, even where there are scandalous allegations in the pleadings[5]. If the claim is tried the defendant's fair fame will be cleared, should it deserve to be cleared; if the claim is not tried his fair fame is not assailed[6]. As to the second head of damage, no civil claim will result in damage to the person, in the sense of loss of life, limb or liberty[7]. As regards the third head of damage (that is damage to property), the court in the original claim will by its judgment give the defendant such costs as he is entitled to[8]. In practice, therefore, malicious institution of proceedings in tort or for breach of contract is not actionable[9]. The abuses of proceedings in respect of which the law acknowledges that damages can be recovered are malicious institution of bankruptcy or winding-up proceedings[10], malicious arrest[11], malicious execution[12], and malicious arrest of a ship[13].

1   See PARA 733. See also DAMAGES vol 29 (2014) PARAS 362–363.

2   *Quartz Hill Consolidated Gold Mining Co v Eyre* (1883) 11 QBD 674 at 688–689, CA, per Bowen LJ. There are some cases in which damage is necessarily involved, e g where a petition is maliciously presented to wind up a company (at least a trading company), for the presentation of such a petition must injure the credit of the company (*Quartz Hill Gold Consolidated Mining Co v Eyre* (1883) 11 QBD 674 at 691–693, CA), or where the proceedings affect or endanger a person's liberty (*Quartz Hill Consolidated Gold Mining Co v Eyre* (1883) 11 QBD 674 at 683, CA, per Brett MR, and at 689 per Bowen LJ, citing *Savile v Roberts* (1698) 1 Ld Raym 374 at 378), or where the proceedings result in the detention of goods (*The Walter D Wallet* [1893] P 202 at 207 per Sir Francis H Jeune P, applying *Chandler v Doulton* (1865) 3 H & C 553 (excessive distress)). See also *The St Clair (Owners) v The Audny (Owners)* 1922 SC 85 (excessive bail for ship).

3   *Quartz Hill Consolidated Gold Mining Co v Eyre* (1883) 11 QBD 674 at 689–690, CA, per Bowen LJ. Early cases, however, appear to favour the right to bring such a claim where damage could be proved: see *Waterer v Freeman* (1617) Hob 205 at 266–267 per Hobart CJ. In *Savile v Roberts* (1698) 1 Ld Raym 374, relied on by the court in *Quartz Hill Consolidated Gold*

Mining Co v Eyre (1883) 11 QBD 674, CA, it was held that if one person fancies he has a right against another he may bring a civil claim; but if the claim is one of mere vexation, the person sued cannot bring a claim for damages merely because the first claim was brought maliciously, since he must prove some special damage, eg that he was held to excessive bail. As to these two cases see *Wren v Weild* (1869) LR 4 QB 730 at 736 per Blackburn J. See also *Atwood v Monger* (1653) Sty 378.

4 *Quartz Hill Consolidated Gold Mining Co v Eyre* (1883) 11 QBD 674 at 689–690, CA, per Bowen LJ. As to the requirement for damage to be to reputation, person or property see *Savile v Roberts* (1698) 1 Ld Raym 374; and PARA 733.

5 *Quartz Hill Consolidated Gold Mining Co v Eyre* (1883) 11 QBD 674 at 689, CA, per Bowen LJ.

6 *Quartz Hill Consolidated Gold Mining Co v Eyre* (1883) 11 QBD 674 at 689–690, CA, per Bowen LJ. The passage in the judgment of Bowen LJ upon which the statement in the text is based was not necessary for the decision of the case, and it is submitted that, so far as it relates to a man's fame, it is not universally applicable. Serious damage might be caused to a person by the publication in interlocutory proceedings, or in the course of a long trial, of injurious allegations which he would have no immediate opportunity of contradicting.

7 See *Quartz Hill Consolidated Gold Mining Co v Eyre* (1883) 11 QBD 674 at 690, CA, per Bowen LJ.

8 *Quartz Hill Consolidated Gold Mining Co v Eyre* (1883) 11 QBD 674 at 690, CA, per Bowen LJ. The extra costs that the successful party is left to pay after recovery of party and party costs from the loser are not recoverable damage because they are deemed not to be caused by the unjust litigation: *Quartz Hill Consolidated Gold Mining Co v Eyre* (1883) 11 QBD 674 at 682–683, CA, per Brett MR. The only costs which are acknowledged for the purpose of a claim for malicious institution of proceedings are the costs allowed in the original claim, although there is judicial recognition of the fact that the award of costs in a civil claim is not adequate compensation for the costs actually incurred: see *Berry v British Transport Commission* [1962] 1 QB 306, [1961] 3 All ER 65, CA (costs in criminal and civil proceedings distinguished and full criminal outgoings awarded since there is no presumption that a successful party in criminal proceedings will be awarded costs).

9 *Quartz Hill Consolidated Gold Mining Co v Eyre* (1883) 11 QBD 674 at 688–690, CA, per Bowen LJ. But see *Crawford Adjusters (Cayman) Ltd v Sagicor General Insurance (Cayman) Ltd* [2013] UKPC 17, [2014] AC 366, [2013] 4 All ER 8; and PARAS 716, 748.

10 See PARA 751.

11 See PARAS 752–753.

12 See PARA 754.

13 See PARA 755.

751. Malicious institution of bankruptcy or winding-up proceedings.

A claim may be brought in respect of damage caused by maliciously[1] and without reasonable and probable cause[2] commencing bankruptcy proceedings against an individual or winding-up proceedings against a company provided that the proceedings terminated favourably to the claimant[3].

If, by false evidence, a person maliciously and without reasonable and probable cause procures an adjudication in bankruptcy, it will be no answer to a claim for damages brought after annulment that, even if the evidence were true, an adjudication could not have been properly made[4].

An action will lie for falsely and maliciously and without reasonable or probable cause presenting a bankruptcy or winding-up petition even though no pecuniary loss or special damage to the company can be proved, for the presentation of the petition is, from its very nature, calculated to injure the credit of the company[5].

1 Malice, which is a question of fact, may be inferred from the absence of reasonable and probable cause: *Mitchell v Jenkins* (1833) 5 B & Ad 588; and see PARA 737 (malicious prosecution). There was evidence of malice where the proceedings were taken, not to procure equal distribution of the debtor's assets, but to coerce him into the admission of a debt: *Johnson v Emerson and Sparrow* (1871) LR 6 Exch 329 at 355. Cf *Partizan Ltd v OJ Kilkenny & Co Ltd* [1998] 1 BCLC 157, [1998] BCC 912 (malice not proved). There will be strong, if not conclusive, evidence of malice where the bankruptcy proceedings were an abuse of the process

of the court, or were taken for the purpose of extortion, or of putting an improper pressure on the debtor, eg where the object was to stay an action against a third person (*Re Kemp, ex p Kemp* (1841) 1 Mont D & De G 657), or, in violation of good faith, to put an end to a valuable lease (*Re Gallimore, ex p Gallimore* (1816) 2 Rose 424), or to dissolve a partnership between the petitioning creditor and the debtor (*Re Browne, ex p Browne* (1810) 1 Rose 151; *Re Christie, ex p Saunders* (1833) Mont & B 329; *Re Johnson, ex p Johnson* (1842) 2 Mont D & De G 678; *Re Coulson and Phipps, ex p Phipps* (1844) 3 Mont D & De G 505), or where, there being no assets, the sole object was to defeat an action (*Re Bourne, ex p Bourne* (1826) 2 Gl & J 137). See also *Re Davis, ex p King* (1876) 3 ChD 461, CA, where a petition presented for the purpose of extorting money from the debtor was dismissed; *Re Adams, ex p Griffin* (1879) 12 ChD 480, CA, where the petitioner purchased a debt so as to obtain an adjudication for a fraudulent purpose. However, it seems that the existence of a mere bye motive, not affected with fraud, will not render bankruptcy proceedings an abuse of the process of the court. Thus proceedings were not avoided where the object of the petitioning creditor was to get the bankrupt out of a firm with which the petitioner had extensive dealings, there being no fraud on the part of the petitioner or concert with the other partners: *Re Wilbeam, ex p Wilbeam* (1820) Buck 459, sub nom *Re Wilbran, ex p Wilbran* 5 Madd 1 (approved in *King v Henderson* [1898] AC 720, PC). See also *Re Christie, ex p Saunders* (1833) Mont & B 329 at 351; and BANKRUPTCY AND INDIVIDUAL INSOLVENCY vol 5 (2013) PARA 189.

2   *Whitworth v Hall* (1831) 2 B & Ad 695, approved in *Metropolitan Bank Ltd v Pooley* (1885) 10 App Cas 210, HL. As to evidence of want of reasonable and probable cause in proceedings for malicious prosecution see PARAS 741–744. See also *Cotton v James* (1830) 1 B & Ad 128; *Hay v Weakley* (1832) 5 C & P 361 (annulment of adjudication not sufficient evidence); *Johnson v Emerson and Sparrow* (1871) LR 6 Exch 329 at 351–353 per Cleasby B; *Cox v English, Scottish and Australian Bank* [1905] AC 168, PC; *Partizan Ltd v OJ Kilkenny & Co Ltd* [1998] 1 BCLC 157, [1998] BCC 912 (absence of reasonable and probable cause not proved).

3   *Whitworth v Hall* (1831) 2 B & Ad 695; *Johnson v Emerson and Sparrow* (1871) LR 6 Exch 329 at 344 per Cleasby B; *Metropolitan Bank v Ltd Pooley* (1885) 10 App Cas 210, HL; *Beechey v William Hill (Park Lane) Ltd* [1956] CLY 5442, (1956) Times, 9 February. As to criminal proceedings terminating in favour of the claimant cf PARAS 726–727.

4   *Farley v Danks* (1855) 4 E & B 493; *Johnson v Emerson and Sparrow* (1871) LR 6 Exch 329 at 341 per Cleasby B. See also *Quartz Hill Consolidated Gold Mining Co v Eyre* (1883) 11 QBD 674 at 684, CA, per Brett MR.

5   *Quartz Hill Consolidated Gold Mining Co v Eyre* (1883) 11 QBD 674, CA. The court treated a winding-up petition as equivalent to a bankruptcy petition for these purposes, noting that the petition was required to be made public before such time as the company could defend itself against the imputations made against it: *Quartz Hill Consolidated Gold Mining Co v Eyre* (1883) 11 QBD 674 at 685, CA, per Brett MR. Cf *Wyatt v Palmer* [1899] 2 QB 106, CA, declining to stop as frivolous and vexatious a claim brought without special damage for the presentation of a malicious and unfounded bankruptcy petition which had been dismissed.

752. Malicious arrest or detention of a person. A claim may be brought for malicious arrest where a person maliciously and without reasonable and probable cause procures the arrest of a person[1]. The arrest constitutes sufficient damage for this tort[2]. Although no claim lies against a witness for words spoken in giving evidence in court[3], the gist of a claim for malicious arrest is that process was instituted as a result of which the court was induced to order the arrest of the claimant, and the claim will not be defeated because the giving of evidence was merely a step in bringing about the arrest[4]. A claim may also be brought for malicious detention of a person[5].

1   *Daniels v Fielding* (1846) 16 M & W 200; *Ross v Norman* (1850) 5 Exch 359; *Melia v Neate* (1863) 3 F & F 757; *Johnson v Emerson and Sparrow* (1871) LR 6 Exch 329; *Roy v Prior* [1971] AC 470, [1970] 2 All ER 729, HL (arrest to compel witness to give evidence). Cf *Revis v Smith* (1856) 18 CB 126. A person who makes default in payment of a sum adjudged to be paid by a conviction or by specified orders of a magistrates' court is liable to be committed to prison: see eg the Magistrates' Courts Act 1980 ss 76, 92; and MAGISTRATES vol 71 (2013) PARA 667. As to debts due to the Crown see further CIVIL PROCEDURE vol 12 (2009) PARA 1239. As to the arrest of debtors subject to bankruptcy proceedings see BANKRUPTCY AND INDIVIDUAL

INSOLVENCY vol 5 (2013) PARA 217. For an example of a claim for malicious arrest under emergency powers see *Pike v Waldrum and Peninsular and Oriental Steam Navigation Co* [1952] 1 Lloyd's Rep 431.

2   *Roy v Prior* [1971] AC 470, [1970] 2 All ER 729, HL. See PARA 750.
3   As to the protection given to witnesses in respect of evidence given in proceedings see CIVIL PROCEDURE vol 11 (2009) PARA 978; DEFAMATION vol 32 (2012) PARA 597 et seq.
4   See *Roy v Prior* [1971] AC 470 at 479–480, [1970] 2 All ER 729 at 735, HL, per Lord Morris, and at 480 and 736 per Lord Wilberforce. Thus a solicitor is liable where his evidence in open court on his applying for the warrant of arrest causes the arrest to be made: *Roy v Prior* [1971] AC 470, [1970] 2 All ER 729, HL, which also establishes that the tort may be committed even though a judge's order was necessary for the arrest. Cf *Daniels v Fielding* (1846) 16 M & W 200 at 207 per Rolfe B.
     It has been held that it is not essential to produce the warrant in order to prove that an arrest was made: *Crook v Dowling* (1782) 3 Doug KB 75; *Arundell v White* (1811) 14 East 216; *Casburn v Reid* (1818) 2 Moore CP 60; *Petrie v Lamont* (1842) 3 Man & G 702.
5   *Moore v Guardner* (1847) 16 M & W 595, where a debtor was not released after paying the costs he owed and for non-payment of which he was in custody under an attachment.

753. Arrest of privileged persons. A person privileged from arrest by reason of his having been ordered as a witness to attend a court, or by reason of any other court order, cannot, if arrested, recover damages on the strength of the privilege, even though the arrest was made maliciously and with knowledge of the privilege[1]. The privilege is that of the court which made the order[2], and the remedy is to apply to the court for release and to have the person making the arrest punished for contempt[3].

1   *Magnay v Burt* (1843) 5 QB 381, where a witness was arrested on returning from an examination order by the court; *Yearsley v Heane* (1845) 14 M & W 322, where a person was arrested after a protection order had been made under the Insolvent Debtors Act 1842 (repealed).
2   *Magnay v Burt* (1843) 5 QB 381. See also *Re Hunt* [1959] 2 QB 69, [1959] 2 All ER 252, CA.
3   *Magnay v Burt* (1843) 5 QB 381; *Yearsley v Heane* (1845) 14 M & W 322. See also *Watson v Carrol* (1839) 4 M & W 592; *Philips v Naylor* (1858) 3 H & N 14 (affd (1859) 4 H & N 565); and CONTEMPT OF COURT vol 22 (2012) PARA 42.

754. Malicious execution. A claim may be brought where a person maliciously and without reasonable and probable cause procures execution to be levied on a person's goods, causing him damage[1]. A claim may be brought if a judgment creditor maliciously takes out execution for the full amount when part of the debt has been paid[2], or if he refuses a tender of the debt and proceeds to execution[3]. From the nature of the claim, the claimant does not have to prove that the proceedings terminated in his favour[4].

1   *Churchill v Siggers* (1854) 3 E & B 929 at 937–938 per Lord Campbell. See also PARA 750. If judgment has been improperly obtained it should be set aside and any seizure in pursuance of it will be trespass: see *Bates v Pilling* (1826) 6 B & C 38; *Brown v Jones* (1846) 15 M & W 191.
2   *Churchill v Siggers* (1854) 3 E & B 929.
3   *Gilding v Eyre* (1861) 10 CBNS 592. If a creditor levies execution under a void warrant, or when he is unaware that the debt has been paid, the remedy is in trespass, not malicious execution: *Clissold v Cratchley* [1910] 2 KB 244, CA. See also CIVIL PROCEDURE vol 12 (2009) PARA 1375 et seq.
4   *Gilding v Eyre* (1861) 10 CBNS 592.

755. Maliciously procuring arrest of ship. A claim may be brought against a person who maliciously and without reasonable and probable cause procures, by means of Admiralty proceedings, the arrest of a ship, if the ship has been released and the proceedings have terminated in favour of the person aggrieved by the arrest[1]. The general rule that the cause of action does not accrue until there has been a prior determination in favour of the claimant does not apply in cases where the action is ancillary to the main proceedings and there is no risk of inconsistent findings or collateral attack[2].

In a claim for the malicious arrest of a ship, no actual or special damage need be proved; the claimant, if he succeeds, is entitled to at least nominal damages[3].

Where actual damage has been sustained, the Admiralty Court will not, if the facts are properly brought to its knowledge, which may be done by sworn statement or affidavit[4], put the injured party to the necessity of bringing a fresh claim, but will, in the original claim, award him damages for the wrongful arrest[5], usually in the nature of demurrage[6].

1 *Castrique v Behrens* (1861) 3 E & E 709; *Redway v McAndrew* (1873) LR 9 QB 74; *The Strathnaver* (1875) 1 App Cas 58 at 67, PC; *The Collingrove, The Numida* (1885) 10 PD 158; *The Walter D Wallet* [1893] P 202. The sentence in the text was considered in *Congentra AG v Sixteen Thirteen Marine SA, The Nicholas M* [2008] EWHC 1615 (Comm) at [35]–[44], [2009] 1 All ER (Comm) 479 at [35]–[44], [2008] 2 Lloyd's Rep 602 at [35]–[44] per Flaux J. As to proceedings terminating in favour of the claimant in cases of malicious prosecution see PARAS 726–727. As to the practice in Admiralty see SHIPPING AND MARITIME LAW vol 93 (2008) PARA 157 et seq.

2 *Congentra AG v Sixteen Thirteen Marine SA, The Nicholas M* [2008] EWHC 1615 (Comm), [2009] 1 All ER (Comm) 479, [2008] 2 Lloyd's Rep 602, citing *Gilding v Eyre* (1861) 10 CBNS 592 as an example. See also PARA 754.

3 *The Walter D Wallet* [1893] P 202. At least nominal damages must be awarded for the detention of the ship. The reasoning of this case seems relevant for the detention of any property, not merely ships. Where the defendant caused the claimant's ship to be wrongfully arrested in breach of contract by the defendant, and the claimant incurred bank interest charges in providing a bank guarantee for the purpose of releasing the ship, those interest charges were not a foreseeable consequence of the wrongful arrest and so were not recoverable damages: *Compania Financiera Soleada SA v Hamoor Tanker Corpn Inc, The Borag* [1981] 1 All ER 856, [1981] 1 WLR 274, CA. As to nominal damages see DAMAGES vol 29 (2014) PARAS 319–320.

4 *The Collingrove, The Numida* (1885) 10 PD 158 at 161 per Sir James Hannen P.

5 *The Evangelismos* (1858) 12 Moo PCC 352 at 359, PC, approved in *The Strathnaver* (1875) 1 App Cas 58, PC; *The Collingrove, The Numida* (1885) 10 PD 158 at 160 per Sir James Hannen P, following *The Orion* (1852) 12 Moo PCC 356n. See also *The Nautilus* (1856) Sw 105; *The Glasgow (otherwise The Ya Macraw)* (1856) Sw 145, where the element of malice seems to have been wanting. From the language of the court in *The Collingrove, The Numida* (1885) 10 PD 158 at 161, it might be inferred that to entitle the owner of a ship to damages for her arrest without cause it is enough to show something less than malice, namely 'that it was the result of gross negligence', but a reference to the authority on which this language is founded shows that the negligence must be that crassa negligentia from which the law implies malice: *The Evangelismos* (1858) 12 Moo PCC 352, PC.

6 *The Orion* (1852) 12 Moo PCC 356n; *The Nautilus* (1856) Sw 105; *The Glasgow (otherwise The Ya Macraw)* (1856) Sw 145. See SHIPPING AND MARITIME LAW vol 93 (2008) PARA 161 et seq.

(4) IMPROPER REGISTRATION OF JUDGMENTS

756. When a claim for improper registration of judgment may be brought. The improper registration of a judgment or order for the payment of money, by which the party against whom it has been obtained is prejudiced in disposing of his land[1], is not actionable without proof of malice and want of reasonable and probable cause[2].

1 As to writs and orders affecting land see REAL PROPERTY AND REGISTRATION vol 87 (2012) PARA 746.

2 *Gibbs v Pike* (1842) 9 M & W 351. As to the requirement of malice (in the context of malicious prosecution) see PARAS 728, 737 et seq. As to reasonable and probable cause (in the context of malicious prosecution) see PARAS 729–730.

(5) ABUSE OF PROCESS

757. When a claim for abuse of process lies. It is a tort to use legal process in its proper form in order to accomplish a purpose other than that for which it was designed and, as a result, to cause damage[1]. The claimant need not prove want of reasonable and probable cause, nor need the proceedings have terminated in his favour[2]. He must show that the defendant has used the proceedings for some improper purpose[3]. Proper process may become wrongful if unduly and unnecessarily repeated[4]. It has been said that liability for malicious abuse of process too closely resembles liability for malicious proceedings to be treated separately[5].

1   *Grainger v Hill* (1838) 4 Bing NC 212, where the defendant was held liable when he had the plaintiff arrested, ostensibly for non-payment of a debt, but in fact in order illegally to compel him to surrender the register of a vessel without which the plaintiff could not take the vessel out to sea. See also *Parton v Hill* (1846) 10 LT 414; *Churchill v Siggers* (1854) 3 E & B 929 at 937 per Lord Campbell; *Goldsmith v Sperrings Ltd* [1977] 2 All ER 566 at 574, [1977] 1 WLR 478 at 489, CA, per Lord Denning MR (dissenting), at 582 and 498–499 per Scarman LJ, and at 585 and 503 per Bridge LJ; *Re Marjory, a Debtor (No 757 of 1954)* [1955] Ch 600 at 623, [1955] 2 All ER 65 at 78, CA, per Lord Evershed MR. It seems that the claimant need not be a party to the abusive proceedings, and collusive proceedings involving others but designed to harm him may ground a claim: *Smith v Tunstall* (1687) Carth 3.

2   *Grainger v Hill* (1838) 4 Bing NC 212. See also *Speed Seal Products Ltd v Paddington* [1986] 1 All ER 91, [1985] 1 WLR 1327, CA. In *Smith v East Elloe RDC* [1956] AC 736, [1956] 1 All ER 855, HL, it was held that there was jurisdiction to hear a claim that a clerk of the council knowingly and in bad faith wrongfully procured a compulsory purchase order to be made and confirmed by a minister, even though a statute precluded the plaintiff from challenging the validity of the order itself on the grounds of bad faith. As to reasonable and probable cause in the context of malicious prosecution see PARAS 729–730. As to the requirement that proceedings terminated in the claimant's favour for a case of malicious prosecution to succeed see PARAS 726–727.

3   *Clissold v Cratchley* [1910] 2 KB 244, CA. Therefore, a defendant who by mistake issues civil process note for a debt which has already been paid is not liable: *Corbett v Burge, Warren and Ridgley Ltd* (1932) 48 TLR 626.

4   *Heywood v Collinge* (1838) 9 Ad & El 268 at 273–274 per Lord Denman CJ. If a person habitually, persistently and unreasonably institutes vexatious legal proceedings then, on application by the Attorney General, the High Court may direct that no legal proceedings be commenced or continued in any court without leave of the High Court: see the Senior Courts Act 1981 s 42 (amended by the Prosecution of Offences Act 1985 s 24); and CIVIL PROCEDURE vol 11 (2009) PARA 258. A court may not discharge the order but there may be an appeal to the Court of Appeal, limited to whether the order should have been made in the first place: *Rohrberg v Charkin* [1985] NLJ Rep 185, CA. The High Court has an inherent jurisdiction to prevent the institution of civil proceedings which are likely to constitute an abuse of the process of the court: *Ebert v Venvil, Ebert v Birch* [2000] Ch 484, [1999] 3 WLR 670, CA. An order made in the High Court prohibiting commencement of proceedings without leave may also extend to proceedings in the county court, but the county court should not purport to bind the High Court: *Ebert v Venvil, Ebert Birch* [2000] Ch 484, [1999] 3 WLR 670, CA. See also *Grepe v Loam* (1887) 37 ChD 168, CA; *Landi Den Hartog BV v Sea Bird (Clean Air Fuel Systems) Ltd* [1976] FSR 489; *Bhamjee v Forsdick (No 2)* [2003] EWCA Civ 1113, [2004] 1 WLR 88.

5   *Gregory v Portsmouth City Council* [2000] 1 AC 419 at 427, [2000] 1 All ER 560 at 565, HL, per Lord Steyn.

(6) PERJURY

758. Perjury. A claimant who is imprisoned in consequence of false evidence given by the defendant on oath at the claimant's trial has no cause of action; perjury is a crime but not a tort[1].

1 *Hargreaves v Bretherton* [1959] 1 QB 45, [1958] 3 All ER 122, approved obiter in *Roy v Prior* [1971] AC 470 at 477, [1970] 2 All ER 729 at 733, HL, per Lord Morris. The Court of Appeal held in *Marrinan v Vibart* [1963] 1 QB 528, [1962] 3 All ER 380 that the rule is not circumvented by alleging a conspiracy between witnesses to make false statements, but this may now be open to reconsideration in the light of the decision of the House of Lords in *Revenue and Customs Comrs v Total Network SL* [2008] UKHL 19, [2008] 1 AC 1174, [2008] 2 All ER 413 (criminal offence not involving commission of a tort sufficient to make out conspiracy to injure by unlawful means). See also PARA 714. As to the immunity of witnesses in tort, even for statements made before prosecution if made for the purpose of a possible prosecution, see *Evans v London Hospital Medical College* [1981] 1 All ER 715, [1981] 1 WLR 184; *Taylor v Serious Fraud Office* [1999] 2 AC 177, [1998] 4 All ER 801, HL; *Westcott v Westcott* [2008] EWCA Civ 818, [2009] QB 407, [2009] 1 All ER 727. As to perjury see CRIMINAL LAW vol 26 (2010) PARA 668.

10. TORT AND EMPLOYMENT

(1) EMPLOYER'S LIABILITIES TO EMPLOYEE

(i) Employer's Liabilities at Common Law

759. Employer's common law duty to employee. The common law has from early times imposed a duty on an employer to take reasonable care to see that his employees, jointly engaged with him in carrying on his work or industry, do not suffer injury in consequence of his personal negligence, including his failure properly to superintend and control the undertaking in which he and they are mutually engaged[1].

A breach of this duty causing personal injury has always given the employee a right of action. For his own personal negligence an employer was always, and still is, liable at common law[2]. A liability for personal negligence may arise not only where the employer actually takes part in the work himself[3] but also where, whether through his own acts and omissions or those of his agent, he fails to discharge his non-delegable duty of care to employees[4]. Alternatively the employer may be vicariously liable for the breach of duty of one employee who injures another[5].

1   See *Wilsons and Clyde Coal Co Ltd v English* [1938] AC 57, [1937] 3 All ER 628, HL. The duty is also an implied term in the contract of employment, so that an action for breach of the duty can be brought either in contract or in tort: see *Matthews v Kuwait Bechtel Corpn* [1959] 2 QB 57, [1959] 2 All ER 345, CA. For the employer's duty as to the safety of employment see HEALTH AND SAFETY AT WORK vol 52 (2014) PARA 376 et seq.

2   *Thomas v Quartermaine* (1887) 18 QBD 685 at 691, CA, per Bowen LJ. Claims are frequently brought in which damages are claimed first at common law and secondly for breach of statutory duty: see eg *Bath v British Transport Commission* [1954] 2 All ER 542, [1954] 1 WLR 1013, CA. As to negligence in general see NEGLIGENCE.

3   *Ashworth v Stanwix* (1861) 3 E & E 701.

4   As to non-delegable duties of care see PARA 794 et seq.

5   As to vicarious liability see PARA 767 et seq. As to the employer's right to recover an indemnity from the employee for whose fault he has been made vicariously liable see EMPLOYMENT vol 39 (2014) PARA 39.

760. Abolition of common employment: avoidance of contracting out. The doctrine of common employment[1] was that if the person occasioning and the person suffering an injury were fellow employees engaged in a common employment for and under the same employer, the employer, where he had taken reasonable care to select proper and competent employees, was not liable at common law for the consequences of the injury[2]. This doctrine is no longer a defence[3].

Moreover any provision contained in a contract of employment or apprenticeship or any collateral agreement is void in so far as it would have the effect of excluding or limiting the employer's liability in respect of personal injuries[4] caused to the person employed or apprenticed by the negligence of persons in common employment with him[5].

1   See the judgment of Abinger CB in *Priestley v Fowler* (1837) 3 M & W 1. The doctrine was established in the law of Scotland in *Bartonshill Coal Co v Reid* (1858) 3 Macq 266, HL, and *Bartonshill Coal Co v Maguire* (1858) 3 Macq 300, HL. See also *Graham (or Miller) v Glasgow Corpn* [1947] AC 368 at 372, [1947] 1 All ER 1 at 2–3, HL, per Viscount Simon. The last reported case before the House of Lords on the doctrine was *Glasgow Corpn v Bruce (or Neilson)* [1948] AC 79, [1947] 2 All ER 346, HL.

2 See *Priestley v Fowler* (1837) 3 M & W 1; *Wilson v Merry* (1868) LR 1 Sc & Div 326, HL. See also the cases cited in note 1.

3 See the Law Reform (Personal Injuries) Act 1948 ss 1(1), 3, 6(2). The Act binds the Crown: s 4. The Act was passed to remedy what had come to be regarded as a hardship to the injured employee by making the employer vicariously liable for injuries caused tortiously by a fellow employee: *Lindsay v Charles Connell & Co Ltd* 1951 SC 281, Ct of Sess at 285 per Lord Blades.

4 'Personal injury' includes any disease and any impairment of a person's physical or mental condition, and 'injured' must be construed accordingly: Law Reform (Personal Injuries) Act 1948 s 3.

5 See the Law Reform (Personal Injuries) Act 1948 s 1(3); and *Smith v British European Airways Corpn* [1951] 2 KB 893, [1951] 2 All ER 737 (a rule of a pension scheme void in so far as it excluded such liability). See also the provisions of the Unfair Contract Terms Act 1977 s 2(1), (2), which restrict avoidance of liability for negligence by a contract term. These provisions extend to a contract of employment only in favour of an employee: s 1(2), Sch 1 para 4. See further CONTRACT vol 22 (2012) PARAS 407–410.

(ii) Employer's Liability for Breach of Statutory Duty

761. Claim against employer for breach of statutory duty. Apart from the duty cast upon an employer at common law[1] there is a vast body of statute law imposing duties upon him in relation to the safety of working conditions which carry the sanctions of the criminal law[2].

Breach of a duty imposed by a statutory instrument containing (whether alone or with other provision) health and safety regulations is not actionable except to the extent that regulations under the Health and Safety at Work etc Act 1974[3] so provide[4]. Similarly, breach of a duty imposed by an existing statutory provision is not actionable except to the extent that such regulations[5] so provide (including by modifying any of the existing statutory provisions)[6]. Such regulations[7] may include provision for a defence to be available in any action for breach of the duty[8], or may include provision for any term of an agreement which purports to exclude or restrict any liability for such a breach to be void[9].

An employee may also maintain independently a civil claim in the common law tort of breach of statutory duty if it is shown that the provisions in question were intended to impose, in addition to a public duty, a duty enforceable by a person aggrieved by the contravention of the provisions[10], and that the damage or injury suffered by the employee was caused or materially contributed to by the breach[11].

1 See PARA 759.

2 For such provisions relating to agriculture, factories, mines and quarries see AGRICULTURAL PRODUCTION AND MARKETING vol 1 (2008) PARA 1246 et seq; HEALTH AND SAFETY AT WORK; MINES, MINERALS AND QUARRIES vol 76 (2013) PARA 511 et seq. Statutory regulations do not supersede the employer's common law duties, and the regulations ought not to be expected to cover every kind of danger: *Bux v Slough Metals Ltd* [1974] 1 All ER 262, [1973] 1 WLR 1358, CA. Irrespective of any liability or breach of duty on the part of his employer, an injured employee may be entitled to benefit under the state system of national insurance or of insurance against industrial injuries: see WELFARE BENEFITS AND STATE PENSIONS vol 104 (2014) PARA 174 et seq.

3 Ie the Health and Safety at Work etc Act 1974 s 47: see HEALTH AND SAFETY AT WORK vol 52 (2014) PARA 388.

4 Health and Safety at Work etc Act 1974 s 47(2) (substituted by the Enterprise and Regulatory Reform Act 2013 s 69(1), (3)). As to the making of health and safety regulations see the Health and Safety at Work etc Act 1974 s 15; and HEALTH AND SAFETY AT WORK vol 52 (2014) PARA 388. See also PARA 509.

5 Ie regulations under the Health and Safety at Work etc Act 1974 s 47.

6 Health and Safety at Work etc Act 1974 s 47(2A) (s 47(2A), (2B) added by the Enterprise and Regulatory Reform Act 2013 s 69(1), (3)).

7   Ie regulations under the Health and Safety at Work etc Act 1974 s 47.

8   Ie breach of the duty mentioned in the Health and Safety at Work etc Act 1974 s 47(2) or
     s 47(2A).

9   Health and Safety at Work etc Act 1974 s 47(2B) (as added: see note 6). See the Health and
     Safety at Work etc Act 1974 (Civil Liability) (Exceptions) Regulations 2013, SI 2013/1667; and
     HEALTH AND SAFETY AT WORK vol 52 (2014) PARA 380.

10   The courts have leaned in favour of conferring on employees a right to claim damages for breach
     of statutory duty imposed on their employers or the occupiers of factories in which they work:
     see *Solomons v R Gertzenstein Ltd* [1954] 2 QB 243 at 255, [1954] 2 All ER 625 at 631, CA,
     per Somervell LJ. As to the matters to be considered in construing a statute to ascertain whether
     a claim may be brought see PARA 504 et seq.

11   As to breach of statutory duty see PARA 500 et seq. As to defences to an action for breach of
     statutory duty see PARAS 516–521. As to causation see PARAS 514–515; and DAMAGES vol 29
     (2014) PARA 364 et seq.

762.   Claim against employer for injury caused by defective equipment.

Where an employee[1] suffers personal injury[2] in the course of his employment[3] in
consequence of a defect in equipment[4] provided by his employer for the purpose
of the employer's business[5] and the defect is attributable wholly or partly to the
fault[6] of a third party[7], the injury is deemed to be also attributable to negligence
on the part of the employer[8]. This is without prejudice to the law relating to
contributory negligence and to any remedy by way of contribution or in contract
or otherwise which is available to the employer in respect of the injury[9]. These
provisions bind the Crown[10]. Any agreement is void in so far as it purports to
exclude or limit this liability[11].

1   'Employee' means a person who is employed by another person under a contract of service or
     apprenticeship and is so employed for the purposes of a business carried on by that other
     person; and 'employer' is construed accordingly: Employer's Liability (Defective Equipment)
     Act 1969 ss 1(3), 2(1). The Employers' Liability (Compulsory Insurance) Act 1969 requires
     employers to insure against this liability (see INSURANCE vol 60 (2011) PARA 666), but directors
     of an insolvent company which failed to insure have been held not personally liable: *Richardson
     v Pitt-Stanley* [1995] QB 123, [1995] 1 All ER 460, CA.

2   'Personal injury' includes loss of life, any impairment of a person's physical or mental condition
     and any disease: Employer's Liability (Defective Equipment) Act 1969 s 1(3). The Act only
     applies to injuries suffered after its commencement (ie 25 October 1969): ss 1(1), 2(2).

3   As to the liability of an employer depending on the employee having acted 'in the course of his
     employment' see PARA 780.

4   'Equipment' includes any plant and machinery, vehicle, aircraft and clothing: Employer's
     Liability (Defective Equipment) Act 1969 s 1(3). For these purposes, 'equipment' includes a ship,
     even though ships are not mentioned in the clarifying definition in s 1(3): *Coltman v Bibby
     Tankers Ltd, The Derbyshire* [1988] AC 276, [1987] 3 All ER 1068, HL. See also *Knowles v
     Liverpool City Council* [1993] 4 All ER 321, [1993] 1 WLR 1428, HL (equipment includes
     material (on the facts, a paving stone) on which the employee is working).

5   'Business' includes the activities carried on by any public body: Employer's Liability (Defective
     Equipment) Act 1969 s 1(3).

6   'Fault' means negligence, breach of statutory duty or other act or omission which gives rise to
     liability in tort: Employer's Liability (Defective Equipment) Act 1969 s 1(3).

7   It is immaterial whether the third party is identified or not: Employer's Liability (Defective
     Equipment) Act 1969 s 1(1)(b).

8   Employer's Liability (Defective Equipment) Act 1969 s 1(1). It is immaterial whether or not the
     employer is otherwise liable in respect of the injury: s 1(1).

9   Employer's Liability (Defective Equipment) Act 1969 s 1(1). See also *James v Durkin (Civil
     Engineering Contractors)* (1983) Times, 25 May. As to contributory negligence see PARAS 518,
     764; and DAMAGES vol 29 (2014) PARA 382 et seq; NEGLIGENCE vol 78 (2010) PARA 75 et seq.

10   Employer's Liability (Defective Equipment) Act 1969 s 1(4). For these purposes, persons in the
     service of the Crown are treated as employees of the Crown: s 1(4).

11   Employer's Liability (Defective Equipment) Act 1969 s 1(2).

(iii) Defences available to Employers

763. Volenti non fit injuria. The defence of volenti non fit injuria is available to an employer as it is to any other defendant sued in tort[1], but for the defence to succeed it must be shown not only that the employee fully understood and appreciated the risk and danger of the work, but also that in carrying it out he acted as a volunteer in the strictest sense. In practice, therefore, the defence rarely succeeds where the employee is going about his usual work[2].

The principle volenti non fit injuria is not generally a defence to a claim for breach of a statutory duty intended to protect the employee[3], but the defence may be applicable where the employer is not personally in breach of the statute[4].

1 As to the defence of volenti non fit injuria see PARA 465; and NEGLIGENCE vol 78 (2010) PARA 69 et seq.

2 See *Bowater v Rowley Regis Corpn* [1944] KB 476, [1944] 1 All ER 465, CA, where the defence was held inapplicable in a case where a carter under protest drove a horse known to be unsafe which injured him. See also *Clarke v Holmes* (1862) 7 H & N 937; *Yarmouth v France* (1887) 19 QBD 647, DC; *Smith v Baker & Sons* [1891] AC 325, HL (where Lord Herschell, at 366, criticised the Court of Appeal's application of the defence in *Thomas v Quartermaine* (1887) 18 QBD 685, CA); *Monaghan v WH Rhodes & Son* [1920] 1 KB 487; *Baker v James* [1921] 2 KB 674; *D'Urso v Sanson* [1939] 4 All ER 26; *Hyett v Great Western Rly Co* [1948] 1 KB 345, [1947] 2 All ER 264; *Merrington v Ironbridge Metal Works Ltd* [1952] 2 All ER 1101, 117 JP 23; *Weir v Andrew Barclay & Co Ltd* 1955 SLT (Notes) 56, Ct of Sess; *General Cleaning Contractors Ltd v Christmas* [1953] AC 180, [1952] 2 All ER 1110, HL (a workman is not expected to initiate safety measures, and his continued work in an established dangerous system does not afford the employer a defence). The defence was applicable in *Taylor v Sims* [1942] 2 All ER 375; *Imperial Chemical Industries Ltd v Shatwell* [1965] AC 656, [1964] 2 All ER 999, HL; *O'Reilly v National Rail and Tramway Appliances Ltd* [1966] 1 All ER 499 (obiter).

3 *Baddeley v Earl Granville* (1887) 19 QBD 423, DC; *Davies v Thomas Owen & Co* [1919] 2 KB 39; *Wheeler v New Merton Board Mills Ltd* [1933] 2 KB 669, CA; *Alford v National Coal Board* [1952] 1 All ER 754 at 757, HL, per Lord Normand. See also PARA 519.

4 See *Imperial Chemical Industries Ltd v Shatwell* [1965] AC 656, [1964] 2 All ER 999, HL (employees in breach of statutory duty laid on them personally being volens could not hold employers liable for fellow workers' breaches). See also *Hugh v National Coal Board* 1972 SC 252, Ct of Sess.

764. Employee's contributory negligence. Even if an employee succeeds in establishing that his employer's breach of duty was a cause of his injuries, the employee may nevertheless be guilty of contributory negligence if there has been an act or omission on his part, amounting to want of reasonable care for his own safety, which has caused or contributed to the damage of which he complains[1].

Where the breach of duty on the part of the employer and the employee's own negligence are found to be material causes of the employee's injury, responsibility will be apportioned[2] between them[3] upon general principles which are dealt with elsewhere in this work[4].

1 As to contributory negligence see PARA 518; DAMAGES vol 29 (2014) PARA 382 et seq; NEGLIGENCE vol 78 (2010) PARA 75 et seq. As to the test for determining who is responsible for an accident see eg *Stapley v Gypsum Mines Ltd* [1953] AC 663 at 681, [1953] 2 All ER 478 at 485–486, HL, per Lord Reid. It was said in *Flower v Ebbw Vale Steel, Iron and Coal Co Ltd* [1934] 2 KB 132 at 140 per Lawrence J (at first instance in an action against an employer for breach of statutory duty) that an employee ought not to be held guilty of contributory negligence for every risky thing which he may do in his familiarity with the machine upon which he is working. This statement was approved in the same case in the House of Lords ([1936] AC 206 at 214, HL, per Lord Wright), and in *Caswell v Powell Duffryn Associated Collieries Ltd* [1940] AC 152 at 166, [1939] 3 All ER 722 at 731, HL, per Lord Atkin, and at 175 and 737 per Lord Wright; see also *Stringer v Automatic Woodturning Co Ltd* [1956] 1 All ER 327 at 332, 336, CA (action for breach of statutory duty). It has, however, been doubted how far the principle stated by Lawrence J in *Flower v Ebbw Vale Steel, Iron and Coal Co Ltd* [1934] 2 KB

132 applies in the case of an ordinary common law claim where there is no evidence of employees performing repetitive work under strain or for long hours at dangerous machines: see *Staveley Iron and Chemical Co Ltd v Jones* [1956] AC 627 at 642, 647, [1956] 1 All ER 403 at 408, 413, HL. Failure to ask for something which the employer is under a duty to provide may constitute contributory negligence: see *Clifford v Charles H Challen & Son Ltd* [1951] 1 KB 495, [1951] 1 All ER 72, CA. The mere fact that an employee suffered injury while trespassing on his employer's property does not make him guilty of contributory negligence: *Westwood v Post Office* [1974] AC 1, [1973] 3 All ER 184, HL.

2   Ie under the Law Reform (Contributory Negligence) Act 1945 s 1. As to apportionment of liability see DAMAGES vol 29 (2014) PARA 620 et seq; NEGLIGENCE vol 78 (2010) PARA 75 et seq.

3   See eg *Stapley v Gypsum Mines Ltd* [1953] AC 663, [1953] 2 All ER 478, HL (failure to fetch down insecure roof in mine; employee 80% to blame); *National Coal Board v England* [1954] AC 403, [1954] 1 All ER 546, HL (negligent shot-firing; employee 25% to blame); *Williams v Sykes and Harrison Ltd* [1955] 3 All ER 225, [1955] 1 WLR 1180, CA (unfenced machinery, employee 80% to blame); *Hodkinson v Henry Wallwork & Co Ltd* [1955] 3 All ER 236, [1955] 1 WLR 1195, CA (unfenced transmission machinery, employee 90% to blame). In all these cases the apportionment of the trial judge was altered on appeal. Normally an appellate court is loath to interfere with the discretion exercised by the trial judge (*National Coal Board v England* [1954] AC 403 at 427, [1954] 1 All ER 546, at 557, HL, per Lord Reid, and at 427–428 and 557 per Lord Tucker).

4   See DAMAGES vol 29 (2014) PARA 620 et seq; NEGLIGENCE vol 78 (2010) PARA 75 et seq.

(iv) Claims in respect of Employee's Death

765. Claim for breach of duty survives employee's death. A claim by an employee against his employer for breach of duty may survive the employee's death, since causes of action subsisting in him at his death survive for the benefit of his estate[1].

The damages recoverable include damages for medical expenses and pain and suffering undergone by the deceased before his death[2], but they do not extend to any loss to the deceased's estate in consequence of his death[3].

1   See the Law Reform (Miscellaneous Provisions) Act 1934 s 1(1); and WILLS AND INTESTACY vol 103 (2010) PARAS 12791280. Claims for defamation do not survive (see s 1(1) proviso (amended by the Law Reform (Miscellaneous Provisions) Act 1970 s 7, Schedule; and the Administration of Justice Act 1982 ss 4(2), 75, Sch 9 P I)), nor do claims for exemplary damages (see the Law Reform (Miscellaneous Provisions) Act 1934 s 1(2)(a)(i) (substituted by the Administration of Justice Act 1982 ss 4(2), 73(3), (4))), nor claims under the Fatal Accidents Act 1976 s 1A (see PARA 488; and DAMAGES vol 29 (2014) PARA 489 et seq; NEGLIGENCE vol 78 (2010) PARA 25 et seq) for bereavement damages (see the Law Reform (Miscellaneous Provisions) Act 1934 s 1(1A) (added by the Administration of Justice Act 1982 ss 4(1), 73(1))).

2   *Rose v Ford* [1936] 1 KB 90, CA; on appeal [1937] AC 826, [1937] 3 All ER 359, HL (where the decision that damages for pain and suffering were recoverable was in effect upheld in the House of Lords). As to damages for non-pecuniary loss (including pain and suffering) see DAMAGES vol 29 (2014) PARA 435 et seq.

3   See the Law Reform (Miscellaneous Provisions) Act 1934 s 1(2)(c). A sum for funeral expenses may, however, be included: see s 1(2)(c). See further WILLS AND INTESTACY vol 103 (2010) PARA 1282.

766. Claim for benefit of employee's dependants. A claim in respect of a wrongful act, neglect or default causing an employee's death may be brought by his personal representatives, as in the case of any other person whose death is so caused, for the benefit of his dependants[1]. This right is additional to the rights conferred by the survival of the cause of action previously mentioned[2].

1   See the Fatal Accidents Act 1976; PARA 488; and DAMAGES vol 29 (2014) PARA 489 et seq; NEGLIGENCE vol 78 (2010) PARA 25 et seq.

2   See the Law Reform (Miscellaneous Provisions) Act 1934 s 1(5) (amended by the Carriage by Air Act 1961 s 14(3), Sch 2); and WILLS AND INTESTACY vol 103 (2010) PARA 1282. As to the survival of the cause of action see PARA 765.

(2) EMPLOYER'S VICARIOUS LIABILITY

(i) General Principles of Vicarious Liability

767. Employer vicariously liable in tort independent of personal fault. Independently of personal fault, an employer[1] will be vicariously liable for a tort[2] committed by an employee[3] in the course of employment[4].

1　As to the specific position of corporations, public authorities, trustees and the Crown see PARA 786 et seq.
2　As to the commission of a tort by the employee see PARA 768 et seq.
3　As to the employer's liability for torts committed by another person's employee whom he has temporarily hired see PARA 800 et seq. As to the employer's liability as principal for torts committed by an agent see PARA 791 et seq. As to the employer's liability for torts committed by an independent contractor in those exceptional circumstances where a personal and non-delegable duty arises see PARA 794 et seq. Certain relationships, while not strictly within the bounds of an employment contract, may be akin to the employer/employee relationship and therefore may be subject to the principles of vicarious liability: see *Various Claimants v Catholic Child Welfare Society* [2012] UKSC 56, [2013] 2 AC 1, [2013] 1 All ER 670; *JGE v Trustees of the Portsmouth Roman Catholic Diocesan Trust* [2012] EWCA Civ 938, sub nom *E v English Province of Our Lady of Charity* [2013] QB 722, [2012] 4 All ER 1152; and PARA 773.
4　See PARA 778 et seq.

(ii) Commission of a Tort by the Employee

768. Tort committed by the employee. To render an employer vicariously liable it is necessary to prove that his employee has been guilty of a tort towards the person injured[1]. The employer is not responsible where the injury is occasioned without the commission of a tort[2]. Where, although his employee has been negligent, one of the causes of the injury is contributory negligence of the person injured, liability will be apportioned[3].

1　*Majrowski v Guy's and St Thomas's NHS Trust* [2006] UKHL 34 at [15], [2007] 1 AC 224 at [15], [2006] 4 All ER 395 at [15] per Lord Nicholls, rejecting the 'employer's tort' theory whereby it is only the employee's acts, and not his torts, that are attributed to the employer. See also *Crédit Lyonnais Bank Nederland NV (now known as Generale Bank Nederland NV) v Export Credits Guarantee Department* [2000] 1 AC 486, [1999] 1 All ER 929, HL (all the elements of a tort must occur within the course of employment; the employer is not liable if what is done within the course of employment is not a complete tort and completion by the employee would lie outside the course of employment, even if what is done in the course of employment would assist a third party to commit a tort); *Armstrong v Strain* [1952] 1 KB 232, [1952] 1 All ER 139, CA; *Esso Petroleum Co Ltd v Southport Corpn* [1956] AC 218, [1955] 3 All ER 864, HL; *Staveley Iron and Chemical Co Ltd v Jones* [1956] AC 627 at 639, [1956] 1 All ER 403 at 406, HL, per Lord Morton. The employer's vicarious liability, if any, is of course distinct from his liability for any personal breach of duty by him arising out of the same facts: *Staveley Iron and Chemical Co Ltd v Jones* [1956] AC 627 at 639, [1956] 1 All ER 403 at 406, HL, per Lord Morton. See also *Port Swettenham Authority v TW Wu & Co* [1979] AC 580, [1978] 3 All ER 337, PC.
2　*Aston v Heaven* (1797) 2 Esp 533; *Christie v Griggs* (1809) 2 Camp 79; *Crofts v Waterhouse* (1825) 3 Bing 319; *Holmes v Mather* (1875) LR 10 Exch 261.
3　Ie under the Law Reform (Contributory Negligence) Act 1945 s 1. As to contributory negligence see PARAS 518, 764; DAMAGES vol 29 (2014) PARA 382 et seq; NEGLIGENCE vol 78 (2010) PARA 75 et seq.

769. Nature of tort immaterial for purposes of establishing vicarious liability. For the purposes of establishing vicarious liability, the nature of the tort committed by the employee is immaterial and the employer is liable whether the tort is an assault[1], a false imprisonment[2], a conversion[3], a trespass to land[4], an infringement of a patent or trade mark[5], a nuisance[6] or a breach of statutory duty[7]. An employer, including a corporation[8], is liable even where the tort involves malice or guilty knowledge, as, for instance, in the case of malicious prosecution[9], libel or slander[10] or fraud[11]. It must, however, be proved in every case that the conduct in question was within the scope of the employee's authority or employment[12].

1   *Seymour v Greenwood* (1861) 7 H & N 355, Ex Ch; *Eastern Counties Rly Co v Broom* (1851) 6 Exch 314 (corporation); *Bayley v Manchester, Sheffield and Lincolnshire Rly Co* (1873) LR 8 CP 148, Ex Ch (corporation); *Dyer v Munday* [1895] 1 QB 742, CA. See also PARA 784. The employer is not liable if the assault was an act of private vengeance on the part of the employee, not committed in the course of, or otherwise closely connected with, his employment: *Warren v Henlys Ltd* [1948] 2 All ER 935; cf *Mattis v Pollock (t/a Flamingos Nightclub)* [2003] EWCA Civ 887, [2004] 4 All ER 85, [2003] 1 WLR 2158; *Gravil v Carroll* [2008] EWCA Civ 689, [2008] ICR 1222, [2008] IRLR 829. See also *Weddall v Barchester Healthcare Ltd; Wallbank v Wallbank Fox Designs Ltd* [2012] EWCA Civ 25, [2012] IRLR 307, [2012] All ER (D) 01 (Feb) (an employer may be vicariously liable where an employee reacts to a reasonable instruction with violence, unless the request was a pretext for violence unconnected with the work).
    As to the course of employment see PARA 780. As to actions for assault see PARA 528 et seq.
2   *Goff v Great Northern Rly Co* (1861) 3 E & E 672; *Walker v South Eastern Rly Co, Smith v South Eastern Rly Co* (1870) LR 5 CP 640; *Moore v Metropolitan Rly Co* (1872) LR 8 QB 36.
3   *Lloyd v Grace, Smith & Co* [1912] AC 716, HL; *Jones v Hart* (1698) 2 Salk 441; *Yarborough v Bank of England* (1812) 16 East 6 (corporation); *Giles v Taff Vale Rly Co* (1853) 2 E & B 822, Ex Ch (corporation). See PARA 604 et seq.
4   *Gregory v Piper* (1829) 9 B & C 591; *Lyons v Martin* (1838) 8 Ad & El 512. See also PARA 563 et seq. Cf *Huzzey v Field* (1835) 2 Cr M & R 432 (infringement of right of ferry); and see HIGHWAYS, STREETS AND BRIDGES vol 55 (2012) PARA 201.
5   *Betts v Neilson, Betts v De Vitre* (1868) 3 Ch App 429 at 441–442 per Lord Chelmsford LC (corporation) (affd sub nom *Neilson v Betts* (1871) LR 5 HL 1). See also PATENTS AND REGISTERED DESIGNS vol 79 (2014) PARA 499 et seq. As to the liability of an employer for an infringement of copyright by his employees see COPYRIGHT vol 23 (2013) PARA 883.
6   *Rapier v London Tramways Co* [1893] 2 Ch 588, CA (corporation); and see NUISANCE.
7   *Majrowski v Guy's and St Thomas's NHS Trust* [2006] UKHL 34, [2007] 1 AC 224, [2006] 4 All ER 395; and see PARA 512. As to breach of statutory duty generally see PARA 500 et seq.
8   See the cases cited in the other notes to this paragraph. See also CORPORATIONS vol 24 (2010) PARA 478. For the principle that a corporation is not liable if the act is one which it could not in any circumstances have authorised an employee to commit see PARA 786.
9   *Bank of New South Wales v Owston* (1879) 4 App Cas 270, PC (corporation); *Edwards v Midland Rly Co* (1880) 6 QBD 287 (corporation); *Cornford v Carlton Bank Ltd* [1899] 1 QB 392 (affd [1900] 1 QB 22, CA) (corporation). See also PARA 722.
10 *Whitfield v South Eastern Rly Co* (1858) EB & E 115 (corporation); *Citizens' Life Assurance Co Ltd v Brown* [1904] AC 423, PC (corporation; where the defence of privilege was rebutted on proof of actual malice in the employee); cf *Nevill v Fine Arts and General Insurance Co* [1895] 2 QB 156, CA (affd [1897] AC 68, HL). See also DEFAMATION.
11 *Lloyd v Grace, Smith & Co* [1912] AC 716, HL; *Barwick v English Joint Stock Bank* (1867) LR 2 Exch 259, Ex Ch (corporation); *Mackay v Commercial Bank of New Brunswick* (1874) LR 5 PC 394, PC (corporation); *Houldsworth v City of Glasgow Bank* (1880) 5 App Cas 317, HL (corporation). See also PARA 784; and MISREPRESENTATION vol 76 (2013) PARA 754 et seq.
12 As to the scope of authority see PARA 779. As to what acts are in the course of employment see PARA 780.

770. Employee's liability as tortfeasor is independent of contract of employment. As a general rule an employee who commits a tort is liable in damages to the person injured[1], and his liability is not affected by the existence of a contract of employment[2] or, where he commits the tort in the course of his employment and within the scope of his authority, by the existence of the corresponding liability of his employer for the same tort[3], since he is the actual tortfeasor[4]. An employee cannot, therefore, excuse himself from liability for his own act on the ground that he did it solely in his capacity as the employee of another and in obedience to his employer's express orders[5], or that his employer subsequently adopted or ratified it, unless the act is thereby deprived of its tortious character[6]. Similarly, it is no defence that he acted solely on his employer's behalf and in his employer's interest[7]; nor can he escape responsibility on the ground that he did not know and had no reason to know or to suspect that the act in question was tortious[8], unless the act is incapable of being regarded as a tort in the absence of actual or imputed knowledge that it is wrongful[9].

1 As to the cases in which the employer is also liable see PARA 768 et seq.

2 *Lane v Cotton* (1701) 12 Mod Rep 472 at 488 per Holt CJ; *Sands v Child* (1693) 3 Lev 351 at 352; *Adler v Dickson* [1955] 1 QB 158, [1954] 3 All ER 397, CA; *Fairline Shipping Corpn v Adamson* [1975] QB 180, [1974] 2 All ER 967. Where liability turns on assumption of responsibility, it may be necessary to inquire whether the employee was assuming responsibility personally or only on behalf of the company (in which case the employee commits no tort): compare *Williams v Natural Life Health Foods* [1998] 2 All ER 577, [1998] 1 WLR 830 with *Merrett v Babb* [2001] EWCA Civ 214, [2001] QB 1174, 80 ConLR 43.

3 In such a case he may, however, be entitled to be indemnified by his employer, if he is not in pari delicto: *Dixon v Fawcus* (1861) 3 E & E 537; *Toplis v Grane* (1839) 5 Bing NC 636; *Adamson v Jarvis* (1827) 4 Bing 66.

4 A judgment against the employer is not a bar to an action against his employee or vice versa: see the Civil Liability (Contribution) Act 1978 s 3; and DAMAGES vol 29 (2014) PARA 620. As to the circumstances in which an employee is liable to indemnify his employer against liability incurred by his employer as a result of the employee's breach of his implied duty of care see EMPLOYMENT vol 39 (2014) PARA 53.

5 *Sands v Child* (1693) 3 Lev 351 at 352; *Perkins v Smith* (1752) Say 40; *Mill v Hawker* (1874) LR 9 Exch 309; affd (1875) LR 10 Exch 92.

6 *Hull v Pickersgill* (1819) 1 Brod & Bing 282; *Whitehead v Taylor* (1839) 10 Ad & El 210; cf *Sykes v Sykes* (1870) LR 5 CP 113. See also AGENCY vol 1 (2008) PARA 59.

7 *Stephens v Elwall* (1815) 4 M & S 259; *Wilson v Peto* (1821) 6 Moore CP 47; *Cranch v White* (1835) 1 Bing NC 414.

8 *Stephens v Elwall* (1815) 4 M & S 259; cf *Consolidated Co v Curtis & Son* [1892] 1 QB 495.

9 Cf *Day v Bream* (1837) 2 Mood & R 54; *Emmens v Pottle* (1885) 16 QBD 354, CA. See AGENCY vol 1 (2008) PARA 59.

771. Employee not entitled to benefit of provisions excluding employer's liability. Where in a contract between an employer and a third person there is a provision excluding the employer's liability, an employee, not being party to the contract, is not entitled to its protection at common law[1]. However, a third party to the contract, including an employee, can avail himself of an exclusion[2] in it under the Contracts (Rights of Third Parties) Act 1999[3] if the contract expressly provides that he may or, unless on a proper construction of the contract it appears that the parties did not intend the term to be enforceable by him, the exclusion purports to benefit him[4].

1 *Scruttons Ltd v Midland Silicones Ltd* [1962] AC 446, [1962] 1 All ER 1, HL. See also *Cosgrove v Horsfall* (1945) 175 LT 334; *Adler v Dickson* [1955] 1 QB 158, [1954] 3 All ER 397, CA; *Gore v Van der Lann* [1967] 2 QB 31, [1967] 1 All ER 360, CA; *Wilson v Darling Island Stevedoring and Lighterage Co Ltd* [1956] 1 Lloyd's Rep 346, Aust HC. For exceptions see *Elder, Dempster & Co Ltd v Paterson, Zochonis & Co Ltd* [1924] AC 522, HL (criticised in *Scruttons Ltd v Midland Silicones Ltd* [1962] AC 446 at 468–471, [1962] 1 All ER 1 at 7–9, HL, per Viscount Simonds); *New Zealand Shipping Co v AM Satterthwaite & Co Ltd, The Eurymedon* [1975] AC 154, [1974] 1 All ER 1015, PC; *Port Jackson Stevedoring Pty Ltd v Salmond & Spraggon (Australia) Pty Ltd, The New York Star* [1980] 3 All ER 257, [1981] 1 WLR 138, PC; *Norwich City Council v Harvey* [1989] 1 All ER 1180, [1989] 1 WLR 828, CA (provision that building owner bears risk of fire exempts third party sub-contractor; not such a close and direct relationship between them for the subcontractor to owe the building owner a duty of care).

2 See the Contracts (Rights of Third Parties) Act 1999 s 1(6); and CONTRACT vol 22 (2012) PARA 343.

3   The Act does not apply in relation to a contract entered into before 11 May 2000, unless the contract is entered into on or after 11 November 1999 and expressly provides for the application of the Contracts (Rights of Third Parties) Act 1999: see s 10(2), (3); and CONTRACT vol 22 (2012) PARA 342.
4   See the Contracts (Rights of Third Parties) Act 1999 s 1(1), (2); and CONTRACT vol 22 (2012) PARA 343. The employee must be expressly identified in the contract by name, as a member of a class or as answering a particular description but need not be in existence when the contract is entered into: s 1(3). The Unfair Contract Terms Act 1977 s 2(2) (restriction on exclusion etc of liability for negligence in respect of loss or damage other than death or personal injury) does not apply where the negligence consists of the breach of an obligation arising from a term of a contract and the person seeking to enforce it is a third party acting in reliance on the above provisions: Contracts (Rights of Third Parties) Act 1999 s 7(2); and CONTRACT vol 22 (2012) PARA 345. See also CONTRACT vol 22 (2012) PARAS 347, 410.

772.   Employee not liable if his act would have been justifiable if done by employer.   An employee may justify the commission of an act which is prima facie tortious where it is committed in defence of his employer's person[1] or property[2], provided the act is one which would have been justifiable if committed by the employer himself. Thus an employee is entitled to evict a trespasser from his employer's land, and for that purpose to make use of such force as may be necessary and unavoidable[3].

1   *Leewerd v Basilee* (1695) 1 Salk 407; and see EMPLOYMENT.
2   *Ewer v Jones* (1846) 9 QB 623. As to defences to actions of tort see PARA 456 et seq.
3   *Piggott v Kemp* (1832) 1 Cr & M 197.

(iii) Employer's Relationship with Primary Tortfeasor

773.   Whether contract of employment required to establish vicarious liability.   The employer's vicarious liability is normally conditional on the existence of a relationship of employer and employee between himself and the person for whose tort it is sought to hold him liable[1]. There is no single test for determining whether such a relationship exists and the court must form a rounded view in the light of a range of relevant factors, including the extent of the employer's control of the work done, the mutuality of obligation between the parties, the extent of the worker's integration into the employer's business, the ownership of any tools and equipment, the incidence of risk and the chance of profit[2].

Certain relationships, while not strictly between employer and employee, may give rise to vicarious liability where the relationship itself directly facilitates the commission of the tort by placing the tortfeasor in a position to commit the tort[3]. This has been shown where members of a church or religious order had abused children in the course of carrying out activities in that capacity[4].

An employer will not generally be held liable for a tort committed by his independent contractor[5].

1   See, however, the text and notes 3–4. As to the general principles of the employer's vicarious liability see PARA 767.
2   See EMPLOYMENT vol 39 (2014) PARA 4.
3   See the text and note 4.
4   See *Various Claimants v Catholic Child Welfare Society* [2012] UKSC 56, [2013] 2 AC 1, [2013] 1 All ER 670. The claimants had had difficulty in establishing the conventional relationship of employer/employee but it was found that the relationship had facilitated the commission of the abuse by placing the abusers in a position where they enjoyed both physical proximity to their victims and the influence of authority over them both as teachers and as men of God (*Various Claimants v Catholic Child Welfare Society* above at [84]). The essential closeness of connection between the relationship between the defendant and the tortfeasor and the acts of abuse involves a strong causative link [at 86], and while creation of risk is not enough, of itself, to give rise to vicarious liability for abuse it is always likely to be an important element in the facts that give

rise to such liability (at 87]). See also *JGE v Trustees of the Portsmouth Roman Catholic Diocesan Trust* [2012] EWCA Civ 938, sub nom *E v English Province of Our Lady of Charity* [2013] QB 722, [2012] 4 All ER 1152.

5 See PARA 777.

774. Dual vicarious liability. It is possible for two different defendants each to be vicariously liable for the single tortious act of the tortfeasor[1]. This may happen, for example, where an employer's employee is hired out to another temporarily for work so that there is, in effect, shared control of the employee[2].

1 *Viasystems (Tyneside) Ltd v Thermal Transfer (Northern) Ltd* [2005] EWCA Civ 1151, [2006] QB 510, [2005] 4 All ER 1181.

2 If, on the facts of the case, the core question is who was entitled, and in theory obliged, to control the employee's relevant negligent act so as to prevent it, there will be some cases in which the sensible answer would be each of the two 'employers': *Viasystems (Tyneside) Ltd v Thermal Transfer (Northern) Ltd* [2005] EWCA Civ 1151 at [49], [2006] QB 510 at [49], [2005] 4 All ER 1181 at [49]. See also *Penny v Wimbledon UDC* [1899] 2 QB 72, CA; and PARA 777. As to the employment of another person's employees see further PARA 800 et seq.

775. Restriction on choice of employee. An employer is not exempt from liability for his employee's torts merely on the ground that he is required by law to employ a person who is a member of a particular class or who possesses a particular qualification[1]. It is immaterial that the employer's power of selection is in consequence restricted or even that he is prohibited from himself doing the work for which the employee is employed[2].

1 *Martin v Temperley* (1843) 4 QB 298 (lightermen on the Thames).

2 *Martin v Temperley* (1843) 4 QB 298 at 312–313 per Coleridge J.

776. Superior and inferior employees. A superior employee is not, as such, vicariously liable in respect of the torts of an inferior employee[1], but may incur personal liability as a joint tortfeasor by co-operating in or ordering the commission of a tort[2].

1 This applies to both Crown servants and those in private employment and whether or not the superior can appoint, dismiss and control the work of the inferior: *Lane v Cotton* (1701) 1 Ld Raym 646; *Stone v Cartwright* (1795) 6 Term Rep 411; *Whitfield v Lord Le Despencer* (1778) 2 Cowp 754; *The Mentor* (1799) 1 Ch Rob 179; *Nicholson v Mouncey* (1812) 15 East 383; *Blaikie v Stembridge* (1859) 6 CBNS 894; *Tobin v R* (1864) 16 CBNS 310 at 351 per Erle CJ; *Raleigh v Goschen* [1898] 1 Ch 73; *Bainbridge v Postmaster-General* [1906] 1 KB 178. As to company directors see *Weir v Bell* (1878) 3 ExD 238; *Cargill v Bower* (1878) 10 ChD 502; *Bear v Stevenson* (1874) 30 LT 177.

2 *Kinsella v Hamilton* (1890) 26 LR Ir 671. He may, perhaps, also incur personal liability by ratification: *Weir v Bell* (1878) 3 ExD 238. Delegation of work by the superior could also be in itself negligent: cf *Re City Equitable Fire Insurance Co Ltd* [1925] Ch 407.

777. Employer not generally liable for independent contractor's tort. The liability of an employer for the tort of a person in his employment generally depends upon the existence of the relationship of employer and employee between them and does not arise merely from the fact that a person is engaged to do work on the employer's behalf[1]. If the person employed to do particular work is not in the position of an employee, but is an independent contractor, the employer is not, as a rule, responsible for any tort committed by him in the course of his employment[2], or by the employees whom he may have engaged for the actual performance of the work[3], and any person injured thereby must look to the independent contractor for compensation[4].

There are, however, certain cases in which the employer may be liable for the torts committed by an independent contractor or by the contractor's employees[5]. The mere fact that the contractor is liable does not of itself free the employer from liability[6].

1   *Milligan v Wedge* (1840) 12 Ad & El 737 at 742; *Sadler v Henlock* (1855) 4 E & B 570; *Randleson v Murray* (1838) 8 Ad & El 109; *Holmes v Onion* (1857) 2 CBNS 790. See also *Pickard v Smith* (1861) 10 CBNS 470 at 480 per Williams J. Certain relationships, while not strictly within the bounds of an employment contract, may be akin to the employer/employee relationship and therefore may be subject to the principles of vicarious liability: see *Various Claimants v Catholic Child Welfare Society* [2012] UKSC 56, [2013] 2 AC 1, [2013] 1 All ER 670; *JGE v Trustees of the Portsmouth Roman Catholic Diocesan Trust* [2012] EWCA Civ 938, sub nom *E v English Province of Our Lady of Charity* [2013] QB 722, [2012] 4 All ER 1152; and PARA 773.
      As to vicarious liability for employees see PARA 767. As to the difference between an employee and an independent contractor see PARA 773; and EMPLOYMENT vol 39 (2014) PARA 4.
2   *Rapson v Cubitt* (1842) 9 M & W 710. Cf *Gregory v Shepherds (a firm)* [2000] PNLR 769, CA (liability for personal negligence). A person may be an employee of the employer for one purpose and a contractor for another purpose: *Knight v Fox* (1850) 5 Exch 721. There is clearly no liability when the tort falls outside the scope of the employment: *Pickard v Smith* (1861) 10 CBNS 470 at 480 per Williams J. See also PARA 781. As to scope of employment see PARA 780.
3   *Milligan v Wedge* (1840) 12 Ad & El 737; *Murray v Currie* (1870) LR 6 CP 24.
4   *Waldock v Winfield* [1901] 2 KB 596, CA; *Morgan v Incorporated Central Council of Girls' Friendly Society* [1936] 1 All ER 404; *Riden v AC Billings & Sons Ltd* [1957] 1 QB 46, [1956] 3 All ER 357, CA (affd sub nom *AC Billings & Sons Ltd v Riden* [1958] AC 240, [1957] 3 All ER 1, HL, overruling *Malone v Laskey* [1907] 2 KB 141, CA, so far as it dealt with negligence). As to the liability of an employer who is also an occupier of premises for damage suffered by visitors to the premises see the Occupiers' Liability Act 1957 ss 1, 3; and NEGLIGENCE vol 78 (2010) PARA 29 et seq. As to the circumstances in which it is a defence for the occupier that he entrusted work to an independent contractor see s 2(4)(b); and LANDLORD AND TENANT vol 62 (2012) PARA 628; NEGLIGENCE. As to the liability of a landlord see the Defective Premises Act 1972 s 4; and LANDLORD AND TENANT vol 62 (2012) PARA 623.
5   As to the position where the employer becomes the employer pro hac vice of the contractor's employee see PARAS 801–802.
6   *Penny v Wimbledon UDC* [1899] 2 QB 72, CA. As to dual vicarious liability see PARA 774.

(iv) Employer's Relationship with the Tortious Conduct

778.   Employer's vicarious liability for acts expressly authorised.   Where an employer expressly authorises his employee to do a particular act which is in itself a tort[1], or which necessarily results in a tort[2], the employer is liable to an action in tort at the suit of the person injured[3]. His liability is equally clear where he ratifies a tort committed by his employee without his authority[4].

Where the act which the employee is expressly authorised to do is lawful, the employer may nevertheless be responsible for the manner in which the employee executes his authority[5]. If, therefore, the employee does the act in such a manner as to occasion injury to a third person, the employer cannot escape liability merely on the ground that he did not actually authorise the particular manner in which the act was done[6], or even that the employee was acting on his own behalf and not on that of his employer[7].

1   *Campbell v Paddington Corpn* [1911] 1 KB 869, DC; *Mill v Hawker* (1874) LR 9 Exch 309 (for subsequent proceedings see (1875) LR 10 Exch 92); *Ellis v Sheffield Gas Consumers Co* (1853) 2 E & B 767 (independent contractor); *Hatch v Hale* (1850) 15 QB 10 (distress).
2   *Gregory v Piper* (1829) 9 B & C 591.
3   As to the defences open in a tort claim see PARA 456 et seq; and NEGLIGENCE.
4   *Wilson v Tunman* (1843) 6 Man & G 236 at 242–243 per Tindal CJ; *Lewis v Read* (1845) 13 M & W 834; *Hilbery v Hatton* (1864) 2 H & C 822 (even if unaware the act ratified is

unlawful); *Carter v Vestry of St Mary Abbotts, Kensington* (1900) 64 JP 548, CA. See also PARA 780. As to the requisites of ratification see AGENCY vol 1 (2008) PARA 66.

5   *Limpus v London General Omnibus Co* (1862) 1 H & C 526, Ex Ch; *Hatch v Hale* (1850) 15 QB 10. Apart from the relation of employer and employee, or of principal and agent, a person directing another to do a particular act is not necessarily responsible as to the manner in which it is done: *Lucas v Mason* (1875) LR 10 Exch 251.

6   See PARA 781. See also *Limpus v London General Omnibus Co* (1862) 1 H & C 526, Ex Ch; *Goh Choon Seng v Lee Kim Soo* [1925] AC 550, PC; *Canadian Pacific Rly Co v Lockhart* [1942] AC 591, [1942] 2 All ER 464, PC (unauthorised use of uninsured car on authorised journey); *McKean v Raynor Bros Ltd (Nottingham)* [1942] 2 All ER 650 (use of private car instead of employer's lorry); *LCC v Cattermoles (Garages) Ltd* [1953] 2 All ER 582, [1953] 1 WLR 997, CA (garage hand moving car by driving instead of pushing it); cf *Goodman v Kennell* (1827) 3 C & P 167 (use of horse by employee sent on errand on foot; no vicarious liability). For the liability of bailees and carriers for the acts of their employees see BAILMENT AND PLEDGE vol 4 (2011) PARA 148; CARRIAGE AND CARRIERS vol 7 (2015) PARAS 39, 84–85. As to the liability of an employer for infringement of copyright committed by his employees see COPYRIGHT vol 23 (2013) PARA 883.

7   *Lloyd v Grace, Smith & Co* [1912] AC 716, HL. See also *Hambro v Burnand* [1904] 2 KB 10, CA (principal and agent); *Bernard v A-G of Jamaica* [2004] UKPC 47, [2005] IRLR 398; and see PARA 780.

779. Employer's vicarious liability for acts done with implied authority. The liability of an employer extends to all torts committed by his employee when purporting to act in the course of such business as the employee was authorised or held out as authorised to transact on his employer's account[1]. It is not necessary to prove an express command[2]. If the employee is acting within the scope of his authority his employer is liable whether he receives the benefit of the wrongful act or not[3]. If the employer accepts the benefit of the wrongful act he is liable on the further ground that he has adopted and ratified the employee's act[4]. Where a tort committed by the employee falls within the scope of the authority to be implied from his employment, the employer cannot escape liability on the ground that he gave his employee no authority to commit torts[5], or even on the ground that he had expressly prohibited the employee from committing the tort in question[6]. The employer has put the employee into a position to do a particular class of acts on his behalf[7], and he must therefore accept responsibility for the manner in which the employee conducts himself in the performance of any such act[8].

1   *Lloyd v Grace, Smith & Co* [1912] AC 716 at 725, HL, per Earl Loreburn.

2   *Barwick v English Joint Stock Bank* (1867) LR 2 Exch 259 at 265 per Willes J.

3   *Irwin v Waterloo Taxi-Cab Co Ltd* [1912] 3 KB 588, CA; *Lloyd v Grace, Smith & Co* [1912] AC 716 at 738, HL, per Lord Macnaghten; *Uxbridge Permanent Benefit Building Society v Pickard* [1939] 2 KB 248, [1939] 2 All ER 344, CA.

4   *Lloyd v Grace, Smith & Co* [1912] AC 716 at 738, HL, per Lord Macnaghten.

5   *Lloyd v Grace, Smith & Co* [1912] AC 716, HL; *United Africa Co Ltd v Saka Owoade* [1955] AC 130, [1957] 3 All ER 216, PC; *Morris v CW Martin & Sons Ltd* [1966] 1 QB 716, [1965] 2 All ER 725, CA.

6   *Limpus v London General Omnibus Co* (1862) 1 H & C 526, Ex Ch; *Canadian Pacific Rly Co v Lockhart* [1942] AC 591, [1942] 2 All ER 464, PC; *LCC v Cattermoles (Garages) Ltd* [1953] 2 All ER 582, [1953] 1 WLR 997, CA; *Ilkiw v Samuels* [1963] 2 All ER 879, [1963] 1 WLR 991, CA; *East v Beavis Transport Ltd* [1969] 1 Lloyd's Rep 302, CA; *Rose v Plenty* [1976] 1 All ER 97, [1976] 1 WLR 141, CA. The employer may, however, by the orders he gives, limit the scope of the employee's authority: *Twine v Bean's Express Ltd* (1946) 62 TLR 458, CA; *Conway v George Wimpey & Co Ltd* [1951] 2 KB 266, [1951] 1 All ER 363, CA; *Iqbal v London Transport Executive* (1973) 16 KIR 329, CA. It may be that a claimant who knows of a prohibition and could have avoided the danger cannot recover: *Stone v Taffe* [1974] 3 All ER 1016 at 1022, [1974] 1 WLR 1575 at 1581–1582, CA, per Stephenson LJ. See also PARA 783.

7   But note that vicarious liability is not limited to acts that the employee is authorised to do: *Dubai Aluminium Co Ltd v Salaam (Livingstone, third parties)* [2002] UKHL 48 at [21]–[22], [2003] 2 AC 366 at [21]–[22], [2003] 1 All ER 97 at [21]–[22] per Lord Nicholls.

8   *Barwick v English Joint Stock Bank* (1867) LR 2 Exch 259 at 266 per Willes J.

780.   Employer's liability for acts done 'in the course of employment'.
Vicarious liability is not strictly confined to acts done with the employer's authority but extends to acts so closely connected with acts the employee was authorised to do that, for the purpose of the liability of the employer to third parties, the wrongful conduct may fairly and properly be regarded as done in the ordinary course of the employee's employment[1]. An employer is liable for the wrongful acts of his employee authorised by him or for wrongful modes of doing authorised acts[2]. The liability may therefore arise where the act is one which, if lawful[3], would have fallen within the scope of the employee's employment as being in the discharge of his duties[4] or the preservation of the employer's interests[5] or property[6], or otherwise incidental to the purposes of his employment[7]. The act need not be part of the employee's ordinary employment but may be necessary because of the exigencies of the particular occasion[8]. If, on the other hand, the act is one which, even if lawful, would not have fallen within the scope of the employee's employment[9], the employer is not liable[10] unless the act is capable of being ratified[11] and is in fact ratified by him[12]. The fact that the act which the employee has done would only be covered by his authority on the supposition that certain facts existed, but which did not in fact exist, does not excuse the employer, provided the employee acted on the belief that they did exist[13]. On the other hand, the employer is not liable merely because the employee, in doing the act, honestly believed that he was acting in his employer's interests and intended the act to be for the employer's benefit[14]. Time of work and travelling arrangements may be relevant to the limits of course of employment[15], as may spatial limits[16].

There is therefore no definitive test of when a tort is committed by the employee tortfeasor in the course of his employment[17]. Courts have used various expressions and concepts to express the test of when a tort is or is not committed 'in the course of the employee tortfeasor's employment'. The most generalised test is whether the tort is so closely connected with the employment (that is what was authorised or expected of the employee) that it would be fair and just to hold the employer vicariously responsible[18]. The various different formulations have to be considered in the context of the particular facts of the case in hand[19].

1   *Lister v Hesley Hall Ltd* [2001] UKHL 22 at [28], [2002] 1 AC 215 at [28], [2001] 2 All ER 769 at [28] per Lord Steyn, and at [70] per Lord Millett; *Dubai Aluminium Co Ltd v Salaam (Livingstone, third parties)* [2002] UKHL 48 at [21]–[22], [2003] 2 AC 366 at [21]–[22], [2003] 1 All ER 97 at [21]–[22] per Lord Nicholls. See also *Mohamud v WM Morrison Supermarkets plc* [2014] EWCA Civ 116, [2014] 2 All ER 990, [2014] IRLR 386 (employer not liable for employee's assault on customer; the fact that the employee's job included interaction with the public did not, by itself, provide the requisite connection between the tort and the circumstances of the employment: see PARA 784); *Vaickuviene v J Sainsbury plc* [2013] CSIH 67, [2013] IRLR 792 (employer not vicarious liable where employee murdered colleague, despite prior course of harassment, as act not sufficiently closely connected with employment: see PARA 784).

     Some authorities prefer to speak of the scope, rather than course, of employment: see e g *Lister v Hesley Hall Ltd* [2001] UKHL 22 at [40], [2002] 1 AC 215 at [40], [2001] 2 All ER 769 at [40] per Lord Clyde. The interpretations given to such phrases as 'in the course of employment' under statute may differ from its interpretation in deciding upon vicarious liability at common law: *Tower Boot Co Ltd* [1997] 2 All ER 406, [1997] ICR 254, CA (race discrimination).

An employer is not liable where an employee performs a lawful act within his employment which, when linked with other acts not performed in the course of his employment, is tortious: *Crédit Lyonnais Bank Nederland NV (now known as Generale Bank Nederland NV) v Export Credits Guarantee Department* [2000] 1 AC 486, [1999] 1 All ER 929, HL.

2   *Poland v John Parr & Sons* [1927] 1 KB 236 at 240, CA, per Bankes LJ; *Canadian Pacific Rly Co v Lockhart* [1942] AC 591 at 599, [1942] 2 All ER 464 at 467, PC; *LCC v Cattermoles (Garages) Ltd* [1953] 2 All ER 582 at 584–585, [1953] 1 WLR 997 at 998, CA, per Lord Evershed MR; *Ilkiw v Samuels* [1963] 2 All ER 879 at 884, [1963] 1 WLR 991 at 997, CA, per Willmer LJ, and at 889 and 1004 per Diplock LJ; *Kay v ITW Ltd* [1968] 1 QB 140 at 153–154, [1967] 3 All ER 22 at 26–27, CA, per Sellers LJ; *General Engineering Services Ltd v Kingston and St Andrew Corpn* [1988] 3 All ER 867 at 869, [1989] 1 WLR 69 at 72, PC; *Lister v Hesley Hall Ltd* [2001] UKHL 22 at [36], [2002] 1 AC 215 at [36], [2001] 2 All ER 769 at [36] per Lord Clyde ('a classic test'), and at [59] per Lord Hobhouse ('classic'); *Dubai Aluminium Co Ltd v Salaam (Livingstone, third parties)* [2002] UKHL 48 at [30], [2003] 2 AC 366 at [30], [2003] 1 All ER 97 at [30] per Lord Nicholls of Birkenhead. In *Lister v Hesley Hall Ltd* [2001] UKHL 22, [2002] 1 AC 215, [2001] 2 All ER 769, the House of Lords admitted the practical utility of the test, but observed that it should not be applied mechanically, especially where intentional misconduct was involved: see especially at [20] per Lord Steyn, at [60] per Lord Hobhouse and at [67], [70] per Lord Millett. See also *Dubai Aluminium Co Ltd v Salaam (Livingstone, third parties)* [2002] UKHL 48 at [128], [2003] 2 AC 366 at [128], [2003] 1 All ER 97 at [128] per Lord Millett; *Bernard v A-G of Jamaica* [2004] UKPC 47 at [18], [2005] IRLR 398 at [18].

3   See PARA 772. As to liability for the employee's criminal acts see PARA 784.

4   *Great Western Rly Co v Bunch* (1888) 13 App Cas 31, HL; *Ashton v Spiers and Pond* (1893) 9 TLR 606; cf *Houghton v Pilkington* [1912] 3 KB 308, DC. It is sufficient if the act, though not strictly falling within the employee's ordinary duties, is habitually done by him, to the knowledge of the employer, without question: *Milner v Great Northern Rly Co* (1884) 50 LT 367; *Aitchison v Page Motors Ltd* (1935) 154 LT 128.

5   *Moore v Metropolitan Rly Co* (1872) LR 8 QB 36; *Bayley v Manchester, Sheffield and Lincolnshire Rly Co* (1873) LR 8 CP 148, Ex Ch; *Burns v Poulsom* (1873) LR 8 CP 563. Cf the cases cited in note 14.

6   *Poland v John Parr & Sons* [1927] 1 KB 236, CA.

7   *Bayley v Manchester, Sheffield and Lincolnshire Rly Co* (1873) LR 8 CP 148, Ex Ch; *Lowe v Great Northern Rly Co* (1893) 62 LJQB 524, DC.

8   *Bank of New South Wales v Owston* (1879) 4 App Cas 270, PC. Cf where the exigency no longer exists: *Allen v London and South Western Rly Co* (1870) LR 6 QB 65, *Abrahams v Deakin* [1891] 1 QB 516, CA; *Hanson v Waller* [1901] 1 KB 390, DC.

9   *Glasgow Corpn v Lorimer* [1911] AC 209, HL; *Edwards v London and North Western Rly Co* (1870) LR 5 CP 445; *Walker v South Eastern Rly Co, Smith v South Eastern Rly Co* (1870) LR 5 CP 640; *Houghton v Pilkington* [1912] 3 KB 308, DC. A relevant consideration may be that the task performed was part of another employee's job description and not that of the employee who undertook it: see *Iqbal v London Transport Executive* (1973) 16 KIR 329, CA; *Beard v London General Omnibus Co* [1900] 2 QB 530, CA. Cf *Ricketts v Thos Tilling Ltd* [1915] 1 KB 644, CA; *Ilkiw v Samuels* [1963] 2 All ER 879, [1963] 1 WLR 991, CA.

10 In the case of a corporation, where the act done is lawful but is ultra vires the corporation, it is not liable: see PARA 786; and CORPORATIONS vol 24 (2010) PARA 435. Cf *Campbell v Paddington Corpn* [1911] 1 KB 869, DC.

11 As to the requisites of ratification see AGENCY vol 1 (2008) PARA 66.

12 *Lewis v Read* (1845) 13 M & W 834; *Eastern Counties Rly Co v Broom* (1851) 6 Exch 314, Ex Ch; *Roe v Birkenhead, Lancashire and Cheshire Junction Rly Co* (1851) 7 Exch 36; *Carter v Vestry of St Mary Abbotts, Kensington* (1900) 64 JP 548, CA; and PARA 778.

13 *Seymour v Greenwood* (1861) 7 H & N 355, Ex Ch; *Bayley v Manchester, Sheffield and Lincolnshire Rly Co* (1873) LR 8 CP 148, Ex Ch; *Bank of New South Wales v Owston* (1879) 4 App Cas 270, PC; *Lambert v Great Eastern Rly Co* [1909] 2 KB 776, CA.

14 *Lord Bolingbroke v Swindon Local Board* (1874) LR 9 CP 575; *Kay v ITW Ltd* [1968] 1 QB 140 at 154, [1967] 3 All ER 22 at 26, CA, per Sellers LJ. Cf the cases cited in note 5.

15 The course of employment normally starts when the employee enters his place of work: *Compton v McClure* [1975] ICR 378. Leaving work may be included: *Bell v Blackwood Morton & Sons Ltd* 1960 SC 11, Ct of Sess. Travelling to and from work is not normally within the course of employment unless the employee is required to use the transport or travelling in work time: *Smith v Stages* [1989] AC 928, [1989] 1 All ER 833, HL; *Vandyke v Fender* [1970] 2 QB 292, [1970] 2 All ER 335, CA, distinguished in *Nottingham v Aldridge* [1971] 2 QB 739, [1971] 2 All ER 751; *Elleanor v Cavendish Woodhouse Ltd and Comerford* [1973] 1 Lloyd's

Rep 313, CA. Note that an employee may be acting in the course of his employment even though he has finished his day's work: see *Staton v National Coal Board* [1957] 2 All ER 667, [1957] 1 WLR 893 (act done by employee on employer's premises while on way to collect wages); distinguished in *British Transport Commission v Maxine & Co Ltd* (1963) 107 Sol Jo 1024. As to meal and refreshment breaks see the cases in PARA 781 note 5.

16 *Lyons v Martin* (1838) 8 Ad & El 512; *Lewis v Read* (1845) 13 M & W 834; *Stevens v Woodward* (1881) 6 QBD 318 (use of washroom within or outside course of employment depending on whether use allowed or forbidden by employer); *Joseph Rand Ltd v Craig* [1919] 1 Ch 1, CA (fly-tipping).

17 *Weddall v Barchester Healthcare Ltd; Wallbank v Wallbank Fox Designs Ltd* [2012] EWCA Civ 25 at [65], [2012] IRLR 307 at [65], [2012] All ER (D) 01 (Feb) at [65].

18 *Gravil v Carroll* [2008] EWCA Civ 689 at [21], [2008] ICR 1222 at [21], [2008] IRLR 829 at [21] per Sir Anthony Clarke MR (cited in *Weddall v Barchester Healthcare Ltd; Wallbank v Wallbank Fox Designs Ltd* [2012] EWCA Civ 25 at [65], [2012] IRLR 307 at [65], [2012] All ER (D) 01 (Feb) at [65]).

19 *Weddall v Barchester Healthcare Ltd; Wallbank v Wallbank Fox Designs Ltd* [2012] EWCA Civ 25 at [65], [2012] IRLR 307 at [65], [2012] All ER (D) 01 (Feb) at [65].

781.   Employer's liability for acts incidental to the employment.   In order for an employer to be vicariously liable for the torts of his employee, it is not sufficient that the employment merely gave the employee the opportunity to commit the tort[1], or even that the act in the doing of which the third person was injured was done on the employer's behalf[2]. There must be a close connection between the employee's tortious conduct and the employer's business[3]. However, liability extends beyond the performance of duties that the employee was engaged to perform and extends to acts that are reasonably incidental to the employment[4], even if done for the employee's convenience and not for the employer's benefit[5]. The employer is not liable where the act which gave rise to the injury was an independent act unconnected with the employee's employment, or took place while the employee was engaged on his own and not his employer's business[6].

1 *Heasmans v Clarity Cleaning Co Ltd* [1987] ICR 949, [1987] IRLR 286, CA. However, see *Brink's Global Services Inc v Igrox Ltd* [2010] EWCA Civ 1207, [2011] IRLR 343, [2010] All ER (D) 260 (Oct) (doubting *Heasmans v Clarity Cleaning Co Ltd*), where an employee returned to work to steal silver while carrying out fumigation duties. In evaluating the closeness of the connection between the tort and the purposes for which the tortfeasor was employed, the court confirmed that all the circumstances had to be taken into account and, when making that evaluation, it was appropriate to consider whether the wrongful act could fairly be regarded as a risk reasonably incidental to the purpose for which the tortfeasor was employed (at [29]). Theft by an employee from the very container which he was instructed to fumigate was a risk reasonably incidental to the purpose for which he was employed (at [30]).

   Even though the employment has merely given the employee the opportunity to commit the tort, the employer may still be liable on the basis of personal negligence if he has failed to check the good character or otherwise of the employee: *Adams (Durham) v Trust Houses* [1960] 1 Lloyd's Rep 380; *Nahhas v Pier House (Cheyne Walk) Management* (1984) 270 Estates Gazette 328; *Williams v Curzon Syndicate Ltd* (1919) 35 TLR 475, CA; *De Parrell v Walker* (1932) 49 TLR 37; *Port Swettenham Authority v TW Wu & Co* [1979] AC 580, [1978] 3 All ER 337, PC.

2 *Joseph Rand Ltd v Craig* [1919] 1 Ch 1, CA; *Kay v ITW Ltd* [1968] 1 QB 140 at 154, [1967] 3 All ER 22 at 26, CA, per Sellers LJ; and PARA 780.

3 The fact that the employee's job includes interaction with the public does not, by itself, provide the requisite connection between the tort and the circumstances of the employment (where an employee assaulted a customer while on duty): *Mohamud v WM Morrison Supermarkets plc* [2014] EWCA Civ 116, [2014] 2 All ER 990, [2014] IRLR 386; and see PARAS 780, 784.

4 *Burns v Poulsom* (1873) LR 8 CP 563; *Thomson v British Steel Corpn* 1977 SLT 26, Ct of Sess (employer liable for negligent driving of employee where driving was incidental to his employment); *Heasmans v Clarity Cleaning Co Ltd* [1987] ICR 949, [1987] IRLR 286, CA (no nexus between tortious or criminal act and circumstances of employment); *Irving and Irving v Post Office* [1987] IRLR 289, CA.

5   *Ruddiman & Co v Smith* (1889) 60 LT 708, DC (use of lavatory); *Smith v Martin and Kingston-upon-Hull Corpn* [1911] 2 KB 775, CA; *Jefferson v Derbyshire Farmers Ltd* [1921] 2 KB 281, CA; *Century Insurance Co Ltd v Northern Ireland Road Transport Board* [1942] AC 509, [1942] 1 All ER 491, HL (cases of employees smoking while handling petrol in course of duties); contrast *Williams v Jones* (1865) 3 H & C 602, Ex Ch; *Kirby v National Coal Board* 1957 SLT 367 (affd 1958 SC 514). Collecting wages has been regarded as within the course of employment (*Staton v National Coal Board* [1957] 2 All ER 667, [1957] 1 WLR 893), as has leaving work (*Bell v Blackwood Morton & Sons Ltd* 1960 SC 11, Ct of Sess). As to meal and refreshment breaks see *Higbid v RC Hammett Ltd* (1932) 49 TLR 104, CA; *Crook v Derbyshire Stone Ltd* [1956] 2 All ER 447, [1956] 1 WLR 432; *Harvey v RG O'Dell Ltd* [1958] 2 QB 78, [1958] 1 All ER 657; *Hilton v Thomas Burton (Rhodes) Ltd* [1961] 1 All ER 74, [1961] 1 WLR 705; *Stewarts (Edinburgh) Holdings Ltd v Lord Advocate* 1966 SLT 86, Sh Ct. As regards practical jokes played on a fellow employee see *Coddington v International Harvester Co of Great Britain Ltd* (1969) 6 KIR 146; *Chapman v Oakleigh Animal Products Ltd* (1970) 8 KIR 1063, CA; *Harrison v Michelin Tyre Co Ltd* [1985] 1 All ER 918, [1985] ICR 696. As regards the employer's personal liability in respect of practical jokers compare *Smith v Crossley Brothers* (1951) 95 Sol Jo 655, CA, with *Hudson v Ridge Manufacturing Co Ltd* [1957] 2 QB 348, [1957] 2 All ER 229.

6   See PARA 785.

782. Employer's liability where acts delegated to others. An employer may be vicariously liable for the default of his employee acting in the course of the employee's employment, even though the act which caused injury was performed by a stranger[1] or by another employee acting outside his employment, where the employee for whose default it is sought to make the employer liable allowed the act to be performed, for example where he permitted a vehicle of which he was the driver to be driven by or left in the charge of another person[2]. In such a case, the employer is not liable unless the employee for whose default it is sought to make the employer liable was himself guilty of negligence or some other tort in allowing the act to be done[3], and this conduct was within the scope of his employment[4] and the effective cause of the injury[5].

1   *Booth v Mister* (1835) 7 C & P 66; *Engelhart v Farrant & Co* [1897] 1 QB 240, CA; *Trust Co Ltd v de Silva* [1956] 1 WLR 376, [1956] 1 Lloyd's Rep 309, PC; *East v Beavis Transport Ltd* [1969] 1 Lloyd's Rep 302, CA. Cf *Mann v Ward* (1892) 8 TLR 699, CA. As to what qualifies as an act done 'in the course of employment' see PARA 780 et seq.
2   *Engelhart v Farrant & Co* [1897] 1 QB 240, CA; *Beard v London General Omnibus Co* [1900] 2 QB 530, CA; *Ilkiw v Samuels* [1963] 2 All ER 879, [1963] 1 WLR 991; *East v Beavis Transport Ltd* [1969] 1 Lloyd's Rep 302, CA.
3   *Ricketts v Thos Tilling Ltd* [1915] 1 KB 644, CA. Cf *Trust Co Ltd v de Silva* [1956] 1 WLR 376, [1956] 1 Lloyd's Rep 309, PC.
4   See *Gwilliam v Twist* [1895] 2 QB 84, CA; *Coogan v Dublin Motor Co* (1914) 49 ILT 24. Cf *Ilkiw v Samuels* [1963] 2 All ER 879, [1963] 1 WLR 991, CA. As to the scope of employment see PARA 780 et seq.
5   *Engelhart v Farrant & Co* [1897] 1 QB 240, CA.

783. Employer liable for employee's act even when act was prohibited by employer. The employer cannot escape responsibility where the act is otherwise one for which he is responsible, on the ground that he had forbidden the employee to do the act in the manner which produced the injury[1]. The employer may, however, by the orders he gives, limit the scope of the employee's employment, rather than merely prescribing the ways in which the employment may or may not be performed[2].

1   *Limpus v London General Omnibus Co* (1862) 1 H & C 526, Ex Ch; *Whatman v Pearson* (1868) LR 3 CP 422; *Canadian Pacific Rly Co v Lockhart* [1942] AC 591, [1942] 2 All ER 464, PC; *LCC v Cattermoles (Garages) Ltd* [1953] 2 All ER 582, [1953] 1 WLR 997, CA; *Ilkiw v Samuels* [1963] 2 All ER 879, [1963] 1 WLR 991, CA; *East v Beavis Transport Ltd* [1969] 1 Lloyd's Rep 302, CA; *Rose v Plenty* [1976] 1 All ER 97, [1976] 1 WLR 141, CA. Aliter where

the fact that the act was forbidden showed that it was outside the scope of the employee's authority: see cases in note 2. Cf *Harris v Perry & Co* [1903] 2 KB 219, CA (where the act, though purportedly forbidden, was tacitly allowed). See also PARA 779. As to the principles of vicarious liability see PARA 767 et seq.

2   *Plumb v Cobden Flour Mills Co Ltd* [1914] AC 62 at 67, HL, per Lord Dunedin; *Ilkiw v Samuels* [1963] 2 All ER 879 at 890, [1963] 1 WLR 991 at 1004, CA, per Diplock LJ. See also *Stevens v Woodward* (1881) 6 QBD 318, DC; *Twine v Bean's Express Ltd* (1946) 62 TLR 458, CA; *Conway v George Wimpey & Co Ltd* [1951] 2 KB 266, [1951] 1 All ER 363, CA; *Daniels v Whetstone Entertainments Ltd* [1962] 2 Lloyd's Rep 1, CA; *Iqbal v London Transport Executive* (1973) 16 KIR 329, CA.

784.   Employer's liability in tort for employee's criminal act.   In accordance with the principle that an employer is liable for the acts of an employee when acting within the scope of his authority, an employer is not exempt from liability in tort because his employee's act amounts to a crime, provided it is an act that is sufficiently connected with the employment[1]. The employer may thus be liable, irrespective of personal negligence[2], when an employee steals goods entrusted to the employer by a third party[3], or defrauds the employer's client or business partner while in a position of trust[4], or commits an assault[5] (even a sexual assault[6]) in the course of employment. However, it is not sufficient to give rise to vicarious liability that the employee used his employment to gain the opportunity to commit the offence[7]. For example, the fact that an assault takes place at the employee's place of work and at a time when he is on duty is relevant, but not conclusive, to establishing vicarious liability; a greater connection between the tort and the circumstances of the employment may be required[8].

1   *Osborn v Gillett* (1873) LR 8 Exch 88; *Dyer v Munday* [1895] 1 QB 742; CA; *Morris v CW Martin & Sons Ltd* [1966] 1 QB 716, [1965] 2 All ER 725, CA.
2   Eg in appointing or supervising his employees: *Adams (Durham) v Trust Houses* [1960] 1 Lloyd's Rep 380; *Nahhas v Pier House (Cheyne Walk) Management Ltd* (1984) 270 Estates Gazette 328; *Williams v Curzon Syndicate Ltd* (1919) 35 TLR 475, CA; *De Parrell v Walker* (1932) 49 TLR 37.
3   *United Africa Co Ltd v Saka Owoade* [1955] AC 130, [1957] 3 All ER 216, PC (applying *Lloyd v Grace, Smith & Co* [1912] AC 716, HL); *Morris v CW Martin & Sons Ltd* [1966] 1 QB 716, [1965] 2 All ER 725, CA; *Frans Maas (UK) Ltd v Samsung Electronics (UK) Ltd* [2004] EWHC 1502 (Comm), [2005] 2 All ER (Comm) 783, [2004] 2 Lloyd's Rep 251. See also *Brink's Global Services Inc v Igrox Ltd* [2010] EWCA Civ 1207, [2011] IRLR 343 (employer vicariously liable when employee returned to compound out of work hours to commit theft); and PARA 781. As to where the employee's negligence facilitates the theft, compare *Abraham v Bullock* (1902) 86 LT 796, CA, with *Cobb v Great Western Rly Co* [1893] 1 QB 459, CA.
4   *Lloyd v Grace, Smith & Co* [1912] AC 716, HL; *Uxbridge Permanent Benefit Building Society v Pickard* [1939] 2 KB 248, [1939] 2 All ER 344, CA; *Dubai Aluminium Co Ltd v Salaam (Livingstone, third parties)* [2002] UKHL 48, [2003] 2 AC 366, [2003] 1 All ER 97. Cf *Slingsby v District Bank Ltd* [1931] 2 KB 588; *Armagas Ltd v Mundogas SA, The Ocean Frost* [1986] AC 717, [1986] 2 All ER 385, HL; *JJ Coughlan Ltd v Ruparelia* [2003] EWCA Civ 1057, [2004] PNLR 4. As to the employee's negligent facilitation of fraud see *HSBC Bank plc v So* [2009] EWCA Civ 296, [2009] 1 CLC 503, [2009] All ER (D) 82 (May). See also PARA 769.
5   *Seymour v Greenwood* (1861) 7 H & N 355, Ex Ch; *Eastern Counties Rly Co v Broom* (1851) 6 Exch 314; *Bayley v Manchester, Sheffield and Lincolnshire Rly Co* (1873) LR 8 CP 148, Ex Ch; *Dyer v Munday* [1895] 1 QB 742, CA; *Fennelly v Connex South Eastern Ltd* [2001] IRLR 390, CA; *Mattis v Pollock (t/a Flamingos Nightclub)* [2003] EWCA Civ 887, [2004] 4 All ER 85, [2003] 1 WLR 2158; *Bernard v A-G of Jamaica* [2004] UKPC 47, [2005] IRLR 398; *Gravil v Carrol* [2008] EWCA Civ 689, [2008] ICR 1222, [2008] IRLR 829. See also PARA 769. The employer is not liable if the assault was an act of private vengeance on the part of the employee, not committed in the course of, or otherwise closely connected with, his employment: *Warren v Henlys Ltd* [1948] 2 All ER 935; *Daniels v Whetstone Entertainments* [1962] 2 Lloyd's Rep 1; *Keppel Bus Co Ltd v Sa'ad Bin Ahmed* [1974] 2 All ER 700, [1974] 1 WLR 1082, PC; *A-G of the British Virgin Islands v Hartwell* [2004] UKPC 12, [2004] 1 WLR 1273. See also *Richards v West Middlesex Waterworks Co* (1885) 15 QBD 660. In an exceptional case, vicarious liability may arise even in respect of the use of a firearm: see *Bernard v A-G of Jamaica* [2004] UKPC

47, [2005] IRLR 398; *Brown v Robinson* [2004] UKPC 56, [2004] All ER (D) 208 (Dec), distinguishing *A-G of the British Virgin Islands v Hartwell* [2004] UKPC 12, [2004] 1 WLR 1273 (all cases involving police officers). As to harassment see *Majrowski v Guy's and St Thomas's NHS Trust* [2006] UKHL 34, [2007] 1 AC 22, [2006] 4 All ER 395.

6   *Lister v Hesley Hall Ltd* [2001] UKHL 22, [2002] 1 AC 215, [2001] 2 All ER 769. Cf *Makanjuola v Metropolitan Police Comr* (1989) 2 Admin LR 214, 154 LG Rev 248; *N v Chief Constable of Merseyside* [2006] EWHC 3041 (QB), [2006] Po LR 160. For cases finding vicarious liability for sexual assault by tortfeasor not strictly in employer/employee relationship with defendant see *Various Claimants v Catholic Child Welfare Society* [2012] UKSC 56, [2013] 2 AC 1, [2013] 1 All ER 670; *JGE v Trustees of the Portsmouth Roman Catholic Diocesan Trust* [2012] EWCA Civ 938, sub nom *E v English Province of Our Lady of Charity* [2013] QB 722, [2012] 4 All ER 1152; and PARA 773.

7   *N v Chief Constable of Merseyside* [2006] EWHC 3041 (QB), [2006] Po LR 160 (police officer off duty but in uniform, showed warrant card).

8   *Mohamud v WM Morrison Supermarkets plc* [2014] EWCA Civ 116, [2014] 2 All ER 990, [2014] IRLR 386 (employer not vicariously liable for unprovoked assault by employee on customer). See also *Vaickuviene v J Sainsbury plc* [2013] CSIH 67, [2013] IRLR 792 (employer not vicarious liable where employee murdered colleague, despite prior course of harassment, as act not sufficiently closely connected with employment).

785.   No vicarious liability where employee engaged on his own business. If at the time when the injury takes place the employee is engaged, not on his employer's business, but on his own, the employer's vicarious liability does not arise because the employee is not acting in the course of employment[1]. In such a case it is immaterial whether the employee is using his employer's property with his employer's permission[2], so long as he is clearly acting on his own business[3], or whether he is using it surreptitiously, and is therefore, as regards his employer, a trespasser[4]. Where, however, the employee, whilst using his employer's property in the course of his employment, embarks upon business of his own, and the injury is occasioned afterwards, the employer's liability continues[5] unless the employee, in deviating from the business which he was employed to perform, can no longer be considered to be acting in the course of his employment, and must be regarded as engaged in a separate transaction[6].

1   *Storey v Ashton* (1869) LR 4 QB 476; *Sanderson v Collins* [1904] 1 KB 628, CA; *Kooragang Investments Pty Ltd v Richardson and Wrench Ltd* [1982] AC 462, [1981] 3 All ER 65, PC (moonlighting). See also *General Engineering Services Ltd v Kingston and St Andrew Corpn* [1988] 3 All ER 867, [1989] 1 WLR 69, PC (firemen deliberately delaying arrival at fire as part of campaign of industrial action). But note that an employer will be vicariously liable notwithstanding that the employee was acting exclusively for his own benefit if the unlawful act was sufficiently connected with his employment: *Bernard v A-G of Jamaica* [2004] UKPC 47, [2005] IRLR 398.

2   *Cormack v Digby* (1876) IR 9 CL 557, where the employee had borrowed his employer's cart for his own purposes, and it was held that the employer was not liable although the employee had offered to bring back certain goods on his employer's behalf and the employer had agreed; *Higbid v RC Hammett Ltd* (1932) 49 TLR 104, CA; *Hilton v Thomas Burton (Rhodes) Ltd* [1961] 1 All ER 74, [1961] 1 WLR 705.

3   *Sanderson v Collins* [1904] 1 KB 628, CA. But a criminal act may be sufficiently connected with the employment as to give rise to vicarious liability: see PARA 784.

4   *Joel v Morison* (1834) 6 C & P 501 ('going on a frolic of his own'); *Rayner v Mitchell* (1877) 2 CPD 357, where it was held to be immaterial that the employee, after taking his employer's cart for his own purposes, had called on his return journey for certain goods belonging to his employer; *Sanderson v Collins* [1904] 1 KB 628, CA (distinguishing *Coupé Co v Maddick* [1891] 2 QB 413, DC). Cf *Morris v CW Martin & Sons Ltd* [1966] 1 QB 716, [1965] 2 All ER 725, CA; *Aitchison v Page Motors Ltd* (1935) 180 LT 128; *Central Motors (Glasgow) Ltd v Cessnock Garage and Motor Co* 1925 SC 796, Ct of Sess; *Adams (Durham) Ltd and Day v Trust Houses* [1960] 1 Lloyd's Rep 380.

5   *Patten v Rea* (1857) 2 CBNS 606, where the employee, who was driving a pig, was going on a journey partly on his employer's business and partly on private business of his own; *Sleath v Wilson* (1839) 9 C & P 607; *Venables v Smith* (1877) 2 QBD 279; *Higbid v RC Hammett Ltd* (1932) 49 TLR 104, CA.

6   It is a question of degree as to how far the deviation should be considered a separate transaction: *Storey v Ashton* (1869) LR 4 QB 476 at 480 per Cockburn CJ. Cf *Williams v A and W Hemphill Ltd* 1965 SLT 200.

(v) Particular Parties subject to Vicarious Liability

786. Vicarious liability of corporations. Where an employee of a corporation commits a tortious act, the corporation is not liable if the act is one which it could not in any circumstances have authorised an employee to commit[1]. Where, however, the act is not ultra vires the corporation, and is committed by the employee within the scope of his authority and in the course of his employment by the corporation, the corporation is liable[2] and cannot escape liability on the ground that, being a corporation, it cannot commit torts[3].

1   *Poulton v London and South Western Rly Co* (1867) LR 2 QB 534; *Ormiston v Great Western Rly Co* [1917] 1 KB 598. But cf *Campbell v Paddington Corpn* [1911] 1 KB 869, DC. In favour of a person dealing in good faith with a company the power of the directors to bind the company or authorise others to do so is free of any limitation under the constitution of the company: see the Companies Act 2006 s 40; and COMPANIES vol 14 (2009) PARA 263.

2   See PARA 780. See also CORPORATIONS vol 24 (2010) PARA 478 et seq. As to the statutory exception relating to transactions in favour of persons dealing with a company see note 1.

3   *Barwick v English Joint Stock Bank* (1867) LR 2 Exch 259, Ex Ch. A corporation will not be liable for a tort committed by an employee of a wholly owned subsidiary: *R v Waverley Construction Co Ltd* (1972) 30 DLR (3d) 224. As to the principle that the corporation may be liable even though the tort committed involves malice or guilty knowledge see PARA 769. As to the criminal liability of corporations see CORPORATIONS vol 24 (2010) PARA 482; CRIMINAL LAW vol 25 (2010) PARA 37.

787. Vicarious liability of unincorporated associations. It is possible for an unincorporated association to be vicariously liable for the tortious acts of one or more of its members[1].

1   *Heatons Transport (St Helens) Ltd v Transport and General Workers Union, Craddock Bros v Transport and General Workers Union, Panalpina Services Ltd v Transport and General Workers Union* [1972] 3 All ER 101 at 109, [1973] AC 15 at 99; *Thomas v National Union of Mineworkers (South Wales Area)* [1985] 2 All ER 1 at 24, [1986] Ch 20 at 66–67; *Dubai Aluminium Co Ltd v Salaam* [2002] UKHL 48, [2003] 1 All ER 97, [2003] 2 AC 366. As to the general principles of the employer's vicarious liability see PARA 767.

788. Vicarious liability of trustees. The liability of private trustees and personal representatives for the acts of their employees is considered elsewhere in this work[1].

Trustees who have the management and control of property for public purposes are not exempt from liability for the acts or defaults of any person employed for the purpose of carrying out their duties on the ground that they act gratuitously[2]. They may be able to exempt themselves from liability by dispelling any inference that the act or default complained of amounted to a breach of any duty imposed upon them as regards the person injured[3], or that the relation of employer and employee, or of principal and agent, existed between themselves and the person actually at fault[4].

1   See TRUSTS AND POWERS vol 98 (2013) PARA 665 et seq; WILLS AND INTESTACY vol 103 (2010) PARA 1214 et seq.

2 *Mersey Docks and Harbour Board Trustees v Gibbs* (1866) LR 1 HL 93 (applying *Parnaby v Lancaster Canal Co* (1839) 11 Ad & El 223, Ex Ch, and reviewing the earlier conflicting cases); *Coe v Wise* (1866) LR 1 QB 711.
3 *Forbes v Lee Conservancy Board* (1879) 4 ExD 116.
4 *Metcalfe v Hetherington* (1860) 5 H & N 719, Ex Ch.

789. Vicarious liability of public authorities. Although in general a public authority is responsible for the acts of its employees, it is not liable when the tort is committed by the employee in the discharge of a duty which he is required to perform as a public duty imposed upon himself, and not as a duty imposed upon the authority to be performed through its employee[1].

It has been observed that the liability of a chief officer of police for unlawful acts by constables[2] is more extensive than the vicarious liability of an employer[3].

1 See eg *Stanbury v Exeter Corpn* [1905] 2 KB 838, DC. See CONSTITUTIONAL AND ADMINISTRATIVE LAW vol 20 (2014) PARA 648. As to public authorities see PARAS 807–810.
2 The chief officer of police for a police area is liable for any unlawful conduct of constables under his direction and control in the performance or purported performance of their functions in like manner as a master is liable in respect of any unlawful conduct of his servants in the course of their employment, and accordingly is, in the case of a tort, to be treated for all purposes as a joint tortfeasor: see the Police Act 1996 s 88(1); and POLICE AND INVESTIGATORY POWERS vol 84 (2013) PARA 5.
3 See *Weir v Bettison (sued as Chief Constable of Merseyside Police)* [2003] EWCA Civ 111 at [11], [2003] ICR 708 at [11] per Sir Denis Henry. Cf *Makanjuola v Metropolitan Police Comr* (1989) 2 Admin LR 214, 154 LG Rev 248; *N v Chief Constable of Merseyside* [2006] EWHC 3041 (QB), [2006] Po LR 160.

790. Crown's liability for its employees' torts. Subject to certain savings and limitations[1] the Crown is liable to the same extent as if it were a private individual of full age and capacity for torts committed by its employees and agents, and is also liable in respect of torts committed by its officers in the performance or purported performance of functions conferred on them as such as if those functions had been imposed solely by instructions from the Crown[2].

1 For the savings and limitations in question see generally CONSTITUTIONAL AND ADMINISTRATIVE LAW vol 20 (2014) PARA 192.
2 See the Crown Proceedings Act 1947 s 2; and CONSTITUTIONAL AND ADMINISTRATIVE LAW vol 20 (2014) PARAS 191–192. As to the procedure in actions against the Crown, and the special provisions applying to such proceedings, see CROWN AND CROWN PROCEEDINGS vol 29 (2014) PARA 93 et seq.

(vi) Principals and Agents

791. Vicarious liability for agents. As the function of an agent is to create contractual relations and transact dispositions of property between his principal and a third party in accordance with authority or on the basis of ratification[1], this may involve torts of deceit[2], misrepresentation[3] and conversion[4]. The liability of the principal in respect of these torts will depend on scope of authority or ratification[5] rather than on course of employment[6]. Agents may also be employees or independent contractors and their employer-principals will be liable for torts committed in these capacities as for employees and independent contractors who are not agents[7].

There may also be agency liability in respect of persons not ordinarily regarded as employees or independent contractors. These include partners[8], solicitors[9], sheriffs and bailiffs[10] and persons using vehicles for the common purposes of the owner and the user[11].

If a person without actual or apparent authority, or acting in excess of the authority that he has, professes to a third party to have authority and his action is not ratified but disowned by the alleged principal, the purported agent will be liable for the breach of warranty of authority to the third party for loss caused by the lack of authority[12]. Such a claim is primarily regarded as contractual[13] but if the misrepresentation of authority was made deliberately or recklessly the claim could be brought in deceit[14] and be subject to the measure of damages applicable in tort[15].

1   See AGENCY vol 1 (2008) PARA 29 et seq. As to ratification see AGENCY vol 1 (2008) PARA 57 et seq.

2   *Briess v Woolley* [1954] AC 333, [1954] 1 All ER 909, HL.

3   *Esso Petroleum Co Ltd v Mardon* [1976] QB 801, [1976] 2 All ER 5, CA; *Howard Marine and Dredging Co v A Odgen & Sons Ltd* [1978] QB 574, [1978] 2 All ER 1134, CA; *WB Anderson & Sons Ltd v Rhodes (Liverpool) Ltd* [1967] 2 All ER 850. An agent will not be liable under the Misrepresentation Act 1967 s 2(1) (see MISREPRESENTATION vol 76 (2013) PARA 800) for negligent misrepresentation but could be liable at common law: see *Resolute Maritime Inc v Nippon Kaiji Kyokai, The Skopas* [1983] 2 All ER 1, [1983] 1 WLR 857.

4   *Hilbery v Hatton* (1864) 2 H & C 822.

5   *Armagas Ltd v Mundogas SA, The Ocean Frost* [1986] AC 717, [1986] 2 All ER 385, HL.

6   See Atiyah *Vicarious Liability* (1967).

7   See Atiyah *Vicarious Liability* (1967).

8   See the Partnership Act 1890 ss 10, 11; and PARTNERSHIP vol 79 (2014) PARAS 66, 69.

9   A client may be liable for the torts of a solicitor in issuing legal process or perhaps in continuing proceedings when it was clear they were ill-founded: *Bate v Pilling* (1826) 6 B & C 38; *Jarmain v Hooper* (1843) 6 Man & G 827; *Morris v Salberg* (1889) 22 QBD 614, CA; *Clissold v Cratchley* [1910] 2 KB 244, CA; *Lee v Rumilly* (1891) 55 JP 519. See LEGAL PROFESSIONS vol 66 (2015) PARAS 623, 651–652.

10 A sheriff in levying execution is not generally an agent of the judgment creditor, who will only be liable if he gives specific instructions to carry out tortious acts: *Barclays Bank Ltd v Roberts* [1954] 3 All ER 107, [1954] 1 WLR 1212, CA. See also *Wilson v Tumman* (1843) 6 Man & G 236; *Morris v Salberg* (1889) 22 QBD 614, CA. A sheriff is liable for the acts of his officers, and the scope of their authority and course of employment has been interpreted widely: *Smith v Pritchard* (1849) 8 CB 565; *Smart v Hutton* (1833) 8 Ad & El 568n. A landlord may be liable for a bailiff levying distress on the basis of specific authority or ratification (e g *Carter v Vestry of St Mary Abbots Kensington* (1899) 63 JP 487) or scope of authority (e g *Perring & Co v Emerson* [1906] 1 KB 1, DC). As to sheriffs generally see LOCAL GOVERNMENT vol 69 (2009) PARA 115.

11 *Ormrod v Crosville Motor Services Ltd* [1953] 2 All ER 753, [1953] 1 WLR 1120, CA; *The Thelma* [1953] 2 Lloyd's Rep 613, HL; *Carberry v Davies* [1968] 2 All ER 817, [1968] 1 WLR 1103, CA; *Vandyke v Fender* [1970] 2 QB 292, [1970] 2 All ER 335, CA; *Nelson v Raphael* [1979] RTR 437. There must be an element of joint enterprise, hence returning a car (*Klein v Caluori* [1971] 2 All ER 701, [1971] 1 WLR 619), and household shopping (*Norwood v Navan* [1981] RTR 457, CA) are not sufficient common purposes for owner's liability. See also PARA 792.

12 See AGENCY vol 1 (2008) PARAS 160–161. See also *Collen v Wright* (1857) 8 E & B 647. The purported agent will not be liable if apparent or ostensible authority existed (*Rainbow v Howkins* [1904] 2 KB 322 at 326), or the agent is an agent of the Crown (*Dunn v Macdonald* [1897] 1 QB 555, CA). See also *Rashdall v Ford* (1866) LR 2 Eq 750 (misrepresentation of law).

13 *Dickson v Reuter's Telegram Co Ltd* (1877) 3 CPD 1 at 5, CA, per Bramwell LJ; *The Piraeus* [1974] 2 Lloyd's Rep 266, CA; *SEB Trygg Liv Holding AB v Manches* [2005] EWCA Civ 1237 at [60], [2006] 1 All ER 437 at [60], [2006] 1 WLR 2276 at [60] per Buxton LJ; *OBG Ltd v Allan* [2007] UKHL 21, [2008] 1 AC 1, [2007] 4 All ER 545 at [93] per Lord Hoffmann. See also PARA 408. As to liability in contract see CONTRACT.

14 *Polhill v Walter* (1832) 3 B & Ad 114.

15 *Doyle v Olbey (Ironmongers) Ltd* [1969] 2 QB 158, [1969] 2 All ER 119, CA; *Smith New Court Securities Ltd v Citibank NA* [1997] AC 254, sub nom *Smith New Court Securities Ltd v Scrimgeour Vickers (Asset Management) Ltd* [1996] 4 All ER 769, HL (all direct consequences, not merely those foreseeable). As to the measure of damages in tort see DAMAGES vol 29 (2014) PARA 408 et seq.

792. Liability for drivers of vehicles. If the driver of a vehicle is an employee or independent contractor the general rules of vicarious liability apply[1]. If the owner of the vehicle authorises a person who is neither an employee nor an independent contractor to drive the vehicle partly for the owner's purposes, or partly for the owner's purposes and partly for his own purposes, the owner will be liable for torts incidental to that use[2]. Mere permission to use the vehicle is not enough[3].

1   As to the principles of vicarious liability see PARA 767 et seq. As to employees see e g *Limpus v London General Omnibus Co* (1862) 1 H & C 526, Ex Ch; *Beard v London General Omnibus Co* [1900] 2 QB 530, CA; *Ricketts v Thos Tilling Ltd* [1915] 1 KB 644; *Canadian Pacific Rly Co v Lockhart* [1942] AC 591, [1942] 2 All ER 464, PC; *LCC v Cattermoles (Garages) Ltd* [1953] 2 All ER 582, [1953] 1 WLR 997, CA; *Ilkiw v Samuels* [1963] 2 All ER 879, [1963] 1 WLR 991, CA; *Kay v ITW Ltd* [1968] 1 QB 140, [1967] 3 All ER 22, CA; *Nottingham v Aldridge* [1971] 2 QB 739, [1971] 2 All ER 751; *Iqbal v London Transport Executive* (1973) 16 KIR 329, CA; *Rose v Plenty* [1976] 1 All ER 97, [1976] 1 WLR 141, CA; *Smith v Stages* [1989] AC 928, [1989] 1 All ER 833, HL. As to independent contractors see *Rogers v Night Riders* [1983] RTR 324, CA.
2   *Ormrod v Crosville Motor Services Ltd* [1953] 2 All ER 753, [1953] 1 WLR 1120, CA (car driven for holiday for owner and driver); *The Thelma* [1953] 2 Lloyd's Rep 613 (boat); *Carberry v Davies* [1968] 2 All ER 817, [1968] 1 WLR 1103, CA; *Vandyke v Fender* [1970] 2 QB 292, [1970] 2 All ER 335, CA; *Nelson v Raphael* [1979] RTR 437, CA. In such cases the drivers have been termed 'agents' of the person held vicariously liable: *Ormrod v Crosville Motor Services Ltd* [1953] 2 All ER 753, [1953] 1 WLR 1120, CA. Such cases were once determined on control or the right to control, giving a wider liability than arises in the current law: see *Samson v Aitchinson* [1912] AC 844, PC; *Pratt v Patrick* [1924] 1 KB 488; *Parker v Miller* (1926) 42 TLR 408, CA. Cf *Chowdhary v Gillot* [1947] 2 All ER 541 (employee driving claimant's vehicle).
3   *Morgans v Launchbury* [1973] AC 127, [1972] 2 All ER 606, HL (wife allowing husband to use car); *Higbid v RC Hammett Ltd* (1932) 49 TLR 104, CA; *Hewitt v Bonvin* [1940] 1 KB 188, CA. Hence an owner is not liable for a driver returning a borrowed car (*Klein v Caluori* [1971] 2 All ER 701, [1971] 1 WLR 619) or for a spouse going shopping (*Norwood v Navan* [1981] RTR 457, CA). The decision in *Scarsbrook v Mason* [1961] 3 All ER 767, where a passenger was held liable for the driver's negligence on the basis of joint enterprise, seems hard to reconcile with the principle that a mere permission to drive does not make the owner liable for the driver's negligence (*Morgans v Launchbury* [1973] AC 127, [1972] 2 All ER 606, HL) and the correctness of the decision has been doubted (*S v Walsall Metropolitan Borough Council* [1985] 1 WLR 1150 at 1153, CA, per Oliver LJ).

793. Vicarious liability of employer does not preclude personal liability of agent. The employer's vicarious liability in tort does not preclude the personal liability of the agent (despite this being inconsistent with the position of the agent in contract). An agent, including a public agent[1], who commits a wrongful act[2] in the course of his employment, is personally liable to any third person who suffers loss or damage thereby[3], notwithstanding that the act was expressly authorised or ratified by the principal[4], unless it was thereby deprived of its wrongful character[5]. It is immaterial that the agent did the act innocently and without knowledge that it was wrongful[6], except in cases where actual malice is essential to constitute the wrong[7].

An agent cannot generally rely upon an exclusion clause contained in the contract between the principal and the third party[8], unless on the wording of the contract the principal has contracted not only on his own behalf, but also on behalf of his agent[9].

1   *Entick v Carrington* (1765) 19 State Tr 1029; *Adams v Naylor* [1946] AC 543, [1946] 2 All ER 241, HL (decided before the passing of the Crown Proceedings Act 1947; as to the remedies thereby conferred see PARA 418). At common law a public agent could not be sued in his official capacity: *Raleigh v Goschen* [1898] 1 Ch 73; *Bainbridge v Postmaster General* [1906] 1 KB 178, CA. As to the liability of Crown servants and as to proceedings against government

departments see CONSTITUTIONAL AND ADMINISTRATIVE LAW vol 20 (2014) PARA 197. As to the immunity from legal process of diplomatic agents of foreign governments see INTERNATIONAL RELATIONS LAW.

2   An agent is liable only for his personal act and not for the acts of his co-agents (*Re Denham & Co* (1883) 25 ChD 752) or sub-agents (*Stone v Cartwright* (1795) 6 Term Rep 411), unless he is a partner (*Weir v Bell* (1878) 3 ExD 238 at 244, CA, per Bramwell LJ), or has otherwise made himself a principal in the transaction (*Cargill v Bower* (1878) 10 ChD 502 at 514 per Fry J; *Weir v Bell* (1878) 3 ExD 238 at 249, CA, per Cockburn CJ), or unless he is made liable by statute.

3   *Bennett v Bayes, Pennington and Harrison* (1860) 5 H & N 391; *Swift v Jewsbury and Goddard* (1874) LR 9 QB 301; *Lowe v Dorling & Son* [1906] 2 KB 772, CA; *Cope v Sharpe (No 2)* [1912] 1 KB 496, CA.

4   *Johnson v Emerson and Sparrow* (1871) LR 6 Exch 329 (attorney). As to the liability of the principal see generally AGENCY vol 1 (2008) PARAS 150–154. As to the right of the third party to rescission of contracts made as a result of a misrepresentation by the agent see AGENCY vol 1 (2008) PARA 135; MISREPRESENTATION vol 76 (2013) PARAS 725, 811 et seq. As to the right of action in respect of misrepresentation see AGENCY vol 1 (2008) PARAS 135, 152–153; and see generally MISREPRESENTATION. For a consideration of the tort of conversion by an agent see AGENCY vol 1 (2008) PARA 165. As to conversion see PARA 604 et seq.

5   *Hull v Pickersgill* (1819) 1 Brod & Bing 282; *Anderson v Watson* (1827) 3 C & P 214; *Sykes v Sykes* (1870) LR 5 CP 113; and contrast *Sharland v Mildon* (1846) 5 Hare 469; *Padget v Priest* (1787) 2 Term Rep 97.

6   *Baschet v London Illustrated Standard Co* [1900] 1 Ch 73.

7   *Eaglesfield v Marquis of Londonderry* (1878) 38 LT 303, HL; *Tims v John Lewis & Co Ltd* [1951] 2 KB 459, CA; revsd sub nom *John Lewis & Co Ltd v Tims* [1952] AC 676, [1952] 1 All ER 1203, HL, but approved on this point at 683 and 1206 per Lord Porter. See also *Egger v Viscount Chelmsford* [1965] 1 QB 248, [1964] 3 All ER 406, CA (agent relying on qualified privilege was held not to be affected by malice of principal).

8   *Adler v Dickson* [1955] 1 QB 158, [1954] 3 All ER 397, CA; *Scruttons Ltd v Midland Silicones Ltd* [1962] AC 446, [1962] 1 All ER 1, HL; *Canadian General Electric Co Ltd v The Lake Bosomtwe and Pickford and Black Ltd* [1970] 2 Lloyd's Rep 81. For exceptions see *New Zealand Shipping Co Ltd v AM Satterthwaite & Co Ltd, The Eurymedon* [1975] AC 154, [1974] 1 All ER 1015, PC; *Port Jackson Stevedoring Pty v Salmond and Spraggon (Australia) Pty* [1980] 3 All ER 257, [1981] 1 WLR 138, PC; *Norwich City Council v Harvey* [1989] 1 All ER 1180, [1989] 1 WLR 828, CA; and CARRIAGE AND CARRIERS vol 7 (2015) PARA 85.

9   A third party to a contract can avail himself of an exclusion in it if the contract expressly provides that he may or, unless on a proper construction of the contract it appears that the parties did not intend the term to be enforceable by him, the exclusion purports to benefit him: see the Contracts (Rights of Third Parties) Act 1999; and PARA 771. As to the common law see *Pyrene Co Ltd v Scindia Navigation Co Ltd* [1954] 2 QB 402, [1954] 2 All ER 158; *Alsey Steam Fishing Co Ltd v Hillman (Owners), The Kirknes* [1957] P 51, [1957] 1 All ER 97. The limitations on liability of shipowners and carriers by air conferred by statute extend also to their servants and agents acting in the course of their employment: see e g CARRIAGE AND CARRIERS vol 7 (2015) PARAS 155 et seq, 640 et seq; SHIPPING AND MARITIME LAW vol 93 (2008) PARAS 195–197.

(vii) Non-delegable Duties

794. Non-delegable duty to ensure that care is taken. An employer is not generally liable for torts committed by his independent contractor[1] but liability may arise where the law imposes on him a non-delegable duty not merely to take care but to ensure that care is taken[2]. Where such a duty exists, it is not discharged by delegating its performance[3] to a contractor if the latter in fact performs it negligently[4].

English law has long recognised that non-delegable duties exist, but there has been no single theory to explain when or why[5]. However, two broad categories of case have been identified in which such a duty has been held to have arisen[6]. These are:

(1)   where the defendant employs an independent contractor to perform some function which is either inherently hazardous or liable to become so in the course of his work[7]; and

(2)   where the common law imposes a duty upon the defendant arising from an antecedent relationship between the defendant and the claimant[8].

It should be noted that an employer who employs an independent contractor to execute work which is in itself unlawful is responsible to third persons for any injuries sustained by them in consequence of the execution of the work by the independent contractor[9].

1   See PARA 799.
2   Liability for breach of a non-delegable duty is to be contrasted with liability as a joint tortfeasor for authorising the commission of a tort (*Quarman v Burnett* (1840) 6 M & W 499 at 507 per Parke B; *M'Laughlin v Pryor* (1842) 4 Man & G 48; *Burgess v Gray* (1845) 1 CB 578) or ratifying the tortious conduct (*Jolliffe v Willmett & Co* [1971] 1 All ER 478).

    As to contributions between the employer and the contractor in such cases see the Civil Liability (Contribution) Act 1978; and DAMAGES vol 29 (2014) PARA 620 et seq. See also *Daniel v Rickett, Cockerell & Co Ltd and Raymond* [1938] 2 KB 322, [1938] 2 All ER 631. As to contribution between joint tortfeasors generally see PARA 447 et seq; and DAMAGES vol 29 (2014) PARA 620 et seq.
3   As to the distinction between discharge of the duty and delegation of its performance see *Davie v New Merton Board Mills Ltd* [1959] AC 604, [1959] 1 All ER 346, HL (which should now be considered in the light of the Employers Liability (Defective Equipment) Act 1969: see EMPLOYMENT vol 39 (2014) PARA 33).
4   See e g *Dalton v Angus & Co* (1881) 6 App Cas 740 at 829, HL, per Lord Blackburn; *Cassidy v Ministry of Health* [1951] 2 KB 343 at 363, [1951] 1 All ER 574 at 587, CA, per Denning LJ. Examples of such non-delegable duties include the duties of a bailee for reward (*Morris v CW Martin & Sons Ltd* [1966] 1 QB 716, [1965] 2 All ER 725, CA; *British Road Services Ltd v Arthur V Crutchley* [1968] 1 All ER 811, [1968] 1 Lloyd's Rep 271, CA), and the duty not to let one's land cause a nuisance to a neighbour (*Dalton v Angus & Co* (1881) 6 App Cas 740, HL; *Hughes v Percival* (1883) 8 App Cas 443 at 446, HL; *Lemaitre v Davis* (1881) 19 ChD 281; *Matania v National Provincial Bank Ltd and Elevenist Syndicate Ltd* [1936] 2 All ER 633, CA; *Alcock v Wraith* (1991) 59 BLR 20, CA). It has been held that there is no comparable duty to ensure a contractor on one's land takes reasonable care not to cause personal injury: *Rapson v Cubitt* (1842) 9 M & W 710; *Green v Fibreglass Ltd* [1958] 2 QB 245, [1958] 2 All ER 521.
5   *Woodland v Essex County Council* [2013] UKSC 66 at [6], [2014] AC 537 at [6], [2014] 1 All ER 482 at [6].
6   *Woodland v Essex County Council* [2013] UKSC 66 at [6], [2014] AC 537 at [6], [2014] 1 All ER 482 at [6].
7   *Woodland v Essex County Council* [2013] UKSC 66 at [6], [2014] AC 537 at [6], [2014] 1 All ER 482 at [6]. As to this category of non-delegable duty see PARA 795.
8   *Woodland v Essex County Council* [2013] UKSC 66 at [6], [2014] AC 537 at [6], [2014] 1 All ER 482 at [6]. As to this category of non-delegable duty see PARA 796.
9   *Ellis v Sheffield Gas Consumers Co* (1853) 2 E & B 767.

795.   Non-delegable duties in relation to hazardous activities.   The first category of cases in which there are non-delegable duties[1] is where the defendant employs an independent contractor to perform some function which is either inherently[2] hazardous or liable to become so in the course of his work[2]. These cases have often been concerned with the creation of hazards in a public place, generally in circumstances which apart from statutory authority would constitute a public nuisance[3].

An employer who employs an independent contractor to execute inherently dangerous work from which, in the natural course of things, injurious consequences to others must be expected to arise unless measures are adopted by which such consequences may be prevented, is bound to see that everything is done which is reasonably necessary to avoid those consequences[4]. He cannot, therefore, relieve himself of his responsibility in such a case by proving that he had delegated the performance of this duty to the contractor employed to do the work, or to some independent person[5], however competent the contractor or delegate may be[6]. In accordance with the same principle, where the work which the independent contractor is employed to do is of a character that is inherently dangerous to the public unless done with proper precautions, the employer is responsible to any member of the public who sustains injury in consequence of the manner in which the work is done[7].

Performing operations on or near a highway by its very nature carries a risk of serious harm to highway-users, and there have been numerous cases where non-delegable duties of care have been identified in such situations[8]. With regard to highways, a distinction must be drawn between the exercise of the public right to pass and repass, on the one hand, and the execution of work upon the highway, on the other[9].

It has been said that the non-delegable duty in respect of inherently dangerous work arises only in respect of activities that are exceptionally dangerous whatever precautions are taken[10]. The inquiry is into the intrinsic quality of the operation in question, disregarding circumstances that may have increased the danger on the facts of the individual case[11]. In such cases it is a duty not merely to take care but to provide that care is taken so that if there is negligence on the part of the contractor, the duty on the employer is broken[12]. However, this requirement for exceptional danger has been criticised in the Supreme Court[13].

1   As to non-delegable duties see PARA 794.

2   *Woodland v Essex County Council* [2013] UKSC 66 at [6], [2014] AC 537 at [6], [2014] 1 All ER 482 at [6].

3   *Woodland v Essex County Council* [2013] UKSC 66 at [6], [2014] AC 537 at [6], [2014] 1 All ER 482 at [6], citing *Pickard v Smith* (1861) 10 CB (NS) 470; *Penny v Wimbledon UDC* [1898] 2 QB 212, 62 JP 582, 67 LJQB 754, 78 LT 748; *Holliday v National Telephone Co* [1899] 2 QB 392, 68 LJQB 1016, 47 WR 658. See also *Honeywill and Stein Ltd v Larkin Brothers (London's Commercial Photographers) Ltd* [1934] 1 KB 191, 103 LJKB 74, [1933] All ER Rep 77 (applying the principle more broadly to 'extra-hazardous' operations generally).

4   *Bower v Peate* (1876) 1 QBD 321; *Pendlebury v Greenhalgh* (1875) 1 QBD 36, CA; *Hughes v Percival* (1883) 8 App Cas 443; *Black v Christchurch Finance Co Ltd* [1894] AC 48, PC; *Honeywill and Stein Ltd v Larkin Bros (London's Commercial Photographers) Ltd* [1934] 1 KB 191, CA; *Balfour v Barty-King (Hyder & Sons (Builders) Ltd, third parties)* [1957] 1 QB 496, [1957] 1 All ER 156, CA; *Johnson (t/a Johnson Butchers) v BJW Property Developments Ltd* [2002] EWHC 1131 (TCC), [2002] 3 All ER 574, 86 ConLR 74. The employer's duty is not absolute but merely a duty to ensure that reasonable care is taken by the contractor: *Bower v Peate* (1876) 1 QBD 321 at 327 per Cockburn CJ; *Hughes v Percival* (1883) 8 App Cas 443 at 446 per Lord Blackburn; *Dalton v Angus & Co* (1881) 6 App Cas 740 at 829, HL, per Lord Blackburn; *Penny v Wimbledon UDC* [1899] 2 QB 72 at 78, CA, per Romer LJ; *The Pass of Ballater* [1942] P 112 at 117, [1942] 2 All ER 79 at 84 per Langton J.

5   *Bower v Peate* (1876) 1 QBD 321 at 326 per Cockburn CJ.

6   It is immaterial that the employer has stipulated for proper precautions to be taken: *Bower v Peate* (1876) 1 QBD 321; *Black v Christchurch Finance Co Ltd* [1894] AC 48, PC. The liability does not extend to collateral acts of negligence on the part of the contractor or his employees: see PARA 797.

7   *Pickard v Smith* (1861) 10 CBNS 470; *Blake v Thirst* (1863) 2 H & C 20; *Gray v Pullen* (1864) 5 B & S 970, Ex Ch; *Tarry v Ashton* (1876) 1 QBD 314; *Penny v Wimbledon UDC* [1899] 2 QB 72, CA; *Hill v Tottenham UDC* (1898) 79 LT 495; *The Snark* [1900] P 105, CA; *Daniel v Rickett, Cockerell & Co Ltd and Raymond* [1938] 2 KB 322 at 324–325, [1938] 2 All ER 631 at 632–633 per Hilbery J; *Robinson v Beaconsfield RDC* [1911] 2 Ch 188, CA.

8   See eg *Tarry v Ashton* (1876) 1 QBD 314; *Hardaker v Idle District Council* [1896] 1 QB 335 at 351, CA; *Holliday v National Telephone Co* [1899] 2 QB 392 at 398, CA; *Penny v Wimbledon UDC* [1899] 2 QB 72, CA; *The Snark* [1900] P 105 at 110, CA (concerning a navigable waterway rather than a highway); *Maxwell v British Thomson-Houston Co Ltd* (1902) 18 TLR

278, CA; *Daniel v Rickett, Cockerell & Co Ltd and Raymond* [1938] 2 KB 322, [1938] 2 All ER 631; *Walsh v Holst & Co Ltd* [1958] 3 All ER 33, [1958] 1 WLR 800, CA; *Clarke v J Sugrue & Sons Ltd* (1959) Times, 29 May.

9   It has long been settled that the employer is liable for his contractor's stationary works which obstruct or endanger the public right of passage: *Bush v Steinman* (1799) 1 Bos & P 404.

10 *Biffa Waste Services Ltd v Maschinenfabrik Ernst Hese GmbH* [2008] EWCA Civ 1257 at [78], [2009] QB 725 at [78], 122 ConLR 1 at [78].

11 *Biffa Waste Services Ltd v Maschinenfabrik Ernst Hese GmbH* [2008] EWCA Civ 1257 at [81], [2009] QB 725 at [81], 122 ConLR 1 at [81].
    Examples of special dangers that have been recognised in decided cases include: dangerous building operations (see eg *Hughes v Percival* (1883) 8 App Cas 443, HL; *Alcock v Wraith* (1991) 59 BLR 20, CA; *Stewart v Malik* [2009] CSIH 5, 2009 SC 265. Contrast *Green v Fibreglass Ltd* [1958] 2 QB 245, [1958] 2 All ER 521; *Cook v Broderip* (1968) 112 Sol Jo 193; *Bluett v King Core Demolition Services* (1973) 227 Estates Gazette 503), the blasting of rock (*Paterson v Lindsay* (1885) 23 Sc LR 180), work adjacent to gas pipes (*Hardaker v Idle District Council* [1896] 1 QB 335, CA; *Rapson v Cubitt* (1842) 9 M & W 710; *Brooke v Bool* [1928] 2 KB 578, DC), the use of a benzoline lamp which exploded on the highway (*Holliday v National Telephone Co* [1899] 2 QB 392, CA; cf *Biffa Waste Services Ltd v Maschinenfabrik Ernst Hese GmbH* [2008] EWCA Civ 1257 at [71], [2009] QB 725 at [71], 122 ConLR 1 at [71]), photography by magnesium flash (*Honeywill and Stein Ltd v Larkin Bros (London's Commercial Photographers) Ltd* [1934] 1 KB 191, CA), and the use of an oxy-acetylene burner in an oil-tank ship (*The Pass of Ballater* [1942] P 112, [1942] 2 All ER 79).
    However, it has been decided that welding is not an exceptionally dangerous activity giving rise to a non-delegable duty on the employer commissioning its performance: see *Biffa Waste Services Ltd v Maschinenfabrik Ernst Hese GmbH* [2008] EWCA Civ 1257, [2009] QB 725, 122 ConLR 1.
    Cases where employers of contractors were held liable for escapes of fire under the rule in *Rylands v Fletcher* (1868) LR 3 HL 330, include *Black v Christchurch Finance Co Ltd* [1894] AC 48, PC; *Balfour v Barty-King (Hyder & Sons (Builders) Ltd, third parties)* [1957] 1 QB 496, [1957] 1 All ER 156, CA; *Johnson (t/a Johnson Butchers) v BJW Property Developments Ltd* [2002] EWHC 1131 (TCC), [2002] 3 All ER 574, 86 ConLR 74. See now *Stannard (t/a Wyvern Tyres) v Gore* [2012] EWCA Civ 1248, [2014] QB 1, [2013] 1 All ER 694, doubting this type of liability; and PARA 597.
    As to liability in nuisance for damage by fire see *Spicer v Smee* [1946] 1 All ER 489. As to an occupier's liability for fire see generally FIRE AND RESCUE SERVICES vol 51 (2013) PARA 1 et seq.

12 *The Pass of Ballater* [1942] P 112 at 117, [1942] 2 All ER 79 at 84 per Langton J.

13 *Woodland v Essex County Council* [2013] UKSC 66 at [6], [2014] AC 537 at [6], [2014] 1 All ER 482 at [6] per Lord Sumption who observed: 'Many of these decisions are founded on arbitrary distinctions between ordinary and extraordinary hazards which may be ripe for re-examination. Their justification, if there is one, should probably be found in a special public policy for operations involving exceptional danger to the public'.

796.   Non-delegable duties where there is an existing relationship between employer and tortfeasor.   The second category of non-delegable duty[1] comprises cases where the common law imposes a duty upon the defendant which has three critical characteristics:

(1)   The duty arises not from the negligent character of the act itself but because of an antecedent relationship between the defendant and the claimant[2].

(2)   The duty is a positive or affirmative duty to protect a particular class of persons against a particular class of risks, and not simply a duty to refrain from acting in a way that foreseeably causes injury[3].

(3)   The duty is, by virtue of that relationship, personal to the defendant[4].

The work required to perform such a duty may well be delegable, and usually is, but the duty itself remains the defendant's. Its delegation makes no difference to his legal responsibility for the proper performance of a duty which is in law his own[5]. In these cases, the defendant is assuming a liability analogous to that assumed by a person who contracts to do work carefully[6].

Examples of such situations will often occur in the public sector, where free-of-charge services mean that remedies will be available in tort rather than contract[7]. NHS hospitals owe their patients non-delegable duties of care which cannot be evaded by relying on skilled health care providers[8] even if the negligent treatment is provided by an independent contractor[9]. The same principle applies where an education authority undertakes to protect pupils from injury, even when they entrust the care of children to independent contractors[10], and it could logically be extended to prisoners in custody or residents in a care home[11].

The defining features of this category of non-delegable duty of care are as follows:

(a) The claimant is a patient or a child, or for some other reason is especially vulnerable or dependent on the protection of the defendant against the risk of injury[12].

(b) There is an antecedent relationship between the claimant and the defendant, independent of the negligent act or omission itself which places the claimant in the actual custody, charge or care of the defendant, and from which it is possible to impute to the defendant the assumption of a positive duty to protect the claimant from harm, and not just a duty to refrain from conduct which will foreseeably damage the claimant[13].

(c) The claimant has no control over how the defendant chooses to perform those obligations (whether personally or through employees or through third parties)[14].

(d) The defendant has delegated to a third party some function which is an integral part of the positive duty which he has assumed towards the claimant; and the third party is exercising, for the purpose of the function thus delegated to him, the defendant's custody or care of the claimant and the element of control that goes with it[15].

(e) The third party has been negligent not in some collateral respect[16] but in the performance of the very function assumed by the defendant and delegated by the defendant to him[17].

However, the Supreme Court has warned that the courts should be sensitive about imposing unreasonable financial burdens on those providing critical public services, and a non-delegable duty of care should be imputed to schools only so far as it would be fair, just and reasonable to do so[18]. Schools are liable for the negligence of independent contractors only if and so far as the latter are performing functions which the school has assumed for itself a duty to perform, generally in school hours and on school premises (or at other times or places where the school may carry out its educational functions)[19].

1   As to non-delegable duties see PARA 794.
2   *Woodland v Essex County Council* [2013] UKSC 66 at [7], [2014] AC 537 at [7], [2014] 1 All ER 482 at [7].
3   *Woodland v Essex County Council* [2013] UKSC 66 at [7], [2014] AC 537 at [7], [2014] 1 All ER 482 at [7].
4   *Woodland v Essex County Council* [2013] UKSC 66 at [7], [2014] AC 537 at [7], [2014] 1 All ER 482 at [7].
5   *Woodland v Essex County Council* [2013] UKSC 66 at [7], [2014] AC 537 at [7], [2014] 1 All ER 482 at [7].
6   *Woodland v Essex County Council* [2013] UKSC 66 at [7], [2014] AC 537 at [7], [2014] 1 All ER 482 at [7]. The contracting party will normally be taken to contract that the work will be done carefully by whomever he may get to do it: see *Photo Production Ltd v Securicor Transport Ltd* [1980] AC 827 at 848, [1980] 1 All ER 556 at 566, HL, per Lord Diplock (cited in *Woodland v Essex County Council* at [7]).

7   See *Gold v Essex County Council* [1942] 2 KB 293 at 301–302, [1942] 2 All ER 237 at 242–243, CA, per Lord Greene MR.

8   *Gold v Essex County Council* [1942] 2 KB 293 at 301–302, [1942] 2 All ER 237 at 242–243, CA, per Lord Greene MR ('The first task is to discover the extent of the obligation assumed by the person whom it is sought to make liable. Once this is discovered, it follows of necessity that the person accused of a breach of the obligation cannot escape liability because he has employed another person, whether a servant or agent, to discharge it on his behalf, and this is equally true whether or not the obligation involves the use of skill'). See also *Cassidy v Ministry of Health* [1951] 2 KB 343, at 362–3, [1951] 1 All ER 574 at 586–587, CA, per Denning (hospital authority in charge of a casualty department had an obligation to provide proper medical and nursing care for patients); *Barnett v Chelsea and Kensington Hospital Management Committee* [1969] 1 QB 428, [1968] 1 All ER 1068. See also *X (Minors) v Bedfordshire County Council* [1995] 2 AC 633, [1995] 3 All ER 353, HL; *Farraj v King's Healthcare NHS Trust* [2009] EWCA Civ 1203, [2010] 1 WLR 2139, [2009] All ER (D) 158 (Nov).

9   *M v Calderdale and Kirklees Health Authority* [1998] Lloyd's Rep Med 157, County Court.

10 *Woodland v Essex County Council* [2013] UKSC 66, [2014] AC 537, [2014] 1 All ER 482, where the local authority had delegated the care and control of the claimant pupil to third parties (an unincorporated business) to carry out swimming lessons at a local pool as an integral part of its teaching function. The claimant sustained serious brain injury during a swimming lesson. It was held that the local authority owed a non-delegable duty of care to its pupils. Therefore, if it was found that the third parties had been negligent then the authority would be in breach of that duty.

11 *Woodland v Essex County Council* [2013] UKSC 66 at [23], [2014] AC 537 at [23], [2014] 1 All ER 482 at [23].

12 *Woodland v Essex County Council* [2013] UKSC 66 at [23], [2014] AC 537 at [23], [2014] 1 All ER 482 at [23].

13 *Woodland v Essex County Council* [2013] UKSC 66 at [23], [2014] AC 537 at [23], [2014] 1 All ER 482 at [23]. It is characteristic of such relationships that they involve an element of control over the claimant, which varies in intensity from one situation to another, but is clearly very substantial in the case of schoolchildren: *Woodland v Essex County Council* at [23].

14 *Woodland v Essex County Council* [2013] UKSC 66 at [23], [2014] AC 537 at [23], [2014] 1 All ER 482 at [23].

15 *Woodland v Essex County Council* [2013] UKSC 66 at [23], [2014] AC 537 at [23], [2014] 1 All ER 482 at [23].

16 As to collateral acts of negligence on the part of the contractor or his employees: see PARA 797.

17 *Woodland v Essex County Council* [2013] UKSC 66 at [23], [2014] AC 537 at [23], [2014] 1 All ER 482 at [23].

18 *Woodland v Essex County Council* [2013] UKSC 66 at [25], [2014] AC 537 at [25], [2014] 1 All ER 482 at [25].

19 *Woodland v Essex County Council* [2013] UKSC 66 at [25], [2014] AC 537 at [25], [2014] 1 All ER 482 at [25]. They will not be liable for the defaults of independent contractors providing extra-curricular activities outside school hours, such as school trips in the holidays. Nor will they be liable for the negligence of those to whom no control over the child has been delegated, such as bus drivers or the theatres, zoos or museums to which children may be taken by school staff in school hours: *Woodland v Essex County Council* at [25].

797.   Employer not liable for 'collateral negligence' of independent contractor.
Even in those cases where the employer is under a personal or non-delegable duty[1] he is not liable for every negligent act of an independent contractor. The employer is responsible only where the contract which he has made is one by which he entrusts performance of his duty to the independent contractor[2]. The danger must be inherent in the work itself in order for the employer to be liable; negligent performance by the contractor of an otherwise low-risk activity is not sufficient. Employers have been held not liable for damage resulting from the casual or collateral negligence of an independent contractor, or of the latter's employees[3], while doing the work contracted to be done[4]. Negligence is said to be casual or collateral when it arises incidentally in the course of the performance of, and not directly from, the act authorised[5].

1   See PARA 794.
2   *Thomson v Cremin* (1941) [1953] 2 All ER 1185 at 1191, [1956] 1 WLR 103n at 110, HL, per
    Lord Wright; *Pickard v Smith* (1861) 10 CBNS 470 at 480 per curiam; *Cook v Square D Ltd*
    [1992] ICR 262, sub nom *Square D Ltd v Cook*, [1992] IRLR 34, CA. The occupier of a ship
    did not delegate his former common law duty towards an invitee to an intending purchaser who
    contracted for a trip (*Hobson v Bartram & Sons Ltd* [1950] 1 All ER 412, CA); and see *Daniel
    v Metropolitan Rly Co* (1871) LR 5 HL 45; *The Bearn* [1906] P 48, CA; *Davie v New Merton
    Board Mills Ltd* [1959] AC 604, [1959] 1 All ER 346, HL.
3   *Quarman v Burnett* (1840) 6 M & W 499; *Dalton v Angus & Co* (1881) 6 App Cas 740 at
    829, HL.
4   An example of casual negligence is letting a stone or tool fall upon the highway: *Reedie v
    London and North Western Rly Co* (1849) 4 Exch 244; *Penny v Wimbledon UDC* [1899] 2 QB
    72 at 76, CA, per A L Smith LJ; *Padbury v Holliday and Greenwood Ltd* (1912) 28 TLR
    494, CA ('[B]efore a superior employer could be held liable for the negligent act of a servant of
    a sub-contractor it must be shown that the work which the sub-contractor was employed to do
    was work the nature of which, and not merely the performance of which, cast on the superior
    employer the duty of taking precautions': at 495 per Fletcher Moulton LJ). See also *Rowe v
    Herman* [1997] 1 WLR 1390, 58 ConLR 33, CA (metal plates laid on highway not an essential
    part of contract work and risk).
        However, the contractor's negligence in the following cases was held to be not casual:
    Holliday v National Telephone Co [1899] 2 QB 392, CA (use of benzoline lamp with faulty
    safety valve); *Penny v Wimbledon UDC* [1899] 2 QB 72, CA (unguarded heaps of soil
    negligently left on highway) (but see *Peachey v Rowland* (1853) 13 CB 182; cf *Hardaker v Idle
    District Council* [1896] 1 QB 335, CA; *Robinson v Beaconsfield RDC* [1911] 2 Ch 188 at
    198, CA, per Buckley LJ); *Maxwell v British Thomson-Houston Co Ltd* (1902) 18 TLR
    278, CA (leaving the movable derrick used for working at an electric tram standard so near the
    lines as to injure a passenger on a tram). It is submitted that these cases would now be likely to
    be considered to fall under the first category of non-delegable duties (ie in relation to hazardous
    activities) as expressed in *Woodland v Essex County Council* [2013] UKSC 66, [2014] AC 537,
    [2014] ICR 482: see PARA 795.
5   *Hole v Sittingbourne and Sheerness Rly Co* (1861) 6 H & N 488 at 497 per Pollock CB; *Pickard
    v Smith* (1861) 10 CBNS 470 at 480 per Williams J; *Gray v Pullen* (1864) 5 B & S 970 at 985,
    Ex Ch, per Erle CJ; *Cassidy v Ministry of Health* [1951] 2 KB 343 at 364, [1951] 1 All ER 574
    at 587, CA, per Denning LJ; *Walsh v Holst & Co Ltd* [1958] 3 All ER 33 at 36, [1958] 1 WLR
    800, CA, per Hodson LJ.

798.   Employer under statutory obligation to execute work.   An employer who
is under a statutory obligation to execute particular work and who entrusts the
execution of it to an independent contractor is responsible to third persons for
any injury sustained by them in consequence of the improper execution of the
work by the independent contractor[1]. The employers may, however, be exempt
from liability under the terms of the statute imposing the duty[2].

1   *Hole v Sittingbourne and Sheerness Rly Co* (1861) 6 H & N 488; *Gray v Pullen* (1864) 5
    B & S 970, Ex Ch; *Hyams v Webster* (1867) LR 2 QB 264 (affd (1868) LR 4 QB 138, Ex Ch);
    Hardaker v Idle District Council [1896] 1 QB 335, CA; *Robinson v Beaconsfield RDC* [1911]
    2 Ch 188, CA; *Smith v Cammell Laird & Co Ltd* [1940] AC 242, [1939] 4 All ER 381, HL;
    Hosking v De Havilland Aircraft Co Ltd [1949] 1 All ER 540.
2   *Howitt v Nottingham Tramways Co* (1883) 12 QBD 16, DC. See also *Barham v Ipswich Dock
    Comrs* (1885) 54 LT 23.

(3)   LIABILITY FOR INDEPENDENT CONTRACTORS AND OTHER PERSON'S EMPLOYEES

(i)   Liability for Independent Contractors

**799.   Liability of employer in respect of personal duties delegated to
independent contractors.**   If an employer entrusts the execution of the personal
non-delegable duties he owes with regard to his employees at common law[1] to an

independent contractor appointed for the purpose, the employer is liable for any negligence on the part of the contractor or the contractor's employees or agents[2].

So, too, where statute imposes a duty on an employer of labour for the protection of his workers, the employer usually remains liable, unless statute otherwise provides, for any breach of the duty even though he has delegated its performance to another[3].

1 *Wilsons and Clyde Coal Co Ltd v English* [1938] AC 57, [1937] 3 All ER 628, HL; *Davie v New Merton Board Mills Ltd* [1959] AC 604, [1959] 1 All ER 346, HL (the specific decision in this case reversed by the Employer's Liability (Defective Equipment) Act 1969: see EMPLOYMENT; HEALTH AND SAFETY AT WORK vol 52 (2014) PARA 377); *McDermid v Nash Dredging and Reclamation Co Ltd* [1987] AC 906, [1987] 2 All ER 878, HL. See also PARA 762. As to non-delegable duties of employers see PARA 794 et seq.

2 See *Wilsons and Clyde Coal Co Ltd v English* [1938] AC 57 at 83–84, [1937] 3 All ER 628 at 643, HL, per Lord Wright; *McDermid v Nash Dredging and Reclamation Co Ltd* [1987] AC 906, [1987] 2 All ER 878, HL. See also *Paine v Colne Valley Electricity Supply Co Ltd* [1938] 4 All ER 803; *Pratt v Richards* [1951] 2 KB 208, [1951] 1 All ER 90n; *Morris v Breaveglen Ltd* [1993] ICR 766, [1993] IRLR 350; *Johnson v Coventry Churchill International Ltd* [1992] 3 All ER 14 (liability for safe system abroad); cf *Cook v Square D Ltd* [1992] ICR 262, sub nom *Square D Ltd v Cook* [1992] IRLR 34, CA.

3 See PARA 798; and HEALTH AND SAFETY AT WORK vol 52 (2014) PARA 383. As to statutory liability under the Employer's Liability (Defective Equipment) Act 1969 see PARA 762; and EMPLOYMENT; HEALTH AND SAFETY AT WORK vol 52 (2014) PARA 377. As regards civil liability for breach of statutory duty see PARA 761 et seq.

(ii) Employment of Another Person's Employees

800. Liability for torts of another person's employees. The general, as distinguished from the special or temporary, employer is normally[1] liable for all torts committed by his employees in the course of their employment and within the scope of their employment, and his liability is not affected by the existence of a contract between him and some other person for the temporary employment of the employees in work for that person or for the hiring of the employees to that person[2]. The general employer is, therefore, normally responsible for the acts of his employees, not only to third persons, but also to the person with whom he contracted[3], provided the employee who commits the tort is acting in the course of his employment[4].

Exceptionally, where there is shared control of the hired employee, there may be a dual vicarious liability on both the general employer and the hirer[5].

1 For circumstances where the temporary and not the general employer is liable, see PARA 801.

2 *Dalyell v Tyrer* (1858) EB & E 899; *Mersey Docks and Harbour Board v Coggins and Griffiths (Liverpool) Ltd* [1947] AC 1, [1946] 2 All ER 345, HL; *Kauppan Bhoomidas v Port of Singapore Authority* [1978] 1 All ER 956, [1978] 1 WLR 189, PC. It is easier to show that a full transfer has taken place when an unskilled worker is borrowed rather than when a worker together with vehicle or machinery has been lent: see *Denham v Midland Employers' Mutual Assurance Ltd* [1955] 2 QB 437 at 444, [1955] 2 All ER 561 at 564, CA, per Denning LJ; and compare *Gibb v United Steel Cos Ltd* [1957] 2 All ER 110, [1957] 1 WLR 668 with *Brady v Giles* (1835) 1 Mood & R 494 and *Sykes v Millington* [1953] 1 QB 770, [1953] 1 All ER 1098, DC; but see *McGregor v JS Duthie & Sons & Co Ltd* 1966 SLT 133, Ct of Sess (transfer even though general employer was in lorry with loaned employee). A contractual term transferring the employee's employment from the general employer to a hirer may act, as regards the general employer, as an exclusion of liability and so be subject to the Unfair Contract Terms Act 1977: *Phillips Products Ltd v Hyland* [1987] 2 All ER 620, [1987] 1 WLR 659n, CA. Cf *Thompson v T Lohan (Plant Hire) Ltd* [1987] 2 All ER 631, [1987] 1 WLR 649, CA (contractual transfer to hirer of general employer's liability, but not the employment; not an exclusion clause within Unfair Contract Terms Act 1977).

3 *Holmes v Onion* (1857) 2 CBNS 790.

4   There is no liability if the relationship of employer and employee does not exist between the supplier of the labour and the person whose labour is supplied and who does the wrongful act: *Hall v Lees* [1904] 2 KB 602, CA.

5   *Viasystems (Tyneside) Ltd v Thermal Transfer (Northern) Ltd* [2005] EWCA Civ 1151, [2006] QB 510, [2005] 4 All ER 1181. Cf *Hawley v Luminar Leisure Ltd* [2006] EWCA Civ 18, [2006] Lloyd's Rep IR 307, [2006] IRLR 817; *Biffa Waste Services Ltd v Maschinenfabrik Ernst Hese GmbH* [2008] EWCA Civ 1257, [2009] QB 725, 122 ConLR 1. See PARA 774. As to contribution between joint tortfeasors see the Civil Liability (Contribution) Act 1978; PARA 449 et seq; and DAMAGES vol 29 (2014) PARA 620 et seq.

801.   Circumstances in which temporary and not general employer is liable.   In order to absolve the general employer from liability and to make the person with whom he has contracted for the execution of work or the hire of an employee vicariously liable for the acts of the general employer's employee[1], it is necessary to prove that the relationship of employer and employee has been temporarily constituted between that person and the general employer's employee and that it existed at the time when the tort was committed[2].

1   The general employer may be personally liable if he lends an incompetent worker: *McConkey v Amec plc* (1990) 27 Con LR 88, CA. In certain circumstances a person may also be under a personal, and not merely a vicarious, liability for the acts of an independent contractor or the contractor's employees by reason of the principle that a person who procures the execution of inherently dangerous work which is likely to have injurious consequences unless proper precautions are observed cannot relieve himself from responsibility by delegating its performance to an independent contractor: see PARA 794 et seq. As to the liability of a person who employs an independent contractor to perform unlawful work see PARA 794; as to the liability of a person who, where he is under a statutory duty to execute work, employs a contractor see PARA 798. A situation may arise whereby the hirer of an employee may become liable as a joint tortfeasor if he intervenes without authority to give directions how the work should be done and damage is thereby caused, although he is not *pro hac vice* the employer of the man in question: see *Mersey Docks and Harbour Board v Coggins and Griffith (Liverpool) Ltd* [1947] AC 1 at 12, [1946] 2 All ER 345 at 349, HL, per Viscount Simon. See also *Hardaker v Idle District Council* [1896] 1 QB 335 at 344, CA.

2   As to cases where vicarious responsibility was considered to rest on the general employer see PARA 802 note 9. As to cases were vicarious responsibility was considered to rest on the hirer see PARA 802 note 8. As to dual vicarious liability see PARAS 774, 800.

802.   Transfer of employee; onus of proof.   The presumption is against a transfer of an employee of such a kind as to make the hirer or person on whose behalf the employee is temporarily working responsible for the employee's acts, and a heavy burden rests upon the party seeking to establish that the relationship of employer and employee has been constituted, for the time being[1], between the temporary employer and the general employer's employee[2]. It seems that the onus may be easier to discharge if labour only, particularly unskilled labour, and not both machinery and labour to operate it, are supplied by the general employer[3].

The fact that a term of the contract between the hirer and the supplier of a workman purports to lay down whose employee the workman concerned is to be deemed to be does not conclude the question who is liable for injury caused by the workman's negligence[4].

The questions of by whom the negligent employee was engaged, who paid him, and who had power to dismiss him do not determine the matter, but may be relevant considerations[5]. To succeed in discharging the burden, it must be shown that *pro hac vice* the temporary employer had the right[6] to control how the work should be done[7]. Whether[8] or not[9] the temporary employer had such a right in any particular case is a question of fact[10].

If it can be shown that the relationship of employer and employee exists *pro hac vice*, the liability of the temporary employer is the same whether the lending of the employee is gratuitous or for reward[11].

1   See *Savory v Holland, Hannen and Cubitts (Southern) Ltd* [1964] 3 All ER 18 at 20, [1964] 1 WLR 1158 at 1162, CA, per Lord Denning MR.

2   *Century Insurance Co v Northern Ireland Road Transport Board* [1942] AC 509, [1942] 1 All ER 491, HL (no transfer of independent contractor's employees, but merely a transfer of the benefit of their services); *Mersey Docks and Harbour Board v Coggins and Griffith (Liverpool) Ltd* [1947] AC 1 at 10, [1946] 2 All ER 345 at 348, HL, per Viscount Simon, at 13 and 349 per Lord Macmillan, and at 21 and 353 per Lord Uthwatt; *Viasystems (Tyneside) Ltd v Thermal Transfer (Northern) Ltd* [2005] EWCA Civ 1151 at [7], [2006] QB 510 at [7], [2005] 4 All ER 1181 at [7] per May LJ. In *Holt v WH Rhodes & Sons Ltd* [1949] 1 All ER 478 at 480, CA, per Lord Merriman P, it was said that the same heavy onus is placed on an employee seeking to establish that a temporary employer owes him a duty to provide a reasonably safe system of working.

3   See *Mersey Docks and Harbour Board v Coggins and Griffiths (Liverpool) Ltd* [1947] AC 1 at 17, [1946] 2 All ER 345 at 351, HL, per Lord Porter, and at 22 and 354 per Lord Uthwatt; *Garrard v AE Southey & Co and Standard Telephones and Cables Ltd* [1952] 2 QB 174 at 179, [1952] 1 All ER 597 at 600 per Parker J; *Denham v Midland Employers' Mutual Assurance Ltd* [1955] 2 QB 437, [1955] 2 All ER 561, CA; *Gibb v United Steel Cos Ltd* [1957] 2 All ER 110, [1957] 1 WLR 668.

4   *Mersey Docks and Harbour Board v Coggins and Griffiths (Liverpool) Ltd* [1947] AC 1 at 10, [1946] 2 All ER 345 at 348, HL, per Viscount Simon, at 13–14 and 349–350 per Lord Macmillan, at 15 and 350 per Lord Porter, at 20 and 353 per Lord Simonds, and at 22 and 354 per Lord Uthwatt. An employee's contract of employment cannot be transferred without his consent: *Mersey Docks and Harbour Board v Coggins and Griffiths (Liverpool) Ltd* [1947] AC 1, [1946] 2 All ER 345, HL; *Denham v Midland Employers' Mutual Assurance Ltd* [1955] 2 QB 437, [1955] 2 All ER 561, CA. A term in the contract between the hirer and the contractor may, however, determine the liability of the hirer and contractor as between themselves for the acts of the workman: *Mersey Docks and Harbour Board v Coggins and Griffiths (Liverpool) Ltd* [1947] AC 1 at 15, [1946] 2 All ER 345 at 350, HL, per Lord Porter; *Herdman v Walker (Tooting) Ltd (City Plant Hirers Ltd, third party)* [1956] 1 All ER 429, [1956] 1 WLR 209 (hirers of crane and driver liable to indemnify owners of crane); *Thompson v T Lohan (Plant Hire) Ltd* [1987] 2 All ER 631, [1987] 1 WLR 649, CA.

5   *Mersey Docks and Harbour Board v Coggins and Griffiths (Liverpool) Ltd* [1947] AC 1 at 10, [1946] 2 All ER 345 at 347, HL, per Viscount Simon, and at 17 and 351 per Lord Porter; *Viasystems (Tyneside) Ltd v Thermal Transfer (Northern) Ltd* [2005] EWCA Civ 1151 at [7], [2006] QB 510 at [7], [2005] 4 All ER 1181 at [7] per May LJ. See also *Quarman v Burnett* (1840) 6 M & W 499; *Reedie v London and North Western Rly Co, Hobbit v London and North Western Rly Co* (1849) 4 Exch 244; *Ready Mixed Concrete (East Midlands) Ltd v Yorkshire Traffic Area Licensing Authority* [1970] 2 QB 397, [1970] 1 All ER 890, DC.

6   As to the liability of a hirer who interferes without authority in the way work is done see PARA 801 note 1.

7   See *Donovan v Laing, Wharton and Down Construction Syndicate Ltd* [1893] 1 QB 629 at 633–634, CA, per Bowen LJ; *Mersey Docks and Harbour Board v Coggins and Griffiths (Liverpool) Ltd* [1947] AC 1 at 10–12, [1946] 2 All ER 345 at 348–349, HL, per Viscount Simon, at 14 and 350 per Lord Macmillan, at 16 and 351 per Lord Porter, at 18 and 352 per Lord Simonds, and at 21 and 354 per Lord Uthwatt; *Savory v Holland, Hannen and Cubitts (Southern) Ltd* [1964] 3 All ER 18 at 20, [1964] 1 WLR 1158 at 1163, CA, per Lord Denning M; *Viasystems (Tyneside) Ltd v Thermal Transfer (Northern) Ltd* [2005] EWCA Civ 1151 at [7], [2006] QB 510 at [7], [2005] 4 All ER 1181 at [7] per May LJ. In situations of joint control, dual vicarious liability may arise: see PARAS 774, 800. For a general discussion of the indicia of the relationship of employer and employee see EMPLOYMENT vol 39 (2014) PARA 2 et seq. The test has sometimes been concisely expressed as whether the employee or the benefit of his work was transferred: *Moore v Palmer* (1886) 2 TLR 781 at 782, CA, per Bowen LJ; *Century Insurance Co v Northern Ireland Road Transport Board* [1942] AC 509, [1942] 1 All ER 491, HL; *Ready Mixed Concrete (East Midlands) Ltd v Yorkshire Traffic Area Licensing Authority* [1970] 2 QB 397, [1970] 1 All ER 890, DC.

8   For instances in which temporary employers have stood in the relation of employers and employees with the persons employed see eg *Murray v Currie* (1870) LR 6 CP 24 (cf *Union Steamship Co Ltd v Claridge* [1894] AC 185, PC, cited in note 9); *Rourke v White Moss*

Colliery Co (1877) 2 CPD 205, CA; *Baumwoll Manufactur von Carl Scheibler v Furness* [1893] AC 8, HL; *Donovan v Laing, Wharton and Down Construction Syndicate Ltd* [1893] 1 QB 629, CA (hire of crane and driver; doubted and distinguished in *Mersey Docks and Harbour Board v Coggins and Griffiths (Liverpool) Ltd* [1947] AC 1, [1946] 2 All ER 345, HL); *Jones v Scullard* [1898] 2 QB 565; *Wilmerson v Lynn and Hamburg Steamship Co Ltd* [1913] 3 KB 931, CA; *Bain v Central Vermont Rly Co* [1921] 2 AC 412, PC; *AH Bull & Co v West African Shipping Agency and Lighterage Co* [1927] AC 686, PC; *Clinker v Stevens* (1943) 78 Ll L Rep 501n; *Gibb v United Steel Cos Ltd* [1957] 2 All ER 110, [1957] 1 WLR 668; *McGregor v JS Duthie & Sons & Co Ltd* 1966 SLT 133, Ct of Sess; *Hawley v Luminar Leisure Ltd* [2006] EWCA Civ 18, [2006] Lloyd's Rep IR 307, [2006] IRLR 817. See also the cases cited in PARA 803 note 1. As to agency staff see *McMeechan v Secretary of State for Employment* [1997] ICR 549, [1997] IRLR 353, CA; *Clark v Oxfordshire Health Authority* [1998] ICR 125, [1998] IRLR 125, CA; *Dacas v Brook Street Bureau (UK) Ltd* [2004] EWCA Civ 217, [2004] ICR 1437, [2004] IRLR 358.

9   For instances in which temporary employers have been held not to have become the employer *pro hac vice* of persons in the general employment of others see eg *Laugher v Pointer* (1826) 5 B & C; *Quarman v Burnett* (1840) 6 M & W 499; *Dalyell v Tyrer* (1858) EB & E 899; *Innocent v Peto* (1864) 4 F & F 8; *Moore v Palmer* (1886) 2 TLR 781, CA; *Waldock v Winfield* [1901] 2 KB 596, CA; *Union Steamship Co Ltd v Claridge* [1894] AC 185, PC (cf *Murray v Currie* (1870) LR 6 CP 24); *Willard v Whiteley Ltd* [1938] 3 All ER 779, CA; *Dowd v Boase & Co Ltd* [1945] KB 301, [1945] 1 All ER 605, CA; *Johnson v AH Beaumont Ltd and Ford Motor Co* [1953] 2 QB 184, [1953] 2 All ER 106; *The Panther and The Ericbank* [1957] P 143, [1957] 1 All ER 641 (tug involved in collision in course of towage contract; officer in charge of tug employee of tug owners not of owners of tow); *Savory v Holland, Hannen and Cubitts (Southern) Ltd* [1964] 3 All ER 18, [1964] 1 WLR 1158, CA; *Ready Mixed Concrete (East Midlands) Ltd v Yorkshire Traffic Area Licensing Authority* [1970] 2 QB 397, [1970] 1 All ER 890, DC; *Biffa Waste Services Ltd v Maschinenfabrik Ernst Hese GmbH* [2008] EWCA Civ 1257, [2009] QB 725, 122 ConLR 1.

10 *Brady v Giles* (1835) 1 Mood & R 494; *M'Cartan v Belfast Harbour Comrs* [1911] 2 IR 143 at 151–152, HL, per Lord Dunedin; *Century Insurance Co v Northern Ireland Road Transport Board* [1942] AC 509 at 515, [1942] 1 All ER 491 at 495, HL, per Lord Wright; *Mersey Docks and Harbour Board v Coggins and Griffiths (Liverpool) Ltd* [1947] AC 1 at 21, [1946] 2 All ER 345 at 354, HL, per Lord Uthwatt.

11 *Donovan v Laing, Wharton and Down Construction Syndicate Ltd* [1893] 1 QB 629 at 633, CA, per Lord Esher MR.

803. Duty of hirer and temporary employer towards employee. If the general employer has parted for the time being with his rights of control as employer and those rights have been assumed by the temporary employer, the latter has all the responsibilities attaching to the relationship of employer and employee towards the employee[1].

Even if the relationship does not amount to one of temporary employment, the hirer will be liable if in all the circumstances he failed to use reasonable care for the safety of the employee[2].

1 *Garrard v AE Southey & Co and Standard Telephones and Cables Ltd* [1952] 2 QB 174, [1952] 1 All ER 597; *Holt v WH Rhodes & Son Ltd* [1949] 1 All ER 478 at 480, CA, per Lord Merriman P; *Gibb v United Steel Cos Ltd* [1957] 2 All ER 110, [1957] 1 WLR 668. As to the duties of an employer to his employee generally see EMPLOYMENT vol 39 (2014) PARA 21 et seq.

2 *Savory v Holland, Hannen and Cubitts (Southern) Ltd* [1964] 3 All ER 18, [1964] 1 WLR 1158, CA. See also *Mulready v JH and W Bell Ltd* [1953] 2 QB 117, [1953] 2 All ER 215, CA.

(4) LIABILITIES OF THIRD PERSONS

(i) Liability to Employer for Injury to Employee

804. Employer has no right to recover in respect of injury to employee. An employer has no right to recover damages against the wrongdoer in respect of the loss of services which he sustains when an employee is injured[1]. The former exception to this rule in the case of domestic servants in the action known as per quod servitium amisit was abolished by statute[2].

1 *Taylor v Neri* (1795) 1 Esp 385 (manager of place of entertainment not entitled to recover for loss of services of performer); *A-G for New South Wales v Perpetual Trustee Co (Ltd)* [1955] AC 457, [1955] 1 All ER 846, PC; *IRC v Hambrook* [1956] 2 QB 641, [1956] 3 All ER 338, CA; *Metropolitan Police District Receiver v Croydon Corpn, Monmouthshire County Council v Smith* [1957] 2 QB 154, [1957] 1 All ER 78, CA; *Lee v Sheard* [1956] 1 QB 192, [1955] 3 All ER 777, CA; *West Bromwich Albion Football Club Ltd v El-Safty* [2006] EWCA Civ 1299, 92 BMLR 179, [2007] PIQR P76.
2 See the Administration of Justice Act 1982 s 2(c)(i); and PARA 429.

(ii) Liability to Employee

805. Nature of employee's rights. An employee who has suffered injury resulting from the act or omission of a third person can recover damages in tort against that person provided only that he can show that the third person has been guilty of a tort to him personally[1]. Thus if an employee is injured by reason of a latent defect in a tool purchased by his employer for his use, he may be entitled to recover damages against the manufacturers of the tool on the principle[2] that if a manufacturer sells an article in such form as to show that it is intended to reach the ultimate user in the form in which it left the manufacturer with no reasonable possibility of intermediate examination, the manufacturer owes a duty to the ultimate user to take reasonable care in the manufacture of the article so that it will not result in injury to the user[3]. Where, however, the third person owes a duty to the employer only, its violation confers no rights upon the employee even though he may sustain injury thereby. Thus an employee who is in occupation of premises on his employer's behalf cannot maintain an action against a trespasser, since the employee has himself no estate in the premises, it being immaterial that he may have been allowed by his employer to use the premises for his own business[4].

1 *Thrussell v Handyside* (1888) 20 QBD 359, DC; *Parry v Smith* (1879) 4 CPD 325. The fact of the employee's employment may affect the measure of the damages which he is entitled to recover: see eg *Lee v Sheard* [1956] 1 QB 192, [1955] 3 All ER 777, CA (plaintiff held entitled to recover, as damages for negligence, decrease in remuneration from limited company owing to its profits being diminished by reason of his absence owing to defendant's negligence). For the right to recover loss of earnings in an action for personal injuries see DAMAGES vol 29 (2014) PARA 441 et seq. As to pecuniary loss generally see DAMAGES vol 29 (2014) PARA 439 et seq. As to the deduction from such damages of tax which the employee would have had to pay if he had received the earnings see EMPLOYMENT vol 40 (2014) PARA 786.
2 See eg *M'Alister (or Donoghue) v Stevenson* [1932] AC 562, HL; and NEGLIGENCE vol 78 (2010) PARA 47 et seq.
3 See eg *Davie v New Merton Board Mills Ltd* [1958] 1 QB 210, [1958] 1 All ER 67, CA; affd [1959] AC 604, [1959] 1 All ER 3 46, HL. For the employer's statutory liability in such circumstances see the Employer's Liability (Defective Equipment) Act 1969 s 1(1); and PARA 762.
4 *White v Bayley* (1861) 10 CBNS 227.

806. Circumstances in which the employee must have been acting in the course of his employment. In order to establish a breach of duty towards the employee it may in certain cases be necessary to consider whether he was acting in the course of his employment. The facts of the case may show that the third person owed a duty not only to the employer but also to the employees engaged on his behalf[1].

1   *Parry v Smith* (1879) 4 CPD 325; *Elliott v Hall* (1885) 15 QBD 315, DC. Where the employee is sent to work on the premises of another, the care that the latter must exercise as occupier is to be assessed in the light of the expectation that a person in the exercise of his calling will appreciate and guard against any risks ordinarily incident to it: see the Occupiers' Liability Act 1957 s 2(3)(b); *Roles v Nathan* [1963] 2 All ER 908, [1963] 1 WLR 1117, CA; and NEGLIGENCE vol 78 (2010) PARA 32. In such a case, the employer remains under an obligation to provide a safe system of work (*Garcia v Harland & Wolff Ltd* [1943] 1 KB 731, [1943] 2 All ER 477), and may incur a joint liability with the occupier for the employee's injury.

11. PUBLIC AUTHORITIES

807. Liability of public authorities for torts. Unless the contrary is provided by statute[1], public authorities[2] have the same duties and are subject to the same liabilities as the general law imposes on private persons doing the same things[3], as well as certain additional duties and liabilities that are imposed on them by common law or statute[4], notably the common law tort of misfeasance in public office[5] and the duty of a 'public authority' to act in a way which is compatible with specified rights guaranteed by the Convention for the Protection of Human Rights and Fundamental Freedoms (1950)[6] under the Human Rights Act 1998[7].

Though public servants, agents and officers are not liable in a representative capacity for their torts, they remain personally liable for their tortious acts or omissions[8] and their employer[9] may be vicariously liable if such acts or omissions are done in the exercise of their authority or course of their employment[10].

1 As to statutory authority generally see PARA 457.
2 The term 'public authority' is used here to include any person certain of whose functions are functions of a public nature, as it is in the Human Rights Act 1998 s 6(3), where 'public authority' includes a court or tribunal, and any person certain of whose functions are functions of a public nature, but does not include either House of Parliament or a person exercising functions in connection with proceedings in Parliament. As to the liability of the Crown see the Crown Proceedings Act 1947; and PARA 418.
3 *Mersey Docks and Harbour Board Trustees v Gibbs* (1866) LR 1 HL 93. See PARA 419; and CONSTITUTIONAL AND ADMINISTRATIVE LAW vol 20 (2014) PARA 606.
4 As to the liability of public authorities in respect of the exercise of statutory powers see PARAS 809–810.
5 As to misfeasance in public office see PARA 808.
6 See the Convention for the Protection of Human Rights and Fundamental Freedoms (Rome, 4 November 1950; TS 71 (1953); Cmd 8969) (the 'European Convention on Human Rights'); PARA 810; and RIGHTS AND FREEDOMS vol 88A (2013) PARAS 23 et seq, 88.
7 See PARA 810.
8 *Raleigh v Goschen* [1898] 1 Ch 73; *Mackenzie-Kennedy v Air Council* [1927] 2 KB 517 at 532, CA, per Atkin LJ.
9 Vicarious liability also rests on the Crown for torts committed by Crown servants or agents (see the Crown Proceedings Act 1947 s 2(1)(a); and PARA 790) and on the chief officer of police for a police area for torts committed by constables under his direction and control in the performance or purported performance of their functions (see the Police Act 1996 s 88(1); and PARA 789).
10 As to vicarious liability for employees generally see PARA 767 et seq.

808. Misfeasance in public office. The elements of the tort of misfeasance in public office are[1]:

(1) the defendant is a public officer[2];
(2) the exercise of power as a public officer[3];
(3) the defendant's state of mind is such as to constitute either targeted malice (that is, conduct specifically intended to injure a person or persons)[4], or knowledge[5] that he has no power to do the act complained of and that the act will probably injure the claimant[6];
(4) the claimant has a sufficient interest to found a legal standing to sue[7];
(5) causation[8];
(6) the claimant suffers loss[9] that the defendant actually foresaw as a probable consequence[10].

1 See *Three Rivers District Council v Bank of England (No 3)* [2003] 2 AC 1 at 191–196, [2000] 3 All ER 1 at 8–12, HL, per Lord Steyn. See also *Three Rivers District Council v Bank of England (No 3)* [2001] UKHL 16 at [42], [2003] 2 AC 1 at [42], [2001] 2 All ER 513 at [42]

per Lord Hope, and at [121] per Lord Hutton. The liability may be traced back to *Turner v Sterling* (1671) 2 Vent 25. The tort was considered well-established in *Dunlop v Woollahra Municipal Council* [1982] AC 158 at 172, [1981] 1 All ER 1202 at 1210, PC.

2 'Public officer' includes a public body: *Three Rivers District Council v Bank of England (No 3)* [2003] 2 AC 1 at 142, [2000] 3 All ER 1 at 8, HL, per Lord Steyn; *Three Rivers District Council v Bank of England (No 3)* [2001] UKHL 16 at [126], [2003] 2 AC 1 at [126], [2001] 2 All ER 513 at [126] per Lord Hutton. See also *Henly v Mayor and Burgesses of Lyme* (1828) 5 Bing 91 at 107–108 per Best CJ; *Dunlop v Woollahra Municipal Council* [1982] AC 158, [1981] 1 All ER 1202, PC; *Jones v Swansea City Council* [1990] 3 All ER 737, [1990] 1 WLR 1453, HL (local authority exercising private law functions as a landlord). A public body may also be liable vicariously for the misfeasance of its employee: *Racz v Home Office* [1994] 2 AC 45, [1994] 1 All ER 97, HL.

A public officer is a person who exercises governmental power and the term does not apply to a commercial operation concerned with the internal commercial interests of its own members, even if it regulates its members' activities: *Society of Lloyd's v Henderson* [2007] EWCA Civ 930, [2008] 1 WLR 2255, [2008] Lloyd's Rep IR 317.

3 The exercise of power includes the procuring of the making of a compulsory purchase order (*Smith v East Elloe RDC* [1956] AC 736 at 752–753, [1956] 1 All ER 855 at 859–860, HL, per Viscount Simonds), and the refusal or cancellation, or procuring of the cancellation, of a licence (*David v Abdul Cader* [1963] 3 All ER 579, [1963] 1 WLR 834, PC; *Roncarelli v Duplessis* [1952] 1 DLR 680; for further proceedings see [1959] SCR 121, 16 DLR (2d) 689, Can SC). But a police officer who makes a false report about the suspect of an investigation is not exercising a power, so cannot be liable for misfeasance in public office, though he may incur liability in defamation: *Calveley v Chief Constable of the Merseyside Police* [1989] AC 1228 at 1240–1241, [1989] 1 All ER 1025 at 1032, HL, per Lord Bridge.

The exercise of power may be by positive act or omission, but in the case of an omission there must be a legal duty to act and a failure to act which amounts to an unlawful breach of that duty; mere inadvertence or oversight is insufficient: *Three Rivers District Council v Bank of England (No 3)* [2003] 2 AC 1 at 228, [2000] 3 All ER 1 at 41, HL, per Lord Hutton, at 230 and 43 per Lord Hobhouse, and at 237–238 and 49 per Lord Millett. See e g *Henly v Mayor and Burgesses of Lyme* (1828) 5 Bing 91. It is not necessary to show a conscious decision not to act; a deliberate or wilful failure to take a decision will also suffice: *Three Rivers District Council v Bank of England (No 3)* [2001] UKHL 16 at [69], [2003] 2 AC 1 at [69], [2001] 2 All ER 513 at [69] per Lord Hope.

4 Targeted malice involves bad faith in the sense of the exercise of public power for an improper or ulterior motive: *Three Rivers District Council v Bank of England (No 3)* [2003] 2 AC 1 at 191, [2000] 3 All ER 1 at 7, HL, per Lord Steyn. The intention may be directed at the claimant individually or as a member of a class: *Three Rivers District Council v Bank of England (No 3)* [2003] 2 AC 1 at 193, [2000] 3 All ER 1 at 9, HL, per Lord Steyn. Cf *Weir v Secretary of State for Transport* [2005] EWHC 2192 (Ch), [2005] All ER (D) 160 (Oct) ('targeted malice' not proved).

5 Reckless indifference as to consequences is sufficient: *Three Rivers District Council v Bank of England (No 3)* [2003] 2 AC 1, [2000] 3 All ER 1, HL. Reckless indifference in a subjective rather than objective sense is required: *Three Rivers District Council v Bank of England (No 3)* [2003] 2 AC 1 at 193, [2000] 3 All ER 1 at 9, HL, per Lord Steyn; *Society of Lloyd's v Henderson* [2007] EWCA Civ 930, [2008] 1 WLR 2255, [2008] Lloyd's Rep IR 317; *Dennett v Southwark London Borough Council* [2007] EWCA Civ 1091, [2008] LGR 94, [2008] HLR 23. Subjective recklessness entails wilful disregard of the risk: *Three Rivers District Council v Bank of England (No 3)* [2003] 2 AC 1 at 231, [2000] 3 All ER 1 at 44, HL, per Lord Hobhouse. See also *Three Rivers District Council v Bank of England (No 3)* [2001] UKHL 16 at [46], [2003] 2 AC 1 at [46], [2001] 2 All ER 513 at [46] per Lord Hope. An institution can only be reckless subjectively if one or more individuals acting on its behalf are subjectively reckless, and their subjective state of mind needs to be established; to that end, they need to be identified: *Southwark London Borough Council v Dennett* [2007] EWCA Civ 1091 at [21], [2008] LGR 94 at [21], [2008] HLR 369 at [21] per May LJ. See also *Society of Lloyd's v Henderson* [2007] EWCA Civ 930 at [49], [2008] 1 WLR 2255 at [49], [2008] Lloyd's Rep IR 317 at [49] per Buxton LJ.

6 This state of mind involves bad faith in as much as the public officer does not have an honest belief that his act is lawful: *Three Rivers District Council v Bank of England (No 3)* [2003] 2 AC 1 at 191, [2000] 3 All ER 1 at 7, HL, per Lord Steyn. See also at 223 and 36 per Lord Hutton, at 231 and 43–44 per Lord Hobhouse. Cf at 235 and 48 per Lord Millett, who considered that the element of knowledge was a way of establishing by inference the necessary intention to injure, not a substitute for it. Cases falling into this category include *Ashby v White*

(1703) 2 Ld Raym 938 and subsequent cases on the discretionary refusal of voting rights (see *Drewe v Coulton* (1787) 1 East 563; *Cullen v Morris* (1819) 2 Stark 577; *Tozer v Child* (1857) 7 E & B 377) and several cases involving malicious acts of inferior court judges within their jurisdiction (see *Harman v Tappenden* (1801) 1 East 555; *Ackerley v Parkinson* (1815) 3 M & S 411; *Taylor v Nesfield* (1854) 3 E & B 724). See also *Bourgoin SA v Minister of Agriculture, Fisheries and Food* [1986] QB 716, [1985] 3 All ER 585, CA.

The term 'dishonesty' is sometimes used by way of alternative to 'bad faith' but the former in some contexts implies a financial motive, so the latter is preferable: *Three Rivers District Council v Bank of England (No 3)* [2003] 2 AC 1 at 227–228, [2000] 3 All ER 1 at 40–41, HL, per Lord Hutton.

7 If the public officer knows that his unlawful conduct will probably injure another person, or is reckless as to the consequence, the claimant does not need to show any other link or relationship between himself and the officer before liability can arise: *Three Rivers District Council v Bank of England (No 3)* [2003] 2 AC 1 at 228, [2000] 3 All ER 1 at 41, HL, per Lord Hutton. In such a case, it is immaterial whether the defendant knows at the relevant time of the risk to the claimant or to a particular class of which the claimant is or becomes a member; what matters is his knowledge of the risk to someone: *Akenzua v Secretary of State for the Home Department* [2002] EWCA Civ 1470, [2003] 1 All ER 35, [2003] 1 WLR 741.

8 Causation is a question of fact: *Three Rivers District Council v Bank of England (No 3)* [2003] 2 AC 1 at 194, [2000] 3 All ER 1 at 9, HL, per Lord Steyn. As to causation generally see PARA 417.

9 The tort of misfeasance in public office is not actionable per se: *Watkins v Secretary of State for the Home Department* [2006] UKHL 17, [2006] 2 AC 395, [2006] 2 All ER 353. The claimant must suffer damage that is specific to him and not suffered in common with the public in general: *Three Rivers District Council v Bank of England (No 3)* [2003] 2 AC 1 at 231, [2000] 3 All ER 1 at 44, HL, per Lord Hobhouse. Actionable damage includes not just physical harm (*Akenzua v Secretary of State for the Home Department* [2002] EWCA Civ 1470, [2003] 1 All ER 35, [2003] 1 WLR 741), but also pure economic loss (*Three Rivers District Council v Bank of England (No 3)* [2003] 2 AC 1, [2000] 3 All ER 1, HL) and loss of liberty, including the residual liberty of a person who is lawfully imprisoned (*Karagozlu v Metropolitan Police Comr* [2006] EWCA Civ 1691, [2007] 2 All ER 1055, [2007] 1 WLR 1881). Mental injury falling short of a psychiatric condition will not suffice: *Hussain v Chief Constable of West Mercia Constabulary* [2008] EWCA Civ 1205, (2008) Times, 17 November, [2008] All ER (D) 06 (Nov). The mere invasion of a constitutional right does not constitute actionable damage: *Watkins v Secretary of State for the Home Department* [2006] UKHL 17, [2006] 2 AC 395, [2006] 2 All ER 353.

10 It is not sufficient that the loss was a reasonably foreseeable consequence of the relevant acts or omissions: *Three Rivers District Council v Bank of England (No 3)* [2003] 2 AC 1 at 194–195, [2000] 3 All ER 1 at 11, HL, per Lord Steyn, and at 236 and 49 per Lord Millett.

809. Negligence in relation to a public authority's statutory powers. A public authority's negligence may give rise to a cause of action in the tort of negligence[1], in circumstances where a duty of care is owed[2], or take away a defence of statutory authority that would otherwise have arisen in respect of some other tortious cause of action[3]. No liability in tort can arise from acts done in pursuance, and within the scope, of statutory powers where the powers are exercised in good faith, reasonably, without negligence and for the purpose for which, and in the manner which, the statute provides[4]. The protection of the statute is lost, however, if the public authority fails to exercise its powers with reasonable care[5] so as to avoid unnecessary interference with private rights[6].

1 As to liability in the tort of negligence generally see NEGLIGENCE.
2 As to the circumstances when a public authority will owe a duty of care in respect of its statutory duties and powers see NEGLIGENCE vol 78 (2010) PARA 17 et seq. As to liability in the tort of negligence for failure to exercise a statutory power see NEGLIGENCE vol 78 (2010) PARA 19. As to liability for breach of statutory duty see PARA 500 et seq, with particular reference to public authorities at PARA 508.
3 As to statutory authority see also PARA 457.
4 *Vaughan v Taff Vale Rly Co* (1860) 5 H & N 679; *Hammersmith and City Rly Co v Brand* (1869) LR 4 HL 171; *Dunne v North Western Gas Board* [1964] 2 QB 806, [1963] 3 All ER 916, CA; *Allen v Gulf Oil Refining Ltd* [1981] AC 1001, [1981] 1 All ER 353.

5 As to reasonable care see NEGLIGENCE vol 78 (2010) PARAS 21–22.
6 *Geddis v Proprietors of Bann Reservoir* (1878) 3 App Cas 430, HL; *Metropolitan Asylum District Managers v Hill* (1881) 6 App Cas 193, HL. As to the defence of statutory authority in the law of nuisance see NUISANCE vol 78 (2010) PARA 192.

810–900. Liability of public authorities under the Human Rights Act 1998.

Under the Human Rights Act 1998[1], it is unlawful for a 'public authority'[2] to act in a way which is incompatible with a right guaranteed by the Convention for the Protection of Human Rights and Fundamental Freedoms (1950)[3] which is appended to the Act[4]. A person who claims that a public authority has acted (or proposes to act) in a way which is made unlawful as described above may bring proceedings against the authority in the appropriate court or tribunal, but only if he is (or would be) a victim of the unlawful act[5]. In relation to any act (or proposed act) of a public authority which the court finds is (or would be) unlawful, it may grant such relief or remedy, or make such order, within its powers as it considers just and appropriate[6]. But no award of damages may be made unless, taking account of all the circumstances of the case, the court is satisfied that the award is necessary to afford just satisfaction to the person in whose favour it is made[7].

In some circumstances, the Human Rights Act 1998 imposes a positive obligation on public authorities to take steps to protect the Convention rights by intervening to prevent one person from causing harm to another, as where there is a real and immediate risk to life, and liability may be imposed under the Act where there is an unreasonable failure to comply with this positive obligation[8].

1 Human Rights Act 1998 s 6(1). The relevant provisions of the Act came into effect on 2 October 2000: see the Human Rights Act 1998 (Commencement No 2) Order 2000, SI 2000/1851, art 2.
2 Under the Human Rights Act 1998, 'public authority' includes a court or tribunal, and any person certain of whose functions are functions of a public nature, but does not include either House of Parliament or a person exercising functions in connection with proceedings in Parliament: s 6(3).
3 Ie the Convention for the Protection of Human Rights and Fundamental Freedoms (Rome, 4 November 1950; TS 71 (1953); Cmd 8969) (the 'European Convention on Human Rights'). See further RIGHTS AND FREEDOMS vol 88A (2013) PARA 88.
4 See the Human Rights Act 1998 s 1, Sch 1; and RIGHTS AND FREEDOMS vol 88A (2013) PARAS 14, 23 et seq. These rights are in addition to, and not in substitution for, existing rights: see the Human Rights Act 1998 s 11; and RIGHTS AND FREEDOMS vol 88A (2013) PARA 27.
5 See the Human Rights Act 1998 s 7(1); and RIGHTS AND FREEDOMS vol 88A (2013) PARA 28. For the purposes of s 7, a person is a victim of an unlawful act only if he would be a victim for the purposes of the Convention for the Protection of Human Rights and Fundamental Freedoms art 34 if proceedings were brought in the European Court of Human Rights in respect of that act: Human Rights Act 1998 s 7(7). Damages may be awarded only by a court which has power to award damages, or to order the payment of compensation, in civil proceedings: s 7(2).
6 See the Human Rights Act 1998 s 8(1); and RIGHTS AND FREEDOMS vol 88A (2013) PARA 29.
7 See the Human Rights Act 1998 s 8(3); and RIGHTS AND FREEDOMS vol 88A (2013) PARA 29. See further *Anufrijeva v Southwark London Borough Council* [2003] EWCA Civ 1406, [2004] QB 1124, [2004] 1 All ER 833.
8 The real and immediate risk test adopted by the European Court of Human Rights in *Osman v United Kingdom* (App no 23452/94) (2000) 29 EHRR 245 was applied and considered in *Van Colle v Chief Constable of the Hertfordshire Police* [2008] UKHL 50, [2009] 1 AC 225, [2008] 3 All ER 977 (police); *Savage v South Essex Partnership NHS Foundation Trust* [2008] UKHL 74, [2009] 1 AC 691, [2009] 1 All ER 1053 (suicide by person detained under mental health legislation); *Mitchell v Glasgow City Council* [2009] UKHL 11, [2009] 1 AC 874, [2009] 3 All ER 205 (fatal quarrel between neighbours in local authority accommodation). However, see Application 7678/09 *Van Colle v United Kingdom* [2012] ECHR 7678/09, (2013) Times, 22 January, ECtHR (where it was not obvious that the life of a witness was in immediate danger, the right to life was not breached where, although made aware of threats, police failed to take steps to protect witness from fatal attack).

310–600 Liability of public authorities under the Human Rights Act 1998.

TRADE AND INDUSTRY

1. ADMINISTRATION

(1) CENTRAL GOVERNMENT

901. Government responsibility for trade and industry. Government responsibility in relation to matters of trade and industry is vested in the Department for Business, Innovation and Skills[1]. Certain functions, in so far as they are exercisable in relation to Wales, have been transferred to, or are now exercisable concurrently with, the National Assembly for Wales and the Welsh Ministers[2].

1   As to the Department for Business, Innovation and Skills see PARA 902.
2   See PARA 902 note 21.

902. Transfers of functions between government departments, the Secretary of State and the Welsh Ministers. Matters relating to trade were originally within the general jurisdiction of the Board of Trade[1]. Subsequently, specialised ministries were established such as those relating to technology, power, science[2] and aviation. In 1970 certain powers previously exercised by such ministries were transferred to the Secretary of State[3], which in practice meant the Secretary of State for Trade and Industry[4], who was also empowered to exercise concurrently the powers of the Board of Trade[5]. This device of assigning powers simply to 'the Secretary of State' was used again in 1974 when the Department of Trade and Industry was divided and its functions transferred en bloc to the Secretary of State[6] and distributed by administrative arrangements[7] among the four successor Departments of Trade, Industry, Energy[8] and Prices and Consumer Protection[9].

In 1983 the Departments of Trade and of Industry were once again amalgamated to form a single department, known as the Department of Trade and Industry, and the functions of the Secretary of State for Trade and the Secretary of State for Industry were transferred en bloc to the Secretary of State for Trade and Industry[10], who could also use the title 'President of the Board of Trade'[11]. Following the May 2005 general election the name of the Department of Trade and Industry was changed to the Department for Productivity, Energy and Industry but the old name was almost immediately reinstated. The Department of Trade and Industry was replaced by the Department for Business, Enterprise and Regulatory Reform and the Department for Innovation, Universities and Skills on 28 June 2007, which in turn were merged on 5 June 2009 to form the Department for Business, Innovation and Skills[12]. The Secretary of State for Business, Innovation and Skills is now the relevant Secretary of State and President of the Board of Trade.

Certain functions of the Board of Trade relating to employment were transferred to the Minister of Labour in 1916[13] and from him to the Secretary of State for Employment and Productivity on the dissolution of the Ministry of Labour in 1968[14]. The title of that Secretary of State was changed in 1970 to Secretary of State for Employment and in 2002 to Secretary of State for Work and Pensions[15], but a number of employment functions are now exercisable by the Secretary of State for Business, Innovation and Skills[16]. Functions relating to tourism were transferred from the Secretary of State for Trade and Industry to the Secretary of State for Employment in 1985[17] but subsequently transferred to the Secretary of State for National Heritage[18]; and functions relating to small businesses also transferred to him in 1985 were subsequently transferred to the

Secretary of State for Trade and Industry[19]. The functions of the Secretary of State for Employment relating to general indices of retail prices and the family expenditure survey were transferred to the Chancellor of the Exchequer in 1989[20].

Functions relating to Wales are now mainly the responsibility of the Welsh Ministers[21].

1 As to the Board of Trade see CONSTITUTIONAL AND ADMINISTRATIVE LAW vol 20 (2014) PARA 162. The Board of Trade is still mentioned in many statutes and still theoretically exists. However, in time its functions came to be exercised mainly by its President. The office of President of the Board of Trade was held by the Secretary of State for Trade and Industry, who exercised the President's functions concurrently and could use the title (see text and note 11): Secretary of State for Trade and Industry Order 1970, SI 1970/1537, art 2(1)(b) (lapsed). The Secretary of State for Business, Innovation and Skills has now taken over the functions of the Secretary of State for Trade and Industry: see text and note 12. Certain functions of the Board of Trade and Secretary of State are now exercisable concurrently with the Chancellor of the Exchequer: Transfer of Functions (Economic Statistics) Order 1989, SI 1989/992, art 2. Others are exercisable concurrently with or transferred to the Treasury: see the Transfer of Functions (Financial Services) Order 1992, SI 1992/1315. In England, Wales and Northern Ireland, only 'designated' Ministers and departments can exercise the powers conferred by the European Communities Act 1972 s 2(2) to make orders, rules, regulations and schemes. In relation to financial assistance for industry the 'Secretary of State' is so designated in respect of matters related to listing securities on a stock exchange: see the European Communities (Designation) Order 2012, SI 2012/1759, arts 2, 8, Sch 1 (revoking the previous designation of the Treasury in the Transfer of Functions (Financial Services) Order 1992, SI 1992/1315).

2 Certain functions of this minister were transferred to the Secretary of State for Education and Science by virtue of the Secretary of State for Education and Science Order 1964, SI 1964/490, and subsequently to the former Minister of Technology by virtue of the Minister of Technology Order 1964, SI 1964/2048 (lapsed). Other functions were transferred to the Secretary of State for Education and Science in 1964 and retained by him until 1992, when his title was changed to Secretary of State for Education: see the Transfer of Functions (Science) Order 1992, SI 1992/1296. The Secretary of State for Business, Innovation and Skills now exercises functions under the Science and Technology Act 1965 (see NATIONAL CULTURAL HERITAGE vol 77 (2010) PARA 967 et seq): Transfer of Functions (Science) Order 1995, SI 1995/2985; and see the Transfer of Functions (Scientific Research) Order 1999, SI 1999/2785.

3 See the Secretary of State for Trade and Industry Order 1970, SI 1970/1537 (amended by SI 1971/716; and by the Supply Powers Act 1975 s 8(1), Sch 2 Pt II) (lapsed).

4 See the Secretary of State for Trade and Industry Order 1970, SI 1970/1537, art 2(1)(a) (lapsed). The Secretaryship of State is theoretically one office and a reference simply to the Secretary of State means one of Her Majesty's Principal Secretaries of State, without being specific: see the Interpretation Act 1978 s 5, Sch 1; and CONSTITUTIONAL AND ADMINISTRATIVE LAW vol 20 (2014) PARA 153.

5 See the Secretary of State for Trade and Industry Order 1970, SI 1970/1537, art 2(1)(a) (lapsed).

6 See the Secretary of State (New Departments) Order 1974, SI 1974/692 (amended by SI 1976/1775) (lapsed).

7 See 871 HC Official Report (5th series) written answers col 178.

8 In 1992 the former functions of the Department of Energy were transferred to the Secretary of State for Trade and Industry, except for energy efficiency functions which were transferred to the Secretary of State for the Environment: see the Transfer of Functions (Energy) Order 1992, SI 1992/1314.

9 In 1979 the remaining functions of the Secretary of State for Prices and Consumer Protection were transferred to the Secretary of State for Trade: see the Secretary of State for Trade Order 1979, SI 1979/578.

10 See the Transfer of Functions (Trade and Industry) Order 1983, SI 1983/1127, art 2(1). The civil aviation and shipping functions of the Secretary of State for Trade were transferred to the Secretary of State for Transport: art 2(3).

11 See e g Department of Trade and Industry Press Notice P/92/241, dated 15 April 1992.

12 See the Department for Business, Enterprise and Regulatory Reform Annual Report and Accounts 2008–2009 para 1.1.

13 See the New Ministries and Secretaries Act 1916 s 1 (repealed).

14 See the Secretary of State for Employment and Productivity Order 1968, SI 1968/729 (lapsed).

15 See the Secretaries of State for Education and Skills and for Work and Pensions Order 2002, SI 2002/1397.

16 See the Secretary of State for Trade and Industry Order 1970, SI 1970/1537 (lapsed); and the Transfer of Functions (Education and Employment) Order 1995, SI 1995/2986. The employment functions of this Secretary of State are now exercisable by the Department for Business, Innovation and Skills.

17 See the Transfer of Functions (Tourism and Small Businesses) Order 1985, SI 1985/1778.

18 See the Transfer of Functions (National Heritage) Order 1992, SI 1992/1311. The Secretary of State for National Heritage is now the Secretary of State for Culture, Media and Sport: see the Secretary of State for Culture, Media and Sport Order 1997, SI 1997/1744. (Note that, in connection with the 2012 Olympic Games, there was a temporary change of title and expansion of functions: see the Secretary of State for Culture, Olympics, Media and Sport Order 2010, SI 2010/1551; and the Transfer of Functions (Secretary of State for Culture, Media and Sport) Order 2012, SI 2012/2590).

19 See the Transfer of Functions (Tourism and Small Businesses) Order 1985, SI 1995/1778; and the Transfer of Functions (Small Businesses) Order 1992, SI 1992/1297.

20 See the Transfer of Functions (Economic Statistics) Order 1989, SI 1989/992.

21 Pursuant to the establishment of the Welsh Assembly Government under the Government of Wales Act 2006 Pt 2 (ss 45–92) (see CONSTITUTIONAL AND ADMINISTRATIVE LAW vol 20 (2014) PARA 351 et seq), statutory functions relating to trade and industry, including functions under subordinate legislation, so far as exercisable in relation to Wales, are now almost exclusively the responsibility of Welsh Ministers (ie the First Minister and the Welsh Ministers established under ss 46, 48: see s 45(2); and CONSTITUTIONAL AND ADMINISTRATIVE LAW vol 20 (2014) PARAS 374–375). These functions were previously transferred to the National Assembly for Wales by Order in Council under the Government of Wales Act 1998 s 22 (see the National Assembly for Wales (Transfer of Functions) Order 1999, SI 1999/672, arts 2, 3, Sch 1). Relevant functions were transferred from the Assembly to the Welsh Ministers by the Government of Wales Act 2006 s 162, Sch 11 para 30. Further transfers of ministerial functions to the Welsh Ministers may be effected by Order in Council pursuant to s 58, Sch 3 paras 1–8. As to the exercise of transferred functions and the bringing of subordinate legislation made by the Welsh Ministers before the National Assembly for Wales see Sch 11 paras 33–35 (in the case of functions transferred to the Assembly by Order in Council under the Government of Wales Act 1998 s 22) or the Government of Wales Act 2006 Sch 3 para 9 (in the case of functions transferred to the Welsh Ministers by Order in Council under s 58).

Few functions relevant to this title have actually been so transferred; those which have, or are now exercisable concurrently, relate to:

(1)   industrial designs (see the Industrial Organisation and Development Act 1947 s 11; and PARA 1035);

(2)   the development of tourism (see the Development of Tourism Act 1969 ss 1(2), (6), 2(8), (8A), 4(1), (4), 6(1)–(4), 17(1), (4); the Tourism (Overseas Promotion) (Wales) Act 1992; the Wales Tourist Board (Transfer of Functions to the National Assembly for Wales and Abolition) Order 2005, SI 2005/3225; and PARA 1028 et seq);

(3)   the Welsh Development Agency (see the Welsh Development Agency Act 1975, and the Welsh Development Agency (Transfer of Functions to the National Assembly for Wales and Abolition) Order 2005, SI 2005/3226; and PARA 1051 et seq);

(4)   industrial development generally (see the Industrial Development Act 1982; and PARA 1036 et seq).

As to the National Assembly for Wales and the Welsh Ministers generally see CONSTITUTIONAL AND ADMINISTRATIVE LAW vol 20 (2014) PARA 351 et seq.

(2)   INQUIRIES AND ARBITRATIONS

903.   Inquiries by the Secretary of State.   Where under any special Act[1] the Secretary of State[2] is required or authorised to sanction, approve, confirm or determine any appointment, matter or thing, or make any order or do any other act for the purpose of the special Act, he may make such inquiries as he thinks necessary to enable him to comply with that requirement or exercise that authority[3]. An inquiry by the Secretary of State under any Act may be held by any person duly authorised by him, and if so held is deemed to be duly held[4].

1 'Special Act' means a local or local and personal Act, or an Act of a local and personal nature, and includes a provisional order of the Secretary of State confirmed by Act of Parliament: Board of Trade Arbitrations, etc Act 1874 s 4 (amended by the Statute Law (Repeals) Act 1976 s 1(1), Sch 1 Pt XXI).

2 As to the office of the Secretary of State see PARA 902. These powers were originally vested in the Board of Trade, but are now exercisable by the Secretary of State: see PARA 902; and CONSTITUTIONAL AND ADMINISTRATIVE LAW vol 20 (2014) PARA 162. In relation to railways, light railways, tramways, canals, waterways and inland navigation, these powers are exercisable by the Secretary of State for Transport or the Secretary of State for Environment, Food and Rural Affairs. As to the Principal Secretaries of State see CONSTITUTIONAL AND ADMINISTRATIVE LAW vol 20 (2014) PARA 153.

3 Board of Trade Arbitrations, etc Act 1874 s 2.

4 See the Board of Trade Arbitrations, etc Act 1874 s 2.

904. Expenses of inquiries and arbitrations.

When application is made to the Secretary of State[1] in pursuance of a special Act[2] to be arbitrator or to appoint any arbitrator or other person, or to hold an inquiry, or do any other thing for the purpose of the special Act, all expenses of the Secretary of State must be defrayed by the parties to the application to such an amount as he may certify by order to be due; and, subject to any provision in the special Act, the expenses must be defrayed by such of the parties as he may by order direct, or, if so directed, be paid as the costs of the arbitration[3]. The Secretary of State may require payment on account or security for payment on demand[4]. His certificate is conclusive as to amount, which may be recovered as a debt, and, if payable to him, as a debt due to the Crown[5].

1 As to the Secretary of State see PARA 902.

2 As to the meaning of 'special Act' see PARA 903 note 1.

3 Board of Trade Arbitrations, etc Act 1874 s 3.

4 Board of Trade Arbitrations, etc Act 1874 s 3.

5 Board of Trade Arbitrations, etc Act 1874 s 3. As to the recovery of debts due to the Crown see CROWN AND CROWN PROCEEDINGS vol 29 (2014) PARAS 90–92.

2. LEGISLATIVE CONTROLS

(1) GENERAL TRADE CONTROLS

(i) Control of Supply

905. Supply powers of the Secretary of State. The Secretary of State[1] has power to acquire, produce or process articles required for the public service[2] or articles to be exchanged for such articles; to sell, exchange or otherwise dispose of any such articles or any government surplus materials[3]; to store and transport any such articles and materials; and to do all such things in the exercise of these powers (including the erection of buildings and the execution of works) as appear to him necessary or expedient for the exercise of these powers[4]. He may also make payments by way of grant or loan, in accordance with arrangements approved by the Treasury[5], to any person producing, dealing in or having control of any article required for the public service and to any person carrying on the business of storing goods, for the purpose of inducing the augmentation of stocks of that article or of any other article which can conveniently be used for or in connection with its production, or the improvement of facilities available for the storage of any such stocks or any articles required for the public service[6].

The Secretary of State may also by notice in writing require any person producing, dealing in or having control of any article required for the public service to make periodical and other returns, at such times, and containing such particulars as may be specified in the notice, as to:

(1)   the stocks of that article for the time being held by him and the quantities of any such article which by virtue of any contract are to be delivered by or to him and the date of such delivery; and

(2)   the facilities available for producing that article or storing stocks of it[7].

He may by the like notice require any person carrying out works required for the public service[8], or carrying on a business which in the opinion of the Secretary of State is suitable for or can be adapted to carrying out such works, or who has under his control accommodation suitable for the storage of any articles required for that service, to make periodical and other returns, at times specified in the notice and containing particulars so specified, as to:

(a)   the facilities for carrying out such works[9]; or

(b)   the nature and extent of the accommodation, the period for which any part of it is already required and its purpose, and the facilities available for making use of it[10].

Her Majesty may by Order in Council apply in relation to the Secretary of State[11] any of the provisions of certain specified enactments[12] for the purpose of conferring on him any powers, rights and privileges in relation to the acquisition and holding of land for the purpose of discharging any of his functions, and in relation to the management, use and disposal in any manner of land acquired for that purpose, which under those enactments are vested in the Secretary of State for Defence for any purpose[13]. No recommendation may, however, be made to make such an order unless a draft of the order has been laid before Parliament and has been approved by a resolution of each House of Parliament[14]; and any such order may be varied or revoked by a subsequent order[15].

1   As to the Secretary of State see PARA 902.
2   As to the meaning of 'articles required for the public service' see PARA 906.

3   'Government surplus materials' means surplus articles of any government department and surplus articles of the government of any country outside the United Kingdom to be disposed of by Her Majesty's government in the United Kingdom in pursuance of an agreement between those governments: Supply Powers Act 1975 s 7. 'Articles' includes substances and 'government department' includes a Northern Ireland department: s 7. As to the meaning of 'United Kingdom' see PARA 906 note 7.

4   Supply Powers Act 1975 s 1(1). Without prejudice to his powers of inspection under s 1(1), the Secretary of State may, at the request of the parties concerned, carry out or supervise the carrying out of any inspection for the purposes of or in connection with the production of any articles where the inspection can conveniently be carried out or supervised by him in connection with the exercise of his functions: s 1(2).

5   As to the Treasury see CONSTITUTIONAL AND ADMINISTRATIVE LAW vol 20 (2014) PARA 262 et seq.

6   Supply Powers Act 1975 s 3. As to untrue statements etc for the purpose of obtaining such a payment see PARA 907.

7   Supply Powers Act 1975 s 4(1). Where a government department or any body or person has, by virtue of any Act, power to obtain for any purpose information as to matters with respect to which the Secretary of State is empowered by s 4(1)–(3) to require returns to be made:
    (1)   that department or body must, if so required by him, exercise that power for the purpose of assisting him in obtaining any such information (s 4(4)(a)); and
    (2)   any such information obtained by that department or body may, whether upon a requisition of the Secretary of State or otherwise, notwithstanding anything in any enactment, be furnished to him (s 4(4)(b)).
    As to unauthorised disclosure of information see PARA 907.

8   As to the meaning of 'works required for the public service' see PARA 906.

9   Supply Powers Act 1975 s 4(2). See also note 7.

10   Supply Powers Act 1975 s 4(3). See also note 7.

11   References in the Supply Powers Act 1975 s 2 to the Secretary of State do not include the Secretary of State for Defence: s 2(6). As to the Secretary of State for Defence see CONSTITUTIONAL AND ADMINISTRATIVE LAW vol 20 (2014) PARA 266.

12   Ie the enactments specified in the Supply Powers Act 1975 Sch 1 Pt I: s 2(1). The specified enactments are the Defence Acts 1842–1873; the Ordnance Board Transfer Act 1855; the Lands Clauses Consolidation Acts Amendment Act 1860 s 7; the Militia (Lands and Buildings) Act 1873 s 7; the Municipal Corporations Act 1882 s 254; and the Military Lands Act 1892 Pt II (ss 14–18) (see ARMED FORCES vol 3 (2011) PARAS 402, 403): Supply Powers Act 1975 Sch 1 Pt I. Any of the provisions of the Harbours, Docks and Piers Clauses Act 1847 s 28 (see PORTS AND HARBOURS vol 85 (2012) PARA 73), with any necessary modifications or adaptations, may also be applied by Order in Council in relation to the Secretary of State acting in the discharge of any of his functions under the Supply Powers Act 1975 or to property for the time being vested in or under his control for the purpose of discharging any of those functions: s 2(2), Sch 1 Pt II (Sch 1 Pt II amended by the Transport and Works Act 1992 s 68(1), Sch 4 Pt I).

13   Supply Powers Act 1975 s 2(1).

14   Supply Powers Act 1975 s 2(4). If, at any time when Parliament is dissolved or prorogued or when both Houses of Parliament are adjourned for more than 14 days, it is shown to the satisfaction of the Secretary of State that the making of an Order in Council under s 2 is urgently necessary, a draft of the order need not be laid before Parliament, but the order ceases to have effect, except as respects things previously done or omitted to be done, at the expiration of the period of 28 days beginning with the date on which the House of Commons first sits after the making of the order unless within that period resolutions approving the order are passed by both Houses of Parliament: s 2(5). As to the laying of instruments before Parliament see STATUTES AND LEGISLATIVE PROCESS vol 96 (2012) PARA 1052 et seq.

15   Supply Powers Act 1975 s 2(3). At the date at which this volume states the law no such order had been made.

906.   Articles and works required for the public service.   'Articles required for the public service' means:
    (1)   articles[1] required for the discharge of its functions by any government department[2], the United Kingdom Atomic Energy Authority[3], the Civil Aviation Authority[4] or any research council[5];
    (2)   articles required for the defence of any part of the Commonwealth[6],

including any territory under Her Majesty's protection or in which she has jurisdiction, or for the maintenance or restoration of peace and security in any part of the world or for any measures arising out of a breach or apprehended breach of peace in any part of the world;

(3)   articles required by any international organisation of which the United Kingdom[7] is a member or (where the relevant international agreement so provides) by any other member of such an organisation;

(4)   articles which in the opinion of the Secretary of State[8] would be essential for the needs of the community in the event of war;

(5)   articles for supply to a person carrying on an undertaking which includes the production of articles of that or any other description where that person requests the Secretary of State to supply those articles, and the Secretary of State is satisfied that the supply will serve the interests of the community; and

(6)   anything which, in the opinion of the Secretary of State, is or is likely to be necessary for or in connection with the production of any such articles as are mentioned in heads (1) to (5) above[9].

'Works required for the public service' is to be construed accordingly[10].

1   'Articles' includes substances: Supply Powers Act 1975 s 7.
2   As to the meaning of 'government department' see PARA 905 note 3.
3   As to the United Kingdom Atomic Energy Authority see ENERGY AND CLIMATE CHANGE vol 44 (2011) PARA 787 et seq.
4   As to the Civil Aviation Authority see AIR LAW vol 2 (2008) PARA 50 et seq.
5   Ie any research council within the meaning of the Science and Technology Act 1965 (see s 1; and NATIONAL CULTURAL HERITAGE vol 77 (2010) PARA 967 et seq): Supply Powers Act 1975 s 7.
6   As to the Commonwealth see generally COMMONWEALTH.
7   'United Kingdom' means Great Britain and Northern Ireland: Interpretation Act 1978 s 5, Sch 1. 'Great Britain' means England, Scotland and Wales: Union with Scotland Act 1706 preamble art I; Interpretation Act 1978 s 22(1), Sch 2 para 5(a). Neither the Channel Islands nor the Isle of Man is within the United Kingdom. See further CONSTITUTIONAL AND ADMINISTRATIVE LAW vol 20 (2014) PARA 3. 'England' means, subject to any alteration of boundaries under the Local Government Act 1972 Pt IV (ss 53–78), the area consisting of the counties established by s 1 (see LOCAL GOVERNMENT vol 69 (2009) PARAS 5, 24, 27), Greater London and the Isles of Scilly: Interpretation Act 1978 s 5, Sch 1. 'Wales' means the combined area of the counties which were created by the Local Government Act 1972 s 20 (see LOCAL GOVERNMENT vol 69 (2009) PARAS 5, 37, 41), but subject to any alteration made under s 73 (consequential alteration of boundary following alteration of watercourse) (see LOCAL GOVERNMENT vol 69 (2009) PARA 90): Interpretation Act 1978 Sch 1 (definition substituted by the Local Government (Wales) Act 1994 s 1(3), Sch 2 para 9). As to Greater London see LONDON GOVERNMENT vol 71 (2013) PARA 14.
8   As to the Secretary of State see PARA 902.
9   Supply Powers Act 1975 s 7.
10   Supply Powers Act 1975 s 7.

907. Disclosure of information, offences and penalties. No information with respect to an individual business which has been obtained under or by virtue of the Supply Powers Act 1975 may be disclosed without the consent of the person carrying on that business[1], but this does not apply to the disclosure of any information to a government department[2], or any person authorised by a government department, requiring that information for the purpose of the discharge of that department's functions, or any disclosure for the purposes of any prosecution for an offence under that Act[3].

If any person knowingly or recklessly makes any untrue statement or untrue representation for the purpose of obtaining a payment, either for himself or for another person, for the creation of a reserve[4], or discloses any information in contravention of the above provisions, he is guilty of an offence[5].

If any person fails to make any return which he is required[6] to make, or knowingly or recklessly makes any untrue statement in any such return, he is guilty of an offence[7].

Where any of the above offences committed by a body corporate is proved to have been committed with the consent or connivance of any director, manager, secretary or other officer of that body, he, as well as the body corporate, is guilty of the offence and is liable to be proceeded against and punished accordingly[8].

1 Supply Powers Act 1975 s 5(1).
2 As to the meaning of 'government department' see PARA 905 note 3.
3 Supply Powers Act 1975 s 5(2). Offences under the Supply Powers Act 1975 are set out in s 6.
4 Ie a payment under the Supply Powers Act 1975 s 3 (see PARA 905): s 6(1).
5 Supply Powers Act 1975 s 6(1). A person guilty of such an offence is liable on summary conviction to imprisonment for a term not exceeding three months or to a fine not exceeding the prescribed sum, or to both, or on conviction on indictment to imprisonment for term not exceeding two years or to a fine, or to both: s 6(1)(a), (b) (amended by virtue of the Criminal Law Act 1977 s 32(1); and the Magistrates' Courts Act 1980 s 32(2)). As to the prescribed sum see SENTENCING AND DISPOSITION OF OFFENDERS vol 92 (2010) PARA 141.
6 Ie under the Supply Powers Act 1975 s 4 (see PARA 905): s 6(2)(a).
7 Supply Powers Act 1975 s 6(2). A person guilty of such an offence is liable on summary conviction to a fine not exceeding level 3 on the standard scale: s 6(2) (amended by virtue of the Criminal Justice Act 1982 ss 38, 46). Where the failure continues after conviction, he is guilty of a further offence and liable on summary conviction to a fine not exceeding £50 for each day on which the failure continues: Supply Powers Act 1975 s 6(2). As to the standard scale see SENTENCING AND DISPOSITION OF OFFENDERS vol 92 (2010) PARA 142.
8 Supply Powers Act 1975 s 6(3).

(ii) Control of Imports and Exports

A. CONTROL OF IMPORTS AND EXPORTS IN GENERAL

908. General legislative powers of control. The import and export of goods is subject to general control under legislation now largely consolidated in the Customs and Excise Acts 1979[1]. The import of certain goods is specifically prohibited under the Customs Consolidation Act 1876 and other enactments[2]. However, in addition, under the Import, Export and Customs Powers (Defence) Act 1939 the Secretary of State[3] may by order[4] regulate or prohibit the import into the United Kingdom[5], or any specified part of it, of any goods[6]. This power was originally conferred on the basis that it would expire at the end of the wartime emergency which necessitated it[7] but it was never withdrawn and is now exercisable on a permanent basis[8]. The Export Control Act 2002 enables controls to be imposed on the export of goods, the transfer of technology, the provision of technical assistance overseas and activities connected with trade in controlled goods[9].

1 The Acts which may be cited together as the Customs and Excise Acts 1979 are the Customs and Excise Duties (General Reliefs) Act 1979, the Alcoholic Liquor Duties Act 1979, the Hydrocarbon Oil Duties Act 1979, the Tobacco Products Duty Act 1979, and the Customs and Excise Management Act 1979: ss 1(1), 178(2) (both amended by the Finance (No 2) Act 1992 s 82, Sch 18 Pt II). Also 'the Customs and Excise Acts' means the Customs and Excise Acts 1979 and any other enactment for the time being in force relating to customs or excise: Customs and Excise Management Act 1979 s 1(1). As to customs duties generally see CUSTOMS AND EXCISE vol 30 (2012) PARA 1 et seq; and as to free movement of goods within the European Union see EUROPEAN UNION vol 47A (2014) PARA 301.
2 See the Customs Consolidation Act 1876 s 42 (amended by the Statute Law Revision Act 1883; the Revenue Act 1883 s 19, Schedule; the Finance Act 1896 s 5; the Copyright Act 1911 s 36, Sch 2; the Finance Act 1917 s 6; the Finance Act 1929 ss 5, 6, Schedule; the Finance Act 1946 ss 2(1), 67(10), Sch 12 Pt I; the Isle of Man (Customs) Act 1946 s 1(1); the Customs and Excise

Act 1952 s 320, Sch 12 Pt I; the Hallmarking Act 1973 s 23, Sch 7 Pt I; the Diseases of Animals Act 1975 s 4(3), Sch 2; the Forgery and Counterfeiting Act 1981, Schedule Pt II; the Statute Law (Repeals) Act 1993; and the Statute Law (Repeals) Act 2008. As to restrictions on the import and export of animals see ANIMALS vol 2 (2008) PARAS 966 et seq, 1081 et seq; as to restrictions on the import and export of certain cultural objects see NATIONAL CULTURAL HERITAGE vol 77 (2010) PARAS 1092, 1093 and PARA 916; as to restrictions on the import and export of certain plants see OPEN SPACES AND COUNTRYSIDE vol 78 (2010) PARA 716 et seq; and as to restrictions on the import of controlled drugs see MEDICAL PRODUCTS AND DRUGS vol 75 (2013) PARA 491. As to the licensing scheme controlling the import of timber and timber products see the Forest Law Enforcement, Governance and Trade Regulations 2012, SI 2012/178; and FORESTRY vol 52 (2014) PARA 4. As to drug trafficking offences see CRIMINAL LAW vol 26 (2010) PARA 725 et seq.

3   Powers under the Import, Export and Customs Powers (Defence) Act 1939 were originally vested in the Board of Trade, but are now exercisable by the Secretary of State for Business, Innovation and Skills (who is President of the Board of Trade at the date at which this volume states the law): see PARA 902.

4   See the Import of Goods (Control) Order 1954, SI 1954/23; and PARA 915.

5   For the purposes of the Import, Export and Customs Powers (Defence) Act 1939, the Isle of Man forms part of the United Kingdom: s 8(1)(a). As to the meaning of 'United Kingdom' generally see PARA 906 note 7.

6   See the Import, Export and Customs Powers (Defence) Act 1939 s 1(1) (amended by the Export Control Act 2002 s 15(2)(a)); and CUSTOMS AND EXCISE vol 31 (2012) PARA 994. 'Goods' includes stores and containers; 'stores' means goods for use in a ship or aircraft and includes fuel and spare parts and other articles of equipment, whether or not for immediate fitting; 'container' includes any bundle or package and any baggage, box, cask or other receptacle whatsoever and 'ship' includes any boat or other vessel whatsoever and any hovercraft: Customs and Excise Management Act 1979 s 1(1), (2), (4), (4B) (definition of 'goods' amended by the Finance Act 2013 s 225; definition of 'container' amended by the Finance Act 2008 s 117(2); Customs and Excise Management Act 1979 s 1(4), (4B) substituted by the Finance Act 1999 s 10(1); Customs and Excise Management Act 1979 s 1(4) amended by the Finance Act 2014 Sch 21 para 1(2); applied by the Import, Export and Customs Powers (Defence) Act 1939 s 9(2) (amended by the Customs and Excise Management Act 1979 Sch 4 para 12, Table Pt I). An order under the Import, Export and Customs Powers (Defence) Act 1939 s 1 may suspend wholly or in part the operation of any enactment, proclamation, Order in Council or order prohibiting or regulating the import of any goods and may contain such provisions (including penal provisions) as appear to the Secretary of State necessary for securing the operation and enforcement of the order: see s 1(3) (amended by the Export Control Act 2002 s 15(2)(b)). The order may be varied or revoked by a subsequent order: Import, Export and Customs Powers (Defence) Act 1939 s 1(2). Without prejudice to the provisions of enactments for the time being in force relating to customs or excise with respect to ships and aircraft, the taking into the United Kingdom of ships or aircraft may be prohibited or regulated by an order under s 1 as an import of goods, notwithstanding that the ships or aircraft are conveying goods or passengers, and whether or not they are moving under their own power: s 1(4) (amended by the Customs and Excise Management Act 1979 Sch 4 para 12, Table Pt I; and the Export Control Act 2002 s 15(2)(c)). Notwithstanding anything in the Customs and Excise Management Act 1979 s 145 (see CUSTOMS AND EXCISE vol 31 (2012) PARA 1193), a prosecution for an offence under such an order may be instituted by or under the authority of the Secretary of State: Import, Export and Customs Powers (Defence) Act 1939 s 1(5) (amended by the Customs and Excise Management Act 1979 Sch 4 para 12, Table Pt I).

Nothing in any order made under the Import, Export and Customs Powers (Defence) Act 1939 s 1 applies to the importation into the United Kingdom of any cocoa beans and such products as are for the time being defined as cocoa products for the purposes of the International Cocoa Agreement (New York, 15 November 1972): International Cocoa Agreement Act 1973 s 1(1), (6), (7). Such goods may only be imported under a licence granted by the Secretary of State under that Act which may be revoked or varied at any time, and may be granted subject to conditions, which may include a condition requiring the production of evidence that any contribution chargeable under the International Cocoa Agreement has been paid or secured: see the International Cocoa Agreement Act 1973 s 1(2)–(4). Any person who, for the purpose of obtaining such a licence, makes a statement or furnishes any document or information which to his knowledge is false in a material particular or recklessly makes a statement which is false in a material particular is liable on summary conviction to a fine not exceeding level 5 on the standard scale: s 1(5) (amended by virtue of the Criminal Justice Act 1982 ss 38, 46). As to the standard scale see SENTENCING AND DISPOSITION OF OFFENDERS vol 92 (2010) PARA 142.

7 See the Import, Export and Customs Powers (Defence) Act 1939 s 9(3) (repealed) whereby the Act was to continue in force until such date as Her Majesty might by Order in Council declare to be the date on which the emergency that was the occasion of the passing of the Act came to an end, and was then to expire. No such order had been made at the date at which that provision was repealed: see note 8.

8 See the Import and Export Control Act 1990 s 1 (repealing the Import, Export and Customs Powers (Defence) Act 1939 s 9(3) (cited in note 7) with effect from 6 December 1990).

9 See PARAS 911–914.

909. Power to impose charges. In connection with any scheme of control contained in an order made by the Secretary of State[1], the Treasury[2] may by order provide for imposing and recovering such charges as may be specified in the first mentioned order[3]. Any charges so recovered must be paid either into the Exchequer[4] or into such public fund or account as may be specified in the Treasury order[5].

1 Ie an order made under the Import, Export and Customs Powers (Defence) Act 1939 s 1 (see PARA 908): s 2(1). As to the Secretary of State see PARA 902. See also PARA 908 note 3.

2 As to the Treasury see CONSTITUTIONAL AND ADMINISTRATIVE LAW vol 20 (2014) PARA 262 et seq.

3 Import, Export and Customs Powers (Defence) Act 1939 s 2(1). Any such order must be laid before the House of Commons: see s 2(3) (amended by the Statute Law (Repeals) Act 1986); the Statutory Instruments Act 1946 s 4; and STATUTES AND LEGISLATIVE PROCESS vol 96 (2012) PARA 1045 et seq. It may be varied or revoked by a subsequent order by the Treasury: see the Import, Export and Customs Powers (Defence) Act 1939 s 2(1). Such an order imposing or increasing a charge ceases to have effect on the expiration of 28 days (not counting any time when Parliament is dissolved or prorogued, or during which the House of Commons is adjourned for more than four days) from the date of the making of the order unless at some time before the expiration of that period it has been approved by a resolution of the House of Commons, without prejudice, however, to the validity of anything previously done under the order or to the making of a new order: see s 2(4); and cf the Statutory Instruments Act 1946 s 4(3); and STATUTES AND LEGISLATIVE PROCESS vol 96 (2012) PARA 1048. At the date at which this volume states the law, no order had been made under this power. As to the dissolution or prorogation of Parliament see PARLIAMENT vol 78 (2010) PARAS 1018 et seq, 1021 et seq.

4 As to the Exchequer see CONSTITUTIONAL AND ADMINISTRATIVE LAW vol 20 (2014) PARA 480.

5 Import, Export and Customs Powers (Defence) Act 1939 s 2(2).

910. Offences relating to imports, exports and trading with the enemy. If any goods[1] are imported in contravention either of an order made under the Import, Export and Customs Powers (Defence) Act 1939[2], or of the law relating to trading with the enemy[3], those goods are to be deemed prohibited goods and forfeited[4].

1 As to the meaning of 'goods' see PARA 908 note 6.

2 Ie an order made under the Import, Export and Customs Powers (Defence) Act 1939 s 1 (see PARA 908): see s 3(1)(a).

3 See in particular the Trading with the Enemy Act 1939; and ARMED CONFLICT AND EMERGENCY vol 3 (2011) PARA 197 et seq. 'Enemy' means: (1) any state, or sovereign of a state, at war with Her Majesty; (2) any individual resident in enemy territory; (3) any body of persons (whether corporate or unincorporate) carrying on business in any place, if and so long as the body is controlled by a person who, under this provision, is an enemy; (4) any body of persons constituted or incorporated in, or under the laws of, a state at war with Her Majesty; or (5) any other person who for the purposes of any Act relating to trading with the enemy is to be deemed to be an enemy; but does not include any person by reason only that he is an enemy subject: Import, Export and Customs Powers (Defence) Act 1939 s 8(1)(b). 'Enemy territory' means any area which is under the sovereignty of, or in the occupation of, a power with whom Her Majesty is at war, not being an area in the occupation of Her Majesty or of a power allied with Her Majesty: s 8(1)(d). 'Enemy subject' means: (a) an individual who, not being either a British subject or a British protected person, possesses the nationality of a state at war with Her Majesty; or (b) a body of persons constituted or incorporated in, or under the laws of, any such

state: s 8(1)(c). As to the meanings of 'British subject' and 'British protected person' for these purposes see BRITISH NATIONALITY vol 4 (2011) PARAS 469, 476.

A certificate of a Secretary of State that any area is or was under the sovereignty of, or in the occupation of, any power, or as to the time at which any area became or ceased to be under such sovereignty or in such occupation is for these purposes conclusive evidence of the facts stated in the certificate: s 8(2). As to the Secretary of State see PARA 902. See also PARA 908 note 3.

4   Import, Export and Customs Powers (Defence) Act 1939 s 3(1) (amended by the Export Control Act 2002 s 15(1), (3)(a)).

If any goods are imported, an officer of revenue and customs may require any person possessing or having control of the goods to furnish proof that the importation is not unlawful by virtue either of an order or of the law relating to trading with the enemy (see note 3) and if such proof is not furnished to the satisfaction of the Commissioners for Revenue and Customs, then, unless the contrary is proved, the goods are deemed to be prohibited goods and are to be forfeited: Import, Export and Customs Powers (Defence) Act 1939 s 3(3) (amended by the Customs and Excise Act 1952 Sch 12 Pt I; the Emergency Laws (Miscellaneous Provisions) Act 1953 s 1, Sch 1 para 5; and the Export Control Act 2002 s 15(1), (3)(c); and by virtue of the Commissioners for Revenue and Customs Act 2005 s 50(1), (2), (7)). As to proceedings under the customs and excise enactments see the Customs and Excise Management Act 1979 ss 145, 146, 146A, 147–152, 154–156, 171; and CUSTOMS AND EXCISE vol 31 (2012) PARA 1193 et seq. As to the Commissioners for Revenue and Customs see CUSTOMS AND EXCISE vol 31 (2012) PARA 921 et seq.

B. EXPORT, TRANSFER OF TECHNOLOGY, TECHNICAL ASSISTANCE AND TRADE CONTROL

911. Control powers. The Secretary of State[1] may by order[2] make provision for or in connection with the imposition of: (1) export controls in relation to goods of any description[3]; (2) transfer controls in relation to technology of any description[4]; (3) technical assistance controls in relation to technical assistance of any description[5]; (4) trade controls in relation to goods of any description[6].

'Export controls', in relation to any goods[7], means the prohibition or regulation of their exportation from the United Kingdom[8] or their shipment as stores[9].

'Transfer controls', in relation to any technology[10], means the prohibition or regulation of its transfer[11]: (a) by a person or from a place[12] within the United Kingdom to a person or place outside the United Kingdom[13]; (b) by a person or from a place outside the United Kingdom to a person who, or a place which, is also outside the United Kingdom, but only where the transfer is by, or within the control of, a United Kingdom person[14]; (c) by a person or from a place within the United Kingdom to a person who, or a place which, is also within the United Kingdom, but only where there is reason to believe that the technology may be used outside the United Kingdom[15]; or (d) by a person or from a place outside the United Kingdom to a person or place within the United Kingdom, but only where the transfer is by, or within the control of, a United Kingdom person and there is reason to believe that the technology may be used outside the United Kingdom[16].

'Technical assistance controls', in relation to any technical assistance, means the prohibition or regulation of participation in the provision outside the United Kingdom of that technical assistance[17]. 'Technical assistance' means services which are provided or used, or which are capable of being used, in connection with the development, production or use of any goods or technology[18]. Technical assistance may be described in the order wholly or partly by reference to the uses to which it, or the goods or technology in question, may be put[19]. A person participates in the provision of technical assistance outside the United Kingdom if he provides technical assistance outside the United Kingdom or agrees to do so, or if he makes arrangements under which another person provides technical assistance outside the United Kingdom or agrees to do so[20]. Technical assistance controls may be imposed on acts done outside the United Kingdom, but only if they are done by a person who is, or is acting under the control of, a United Kingdom person[21].

'Trade controls', in relation to any goods, means the prohibition or regulation of their acquisition or disposal, their movement or activities which facilitate or are otherwise connected with their acquisition, disposal or movement[22]. Goods may be described in the order wholly or partly by reference to the uses to which the goods, or any information recorded on or derived from them, may be put[23]. A person acquires goods if he buys, hires or borrows them or accepts them as a gift, and a person disposes of goods if he sells, lets on hire, lends or gives them[24]. The making of an agreement with another to acquire, dispose of or move goods, and the making of arrangements under which another person acquires, disposes of or moves goods or agrees with a third person to acquire, dispose of or move goods, are activities which facilitate the acquisition, disposal or movement of the goods[25].

The Secretary of State may by order make provision in connection with any controls that may be imposed by a directly applicable EU provision[26] on the exportation of goods[27], the transfer of technology[28], participation in the provision of technical assistance[29], the acquisition, disposal or movement of goods, or on activities which facilitate or are otherwise connected with the acquisition, disposal or movement of goods[30].

The Secretary of State has power to make similar provision under European Union law[31].

1   As to the Secretary of State see PARA 902.
2   Such an order must be made by statutory instrument and is subject to annulment in pursuance of a resolution of either House of Parliament: Export Control Act 2002 s 13(1), (5)(a). See STATUTES AND LEGISLATIVE PROCESS vol 96 (2012) PARA 1045 et seq. As to orders made under these powers see the Export of Objects of Cultural Interest (Control) Order 2003, SI 2003/2759 (made under the Export Control Act 2002 ss 1, 5, 7; see also PARA 916); the Export of Radioactive Sources (Control) Order 2006, SI 2006/1846 (made under the Export Control Act 2002 ss 1, 5, 7); and the Export Control Order 2008, SI 2008/3231 (made under the Export Control Act 2002 ss 1–5, 7; see also PARA 917 et seq). Orders have been made under the Export Control Act 2002 ss 1–5, 7 (see text and notes 1, 3–30, PARAS 912, 913) and the European Communities Act 1972 s 2(2), Sch 2 para 1A (see CONSTITUTIONAL AND ADMINISTRATIVE LAW vol 20 (2014) PARA 156) in relation to specific countries (see the Export Control (Guinea) Order 2010, SI 2010/364; the Export Control (Somalia) Order 2011, SI 2011/146; the Export Control (Libya) Order 2011, SI 2011/825; the Export Control (Eritrea and Miscellaneous Amendments) Order 2011, SI 2011/1296; the Export Control (Belarus) and (Syria Amendment) Order 2011, SI 2011/2010; the Export Control (Iran Sanctions) Order 2012, SI 2012/1243; the Export Control (Syria Sanctions) Order 2013, SI 2013/2012; and the Export Control (North Korea and Ivory Coast Sanctions and Syria Amendment) Order 2013, SI 2013/3182) and under the Export Control Act 2002 ss 3–5, 7 and the European Communities Act 2002 s 2(2) (see the Export Control (Democratic Republic of Congo) Order 2005, SI 2005/1677; and the Export Control (Liberia) Order 2011, SI 2011/145).
3   Export Control Act 2002 s 1(1).
4   Export Control Act 2002 s 2(1).
5   Export Control Act 2002 s 3(1).
6   Export Control Act 2002 s 4(1). There is to be paid out of money provided by Parliament any expenses of a government department incurred in consequence of the Export Control Act 2002, and any increase attributable to the Act in the sums payable out of such money under any other Act: s 14. Nothing in the Act affects Her Majesty in her private capacity within the meaning of the Crown Proceedings Act 1947 (see CROWN AND CROWN PROCEEDINGS vol 29 (2014) PARA 84 et seq): Export Control Act 2002 s 16(7). Her Majesty may by Order in Council direct that any of the provisions of the Act, or of any order under the Act, are to extend, with such exceptions and modifications as appear to Her Majesty to be appropriate, to the Isle of Man or to any British overseas territory: s 16(5). See the Export of Goods, Transfer of Technology and

Provision of Technical Assistance (Control) (Overseas Territories) Order 2004, SI 2004/3101; the Trade in Goods (Control) (Overseas Territories) Order 2004, SI 2004/3102; the Trade in Controlled Goods (Embargoed Destinations) (Overseas Territories) Order 2004, SI 2004/3103; and the Judicial Proceedings in Specified Overseas Territories (Restrictive Measures) Order 2009, SI 2009/888. As to the approach of the court when sentencing an offender for an evasion of a control order see *R v Knight* [2008] EWCA Crim 478, [2008] 2 Cr App Rep (S) 425, [2008] All ER (D) 100 (Feb). See also *R (on the application of Melli Bank plc) v HM Treasury* [2008] EWHC 1661 (Admin), [2008] All ER (D) 119 (Jul), DC (validity of freezing of assets of English subsidiary of Iranian bank pursuant to control order).

7   Goods may be described in the order wholly or partly by reference to the uses to which the goods, or any information recorded on or derived from them, may be put: Export Control Act 2002 s 1(3).

8   As to the meaning of 'United Kingdom' see PARA 906 note 7.

9   Export Control Act 2002 s 1(2). Export controls may be imposed in relation to the removal from the United Kingdom of vehicles, vessels and aircraft as an exportation of goods, whether or not they are moving under their own power or carrying goods or passengers: s 1(6). The removal of goods to the Isle of Man is not to be regarded as an exportation of those goods: s 11(3). The Act, so far as it relates to the imposition of export controls, is an Act relating to customs for the purposes of the definition of 'the Customs and Excise Acts' in the Customs and Excise Management Act 1979 s 1 (see PARA 908 note 1): Export Control Act 2002 s 11(4). The power to impose export controls is subject to s 5 (see PARA 912): s 1(4).

10   'Technology' means information, including information comprised in software, that is capable of use in connection with: (1) the development, production or use of any goods or software; (2) the development of, or the carrying out of, an industrial or commercial activity or an activity of any other kind whatsoever: Export Control Act 2002 s 2(6). Technology may be described in the order wholly or partly by reference to the uses to which it may be put: s 2(3).

11   'Transfer', in relation to any technology, means a transfer by any means, or combination of means, including oral communication and the transfer of goods on which the technology is recorded or from which it can be derived, other than the exportation of such goods: Export Control Act 2002 s 2(6).

12   'Place' includes a vehicle, vessel or aircraft: Export Control Act 2002 s 11(1).

13   Export Control Act 2002 s 2(2)(a). The power to impose transfer controls is subject to s 5 (see PARA 912): s 2(4).

14   Export Control Act 2002 s 2(2)(b). See also note 13. 'United Kingdom person' means a United Kingdom national, a Scottish partnership or a body incorporated under the law of any part of the United Kingdom: s 11(1). A United Kingdom national for these purposes is an individual who is a British citizen, a British overseas territories citizen, a British national (overseas), a British overseas citizen, a person who under the British Nationality Act 1981 is a British subject, or a British protected person within the meaning of the 1981 Act: Export Control Act 2002 s 11(2). As to British citizenship, British overseas territories citizenship, British national (overseas) status, British overseas citizenship, British subject status and British protected person status, see BRITISH NATIONALITY vol 4 (2011) PARA 421 et seq.

15   Export Control Act 2002 s 2(2)(c). See also note 13.

16   Export Control Act 2002 s 2(2)(d). See also note 13.

17   Export Control Act 2002 s 3(2). The power to impose technical assistance controls may only be exercised for the purpose of imposing controls corresponding to or connected with any export controls or transfer controls imposed under s 1 or 2 (see text and notes 7–16), or any controls imposed by a directly applicable EU provision on the exportation of goods or the transfer of technology: s 3(4)(a) (amended by SI 2011/1043). 'EU provision' means a provision of a directive or regulation within the meaning of the Treaty on the Functioning of the European Union (Rome, 25 March 1957; TS 1 (1973); Cmnd 5179) art 288: Export Control Act 2002 s 11(1) (definition amended by SI 2011/1043; SI 2012/1809). As to the Treaty on the Functioning of the European Union see EUROPEAN UNION vol 47A (2014) PARA 6). The power to impose technical assistance controls is subject to the Export Control Act 2002 s 5 (see PARA 912): s 3(4)(b).

18   Export Control Act 2002 s 3(2).

19   Export Control Act 2002 s 3(3).

20   Export Control Act 2002 s 3(5).

21   Export Control Act 2002 s 3(7).

22   Export Control Act 2002 s 4(2). The power to impose trade controls may only be exercised for the purpose of imposing controls corresponding to or connected with any export controls or transfer controls imposed under s 1 or s 2 (see text and notes 7–16), or any controls imposed by a directly applicable EU provision on the exportation of goods or the transfer of technology:

s 4(4)(a) (amended by SI 2011/1043). The power to impose trade controls is subject to the Export Control Act 2002 s 5 (see PARA 912): s 4(4)(b). Trade controls may be imposed on acts done outside the United Kingdom and the Isle of Man, but only if they are done by a person who is, or is acting under the control of, a United Kingdom person: s 4(8).

23 Export Control Act 2002 s 4(3).
24 Export Control Act 2002 s 4(6).
25 Export Control Act 2002 s 4(7).
26 As to direct applicability of EU provisions see note 17; and EUROPEAN UNION vol 47A (2014) PARA 10.
27 Export Control Act 2002 s 1(5). See the Export Control (Guinea) Order 2010, SI 2010/364; the Export Control (Uzbekistan) Order 2010, SI 2010/615; the Export Control (Somalia) Order 2011, SI 2011/146; the Export Control (Libya) Order 2011, SI 2011/825.
28 Export Control Act 2002 s 2(5).
29 Export Control Act 2002 s 3(6).
30 Export Control Act 2002 s 4(5).
31 Ie under the European Communities Act 1972 s 2(2). See the Zimbabwe (Sale, Supply, Export, Technical Assistance, Financing and Financial Assistance and Shipment of Equipment) (Penalties and Licences) Regulations 2004, SI 2004/559; the Lebanon (Technical Assistance, Financing and Financial Assistance) (Penalties and Licences) Regulations 2006, SI 2006/2681; and the Export Control (Sudan, South Sudan and Central African Republic Sanctions) Regulations 2014, SI 2014/3258.

See also the Zimbabwe (Financial Sanctions) Regulations 2009, SI 2009/847; the Liberia (Asset-Freezing) Regulations 2012, SI 2012/1516; the Iran (European Union Financial Sanctions) Regulations 2012, SI 2012/925; the Ukraine (European Union Financial Sanctions) Regulations 2014, SI 2014/507; the Central African Republic (European Union Financial Sanctions) Regulations 2014, SI 2014/587; the Ukraine (European Union Financial Sanctions) (No 2) Regulations 2014, SI 2014/693; the Sudan (European Union Financial Sanctions) Regulations 2014, SI 2014/1826; the South Sudan (European Union Financial Sanctions) Regulations 2014, SI 2014/1827; the Ukraine (European Union Financial Sanctions) (No 3) Regulations 2014, SI 2014/2054; and the Yemen (European Union Financial Sanctions) Regulations 2014, SI 2014/3349.

912. Restriction on control powers. Controls of any kind may only be imposed for the purpose of giving effect to any EU provision[1] or other international obligation[2] of the United Kingdom[3], and as described below[4]. Export controls[5] and trade controls[6] may be imposed in relation to: (1) military equipment[7]; (2) goods on which military technology[8] is recorded or from which it can be derived; or (3) goods intended, designed or adapted for use in the development or production of military equipment or military technology[9]. Transfer controls[10] may be imposed in relation to: (a) military technology; or (b) technology intended, designed or adapted for use in the development or production of military technology[11]. Technical assistance controls[12] may be imposed in relation to any services connected with the development, production or use of goods falling within head (1), (2) or (3), or any technology falling within head (a) or (b)[13].

Further, export controls may be imposed in relation to any goods the exportation or use of which is capable of having a relevant consequence[14]; transfer controls may be imposed in relation to any technology the transfer[15] or use of which is capable of having such a consequence[16]; technical assistance controls may be imposed in relation to any technical assistance[17] the provision or use of which is capable of having such a consequence[18]; and trade controls may be imposed in relation to any goods the acquisition, disposal, movement or use of which is capable of having such a consequence[19].

However, the restrictions described above do not apply to the power to impose any controls if the control order[20] which imposes them provides for its expiry no later than the end of the period of 12 months beginning with the day on which it is made[21]. Further, the restrictions do not apply in relation to

provisions of a control order which amend an earlier control order[22] or revoke
and re-enact, with or without modifications, provisions of an earlier control
order, unless they impose new controls or strengthen the controls previously
imposed[23].

1   As to the meaning of 'EU provision' see PARA 911 note 17.
2   'International obligation' includes an obligation relating to a joint action or common position
    adopted, or a decision taken, by the Council of the European Union under provisions of the
    Treaty on European Union (Maastricht, 7 February 1992; TS 12 (1994); Cm 2485; ECS 3
    (1992); Cm 1934) on a common foreign and security policy: Export Control Act 2002 s 5(3)
    (amended by SI 2012/1809). As to the Council of the European Union see EUROPEAN UNION
    vol 47A (2014) PARA 44–47; and as to the Treaty on European Union see EUROPEAN UNION
    vol 47A (2014) PARA 2.
3   As to the meaning of 'United Kingdom' see PARA 906 note 7.
4   Export Control Act 2002 s 5(1), (2) (s 5(2) amended by SI 2011/1043).
5   As to the meaning of 'export controls' see PARA 911.
6   As to the meaning of 'trade controls' see PARA 911.
7   'Military equipment' includes firearms and other weapons, whether or not intended, designed or
    adapted for military use or in military use, and goods intended, designed or adapted for military
    use, whether or not in military use: Export Control Act 2002 Schedule para 1(4). The reference
    to firearms and other weapons includes a reference to component parts of firearms or other
    weapons, accessories for use with firearms or other weapons, and ammunition, missiles or
    projectiles of any kind which are intended, designed or adapted for use with firearms or other
    weapons: Schedule para 1(5).
        The Secretary of State may by order made by statutory instrument modify the provisions of
    the Schedule: ss 12(1), 13(1). Such an order may make transitional provision in connection with
    any modification made by the order: s 12(2). A statutory instrument containing such an order
    may not be made unless a draft of it has been laid before and approved by a resolution of each
    House of Parliament: s 13(4). See STATUTES AND LEGISLATIVE PROCESS vol 96 (2012) PARA 1045
    et seq. At the date at which this volume states the law no such order had been made. As to the
    Secretary of State see PARA 902.
8   'Military technology' includes technology intended, designed or adapted for military use,
    whether or not in military use, and technology intended, designed or adapted for use in
    connection with the development, production or use of military equipment or goods falling
    within head (3) of the text: Export Control Act 2002 Schedule para 1(4). See also note 7. As to
    the meaning of 'technology' see PARA 911 note 10.
9   Export Control Act 2002 s 5(4), (7), Schedule para 1(1). Export controls may also be imposed in
    relation to objects of cultural interest: Schedule para 4. See also note 7. 'Objects of cultural
    interest' includes objects of historical or scientific interest: s 11(1). See the Export of Objects of
    Cultural Interest (Control) Order 2003, SI 2003/2759 (see PARA 916); the Export of Radioactive
    Sources (Control) Order 2006, SI 2006/1846; and the Export Control Order 2008,
    SI 2008/3231 (see PARA 917 et seq). As to orders made in relation to specific countries see PARA
    911 note 2.
10 As to the meaning of 'transfer controls' see PARA 911.
11 Export Control Act 2002 s 5(5), Schedule para 1(2). See also notes 7, 9.
12 As to the meaning of 'technical assistance controls' see PARA 911.
13 Export Control Act 2002 s 5(6), Schedule para 1(3). See also notes 7, 9.
14 Export Control Act 2002 s 5(4), Schedule para 2(1). A relevant consequence, in relation to any
    activity, is a consequence, direct or indirect, of a kind relating to: (1) the national security of the
    United Kingdom, any dependency, any member state or any other friendly state; (2) the peace,
    security or stability in any region of the world or within any country; (3) weapons of mass
    destruction; (4) breaches of international law and human rights; (5) terrorism and crime:
    Schedule para 3(1), (2). 'Dependency' means the Isle of Man, any of the Channel Islands or a
    British overseas territory; and 'country' includes a territory but does not include the United
    Kingdom or the Isle of Man: Schedule para 3(4). The question whether an activity involving
    goods, technology or technical assistance of any particular description is capable of having a
    relevant consequence is to be determined by the Secretary of State at the time the order imposing
    the controls is made: Schedule para 3(3). See also notes 7, 9.
15 As to the meaning of 'transfer' see PARA 911 note 11.
16 Export Control Act 2002 s 5(5), Schedule para 2(2). See also notes 7, 9.
17 As to the meaning of 'technical assistance' see PARA 911.
18 Export Control Act 2002 s 5(6), Schedule para 2(3). See also notes 7, 9.

19 Export Control Act 2002 s 5(7), Schedule para 2(4). See also notes 7, 9.
20 'Control order' means an order under the Export Control Act 2002 ss 1(1), 2(1), 3(1) or 4(1)
    (see PARA 911): s 11(1).
21 Export Control Act 2002 s 6(1). See the Export Control (Amendment) (No 2) Order 2011,
    SI 2011/580 (which ceased to have effect on 1 March 2012: art 1(3)). A statutory instrument
    containing a control order made by virtue of s 6(1) must be laid before Parliament after being
    made but, unless it is approved by a resolution of each House before the end of the period of 40
    days beginning with the day on which it is made, ceases to have effect at the end of that period:
    s 13(2). In reckoning that period no account is to be taken of any time during which Parliament
    is dissolved or prorogued or during which either House is adjourned for more than four days:
    s 13(3). As to the dissolution or prorogation of Parliament see PARLIAMENT vol 78 (2010) PARAS
    1018 et seq, 1021 et seq.
22 An 'earlier control order' does not include an order made by virtue of the Export Control
    Act 2002 s 6(1): s 6(3).
23 Export Control Act 2002 s 6(2).

913.   Use of control powers. An order[1] may, without prejudice to the
generality of the power under which it is made, make provision: (1) for an
activity to be prohibited unless a specified person[2] has granted a licence
authorising that activity[3]; (2) creating exceptions from any provision of the
order[4]; (3) requiring persons to keep, and produce, records[5]; (4) requiring
persons to provide information to any specified person[6]; (5) about the purposes
for which information held in connection with anything done under or by virtue
of the order may be used[7]; (6) about the persons to whom any such information
may be disclosed[8]; (7) creating offences[9]; and (8) for the enforcement of the
order, including provision as to the powers and duties of any person who is to
enforce it[10].

Such an order may: (a) make provision binding the Crown[11]; (b) amend,
repeal or revoke, or apply, with or without modifications, provisions of any Act
or subordinate legislation[12]; (c) provide for any reference in the order to a
document, including a technical list by reference to which any EU provision[13] or
international obligation[14] operates, to take effect as a reference to that document
as revised or re-issued from time to time[15]; (d) make incidental, supplementary
and transitional provision[16]; and (e) make different provision for different cases
and different circumstances[17].

The Secretary of State[18] may not make a control order[19] which has the effect
of prohibiting or regulating the communication of information in the ordinary
course of scientific research, the making of information generally available to the
public, or the communication of information that is generally available to the
public, unless the interference by the order in the freedom to carry on the activity
in question is necessary, and no more than is necessary[20].

1   Ie an order made under the Export Control Act 2002 ss 1–6 (see PARAS 911–912): s 7(1).
2   Ie a person specified in the order: Export Control Act 2002 s 7(1)(a).
3   Export Control Act 2002 s 7(1)(a).
4   Export Control Act 2002 s 7(1)(b).
5   Export Control Act 2002 s 7(1)(c).
6   Export Control Act 2002 s 7(1)(d). The reference to a person specified is to a person specified in
    the order: s 7(1)(d).
7   Export Control Act 2002 s 7(1)(e).
8   Export Control Act 2002 s 7(1)(f).
9   Export Control Act 2002 s 7(1)(g). Such offences may be indictable, summary or triable either
    way, subject to the limitation that no offence so created may be punishable on indictment with
    imprisonment for a term exceeding 10 years: s 7(1)(g). As to classification of offences see
    CRIMINAL PROCEDURE vol 27 (2010) PARA 160 et seq.
10 Export Control Act 2002 s 7(1)(h).
11 Export Control Act 2002 s 7(2)(a).

12　Export Control Act 2002 s 7(2)(b).
13　As to the meaning of 'EU provision' see PARA 911 note 17.
14　As to the meaning of 'international obligation' see PARA 912 note 2.
15　Export Control Act 2002 s 7(2)(c) (amended by SI 2011/1043).
16　Export Control Act 2002 s 7(2)(d).
17　Export Control Act 2002 s 7(2)(e).
18　As to the Secretary of State see PARA 902.
19　As to the meaning of 'control order' see PARA 912 note 20.
20　Export Control Act 2002 s 8(1). The question whether any such interference is necessary is to be determined by the Secretary of State by reference to the circumstances prevailing at the time the order is made and having considered the reasons for seeking to control the activity in question and the need to respect the freedom to carry on that activity: s 8(2).

914.　Guidance about the exercise of functions under control orders; annual reports.　The Secretary of State[1] may give guidance[2] about any matter relating to the exercise of licensing powers or other functions[3], but must give guidance about the general principles to be followed when exercising such licensing powers[4]. Any person exercising such a licensing power or other function must have regard to any guidance which relates to that power or function[5].

The Secretary of State must lay before Parliament in respect of each year a report on the operation during the year of an export order so far as relating to the export of objects of cultural interest[6] and a report on other matters relating to the operation of the Export Control Act 2002, and any order made under it, during the year[7].

1　As to the Secretary of State see PARA 902.
2　'Guidance' means guidance stating that it is given under the Export Control Act 2002 s 9: s 9(7). A copy of any guidance must be laid before Parliament and published in such manner as the Secretary of State may think fit: s 9(6).
3　Export Control Act 2002 s 9(2). The licensing powers and other functions referred to are those conferred by a control order on any person in connection with controls imposed under the Export Control Act 2002: s 9(1). As to the meaning of 'control order' see PARA 912 note 20.
4　Export Control Act 2002 s 9(3). The guidance required by s 9(3) must include, but is not restricted to, guidance about the consideration, if any, to be given, when exercising such powers, to issues relating to sustainable development, and issues relating to any possible consequences of the activity being controlled that are relevant consequences: s 9(4). As to the meaning of 'relevant consequence' see PARA 912 note 14.
5　Export Control Act 2002 s 9(5). The consolidated criteria relating to export licensing decisions announced to Parliament by the Secretary of State on 26 October 2000 must, until withdrawn or varied under s 9, be treated as guidance which is given and published under s 9, and fulfils the duty imposed by s 9(3) in respect of any export controls and transfer controls which may be imposed in relation to goods or technology of a description falling within the Schedule para 1 or para 2 (see PARA 912): s 9(8). As to the meaning of 'export controls' and 'transfer controls' see PARA 911; and as to the meaning of 'technology' see PARA 911 note 10.
6　As to the meaning of 'objects of cultural interest' see PARA 912 note 9.
7　Export Control Act 2002 s 10(1). A report required by s 10(1) must be laid before Parliament as soon as practicable after the end of the year to which it relates: s 10(2).

(iii)　Particular Controls

A.　IMPORT OF GOODS

915.　Import licences.　All goods[1], other than goods which are proved to the satisfaction of the Commissioners for Revenue and Customs[2] to have been consigned from the Channel Islands[3], are prohibited from being imported into the United Kingdom[4] except under the authority of a licence[5] granted by the Secretary of State[6] and in accordance with any condition[7] attached to the licence[8]. The Secretary of State may modify or revoke the licence at any time[9].

Any licence which may have been granted in connection with an application for which any person makes any statement or furnishes any document or information which to his knowledge is false in a material particular, or recklessly makes any statement which is false in a material particular, is void as from the time the licence was granted[10].

1 Unless otherwise specified, 'goods' means both used and unused goods: Import of Goods (Control) Order 1954, SI 1954/23, art 6(1). The order was made in the exercise of powers under the Import, Export and Customs Powers (Defence) Act 1939 s 1 (see PARA 908) and came into operation on 21 January 1954 (see the Import of Goods (Control) Order 1954, SI 1954/23, art 8). As to the meaning of 'goods' for the purposes of the Import, Export and Customs Powers (Defence) Act 1939 see PARA 908 note 6.

2 As to the Commissioners for Revenue and Customs see CUSTOMS AND EXCISE vol 31 (2012) PARA 921 et seq.

3 See the Import of Goods (Control) Order 1954, SI 1954/23, art 3 (amended by virtue of the Commissioners for Revenue and Customs Act 2005 s 50(1), (7)). This exception does not, however, extend to: (1) the following dyes, dyestuffs and intermediates: (a) synthetic organic dyestuffs, including pigment dyestuffs, whether soluble or insoluble; (b) compounds, preparations and articles manufactured from any such dyestuffs, except any such compounds, preparations and articles as are not suitable for use in dyeing; (c) organic intermediate products used in the manufacture of any such dyestuffs; (2) the following arms and ammunition: (a) lethal firearms, including any lethal barrelled weapon of any description from which any shot, bullet or other missile can be discharged and other weapons of whatever description designed or adapted for the discharge of any noxious liquid, gas or other thing; (b) component parts of any such firearm or such other weapon, any accessory to any such firearm or other weapon designed or adapted to diminish the noise or flash caused by firing the weapon; (c) ammunition, including grenades, bombs and other like missiles, and any ammunition containing or designed or adapted to contain any noxious liquid, gas or other thing, and component parts of any such ammunition; and (3) plumage, other than plumage of birds imported alive and other than plumage of birds ordinarily used in the United Kingdom as articles of diet: Import of Goods (Control) Order 1954, SI 1954/23, art 3.

4 Import of Goods (Control) Order 1954, SI 1954/23, art 1. As to the meaning of 'United Kingdom' see PARA 906 note 7; but cf PARA 908 note 5.

5 Licences may be individual (ie enabling specified individuals or classes to import specified goods) or general (ie enabling persons generally to import certain goods from certain countries without the need to apply for an individual licence).

6 As to the Secretary of State see PARAS 902, 908 note 3.

7 A licence granted under the Import of Goods (Control) Order 1954, SI 1954/23, art 2 permitting goods to be imported for transit or transhipment may be granted subject to either or both of the following conditions: (1) that the goods be exported to a specified destination; (2) that they be exported within a specified time: art 2A(1) (art 2A added by SI 1978/806). If goods are imported under the authority of such a licence and any such condition imposed by the licence is contravened or not complied with, the goods are liable to forfeiture: Import of Goods (Control) Order 1954, SI 1954/23, art 2A(2) (art 2A as so added).

8 Import of Goods (Control) Order 1954, SI 1954/23, art 2. As to the compatibility of import licences with European Union law see CUSTOMS AND EXCISE vol 30 (2012) PARA 16.

9 Import of Goods (Control) Order 1954, SI 1954/23, art 5(1).

10 Import of Goods (Control) Order 1954, SI 1954/23, art 4. In addition, that person commits an offence for which he is liable on summary conviction to a fine not exceeding £500 or to imprisonment for a term not exceeding six months, or to both: art 4.

B. EXPORT OF GOODS

(A) Objects of Cultural Interest

916. Export of objects of cultural interest. Subject to the provisions of the Export of Objects of Cultural Interest (Control) Order 2003[1], all objects[2] are prohibited to be exported to any destination except under the authority of a licence in writing granted by the Secretary of State[3], and in accordance with all the conditions attached to the licence[4]. The Secretary of State may also grant an

EU licence[5] under the relevant European Union law. An EU licence or a licence granted by the Secretary of State may be: (1) general or specific; (2) unlimited or limited so as to expire on a specified date unless renewed; and (3) subject to or without conditions, and any such condition may require any act or omission before or after the exportation of objects under the licence[6]. Any such licence may be varied, suspended or revoked by the Secretary of State at any time and in such circumstances and on such terms as the Secretary of State thinks fit, by serving a notice to that effect on the holder of the licence[7].

Where for the purpose of obtaining a licence under the 2003 Order or an EU licence, any person either: (a) makes any statement or furnishes any document or information which to his knowledge is false in a material particular; or (b) recklessly makes any statement or furnishes any document or information which is false in a material particular, he is guilty of an offence[8].

Any person who has done any act under the authority of a licence granted under the 2003 Order or an EU licence and fails to comply with any condition attaching to that licence, is guilty of an offence[9]. However, no person is guilty of such an offence where: (i) the licence condition in question had been previously modified by the Secretary of State; and (ii) the alleged failure to comply would not have been a failure had the licence not been so modified; and (iii) the condition with which he failed to comply was modified, otherwise than with his consent, by the Secretary of State after the doing of the act authorised by the licence[10].

Any person who exports or ships objects or cultural goods[11] must, if so required by the Commissioners for Revenue and Customs[12], furnish within such time as the Commissioners may determine, evidence of the destination to which the objects or cultural goods were delivered and, if he fails to do so, he is guilty of an offence[13].

It is the duty of the Commissioners to take such action as they consider appropriate to secure the enforcement of the 2003 Order[14] and of the relevant European Union legislation in respect of the export of cultural goods[15].

Information[16] which is held by the Secretary of State or the Commissioners in connection with the operation of controls imposed by the 2003 Order or by any directly applicable EU provision on the exportation of cultural goods[17] may be used for the purposes of, or for any purposes connected with: (A) the exercise of functions in relation to any control imposed by the 2003 Order or by any order made under the Export Control Act 2002[18]; (B) giving effect to any EU or other international obligation of the United Kingdom; (C) facilitating the exercise by an authority or international organisation outside the United Kingdom of functions which correspond to functions conferred by or in connection with any activity subject to any control by the 2003 Order or by any order made under the Export Control Act 2002, and may be disclosed to any person for use for these purposes[19]. No disclosure of information may be made by virtue of this provision unless the Secretary of State is, or the Commissioners are, satisfied that the making of the disclosure is proportionate to what is sought to be achieved by it[20]. Nothing in these provisions is to be taken to prejudice any power to disclose information which exists apart from them[21].

1   Ie the Export of Objects of Cultural Interest (Control) Order 2003, SI 2003/2759. The Order came into force on 1 May 2004: see art 1(1).
2   'Objects' means objects of cultural interest of a description specified in and not excluded from the Export of Objects of Cultural Interest (Control) Order 2003, SI 2003/2759, Schedule: art 1(2). The objects so specified are any objects of cultural interest manufactured or produced more than 50 years before the date of exportation except: (1) postage stamps and other articles

of philatelic interest; (2) birth, marriage or death certificates or other documents relating to the personal affairs of the exporter or the spouse of the exporter; (3) letters or other writings written by or to the exporter or the spouse of the exporter; and (4) goods exported by, and being the personal property of, the manufacturer or producer thereof, or the spouse, widow or widower of that person: Schedule. 'Exportation' includes shipment as stores and, unless the context otherwise requires, means exportation from the United Kingdom to any destination except for the Isle of Man: Export of Objects of Cultural Interest (Control) Order 2003, SI 2003/2759, art 1(2). As to the meaning of 'United Kingdom' see PARA 906 note 7.

3 The Secretary of State here concerned is the Secretary of State for Culture, Media and Sport. As to the Secretary of State in relation to trade and industry in general see PARA 902.

4 Export of Objects of Cultural Interest (Control) Order 2003, SI 2003/2759, art 2.

5 'EU licence' means an authorisation granted by the Secretary of State (whether before or after commencement of the Export of Objects of Cultural Interest (Control) Order 2003, SI 2003/2759 (see note 1)) under Council Regulation (EC) 116/2009 (OJ L39, 10.2.2009, p 1) on the export of cultural goods: see the Export of Objects of Cultural Interest (Control) Order 2003, SI 2003/2759, art 1(2) (amended by SI 2011/1043).

6 Export of Objects of Cultural Interest (Control) Order 2003, SI 2003/2759, art 3(1) (amended by SI 2011/1043).

7 Export of Objects of Cultural Interest (Control) Order 2003, SI 2003/2759, art 3(2).

8 Export of Objects of Cultural Interest (Control) Order 2003, SI 2003/2759, art 4(1). A person guilty of such an offence is liable, on summary conviction, to a fine of the prescribed sum and, on conviction on indictment, to a fine of any amount, or imprisonment for a term not exceeding two years, or to both, and any licence which may have been granted in connection with the application for which the false statement was made or the false document or information furnished, is void as from the time it was granted: art 4(2). As to the prescribed sum see SENTENCING AND DISPOSITION OF OFFENDERS vol 92 (2010) PARA 141.

9 Export of Objects of Cultural Interest (Control) Order 2003, SI 2003/2759, art 5(1) (amended by SI 2011/1043). A person guilty of such an offence is liable, on summary conviction to a fine of the prescribed sum and, on conviction on indictment to a fine of any amount, or imprisonment for a term not exceeding two years, or to both: Export of Objects of Cultural Interest (Control) Order 2003, SI 2003/2759, art 5(2).

10 Export of Objects of Cultural Interest (Control) Order 2003, SI 2003/2759, art 5(3).

11 'Cultural goods' has the same meaning as that given in Council Regulation (EC) 116/2009 (OJ L39, 10.2.2009, p 1) (see Annex I which lists categories of cultural objects): Export of Objects of Cultural Interest (Control) Order 2003, SI 2003/2759, art 1(2).

12 As to the Commissioners for Revenue and Customs see CUSTOMS AND EXCISE vol 31 (2012) PARA 921 et seq.

13 Export of Objects of Cultural Interest (Control) Order 2003, SI 2003/2759, arts 1(2), 6(1) (art 1(2) amended by virtue of the Commissioners for Revenue and Customs Act 2005 s 50(1), (7)). Any person guilty of such an offence is liable on summary conviction to a fine not exceeding level 4 on the standard scale: Export of Objects of Cultural Interest (Control) Order 2003, SI 2003/2759, art 6(2). As to the standard scale see SENTENCING AND DISPOSITION OF OFFENDERS vol 92 (2010) PARA 142.

14 Export of Objects of Cultural Interest (Control) Order 2003, SI 2003/2759, art 7(1).

15 Export of Objects of Cultural Interest (Control) Order 2003, SI 2003/2759, art 7(2).

16 For these purposes, 'information' is any information that relates to a particular business or other activity carried on by a person: Export of Objects of Cultural Interest (Control) Order 2003, SI 2003/2759, art 8(4). The information that may be disclosed by virtue of art 8 includes information obtained before the commencement of the 2003 Order (see note 1): art 8(6).

17 Export of Objects of Cultural Interest (Control) Order 2003, SI 2003/2759, art 8(1) (amended by SI 2011/1043).

18 See PARA 911 et seq.

19 Export of Objects of Cultural Interest (Control) Order 2003, SI 2003/2759, art 8(2) (amended by SI 2011/1043).

20 Export of Objects of Cultural Interest (Control) Order 2003, SI 2003/2759, art 8(3).

21 Export of Objects of Cultural Interest (Control) Order 2003, SI 2003/2759, art 8(5).

(B) Prohibitions and Controls

917.   Prohibited goods. In exercise of his power to regulate the export of goods[1], the Secretary of State[2] has imposed export and transfer controls on specified categories of goods, including technical assistance[3], which could be used for capital punishment, torture or other cruel, inhuman or degrading treatment or punishment, and on trade in dual-use items[4], including the transmission of software[5] or technology[6] in intangible form[7].

To the extent that a person may not export goods pursuant to the following provisions, the exportation of the goods in question is prohibited[8].

Subject to exceptions[9], no person may export[10] military[11] goods or transfer[12] military software or technology by electronic means[13].

Subject to exceptions[14], no person may export UK controlled[15] dual-use goods or transfer UK controlled dual-use software or technology by electronic means[16]: (1) to a destination specified[17] as a prohibited destination in relation to the goods, software or technology in question[18]; or (2) where the destination is not a prohibited destination but the exporter or transferor knows both that the final destination of the goods, software or technology is a prohibited destination and that no processing or working is to be performed on the goods, software or technology in question before they are exported or transferred to that final destination[19].

Subject to exceptions[20], no person may export a human or veterinary medicinal product containing the active ingredient pancuronium bromide or propofol where the product is in a form suitable for injection or for preparation of an injection[21] and the destination of the product is the United States of America[22], or, where the destination is not the United States of America, the exporter knows that the final destination of the product is the United States of America[23].

1 Ie under the Export Control Act 2002: see PARA 911.
2 As to the Secretary of State see PARA 902.

3 'Technical assistance' means any technical support related to repairs, development, manufacture, assembly, testing, use, maintenance or any other technical service: Export Control Order 2008, SI 2008/3231, art 2(1).

4 'Dual-use' in relation to goods, software or technology (see notes 5, 6), means usable for both civil and military purposes: Export Control Order 2008, SI 2008/3231, art 2(1). Except in the definition of category C goods (see PARA 925 note 21), tangible storage media on which dual-use software or technology is recorded are taken to be dual-use goods: art 2(2).

5 'Software' means one or more programmes or microprogrammes fixed in any tangible medium of expression; 'programme' means a sequence of instructions to carry out a process in, or convertible into, a form executable by an electronic computer; and 'microprogramme' means a sequence of elementary instructions, maintained in a special storage, the execution of which is initiated by the introduction of its reference instruction into an instruction register: Export Control Order 2008, SI 2008/3231, art 2(1).

6 'Technology' means information (including but not limited to information comprised in software and documents such as blueprints, manuals, diagrams and designs) that is capable of use in connection with the development, production or use of any goods: Export Control Order 2008, SI 2008/3231, art 2(1).

7 See the Export Control Order 2008, SI 2008/3231, Pt 2 (arts 3–18) (see text and notes 9–23; and PARAS 918–923). The Order came into force on 6 April 2009: see art 1. It does not apply to:
    (1) any export of goods, transfer of technology or participation in the provision of technical assistance; or
    (2) any activity which facilitates, or is otherwise connected with, the acquisition, disposal or movement of goods,
    that takes place in accordance with the terms of a licence granted before 6 April 2009 under the legislation revoked by art 45(1), Sch 6, or under the Dual-use Regulation or the Torture Regulation, or to any such licence: Export Control Order 2008, SI 2008/3231, art 45(2). To the extent that, owing to art 45(2), the 2008 Order does not apply, the revoked legislation continues to apply: art 45(3).
    'Dual-use Regulation' means Council Regulation (EC) 428/2009 (OJ L134, 29.5.2009, p 1) as amended from time to time; and 'Torture Regulation' means Council Regulation (EC)

1236/2005 (OJ L200, 30.7.2005, p 1) as amended from time to time: see the Export Control Order 2008, SI 2008/3231, art 2(1) (definition 'Dual-use Regulation' substituted by SI 2009/2151).

8   See the Export Control Order 2008, SI 2008/3231, art 9A (added by SI 2009/1852).

9   Ie subject to the Export Control Order 2008, SI 2008/3231, arts 13–18, 26 (see PARAS 920–923, 927): art 3.

10 'Exportation' is to be construed as follows: (1) unless the context otherwise requires, it only includes removal from the United Kingdom to a destination outside the United Kingdom and the Isle of Man; (2) it includes shipment as stores; (3) in relation to a vessel, vehicle, submersible vehicle or aircraft, it includes taking it out of the United Kingdom, notwithstanding that it is conveying goods or passengers and whether or not it is moving under its own power, and cognate expressions are to be construed accordingly: Export Control Order 2008, SI 2008/3231, art 2(1). As to the meaning of 'United Kingdom' see PARA 906 note 7. As to the meanings of 'shipment' (and cognate expressions) see the Customs and Excise Management Act 1979 s 1(1) (see PARA 939 note 9); and as to the meaning of 'stores' see the Customs and Excise Management Act 1979 s 1(1), (4)–(4B) (see PARA 908 note 6) (definitions applied by the Export Control Order 2008, SI 2008/3231, art 2(1)). 'Vessel' includes any ship, surface effect vehicle, vessel of small waterplane area or hydrofoil, and the hull or part of the hull of a vessel; 'surface effect vehicle' means any air cushion vehicle (whether side wall or skirted) and any vehicle using the wing-in-ground effect for positive lift; 'vehicle' includes a railway carriage; and 'aircraft' means a fixed wing, swivel wing, rotary wing, tilt rotor or tilt wing vehicle or helicopter: art 2(1).

11 'Military' in relation to goods, software and technology, means listed in the Export Control Order 2008, SI 2008/3231, Sch 2: art 2(1). Except in the definition of category C goods (see PARA 925 note 21), tangible storage media on which military software or technology is recorded are taken to be military goods: art 2(2). The items listed in Sch 2 are military, security and para-military goods, software and technology and arms, ammunition and related materiel: Sch 2 (substituted by SI 2014/1069). The Export Control Order 2008, SI 2008/3231, Sch 2 is not set out in detail in this work; it is based on the Wassenaar Arrangement military list.

12 'Transfer', in relation to software or technology, means transfer by electronic or non-electronic means (or any combination of electronic and non-electronic means) from a person or place within the United Kingdom to a person or place outside the United Kingdom, except in the Export Control Order 2008, SI 2008/3231, arts 10, 11 (see PARA 919) where the limitations as to the origin and destination of the transfer do not apply, and cognate expressions are to be construed accordingly: art 2(1). 'Transfer by electronic means', in relation to software and technology, means transmission by facsimile, telephone or other electronic media and includes the transmission of technology by describing it orally over the telephone: art 2(1) (definition substituted by SI 2009/2151). 'Transfer by non-electronic means', in relation to software or technology, means disclosure of software or technology by any means (or combination of means), including oral communication, other than as the exportation of goods or the transfer by electronic means: Export Control Order 2008, SI 2008/3231, art 2(1).

13 See the Export Control Order 2008, SI 2008/3231, art 3.

14 Ie subject to the Export Control Order 2008, SI 2008/3231, arts 13, 14, 17, 18, 26 (see PARAS 920, 922, 923, 927): art 4(1) (art 4 as substituted: see note 16).

15 'UK controlled' in relation to dual-use goods, software and technology, means listed in the Export Control Order 2008, SI 2008/3231, Sch 3: art 2(1). Such goods are specified explosive-related goods and technology; materials, chemicals, micro-organisms and toxins; telecommunications and related technology; detection equipment; vessels and related software and technology; and aircraft and related technology: see Sch 3 (substituted by SI 2010/2007; and amended by SI 2012/1910; SI 2014/121). The Export Control Order 2008, SI 2008/3231, Sch 3 is not set out in detail in this work.

16 See the Export Control Order 2008, SI 2008/3231, art 4(1) (art 4 substituted by SI 2010/121). The Export Control Order 2008, SI 2008/3231, art 4 binds the Crown, although the Crown is not criminally liable as a result of a contravention of it: art 2A(1)(a). This does not affect the application of art 4 to persons in the public service of the Crown. As to Crown proceedings see CROWN AND CROWN PROCEEDINGS vol 29 (2014) PARA 84 et seq.

17 Ie specified in the Export Control Order 2008, SI 2008/3231, Sch 3 (see note 15): art 4(2) (art 4 as substituted: see note 16).

18 See the Export Control Order 2008, SI 2008/3231, art 4(2) (art 4 as substituted: see note 16).

19 See the Export Control Order 2008, SI 2008/3231, art 4(3) (art 4 as substituted: see note 16).

20 Ie subject to the Export Control Order 2008, SI 2008/3231, arts 17, 26 (see PARAS 922, 927): art 4A(1) (art 4A as added: see note 21).

21 See the Export Control Order 2008, SI 2008/3231, art 4A(1) (art 4A added by SI 2012/929; Export Control Order 2008, SI 2008/3231, art 4A(1) amended by SI 2012/1910).

22 See the Export Control Order 2008, SI 2008/3231, art 4A(2) (art 4A as added: see note 21).

23 See the Export Control Order 2008, SI 2008/3231, art 4A(3) (art 4A as added: see note 21).

918. Export or transfer to a destination outside the customs territory and goods in transit. Where a person (the 'inquirer') has grounds for suspecting that dual-use[1] goods, software[2] or technology[3] are or may be intended, in their entirety or in part, for WMD purposes[4] and the goods, software or technology in question are not specified in the Dual-use Regulation[5], then, subject to the licensing provisions[6], the inquirer must not export[7] the goods in question or transfer the software or technology in question by electronic means[8], to a destination outside the customs territory[9] unless, having made all reasonable inquiries as to the proposed use of the goods, software or technology in question, the inquirer is satisfied that they will not be used for WMD purposes[10].

Where: (1) a person (the 'relevant person') knows that the final destination of dual-use goods, software or technology is outside the customs territory, and that no processing or working is to be performed on the goods, software or technology in question within the customs territory[11]; (2) the relevant person would only be permitted to export or transfer the goods, software or technology in question to a destination outside the customs territory to the extent authorised to do so under the Dual-use Regulation[12]; and (3) the goods, software or technology in question are not specified in the Dual-use Regulation[13], then, subject to exceptions[14], the relevant person must not export the goods in question, or transfer the software or technology in question by electronic means, to a destination within the customs territory[15].

Subject to exceptions[16], no person may export specified goods[17] where the goods in question are non-Community goods[18] which are entering and passing through the customs territory with a final destination outside the customs territory[19]. Where a person (the 'exporter') has been informed by a competent authority[20] that dual-use goods are or may be intended, or is aware that dual-use goods specified are or may be intended, in their entirety or in part, for purposes referred to in the Dual-use Regulation[21], and the dual-use goods in question are non-Community goods which are not listed in the Dual-use Regulation[22] and are entering and passing through the customs territory with a final destination outside the customs territory, then, subject to the licensing provisions[23], the exporter must not export the goods in question[24].

Subject to the licensing provisions[25], no person may export: (a) gangchains and leg-irons specially designed for restraining human beings; (b) electric-shock belts designed for restraining human beings[26]; or (c) portable electric shock devices designed for the purpose of riot control or self-protection[27], to a destination within the customs territory[28]; nor may any person export goods within head (a) or (c) above in relation to which there is no export authorisation requirement under the Torture Regulation[29] because the goods are in transit[30].

1 As to the meaning of 'dual-use' see PARA 917 note 4.

2 As to the meaning of 'software' see PARA 917 note 5.

3 As to the meaning of 'technology' see PARA 917 note 6.

4 'WMD purposes' means use in connection with the development, production, handling, operation, maintenance, storage, detection, identification or dissemination of chemical, biological or nuclear weapons or other nuclear explosive devices, or the development, production, maintenance or storage of missiles capable of delivering such weapons: Export Control Order 2008, SI 2008/3231, art 2(1).

5 Ie not specified in Council Regulation (EC) 428/2009 (OJ L134, 29.5.2009, p 1) Annex I: Export Control Order 2008, SI 2008/3231, art 6(1)(b).

6 Ie the Export Control Order 2008, SI 2008/3231, art 26 (see PARA 927): art 6(2).

7 As to the meaning of 'exportation' see PARA 917 note 10.

8 As to the meaning of 'transfer by electronic means' see PARA 917 note 12.

9 'Customs territory' means the customs territory described in Council Regulation (EEC) 2913/92 (OJ L302, 19.10.1992, p 1) art 3 as amended from time to time until its repeal by Council Regulation (EC) 450/2008 (OJ L145, 4.6.2008, p 1) and then the customs territory described in art 3 of the latter Regulation as amended from time to time: Export Control Order 2008, SI 2008/3231, art 2(1). 'Customs territory' is now defined in European Parliament and Council Regulation (EU) 952/2013 (OJ L269, 10.10.2013, p 1) art 4, replacing Council Regulation (EEC) 2913/92 (OJ L302, 19.10.1992, p 1) art 3 as amended by Council Regulation (EC) 450/2008 (OJ L145, 4.6.2008, p 1).

10 See the Export Control Order 2008, SI 2008/3231, art 6. Articles 6–9 bind the Crown, although the Crown is not criminally liable as a result of a contravention of it: art 2A(1)(b). This does not affect the application of arts 6–9 to persons in the public service of the Crown. As to Crown proceedings see CROWN AND CROWN PROCEEDINGS vol 29 (2014) PARA 84 et seq.

11 See the Export Control Order 2008, SI 2008/3231, art 7(1)(a).

12 See the Export Control Order 2008, SI 2008/3231, art 7(1)(b). The extent authorised is such as is set out in Council Regulation (EC) 428/2009 art 3 (controls on listed goods) or art 4 (end-use controls): Export Control Order 2008, SI 2008/3231, art 7(1)(b).

13 See the Export Control Order 2008, SI 2008/3231, art 7(1)(c). The goods, software or technology are specified in Council Regulation (EC) 428/2009 Annex IV: Export Control Order 2008, SI 2008/3231, art 7(1)(c).

14 Ie subject to the Export Control Order 2008, SI 2008/3231, arts 17, 26 (see PARAS 922, 927): art 7(2).

15 Export Control Order 2008, SI 2008/3231, art 7(2). See also note 10.

16 Ie subject to the Export Control Order 2008, SI 2008/3231, arts 17, 26 (see PARAS 922, 927): art 8(1) (art 8 as substituted: see note 19).

17 Ie specified in Council Regulation (EC) 428/2009 Annex I: Export Control Order 2008, SI 2008/3231, art 8(1) (art 8 as substituted: see note 19).

18 'Non-Community goods' means non-Community goods described in Council Regulation (EEC) 2913/92 (OJ L302, 19.10.1992, p 1) art 4(8) as amended from time to time until its repeal by Council Regulation (EC) 450/2008 (OJ L145, 4.6.2008, p 1) and then non-Community goods described in art 4(19) as amended from time to time: Export Control Order 2008, SI 2008/3231, art 2(1) (definition added by SI 2009/2151).

19 See the Export Control Order 2008, SI 2008/3231, art 8(1) (art 8 substituted by SI 2009/2151). See also note 10.

20 'Competent authority' means the Secretary of State or any other authority that is from time to time empowered to grant authorisations under Council Regulation (EC) 428/2009: Export Control Order 2008, SI 2008/3231, art 2(1).

21 Ie under Council Regulation (EC) 428/2009 art 4(1) (WMD purposes end-use control): Export Control Order 2008, SI 2008/3231, art 8(2) (art 8 as substituted: see note 19).

22 Ie listed in Council Regulation (EC) 428/2009 Annex I: Export Control Order 2008, SI 2008/3231, art 8(2) (art 8 as substituted: see note 19).

23 See note 6.

24 See the Export Control Order 2008, SI 2008/3231, art 8(2), (3) (art 8 as substituted: see note 19). See also note 10.

25 See note 6.

26 Ie goods within Council Regulation (EC) 1236/2005 (OJ L200, 30.7.2005, p 1) Annex II item 2.1: Export Control Order 2008, SI 2008/3231, art 9(1)(b).

27 Ie goods within Council Regulation (EC) 1236/2005 (OJ L200, 30.7.2005, p 1) Annex III item 2.1: Export Control Order 2008, SI 2008/3231, art 9(1)(c).

28 See the Export Control Order 2008, SI 2008/3231, art 9(1), (2). See also note 10.

29 Ie no export authorisation requirement under Council Regulation (EC) 1236/2005 (OJ L200, 30.7.2005, p 1) art 5: Export Control Order 2008, SI 2008/3231, art 9(3).

30 See the Export Control Order 2008, SI 2008/3231, art 9(3). See also note 10. 'In transit' means imported into the United Kingdom for transit or transhipment; and 'transit or transhipment', in relation to goods, means transit through the United Kingdom or transhipment with a view to re-exportation of the goods or transhipment of the goods for use as stores: art 2(1). As to the meaning of 'United Kingdom' see PARA 906 note 7. As to the meaning of 'stores' see PARA 908 note 6; definition applied by the Alcoholic Liquor Duties Act 1979 s 4(3).

919.   Transfers of technology.   Subject to exceptions[1], where:

(1)   a person (the 'transferor') has been informed by the Secretary of State[2] that software[3] or technology[4] is or may be intended, in its entirety or in part, for WMD purposes[5], or is aware that software or technology is intended, in its entirety or in part, for WMD purposes, the transferor must not transfer[6] the software or technology in question:

    (a)   to a person or place within the United Kingdom[7] if he knows that the software or technology may be or is intended to be used outside the customs territory[8] or has been informed by the Secretary of State that it may be or is intended to be so used[9];

    (b)   by non-electronic means[10] to a destination outside the customs territory[11];

    (c)   to a destination within the customs territory if he knows that the final destination of the software or technology is outside the customs territory and that no processing or working is to be performed on the software or technology within the customs territory[12];

(2)   a United Kingdom person (the 'transferor') has been informed by a competent authority[13] that software or technology is or may be intended, in its entirety or in part, for WMD purposes, or is aware that software or technology is intended, in its entirety or in part, for WMD purposes[14], then the transferor must not transfer the software or technology in question from a place outside the customs territory to:

    (a)   a destination outside the customs territory[15]; or

    (b)   a destination within the customs territory if the transferor: (i) knows that the final destination of the software or technology is outside the customs territory and knows that no processing or working is to be performed on the software or technology within the customs territory[16]; or (ii) if the destination is the United Kingdom, knows that the software or technology may be or is intended to be used outside the customs territory or has been informed by the Secretary of State that it may be or is intended to be so used[17].

1   Ie subject to the Export Control Order 2008, SI 2008/3231, arts 18, 26 (see PARAS 923, 927): see arts 10(2), 11(2), 12(2).
2   As to the Secretary of State see PARA 902.
3   As to the meaning of 'software' see PARA 917 note 5.
4   As to the meaning of 'technology' see PARA 917 note 6.
5   As to the meaning of 'WMD purposes' see PARA 918 note 4.
6   As to the meaning of 'transfer' see PARA 917 note 12.
7   As to the meaning of 'United Kingdom' see PARA 906 note 7.
8   As to the meaning of 'customs territory' see PARA 918 note 9.

9   See the Export Control Order 2008, SI 2008/3231, art 10.
10 As to the meaning of 'transfer by non-electronic means' see PARA 917 note 12.

11 See the Export Control Order 2008, SI 2008/3231, art 12(1), (2)(a).

12 See the Export Control Order 2008, SI 2008/3231, art 12(1), (2)(b).
13 As to the meaning of 'competent authority' see PARA 918 note 20.

14 See the Export Control Order 2008, SI 2008/3231, art 11(1).

15 See the Export Control Order 2008, SI 2008/3231, art 11(2)(a).

16 See the Export Control Order 2008, SI 2008/3231, art 11(2)(b).

17 See the Export Control Order 2008, SI 2008/3231, art 11(2).

920. Exceptions from prohibition: aircraft, vessels and historic military vehicles. Nothing in the restrictions on the export of military[1] goods and the transfer[2] of military software[3] or technology[4] by electronic means[5] is to be taken to prohibit the exportation[6] of:

(1) any aircraft[7] which is being exported (except to a specified[8] country[9] or destination) after temporary importation[10] into the United Kingdom, provided that there has been no change of ownership or registration since such importation and no military goods have been incorporated into the aircraft since such importation other than by way of replacement for a component essential for the departure of the aircraft[11]; or

(2) any vessel registered or constructed outside the United Kingdom which is being exported (except to a specified[12] country or destination) after temporary importation into the United Kingdom provided that no military goods have been incorporated into the vessel since such importation other than by way of replacement for a component essential for the departure of the vessel[13].

Nothing in the prohibitions on the movement of UK-controlled[14] dual-use[15] goods[16] is to be taken to prohibit the exportation of:

(a) any aircraft the immediately preceding importation of which was on a scheduled journey[17] and which is intended for further scheduled journeys[18];

(b) any aircraft on a scheduled journey[19]; or

(c) any vessel proceeding on a journey providing transport services in the ordinary course of business[20].

Nothing in the restrictions on the export of military goods and the transfer of military software or technology by electronic means[21] or the prohibitions on the movement of UK controlled dual-use goods[22] is to be taken to prohibit the exportation of any aircraft or vessel departing temporarily from the United Kingdom on trials[23].

The prohibition on the export of military goods[24] does not apply to the export of a ground vehicle or component[25] where[26]: (i) the vehicle or component was manufactured more than 50 years before the date of exportation[27]; (ii) the exportation is to a destination in Belgium, France or Germany[28]; (iii) the exportation is for the purposes of a military re-enactment, commemorative event or recreational activity[29]; and (iv) the vehicle or component is to be returned to the United Kingdom within three months of the date of exportation[30].

1 As to the meaning of 'military' see PARA 917 note 11.
2 As to the meaning of 'transfer' see PARA 917 note 12.
3 As to the meaning of 'software' see PARA 917 note 5.
4 As to the meaning of 'technology' see PARA 917 note 6.
5 Ie the Export Control Order 2008, SI 2008/3231, art 3 (see PARA 917): Export Control Order 2008, SI 2008/3231, arts 13(2), 14(1). As to the meaning of 'transfer by electronic means' see PARA 917 note 12.
6 As to the meaning of 'exportation' see PARA 917 note 10.
7 As to the meaning of 'aircraft' see PARA 917 note 10.
8 Ie specified in the Export Control Order 2008, SI 2008/3231, Sch 4 Pt 1, 2 or 3: (see PARAS 922 note 24, 925 note 7): art 13(2).

9 'Country' includes territory: Export Control Order 2008, SI 2008/3231, art 2(1).

10 'Importation' in relation to a vessel, vehicle, submersible vehicle or aircraft means taking it into the United Kingdom, notwithstanding that it is conveying goods or passengers and whether or not it is moving under its own power and cognate expressions are to be construed accordingly:

Export Control Order 2008, SI 2008/3231, art 2(1). As to the meaning of 'vessel' and the meaning of 'vehicle' see PARA 917 note 10. As to the meaning of 'United Kingdom' see PARA 906 note 7.

11 See the Export Control Order 2008, SI 2008/3231, art 13(2).
12 See note 8.
13 See the Export Control Order 2008, SI 2008/3231, art 14(1).
14 As to the meaning of 'UK controlled' see PARA 917 note 15.
15 As to the meaning of 'dual-use' see PARA 917 note 4.
16 Ie the Export Control Order 2008, SI 2008/3231, art 4 (see PARA 917): Export Control Order 2008, SI 2008/3231, arts 13(1), 14(2).
17 'Scheduled journey' means one of a series of journeys which are undertaken between the same two places and which together amount to a systematic service operated in such a manner that its benefits are available to members of the public from time to time seeking to take advantage of it: Export Control Order 2008, SI 2008/3231, art 2(1).
18 See the Export Control Order 2008, SI 2008/3231, art 13(1) (amended by SI 2010/121).
19 See the Export Control Order 2008, SI 2008/3231, art 13(3) (amended by SI 2010/121).
20 See the Export Control Order 2008, SI 2008/3231, art 14(2) (amended by SI 2010/121).
21 See note 5.
22 See note 16.
23 See the Export Control Order 2008, SI 2008/3231, arts 13(4), 14(3) (both amended by SI 2010/121).
24 Ie the Export Control Order 2008, SI 2008/3231, art 3(a) (see PARA 917): art 14A(1).
25 Ie a vehicle or component falling within the Export Control Order 2008, SI 2008/3231 Sch 2, para ML6 (as to Sch 2 see PARA 917 note 11): art 14A(1).
26 Export Control Order 2008, SI 2008/3231, art 14A(1) (art 14A added by SI 2012/1910).
27 Export Control Order 2008, SI 2008/3231, art 14A(2)(a) (art 14A as added: see note 26).
28 Export Control Order 2008, SI 2008/3231, art 14A(2)(b) (art 14A as added: see note 26).
29 Export Control Order 2008, SI 2008/3231, art 14A(2)(c) (art 14A as added: see note 26).
30 Export Control Order 2008, SI 2008/3231, art 14A(2)(d) (art 14A as added: see note 26).

921. Exceptions from prohibition: firearms. Nothing in the restrictions on the export of military[1] goods and the transfer[2] of military software[3] or technology[4] by electronic means[5] is to be taken to prohibit the exportation[6] of any firearm falling within a specified category[7] under the Firearms Directive[8], related ammunition and sight using non-electronic image enhancement for use with such a firearm to any destination in a member state if the following apply[9]:

(1)   the firearm, ammunition and sight using non-electronic image enhancement form part of the personal effects of a person (the 'holder') who is in possession of either a European firearms pass which has been issued to the holder[10] or a document which has been issued to the holder under the corresponding provisions of the law of a member state, which, in either case, relates to the firearm[11]; and

(2)   either: (a) the pass or document referred to in head (1) contains authorisation for the possession of the firearm from the member state of destination and any other member state through which the holder intends that the firearm will pass on its way to that destination; or (b) the holder on request satisfies the proper[12] officer of Her Majesty's Revenue and Customs at the place of exportation that: (i) the exportation of the firearm is necessary to enable the holder to participate in a specified activity as a hunter or marksman[13]; (ii) the firearm falls within the category appropriate to that activity in accordance with the Firearms Directive; and (iii) the exportation or passage of the firearm is not to or through a member state which prohibits or requires an authorisation for the acquisition or possession of the firearm[14].

An exception also applies in respect of firearms authorised to be possessed or, as the case may be, purchased or acquired by a firearm certificate or shot gun certificate[15] or a visitor's firearm or shot gun permit[16]. Nothing in the restrictions on the export of military goods and the transfer of military software or technology by electronic means[17] is to be taken to prohibit the exportation of any firearm to which this exemption applies, related ammunition and sight using non-electronic image enhancement for use with such a firearm to: (A) any destination in a member state by a specified[18] person or body or by the holder of a firearm certificate granted in the Isle of Man[19]; or (B) any other destination other than a specified[20] country or destination[21]. The exception only applies, however, if the firearm, related ammunition and sight using non-electronic image enhancement form part of the personal effects of the holder of the relevant certificate or permit and, in a case to which head (B) applies, the certificate or permit is produced by the holder, or the holder's duly authorised agent, with the firearm and, if carried, ammunition and sight to the proper officer of Her Majesty's Revenue and Customs at the place of exportation[22].

1   As to the meaning of 'military' see PARA 917 note 11.
2   As to the meaning of 'transfer' see PARA 917 note 12.
3   As to the meaning of 'software' see PARA 917 note 5.
4   As to the meaning of 'technology' see PARA 917 note 6.
5   Ie the Export Control Order 2008, SI 2008/3231, art 3 (see PARA 917): art 15(1). As to the meaning of 'transfer by electronic means' see PARA 917 note 12.
6   As to the meaning of 'exportation' see PARA 917 note 10.
7   Ie falling within category B, C or D (see PARA 925) of Annex I to the Firearms Directive (see note 8): Export Control Order 2008, SI 2008/3231, art 15(1).
8   The Firearms Directive is Council Directive (EEC) 91/477 (OJ L256, 13.9.1991, p 51) on control of the acquisition and possession of weapons: Export Control Order 2008, SI 2008/3231, art 2(1).
9   Export Control Order 2008, SI 2008/3231, art 15(1).
10 Ie a European firearms pass which has been issued to the holder under the Firearms Act 1968 s 32A (see CRIMINAL LAW vol 26 (2010) PARA 641): Export Control Order 2008, SI 2008/3231, art 15(2)(a).
11 Export Control Order 2008, SI 2008/3231, art 15(2).
12 'Proper', in relation to the person by, with or to whom, or the place at which, anything is to be done, means the person or place appointed or authorised in that behalf by the Commissioners for Revenue and Customs: Customs and Excise Management Act 1979 s 1(1) (definition applied by the Export Control Order 2008, SI 2008/3231, art 2(1)). As to the Commissioners for Revenue and Customs see CUSTOMS AND EXCISE vol 31 (2012) PARA 921 et seq.
13 Ie one of the activities specified in Council Directive (EEC) 91/477 (OJ L256, 13.9.1991, p 51) art 12(2): Export Control Order 2008, SI 2008/3231, art 15(3)(b)(i).
14 Export Control Order 2008, SI 2008/3231, art 15(3).
15 Ie a firearm certificate or shot gun certificate granted under the Firearms Act 1968 (see CRIMINAL LAW vol 26 (2010) PARAS 582–583): Export Control Order 2008, SI 2008/3231, art 16(1)(a).
16 See the Export Control Order 2008, SI 2008/3231, art 16(1). The reference is to a visitor's firearm or shot gun permit granted under the Firearms (Amendment) Act 1988 s 17 (see CRIMINAL LAW vol 26 (2010) PARA 607): Export Control Order 2008, SI 2008/3231, art 16(1)(b).
17 See note 5; and the Export Control Order 2008, SI 2008/3231, art 16(2).
18 Ie specified in the Firearms Directive art 2(2): Export Control Order 2008, SI 2008/3231, art 16(2)(a)(i).
19 See note 15.
20 Ie specified in the Export Control Order 2008, SI 2008/3231 Sch 4 Pt 1, 2 or 3 (see PARAS 922 note 24, 925 note 7): Export Control Order 2008, SI 2008/3231, art 16(2)(b).
21 See the Export Control Order 2008, SI 2008/3231, art 16(2).
22 See the Export Control Order 2008, SI 2008/3231, art 16(3).

922. Exceptions from prohibition: transit or transhipment. Subject to the following exceptions, nothing in the restrictions on the export of military[1] goods and the transfer[2] of military software[3] or technology[4] by electronic means[5], or the prohibitions or controls on the movement of dual-use[6] goods[7] or the movement of certain medicinal products to the United States of America[8], is to be taken to prohibit the exportation[9] of any goods which are goods in transit[10], provided that the following conditions are met[11]. The conditions are that:

(1) the goods in question either: (a) remain on board a vessel[12], aircraft[13] or vehicle[14] for the entire period that they remain in the United Kingdom[15] or are goods on a through bill of lading, through air waybill or single transport contract and in any event are exported before the end of the period of 30 days beginning with the date of their importation[16]; or (b) are European military items which were originally exported from a member state and the destination of the goods following exportation from the United Kingdom is within the EU[17];

(2) the destination of the goods in question following exportation from the United Kingdom has been determined in the country from which they were originally exported prior to their original exportation in connection with the transaction which has given rise to transit or transhipment and has not been changed prior to their exportation from the United Kingdom, or the goods are being returned to that country[18]; and

(3) the goods in question were exported from that country in accordance with any laws or regulations relating to the exportation of goods applying there at the time of exportation of the goods[19].

The above does not apply to: (i) anti-personnel landmines and components specially designed for them[20]; (ii) category A goods[21]; (iii) equipment, software or technology falling within specified entry levels[22]; (iv) goods being exported to a specified destination[23]; (v) military goods being exported to any specified country or destination[24]; or (vi) category B goods[25] being exported to any specified country or destination[26]. Nor does it apply to the extent that: (A) the exporter, or, if the exporter is not within the United Kingdom, any agent of the exporter within the United Kingdom concerned in the exportation or intended exportation, has been informed by a competent authority[27] that the goods are or may be intended, in their entirety or in part, for WMD purposes[28]; (B) the exporter is aware that the goods are intended, in their entirety or in part, for WMD purposes[29]; or (C) the exporter has grounds for suspecting that the goods are or may be intended, in their entirety or in part, for WMD purposes, unless the exporter had made all reasonable inquiries as to their proposed use and is satisfied that they will not be so used[30].

1 As to the meaning of 'military' see PARA 917 note 11.
2 As to the meaning of 'transfer' see PARA 917 note 12.
3 As to the meaning of 'software' see PARA 917 note 5.
4 As to the meaning of 'technology' see PARA 917 note 6.
5 Ie the Export Control Order 2008, SI 2008/3231, art 3 (see PARA 917): art 17(1) (as amended: see note 11). As to the meaning of 'transfer by electronic means' see PARA 917 note 12.
6 As to the meaning of 'dual-use' see PARA 917 note 4.
7 Ie the Export Control Order 2008, SI 2008/3231, arts 4, 7, 8(1) (see PARAS 917, 918): art 17(1) (as amended: see note 11).
8 Ie the Export Control Order 2008, SI 2008/3231, art 4A (see PARA 917): art 17(1) (as amended: see note 11).
9 As to the meaning of 'exportation' see PARA 917 note 10.
10 As to the meaning of 'in transit' see PARA 918 note 30.
11 See the Export Control Order 2008, SI 2008/3231, art 17(1) (amended by SI 2010/121; SI 2012/929; and by virtue of SI 2010/2843).
12 As to the meaning of 'vessel' see PARA 917 note 10.
13 As to the meaning of 'aircraft' see PARA 917 note 10.

14 As to the meaning of 'vehicle' see PARA 917 note 10.

15 As to the meaning of 'United Kingdom' see PARA 906 note 7.

16 As to the meaning of 'importation' see PARA 920 note 10.

17 Export Control Order 2008, SI 2008/3231, art 17(4)(a) (substituted by SI 2012/1910). As to the EU see EUROPEAN UNION.

18 Export Control Order 2008, SI 2008/3231, art 17(4)(b).

19 Export Control Order 2008, SI 2008/3231, art 17(4)(c).

20 Export Control Order 2008, SI 2008/3231, art 17(2)(a).

21 Export Control Order 2008, SI 2008/3231, art 17(2)(b). As to the meaning of 'category A goods' see PARA 925 note 10.

22 Export Control Order 2008, SI 2008/3231, art 17(2)(c). The reference is to equipment, software or technology falling within Sch 2, entries ML18, ML21 or ML22 (production equipment and components, software or technology specifically related to anti-personnel landmines or category A goods): art 17(2)(c).

23 Export Control Order 2008, SI 2008/3231, art 17(2)(d). The reference is to goods being exported to a destination specified in Sch 4 Pt 1 (see PARA 925 note 7): art 17(2)(d).

24 Export Control Order 2008, SI 2008/3231, art 17(2)(e). The reference is to military goods being exported to any destination specified in Sch 4 Pt 2 (see PARA 925 note 7) or Pt 3 (Afghanistan, Argentina, Burundi, China (People's Republic other than the Special Administrative Regions), Iraq, Liberia, Macao Special Administrative Region, Rwanda, Sierra Leone, Somalia, Tanzania and Uganda): art 17(2)(e).

25 As to the meaning of 'category B goods' see PARA 925 note 13.

26 Export Control Order 2008, SI 2008/3231, art 17(2)(f). The reference to any specified country or destination is to any country or destination specified in Sch 4 Pt 4 (amended by SI 2009/1305; SI 2009/2969; SI 2010/615; SI 2010/2007; SI 2011/825; SI 2011/1304; SI 2011/2010; SI 2013/3182; SI 2014/2357) (Albania, Angola, Benin, Bosnia/Herzegovina, Burkina Faso, Cameroon, Cape Verde, Central African Republic, Chad, Colombia, Congo (Brazzaville), Dubai, East Timor (Timor-Leste), Ethiopia, Gambia, Georgia, Ghana, Guinea Bissau, Haiti, Hong Kong Special Administrative Region, Jamaica, Kenya, Krygyzstan, Mali, Mauritania, Moldova, Montenegro, Morocco, Namibia, Nepal, Niger, Nigeria, Oman, Pakistan, Senegal, Serbia, Sri Lanka, Syria, Taiwan, Tajikistan, Togo, Trinidad & Tobago, Turkmenistan, Ukraine, Uzbekistan, Venezuela and Yemen).

27 As to the meaning of 'competent authority' see PARA 918 note 20.

28 Export Control Order 2008, SI 2008/3231, art 17(3)(a). As to the meaning of 'WMD purposes' see PARA 918 note 4.

29 Export Control Order 2008, SI 2008/3231, art 17(3)(b).

30 Export Control Order 2008, SI 2008/3231, art 17(3)(c).

923. Exceptions from prohibition: software and technology. Nothing in the restrictions on the export of military[1] goods and the transfer[2] of military software[3] or technology[4] by electronic means[5] or the prohibitions on the movement of UK controlled[6] dual-use[7] goods[8] is to be taken to prohibit the transfer of technology: (1) that is in the public domain[9]; (2) that is the minimum technology required for: (a) the installation, operation, maintenance or repair of goods or software that are not military goods or software or UK controlled dual-use goods or software; or (b) a patent application[10]; or (3) in the course of basic scientific research[11].

Nothing in the restrictions on transfer of software or technology for WMD purposes[12] is to be taken to prohibit the transfer of software or technology in the public domain[13].

1 As to the meaning of 'military' see PARA 917 note 11.

2 As to the meaning of 'transfer' see PARA 917 note 12.

3 As to the meaning of 'software' see PARA 917 note 5.

4 As to the meaning of 'technology' see PARA 917 note 6.

5 Ie the Export Control Order 2008, SI 2008/3231, art 3 (see PARA 917): art 18(1) (as amended: see note 9). As to the meaning of 'transfer by electronic means' see PARA 917 note 12.

6 As to the meaning of 'UK controlled' see PARA 917 note 15.

7 As to the meaning of 'dual-use' see PARA 917 note 4.

8   Ie the Export Control Order 2008, SI 2008/3231, art 4 (see PARA 917): art 18(1) (as amended: see note 9).
9   Export Control Order 2008, SI 2008/3231, art 18(1)(a) (art 18(1) amended by SI 2010/121). 'In the public domain' means available without restriction upon further dissemination (no account being taken of restrictions arising solely from copyright): Export Control Order 2008, SI 2008/3231, art 2(1).
10 Export Control Order 2008, SI 2008/3231, art 18(1)(b). As to patent applications see PATENTS AND REGISTERED DESIGNS vol 79 (2014) PARA 314 et seq.
11 Export Control Order 2008, SI 2008/3231, art 18(1)(c). 'Basic scientific research' in art 18 means experimental or theoretical work undertaken principally to acquire new knowledge of the fundamental principles of phenomena or observable facts and not primarily directed towards a specific practical aim or objective: art 18(3).
12 Ie the Export Control Order 2008, SI 2008/3231, arts 10, 11 or 12 (see PARA 919): art 18(2).
13 Export Control Order 2008, SI 2008/3231, art 18(2).

924.   Technical assistance controls.   Subject to the obtaining of a licence[1], no person may directly or indirectly provide to a person or place outside the customs territory[2], and no United Kingdom[3] person may directly or indirectly provide from a place outside the customs territory to any person or place outside the customs territory[4], any technical assistance[5] related to the supply, delivery, manufacture, maintenance or use of anything which that person has been informed by the Secretary of State[6] is or may be intended, in its entirety or in part, for WMD purposes[7] or which that person is aware is intended, in its entirety or in part, for WMD purposes[8].

1   Ie subject to the Export Control Order 2008, SI 2008/3231, art 26 (see PARA 927): art 19(1), (2).
2   See the Export Control Order 2008, SI 2008/3231, art 19(1). As to the meaning of 'customs territory' see PARA 918 note 9.
3   As to the meaning of 'United Kingdom' see PARA 906 note 7.
4   See the Export Control Order 2008, SI 2008/3231, art 19(2).
5   As to the meaning of 'technical assistance' see PARA 917 note 3. For the purposes of the Export Control Order 2008, SI 2008/3231, art 19(1), (2), directly providing technical assistance includes providing technical assistance or agreeing to do so, and indirectly providing technical assistance includes making arrangements under which another person provides technical assistance or agrees to do so: art 19(3).
6   As to the Secretary of State see PARA 902.
7   As to the meaning of 'WMD purposes' see PARA 918 note 4.
8   See the Export Control Order 2008, SI 2008/3231, art 19(1), (2).

925.   Trade controls.   Subject to the obtaining of a licence[1] and to the exception for activities carried out in the Isle of Man[2], no person carrying out activities in the United Kingdom[3] and no United Kingdom person[4] may directly or indirectly: (1) supply or deliver; (2) agree to supply or deliver; or (3) do any act calculated to promote the supply or delivery of, any goods subject to trade controls[5] from one third country[6] to another third country that is an embargoed destination[7].

Subject to the obtaining of a licence and to the exceptions for the movement of goods within the customs territory[8] and for activities carried out in the Isle of Man, no person carrying out activities in the United Kingdom and no United Kingdom person[9] may directly or indirectly: (a) supply or deliver; (b) agree to supply or deliver; or (c) do any act calculated to promote the supply or delivery of, any category A goods[10], where that person knows or has reason to believe that such action or actions will, or may, result in the removal of those goods from one third country to another third country[11].

Subject to the obtaining of a licence and to the exception for activities carried out in the Isle of Man, no person carrying out activities in the United Kingdom and no United Kingdom person[12] may directly or indirectly: (i) supply or deliver;

(ii) agree to supply or deliver; or (iii) do any act calculated to promote the supply or delivery of, any category B goods[13], where that person knows or has reason to believe that such action or actions will, or may, result in the removal of those goods from one third country to another third country[14]. However, nothing in these provisions is to be taken to prohibit the provision of financing or financial services, insurance or reinsurance services or general advertising or promotion services by a person whose only involvement in the activities described above is to provide or agree to provide such services[15]. A person (the 'transporter') whose only involvement in such activities is to provide or agree to provide transportation services in relation to category B goods (the 'relevant goods') only contravenes the prohibition if[16] the transporter arranges the removal of the relevant goods from one third country to another third country[17], or if the transporter, otherwise than in the course of providing services to another person to whom the prohibition applies and who has agreed to provide transportation services in relation to the relevant goods, removes or agrees to remove the relevant goods from one third country to another third country[18]. Nor is anything in these provisions to be taken to prohibit any contract promotion activity[19] that is carried out otherwise than for payment[20].

Subject to the obtaining of a licence and to the exceptions for the movement of goods within the customs territory and for activities carried out in the Isle of Man, no person may directly or indirectly agree to supply or deliver, or do any act calculated to promote the supply or delivery of, any category C goods[21], where that person knows or has reason to believe that such action or actions will, or may, result in the removal of those goods from one third country to another third country[22]. However, this is not to be taken to prohibit the provision of transportation services, financing or financial services, insurance or reinsurance services or general advertising or promotion services, by a person whose only involvement in the activities described above is to provide or agree to provide such services[23], or to prohibit any contract promotion activity that is carried out otherwise than for payment[24].

1 Ie subject to the Export Control Order 2008, SI 2008/3231, art 26 (see PARA 927): art 20(2).
2 Ie the Export Control Order 2008, SI 2008/3231, art 25 (see PARA 926): art 20(2).
3 As to the meaning of 'United Kingdom' see PARA 906 note 7.
4 See the Export Control Order 2008, SI 2008/3231, art 20(1).
5 'Goods subject to trade controls' means goods that are category A goods, category B goods or category C goods (see notes 10, 13, 21 respectively): Export Control Order 2008, SI 2008/3231, art 2(1).
6 'Third country' means any country that is not the United Kingdom or the Isle of Man except that, for the purposes of the Export Control Order 2008, SI 2008/3231, Pt 4 (arts 20–25), goods that are goods in transit are considered to be located in a third country: art 2(1). As to the meaning of 'in transit' see PARA 918 note 30.
7 See the Export Control Order 2008, SI 2008/3231, art 20(2). 'Embargoed destination' means a country listed in Sch 4 Pt 1 (Embargoed and No Exception for Transit) or Pt 2 (Embargoed and Subject to Transit Control for Military Goods): art 2(1). The countries so listed are the Democratic People's Republic of Korea and Iran (Sch 4 Pt 1); and Armenia, Azerbaijan, Belarus, Burma (Myanmar), Democratic Republic of the Congo, Eritrea, Guinea, Ivory Coast (Côte d'Ivoire), Lebanon, Libya, Russia, South Sudan, Sudan, Syria, Zimbabwe (Sch 4 Pt 2 (amended by SI 2009/2969; SI 2010/2007; SI 2011/825; SI 2011/2010; SI 2011/2925; SI 2014/2357)).
8 Ie the Export Control Order 2008, SI 2008/3231, art 24 (see PARA 926): art 21(2).
9 See the Export Control Order 2008, SI 2008/3231, art 21(1).
10 'Category A goods' means goods specified in the Export Control Order 2008, SI 2008/3231, Sch 1 Pt 1: art 2(1). Such goods are:
   (1) certain security and para-military police equipment, ie: (a) goods designed for the execution of human beings, as follows: (i) gallows and guillotines; (ii) electric chairs; (iii) air-tight vaults made of eg steel and glass, designed for the purpose of execution of

human beings by the administration of lethal gas or substance; (iv) automatic drug injection systems designed for the purpose of execution of human beings by the administration of a lethal chemical substance (Sch 1 Pt 1 para 1 (Sch 1 substituted by SI 2010/2007)); (b) restraints specially designed for restraining human beings, as follows: (i) leg-irons, gangchains, shackles and individual cuffs or shackle bracelets except those that are 'ordinary handcuffs'; (ii) restraint chairs unless designed for disabled persons; (iii) shackle boards; (iv) thumb-cuffs and thumb-screws, including serrated thumb-cuffs; (v) electric shock belts (Export Control Order 2008, SI 2008/3231, Sch 1 Pt 1 para 2 (Sch 1 as so substituted)); (c) portable devices designed or modified for the purpose of riot control or self-protection by the administration of an electric shock (eg electric-shock batons, electric-shock shields, stun-guns and electric-shock dart-guns) (Sch 1 Pt 1 para 3 (Sch 1 as so substituted)); (d) components specially designed or modified for the devices in head (c) (Sch 1 Pt 1 para 4 (Sch 1 as so substituted)); (e) hand-held, spiked batons (Sch 1 Pt 1 para 5 (Sch 1 as so substituted));

(2) cluster munitions, explosive submunitions and explosive bomblets, as follows: (a) conventional munitions designed to disperse or release explosive submunitions (see head (c) below), not including: (i) munitions or submunitions designed to dispense flares, smoke, pyrotechnics or chaff; or munitions designed exclusively for an air defence role; (ii) munitions or submunitions designed to produce electrical or electronic effects; (iii) munitions that have all of the following characteristics: (A) each munition contains fewer than ten explosive submunitions; (B) each explosive submunition weighs more than 4 kilograms; (C) each explosive submunition is designed to detect and engage a single target object; (D) each explosive submunition is equipped with an electronic self-destruction mechanism; (E) each explosive submunition is equipped with an electronic self-deactivating feature ('cluster munitions') (Sch 1 Pt 1 para 6(a) (Sch 1 as so substituted)); (b) conventional munitions, weighing less than 20 kilograms each, which are not self-propelled and which, in order to perform their task, are designed to be dispersed or released by a dispenser affixed to an aircraft, and are designed to function by detonating an explosive charge prior to, on or after impact ('explosive bomblets') (Sch 1 Pt 1 para 6(b) (Sch 1 as so substituted)); (c) conventional munitions, weighing less than 20 kilograms each, which, in order to perform their task, are dispersed or released by a cluster munition and are designed to function by detonating an explosive charge prior to, on or after impact ('explosive submunitions') (Sch 1 Pt 1 para 7 (Sch 1 as so substituted)); (d) components specially designed for cluster munitions, explosive submunitions or explosive bomblets (Sch 1 Pt 1 para 8 (Sch 1 as so substituted)).

'Ordinary handcuffs' means handcuffs which have an overall dimension including chain, measured from the outer edge of one cuff to the outer edge of the other cuff, between 150 mm and 240 mm which locked and have not been modified to cause physical pain or suffering; 'self-deactivating feature' means one which automatically renders a munition inoperable by means of the irreversible exhaustion of a component, eg a battery, that is essential to the operation of the munition; and 'self-destruction mechanism' means an incorporated, automatically-functioning mechanism which is in addition to the primary initiating mechanism of a munition and which secures the destruction of the munition into which it is incorporated: Sch 1 definitions.

11 See the Export Control Order 2008, SI 2008/3231, art 21(2).

12 See the Export Control Order 2008, SI 2008/3231, art 22(1).

13 'Category B goods' means goods specified in the Export Control Order 2008, SI 2008/3231, Sch 1 Pt 2: art 2(1). Such goods are:

(1) goods specified in entry ML1.a., ML1.b., ML1.c. or ML2.a. in Sch 2 that are designed to be carried, operated and fired by an individual or by three or fewer individuals acting together, other than mortars with a calibre of 100 mm or more (Sch 1 Pt 2 para 9 (Sch 1 as substituted: see note 10 head (1); Sch 1 Pt 2 substituted by SI 2014/702));

(2) the following goods: (a) accessories specified in entry ML1.d or ML2.c. in the Export Control Order 2008, SI 2008/3231, Sch 2 that are capable of being used in connection with weapons falling within head (1); (b) weapon sights specified in entry ML5.a. in Sch 2 that are designed for use within weapons falling within head (1); and (c) ammunition that is capable of being fired or launched by weapons falling within head (1) (Sch 1 Pt 2 para 10 (as so substituted));

(3) equipment specified in entry ML4.b in Sch 2 that is: (a) specially designed for firing or launching rockets, grenades, missiles or other explosive devices; and (b) designed to be carried, operated and fired by an individual or by three or fewer individuals acting together (Sch 1 Pt 2 para 11) (as so substituted));

(4)   rockets, grenades, missiles and other explosive devices that are: (a) specified in entry ML4 in Sch 2; and (b) capable of being fired or launched from equipment falling within head (3) (Sch 1 Pt 2 para 12 (as so substituted));

(5)   grenades specified in entry ML4 in Sch 2 that are designed to be thrown (Sch 1 Pt 2 para 13 (as so substituted));

(6)   to the extent they do not fall within head (3) or (4), the following goods: (a) man-portable air defence systems (MANPADS), as follows: (i) surface-to-air missile systems designed to be man-portable and operated and fired by a single individual; (ii) surface-to-air missile systems designed to be operated and fired by more than one individual acting as a crew and portable by several individuals; (b) missiles for MANPADS; (c) production equipment specially designed for MANPADS; (d) field test equipment specially designed for MANPADS; (e) specialised training equipment and simulators for MANPADS (Sch 1 Pt 2 para 14 (as so substituted));

(7)   missiles capable of a range of 300 km or more that fall within Sch 2 (Sch 1 Pt 2 para 15 (as so substituted));

(8)   land mines designed to be placed under, on or near the ground or other surface area and to be exploded by the presence, proximity or contact of a vehicle (Sch 1 Pt 2 para 16 (as so substituted));

(9)   components specially designed for goods falling within any of heads (1) to (8) (Sch 1 Pt 2 para 17 (as so substituted));

(10)   vehicles specified in entry ML6.a in Sch 2 as follows: (a) tracked or wheeled self-propelled armoured fighting vehicles with an unladen weight of 16.5 metric tonnes or more and with a main gun with a calibre of 75 mm or more; (b) tracked, semi-tracked or wheeled self-propelled vehicles, with armoured protection, as follows: (i) designed and equipped to transport a squad of four or more infantrymen; or (ii) armed with an integral weapon with a calibre of 12.5 mm or more or a missile launcher (Sch 1 Pt 2 para 18 (as so substituted));

(11)   to the extent that they do not fall within head (1) or (3), the following goods: (a) guns or howitzers specified in entry ML2.a of Sch 2 with a calibre of 75 mm or more; (b) mortars specified in entry ML2.a of Sch 2 with a calibre of 100 mm or more; and (c) multiple-launch rocket systems specified in entry ML4.b of Sch 2 with a calibre of 75 mm or more (Sch 1 Pt 2 para 19 (as so substituted));

(12)   combat aircraft (ie fixed-wing or variable geometry wing aircraft designed, equipped or modified to engage targets by employing guided missiles, unguided rockets, bombs, guns, cannons or other weapons of destruction, including versions of these aircraft which perform specialised electronic warfare, suppression of air defence or reconnaissance missions, not including primary trainer aircraft unless so designed, equipped or modified) and attack helicopters (ie rotary-wing aircraft designed, equipped or modified to engage targets by employing guided or unguided anti-armour, air-to-surface, air-to-subsurface, or air-to-air weapons and equipped with an integrated fir control and aiming system for these weapons, including versions of these aircraft which perform specialised reconnaissance or electronic warfare missions) specified in entry ML10.a or ML10.c of Sch 2 (Sch 1 definitions, Pt 2 para 20 (definitions 'attack helicopter' and 'combat aircraft' added by SI 2014/702; Export Control Order 2008, SI 2008/3231, Sch 1 and Sch 1 Pt 2 as so substituted));

(13)   vessels and submarines specified in entry ML9.a of the Export Control Order 2008, SI 2008/3231, Sch 2 having a standard displacement of 500 metric tons or above, or of less than 500 metric tons and equipped for launching missiles or torpedoes with a range of 25 km or more (Sch 1 Pt 2 para 21 (as so substituted));

(14)   to the extent not covered in heads (1)–(13), the following goods specified in entry ML4 of Sch 2: (a) rockets or missiles capable of a range of 25 km or more other than ground-to-air missiles (ie those surface-to-air missiles which are mounted on fixed land sites or on wheeled or tracked mobile launchers); (b) equipment designed or modified for launching missiles or rockets in head (a) (Sch 1 Pt 2 para 22 (as so substituted)).

'Production' has the same meaning as in Sch 2 (ie all production stages, eg product engineering, manufacture, integration, assembly (mounting), inspection, testing, quality assurance: Sch 2 definitions): Sch 1 definitions (Sch 1 as so substituted). As to Sch 2 see PARA 917 note 11.

14 See the Export Control Order 2008, SI 2008/3231, art 22(2).
15 Export Control Order 2008, SI 2008/3231, art 22(3).
16 Export Control Order 2008, SI 2008/3231, art 22(4).
17 Export Control Order 2008, SI 2008/3231, art 22(5).
18 Export Control Order 2008, SI 2008/3231, art 22(6).

19 'Contract promotion activity' means any act calculated to promote the arrangement or negotiation of a contract for the acquisition, disposal or movement of goods or any agreement to do such an act: Export Control Order 2008, SI 2008/3231, art 2(1).
20 Export Control Order 2008, SI 2008/3231, art 22(7). 'Payment' includes a payment in money or money's worth or in kind whether referable to a particular act or made from time to time but does not include a payment made by way of wages or salary: art 2(1).
21 'Category C goods' means: (1) military goods other than goods specified in the Export Control Order 2008, SI 2008/3231, Sch 1 (see notes 10, 13); (2) portable devices for the purpose of riot control or self-protection by the administration or dissemination of an incapacitating chemical substance; (3) pelargonic acid vanillylamide (PAVA); (4) oleoresin capsicum (OC): art 2(1).
22 See the Export Control Order 2008, SI 2008/3231, art 23(1).
23 Export Control Order 2008, SI 2008/3231, art 23(2).
24 Export Control Order 2008, SI 2008/3231, art 23(3).

926. Trade controls: exceptions. Nothing in the restrictions on trade in category A or category C goods[1] is to be taken to prohibit activities related to the movement of the following goods within the customs territory[2]:

(1) certain goods designed for the execution of human beings[3];

(2) individual cuffs[4];

(3) shackles except those shackles which have an overall dimension including chain, when measured from the outer edge of one cuff to the outer edge of the other cuff, of between 240 mm and 280 mm when locked and have not been modified to cause physical pain or suffering[5];

(4) certain restraints specially designed for restraining human beings and components specially designed or modified for devices designed or modified for the purposes of riot control or self-protection by the administration of an electric shock[6];

(5) portable devices for the purpose of riot control or self-protection by the administration or dissemination of an incapacitating chemical substance[7];

(6) pelargonic acid vanillylamide (PAVA)[8];

(7) oleoresin capsicum (OC)[9].

Nothing in provisions on trade controls[10] is to be taken to prohibit activities carried out in the Isle of Man[11].

1 Ie nothing in the Export Control Order 2008, SI 2008/3231, art 21 or art 23 (see PARA 925): art 24. As to the meaning of 'category A goods' and 'category C goods' see PARA 925 notes 10, 21 respectively.
2 As to the meaning of 'customs territory' see PARA 918 note 9.
3 Export Control Order 2008, SI 2008/3231, art 24(a). The reference to goods designed for the execution of human beings is to those listed in Sch 1 para 1 (see PARA 925 note 10 head (1)(a): art 24(a).
4 Export Control Order 2008, SI 2008/3231, art 24(b).
5 Export Control Order 2008, SI 2008/3231, art 24(c).
6 Export Control Order 2008, SI 2008/3231, art 24(d). The reference to restraints and components is to those listed in Sch 1 paras 2(b), (c), (d), 4 (see PARA 925 note 10 head (1)(b)(ii), (iii), (iv), (d)): art 24(d).
7 Export Control Order 2008, SI 2008/3231, art 24(e).
8 Export Control Order 2008, SI 2008/3231, art 24(f).
9 Export Control Order 2008, SI 2008/3231, art 24(g).
10 Ie the Export Control Order 2008, SI 2008/3231 Pt 4 (arts 20–25) (see text and notes 1–9, 11, PARA 925): art 25.
11 Export Control Order 2008, SI 2008/3231, art 25.

927. Export licences. Nothing in the export or transfer controls, the technical assistance controls or the trade controls under the Export Control Order 2008[1] prohibits an activity that is carried out under the authority of a UK licence[2].

Unless it provides otherwise, a UK licence to export[3] military[4] goods also authorises the export or transfer[5] of the minimum technology[6] required for the installation, operation, maintenance and repair of the goods to the same destination as the goods[7]. A UK licence to supply or deliver goods subject to trade controls also authorises agreeing to supply or deliver, or doing any act calculated to promote the supply or delivery of, the goods[8].

For the purposes of the rules about authorisations in the Dual-use Regulation[9], the Secretary of State is empowered to grant authorisations[10]. The authorisation required by that Regulation[11] for exportation or transfer of goods, software[12] or technology from the United Kingdom[13] is a licence granted by the Secretary of State[14].

A licence[15] granted by the Secretary of State may be: (1) either general[16] or granted to a particular person (except that a licence granted under the Torture Regulation[17] may not be a general licence); (2) limited so as to expire on a specified date unless renewed; (3) subject to, or without, conditions and any such condition may require any act or omission before or after the doing of the act authorised by the licence[18].

The exportation of goods to any destination outside the customs territory[19] is to be regarded as being under the authority of a UK licence to, or for the benefit of, a particular person (the 'licence holder') only if: (a) the licence holder is the person on whose behalf the exportation declaration is made; and (b) the licence holder is established within the customs territory and either the licence holder is the owner of the goods or has a similar right of disposal over them or, if no person who is the owner of the goods or has a similar right of disposal over them is established within the customs territory, the licence holder is a party to one or more contracts under which the ownership of the goods or a similar right of disposal over them has passed to a person not established within the customs territory and pursuant to which the goods are to be, are being or have been exported from the customs territory[20]. This does not apply, however, if no person falls within head (b) above or if the exportation is of goods imported into the United Kingdom for transit or transhipment[21].

1   Ie the Export Control Order 2008, SI 2008/3231, Pt 2 (arts 3–18) (see PARAS 917–923), Pt 3 (art 19) (see PARA 924) or Pt 4 (arts 20–25) (see PARAS 925, 926): art 26(1).
2   Export Control Order 2008, SI 2008/3231, art 26(1). 'UK licence' means a licence in writing granted by the Secretary of State that authorises an act or acts that would otherwise be prohibited by the 2008 Order: art 2(1). As to the Secretary of State see PARA 902.
3   As to the meaning of 'export' see PARA 917 note 10.
4   As to the meaning of 'military' see PARA 917 note 11.
5   As to the meaning of 'transfer' see PARA 917 note 12.
6   As to the meaning of 'technology' see PARA 917 note 6.
7   Export Control Order 2008, SI 2008/3231, art 26(2).
8   Export Control Order 2008, SI 2008/3231, art 26(3).
9   Ie Council Regulation (EC) 428/2009 (OJ L134, 29.5.2009, p 1) art 9. As to the meaning of 'dual-use' see PARA 917 note 4.
10 Export Control Order 2008, SI 2008/3231, art 26(4) (amended by SI 2009/2151).
11 Ie by Council Regulation (EC) 428/2009 art 22(1).
12 As to the meaning of 'software' see PARA 917 note 5.
13 As to the meaning of 'United Kingdom' see PARA 906 note 7.
14 Export Control Order 2008, SI 2008/3231, art 26(5) (amended by SI 2009/2151).
15 'Licence' means a UK licence or an authorisation granted under Council Regulation (EC) 428/2009 (the Dual-use Regulation) or Council Regulation (EC) 1236/2005 (OJ L200, 30.7.2005, p 1) (the Torture Regulation): Export Control Order 2008, SI 2008/3231, art 2(1).
16 'General' in relation to a licence, means not granted to a particular person but available for use generally: Export Control Order 2008, SI 2008/3231, art 2(1).
17 See note 15.

18 Export Control Order 2008, SI 2008/3231, art 26(6).
19 As to the meaning of 'customs territory' see PARA 918 note 9.
20 Export Control Order 2008, SI 2008/3231, art 27(1).
21 Export Control Order 2008, SI 2008/3231, art 27(2). As to the meaning of 'transit or transhipment' see PARA 918 note 30.

928. Export licences: amendment, suspension, revocation and refusal. The Secretary of State[1] may by notice amend, suspend or revoke a licence[2] granted by the Secretary of State, or suspend or revoke a general licence[3] granted by the Secretary of State as it applies to a particular licence user[4]. Such a notice, or a notice of suspension or revocation of authorisation under the Dual-use Regulation[5] or the Torture Regulation[6], is not to take effect until: (1) in the case of a notice affecting all users of a general licence, it has been published in a manner appearing to the Secretary of State to be suitable for securing that the notice is seen by persons likely to be affected by it; (2) in any other case, it has been served on the holder of the licence or on the licence user affected[7].

In the event that the Secretary of State decides not to grant a licence to any person who has applied for one, the applicant must be provided with a written notification setting out the reason or reasons for the decision[8]. In the event that the Secretary of State decides to: (a) suspend a licence other than a general licence, or to suspend a general licence as it applies to a particular licence user[9]; (b) revoke a licence other than a general licence, or to revoke a licence as it applies to a particular licence user[10]; (c) amend a licence other than a general licence, and does not do so at the request of the licence holder[11], the licence holder or licence user must be provided with a written notification setting out the terms of the suspension, where relevant, and the reason or reasons for the decision[12].

Any person who has a right under any of the above provisions to a written notification in respect of a decision made by the Secretary of State has 28 days beginning with the date of the written notification in which to submit an appeal against the decision in writing to the Secretary of State, Export Control Organisation, Department for Business, Innovation and Skills[13]. Any appeal so submitted must specify the grounds on which that appeal is made and may provide further information or arguments in support of the appeal[14]. Pending determination of any such appeal, any decision taken by the Secretary of State continues to have effect[15].

1   As to the Secretary of State see PARA 902.
2   As to the meaning of 'licence' see PARA 927 note 15.
3   As to the meaning of 'general' in relation to a licence see PARA 927 note 16.
4   Export Control Order 2008, SI 2008/3231, art 32(1). 'Licence user' means a person who is registered under art 28 (see PARA 931) to use a general licence or who is entitled to use a general licence without registration owing to the terms of that general licence: art 2(1).
5   Ie a notice under Council Regulation (EC) 428/2009 (OJ L134, 29.5.2009, p 1) art 13(1), (4) (suspension, revocation, etc of authorisations and suspension, revocation, etc of authorisations for brokering services respectively): Export Control Order 2008, SI 2008/3231, art 32(2) (as amended: see note 7).
6   Ie a notice under Council Regulation (EC) 1236/2005 (OJ L200, 30.7.2005, p 1) art 9(4) (suspension, revocation, etc of authorisations): Export Control Order 2008, SI 2008/3231, art 32(2) (as amended: see note 7).
7   Export Control Order 2008, SI 2008/3231, art 32(2) (amended by SI 2009/2151).
8   Export Control Order 2008, SI 2008/3231, art 33(1).
9   See the Export Control Order 2008, SI 2008/3231, art 33(2).
10   See the Export Control Order 2008, SI 2008/3231, art 33(3).
11   See the Export Control Order 2008, SI 2008/3231, art 33(4).
12   See the Export Control Order 2008, SI 2008/3231, art 33(2)–(4).

13 Export Control Order 2008, SI 2008/3231, art 33(5) (amended by SI 2009/2748).
14 Export Control Order 2008, SI 2008/3231, art 33(6).
15 Export Control Order 2008, SI 2008/3231, art 33(7).

929. European military items. The Secretary of State[1] is empowered[2] to grant certificates to recipients established in the United Kingdom[3] of European military items[4] under authorisations granted by competent authorities[5] in other member states[6].

Before granting a certificate, the Secretary of State must establish the reliability of the recipient undertaking and in particular its capacity to observe limitations on the export[7] of European military items which are received under an authorisation granted by a competent authority in another member state[8].

Such a certificate must contain: (1) the name of the competent authority issuing the certificate[9]; (2) the name and address of the recipient[10]; (3) a statement of the recipient's conformity with assessment criteria[11]; (4) the date of issue and the period of validity of the certificate[12]. It may be subject to conditions relating to the provision of information necessary to verify compliance with assessment criteria[13] or to its suspension or revocation[14].

The Secretary of State may by notice amend, suspend or revoke a certificate[15]. If the Secretary of State decides to amend, suspend or revoke a certificate[16], or decides not to grant a certificate to an applicant[17], the certificate holder or applicant must be provided with a written notification setting out the reason for the decision[18]. A person who has a right to such a written notification may within 28 days beginning with the date of the written notification submit an appeal against the decision by notice in writing to the Secretary of State, Export Control Organisation, Department for Business, Innovation and Skills[19]. Pending determination of an appeal the Secretary of State's decision continues to have effect[20].

1 As to the Secretary of State see PARA 902.
2 Ie empowered for the purposes of the Defence-related Products Directive art 9(1): Export Control Order 2008, SI 2008/3231, art 28A(1) (art 28A as added: see note 6). The Defence-related Products Directive is European Parliament and Council Directive (EC) 2009/43 (OJ L146, 10.6.2009, p 1) simplifying terms and conditions of transfers of defence-related products within the European Union: Export Control Order 2008, SI 2008/3231, art 2(1) (definition added by SI 2012/1910).
3 As to the meaning of 'United Kingdom' see PARA 906 note 7.
4 'European military items' means goods, software or technology listed in the Export Control Order 2008, SI 2008/3231, Sch 2 (see PARA 917 note 11) except in entry PL5017 or PL5001: art 2(1) (definition added by SI 2012/1910). As to the meaning of 'software' see PARA 917 note 5; and as to the meaning of 'technology' see PARA 917 note 6.
5 As to the meaning of 'competent authority' see PARA 918 note 20.
6 Export Control Order 2008, SI 2008/3231, art 28A(1) (art 28A added by SI 2012/1910).
7 As to the meaning of 'export' see PARA 917 note 10.
8 Export Control Order 2008, SI 2008/3231, art 28A(2) (art 28A as added: see note 6). The recipient's reliability must be assessed according to the following criteria:
    (1)   proven experience in defence activities, taking into account in particular the undertaking's record of compliance with export restrictions including any relevant court decisions, any authorisation held by the undertaking to produce or market European military items, and the employment of experienced management staff by the recipient (art 28A(2)(a) (art 28A as so added));
    (2)   relevant industrial activity in European military items within the EU and in particular capacity for system or sub-system integration (art 28A(2)(b) (art 28A as so added));
    (3)   the appointment of a senior executive as the dedicated officer personally responsible for exports and transfers (art 28A(2)(c) (art 28A as so added));
    (4)   the provision of a written undertaking, signed by the senior executive referred to in head (3), that the undertaking will: (a) take all necessary steps to observe and enforce any specific condition of an authorisation granted by a competent authority in another

member state relating to end-use and re-export of any specific component or product received (art 28A(2)(d) (art 28A as so added)); and (b) provide to the Secretary of State upon request detailed information concerning the end-users or end-use of all European military items exported, transferred or received under an authorisation granted by a competent authority in another member state (art 28A(2)(e) (art 28A as so added));

(5)   the provision of a written description, signed by the senior executive referred to in head (3), of the undertaking's internal compliance programme or export and transfer management systems, such description providing details of the organisational, human and technical resources allocated to the management of exports and transfers, the chain of responsibility within the undertaking, internal audit procedures, awareness-raising and staff-training, physical and technical security arrangements, record-keeping and traceability of exports and transfers (art 28A(2)(f) (art 28A as so added)).

As to the EU see EUROPEAN UNION. As to the meaning of 'transfer' see PARA 917 note 12.

9   Export Control Order 2008, SI 2008/3231, art 28A(3)(a) (art 28A as added: see note 6).
10 Export Control Order 2008, SI 2008/3231, art 28A(3)(b) (art 28A as added: see note 6).
11 Export Control Order 2008, SI 2008/3231, art 28A(3)(c) (art 28A as added: see note 6). The reference to assessment criteria is to the criteria referred to in art 28A(2) (see note 8): art 28A(3)(c) (art 28A as so added).
12 Export Control Order 2008, SI 2008/3231, art 28A(3)(d) (art 28A as added: see note 6). The period of validity of a certificate granted by the Secretary of State must not exceed five years: art 28A(4) (art 28A as so added).
13 See note 11.
14 Export Control Order 2008, SI 2008/3231, art 28A(5) (art 28A as added: see note 6).
15 Export Control Order 2008, SI 2008/3231, art 28A(6) (art 28A as added: see note 6).
16 Export Control Order 2008, SI 2008/3231, art 33A(2) (art 33A added by SI 2012/1910).
17 Export Control Order 2008, SI 2008/3231, art 33A(1) (art 33A as added: see note 16).
18 Export Control Order 2008, SI 2008/3231, art 33A(1), (2) (art 33A as added: see note 16).
19 Export Control Order 2008, SI 2008/3231, art 33A(3) (art 33A as added: see note 16). A notice of appeal must specify the grounds on which it is made and may provide further information or arguments in support of the appeal: art 33A(4) (art 33A as so added).
20 Export Control Order 2008, SI 2008/3231, art 33A(5) (art 33A as added: see note 16).

930.   Record keeping.   The following must keep detailed registers or records:

(1)   a person who acts under the authority of a general licence[1] granted by the Secretary of State[2];

(2)   a person who acts under the authority of the Union General Export Authorisation[3] while established in the United Kingdom[4]; and

(3)   a person who acts under the authority or an individual licence to export[5] or transfer[6] European military items[7] within the EU[8].

The registers or records must contain sufficient detail as may be necessary to allow specified information[9], where appropriate, to be identified in relation to each act carried out under the authority of the licence or authorisation[10]. They must be kept:

(a)   in the case of a general licence authorising an activity that would otherwise be prohibited by trade controls[11], for at least four years from the end of the calendar year in which the authorised act took place;

(b)   in any other case, for at least three years from the end of the calendar year in which the authorised act took place,

or for such longer period as may be specified in the licence or authorisation[12].

Not later than 30 days after[13] the first exportation or transfer of particular information security items[14] from the United Kingdom under the authority of the Union General Export Authorisation by any person, that person must (in addition to any particulars already given to the Secretary of State[15]) give to the Secretary of State in relation to those goods or that software or technology written notice[16] of such of the required information[17] as is in their possession and such other of that information as they can reasonably be expected to obtain within that time[18]. A person who has given to the Secretary of State such written notice of information must, not later than 30 days after any change in that information, give to the Secretary of State written notice of the changed information[19]. A person who exports or transfers non-specified[20] information security items to a destination within the customs territory[21] must maintain registers or records in relation to each such exportation or transfer that contain such of the required information[22] as they can reasonably be expected to obtain and such other of that information as comes into their possession[23].

1 As to the meaning of 'general licence' see PARA 927 note 16. As to licences generally see PARA 927.

2 Export Control Order 2008, SI 2008/3231, art 29(1)(a) (art 29(1) substituted by SI 2012/1910). As to the Secretary of State see PARA 902.

3 'Union General Export Authorisation' has the same meaning as in Council Regulation (EC) 428/2009 (OJ L134, 29.5.2009, p 1) art 2(9) (ie the authorisation constituted by Council Regulation (EC) 1334/2000 (OJ L159, 30.6.2000, p 1) art 6(1), Annex II: European Union (Amendment) Act 2008 s 3(6)): Export Control Order 2008, SI 2008/3231, art 2(1) (definition added by SI 2012/1910).

4 Export Control Order 2008, SI 2008/3231, art 29(1)(b) (art 29(1) as substituted: see note 2). As to the meaning of 'United Kingdom' see PARA 906 note 7.

5 As to the meaning of 'export' see PARA 917 note 10.

6 As to the meaning of 'transfer' see PARA 917 note 12.

7 As to the meaning of 'European military items' see PARA 929 note 4.

8 Export Control Order 2008, SI 2008/3231, art 29(1)(c) (art 29(1) as substituted: see note 2). As to the EU see EUROPEAN UNION.

9 The information to be identified is: (1) a description of the act; (2) a description of the goods, software or technology to which the act relates; (3) the date of the act or the dates between which the act took place; (4) the quantity of the goods (if any) to which the act relates; (5) the name and address of the person referred to in the Export Control Order 2008, SI 2008/3231, art 29(1); (6) the name and address of any consignee of the goods to which the act relates or any recipient of the software or technology to which the act relates; (7) in so far as it is known to the person referred to in art 29(1), the name and address of the end-user of the goods, software or technology to which the act relates; (8) if different from the person referred to in art 29(1), the name and address of the supplier of the goods (if any) to which the act relates; (9) any further information required by the licence or authorisation referred to in art 29(1): art 29(2)(a)–(i). The documents and records to be kept in accordance with Council Regulation (EC) 428/2009 art 22(8) (records of exportation and transfer of listed items within the customs territory) are the registers or records referred to in the Export Control Order 2008, SI 2008/3231, art 29(2)(a)–(i): art 29(4) (amended by SI 2009/2151). As to the meaning of 'software' and 'technology' see PARA 917 notes 5, 6.

10 See the Export Control Order 2008, SI 2008/3231, art 29(2).

11 Ie by the Export Control Order 2008, SI 2008/3231, Pt 4 (arts 21–25) (see PARAS 925, 926): art 29(3)(a).

12 Export Control Order 2008, SI 2008/3231, art 29(3).

13 Any reference in the Export Control Order 2008, SI 2008/3231, to time after an event is a reference to a period of that length of time beginning on the day of that event: art 2(3).

14 Ie information security systems not specified in the Export Control Order 2008, SI 2008/3231, Sch 5. 'Information security items' means goods, software and technology specified in Council Regulation (EC) 428/2009 (OJ L134, 29.5.2009, p 1) Annex I Pt 2 Category 5: Export Control Order 2008, SI 2008/3231, art 2(1). The information security items specified in Sch 5 are the following software and technology, to the extent that such software or technology is for an intra-group or collaborative end-use: (1) cryptography development software specified in Council Regulation (EC) 428/2009 (OJ L134, 29.5.2009, p 1) Annex I, Pt 2, Category 5, item 5D002, other than software having the characteristics, or performing or simulating the functions, of equipment designed or modified to perform cryptanalytic functions; (2) cryptography development technology specified in Annex I entry 5E002, other than technology for the development, production or use of: (a) equipment designed or modified to perform cryptanalytic functions; or (b) software having the characteristics, or performing or simulating the functions, of equipment designed or modified to perform cryptanalytic functions: Export Control Order 2008, SI 2008/3231, Sch 5 para 2. 'Development' has the same meaning as in Sch 2 (ie all stages prior to production eg design, design research, design analyses, design concepts, assembly and testing of prototypes, pilot production schemes, design data, process of

transforming design data into goods or software, configuration design, integration design, layouts: Sch 2 definitions): Sch 5 para 1. As to Sch 2 see PARA 917 note 11. 'Intra-group or collaborative end-use' means: (i) use by the exporter, or a subsidiary undertaking or parent undertaking of the exporter, in that person's own commercial cryptographic goods; or (ii) use by a business or academic collaborator of the exporter in that person's own commercial cryptographic goods in accordance with the terms of a collaboration agreement with the exporter: Sch 5 para 1. 'Parent undertaking' and 'subsidiary undertaking' have the same meanings as in the Companies Act 2006 (see s 1162, Sch 7; and COMPANIES vol 14 (2009) PARA 26); 'collaboration agreement' means an agreement for the carrying out of work comprising or related to research into the development of cryptography or cryptographic goods or software; and 'business or academic collaborator', in relation to an exporter, means a person who is either: (A) working by way of business in research and development of cryptography or cryptographic goods or software; or (B) teaching, or undertaking research as a member of or at a university or institution of higher education into, cryptography or cryptographic goods or software, and with whom the exporter has previously entered into a collaboration agreement: Export Control Order 2008, SI 2008/3231, Sch 5 para 1. 'Production', 'technology' and 'use' have the same meanings as in Sch 2: Sch 5 para 1. As to the meaning of 'production' so defined see PARA 925 note 13. 'Technology' means specific information necessary for the development, production or use of goods or software; and 'use' means operation, installation (eg on-site installation), maintenance, checking, repair, overhaul and refurbishing: Sch 2 definitions. 'Information' may take forms including, not limited to: blueprints, plans, diagrams, models, formulae, tables, source code, engineering designs and specifications, manuals and instructions written or recorded on other media or devices; and 'source code' is a convenient expression of one or more processes which may be turned by a programming system into equipment executable form: Sch 2 definitions.

15 Ie given under the Export Control Order 2008, SI 2008/3231, art 28(1) (see PARA 931): art 30(1).

16 Any notice to be given to the Secretary of State by a person under the Export Control Order 2008, SI 2008/3231, may be given by an agent of that person; and must be sent by post or delivered to the Secretary of State at the Export Control Organisation, Department for Business, Innovation and Skills: art 44 (amended by SI 2009/2748). As to agency see AGENCY vol 1 (2008) PARA 1 et seq.

17 Ie the information specified in the Export Control Order 2008, SI 2008/3231, Sch 5. The information so specified is: (1) a general description of the goods, software or technology, such as might be contained in a product brochure; (2) descriptions of all relevant encryption algorithms and key management schemes, and descriptions of how they are used by the goods, software or technology (eg which algorithm is used for authentication, which for confidentiality and which for key exchange); and details (eg source code) of how they are implemented (eg how keys are generated and distributed, how key length is governed and how the algorithm and keys are called by the software); (3) details of any measures taken to preclude user modification of the encryption algorithm, key management scheme or key length; (4) details of pre- or post-processing of data, such as compression of plain text or packetisation of encrypted data; (5) details of programming interfaces that can be used to gain access to the cryptographic functionality of the goods, software or technology; and (6) a list of any protocols to which the goods, software or technology adhere: Sch 5 para 3.

18 Export Control Order 2008, SI 2008/3231, art 30(1) (amended by SI 2012/1910).

19 Export Control Order 2008, SI 2008/3231, art 30(2).

20 Ie not specified in Council Regulation (EC) 428/2009 (OJ L134, 29.5.2009, p 1) Annex IV: Export Control Order 2008, SI 2008/3231, art 30(3).

21 As to the meaning of 'customs territory' see PARA 918 note 9.

22 See note 17.

23 Export Control Order 2008, SI 2008/3231, art 30(3). The registers or records referred to in art 30(3) must be kept for at least three years from the end of the calendar year in which the exportation or transfer took place: art 30(4).

931. Inspection of records. Not later than 30 days after[1]:

(1)   any person first does any act under the authority of a general licence[2] granted by the Secretary of State[3] that does not provide otherwise; or

(2)   any person established in the United Kingdom[4] first does any act under the authority of the Union General Export Authorisation[5],

the person in question must give written notice to the Secretary of State[6] of the name and the address at which copies of the records required to be kept under the Export Control Order 2008[7] may be inspected by any person authorised by the Secretary of State or by the Commissioners for Revenue and Customs[8]. A person (a 'relevant person') who is required[9] to keep registers, records or documents ('compulsory records') must permit those compulsory records to be inspected and copied by a person so authorised[10].

A person authorised by the Secretary of State or the Commissioners who produces, if required to do so, a duly authenticated document showing their authority, has the right at any reasonable hour to enter for the purpose of inspection:

(a)   in the case of compulsory records required to be kept under the Export Control Order 2008[11], the premises the address of which has been most recently notified to the Secretary of State[12] in relation to the records; or

(b)   in the case of compulsory records required to be kept under the Dual-use Regulation[13], the premises the address of which has been most recently notified to the Secretary of State[14] in relation to the records or, if none, such other premises the address of which has been notified for this purpose[15].

Where a relevant person keeps compulsory records in a form which is not legible, the relevant person must at the request of a person authorised by the Secretary of State or the Commissioners reproduce the relevant records in a legible form[16].

1   As to references to time after an event see PARA 930 note 13.
2   As to the meaning of 'general licence' see PARA 927 note 16; and as to licences generally see PARA 927.
3   As to the Secretary of State see PARA 902.
4   As to the meaning of 'United Kingdom' see PARA 906 note 7.
5   As to the meaning of 'Union General Export Authorisation' see PARA 930 note 3.
6   As to the giving of notice to the Secretary of State see PARA 930 note 16.
7   Ie required under the Export Control Order 2008, SI 2008/3231, art 29 or 30 (see PARA 930) or under Council Regulation (EC) 1334/2000 (OJ L159, 30.6.2000, p 1) art 20 (record-keeping): art 28(1) (as amended: see note 8).
8   See the Export Control Order 2008, SI 2008/3231, art 28(1) (amended by SI 2009/2151; SI 2012/1910). The reference to any person authorised is to any person authorised under the Export Control Order 2008, SI 2008/3231, art 31 (see text and notes 9–16): art 28(1). As to the Commissioners for Revenue and Customs see CUSTOMS AND EXCISE vol 31 (2012) PARA 921 et seq. A person who has given to the Secretary of State such notice must give notice of any change in the particulars provided, no later than 30 days after the change: art 28(2).
9   Ie under the Export Control Order 2008, SI 2008/3231, art 29 or 30 (see PARA 930) or Council Regulation (EC) 428/2009 (OJ L134, 29.5.2009, p 1) art 20 (record-keeping) or art 22(8) (records of exportation and transfer of listed items within the customs territory): art 31(1) (as amended: see note 10).
10   See the Export Control Order 2008, SI 2008/3231, art 31(1) (amended by SI 2009/2151).
11   Ie under the Export Control Order 2008, SI 2008/3231, art 29 or 30 (PARA 930): art 31(2)(a) (art 31(2) as amended: see note 15).
12   Ie under the Export Control Order 2008, SI 2008/3231, art 28 (see text and notes 1–8): art 31(2)(a) (art 31(2) as amended: see note 15).
13   Ie under Council Regulation (EC) 428/2009 (OJ L134, 29.5.2009, p 1) art 20 or art 22(8): art 31(2)(b) (art 31(2) as amended: see note 15).
14   See note 12.
15   Export Control Order 2008, SI 2008/3231, art 31(2) (amended by SI 2009/2151).
16   Export Control Order 2008, SI 2008/3231, art 31(3).

932.   Customs powers.   Where a person (the 'exporter') has exported[1] goods and required a licence[2] to do so[3], the Commissioners for Revenue and Customs[4] may require the exporter to provide within such time as the Commissioners may determine evidence of the destination to which the goods in question were delivered[5].

Goods in relation to which a licence has not been granted and which are brought to any place in the United Kingdom[6] for the purpose of being exported may be detained by the proper[7] officer of Her Majesty's Revenue and Customs as if they were liable to forfeiture, if and so long as that officer has reason to believe that a competent authority[8] (after, if necessary, having had the impending exportation brought to its attention) might inform the exporter: (1) that the goods are or may be intended, in their entirety or in part, for WMD purposes[9]; or (2) as provided[10] in the Dual-use Regulation[11].

Any dual-use goods[12] in relation to which a licence has been granted which are brought to any place in the United Kingdom for the purpose of being exported to a destination outside the customs territory[13] may be detained by a proper officer of Her Majesty's Revenue and Customs for a period of ten working days[14] as if they were liable to forfeiture where that officer or the Secretary of State[15] has grounds for suspicion that: (a) relevant information was not taken into account when the licence was granted; or (b) circumstances have materially changed since the issue of the licence[16]. The period may be extended to 30 working days where the Secretary of State certifies that a request for such an extension[17] has been received from the member state which granted the licence[18].

Where the Commissioners for Revenue and Customs investigate or propose to investigate any matter with a view to determining: (i) whether there are grounds for believing that an offence has been committed by reason of a contravention of specified provisions of the Export Control Order 2008[19] or the Dual-use Regulation or the Torture Regulation[20]; (ii) whether a person should be prosecuted for such an offence, the matter must be treated as an assigned matter[21]. Specified provisions of the Customs and Excise Management Act 1979 apply with modifications[22].

1   As to the meaning of 'export' see PARA 917 note 10.
2   As to the meaning of 'licence' see PARA 927 note 15.
3   Export Control Order 2008, SI 2008/3231, art 39(1).
4   As to the Commissioners for Revenue and Customs see CUSTOMS AND EXCISE vol 31 (2012) PARA 921 et seq.
5   Export Control Order 2008, SI 2008/3231, art 39(2). A person who fails to comply with a requirement imposed by the Commissioners under art 39(2) commits an offence and is liable on summary conviction to a fine not exceeding level 4 on the standard scale: art 39(3). As to the standard scale see SENTENCING AND DISPOSITION OF OFFENDERS vol 92 (2010) PARA 142.
6   As to the meaning of 'United Kingdom' see PARA 906 note 7.
7   As to the meaning of 'proper' see PARA 921 note 12.
8   As to the meaning of 'competent authority' see PARA 918 note 20.
9   As to the meaning of 'WMD purposes' see PARA 918 note 4.
10 Ie provided in Council Regulation (EC) 428/2009 (OJ L134, 29.5.2009, p 1) art 4(2) (military end-use control) or 4(3) (end-use control relating to use in items exported or transferred without authorisation): Export Control Order 2008, SI 2008/3231, art 40(1)(b).
11 Export Control Order 2008, SI 2008/3231, art 40(1). 'Dual-use Regulation' means Council Regulation (EC) 428/2009 (OJ L134, 29.5.2009, p 1) as amended from time to time: see the Export Control Order 2008, SI 2008/3231, art 2(1) (definition substituted by SI 2009/2151).
12 Ie goods listed in Council Regulation (EC) 428/2009 (OJ L134, 29.5.2009, p 1) Annex I: Export Control Order 2008, SI 2008/323, art 40(2) (as amended: see note 16). As to the meaning of 'dual-use' see PARA 917 note 4.
13 As to the meaning of 'customs territory' see PARA 918 note 9.
14 For these purposes, 'working day' means a day that is not a Saturday or Sunday, Christmas Day, Good Friday or any day that is a bank holiday under the Banking and Financial Dealings

Act 1971 (see TIME vol 97 (2015) PARA 321) in the part of the United Kingdom where the goods referred to in the Export Control Order 2008, SI 2008/3231, art 40(2) have been detained: art 40(3).

15 As to the Secretary of State see PARA 902.

16 Export Control Order 2008, SI 2008/3231, art 40(2) (amended by SI 2009/2151).

17 Ie in accordance with Council Regulation (EC) 1334/2000 (OJ L159, 30.6.2000, p 1) art 16(4) (customs procedures): Export Control Order 2008, SI 2008/3231, art 40(2) (as amended: see note 16).

18 Export Control Order 2008, SI 2008/3231, art 40(2) (as amended: see note 16).

19 Ie the Export Control Order 2008, SI 2008/3231, art 3, 4, 4A, 6, 7, 8, 9, 11, 12, 19, 20, 21, 22, 23, 37, 38 or 39 (see PARAS 917, 918, 919, 924, 925, 932, 934), or art 31 so far as it relates to the powers of the Commissioners (see PARA 931): art 41(1) (as amended: see note 21).

20 'Torture Regulation' means Council Regulation (EC) 1236/2005 (OJ L200, 30.7.2005, p 1) as amended from time to time: see the Export Control Order 2008, SI 2008/3231, art 2(1).

21 Export Control Order 2008, SI 2008/3231, art 41(1) (amended by SI 2010/121; SI 2010/2843; SI 2011/580; SI 2012/929). As to assigned matters see CUSTOMS AND EXCISE vol 31 (2012) PARA 1164.

22 The application is as follows:
    (1)   the Customs and Excise Management Act 1979 s 77A (provision as to information powers) (see CUSTOMS AND EXCISE vol 31 (2012) PARA 1045) applies to a person concerned in an activity which, if not authorised by a licence, would contravene: (a) the Export Control Order 2008, SI 2008/3231, art 3, 4, 4A, 6, 7, 8, 9, 11, 12, 19, 20, 21, 22 or 23 (see PARAS 917, 918, 919, 924, 925); (b) the Dual-use Regulation; or (c) the Torture Regulation, and accordingly references in the Customs and Excise Management Act 1979 s 77A to exportation are to be read as including any such activity (Export Control Order 2008, SI 2008/3231, art 41(2) (amended by SI 2010/121; SI 2010/2843; SI 2011/580; SI 2012/929));
    (2)   the Customs and Excise Management Act 1979 s 138 (provision as to arrest of persons) (see CUSTOMS AND EXCISE vol 31 (2012) PARA 1149) applies to the arrest of a person for an offence under the Export Control Order 2008, SI 2008/3231, as it applies to the arrest of a person for an offence under the Customs and Excise Acts (Export Control Order 2008, SI 2008/3231, art 41(3));
    (3)   the Customs and Excise Management Act 1979 ss 145, 146, 146A, 147, 148, 150, 151, 152, 154, and 155 (proceedings for offences, mitigation of penalties, proof and other matters) (see CUSTOMS AND EXCISE vol 31 (2012) PARAS 1184, 1185, 1193 et seq, 1198) apply in relation to offences and penalties under the Export Control Order 2008, SI 2008/3231, as they apply in relation to offences and penalties under the Customs and Excise Acts (Export Control Order 2008, SI 2008/3231, art 41(4));
    (4)   for the purposes of the application of the Customs and Excise Management Act 1979 s 145 (see CUSTOMS AND EXCISE vol 31 (2012) PARA 1193) to the Export Control Order 2008, SI 2008/3231, only offences related to contraventions of the provisions referred to in art 41(1)(a) (see notes 19–21) are offences under the Customs and Excise Acts (Export Control Order 2008, SI 2008/3231, art 41(5));
    (5)   in the case of an offence committed in connection with a prohibition or restriction on exportation in the Export Control Order 2008, SI 2008/3231, Pt 2 (arts 3–18) (see PARAS 917–923), the Dual-use Regulation or the Torture Regulation, the Customs and Excise Management Act 1979 ss 68(3)(b) and 170(3)(b) (see CUSTOMS AND EXCISE vol 31 (2012) PARAS 1027, 1175) have effect as if for the words '7 years' there were substituted the words '10 years' (Export Control Order 2008, SI 2008/3231, art 42).
    'Customs and Excise Acts' has the same meaning as in the Customs and Excise Management Act 1979 s 1 (see PARA 908 note 1): Export Control Order 2008, SI 2008/3231, art 2(1).

933. Offences in connection with prohibitions and restrictions.

A person who contravenes or fails to comply with any of the following commits an offence and is liable on summary conviction to a fine not exceeding level 3 on the standard scale[1]:

    (1)   a prohibition relating to export and transfer controls[2] or trade controls[3];

    (2)   a prohibition or restriction in the provisions of the Dual-use Regulation[4] dealing with controls on listed goods[5], military end-use[6], end-use in

items exported or transferred without authorisation[7] or on the exportation or transfer of sensitive items within the customs territory[8];

(3) the requirements of the Dual-use Regulation as to records and documents[9];

(4) an export prohibition or restriction in the Torture Regulation[10] in respect of the supply of technical assistance[11] as defined in that Regulation[12];

(5) an import prohibition or restriction in the Torture Regulation in respect of the acceptance of technical assistance[13] as defined in that Regulation[14].

A person who does any of the following commits and offence and may be arrested:

(a) contravenes a prohibition relating to export and transfer controls[15] or technical assistance controls[16] that is engaged because the person has been informed, is aware, or has grounds for suspecting, that goods, software[17] or technology[18] are or may be intended, in their entirety or in part, for WMD purposes[19];

(b) is knowingly concerned in activity prohibited by export and transfer controls[20], technical assistance controls[21] or trade controls[22] with intent to evade the relevant prohibition[23];

(c) contravenes a prohibition or restriction in the Dual-use Regulation relating to end-use control for WMD purposes[24] or brokering services[25];

(d) fails to comply with the requirement in that Regulation to notify the competent authority[26] in the case of awareness of end-use for certain military or WMD purposes[27];

(e) is knowingly concerned in an activity prohibited or restricted by any of the provisions of the Dual-use Regulation mentioned in heads (2), (c)[28] with intent to evade the relevant prohibition or restriction[29];

(f) is knowingly concerned in the provision of technical assistance as defined in the Torture Regulation with intent to evade the prohibition on the provision of technical assistance in that Regulation[30];

(g) is knowingly concerned in the acceptance of technical assistance as defined in the Torture Regulation with intent to evade the prohibition on the acceptance of technical assistance in that Regulation[31].

A person guilty of one of the offences listed in heads (a) to (g) is liable:

(i) on summary conviction, to a fine not exceeding the statutory maximum[32] or to imprisonment for a term not exceeding:

(A) in the case of the offences described in heads (a) to (f), six months[33]; or

(B) in the case of the offence described in head (g), three months,

or to both a fine and imprisonment; or

(ii) on indictment, to a fine or to imprisonment for a term not exceeding:

(A) in the case of the offences described in heads (a) to (d), (g), two years; or

(B) in the case of the offences described in heads (e), (f), ten years,

or to both a fine and imprisonment[34].

1 As to the standard scale see SENTENCING AND DISPOSITION OF OFFENDERS vol 92 (2010) PARA 142.

2 Ie a prohibition in the Export Control Order 2008, SI 2008/3231, Pt 2 (arts 3–18) (see PARAS 917–923): art 34(1). Article 34(1), (5) (see heads (1), (b) above) does not create an offence

related to prohibitions on the exportation of goods (see the Customs and Excise Management Act 1979; and CUSTOMS AND EXCISE vol 31 (2012) PARA 1026 et seq): Export Control Order 2008, SI 2008/3231, art 34(7).

3   See the Export Control Order 2008, SI 2008/3231, art 34(1). The reference to a prohibition is to a prohibition in the Export Control Order 2008, SI 2008/3231, Pt 4 (arts 20–25) (see PARAS 925, 926): art 34(1). See also note 2. A person is not guilty of such an offence by reason or a contravention of the prohibition in art 20 (see PARA 925) however, if they: (1) did not know, and had no reason to suppose, that the goods referred to in art 20 were destined for an embargoed destination; and (2) are able to show the matters stated in head (1): see art 34(2). As to the meaning of 'embargoed destination' see PARA 925 note 7.

4   'Dual-use Regulation' means Council Regulation (EC) 428/2009 (OJ L134, 29.5.2009, p 1) as amended from time to time: see the Export Control Order 2008, SI 2008/3231, art 2(1) (definition substituted by SI 2009/2151).

5   Ie a prohibition or restriction in Council Regulation (EC) 428/2009 (OJ L134, 29.5.2009, p 1) art 3(1): Export Control Order 2008, SI 2008/3231, art 35(1) (as amended: see note 8). Article 35(1), (4) (see heads (2), (c) above) does not create an offence related to prohibitions or restrictions on the exportation of goods from the United Kingdom (see the Customs and Excise Management Act 1979; and CUSTOMS AND EXCISE vol 31 (2012) PARA 1026 et seq): Export Control Order 2008, SI 2008/3231, art 35(8). As to the meaning of 'United Kingdom' see PARA 906 note 7.

6   Ie in Council Regulation (EC) 428/2009 (OJ L134, 29.5.2009, p 1) art 4(2): Export Control Order 2008, SI 2008/3231, art 35(1) (as amended: see note 8). See also note 5.

7   Ie in Council Regulation (EC) 428/2009 (OJ L134, 29.5.2009, p 1) art 4(3): Export Control Order 2008, SI 2008/3231, art 35(1) (as amended: see note 8). See also note 5.

8   Export Control Order 2008, SI 2008/3231, art 35(1) (amended by SI 2009/2151). The prohibitions and restrictions on the exportation or transfer of sensitive items are in Council Regulation (EC) 428/2009 (OJ L134, 29.5.2009, p 1) art 22(1): Export Control Order 2008, SI 2008/3231, art 35(1) (as so amended). See also note 5. As to the meaning of 'customs territory' see PARA 918 note 9.

9   See the Export Control Order 2008, SI 2008/3231, art 35(7) (substituted by SI 2009/2151). The requirements are in Council Regulation (EC) 428/2009 (OJ L134, 29.5.2009, p 1) art 20 (record-keeping), 22(8) (records of exportation and transfer of listed items within the customs territory) or 22(10) (requirement in relation to commercial documents for exportation and transfer of listed items within the customs territory): Export Control Order 2008, SI 2008/3231, art 35(7) (as so substituted).

10   'Torture Regulation' means Council Regulation (EC) 1236/2005 (OJ L200, 30.7.2005, p 1) as amended from time to time: see the Export Control Order 2008, SI 2008/3231, art 2(1).

11   Ie a prohibition or restriction in Council Regulation (EC) 1236/2005 (OJ L200, 30.7.2005, p 1) art 3(1) (export prohibition): Export Control Order 2008, SI 2008/3231, art 36(1).

12   See the Export Control Order 2008, SI 2008/3231, art 36(1).

13   Ie a prohibition or restriction in Council Regulation (EC) 1236/2005 (OJ L200, 30.7.2005, p 1) art 4(1) (import prohibition): Export Control Order 2008, SI 2008/3231, art 36(4).

14   See the Export Control Order 2008, SI 2008/3231, art 36(4).

15   See note 2.

16   Ie a prohibition in the Export Control Order 2008, SI 2008/3231, Pt 3 (art 19) (see PARA 924): art 34(3).

17   As to the meaning of 'software' see PARA 917 note 5.

18   As to the meaning of 'technology' see PARA 917 note 6.

19   See the Export Control Order 2008, SI 2008/3231, art 34(3). As to the meaning of 'WMD purposes' see PARA 918 note 4.

20   See note 2.

21   See notes 2, 16.

22   Ie a prohibition in the Export Control Order 2008, SI 2008/3231, Pt 4 (arts 20–25) (see PARAS 925, 926): art 34(5).

23   See the Export Control Order 2008, SI 2008/3231, art 34(5).

24   Ie a prohibition or restriction in Council Regulation (EC) 428/2009 (OJ L134, 29.5.2009, p 1) art 4(1): Export Control Order 2008, SI 2008/3231, art 35(2)(a) (as amended: see note 25).

25   See the Export Control Order 2008, SI 2008/3231, art 35(2)(a) (amended by SI 2009/2151). The prohibitions and restrictions are in Council Regulation (EC) 428/2009 (OJ L134, 29.5.2009, p 1) art 5(1): Export Control Order 2008, SI 2008/3231, art 35(2)(a) (as so amended).

26   As to the meaning of 'competent authority' see PARA 918 note 20.

27 See the Export Control Order 2008, SI 2008/3231, art 35(2)(b) (amended by SI 2009/1305). Ie the requirement in Council Regulation (EC) 428/2009 (OJ L134, 29.5.2009, p 1) art 4(4): Export Control Order 2008, SI 2008/3231, art 35(2)(b) (as so amended).

28 Ie Council Regulation (EC) 428/2009 (OJ L134, 29.5.2009, p 1) art 3(1), 4(1), 4(2), 4(3), 5(1) or 22(1): Export Control Order 2008, SI 2008/3231, art 35(4) (as amended: see note 29). See also note 5.

29 See the Export Control Order 2008, SI 2008/3231, art 35(4) (amended by SI 2009/2151).

30 See the Export Control Order 2008, SI 2008/3231, art 36(2). The relevant prohibition is in Council Regulation (EC) 1236/2005 (OJ L200, 30.7.2005, p 1) art 3(1) (export prohibition): Export Control Order 2008, SI 2008/3231, art 36(2).

31 See the Export Control Order 2008, SI 2008/3231, art 36(5). The relevant prohibition is in Council Regulation (EC) 1236/2005 (OJ L200, 30.7.2005, p 1) art 4(1) (import prohibition): Export Control Order 2008, SI 2008/3231, art 36(5).

32 As to the statutory maximum see SENTENCING AND DISPOSITION OF OFFENDERS vol 92 (2010) PARA 140.

33 In the case of an offence committed after the Criminal Justice Act 2003 s 154(1) comes into force, the reference to 'six months' should be substituted by a reference to '12 months': Export Control Order 2008, SI 2008/3231, arts 34(4)(a)(i), (6)(a)(i), (8), 35(3)(a)(i), (5)(a)(i), (9), 36(3)(a)(i), (8). At the date at which this volume states the law, no day had been appointed for the coming into force of the Criminal Justice Act 2003 s 154(1).

34 See the Export Control Order 2008, SI 2008/3231, arts 34(4), (6), 35(3), (5), 36(3), (6).

934. Offences in connection with export licences or authorisations. Where for the purpose of obtaining a licence[1] or certificate[2] a person (the 'applicant') either:

(1) makes a statement or furnishes a document or information which to the applicant's knowledge is false in a material particular; or

(2) recklessly makes a statement or furnishes a document or information which is false in a material particular,

the applicant commits an offence and any licence or certificate that has been granted in connection with the application for which the false statement was made or the false document or information was furnished is void as from the time it was granted[3].

A person who, having acted under the authority of a licence or the Union General Export Authorisation[4], fails to comply with: (a) any of the requirements or conditions to which the licence or the Union General Export Authorisation is subject; or (b) any obligation as to registration or the keeping of records[5], commits an offence unless[6]: (i) the licence was modified after the completion of the act authorised; and (ii) the alleged failure to comply would not have been a failure had the licence not been so modified[7].

A person who fails to comply with the requirements of the Dual-use Regulation[8] to provide relevant information for licence applications[9] commits an offence and any licence which may have been granted in connection with the application is void as from the time it was granted[10].

A person who fails to comply with the requirement of the Torture Regulation[11] to provide relevant information for licence applications[12] commits an offence and any licence which may have been granted in connection with the application is void as from the time it was granted[13].

1 As to the meaning of 'licence' see PARA 927 note 15. As to licences generally see PARA 927.

2 As to certificates see PARA 929.

3 Export Control Order 2008, SI 2008/3231, art 37(1) (art 37 amended by SI 2012/1910). A person guilty of an offence under the Export Control Order 2008, SI 2008/3231, art 37(1) is liable: (1) on summary conviction, to a fine not exceeding the statutory maximum or to imprisonment for a term not exceeding three months, or to both; or (2) on conviction on

indictment, to a fine or to imprisonment for a term not exceeding two years, or to both: art 37(2). As to the statutory maximum see SENTENCING AND DISPOSITION OF OFFENDERS vol 92 (2010) PARA 140.

4 As to the meaning of 'the Union General Export Authorisation' see PARA 930 note 3.

5 Ie any obligation under the Export Control Order 2008, SI 2008/3231, art 28, 29, 30 or 31 (see PARAS 930, 931): art 38(1)(b) (art 38(1) as amended: see note 6).

6 Export Control Order 2008, SI 2008/3231, art 38(1) (amended by SI 2012/1910). A person guilty of an offence under the Export Control Order 2008, SI 2008/3231, art 38(1) is liable: (1) on summary conviction, to a fine not exceeding the statutory maximum or to imprisonment for a term not exceeding three months, or to both; or (2) on conviction on indictment, to a fine or to imprisonment for a term not exceeding two years, or to both: art 38(3).

7 Export Control Order 2008, SI 2008/3231, art 38(2).

8 'Dual-use Regulation' means Council Regulation (EC) 428/2009 (OJ L134, 29.5.2009, p 1) as amended from time to time: see the Export Control Order 2008, SI 2008/3231, art 2(1) (definition substituted by SI 2009/2151).

9 Ie the requirements in Council Regulation (EC) 1334/2000 (OJ L159, 30.6.2000, p 1) art 9(2) (provision of relevant information for export authorisation applications) or 10(2) (provision of relevant information for authorisation applications for brokering services): Export Control Order 2008, SI 2008/3231, art 35(6) (as amended: see note 10).

10 Export Control Order 2008, SI 2008/3231, art 35(6) (amended by SI 2009/2151). A person guilty of such an offence is liable on summary conviction to a fine not exceeding level 3 on the standard scale: Export Control Order 2008, SI 2008/3231, art 35(6) (as so amended). As to the standard scale see SENTENCING AND DISPOSITION OF OFFENDERS vol 92 (2010) PARA 142.

11 'Torture Regulation' means Council Regulation (EC) 1236/2005 (OJ L200, 30.7.2005, p 1) as amended from time to time: see the Export Control Order 2008, SI 2008/3231, art 2(1).

12 Ie the requirement in Council Regulation (EC) 1236/2005 (OJ L200, 30.7.2005, p 1) art 8(2) (provision of relevant information for licence applications): Export Control Order 2008, SI 2008/3231, art 36(7).

13 Export Control Order 2008, SI 2008/3231, art 36(7). A person guilty of such an offence is liable on summary conviction to a fine not exceeding level 3 on the standard scale: art 36(7).

935. Use and disclosure of information. Restrictions apply to information[1] which is held from time to time by the Secretary of State[2] or the Commissioners for Revenue and Customs[3] in connection with the operation of controls imposed by the Export Control Order 2008[4] or by any directly applicable EU provision on the export[5] of goods, the transfer[6] of software[7] or technology[8], participation in the provision of technical assistance, or activities which facilitate, or are otherwise connected with, the acquisition, disposal or movement of goods[9]. Such information may be used for the purposes of, or for any purposes connected with:

(1) the exercise of functions in relation to any control imposed by the Export Control Order 2008 or by any other order made under the Export Control Act 2002;

(2) giving effect to any EU provision or other international obligation of the United Kingdom[10];

(3) facilitating the exercise by an authority or international organisation outside the United Kingdom of functions which correspond to functions conferred by or in connection with any activity subject to control by the Export Control Order 2008 or any other order made under the Export Control Act 2002,

and may be disclosed to any person for use for these purposes[11].

No disclosure of information may be made by virtue of the above provisions unless the making of the disclosure is proportionate to the object of the disclosure[12]; and nothing in these provisions affects any power to disclose information that exists apart from these provisions[13].

The information that may be disclosed by virtue of these provisions includes information obtained before the 2008 Order came into force[14].

1 For these purposes, 'information' is any information that relates to a particular business or other activity carried on by a person: Export Control Order 2008, SI 2008/3231, art 43(4).
2 As to the Secretary of State see PARA 902.
3 As to the Commissioners for Revenue and Customs see CUSTOMS AND EXCISE vol 31 (2012) PARA 921 et seq.
4 Ie the Export Control Order 2008, SI 2008/3231: see PARA 917 et seq.
5 As to the meaning of 'export' see PARA 917 note 10.
6 As to the meaning of 'transfer' see PARA 917 note 12.
7 As to the meaning of 'software' see PARA 917 note 5.
8 As to the meaning of 'technology' see PARA 917 note 6.
9 Export Control Order 2008, SI 2008/3231, art 43(1) (amended by SI 2011/1043).
10 As to the meaning of 'United Kingdom' see PARA 906 note 7.
11 Export Control Order 2008, SI 2008/3231, art 43(2) (amended by SI 2011/1043).
12 Export Control Order 2008, SI 2008/3231, art 43(3).
13 Export Control Order 2008, SI 2008/3231, art 43(5).
14 Export Control Order 2008, SI 2008/3231, art 43(6). As to the commencement of the Order see PARA 917 note 7.

936. Review of controls by Secretary of State. The Secretary of State[1] must from time to time:

(1) carry out a review of provisions of the Export Control Order 2008[2] to the extent that they implement the Defence-related Products Directive[3];

(2) set out the conclusion of the review in a report; and

(3) publish the report[4].

The report must in particular:

(a) set out the objectives intended to be achieved by the regulatory system established by the relevant provisions of the Export Control Order 2008[5] to the extent that the implement the Defence-related Products Directive;

(b) assess the extent to which those objectives are achieved; and

(c) assess whether those objectives remain appropriate and, if so, the extent to which they could be achieved with a system that imposes less regulation[6].

1 As to the Secretary of State see PARA 902.
2 Ie the Export Control Order 2008, SI 2008/3231, arts 3, 17, 26, 28, 28A, 29, 31, 33A, 34, 37, 38 and 41 (see PARAS 917, 922, 927, 929–934): art 46(1)(a) (art 46 as added: see note 3).
3 In carrying out the review the Secretary of State must, so far as reasonable, have regard to how the Defence-related Products Directive is implemented in other member states: Export Control Order 2008, SI 2008/3231, art 46(2) (art 46 added by SI 2012/1910). The Defence-related Products Directive is European Parliament and Council Directive (EC) 2009/43 simplifying terms and conditions of transfers of defence-related products within the European Union (OJ L146, 10.6.2009, p 1): Export Control Order 2008, SI 2008/3231, art 2(1) (definition added by SI 2012/1910).
4 Export Control Order 2008, SI 2008/3231, art 46(1) (art 46 as added: see note 3). The first such report was required to be published before the end of the period of five years beginning with 30 June 2012 and are to be published at intervals not exceeding five years: art 46(4), (5) (art 46 as so added).
5 See note 2.
6 Export Control Order 2008, SI 2008/3231, art 46(3) (art 46 as added: see note 3).

C. PARTICULAR GOODS

937. Control under particular enactments. In addition to general controls on imports and exports, many enactments place restrictions on the importation or exportation of particular goods. Most of these restrictions, which are dealt with specifically elsewhere in this work, are on importation, often with a view to the prevention of the spread of disease or the control of dangerous things[1]. Such restrictions may, however, be modified so as to allow the importation of goods from other EU member states[2]. The export of dangerous chemicals is controlled under European Union law[3].

Restrictions may also be imposed by Order in Council under the United Nations Act 1946[4] in order to give effect to sanctions imposed by the United Nations Security Council[5]; and the Secretary of State[6] has power to require persons carrying on business in the United Kingdom[7] to give him notice of any requirement or prohibition imposed or threatened to be imposed on those persons by measures by or under the law of any overseas country for regulating or controlling international trade which may be damaging to the trading interests of the United Kingdom, and to prohibit compliance with any such measures[8]. Certain types of assistance to specified countries relating to military activities are subject to controls and criminal penalties[9].

1 See eg the Trade in Animals and Related Products Regulations 2011, SI 2011/1197; Trade in Animals and Related Products (Wales) Regulations 2011, SI 2011/2379; and ANIMALS vol 2 (2008) PARA 1084; the Genetically Modified Organisms (Transboundary Movements) (England) Regulations 2004, SI 2004/2692, and the Genetically Modified Organisms (Transboundary Movements) (Wales) Regulations 2005, SI 2005/1912, which implement European Parliament and Council Regulation (EC) 1946/2003 (OJ L287, 5.11.2003, p 1) on transboundary movements of genetically modified organisms; and FOOD AND DRINK vol 51 (2013) PARA 732. See also the Environmental Protection Act 1990 s 140 (power to prohibit or restrict the importation, use, supply or storage of injurious substances or articles); and ENVIRONMENTAL QUALITY AND PUBLIC HEALTH vol 46 (2010) PARA 790.

2 Eg the definition of 'transboundary movement' in European Parliament and Council Regulation (EC) 1946/2003 (OJ L287, 5.11.2003, p 1) art 3(14) excludes intentional movements of genetically modified organisms between parties within the European Union.

3 See the Biocidal Products and Chemicals (Appointment of Authorities and Enforcement) Regulations 2013, SI 2013/1506, made by the Secretary of State in exercise of powers conferred by the European Communities Act 1972 s 2(2) to provide for the appointment of designated national authorities in relation to, and the enforcement in respect of the United Kingdom of, European Parliament and Council Regulation (EU) 649/2012 concerning the export and import of hazardous chemicals (OJ L201, 27.7.12, p 60) (the 'PIC Regulation'), which implements a common system of notification and information for imports from and exports to countries which are not member states; and HEALTH AND SAFETY AT WORK vol 53 (2014) PARA 533. The Health and Safety Executive is the designated national authority to act for the performance of the administrative functions required by the PIC Regulation, in accordance with art 4, and has the responsibility of controlling the import and export of chemicals listed in Annex I, in accordance with art 18: Biocidal Products and Chemicals (Appointment of Authorities and Enforcement) Regulations 2013, SI 2013/1506, regs 4(1), 7. As to the Health and Safety Executive see HEALTH AND SAFETY AT WORK vol 52 (2014) PARA 326 et seq.

4 Ie under the United Nations Act 1946 s 1: see INTERNATIONAL RELATIONS LAW vol 61 (2010) PARA 526.

5 See eg the Libya (United Nations Sanctions) Order 1993, SI 1993/2807; the Iran (United Nations Sanctions) Order 2009, SI 2009/886; and CONSTITUTIONAL AND ADMINISTRATIVE LAW vol 20 (2014) PARA 558.

6 As to the Secretary of State see PARA 902.

7 As to the meaning of 'United Kingdom' see PARA 906 note 7.

8 See the Protection of Trading Interests Act 1980 s 1; and INTERNATIONAL RELATIONS LAW vol 61 (2010) PARA 235.

9 See eg the Export Control (Sudan, South Sudan and Central African Republic Sanctions) Regulations 2014, SI 2014/3258; and the Export Control (Liberia) Order 2011, SI 2011/145.

(2) EXCISE RESTRICTIONS

938. Excise licences. An excise licence[1] must be in such form and contain such particulars as the Commissioners for Revenue and Customs[2] direct and, subject to any enactment relating to the licence or trade in question, may be granted by the proper officer[3] on payment of any appropriate duty[4]. If any person who is the holder of an excise licence to carry on any trade or to manufacture or sell any goods fails to produce his licence for examination within one month after being so requested by an officer, his failure attracts a penalty[5].

1   As to excise licences generally see CUSTOMS AND EXCISE vol 31 (2012) PARA 609 et seq.

2   As to the Commissioners for Revenue and Customs see CUSTOMS AND EXCISE vol 31 (2012) PARA 921 et seq.

3   Subject to the Customs and Excise Management Act 1979 s 8(2), which enables any person to be engaged in revenue and customs duties, 'officer' means a person commissioned by the Commissioners for Revenue and Customs. As to the meaning of 'proper' see PARA 921 note 12.

4   Customs and Excise Management Act 1979 s 101(1) (amended by the Finance Act 1986 Sch 5 para 1(a); and by virtue of the Commissioners for Revenue and Customs Act 2005 s 50(1), (7)). An excise licence for the carrying on of a trade is to be granted in respect of one set of premises only, but a licence for the same trade may be granted to the same person in respect of each of two or more sets of premises: Customs and Excise Management Act 1979 s 101(2). Where an excise licence trade is carried on at any set of premises by two or more persons in partnership, then, subject to the provisions of any enactment relating to the licence or trade in question, not more than one licence is required to be held by those persons in respect of those premises at any one time: s 101(3) (amended by the Finance Act 1986 Sch 5 para 1(b)).

5   Customs and Excise Management Act 1979 s 101(4) (amended by the Finance Act 1994 Sch 4 para 5). This is without prejudice to any other requirement as to the production of licences contained in the Customs and Excise Acts 1979: s 101(4). As to the meaning of 'the Customs and Excise Acts 1979' see PARA 908 note 1. The penalty is under the Finance Act 1994 s 9: see CUSTOMS AND EXCISE vol 31 (2012) PARA 1213.

939. Hydrocarbon oils. With a view to the protection of the revenue[1] the Commissioners for Revenue and Customs[2] may make regulations: (1) prohibiting the production of hydrocarbon oil[3] except by a person holding a licence; (2) specifying the circumstances in which any such licence may be surrendered or revoked; (3) regulating the production, storage and warehousing[4] of hydrocarbon oil and the removal of any such oil to or from premises used in its production; (4) prohibiting the refining of hydrocarbon oil elsewhere than in a refinery[5]; (5) prohibiting the incorporation of gas in hydrocarbon oil elsewhere than in a refinery; and (6) regulating the use and storage of hydrocarbon oil in a refinery[6]. They may also protect the revenue by: (a) regulating or prohibiting the removal to a refinery of hydrocarbon oil in respect of which any rebate[7] has been allowed; (b) regulating the removal of imported hydrocarbon oil to a refinery without payment of the excise duty on such oil; (c) making provision for securing payment of the excise duty on any imported hydrocarbon oil received into a refinery; (d) relieving from the excise duty chargeable on hydrocarbon oil produced in the United Kingdom[8] any such oil intended for exportation or shipment[9] as stores[10]; (e) conferring power to require information relating to the supply or use of aviation gasoline[11] to be given by producers, dealers and users; and (f) requiring producers and users of and dealers in aviation gasoline to keep and produce records relating to aviation gasoline[12].

Where any person contravenes or fails to comply with such a regulation his contravention or failure to comply attracts a penalty[13] and any goods[14] in respect of which any person contravenes or fails to comply with any such regulation are liable to forfeiture[15].

In addition to the above provisions, the Secretary of State[16] is empowered to make regulations for the implementation of the EU Treaty[17] obligations in relation to the conditions for granting and using authorisations for the prospection, exploration and production of hydrocarbons[18].

1   As to revenue and excise duties on hydrocarbon oil see CUSTOMS AND EXCISE vol 30 (2012) PARA 498 et seq.

2   As to the Commissioners for Revenue and Customs see CUSTOMS AND EXCISE vol 31 (2012) PARA 921 et seq.

3   'Hydrocarbon oil' means petroleum oil, coal tar and oil produced from coal, shale, peat or any other bituminous substance, and all liquid hydrocarbons, but does not include such hydrocarbons or bituminous or asphaltic substances as are: (1) solid or semi-solid at a temperature of 15° C; or (2) gaseous at a temperature of 15° C and under a pressure of 1013.25 millibars: Hydrocarbon Oil Duties Act 1979 ss 1(2), 27(1).

4   'Warehouse', except in the expressions 'Queen's warehouse' and 'distiller's warehouse', means a place of security approved by the Commissioners for Revenue and Customs under the Customs and Excise Management Act 1979 s 92(1) (excise warehouse) or s 92(2) (customs warehouse) or both s 92(1) and s 92(2) (see CUSTOMS AND EXCISE vol 31 (2012) PARAS 692, 717) and, except in s 92, also includes a distiller's warehouse; and 'warehoused' and cognate expressions are, subject to s 92(4) and any regulations made by virtue of s 93(2)(da)(i) or (e) or (4), construed accordingly: s 1(1) (amended by the Finance (No 2) Act 1992 Sch 2 para 1(b); and by virtue of the Commissioners for Revenue and Customs Act 2005 s 50(1), (7)); definition applied by the Hydrocarbon Oil Duties Act 1979 s 27(3).

5   'Refinery' means any premises which: (1) are approved by the Commissioners for Revenue and Customs for the treatment of hydrocarbon oil; or (2) are approved by them for the production of energy for use in the treatment of hydrocarbon oil at such approved premises or in the production of hydrocarbon oil at other premises used for the production of such oil; and the commissioners may approve any such premises if it appears to them that more than one-third of the energy will be produced for such use: Hydrocarbon Oil Duties Act 1979 s 27(1) (definition substituted by the Finance Act 1981 s 5(3)). If in the case of any premises which the Commissioners can approve it appears to them appropriate to do so, they may direct that the provisions of the Hydrocarbon Oil Duties Act 1979 (other than the definition of 'refinery') applies to them as if, instead of being a refinery, they were other premises used for the production of hydrocarbon oil: s 27(1A) (added by the Finance Act 1981 s 5(4)).

6   Hydrocarbon Oil Duties Act 1979 s 21(1)(a), Sch 3 Pt I paras 1–6 (Sch 3 Pt I para 2 substituted by the Finance Act 1986 Sch 5 para 4). In the case of regulations made for the purposes of the Hydrocarbon Oil Duties Act 1979 Sch 3 Pt I (paras 1–11), different regulations may be made for different classes of hydrocarbon oil; and the power to make such regulations must include power to make regulations: (1) regulating the allowance and payment of drawback under or by virtue of the Hydrocarbon Oil Duties Act 1979 s 15 (drawback of duty on exportation etc of certain goods) (see CUSTOMS AND EXCISE vol 30 (2012) PARA 537); and (2) for making the allowance and payment of drawback by virtue of an order under s 15(2) subject to such conditions as the Commissioners see fit to impose for the protection of the revenue: s 21(2). Any power to make regulations under the Hydrocarbon Oil Duties Act 1979 is exercisable by statutory instrument, subject to annulment in pursuance of a resolution of either House of Parliament: s 25. See STATUTES AND LEGISLATIVE PROCESS vol 96 (2012) PARA 1045 et seq. See the Hydrocarbon Oil Regulations 1973, SI 1973/1311; and CUSTOMS AND EXCISE vol 30 (2012) PARA 570 et seq. The Hydrocarbon Oil Regulations 1973, SI 1973/1311 were originally made under the Hydrocarbon Oil (Customs and Excise) Act 1971 (repealed) but now have effect under the Hydrocarbon Oil Duties Act 1979 ss 21, 24, Sch 3 Pts I, II, Sch 4 by virtue of s 28(6) and the Interpretation Act 1978 s 17(2)(b). By virtue of the Hydrocarbon Oil Duties Act 1979 ss 20AA, 24 (see CUSTOMS AND EXCISE vol 30 (2012) PARA 565; CUSTOMS AND EXCISE vol 31 (2012) PARA 636), the regulations also cover the granting of reliefs, the mixing of oil, the marking of oil, the control of storage and supply of oil, the keeping of records and the entry of premises: CUSTOMS AND EXCISE vol 30 (2012) PARA 538. The sampling of oil is governed by the Hydrocarbon Oil Duties Act 1979 s 24(5), Sch 5: see CUSTOMS AND EXCISE vol 30 (2012) PARA 567.

7   'Rebate' means rebate of duty under the Hydrocarbon Oil Duties Act 1979 s 11, 13ZA, 13AA, 14, 14A, 14B or 20AB (see CUSTOMS AND EXCISE vol 30 (2012) PARA 525 et seq) and 'rebated' has a corresponding meaning: Hydrocarbon Oil Duties Act 1979 s 27(1) (definition amended by the Finance Act 1987 s 1(3); the Finance Act 2001 s 3(3); the Finance Act 2002 Sch 3 Pt 2 para 9; and the Finance Act 2008 s 13(9)(a), Sch 5 para 22(2)(d), Sch 6 Pt 2 para 32).

8   As to the meaning of 'United Kingdom' see PARA 906 note 7.

9   'Shipment' includes loading into an aircraft, and 'shipped' and cognate expressions must be construed accordingly: Customs and Excise Management Act 1979 s 1(1); definitions applied by the Hydrocarbon Oil Duties Act 1979 s 27(3).

10 As to the meaning of 'stores' see PARA 908 note 6; definition applied by the Hydrocarbon Oil Duties Act 1979 s 27(3).

11 'Aviation gasoline' means light oil which: (1) is specially produced as fuel for aircraft; (2) at 37.8° C, has a Reid Vapour Pressure of not less than 38 kPa and not more than 49 kPa; and (3) is delivered for use solely as fuel for aircraft: Hydrocarbon Oil Duties Act 1979 ss 1(3D), 27(1) (s 1(3D) added by the Finance Act 2008 Sch 6 Pt 1 para 2; definition in the Hydrocarbon Oil Duties Act 1979 s 27(1) added by the Finance Act 1982 s 4(4); and amended by the Finance Act 2008 Sch 6 Pt 1 para 6). 'Light oil' means hydrocarbon oil of which at least 90% by volume distils at a temperature not exceeding 210° C, or which gives off an inflammable vapour at a temperature of less than 23° C when tested in the manner prescribed by the Acts relating to petroleum: Hydrocarbon Oil Duties Act 1979 ss 1(3), 27(1). 'Road vehicle' means a vehicle constructed or adapted for use on roads but does not include any vehicle which is an 'excepted vehicle' within the meaning given by Sch 1 (excepted vehicles): s 27(1) (definitions amended and added respectively by the Finance Act 2008 Sch 5 para 22(2)(b), (e)).

12 Hydrocarbon Oil Duties Act 1979 Sch 3 Pt I paras 7–10C (paras 10A–10C added by the Finance Act 1982 s 4(5); the Hydrocarbon Oil Duties Act 1979 Sch 3 para 10A substituted by the Finance Act 1990 s 3(5); and repealed by the Finance Act 2008 Sch 6 Pt 1 para 7). Power is also conferred for securing and collecting the excise duty chargeable on hydrocarbon oil: see the Hydrocarbon Oil Duties Act 1979 Sch 3 Pt I para 11 (amended by the Finance Act 1985 s 98(6), Sch 4 para 4, Sch 27 Pt I). See CUSTOMS AND EXCISE vol 30 (2012) PARA 561.

13 Ie a penalty under the Finance Act 1994 s 9 (civil penalties): see CUSTOMS AND EXCISE vol 31 (2012) PARA 1213.

14 As to the meaning of 'goods' see PARA 908 note 6; definition applied by the Hydrocarbon Oil Duties Act 1979 s 27(3).

15 Hydrocarbon Oil Duties Act 1979 s 21(3) (amended by the Finance Act 1994 Sch 4 Pt III para 55).

16 As to the Secretary of State see PARA 902.

17 Ie the Treaty on the Functioning of the European Union (Rome, 25 March 1957; TS 1 (1973); Cmnd 5179). The Treaty was formerly known as the Treaty establishing the European Community (Rome, 25 March 1957; TS 1 (1973); Cmnd 5179) ('EC Treaty): see EUROPEAN UNION vol 47A (2014) PARA 6).

18 See the European Communities (Designation) (No 2) Order 1994, SI 1994/1327, made under the European Communities Act 1972 s 2(2).

940. Licence to manufacture or deal wholesale in denatured alcohol. Any distiller[1], rectifier[2] or compounder[3] may be authorised by the Commissioners for Revenue and Customs[4] to denature dutiable alcoholic liquor[5], and no person other than a denaturer so authorised may denature dutiable alcoholic liquor or deal wholesale[6] in denatured alcohol unless he holds an excise licence as a denaturer[7] or in the case of dealing wholesale is exempted by regulations from holding such a licence[8]. The Commissioners may at any time revoke or suspend any such authorisation or licence[9].

1 'Distiller' means a person holding a distiller's licence under the Alcoholic Liquor Duties Act 1979 s 12 (see CUSTOMS AND EXCISE vol 30 (2012) PARA 412): Alcoholic Liquor Duties Act 1979 s 4(1).

2 'Rectifier' means a person holding a licence as a rectifier under the Alcoholic Liquor Duties Act 1979 s 18 (see CUSTOMS AND EXCISE vol 30 (2012) PARA 419): s 4(1).

3 'Compounder' means a person holding a licence as a compounder under the Alcoholic Liquor Duties Act 1979 s 18 (see CUSTOMS AND EXCISE vol 30 (2012) PARA 419): s 4(1).

4 As to the Commissioners for Revenue and Customs see CUSTOMS AND EXCISE vol 31 (2012) PARA 921 et seq.

5 Alcoholic Liquor Duties Act 1979 s 75(1) (amended by the Finance Act 1995 Sch 2 para 5(a), (c), (d)). Any person so authorised is referred to as an 'authorised denaturer': Alcoholic Liquor Duties Act 1979 ss 4(1), 75(1) (definition in s 4(1) added by the Finance Act 1995 Sch 2 paras 1(a); s 75(1) as so amended). 'Dutiable alcoholic liquor' means any of the liquors mentioned in the Alcoholic Liquor Duties Act 1979 s 1(1) (see CUSTOMS AND EXCISE vol 30 (2012) PARA 392): see ss 1(1), 4(1).

6 'Dealing wholesale' means the sale at any one time to any one person of a quantity of denatured alcohol of not less than 20 litres or such smaller quantity as the Commissioners for Revenue and Customs may by regulations specify: Alcoholic Liquor Duties Act 1979 s 75(7) (amended by the Finance Act 1995 Sch 2 para 5(d); and by SI 1979/241). At the date at which this volume states the law, no such regulations had been made. 'Denatured alcohol' means denatured alcohol

within the meaning of the Finance Act 1995 s 5 and references to denaturing a liquor are references to subjecting it to any process by which it becomes denatured alcohol: Alcoholic Liquor Duties Act 1979 s 4(1) (definition added by the Finance Act 1995 Sch 2 para 1(c)).

7　Alcoholic Liquor Duties Act 1979 s 75(2) (amended by the Finance Act 1995 Sch 2 para 5(a), (c), (d)). Where any person, not being an authorised denaturer, denatures dutiable alcoholic liquor otherwise than under and in accordance with a licence under the Alcoholic Liquor Duties Act 1979 s 75 (see CUSTOMS AND EXCISE vol 30 (2012) PARA 496) his doing so will attract a penalty under the Finance Act 1994 s 9 (civil penalties) (see CUSTOMS AND EXCISE vol 31 (2012) PARA 1213): Alcoholic Liquor Duties Act 1979 s 75(5) (amended by the Finance Act 1994 Sch 4 para 45; and the Finance Act 1995 Sch 2 para 5(a), (c)). As to excise licences generally see PARA 938.

8　See the Alcoholic Liquor Duties Act 1979 s 77(1)(d) (amended by the Finance Act 1981 Sch 8 Pt II para 23(a); and the Finance Act 1995 Sch 2 para 5(d)); and PARA 941. As to the penalties for failing to comply with regulations made under the Alcoholic Liquor Duties Act 1979 s 77 see PARA 941.

9　Alcoholic Liquor Duties Act 1979 s 75(6).

941. Production, storage and transfer etc of denatured alcohol. With a view to the protection of the revenue[1] the Commissioners for Revenue and Customs[2] may make regulations[3]:

(1)　regulating the denaturing of dutiable alcoholic liquor[4] and the supply, storage, removal, sale, delivery, receipt, use and exportation or shipment[5] as stores[6] of denatured alcohol[7];

(2)　permitting dutiable alcoholic liquor to be denatured in warehouse[8];

(3)　permitting dealing wholesale[9] without a licence in specified denatured alcohol[10];

(4)　regulating the importation, receipt, removal, storage and use of dutiable alcoholic liquor for denaturing[11];

(5)　regulating the storage and removal of substances to be used in denaturing dutiable alcoholic liquor[12];

(6)　prescribing the manner in which account is to be kept of stocks of denatured alcohol in the possession of authorised or licensed denaturers[13] and of retailers[14] of denatured alcohol[15];

(7)　for securing any duty[16] chargeable in respect of denatured alcohol of any class[17].

If any person contravenes or fails to comply with any such regulation, or with any condition, restriction or requirement imposed under such a regulation, his contravention or failure to comply attracts a penalty[18]. If, save as permitted by any regulation, any person deals wholesale in denatured alcohol otherwise than under and in accordance with a licence[19], his doing so attracts a penalty[20], and any dutiable alcoholic liquor or denatured alcohol in respect of which there is such a contravention or failure to comply or any such dealing is liable to forfeiture[21].

If any person:

(a)　supplies to another, in contravention of any regulations, any denatured alcohol containing dutiable alcoholic liquor of any description; or

(b)　uses any such denatured alcohol in contravention of any such regulations,

that person must, on demand by the Commissioners, pay on the amount of dutiable alcoholic liquor of that description comprised, at the time of its supply or use, in the denatured alcohol that is so supplied or used, or on such part of it as the Commissioners may specify, the duty payable on dutiable alcoholic liquor of that description[22].

1   As to revenue and excise duties on denatured alcohol see CUSTOMS AND EXCISE vol 30 (2012) PARAS 409, 496 et seq.

2   As to the Commissioners for Revenue and Customs see CUSTOMS AND EXCISE vol 31 (2012) PARA 921 et seq.

3   The power to make regulations is exercisable by statutory instrument (Alcoholic Liquor Duties Act 1979 s 90(1)), and any such statutory instrument is subject to annulment in pursuance of a resolution of either House of Parliament (s 90(2); and see STATUTES AND LEGISLATIVE PROCESS vol 96 (2012) PARA 1045 et seq). Different regulations may be made under s 77 with respect to different classes of denatured alcohol or different kinds of denatured alcohol of any class: s 77(2) (amended by the Finance Act 1995 Sch 2 paras 5(a), (d), 6; and the Finance Act 1981 Sch 8 Pt II para 23(b)). Without prejudice to the generality of the Alcoholic Liquor Duties Act 1979 s 77(1), regulations may: (1) provide for the imposition of conditions and restrictions relating to the matters there mentioned; (2) frame any provision of the regulations with respect to the supply, receipt or use of denatured alcohol by reference to matters to be contained from time to time in a notice published in accordance with the regulations by the Commissioners for Revenue and Customs and having effect until withdrawn in accordance with the regulations; and (3) impose or provide for the imposition of requirements on authorised or licensed denaturers and on retailers of denatured alcohol to keep and preserve records relating to their businesses as such and to produce them to an officer when required to do so for the purposes of allowing him to inspect them, copy or take extracts from them or remove them at a reasonable time and for a reasonable period: s 77(2) (as so amended). Where documents removed under this power are lost or damaged, the Commissioners are liable to compensate their owner for any expenses reasonably incurred by him in replacing or repairing them: s 77(2A) (added by the Finance Act 1981 Sch 8 Pt II para 23(c)).

   In exercise of the power conferred by the Alcoholic Liquor Duties Act 1979 s 77, the Denatured Alcohol Regulations 2005, SI 2005/1524 have been made, which make provision as to classes of denatured alcohol and formulations (Pt 2 (regs 4–7), Schedule), producers and distributors of denatured alcohol (Pt 3 (regs 8–11)), the receipt, use and supply of denatured alcohol (Pt 4 (regs 12–15)), the recovery of alcohol (reg 16), the disposal of stocks of denatured alcohol (reg 17), and importing and exporting denatured alcohol (reg 18). See also CUSTOMS AND EXCISE vol 30 (2012) PARAS 409, 496 et seq.

4   As to the meaning of 'denaturing a liquor' see PARA 940 note 6; and as to the meaning of 'dutiable alcoholic liquor' see PARA 940 note 5.

5   As to the meanings of 'shipment' and 'shipped' see PARA 939 note 9; definitions applied by the Alcoholic Liquor Duties Act 1979 s 4(3).

6   As to the meaning of 'stores' see PARA 908 note 6; definition applied by the Alcoholic Liquor Duties Act 1979 s 4(3).

7   Alcoholic Liquor Duties Act 1979 s 77(1)(a) (s 77(1) amended by the Finance Act 1995 Sch 2 para 5). As to the meaning of 'denatured alcohol' see PARA 940 note 6. See also note 3; the Excise Goods (Holding, Movement and Duty Point) Regulations 2010, SI 2010/593; and CUSTOMS AND EXCISE vol 31 (2012) PARA 639 et seq.

8   Alcoholic Liquor Duties Act 1979 s 77(1)(c) (s 77(1) as amended: see note 7). See also note 3. As to the meaning of 'warehouse' see PARA 939 note 4; definition applied by s 4(3).

9   Ie dealing wholesale within the meaning of the Alcoholic Liquor Duties Act 1979 s 75 (see PARA 940): s 77(1)(d).

10   Alcoholic Liquor Duties Act 1979 s 77(1)(d) (s 77(1) as amended: see note 7; s 77(1)(d) amended by the Finance Act 1981, Sch 8 Pt II para 23(a)). See also note 3.

11   Alcoholic Liquor Duties Act 1979 s 77(1)(e) (s 77(1) as amended: see note 7). See also note 3; the Excise Goods (Holding, Movement and Duty Point) Regulations 2010, SI 2010/593; and CUSTOMS AND EXCISE vol 31 (2012) PARA 639 et seq.

12   Alcoholic Liquor Duties Act 1979 s 77(1)(f) (s 77(1) as amended: see note 7). See also note 3.

13   As to the meaning of 'authorised denaturer' see PARA 940 note 5. 'Licensed denaturer' means a person holding a licence under Alcoholic Liquor Duties Act 1979 s 75(2) (see PARA 940): s 4(1) (definition substituted by the Finance Act 1995 Sch 2 para 1(d)).

14   'Retailer' means, in relation to dutiable alcoholic liquor, a person who sells such liquor by retail: Alcoholic Liquor Duties Act 1979 s 4(1) (definition amended by the Finance Act 1981 s 139(6), Sch 13 Pt III).

15   Alcoholic Liquor Duties Act 1979 s 77(1)(g) (s 77(1) as amended: see note 7). See also note 3.

16   'Duty' means excise duty: Alcoholic Liquor Duties Act 1979 ss 1(1), 4(1). As to the duty payable on alcohol see CUSTOMS AND EXCISE vol 30 (2012) PARA 391 et seq.

17   Alcoholic Liquor Duties Act 1979 s 77(1)(h) (s 77(1) as amended: see note 7). See also note 3.

18 Alcoholic Liquor Duties Act 1979 s 77(3) (amended by the Finance Act 1981 Sch 8 para 23(d); and the Finance Act 1994 Sch 4 Pt II para 46(1)). The penalty is under the Finance Act 1994 s 9 (civil penalties): see CUSTOMS AND EXCISE vol 31 (2012) PARA 1213.
19 Ie a licence under the Alcoholic Liquor Duties Act 1979 s 75 (see PARA 940): see s 77(4).
20 Alcoholic Liquor Duties Act 1979 s 77(4) (amended by the Finance Act 1981 s 139(6), Sch 8 para 23(d), Sch 19 Pt III; the Finance Act 1994 Sch 4 Pt II para 46(2) and the Finance Act 1995 Sch 2 para 5(d)). The penalty is under the Finance Act 1994 s 9 (civil penalties): see CUSTOMS AND EXCISE vol 31 (2012) PARA 1213.
21 Alcoholic Liquor Duties Act 1979 s 77(5) (amended by the Finance Act 1994 Sch 4 Pt II para 46(3); and the Finance Act 1995 Sch 2 para 5(c), (d)).
22 Alcoholic Liquor Duties Act 1979 s 78(5) (s 78 substituted by the Finance Act 1995 Sch 2 para 7). Any supply of denatured alcohol to a person who: (1) by virtue of any regulations under the Alcoholic Liquor Duties Act 1979 s 77 is prohibited from receiving it unless authorised to do so by or under the regulations; and (2) is not so authorised in the case of the denatured alcohol supplied to him, is to be taken for the purposes of s 78(5) to be a supply in contravention of those regulations: s 78(6) (s 78 as so substituted). A demand made for the purposes of s 78(5) must be combined, as if there had been a default such as is mentioned in that section, with an assessment and notification under the Finance Act 1994 s 12 (assessments to excise duty: see CUSTOMS AND EXCISE vol 31 (2012) PARAS 1226, 1227) of the amount of duty due in consequence of the making of the demand: Alcoholic Liquor Duties Act 1979 s 78(7) (s 78 as so substituted).

942. Liability for defaults in respect of denatured alcohol. If, at any time when an account is taken and a balance struck of the quantity of any kind of denatured alcohol[1] in the possession of an authorised or licensed denaturer[2], there is a difference between:

(1)   the quantity (the 'actual amount') of the dutiable alcoholic liquor[3] of any description in the denatured alcohol in his possession; and

(2)   the quantity (the 'proper amount') of dutiable alcoholic liquor of that description which, according to any such accounts as are required to be kept by virtue of any regulations[4], ought to be in the denatured alcohol in his possession[5],

and if the actual amount exceeds the proper amount, the relevant amount of any dutiable alcoholic liquor of the description in question which is in the possession of the denaturer is liable to forfeiture; and for this purpose the relevant amount is the amount corresponding to the amount of the excess or such part of that amount as the Commissioners for Revenue and Customs[6] consider appropriate[7]. If the actual amount is less than the proper amount, the denaturer must, on demand by the Commissioners, pay on the amount of the deficiency, or on such part of it as the Commissioners may specify in the demand, the duty[8] payable on dutiable alcoholic liquor of the description comprised in the deficiency[9].

These provisions do not apply if the difference constitutes:

(a)   an excess of the actual amount over the proper amount of not more than 1 per cent of the aggregate of: (i) the quantity of dutiable alcoholic liquor of the description in question in the balance of dutiable alcoholic liquor struck when an account was last taken; and (ii) the quantity of dutiable alcoholic liquor of that description which has since been lawfully added to the denaturer's stock; or

(b)   a deficiency such that the actual amount is less than the proper amount by not more than 2 per cent of that aggregate[10].

1 As to the meaning of 'denatured alcohol' see PARA 940 note 6.
2 As to the meaning of 'authorised denaturer' PARA 940 note 5; and as to the meaning of 'licensed denaturer' see PARA 941 note 13.
3 As to the meaning of 'dutiable alcoholic liquor' see PARA 940 note 5.
4 Ie any regulations under the Alcoholic Liquor Duties Act 1979 s 77 (see PARA 941): s 78(1)(b) (s 78 as substituted: see note 5).

5   Alcoholic Liquor Duties Act 1979 s 78(1) (s 78 substituted by the Finance Act 1995 Sch 2 para 7).
6   As to the Commissioners for Revenue and Customs see CUSTOMS AND EXCISE vol 31 (2012) PARA 921 et seq.
7   Alcoholic Liquor Duties Act 1979 s 78(3) (s 78 as substituted: see note 5).
8   As to the meaning of 'duty' see PARA 941 note 16.
9   Alcoholic Liquor Duties Act 1979 s 78(4) (s 78 as substituted: see note 5). A demand made for the purposes of s 78(4) must be combined, as if there had been a default such as is mentioned in that section, with an assessment and notification under the Finance Act 1994 s 12 (assessments to excise duty: see CUSTOMS AND EXCISE vol 31 (2012) PARAS 1226, 1227) of the amount of duty due in consequence of the making of the demand: Alcoholic Liquor Duties Act 1979 s 78(7) (s 78 as so substituted).
10 Alcoholic Liquor Duties Act 1979 s 78(2) (s 78 as substituted: see note 5).

943.   Inspection and examination of denatured alcohol. An officer[1] of Revenue and Customs[2] may, in the daytime, enter and inspect the premises of any person authorised[3] to received denatured alcohol[4]. He may inspect and examine any denatured alcohol on the premises and take samples of any denatured alcohol, or of any goods[5] containing denatured alcohol, paying a reasonable price for each sample[6].

1   As to the meaning of 'officer' see PARA 938 note 3; definition applied by the Alcoholic Liquor Duties Act 1979 s 4(3).
2   As to officers of Revenue and Customs see CUSTOMS AND EXCISE vol 31 (2012) PARA 921 et seq; and as to the general powers of search of such officers see CUSTOMS AND EXCISE vol 31 (2012) PARA 1141 et seq.
3   Ie authorised by regulations under the Alcoholic Liquor Duties Act 1979 s 77 (see PARA 941): s 79 (as amended: see note 4).
4   Alcoholic Liquor Duties Act 1979 s 79 (amended by the Finance Act 1995 Sch 2 para 5(d)). As to the meaning of 'denatured alcohol' see PARA 940 note 6.
5   As to the meaning of 'goods' see PARA 908 note 6; definition applied by the Alcoholic Liquor Duties Act 1979 s 4(3).
6   Alcoholic Liquor Duties Act 1979 s 79 (as amended: see note 4). The powers conferred by s 79 are without prejudice to any other power conferred by the Customs and Excise Acts 1979 (as to which see PARA 908): Alcoholic Liquor Duties Act 1979 s 79. As to the general power to take samples see CUSTOMS AND EXCISE vol 31 (2012) PARA 1142.

944.   Prohibition of denatured alcohol as a beverage. With certain exceptions[1] it is prohibited:
   (1)   to prepare, or attempt to prepare, any denatured alcohol[2], methyl alcohol or any mixture containing either of these liquors[3] as a beverage or as a mixture with a beverage[4];
   (2)   to sell any such liquor, whether so prepared or not, as a beverage or mixed with a beverage[5];
   (3)   to use any such liquor or any derivative of it in the preparation of any article capable of being used wholly or partially as a beverage or internally as a medicine[6];
   (4)   to sell or possess any such articles in the preparation of which any such liquor or any derivative of it has been used[7]; or
   (5)   except as permitted by the Commissioners for Revenue and Customs and in accordance with any conditions imposed by them, to purify or attempt to purify any such liquor or, after any such liquor has once been used, to recover or attempt to recover the spirit or alcohol contained in it by distillation or condensation or in any other manner[8].

Any person committing such acts contrary to the above provisions is liable on summary conviction to a penalty[9], and the liquor in respect of which the offence was committed is liable to forfeiture[10].

1 Nothing in these prohibitions affects the use of any denatured alcohol, methyl alcohol or mixtures containing denatured alcohol or methyl alcohol, or any derivative of those substances: (1) in the preparation for use as a medicine of sulphuric ether, chloroform or any other article which the Commissioners for Revenue and Customs may by order specify; or (2) in the making for external use only of any article sold or supplied in accordance with regulations made by the commissioners under the Alcoholic Liquor Duties Act 1979 s 77 (see PARA 941); or (3) in any art or manufacture: s 80(2)(a)–(c), (3) (s 80(3) amended by the Finance Act 1995 Sch 2 para 5(d)). The prohibition does not affect the sale or possession of any article permitted to be prepared or made as stated in head (1) or head (2) above where the article is sold or possessed for use as mentioned in those heads: Alcoholic Liquor Duties Act 1979 s 80(2). As to the Commissioners for Revenue and Customs see CUSTOMS AND EXCISE vol 31 (2012) PARA 921 et seq.

2 As to the meaning of 'denatured alcohol' see PARA 940 note 6.

3 Alcoholic Liquor Duties Act 1979 s 80(3) (as amended: see note 1).

4 Alcoholic Liquor Duties Act 1979 s 80(1)(a).

5 Alcoholic Liquor Duties Act 1979 s 80(1)(b).

6 Alcoholic Liquor Duties Act 1979 s 80(1)(c).

7 Alcoholic Liquor Duties Act 1979 s 80(1)(d).

8 Alcoholic Liquor Duties Act 1979 s 80(1)(e).

9 The penalty must not exceed level 3 on the standard scale: Alcoholic Liquor Duties Act 1979 s 80(1) (amended by virtue of the Criminal Justice Act 1982 ss 38, 46). As to the standard scale see SENTENCING AND DISPOSITION OF OFFENDERS vol 92 (2010) PARA 142.

10 Alcoholic Liquor Duties Act 1979 s 80(1).

945. Petrol substitutes.

Where any person:

(1) puts to a chargeable use[1] any liquid[2] which is not hydrocarbon oil; and

(2) knows or has reasonable cause to believe that there is duty charged[3] on that liquid which has not been paid and is not lawfully deferred,

his putting the liquid to that use attracts a penalty[4], and any goods in respect of which any person contravenes this provision are liable to forfeiture[5].

Likewise, where any person:

(a) puts any biodiesel[6] or bioethanol[7] to a chargeable use[8]; and

(b) knows or has reasonable cause to believe that there is duty charged[9] on that biodiesel or bioethanol which has not been paid and is not lawfully deferred,

his putting the biodiesel or bioethanol to that use attracts a penalty[10], and any goods in respect of which any person contravenes this provision are liable to forfeiture[11].

1 Ie within the meaning of the Hydrocarbon Oil Duties Act 1979 s 6A (see CUSTOMS AND EXCISE vol 30 (2012) PARA 510): s 22(1)(a) (s 22(1) as amended: see note 5).

2 For these purposes, 'liquid' does not include any substance which is gaseous at a temperature of 15° C and under a pressure of 1013.25 millibars: Hydrocarbon Oil Duties Act 1979 s 22(2).

3 Ie under the Hydrocarbon Oil Duties Act 1979 s 6A (see CUSTOMS AND EXCISE vol 30 (2012) PARA 510): s 22(1)(b) (s 22(1) as amended: see note 5).

4 Ie under the Finance Act 1994 s 9 (civil penalties) (see CUSTOMS AND EXCISE vol 31 (2012) PARA 1213): s 22(1) (s 22(1) as amended: see note 5).

5 Hydrocarbon Oil Duties Act 1979 s 22(1) (amended by the Finance Act 1993 s 11(3); and the Finance Act 1994 Sch 4 Pt III para 56(1)). The Finance Act 1994 s 10 (exception for cases of reasonable excuse) (see CUSTOMS AND EXCISE vol 31 (2012) PARA 1213) does not apply in relation to conduct attracting a penalty by virtue of the Hydrocarbon Oil Duties Act 1979 s 22(1), (1AA) or (1AB): s 22(1A) (added by the Finance Act 1994 Sch 4 Pt III para 56(2); amended by the Finance Act 2004 s 10(8)(b)).

6 As to the meaning of 'biodiesel' see the Hydrocarbon Oil Duties Act 1979 s 2AA; and CUSTOMS AND EXCISE vol 30 (2012) PARA 506.

7 As to the meaning of 'bioethanol' see the Hydrocarbon Oil Duties Act 1979 s 2AB; and CUSTOMS AND EXCISE vol 30 (2012) PARA 508.

8 Ie within the meaning of the Hydrocarbon Oil Duties Act 1979 s 6AA or 6AD (see CUSTOMS AND EXCISE vol 30 (2012) PARAS 506, 508): s 22(1AA), (1AB) (as added: see note 11).

9 Ie under the Hydrocarbon Oil Duties Act 1979 s 6AA or 6AD (see CUSTOMS AND EXCISE vol 30 (2012) PARAS 506, 508): s 22(1AA), (1AB) (as added: see note 11).

10　Ie under the Finance Act 1994 s 9 (civil penalties) (see CUSTOMS AND EXCISE vol 31 (2012) PARA 1213): s 22(1AA), (1AB) (as added: see note 11).
11　Hydrocarbon Oil Duties Act 1979 s 22(1AA), (1AB) (s 22(1AA) added by the Finance Act 2002 Sch 2 para 5(7); Hydrocarbon Oil Duties Act 1979 s 22(1AB) added by the Finance Act 2004 s 10(8)(a)). See also note 5.

(3) REGULATION OF PARTICULAR TRADES

(i) Regulated Trades

946.   Miscellaneous restrictions on trade. Particular statutory restrictions, which are considered subsequently in this title, exist in respect of:

(1)　dealing in scrap metal[1];
(2)　hairdressers and barbers[2];
(3)　employment agencies[3];
(4)　the provision of security industry services[4]; and
(5)　sunbed businesses[5].

Particular restrictions, which are considered elsewhere in this work, also exist in relation to pyramid selling schemes[6], acupuncturists and tattooists[7], trading stamps[8], certain offensive and dangerous trades[9], motor salvage operators[10] and vehicle registration plate suppliers[11].

There are a variety of restrictions, which are considered elsewhere in this work, governing the use of premises for certain trades and industries. In particular, such restrictions exist in relation to:

(a)　pet shops[12];
(b)　bookmakers[13];
(c)　slaughterhouses[14];
(d)　inns and hotels[15];
(e)　massage parlours and establishments for special treatment[16];
(f)　pharmaceutical chemists[17];
(g)　food premises[18];
(h)　mines and quarries[19]; and
(i)　cinemas, sex cinemas and sex shops[20].

Examples of commercial activities which are subject to control by licence (and which are considered elsewhere in this work) include: (i) the manufacture of explosives[21]; (ii) the manufacture, assembly, sale, supply, import or export of medicinal products[22]; and (iii) street trading[23].

1　See PARA 954 et seq.
2　See PARA 966 et seq.
3　See PARA 974 et seq.
4　See PARA 980 et seq.
5　See PARA 1004 et seq.
6　See CONSUMER PROTECTION vol 21 (2011) PARA 593 et seq.
7　See ENVIRONMENTAL QUALITY AND PUBLIC HEALTH vol 46 (2010) PARA 973 et seq.
8　See VALUE ADDED TAX vol 99 (2012) PARA 272.
9　See eg BUILDING vol 6 (2011) PARA 140 et seq (storage of celluloid and cinematograph film); and ENERGY AND CLIMATE CHANGE vol 44 (2011) PARA 1046 (searching for and getting petroleum).
10　See ENVIRONMENTAL QUALITY AND PUBLIC HEALTH vol 46 (2010) PARA 750.
11　See ROAD TRAFFIC vol 89 (2011) PARA 325.
12　See ANIMALS vol 2 (2008) PARAS 936, 937.
13　See LICENSING AND GAMBLING vol 67 (2008) PARA 460 et seq.
14　See FOOD AND DRINK vol 51 (2013) PARA 931 et seq.
15　See LICENSING AND GAMBLING vol 67 (2008) PARA 183 et seq.
16　See ENVIRONMENTAL QUALITY AND PUBLIC HEALTH vol 46 (2010) PARA 978.

17 See MEDICAL PROFESSIONS vol 74 (2011) PARA 784 et seq.
18 See FOOD AND DRINK vol 51 (2013) PARA 677 et seq.
19 See MINES, MINERALS AND QUARRIES vol 76 (2013) PARA 511 et seq.
20 See LICENSING AND GAMBLING vol 67 (2008) PARAS 31, 254 et seq, 301 et seq.
21 See EXPLOSIVES vol 47 (2014) PARA 466 et seq.
22 See MEDICAL PRODUCTS AND DRUGS vol 75 (2013) PARAS 35 et seq, 141 et seq.
23 See MARKETS vol 71 (2013) PARA 913 et seq.

(ii) The Iron and Steel Industry

947. Privatisation of the iron and steel industry: creation of British Steel plc.
After its initial nationalisation in 1949 and denationalisation in 1953[1], the iron
and steel industry was largely renationalised in 1967 under the control of the
British Steel Corporation[2]. However, as from 5 September 1988[3] all the property,
rights and liabilities of the corporation became vested in British Steel plc[4], the
successor company nominated by the Secretary of State[5] under the British Steel
Act 1988[6].

The company was wholly owned by the Crown on the appointed day, but
provision was made for the issue and allotting of shares in it, with a view to it
ceasing to be wholly owned by the Crown[7]. The Secretary of State was
thereupon required to fix a target investment limit for government shareholding
in the company; a new such limit may by order be fixed from time to time,
provided that each new limit is lower than the one it replaces, and that no order
may be revoked except by an order fixing a new limit[8].

The British Steel Corporation continues to exist in order to carry out
transitional functions[9]. When the Secretary of State is satisfied that nothing
further remains to be done by the corporation under the transitional provisions
he may, after consulting the corporation and British Steel plc, by order dissolve
the corporation as from a day specified in the order[10].

No information, and nothing contained in a forecast, obtained under the Iron
and Steel Act 1982[11] or any of its predecessors[12] may be disclosed except by
consent, or in summary form relating to a number of businesses, or for the
institution or other purposes of criminal proceedings under the Act or its
predecessors[13]. Disclosure in contravention of this prohibition is an offence
punishable on summary conviction by imprisonment for up to three months or a
fine not exceeding the statutory maximum, or both, and on conviction on
indictment to imprisonment for up to two years or a fine, or both[14]. Where such
an offence committed by a body corporate is proved to have been committed
with the consent or connivance of, or to be attributable to any neglect on the
part of, any director[15], manager, secretary or other similar officer of the body
corporate, or any person purporting to act in any such capacity, he as well as the
body corporate is guilty of the offence and liable to be proceeded against and
punished accordingly[16].

1 See the Iron and Steel Acts 1949 and 1953 (both repealed).
2 See the Iron and Steel Act 1967 (repealed). The former legislation was consolidated in the Iron
   and Steel Act 1982, which has been largely repealed by the British Steel Act 1988. See text and
   notes 3–10.
3 See the British Steel Act 1988 (Appointed Day) Order 1988, SI 1988/1375, made under the
   British Steel Act 1988 s 1(1). On the date mentioned in the text the repeal of most of the Iron
   and Steel Act 1982 came into force: British Steel Act 1988 Sch 2 Pt I. The full repeal of the Iron
   and Steel Act 1982 s 1 and Sch 1 will take effect as from the date of dissolution of the
   corporation (see text and notes 9–10): British Steel Act 1988 Sch 2 Pt II. After that date, the only

provisions of the Iron and Steel Act 1982 remaining in force will be s 33 and s 34 (both amended by the British Steel Act 1988 Sch 2 Pt I) (disclosure of information, and offences relating thereto: see text and notes 11–16).

4   See the British Steel Act 1988 (Nominated Company) Order 1988, SI 1988/1376, made under the British Steel Act 1988 s 1(2) (repealed). As to provisions relating to the financial structure of the company see s 7. The Secretary of State was empowered, before the company ceased to be wholly owned by the Crown, to make loans to the company: see s 8; see also s 9 (temporary restrictions on borrowings). On 6 October 1999, British Steel plc merged with the Dutch company Koninklijke Hoogovens to become the Corus Group, which in turn became part of the Tata Steel Group (a subsidiary of the Tata Group of India) on 30 January 2007.

5   Ie the Secretary of State for Business, Innovation and Skills. The expenses of the Secretary of State under the British Steel Act 1988 are payable out of money provided by Parliament: s 14. As to the Secretary of State see PARA 902.

6   British Steel Act 1988 s 1 (s 1(2), (5) repealed by the Statute Law (Repeals) Act 2004); and see the British Steel Act 1988 Sch 1 for supplementary provisions relating to the vesting. Provision was made for the reduction and extinguishment of liabilities of the British Steel Corporation prior to the appointed day: see s 2 (repealed). Provision may be made for such amendment of enactments as may be necessary or expedient in connection with references to the corporation: s 16(2). Any order under the British Steel Act 1988 must be made by statutory instrument: s 13(1). Orders under s 6 or s 16(2) are subject to annulment in pursuance of a resolution of either House of Parliament: s 13(2). See STATUTES AND LEGISLATIVE PROCESS vol 96 (2012) PARA 1045 et seq.

7   See the British Steel Act 1988 ss 3, 4, 15(2) (s 3(1)–(4) repealed by the Statute Law (Repeals) Act 2004). Powers of the Secretary of State or the Treasury are exercisable by duly appointed nominees: British Steel Act 1988 s 5. As to the Treasury see CONSTITUTIONAL AND ADMINISTRATIVE LAW vol 20 (2014) PARA 262 et seq.

8   See the British Steel Act 1988 s 6(1)–(4). The target investment limit was fixed by the British Steel Act 1988 (Government Shareholding) Order 1989, SI 1989/824, at 0.0472% of the voting rights exercisable in all circumstances at general meetings of British Steel plc: see art 2. It is the duty of the Treasury and the Secretary of State to ensure that the government shareholding does not exceed that limit, but subject to this, the Treasury and Secretary of State may exercise their powers to take up rights available to them, or to direct their nominees to do so: British Steel Act 1988 s 6(5), (6). The temporary suspension of voting rights is disregarded: s 6(7). As to the power to make orders under s 6 see note 6.

     Provision is made in relation to the liability of British Steel plc to corporation tax (see INCOME TAXATION vol 58A (2014) PARA 1018 et seq): see the British Steel Act 1988 s 11 (amended by the Taxation of Chargeable Gains Act 1992 Sch 10 para 15; the Finance Act 1996 Sch 14 para 55; and the Corporation Tax Act 2009 Sch 1 Pt 2 para 329).

9   British Steel Act 1988 s 10(1). As to the transitional functions see Sch 3 paras 2–12. The period from the appointed day (ie 5 September 1988: see text and notes 3–6) and the day specified as the day of dissolution is the transitional period: s 10(1).

10   British Steel Act 1988 s 10(2). At the date at which this volume states the law not such order had been made. As to the constitution and composition of the corporation, and other provisions relating to the performance of its functions see the Iron and Steel Act 1982 s 1, Sch 1 (prospectively repealed (see note 3); both amended, in relation to the transitional period, by the British Steel Act 1988 Sch 3 para 1).

11   See notes 2–3.

12   The predecessors of the Iron and Steel Act 1982 are the Iron and Steel Act 1949, the Iron and Steel Act 1953, the Iron and Steel Act 1967 and the Iron and Steel Act 1975: Iron and Steel Act 1982 s 33(4). See notes 1–2.

13   Iron and Steel Act 1982 s 33(1), (2) (amended by the British Steel Act 1988 Sch 2 Pt I).

14   Iron and Steel Act 1982 s 33(3). As to the statutory maximum see SENTENCING AND DISPOSITION OF OFFENDERS vol 92 (2010) PARA 140.

15   In relation to the British Steel Corporation, or a body corporate established to carry on a nationalised industry and managed by its members, 'director' means a member of the corporation or body in question: Iron and Steel Act 1982 s 34(2).

16   Iron and Steel Act 1982 s 34(1) (amended by the British Steel Act 1988 Sch 2 Pt I).

(iii) The Sugar Industry

948. Deregulation of the sugar industry. The sugar industry was formerly subject to considerable regulation by the Sugar Act 1956, which gave the Sugar

Board[1] powers to buy sugar from abroad (pursuant to the Commonwealth Sugar Agreement[2]), and the British Sugar Corporation Ltd[3] powers to buy domestically grown sugar beet. However, this statutory system of regulation was substantially repealed by the European Communities Act 1972 and the Agriculture (Miscellaneous Provisions) Act 1976[4]. The Sugar Board was dissolved on 15 February 1977[5], and the corporation no longer exercises major statutory powers. There remains, as an exception, one area of statutory control, namely a ministerial reserve power to arrange the setting of the price in any year of home-grown beet[6] in default of agreement between growers and processors[7].

1 The Sugar Board was established by the Sugar Act 1956 s 1(1) (repealed).
2 The Commonwealth Sugar Agreement dated 21 December 1951 was made between the Minister of Food on behalf of the United Kingdom government and representatives of the sugar industries and exporters in Australia, the British West Indies, Fiji, Mauritius and the Union of South Africa: see the Sugar Act 1956 s 1(9), Sch 1 (repealed).
3 The British Sugar Corporation was originally formed under the Sugar Industry (Reorganisation) Act 1936 s 3 (repealed).
4 The major repeals were effected by the European Communities Act 1972 s 4(1), (2), Sch 3 Pt II, by a series of orders fixing appointed days for the repeals to come into effect, namely the Sugar Act 1956 (Repeals) (Appointed Day) (No 1) Order 1973, SI 1973/135; the Sugar Act 1956 (Repeals) (Appointed Day) (No 2) Order 1973, SI 1973/1019; the Sugar Act 1956 (Repeals) (Appointed Day) (No 3) Order 1975, SI 1975/1164; the Sugar Act 1956 (Repeals) (Appointed Day) (No 4) Order 1976, SI 1976/548; the Sugar Act 1956 (Repeals) (Appointed Day) (No 5) Order 1976, SI 1976/2016; and the Sugar Act 1956 (Repeals) (Appointed Day) (No 6) Order 1981, SI 1981/1192. The repeals contained in the Agriculture (Miscellaneous Provisions) Act 1976 Sch 4 Pt I were principally to dissolve the Sugar Board, and under s 27(4) (repealed) came into effect with the coming into force on 15 February 1977 of the Sugar Board (Dissolution) Order 1977, SI 1977/224 (lapsed).
5 See the Agriculture (Miscellaneous Provisions) Act 1976 s 1(4) (repealed); the Sugar Board (Dissolution) Order 1977, SI 1977/224 (lapsed); and note 4. On 1 December 1976 the property, rights and liabilities of the Sugar Board became vested in the Minister of Agriculture, Fisheries and Food (now the Secretary of State for Environment, Food and Rural Affairs): Sugar Board (Transfer of Property etc) (Appointed Day) Order 1976, SI 1976/1963, art 2 (lapsed).
6 As to the meaning of 'home-grown beet' see PARA 949 note 2.
7 See PARA 949.

949. Determination of price of home-grown beet. If in any year it is made to appear to the ministers[1] by the processors of home-grown beet[2] or by a body which is in their opinion substantially representative of the growers of home-grown beet, that the processors and that body are unable to agree on the prices and other terms and conditions for the purchase of home-grown beet by the processors, the ministers may determine (or designate a person to determine) those prices, terms and conditions[3]. Any purchase by processors for which prices, terms and conditions have been so determined, or a contract for such a purchase, takes effect as a purchase or contract at those prices and on those terms and conditions[4].

For the purpose of facilitating:

(1) the making of such a determination as described above; or

(2) the preparation or conduct of discussions concerning EU arrangements for or relating to the regulation of the market for sugar[5],

the appropriate minister[6] may serve on any processor of home-grown beet a notice requiring him to furnish specified information in writing within a specified period[7]. Information so obtained may not be disclosed except with the previous written consent of the person who furnished it, and a person who contravenes this prohibition is liable on conviction on indictment to a fine or imprisonment for up to two years or both, or on summary conviction to a fine not exceeding the statutory maximum[8] or imprisonment for up to three months or both[9]. However, this does not restrict the disclosure of:

(a)   information to any of the ministers[10]; or

(b)   information obtained under head (1) above to a person designated to make a determination as described above or to a body which substantially represents the growers of home-grown beet[11]; or

(c)   the disclosure of information obtained under head (2) above to the EU institution concerned[12].

1   'Ministers' means the Secretary of State for Environment, Food and Rural Affairs, the Secretary of State for Scotland and the Welsh Ministers, acting jointly: Food Act 1984 s 69(3) (amended by the Food Safety Act 1990 Sch 2 para 14; and by virtue of SI 1999/672; and the Government of Wales Act 2006 s 162, Sch 11 para 32). As to the Secretary of State for Environment, Food and Rural Affairs see ENVIRONMENTAL QUALITY AND PUBLIC HEALTH vol 45 (2010) PARA 58 et seq; as to the Secretary of State for Scotland see CONSTITUTIONAL AND ADMINISTRATIVE LAW vol 20 (2014) PARA 69; and as to the Welsh Ministers see CONSTITUTIONAL AND ADMINISTRATIVE LAW vol 20 (2014) PARA 380.

2   'Home-grown beet' means sugar beet grown in Great Britain: Food Act 1984 s 69(3) (as amended (see note 1); definition added by SI 2003/1281). As to the meaning of 'Great Britain' see PARA 906 note 7.

3   Food Act 1984 s 69(1).

4   Food Act 1984 s 69(2).

5   As to the common organisation of the market in sugar see AGRICULTURAL PRODUCTION AND MARKETING vol 1 (2008) PARA 711.

6   'Appropriate minister' means, in relation to England, the Secretary of State for Environment, Food and Rural Affairs (see note 1); in relation to Scotland, the Secretary of State; and, in relation to Wales, the Welsh Ministers: Food Act 1984 s 69A(4) (s 69A added by the Food Safety Act 1990 Sch 2 para 15; definition amended by virtue of SI 1999/672; and the Government of Wales Act 2006 s 162, Sch 11 para 32).

7   Food Act 1984 s 69A(1) (s 69A as added: see note 6).

8   As to the statutory maximum see SENTENCING AND DISPOSITION OF OFFENDERS vol 92 (2010) PARA 140.

9   Food Act 1984 s 69A(2) (s 69A as added: see note 6).

10   Food Act 1984 s 69A(3) (s 69A as added: see note 6).

11   Food Act 1984 s 69A(3)(a) (s 69A as added: see note 6).

12   Food Act 1984 s 69A(3)(b) (s 69A as added: see note 6).

(iv) The Cinematograph Industry

950.   The British Film Institute and deregulation of the cinematograph industry.   There was formerly in existence a system under which a statutory body, the British Film Fund Agency[1], was empowered to impose a levy on film exhibitors and to make payments out of the proceeds of the levy to another statutory body, the National Film Finance Corporation[2], and others, to provide finance for the production and distribution of films[3]. That system was discontinued by the Films Act 1985 and regulations made thereunder[4], and the two statutory bodies were abolished[5]. The remaining statutory provisions relating to the cinematograph industry empower the Secretary of State to give financial assistance for the production of films[6] and to make grants to the British Film Institute[7].

1   The British Film Fund Agency was established by the Cinematograph Films Act 1957 s 1 (repealed) and continued by the Film Levy Finance Act 1981 s 1(1) (repealed).

2   The National Film Finance Corporation was established by the Cinematograph Film Production (Special Loans) Act 1949 (repealed) and continued by the National Film Finance Corporation Act 1981 s 1(1) (repealed).

3   This system was operated under the Film Levy Finance Act 1981 and the National Film Finance Corporation Act 1981 (both repealed). As to the licensing etc of cinemas and the showing of films see LICENSING AND GAMBLING vol 67 (2008) PARAS 31, 254 et seq.

4 See the Films Act 1985 s 2(4) (repealed); and the Films (Ending of Final Levy and Final Distribution Periods) Order 1985, SI 1985/811 (spent).
5 See the British Film Fund Agency (Dissolution) Order 1988, SI 1988/37 (lapsed); and the National Film Finance Corporation (Dissolution) Order 1985, SI 1985/1943 (lapsed).
6 See LICENSING AND GAMBLING vol 67 (2008) PARA 261.
7 The Secretary of State may from time to time make grants to the British Film Institute of such amounts as he thinks fit out of money provided by Parliament: British Film Institute Act 1949 s 1 (amended by the Sunday Cinema Act 1972 s 4, Schedule; and by SI 1992/1311). This function is exercisable by the Secretary of State for Culture, Media and Sport: see the Transfer of Functions (National Heritage) Order 1992, SI 1992/1311 (amended by SI 1997/1744). The British Film Institute is a company incorporated for the purpose of encouraging the use and development of the cinematograph as a means of entertainment and instruction: see the Report of the Committee on the British Film Institute (1948) (Cmd 7361) para 3, App III. As to cinemas generally see LICENSING AND GAMBLING vol 67 (2008) PARA 254 et seq.

(v) Shipbuilding

951. Privatisation of British shipbuilding industry. The British shipbuilding industry was formerly owned and managed by British Shipbuilders, a public corporation established in 1977[1]. Over time the assets of British Shipbuilders were re-privatised, and its main function became that of managing the commitments and liabilities arising from its former manufacture of ships and marine engines[2]. British Shipbuilders was abolished[3], and its property, rights and liabilities were transferred to the Secretary of State[4], on 22 March 2013[5].

1 British Shipbuilders was established by the Aircraft and Shipbuilding Industries Act 1977 s 1(1)(b) (repealed). The assets of the companies previously involved in the shipbuilding industry were vested in British Shipbuilders: see the Aircraft and Shipbuilding Industries Act 1977 ss 19, 20, Sch 2 Pt I (repealed). Compensation for the securities of companies vested in British Shipbuilders was to be paid by the issue of government stock, referred to as 'compensation stock' (see the Aircraft and Shipbuilding Industries Act 1977 ss 35–39, Sch 5 (repealed)), the rate of interest of which, as well as conditions as to repayment, redemption and other matters, were determined by the Treasury (see s 40). The procedure for the issue of stock was governed by the Aircraft and Shipbuilding Industries (Issue of Compensation Stock) Regulations 1977, SI 1977/754 (revoked). British Shipbuilders had power to establish and maintain pensions schemes (see the Aircraft and Shipbuilding Industries Act 1977 s 49 (repealed); and the Shipbuilding Industry (Pensions Schemes) Regulations 1978, SI 1978/232 (revoked)); and provision was made regarding the payment of compensation for loss by employees of employment, emoluments or pension rights (see the Aircraft and Shipbuilding Industries Act 1977 s 50 (repealed)). As to the Treasury see CONSTITUTIONAL AND ADMINISTRATIVE LAW vol 20 (2014) PARA 262 et seq.
   The Aircraft and Shipbuilding Industries Act 1977 also took into public ownership the companies engaged in the manufacture of aircraft, whose assets were vested in the other corporation established by the Act, British Aerospace: see s 1(1)(a) (repealed). This policy was, however, reversed in relation to aircraft by the British Aerospace Act 1980, which dissolved British Aerospace as from 31 December 1981: s 10(9); British Aerospace (Dissolution) Order 1981, SI 1981/1793, art 2. See further PARA 953.
   A tribunal known as the Aircraft and Shipbuilding Industries Arbitration Tribunal was established to determine any question or dispute expressly required by the Aircraft and Shipbuilding Industries Act 1977 to be determined by or referred to arbitration under the Act, or any matter in respect of which the Act gave jurisdiction to the tribunal: see the Aircraft and Shipbuilding Industries Act 1977 s 42(1) (repealed). The tribunal was under the direct supervision of the Administrative Justice and Tribunals Council: see the Tribunals and Inquiries Act 1992 Sch 1 para 2 (repealed); and the Tribunals, Courts and Enforcement Act 2007 s 45 (repealed). Both the tribunal and the council have now been abolished: see the Public Bodies (Abolition of the Aircraft and Shipbuilding Industries Arbitration Tribunal) Order 2013, SI 2013/686; and the Public Bodies (Abolition of Administrative Justice and Tribunals Council) Order 2013, SI 2013/2042 (both made under the Public Bodies Act 2011 ss 1(1), 6(1), (5), 35(2)).

2   For example, personal injury claims relating to mesothelioma contracted after being exposed to
    asbestos dust while working for British Shipbuilders. As to employers' liabilities for exposure of
    employees to harmful substances see HEALTH AND SAFETY AT WORK vol 52 (2014) PARA 376.
3   See the Public Bodies Act 2011 s 1, Sch 1; and the Public Bodies (Abolition of British
    Shipbuilders) Order 2013, SI 2013/687, art 4.
4   As to the Secretary of State see PARA 902.
5   See the Public Bodies Act 2011 ss 6, 23, 24(1), 35(2); and the Public Bodies (Abolition of British
    Shipbuilders) Order 2013, SI 2013/687, arts 1(2), 2, 3.

952.   Construction credits.   The Secretary of State[1], with the consent of the
Treasury[2], may guarantee the payment by any person who is an individual
resident in, or a body corporate incorporated under the law of any part of the
United Kingdom[3], any of the Channel Islands or the Isle of Man of any sum
payable by that person in respect of principal or interest under arrangements
(whether by way of loan or otherwise) entered into by that person for the
purpose of financing the construction[4] to the order of that person in any member
state of the European Union of a ship[5] or mobile offshore installation[6] of the
qualifying size[7], and its equipment[8] to his order[9]. The aggregate of the liability of
the Secretary of State under the guarantees together with the guarantees given
under superseded legislation[10] may not exceed £1,400 million, less the amounts
which have been paid by him to meet a liability and have not been repaid to
him[11].

The Secretary of State may make a loan to any person who is a creditor in
respect of a sum the payment of which has been so guaranteed by the Secretary
of State[12]. The aggregate of the loans outstanding may not at any time exceed the
limit with respect to guarantees, less the amounts which have been paid by him
to meet a liability and have not been repaid to him[13].

1   As to the Secretary of State see PARA 902.
2   As to the Treasury see CONSTITUTIONAL AND ADMINISTRATIVE LAW vol 20 (2014) PARA 262 et
    seq.
3   As to the meaning of 'United Kingdom' see PARA 906 note 7.
4   'Construction' includes the completion of a partially constructed ship or installation and the
    alteration of a ship or installation and of a partially constructed ship or installation: Industry
    Act 1972 s 10(9) (amended by the Industry Act 1975 s 24(3); the Shipbuilding Act 1979 s 2; and
    SI 2009/1941).
5   'Ship' includes every description of vessel used in navigation: Industry Act 1972 s 12(1).
6   'Mobile offshore installation' means any installation intended for underwater exploitation of
    mineral resources or exploration with a view to such exploitation and which can move by water
    from place to place without major dismantling or modification, whether or not it has its own
    motive power: Industry Act 1972 s 12(1).
7   A ship other than a tug is of the qualifying size if its gross tonnage, ascertained in accordance
    with regulations under the Merchant Shipping Act 1995 s 19 (see SHIPPING AND MARITIME LAW
    vol 93 (2008) PARA 248) is not less than 100 tons (Industry Act 1972 s 12(2)(a) (amended by the
    Merchant Shipping Act 1995 Sch 13 para 47)); a tug is of the qualifying size if it is of not less
    than 500 brake horsepower (Industry Act 1972 s 12(2)(b)); and an installation is of the
    qualifying size if it weighs not less than 100 tons excluding fuel and water (s 12(2)(c)).
8   'Equipment', in relation to a ship or installation, means the installation on or in it, or the
    provision for it, of fixed or movable equipment, or apparatus or furnishings of any kind:
    Industry Act 1972 s 12(1).
9   Industry Act 1972 s 10(1) (amended by SI 1987/1807). A guarantee or loan may be given on
    such terms and conditions as may be specified with the approval of the Treasury: Industry
    Act 1972 s 10(7). The Secretary of State, with the consent of the Treasury, may renew such a
    guarantee (including a guarantee previously so renewed) on the transfer of the liability to which
    it relates, or any part of that liability, from one body corporate to another within the same
    group: s 10(7A) (s 10(7A), (7B) added by the Industry Act 1975 s 24(2)). Two bodies corporate
    are in the same group for this purpose if one is the other's holding company or both are
    subsidiaries of a third body corporate: Industry Act 1972 s 10(7B) (as so added). In addition to
    construction credits (by way of guarantee) s 11 also provided for the making of grants by the

Secretary of State towards the costs paid in the years 1972–1974 of the construction of certain ships. 'Holding company' and 'subsidiary' have the meanings assigned to them by the Companies Act 2006 s 1159 (see COMPANIES vol 14 (2009) PARA 25): Industry Act 1972 s 10(9) (as amended: see note 4).

10 Ie under the Shipbuilding Industry Act 1967 s 7 (repealed).

11 Industry Act 1972 s 10(2), (3) (s 10(2) amended by the Industry Act 1975 s 24(1); Industry Act 1972 s 10(3) amended by the Industry Act 1975 s 23); Ships and Mobile Offshore Installations Construction Credits (Increase of Limit) Order 1975, SI 1975/138, art 2. The maximum limit may be raised to £1,800 million by the Secretary of State by order contained in a statutory instrument approved by a resolution of the House of Commons: Industry Act 1972 s 10(3), (4) (s 10(3) as so amended).At the date at which this volume states the law no such order had been made. The liabilities of the Secretary of State do not include liability in respect of interest on any money which is the subject of a guarantee: s 10(8).

12 Industry Act 1972 s 10(5). Grants may be made by the Secretary of State with the consent of the Treasury, on such terms and conditions as he may determine, to any person who is or has been a creditor for the purpose of supplementing the interest receivable or received on the principal money the payment of which has been guaranteed under s 10 or under the Shipbuilding Industry Act 1967 s 7 (repealed): Industry Act 1972 s 10A (added by the Industry Act 1975 s 25).

13 Industry Act 1972 s 10(6) (amended by the Industry Act 1975 s 24(1)).

(vi) Aircraft Manufacture

953. Privatisation of aircraft manufacturing industry: creation of British Aerospace Ltd. Under the Aircraft and Shipbuilding Industries Act 1977, the manufacture of aircraft and ships was taken into public ownership and two corporations, British Shipbuilders[1] and British Aerospace, were formed[2]. The British Aerospace Act 1980, however, made provision for the vesting of the property, rights, liabilities and obligations of British Aerospace in a successor company, British Aerospace Ltd[3], as from the appointed day, that is, 1 January 1981[4], and for the dissolution of British Aerospace as from 31 December 1981[5].

The successor company was wholly owned by the Crown at the appointed day[6], and provision was made as to the initial government shareholding in the company[7], and the financial structure of the company and its subsidiaries (including the establishment and application of a 'statutory reserve', being the amount by which the government investment in British Aerospace exceeded the initial share capital of the successor company)[8].

The Secretary of State[9] was empowered to acquire voting shares in the successor company, or rights to subscribe for ordinary shares, or securities which could be converted into, or carry, rights to subscribe for shares, but was not permitted to dispose of them without the consent of the Treasury[10]. The Secretary of State was required to set a target investment limit for the government shareholding in the company as soon as it ceased to be wholly owned by the Crown, and was empowered from time to time, by order made by statutory instrument, to fix a new limit[11].

If a resolution is passed for the voluntary winding up of the successor company, or a winding-up order has been made by the court[12], the Secretary of State is liable, on the commencement of the winding up[13], to discharge certain outstanding liabilities of the successor company[14], and he becomes a creditor of the company to the extent of the amount he has paid[15].

Employment by British Aerospace was declared to be uninterrupted by the transfer to British Aerospace Ltd, and pension rights were expressly preserved[16].

1 Now abolished; see PARA 951.

2 British Aerospace was formed of the companies mentioned in the Aircraft and Shipbuilding Industries Act 1977 s 19(1), Sch 1 Pt I. References in that Act to British Aerospace were generally removed by the British Aerospace Act 1980 s 10(1), Sch 3 (s 10 repealed).

3   See the British Aerospace Act 1980 s 1(1), (2), 14(1) (s 1(2) repealed); and the British Aerospace (Nominated Company) Order 1980, SI 1980/1989 (lapsed).

4   See the British Aerospace Act 1980 ss 1, 14, Sch 1 (s 1 amended by the Statute Law (Repeals) Act 2004; Sch 1 amended by the Industrial Development Act 1982 Sch 2 Pt II para 15); and the British Aerospace (Appointed Day) Order 1980, SI 1980/1988. Provision was made for the continuation in force or effect after the appointed day of agreements and transactions entered into before that day (British Aerospace Act 1980 s 1(3), (6), Sch 1 para 1), for the continuity of certain proceedings (s 1(4) (repealed)), and for the liability of the successor company under judgments or orders made before the appointed day (s 8 (repealed)). Specified government investment in British Aerospace was extinguished immediately before the appointed day: see s 2 (repealed).

       Provision is made in relation to the liability of the successor company to corporation tax (see INCOME TAXATION vol 58A (2014) PARA 1018 et seq), and development land tax (now abolished): see the British Aerospace Act 1980 s 12 (amended by the Taxation of Chargeable Gains Act 1992 Sch 10 para 4).

5   See the British Aerospace Act 1980 s 10 (repealed); and the British Aerospace (Dissolution) Order 1981, SI 1981/1793 (lapsed). Transitional provision was also made: see the British Aerospace Act 1980 s 10, Sch 2 (repealed).

6   See the British Aerospace Act 1980 s 1(2) (repealed).

7   See the British Aerospace Act 1980 s 3 (repealed), which provided for the issue of shares under the direction of the Secretary of State. As to the Secretary of State see PARA 902. Any administrative expenses of the Secretary of State are paid out of money provided by Parliament: British Aerospace Act 1980 s 13.

8   See the British Aerospace Act 1980 s 4 (amended by SI 2008/948).

9   The Secretary of State's functions in relation to the acquisition and disposal of shares, etc could be discharged by a nominee, who did so under the direction of the Secretary of State with the consent of the Treasury: see the British Aerospace Act 1980 s 6 (repealed). As to the Treasury see CONSTITUTIONAL AND ADMINISTRATIVE LAW vol 20 (2014) PARA 262 et seq.

10   British Aerospace Act 1980 s 5(1)–(3) (repealed). The Secretary of State's expenses were met out of money provided by Parliament: s 5(4) (repealed). Any dividend or other sums received by him as a result of such acquisition had to be paid into the Consolidated Fund: s 5(5) (repealed). As to the Consolidated Fund see CONSTITUTIONAL AND ADMINISTRATIVE LAW vol 20 (2014) PARA 480 et seq; PARLIAMENT vol 78 (2010) PARAS 1028–1031.

11   See the British Aerospace Act 1980 s 7 (repealed). Any such limit was required to be lower than the one which it replaced: s 7(4)(a) (repealed). The most recent limit was set by the British Aerospace Act 1980 (Government Shareholding) Order 1986, SI 1986/848 (lapsed), setting a target investment limit of nil: see art 2 (lapsed).

12   As to winding up generally see COMPANY AND PARTNERSHIP INSOLVENCY vol 16 (2011) PARA 380 et seq.

13   Ie on the passing of the resolution or, as the case may be, on the making of the order: British Aerospace Act 1980 s 9(6).

14   British Aerospace Act 1980 s 9(1), (2) (s 9(1) amended by the Insolvency Act 1986 Sch 14; British Aerospace Act 1980 s 9(2) amended by the Statute Law (Repeals) Act 2004). The liabilities are any obligation transferred to the successor company on the appointed day: British Aerospace Act 1980 s 9(2) (as so amended). Any sums required by the Secretary of State to discharge any such liability are paid out of money provided by Parliament: s 9(3).

15   British Aerospace Act 1980 s 9(4), which further provides that the Secretary of State's claim is to be treated for the purposes of the winding up as a claim against the original liability. Any sums received by the Secretary of State in the winding up must be paid into the Consolidated Fund: s 9(5).

16   British Aerospace Act 1980 Sch 1 para 2. In the period during which the aircraft industry was in public ownership the same powers to establish and maintain pension schemes existed as have been previously described in relation to shipbuilding: see the Aircraft and Shipbuilding Industries Act 1977 s 49 (repealed); and PARA 951. See also the Aircraft Industry (Pension Schemes) Regulations 1977, SI 1977/1329 (lapsed), made under the Aircraft and Shipbuilding Industries Act 1977 s 49 (repealed).

(vii) Scrap Metal Dealers

954. Licensing of scrap metal dealers. No person may carry on business as a scrap metal dealer[1] unless authorised by a licence[2]. To do so is an offence[3].

A scrap metal licence, issued by a local authority[4], must be one of two types[5]:

(1)   a site licence, authorising the licensee to carry on business at any site[6] in the authority's area as defined in the licence[7], which must name the licensee and the authority, identify all the sites in the authority's area at which the licensee is authorised to carry on business, name the site manager[8] of each site and state the date on which it is due to expire[9];

(2)   a collector's licence, authorising the licensee to carry on business as a mobile collector[10] in the authority's area[11], which must name the licensee and the authority, and state the date on which it is due to expire[12].

A licence must be in in a form that complies with heads (1) and (2) and enables the licensee to comply with requirements regarding its display[13]. The Secretary of State may prescribe further requirements as to the form and content of licence in regulations[14].

A scrap metal dealer who holds a site licence must display a copy of the licence in a prominent place in an area accessible to the public at each site identified in the licence[15]. A scrap metal dealer who holds a collector's licence must display a copy of the licence on any vehicle being used in the course of the dealer's business[16], in a manner which enables it to be easily read by a person outside the vehicle[17]. To fail to display a licence is an offence[18].

1   A person carries on a business as a scrap metal dealer for these purposes if he carries on a business which consists wholly or partly of buying or selling scrap metal, whether in the form in which it was bought or not, or if he carries on business as a motor salvage operator, so far as that does not constitute carrying on a business which consists wholly or partly of buying or selling scrap metal: Scrap Metal Dealers Act 2013 s 21(2). 'Scrap metal dealer' means a person who is for the time being carrying on business as a scrap metal dealer, whether or not authorised by a licence: s 21(5). 'Scrap metal', subject to amendment by the Secretary of State by order, includes any old, waste or discarded metal or metallic material and any product, article or assembly which is made from or contains metal and is broken, worn out or regarded by its last holder as having reached the end of its useful life, but does not include gold, silver or any alloy of which two per cent or more by weight is attributable to gold or silver: s 21(6)–(8). As to the Secretary of State see PARA 902.
      Power under the Scrap Metal Dealers Act 2013 to make an order or regulations is exercisable by statutory instrument subject to annulment in pursuance of a resolution of either House of Parliament (other than an order under s 12(2) (see PARA 963 note 6) or s 21(8) which may not be made unless a draft of the instrument has been laid before and approved by a resolution of each House of Parliament): s 20(1)–(3). Any power to make an order or regulations under the Act may be executed so as to make different provisions for different purposes and includes power to make such incidental, supplementary, consequential, transitory, transitional or saving provision as the Secretary of State considers appropriate: s 20(4). See STATUTES AND LEGISLATIVE PROCESS vol 96 (2012) PARAS 1032, 1045 et seq.
      A person who manufactures articles is not regarded as selling scrap metal if they do so only as a by-product of manufacturing articles or as surplus materials not required for manufacturing them: s 21(3). A person carries on business as a motor salvage operator if they carry on a business which consists: (1) wholly or partly in recovering salvageable parts from motor vehicles for re-use or sale and subsequently selling or otherwise disposing of the rest of the vehicle for scrap; (2) wholly or mainly in buying written-off vehicles and subsequently repairing and reselling them; (3) wholly or mainly in buying or selling motor vehicles which are to be the subject, whether immediately or on a subsequent resale, of any of the activities mentioned in heads (1) and (2); or (4) wholly or mainly in activities falling within heads (2) and (3): s 21(4).
2   Scrap Metal Dealers Act 2013 s 1(1). Subject to revocation (see s 4; and PARA 958) a licence expires at the end of the period of three years beginning with the day on which it is issued, but can be renewed on application to do so if the application is received before the licence expires, in which case the renewed licence expires at the end of the period of three years beginning with the day on which it is renewed or, if renewed more than once, the day on which it was last renewed: see Sch 1 para 1(1), (2)(c), (3). If the application for renewal is withdrawn, the licence expires at the end of the day on which the application is withdrawn and if the application is refused the licence expires when no appeal under Sch 1 para 9 (see PARA 956) is possible in relation to the refusal or any such appeal is finally determined or withdrawn: Sch 1 para 1(2)(a),

    (b). The Secretary of State may by order substitute different periods for the periods specified in Sch 1 para 1(1), (2)(c): Sch 1 para 1(4). At the date at which this volume states the law no such order had been made. As to applications for licences see PARA 955.

3   Scrap Metal Dealers Act 2013 s 1(3). A person guilty of such an offence is liable on summary conviction to a fine not exceeding level 5 on the standard scale: s 1(3). As to the standard scale see SENTENCING AND DISPOSITION OF OFFENDERS vol 92 (2010) PARA 142.

    Where an offence under the Scrap Metal Dealers Act 2013 is committed by a body corporate and is proved to have been committed with the consent or connivance of a director, manager, secretary or other similar officer, or to be attributable to any neglect on the part of any such individual, the individual as well as the body corporate is guilty of the offence and is liable to proceeded against and punished accordingly: s 17(1). Where the affairs of a body corporate are managed by its members, this applies in relation to the acts and omissions of a member in connection with that management as if the member were a director of the body corporate: s 17(2).

4   Scrap Metal Dealers Act 2013 s 2(1). 'Local authority', in relation to England, means the council of a district, the Common Council of the City of London or the council of a London borough and, in relation to Wales, means the council of a county or a county borough: s 22(3). As to local government areas and authorities in England and Wales see LOCAL GOVERNMENT vol 69 (2009) PARA 22 et seq; as to the London boroughs and their councils see LONDON GOVERNMENT vol 71 (2013) PARAS 15, 20–22, 55 et seq; and as to the Common Council of the City of London see LONDON GOVERNMENT vol 71 (2013) PARA 34 et seq. As to the issuing of a licence see PARA 957.

    A person may hold more than one licence issued by different local authorities, but may not hold more than one licence issued by any one authority: s 2(9).

5   See the Scrap Metal Dealers Act 2013 s 2(2). A local authority may, on an application, very a licence by changing it from one type to the other: Sch 1 para 3(1). The authority must, within 28 days of such variation, notify the relevant environment body of the variation and the relevant environmental body must amend the register under s 7 (see PARA 959) accordingly: s 8(6)(b), (8). 'Relevant environmental body' means, for an authority in England, the Environment Agency and, for an authority in Wales, the Natural Resources Body for Wales: s 8(11). As to the Environment Agency see ENVIRONMENTAL QUALITY AND PUBLIC HEALTH vol 45 (2010) PARA 68 et seq; and as to the Natural Resources Body for Wales see FORESTRY vol 52 (2014) PARA 38. As to such applications see PARA 955.

6   'Site' means any premises used in the course of carrying on business as a scrap metal dealer, whether or not metal is kept there: Scrap Metal Dealers Act 2013 s 22(9). 'Premises' includes any land or other place, whether enclosed or not: s 22(6).

7   Scrap Metal Dealers Act 2013 s 2(3).

8   'Site manager', in relation to a site at which a scrap metal dealer carries on business, means the individual who exercise day-to-day control and management of activities at the site: Scrap Metal Dealers Act 2013 s 22(10). An individual may be named in a licence as site manager at more than one site, but no site may have more than one site manager named in relation to it: s 22(11).

9   Scrap Metal Dealers Act 2013 s 2(4).

10   'Mobile collector' means a person who carries on business as a scrap metal dealer otherwise than at a site and who regularly engages, in the course of that business, in collecting waste materials and old, broken, worn out or defaced articles by means of visits from door to door: Scrap Metal Dealers Act 2013 s 22(4).

11   Scrap Metal Dealers Act 2013 s 2(5).

12   Scrap Metal Dealers Act 2013 s 2(6).

13   Scrap Metal Dealers Act 2013 s 2(7). The reference to requirements regarding its display is to the requirements in s 10 (see text and notes 15–18): s 2(7)(b).

14   Scrap Metal Dealers Act 2013 s 2(8). At the date at which this volume states the law no such regulations had been made.

15   Scrap Metal Dealers Act 2013 s 10(1), (2).

16   Scrap Metal Dealers Act 2013 s 10(3).

17   Scrap Metal Dealers Act 2013 s 10(4).

18   Scrap Metal Dealers Act 2013 s 10(5). A person guilty of such an offence is liable on summary conviction to a fine not exceeding level 3 on the standard scale: s 10(5).

955. Scrap metal licence applications. Scrap metal[1] licences are issued[2] or renewed[3] on application[4].

    If there is a change in the name of the licensee[5], the sites[6] in the local authority's area at which the licensee is authorised to carry on business[7] or the site manager[8] of each site[9], the licensee must make an application to vary the licence accordingly[10] or else be guilty of an offence[11]. Such an application must be made to the local authority that issued the licence[12] and must contain particulars of the changes to be made to the licence[13].

Either when the application is made or later, the local authority may request that the applicant provide such further information as the authority considers relevant for the purpose of considering the application[14] and if the applicant fails to provide the information so requested the authority may decline to proceed with the application[15].

It is an offence to make a statement knowing it to be false in a material particular, or recklessly make a statement which is false in a material particular, in an application or a response to a request for further information from a local authority[16].

1 As to the meaning of 'scrap metal' see PARA 954 note 1.
2 As to the issuing of such licences see PARA 957.
3 As to the renewal of such licences see PARA 954 note 2.
4 Scrap Metal Dealers Act 2013 Sch 1 para 2(1). The details that must accompany an application are set out in Sch 1 para 2(1)–(3). They may be altered by the Secretary of State by order: Sch 1 para 2(4). As to the Secretary of State see PARA 902. As to the making of orders or regulations under the Scrap Metal Dealers Act 2013 generally see PARA 954 note 1. An applicant for a scrap metal licence, or for the renewal or variation of a licence, must notify the authority to which the application was made of any changes which materially affect the accuracy of the information which the applicant has provided in connection with the application: s 8(1). A person who fails to comply with a notification requirement under s 8 is guilty of an offence and liable on summary conviction to a fine not exceeding level 3 on the standard scale: s 8(9). As to the standard scale see SENTENCING AND DISPOSITION OF OFFENDERS vol 92 (2010) PARA 142. It is a defence for a person charged with such an offence to prove that the person took all reasonable steps to avoid committing the offence: s 8(10).

   Applications must also be accompanied by a fee set by the local authority issuing the licence: Sch 1 para 6(1). In setting such a fee the authority must have regard to any guidance issued from time to time by the Secretary of State with the approval of the Treasury: Sch 1 para 6(2). As to the meaning of 'local authority' see PARA 954 note 4. As to the Treasury see CONSTITUTIONAL AND ADMINISTRATIVE LAW vol 20 (2014) PARA 262 et seq.

5 Ie a change to the matters mentioned in the Scrap Metal Dealers Act 2013 s 2(4)(a), (6)(a) (see PARA 954): Sch 1 para 3(2).
6 As to the meaning of 'site' see PARA 954 note 6.
7 Ie a change to the matters mentioned in the Scrap Metal Dealers Act 2013 s 2(4)(c) (see PARA 954): Sch 1 para 3(2).
8 As to the meaning of 'site manager' see PARA 954 note 8.
9 Ie a change to the matters mentioned in the Scrap Metal Dealers Act 2013 s 2(4)(d) (see PARA 954): Sch 1 para 3(2). As to the fee to accompany an application see note 4.
10 Scrap Metal Dealers Act 2013 Sch 1 para 3(2). The power to change the name of the licensee does not however include the power to transfer the licence from one person to another: Sch 1 para 3(3).
11 Scrap Metal Dealers Act 2013 Sch 1 para 3(5). A person guilty of such an offence is liable on summary conviction to a fine not exceeding level 3 on the standard scale: Sch 1 para 3(5). It is a defence for a person charged with such an offence to prove that the person took all reasonable steps to avoid committing the offence: Sch 1 para 3(6). As to offences committed by a body corporate see PARA 954 note 3.
12 Scrap Metal Dealers Act 2013 Sch 1 para 3(4)(a).
13 Scrap Metal Dealers Act 2013 Sch 1 para 3(4)(b). As to the notification obligation on the local authority when a licence is varied see PARA 954 note 5.
14 Scrap Metal Dealers Act 2013 Sch 1 para 4(1).
15 Scrap Metal Dealers Act 2013 Sch 1 para 4(2). As to the notification requirement when any information provided in connection with an application has changed see note 4.
16 Scrap Metal Dealers Act 2013 Sch 1 para 5. A person guilty of such an offence is liable on summary conviction to a fine not exceeding level 3 on the standard scale: Sch 1 para 5.

956. Refusals, representations and appeals. If a local authority[1] proposes to refuse an application for a scrap metal[2] licence or for variation of such a licence[3] or to revoke or vary such a licence[4], the authority must give the applicant or licensee ('A') a notice setting out what the authority proposes to do and the reasons for it[5]. The notice must also state that, within a specified period[6], A may make representations about the proposal or may inform the authority that he wishes to make representations[7].

If A does not make any representations, has not informed the authority within the specified period that he intends to make any representations, or has informed the authority within the specified period that he does not wish to make any representations, the authority may refuse the application or revoke or vary the licence[8].

If A does inform the authority within the specified period that he wishes to make representations, the authority must allow A a further reasonable period to make such representation, and may refuse the application, or revoke or vary the order if A fails to make representations within that further period[9]. If A does make representations within either the specified period or the further period, the authority must consider the representations[10].

If the authority refuses the application, or revokes or varies the licence, it must give A a notice setting out the decision and the reasons for it, stating that A may appeal against the decision and the time within which such an appeal may be brought, and, in the case of a revocation or variation, stating the date on which the revocation or variation is to take effect[11].

An applicant may appeal to a magistrates' court against the refusal of an application for a scrap metal licence or for a variation of such a licence[12]. A licensee may appeal to a magistrates' court against the inclusion in a licence of a condition[13] or against the revocation or variation of a licence[14]. An appeal must be made within the period of 21 days beginning with the day on which notice of the decision to refuse the application, to include the condition, or to revoke or vary the licence, was given[15]. On an appeal, the magistrates' court may confirm, vary or reverse the authority's decision and give such directions as it considers appropriate[16]. The authority must comply with any such directions[17], but need not do so until the time for making an application by way of case stated[18] has passed[19] or, if such application is made, until the application is finally determined or withdrawn[20].

1   As to the meaning of 'local authority' see PARA 954 note 4.
2   As to the meaning of 'scrap metal' see PARA 954 note 1.
3   Ie an application under the Scrap Metal Dealers Act 2013 Sch 1 para 2 or para 3 (see PARA 955): Sch 1 para 7(1)(a).
4   Ie revoke or vary a licence under the Scrap Metal Dealers Act 2013 s 4 (see PARA 958): Sch 1 para 7(1)(b).
5   Scrap Metal Dealers Act 2013 Sch 1 para 7(1).
6   The period specified must be not less than 14 days beginning with the date on which the notice is given to A: Scrap Metal Dealers Act 2013 Sch 1 para 7(4).
7   Scrap Metal Dealers Act 2013 Sch 1 para 7(3).
8   Scrap Metal Dealers Act 2013 Sch 1 para 7(5).
9   Scrap Metal Dealers Act 2013 Sch 1 para 7(6).
10   Scrap Metal Dealers Act 2013 Sch 1 para 7(7). If A informs the authority that he wishes to make representations orally, the authority must give him the opportunity of appearing before, and being heard by, a person appointed by the authority: Sch 1 para 7(8).
11   Scrap Metal Dealers Act 2013 Sch 1 para 8.
12   Scrap Metal Dealers Act 2013 Sch 1 para 9(1).
13   Ie a condition under the Scrap Metal Dealers Act 2013 s 3(8) (see PARA 957 note 6): Sch 1 para 9(2)(a).

14 Scrap Metal Dealers Act 2013 Sch 1 para 9(2).
15 Scrap Metal Dealers Act 2013 Sch 1 para 9(3). The procedure on such an appeal is by way of complaint for an order, and the Magistrates' Courts Act 1980 (see MAGISTRATES vol 71 (2013) PARA 510 et seq) applies to the proceedings: Sch 1 para 9(5). For the purposes of the time limit, the making of the complaint is to be treated as the making of the appeal: Sch 1 para 9(5).
16 Scrap Metal Dealers Act 2013 Sch 1 para 9(6). The reference to what the court considers appropriate is to what the court considers appropriate having regard to the provisions of the Scrap Metal Dealers Act 2013: Sch 1 para 9(6)(b).
17 Scrap Metal Dealers Act 2013 Sch 1 para 9(7).
18 Ie an application under the Magistrates' Courts Act 1980 s 111 (see MAGISTRATES vol 71 (2013) PARA 703 et seq): Scrap Metal Dealers Act 2013 Sch 1 para 9(8)(a).
19 Scrap Metal Dealers Act 2013 Sch 1 para 9(8)(a).
20 Scrap Metal Dealers Act 2013 Sch 1 para 9(8)(b).

957. Issuing of scrap metal licences. A local authority[1] must not issue or renew a scrap metal[2] licence[3] unless it is satisfied that the applicant is a suitable person to carry on business as a scrap metal dealer[4]. In determining whether an applicant is a suitable person, the authority may have regard to any information it considers relevant, in particular:

(1) whether the applicant or any site manager[5] has been convicted of any relevant offence[6];

(2) whether the applicant or any site manager has been the subject of any relevant enforcement action[7];

(3) any previous refusal of an application for the issue or renewal of a scrap metal licence, and the reasons for that refusal[8];

(4) any previous refusal of an application for a relevant environmental permit or registration[9], and the reasons for that refusal[10];

(5) any previous revocation of a scrap metal licence, and the reasons for that revocation[11];

(6) whether the applicant has demonstrated that there will be in place adequate procedures to ensure that provisions relating the regulations of scrap metal dealers[12] will be complied with[13].

In determining whether a company is a suitable person to carry on business as a scrap metal dealer, a local authority must have regard, in particular as to whether any director, secretary or shadow director[14] of the company is a suitable person[15].

In determining whether a partnership is a suitable person to carry on business as a scrap metal dealer, a local authority is to have regard, in particular, to whether each of the partners is a suitable person[16].

When determining suitability a local authority may have regard to any guidance issued for such purpose by the Secretary of State[17] and may consult other persons including, in particular, any other local authority, the Environment Agency[18], the Natural Resources Body for Wales[19] or an officer of a police force[20].

1 As to the meaning of 'local authority' see PARA 954 note 4.
2 As to the meaning of 'scrap metal' see PARA 954 note 1.
3 As to the form and requirements of such a licence see PARA 954.
4 Scrap Metal Dealers Act 2013 s 3(1). As to the meanings of 'scrap metal dealer' and 'carry on business as a scrap metal dealer' see PARA 954 note 1.
5 As to the meaning of 'site manager' see PARA 954 note 8. For these purposes, the definition includes an individual proposed to be named in the licence as a site manager: Scrap Metal Dealers Act 2013 s 3(3)(a).
6 Scrap Metal Dealers Act 2013 s 3(2)(a). 'Relevant offence' means an offence set out in the Scrap Metal Dealers Act 2013 (Prescribed Relevant Offences and Relevant Enforcement Action) Regulations 2013, SI 2013/2258, Schedule and includes any offence of: (1) attempting or

conspiring to commit any offence falling within that Schedule; (2) inciting or aiding, abetting, counselling or procuring the commission of any offence falling within that Schedule; and (3) an offence under the Serious Crime Act 2007 Pt 2 (ss 44–67) (encouraging or assisting crime) (see CRIMINAL LAW vol 25 (2010) PARA 64 et seq) committed in relation to any offence falling within the Scrap Metal Dealers Act 2013 (Prescribed Relevant Offences and Relevant Enforcement Action) Regulations 2013, SI 2013/2258, Schedule: Scrap Metal Dealers Act 2013 s 3(3)(b); Scrap Metal Dealers Act 2013 (Prescribed Relevant Offences and Relevant Enforcement Action) Regulations 2013, SI 2013/2258, reg 2. As to the Secretary of State see PARA 902. As to the making of orders or regulations under the Scrap Metal Dealers Act 2013 generally see PARA 954 note 1.

If the applicant or site manager has been convicted of a relevant offence, the authority may include one or both of the following conditions: (1) that the dealer must not receive scrap metal except between 9am and 5pm on any day; or (2) that all scrap metal received must be kept in the form in which it is received for a period specified in the condition, not exceeding 72 hours, beginning with the time when it is received: s 3(8), (9).

7   Scrap Metal Dealers Act 2013 s 3(2)(b). For these purposes, a person is the subject of 'relevant enforcement action' if: (1) the person has been charged with an offence specified in the Scrap Metal Dealers Act 2013 (Prescribed Relevant Offences and Relevant Enforcement Action) Regulations 2013, SI 2013/2258, Schedule, and criminal proceedings in respect of that offence have not yet concluded; or (2) an environmental permit granted in respect of the person under the Environmental Permitting (England and Wales) Regulations 2010, SI 2010/675 (see ENVIRONMENTAL QUALITY AND PUBLIC HEALTH vol 46 (2010) PARAS 662–692) has been revoked in whole, or partially revoked, to the extent that the permit no longer authorises the recovery of metal: Scrap Metal Dealers Act 2013 s 3(3)(c); Scrap Metal Dealers Act 2013 (Prescribed Relevant Offences and Relevant Enforcement Action) Regulations 2013, SI 2013/2258, reg 3.

8   Scrap Metal Dealers Act 2013 s 3(2)(c).

9   'Relevant environmental permit or registration', in relation to an application made to a local authority, means: (1) any environmental permit under the Environmental (Permitting) Regulations 2010, SI 2010/675, reg 13 (see ENVIRONMENTAL QUALITY AND PUBLIC HEALTH vol 46 (2010) PARA 664) authorising any operation by the applicant in the local authority's area; (2) any registration of the applicant under Sch 2 (see ENVIRONMENTAL QUALITY AND PUBLIC HEALTH vol 46 (2010) PARA 663) in relation to an exempt waste operation within the meaning of reg 5 (see ENVIRONMENTAL QUALITY AND PUBLIC HEALTH vol 46 (2010) PARA 663) carried on in that area; (3) any registration of the application under the Waste (England and Wales) Regulations 2011, SI 2011/988, Pt 8 (regs 24–34) (carriers, brokers and dealers of controlled waste) (see ENVIRONMENTAL QUALITY AND PUBLIC HEALTH vol 45 (2010) PARA 33): Scrap Metal Dealers Act 2013 s 22(7).

10   Scrap Metal Dealers Act 2013 s 3(2)(d).

11   Scrap Metal Dealers Act 2013 s 3(2)(e).

12   Ie the Scrap Metal Dealers Act 2013: s 3(2)(f).

13   Scrap Metal Dealers Act 2013 s 3(2)(f).

14   Ie any person in accordance with whose directions or instructions the directors of the company are accustomed to act: Scrap Metal Dealers Act 2013 s 3(4)(c).

15   Scrap Metal Dealers Act 2013 s 3(4).

16   Scrap Metal Dealers Act 2013 s 3(5).

17   Scrap Metal Dealers Act 2013 s 3(6).

18   As to the Environment Agency see ENVIRONMENTAL QUALITY AND PUBLIC HEALTH vol 45 (2010) PARA 68 et seq.

19   As to the Natural Resources Body for Wales see FORESTRY vol 52 (2014) PARA 38.

20   Scrap Metal Dealers Act 2013 s 3(7). 'Officer of a police force' includes a constable of the British Transport Police Force: s 22(5). As to police forces see POLICE AND INVESTIGATORY POWERS vol 84 (2013) PARAS 7, 8; and as to the British Transport Police Force see RAILWAYS AND TRAMWAYS vol 86 (2013) PARA 285 et seq. If another local authority, the Environment Agency, the Natural Resources Body for Wales or an officer of a police force requests, for purposes relating to the Scrap Metal Dealers Act 2013, information that has been supplied to a local authority under the Act and that relates to a scrap metal licence or to an application for or relating to a licence, the local authority must supply it: s 6(1), (2). This does not limit any other power the authority has to supply that information: s 6(3).

958.   Revocation of and imposition of conditions on scrap metal licences.   A local authority[1] that has issued a scrap metal[2] licence[3] may revoke the licence if:

(1)   it is satisfied that the licensee does not carry on business at any of the sites[4] identified in the licence[5];

(2)   it is satisfied that a site manager[6] named in the licence does not act as site manager at any of the sites identified in the licence[7]; or

(3)   it is no longer satisfied that the licensee is a suitable person to carry on business as a scrap metal dealer[8].

The authority may vary a licence[9] if the licensee or any site manager named in the licence is convicted of a relevant offence[10].

Such a revocation or variation comes into effect when no appeal[11] is possible in relation to it, or when any such appeal is finally determined or withdrawn[12]. However, if the authority considers that a licence should not continue in force without conditions, it may by notice provide that the licence is subject to conditions[13] until its revocation comes into effect, or that a variation[14] comes into effect immediately[15].

1   As to the meaning of 'local authority' see PARA 954 note 4.
2   As to the meaning of 'scrap metal' see PARA 954 note 1.
3   As to the issuing of such licences see PARA 957.
4   As to the meaning of 'site' see PARA 954 note 6.
5   Scrap Metal Dealers Act 2013 s 4(1). A licensee who is not carrying on business as a scrap metal dealer in the area of the authority that issued the licence must, within 28 days of the beginning of the period in which the licensee is not carrying on business in that area while licensed, notify the authority of that fact: s 8(2), (3). As to the offence of failing to comply with this requirement see PARA 955 note 4. An authority must, within 28 days of such notification, notify the relevant environment body of the notification given to it and the relevant environmental body must amend the register under s 7 (see PARA 959) accordingly: s 8(6)(a), (8). As to the meaning of 'relevant environmental body' see PARA 954 note 5. See also note 8.
6   As to the meaning of 'site manager' see PARA 954 note 8.
7   Scrap Metal Dealers Act 2013 s 4(2). See also note 8.
8   Scrap Metal Dealers Act 2013 s 4(3). As to the meaning of 'scrap metal dealer' see PARA 954 note 1. Section 3(2)–(7) (see PARA 957) applies for the purposes of determining whether an authority continues to be satisfied that a person is a suitable person or not: s 4(4). An authority must, within 28 days of revocation of a licence, notify the relevant environment body of the revocation and the relevant environmental body must amend the register under s 7 (see PARA 959) accordingly: s 8(6)(c), (8).
9   Such variation must be by adding one or both of the conditions set out in the Scrap Metal Dealers Act 2013 s 3(8) (see PARA 957 note 6): s 4(5).
10   Scrap Metal Dealers Act 2013 s 4(5). As to the meaning of 'relevant offence' see PARA 957 note 6.
11   Ie an appeal under the Scrap Metal Dealers Act 2013 Sch 1 para 9 (see PARA 956): s 4(6).
12   Scrap Metal Dealers Act 2013 s 4(6).
13   Ie one or both of the conditions set out in the Scrap Metal Dealers Act 2013 s 3(8) (see PARA 957 note 6): s 4(7)(a).
14   Ie a variation under the Scrap Metal Dealers Act 2013 s 4: s 4(7)(b).
15   Scrap Metal Dealers Act 2013 s 4(7).

959.   Register of scrap metal licences.   The Environment Agency[1] must maintain a register of scrap metal[2] licences issued[3] by local authorities[4] in England[5], and the Natural Resources Body for Wales[6] must maintain a register of scrap metal licences issued by local authorities in Wales[7]. The registers must be open to the public[8], may be combined with any other registers maintained by the Environment Agency or the Natural Resources Body for Wales as appropriate[9], and each entry in them must record:

(1)   the name of the authority that issued the licence[10];

(2)   the name and any trading name of the licensee[11];

(3)   the address of any site[12] identified in the licence[13];

(4)   the type of licence[14]; and

(5)   the date on which the licence is due to expire[15].

1   As to the Environment Agency see ENVIRONMENTAL QUALITY AND PUBLIC HEALTH vol 45 (2010) PARA 68 et seq.
2   As to the meaning of 'scrap metal' see PARA 954 note 1.
3   As to the issuing of scrap metal licences see PARA 957.
4   As to the meaning of 'local authority' see PARA 954 note 4.
5   Scrap Metal Dealers Act 2013 s 7(1).
6   As to the Natural Resources Body for Wales see FORESTRY vol 52 (2014) PARA 38.
7   Scrap Metal Dealers Act 2013 s 7(2).
8   Scrap Metal Dealers Act 2013 s 7(4).
9   Scrap Metal Dealers Act 2013 s 7(5).
10   Scrap Metal Dealers Act 2013 s 7(3)(a).
11   Scrap Metal Dealers Act 2013 s 7(3)(b), (c). If a licensee carries on business under a trading name he must, within 28 days of the change occurring, notify the authority that issued the licence of any such change: s 8(4), (5). As to the offence of failing to comply with this requirement see PARA 955 note 4.
12   As to the meaning of 'site' see PARA 954 note 6.
13   Scrap Metal Dealers Act 2013 s 7(3)(d).
14   Scrap Metal Dealers Act 2013 s 7(3)(e). As to the two types of licence see PARA 954.
15   Scrap Metal Dealers Act 2013 s 7(3)(f). As to the duration of a licence see PARA 954 note 2.

960.   Closure of unlicensed scrap metal sites: closure notices. If a constable or the local authority[1] is satisfied that premises[2] are being used by a scrap metal dealer[3] in the course of business and that the premises is not a licensed site[4], unless the premises are residential premises[5] the constable or authority may issue a closure notice which:

(1)   states that the constable or authority is so satisfied, giving reasons[6];
(2)   states that the constable or authority may apply to the court for a closure order[7]; and
(3)   specifies the steps which may be taken to ensure that the alleged use of the premises ceases[8].

The closure notice must be given to the person who appears to the constable or authority to be the site manager[9] of the premises[10] and any person, other than that person, who appears to the constable or authority to be a director, manager or other officer of the business in question[11]. It must also be given to a person who occupies another part of any building or structure of which the premises form part and who the constable or authority reasonably believes, at the time of giving the closure notice, that the person's access to the other part would be impeded if a closure order were made in respect of the premises[12].

A closure notice may be cancelled by a cancellation notice issued by a constable or the local authority[13] which takes effect when it is given to any one of the persons to whom the closure notice was given[14].

1   As to the meaning of 'local authority' see PARA 954 note 4.
2   As to the meaning of 'premises' see PARA 954 note 6. In the case of a local authority, the powers conferred by the Scrap Metal Dealers Act 2013 Sch 2 are exercisable only in relation to premises in the authority's area, and 'the local authority' in relation to any premises is to be read accordingly: Sch 2 para 1(2).
3   As to the meanings of 'scrap metal' and 'scrap metal dealer' see PARA 954 note 1.
4   Scrap Metal Dealers Act 2013 Sch 2 para 2(1). As to the meaning of 'site' see PARA 954 note 6.
5   Scrap Metal Dealers Act 2013 Sch 2 para 2(2).
6   Scrap Metal Dealers Act 2013 Sch 2 para 2(3)(a), (b).
7   Scrap Metal Dealers Act 2013 Sch 2 para 2(3)(c). As to such application to the court see PARA 961.
8   Scrap Metal Dealers Act 2013 Sch 2 para 2(3)(d).
9   As to the meaning of 'site manager' see PARA 954 note 8.
10   Scrap Metal Dealers Act 2013 Sch 2 para 2(4)(a).

11   Scrap Metal Dealers Act 2013 Sch 2 para 2(4)(b). The constable or authority may also give the notice to any person who has an interest in the premises: Sch 2 para 2(5). For these purposes, a person has an interest in premises if the person is the owner, leaseholder or occupier of the premises: Sch 2 para 1(1).

12   Scrap Metal Dealers Act 2013 Sch 2 para 2(6), (7).

13   Scrap Metal Dealers Act 2013 Sch 2 para 3(1).

14   Scrap Metal Dealers Act 2013 Sch 2 para 3(2). The cancellation notice must also be given to any other person to whom the closure notice was given: Sch 2 para 3(3).

961.   Closure of unlicensed scrap metal sites: closure orders. Where a closure notice[1] has been given[2], a constable or the local authority[3] may make a complaint to a justice of the peace[4] for a closure order[5]. Such complaint may not be made less than seven days after or more than six months after the date on which the closure notice was given[6]. Nor may a complaint be made if the constable or authority is satisfied that the premises[7] are not, or are no longer, being used by a scrap metal dealer[8] in the course of business and that there is no reasonable likelihood that the premises will be so used in the future[9].

Where such a complaint has been made, the justice may issue a summons to answer to the complaint[10].

If, on hearing such a complaint, the court is satisfied that the closure notice was given[11] and that the premises continue to be used by a scrap metal dealer in the course of business or there is a reasonable likelihood that the premises will be so used in the future[12], the court may make such order as it considers appropriate for the closure of the premises (a 'closure order')[13]. Such order may in particular require:

(1)   that the premises be closed immediately to the public and remain closed until a constable or the local authority makes a certificate for termination of the closure order[14];

(2)   that the use of the premises by a scrap metal dealer in the course of business be discontinued immediately[15];

(3)   that any defendant pay into court such sum as the court determines and that the sum will not be released by the court to that person until the other requirements of the order are met[16],

and may include such provision as the court considers appropriate for dealing with the consequences if the order should cease to have effect[17]. As soon as practicable after a closure order is made the complainant must fix a copy of it in a conspicuous position on the premises in respect of which it was made[18]. A constable or authorised person[19] may, using reasonable force if necessary, enter any premises in respect of which a closure order has been made at any reasonable time and, having entered the premises, do anything reasonably necessary for the purposes of securing compliance with the order[20].

It is an offence to permit premises to be open in contravention of a closure order or otherwise fail to comply with, or do an act in contravention of, a closure order, without reasonable excuse[21].

Where a closure order has been made, but a constable or the local authority is satisfied that the need for the order has ceased[22], the constable or authority may make a certificate to that effect[23]. The closure order ceases to have effect when the certificate is made[24]. As soon as practicable after making a certificate the constable or authority must give a copy of it to any person against whom the closure order was made[25] and to the designated officer for the court that made the order[26], and must fix a copy of the certificate in a conspicuous position on the premises in respect of which the order was made[27].

1   As to closure notices see PARA 960.
2   Ie given under the Scrap Metal Dealers Act 2013 Sch 2 para 2(4) (see PARA 960): Sch 2 para 4(1).
3   As to the meaning of 'local authority' see PARA 954 note 4.
4   As to justices of the peace see MAGISTRATES vol 71 (2013) PARA 401 et seq.
5   Scrap Metal Dealers Act 2013 Sch 2 para 4(1). The procedure on such a complaint must be in accordance with the Magistrates' Courts Act 1980 (see MAGISTRATES vol 71 (2013) PARA 510 et seq): Sch 2 para 4(7).
6   Scrap Metal Dealers Act 2013 Sch 2 para 4(2).
7   As to the meaning of 'premises' see PARA 954 note 6.
8   As to the meanings of 'scrap metal' and 'scrap metal dealer' see PARA 954 note 1.
9   Scrap Metal Dealers Act 2013 Sch 2 para 4(3).
10   Scrap Metal Dealers Act 2013 Sch 2 para 4(4). The summons must be directed to any person to whom the closure notice was given under Sch 2 para 2(4) (see PARA 960): Sch 2 para 4(5). If such a summons is issued, notice of the date, time, and place at which the complaint will be heard must be given to all the persons to whim the closure notice was given under Sch 2 para 2(5), (7) (see PARA 960): Sch 2 para 4(6).
11   Ie given under the Scrap Metal Dealers Act 2013 Sch 2 para 2(4) (see PARA 960): Sch 2 para 5(1).
12   Scrap Metal Dealers Act 2013 Sch 2 para 5(1).
13   Scrap Metal Dealers Act 2013 Sch 2 para 5(2).
14   Scrap Metal Dealers Act 2013 Sch 2 para 5(3)(a). The reference to a certificate is to a certificate under Sch 2 para 6 (see text and notes 22–27): Sch 2 para 5(3)(a). A closure order including such a requirement may, in particular, include such conditions as the court considers appropriate relating to the admission of persons onto the premises and the access by persons to another part of any building or other structure of which the premises form part: Sch 2 para 5(4).
15   Scrap Metal Dealers Act 2013 Sch 2 para 5(3)(b).
16   Scrap Metal Dealers Act 2013 Sch 2 para 5(3)(c). A sum which has been ordered to be paid into court under a closure order is to be paid to the designated officer for the court: Sch 2 para 5(7). As to designated officers see MAGISTRATES vol 71 (2013) PARA 505.
17   Scrap Metal Dealers Act 2013 Sch 2 para 5(5). The reference to the order ceasing to have effect is to its ceasing to have effect under Sch 2 para 6 (see text and notes 22–27): Sch 2 para 5(5).
18   Scrap Metal Dealers Act 2013 Sch 2 para 5(6).
19   Ie authorised for these purposes by the local authority: Scrap Metal Dealers Act 2013 Sch 2 para 9(7).
20   Scrap Metal Dealers Act 2013 Sch 2 para 9(2). If the owner, occupier or other person in charge of the premises requires an officer seeking to exercise these power to produce evidence of the officer's identity or evidence of the officer's authority to exercise the powers, the officer must produce that evidence: Sch 2 para 9(4). A person who intentionally obstructs a constable or an authorised person in the exercise of these powers is guilty of an offence and liable on summary conviction to a fine not exceeding level 5 on the standard scale: Sch 2 para 9(5), (6). As to the standard scale see SENTENCING AND DISPOSITION OF OFFENDERS vol 92 (2010) PARA 142. As to offences committed by a body corporate see PARA 954 note 3.
21   Scrap Metal Dealers Act 2013 Sch 2 para 9(1). A person guilty of such an offence is liable on summary conviction to a fine not exceeding level 5 on the standard scale: Sch 2 para 9(6).
22   Scrap Metal Dealers Act 2013 Sch 2 para 6(1).
23   Scrap Metal Dealers Act 2013 Sch 2 para 6(2).
24   Scrap Metal Dealers Act 2013 Sch 2 para 6(3). If the order includes a requirement under Sch 2 para 5(3)(c) that a defendant pay money into court (see text and note 16), any such money is to be released by the court to the defendant, whether or not the court has made provision to that effect under Sch 2 para 5(5) (see text and note 17): Sch 2 para 6(4).
25   Scrap Metal Dealers Act 2013 Sch 2 para 6(5)(a). The constable or authority must also give a copy of the certificate to any person who requests one: Sch 2 para 6(6).
26   Scrap Metal Dealers Act 2013 Sch 2 para 6(5)(b).
27   Scrap Metal Dealers Act 2013 Sch 2 para 6(5)(c).

962. Closure of unlicensed scrap metal sites: discharge and appeal. A complaint to a justice of the peace[1] for an order that a closure order[2] be discharged (a 'discharge order') may be made by any person to whom the relevant closure notice[3] was given[4] or who has an interest in the premises[5] but to whom the closure notice was not given[6]. Where such a complaint is made the justice may issue a summons directed to such constable as the justice considers appropriate or the local authority[7] requiring that person to appear before the magistrates' court[8] to answer to the complaint[9]. The court may not make a discharge order unless it is satisfied that there is no longer a need for the closure order[10].

An appeal may be made to the Crown Court[11]: (1) by any person to whom the relevant closure notice was given, or who has an interest in the premises but to whom the closure notice was not given, against a closure order or a decision not to make a discharge order[12]; or (2) by a constable or, as the case may be, the local authority against a discharge order or a decision not to make a closure order[13]. On such an appeal the Crown Court may make such order as it considers appropriate[14].

1 As to justices of the peace see MAGISTRATES vol 71 (2013) PARA 401 et seq.
2 As to closure orders see PARA 961.
3 As to closure notices see PARA 960.
4 Scrap Metal Dealers Act 2013 Sch 2 para 7(1)(a). The reference to notice having been given is to its having been given under Sch 2 para 2 (see PARA 960): Sch 2 para 7(1)(a).
5 As to the meaning of 'premises' see PARA 954 note 6; and as to the meaning of having an interest in premises see PARA 960 note 11.
6 Scrap Metal Dealers Act 2013 Sch 2 para 7(1)(b). The procedure on such a complaint must be in accordance with the Magistrates' Courts Act 1980 (see MAGISTRATES vol 71 (2013) PARA 510 et seq): Scrap Metal Dealers Act 2013 Sch 2 para 7(5).
7 As to the meaning of 'local authority' see PARA 954 note 4.
8 As to the magistrates' court see MAGISTRATES vol 71 (2013) PARA 470 et seq.
9 Scrap Metal Dealers Act 2013 Sch 2 para 7(3). If such a summons is issued, notice of the date, time and place at which the complaint will be heard must be given to all the persons, other than the complainant, to whom the closure notice was given under Sch 2 para 2 (see PARA 960): Sch 2 para 7(4).
10 Scrap Metal Dealers Act 2013 Sch 2 para 7(2).
11 As to the Crown Court see COURTS AND TRIBUNALS vol 24 (2010) PARA 716 et seq.
12 See the Scrap Metal Dealers Act 2013 Sch 2 para 8(1)(a), (d), (3). Any appeal under Sch 2 para 8 must be made before the end of the period of 21 days beginning with the day on which the order or the decision in question was made: Sch 2 para 8(2).
13 See the Scrap Metal Dealers Act 2013 Sch 2 para 8(1)(b), (c), (4). See also note 12.
14 Scrap Metal Dealers Act 2013 Sch 2 para 8(5).

963. Scrap dealing offences. A scrap metal dealer[1] must not:
(1) receive scrap metal from a person without verifying, by reference to documents, data or other information obtained from a reliable and independent source[2], the person's full name and address[3];
(2) pay[4] for scrap metal except by a cheque[5] or by an electronic transfer of funds[6].

If a scrap metal dealer receives scrap metal in breach of head (1) or pays for scrap metal in breach of head (2), each of:
(a) the scrap metal dealer;
(b) if the metal is received at a site[7], the site manager[8]; and
(c) in the case of a breach of head (1), any person who, under arrangements made by a person in head (a) or (b), has responsibility for verifying the name and address or, in the case of a breach of head (2), any person who makes the payment acting for the dealer,
is guilty of an offence[9].

A person who gives a false name or false address on delivering scrap metal to a scrap metal dealer is guilty of an offence[10].

1 As to the meanings of 'scrap metal' and 'scrap metal dealer' see PARA 954 note 1.
2 Scrap Metal Dealers Act 2013 s 11(2).

3   Scrap Metal Dealers Act 2013 s 11(1). The Secretary of State may prescribe documents, data or other information which are not sufficient for this purpose, and has prescribed documents and information sufficient for this purpose: see s 11(3); and the Scrap Metal Dealers Act 2013 (Prescribed Documents and Information for Verification of Name and Address) Regulations 2013, SI 2013/2276. As to the Secretary of State see PARA 902. As to the making of orders or regulations under the Scrap Metal Dealers Act 2013 generally see PARA 954 note 1.

4   For these purposes, 'pay' includes pay in kind with goods or services: Scrap Metal Dealers Act 2013 s 12(3).

5   Ie a cheque which under the Bills of Exchange Act 1882 s 81A (see FINANCIAL SERVICES AND INSTITUTIONS vol 49 (2008) PARA 1500) is not transferable: Scrap Metal Dealers Act 2013 s 12(1)(a).

6   Scrap Metal Dealers Act 2013 s 12(1). The Secretary of State may by order amend s 12(1) to permit other methods of payment: s 12(2). At the date at which this volume states the law no such order had been made.

7   As to the meaning of 'site' see PARA 954 note 6.

8   As to the meaning of 'site manager' see PARA 954 note 8.

9   Scrap Metal Dealers Act 2013 ss 11(4), 12(4). A person guilty of such an offence is liable on summary conviction to a fine not exceeding level 3 on the standard scale if the offence relates to a breach of head (1) and not exceeding level 5 on the standard scale if the offence relates to a breach of head (2): ss 11(6), 12(6). As to the standard scale see SENTENCING AND DISPOSITION OF OFFENDERS vol 92 (2010) PARA 142. It is a defence for a scrap metal dealer or a site manager charged with such an offence to prove that they made arrangements to ensure that the metal was not received in breach of the relevant provision and took all reasonable steps to ensure that those arrangements were complied with: ss 11(5), 12(5). As to offences committed by a body corporate see PARA 954 note 3.

10 Scrap Metal Dealers Act 2013 s 11(7). A person guilty of such an offence is liable on summary conviction to a fine not exceeding level 3 on the standard scale: s 11(7).

964. Records of dealings in scrap metal. If a scrap metal dealer[1] receives or disposes[2] of any scrap metal in the course of his business[3], he must record:

(1)   the description of the metal, including its type, or types if mixed, form and weight and, for scrap metal that is being received, its condition and any marks identifying previous owners or other distinguishing features[4];

(2)   the date and time of its receipt or disposal[5];

(3)   in relation to scrap metal that is being received: (a) if it is delivered on a vehicle, the registration mark[6] of the vehicle[7]; (b) if the metal is received from a person, the full name and address of that person[8]; and (c) if the dealer pays for the metal, the full name of the person who makes the payment acting for the dealer[9];

(4)   in relation to scrap metal that is being disposed of: (a) if the disposal is to another person, the full name and address of that person[10]; (b) if the dealer receives payment for the metal, whether by way of sale or exchange, the price or other consideration received[11].

The dealer must keep the information and other records so required[12] for a period of three years beginning with the day on which the metal is received or disposed of[13].

If a dealer fails to fulfil the record-keeping requirements[14], each of: (i) the scrap metal dealer; (ii) if the metal is received at or despatched from a site, the site manager[15]; and (iii) any person who, under arrangements made by a person within head (i) or (ii), has responsibility for fulfilling the requirement, is guilty of an offence[16].

1   As to the meanings of 'scrap metal' and 'scrap metal dealer' see PARA 954 note 1.

2   For these purposes, metal is disposed of whether or not: (1) it is in the same form in which it was received; (2) the disposal is to another person; or (3) the metal is despatched from a site: Scrap Metal Dealers Act 2013 s 14(2). As to the meaning of 'site' see PARA 954 note 6.

3 Scrap Metal Dealers Act 2013 ss 13(1), 14(1). Where the disposal is in the course of business under a collector's licence, the dealer must record the date and time of the disposal and, if the disposal is to another person, the full name and address of that person: s 14(4). As to the types of licence see PARA 954.

4 Scrap Metal Dealers Act 2013 ss 13(2)(a), 14(3)(a). The information mentioned in ss 13(2), (5), 14(3), (4) must be recorded in a manner which allows the information and the scrap metal to which it relates to be readily identified by reference to each other: s 15(1). As to a discussion of what constituted a description of scrap metal as required under the previous legislation, the Scrap Metal Dealers Act 1964 s 2 (repealed), see *Jenkins v A Cohen & Co Ltd* [1971] 2 All ER 1384, [1971] 1 WLR 1280.

5 Scrap Metal Dealers Act 2013 ss 13(2)(b), 14(3)(b). See also note 4.

6 Ie the registration mark within the meaning of the Vehicle Excise and Registration Act 1994 s 23 (see ROAD TRAFFIC vol 89 (2011) PARA 366): Scrap Metal Dealers Act 2013 s 13(2)(c).

7 Scrap Metal Dealers Act 2013 s 13(2)(c). See also note 4.

8 Scrap Metal Dealers Act 2013 s 13(2)(d). If the dealer receives the metal from a person, the dealer must keep a copy of any document which the dealer uses to verify the name and address of that person: s 13(3). The records mentioned in s 13(3), (4) must be marked so as to identify the scrap metal to which they relate: s 15(2). As to verification of names and addresses see PARA 963.

9 Scrap Metal Dealers Act 2013 s 13(2)(e). See also note 4. If the dealer pays for the metal by cheque, the dealer must keep a copy of the cheque: s 13(4). See also note 8. If the dealer pays for the metal by electronic transfer, the dealer must keep the receipt identifying the transfer or, if no such receipt was obtained, the dealer must record particulars identifying the transfer: s 13(5). See also note 4. As to regulation of payment for scrap metal see PARA 963.

10 Scrap Metal Dealers Act 2013 s 14(3)(c). See also note 4.

11 Scrap Metal Dealers Act 2013 s 14(3)(d). See also note 4.

12 Ie required under the Scrap Metal Dealers Act 2013 ss 13(2)–(5), 14(3), (4): s 15(3).

13 Scrap Metal Dealers Act 2013 s 15(3).

14 Ie the requirements under the Scrap Metal Dealers Act 2013 ss 13–15.

15 As to the meaning of 'site manager' see PARA 954 note 8.

16 Scrap Metal Dealers Act 2013 s 15(4). A person guilty of such an offence is liable on summary conviction to a fine not exceeding level 5 on the standard scale: s 15(6). As to the standard scale see SENTENCING AND DISPOSITION OF OFFENDERS vol 92 (2010) PARA 142. It is a defence for a scrap metal dealer or site manager charged with such an offence to prove that they made arrangements to ensure that the requirement was fulfilled, and took all reasonable steps to ensure that those arrangements were complied with: s 15(5). As to offences committed by a body corporate see PARA 954 note 3.

965. Right to enter and inspect premises of scrap metal dealers. A constable or an officer of a local authority[1] may enter[2] and inspect a licensed site[3] other than residential premises[4] at any reasonable time on notice to the site manager[5], or otherwise than on notice to the site manager if reasonable attempts to give such notice have been made and failed[6], or if entry to the site is reasonably required for the purposes of ascertaining whether provisions regulating the activities of scrap metal dealers[7] are being complied with or for investigating offences under such provisions and in either case the giving of notice would defeat that purpose[8].

A justice of the peace[9] may issue a warrant[10] authorising entry[11] to any premises[12] if the justice is satisfied by information on oath that there are reasonable grounds for believing that entry to the premises is reasonably required for the purposes of securing compliance with the provisions regulating the activities of scrap metal dealers[13], or ascertaining whether those provisions are being complied with[14].

A constable or an officer of a local authority may require production of an inspect any scrap metal kept at any premises they have entered under these provisions, require production of and inspect any records[15] and take copies or extracts from such records[16].

1 As to the meaning of 'local authority' see PARA 954 note 4.

2 Force may not be used to enter premises under the Scrap Metal Dealers Act 2013 s 16(1), (2): see s 16(4). As to the meaning of 'premises' see PARA 954 note 6.

3 As to the meaning of 'site' see PARA 954 note 6. An officer of a local authority may only exercise the powers under the Scrap Metal Dealers Act 2013 s 16 in relation to premises in the area of the authority: s 16(12).

4 Scrap Metal Dealers Act 2013 s 16(3).

5 Scrap Metal Dealers Act 2013 s 16(1). As to the meaning of 'site manager' see PARA 954 note 8.

6 Scrap Metal Dealers Act 2013 s 16(2)(a).

7 Ie the Scrap Metal Dealers Act 2013 (see PARA 954 et seq): s 16(2)(b). As to the meanings of 'scrap metal' and 'scrap metal dealer' see PARA 954 note 1.

8 Scrap Metal Dealers Act 2013 s 16(2)(b). If the owner, occupier or other person in charge of the premises requires an officer seeking to exercise these powers to produce evidence of the officer's identity or evidence of the officer's authority to exercise the powers, the officer must produce that evidence: s 16(10), (11). A person who obstructs the exercise of a right of entry or inspection under s 16 is guilty of an offence and liable on summary conviction to a fine not exceeding level 3 on the standard scale: s 16(13)(a). As to the standard scale see SENTENCING AND DISPOSITION OF OFFENDERS vol 92 (2010) PARA 142. As to offences committed by a body corporate see PARA 954 note 3.

9 As to justices of the peace see MAGISTRATES vol 71 (2013) PARA 401 et seq.

10 Such a warrant is a warrant signed by the justice specifying the premises concerned and authorising a constable or an officer of a local authority to enter and inspect the premises at any time within one month from the date of the warrant: Scrap Metal Dealers Act 2013 s 16(7).

11 Reasonable force may, if necessary, be used to enter premises under such a warrant: Scrap Metal Dealers Act 2013 s 16(8).

12 Premises are within this provision if the premises are a licensed site or the premises are not a licensed site but there are reasonable grounds for believing that the premises are being used by a scrap metal dealer in the course of business: Scrap Metal Dealers Act 2013 s 16(6). See also note 3.

13 See note 7.

14 Scrap Metal Dealers Act 2013 s 16(5). See also note 8.

15 Ie any records kept in accordance with the Scrap Metal Dealers Act 2013 s 13 or s 14 (see PARA 964) and any other records relating to payment for scrap metal: s 16(9)(b).

16 Scrap Metal Dealers Act 2013 s 16(9). A person who fails to produce a record required to be produced under s 16 is guilty of an offence and liable on summary conviction to a fine not exceeding level 3 on the standard scale: s 16(13)(b).

(viii) Hairdressers and Barbers

A. REGULATION OF HAIRDRESSERS AND BARBERS

966. Registration in London. The council of a London borough[1] or the Common Council of the City of London[2] may by resolution appoint a day[3] after which no person may carry on the business[4] of a hairdresser or barber on any premises within the borough or, as the case may be, the City unless he is registered by the council in respect of those premises[5]. The council must register an applicant who provides particulars of his name and residence and the premises in respect of which he desires to be registered, and must issue to him a certificate of registration[6]. A person so registered must keep a copy of the certificate prominently displayed in the premises along with a copy of any relevant byelaws[7].

1 As to London boroughs see LONDON GOVERNMENT vol 71 (2013) PARA 15.

2 As to the Common Council of the City of London see LONDON GOVERNMENT vol 71 (2013) PARA 34 et seq. The Common Council is included by virtue of the Greater London Council (General Powers) Act 1967 s 20(1).

3 'Appointed day' in relation to a borough, or as the case may be, the City, means such day as may be fixed by resolution of the council: Greater London Council (General Powers) Act 1967 s 21(7)(a). The council must cause to be published in a local newspaper circulating in the borough or the City notice of the passing of the resolution and of the day fixed by it, and of the general effect of the provisions of s 21(1)–(6) (see text and notes 4–7), and the day so fixed must

not be earlier than the expiration of one month from the date of publication of the notice: s 21(7)(b). Either a copy of a newspaper containing any such notice, or a certified reproduction of part of it bearing the date of its publication and containing the notice, is evidence of the publication of the notice and of the date of publication: see s 21(8).

4　A person is not deemed to carry on the business of a hairdresser or barber on any premises solely by reason that he visits those premises only by prior appointment with a customer who resides at or is an inmate of them for the purpose of attending to that customer: Greater London Council (General Powers) Act 1967 s 21(1) proviso.

5　Greater London Council (General Powers) Act 1967 s 21(1), (7)(a). If any person carries on business in contravention of s 21(1), he is liable on summary conviction to a fine not exceeding level 3 on the standard scale, and a daily fine not exceeding £5 for each day on which an offence is continued after conviction: ss 20(1), 21(3) (s 21(3) amended by the Greater London Council (General Powers) Act 1983 s 3, Schedule; and by virtue of the Criminal Justice Act 1982 s 46(1), (4)). As to the standard scale see SENTENCING AND DISPOSITION OF OFFENDERS vol 92 (2010) PARA 142.

6　See the Greater London Council (General Powers) Act 1967 s 21(2). The obligation upon the council to register an applicant does not apply where planning permission is required for the carrying on of the business and has not been granted: see s 21(2) proviso.

7　See the Greater London Council (General Powers) Act 1967 s 21(4). Relevant byelaws are those made under the Public Health Act 1961 s 77, for the purpose of securing cleanliness of premises, instruments, equipment, clothing etc in a hairdresser's or barber's business: see the Greater London Council (General Powers) Act 1967 s 21(4); and PARA 967. Failure to so display the certificate renders a person liable on summary conviction to a fine not exceeding level 2 on the standard scale and a daily fine not exceeding 50p for each day on which an offence is continued after conviction: s 21(4) (amended by the Greater London Council (General Powers) Act 1983 s 3, Schedule; and by virtue of the Criminal Justice Act 1982 s 46(1), (4)). Where an offence punishable under the Greater London Council (General Powers) Act 1967 s 21 which has been committed by a body corporate is proved to have been committed with the consent or connivance of, or to be attributable to any neglect on the part of, any director, manager, secretary or other similar officer of the body corporate, or any person purporting to act in such capacity, he as well as the body corporate is deemed to be guilty of that offence: s 21(5). The Public Health Act 1936 ss 287, 288, 341 (which relate respectively to powers of entry, penalties for obstruction and the application of the Act to Crown property: see ENVIRONMENTAL QUALITY AND PUBLIC HEALTH vol 45 (2010) PARAS 108, 114–115), have effect as if the Greater London Council (General Powers) Act 1967 s 21 was contained in the Public Health Act 1936: Greater London Council (General Powers) Act 1967 s 21(6).

967. Regulation by local authorities. A local authority[1] may make byelaws for securing the cleanliness of premises[2] on which a hairdresser's or barber's business is carried on and the instruments, towels, materials and equipment used in that business, and the cleanliness of the hairdressers or barbers working in those premises in regard to themselves and their clothing[3]. The Secretary of State[4] is the confirming authority as respects these byelaws[5], and it is the duty of the local authority to enforce the byelaws it makes[6]. For the purpose of enforcing the byelaws the local authority has power of entry into premises[7].

1　'Local authority' in this context means the council of a district or London borough, the Common Council of the City of London, the Sub-Treasurer of the Inner Temple or the Under Treasurer of the Middle Temple, and includes the Council of the Isles of Scilly: Public Health Act 1961 s 2(3) (amended by the London Government Act 1963 s 40(2), Sch 11 Pt I para 33; and the Local Government Act 1972 Sch 30). As to the London boroughs and their councils see LONDON GOVERNMENT vol 71 (2013) PARAS 15, 20–22, 55 et seq. As to the Common Council of the City of London and the Sub-Treasurer of the Inner Temple and the Under Treasurer of the Middle Temple see LONDON GOVERNMENT vol 71 (2013) PARA 34 et seq. As to the Council of the Isles of Scilly see LOCAL GOVERNMENT vol 69 (2009) PARA 36.

2　'Premises' includes messuages, buildings, land, easements and hereditaments of any tenure: Public Health Act 1936 s 343(1) (definition applied by the Public Health Act 1961 s 1(4)).

3　Public Health Act 1961 s 77(1). A hairdresser registered by a London borough council or the Common Council must display a copy of any such byelaws on his premises: see PARA 966 text and note 7.

4   As to the Secretary of State in the context of the Public Health Acts 1936 and 1961 see
ENVIRONMENTAL QUALITY AND PUBLIC HEALTH vol 45 (2010) PARA 58. As to the transfer of
functions of the Secretary of State relating to public health, so far as exercisable in relation to
Wales, to the Welsh Ministers see ENVIRONMENTAL QUALITY AND PUBLIC HEALTH vol 45 (2010)
PARA 59.
5   Public Health Act 1961 s 77(3).
6   Public Health Act 1961 s 77(1).
7   See the Public Health Act 1961 s 77(2), applying the Public Health Act 1936 s 287 (see
ENVIRONMENTAL QUALITY AND PUBLIC HEALTH vol 45 (2010) PARA 114).

B. VOLUNTARY REGISTRATION

968. The Hairdressing Council. A body known as the Hairdressing Council[1]
is established in relation to the voluntary registration of hairdressers[2]. It consists
of 15 members[3], comprising:

(1)   four employers of persons engaged in hairdressing[4] or self-employed
persons engaged in hairdressing who are registered persons[5];

(2)   four employees engaged in hairdressing who are registered persons[6];

(3)   one person appointed by the President of the British Medical
Association[7];

(4)   one person appointed by the President of the Royal College of
Physicians of London[8]; and

(5)   five persons appointed by the members appointed under heads (1) and
(2) from among persons appearing those members to have had wide
experience of and shown capacity in industry, commerce,
administration, finance or the practice of law or to have in some other
respect special knowledge or experience which would be of value to the
council in the exercise and performance of its functions[9].

The council has power to do anything calculated to facilitate the proper
discharge of its functions[10]. Its powers may be exercised notwithstanding any
vacancy[11], and proceedings are not invalidated by any defect in the appointment
of a member[12]. The council may make regulations with regard to its meetings
and procedure[13].

The council must keep audited accounts of all sums received or paid by it[14]. It
must set up an investigating committee and a disciplinary committee[15] and
appoint a registrar[16], and may appoint other officers and servants[17].

It may pay fees for attendance at meetings, and travelling and other
allowances to members[18], pay remuneration, pensions and gratuities to officers
and servants, and provide or maintain superannuation schemes for them[19]. The
council has no powers, however, as regards negotiating questions of service,
charges, wages or conditions of employment of hairdressers as between employer
and employees or otherwise[20].

1   Although the legislation refers to the 'Hairdressing Council' the Council refers to itself on its
website as the Hair Council. At the date at which this volume states the law the Hairdressing
Council's website address was www.haircouncil.org.uk.
2   Hairdressers (Registration) Act 1964 s 1(1). The council is constituted in accordance with Sch 1
Pt I (paras 1–3); and the supplementary provisions contained in Sch 1 Pt II (paras 4–12) (relating
to constitution, term of office, validity of proceedings), have effect with respect to the council:
s 1(2). The council is a body corporate with perpetual succession and a common seal: Sch 1
para 4.
3   As to the tenure of office of members see the Hairdressers (Registration) Act 1964 Sch 1
paras 6, 7 (Sch 1 para 6 amended by the Statute Law (Repeals) Act 2004). As to the first
members appointed see Hairdressers (Registration) Act 1964 Sch 1 paras 2, 5, 6(1) (Sch 1
paras 2, 5 repealed). A member may resign at any time by notice addressed to the registrar (see
text and note 16): Sch 1 para 8. A person appointed to fill a casual vacancy holds office during

the remainder of the term in office of the person whom he has replaced (Sch 1 para 9(1)); a vacancy other than a casual vacancy must be filled before the date on which the vacancy will occur (Sch 1 para 9(2)). The Hairdressing Council currently has 17 members, including a Chair and Registrar: see the Hairdressing Council website (see note 1).

4 'Hairdressing' means shaving, cutting, shampooing, tinting, dyeing, bleaching, waving, curling, straightening, setting, or dressing of the hair, upon the scalp or face, with or without the aid of any apparatus or appliance, preparation or substance; and the hand or vibro massage of the scalp or face: Hairdressers (Registration) Act 1964 s 15.

5 Hairdressers (Registration) Act 1964 Sch 1 para 1(1) (amended by the Statute Law (Repeals) Act 2004). Two of the four employers or self-employed persons must be appointed by the National Hairdressers' Federation and two by the Incorporated Guild of Hairdressers, Wigmakers and Perfumers: Hairdressers (Registration) Act 1964 Sch 1 para 1(1). Before those bodies make appointments they must consult together and ensure that not less than two of the appointees are engaged in ladies' hairdressing: Sch 1 para 3(1). 'Registered person' means a person who is registered under s 3 (see PARA 970): s 15.

6 Hairdressers (Registration) Act 1964 Sch 1 para 1(2) (amended by the Statute Law (Repeals) Act 2004). These persons must be appointed by the Union of Shop, Distributive and Allied Workers: Hairdressers (Registration) Act 1964 Sch 1 para 1(2). Not less than two of these appointees must be engaged in ladies' hairdressing: Sch 1 para 3(2).

7 Hairdressers (Registration) Act 1964 Sch 1 para 1(3).

8 Hairdressers (Registration) Act 1964 Sch 1 para 1(4). As to the Royal College of Physicians of London see MEDICAL PROFESSIONS vol 74 (2011) PARA 252.

9 Hairdressers (Registration) Act 1964 Sch 1 para 1(5) (amended by the Statute Law (Repeals) Act 2004). 'Functions' includes powers and duties: Hairdressers (Registration) Act 1964 s 15.

10 Hairdressers (Registration) Act 1964 Sch 1 para 10(1).

11 However, no business may be conducted unless there are at least five members present: Hairdressers (Registration) Act 1964 Sch 1 para 12.

12 Hairdressers (Registration) Act 1964 Sch 1 para 10(3).

13 Hairdressers (Registration) Act 1964 Sch 1 para 11. Such regulations are not made by statutory instrument and are not dealt with in this title.

14 Hairdressers (Registration) Act 1964 s 13(1). The accounts are audited by auditors appointed by the council: s 13(1). No person may be appointed as auditor unless he is eligible for appointment as a statutory auditor under the Companies Act 2006 Pt 42 (ss 1209–1264) (see COMPANIES vol 15 (2009) PARA 958): Hairdressers (Registration) Act 1964 s 13(2) (amended by SI 1991/1997; and SI 2008/948). Copies of the council's accounts must be furnished to any person on application and on payment of such reasonable sum as the council may determine: Hairdressers (Registration) Act 1964 s 13(3).

15 See the Hairdressers (Registration) Act 1964 s 8; and PARA 972.

16 Hairdressers (Registration) Act 1964 s 12. The registrar holds and vacates office in accordance with the terms of his appointment: s 12(1).

17 See the Hairdressers (Registration) Act 1964 Sch 1 para 10(2)(a).

18 See the Hairdressers (Registration) Act 1964 Sch 1 para 10(2)(b).

19 See the Hairdressers (Registration) Act 1964 Sch 1 para 10(2)(c), (d).

20 Hairdressers (Registration) Act 1964 s 14.

969. Register of hairdressers.

The Hairdressing Council[1] must maintain a register of hairdressers[2], which it must publish as often as it thinks fit[3]. If the register is not published in any year the council must publish within that year any alterations in the register which have been made since its last publication[4].

The council may make rules with respect to the form and keeping of the register and the making of entries, alterations and corrections in it and, in particular:

(1) regulating the making of applications for registration and the supporting evidence[5];

(2) providing for the notification to the council of any change in the particulars entitling a person to be registered[6];

(3) prescribing fees[7] for entry in, restoration to, and retention in, the register[8];

(4) authorising the registrar of the council to refuse to enter a name in or

restore it to the register until the fee has been paid and to remove a name on non-payment of the retention fee after prescribed notices and warnings[9];

(5) prescribing anything required or authorised to be prescribed by the provisions of the Hairdressers (Registration) Act 1964 relating to the register[10].

1 As to the council see PARA 968.
2 Hairdressers (Registration) Act 1964 s 2 (amended by the Statute Law (Repeals) Act 2004). That provision before its partial repeal also provided for the establishment of the register at the time when the Act was passed. The register must contain the names, addresses, qualifications and such other particulars as may be prescribed of all persons who are entitled under the provisions of the Act to be registered and who apply in the prescribed manner to be so registered, and the form of hairdressing which such persons are qualified to practise: Hairdressers (Registration) Act 1964 s 2. 'Prescribed' means prescribed by rules under the Act: s 15. Such rules are not made by statutory instrument and are not dealt with in this title. As to the meaning of 'hairdressing' see PARA 968 note 4.
3 Hairdressers (Registration) Act 1964 s 7(1) (amended by the Statute Law (Repeals) Act 2004), which before its partial repeal additionally provided for the initial publication of the register within six months of 1 January 1966.
4 Hairdressers (Registration) Act 1964 s 7(2).
5 Hairdressers (Registration) Act 1964 s 6(1)(a).
6 Hairdressers (Registration) Act 1964 s 6(1)(b).
7 Rules which prescribe fees may provide for the charging of different fees in different classes of cases: Hairdressers (Registration) Act 1964 s 6(3). Such rules are not made by statutory instrument and are not dealt with in this title.
8 Hairdressers (Registration) Act 1964 s 6(1)(c), (d).
9 Hairdressers (Registration) Act 1964 s 6(1)(e). Rules under s 6 which provide for the erasure of a name from the register on failure to pay a fee must provide for its restoration to the register on the making of the prescribed application in that behalf and on payment of that fee and any additional fee prescribed in respect of the restoration: s 6(2). See also note 7. Such rules are not made by statutory instrument and are not dealt with in this title.
10 Hairdressers (Registration) Act 1964 s 6(1)(f).

970. Qualifications for registration. A person is entitled[1] to be registered by the Hairdressing Council[2] if he applies for registration and satisfies the council that he has:

(1) served a period of apprenticeship, or attended an approved[3] course of training conducted at an approved[4] institution, or partly at one such institution and partly at another or others[5]; and

(2) attained a reasonable and sufficient standard to qualify him to practise the form of hairdressing[6] in respect of which the application was made[7].

On registering any person the council must issue to him a certificate of registration[8].

1 Ie subject to the provisions of the Hairdressers (Registration) Act 1964 and any rules made under s 6 (see PARA 969): s 3(1) (as amended: see note 5).
2 As to the council see PARA 968.
3 Ie approved by the council under the Hairdressers (Registration) Act 1964 s 4 (see PARA 971): s 3(1)(a)(ii).
4 See note 3.
5 Hairdressers (Registration) Act 1964 s 3(1)(a) (s 3(1) amended by the Statute Law (Repeals) Act 2004).
6 As to the meaning of 'hairdressing' see PARA 968 note 4.
7 Hairdressers (Registration) Act 1964 s 3(1)(b) (s 3(1) as amended: see note 5).
8 Hairdressers (Registration) Act 1964 s 3(3).

971. Approval of courses, qualifications and institutions. The Hairdressing Council[1] may approve:

(1)   any course of training which it considers is designed to confer sufficient knowledge and skill for the practice of hairdressing[2] on persons completing it[3];

(2)   any qualification which, as a result of an examination taken in conjunction with such an approved course, is granted to candidates reaching a standard indicating, in the council's opinion, sufficient knowledge and skill to practise hairdressing[4]; and

(3)   any institution it considers properly organised and equipped for conducting the whole or any part of an approved course[5].

The council may refuse its approval or withdraw an approval previously given[6].

The power of approval conferred on the council includes power to approve: (a) a course of training prepared by it and conducted either under arrangements made by it or otherwise; (b) a qualification awarded by it as a result of an examination held under arrangements made by it[7]. If the council withdraws its approval this does not prejudice the registration or entitlement to registration of any person who was registered or entitled to registration by virtue of that approval immediately before it was withdrawn[8].

It is the council's duty to keep itself informed of the nature of the instruction given at approved institutions to persons attending approved courses and the examinations the passing of which may be prescribed[9] by it as being a condition of registration[10].

1   As to the council see PARA 968.
2   As to the meaning of 'hairdressing' see PARA 968 note 4.
3   Hairdressers (Registration) Act 1964 s 4(1)(a).
4   Hairdressers (Registration) Act 1964 s 4(1)(b).
5   Hairdressers (Registration) Act 1964 s 4(1)(c).
6   Hairdressers (Registration) Act 1964 s 4(1). Notice of the giving, refusal or withdrawal of such an approval must be served by the council on the body or person affected: s 4(1). Any reference in s 4 to a body or person affected, in relation to an approval, is a reference to the body or person who applied for the approval: s 4(4).
7   Hairdressers (Registration) Act 1964 s 4(2).
8   Hairdressers (Registration) Act 1964 s 4(3).
9   As to the meaning of 'prescribed' see PARA 969 note 2.
10   Hairdressers (Registration) Act 1964 s 5.

972.   Investigating and disciplinary committees.   The Hairdressing Council[1] must set up two committees:

(1)   an investigating committee, charged with the duty of conducting a preliminary investigation into any case where it is alleged that a person registered by the council is liable to have his name removed from the register[2] and of deciding whether the case should be referred to the disciplinary committee[3]; and

(2)   a disciplinary committee, charged with the duty of considering and determining any case referred to it by the investigating committee and any other case of which the disciplinary committee has cognisance[4].

Rules regulating the membership of each committee, the times and places of meetings, quorum and mode of summoning members of the disciplinary committee, are to be made by the council, but a person is not eligible for membership of either committee unless he is a member of the council[5]. The rules must ensure that no person who acted as a member of the investigating committee in respect of any case acts as a member of the disciplinary committee with respect to that case[6].

The council must make rules as to the procedure to be followed and the rules of evidence to be observed in proceedings before the disciplinary committee[7]. To advise the disciplinary committee on questions of law there must in all proceedings before it be an assessor who must be a person who has a ten year general qualification[8].

1   As to the council see PARA 968.
2   'Register' means the register of hairdressers to be maintained in pursuance of the Hairdressers (Registration) Act 1964 s 2 (see PARA 969): s 15.
3   Hairdressers (Registration) Act 1964 s 8(1)(a).
4   Hairdressers (Registration) Act 1964 s 8(1)(b). The committee has cognisance of other cases by virtue of s 9(3): see PARA 973.
5   Hairdressers (Registration) Act 1964 Sch 2 para 1(1). Rules under the Hairdressers (Registration) Act 1964 are not made by statutory instrument, and are not dealt with in this work.
6   Hairdressers (Registration) Act 1964 Sch 2 para 1(2).
7   Hairdressers (Registration) Act 1964 Sch 2 para 2(1). In particular, rules must be made for:
    (1)   securing that notice that the proceedings are to be brought is given at the specified time and in the specified manner, to the person alleged to be liable to have his name removed from the register (Sch 2 para 2(1)(a));
    (2)   determining who, in addition to that person, is to be a party to the proceedings (Sch 2 para 2(1)(b));
    (3)   securing that any party may be heard by the committee (Sch 2 para 2(1)(c));
    (4)   enabling any party to be represented by counsel or solicitor or (if the rules so provide and the party so elects) by a person of some other specified description (Sch 2 para 2(1)(d)); and
    (5)   requiring proceedings before the committee to be held in public except so far as may be provided by the rules (Sch 2 para 2(1)(e)).
    As respects proceedings for the registration of a person whose name was previously removed from the register by direction of the disciplinary committee, the council has power to make rules with respect to all or any of the matters mentioned in heads (1)–(5), but is not required to do so; and separate rules may be made as respects such proceedings: Sch 2 para 2(2).
8   Hairdressers (Registration) Act 1964 Sch 2 para 3(1) (amended by the Courts and Legal Services Act 1990 s 72(1), Sch 10 para 23). As to the meaning of a 'ten year general qualification' see the Courts and Legal Services Act 1990 s 71; and LEGAL PROFESSIONS vol 65 (2015) PARA 540. The power of appointing an assessor for the disciplinary committee is exercisable by the council, but if no assessor appointed by it is available to act in any particular proceedings the committee may itself appoint an assessor: Hairdressers (Registration) Act 1964 Sch 2 para 3(2). Except in the case of an assessor so appointed by the committee, an assessor may be appointed under this provision either generally or for any particular proceedings or class of proceedings, and holds and vacates office in accordance with the terms of the instrument under which he is appointed: Sch 2 para 3(3).

973.   Removal from the register.   The disciplinary committee[1] may direct that a person's name be removed from the register[2] where he is convicted by any court in the United Kingdom[3] of a criminal offence which in the committee's opinion renders him unfit to be registered, or if it judges him guilty of serious negligence in any professional respect, or if it is satisfied that his name has been fraudulently entered[4]. The committee must serve the person whose name is to be removed with notice[5] of the direction[6]. Where the name of any person is so removed from the register, he must deliver up to the Hairdressing Council[7] his certificate of registration within seven days of receiving notice of the removal[8].

A person whose name is removed is not entitled to be registered again except in pursuance of a direction given by the committee on his application[9].

1   As to the disciplinary committee see PARA 972.
2   As to the meaning of 'register' see PARA 972 note 2.
3   As to the meaning of 'United Kingdom' see PARA 906 note 7.
4   Hairdressers (Registration) Act 1964 s 9(1).

5　'Notice' means a notice in writing: Hairdressers (Registration) Act 1964 s 11(1). Any notice authorised or required to be served under the Hairdressers (Registration) Act 1964 may, without prejudice to any other method of service but subject to any provision to the contrary in rules under the Act, be served by post; and for the purpose of the application of s 11(2) to what is now the Interpretation Act 1978 s 7 (which relates to service by post; see STATUTES AND LEGISLATIVE PROCESS vol 96 (2012) PARA 1219), the proper address of a person to whose registration such a notice relates is his address on the register: Hairdressers (Registration) Act 1964 s 11(2).

6　Hairdressers (Registration) Act 1964 s 9(2).

7　As to the council see PARA 968.

8　Hairdressers (Registration) Act 1964 s 10.

9　Hairdressers (Registration) Act 1964 s 9(3). A direction under s 9 for the removal of a person's name from the register may prohibit an application under s 9(3) by that person until the expiration of a specified period from the date of the direction (and, where he has duly made such an application, from the date of his last application): s 9(3).

(ix) Employment Agencies

974. Meaning of 'employment agency' and 'employment business'.
'Employment agency' means the business (whether or not carried on with a view to profit and whether or not carried on in conjunction with any other business) of providing services[1] (whether by the provision of information or otherwise) for the purpose of finding persons employment[2] with employers or of supplying employers with persons for employment by them[3].

'Employment business' means the business (whether or not carried on with a view to profit and whether or not carried on in conjunction with any other business) of supplying persons (being persons in the employment of the person carrying on the business) to act for and under the control of other persons in any capacity[4].

However, neither 'employment agency' nor 'employment business' includes any arrangements, services, functions or business to which the Employment Agencies Act 1973 does not apply by virtue of certain specified exemptions[5].

1　This reference to providing services does not include a reference: (1) to publishing a newspaper or other publication unless it is published wholly or mainly for the purpose mentioned in the text; (2) to the display by any person of advertisements on premises occupied by him otherwise than for that purpose; or (3) to providing a programme service within the meaning of the Broadcasting Act 1990 (see BROADCASTING vol 4 (2011) PARA 507): Employment Agencies Act 1973 s 13(4) (amended by the Broadcasting Act 1990 Sch 20 para 18).

2　'Employment' includes: (1) employment by way of a professional engagement or otherwise under a contract for services; (2) the reception in a private household of a person under an arrangement by which that person is to assist in the domestic work of the household in consideration of receiving hospitality and pocket money or hospitality only: Employment Agencies Act 1973 s 13(1). 'Worker' and 'employer' must be construed accordingly: s 13(1).

3　Employment Agencies Act 1973 s 13(1), (2) (s 13(2) amended by the Employment Relations Act 1999 Sch 7 para 7).

4　Employment Agencies Act 1973 s 13(1), (3). Where elements of control are divided between different persons, the natural meaning of control is the predominant practical control over what the transferred employee does: *Accenture Services Ltd v Revenue and Customs Comrs; Barclays Bank plc v Revenue and Customs Comrs* [2009] EWHC 857 (Admin), [2009] STC 1503, [2009] All ER (D) 223 (Apr) (staff supplied had not come under the predominant control of any person other than the agency).

5　Employment Agencies Act 1973 s 13(1). These exceptions are those that arise by virtue of s 13(7): see PARA 976.

975. Prohibition orders. On application by the Secretary of State[1], an employment tribunal[2] may by order prohibit a person from carrying on, or being concerned with the carrying on of any employment agency[3] or employment business[4], or any specified[5] description of employment agency or employment business[6]. Such an order (a 'prohibition order') may either prohibit a person from engaging in an activity altogether or prohibit him from doing so otherwise than in accordance with specified conditions[7]. A prohibition order must be made for a period beginning with the date of the order and ending on a specified date, or on the happening of a specified event, and in either case, not more than ten years later[8].

An employment tribunal may not make a prohibition order in relation to any person unless it is satisfied that he is, on account of his misconduct or for any other sufficient reason, unsuitable to do what the order prohibits[9].

Any person who, without reasonable excuse, fails to comply with a prohibition order is guilty of an offence[10].

On application by the person to whom a prohibition order applies, an employment tribunal may vary or revoke the order if it is satisfied that there has been a material change of circumstances since the order was last considered[11]. On such an application a tribunal may not so vary a prohibition order as to make it more restrictive[12].

An appeal lies to the Employment Appeal Tribunal[13] on a question of law arising from any decision of, or arising in proceedings before, an employment tribunal in relation to the making of a prohibition order or the disposition of an application for variation or revocation of a prohibition order[14].

1   As to the Secretary of State see PARA 902.
2   As to employment tribunals see **EMPLOYMENT** vol 41A (2014) PARA 1399 et seq.
3   As to the meaning of 'employment agency' see PARA 974.
4   As to the meaning of 'employment business' see PARA 974.
5   'Specified', in relation to a prohibition order, means specified in the order: Employment Agencies Act 1973 s 3A(9) (ss 3A–3D added by the Deregulation and Contracting Out Act 1994 Sch 10 para 1(3)).
6   Employment Agencies Act 1973 s 3A(1) (s 3A as added (see note 5); s 3A(1), (4)–(6) amended by virtue of the Employment Rights (Dispute Resolution) Act 1998 s 1(2)(a)).
7   Employment Agencies Act 1973 s 3A(2) (s 3A as added: see note 5).
8   Employment Agencies Act 1973 s 3A(3) (s 3A as added: see note 5).
9   Employment Agencies Act 1973 s 3A(4) (s 3A as added (see note 5); s 3A(4) as amended (see note 6)). An employment tribunal may however make a prohibition order in relation to:
    (1)   a body corporate, if it is satisfied that: (a) any director, secretary, manager or similar officer of the body corporate; (b) any person who performs on behalf of the body corporate the functions of a director, secretary, manager or similar officer; or (c) any person in accordance with whose directions or instructions the directors of the body corporate are accustomed to act, is unsuitable to do what the order prohibits;
    (2)   a partnership, if it is satisfied that any member of the partnership, or any manager employed by the partnership, is unsuitable to do what the order prohibits,
and the unsuitability is on account of the person's misconduct of for any other sufficient reason: s 3A(5), (6) (s 3A as so added; s 3A(5), (6) as amended (see note 6)). A person is not deemed to fall within head (1)(c) by reason only that the directors act on advice given by him in a professional capacity: s 3A(8) (s 3A as so added). 'Director', in relation to a body corporate whose affairs are controlled by its members, means a member of the body corporate: s 3A(9) (s 3A as so added).
    For the purposes of s 3A(4), where an employment agency or employment business has been improperly conducted, each person who was carrying on, or concerned with the carrying on of, the agency or business at the time, is deemed to have been responsible for what happened unless he can show that it happened without his connivance or consent and was not attributable to any neglect on his part: s 3A(7) (s 3A as so added).
10   Employment Agencies Act 1973 s 3B (as added (see note 5); amended by the Employment Act 2008 s 15). A person guilty of such an offence is liable, on conviction on indictment, to a fine and, on summary conviction, to a fine not exceeding the statutory maximum: Employment Agencies Act 1973 s 3B (as so added and amended). Where any offence committed under the Employment Agencies Act 1973 by a body corporate is proved to have been committed with the

consent or connivance of, or to have been attributable to any neglect on the part of, any director, manager, secretary or similar officer, or a person who was purporting to act in any such capacity, he as well as the body corporate is guilty of the offence and is liable to be proceeded against and punished accordingly: s 11(1) (numbered as such by the Employment Act 2008 s 17(a)). As to the statutory maximum see SENTENCING AND DISPOSITION OF OFFENDERS vol 92 (2010) PARA 140.

The court in which a person is convicted of an offence under the Employment Agencies Act 1973 may order him to pay to the Secretary of State a sum which appears to the court not to exceed the costs of the investigation which resulted in the conviction: s 11B (added by the Employment Relations Act 1999 Sch 7 para 5).

11 Employment Agencies Act 1973 s 3C(1) (s 3C as added (see note 5); s 3C(1)–(4) amended by virtue of the Employment Rights (Dispute Resolution) Act 1998 s 1(2)(a)). The Secretary of State is a party to any proceedings before a tribunal with respect to such an application, and is entitled to appear and be heard accordingly: Employment Agencies Act 1973 s 3C(3) (s 3C as so added; s 3C(3) as so amended).

When making a prohibition order or disposing of an application under s 3C, an employment tribunal may, with a view to preventing the making of vexatious or frivolous applications, by order prohibit the making of such an application, or further application, in relation to the prohibition order before such date as the tribunal may specify: s 3C(4) (s 3C as so added; s 3C(4) as so amended).

12 Employment Agencies Act 1973 s 3C(2) (s 3C as added (see note 5); s 3C(2) as amended (see note 11)).

13 As to the Employment Appeal Tribunal see EMPLOYMENT vol 41A (2014) PARA 1422 et seq.

14 Employment Agencies Act 1973 s 3D(1) (s 3D as added (see note 5); s 3C(1), (2) amended by virtue of the Employment Rights (Dispute Resolution) Act 1998 s 1(2)(a)). No other appeal lies from a decision of an employment tribunal under the Employment Agencies Act 1973 s 3A or s 3C and the Tribunals and Inquiries Act 1992 s 11 (appeals from certain tribunals to the High Court: see CIVIL PROCEDURE vol 12 (2009) PARA 1691) does not apply to proceedings before an employment tribunal under those provisions: Employment Agencies Act 1973 s 3D(2) (s 3D as so added; s 3D(2) as so amended).

976.   Exemptions from the Employment Agencies Act 1973. The following businesses, agencies and services are exempted from the application of the Employment Agencies Act 1973:

(1)   any business which is carried on exclusively for the purpose of obtaining employment[1] for persons formerly in the armed forces[2] or persons released from a custodial sentence passed by a criminal court in the United Kingdom, the Channel Islands or the Isle of Man[3];

(2)   an early years childminder agency or a later years childminder agency[4];

(3)   services which are ancillary to the letting on hire of any aircraft, vessel, vehicle, plant or equipment[5];

(4)   the exercise by a local authority[6] or a joint authority[7] of any of its functions[8];

(5)   the exercise by a joint waste authority[9] established for an area in England of any of its functions[10];

(6)   the exercise by an economic prosperity board[11] or a combined authority[12] of any of its functions[13];

(7)   the exercise by a police and crime commissioner[14], the Mayor's Office for Policing and Crime[15], a chief constable[16] or the Commissioner of Police for the Metropolis[17] of any of their functions[18];

(8)   the exercise by the Broads Authority[19] of any of its functions[20];

(9)   the exercise by a national park authority[21] of any of its functions[22];

(10)   the exercise by the London Fire and Emergency Planning Authority[23] of any of its functions[24];

(11)   services provided by any organisation[25] of employers[26] or of workers[27] for its members[28];

(12) services provided in pursuance of arrangements made or a direction given under the Employment and Training Act 1973[29];

(13) services provided by an appointments board or service controlled by one or more universities[30]; and

(14) any prescribed[31] business or service, or prescribed class of business or service or business or service carried on or provided by prescribed persons or classes of person[32].

1 As to the meaning of 'employment' see PARA 974 note 2.

2 As to the armed forces generally see ARMED FORCES.

3 See the Employment Agencies Act 1973 s 13(7)(a) (amended by the Criminal Justice Act 1988 Sch 8 Pt I para 7). The business must be certified annually by or on behalf of the appropriate board of the Defence Council or the Secretary of State, as the case may be: see the Employment Agencies Act 1973 s 13(7)(a). As to the meaning of 'United Kingdom' see PARA 906 note 7. As to the Secretary of State see PARA 902. As to the Defence Council see ARMED FORCES vol 3 (2011) PARA 302; CONSTITUTIONAL AND ADMINISTRATIVE LAW vol 20 (2014) PARA 562 et seq.

4 Employment Agencies Act 1973 s 13(7)(ca) (added by the Children and Families Act 2014 Sch 4 Pt 6 para 64). Such childminding is defined in the Childcare Act 2006 s 98 (see CHILDREN AND YOUNG PERSONS vol 10 (2012) PARA 1099A): Employment Agencies Act 1973 s 13(7)(ca) (as so added).

5 Employment Agencies Act 1973 s 13(7)(d).

6 'Local authority', in relation to England, means a county council, the Common Council of the City of London, a district council or a London borough council and in relation to Wales, means a county council or a county borough council: Employment Agencies Act 1973 s 13(1) (definition amended by the Local Government Act 1985 Sch 17; and the Local Government (Wales) Act 1994 Sch 16 para 41, Sch 18). As to the Common Council of the City of London and London boroughs see LONDON GOVERNMENT vol 71 (2013) PARAS 15, 34 et seq; and as to county councils and county borough councils in Wales see LOCAL GOVERNMENT vol 69 (2009) PARAS 5, 37, 41.

7 Ie a joint authority established under the Local Government Act 1985 Pt IV (ss 23–42) (see LOCAL GOVERNMENT vol 69 (2009) PARA 47 et seq): Employment Agencies Act 1973 s 13(7)(f) (as amended: see note 8).

8 Employment Agencies Act 1973 s 13(7)(f) (amended by the Local Government Act 1985 Sch 14 Pt II para 50; the Education Reform Act 1988 s 237(2), Sch 13 Pt I; the Police and Magistrates' Courts Act 1994 Sch 4 Pt II para 50; the Police Act 1996 Sch 7 Pt I para 1(2)(i); the Police Act 1997 Sch 9 para 26; and the Serious Organised Crime and Police Act 2005 Sch 4 para 19, Sch 17 Pt 2).

9 Ie a joint waste authority established under the Local Government and Public Involvement in Health Act 2007 s 207 (joint waste authorities) (see ENVIRONMENTAL QUALITY AND PUBLIC HEALTH vol 46 (2010) PARA 621): Employment Agencies Act 1973 s 13(7)(fza) (as added: see note 10).

10 Employment Agencies Act 1973 s 13(7)(fza) (added by the Local Government and Public Involvement in Health Act 2007 Sch 13 Pt 2 para 30).

11 Ie an economic prosperity board established under the Local Democracy, Economic Development and Construction Act 2009 s 88 (see PARA 1086 et seq): Employment Agencies Act 1973 s 13(7)(fzb) (as added: see note 13).

12 Ie a combined authority established under the Local Democracy, Economic Development and Construction Act 2009 s 103 (see PARA 1092 et seq): Employment Agencies Act 1973 s 13(7)(fzc) (as added: see note 13).

13 Employment Agencies Act 1973 s 13(7)(fzb), (fzc) (added by the Local Democracy, Economic Development and Construction Act 2009 Sch 6 para 40).

14 As to police and crime commissioners see POLICE AND INVESTIGATORY POWERS vol 84 (2013) PARA 85.

15 As to the Mayor's Office for Policing and Crime see POLICE AND INVESTIGATORY POWERS vol 84 (2013) PARA 78.

16 Ie a chief constable established under the Police Reform and Social Responsibility Act 2011 s 2 (see): Employment Agencies Act 1973 s 13(7)(fc) (as added: see note 18).

17 As to the Metropolitan Police Commissioner see POLICE AND INVESTIGATORY POWERS vol 84 (2013) PARA 117 et seq.

18 Employment Agencies Act 1973 s 13(7)(fa)–(fd) (s 13(7)(fa) added by the Greater London Authority Act 1999 Sch 27 para 37; the Employment Agencies Act 1973 s 13(7)(fa) substituted, s 13(7)(fb)–(fd) added, by the Police Reform and Social Responsibility Act 2011 Sch 16 Pt 3 para 118(b)).

19 As to the Broads Authority see WATER AND WATERWAYS vol 101 (2009) PARA 734.

20 Employment Agencies Act 1973 s 13(7)(ff) (added by the Norfolk and Suffolk Broads Act 1988 Sch 6 para 11).

21 As to national park authorities see OPEN SPACES AND COUNTRYSIDE vol 78 (2010) PARA 526 et seq.

22 Employment Agencies Act 1973 s 13(7)(fg) (added by the Environment Act 1995 Sch 10 para 11).

23 As to the London Fire and Emergency Planning Authority see FIRE AND RESCUE SERVICES vol 51 (2013) PARA 17; LONDON GOVERNMENT vol 71 (2013) PARA 315.

24 Employment Agencies Act 1973 s 13(7)(fh) (added by the Greater London Authority Act 1999 Sch 29 Pt I para 22).

25 'Organisation' includes an association of organisations: Employment Agencies Act 1973 s 13(1).

26 'Organisation of employers' means an organisation which consists wholly or mainly of employers and whose principal objects include the regulation of relations between employers and workers or organisations of workers: Employment Agencies Act 1973 s 13(1). As to the meanings of 'employer' and 'worker' see PARA 974 note 2.

27 'Organisation of workers' means an organisation which consists wholly or mainly of workers and whose principal objects include the regulation of relations between workers and employers or organisations of employers: Employment Agencies Act 1973 s 13(1). The organisation must genuinely be an organisation of workers, not merely a co-operative employment agency: see *McCabe v Edwards* [1981] ICR 468, DC.

28 Employment Agencies Act 1973 s 13(7)(g).

29 Employment Agencies Act 1973 s 13(7)(ga) (added by the Trade Union Reform and Employment Rights Act 1993 s 49(2), Sch 8 para 4). This exception applies to arrangements made or a direction given under the Employment and Training Act 1973 s 10 (see EMPLOYMENT vol 40 (2014) PARA 640): Employment Agencies Act 1973 s 13(7)(ga) (as so added).

30 Employment Agencies Act 1973 s 13(7)(h).

31 'Prescribed' means prescribed by regulations made under the Employment Agencies Act 1973 by the Secretary of State: s 13(1). The Secretary of State has power, exercisable by statutory instrument, to make regulations for prescribing anything which is to be prescribed under the Employment Agencies Act 1973: s 12(1), (4). Regulations may make different provision in relation to different cases or classes of cases: s 12(3). Before making regulations he must consult with such bodies as appear to him to be representative of the interests concerned: s 12(2). After consultation with such bodies as appear to him to be concerned the Secretary of State may by order repeal or amend provisions of local Acts which appear to him to be unnecessary or inconsistent with the Employment Agencies Act 1973: see s 14(3). Such orders, being local in nature, are not recorded in this work.

Regulations under s 13(7)(i) (see text and note 32) or an order under s 14(3), are subject to annulment in pursuance of a resolution of either House of Parliament: s 12(6) (substituted by the Employment Relations Act 1999 Sch 7 para 6). See also STATUTES AND LEGISLATIVE PROCESS vol 96 (2012) PARA 1045 et seq.

32 Employment Agencies Act 1973 s 13(7)(i) (substituted by the Employment Relations Act 1999 Sch 7 para 8). The following bodies have been exempted under this head:
(1) certain colleges for teacher training, other institutions of further education, charities, bodies comprising representatives of industrial training boards (defined in the Industrial Training Act 1982 s 1(2): see EMPLOYMENT vol 40 (2014) PARA 658), together with representatives of any one or more of an organisation of employers, an organisation of workers or a body comprising representatives of two or more such organisations, and the British Council (see the Employment Agencies Act 1973 (Exemption) Regulations 1976, SI 1976/710);
(2) the Crown Agents for Oversea Governments and Administrations, or any of its wholly owned subsidiaries (see the Employment Agencies Act 1973 (Exemption) (No 2) Regulations 1979, SI 1979/1741 (amended by SI 1984/978));
(3) the Association of Dispensing Opticians Ltd, the Association of Meat Inspectors (Great Britain) Ltd, the Chartered Institute of Patent Agents, the Faculty of Actuaries in Scotland, the General Pharmaceutical Council, the Incorporated Brewers' Guild, the Institute of Actuaries, the Institute of Chartered Accountants in England and Wales, the Institute of Chartered Accountants of Scotland, the Institute of Chartered Secretaries and Administrators, the Institute of Legal Executives, the Institute of Marketing, the

Institute of the Motor Industry, the Institute of Personnel Management, the Institute of Qualified Private Secretaries Ltd, the Law Society of Scotland, local law societies in England and Wales, the Pensions Management Institute, the Royal Society of Chemistry, the Society of Architectural and Associated Technicians, the Society of Business Economists, the Society of Chiropodists, the Law Society and Law Society Services Ltd (see the Employment Agencies Act 1973 (Exemption) (No 2) Regulations 1984, SI 1984/978 (amended by SI 2010/1621)).

977. Conduct of employment agencies and employment businesses. The Secretary of State[1] may make regulations to secure the proper conduct of employment agencies[2] and employment businesses[3] and to protect the interests of persons availing themselves of the services of such agencies and businesses[4]. Any person who contravenes or fails to comply with such regulations is guilty of an offence[5].

Regulations made under this power[6] provide that employment agencies and employment businesses must abide by certain general obligations relating to their dealings with work-seekers[7] and hirers[8], must notify work-seekers of their charges and of the terms of any offers or gifts made to induce work-seekers to engage a particular agency or employment business[9], must obtain the agreement of work-seekers and hirers to the terms which apply or will apply as between the particular agency or employment business and the work-seeker or hirer[10], must satisfy specified requirements in relation to the introduction or supply of work-seekers to hirers[11], and must comply with certain requirements as to advertising[12], client accounts[13], charges to work-seekers[14], confidentiality[15] and the keeping of records[16]. Special provision is made for situations where more than one agency or employment business is involved[17], and where work-seekers are provided with travel or required to live away from home[18].

Any officer duly authorised in that behalf by the Secretary of State may, at all reasonable times, and on producing written evidence of his authority, if so required:

(1) enter any relevant business premises[19];

(2) inspect those premises and: (a) any records or documents[20] kept in pursuance of the Employment Agencies Act 1973 or any regulations made under that Act; and (b) any financial records or other financial documents not falling within head (a) which he may reasonably require to inspect for the purpose of ascertaining whether the provisions of the Act and of any regulations made under it are being complied with or of enabling the Secretary of State to exercise his functions under the Act[21]; and

(3) require any person on those premises to furnish him with information which he may reasonably require for ascertaining whether the provisions of the Act or of any regulations made under it are being complied with or for enabling the Secretary of State to exercise his functions[22].

Restrictions are placed upon the disclosure of any information obtained in the exercise of these powers[23].

1 As to the Secretary of State see PARA 902.
2 As to the meaning of 'employment agency' see PARA 974.
3 As to the meaning of 'employment business' see PARA 974.
4 Employment Agencies Act 1973 s 5(1). As to the purposes for which regulations may be made see s 5(1)(a)–(ec), (1A) (s 5(1)(ea)–(ec), (1A) added by the Employment Relations Act 1999 Sch 7 para 2(2), (3)). As to the making of regulations and orders under the Employment Agencies Act 1973 generally see PARA 976 note 31. In the case of regulations under s 5(1), a draft must

have been laid before and approved by each House of Parliament: s 12(5) (substituted by the Employment Relations Act 1999 Sch 7 para 6). See also STATUTES AND LEGISLATIVE PROCESS vol 96 (2012) PARA 1045 et seq.

Any person who makes or causes to be made or knowingly allows to be made any entry in a record or other document required to be kept in pursuance of the Employment Agencies Act 1973 or of any regulations made under it which he knows to be false in a material particular is guilty of an offence: s 10(2). A person who commits such an offence is liable on summary conviction to a fine not exceeding level 5 on the standard scale: s 10(3) (amended by virtue of the Criminal Justice Act 1982 ss 38, 46). As to the standard scale see SENTENCING AND DISPOSITION OF OFFENDERS vol 92 (2010) PARA 142.

Notwithstanding the Magistrates' Courts Act 1980 s 127(1) (information to be laid within six months of offence: see MAGISTRATES vol 71 (2013) PARA 526) an information relating to a relevant offence which is triable by a magistrates' court in England and Wales may be so tried if it is laid at any time within three years after the date of the commission of the offence, and within six months after the date on which evidence sufficient in the opinion of the Secretary of State to justify the proceedings came to his knowledge: Employment Agencies Act 1973 s 11A(2) (s 11A added by the Employment Relations Act 1999 Sch 7 para 5). For this purpose a certificate of the Secretary of State as to the date on which evidence came to his knowledge is conclusive evidence: Employment Agencies Act 1973 s 11A(4) (as so added). A relevant offence is one under s 9(4)(b) (see note 23) or s 10(2), for which proceedings are instituted by the Secretary of State: s 11A(1) (as so added; amended by the Employment Act 2008 Schedule Pt 5).

The Agency Workers Regulations 2010, SI 2010/93 (see EMPLOYMENT vol 39 (2014) PARA 97 et seq), implementing European Parliament and Council Directive (EC) 2008/104 on temporary agency work (OJ L327, 5.12.2008, p 9), do not affect the rules as to the conduct of employment agencies.

See also the Merchant Shipping (Maritime Labour Convention) (Recruitment and Placement) Regulations 2014, SI 2014/1615, made under the European Communities Act 1972 s 2(2), which implement part of the Maritime Labour Convention 2006 reg 1.4 by imposing obligations on employment agencies and employment businesses in respect of the provision of their services as regards seafarer employment agreements, in particular to provide a financial system of protection for persons they have introduced or supplied for work as a seafarer and who have been employed as such: see the Merchant Shipping (Maritime Labour Convention) (Recruitment and placement) Regulations 2014, SI 2014, regs 4–7. 'Seafarer employment agreement' means the written agreement required by the Merchant Shipping (Maritime Labour Convention) (Minimum Requirements for Seafarers etc) Regulations 2014, SI 2014/1613 reg 9 (see SHIPPING AND MARITIME LAW vol 93 (2008) PARA 457A) where the seafarer works on a United Kingdom ship or the agreement governing the seafarer's work on the sip where the seafarer works on a ship which is not a United Kingdom ship: Merchant Shipping (Maritime Labour Convention) (Recruitment and Placement) Regulations 2014, SI 2014/1615 reg 3. 'Seafarer' means any person who is employed or engaged or who works in any capacity on board a ship and whose normal place of work is on a ship; and 'United Kingdom ship' means a United Kingdom ship within the meaning of the Merchant Shipping Act 1995 s 85(2) (see SHIPPING AND MARITIME LAW vol 94 (2008) PARA 591), a government ship within the meaning of s 308(4) (SHIPPING AND MARITIME LAW vol 93 (2008) PARA 20) which is ordinarily engaged in commercial maritime operations, or a hovercraft registered under the Hovercraft Act 1968 (see SHIPPING AND MARITIME LAW vol 93 (2008) PARA 390): Merchant Shipping (Maritime Labour Convention) (Recruitment and Placement) Regulations 2014, SI 2014/1615, reg 2(1).

5 Employment Agencies Act 1973 s 5(2) (amended by the Employment Act 2008 s 15). A person guilty of such an offence is liable, on conviction on indictment, to a fine and, on summary conviction to a fine not exceeding the statutory maximum: Employment Agencies Act 1973 s 5(2) (as so amended). As to the statutory maximum see SENTENCING AND DISPOSITION OF OFFENDERS vol 92 (2010) PARA 140. See also PARA 975 note 10. In addition, without prejudice to any right of action and any defence which exists or may be available apart from the provisions of the 1973 Act and the Conduct of Employment Agencies and Employment Businesses Regulations 2003, SI 2003/3319, contravention of, or failure to comply with, any of the provisions of the Act or of the regulations by an agency or employment business, so far as it causes damage, is actionable: reg 30(1). For this purpose, 'damage' includes the death of, or injury to, any person (including any disease and any impairment of that person's physical or mental condition): reg 30(2). Where any term of a contract is prohibited or made unenforceable by the regulations, the contract continues to bind the parties to it if it is capable of continuing in existence without that term: reg 31(1). Where a hirer (see note 8) pays any money pursuant to a contractual term which is unenforceable by virtue of reg 10 (see note 8), the hirer is entitled to recover that money: reg 31(2).

6 Ie the Conduct of Employment Agencies and Employment Businesses Regulations 2003, SI 2003/3319. Note that these regulations do not govern the employment status of agency workers, which remains a matter of common law (see EMPLOYMENT vol 39 (2014) PARA 11); nor are these regulations affected by the Agency Worker Regulations 2010, SI 2010/93 (see EMPLOYMENT vol 39 (2014) PARA 97 et seq).

7 'Work-seeker' means a person to whom an agency or employment business provides or holds itself out as being capable of providing work-finding services: Conduct of Employment Agencies and Employment Businesses Regulations 2003, SI 2003/3319, reg 2. 'Work-finding services' means services, whether by the provision of information or otherwise, provided: (1) by an agency to a person for the purpose of finding that person employment or seeking to find that person employment; (2) by an employment business to an employee of the employment business for the purpose of finding or seeking to find another person, with a view to the employee acting for and under the control of that other person; (3) by an employment business to a person for the purpose of finding or seeking to find another person, with a view to the first person becoming employed by the employment business and acting for and under the control of the second person: Conduct of Employment Agencies and Employment Businesses Regulations 2003, SI 2003/3319, reg 2. 'Agency' means an employment agency as defined in the Employment Agencies Act 1973 s 13(1), (2) (see PARA 974) and includes a person carrying on an agency, and in the case of a person who carries on both an agency and an employment business means such a person in his capacity in carrying on the agency; and 'employment business' means an employment business as defined in s 13(1), (3) (see PARA 974) and includes a person carrying on an employment business, and in the case of a person who carries on both an employment business and an agency means such a person in his capacity in carrying on the employment business: Conduct of Employment Agencies and Employment Businesses Regulations 2003, SI 2003/3319, reg 2.

8 See the Conduct of Employment Agencies and Employment Businesses Regulations 2003, SI 2003/3319, regs 5–12. 'Hirer' means a person (including an employment business) to whom an agency or employment business introduces or supplies or holds itself out as being capable of introducing or supplying a work-seeker: reg 2. The general obligations cover restrictions on requiring work-seekers to use additional services of the agency or employment business (see reg 5 (amended by SI 2007/3575)), on taking detrimental action relating to work-seekers working elsewhere (see the Conduct of Employment Agencies and Employment Businesses Regulations 2003, SI 2003/3319, reg 6), on providing work-seekers in industrial disputes (see reg 7), on paying work-seekers' remuneration (see reg 8), on agencies and employment businesses purporting to act on a different basis to work-seekers and hirers (see reg 9) and on charges to hirers (see reg 10), and prohibitions on entering into a contract on behalf of a client (see reg 11) and on employment businesses withholding payment to work-seekers on certain grounds (see reg 12).

The regulations apply equally, with modifications, to a work-seeker which is a company: see reg 32 (amended by SI 2007/3575; and SI 2010/1782).

9 See the Conduct of Employment Agencies and Employment Businesses Regulations 2003, SI 2003/3319, reg 13 (amended by SI 2007/3575; and SI 2010/1782). As to the requirements relating to notification see the Conduct of Employment Agencies and Employment Businesses Regulations 2003, reg 33.

10 See the Conduct of Employment Agencies and Employment Businesses Regulations 2003, SI 2003/3319, regs 14–17.

11 See the Conduct of Employment Agencies and Employment Businesses Regulations 2003, SI 2003/3319, regs 18–22. Such requirements include obtaining specified information from a hirer (see reg 18), confirming the identity of a work-seeker and that he has the necessary qualifications, experience, etc and is willing to work in the position which the hirer seeks to fill (see reg 19 (substituted by SI 2010/1782)), taking steps for the protection of the work-seeker and the hirer (see the Conduct of Employment Agencies and Employment Businesses Regulations 2003, reg 20), providing information to work-seekers and hirers (see reg 21 (amended by SI 2007/3575)) and fulfilling additional requirements where professional qualifications are required or where work-seekers are to work with vulnerable persons (see the Conduct of Employment Agencies and Employment Businesses Regulations 2003, reg 22 (substituted by SI 2010/1782)).

12 See the Conduct of Employment Agencies and Employment Businesses Regulations 2003, SI 2003/3319, reg 27 (amended by SI 2010/1782).

13 See the Conduct of Employment Agencies and Employment Businesses Regulations 2003, SI 2003/3319, reg 25, Sch 2.

14 See the Conduct of Employment Agencies and Employment Businesses Regulations 2003, SI 2003/3319, reg 26, Sch 3 (Sch 3 amended by SI 2010/1782); and PARA 978.

15 See the Conduct of Employment Agencies and Employment Businesses Regulations 2003, SI 2003/3319, reg 28 (amended by SI 2007/3575).

16 See the Conduct of Employment Agencies and Employment Businesses Regulations 2003, SI 2003/3319, reg 29, Schs 4–6. As to the making of false entries in records see note 4.

17 See the Conduct of Employment Agencies and Employment Businesses Regulations 2003, SI 2003/3319, reg 23.

18 See the Conduct of Employment Agencies and Employment Businesses Regulations 2003, SI 2003/3319, reg 24.

19 Employment Agencies Act 1973 s 9(1)(a) (s 9(1) amended by the Employment Protection Act 1975 Sch 13 para 6(1); the Employment Agencies Act 1973 s 9(1)(a) amended by the Employment Relations Act 1999 Sch 7 para 4(2)(a)). 'Relevant business premises' means premises: (1) which are used, have been used or are to be used for or in connection with the carrying on of an employment agency or employment business; (2) which the officer has reasonable cause to believe are used or have been used for or in connection with the carrying on of an employment agency or employment business; or (3) which the officer has reasonable cause to believe are used for the carrying on of a business by a person who also carries on or has carried on an employment agency or employment business, if the officer also has reasonable cause to believe that records or other documents which relate to the employment agency or employment business are kept there: Employment Agencies Act 1973 s 9(1B) (s 9(1A), (1B), (1C) added by the Employment Relations Act 1999 Sch 7 para 4(3)).

A person who obstructs an officer in the exercise of his powers under the Employment Agencies Act 1973 s 9(1)(a) or (b), (1AD) or (1AE), or who, without reasonable excuse, fails to comply with a requirement under s 9(1)(c), (1A), (1AA) or (1AB), is guilty of an offence and liable on summary conviction to a fine not exceeding level 3 on the standard scale: see the Employment Agencies Act 1973 s 9(3) (amended by virtue of the Criminal Justice Act 1982 ss 38, 46; and the Employment Act 2008 s 16(8)).

20 'Document' includes information recorded in any form: Employment Agencies Act 1973 s 9(1C)(a) (s 9(1C) as added (see note 19); and amended by the Employment Act 2008 s 16(7)). An officer may take copies of any record or other document inspected by or furnished to him under the Employment Agencies Act 1973 s 9 and may, for this purpose, remove a record or other document from the premises where it is inspected by or furnished to him; but he must return it as soon as reasonably practicable: s 9(1AD), (1AE) (added by the Employment Act 2008 s 16(6)).

21 Employment Agencies Act 1973 s 9(1)(b) (s 9(1) as amended (see note 19); s 9(1)(b) amended by the Employment Act 2008 s 16(2)).

If an officer seeks to inspect or acquire, in accordance with the Employment Agencies Act 1973 s 9(1)(b) or (c), a record or other document or information which is not kept at the premises being inspected, the officer may by notice in writing require the person carrying on the employment agency or employment business to furnish him with the record or other document or information at such time and place as he may specify: s 9(1A) (as added (see note 19); and amended by the Employment Act 2008 s 16(4)). Information is kept at premises if it is accessible from them: Employment Agencies Act 1973 s 9(1C)(b) (s 9(1C) as added (see note 19) and amended (see note 20)). Where a person carrying on an employment agency or employment business fails to comply with s 9(1A) in relation to: (1) any record or other document or information and the officer has reasonable cause to believe that the record or other document or information is kept by a person concerned, or formerly concerned, with the carrying on of the employment agency or employment business; (2) any financial record or other financial document which is kept by a bank, the officer may by notice in writing require that person to furnish him with the record or other document or information at such time and place as he may specify: s 9(1AA), (1AB) (s 9(1AA)–(1AC) added by the Employment Act 2008 s 16(5)). For this purpose, 'bank' means a person who has permission under the Financial Services and Markets Act 2000 Pt 4A (ss 55A–55Z4) (see FINANCIAL SERVICES AND INSTITUTIONS vol 48 (2008) PARA 348A) to accept deposits: Employment Agencies Act 1973 s 9(1AC) (as so added; and amended by the Financial Services Act 2012 Sch 18 Pt 2 para 36).

22 Employment Agencies Act 1973 s 9(1)(c) (s 9(1) as amended (see note 19); s 9(1)(c) amended by the Employment Protection Act 1975 Sch 13 para 6(2)). See also note 20. Nothing in the Employment Agencies Act 1973 s 9 requires a person to produce, provide access to or make arrangements for the production of anything which he could not be compelled to produce in civil proceedings before the High Court: s 9(2) (s 9(2) substituted and s 9(2A), (2B) added by the Employment Relations Act 1999 Sch 7 para 4(4)). A statement made by a person in compliance with a requirement under the Employment Agencies Act 1973 s 9 may be used in evidence against him in criminal proceedings: s 9(2A) (as so added). However, except in proceedings for an offence under the Perjury Act 1911 s 5 (false statements made otherwise than on oath: see

CRIMINAL LAW vol 26 (2010) PARA 673), no evidence relating to the statement may be adduced, and no question relating to it may be asked, by or on behalf of the prosecution unless evidence relating to it is adduced, or a question relating to it is asked, by or on behalf of the person who made the statement: Employment Agencies Act 1973 s 9(2B) (as so added).

23 See the Employment Agencies Act 1973 s 9(4) (amended by the Employment Protection Act 1975 Sch 13 para 6(3), Sch 18; the Deregulation and Contracting Out Act 1994 Sch 10 Pt I para 1(4); the Employment Act 2008 ss 16(9), 18(2), Schedule Pt 5; by virtue of the Criminal Justice Act 1982 ss 38, 46; and by SI 2009/2999). As from a day to be appointed the Employment Agencies Act 1973 s 9(4) is amended without changing the substance of the provision by the Employment Relations Act 1999 Sch 7 para 4(6), Sch 9. At the date at which this volume states the law no day for the coming into force of the amendment had been appointed. No information so obtained, or obtained pursuant to the National Minimum Wage Act 1998 s 15(5A) (see EMPLOYMENT vol 39 (2014) PARA 239), may be disclosed except:

  (1) with the consent of the person furnishing the information, or, where furnished on behalf of another person, with the consent of that other person or with the consent of the person carrying on or proposing to carry on the employment agency or employment business concerned (Employment Agencies Act 1973 s 9(4)(a)(i)); or

  (2) to the Secretary of State, or an officer or servant appointed by him, or a person exercising functions on his behalf, for the purposes of the exercise of their respective functions under the Act (s 9(4)(a)(ii)); or

  (3) by the Secretary of State or such an officer, servant or person to the person carrying on or proposing to carry on the employment agency or employment business concerned, to any person in his employment, or, in the case of information relating to a person availing himself of the services of such an agency or business, to that person (Employment Agencies Act 1973 s 9(4)(a)(iii)); or

  (4) with a view to the institution of, or otherwise for the purposes of, any criminal proceedings pursuant to or arising out of the Act or for the purposes of any proceedings under the Employment Agencies Act 1973 s 3A, 3C or 3D (see PARA 975) (s 9(4)(a)(iv));

  (5) to an officer acting for the purposes of the National Minimum Wage Act 1998 for any purpose relating to that Act (Employment Agencies Act 1973 s 9(4)(a)(v)); or

  (6) to an authority in another EEA state pursuant to the Provision of Services Regulations 2009, SI 2009/2999 (see SALE OF GOODS AND SUPPLY OF SERVICES vol 91 (2012) PARA 321 et seq).

As to the European Economic Area (EEA) see the Agreement on the European Economic Area (Oporto, 2 May 1992; EC 7 (1992); Cm 2183) as adjusted by the Protocol (Brussels, 17 March 1993; EC 2 (1993); Cm 2183); and CUSTOMS AND EXCISE vol 30 (2012) PARA 5.

Any person who contravenes the Employment Agencies Act 1973 s 9(4)(a) is guilty of an offence and liable on summary conviction to a fine not exceeding level 5 on the standard scale: s 9(4)(b) (amended by virtue of the Criminal Justice Act 1982 ss 38, 46). See also PARA 975 note 10.

978. Charging of fees. Except in such cases or classes of case as the Secretary of State[1] may prescribe[2]: (1) a person carrying on an employment agency[3] may not request or directly or indirectly receive any fee[4] from any person for providing services (whether by the provision of information or otherwise) for the purpose of finding him employment or seeking to find him employment[5]; (2) a person carrying on an employment business[6] may not request or directly or indirectly receive any fee from an employee for providing services (whether by the provision of information or otherwise) for the purpose of finding or seeking to find another person, with a view to the employee acting for and under the control of that other person; (3) a person carrying on an employment business may not request or directly or indirectly receive any fee from a second person for providing services (whether by the provision of information or otherwise) for the purpose of finding or seeking to find a third person, with a view to the second person becoming employed by the first person and acting for and under the control of the third person[7]. Any person contravening this prohibition is guilty of an offence[8].

The regulations prescribing exceptions provide that fees may be charged by agents for finding work for persons in specified professions[9], except where the agent also charges a fee to the hirer in question[10], or where the agent and the employer are connected with each other[11] unless the agency informs the work-seeker of the fact that it is connected with the hirer[12]. Where the agent is allowed to charge a fee, any fee charged by the agency may consist only of a charge or commission payable out of the work-seeker's earnings in any such employment which the agency has found for him[13]. In addition, the restrictions on charging fees to work-seekers do not apply to any fee consisting of a charge to a work-seeker in respect of the purchase of or subscription for a publication containing information about employers, provided that certain conditions are met[14], or in respect of a fee charged by an agency for the service provided by it of finding or seeking to find a work-seeker employment where the work-seeker in question is a company and the employment is in an occupation other than any of the specified occupations[15].

1 As to the Secretary of State see PARA 902.
2 As to the cases so prescribed see the text and notes 9–15. As to the meaning of 'prescribed' see PARA 976 note 31; and as to bodies completely exempted from the application of the Employment Agencies Act 1973 see PARA 976.
3 As to the meaning of 'employment agency' see PARA 974.
4 'Fee' includes any charge however described: Employment Agencies Act 1973 s 13(1). As to the meaning of 'demand' in relation to a fee see *First Point International Ltd v Department of Trade and Industry* (1999) 164 JP 89, DC.
5 The collection and assessment of appraisal information is part of the process of seeking to find employment for a client, if the seeking of information is sufficiently proximate to what happens thereafter: see *First Point International Ltd v Department of Trade and Industry* (1999) 164 JP 89, DC.
6 As to the meaning of 'employment business' see PARA 974.
7 Employment Agencies Act 1973 s 6(1) (substituted by the Employment Relations Act 1999 Sch 7 para 3).
     As to the making of regulations and orders under the Employment Agencies Act 1973 generally see PARA 976 note 31. In the case of regulations under s 5(1), a draft must have been laid before and approved by each House of Parliament: s 12(5) (substituted by the Employment Relations Act 1999 Sch 7 para 6). See also STATUTES AND LEGISLATIVE PROCESS vol 96 (2012) PARA 1045 et seq.
8 Employment Agencies Act 1973 s 6(2) (amended by the Employment Act 2008 s 15). A person guilty of such an offence is liable, on conviction on indictment, to a fine and, on summary conviction to a fine not exceeding the statutory maximum: Employment Agencies Act 1973 s 6(2) (as so amended). See also PARA 975 note 10. As to the statutory maximum see SENTENCING AND DISPOSITION OF OFFENDERS vol 92 (2010) PARA 140.
9 See the Conduct of Employment Agencies and Employment Businesses Regulations 2003, SI 2003/3319, reg 26(1). The specified professions are:
     (1) actor, musician, singer, dancer, background artist, extra, walk-on or other performer;
     (2) composer, writer, artist, director, production manager, lighting cameraman, camera operator, make up artist, clothes, hair or make up stylist, film editor, action arranger or co-ordinator, stunt arranger, costume or production designer, recording engineer, property master, film continuity person, sound mixer, photographer, stage manager, producer, choreographer, theatre designer;
     (3) photographic or fashion model;
     (4) professional sports person: Sch 3 (amended by SI 2007/3575; SI 2010/1782).
10 See the Conduct of Employment Agencies and Employment Businesses Regulations 2003, SI 2003/3319, reg 26(3).
11 For these purposes a person is connected with:
     (1) their spouse or civil partner or minor child or stepchild (Conduct of Employment Agencies and Employment Businesses Regulations 2003, SI 2003/3319, reg 3(1)(a) (amended by SI 2005/2114));
     (2) any individual who employs him or is his employee (Conduct of Employment Agencies and Employment Businesses Regulations 2003, SI 2003/3319, reg 3(1)(b));
     (3) any person who is in partnership with him (reg 3(1)(c));
     (4) any company of which he is a director or other officer and any company connected with that company (reg 3(1)(d));

(5)   in the case of a company: (a) any person who is a director or other officer of that company; (b) any subsidiary or holding company, both as defined in the Companies Act 2006 s 1159 (see COMPANIES vol 14 (2009) PARA 25), of that company and any person who is a director or other officer, or an employee of any such subsidiary or holding company; (c) any company of which the same person or persons have control (Conduct of Employment Agencies and Employment Businesses Regulations 2003, SI 2003/3319, reg 3(1)(e) (amended by virtue of the Companies Act 2006 s 1297(5))); and

(6)   in the case of a trustee of a trust, a beneficiary of the trust, and any person to whom the terms of the trust confer a power that may be exercised for that person's benefit (Conduct of Employment Agencies and Employment Businesses Regulations 2003, SI 2003/3319, reg 3(1)(f)).

For these purposes a person is to be taken as having control of a company if: (i) he or any person with whom he is connected is a director of that company or of another company which has control of it; (ii) the directors of that company or another company which has control of it (or any of them) are accustomed to act in accordance with his directions or instructions; or (iii) he is entitled to exercise, or control the exercise of, one third or more of the voting power at any general meeting of the company or of another company which has control of it: reg 3(2). 'Company' includes any body corporate (whether incorporated in Great Britain or elsewhere) and references to directors and other officers of a company and to voting power at any general meeting of a company have effect in the case of a company incorporated outside Great Britain with any necessary modifications: reg 2. As to the meaning of 'Great Britain' see PARA 906 note 7.

12 See the Conduct of Employment Agencies and Employment Businesses Regulations 2003, SI 2003/3319, reg 26(4).

13 Conduct of Employment Agencies and Employment Businesses Regulations 2003, SI 2003/3319, reg 26(2). This does not apply to any fee charged to a work-seeker, who is not a work-seeker seeking employment as a photographic or fashion model, by an agency in respect of the inclusion of information about the work-seeker in a publication provided that:

(1)   the publication is wholly for one or both of the following purposes, namely the purpose of finding work-seekers employment in, or providing hirers with information about work-seekers in relation to, any of the occupations listed in Sch 3 (see note 9), other than photographic or fashion model (reg 26(5)(a) (reg 26(5) amended by SI 2010/1782)); and

(2)   either: (a) the only work-finding service provided by the agency or any person connected with it to the work-seeker is the service described in this note; or (b) the fee charged to the work-seeker amounts to no more than a reasonable estimate of the cost of production and circulation of the publication attributable to the inclusion of information about that work-seeker in the publication (Conduct of Employment Agencies and Employment Businesses Regulations 2003, SI 2003/3319, reg 26(5)(b) (as so amended)); and

(3)   in addition to the requirements in regs 13 and 16, in so far as they are applicable, the agency has, before it entered into the contract with the work-seeker by reference to which the fee is to be charged, made available to him a copy of a current edition of the publication (or, where the publication exists only in electronic form, given him access to a current edition of the publication) in which it is offering to include information about him (reg 26(5)(c) (as so amended)); and

(4)   in relation to a work-seeker who is not seeking employment as an actor, background artist, dancer, extra, musician, singer or other performer, where an agency proposes to include information about the work-seeker in a publication, for seven days from the date of the agency and work-seeker entering into a contract for such a service, whether written or oral and whether or not expressly mentioning fees permitted under the Conduct of Employment Agencies and Employment Businesses Regulations 2003, SI 2003/3319, reg 26(5): (a) the agency may not charge such a permitted fee to a work-seeker; (b) the work-seeker is entitled without detriment or penalty to cancel or withdraw from any such contract with immediate effect by informing the agency of such cancelation or withdrawal; and (c) the agency may not include the information in the publication, and before entering into any such contract the agency must inform the work-seeker of the right to cancel or withdraw from any such contract and the time limit for exercising that right (reg 26(5)(d) (reg 26(5) as so amended));

(5)   where an agency proposes to include information about a work-seeker seeking employment as an actor, background artist, dancer, extra, musician, singer or other performer in a publication, for 30 days from the date of the agency and the work-seeker

entering into a contract for such a service, whether written or oral and whether or not expressly mentioning fees permitted under the Conduct of Employment Agencies and Employment Businesses Regulations 2003, SI 2003/3319, reg 26(5): (a) the agency may not charge such a permitted fee to a work-seeker; and (b) the work-seeker is entitled without detriment or penalty to cancel or withdraw from any such contract with immediate effect by informing the agency of such cancellation or withdrawal, and before entering into any such contract the agency must inform the work-seeker of the right to cancel or withdraw from any such contract and the time limit for exercising that right (reg 26(5)(e) (as so amended));

(6)   where an agency proposes to include information about a work-seeker referred to in head (5) in a publication, after the date of the agency and the work-seeker entering into the contract referred to in that head, the agency must make available to the work-seeker a copy of the information and at the same time must inform the work-seeker of the right to object, its effect and the time limit for exercising that right and for seven days from the date on which the agency first makes available a copy of the information to the work-seeker: (a) the agency must not charge a fee permitted by the Conduct of Employment Agencies and Employment Businesses Regulations 2003, SI 2003/3319, reg 26(5) to a work-seeker; (b) the agency may not include the information in the publication; and (c) the work-seeker is entitled to object to any aspect of the information relating to the work-seeker to be included in the publication by informing the agency of the objection (reg 26(5)(f) (as so amended));

(7)   where head (6) applies and the work-seeker informs the agency of an objection, the agency may not charge a fee or include the information in the publication until the work-seeker's reasonable requirements have been addressed (even if addressing the requirements takes longer than the period referred to in that head) (reg 26(5)(g) (as so amended)); and

(8)   where an agency includes, or proposes to include, information about a work-seeker in a publication, the work-seeker is entitled to a full refund of the fees paid if the publication including that information is not produced and made available to potential hirers within 60 days from the date on which payment is made by the work-seeker (reg 16(5)(h) (as so amended)).

As to the meanings of 'agency', 'work-seeker' and work-finding services' see PARA 977 note 7. As to the meaning of 'hirer' see PARA 977 note 8. 'Publication' means any publication whether in paper or electronic form other than a programme service within the meaning of the Broadcasting Act 1990 (see BROADCASTING vol 4 (2011) PARA 507): Conduct of Employment Agencies and Employment Businesses Regulations 2003, SI 2003/3319, reg 2.

Where an agency makes a copy of the information referred to in head (6) available to the work-seeker: (i) during the period referred to in head (5), where the period referred to in head (6) has elapsed without an objection or where the reasonable requirements of the work-seeker have been addressed, head (5) continues to apply; or (ii) after the period referred to in head (5) has elapsed, head (6) applies until the later of the date on which the period referred to in head (6) has elapsed or, following an objection, the date on which the reasonable requirements of the work-seeker have been addressed: reg 26(5A) (reg 26(5A)–(5C) added by SI 2010/1782). Any reference in heads (1)–(8) to the inclusion of information about a work-seeker in a publication includes the inclusion of a photographic image or audio or video recording of the work-seeker in a publication, although this should not be construed, when read with heads (1)–(8), as preventing an agency producing a photographic image or audio or video recording for the purpose of providing a copy of the image or recording to the work-seeker: Conduct of Employment Agencies and Employment Businesses Regulations 2003, SI 2003/3319, reg 26(5B), (5C) (as so added).

14 See the Conduct of Employment Agencies and Employment Businesses Regulations 2003, SI 2003/3319, reg 26(6).

15 Conduct of Employment Agencies and Employment Businesses Regulations 2003, SI 2003/3319, reg 26(7).

979.   Discrimination and harassment by employment agencies. A person concerned with the provision of a service for finding employment[1] for persons or the provision of a service for supplying employers with persons to do work (a 'service-provider')[2] must not discriminate[3] against or victimise[4] a person:

(1)   in the arrangements the service-provider makes for selecting persons to whom to provide, or to whom to offer to provide, the service;

(2)   as to the terms on which the service-provider offers to provide the service to the person;

(3)   by not offering to provide the service to the person[5].

The service provider must also not, in relation to the provision of the service:

(a)   as to the terms on which they provide the service to the person;

(b)   by not providing the service to the person;

(c)   by terminating the provision of the service to the person; or

(d)   by subjecting the person to any other detriment[6].

In addition, such a service-provider must also not, in relation to the provision of the service, harass[7] a person who asks them to provide the service or for whom they are providing the service[8].

It is unlawful for an employment agency to refuse a person any of its services:

(i)   because he is, or is not, a member of a trade union; or

(ii)   because he is unwilling to accept a requirement to take steps to become or cease to be, or to remain or not to become a member of a trade union[9].

1   'Employment' for these purposes means: (1) employment under a contract of employment, a contract of apprenticeship or a contract personally to do work; (2) Crown employment; (3) employment as a relevant member of the House of Commons staff or the House of Lords staff: Equality Act 2010 s 83(1), (2). See also DISCRIMINATION vol 33 (2013) PARA 110. 'Crown employment' has the meaning given in the Employment Rights Act 1996 s 191 (see EMPLOYMENT vol 39 (2014) PARA 163): Equality Act 2010 s 83(9). As to the meanings of 'relevant member of the House of Commons staff' and 'relevant member of the House of Lords staff' see the Employment Rights Act 1996 ss 194, 195; Equality Act 2010 s 83(5), (6); EMPLOYMENT vol 39 (2014) PARAS 164, 165; and DISCRIMINATION vol 33 (2013) PARA 110.

2   See the Equality Act 2010 s 56(1), (2)(d), (e).

3   As to discrimination see the Equality Act 2010 Pt 2 Ch 2 (ss 13–19); and DISCRIMINATION vol 33 (2013) PARA 65 et seq.

4   As to victimisation see the Equality Act 2010 s 27; and DISCRIMINATION vol 33 (2013) PARA 75.

5   See the Equality Act 2010 s 55(1), (4).

6   See the Equality Act 2010 s 55(2), (5).

7   As to harassment see the Equality Act 2010 s 26; and DISCRIMINATION vol 33 (2013) PARAS 73, 74.

8   Equality Act 2010 s 55(3).

9   See the Trade Union and Labour Relations (Consolidation) Act 1992 s 138(1); and EMPLOYMENT vol 41 (2014) PARA 1043.

(x) Security Industry

A. THE SECURITY INDUSTRY AUTHORITY

980.   Functions and powers of the Security Industry Authority. There is a body corporate called the Security Industry Authority (the 'Authority')[1]. The functions of the Authority are:

(1)   to carry out functions relating to licensing and approvals[2];

(2)   to keep under review generally the provision of security industry services[3] and other services involving the activities of security operatives[4];

(3)   for the purpose of protecting the public, to monitor the activities and effectiveness of persons carrying on businesses providing any security industry services or other services involving the activities of security operatives[5];

(4)   to ensure the carrying out of such inspections as it considers necessary

of the activities and businesses of: (a) persons engaged in licensable conduct[6]; and (b) persons registered[7] as approved providers of security industry services[8];

(5)   to set or approve standards of conduct, training and levels of supervision for adoption by: (a) those who carry on businesses providing security industry services or other services involving the activities of security operatives; and (b) those who are employed for the purposes of such businesses[9];

(6)   to make recommendations and proposals for the maintenance and improvement of standards in the provision of security industry services and other services involving the activities of security operatives[10];

(7)   to keep under review the operation of the Private Security Industry Act 2001[11].

The Authority has the power to do anything that it considers is calculated to facilitate, or is incidental or conducive to, the carrying out of any of its functions[12]. In carrying out its functions the Authority must comply with any general or specific directions given to it in writing by the Secretary of State[13], and provide him with such information[14] about its activities as he may request[15].

The Authority is not to be regarded as the servant or agent of the Crown, or as enjoying any status, immunity or privilege of the Crown, and its property is not to be regarded as property of, or property held on behalf of, the Crown[16]. The Authority's members are disqualified from membership of the House of Commons[17]. The Authority is subject to investigation by the Parliamentary Commissioner for Administration[18], and its records are public records[19].

1   Private Security Industry Act 2001 s 1(1).
2   Private Security Industry Act 2001 s 1(2)(a). As to licensing and approvals see PARAS 995–1002.
3   'Security industry services' means services which are provided under a contract for services and in the course of which the person providing the services secures: (1) that the activities of a security operative are carried out; or (2) that a person is made available to carry out, under directions given by or on behalf of another person, any activities which will or are likely to consist of or include the activities of a security operative: Private Security Industry Act 2001 s 25(1). As to the activities of a security operative see PARAS 986 note 3, 987–991.
4   Private Security Industry Act 2001 s 1(2)(b).
5   Private Security Industry Act 2001 s 1(2)(c).
6   As to the meaning of 'licensable conduct' see PARA 986.
7   Ie registered under the Private Security Industry Act 2001 s 14 (see PARA 1000): s 1(2)(d)(ii).
8   Private Security Industry Act 2001 s 1(2)(d).
9   Private Security Industry Act 2001 s 1(2)(e).
10   Private Security Industry Act 2001 s 1(2)(f).
11   Private Security Industry Act 2001 s 1(2)(g).
12   Private Security Industry Act 2001 s 1(3). In particular, the Authority may, for any purpose connected with the carrying out of its functions: (1) make proposals to the Secretary of State for the modification of any provision contained in or made under the Private Security Industry Act 2001; and (2) undertake, or arrange for or support, whether financially or otherwise, the carrying out of research relating to the provision of security industry services and of other services involving the activities of security operatives: s 1(4). 'Modification' includes amendments, additions and omissions: s 25(1). As to the Secretary of State see PARA 902.
      The Authority has the power to bring prosecutions for offences under the Private Security Industry Act 2001: *R (on the application of Securiplan plc) v Security Industry Authority* [2008] EWHC 1762 (Admin), [2009] 2 All ER 211. As to such offences see PARAS 986 et seq, 994, 996, 1001, 1003.
13   Private Security Industry Act 2001 s 2(1). Before giving directions under s 2(1), the Secretary of State must consult the Authority: s 2(2)(a) (numbered as such by the Serious Organised Crime and Police Act 2005 Sch 15 para 2(a)).
14   'Information' includes reports, references and other documents, photographs and data of any description: Private Security Industry Act 2001 s 25(1).

15 Private Security Industry Act 2001 s 2(3)(a) (numbered as such by the Serious Organised Crime
     and Police Act 2005 Sch 15 para 2(b)).
16 Private Security Industry Act 2001 s 1(5).
17 House of Commons Disqualification Act 1975 s 1(1)(f), Sch 1 Pt II (amended by the Private
     Security Industry Act 2001 Sch 1 para 21) (see PARLIAMENT vol 78 (2010) PARA 908).
18 See the Parliamentary Commissioner Act 1967 s 4(1), Sch 2 (s 4 substituted by the
     Parliamentary and Health Service Commissioners Act 1987 s 1(1); Parliamentary Commissioner
     Act 1967 Sch 4 substituted by SI 2011/2986); and CONSTITUTIONAL AND ADMINISTRATIVE LAW
     vol 20 (2014) PARA 634.
19 Ie for the purposes of the Public Records Act 1958: see s 10, Sch 1 para 3 Table Pt II (amended
     by the Private Security Industry Act 2001 Sch 1 para 18).

981. Constitution and members. The Security Industry Authority[1] consists of such number of members as the Secretary of State[2] may determine[3], and those members are appointed by the Secretary of State[4]. A member holds and vacates office in accordance with the terms of his appointment[5]. A person must not be appointed as a member for more than five years[6]. A person may at any time resign his office as a member by notice in writing to the Secretary of State[7]. The Secretary of State may remove a person from office as a member or as chairman[8] of the Authority if satisfied that: (1) he has without reasonable excuse failed, for a continuous period of three months, to carry out his functions as a member or, as the case may be, as chairman[9]; (2) he has without reasonable excuse been absent from three consecutive meetings of the Authority[10]; (3) he has been convicted, whether before or after his appointment, of a criminal offence[11]; (4) he is an undischarged bankrupt or his estate has been sequestrated and he has not been discharged, or he has made an arrangement with, or granted a trust deed for, his creditors[12]; (5) a moratorium period under a debt relief order[13] applies in relation to him[14]; (6) he has failed to comply with the terms of his appointment[15]; or (7) he is otherwise unable or unfit to carry out his functions as a member or, as the case may be, as chairman[16]. A person who ceases, otherwise than by virtue of any reason described in heads (1) to (7), to be a member or the chairman of the Authority is eligible for re-appointment[17].

The Authority must pay to its members such remuneration and allowances as the Secretary of State may determine[18], and must, as regards any of its members or former members in whose case the Secretary of State may so determine, pay or make payments in respect of such pension or gratuity as the Secretary of State may determine[19]. If a person ceases to be a member or ceases to be the chairman of the Authority, and it appears to the Secretary of State that there are special circumstances which make it right that he should receive compensation, the Secretary of State may direct the Authority to make a payment of such amount as he may determine[20].

1 As to the Security Industry Authority see PARA 980.
2 As to the Secretary of State see PARA 902.
3 Private Security Industry Act 2001 Sch 1 para 1(1). The Secretary of State must appoint one of
     the members of the Authority to be to be its chairman, and before appointing the chairman, the
     Secretary of State must consult the Scottish Ministers and the Department of Justice in Northern
     Ireland: Sch 1 para 1(3), (4) (Sch 1 para 1(4) added by the Serious Organised Crime and Police
     Act 2005 Sch 15 para 13(a); and amended by SI 2010/976).
4 Private Security Industry Act 2001 Sch 1 para 1(2).
5 Private Security Industry Act 2001 Sch 1 para 2(1). The chairman also holds and vacates that
     office in accordance with the terms of his appointment: Sch 1 para 2(4)(a).
6 Private Security Industry Act 2001 Sch 1 para 2(2).
7 Private Security Industry Act 2001 Sch 1 para 2(3). The chairman also may resign that office by
     notice in writing to the Secretary of State: Sch 1 para 2(4)(b). The chairman ceases to hold that
     office if he ceases to be a member: Sch 1 para 2(4)(c).

8 Before removing a person from office as chairman of the Authority, the Secretary of State must consult the Scottish Ministers and the Department of Justice in Northern Ireland: Private Security Industry Act 2001 Sch 1 para 3(2) (added by the Serious Organised Crime and Police Act 2005 Sch 15 para 13(b); amended by SI 2010/976).

9 Private Security Industry Act 2001 Sch 1 para 3(1)(a) (Sch 1 para 3(1) numbered as such by the Serious Organised Crime and Police Act 2005 Sch 15 para 13(b)).

10 Private Security Industry Act 2001 Sch 1 para 3(1)(b) (Sch 1 para 3(1) as renumbered: see note 9).

11 Private Security Industry Act 2001 Sch 1 para 3(1)(c) (Sch 1 para 3(1) as renumbered: see note 9).

12 Private Security Industry Act 2001 Sch 1 para 3(1)(d) (Sch 1 para 3(1) as renumbered: see note 9).

13 Ie a debt relief order under the Insolvency Act 1986 Pt VIIA (ss 251A–251X) (see BANKRUPTCY AND INDIVIDUAL INSOLVENCY vol 5 (2013) PARA 101 et seq): Private Security Industry Act 2001 Sch 1 para 3(1)(da) (Sch 1 para 3(1) as renumbered (see note 9); Sch 1 para 3(1)(ea) as added (see note 14)).

14 Private Security Industry Act 2001 Sch 1 para 3(1)(da) (Sch 1 para 3(1) as renumbered (see note 9); Sch 1 para 3(1)(ea) added by SI 2012/2404).

15 Private Security Industry Act 2001 Sch 1 para 3(1)(e) (Sch 1 para 3(1) as renumbered: see note 9).

16 Private Security Industry Act 2001 Sch 1 para 3(1)(f) (Sch 1 para 3(1) as renumbered: see note 9).

17 Private Security Industry Act 2001 Sch 1 para 4.

18 Private Security Industry Act 2001 Sch 1 para 5(1).

19 Private Security Industry Act 2001 Sch 1 para 5(2).

20 Private Security Industry Act 2001 Sch 1 para 5(3).

982. Staff. The Security Industry Authority[1] has a chief executive[2] and such other employees as it may appoint[3]. It must pay to its employees[4] such remuneration and allowances as it may, with the consent of the Secretary of State, determine[5]. Further, the Authority must pay, or make payments in respect of, such pensions or gratuities to or in respect of its employees or former employees as it may, with the consent of the Secretary of State, determine[6]. It must provide and maintain such schemes, whether contributory or not, as it may determine, with the consent of the Secretary of State, for the payment of pensions or gratuities in respect of its employees or former employees[7].

If any person: (1) on ceasing to be employed by the Authority becomes or continues to be one of its members; and (2) was, by reference to his employment, a participant in a pension scheme maintained by the Authority, the Authority may, with the consent of the Secretary of State, make provision for that person to continue to participate in that scheme, on such terms and conditions as it may with the consent of the Secretary of State determine, as if his service as a member were service as an employee[8].

1 As to the Security Industry Authority see PARA 980.

2 Private Security Industry Act 2001 Sch 1 para 6(1)(a). The chief executive has responsibility to the Authority for the carrying out of its functions and the management of its employees: Sch 1 para 6(1)(a). The first appointment of a chief executive was made by the Secretary of State but, subject to obtaining the Secretary of State's consent, subsequent appointments are made by the Authority itself: Sch 1 para 6(2). Before giving such consent, the Secretary of State must consult the Scottish Ministers and the Department of Justice in Northern Ireland: Sch 1 para 6(2A) (added by the Serious Organised Crime and Police Act 2005 Sch 15 para 13(c); amended by SI 2010/976). As to the Secretary of State see PARA 902.

3 Private Security Industry Act 2001 Sch 1 para 6(1)(b). The numbers of such employees and their terms and conditions of service is subject to the approval of the Secretary of State: Sch 1 para 6(1)(b).

4 References to the employees of the Authority include references to its chief executive (whether appointed by the Secretary of State or by the Authority): Private Security Industry Act 2001 Sch 1 para 6(3).

5 Private Security Industry Act 2001 Sch 1 para 7(1). As to payments the Authority is required to pay to its employees see PARA 981 text and notes 18–20.
6 Private Security Industry Act 2001 Sch 1 para 7(2)(a). Employment with the Authority is included among the kinds of employment to which a civil service pension scheme applies: see the Superannuation Act 1972 Sch 1 (amended by the Private Security Industry Act 2001 Sch 1 para 20); and CONSTITUTIONAL AND ADMINISTRATIVE LAW vol 20 (2014) PARA 298).
7 Private Security Industry Act 2001 Sch 1 para 7(2)(b). References to pensions and gratuities in this provision include references to pensions or gratuities by way of compensation to or in respect of employees who suffer loss of employment or loss or diminution of emoluments: Sch 1 para 7(3).
8 Private Security Industry Act 2001 Sch 1 para 7(4). Any such provision is without prejudice to Sch 1 para 5 (see PARA 981 text and notes 18–20): Sch 1 para 7(5).

983. Committees. The Security Industry Authority[1] may establish committees[2]. A person who is not a member of the Authority may be appointed to a committee or sub-committee of the Authority[3]. The Authority may pay to members of its committees or sub-committees who are neither members nor employees of the Authority such remuneration and allowances as the Secretary of State[4] may determine[5]. The Authority may, to such extent as it may determine, delegate[6] any of its functions to any of its committees or any of its employees[7], and any such committee may, to such extent as it may determine, delegate any function conferred on it to any of its sub-committees or to any employee of the Authority[8].

1 As to the Security Industry Authority see PARA 980.
2 Private Security Industry Act 2001 Sch 1 para 8(1). Any such committee may establish one or more sub-committees: Sch 1 para 8(2).
3 Private Security Industry Act 2001 Sch 1 para 8(3).
4 As to the Secretary of State see PARA 902.
5 Private Security Industry Act 2001 Sch 1 para 8(4).
6 'Delegate' includes further delegate: Private Security Industry Act 2001 Sch 1 para 24.
7 Private Security Industry Act 2001 Sch 1 para 9(1). 'Employee' includes the chief executive (see PARA 982): Sch 1 para 6(3).
8 Private Security Industry Act 2001 Sch 1 para 9(2). Any sub-committee may, to such extent as it may determine, delegate any functions conferred on it to any employee of the Authority: Sch 1 para 9(3).

984. Proceedings and evidence. The Security Industry Authority[1] may regulate its own procedure, including quorum, and the procedure, including quorum, of its committees and sub-committees[2]. The quorum for meetings of the Authority must in the first instance be determined by a meeting of the Authority that is attended by at least five of its members[3]. The Authority must make provision for a quorum for meetings of its committees or sub-committees to include at least one member or employee[4] of the Authority[5]. The validity of any proceedings of the Authority, or of any of its committees or sub-committees, is not affected by: (1) any vacancy among the members of the Authority or of members of the committee or sub-committee[6]; (2) any vacancy in the office of the chairman of the Authority[7]; or (3) any defect in the appointment of any one or more members or of the chairman of the Authority[8].

The application of the seal of the Authority is to be authenticated by the signature of any member, or of any other person who has been authorised by the Authority, whether generally or specially, for that purpose[9]. A document purporting to be duly executed by the Authority under its seal, or signed on its behalf, must be received in evidence and, unless the contrary is proved, be taken to be so executed or signed[10].

1 As to the Security Industry Authority see PARA 980.

2 Private Security Industry Act 2001 Sch 1 para 10(1). As to the Authority's committees and sub-committees see PARA 983.
3 Private Security Industry Act 2001 Sch 1 para 10(2).
4 'Employee' includes the chief executive (see PARA 982): Private Security Industry Act 2001 Sch 1 para 6(3).
5 Private Security Industry Act 2001 Sch 1 para 10(3).
6 Private Security Industry Act 2001 Sch 1 para 11(a).
7 Private Security Industry Act 2001 Sch 1 para 11(b).
8 Private Security Industry Act 2001 Sch 1 para 11(c).
9 Private Security Industry Act 2001 Sch 1 para 12.
10 Private Security Industry Act 2001 Sch 1 para 13.

985. Accounts and annual report. The Secretary of State[1] may make payments to the Security Industry Authority[2] out of money provided by Parliament[3], and the Authority must not borrow money except with the consent of the Secretary of State[4].

The Authority may impose such charges as it considers appropriate in connection with the carrying out of any of its functions[5]. The Authority must pay to the Secretary of State all sums received by it[6] in the course of, or in connection with, the carrying out of its functions[7], and any sums so received by the Secretary of State must be paid into the Consolidated Fund[8].

The Authority must keep proper accounts and proper records in relation to the accounts, and prepare a statement of accounts in respect of each financial year[9]. The statement of accounts must be in such form, and must contain such information[10], as the Secretary of State may direct[11]. The Authority must, within such period after the end of each financial year as the Secretary of State may direct, send copies of the statement of accounts relating to that year to the Secretary of State, the Scottish Ministers, the Department of Justice in Northern Ireland and the Comptroller and Auditor General[12]. The Comptroller and Auditor General must examine, certify and report on every statement of accounts sent to him by the Authority, and lay copies of each such statement and of his report on it before each House of Parliament[13].

As soon as practicable after the end of each financial year, the Authority must send to the Secretary of State, the Scottish Ministers and the Department of Justice in Northern Ireland a report on the carrying out of its functions during that year[14], and the Secretary of State must lay a copy of each such report before each House of Parliament[15].

1 As to the Secretary of State see PARA 902.
2 As to the Security Industry Authority see PARA 980.
3 Private Security Industry Act 2001 Sch 1 para 14(1).
4 Private Security Industry Act 2001 Sch 1 para 14(2).
5 Private Security Industry Act 2001 Sch 1 para 15(1).
6 Ie otherwise than under the Private Security Industry Act 2001 Sch 1 para 14.
7 Private Security Industry Act 2001 Sch 1 para 15(2). This requirement does not apply where the Secretary of State so directs: Sch 1 para 15(3).
8 Private Security Industry Act 2001 Sch 1 para 15(4). As to the Consolidated Fund see CONSTITUTIONAL AND ADMINISTRATIVE LAW vol 20 (2014) PARA 480 et seq.
9 Private Security Industry Act 2001 Sch 1 para 16(1). 'Financial year' means the period beginning with the day appointed for the coming into force of s 1 (1 April 2003: see SI 2002/3125 art 3(a)) and ending with the next 31 March, and any subsequent period of 12 months ending with 31 March: Private Security Industry Act 2001 Sch 1 para 24.
10 As to the meaning of 'information' see PARA 980 note 14.
11 Private Security Industry Act 2001 Sch 1 para 16(2).
12 Private Security Industry Act 2001 Sch 1 para 16(3) (amended by the Serious Organised Crime and Police Act 2005 Sch 15 para 13(e); and SI 2010/976). As to the Comptroller and Auditor General see CONSTITUTIONAL AND ADMINISTRATIVE LAW vol 20 (2014) PARAS 494–496.

13 Private Security Industry Act 2001 Sch 1 para 16(4). As to the laying of documents before Parliament see STATUTES AND LEGISLATIVE PROCESS vol 96 (2012) PARA 1052.
14 Private Security Industry Act 2001 Sch 1 para 17(1) (amended by SI 2010/976).
15 Private Security Industry Act 2001 Sch 1 para 17(2).

B. LICENSABLE CONDUCT

986. Conduct prohibited without a licence. It is an offence[1] for a person to engage in any licensable conduct except under and in accordance with a licence[2]. A person engages in licensable conduct if:

(1) he carries out any designated activities[3] for the purposes of, or in connection with, any contract for the supply of services under which:

    (a) he;

    (b) a body corporate of which he is a director[4]; or

    (c) a firm[5] of which he is a partner;

    is or may be required to secure that any such activities are carried out[6];

(2) in the course of any employment of his by any person he carries out any designated activities for the purposes of, or in connection with, any contract for the supply of services under which his employer is or may be so required[7];

(3) he carries out any designated activities in accordance with directions given to him by or on behalf of a person to whom his services are supplied, whether or not for the carrying out of any such activities, by:

    (a) a body corporate of which he is a director;

    (b) a firm of which he is a partner;

    (c) a person by whom he is employed; or

    (d) a person to whom he supplies his services under a contract for the purposes of which, or in connection with which, he is or may be required to work in accordance with the directions of another[8];

(4) he acts:

    (a) in the course of any employment of his by any person; or

    (b) in accordance with any directions[9], as the manager or supervisor[10] of one or more individuals required in the course of their employment to engage in licensable conduct falling within head (2)[11];

(5) he acts:

    (a) in the course of any employment of his by any person; or

    (b) in accordance with any directions[12], as the manager or supervisor of individuals who are required in accordance with any such directions to engage in conduct which would be licensable conduct falling within head (2) if they were required to engage in that conduct as the employees of the person to whom their services are supplied[13];

(6) he is the director of any body corporate or the partner of any firm at a time when another of the directors or partners of the body or firm, or any employee of the body or firm, engages in licensable conduct[14];

(7) he is the employer of an individual who in the course of any employment of his with that employer carries out any designated activities subject to additional controls[15];

(8) in the course of any employment of his, or for purposes connected with his being a director or partner of a body corporate or firm, he carries out designated activities subject to additional controls[16]; or

(9)   in the course of any employment of his by any person he acts as the manager or supervisor of one or more individuals the duties of whose employment involve the carrying out of any designated activities subject to additional controls[17].

1   As to offences by bodies corporate see PARA 993.

2   Private Security Industry Act 2001 s 3(1). 'Licence' means a licence from the Security Industry Authority under the Private Security Industry Act 2001: s 25(1). A person guilty of an offence under the Private Security Industry Act 2001 s 3 is liable, on summary conviction, to imprisonment for a term not exceeding six months or to a fine not exceeding level 5 on the standard scale, or to both: s 3(6). As to the standard scale see SENTENCING AND DISPOSITION OF OFFENDERS vol 92 (2010) PARA 142.

As from a day to be appointed, s 3 is amended by substituting 'an individual' for 'a person' and 'conduct licensable under this section' for 'licensable conduct', and by adding 'under this section' after 'licence' at the end of s 3(1); and the definition of 'licence' is amended by adding '(unless otherwise specified)' after 'means': see the Crime and Security Act 2010 Sch 1 para 3 (not yet in force). At the date at which this volume states the law no such day had been appointed.

As from a day to be appointed the Private Security Industry Act 2001 ss 4A, 4B are added by the Crime and Security Act 2010 s 42(2) (not yet in force) to create the requirement that businesses be licensed before carrying out conduct licensable under the Private Security Industry Act 2001 s 4A, and to provide exemptions from that requirement. At the date at which this volume states the law no such day had been appointed.

3   'Designated activities' means such of the activities of a security operative as are for the time being designated by an order made by the Secretary of State, and such an order may designate different activities for the purposes of different paragraphs of the Private Security Industry Act 2001 s 3(2): ss 3(3), 25(1). As to the prospective amendment of s 3 see note 2. Activities of security operatives are those to which Sch 2 paras 2–6 (see PARAS 987–990) apply (see Sch 2 para 1(1)), and activities under Sch 2 paras 2 (manned guarding; see PARA 987), 3 (repealed), 3A (repealed) and 6 (keyholding; see PARA 990) were so designated by the Private Security Industry Act 2001 (Designated Activities) Order 2006, SI 2006/426 (amended by SI 2006/824; and SI 2006/1804). The Secretary of State may by order amend the Private Security Industry Act 2001 Sch 2 Pt 1 (paras 1–6) for the purpose of adding or excluding any such activities as he thinks fit to or from those that fall to be regarded as the activities of a security operative: Sch 2 para 1(2). See the Private Security Industry Act 2001 (Amendments to Schedule 2) Order 2006, SI 2006/1831, art 2; the Private Security Industry Act 2001 (Amendments to Schedule 2) Order 2007, SI 2007/2201, art 2; and the Private Security Industry Act 2001 (Amendments to Schedule 2) Order 2009, SI 2009/3043, art 2 (each amending the Private Security Industry Act 2001 Sch 2 para 2 (see PARA 987)). The Secretary of State may not make an order containing, with or without any other provision, any provision authorised by Sch 2 para 1(2) unless a draft of the order has been laid before Parliament and approved by a resolution of each House: Sch 2 para 1(3). As to the Secretary of State see PARA 902. As to the laying of documents before Parliament see STATUTES AND LEGISLATIVE PROCESS vol 96 (2012) PARA 1052.

Powers to make orders and regulations under the Private Security Industry Act 2001 are exercisable by statutory instrument: Private Security Industry Act 2001 s 24(2) (amended by the Serious Organised Crime and Police Act 2005 Sch 15 para 11(b)). A statutory instrument containing any order or regulations, other than a commencement order under the Private Security Industry Act 2001 s 26(2), or an order a draft of which has been approved for the purposes of Sch 2 para 1(3) or 7(3) (see PARA 992 note 4), is subject to annulment in pursuance of a resolution of either House of Parliament: s 24(3) (amended by the Serious Organised Crime and Police Act 2005 Sch 15 para 11(c)). See STATUTES AND LEGISLATIVE PROCESS vol 96 (2012) PARA 1045 et seq. Before making any regulations or order (other than an order under the Private Security Industry Act 2001 Sch 2 para 1(2) or 7(2) (see PARA 992 note 4)), or laying any draft order under Sch 2 para 1(2) or 7(2) before Parliament, the Secretary of State must consult the Scottish Ministers, the Department of Justice in Northern Ireland and the Security Industry Authority: s 24(4) (amended by the Serious Organised Crime and Police Act 2005 Sch 15 para 11(e); the Protection of Freedoms Act 2012 Sch 9 Pt 4 para 20(6), Sch 10 Pt 3; and SI 2010/976). Any order or regulations may make different provisions for different cases, and contain such incidental, supplemental, consequential and transitional provision as the Secretary of State thinks fit: Private Security Industry Act 2001 s 24(5) (amended by the Serious Organised Crime and Police Act 2005 Sch 15 para 11(f); and SI 2010/976).

4   'Director', in relation to a company, as defined in the Companies Act 2006 s 1(1) (see
     COMPANIES vol 14 (2009) PARA 24), includes a shadow director; in relation to any such
     company that is a subsidiary of another, includes any director or shadow director of the other
     company; and, in relation to a body corporate whose affairs are managed by its members,
     means a member of that body corporate: Private Security Industry Act 2001 s 25(1) (definition
     amended by SI 2009/1941). 'Shadow director' means a shadow director as defined in the
     Companies Act 2006 s 251 (see COMPANIES vol 14 (2009) PARA 479): Private Security Industry
     Act 2001 s 25(1) (definition amended by SI 2007/2194). 'Subsidiary' means a subsidiary as
     defined in the Companies Act 2006 s 1159 (see COMPANIES vol 14 (2009) PARA 25): Private
     Security Industry Act 2001 s 25(1) (definition amended by SI 2009/1941).
5   References, in relation to a firm, to a member of the firm include references to any person who,
     in relation to that firm, is liable as a partner under the Partnership Act 1890 s 14 (see
     PARTNERSHIP vol 79 (2014) PARA 72): Private Security Industry Act 2001 s 25(2).
6   Private Security Industry Act 2001 s 3(2)(a). As to the prospective amendment of s 3 see note 2.
7   Private Security Industry Act 2001 s 3(2)(b). As to the prospective amendment of s 3 see note 2.
8   Private Security Industry Act 2001 s 3(2)(c). As to the prospective amendment of s 3 see note 2.
9   Ie directions given as mentioned in head (3) above: Private Security Industry Act 2001 s 3(2)(d).
     As to the prospective amendment of s 3 see note 2.
10   A person is not to be treated as acting as the manager or supervisor of an individual by reason
     only of his giving directions to that individual in a case in which: (1) the directions are given on
     behalf of a person to whom the individual's services are provided under a contract for services,
     and (2) the person who under the contract provides the individual's services or another person
     acting on his behalf, acts as the manager or supervisor of that individual in relation to the
     activities carried out by him in accordance with those directions: Private Security Industry
     Act 2001 s 3(4). As to the prospective amendment of s 3 see note 2.
11   Private Security Industry Act 2001 s 3(2)(d). As to the prospective amendment of s 3 see note 2.
12   Ie directions given as mentioned in head (3) above: Private Security Industry Act 2001 s 3(2)(e).
     As to the prospective amendment of s 3 see note 2.
13   Private Security Industry Act 2001 s 3(2)(e). As to the prospective amendment of s 3 see note 2.
14   Private Security Industry Act 2001 s 3(2)(f). As to the prospective amendment of s 3 see note 2.
     The licensable conduct referred to is licensable conduct falling within any of heads (1)–(5) in the
     text: s 3(2)(f).
15   Private Security Industry Act 2001 s 3(2)(g). As to the prospective amendment of s 3 see note 2.
     As to activities subject to additional controls see PARA 991.
16   Private Security Industry Act 2001 s 3(2)(h). As to the prospective amendment of s 3 see note 2.
17   Private Security Industry Act 2001 s 3(2)(i). As to the prospective amendment of s 3 see note 2.

987.   Manned guarding.   Manned guarding activities are:
(1)   guarding premises[1] against unauthorised access[2] or occupation, against
       outbreaks of disorder or against damage[3];
(2)   guarding property against destruction or damage, against being stolen
       or against being otherwise dishonestly taken or obtained[4];
(3)   guarding one or more individuals against assault or against injuries that
       might be suffered in consequence of the unlawful conduct of others[5].
Manned guarding activities do not include:
(a)   activities of an individual who exercises control over the persons
       allowed access to any premises to the extent only of securing, or
       checking, that persons allowed access have paid for admission or have
       invitations or passes allowing admission[6];
(b)   activities of a person who, incidentally to the carrying out of any
       activities in relation to a group of individuals which are neither the
       activities of a security operative[7], nor activities comprising the exercise
       of control as mentioned in head (a), maintains order or discipline
       amongst those individuals[8];
(c)   activities of a person who, incidentally to the carrying out of activities
       which are not wholly or mainly the activities of a security operative,
       responds to a sudden or unexpected occurrence[9];
(d)   other specified activities[10].

1   'Premises' includes any vehicle or moveable structure and any other place whatever, whether or
     not occupied as land: Private Security Industry Act 2001 s 25(1). 'Vehicle' includes any vessel,
     aircraft or hovercraft: s 25(1).
2   References to guarding premises against unauthorised access include references to being wholly
     or partly responsible for determining the suitability for admission to the premises of persons
     applying for admission: Private Security Industry Act 2001 Sch 2 para 2(2).
3   Private Security Industry Act 2001 Sch 2 para 2(1)(a). References to guarding against something
     happening include references to so providing a physical presence, or carrying out any form of
     patrol or surveillance, as to deter or otherwise discourage it from happening, or to provide
     information, if it happens, about what has happened: Sch 2 para 2(3). 'Surveillance' includes
     covertly listening to or recording conversations or other sounds and any method of covertly
     obtaining information: Private Security Industry Act 2001 s 25(1). As to the meaning of
     'information' see PARA 980 note 14.
4   Private Security Industry Act 2001 Sch 2 para 2(1)(b).
5   Private Security Industry Act 2001 Sch 2 para 2(1)(c).
6   Private Security Industry Act 2001 Sch 2 para 2(4).
7   As to the meaning of 'activities of a security operative' see PARA 986 note 3.
8   Private Security Industry Act 2001 Sch 2 para 2(5).
9   Private Security Industry Act 2001 Sch 2 para 2(6).
10   See the Private Security Industry Act 2001 Sch 2 para 2(7) (added by SI 2006/1831; and
     amended by the Offender Management Act 2007 s 13(7); the Police Reform and Social
     Responsibility Act 2011 Sch 16 Pt 3 para 273(2); the Criminal Courts and Justice Act 2015
     Sch 10 Pt 5 para 32; SI 2007/2201; and SI 2009/3043). The specified activities are listed in the
     Private Security Industry Act 2001 Sch 2 para 2(7) (as so added and amended).

988.   Private investigations.   Private investigations activities are any surveillance[1], inquiries or investigations carried out for the purpose of obtaining information[2] about a particular person or about the activities or whereabouts of a particular person[3], or about the circumstances in which or means by which property has been lost or damaged[4].

Private investigations activities do not include:

(1)   activities carried out exclusively for the purposes of market research[5];

(2)   activities carried out exclusively for the purpose of determining whether a particular person is credit-worthy[6];

(3)   any activities of a person with a general qualification[7] which are carried out by him for the purposes of any legal practice carried on by him, by any firm of which he is a partner or by which he is employed[8], or by any body corporate of which he is a director[9] or member or by which he is employed[10];

(4)   any activities of a member of a relevant accountancy body[11] which are carried out by him as such and for the purposes of any accountancy practice carried on by him, by any firm of which he is a partner or by which he is employed, or by any body corporate of which he is a director or member or by which he is employed[12];

(5)   activities carried out for the purpose of obtaining information exclusively with a view to its use, or the use of information to which it relates, for the purposes of or in connection with the publication to the public or to a section of the public of any journalistic, literary or artistic material or of any work of reference[13];

(6)   activities carried out exclusively by means of references to certain documents[14];

(7)   activities carried out with the knowledge or consent of the person about whom, or about whose activities or whereabouts, information is sought, or every person whose interest in any property has been affected by the loss or damage about which information is sought[15];

(8)   activities of any person who carries out any inquiries or investigation

merely incidentally to the carrying out of any activities which are not the activities of a security operative[16].

1   As to the meaning of 'surveillance' see PARA 987 note 3.
2   As to the meaning of 'information' see PARA 980 note 14.
3   Private Security Industry Act 2001 Sch 2 para 4(1)(a).
4   Private Security Industry Act 2001 Sch 2 para 4(1)(b).
5   Private Security Industry Act 2001 Sch 2 para 4(2). 'Market research' includes: (1) discovering whether a person is a potential customer for any goods or services or the extent of his satisfaction with goods or services supplied to him; and (2) obtaining information from any person for the purpose of analysing public opinion on any matter, whether or not relating to the market for any goods or services: Sch 2 para 4(10).
6   Private Security Industry Act 2001 Sch 2 para 4(3).
7   A general qualification refers to a general qualification within the meaning of the Courts and Legal Services Act 1990 s 71 (see LEGAL PROFESSIONS vol 65 (2015) PARA 540): Private Security Industry Act 2001 Sch 2 para 4(4).
8   As to references to a member of a firm see PARA 986 note 5.
9   As to the meaning of 'director' see PARA 986 note 4.
10 Private Security Industry Act 2001 Sch 2 para 4(4).
11 'Relevant accountancy body' means the Institute of Chartered Accountants in England and Wales; the Institute of Chartered Accountants of Scotland; the Institute of Chartered Accountants in Ireland; the Association of Chartered Certified Accountants; the Chartered Institute of Management Accountants; the Chartered Institute of Public Finance and Accountancy: Private Security Industry Act 2001 s 25(1).
12 Private Security Industry Act 2001 Sch 2 para 4(5).
13 Private Security Industry Act 2001 Sch 2 para 4(6).
14 Private Security Industry Act 2001 Sch 2 para 4(7). The documents are: (1) registers or other records that are open to public inspection, whether or not on the payment of a fee; (2) registers or other records which are kept by the person by whom or on whose behalf the activities are carried out or to which that person has a right of access; (3) published works: Sch 2 para 4(7).
15 Private Security Industry Act 2001 Sch 2 para 4(8).
16 Private Security Industry Act 2001 Sch 2 para 4(9). As to the meaning of 'activities of a security operative' see PARA 986 note 3.

989.   Security consultants.   Security consultant activities are the giving of advice about the taking of security precautions in relation to any risk to property or to the person[1], or the acquisition of any services involving the activities of a security operative[2].

Security consultant activities do not include:

(1)   the giving of legal or financial advice or the giving of any advice about the conduct of any business involving the provision of any services involving the activities of a security operative[3];

(2)   any activities of a member of a relevant accountancy body[4] which are carried out by him as such and for the purposes of any accountancy practice carried on by him, by any firm of which he is a partner or by which he is employed[5], or by any body corporate of which he is a director or member or by which he is employed[6];

(3)   the provision of training to persons for the purpose of giving them qualifications, knowledge or skill for use in the carrying out of the activities of a security operative for others[7].

1   Private Security Industry Act 2001 Sch 2 para 5(1)(a).
2   Private Security Industry Act 2001 Sch 2 para 5(1)(b). As to the meaning of 'activities of a security operative' see PARA 986 note 3.
3   Private Security Industry Act 2001 Sch 2 para 5(2).
4   As to the meaning of 'relevant accountancy body' see PARA 988 note 11.
5   As to references to a member of a firm see PARA 986 note 5.
6   Private Security Industry Act 2001 Sch 2 para 5(3).
7   Private Security Industry Act 2001 Sch 2 para 5(4).

990. Keyholding. Keyholding activities are the keeping custody of, or controlling access to, any key or similar device for operating, whether mechanically, electronically or otherwise, any lock[1].

Keyholding activities do not include activities carried out merely incidentally to the provision of any services in connection with a proposal for the sale of any premises or other property to which the key or similar device gives access[2], or the activities of a person who holds a key or other device for obtaining access to any premises for purposes incidental to the provision in relation to those premises, or in relation to an individual present on those premises, of any services that do not consist in or include the carrying out of any of the activities of a security operative[3].

1 Private Security Industry Act 2001 Sch 2 para 6(1). 'Lock' means a lock or similar device, whether operated mechanically, electronically or otherwise, that is designed or adapted: (1) for protecting any premises against unauthorised entry; or (2) for securing any safe or other container specifically designed or adapted to hold valuables: Sch 2 para 6(4).
2 Private Security Industry Act 2001 Sch 2 para 6(2).
3 Private Security Industry Act 2001 Sch 2 para 6(3). As to the meaning of 'activities of a security operative' see PARA 986 note 3.

991. Activities subject to additional controls. Manned guarding activities[1] which are carried out in relation to licensed premises[2], and at or in relation to times when those premises are open to the public[3] are subject to additional controls[4].

'Licensed premises' means:

(1)　any premises in respect of which a premises licence or temporary event notice has effect under the Licensing Act 2003 to authorise either the supply of alcohol[5] for consumption on the premises[6] or the provision of regulated entertainment[7];

(2)　any premises in respect of which a licence of a prescribed[8] description under any prescribed local statutory provision[9] is for the time being in force[10].

For these purposes, premises are not licensed premises:

(a)　if there is in force in respect of the premises a premises licence which authorises regulated entertainment[11];

(b)　in relation to any occasion on which the premises are being used exclusively for the purposes[12] of a club which holds a club premises certificate in respect of the premises, or for regulated entertainment of the kind mentioned in head (a) in circumstances where that use is a permitted temporary activity[13];

(c)　in relation to any occasion on which a casino premises licence or a bingo premises licence is in force in respect of the premises under the Gambling Act 2005 and the premises are being used wholly or mainly for the purposes for which such a licence is required[14];

(d)　in relation to any occasion on which a licence is in force in respect of the premises under the Theatres Act 1968[15] or the Cinemas Act 1985[16] and the premises are being used wholly or mainly for the purposes for which the licence is required[17]; or

(e)　in relation to any such other occasion as may be prescribed for these purposes[18].

The following are not activities subject to additional controls:

(i)　manned guarding activities which only involve the use of closed circuit television equipment[19];

(ii)   the guarding of property against destruction or damage, against being stolen or against being otherwise dishonestly taken or obtained[20] which involves the secure transportation of property in vehicles[21] specially manufactured or adapted so as to have secure transportation as their primary function[22];

(iii)   guarding one or more individuals against assault or against injuries that might be suffered in consequence of the unlawful conduct of others[23].

1   Ie those activities which are activities of a security operative by virtue of the Private Security Industry Act 2001 Sch 2 para 2 (see PARA 987): see Sch 2 para 8(1) (as amended: see note 2).

2   Private Security Industry Act 2001 Sch 2 para 8(1)(a) (Sch 2 para 8(1) amended by SI 2006/1831).

3   Private Security Industry Act 2001 Sch 2 para 8(1)(b) (Sch 2 para 8(1) as amended: see note 2). For these purposes, the times when premises are open to the public are to be taken to include any time when they are open to a section of the public comprising the individuals who qualify for admission to the premises as the members of a particular club, association or group or otherwise as being person to whom a particular description applies or in relation to whom particular conditions are satisfied: Sch 2 para 8(4).

4   See the Private Security Industry Act 2001 s Sch 2 paras 7(1), 8(1). The Secretary of State may by order amend Sch 2 Pt 2 (paras 7–10) for the purpose of adding or excluding any such activities as he thinks fit to or from those that fall to be regarded as activities subject to additional controls: Sch 2 para 7(2). See the Private Security Industry Act 2001 (Amendments to Schedule 2) Order 2006, SI 2006/1831, art 5; the Private Security Industry Act 2001 (Amendments to Schedule 2) Order 2007, SI 2007/2201, art 5; and the Private Security Industry Act 2001 (Amendments to Schedule 2) Order 2009, SI 2009/3043, arts 5–7 (each amending the Private Security Industry Act 2001 Sch 2 para 8 (see text and notes 5–23)). The Secretary of State may not make an order containing, with or without any other provision, any provision authorised by Sch 2 para 7(2) unless a draft of the order has been laid before Parliament and approved by a resolution of each House: Sch 2 para 7(3). As to the Secretary of State see PARA 902. As to the laying of documents before Parliament see STATUTES AND LEGISLATIVE PROCESS vol 96 (2012) PARA 1052. As to the power to make orders or regulations under the Private Security Industry Act 2001 in general see PARA 986 note 3.

5   Ie the supply of alcohol within the meaning of the Licensing Act 2003 s 14 (see LICENSING AND GAMBLING vol 67 (2008) PARA 53): Private Security Industry Act 2001 Sch 2 para 8(2)(a) (as substituted: see note 6).

6   Private Security Industry Act 2001 Sch 2 para 8(2)(a) (Sch 2 para 8(2)(a), (b) substituted by the Licensing Act 2003 Sch 6 para 118(2)). Activities carried out in relation to such premises are only activities subject to additional controls if they are carried out at or in relation to time when alcohol is being supplied (within the meaning of the Licensing Act 2003 s 14 (see note 5) for consumption on the premises: Private Security Industry Act 2001 Sch 2 para 8(1A) (Sch 2 para 8(1A)–(1C) added by SI 2006/1831).

7   Private Security Industry Act 2001 Sch 2 para 8(2)(b) (as substituted: see note 6). Activities carried out in relation to such premises are only activities subject to additional controls if they are carried out at or in relation to times when regulated entertainment is being provided on the premises: Sch 2 para 8(1B) (as added: see note 6).

8   Ie prescribed by regulations made by the Secretary of State, or determined in any such manner and by such person as may be provided for in any such regulations: Private Security Industry Act 2001 s 24(1).

9   'Local statutory provision' means: (1) a provision of any local Act; (2) a provision of any instrument in the nature of a local enactment; (3) a provision of any instrument made under a local statutory provision: Private Security Industry Act 2001 s 25(1).

10 Private Security Industry Act 2001 Sch 2 para 8(2)(e). Such licences and statutory provisions, being local in nature, are not recorded in this work.

11 Private Security Industry Act 2001 Sch 2 para 8(3)(a) (Sch 2 para 8(3) substituted by the Licensing Act 2003 Sch 6 para 118(3)). The reference to regulated entertainment is to regulated entertainment within the Licensing Act 2003 Sch 1 para 2(1)(a), (b) (see LICENSING AND GAMBLING vol 67 (2008) PARA 31).

12 References to the occasion on which any premises are being used for a particular purpose include references to any time on that occasion when the premises are about to be used for that purpose, or have just been used for that purpose: Private Security Industry Act 2001 Sch 2 para 8(5).

13 Private Security Industry Act 2001 Sch 2 para 8(3)(b) (Sch 2 para 8(3) as substituted: see note 11). The reference to a permitted temporary activity is to an activity temporarily permitted by virtue of the Licensing Act 2003 Pt 5 (ss 98–110) (see LICENSING AND GAMBLING vol 67 (2008) PARAS 108–113).

14 Private Security Industry Act 2001 Sch 2 para 8(3)(c) (Sch 2 para 8(3) as substituted (see note 11); Sch 2 para 8(3)(c) substituted by SI 2007/2201). See LICENSING AND GAMBLING vol 67 (2008) PARA 460 et seq.

15 The relevant provisions of the Theatres Act 1968 have been repealed subject to transitional provisions: see the Licensing Act 2003 Sch 6 para 44, Sch 8 Pt 1; and LICENSING AND GAMBLING vol 67 (2008) PARA 26.

16 The Cinemas Act 1985 has been repealed subject to transitional provisions: see the Licensing Act 2003 Sch 6 para 95, Sch 8 Pt 1; and LICENSING AND GAMBLING vol 67 (2008) PARA 26.

17 Private Security Industry Act 2001 Sch 2 para 8(3)(ca), (cb) (Sch 2 para 8(3) as substituted (see note 11); Sch 2 para 8(3)(ca), (cb) added by SI 2007/2201).

18 Private Security Industry Act 2001 Sch 2 para 8(3)(d) (Sch 2 para 8(3) as substituted: see note 11). At the date at which this volume states the law no such other occasions had been prescribed.

19 Private Security Industry Act 2001 Sch 2 para 8(1C)(a) (Sch 2 para 8(1C) as added (see note 6); Sch 2 para 8(1C)(a) numbered as such by SI 2007/2201).

20 Ie activities under the Private Security Industry Act 2001 Sch 2 para 2(1)(b) (see PARA 987): Sch 2 para 8(1C)(b) (as added: see notes 6, 22).

21 As to the meaning of 'vehicle' see PARA 987 note 1.

22 Private Security Industry Act 2001 Sch 2 para 8(1C)(b) (Sch 2 para 8(1C) as added (see note 6); Sch 2 para 8(1C)(b), (c) added by SI 2007/2201).

23 Private Security Industry Act 2001 Sch 2 para 8(1C)(c) (as added: see notes 6, 22). Such activities are the activities under Sch 2 para 2(1)(c) (see PARA 987): Sch 2 para 8(1C)(c) (as so added).

992. Exemptions from the licence requirement. If it appears to the Secretary of State[1] that there are circumstances in which licensable conduct[2] is engaged in only by persons to whom suitable alternative arrangements[3] will apply[4], and the Secretary of State is satisfied that, as a consequence, it is unnecessary for persons engaging in any such conduct in those circumstances to be required to be licensed[5], then he may by regulations[6] prescribing those circumstances provide that a person is not guilty of an offence[7] in respect of any conduct engaged in by him in those circumstances[8].

A person is not guilty of an offence[9] in respect of any activities of his as a security operative if: (1) he carries out those activities in his capacity as the director[10] of a body corporate, the partner of any firm[11] or the employee of any person[12]; (2) he has applied to the Security Industry Authority for the grant of a licence[13] and that application is pending[14]; (3) the licence applied for would authorise him to carry out those activities and is not one he has previously been refused[15]; (4) the body, firm or, as the case may be, the employer is a person who is for the time being registered[16] as an approved provider of security industry services[17]; and (5) the Authority has given notice to the body, firm or employer that it has authorised that body, firm or employer to use directors, partners or employees whose applications are pending to carry out activities that consist in or include those activities[18].

A relevant employee[19] who engages in licensable conduct is not guilty of an offence[20] in respect of that conduct if it is carried out in connection with the use of a certified sports ground or certified sports stand for purposes for which its safety certificate has effect[21]. An employee for a visiting team[22] who engages in licensable conduct is not guilty of an offence[23] in respect of that conduct if: (a) it is carried out in connection with the use of a certified sports ground or certified sports stand for purposes for which its safety certificate has effect; and (b) that visiting team is involved in the activities for which the ground is being used, or which the stand is being used to view[24].

1 As to the Secretary of State see PARA 902.
2 As to the meaning of 'licensable conduct' see PARA 986.
3 References in these provisions to suitable alternative arrangements are references to arrangements that the Secretary of State or, as the case may be, the Security Industry Authority is satisfied are equivalent, for all practical purposes so far as the protection of the public is concerned, to those applying to persons applying for and granted licences: Private Security Industry Act 2001 s 4(3). As to the prospective amendment of s 4 see note 4. As to the Security Industry Authority see PARA 980.
4 Private Security Industry Act 2001 s 4(1)(a). As from a day to be appointed s 4 is amended by substituting references to licensable conduct generally and references to conduct licensable under the Private Security Industry Act 2001 with references to conduct licensable under s 3 (see PARA 986) specifically: see the Crime and Security Act 2010 Sch 1 para 4 (not yet in force). At the date at which this volume states the law no such day had been appointed.
5 Private Security Industry Act 2001 s 4(1)(b). As to the prospective amendment of s 4 see note 4. The reference to a requirement to be licensed is to requirements under the Private Security Industry Act 2001: s 4(1)(b).
6 As to the power to make regulations under the Private Security Industry Act 2001 generally see PARA 986 note 3. Regulations made under s 4 are the Private Security Industry Act 2001 (Exemption) (Aviation Security) Regulations 2010, SI 2010/3018 (amended by SI 2012/1567) and the Private Security Industry Act 2001 (Exemption) (Olympics Security) Regulations 2012, SI 2012/145.
7 Ie an offence under the Private Security Industry Act 2001 s 3 (see PARA 986): s 4(1).
8 Private Security Industry Act 2001 s 4(1). As to the prospective amendment of s 4 see note 4. The provision that may be made by regulations under s 4(1) includes provision that a person is not to be guilty of an offence in respect of any conduct which is engaged in by him in the course of his employment by, or otherwise under the direction of, a person who is certified by the Security Industry Authority in accordance with the regulations to be a person who the Authority is satisfied will secure that suitable alternative arrangements apply: s 4(2).
9 Ie an offence under the Private Security Industry Act 2001 s 3 (see PARA 986): s 4(4). As to the prospective amendment of s 4 see note 4.
10 As to the meaning of 'director' see PARA 986 note 4.
11 As to references to a member of a firm see PARA 986 note 5.
12 Private Security Industry Act 2001 s 4(4)(a). Section 4(4) applies in the case of a person who carries out activities under directions given by or on behalf of another person in pursuance of a contract for the supply of the services of the first person as if the first person were an employee of the other one: s 4(5). As to the prospective amendment of s 4 see note 4.
13 As to when a licence under the Private Security Industry Authority Act 2001 is required see PARA 986.
14 Private Security Industry Act 2001 s 4(4)(b). As to the prospective amendment of s 4 see note 4.
15 Private Security Industry Act 2001 s 4(4)(c). As to the prospective amendment of s 4 see note 4.
16 Ie registered under the Private Security Industry Act 2001 s 14 (see PARA 1000): s 4(4)(d).
17 Private Security Industry Act 2001 s 4(4)(d). As to the prospective amendment of s 4 see note 4. As to the meaning of 'security industry services' see PARA 980 note 3. See also note 12.
18 Private Security Industry Act 2001 s 4(4)(e). As to the prospective amendment of s 4 see note 4. See also note 12.
19 In the Private Security Industry Act 2001 s 4 a 'relevant employee', in relation to a certified sports ground or certified sports stand, means a person employed by:
    (1) the holder of its safety certificate;
    (2) a person who manages the ground or stand or occupies the premises where it is or owns an interest in those premises;
    (3) a company which is in the same group as a company falling within head (2): s 4(9) (s 4(6)–(12) added by the Violent Crime Reduction Act 2006 s 63).
In the Private Security Industry Act 2001 s 4:
    (a) 'certified sports ground' means a sports ground in respect of which a safety certificate is in force; and 'sports ground' has the same meaning as in the Safety of Sports Grounds Act 1975 (see s 17(1); and SPORTS LAW vol 96 (2012) PARA 135);
    (b) 'certified sports stand' means a sports stand in respect of which a safety certificate is in force; and 'sports stand' means a stand within the meaning of the Fire Safety and Safety of Places of Sport Act 1987 Pt III (ss 26–41) (see s 26(11); and SPORTS LAW vol 96 (2012) PARA 147);

- (c) 'safety certificate', 'general safety certificate' and 'special safety certificate' have the same meanings as in the Safety of Sports Grounds Act 1975 (see ss 1(4), 17(1); and SPORTS LAW vol 96 (2012) PARA 136) in relation to a sports ground, and have the same meanings as in the Fire Safety and Safety of Places of Sport Act 1987 Pt III (see s 26(2), (11); and SPORTS LAW vol 96 (2012) PARA 147) in relation to a sports stand;
- (d) 'company', 'holding company' and 'subsidiary' have the same meaning as in the Companies Act 2006 s 1159 (see COMPANIES vol 14 (2009) PARA 25); and
- (e) 'group', in relation to a company, means a holding company and all of its subsidiaries: Private Security Industry Act 2001 s 4(12) (as so added; amended by SI 2009/1941).
  As to the prospective amendment of s 4 see note 4.
20 Ie under the Private Security Industry Act 2001 s 3 (see PARA 986): s 4(6) (as added: see note 19). As to the prospective amendment of s 4 see note 4.
21 Private Security Industry Act 2001 s 4(6) (as added: see note 19). As to the prospective amendment of s 4 see note 4. A reference to the use of a certified sports ground or stand for such purposes is a reference to the use of the ground for activities (in the case of a stand, viewing activities) specified in a general safety certificate in force in respect of that ground or stand, or the use of the ground or stand, on an occasion specified in a special safety certificate which is so in force, for activities (in the case of a stand, viewing activities) specified in the certificate: s 4(10), (11) (as added: see note 19).
22 A reference to a person being an employee for a visiting team in the Private Security Industry Act 2001 s 4 is a reference to his being a relevant employee in relation to the visitors' ground, or in relation to a certified sports stand contained in the visitors' premises, and for these purposes 'visiting team', in relation to a certified sports ground ('the home ground') or a certified sports stand contained in any premises ('the home premises') means a team which uses as its base, or as one of its bases, any premises which are either: (1) a certified sports ground which is not the home ground ('the visitors' ground'); or (2) premises which are not the home premises and which contain a certified sports stand ('the visitors' premises'): s 4(8), (12) (as added: see note 19). As to the prospective amendment of s 4 see note 4.
23 Ie under the Private Security Industry Act 2001 s 3 (see PARA 986): s 4(7) (as added: see note 19). As to the prospective amendment of s 4 see note 4.
24 Private Security Industry Act 2001 s 4(7) (as added: see note 19). As to the prospective amendment of s 4 see note 4.

993. Offences by bodies corporate and unincorporated associations. Where an offence under any of the private security industry provisions[1] is committed by a body coporate[2] and is proved to have been committed with the consent or connivance of, or to be attributable to any neglect on the part of, a director[3], manager, secretary or other similar officer of the body corporate, or any person who was purporting to act in any such capacity, he (as well as the body corporate) is guilty of that offence and liable to be proceeded against and punished accordingly[4].

As from a day to be appointed where an offence under any of the private security industry provisions is committed by an unincorporated association[5] and is proved to have been committed with the consent or connivance of, or to be attributable to any neglect on the part of: (1) in the case of an unincorporated association which is a partnership, a partner or a person purporting to be a partner; or (2) in the case of any other unincorporated association, an officer of the association or any member of it governing body or a person purporting to act in such a capacity, he (as well as the association) is guilty of that offence and liable to be proceeded against and punished accordingly[6].

As from a day to be appointed, proceedings for an offence under any of the private security industry provisions alleged to have been committed by an unincorporated association must be brought against it in its own name[7], and rules of court relating to the service of documents[8] have effect as if the association were a body corporate, and provision relating to the procedure in charges against corporations[9] apply as they apply in relation to a body corporate, for the purpose of such proceedings[10].

1   The private security industry provisions are those of the Private Security Industry Act 2001 (see PARA 980 et seq). The offences are set out in PARAS 986 et seq, 994, 996, 1001, 1003.

2   As to bodies corporate see generally COMPANIES vol 14 (2009) PARA 1; CORPORATIONS.

3   As to the meaning of 'director' see PARA 986 note 4.

4   Private Security Industry Act 2001 s 23(1) (numbered as such by the Serious Organised Crime and Police Act 2005 Sch 15 para 10).

5   As from a day to be appointed, references in the Private Security Industry Act 2001 to an unincorporated association include a partnership which is not regarded as a legal person under the law of the country or territory under which it is formed; and references to a member of an unincorporated association are to be construed, in relation to such a partnership, as references to a partner: s 25(1A) (prospectively added by the Crime and Security Act 2010 s 42(7)). At the date at which this volume states the law no day for the coming into force of the Private Security Industry Act 2001 s 25(1A) had been appointed. As to unincorporated associations generally see CORPORATIONS vol 24 (2010) PARA 301; and as to partnerships see generally PARTNERSHIP.

6   Private Security Industry Act 2001 s 23(3) (prospectively added by the Crime and Security Act 2010 s 42(6)). At the date at which this volume states the law no day for the coming into force of the Private Security Industry Act 2001 s 23(3) had been appointed.

7   Private Security Industry Act 2001 s 23A(1) (s 23A prospectively added by the Crime and Security Act 2010 Sch 1 para 10). At the date at which this volume states the law no day for the coming into force of the Private Security Industry Act 2001 s 23A had been appointed.

8   See CRIMINAL PROCEDURE vol 27 (2010) PARA 116 et seq.

9   The proceedings referenced are the Criminal Justice Act 1925 s 33 and the Magistrates' Court Act 1980 Sch 3 (see CRIMINAL PROCEDURE vol 27 (2010) PARAS 190, 388): Private Security Industry Act 2001 s 23A(b)(i) (s 23A as prospectively added: see note 7).

10 Private Security Industry Act 2001 s 23A(2) (s 23A as prospectively added: see note 7). As from a day to be appointed, where a fine is imposed on an unincorporated association on its conviction for an offence under the Private Security Industry Act 2001, the fine must be paid out of the funds of the association: s 23A(3) (s 23A as so prospectively added).

994. Offence of using unlicensed security operatives and unlicensed wheel-clampers.

A person is guilty of the offence of using an unlicensed security operative if he provides any security industry services[1] to another[2], those services are provided wholly or partly by means of the activities of an individual as a security operative[3], and that individual's activities in connection with the provision of those services involve his engaging in licensable conduct[4] in respect of which he is not the holder of a licence[5]. In proceedings against any person for such an offence, it is a defence for that person to show either that he did not know, and had no reasonable grounds for suspecting, at the time when the activities were carried out, that the individual in question was not the holder of a licence in respect of those activities[6], or that he took all reasonable steps, in relation to the services in question, for securing that that individual would not engage in any licensable conduct in respect of which he was not the holder of a licence[7]. A person is not guilty of such an offence in respect of any services in so far as those services are provided by means of conduct in which a person who is not the holder of a licence is entitled[8] to engage[9].

1   As to the meaning of 'security industry services' see PARA 980 note 3.

2   Private Security Industry Act 2001 s 5(1)(a). As from a day to be appointed s 5 is amended by substituting references to licensable conduct generally and references to conduct licensable under the Private Security Industry Act 2001 with references to conduct licensable under s 3 (see PARA 986) specifically: see the Crime and Security Act 2010 Sch 1 para 6 (not yet in force). At the date at which this volume states the law no day for the coming into force of these amendments had been appointed.

3   Private Security Industry Act 2001 s 5(1)(b). As to the prospective amendment of s 5 see note 2.

4   As to the meaning of 'licensable conduct' see PARA 986.

5   Private Security Industry Act 2001 s 5(1)(c). As to the prospective amendment of s 5 see note 2. As to the meaning of 'licence' see PARA 986 note 2. A person guilty of an offence under the Private Security Industry Act 2001 s 5 is liable, on summary conviction, to imprisonment for a term not exceeding six months or to a fine not exceeding the statutory maximum, or to both,

and, on conviction on indictment, to imprisonment for a term not exceeding five years or to a fine, or to both: s 5(4). As to the statutory maximum see SENTENCING AND DISPOSITION OF OFFENDERS vol 92 (2010) PARA 140. As to the offence of engaging in conduct prohibited without a licence see PARA 986.

6   Private Security Industry Act 2001 s 5(2)(a). As to the prospective amendment of s 5 see note 2.
7   Private Security Industry Act 2001 s 5(2)(b). As to the prospective amendment of s 5 see note 2.
8   Ie entitled by virtue of the Private Security Industry Act 2001 s 4 (see PARA 992): s 5(3). As to the prospective amendment of s 5 see note 2.
9   Private Security Industry Act 2001 s 5(3). As to the prospective amendment of s 5 see note 2.

C. LICENSING FUNCTIONS OF THE SECURITY INDUSTRY AUTHORITY

995.   Licensing criteria.   It is the duty of the Security Industry Authority[1], before granting any licences[2], to prepare and publish a document setting out the criteria which it proposes to apply in determining whether or not to grant a licence[3], and the criteria which it proposes to apply in exercising its powers to revoke or modify[4] a licence[5]. The Authority may from time to time revise the document for the time being setting out the criteria and, if it does so, it must publish the revised document[6]. Criteria or revised criteria do not have effect unless approved by the Secretary of State[7].

The criteria must include such criteria as the Authority considers appropriate for securing that the persons who engage in licensable conduct[8] are fit and proper persons to engage in such conduct[9], may include such criteria as the Authority considers appropriate for securing that those persons have the training and skills necessary to engage in the conduct for which they are licensed[10], and may also include criteria relating to such other matters as the Authority thinks fit[11]. In setting out any criteria or revised criteria, the Authority may provide for different criteria to apply in relation to licences for different descriptions of licensable conduct[12], and in relation to the initial grant of a licence and in relation to a further grant to the same licensee for the purpose of renewing an earlier licence[13].

1   As to the Security Industry Authority see PARA 980.
2   As to the meaning of 'licence' see PARA 986 note 2.
3   Private Security Industry Act 2001 s 7(1)(a).
4   As to the meaning of 'modification' see PARA 980 note 12.
5   Private Security Industry Act 2001 s 7(1)(b). As to the power to modify or revoke a licence see s 10; and PARA 996. The publication in accordance with s 7 of any document setting out any criteria or revised criteria must be in such manner as the Authority considers appropriate for bringing it to the attention of the persons likely to be affected by it: s 7(6).
6   Private Security Industry Act 2001 s 7(2).
7   See the Private Security Industry Act 2001 s 7(5). Before giving such approval, the Secretary of State must consult the Scottish Ministers and the Department of Justice in Northern Ireland: s 7(5A) (added by the Serious Organised Crime and Police Act 2005 Sch 15 para 5; amended by SI 2010/976). As to the Secretary of State see PARA 902.
8   As to the meaning of 'licensable conduct' see PARA 986.
9   Private Security Industry Act 2001 s 7(3)(a).
10 Private Security Industry Act 2001 s 7(3)(b).
11 Private Security Industry Act 2001 s 7(3)(c).
12 Private Security Industry Act 2001 s 7(4)(a).
13 Private Security Industry Act 2001 s 7(4)(b).

996.   Licences to engage in licensable conduct.   The Security Industry Authority[1] may, on an application[2] made to it, grant to the applicant a licence[3] to engage in any such licensable conduct[4] as may be described in the licence[5].

In determining whether or not to grant a licence the Authority must apply the applicable licensing criteria[6]. The Authority may refuse to grant a licence until:

(1) it has been satisfied as to the identity of the applicant in such manner as may be prescribed[7];

(2) the applicant has supplemented his application with such further information, if any, as the Authority may request after receiving the application[8]; and

(3) the Authority has been able to carry out such further inquiries, if any, in relation to the applicant as it considers appropriate[9].

A licence granted by the Authority to engage in any description of licensable conduct must be in such form, must contain such information, and must be granted on such conditions, as may be prescribed in relation to licences to engage in that description of licensable conduct[10], and the Authority may impose such additional conditions as it considers appropriate in relation to the licence in question[11]. The power of the Secretary of State to prescribe the conditions on which a licence must be granted and the power of the Authority to impose additional conditions include the power to prescribe or impose:

(a) conditions containing requirements as to the training, registration and insurances which the licensee[12] is to undergo, or to maintain, while the licence remains in force[13];

(b) conditions as to the manner in which the licensee is to carry out specified activities of a security operative[14] that he is licensed to carry out[15];

(c) conditions imposing obligations as to the production and display of the licence[16];

(d) conditions imposing obligations as to the information to be provided from time to time by the licensee to the Authority[17]; and

(e) such other conditions, whether or not relating to the criteria that would be applied by the Authority in determining whether to grant the licence, as the Secretary of State or the Authority thinks fit[18],

and the conditions that may be prescribed or imposed in relation to any description of licence may include conditions imposing obligations on a licensee by reference to requirements made or directions given by the Authority[19]. Any person who contravenes the conditions of any licence granted to him is guilty of an offence[20].

The Authority may by notice in writing to the licensee modify[21] or revoke any licence granted to him, including any of the conditions of that licence[22]. In determining whether or not to modify or revoke a licence, the Authority must apply the applicable licensing criteria[23].

1 As to the Security Industry Authority see PARA 980.
2 An application to the Authority for the grant of a licence must be in such form, and must be accompanied by such information, as is determined by the Authority: see the Private Security Industry Act 2001 s 8(2); and the Private Security Industry Act 2001 (Licences) Regulations 2007, SI 2007/810, reg 3 (substituted by SI 2011/2156). As to the meaning of 'information' see PARA 980 note 14; and as to the meaning of 'prescribed' see PARA 991 note 8. As to the power to make regulations and orders under the Private Security Industry Act 2001 generally see PARA 986 note 3. On the making of an application for the grant of a licence, the applicant must pay to the Authority a fee of £220 (partly refundable, subject to conditions, where a licence previously granted to the licensee remains valid for a period of at least four months): see the Private Security Industry Act 2001 s 8(7); and the Private Security Industry Act 2001 (Licences) Regulations 2007, SI 2007/810, regs 8, 9 (amended by SI 2011/2917).
3 As to the meaning of 'licence' see PARA 986 note 2.
4 As to the meaning of 'licensable conduct' see PARA 986.
5 Private Security Industry Act 2001 s 8(1). Subject to the Authority's power to revoke or modify a licence (see s 10; and the text and notes 21–23), a licence remains in force for a period of three years beginning with the day on which it is granted or, in any case for which provision as to the

duration of the licence is made by the Secretary of State by order, for such other period beginning with that day as may be specified in the order: s 8(8). As to the Secretary of State see PARA 902. As to the duration of licence issued by way of renewal see the Private Security Industry Act 2001 (Duration of Licence) (No 2) Order 2006, SI 2006/3411, art 4.

As from a day to be appointed, where a licence is granted to an unincorporated association, the licence continues to have effect notwithstanding a change of members of the association, so long as at least one of the persons who was a member before the change remains a member after it: Private Security Industry Act 2001 s 8(9) (prospectively added by the Crime and Security Act 2001 Sch 1 para 8). At the date at which this volume states the law no day for the coming into force of the Private Security Industry Act 2001 s 8(9) had been appointed.

6   Private Security Industry Act 2001 s 8(3). As to the licensing criteria see PARA 995.

7   Private Security Industry Act 2001 s 8(4)(a).

8   Private Security Industry Act 2001 s 8(4)(b). A person is guilty of an offence if for any purposes connected with the carrying out by the Authority of any of its functions under the Private Security Industry Act 2001 he makes any statement to the Authority which he knows to be false in a material particular, or he recklessly makes any statement to the Authority which is false in a material particular: s 22(1). A person guilty of such an offence is liable on summary conviction to imprisonment for a term not exceeding six months or a fine not exceeding level 5 on the standard scale, or to both: s 22(2). As to the standard scale see SENTENCING AND DISPOSITION OF OFFENDERS vol 92 (2010) PARA 142.

9   Private Security Industry Act 2001 s 8(4)(c).

10 Private Security Industry Act 2001 s 8(5). As to the prescribed form of licence in relation to activities subject to additional controls, see the Private Security Industry Act 2001 (Licences) Regulations 2007, SI 2007/810, Schs 2, 3. As to activities subject to additional controls see PARA 991. See also reg 5, which sets out licence conditions, and reg 7 (amended by SI 2007/2504), which states that a person holding a licence for certain types of licensable conduct and in respect of certain categories of licensable activity may perform other specified types of licensable activity without holding a separate licence.

11 See the Private Security Industry Act 2001 s 8(6).

12 In relation to a licence authorising licensable conduct of an employer of an individual who in the course of his employment with that employer carries out any designated activities subject to additional controls, the references in the Private Security Industry Act 2001 s 9(1) to the licensee include references to any of his employees who carry out any designated activities subject to additional controls: s 9(3). As to the meaning of 'designated activities' see PARA 986 note 3.

13 Private Security Industry Act 2001 s 9(1)(a).

14 As to the meaning of 'activities of a security operative' see PARA 986 note 3.

15 Private Security Industry Act 2001 s 9(1)(b).

16 Private Security Industry Act 2001 s 9(1)(c).

17 Private Security Industry Act 2001 s 9(1)(d).

18 Private Security Industry Act 2001 s 9(1)(e).

19 Private Security Industry Act 2001 s 9(2). As from a day to be appointed the conditions that may be prescribed or imposed in relation to any description of licence under s 4A (requirement to license businesses etc (not yet in force): see PARA 986 note 2) include conditions requiring the person to whom the licence is granted to be a member of a nominated body or scheme, and 'nominated body or scheme' means such body or scheme as is for the time being nominated for these purposes by the Authority with the approval of the Secretary of State: Private Security Industry Act 2001 s 9(2A), (2B) (prospectively added by the Crime and Security Act 2010 s 42(4)). At the date at which this volume states the law no day for the coming into force of the Private Security Industry Act 2001 s 9(2A), (2B) had been appointed.

20 Private Security Industry Act 2001 s 9(4). A person guilty of an offence under s 9(4) is liable, on summary conviction, to imprisonment for a term not exceeding six months or to a fine not exceeding level 5 on the standard scale, or to both: s 9(4). In proceedings against any person for an offence under s 9(4) it is a defence for that person to show that he exercised all due diligence to avoid a contravention of the conditions of the licence: s 9(5). 'Contravention' includes a failure to comply: s 25(1). As to the criminal liability of directors and similar corporate officers see PARA 993.

21 As to the meaning of 'modification' see PARA 980 note 12.

22 Private Security Industry Act 2001 s 10(1).

23 Private Security Industry Act 2001 s 10(2). As to the licensing criteria see PARA 995. The modifications that may be made under s 10 include one suspending the effect of the licence for such period as the Authority may determine: s 10(3).

997. Appeals in licensing matters. Where an application for a licence[1] is refused, a licence is granted subject to conditions[2], or a licence is modified[3] or revoked, the applicant or, as the case may be, the holder of the licence may appeal to a magistrates' court against the Security Industry Authority's[4] decision to refuse to grant the licence, to impose those conditions or, as the case may be, to modify or to revoke the licence[5]. Where a magistrates' court makes a decision on such an appeal, an appeal to the Crown Court may be brought against that decision either by the Authority or by the person on whose appeal that decision was made[6].

Where an application for the grant of a licence by way of a renewal is refused or a licence is revoked, the licence to which the application or revocation relates is deemed to remain in force: (1) for the period during which an appeal[7] may be brought[8]; (2) for the period from the bringing of any such appeal until it is determined or abandoned[9]; (3) for the period from any determination on appeal that a licence should be granted until effect is given to that determination, or it is overturned on a further appeal[10]; (4) during any such period as the magistrates' court or the Crown Court may direct, pending an appeal from a determination made on an appeal to the magistrates' court[11].

1   As to applications for licences see PARA 996.
2   Ie conditions under the Private Security Industry Act 2001 s 8(6) (see PARA 996): s 11(1)(b).
3   As to the meaning of 'modification' see PARA 980 note 12.
4   As to the Security Industry Authority see PARA 980.
5   Private Security Industry Act 2001 s 11(1) (amended by the Courts Act 2003 Sch 8 para 395(2)). Such an appeal must be brought before the end of the period of 21 days beginning with the day on which the decision appealed against was first notified to the appellant by the Authority: Private Security Industry Act 2001 s 11(2).
6   Private Security Industry Act 2001 s 11(4). A court to which an appeal is brought under s 11 must determine the appeal in accordance with the criteria for the time being applicable under s 7 (see PARA 995): s 11(5). See also *Security Industry Authority v Stewart; Rahim v Security Industry Authority; R (on the application of Egenti) v Highgate Justices* [2007] EWHC 2338 (Admin), [2008] 2 All ER 1003, [2009] 1 WLR 466 (disapplication or qualification of the criteria in light of an applicant's underlying merits or individual circumstances not authorised by the Act).
7   Ie an appeal under the Private Security Industry Act 2001 s 11(1): s 11(6)(a).
8   Private Security Industry Act 2001 s 11(6)(a).
9   Private Security Industry Act 2001 s 11(6)(b).
10 Private Security Industry Act 2001 s 11(6)(c).
11 Private Security Industry Act 2001 s 11(6)(d) (amended by the Courts Act 2003 Sch 8 para 395(4), Sch 10).

998. Register of licences. It is the duty of the Security Industry Authority[1] to establish and maintain a register of persons licensed under the Private Security Industry Act 2001[2]. The Authority must secure that the register contains particulars of every person who for the time being holds a licence[3]. The particulars that must be recorded in every entry in the register relating to the holder of a licence are: (1) the name of the holder of the licence[4]; (2) an address for the holder of the licence which satisfies the prescribed requirements[5]; (3) the time when the licence will cease to have effect unless renewed[6]; and (4) the terms and other conditions of his licence[7]. It is the duty of the Authority to ensure that such arrangements are in force as it considers appropriate for allowing members of the public and such other persons as it thinks fit to inspect the contents of the register[8] and for securing that such publicity is given to any modification[9] or revocation of a licence as will bring it to the attention of persons likely to be interested in it[10].

1 As to the Security Industry Authority see PARA 980.
2 Private Security Industry Act 2001 s 12(1). As to licences to engage in licensable conduct see PARA 996. As to the meaning of 'licence' see PARA 986 note 2.
3 Private Security Industry Act 2001 s 12(2). As to the offence of providing false information to the Authority see PARA 996 note 8.
4 Private Security Industry Act 2001 s 12(3)(a).
5 Private Security Industry Act 2001 s 12(3)(b). As to the meaning of 'prescribed' see PARA 991 note 8. As to the power to make regulations under the Private Security Industry Act 2001 generally see PARA 986 note 3. As to licence requirements see PARA 996.
6 Private Security Industry Act 2001 s 12(3)(c). As to the duration of a licence see PARA 996 note 5.
7 Private Security Industry Act 2001 s 12(3)(d). As to conditions on licences see PARA 996.
8 Private Security Industry Act 2001 s 12(4)(a). The Authority may impose such fee as it considers reasonable for allowing a person to inspect the register or to take a copy of any part of it: s 12(5).
9 As to the meaning of 'modification' see PARA 980 note 12.
10 Private Security Industry Act 2001 s 12(4)(b).

999.   Licensing at a local authority level. The Secretary of State[1] may by order[2] make provision for local authorities[3] to carry out some or all of the Security Industry Authority's[4] relevant licensing functions[5] in relation to such cases and such areas, and for such purposes, as may be specified or described in the order[6]. Such an order may: (1) impose such conditions and requirements in respect of the carrying out of any of the Authority's relevant licensing functions by a local authority as the Secretary of State thinks fit[7]; (2) provide for any of those conditions or requirements to be framed by reference to directions given by the Secretary of State in accordance with the order[8]; (3) provide for any of the powers exercisable by a local authority by virtue of such an order to be exercisable concurrently in relation to the same case by the Authority and that local authority[9]; and (4) authorise a local authority to retain any fee[10] paid to it[11].

1 As to the Secretary of State see PARA 902.
2 As to the power to make orders under the Private Security Industry Act 2001 generally see PARA 986 note 3. The Secretary of State must consult the Security Industry Authority before making an order under s 13: s 13(6).
3 'Local authority' for this purpose means: (1) the council for any county or district in England other than a metropolitan county the districts comprised in which are districts for which there are councils; (2) the council for any London borough; (3) the Common Council of the City of London; (4) the Council of the Isles of Scilly; (5) the council for any county or county borough in Wales: Private Security Industry Act 2001 s 13(7). As to local government areas and authorities in England and Wales see LOCAL GOVERNMENT vol 69 (2009) PARA 22 et seq; as to the London boroughs and their councils see LONDON GOVERNMENT vol 71 (2013) PARAS 15, 20–22, 55 et seq; as to the Common Council of the City of London see LONDON GOVERNMENT vol 71 (2013) PARA 34 et seq; and as to the Council of the Isles of Scilly see LOCAL GOVERNMENT vol 69 (2009) PARA 36.
4 As to the Security Industry Authority see PARA 980.
5 The Authority's relevant licensing functions are such of its functions under the Private Security Industry Act 2001, other than s 7 (see PARA 995), as relate to the grant, revocation or modification of licences to engage in any such licensable conduct as will or may involve, or relate to, the carrying out of activities to which Sch 2 para 8 (see PARA 991) applies: s 13(2). As to the meaning of 'modification' see PARA 980 note 12. As to the meaning of 'licence' see PARA 986 note 2; and as to the meaning of 'licensable conduct' see PARA 986.
6 Private Security Industry Act 2001 s 13(1). Section 11 (appeals: see PARA 997) applies in relation to a decision made by a local authority in accordance with an order under s 13(1) as it applies in relation to a decision of the Authority, and where s 11 so applies it has effect as if the references in s 11(2) and (4) to the Authority were a reference to the local authority that made the decision in question: s 13(4). The Secretary of State may by order make such provision repealing or modifying the provisions of any local enactment as he considers appropriate in consequence of the coming into force of any of the provisions of the Private Security Industry

Act 2001 or of an order under s 13(1): s 13(5). In exercise of the power under s 3(5) the following orders have been made: the Private Security Industry Act 2001 (Modification of Local Enactments) Order 2004, SI 2004/916 (revoked); the Private Security Industry Act 2001 (Modification of Local Enactments) (No 2) Order 2004, SI 2004/1268 (revoked); the Private Security Industry Act 2001 (Repeal and Revocation) Order 2004, SI 2004/3145; and the Private Security Industry Act 2001 (Repeal and Revocation) Order 2005, SI 2005/248.

7   Private Security Industry Act 2001 s 13(3)(a).

8   Private Security Industry Act 2001 s 13(3)(b).

9   Private Security Industry Act 2001 s 13(3)(c).

10 Ie any fee paid to it by virtue of the Private Security Industry Act 2001 s 8(7) (see PARA 996 note 2).

11 Private Security Industry Act 2001 s 13(3)(d).

D. APPROVED CONTRACTORS

1000.   Register of approved contractors.   It is the duty of the Security Industry Authority[1] to establish and maintain a register of approved providers of security industry services[2]. The Authority must secure that the register contains particulars of every person who is for the time being approved under arrangements for the grant of approvals[3]. The particulars that must be recorded in every entry in the register relating to an approved person are: (1) the name of that person[4]; (2) an address for that person which satisfies the prescribed requirements[5]; (3) the services in respect of which that person is approved[6]; (4) the time when the approval will cease to have effect unless renewed[7]; and (5) the conditions of the approval[8]. It is the duty of the Authority to ensure that such arrangements are in force as it considers appropriate for allowing members of the public to inspect the contents of the register[9] and securing that such publicity is given to any modification[10] or withdrawal of an approval as will bring it to the attention of persons likely to be interested in it[11].

1   As to the Security Industry Authority see PARA 980.

2   Private Security Industry Act 2001 s 14(1). As from a day to be appointed the reference to 'approved providers of security industry services' is substituted by a reference to 'approved persons undertaking security activities' by the Crime and Security Act 2010 s 43(3)(b) (not yet in force). As from a day to be appointed for these purposes a person providing security industry services, and a person who employs an individual to carry out the activities of a security operative on his behalf, undertake security activities: Private Security Industry Act 2001 s 14(1A) (prospectively added by the Crime and Security Act 2010 s 43(3)(c)). At the date at which this volume states the law no day for the coming into force of s 43(3)(c) had been appointed. As to the meaning of 'security industry services' see PARA 980 note 3.

3   Private Security Industry Act 2001 s 14(2). As to such approvals see s 15; and PARA 1001. As to the offence of providing false information to the Authority see PARA 996 note 8.

4   Private Security Industry Act 2001 s 14(3)(a).

5   Private Security Industry Act 2001 s 14(3)(b). As to the meaning of 'prescribed' see PARA 991 note 8. As to the power to make regulations under the Private Security Industry Act 2001 generally see PARA 986 note 3. As to licence requirements see PARA 996.

6   Private Security Industry Act 2001 s 14(3)(c). As from a day to be appointed 'or activities' is added after 'the services' by the Crime and Security Act 2010 s 43(3)(d) (not yet in force). At the date at which this volume states the law no day for the coming into force of s 43(3)(d) had been appointed.

7   Private Security Industry Act 2001 s 14(3)(d).

8   Private Security Industry Act 2001 s 14(3)(e).

9   Private Security Industry Act 2001 s 14(4)(a). The Authority may impose such fee as it considers reasonable for allowing a person to inspect the register or to take a copy of any part of it: s 14(5).

10 As to the meaning of 'modification' see PARA 980 note 12.

11 Private Security Industry Act 2001 s 14(4)(b).

1001. Grant of approvals. It is the duty of the Security Industry Authority[1] to secure that there are arrangements in force for granting approvals to persons who are providing security industry services[2] in the United Kingdom[3] and who seek approval in respect of any such services that they are providing, or are proposing to provide[4]. The arrangements must:

(1) allow for an approval to be granted either in respect of all the services in respect of which it is sought or in respect of only some of them[5];

(2) ensure that an approval is granted to a person in respect of any services only if the condition[6] for the grant of an approval is satisfied[7];

(3) provide for an approval granted to any person to have effect subject to such conditions, whether or not connected with the provision of the services in respect of which the approval is granted, as may be contained in the approval[8];

(4) enable a person to whom the Authority is proposing to grant an approval to refuse it if the proposal is in different terms from the approval which was sought[9];

(5) make provision for the handling of complaints and disputes which: (a) are required by the conditions of an approved person's approval to be dealt with in accordance with a procedure maintained by him in pursuance of those conditions[10]; but (b) are not disposed of by the application of that procedure[11];

(6) provide for an approval to cease to have effect, unless renewed: (a) except in a case to which head (b) below applies, at the end of the period of three years beginning with the day on which it is granted[12]; and (b) in a case for which provision as to the duration of the approval is made by the Secretary of State[13] by order, for such other period beginning with that day as may be specified in the order[14];

(7) provide for the modification[15] and withdrawal of approvals[16].

The Authority may approve the terms in which a person who is for the time being registered[17] as an approved provider of security industry services may hold himself out as so registered[18]. A person is guilty of an offence if he holds himself out as registered[19] as an approved provider of any security industry services when he is not so registered[20], or he is so registered but holds himself out as so registered in terms that have not been approved by the Authority in relation to his case[21].

The Secretary of State may by regulations provide that persons of prescribed descriptions are to be prohibited from providing prescribed security industry services unless they are for the time being approved in respect of those services[22]. As from a day to be appointed, a person who is approved in respect of any security industry services[23], and would be prohibited[24] from providing those services except while for the time being so approved, is guilty of an offence if he contravenes any of the conditions of his approval in respect of those services[25]. The Secretary of State may by regulations make provision in relation to cases in which a person is required by regulations[26] to be approved in respect of any services[27] for the conditions that are to be contained in his approval in relation to the handling of complaints made about the provision of those services[28], and generally in relation to the arrangements[29] that are to be made for such cases[30].

1 As to the Security Industry Authority see PARA 980.
2 As to the meaning of 'security industry services' see PARA 980 note 3.
3 As to the meaning of 'United Kingdom' see PARA 906 note 7.
4 Private Security Industry Act 2001 s 15(1) (amended by the Justice and Security (Northern Ireland) Act 2007 s 49(4)). As from a day to be appointed it is the duty of the Authority to

secure that there are arrangements in force for granting approvals to: (1) a person who provides security industry services and seeks approval in respect of any such services that he is providing or proposes to provide; and (2) a person who employs an individual to carry out the activities of a security operative on his behalf and seeks approval in respect of those activities or other such activities that he proposes to employ an individual to carry out: Private Security Industry Act 2001 s 15(1), (1A) (s 15(1) prospectively substituted, s 15(1A) prospectively added, by the Crime and Security Act 2010 s 43(4)). The Crime and Security Act 2010 s 43(5), (6) (not yet in force) amend, from a day to be appointed, the Private Security Industry Act 2001 s 15 to add the alternative of 'activities' at each reference to 'services'. At the date at which this volume states the law no day for the coming into force of the amendments to s 15 had been appointed.

Where any arrangements under the Private Security Industry Act 2001 s 15 so provide, a person who seeks an approval under the arrangements, applies for a modification of such an approval, is for the time being approved under the arrangements, or has his approval under the arrangements modified wholly or partly in consequence of an application made by him, he must pay to the Authority, at such time or times as may be prescribed, such fee or fees as may be prescribed in relation to that time or those times: Private Security Industry Act 2001 s 15(8).

5   Private Security Industry Act 2001 s 15(2)(a). As to the prospective amendment of s 15 see note 4.

6   The condition referred to is that the Authority is satisfied that the person to whom approval is to be granted: (1) will comply, in providing the services in respect of which he is approved, with such technical and other requirements as may be prescribed (see the Private Security Industry Act 2001 (Approved Contractor Scheme) Regulations 2007, SI 2007/808 (amended by SI 2009/633; and SI 2011/2917)); (2) is a person in relation to whom such other requirements as may be prescribed are, and will continue to be, satisfied; (3) is, and will continue to be, able and willing to comply with any requirements that the Authority is proposing to impose by means of conditions of the approval; and (4) is otherwise a fit and proper person to be approved in respect of those services: Private Security Industry Act 2001 s 15(3). As to the prospective amendment of s 15 see note 4. As to the meaning of 'prescribed' see PARA 991 note 8. As to the power to make regulations under the Private Security Industry Act 2001 generally see PARA 986 note 3. Regulations made by virtue of head (1) or (2) may frame a requirement for the purposes of s 15(3) by reference to the opinion of a person specified in the regulations, or of a person chosen in a manner determined in accordance with the regulations: s 15(4). The requirements which may be imposed by conditions contained in an approval in accordance with the arrangements include: (a) requirements to provide information to such persons, in such form, at such times and in response to such requests as may be specified in or determined under the terms of the condition; (b) requirements framed by reference to the opinion or directions of a person specified in or chosen in accordance with provision contained in the conditions: s 15(5). However, nothing in the arrangements may authorise the imposition, by conditions contained in an approval, of any requirements for: (i) the provision of information; or (ii) the maintenance of a procedure for handling complaints or disputes, in relation to any matter other than one appearing to the Authority to be relevant to the matters mentioned in heads (1)–(4): s 15(6). Any requirement to provide information that is imposed in accordance with the arrangements on any person by the conditions of his approval is enforceable at the suit or instance of the Authority: s 15(7). As to the meaning of 'information' see PARA 980 note 14. As to the offence of providing false information to the Authority see PARA 996 note 8.

7   Private Security Industry Act 2001 s 15(2)(b). As to the prospective amendment of s 15 see note 4.

8   Private Security Industry Act 2001 s 15(2)(c). As to the prospective amendment of s 15 see note 4.

9   Private Security Industry Act 2001 s 15(2)(d). As to the prospective amendment of s 15 see note 4.

10 Private Security Industry Act 2001 s 15(2)(e)(i). As to the prospective amendment of s 15 see note 4.

11 Private Security Industry Act 2001 s 15(2)(e)(ii). As to the prospective amendment of s 15 see note 4.

12 Private Security Industry Act 2001 s 15(2)(f)(i). As to the prospective amendment of s 15 see note 4.

13 As to the Secretary of State see PARA 902.

14 Private Security Industry Act 2001 s 15(2)(f)(ii). At the date at which this volume states the law no such order had been made. As to the power to make orders under the Private Security Industry Act 2001 generally see PARA 986 note 3. As to the prospective amendment of s 15 see note 4.

15 As to the meaning of 'modification' see PARA 980 note 12.

16 Private Security Industry Act 2001 s 15(2)(g). As to the prospective amendment of s 15 see note 4.

17 Ie registered under the Private Security Industry Act 2001 s 14 (see PARA 1000): s 16(1).

18 Private Security Industry Act 2001 s 16(1). As from a day to be appointed the words 'as an approved provider of any security industry services' in s 16(1), (2)(a) are repealed by the Crime and Security Act 2010 s 43(7) (not yet in force). At the date at which this volume states the law no such day had been appointed.

19 References to a person's holding himself out as registered as an approved provider of any services include references to his holding himself out to be a person who is for the time being approved in respect of those services in accordance with arrangements under the Private Security Industry Act 2001 s 15: s 16(4).

20 Private Security Industry Act 2001 s 16(2)(a). As to the prospective amendment of s 16(2)(a) see note 18.

21 Private Security Industry Act 2001 s 16(2)(b). A person guilty of such an offence is liable on summary conviction, to a fine not exceeding the statutory maximum, and on conviction on indictment, to a fine: s 16(3). As to the statutory maximum see SENTENCING AND DISPOSITION OF OFFENDERS vol 92 (2010) PARA 140. As to the criminal liability of directors and similar corporate officers see PARA 993.

22 Private Security Industry Act 2001 s 17(1) (in force for the purpose of making regulations: see the Private Security Industry Act 2001 (Commencement No 1) Order 2002, SI 2002/3125). At the date at which this volume states the law no such regulations had been made. As from a day to be appointed, a person is guilty of an offence if he contravenes any prohibition imposed on him by regulations under the Private Security Industry Act 2001 s 17(1): s 17(2) (in force as from a day to be appointed; at the date at which this volume states the law, no such day had been appointed). As to the meaning of 'contravention' see PARA 996 note 20. A person guilty of an offence under s 17 is liable, on summary conviction, to a fine not exceeding the statutory maximum, and, on conviction on indictment, to a fine: s 17(4). Section 17(4) is in force as from a day to be appointed; at the date at which this volume states the law, no such day had been appointed.

　　As from a day to be appointed the Secretary of State may also provide that persons of prescribed descriptions are to be prohibited from securing that activities of a security operative are carried out on their behalf by an employee unless they are for the time being approved in respect of those activities in accordance with arrangements under s 15 (see text and notes 1–16): s 17(1)(b) (added by the Crime and Security Act 2010 s 43(8)(b)). At the date at which this volume states the law no such day had been appointed.

23 Ie approved in accordance with arrangements under the Private Security Industry Act 2001 s 15 (see text and notes 1–16): s 17(3)(a) (not yet in force: see note 25).

24 Ie prohibited by regulations under the Private Security Industry Act 2001 s 17(1): s 17(3)(b) (not yet in force: see note 25).

25 Private Security Industry Act 2001 s 17(3). Section 17(3) is in force as from a day to be appointed; at the date at which this volume states the law, no such day had been appointed. As from a day to be appointed s 17(3) is amended by the Crime and Security Act 2010 s 43(9) (not yet in force) to add the alternative of 'activities' at each reference to 'services'. At the date at which this volume states the law no such day had been appointed.

26 Ie required by regulations under the Private Security Industry Act 2001 s 17(1): s 17(5) (in force for the purpose of making regulations: see the Private Security Industry Act 2001 (Commencement No 1) Order 2002, SI 2002/3125).

27 Ie approved in accordance with arrangements under the Private Security Industry Act 2001 s 15: s 17(5) (in force for the purpose of making regulations: see the Private Security Industry Act 2001 (Commencement No 1) Order 2002, SI 2002/3125).

28 Private Security Industry Act 2001 s 17(5)(a) (in force for the purpose of making regulations: see the Private Security Industry Act 2001 (Commencement No 1) Order 2002, SI 2002/3125). As to the prospective amendment of the Private Security Industry Act 2001 s 17 see note 22. As from a day to be appointed s 17(5) is amended by the Crime and Security Act 2010 s 43(10) (not yet in force) to add the alternative of 'activities' at each reference to 'services'. At the date at which this volume states the law no such day had been appointed.

29 Ie arrangements under the Private Security Industry Act 2001 s 15: s 17(5) (in force for the purpose of making regulations: see the Private Security Industry Act 2001 (Commencement No 1) Order 2002, SI 2002/3125).

30 Private Security Industry Act 2001 s 17(5)(b) (in force for the purpose of making regulations: see the Private Security Industry Act 2001 (Commencement No 1) Order 2002, SI 2002/3125). See also note 28.

1002. Appeals relating to approvals. Where an application for an approval[1] is refused, conditions are included as conditions of such an approval, or such an approval is modified[2] or withdrawn, the applicant or, as the case may be, the approved person may appeal to a magistrates' court against the Security Industry Authority's[3] decision to refuse to grant the approval, to include those conditions or, as the case may be, to modify or to withdraw the approval[4]. Where a magistrates' court makes a decision on such an appeal, an appeal to the Crown Court may be brought against that decision either by the Authority or by the person on whose appeal that decision was made[5].

Where an application for the grant of an approval by way of a renewal is refused or an approval is withdrawn, the approval to which the application or withdrawal relates is deemed to remain in force: (1) for the period during which an appeal[6] may be brought[7]; (2) for the period from the bringing of any such appeal until it is determined or abandoned[8]; (3) for the period from any determination on appeal that an approval should be granted until effect is given to that determination, or it is overturned on a further appeal[9]; (4) during any such period as the magistrates' court or the Crown Court may direct, pending an appeal from a determination made on an appeal to the magistrates' court[10].

1 Ie an approval under the Private Security Industry Act 2001 s 15 (see PARA 1001): s 18(1)(a).
2 As to the meaning of 'modification' see PARA 980 note 12.
3 As to the Security Industry Authority see PARA 980.
4 Private Security Industry Act 2001 s 18(1) (amended by the Courts Act 2003 Sch 8 para 396(2)). Such an appeal must be brought before the end of the period of 21 days beginning with the day on which the decision appealed against was first notified to the appellant by the Authority: Private Security Industry Act 2001 s 18(2).
5 Private Security Industry Act 2001 s 18(4).
6 Ie an appeal under the Private Security Industry Act 2001 s 18(1): s 18(5)(a).
7 Private Security Industry Act 2001 s 18(5)(a).
8 Private Security Industry Act 2001 s 18(5)(b).
9 Private Security Industry Act 2001 s 18(5)(c).
10 Private Security Industry Act 2001 s 18(5)(d)(i) (numbered as such by the Serious Organised Crime and Police Act 2005 Sch 15 para 9(c); amended by the Courts Act 2003 Sch 8 para 396(4)).

E. POWER TO ENTER AND INSPECT

1003. Powers of entry and inspection. A person authorised in writing for the purpose by the Security Industry Authority[1] may enter any premises[2] owned or occupied by any person appearing to him to be a regulated person[3] other than premises occupied exclusively for residential purposes as a private dwelling[4]. A person exercising such a power must do so only at a reasonable hour[5], and must:

(1) comply with any reasonable request made, whether before or after entry is gained to the premises, by any person present on the premises to do any one or more of the following: (a) state the purpose for which the power is being exercised[6]; (b) show the authorisation by the Authority for his exercise of the power[7]; (c) produce evidence of his identity[8];

(2) make a record of the date and time of his entry, the period for which he remained there and his conduct while there[9]; and

(3) if requested to do so by any person present on the premises at the time of the entry, provide that person with a copy of that record[10].

A person authorised in writing for the purpose by the Authority may require any person appearing to him to be a regulated person to produce to him any documents or other information[11] relating to any matter connected with: (i) any licensable conduct which has been or may be engaged in by the person so appearing[12]; (ii) the provision by the person so appearing of any security industry services[13]; (iii) any matters in respect of which conditions are imposed on the person so appearing by virtue of a licence or of an approval[14].

A person is guilty of an offence if he intentionally obstructs any person in the exercise of such power of entry, fails without reasonable excuse to comply with any such requirement, or makes an unauthorised disclosure[15] of any information disclosed by him in the exercise of any power of entry or as a consequence of the exercise of any such power by another[16].

It is the duty of the Authority to prepare and publish a document containing its guidance as to the manner in which persons authorised to enter premises should exercise that power and conduct themselves after entering premises in exercise of that power[17].

1 As to the Security Industry Authority see PARA 980.
2 As to the meaning of 'premises' see PARA 987 note 1.
3 'Regulated person' means: (1) the holder of any licence granted under the Private Security Industry Act 2001; (2) any person who engages in licensable conduct without being the holder of a licence under the Private Security Industry Act 2001; (3) any person who is for the time being approved in accordance with arrangements under s 15 (see PARA 1001) in respect of any services which regulations under s 17 (see PARA 1001) prohibit him from providing unless so approved; or (4) any person who is not so approved but provides security industry services which he is prohibited by any such regulations from providing: s 19(8). As from a day to be appointed s 19(8) is amended by the Crime and Security Act 2010 Sch 1 para 9 (not yet in force) so that head (2) is replaced by 'any individual who engages in conduct licensable under s 3 without being the holder of a licence under that section; and any person who engages in conduct licensable under s 4A without being the holder of a licence under that section'. As to ss 3, 4A (s 4A not yet in force: see PARA 986 note 2) see PARA 986. At the date at which this volume states the law no such day had been appointed. As to the meaning of 'licence' see PARA 986 note 2; and as to the meaning of 'licensable conduct' see PARA 986. As to the meaning of 'security industry services' see PARA 980 note 3. As to licences to engage in licensable conduct see PARA 996.
4 Private Security Industry Act 2001 s 19(1). As from a day to be appointed, subject to s 19(3), (4) (see text and notes 5, 6), a person authorised in writing for the purpose by the Authority may also enter any premises which appear to him to be premises on which a person engages in conduct licensable under s 4A (requirement to license businesses etc (not yet in force): see PARA 986 note 2), other than premises occupied exclusively for residential purposes as a private dwelling: s 19(1)(b) (prospectively added by the Crime and Security Act 2010 s 42(5)(b)). At the date at which this volume states the law no such day had been appointed.
5 Private Security Industry Act 2001 s 19(3).
6 Private Security Industry Act 2001 s 19(4)(a)(i).
7 Private Security Industry Act 2001 s 19(4)(a)(ii).
8 Private Security Industry Act 2001 s 19(4)(a)(iii).
9 Private Security Industry Act 2001 s 19(4)(b).
10 Private Security Industry Act 2001 s 19(4)(c).
11 As to the meaning of 'information' see PARA 980 note 14.
12 Private Security Industry Act 2001 s 19(2)(a).
13 Private Security Industry Act 2001 s 19(2)(b). As to the meaning of 'security industry services' see PARA 980 note 3.
14 Private Security Industry Act 2001 s 19(2)(c). The reference to an approval is to an approval granted in accordance with arrangements under s 15 (see PARA 1001): s 19(2)(c).
15 For these purposes a disclosure of information is authorised if, and only if, it is made for the purposes of the carrying out by the Authority of any of its functions under the Private Security Industry Act 2001 or for the purposes of any criminal proceedings: s 19(6).
16 Private Security Industry Act 2001 s 19(5). A person guilty of an offence under s 19 is liable, on summary conviction, to imprisonment for a term not exceeding six months or to a fine not exceeding level 5 on the standard scale, or to both: s 19(7). As to the standard scale see SENTENCING AND DISPOSITION OF OFFENDERS vol 92 (2010) PARA 142. As to the offence of providing false information to the Authority see PARA 996 note 8. As to the criminal liability of directors and similar corporate officers see PARA 993.

17 Private Security Industry Act 2001 s 20(1). The Authority may from time to time revise such guidance and, if it does so, the Authority must publish the revised guidance in such manner as appears to the Authority appropriate for bringing the guidance to the attention of persons likely to be affected by it: s 20(2), (3).

(xi) Sunbed Businesses

1004. Regulation of the use of sunbeds. The Sunbeds (Regulation) Act 2010 makes provision about the use or supply of tanning devices that use artificial ultra-violet radiation[1]. It requires a person carrying on a sunbed business to secure that no person aged under 18 uses a sunbed[2].

The Act also gives power to make regulations to make further provision restricting the use, sale or hire of sunbeds[3]. Regulations may make provision requiring a person who carries on a sunbed business ('P') to secure that:

(1) the use of sunbeds to which the business relates is supervised in such manner as the regulations may require[4];

(2) no sunbed to which the business relates is used on domestic premises by a person aged under 18[5];

(3) no offer is made by P or on P's behalf to make a sunbed to which the business relates available for use on domestic premises by a person aged under 18[6].

Regulations may make provision prohibiting or restricting the sale or hire of sunbeds to persons aged under 18[7]. They may also make provision requiring any person who carries on a sunbed business to provide and display prescribed health information to persons who are using or may seek to use a sunbed[8]. Regulations may make provision prohibiting any person who carries on a sunbed business from providing or displaying any material that contains statements relating to the health effects of sunbed use (other than certain excepted statements)[9].

Regulations may make provision requiring any person who carries on a sunbed business to:

(a) secure that protective eyewear meeting prescribed requirements is made available in connection with any use of a sunbed to which the business relates; and

(b) secure as far as reasonably practicable that persons who use a sunbed to which the business relates wear protective eyewear meeting those requirements[10].

1 See the Sunbeds (Regulation) Act 2010, preamble.
2 See the Sunbeds (Regulation) Act 2010 s 2; and CHILDREN AND YOUNG PERSONS vol 9 (2012) PARA 658. There is an exemption in the case of medical treatment in a healthcare establishment: see s 3; and CHILDREN AND YOUNG PERSONS vol 9 (2012) PARA 658. A 'sunbed business' is a business that involves making one or more sunbeds available for use on premises that are occupied by, or are to any extent under the management or control of, the person who carries on the business, and those sunbeds are the sunbeds to which the business relates: Sunbeds (Regulation) Act 2010 s 1(3). 'Sunbed' means an electrically-powered device designed to produce tanning of the human skin by the emission of ultra-violet radiation: s 1(2).
3 See the Sunbeds (Regulation) Act 2010 s 4. The power to make such regulations is exercisable by statutory instrument: see ss 10, 11 (s 10 amended by SI 2015/664). As to such regulations made in relation to Wales see notes 4–10. At the date at which this volume states the law no such regulations had been made in relation to England.
4 Sunbeds (Regulation) Act 2010 s 4(1)(a). Before making regulations under s 4(1)(a), the appropriate national authority must consult persons appearing to the appropriate national authority to have an interest in the subject-matter of the proposed regulations: s 4(3), (4). 'The appropriate national authority' means, in relation to the Secretary of State and, in relation to Wales, the Welsh Ministers. As to the Secretary of State and the Welsh Ministers see PARA 902.

See the Sunbeds (Regulation) Act 2010 (Wales) Regulations 2011, SI 2011/1130, reg 4. It is the duty of local authorities to enforce the provisions of the regulations: see reg 9; and PARA 1005.

5   Sunbeds (Regulation) Act 2010 s 4(1)(b). See the Sunbeds (Regulation) Act 2010 (Wales) Regulations 2011, SI 2011/1130, reg 3. See also note 4.

6   Sunbeds (Regulation) Act 2010 s 4(1)(c). See the Sunbeds (Regulation) Act 2010 (Wales) Regulations 2011, SI 2011/1130, reg 3. See also note 4.

7   Sunbeds (Regulation) Act 2010 s 4(2). Before making regulations under s 4(2), the appropriate national authority must consult persons appearing to the appropriate national authority to have an interest in the subject-matter of the proposed regulations: s 4(3), (4). See the Sunbeds (Regulation) Act 2010 (Wales) Regulations 2011, SI 2011/1130, regs 5, 6. See also note 4.

8   Sunbeds (Regulation) Act 2010 s 5(1). 'Health information' means information about the health risks associated with the use of sunbeds: s 5(2). See the Sunbeds (Regulation) Act 2010 (Wales) Regulations 2011, SI 2011/1130, reg 7, Sch 1, Sch 2. See also note 4.

9   Sunbeds (Regulation) Act 2010 s 5(3). The excepted statements are those containing information prescribed under s 5(1), or statements containing any other information prescribed for the purposes of s 5: see s 5(3). See the Sunbeds (Regulation) Act 2010 (Wales) Regulations 2011, SI 2011/1130, reg 7. See also note 4.

10 Sunbeds (Regulation) Act 2010 s 6. See the Sunbeds (Regulation) Act 2010 (Wales) Regulations 2011, SI 2011/1130, reg 8. See also note 4.

1005. Enforcement of sunbed legislation by local authorities. It is the duty of a local authority to enforce the statutory duty on persons carrying on a sunbed business to secure that no person aged under 18 uses a sunbed in its area, and to appoint authorised officers for that purpose[1]. A person who without reasonable excuse obstructs an authorised officer, acting in the exercise of the officer's functions commits an offence[2]. Further, a person who without reasonable excuse fails to give to an authorised officer, acting in the exercise of the officer's functions, any facilities, assistance or information which the authorised officer reasonably requires of the person for the performance of those functions commits an offence[3]. A person commits an offence if, in purported compliance with any requirement of an authorised officer[4], that person makes a statement which is false or misleading in a material respect, and that person either knows that it is false or misleading or is reckless as to whether it is false or misleading[5].

Where an offence under the Sunbeds (Regulation) Act 2010, or under regulations made under it, is committed by a body corporate, then if the offence is proved to have been committed by, or with the consent or connivance of, or to be attributable to any neglect on the part of:

(1)   any director, manager or secretary of the body corporate; or

(2)   any person who was purporting to act in any such capacity,

that director, manager, secretary or person purporting to act as such (as well as the body corporate) is guilty of the offence and liable to be proceeded against and punished accordingly[6].

1   See the Sunbeds (Regulation) Act 2010 s 7(1), (2), (3), Schedule; and CHILDREN AND YOUNG PERSONS vol 9 (2012) PARA 658. In relation to England, 'local authority' means a district council, a county council for an area for which there is no district council, a London borough council, the Common Council of the City of London, in its capacity as a local authority, the Sub-Treasurer of the Inner Temple, the Under Treasurer of the Middle Temple, or the Council of the Isles of Scilly: s 12(1). In relation to Wales, 'local authority' means a county council or county borough council: s 12(1). As to local government areas and authorities in England and Wales see LOCAL GOVERNMENT vol 69 (2009) PARA 22 et seq. As to the London boroughs and their councils see LONDON GOVERNMENT vol 71 (2013) PARAS 15, 20–22, 55 et seq. As to the Common Council of the City of London see LONDON GOVERNMENT vol 71 (2013) PARA 34 et seq. As to the Sub-Treasurer of the Inner Temple and the Under Treasurer of the Middle Temple see LONDON GOVERNMENT vol 71 (2013) PARA 34 et seq. As to the Council of the Isles of Scilly see LOCAL GOVERNMENT vol 69 (2009) PARA 36.

2   Sunbeds (Regulation) Act 2010 s 8(1). A person guilty of an offence under s 8 is liable on summary conviction to a fine not exceeding level 5 on the standard scale: s 8(4). As to the standard scale see SENTENCING AND DISPOSITION OF OFFENDERS vol 92 (2010) PARA 142. In s 8(1), (2) references to functions under the Sunbeds (Regulation) Act 2010 include references to functions under regulations made under that Act: s 8(5).

3   Sunbeds (Regulation) Act 2010 s 8(2). As to the penalty for this offence see note 2.

4   Ie as mentioned in the Sunbeds (Regulation) Act 2010 s 8(2).

5   Sunbeds (Regulation) Act 2010 s 8(3). As to the penalty for this offence see note 2.

6   Sunbeds (Regulation) Act 2010 s 9(1), (2). The reference to the director, manager or secretary of the body corporate includes a reference to any other similar officer of the body corporate: s 9(3).

3. SHOPS

(1) DEREGULATION OF SHOPS

1006. Former restrictions on shop closing, hours of employment etc. The Shops Act 1950, the Shops (Airports) Act 1962 and the Shops (Early Closing Days) Act 1965 subjected shops to detailed restrictions in relation to hours of closing, conditions of employment, the hours of employment of young persons and relatively strict rules on Sunday trading. Such restrictions have now been abolished[1], except in the case of Sunday trading[2].

1   See the Employment Act 1989 ss 10, 29(4), Sch 3, Sch 7; the Deregulation and Contracting Out Act 1994 ss 23, 24, 81(1), Sch 17 (ss 23, 24 now repealed); and the Sunday Trading Act 1994 ss 1(2), 9(2), Sch 5.
2   As to Sunday trading see PARA 1007 et seq.

(2) SUNDAY TRADING

(i) Opening Hours

1007. Restrictions on Sunday opening of large shops. Formerly, trading on Sunday was severely restricted[1]. The restricting provisions were repealed by the Sunday Trading Act 1994[2] and such restrictions as are now in force relate only to large shops[3]. A large shop must not be open on Sunday for the serving of retail customers[4]; but that prohibition does not apply:

(1)   if it falls within a category of exempt shops[5];
(2)   if it is occupied by persons observing the Jewish Sabbath and a relevant notice has effect[6]; or
(3)   in relation to the opening of a large shop during any continuous period of six hours on a Sunday beginning no earlier than 10 am and ending no later than 6 pm[7].

The above provisions[8] do not apply where the Sunday is Christmas Day[9].

If the above provisions are contravened in relation to a shop, the occupier of the shop is liable on summary conviction to a fine[10]. Where a person is charged with having contravened the above provisions in relation to a large shop which was permitted to be open for the serving of retail customers on the Sunday in question, by reason of his having served a retail customer after the end of the period during which the shop is permitted to be open, it is a defence to prove that the customer was in the shop before the end of that period and left not later than half an hour after the end of that period[11].

1   Ie by the Shops Act 1950 Pt IV (ss 47–67) (repealed).
2   Ie by the Sunday Trading Act 1994 ss 1(2), 9(2), Sch 5. Under the Sunday Trading Act 1994 the Secretary of State may by order made by statutory instrument repeal any provision of a local Act passed before or in the same session as the Sunday Trading Act 1994 if it appears to him that the provision is inconsistent with, or has become unnecessary in consequence of, any provision of the 1994 Act: s 6(1)(a). He may by order made by statutory instrument amend any provision of such a local Act if it appears to him that the provision requires amendment in consequence of any provision of the 1994 Act or any repeal made by virtue of s 6(1)(a): see s 6(1)(b). Before he makes such an order repealing or amending any provision of a local Act, it is the Secretary of State's duty to consult each local authority which he considers would be affected by the repeal or amendment of that provision: Sunday Trading Act 1994 s 6(2). A statutory instrument containing such an order is subject to annulment in pursuance of a resolution of either House of Parliament: s 6(3). See STATUTES AND LEGISLATIVE PROCESS. Such orders, being local in nature, are not recorded in this work. As to the Secretary of State see PARA 902.

For these purposes, 'local authority' means any unitary authority or any district council, so far as it is not a unitary authority: s 8(1). 'Unitary authority' means the council of any county (so far as it is the council for an area for which there are no district councils), the council of any district comprised in an area for which there is no county council, a county borough council, a London borough council, the Common Council of the City of London or the Council of the Isles of Scilly: s 8(2). As to local government areas and authorities see LOCAL GOVERNMENT vol 69 (2009) PARA 22 et seq. As to the London boroughs and their councils see LONDON GOVERNMENT vol 71 (2013) PARAS 15, 20–22, 55 et seq. As to the Common Council of the City of London see LONDON GOVERNMENT vol 71 (2013) PARA 34 et seq. As to the Council of the Isles of Scilly see LOCAL GOVERNMENT vol 69 (2009) PARA 36.

3   For these purposes, 'shop' means any premises where there is carried on a trade or business consisting wholly or mainly of the sale of goods (Sunday Trading Act 1994 s 1(1), Sch 1 para 1); and 'large shop' means a shop which has a relevant floor area exceeding 280 square metres (Sch 1 para 1). 'Relevant floor area', in relation to a shop, means the internal floor area of so much of the shop as consists of, or is comprised in, a building, but excluding any part of the shop which, throughout the week ending with the Sunday in question, is used neither for the serving of customers in connection with the sale of goods nor for the display of goods: Sch 1 para 1. 'Sale of goods' does not include the sale of meals, refreshments or alcohol for consumption on the premises on which they are sold, or the sale of meals or refreshments prepared to order for immediate consumption off those premises: Sch 1 para 1 (amended by the Licensing Act 2003 s 198(1), Sch 6 para 110(1), (2)(b)). 'Alcohol' has the same meaning as in the Licensing Act 2003 (see LICENSING AND GAMBLING vol 67 (2008) PARA 30): Sunday Trading Act 1994 Sch 1 para 1 (definition added by the Licensing Act 2003 Sch 6 para 110(2)(a)).

4   Sunday Trading Act 1994 Sch 1 para 2(1). For these purposes, 'retail customer' means a person who purchases goods retail: Sch 1 para 1. As to the meaning of references to retail purchases see PARA 1009 note 8. A shop may still be a large shop, even though only a small part of the whole shop is open to retail customers: *Haskins Garden Centres Ltd v East Dorset District Council* [1998] EGCS 71, DC.

The Sunday Trading Act 1994 Sch 1 para 2(1) does not apply to any large shop situated in that part of the terminal area of the tunnel system located at the portals of the tunnels in the vicinity of Cheriton, Folkestone, that is within the area shown coloured blue on the deposited plan: Channel Tunnel (Sunday Trading Act 1994) (Disapplication) Order 1994, SI 1994/3286, art 3. 'Deposited plan' means the plan marked 'The Channel Tunnel (Sunday Trading Act 1994) (Disapplication) Order 1994', signed by authority of the Secretary of State for Transport, dated 22 November 1994 and deposited at the Department of the Environment, Transport and the Regions, Parliamentary Library, Room P3/001, 2 Marsham Street, London SW1P 3EB; and 'shop' has the same meaning as in the Sunday Trading Act 1994 (see note 3): Channel Tunnel (Sunday Trading Act 1994) (Disapplication) Order 1994, SI 1994/3286, art 2; Interpretation Act 1978 s 17(2)(a).

5   See the Sunday Trading Act 1994 Sch 1 para 2(2)(a); and PARA 1009.

6   See the Sunday Trading Act 1994 Sch 1 para 2(2)(b); and PARA 1011.

7   See the Sunday Trading Act 1994 Sch 1 para 2(3) (substituted by SI 2004/470); and PARA 1010. The exemption so conferred does not apply where the Sunday is Easter Day: Sunday Trading Act 1994 Sch 1 para 2(4) (amended by the Christmas Day (Trading) Act 2004 s 4(1), (2)(a)).

8   Ie the Sunday Trading Act 1994 Sch 1 para 2(1): see text and note 4.

9   See the Sunday Trading Act 1994 Sch 1 para 2(5) (added by the Christmas Day (Trading) Act 2004 s 4(2)(b)); and PARA 1008.

10   Sunday Trading Act 1994 Sch 1 para 7(1) (amended by SI 2015/664). As to the enforcement of the Sunday Trading Act 1994, and as to the general provisions relating to offences thereunder, see PARAS 1015–1017.

11   Sunday Trading Act 1994 Sch 1 para 8 (substituted by SI 2004/470).

1008. Restrictions on Christmas Day opening of large shops.

A large shop[1] must not be open on Christmas Day for the serving of retail customers[2]. Contravention of this renders the occupier of the shop liable on summary conviction to a fine[3].

Where a shop which is prohibited from opening on Christmas Day is located in a loading control area[4], the occupier of the shop must not load or unload, or permit any other person to load or unload, goods from a vehicle at the shop before 9:00 am on Christmas Day in connection with the trade or business being carried on at the shop, unless the loading or unloading is carried on with the consent⁵ of the local authority for the area in which the shop is situated, and in accordance with any conditions subject to which that consent is granted⁶. A person who contravenes this provision is liable on summary conviction to a fine⁷.

Every local authority⁸ has a duty to enforce these provisions within its area⁹ and, for the purposes of that duty, to appoint inspectors¹⁰.

1 'Large shop' means a shop which has a relevant floor area exceeding 280 square metres; and 'relevant floor area', in relation to a shop, means the internal floor area of so much of the shop as consists of, or is comprised in, a building, but excluding any part of the shop which, throughout the period of seven days ending with the Christmas Day in question, is used neither for the serving of customers in connection with the sale of goods nor for the display of goods: Sunday Trading Act 1994 Sch 1 para 1 (modified by the Christmas Day (Trading) Act 2004 s 1(5)).

2 Christmas Day (Trading) Act 2004 s 1(1). 'Retail customer' has the same meaning as in the Sunday Trading Act 1994 Sch 1 (see PARA 1007 note 4): Christmas Day (Trading) Act 2004 s 1(5). Section 1(1) does not apply to a shop mentioned in the Sunday Trading Act 1994 Sch 1 para 3(1) (see PARA 1009); and 'shop' has the same meaning as in Sch 1 (see PARA 1007 note 3): Christmas Day (Trading) Act 2004 s 1(2), (5). For the purposes of s 1(2), the Sunday Trading Act 1994 Sch 1 para 3(2) (see PARA 1009) has effect as if the reference to weekdays were a reference to days of the year other than Christmas Day, and the reference to Sunday were a reference to Christmas Day: Christmas Day (Trading) Act 2004 s 1(4).

3 Christmas Day (Trading) Act 2004 s 1(3) (amended by SI 2015/664).

4 'Loading control area' means any area designated by a local authority as a loading control area in accordance with the Sunday Trading Act 1994 s 2 (see PARA 1012): Christmas Day (Trading) Act 2004 s 2(4).

5 As to the application of the provisions of the Sunday Trading Act 1994 Sch 3 paras 3–8 (consent required for early Sunday loading and unloading; see PARA 1012) in relation to Christmas Day see PARA 1012 note 5.

6 Christmas Day (Trading) Act 2004 s 2(1).

7 A person who contravenes the Christmas Day (Trading) Act 2004 s 2(1) is liable on summary conviction to a fine not exceeding level 3 on the standard scale: s 2(3). As to the standard scale see SENTENCING AND DISPOSITION OF OFFENDERS vol 92 (2010) PARA 142.

8 'Local authority' has the meaning given by the Sunday Trading Act 1994 s 8 (see PARA 1007 note 2): Christmas Day (Trading) Act 2004 s 3(5).

9 Christmas Day (Trading) Act 2004 s 3(1).

10 Christmas Day (Trading) Act 2004 s 3(2). Such inspectors may be the same persons as those appointed as inspectors by the local authority under the Sunday Trading Act 1994 Sch 2 para 2 (see PARA 1015): Christmas Day (Trading) Act 2004 s 3(2). The Sunday Trading Act 1994 Sch 2 paras 3, 4 (powers of entry and obstruction of inspectors; see PARA 1015) apply in respect of inspectors appointed under the Christmas Day (Trading) Act 2004 s 3(2) as they apply to inspectors appointed under the Sunday Trading Act 1994 Sch 2 para 2 and, for the purposes of Sch 2 para 3 (as so applied), the reference to the provisions of Schs 1, 3 is to be taken as a reference to the provisions of the Christmas Day (Trading) Act 2004 ss 1, 2: see s 3(3). The Sunday Trading Act 1994 Sch 2 paras 5–7 (offences due to fault of other person, offences by body corporate and defence of due diligence; see PARA 1016) apply in respect of the offences under the Christmas Day (Trading) Act 2004 ss 1, 2 as they apply in respect of offences under the Sunday Trading Act 1994: Christmas Day (Trading) Act 2004 s 3(4).

1009. Shops exempt from the prohibition on Sunday opening. The general prohibition on large shops¹ opening on Sunday² does not apply to the following³:

(1) any shop which is at a farm and where the trade or business carried on consists wholly or mainly of the sale of produce from that farm⁴;

(2) any shop where the trade or business carried on consists wholly or mainly of the sale of alcohol⁵;

(3) any shop where the trade or business carried on consists wholly or mainly of the sale of any one or more of the following:
   (a) motor supplies and accessories; or
   (b) cycle supplies and accessories⁶;

(4)   any shop which:
       (a)   is a registered pharmacy[7]; and
       (b)   is not open for the retail sale[8] of any goods other than medicinal
              products[9], veterinary medicinal products[10] and surgical
              appliances[11];
(5)   any shop at a designated airport[12] which is situated in an applicable part
       of the airport[13];
(6)   any shop in a railway station[14];
(7)   any shop at a service area[15];
(8)   any petrol filling station[16];
(9)   any shop which is not open for the retail sale of any goods other than
       food, stores or other necessaries required by any person for a vessel or
       aircraft on its arrival at, or immediately before its departure from, a
       port, harbour or airport[17]; and
(10)   any stand[18] used for the retail sale of goods during the course of an
       exhibition[19].

In determining whether a shop falls within head (1), (2) or (3) above, regard is
to be had to the nature of the trade or business carried on there on weekdays as
well as to the nature of the trade or business carried on there on Sunday[20].

1   As to the meaning of 'large shop' see PARA 1007 note 3.
2   Ie the general prohibition in the Sunday Trading Act 1994 Sch 1 para 2(1): see PARA 1007.
3   Sunday Trading Act 1994 s 1(1), Sch 1 paras 2(2)(a), 3(1).
4   Sunday Trading Act 1994 Sch 1 para 3(1)(a).
5   Sunday Trading Act 1994 Sch 1 para 3(1)(b) (amended by the Licensing Act 2003 s 198(1),
    Sch 6 para 110(1), (3)). As to the meaning of 'alcohol' see PARA 1007 note 3.
6   Sunday Trading Act 1994 Sch 1 para 3(1)(c).
7   For these purposes, 'registered pharmacy' has the same meaning as in the Medicines Act 1968
    (see MEDICAL PRODUCTS AND DRUGS vol 75 (2013) PARA 52): Sunday Trading Act 1994 Sch 1
    para 1.
8   For these purposes, 'retail sale' means any sale other than a sale for use or resale in the course of
    a trade or business; and references to retail purchases are to be construed accordingly: Sunday
    Trading Act 1994 Sch 1 para 1.
9   For these purposes, 'medicinal product' has the same meaning as in the Medicines Act 1968 (see
    MEDICAL PRODUCTS AND DRUGS vol 75 (2013) PARA 25): Sunday Trading Act 1994 Sch 1
    para 1.
10 For these purposes, 'veterinary medicinal product' has the same meaning as in the Veterinary
    Medicines Regulations 2006, SI 2006/2407, reg 2 (revoked; see now the Veterinary Medicines
    Regulations 2013, SI 2013/2033, reg 2; and MEDICAL PRODUCTS AND DRUGS): Sunday Trading
    Act 1994 Sch 1 para 1 (definition added by SI 2006/2407).
11 Sunday Trading Act 1994 Sch 1 para 3(1)(d) (amended by SI 2006/2407).
12 For these purposes, 'designated airport' means an airport designated by an order made by the
    Secretary of State, as being an airport at which there appears to him to be a substantial amount
    of international passenger traffic: Sunday Trading Act 1994 Sch 1 para 3(4). The power to make
    such an order is exercisable by statutory instrument: Sch 1 para 3(5). At the date at which this
    volume states the law no order had been made directly under the Sunday Trading Act 1994
    Sch 1 para 3(4), but orders made under the Shops (Airports) Act 1962 s 1(2) (repealed) and in
    force on 26 August 1994 (ie the commencement date of the Sunday Trading Act 1994 Sch 1: see
    PARA 1013 note 1) have effect, so far as relating to England and Wales, as if made also under the
    Sunday Trading Act 1994 Sch 1 para 3(4), and may be amended or revoked as it has effect for
    these purposes by an order under Sch 1 para 3(4): see Sch 1 para 3(6). As to orders made under
    the Shops (Airports) Act 1962 s 1(2) (repealed) with effect as if made also under the Sunday
    Trading Act 1994 Sch 1 para 3(4) see AIR LAW vol 2 (2008) PARA 320.
13 Sunday Trading Act 1994 Sch 1 para 3(1)(e). For these purposes, the applicable part is every
    part of a designated airport, except any part which is not ordinarily used by persons travelling
    by air to or from the airport: Sch 1 para 3(3).
14 Sunday Trading Act 1994 Sch 1 para 3(1)(f).

15 Sunday Trading Act 1994 Sch 1 para 3(1)(g). The text refers to a service area within the meaning of the Highways Act 1980: see HIGHWAYS, STREETS AND BRIDGES vol 55 (2012) PARA 770.
16 Sunday Trading Act 1994 Sch 1 para 3(1)(h).
17 Sunday Trading Act 1994 Sch 1 para 3(1)(j).
18 For these purposes, 'stand', in relation to an exhibition, means any platform, structure, space or other area provided for exhibition purposes: Sunday Trading Act 1994 Sch 1 para 1.
19 Sunday Trading Act 1994 Sch 1 para 3(1)(k). If a large shop is not exempt, it must comply with the requirements as to the maximum of six hours' opening on a Sunday: see PARAS 1007, 1010.
20 Sunday Trading Act 1994 Sch 1 para 3(2).

1010. Requirement to display notice specifying opening hours. At any time when a large shop[1] is open on Sunday[2] for the serving of retail customers[3], there must be displayed in a conspicuous position inside and outside the shop a notice specifying the permitted Sunday opening hours[4]. If this requirement is contravened, the occupier of the shop is liable on summary conviction to a fine[5].

1 As to the meaning of 'large shop' see PARA 1007 note 3.
2 Ie where the prohibition in the Sunday Trading Act 1994 Sch 1 para 2(1) is excluded only by Sch 1 para 2(3): see PARA 1007. That exemption does not apply where the Sunday is Easter Day or Christmas Day: see Sch 1 para 2(4), (5) (amended and added respectively by the Christmas Day (Trading) Act 2004 s 4(1), (2)(a), (b)).
3 As to the meaning of 'retail customer' see PARA 1007 note 4; and as to the meaning of 'retail sale' see PARA 1009 note 8.
4 Sunday Trading Act 1994 s 1(1), Sch 1 para 6 (amended by SI 2004/470).
5 The fine is one not exceeding level 2 on the standard scale: Sunday Trading Act 1994 Sch 1 para 7(2). As to the standard scale see SENTENCING AND DISPOSITION OF OFFENDERS vol 92 (2010) PARA 142. As to the enforcement of the Sunday Trading Act 1994, and as to the general provisions relating to offences thereunder, see PARAS 1015–1017.

1011. Shops occupied by persons observing the Jewish Sabbath. A person of the Jewish religion[1] who is the occupier[2] of a large shop[3] may give to the local authority[4] for the area in which the shop is situated a notice signed by him stating:

(1)   that he is a person of the Jewish religion; and
(2)   that he intends to keep the shop closed for the serving of customers on the Jewish Sabbath[5].

Such a notice must be accompanied by a certificate signed by an authorised person[6] that the person giving the notice is a person of the Jewish religion[7]. If there is any change in the occupation of the shop in respect of which such a notice has effect, or in any partnership or among the directors of any company by which such a shop is occupied, the notice is to be taken to be cancelled at the end of the period of 14 days beginning with the day on which the change occurred, unless, during that period, or within such further time as the local authority may allow, a fresh notice is given[8] in respect of the shop[9]. A person who, in a notice or certificate given for the above purposes, makes a statement which is false in a material respect and which he knows to be false or does not believe to be true is liable on summary conviction to a fine[10].

Where such a notice is in force, the prohibition on the opening of a large shop on a Sunday does not apply[11].

Every local authority must keep a register containing particulars of the name, if any, and address of every shop in respect of which such a notice has effect[12]; and any register so kept must be open to inspection by members of the public at all reasonable times and may be kept by means of a computer[13].

1 These provisions also apply to persons who are members of any religious body regularly observing the Jewish Sabbath as they apply to persons of the Jewish religion; and accordingly

references to persons of the Jewish religion are to be construed as including any person who is a member of such a body, and in the application of those provisions to such persons, 'authorised person' means a minister of the religious body concerned: Sunday Trading Act 1994 s 1(1), Sch 2 para 9.

2   For these purposes, a shop occupied by a partnership or company is to be taken to be occupied by a person of the Jewish religion if, and only if, the majority of the partners or directors are persons of that religion: Sunday Trading Act 1994 Sch 2 para 8(2). Where the occupier of a shop is a partnership or company any notice under Sch 2 para 8(1) must be given by the majority of the partners or directors and, if not given by all of them, must specify the names of all of the other partners or directors: Sch 2 para 8(4)(a). For these purposes, 'shop' has the same meaning as in Sch 1 (see PARA 1007 note 3): Sch 2 para 8(12).

3   For these purposes, 'large shop' has the same meaning as in the Sunday Trading Act 1994 Sch 1 (see PARA 1007 note 3): Sch 2 para 8(12).

4   As to the meaning of 'local authority' see PARA 1007 note 2.

5   Sunday Trading Act 1994 Sch 2 paras 2(2)(b), 8(1).

6   For these purposes, 'authorised person', in relation to a notice under the Sunday Trading Act 1994 Sch 2 para 8(1), means:
    (1)   the minister of the synagogue of which the person giving the notice is a member;
    (2)   the secretary of that synagogue, within the meaning given in the Marriage Act 1949 Pt IV (ss 53–57) (see REGISTRATION CONCERNING THE INDIVIDUAL vol 88 (2012) PARA 224); or
    (3)   any other person nominated for these purposes by the President of the London Committee of Deputies of the British Jews (otherwise known as the Board of Deputies of British Jews): Sunday Trading Act 1994 Sch 2 para 8(12).

7   Sunday Trading Act 1994 Sch 2 para 8(3). Where the occupier of the shop is a partnership or company, a certificate under Sch 2 para 8(3) is required in relation to each of the persons by whom such a notice is given: Sch 2 para 8(4)(b).

8   Ie under the Sunday Trading Act 1994 Sch 2 para 8(1).

9   Sunday Trading Act 1994 Sch 2 para 8(7). Where a fresh notice is given under Sch 2 para 8(1) by reason of a change of the kind mentioned in Sch 2 para 8(7), the local authority may dispense with the certificate required by Sch 2 para 8(3) in the case of any person in respect of whom such a certificate has been provided in connection with a former notice in respect of that shop or any other shop in the area of the local authority: Sch 2 para 8(8). A notice given under Sch 2 para 8(1) in respect of any shop must be cancelled on application in that behalf being made to the local authority by the occupier of the shop: Sch 2 para 8(9).

10   The fine is one not exceeding level 5 on the standard scale: Sunday Trading Act 1994 Sch 2 para 8(10). As to the standard scale see SENTENCING AND DISPOSITION OF OFFENDERS vol 92 (2010) PARA 142. Where a person is convicted of such an offence, the local authority may cancel any notice under Sch 2 para 8(1) to which the offence relates: Sch 2 para 8(11).
     As to the enforcement of the Sunday Trading Act 1994, and as to the general provisions relating to offences thereunder, see PARAS 1015–1017.

11   See the Sunday Trading Act 1994 Sch 1 para 2(2)(b); and PARA 1007.

12   Sunday Trading Act 1994 Sch 2 para 8(5).

13   Sunday Trading Act 1994 Sch 2 para 8(6).

1012. Control of loading and unloading at large shops on Sunday morning.

A local authority[1] may by resolution designate its area as a loading control area with effect from a date specified in the resolution, which must be a date at least one month after the date on which the resolution is passed[2].

Where a large shop[3] which is permitted to be open on Sunday[4] and which the occupier opens on Sunday for the serving of retail customers is situated in an area so designated, the occupier must not load or unload, or permit any other person to load or unload, goods from a vehicle at the shop before 9:00 am on Sunday in connection with the trade or business carried on in the shop, unless the loading or unloading is carried on with the consent[5] of the local authority for the area in which the shop is situated and in accordance with any conditions[6] subject to which that consent is granted[7].

A person who contravenes the above provisions is liable on summary conviction to a fine[8].

1 As to the meaning of 'local authority' see PARA 1007 note 2.

2 Sunday Trading Act 1994 s 2(1). A local authority may by resolution revoke any designation so made: s 2(2). Before making or revoking any such designation, it is the duty of a local authority to consult persons appearing to it to be likely to be affected by the proposed designation or revocation, whether as the occupiers of shops or as local residents, or persons appearing to the local authority to represent such persons: s 2(3). Where a local authority makes or revokes such a designation, it must publish notice of the designation or revocation in such manner as it considers appropriate: s 2(4).

3 As to the meaning of 'large shop' see PARA 1007 note 3.

4 Ie by virtue of the Sunday Trading Act 1994 Sch 1 para 2(3): see PARA 1007.

5 An application for such consent must be made in writing and must contain such information as the local authority may reasonably require: Sunday Trading Act 1994 s 2(5), Sch 3 para 4. An applicant for such a consent must pay such reasonable fee in respect of his application as the local authority may determine: Sch 3 para 5. Where an application is duly made to the local authority for such a consent, the authority must grant the consent unless it is satisfied that the loading or unloading of goods from vehicles before 9:00 am on Sunday at the shop to which the application relates, in connection with the trade or business carried on at the shop, has caused, or would be likely to cause, undue annoyance to local residents: Sch 3 para 6(1). The authority must determine the application and notify the applicant in writing of its decision within the period of 21 days beginning with the day on which the application is received by the authority (Sch 3 para 6(2)); and, in a case where a consent is granted, such notification must specify the conditions, if any, subject to which the consent is granted (Sch 3 para 6(3)). Where a local authority grants such a consent, it may cause a notice giving details of that consent to be published in a local newspaper circulating in its area: Sch 3 para 8. Where the local authority is satisfied that the loading or unloading authorised by virtue of such a consent has caused undue annoyance to local residents, it may revoke the consent: Sch 3 para 7(b). The provisions of the Sunday Trading Act 1994 Sch 3 paras 3–8 apply as they apply in relation to consent under Sch 3, but as if the reference in Sch 3 para 6(1) to Sunday were a reference to Christmas Day, and the reference in Sch 3 para 7(a) to an offence under Sch 3 para 9 were a reference to an offence under the Christmas Day (Trading) Act 2004 s 2(3) (see PARA 1008 note 7): s 2(2).

6 Such a consent may be granted subject to such conditions as the local authority considers appropriate: Sunday Trading Act 1994 Sch 3 para 3(1). The local authority may at any time vary the conditions subject to which a consent is granted, and must give notice of the variation to the person to whom the consent was granted: Sch 3 para 3(2).

7 Sunday Trading Act 1994 Sch 3 paras 1, 2 (Sch 3 para 1 amended by SI 2004/470). The Sunday Trading Act 1994 Sch 3 para 2 does not apply where the Sunday is Christmas Day (loading and unloading at large shops on Christmas Day being regulated by the Christmas Day (Trading) Act 2004 s 2: see PARA 1008): Sunday Trading Act 1994 Sch 3 para 10 (added by the Christmas Day (Trading) Act 2004 s 4(1), (3)).

8 The fine is one not exceeding level 3 on the standard scale: Sunday Trading Act 1994 Sch 3 para 9. As to the standard scale see SENTENCING AND DISPOSITION OF OFFENDERS vol 92 (2010) PARA 142. Where the occupier of a shop in respect of which such a consent is granted is convicted of an offence under Sch 3 para 9 by reason of his failure to comply with the conditions subject to which the consent was granted, the local authority may revoke the consent: Sch 3 para 7(a). As to the enforcement of the Sunday Trading Act 1994, and as to the general provisions relating to offences thereunder, see PARAS 1015–1017.

1013. Leases entered into before 26 August 1994. Where any lease or agreement, however worded, entered into before 26 August 1994[1] has the effect of requiring the occupier of a shop[2] to keep the shop open for the serving of retail customers[3]:

(1) during normal business hours; or

(2) during hours to be determined otherwise than by or with the consent of the occupier,

that lease or agreement is not to be regarded as requiring, or as enabling any other person to require, the occupier to open the shop on Sunday for the serving of retail customers[4].

1 Ie the date on which the Sunday Trading Act 1994 s 3 came into force. Sections 1, 6–8, 9(1), (3), (4) came into force on 5 July 1994 (ie the date of Royal Assent). Schedules 1, 2 were brought into force on 26 August 1994: ss 1(1), 9(3); Sunday Trading Act 1994 Appointed Day

Order 1994, SI 1994/1841, art 2. The remaining provisions of the Sunday Trading Act 1994 also came into force on 26 August 1994: Sunday Trading Act 1994 s 9(3); Sunday Trading Act 1994 Appointed Day Order 1994, SI 1994/1841, art 2.

2 For these purposes, 'shop' has the same meaning as in the Sunday Trading Act 1994 s 1(1), Sch 1 (see PARA 1007 note 3): s 3(3).

3 For these purposes, 'retail customer' has the same meaning as in the Sunday Trading Act 1994 Sch 1 (see PARA 1007 note 4): s 3(3).

4 Sunday Trading Act 1994 s 3(1). Section 3(1) does not affect any lease or agreement to the extent that it relates specifically to Sunday and would otherwise have the effect of requiring Sunday trading of a kind which before 26 August 1994 would have been lawful by virtue of any provision of the Shops Act 1950 Pt IV (ss 47–67) (repealed): Sunday Trading Act 1994 s 3(2)(a). Nor does s 3(1) affect any lease or agreement to the extent that it is varied by agreement after 26 August 1994: s 3(2)(b).

(ii) Rights of Shop Workers

1014. Statutory protection for shop workers in relation to Sunday working. Special statutory protection is given[1] in relation to Sunday working for shop and betting workers.

Workers qualifying as protected shop workers and protected betting workers, that is to say workers already in employment on 25 August 1994 as shop workers or, as the case may be, on 2 January 1995 as betting workers, or whose contracts do not require Sunday working[2], are protected from being required to work on Sundays[3]. In addition, all shop or betting workers are given an option not to work on Sundays[4].

Protected or opted-out shop or betting workers have a right not to be discriminated against for refusal to work on Sundays[5]; and the dismissal of such a worker for such a refusal is automatically unfair[6], as is any later selection for redundancy on that ground[7].

1 Ie by the Employment Rights Act 1996 Pt IV (ss 36–43): see EMPLOYMENT vol 39 (2014) PARA 298 et seq.

2 See EMPLOYMENT vol 39 (2014) PARA 298.

3 See EMPLOYMENT vol 39 (2014) PARA 299.

4 See EMPLOYMENT vol 39 (2014) PARA 300.

5 See the Employment Rights Act 1996 s 45; and EMPLOYMENT vol 40 (2014) PARA 545.

6 See the Employment Rights Act 1996 s 101; and EMPLOYMENT vol 41 (2014) PARA 743.

7 See the Employment Rights Act 1996 s 105(1), (4); and EMPLOYMENT vol 41 (2014) PARA 738. In addition, dismissal for asserting statutory rights by such a worker is automatically unfair: see s 104; and EMPLOYMENT vol 41 (2014) PARA 748.

(iii) Enforcement of Sunday Trading Law

1015. Appointment of inspectors to check compliance with Sunday trading law. It is the duty of every local authority[1] to enforce within its area the provisions[2] of the Sunday Trading Act 1994[3]. For the purposes of such duties, it is the duty of every local authority to appoint inspectors[4]. An inspector appointed by a local authority has a right, on producing, if so required, some duly authenticated document showing his authority, at all reasonable hours:

(1)   to enter any premises within the area of the local authority, with or without a constable, for the purpose of ascertaining whether there is or has been any contravention of certain provisions[5] of the 1994 Act;

(2)   to require the production of, inspect and take copies of any records, in whatever form they are held, relating to any business carried on on the premises which appear to him to be relevant for the purposes of head (1) above;

(3)   where those records are kept by means of a computer, to require the records to be produced in a form in which they may be taken away; and

(4)   to take such measurements and photographs as he considers necessary for the purposes of head (1) above[6].

Any person who intentionally obstructs an inspector so appointed acting in the execution of his duty is liable on summary conviction to a fine[7].

1   As to the meaning of 'local authority' see PARA 1007 note 2.
2   Ie the provisions of the Sunday Trading Act 1994 ss 1(1), 2(5), Sch 1 (see PARAS 1007–1010), Sch 2 Pt II (paras 8–10) (see PARA 1011) and Sch 3 (see PARA 1012).
3   Sunday Trading Act 1994 Sch 2 para 1.
4   Sunday Trading Act 1994 Sch 2 para 2.
5   Ie the Sunday Trading Act 1994 Schs 1, 3.
6   Sunday Trading Act 1994 Sch 2 para 3.
7   Ie a fine not exceeding level 3 on the standard scale: Sunday Trading Act 1994 Sch 2 para 4. As to the standard scale see SENTENCING AND DISPOSITION OF OFFENDERS vol 92 (2010) PARA 142.

1016.   Offences under the Sunday Trading Act 1994.   Where the commission by any person of any offence under the Sunday Trading Act 1994[1] is due to the act or default of some other person, that other person is guilty of the offence, and a person may be charged with, and convicted of, the offence on that basis, whether or not proceedings are taken against the first-mentioned person[2].

Where an offence committed by a body corporate is proved to have been committed with the consent or connivance of, or to be attributable to any neglect on the part of, any director, manager, secretary or other similar officer of the body corporate, or any person who was purporting to act in any such capacity, he, as well as the body corporate, is guilty of the offence and is liable to be proceeded against and punished accordingly[3].

It is a defence for the person charged with an offence to prove that he took all reasonable precautions and exercised all due diligence to avoid the commission of the offence by himself or by a person under his control[4].

1   The specific offences created by the Sunday Trading Act 1994 are considered in their particular contexts: see PARA 1007 et seq.
2   Sunday Trading Act 1994 Sch 2 para 5.
3   Sunday Trading Act 1994 Sch 2 para 6(1). Where the affairs of a body corporate are managed by its members, Sch 2 para 6(1) applies in relation to the acts and defaults of a member in connection with his functions of management as if he were a director of the body corporate: Sch 2 para 6(2).
4   Sunday Trading Act 1994 Sch 2 para 7(1). If in any case the defence provided by Sch 2 para 7(1) involves the allegation that the commission of the offence was due to the act or default of another person, the person charged is not, without leave of the court, entitled to rely on that defence unless, at least seven clear days before the hearing, he has served on the prosecutor a notice in writing giving such information identifying or assisting in the identification of that other person as was then in his possession: Sch 2 para 7(2).

1017.   Other powers of local authorities to enforce Sunday trading law.
Although given specific powers under the Sunday Trading Act 1994 to enforce the restrictions on Sunday opening[1], a local authority may also use its general power to bring civil proceedings in its own name[2] and apply for an injunction to restrain breaches of the legislation by a particular offender, especially where that offender is deliberately and flagrantly flouting the law and intends to carry on doing so[3].

1   See PARA 1007 et seq.
2   See the Local Government Act 1972 s 222(1); and LOCAL GOVERNMENT vol 69 (2009) PARA 573.

3   *Stoke-on-Trent City Council v B & Q (Retail) Ltd* [1984] AC 754, [1984] 2 All ER 332, HL.
    Although the cases cited here were decided under the Shops Act 1950 (repealed), the principles
    should apply equally to the Sunday Trading Act 1994. There is no need for the council to have
    exhausted its specific criminal powers first: *Runnymede Borough Council v Ball* [1986] 1 All ER
    629, [1986] 1 WLR 353, CA (a planning case). Such an action is not defeated by the defendant's
    claim to have a defence to any criminal proceedings since that goes, not to jurisdiction, but to
    the discretion whether to grant the injunction; further, the court has a discretion to grant such an
    interlocutory injunction without requiring the council to give an undertaking in damages:
    Kirklees Metropolitan Borough Council v Wickes Building Supplies Ltd [1993] AC 227, [1992]
    3 All ER 717, HL. This matter used to be of great significance under the Shops Act 1950 Pt IV
    (ss 47–67) (repealed) governing Sunday trading which was subject to widespread breach and
    was only backed specifically by criminal fines of level 4 on the standard scale, insufficient to
    deter breaches, given the profits to be made. There should now be less likelihood of such cases
    arising given that there is now a more liberal regime on Sunday opening, and that the maximum
    penalty for breach of the current regime is raised (see PARA 1007). As to the standard scale see
    SENTENCING AND DISPOSITION OF OFFENDERS vol 92 (2010) PARA 142.

4. PROMOTION OF TRADE AND ASSISTANCE TO INDUSTRY

(1) PROMOTION OF TRADE

(i) Export and Investment Guarantees

1018. The provision of financial facilities and assistance. The Secretary of State[1] may make arrangements[2] to provide financial facilities and assistance[3] in connection with supplies by persons carrying on business[4] in the United Kingdom[5] of goods or services to persons carrying on business outside the United Kingdom[6], and to make arrangements for the purpose of rendering economic assistance to countries outside the United Kingdom[7]. He may also make arrangements to facilitate the performance of, or to reduce or avoid losses arising under, obligations created or arising in connection with matters as to which he has exercised his powers[8].

1   As to the Secretary of State see PARA 902.
2   Transactions entered into in pursuance of such arrangements, or arrangements of the kinds described in PARAS 1019–1020, may be on such terms as the Secretary of State considers appropriate: Export and Investment Guarantees Act 1991 s 4(1).
3   Such facilities and assistance may be provided in any form, including guarantees, insurance, grants or loans: Export and Investment Guarantees Act 1991 s 1(4). A guarantee includes an indemnity: s 4(3)(b).
4   'Business' includes a profession; a reference to persons 'carrying on business' in relation to things done outside the United Kingdom includes persons carrying on any other activities; and a reference to things done in or outside the United Kingdom is to things done wholly or partly in or, as the case may be, outside the United Kingdom: Export and Investment Guarantees Act 1991 s 4(3)(a), (c), (d). As to the meaning of 'carry on business' see COMPETITION vol 18 (2009) PARAS 370–372.
5   References to the United Kingdom include references to the Isle of Man and the Channel Islands: Export and Investment Guarantees Act 1991 s 4(4). As to the meaning of 'United Kingdom' generally see PARA 906 note 7.
6   Export and Investment Guarantees Act 1991 s 1(1) (substituted by the Industry and Exports (Financial Support) Act 2009 s 2(1)). Such arrangements may be made in connection with goods or services supplied before the arrangements are made or in connection with goods or services which are to be, or which may be, supplied: Export and Investment Guarantees Act 1991 s 1(1A) (added by the Industry and Exports (Financial Support) Act 2009 s 2(1)).
7   Export and Investment Guarantees Act 1991 s 1(2). All the functions of the Secretary of State under ss 1–7, except the power to make orders under ss 5–6, must be exercised and performed through the Export Credits Guarantee Department, which continues to be a department of the Secretary of State: s 13(1). The powers of the Secretary of State under ss 1–3 are exercisable only with the consent of the Treasury; such consent may be given in relation to particular cases or such description of cases as may be specified in the consent: s 4(2). As to the Treasury see CONSTITUTIONAL AND ADMINISTRATIVE LAW vol 20 (2014) PARA 262 et seq.
8   Export and Investment Guarantees Act 1991 s 1(3).

1019. Insurance in respect of overseas losses. The Secretary of State[1] may make arrangements[2] for insuring any person carrying on business in the United Kingdom[3] against risks of losses resulting directly or indirectly from war, expropriation, restrictions on remittances and other similar events, in connection with:

(1)   any investment of resources by the insured in enterprises carried on outside the United Kingdom; or

(2)   guarantees given by the insured in respect of any investment of resources by others in such enterprises in which the insured has any interest[4].

Arrangements may also be made for insuring persons providing such insurance[5].

1 As to the Secretary of State see PARA 902.
2 As to such arrangements see PARA 1018 note 2.
3 As to references to persons carrying on business in the United Kingdom see PARA 1018 note 4.
4 Export and Investment Guarantees Act 1991 s 2(1). References to a person carrying on business in the United Kingdom and to the insured include any company controlled directly or indirectly by him: s 2(3). See also INSURANCE vol 60 (2011) PARA 757. As to the exercise of this power by the Secretary of State see PARA 1018 note 7.
5 Export and Investment Guarantees Act 1991 s 2(2).

1020.   Management of the Export Credits Guarantee Department portfolio.
The Secretary of State[1] may make any arrangements[2] which, in his opinion, are in the interests of the proper financial management of the Export Credits Guarantee Department portfolio (the 'ECGD portfolio')[3]. In pursuance of such arrangements, the Secretary of State may enter into any form of transaction, including lending, and providing and taking out insurance and guarantees[4]. In pursuance of such an arrangement, however, he may not enter into a transaction for the purpose of borrowing money, although he is not precluded from entering into a transaction by reason of its involving borrowing[5].

1 As to the Secretary of State see PARA 902.
2 Such arrangements may be made in anticipation of further rights being acquired or liabilities beings incurred by the Secretary of State: Export and Investment Guarantees Act 1991 s 3(5). As to such arrangements see further PARA 918 note 2.
3 Export and Investment Guarantees Act 1991 s 3(1), which refers simply to 'the ECGD portfolio'. The 'ECGD portfolio' means the rights and liabilities to which the Secretary of State is entitled or subject by virtue of the exercise of his powers under the Export and Investment Guarantees Act 1991 or the old law or in consequence at arrangements made in the exercise of those powers: s 3(6). The 'old law' means the Export and Investment Guarantees Act 1978 (repealed) and any earlier enactment from which any provision of that Act was derived: Export and Investment Guarantees Act 1991 s 15(2).
4 Export and Investment Guarantees Act 1991 s 3(2). The Secretary of State may alter arrangements made under ss 1, 2, (see PARAS 1018–1019) or under the old law (see note 3) or make new or further arrangements: s 3(4). The Secretary of State may certify that any transaction he has entered into or is entering into has been or, as the case may be, is entered into in the exercise of the powers conferred by s 3 and such a certificate is conclusive evidence of the matters stated in it: s 3(7). As to the exercise of these powers by the Secretary of State see PARA 1018 note 7. As to the meaning of 'guarantee' see PARA 1018 note 3.
5 Export and Investment Guarantees Act 1991 s 3(3).

1021.   Information relating to credit and investment insurance.
The Secretary of State[1] may provide, and charge for:
   (1)   information relating to credit or investment insurance;
   (2)   services ancillary to the provision of such credit and insurance; and
   (3)   such other goods and services as may be specified by order[2].

1 As to the Secretary of State see PARA 902.
2 Export and Investment Guarantees Act 1991 s 5(1). The power to make an order is exercisable only with the consent of the Treasury: s 5(2). The power to make an order under the Export and Investment Guarantees Act 1991 s 5 or s 6 (see PARA 1022) is exercisable by statutory instrument, and no such order may be made unless a draft of it has been laid before and approved by resolution of the House of Commons: s 15(3). At the date at which this volume states the law, no such order had been made. As to the Treasury see CONSTITUTIONAL AND ADMINISTRATIVE LAW vol 20 (2014) PARA 262 et seq. As to the laying of drafts before the House of Commons see STATUTES AND LEGISLATIVE PROCESS vol 96 (2012) PARA 1045 et seq.

1022.   Limits to Secretary of State's exports and insurance commitments.
The aggregate amount of the Secretary of State's[1] commitments[2] at any time under

arrangements relating to exports and insurance[3] must not exceed £35,000 million in the case of commitments in sterling, and 30,000 million special drawing rights[4] in the case of foreign currency commitments[5]. The aggregate amount of commitments in connection with the management of the ECGD portfolio[6] must not exceed £15,000 million in the case of commitments in sterling, and 10,000 million special drawing rights in the case of foreign currency commitments[7]. The Secretary of State may by order, with the consent of the Treasury, increase or further increase these limits[8], but may not exercise this power in respect of any limit on more than three occasions[9].

1   As to the Secretary of State see PARA 902.
2   The Secretary of State's commitments under any arrangements are his rights and liabilities relating to those arrangements: Export and Investment Guarantees Act 1991 s 6(5)(a). The amount of any commitments must be ascertained in accordance with the principles determined from time to time by the Secretary of State with the consent of the Treasury: s 6(5)(b). As to the Treasury see CONSTITUTIONAL AND ADMINISTRATIVE LAW vol 20 (2014) PARA 262 et seq.
3   Ie arrangements under the Export and Investment Guarantees Act 1991 ss 1, 2 other than arrangements for giving grants under s 1(3) (see PARA 1018), and arrangements under the old law (as to which see PARA 1020 note 3) other than arrangements for giving grants: s 6(2).
4   The figure was raised to 30,000 million by the Export and Investment Guarantees (Limit on Foreign Currency Commitments) Order 2000, SI 2000/2087. The accounts of the International Monetary Fund have been denominated in special drawing rights since 1972 following the enactment of the International Monetary Fund Act 1968 (repealed). The text of the amendments made to the Articles of Agreement of the Fund relating to special drawing rights is set out in Cmnd 3662. As to the International Monetary Fund see FINANCIAL SERVICES AND INSTITUTIONS vol 49 (2008) PARA 1391.
5   Export and Investment Guarantees Act 1991 s 6(1)(a), (b). 'Foreign currency' means any currency other than sterling, including special drawing rights and any other units of account defined by reference to more than one currency: s 6(5)(c). Whether any commitments are in sterling or foreign currency is to be determined by reference to the currency in which the amount of the commitment is measured, rather than the currency of payment: s 6(5)(d). The equivalent in special drawing rights of the amount of any commitment in foreign currency must be ascertained at intervals determined from time to time by the Secretary of State with the consent of the Treasury, and in accordance with principles so determined: s 6(5)(e). A determination under s 6(5)(e) may provide for leaving out of account for the purposes of the limit in s 6(1)(b) or s 6(3)(b) (see text and note 7) any amount by which the limit would otherwise be exceeded to the extent that the amount is attributable to: (1) a revaluation under s 6(5)(e) of commitments; or (2) the fulfilment of an undertaking which, if fulfilled when it was given, would not have caused the limit to be exceeded: s 6(6).
6   Ie under the Export and Investment Guarantees Act 1991 s 3: see PARA 1020. As to the ECGD portfolio see PARA 1020 note 3.
7   Export and Investment Guarantees Act 1991 s 6(3)(a), (b).
8   Export and Investment Guarantees Act 1991 s 6(4), (7). See note 4. The limits in s 6(1) (see text and notes 1–5) may be increased by a sum not exceeding £5,000 million or 5,000 million special drawing rights, and in s 6(3) (see text and notes 6–7) by a sum not exceeding £3,000 million or 2,000 million special drawing rights: s 6(4)(a), (b). No such order may be made unless a draft of it has been laid before and approved by resolution of the House of Commons: s 15(3).
9   Export and Investment Guarantees Act 1991 s 6(4).

1023.   Secretary of State's annual report on his functions under the Export and Investment Guarantees Act 1991.   The Secretary of State[1] must prepare and lay before Parliament an annual report on the discharge of his functions under the Export and Investment Guarantees Act 1991[2]. A separate return must be prepared as soon as is practicable after 31 March each year showing the aggregate amounts of the commitments in sterling and in foreign currency on that date for the purposes of the relevant statutory limits[3]. That return must also be laid before Parliament[4]. Any such return must also give such further information as to the amounts of the commitments for the purposes of those limits as the Secretary of State may determine for that return[5].

1   As to the Secretary of State see PARA 802.
2   Ie his functions under the Export and Investment Guarantees Act 1991 ss 1–5 (see PARA 1018 et seq): s 7(1), (5).
3   Export and Investment Guarantees Act 1991 s 7(2). The limits referred to are those in s 6(1), (3): see PARA 1022.
4   Export and Investment Guarantees Act 1991 s 7(5).
5   Export and Investment Guarantees Act 1991 s 7(3).

(ii) Transfer or Delegation of Export Credits Guarantee Department Functions

1024.   Functions of the Secretary of State under the Export and Investment Guarantees Act 1991 Pt I. All the functions of the Secretary of State[1] under Part I of the Export and Investment Guarantees Act 1991[2] are exercised and performed through the Export Credits Guarantee Department, which is a department of the Secretary of State[3]. The Secretary of State may, however, make arrangements for certain functions[4] to be exercised on his behalf by any transferee[5] or any other person, instead of through the Export Credits Guarantees Department, on such terms and conditions as he may determine[6].

1   As to the Secretary of State see PARA 902.
2   Ie the Export and Investment Guarantees Act 1991 Pt I (ss 1–7). However, this does not apply to the power to make orders under s 5 or s 6 (see PARAS 1021–1022): s 13(1).
    Any sums required by the Secretary of State for making payments or for defraying his administrative expenses under the Act are paid out of money provided by Parliament, and any sums received by him by virtue of the Act must be paid into the Consolidated Fund: s 14(1). If any sum required by the Secretary of State for fulfilling his liabilities is not so provided, it must be charged on and paid out of the Consolidated Fund: s 14(2). As to the Consolidated Fund see CONSTITUTIONAL AND ADMINISTRATIVE LAW vol 20 (2014) PARA 480 et seq; and PARLIAMENT vol 78 (2010) PARA 1028 et seq.
3   Export and Investment Guarantees Act 1991 s 13(1).
4   Ie the functions to which the Export and Investment Guarantees Act 1991 s 12 applies, namely the Secretary of State's power to make arrangements under s 1 (see PARA 1018) and any of his functions under such arrangements, or arrangements under the old law, including, so far as they relate to any such arrangements, arrangements made by virtue of s 3(4): s 12(2). As to the meaning of 'old law' see PARA 1020 note 3.
5   As to the meaning of 'transferee' see PARA 1025 note 4.
6   Export and Investment Guarantees Act 1991 s 12(1). Section 12 does not affect any requirement for the consent of the Treasury: s 12(3). As to the transfer of functions see PARA 1025. As to the Treasury see CONSTITUTIONAL AND ADMINISTRATIVE LAW vol 20 (2014) PARA 262 et seq.

1025.   Provision for transfer of functions of the Export Credits Guarantee Department. The Secretary of State[1] may make a scheme or schemes for the transfer to any person or persons of such property, rights and liabilities as are specified in or determined in accordance with the scheme[2]. Such a scheme may apply to property wherever situated and to property, rights and liabilities whether or not otherwise capable of being transferred or assigned by the Secretary of State or Her Majesty[3]. A scheme comes into force on a day specified in or determined under the scheme, and the property, rights and liabilities are transferred and vest on that day[4].

No scheme may provide for the transfer of any rights or liabilities relating to a person's employment but specified regulations[5] apply to the transfer of property, rights or liabilities by virtue of such a scheme[6]. Where, by operation of the regulations in relation to a transfer of property, rights or liabilities a person ceases to be employed in the civil service and becomes employed by a transferee, he will not be treated as having retired on redundancy for the purposes of a specified superannuation scheme[7] and his ceasing to be employed in the civil service is not an occasion of redundancy for the purposes of the agreed redundancy procedures of the civil service[8].

1 As to the Secretary of State see PARA 902.
2 Export and Investment Guarantees Act 1991 s 8(1). See PARA 1024. The property, rights and liabilities are those:
   (1) to which the Secretary of State, or, in the case of copyright, Her Majesty, is entitled or subject immediately before the day on which the scheme comes into force (s 8(1)(a)); and
   (2) which then subsisted for the purposes of or in connection with or are otherwise attributable to the exercise of functions under Pt I (ss 1–7) or the old law (as to which see PARA 1020 note 3) (s 8(1)(b)).
   Any property, rights or liabilities are to be taken to fall within s 8(1)(b) if the Secretary of State so certifies: s 8(2).
3 Export and Investment Guarantees Act 1991 s 8(3). The scheme may contain such supplementary, incidental, transitional or consequential provisions as appear to the Secretary of State to be appropriate: s 8(5).
4 Export and Investment Guarantees Act 1991 s 8(4). A certificate by the Secretary of State that anything specified has vested on any day in any person by virtue of a scheme is conclusive for all purposes: s 8(6), Schedule para 1.
      Any agreement made, transaction effected or other thing (not contained in an enactment) which:
   (1) has been made, effected or done by or in relation to the Secretary of State;
   (2) relates to any property, rights or liability transferred under a scheme; and
   (3) is in force or effective immediately before the day on which the scheme comes into force,
   has effect on or after that day as if made, effected or done by the transferee: Schedule para 2(1), (2). References to the Secretary of State relating to or affecting any property, right or liability of the Secretary of State, contained in specified descriptions of documents, are taken on or after that day to refer to the transferee: Schedule para 2(3). 'Transferee' means any person to whom anything is transferred by virtue of a scheme under s 8: s 8(7).
5 Ie the Transfer of Undertakings (Protection of Employment) Regulations 2006, SI 2006/246: see EMPLOYMENT vol 39 (2014) PARA 111 et seq; and EMPLOYMENT 41 (2009) PARAS 1140, 1162 et seq.
6 Export and Investment Guarantees Act 1991 s 9(1) (amended by SI 2006/246). The regulations apply whether or not the transfer would, apart from the Export and Investment Guarantees Act 1991 s 9(1), be a relevant transfer for the purposes of those regulations: s 9(1).
7 Ie any scheme under the Superannuation Act 1972 s 1: see PERSONAL AND OCCUPATIONAL PENSIONS vol 80 (2013) PARA 321.
8 Export and Investment Guarantees Act 1991 s 9(2).

1026. Vehicle companies. In connection with the transfer or delegation of Export Credits Guarantee Department ('ECGD') functions, the Secretary of State[1] may, with the consent of the Treasury[2]:

(1) subscribe for or otherwise acquire shares in or securities of a vehicle company[3] or acquire rights so to subscribe[4];

(2) by direction to a company formed or acquired for the purpose of becoming a transferee, require it, in consequence of the transfer by a scheme of property, rights or liabilities[5], to issue to him or to some other person specified in the direction such shares or securities as may so be specified[6];

(3) from time to time by direction to a vehicle company require it to issue to him or some other person specified in the direction such shares or securities as may be specified[7]; or

(4) make loans to a vehicle company on such terms and conditions as he may determine[8].

He may not subscribe for or otherwise acquire shares in or securities of a vehicle company, or acquire rights so to subscribe, unless all relevant shares[9] are to be held by or on behalf of the Crown[10], or at any time give a direction or make a loan to a vehicle company unless all relevant shares are then held by or on behalf of the Crown[11]. A scheme of transfer of property, rights and liabilities may, as between any vehicle companies or between a vehicle company and the Secretary of State, confer or impose rights and liabilities in connection with any of the matters as to which the Secretary of State may exercise his statutory powers[12].

1   As to the Secretary of State see PARA 902. As to the transfer of ECGD functions see PARA 1025.
2   Export and Investment Guarantees Act 1991 s 10(7). As to the Treasury see CONSTITUTIONAL AND ADMINISTRATIVE LAW vol 20 (2014) PARA 262 et seq.
3   'Vehicle company' means a company formed or acquired for the purpose of becoming a transferor or holding shares in a company formed or acquired for that purpose: Export and Investment Guarantees Act 1991 s 10(1). As to the meaning of 'transferee' see PARA 1025 note 4.
4   Export and Investment Guarantees Act 1991 s 10(2)(a). The Secretary of State may not dispose of any such shares or securities without the consent of the Treasury: s 10(7).
5   Ie under a scheme made under the Export and Investment Guarantees Act 1991 s 8: see PARA 1025.
6   Export and Investment Guarantees Act 1991 s 10(2)(b). A direction under s 10(2)(b) or s 10(2)(c) may require any shares to which it relates to be issued as fully or partly paid up: s 10(3).
7   Export and Investment Guarantees Act 1991 s 10(2)(c); and see note 6.
8   Export and Investment Guarantees Act 1991 s 10(2)(d).
9   'Relevant shares' means the issued shares of a vehicle company or, if it is a subsidiary of another vehicle company, the issued shares of that other company: Export and Investment Guarantees Act 1991 s 10(5)(b).
10   Shares are held by or on behalf of the Crown where the Crown or any person acting on its behalf has a legal interest in them: Export and Investment Guarantees Act 1991 s 10(5)(a).
11   Export and Investment Guarantees Act 1991 s 10(4).
12   Export and Investment Guarantees Act 1991 s 10(6).

1027. Insurance of Secretary of State against losses. In connection with the transfer or delegation of Export Credits Guarantee Department ('ECGD') functions, the Secretary of State[1] may make arrangements with any transferee[2] under which the transferee insures the Secretary of State against risks of losses arising in consequence of arrangements made, before the date on which any scheme of transfer comes into force[3], under the Export and Investment Guarantees Act 1991[4] or under the old law[5].

The Secretary of State must from time to time determine, in relation to such classes of risk determined by him as might be insured by him[6], whether it is expedient in the national interest for him to exercise his powers to make arrangements for reinsuring persons providing insurance for risks of that class[7].

1   As to the Secretary of State see PARA 902. As to the transfer of ECGD functions see PARA 1025.
2   As to the meaning of 'transferee' see PARA 1025 note 4.
3   Ie a scheme under the Export and Investment Guarantees Act 1991 s 8: see PARA 1025.
4   Ie under the Export and Investment Guarantees Act 1991 Pt I (ss 1–7).
5   Export and Investment Guarantees Act 1991 s 11(1). Section 11 is without prejudice to any power of the Secretary of State under Pt I: s 11(3). As to the meaning of 'old law' see PARA 1020 note 3.
6   Ie insured by the Secretary of State under the Export and Investment Guarantees Act 1991 s 1 (see PARA 1018).
7   Export and Investment Guarantees Act 1991 s 11(2). The reference to the Secretary of State's power is to his power under s 1: s 11(2). See also note 5. In exercising his duty under s 11(2) the Secretary of State must consult the Export Guarantees Advisory Council: s 13(4). The Export Guarantees Advisory Council is established under s 13(2), and its function is to give to the Secretary of State, at his request, advice in respect of any matter relating to the exercise of his functions under the Act: s 13(3).

(iii) Development of Tourism

1028. The British Tourist Authority and other tourist bodies. For the purpose of promoting the development of tourism to and within Great Britain[1], four tourist boards[2] were established by the Development of Tourism Act 1969[3]. These bodies have subsequently been reduced to three[4]: the British Tourist Authority ('Visit Britain')[5]; the English Tourist Board ('Visit England')[6]; and Visit Scotland[7]. Each tourist board is a body corporate having perpetual succession and a common seal[8]. Tourism in Wales is promoted by Visit Wales, the Welsh Assembly Government's tourism team within the Department for Heritage[9].

The Greater London Authority is under a duty to promote tourism in Greater London[10].

1 As to the meaning of 'Great Britain' see PARA 906 note 7.
2 'Tourist board' means any body established by the Development of Tourism Act 1969 s 1, namely the three bodies mentioned in the text: s 1(6).
3 See the Development of Tourism Act 1969 s 1(1) (as originally enacted). The four bodies thereby established were the British Tourist Authority, the English Tourist Board, the Scottish Tourist Board and the Wales Tourist Board (as to which see note 9).
4 See the Development of Tourism Act 1969 s 1(1) (amended by the Tourist Boards (Scotland) Act 2006 s 1(2); and by SI 2005/3225).
5 Development of Tourism Act 1969 s 1(1). The British Tourist Authority consists of a chairman and not more than five other members appointed by the Secretary of State, together with the chairmen of the other two tourist boards and a person appointed by the Welsh Ministers: s 1(2) (amended by the Tourist Boards (Scotland) Act 2006 s 1(2); and by SI 2005/3225; and by virtue of the Government of Wales Act 2006 s 162, Sch 11 para 32). The Secretary of State here concerned is the Secretary of State for Culture, Media and Sport. As to the Secretary of State generally see PARA 902 but note that the powers of the Secretary of State for Trade and Industry under this Act were transferred to the Secretary of State for Employment (Transfer of Functions (Tourism and Small Businesses) Order 1985, SI 1985/1778) and then to the Secretary of State for National Heritage (Transfer of Functions (National Heritage) Order 1992, SI 1992/1311). The Department of National Heritage was renamed the Department for Culture, Media and Sport by the Secretary of State for Culture, Media and Sport Order 1997, SI 1997/1744; and the Secretary of State is now styled accordingly.
   As to the appointment and resignation of members of tourist boards and the declaration of offices to be vacant see the Development of Tourism Act 1969 s 1(5), Sch 1 paras 3–5, 18. As to their remuneration and pensions see Sch 1 paras 6–9, 17. Members receiving remuneration are disqualified for membership of the House of Commons: see the House of Commons Disqualification Act 1975 s 1(1)(f), Sch 1 Pt III (amended by SI 2005/3225; and SI 2007/1103); and PARLIAMENT vol 78 (2010) PARA 908.
6 Development of Tourism Act 1969 s 1(1). The English Tourist Board consists of a chairman and not more than six other members appointed by the Secretary of State: s 1(3) (amended by SI 2005/3225). As to the Secretary of State see note 5.
7 Development of Tourism Act 1969 s 1(1) (amended by the Tourist Boards (Scotland) Act 2006 s 1(2)). Visit Scotland consists of a chairman and not more than 11 other members appointed by the Secretary of State for Scotland: Development of Tourism Act 1969 s 1(3) (amended by the Tourist Boards (Scotland) Act 2006 ss 1(2), 2).
8 Development of Tourism Act 1969 Sch 1 paras 1, 15, 16. As to the proceedings of a board see Sch 1 paras 12–14. As to staff see Sch 1 paras 10, 11. A board is not regarded as the servant or agent of the Crown, and is not exempt from taxes etc: see Sch 1 para 2.
9 The functions of the Wales Tourist Board were transferred to the National Assembly for Wales and subsequently to the Welsh Ministers: see the Wales Tourist Board (Transfer of Functions to the National Assembly for Wales and Abolition) Order 2005, SI 2005/3225; and the Government of Wales Act 2006 s 162, Sch 11 para 30. Today, the Welsh Assembly Government's tourism team, within the Department for Heritage, is Visit Wales. As to the National Assembly for Wales and the Welsh Ministers see CONSTITUTIONAL AND ADMINISTRATIVE LAW vol 20 (2014) PARA 373 et seq.
10 See the Greater London Authority Act 1999 s 378; and LONDON GOVERNMENT vol 71 (2013) PARA 282. The Greater London Authority ('GLA') has a duty to advise certain bodies on matters relating to tourism: see the Greater London Authority Act 1999 s 379; and LONDON

GOVERNMENT vol 71 (2013) PARA 282. The GLA's functions under these provisions may be delegated: see s 380. Grants may be paid by the Secretary of State to the Authority for its tourism functions: see s 381; and LONDON GOVERNMENT vol 71 (2013) PARA 283. As to the GLA's functions relating to culture and tourism see further LONDON GOVERNMENT vol 71 (2013) PARA 282 et seq.

1029. Functions of tourist boards. The function of the British Tourist Authority[1] is to encourage people to visit Great Britain[2], to encourage people living in Great Britain to take their holidays there, and to encourage the provision and improvement of tourist amenities and facilities[3] in Great Britain[4]. The other tourist boards[5] and the Welsh Ministers[6] have the same functions as respects their respective countries[7].

The tourist boards (and the Welsh Ministers in relation to Wales) have power to do anything for the purpose of discharging these functions or anything which is incidental or conducive to their discharge[8] and in particular power to:

(1) promote or undertake publicity in any form[9];

(2) provide advisory and information services[10];

(3) promote or undertake research[11];

(4) establish committees to advise them in the performance of their functions[12]; and

(5) contribute to or reimburse expenditure incurred by any other person or organisation carrying on the activities listed in heads (1) to (3) above[13].

None of the tourist boards except the British Tourist Authority has power, otherwise than with the agreement of that Authority, to carry on any activities outside the United Kingdom[14] for the purpose of encouraging people to visit Great Britain or any part of it[15]. Except as otherwise provided[16], none of the tourist boards has power to give financial assistance for the carrying out of, or itself to carry out, any project for providing or improving tourist amenities or facilities in Great Britain[17]. Likewise, except as otherwise provided[18], the Welsh Ministers have no such power under the Development of Tourism Act 1969[19]. Notwithstanding this provision, the Welsh Ministers may carry on activities outside the United Kingdom for the purpose of encouraging people to visit Wales[20].

In discharging their functions, the English Tourist Board, Visit Scotland and the Welsh Ministers must have regard to the desirability of fostering and, in appropriate cases, co-operating with organisations discharging functions corresponding to their functions in relation to particular areas within the countries for which they are respectively responsible[21]. Each tourist board and the Welsh Ministers must also have regard to the desirability of undertaking appropriate consultation with the other tourist boards and, as appropriate, with the Welsh Ministers, and with persons and organisations who have knowledge of, or are interested in, any matters affecting the discharge of their functions[22].

1 As to the British Tourist Authority see PARA 1028.
2 As to the meaning of 'Great Britain' see PARA 906 note 7.
3 'Tourist amenities and facilities' means, in relation to any country, amenities and facilities for visitors to that country and for other people travelling within it on business or pleasure: Development of Tourism Act 1969 s 2(9).
4 Development of Tourism Act 1969 s 2(1).
5 As to the meaning of 'tourist board' see PARA 1028 note 2.
6 As to the Welsh Ministers see CONSTITUTIONAL AND ADMINISTRATIVE LAW vol 20 (2014) PARA 373 et seq.
7 Development of Tourism Act 1969 s 2(1) (amended by the Tourist Boards (Scotland) Act 2006 s 1(2); and by SI 2005/3225; and by virtue of the Government of Wales Act 2006 s 162, Sch 11 para 32).

8 Development of Tourism Act 1969 s 2(2) (amended by SI 2005/3225; and by virtue of the Government of Wales Act 2006 Sch 11 para 32).
9 Development of Tourism Act 1969 s 2(2)(a).
10 Development of Tourism Act 1969 s 2(2)(b).
11 Development of Tourism Act 1969 s 2(2)(c).
12 Development of Tourism Act 1969 s 2(2)(d).
13 Development of Tourism Act 1969 s 2(2)(e) (amended by SI 2005/3225; and by virtue of the Government of Wales Act 2006 Sch 11 para 32). A tourist board may charge for its services and receive contributions towards its expenses in carrying out any of its functions (Development of Tourism Act 1969 s 2(7)), but it may not borrow money except with the consent of the relevant minister and the Treasury (s 2(8)). The Welsh Ministers may charge for their services and receive contributions towards their expenses in carrying out any of their functions under the Development of Tourism Act 1969 as read with the Tourism (Overseas Promotion) (Wales) Act 1992 (see text and note 20) (Development of Tourism Act 1969 s 2(7A) (added by SI 2005/3225; and amended by virtue of the Government of Wales Act 2006 Sch 11 para 32)), and may borrow money for the purposes of exercising their functions under the Development of Tourism Act 1969 as read with the Tourism (Overseas Promotion) (Wales) Act 1992 (Development of Tourism Act 1969 s 2(8A) (added by SI 2005/3225; and amended by virtue of the Government of Wales Act 2006 Sch 11 para 32)). As to the Treasury see CONSTITUTIONAL AND ADMINISTRATIVE LAW vol 20 (2014) PARA 262 et seq.
   'Relevant minister' means, in relation to the British Tourist Authority and the English Tourist Board, the Secretary of State, and, in relation to Visit Scotland, the Secretary of State for Scotland (see the Development of Tourism Act 1969 s 1(6) (amended by the Tourist Boards (Scotland) Act 2006 s 1(2); and by SI 2005/3225); and PARA 1028). After consultation with a tourist board, the relevant minister may give to it directions of a general character as to the exercise of its functions: Development of Tourism Act 1969 s 19(1).
14 As to the meaning of 'United Kingdom' see PARA 906 note 7.
15 Development of Tourism Act 1969 s 2(3). However, this does not prevent a tourist board or the Welsh Ministers from carrying out such activities on behalf of the British Tourist Authority: s 2(3) (amended by SI 2005/3225; and by virtue of the Government of Wales Act 2006 Sch 11 para 32).
16 Ie by the Development of Tourism Act 1969 ss 3, 4: see PARA 1030.
17 Development of Tourism Act 1969 s 2(4).
18 Ie by the Development of Tourism Act 1969 ss 3, 4A: see PARA 1030.
19 Development of Tourism Act 1969 s 2(4A) (added by SI 2005/3225; and amended by virtue of the Government of Wales Act 2006 Sch 11 para 32).
20 Tourism (Overseas Promotion) (Wales) Act 1992 s 1(1) (amended by SI 2005/3225; and by virtue of the Government of Wales Act 2006 Sch 11 para 32). This does not affect the British Tourist Authority's power to carry on activities outside the United Kingdom for the purpose of encouraging people to visit Wales, nor does it prevent the Welsh Ministers from acting on behalf of the Authority as mentioned in the Development of Tourism Act 1969 s 2(3) (see note 15): Tourism (Overseas Promotion) (Wales) Act 1992 s 1(3) (amended by SI 2005/3225; and by virtue of the Government of Wales Act 2006 Sch 11 para 32). The Tourism (Overseas Promotion) (Scotland) Act 1984 (amended by the Tourist Boards (Scotland) Act 2006 s 4 Sch 2 Pt 1 para 4) makes parallel provision for Visit Scotland.
21 Development of Tourism Act 1969 s 2(5) (amended by the Tourist Boards (Scotland) Act 2006 ss 1(2), 4, Sch 2 Pt 1 para 1(a); by SI 2005/3225; and by virtue of the Government of Wales Act 2006 Sch 11 para 32). Without prejudice to the Development of Tourism Act 1969 s 2(1)–(4A), each of the bodies mentioned, and the Welsh Ministers, has power to provide such organisations with financial and other assistance: s 2(5) (as so amended).
22 Development of Tourism Act 1969 s 2(6) (amended by SI 2005/3225; and by virtue of the Government of Wales Act 2006 Sch 11 para 32).

1030. Schemes of financial assistance for tourist projects. After consultation with the other tourist boards[1] and the Welsh Ministers[2], the British Tourist Authority[3] may prepare schemes providing for the giving of financial assistance by those boards and the Welsh Ministers for specified classes of projects which in the Authority's opinion will provide or improve tourist amenities and facilities[4] in Great Britain[5]. Subject to the provisions of any scheme and to certain directions[6], a tourist board and the Welsh Ministers, in making a grant or loan, may impose such terms and conditions as they think fit, including conditions for the repayment of a grant in specified[7] circumstances[8]. Such a scheme must be submitted to the Secretary of State, who may by order confirm it with or without modification[9].

In accordance with arrangements approved by the relevant minister and the Treasury, a tourist board may give financial assistance for the carrying out of any project which in the board's opinion will provide or improve tourist amenities and facilities in the country for which it is responsible[10], and with the approval of the minister and the Treasury may carry out any such project[11].

The Welsh Ministers have power to give financial assistance for the carrying out of any project which in their opinion will provide or improve tourist amenities and facilities in Wales and to carry out any such project[12].

1   As to the meaning of 'tourist board' see PARA 1028 note 2.
2   As to the Welsh Ministers see CONSTITUTIONAL AND ADMINISTRATIVE LAW vol 20 (2014) PARA 373 et seq.
3   As to the British Tourist Authority see PARA 1028.
4   As to the meaning of 'tourist amenities and facilities' see PARA 1029 note 3.
5   Development of Tourism Act 1969 s 3(1) (amended by the Tourist Boards (Scotland) Act 2006 s 1(2); and by SI 2005/3225; and by virtue of the Government of Wales Act 2006 s 162, Sch 11 para 32). As to the meaning of 'Great Britain' see PARA 906 note 7. A scheme under the Development of Tourism Act 1969 s 3 may provide for financial assistance to be given by way of grant or loan by any combination of those methods: s 3(3). Such a scheme may be varied or revoked by a subsequent scheme prepared, submitted and confirmed in like manner or, subject to s 3(6) (see note 9), by an order made by the Secretary of State after consultation with the Authority, the other tourist boards and the Welsh Ministers: s 3(5) (amended by the Tourist Boards (Scotland) Act 2006 s 1(2); and by SI 2005/3225; and by virtue of the Government of Wales Act 2006 Sch 11 para 32). As to the Secretary of State see PARA 1028 note 5.
6   Ie directions under the Development of Tourism Act 1969 s 19: see note 8.
7   Ie specified in the scheme: Development of Tourism Act 1969 s 3(4) (as amended: see note 8).
8   Development of Tourism Act 1969 s 3(4) (amended by SI 2005/3225; and by virtue of the Government of Wales Act 2006 Sch 11 para 32). As to the means of securing compliance with conditions see the Development of Tourism Act 1969 Sch 2.
    Subject to the provisions of the Development of Tourism Act 1969 s 3, the relevant minister (defined in PARA 1029 note 13) may, with the approval of the Treasury, give to a tourist board directions as to:
    (1)   the matters with respect to which that board must be satisfied before making a loan under the scheme (s 19(2)(a) (amended by the Statute Law (Repeals) Act 1998 s 1(1), Sch 1 Pt IV));
    (2)   the terms on which and the conditions subject to which any such loan is to be made (Development of Tourism Act 1969 s 19(2)(b));
    (3)   the conditions to be imposed in making any grant under the scheme (s 19(2)(c) (amended by the Statute Law (Repeals) Act 1998 s 1(1), Sch 1 Pt IV)).
    Such directions may distinguish between different classes of case: Development of Tourism Act 1969 s 19(2). Directions under head (1) may require a tourist board to be satisfied that the applicant cannot obtain a loan for the purpose in question from any other source, whether on terms which are more or less favourable than those of any loan which might be made by the board: s 19(3). A tourist board must give effect to any directions given to it under s 19: s 19(4).
    As to the Treasury see CONSTITUTIONAL AND ADMINISTRATIVE LAW vol 20 (2014) PARA 262 et seq.
9   Development of Tourism Act 1969 s 3(2). If a scheme is so confirmed it then has effect: s 3(2). Any power of the Secretary of State to make orders under s 3 is exercisable by statutory instrument, and any order under s 3(2) must set out the scheme which the order confirms: s 3(6). No order may be made under s 3 except with the consent of the Treasury and unless a draft of the order has been laid before Parliament and approved by a resolution of each House: s 3(6). At the date at which this volume states the law, no such order had been made.
10 Development of Tourism Act 1969 s 4(1)(a). Such financial assistance may be given by way of grant or loan or, if the project is being or is to be carried out by a company incorporated in Great Britain, by subscribing for or otherwise acquiring shares or stock in the company, or by any combination of those methods: s 4(2). In making such a grant or loan a tourist board may, subject to the arrangements, impose such terms and conditions as it thinks fit, including conditions for the repayment of a grant in specified circumstances, and Sch 2 has effect for

securing compliance with such conditions: s 4(3). A tourist board must not dispose of any shares or stock so acquired by it by virtue of s 4 except after consultation with the company in which the shares or stock are held, and with the approval of the relevant minister and (except for the Wales Tourist Board) the Treasury: s 4(4).

11 Development of Tourism Act 1969 s 4(1)(b).

12 Development of Tourism Act 1969 s 4A(1) (s 4A added by SI 2005/3225; and amended by virtue of the Government of Wales Act 2006 Sch 11 para 32). Such financial assistance may be given by way of grant or loan or, if the project is being or is to be carried out by a company incorporated in Great Britain, by subscribing for or otherwise acquiring shares or stock in the company or by any combination of those methods: Development of Tourism Act 1969 s 4A(2) (as so added). In making a grant or loan under these provisions the Welsh Ministers may impose such terms and conditions as they think fit, including conditions for the repayment of a grant in specified circumstances; and Sch 2 has effect for securing compliance with conditions subject to which any such grant is made: s 4A(3) (as so added and amended). The Welsh Ministers must not dispose of any shares or stock acquired by them by virtue of s 4A except after consultation with the company in which the shares or stock are held: s 4A(4) (as so added and amended).

1031. Other duties and powers of tourist boards. It is the duty of a tourist board[1] and the Welsh Ministers to advise any minister or public body[2] on such matters relating to tourism in Great Britain[3] (in the case of the British Tourist Authority), or the part of Great Britain with which the board or the Welsh Ministers is or are concerned (in the case of the other boards and the Welsh Ministers), as the minister or body may refer to it or as the board or the Welsh Ministers may think fit[4].

At the request of any corresponding body established under the law of Northern Ireland, any of the Channel Islands or the Isle of Man[5] and on such terms as may be agreed upon between the British Tourist Authority and that body, the Authority has power to carry on activities outside the United Kingdom[6] and those islands for encouraging people to visit Northern Ireland or those islands[7].

The British Tourist Authority and the Welsh Ministers have power to enter into agreements for the purpose of:

(1) furthering sustainable development in one or more countries[8] outside the United Kingdom;

(2) improving the welfare of the population[9] of one or more such countries; or

(3) alleviating the effects of a natural or man-made disaster or other emergency on the population of one or more such countries[10].

1 As to the meaning of 'tourist board' see PARA 1028 note 2.

2 'Public body' includes any local authority or statutory undertaker, and any trustees, commissioners, board or other persons who, as a public body and not for their own profit, act under any enactment for the improvement of any place or the production or supply of any commodity or service: Development of Tourism Act 1969 s 5(2).

3 As to the meaning of 'Great Britain' see PARA 906 note 7.

4 Development of Tourism Act 1969 s 5(1) (amended by the Tourist Boards (Scotland) Act 2006 s 1(2); and by SI 2005/3225; and by virtue of the Government of Wales Act 2006 s 162, Sch 11 para 32).

5 As to the Channel Islands and the Isle of Man see COMMONWEALTH vol 13 (2009) PARAS 790–800.

6 As to the meaning of 'United Kingdom' see PARA 906 note 7.

7 Development of Tourism Act 1969 s 5(3).

8 'Country' includes any territory or region: International Development Act 2002 s 17(1).

9 References to the population of a country include references to any future population of the country and to any part of the population, present or future: International Development Act 2002 s 17(2).

10 International Development Act 2002 s 9(1), Sch 1 (Sch 1 amended by SI 2005/3225; and by virtue of the Government of Wales Act 2006 Sch 11 para 32). See also HEALTH SERVICES vol 54

(2008) PARA 86. Such an agreement must not make provision for the Authority or ministers to provide financial assistance (see the International Development Act 2002 ss 6, 7): s 9(2). Before entering into such an agreement, the British Tourist Authority must obtain the consent of the Secretary of State: see ss 9(3), (4), 10 (s 9(4) amended by SI 2005/3225; and by virtue of the Government of Wales Act 2006 Sch 11 para 32). The Secretary of State concerned is the Secretary of State for International Development: see CONSTITUTIONAL AND ADMINISTRATIVE LAW vol 20 (2014) PARA 237.

1032.   Tourist boards; accounts and information.   Each tourist board[1] must keep proper accounts and other records in relation to the accounts and must prepare in respect of each of its financial years[2] a statement of account in such form as the relevant minister[3] may with the approval of the Treasury determine[4]. The statement must be submitted to him at such time as he may with such approval direct[5]. Each tourist board must provide him with such information relating to its activities or proposed activities as he from time to time requires[6]. As soon as possible after the end of each financial year, each tourist board must make to the relevant minister a report dealing with its activities during that year, and he must lay a copy of the report before each House of Parliament[7].

1   As to the meaning of 'tourist board' see PARA 1028 note 2.
2   'Financial year' means a 12 month period ending with 31 March in each year: Development of Tourism Act 1969 s 6(7).
3   As to the meaning of 'relevant minister' see PARA 1029 note 13.
4   Development of Tourism Act 1969 s 6(1). As to the Treasury see CONSTITUTIONAL AND ADMINISTRATIVE LAW vol 20 (2014) PARA 262 et seq.
5   Development of Tourism Act 1969 s 6(2). Except in the case of Visit Scotland, the relevant minister must, on or before 30 November in any year, transmit to the Comptroller and Auditor General the statement of account prepared by each tourist board for the last financial year: s 6(3), (8) (s 6(8) added by SSI 2002/176; and amended by the Tourist Boards (Scotland) Act 2006 s 1(2)). The Comptroller and Auditor General must examine and certify each such statement and lay copies before Parliament together with his report: Development of Tourism Act 1969 s 6(4). As to the Comptroller and Auditor General see CONSTITUTIONAL AND ADMINISTRATIVE LAW vol 20 (2014) PARAS 494–496.
6   Development of Tourism Act 1969 s 6(5). For this purpose the board must permit any person authorised in that behalf by the minister to inspect and make copies of its accounts, books, documents or papers and must afford to that person such explanation of each as he may reasonably require: s 6(5).
7   Development of Tourism Act 1969 s 6(6).

1033.   Registration of hotels etc and notification of prices.   Provision may be made by Order in Council[1] for the registration[2] by tourist boards[3] and the Welsh Ministers of hotels and other establishments in Great Britain[4] at which sleeping accommodation is provided by way of trade or business[5]. Such an order may make provision[6] in particular:

(1)   as to the form and contents of the register or registers to be maintained and the establishments to be registered[7];

(2)   for requiring the person carrying on an establishment which is required to be registered to furnish specified information, at specified times, to the body responsible for registering it[8];

(3)   for the charging of annual or other periodical fees for registration[9];

(4)   for the issue and display of certificates of registration and the display of signs indicating that the establishment is registered[10];

(5)   for the inspection of establishments and for powers of entry for that purpose[11];

(6)   for exemptions from any of the requirements of the order[12];

(7)   for securing compliance with any requirement by the imposition of a penalty[13].

Provision may also be made by order for requiring the display by hotels and other establishments of information with respect to the prices charged there for sleeping accommodation or otherwise for securing that such information is brought to the notice of persons seeking to avail themselves of the accommodation[14].

1 Such an order is subject to annulment in pursuance of a resolution of either House of Parliament and may be revoked or varied by a subsequent order: Development of Tourism Act 1969 s 17(6). See STATUTES AND LEGISLATIVE PROCESS. At the date at which this volume states the law, no such order had been made. An order may contain such supplementary and incidental provisions as appear to be necessary or expedient, and may authorise the relevant ministers (defined in PARA 1029 note 13) to make regulations as respects England and Scotland, and the Welsh Ministers as respects Wales, for purposes specified in the order: see s 17(4) (amended by SI 2005/3225; and by virtue of the Government of Wales Act 2006 s 162, Sch 11 para 32).

2 A tourist board maintaining a register has power to publish or make available for publication (gratuitously or for consideration) any information furnished to it, and any information as to any classification or grade accorded to any establishment: Development of Tourism Act 1969 s 17(7). This applies in relation to the Welsh Ministers if they are maintaining such a register as it applies in relation to a tourist board: s 17(7A) (added by SI 2005/3225; and amended by virtue of the Government of Wales Act 2006 Sch 11 para 32).

3 As to the meaning of 'tourist board' see PARA 1028 note 2.

4 As to the meaning of 'Great Britain' see PARA 906 note 7.

5 Development of Tourism Act 1969 s 17(1) (amended by SI 2005/3225; and by virtue of the Government of Wales Act 2006 Sch 11 para 32).

6 An order and any regulations made under it may make different provision for different cases and provision may be made for an order to come into force at different times in relation to, or to different parts of, England, Scotland and Wales respectively: Development of Tourism Act 1969 s 17(5).

7 Development of Tourism Act 1969 s 17(2)(a). If provision is made for the classification or grading of the establishments entered in a register, provision may also be made for:
  (1) requiring the criteria in accordance with which classification or grading is carried out to be determined from time to time by the British Tourist Authority (as to which see PARA 1028) after consultation with the other tourist boards, the Welsh Ministers and other organisations representative of trade and consumer interests likely to be affected (s 17(3)(a) (amended by the Tourist Boards (Scotland) Act 2006 s 1(2); SI 2005/3225; and by virtue of the Government of Wales Act 2006 Sch 11 para 32);
  (2) the publication of any criteria so determined (Development of Tourism Act 1969 s 17(3)(b)); and
  (3) enabling the person carrying on a registered establishment to make representations to the board concerned before any classification or grade is accorded or altered or cancelled (s 17(3)(c) (amended by SI 2005/3225; and by virtue of the Government of Wales Act 2006 Sch 11 para 32)).

8 Development of Tourism Act 1969 s 17(2)(b).

9 Development of Tourism Act 1969 s 17(2)(c).

10 Development of Tourism Act 1969 s 17(2)(d).

11 Development of Tourism Act 1969 s 17(2)(e).

12 Development of Tourism Act 1969 s 17(2)(f).

13 Development of Tourism Act 1969 s 17(2)(g). The penalty must not exceed level 4 on the standard scale: s 17(2)(g) (amended by virtue of the Criminal Justice Act 1982 ss 40, 46). As to the standard scale see SENTENCING AND DISPOSITION OF OFFENDERS vol 92 (2010) PARA 142.

14 Development of Tourism Act 1969 s 18(1). The provisions of s 17(2)(e)–(g), (4)–(6) apply to such an order: s 18(2). At the date at which this volume states the law, no order under this provision is in force.

1034. Financial provisions relating to tourist boards. The relevant minister[1] may pay to a tourist board[2] such sums in respect of its expenditure as he may with the consent of the Treasury determine[3]. Any sums required by a relevant minister for making such payments and any other expenses of his must be defrayed out of money provided by Parliament[4].

Any sums received by a tourist board:

(1)   in repayment of or as interest on any loan made by it;
(2)   in repayment of any grant made by it; or
(3)   as a dividend on or otherwise in respect of any shares or stock acquired
       by it,
must be paid to the relevant minister[5].

1   As to the meaning of 'relevant minister' see PARA 1029 note 13.
2   As to the meaning of 'tourist board' see PARA 1028 note 2.
3   Development of Tourism Act 1969 s 20(1). As to the Treasury see CONSTITUTIONAL AND
     ADMINISTRATIVE LAW vol 20 (2014) PARA 262 et seq.
4   Development of Tourism Act 1969 s 20(2).
5   Development of Tourism Act 1969 s 20(3). Any sums received by a relevant minister under
     s 20(3) must be paid into the Consolidated Fund: s 20(4). As to the Consolidated Fund see
     CONSTITUTIONAL AND ADMINISTRATIVE LAW vol 20 (2014) PARA 480 et seq; and PARLIAMENT
     vol 78 (2010) PARA 1028 et seq.

(iv) Industrial Design

1035.   Furtherance of industrial design.   In order to promote the improvement
of design in the products of British industry, the President of the Board of Trade
in 1944 appointed a Council of Industrial Design[1]. The Secretary of State[2], with
the approval of the Treasury[3], may make grants out of money provided by
Parliament to the council and to any association or body the objects of which
include promoting the improvement of design in any industry or activities
appearing to him to be conducive to it and as to which he is satisfied that it does
not carry on any business for the purposes of making a profit[4].

1   See 406 HC Official Report (5th series) col 1612.
2   As to the Secretary of State see PARA 902. The function under the Industrial Organisation and
     Development Act 1947 s 11 is exercisable by the Welsh Ministers concurrently with the
     Secretary of State: see the National Assembly for Wales (Transfer of Functions) Order 1999,
     SI 1999/672, art 2, Sch 1; the Government of Wales Act 2006 s 162, Sch 11 para 30; and PARA
     902 note 21.
3   As to the Treasury see CONSTITUTIONAL AND ADMINISTRATIVE LAW vol 20 (2014) PARA 262 et
     seq.
4   Industrial Organisation and Development Act 1947 s 11.

(2) ASSISTANCE TO INDUSTRY

(i) Promotion of Local Employment

**1036.   Powers under the Industrial Development Act 1982 for providing
employment.**   The Secretary of State[1] has powers under the Industrial
Development Act 1982[2] for the designation of development areas and
intermediate areas[3], the allocation of financial assistance for industry in assisted
areas[4], premises and sites[5], the improvement of basic services[6], and the
establishment of the Industrial Advisory Board[7].

1   As to the Secretary of State see PARA 902. The functions under the Industrial Development
     Act 1982 (except ss 1, 8(5), (7), 10, 15, 16 (see PARAS 1037, 1041, 1044, 1049)) are exercisable
     by the Welsh Ministers concurrently with the Secretary of State, and the functions of a Minister
     of the Crown under s 13 (see PARA 1046) are exercisable by the Welsh Ministers concurrently
     with the Minister of the Crown by whom they are exercisable: see the National Assembly for
     Wales (Transfer of Functions) Order 1999, SI 1999/672, art 2, Sch 1; the Government of Wales
     Act 2006 s 162, Sch 11 para 30; and PARA 902 note 21.
2   The Industrial Development Act 1982 consolidated, with certain exceptions, the Local
     Employment Act 1972, the Industry Act 1972 Pts I, II, the Industry Act 1980 s 18 and the
     Industry Act 1981 s 6. The Industrial Development Act 1982 was extensively amended by the

Co-operative Development Agency and Industrial Development Act 1984. For transitional provisions see the Co-operative Development Agency and Industrial Development Act (Commencement) Order 1984, SI 1984/1845 (amended by SI 1986/128).

3 See the Industrial Development Act 1982 s 1; and PARA 1037, 1049.
4 See the Industrial Development Act 1982 s 7; and PARAS 1037, 1040–1044, 1049.
5 See the Industrial Development Act 1982 s 14; and PARAS 1045, 1049.
6 See the Industrial Development Act 1982 s 13; and PARAS 1046, 1049.
7 See the Industrial Development Act 1982 s 10; and PARA 1044, 1049.

1037. Development areas. The Secretary of State[1] may by order[2] specify any area of Great Britain[3] as a development area[4]. In making such an order he must have regard to all the circumstances, actual and expected, including the state of employment and unemployment, population changes and migration, and the objectives of regional policies[5].

An order may describe a development area by reference to any of the following kinds of area or any combination of those areas:

(1) wards;
(2) travel to work areas (being areas by reference to which the Secretary of State publishes unemployment records);
(3) any other area which has been created by, or exists or existed for the purposes of, any Act or statutory instrument, whenever passed or made,

and any reference in such an order to a named area or combination of areas is to be construed as a reference to that area as it exists on the date on which the order comes into force[6].

1 The Secretary of State is in practice the Secretary of State for Business, Innovation and Skills: see PARA 903 note 2.
2 An order under the Industrial Development Act 1982 s 1 must be made by statutory instrument subject to annulment in pursuance of a resolution of either House of Parliament: s 1(7). See STATUTES AND LEGISLATIVE PROCESS vol 96 (2012) PARA 1032. At the date at which this volume states the law, the order currently in force under this section is the Assisted Areas Order 2014, SI 2014/1508, which designates development areas in England, Wales and Scotland.
    'Development area' means an area for the time being specified or designated by an order made, or having effect as if made, under the Industrial Development Act 1982 s 1: s 18(1).
3 As to the meaning of 'Great Britain' see PARA 906 note 7.
4 Industrial Development Act 1982 s 1(1)(a).
5 Industrial Development Act 1982 s 1(3).
6 Industrial Development Act 1982 s 1(4) (substituted by the Co-operative Development Agency and Industrial Development Act 1984 s 4; and amended by the Statute Law (Repeals) Act 2004). See also note 2.

1038. Intermediate areas. The Secretary of State[1] may by order[2] specify any area of Great Britain[3] as an intermediate area[4]. In making such an order he must have regard to all the circumstances actual and expected, including the state of employment and unemployment, population changes and migration and the objectives of regional policies[5].

An order may describe an intermediate area by reference to any of the following kinds of area or any combination of those areas:

(1) wards;
(2) travel to work areas (being areas by reference to which the Secretary of State publishes unemployment records);
(3) any other area which has been created by, or exists or existed for the purposes of, any Act or statutory instrument, whenever passed or made,

and any reference in such an order to a named area or combination of areas is to be construed as a reference to that area as it exists on the date on which the order comes into force[6].

1   The Secretary of State is in practice the Secretary of State for Business, Innovation and Skills: see
    PARA 903 note 2.
2   As to the making of such orders see PARA 1037 note 2.
3   As to the meaning of 'Great Britain' see PARA 906 note 7.
4   Industrial Development Act 1982 s 1(1)(b). 'Intermediate area' means an area for the time being
    so specified or designated by an order made, or having effect as if made, under s 1: s 18(1). At
    the date at which this volume states the law no order specifying or designating intermediate
    orders was in force.
        The status as an intermediate area is important as regards the provision of premises and
    basic services (see PARAS 1045–1046) and the amount of grant which may be made for the
    clearance of derelict land (see PARA 1069). However, regional development grants are not
    payable in intermediate areas.
5   Industrial Development Act 1982 s 1(3).
6   Industrial Development Act 1982 s 1(4) (substituted by the Co-operative Development Agency
    and Industrial Development Act 1984 s 4; and amended by the Statute Law (Repeals) Act 2004).

1039. Inner urban areas. The Secretary of State[1] may by order specify as a
designated district any district which includes the whole or part of an inner
urban area in respect of which there exists a special social need[2]. A designated
district authority[3] may then give financial assistance in the form of loans for the
acquisition of or for works on land[4], or loans and grants for the establishment of
common ownership or co-operative enterprises[5].

If the designated district authority by resolution declares an area within the
designated district to be an improvement area[6] the authority may give further
assistance in the form of loans or grants to improve amenities[7] or grants for
converting or improving industrial or commercial buildings[8].

Where the Secretary of State and other ministers concerned consider that a
concerted effort is required to alleviate a special social need in any inner urban
area, they may arrange with the designated district authority[9] and other
appropriate persons what action should be taken[10], and the Secretary of State
may by order specify the area as a special area[11]. The authority may then make
loans for site preparation[12] and grants towards rent[13] or loan interest[14].

Further, the Secretary of State may by order designate an inner urban area as
an urban development area with its own urban development corporation[15], and
the area may be designated as an enterprise zone[16].

1   The Secretary of State is the Secretary of State for the Environment or, in Wales, the Welsh
    Ministers: see PLANNING vol 81 (2010) PARAS 26–27.
2   See the Inner Urban Areas Act 1978 s 1(1). As to orders made in exercise of this power see
    PLANNING vol 83 (2010) PARA 1563.
3   'Designated district authority' in relation to a designated district means the council of that
    district or the council of the county which includes that district, but, in relation to a designated
    district which is a Welsh county or county borough, means the council of that county or county
    borough: Inner Urban Areas Act 1978 s 1(2) (amended by the Local Government etc Scotland
    Act 1994 s 180(1), Sch 13 para 114(2); and the Local Government (Wales) Act 1994 Sch 16
    para 55(1)). As to local government authorities see LOCAL GOVERNMENT vol 69 (2009) PARA 37
    et seq.
4   See the Inner Urban Areas Act 1978 s 2; and PLANNING vol 83 (2010) PARA 1564.
5   See the Inner Urban Areas Act 1978 s 3; and PLANNING vol 83 (2010) PARA 1565.
6   See the Inner Urban Areas Act 1978 s 4, Schedule paras 1–3; and PLANNING vol 83 (2010)
    PARAS 1566, 1569.
7   See the Inner Urban Areas Act 1978 s 5; and PLANNING vol 83 (2010) PARA 1567.
8   See the Inner Urban Areas Act 1978 s 6; and PLANNING vol 83 (2010) PARA 1568.
9   Ie the council of that district or council of the county which includes that district, or both or, as
    respects any such Welsh county or county borough, the council of that county or county
    borough: see the Inner Urban Areas Act 1978 s 7(1)(a) (amended by the Local Government etc
    Scotland Act 1994 Sch 13 para 114(2); and the Local Government (Wales) Act 1994 Sch 16
    para 55(3)).
10 See the Inner Urban Areas Act 1978 s 7; and PLANNING vol 83 (2010) PARA 1570.

11 See the Inner Urban Areas Act 1978 s 8; and PLANNING vol 83 (2010) PARA 1571.
12 See the Inner Urban Areas Act 1978 s 9; and PLANNING vol 83 (2010) PARA 1572.
13 See the Inner Urban Areas Act 1978 s 10; and PLANNING vol 83 (2010) PARA 1573.
14 See the Inner Urban Areas Act 1978 s 11; and PLANNING vol 83 (2010) PARA 1574.
15 See the Local Government, Planning and Land Act 1980 ss 134, 135; and PLANNING vol 83 (2010) PARA 1579 et seq. Where land is in both an urban development area and a designated district the urban development authority has many of the powers of a designated district authority: see the Local Government, Planning and Land Act 1980 s 162; and PLANNING vol 83 (2010) PARA 1588.
16 See the Local Government, Planning and Land Act 1980 s 179, Sch 32; and PLANNING vol 83 (2010) PARA 1640 et seq.

(ii) Financial Assistance for Industry

1040. Provision of financial assistance to provide, maintain or safeguard employment. For specified purposes[1] the Secretary of State[2] may, with the consent of the Treasury[3], provide financial assistance[4] where, in his opinion[5]:

(1) such assistance is likely to provide, maintain or safeguard employment in any part of the assisted areas[6]; and

(2) the undertakings for which the assistance is provided are or will be wholly or mainly in those areas[7].

1 Ie for the purposes set out in the Industrial Development Act 1982 s 7(2): see PARA 1042.
2 As to the Secretary of State see PARA 902. The functions under the Industrial Development Act 1982 s 7 are exercisable by the Welsh Ministers concurrently with the Secretary of State: see the National Assembly for Wales (Transfer of Functions) Order 1999, SI 1999/672, art 2, Sch 1; the Government of Wales Act 2006 s 162, Sch 11 para 30; and PARA 902 note 21. As to the power of the Scottish Ministers to delegate their power under the Industrial Development Act 1982 s 7(1) see s 7(4A)–(4E) (added by the Public Services Reform (Scotland) Act 2010 s 9).
3 As to the Treasury see CONSTITUTIONAL AND ADMINISTRATIVE LAW vol 20 (2014) PARA 262 et seq.
4 As to the nature of this financial assistance see the Industrial Development Act 1982 s 7(3), (4); and PARA 1043.
5 Industrial Development Act 1982 s 7(1).
6 Industrial Development Act 1982 s 7(1)(a). 'Assisted areas' means the development areas, the intermediate areas and Northern Ireland: s 7(6). As to development areas and intermediate areas see PARAS 1037–1038.
7 Industrial Development Act 1982 s 7(1)(b).

1041. Provision of financial assistance for the benefit of the economy. For specified purposes[1] the Secretary of State[2] may, with the consent of the Treasury[3], provide financial assistance[4] where, in his opinion[5]:

(1) the financial assistance is likely to benefit the economy of the United Kingdom, or of any part or area of the United Kingdom[6];

(2) it is in the national interest that financial assistance should be provided on the scale, and in the form and manner, proposed[7]; and

(3) the financial assistance cannot, or cannot appropriately, be so provided otherwise than by him[8].

The aggregate of the sums paid[9] by him, other than sums paid in respect of foreign currency guarantees[10], and his liabilities under any guarantees[11] given by him, less any sum received by him by way of repayment of loans, or repayment of principal sums paid to meet guarantees, may not at any time exceed £12,000 m[12]. The aggregate of his liabilities under foreign currency guarantees[13] and any sums paid by him in respect of such guarantees[14], less any sums received by him by way of repayment of principal sums paid to meet foreign currency guarantees, may not at any time exceed 1,000 million special drawing rights[15].

The sums which the Secretary of State pays or undertakes to pay by way of financial assistance in respect of any one project, excluding sums paid or to be paid in respect of foreign currency guarantees, may not exceed £10 million, except so far as any excess has been authorised by a resolution of the House of Commons[16].

1   Ie for the purposes set out in the Industrial Development Act 1982 s 7(2): see PARA 1042.
2   As to the Secretary of State see PARA 902. The functions under the Industrial Development Act 1982 ss 8, 9 (except s 8(5), (7)) are exercisable by the Welsh Ministers concurrently with the Secretary of State: see the National Assembly for Wales (Transfer of Functions) Order 1999, SI 1999/672, art 2, Sch 1; the Government of Wales Act 2006 s 162, Sch 11 para 30; and PARA 902 note 21.
3   As to the Treasury see CONSTITUTIONAL AND ADMINISTRATIVE LAW vol 20 (2014) PARA 262 et seq.
4   As to the financial assistance which may be given see the Industrial Development Act 1982 s 7(3) (as applied by s 8(2)); and PARA 1043.
5   Industrial Development Act 1982 s 8(1).
6   Industrial Development Act 1982 s 8(1)(a). As to the meaning of 'United Kingdom' see PARA 906 note 7.
7   Industrial Development Act 1982 s 8(1)(b).
8   Industrial Development Act 1982 s 8(1)(c).
9   Ie under the Industrial Development Act 1982 s 8. As to taxation see PARA 1043 note 1.
10 Industrial Development Act 1982 s 8(4)(a). 'Foreign currency guarantee' means a guarantee given under s 8 or under the Industry Act 1972 s 8 (repealed) by the Secretary of State under which his liability is measured in a foreign currency, whether or not it is to be discharged in such a currency; for this purpose a liability measured in sterling but expressed to be subject to a limit in a foreign currency is taken to be measured in such a currency, and a liability measured in foreign currency but expressed to be subject to a limit in sterling is taken to be measured in sterling: Industrial Development Act 1982 s 8(11). 'Foreign currency' means any currency other than sterling, including special drawing rights, and 'guarantee' includes any form of insurance: ss 8(11), 9(7). As to special drawing rights see PARA 1022 note 4.
11 Industrial Development Act 1982 s 8(4)(b). Liabilities in respect of interest on a principal sum so guaranteed are excluded, as are liabilities under foreign currency guarantees: s 8(4)(b).
12 Industrial Development Act 1982 s 8(4), (5) (s 8(5) substituted by the Industry and Exports (Financial Support) Act 2009 s 1(1)). The Secretary of State may, on not more than four occasions, by order made with the consent of the Treasury, increase the limit by a specified sum not exceeding £1,000 million: Industrial Development Act 1982 s 8(5) (as so substituted). Such an order must be made by statutory instrument, a draft of which has been approved by resolution of the House of Commons: s 8(10). At the date at which this volume states the law, no such order had been made.
13 Industrial Development Act 1982 s 8(6)(a). Liability in respect of interest on a principal sum guaranteed under s 8 or under the Industry Act 1972 s 8 (repealed) is excluded: Industrial Development Act 1982 s 8(6)(a).
14 Industrial Development Act 1982 s 8(6)(b).
15 Industrial Development Act 1982 s 8(6), (7); this is subject to the supplementary provisions of s 9 as to limits on foreign currency liabilities: s 8(6). On not more than four occasions the Secretary of State may, by order made with the consent of the Treasury, increase, or further increase, the limit by a specified amount not exceeding 500 million special drawing rights: s 8(7). Such an order must be made by statutory instrument, a draft of which has been approved by resolution of the House of Commons: s 8(10). At the date at which this volume states the law, no such order had been made.
    The amount to be taken into account under s 8(6) at any time in respect of a liability, if the amount of the liability is not expressed in special drawing rights, is the equivalent at that time in special drawing rights of the amount of the liability: s 9(1). That equivalent is determined by the Secretary of State by reference to:
    (1)   the day on which the guarantee is given; and
    (2)   the last day of each quarter at the end of which the guarantee remains in force,
    having regard to what appears to be the appropriate rate of exchange: s 9(2). A determination under head (1) takes effect from the date from which it was made, and remains in force until the end of the quarter in which the guarantee was given, unless it ceases to be required at an earlier date: s 9(3). A determination made under head (2) takes effect as from the end of the quarter

and remains in force throughout the following quarter, unless it ceases to be required at an earlier date: s 9(4). 'Quarter' means a quarter ending with 31 March, 30 June, 30 September or 31 December in any year: s 9(7).

The amount to be taken into account under s 8(6) in respect of a sum paid or received by the Secretary of State otherwise than in special drawing rights is an amount determined by him, by reference to the day of payment or receipt and having regard to what appears to him the appropriate rate of exchange, as being the equivalent in special drawing rights of that sum: s 9(5).

The limit imposed by s 8(6) may be exceeded if the excess is attributable only to, or to a combination of, the following:

(a)   a quarterly revaluation (s 9(6)(a));

(b)   the Secretary of State's liability under a guarantee given in pursuance of a previous undertaking so far as the amount taken into account for the purposes of the limit in respect of the liability exceeds what it would have been if determined by reference to the day on which the undertaking was given (s 9(6)(b));

(c)   a payment made by the Secretary of State under a guarantee, so far as the amount to be taken into account for the purposes of the limit in respect of the payment exceeds what it would have been if determined by reference to the day on which the guarantee was given (s 9(6)(c)).

A quarterly revaluation is a determination made or having effect as if made under head (2): s 9(7).

16 Industrial Development Act 1982 s 8(8). This does not apply where the Secretary of State is satisfied that the payment or undertaking is urgently needed at a time when it is impracticable to obtain the approval of the House of Commons, in which case he must lay a statement concerning the financial assistance before each House of Parliament: s 8(9).

1042. Purposes for which financial assistance for industry may be given.

The specified purposes for which financial assistance for industry[1] may be provided are:

(1)   to promote the development or modernisation of an industry[2];

(2)   to promote the efficiency of an industry[3];

(3)   to create, expand or sustain productive capacity in an industry, or in undertakings in an industry[4];

(4)   to promote the reconstruction, reorganisation or conversion of an industry or of undertakings in an industry[5];

(5)   to encourage the growth of, or the proper distribution of undertakings in, an industry[6]; and

(6)   to encourage arrangements for ensuring that any contraction of an industry proceeds in an orderly way[7].

1 Ie under the Industrial Development Act 1982 s 7(1) (see PARA 1040) or s 8(1) (see PARA 1041).
2 Industrial Development Act 1982 s 7(2)(a). Unless the context otherwise requires, 'industry' includes any description of commercial activity, and references to an industry include references to any section of an industry: s 7(5).
3 Industrial Development Act 1982 s 7(2)(b).
4 Industrial Development Act 1982 s 7(2)(c).
5 Industrial Development Act 1982 s 7(2)(d).
6 Industrial Development Act 1982 s 7(2)(e).
7 Industrial Development Act 1982 s 7(2)(f).

1043. Nature of financial assistance for industry.

Financial assistance for industry[1] may be given on any terms or conditions, and by any description of investment or lending or guarantee, or by making grants[2]. In particular, assistance may be given by:

(1)   investment by acquisition of loan or share capital in any company, including an acquisition effected by the Secretary of State through another company formed for the purpose of giving[3] such assistance[4];

(2)   investment by the acquisition of any undertaking or of any assets[5];

(3)   a loan, whether secured or unsecured, and whether or not carrying interest, or interest at a commercial rate[6]; or

(4)   any form of insurance or guarantee to meet any contingency, and in particular to meet default on payment of a loan, or of interest on a loan, or non-fulfilment of a contract[7].

1   Ie under the Industrial Development Act 1982 s 7(1) or s 8(1): see PARAS 1040–1041. As to the tax treatment of grants under ss 7, 8, see the Corporation Tax Act 2009 s 102; and INCOME TAXATION vol 58 (2014) PARA 173.

2   Industrial Development Act 1982 s 7(3). The Secretary of State may not, however, under s 8 use any money for the acquisition or assistance of banks or insurance companies: s 8(2). As to the Secretary of State see PARA 902. The functions under the Industrial Development Act 1982 s 7 are exercisable by the Welsh Ministers concurrently with the Secretary of State: see the National Assembly for Wales (Transfer of Functions) Order 1999, SI 1999/672, art 2, Sch 1; the Government of Wales Act 2006 s 162, Sch 11 para 30; and PARA 902 note 21.

3   Ie under the Industrial Development Act 1982 Pt III (ss 7–10), or the Industry Act 1972 Pt II (ss 7–9) (repealed).

4   Industrial Development Act 1982 s 7(3)(a). Assistance under this head may not be given unless the Secretary of State is satisfied that it cannot, or cannot appropriately, be given in any other way, and in giving financial assistance under this head he may not acquire any shares or stock in a company without its consent: ss 7(4), 8(3). Such restrictions would not apply to the acquisition of shares or stock under particular powers contained in another Act. See eg the British Leyland Act 1975 (repealed), which authorised the Secretary of State to acquire shares in British Leyland Motor Corporation Ltd up to a maximum expenditure of £265 million.

5   Industrial Development Act 1982 s 7(3)(b).

6   Industrial Development Act 1982 s 7(3)(c).

7   Industrial Development Act 1982 s 7(3)(d).

1044. The Industrial Development Advisory Board. The Industrial Development Advisory Board[1] (the 'board') is an advisory non-departmental public body, sponsored by the Department for Business, Innovation & Skills. It consists of a chairman and not fewer than six nor more than 12 other members[2], and must include persons who appear to the Secretary of State[3] to have wide experience of, and to have shown capacity in, industry, banking, accounting and finance[4]. The board is appointed by the Secretary of State to advise him with respect to the exercise of his functions[5] as to financial assistance for industry[6]. If it makes a recommendation with respect to any matter at his request and he exercises his functions contrary to that recommendation, he must, if the board so requests, lay a statement as to the matter before Parliament[7].

1   The board was originally established on 11 October 1972 under the Industry Act 1972 s 9(1) (repealed), and is continued by the Industrial Development Act 1982 s 10(1).

2   Industrial Development Act 1982 s 10(2).

3   As to the Secretary of State see PARA 902.

4   Industrial Development Act 1982 s 10(3).

5   Ie his functions under the Industrial Development Act 1982 ss 7, 8: see PARA 1040 et seq.

6   Industrial Development Act 1982 s 10(1).

7   Industrial Development Act 1982 s 10(4).

(iii) General Assistance for Industry

1045. Provision of premises and sites to assist industry. In addition to particular powers given to the Welsh Development Agency (now the Welsh Ministers)[1] to provide and manage sites and premises for industrial or commercial undertakings, the Secretary of State[2] has specified powers in order to provide or facilitate the provision of premises in any development area[3] or intermediate area[4] for occupation by undertakings[5] carried on or to be carried on there or for otherwise meeting the requirements of such undertakings, including requirements arising from the needs of persons employed or to be employed in them[6]. These powers are:

(1)   to acquire land[7] by agreement or, if so authorised, compulsorily[8];

(2)   to erect buildings and carry out works on land belonging to the Secretary of State[9]; and

(3)   by agreement with the persons interested in any other land, to erect buildings and carry out works on the land on such terms, including terms as to repayment of expenditure incurred by the Secretary of State, as may be specified in the agreement[10].

Any person duly authorised in writing by the Secretary of State may, at any reasonable time, enter any land to survey it in connection with the exercise of these powers to acquire land[11]. Where land acquired by the Secretary of State under these powers[12] is situated in a locality which is not a development area or an intermediate area, he may exercise in relation to it the following powers[13]:

(a)   to preserve and maintain the land and any buildings or works on it, and to erect buildings and carry out works on it[14];

(b)   where there are buildings on the land, to acquire by agreement other land contiguous or adjacent to it for the purpose of erecting on it extensions to those buildings, or of erecting on it other buildings to be used with buildings on the land already acquired as part of a single undertaking[15];

(c)   to provide means of access, services and other facilities for meeting the requirements of undertakings carried on, or to be carried on, on the land, including requirements arising from the needs of persons employed or to be employed[16].

The Secretary of State may modernise, adapt or reconstruct any buildings or other works on land acquired by him under any of these powers[17].

1   As to the Welsh Development Agency, its functions and the transfer of those functions to the Welsh Ministers, see PARA 1051. See also note 2. The English Industrial Estates Corporation, which was abolished by the Leasehold Reform, Housing and Urban Development Act 1993 s 184(1) (Leasehold Reform, Housing and Urban Development Act 1993 (Commencement Order No 4) 1994, SI 1994/935, art 3), held similar powers. Its role was absorbed by the Urban Regeneration Agency, established by the Leasehold Reform, Housing and Urban Development Act 1993 and subsequently abolished on 1 April 2009: see the Housing and Regeneration Act 2008 s 49; and the Abolition of the Commission for the New Towns and the Urban Regeneration Agency (Appointed Day and Consequential Amendments) Order 2009, SI 2009/801.

2   As to the Secretary of State see PARA 902. The functions under the Industrial Development Act 1982 ss 14, 14A, 17 are exercisable by the Welsh Ministers concurrently with the Secretary of State: see the National Assembly for Wales (Transfer of Functions) Order 1999, SI 1999/672, art 2, Sch 1; the Government of Wales Act 2006 s 162, Sch 11 para 30; and PARA 902 note 21.

3   As to development areas see PARA 1037.

4   As to intermediate areas see PARA 1038.

5   'Undertaking' means any trade or business or any other activity providing employment: Industrial Development Act 1982 s 17(2).

6   Industrial Development Act 1982 s 14(1). Where a locality ceases to be a development area or intermediate area, the fact that it is no longer such an area does not prejudice the completion by the Secretary of State of buildings or works begun before that time in the locality under s 14(1), or the exercise by him in relation to land in the locality of his powers under s 14(1) so far as may be necessary to fulfil any agreement entered into by him before that time: s 17(3)(a). The Secretary of State is in practice the Secretary of State for Business, Innovation and Skills.

7   'Land' includes messuages, tenements and hereditaments, houses and buildings of any tenure: Industrial Development Act 1982 s 17(1).

8   Industrial Development Act 1982 s 14(1)(a). The Secretary of State may not acquire under this power any buildings other than industrial buildings, except for redevelopment or as part of a

larger property which in his opinion would be incomplete without them: s 14(2) (amended by the Housing and Planning Act 1986 s 49, Sch 11 Pt I para 25). Further, the Acquisition of Land Act 1981 applies in relation to the compulsory purchase of land by the Secretary of State under the Industrial Development Act 1982 s 14; but notwithstanding anything in s 14, where at the time of publication of notice of the preparation of a draft compulsory purchase order the land is in use for the purposes of any undertaking, and that undertaking provides employment which is substantial having regard to the extent of the land used for its purposes and the nature of the undertaking, the Secretary of State may not be authorised to acquire compulsorily the interest of the person carrying on the undertaking: s 14(5). 'Industrial building' means a building:

(1) which is used or designed for use for carrying on, in the course of a trade or business, a process for or incidental to:
   (a) the making of any article or part of any article (s 14A(1)(a) (s 14A added by the Housing and Planning Act 1986 Sch 11 Pt I para 25));
   (b) the altering, repairing, ornamenting, finishing, cleaning, washing, freezing, packing or canning, or adapting for sale, or breaking up or demolition, of any article (Industrial Development Act 1982 s 14A(1)(b) (as so added)); or
   (c) the getting, dressing, or preparation for sale of minerals or the extraction or preparation for sale of oil or brine (s 14A(1)(c) (as so added)); or
(2) which is used or designed for use for carrying on, in the course of a trade or business, scientific research (s 14A(1) (as so added)).

Premises which:
(i)   are used or designed for use for providing services or facilities ancillary to the use of other premises for the carrying on of any such process or research as is mentioned above; and
(ii) are or are to be comprised in the same building or the same curtilage as those other premises,

are themselves to be treated as used or designed for use for the carrying on of such a process or, as the case may be, of such research: s 14A(2) (as so added). 'Article' means an article of any description, including a ship or vessel; 'building' includes part of a building; 'minerals' includes all minerals and substances in or under land of a kind ordinarily worked for removal by underground or surface working, except that it does not include peat cut for purposes other than sale; and 'scientific research' means any activity in the fields of natural or applied science for the extension of knowledge: s 14A(3) (as so added).

9   Industrial Development Act 1982 s 14(1)(b).
10 Industrial Development Act 1982 s 14(1)(c).
11 Industrial Development Act 1982 s 14(6) (amended by the Planning (Consequential Provisions) Act 1990 s 4, Sch 2 para 57), which further applies the Town and Country Planning Act 1990 ss 324(8), 325(1)–(6), (8), (9) to such powers of entry as they apply to the Town and Country Planning Act 1990 s 324. See PLANNING vol 81 (2010) PARA 65 et seq.
12 This includes corresponding powers under the Local Employment Act 1972 s 5 (repealed): Industrial Development Act 1982 s 14(4).
13 Industrial Development Act 1982 s 14(4).
14 Industrial Development Act 1982 s 14(4)(a).
15 Industrial Development Act 1982 s 14(4)(b).
16 Industrial Development Act 1982 s 14(4)(c).
17 Industrial Development Act 1982 s 14(3). Where the execution of such work will interrupt the use of the buildings or works by any undertaking, the Secretary of State may acquire other land by agreement, and erect buildings and carry out works on it, or on land previously acquired by him, for the purpose of providing premises for the occupation of that undertaking or of otherwise meeting its requirements: s 14(3).

1046.   Grants or loans for the improvement of basic services. Where it appears to the minister in charge of any government department that adequate provision has not been made for the needs of any development area[1] or intermediate area[2] in respect of a basic service[3] for which the department is responsible, and it is expedient with a view to contributing to the development of industry in that area that the service should be improved, he may, with the consent of the Treasury[4], make grants or loans towards the cost of the improvements to such persons and in such manner as appears to him appropriate[5].

Where at any time a locality ceases to be a development area or an intermediate area, the fact that it is no longer such an area does not prejudice the making of any grant or loan in any case in which the application for the grant or loan was received by the Secretary of State before that time[6].

1 As to development areas see PARA 1037.
2 As to intermediate areas see PARA 1038.
3 'Basic service' means the provision of facilities for transport, whether by road, rail, water or air, or of power, lighting, heating, water, or sewerage and sewage disposal facilities, or any other service or facility on which the development of the area in question, and in particular of industrial undertakings in it, depends: Industrial Development Act 1982 s 13(2). As to the meaning of 'undertaking' see PARA 1045 note 5.
4 As to the Treasury see CONSTITUTIONAL AND ADMINISTRATIVE LAW vol 20 (2014) PARA 262 et seq.
5 Industrial Development Act 1982 s 13(1). These powers are in addition to any other powers of a Minister of the Crown to make grants or loans: s 13(3).
6 Industrial Development Act 1982 s 17(3)(b). Nor does it prejudice the continued operation of any agreement relating to such a grant or loan or of any other agreement relating to grants or loans entered into under Pt IV (ss 11–17), or corresponding provisions of the Local Employment Act 1972: Industrial Development Act 1982 s 17(3)(c). As to the Secretary of State see PARA 902. The functions under the Industrial Development Act 1982 ss 13, 17 are exercisable by the Welsh Ministers concurrently with the Secretary of State or the Minister of the Crown as appropriate: see the National Assembly for Wales (Transfer of Functions) Order 1999, SI 1999/672, art 2, Sch 1; the Government of Wales Act 2006 s 162, Sch 11 para 30; and PARA 902 note 21.

1047. Power of the Secretary of State to give advice to businesses. The Secretary of State[1] may make provision for the giving of advice, whether free of charge or otherwise, to persons carrying on or proposing to carry on a business[2]. Not later than six months after the end of any financial year in which this power is used he must prepare and lay before Parliament a report on the exercise during the year of this power[3].

1 As to the Secretary of State see PARA 902. The functions under the Industrial Development Act 1982 s 11 are exercisable by the Welsh Ministers concurrently with the Secretary of State: see the National Assembly for Wales (Transfer of Functions) Order 1999, SI 1999/672, art 2, Sch 1; the Government of Wales Act 2006 s 162, Sch 11 para 30; and PARA 902 note 21.
2 Industrial Development Act 1982 s 11(1).
3 Industrial Development Act 1982 s 11(2).

1048. Grants or loans for the promotion of careers in industry. The Secretary of State[1] may make such grants[2] or loans[3] to any body as he considers appropriate[4] for the purpose of assisting in:
(1) the promotion of the practice of engineering[5];
(2) the encouragement and improvement of links between industry, or any part of industry, and bodies or individuals concerned with education[6];
(3) the encouragement of young persons and others to take up careers in industry, or in any part of industry, and to pursue appropriate educational courses[7].

He may also, with the approval of the Treasury, guarantee obligations, arising out of loans, incurred by any body established by royal charter[8], and the members of which are appointed by him[9] and which is, in his opinion, concerned with promoting the practice of engineering[10].

1 As to the Secretary of State see PARA 902. The functions under the Industrial Development Act 1982 s 12 are exercisable by the Welsh Ministers concurrently with the Secretary of State: see the National Assembly for Wales (Transfer of Functions) Order 1999, SI 1999/672, art 2, Sch 1; the Government of Wales Act 2006 s 162, Sch 11 para 30; and PARA 902 note 21.

2   Grants may be made on such conditions as the Secretary of State may determine with the approval of the Treasury: Industrial Development Act 1982 s 12(2). As to the Treasury see CONSTITUTIONAL AND ADMINISTRATIVE LAW vol 20 (2014) PARA 262 et seq.
3   Loans may be made at such rates of interest as the Secretary of State may determine with the approval of the Treasury: Industrial Development Act 1982 s 12(2). He may not, however, determine a rate of interest in respect of a loan which is lower than the lowest rate for the time being determined by the Treasury under the National Loans Act 1968 s 5 (see CONSTITUTIONAL AND ADMINISTRATIVE LAW vol 20 (2014) PARA 509), in respect of comparable loans out of the National Loans Fund: Industrial Development Act 1982 s 12(3).
4   Industrial Development Act 1982 s 12(1).
5   Industrial Development Act 1982 s 12(1)(a).
6   Industrial Development Act 1982 s 12(1)(b).
7   Industrial Development Act 1982 s 12(1)(c).
8   Industrial Development Act 1982 s 12(5)(a).
9   Industrial Development Act 1982 s 12(5)(b).
10   Industrial Development Act 1982 s 12(4).
     As to the provision of information in Wales by public bodies for the purposes of the provision of services under s 12 see the Learning and Skills Act 2000 s 138; and EDUCATION vol 36 (2011) PARA 1344.

1049.   Annual reports and statements of account of the Secretary of State.   For each financial year the Secretary of State[1] must prepare and lay before Parliament[2] a report on the discharge of his functions[3]:

(1)   relating to assisted areas[4], financial assistance for industry[5], the provision of premises and sites[6] and the improvement[7] of basic services[8]; and

(2)   in relation to credits and grants for the construction of ships and offshore installations[9], including any function in respect of guarantees given by him under the Shipbuilding Industry Act 1967[10].

The Secretary of State may discharge this duty in any year by making a report on any of his functions mentioned in heads (1) and (2) above and one or more separate reports on the remaining functions[11].

For every financial year the Secretary of State must prepare a statement of accounts, in such form as the Treasury[12] may direct, showing the financial results for the year as respects his activities in the execution of certain of the statutory provisions[13] (other than activities in respect of grants)[14]. He must transmit the statement to the Comptroller and Auditor General[15], on or before 30 November after the financial year in question, for examination and certification[16]. Copies of every such statement, together with the report of the Comptroller and Auditor General, must be laid before Parliament by the Secretary of State[17].

1   As to the Secretary of State see PARA 902.
2   The report must be laid not later than six months after the end of the financial year to which it relates: Industrial Development Act 1982 s 15(1).
3   Such reports must also include information in relation to the exercise by the Welsh Ministers of such functions, and the Welsh Ministers must ensure that all necessary information is supplied to the Secretary of State for this purpose: see the National Assembly for Wales (Transfer of Functions) Order 1999, SI 1999/672, art 2, Sch 1; the Government of Wales Act 2006 s 162, Sch 11 para 30. As to the functions of the Welsh Ministers under the Industrial Development Act 1982 see PARA 1036 note 1; and as to the transfer of certain functions of the Secretary of State relating to this title, so far as exercisable in relation to Wales, to the National Assembly for Wales and subsequently to the Welsh Ministers see PARA 902 note 21. As to the National Assembly for Wales and the Welsh Ministers see CONSTITUTIONAL AND ADMINISTRATIVE LAW vol 20 (2014) PARA 373 et seq.
4   Ie under the Industrial Development Act 1982 Pt I (s 1): see PARAS 1037–1038.
5   Ie under the Industrial Development Act 1982 Pt III (ss 7–10): see PARA 1040 et seq. The report relating to Pt III must contain a statement showing the total amount of the liabilities of the Secretary of State, excluding any liability in respect of interest on a principal sum, under

guarantees given by him under Pt III or the Industry Act 1972 Pt II (ss 7–9) (repealed), or, as the case may be, Pt III (ss 10–12) of that Act, including any liabilities under guarantees given by him under the Shipbuilding Industry Act 1967 s 7 (repealed): Industrial Development Act 1982 s 15(3).

6   Ie under the Industrial Development Act 1982 s 14: see PARA 1045.
7   Ie under the Industrial Development Act 1982 s 13: see PARA 1046.
8   Industrial Development Act 1982 s 15(1)(a) (amended by the Statute Law (Repeals) Act 2004 s 1(2), Sch 2 para 14).
9   Ie under the Industry Act 1972 Pt III (ss 7–10): see PARA 952.
10 Industrial Development Act 1982 s 15(1)(c). A report on the discharge of the Secretary of State's functions under the English Industrial Estates Corporation Act 1981 (repealed) (see PARA 1045 note 1) was also required: see the Industrial Development Act 1982 s 15(1)(d) (repealed, as from a day to be appointed, by the Leasehold Reform, Housing and Urban Development Act 1993 s 187(2), Sch 22). At the date at which this volume states the law, no such day had been appointed.
11 Industrial Development Act 1982 s 15(2) (amended by the Statute Law (Repeals) Act 2004).
12 As to the Treasury see CONSTITUTIONAL AND ADMINISTRATIVE LAW vol 20 (2014) PARA 262 et seq.
13 Ie the Industrial Development Act 1982 ss 13, 14: see PARAS 1045–1046.
14 Industrial Development Act 1982 s 16(1) (amended by the Industrial Development Act 1985 ss 4(2), 6(3), Schedule).
15 As to the Comptroller and Auditor General see CONSTITUTIONAL AND ADMINISTRATIVE LAW vol 20 (2014) PARAS 494–496.
16 Industrial Development Act 1982 s 16(2).
17 Industrial Development Act 1982 s 16(3).

(iv) Promotion of Industrial and Medical Research and Development

1050. Origins of the British Technology Group plc. The National Research Development Corporation ('NRDC') was established in 1948 as a non-departmental government body with the purpose of promoting and developing British technologies by commercialising publicly funded research[1]. Later, the Industry Act 1975 established the National Enterprise Board ('NEB') for:

(1)   the development or assistance of the economy of the United Kingdom or any part of the United Kingdom;

(2)   the promotion in any part of the United Kingdom of industrial efficiency and international competitiveness; and

(3)   the provision, maintenance or safeguarding of productive employment in any part of the United Kingdom[2].

The NRDC and the NEB were merged in 1981 to form the British Technology Group. This was given a statutory basis a decade later by the British Technology Group Act 1991 which transferred the property, rights and liabilities of the NRDC and NEB to the British Technology Group[3] and made provision for the dissolution of the NRDC and NEB[4].

Now a public limited company, the British Technology Group plc's role is to develop and commercialise innovations in the spheres of pharmaceuticals and medical techniques and products.

1   See the Development of Inventions Act 1948 (repealed); Development of Inventions Act 1967 s 1, Schedule (both prospectively repealed by the British Technology Group Act 1991 s 17(2), Sch 2 Pt II, as from the date of dissolution of the National Research Development Corporation appointed in accordance with s 11); National Research Development Corporation Regulations 1986, SI 1986/431.
2   Industry Act 1975 s 2(1) (repealed).
3   British Technology Group Act 1991 s 1, Sch 1; British Technology Group Act 1991 (Appointed Day) Order 1991, SI 1991/2721 (which appointed 6 January 1992 as the day on which the

transfers were made); British Technology Group Act 1991 (Nominated Company) Order 1991, SI 1991/2722 (lapsed); British Technology Group Act 1991 (Government Shareholding) Order 1992, SI 1992/1437 (lapsed).

The British Technology Group Act 1991 also made provision for the financial structure of the successor company (see ss 8, 10) and stated that the successor company is to be treated for the purposes of the Corporation Tax Acts as if it were the same person as the NRDC and the NEB: see s 12.

4   The NRDC and the NEB were to continue in existence after the appointed day until the Secretary of State was satisfied, in the case of either body, that nothing remained to be done under the relevant transitional provisions and, after consulting the body and the successor company, by order dissolved the body in question (this period is referred to as 'the transitional period'): see the British Technology Group Act 1991 s 11; and the National Enterprise Board (Dissolution) Order 1996, SI 1996/1448 (dissolving the NEB on 1 July 1996).

(v) The Welsh Development Agency and the Welsh Industrial Development Advisory Board

A. THE WELSH DEVELOPMENT AGENCY

1051. The Welsh Development Agency, its dissolution and the transfer of its functions to the Welsh Ministers. The Welsh Development Agency was established in 1975[1] for the purpose of:

(1)   furthering the economic development of Wales or any part of Wales;

(2)   promoting industrial efficiency and international competitiveness in Wales;

(3)   promoting, maintaining or safeguarding employment in any part of Wales; and

(4)   furthering the improvement of the environment in Wales (having regard to existing amenity)[2].

Its purposes were later amended, and the agency was abolished and its functions were transferred to the National Assembly for Wales as from 1 April 2006[3]. The current purposes, now the responsibility of the Welsh Ministers[4], are as follows:

(a)   to further the economic and social development of Wales or any part of Wales, and in that connection to provide, maintain and safeguard employment[5];

(b)   to promote efficiency in business and international competitiveness in Wales[6]; and

(c)   to further the improvement of the environment in Wales, having regard to existing amenity[7].

1   See the Welsh Development Agency Act 1975 s 1(1) (as originally enacted). The Welsh Industrial Estates Corporation, which had been established by the Local Employment Act 1960 s 8 (repealed), and continued by the Local Employment Act 1972 s 10 (repealed), was dissolved, and its property, rights and liabilities vested in the agency: Welsh Development Agency Act 1975 s 7(1) (repealed). As to the transfer of staff from the corporation to the agency and compensation for loss of employment see s 7(2), Sch 2 (repealed); and the Welsh Development Agency (Compensation) Regulations 1976, SI 1976/2107 (revoked). Land in Wales held for the purposes of the Local Employment Act 1972 was vested in the agency by the Welsh Development Agency Act 1975 s 8 (repealed).

2   Welsh Development Agency Act 1975 s 1(2) (as originally enacted).

3   See the Welsh Development Agency (Transfer of Functions to the National Assembly for Wales and Abolition) Order 2005, SI 2005/3226; and the Welsh Development Agency Act 1975 s 1(1) (substituted by SI 2005/3226). Except in relation to land in England, the functions and powers of the Secretary of State under the Welsh Development Act 1975 were also transferred to the National Assembly for Wales. As to the functions of the Welsh Ministers see PARA 1052.

4   See the Government of Wales Act 2006 s 162, Sch 11 para 30; and PARA 902 note 21. References to the Assembly are to be construed as references to the Welsh Ministers: see Sch 11 para 32.

5   Welsh Development Agency Act 1975 s 1(2)(a) (amended by the Industry Act 1980 s 1(3)(a);
    and the Government of Wales Act 1998 s 126(2)(a)).
6   Welsh Development Agency Act 1975 s 1(2)(b) (amended by the Government of Wales Act 1998
    s 126(2)(b)). 'Business' includes any industrial, commercial or professional activities (whether or
    not with a view to profit) and the activities of any government department or any local or other
    public authority: Welsh Development Agency Act 1975 s 27(1) (definition added by the
    Government of Wales Act 1998 s 128, Sch 14 para 10).
7   Welsh Development Agency Act 1975 s 1(2)(d).

1052. Functions of the Welsh Ministers in relation to industry. The functions
of the Welsh Ministers[1] under the Welsh Development Agency Act 1975 are[2]:

(1)   to promote Wales as a location for businesses[3], or assist or concert its
      promotion as such a location[4];
(2)   to provide finance for persons carrying on or intending to carry on
      businesses[5];
(3)   to carry on businesses and to establish and carry on new ones[6];
(4)   otherwise to promote or assist the establishment, growth, modernisation
      or development of businesses, or a particular business or particular
      businesses[7];
(5)   to make land available for development[8];
(6)   to provide sites, premises, services and facilities for businesses[9];
(7)   to manage sites and premises for businesses[10];
(8)   to bring derelict land[11] into use or improve its appearance[12],
(9)   to undertake the development and redevelopment of the environment[13];
      and
(10) to promote private ownership of interests in businesses by the disposal
      of securities and other property held by the Welsh Ministers or any of
      their subsidiaries[14].

In exercising their functions under the 1975 Act the Welsh Ministers must
have regard to the requirements of agriculture and efficient land management[15].
They may do anything, whether in Wales or elsewhere, which is calculated to
facilitate the discharge of functions specified above or is incidental or conducive
to their discharge[16]. However, nothing authorises the disregard by the Welsh
Ministers of any enactment or rule of law[17].

After consulting such local authorities[18], national park authorities[19] and other
bodies as appear to them to have an interest, the Welsh Ministers must from time
to time prepare and publish programmes for the performance of such of their
functions under the 1975 Act as they consider appropriate[20].

The Welsh Ministers may establish such committees for giving advice to them
about the discharge of any of their functions under the Welsh Development
Agency Act 1975 as they consider appropriate[21].

The Welsh Ministers have power in connection with their functions under the
1975 Act to:

(a)   make such charge for any of their services as they think fit[22];
(b)   accept any gift made to them for the purpose of any such functions, and
      subject to the terms of the gift and the statutory provisions, apply it for
      those purposes[23]; and
(c)   carry out or commission the carrying out of such inquiries,
      investigations or researches concerning their functions under the Act as
      they may deem necessary or expedient for the performance of such
      functions[24].

1   As to the transfer of powers under the Welsh Development Agency Act 1975 to the Welsh
    Ministers see PARA 1051. As to the transfer of certain functions of the Secretary of State relating

to this title generally, so far as exercisable in relation to Wales, to the National Assembly for Wales and subsequently to the Welsh Ministers see PARA 902 note 21. As to the National Assembly for Wales and the Welsh Ministers see CONSTITUTIONAL AND ADMINISTRATIVE LAW vol 20 (2014) PARA 373 et seq.

2 Welsh Development Agency Act 1975 s 1(3) (amended by SI 2005/3226; and by virtue of the Government of Wales Act 2006 s 162, Sch 11 para 32).

3 As to the meaning of 'business' see PARA 1051 note 6.

4 Welsh Development Agency Act 1975 s 1(3)(a) (amended by the Government of Wales Act 1998 s 126(3)(a)). The Welsh Ministers may appoint a local authority or national park authority, the development corporation of a new town or any other body or person to act as their agent in carrying out their functions under the Welsh Development Agency Act 1975 s 1(3)(a), (da), (f)–(i) (see heads (1), (5)–(9) in the text) or s 21C (see PARA 1055): s 5(1) (amended by the Environment Act 1995 s 78, Sch 10 para 13(2); the Government of Wales Act 1998 Sch 14 para 4; and SI 2005/3226; and by virtue of the Government of Wales Act 2006 Sch 11 para 32). Any such authority, corporation, body or person, on being requested by the Welsh Ministers, may place the services of any of its staff at the ministers' disposal, on such terms as may be agreed with the ministers: Welsh Development Agency Act 1975 s 5(2) (amended by the Environment Act 1995 Sch 10 para 13(2); and SI 2005/3226; and by virtue of the Government of Wales Act 2006 Sch 11 para 32). As to development corporations of new towns see PLANNING vol 83 (2010) PARA 1499 et seq.

5 Welsh Development Agency Act 1975 s 1(3)(b) (amended by the Government of Wales Act 1998 s 126(3)(b)).

6 Welsh Development Agency Act 1975 s 1(3)(c) (amended by the Government of Wales Act 1998 s 126(3)(b)). The Welsh Ministers may only exercise these functions through subsidiaries: Welsh Development Agency Act 1975 s 1(5) (amended by SI 2005/3226; and by virtue of the Government of Wales Act 2006 Sch 11 para 32). 'Subsidiary' means a subsidiary as defined by the Companies Act 2006 s 1159 (see COMPANIES vol 14 (2009) PARA 25): Welsh Development Agency Act 1975 s 27(1) (amended by SI 2009/1941).

7 Welsh Development Agency Act 1975 s 1(3)(d) (amended by the Industry Act 1980 ss 1(3)(c), 21(1), Sch 2; and by the Government of Wales Act 1998 s 126(3)(c)).

8 Welsh Development Agency Act 1975 s 1(3)(da) (added by the Government of Wales Act 1998 s 126(3)(d)). As to the powers of the Welsh Ministers to acquire land see PARA 1053.

9 Welsh Development Agency Act 1975 s 1(3)(f) (amended by the Government of Wales Act 1998 s 126(3)(b)). For the purpose of providing or managing sites and premises for businesses and providing related facilities, or making land available for development, the Welsh Ministers have power to modernise, adapt or reconstruct buildings: Welsh Development Agency Act 1975 s 9(2) (amended by SI 2005/3226; and by virtue of the Government of Wales Act 2006 Sch 11 para 32). The Welsh Ministers may, if they consider there are circumstances which justify the giving of special assistance, provide premises for the occupation of a business free of rent for such time as they think appropriate: see the Welsh Development Agency Act 1975 s 9(3) (substituted by SI 2005/3226; and amended by virtue of the Government of Wales Act 2006 Sch 11 para 32). The Welsh Ministers may also undertake or assist in the provision of means of access or other services or facilities in or for an area where this appears to them to be expedient for the purpose of contributing to or supporting the development of businesses in that area: Welsh Development Agency Act 1975 s 10 (amended by the Government of Wales Act 1998 s 128, Sch 14 para 6; and SI 2005/3226; and by virtue of the Government of Wales Act 2006 Sch 11 para 32).

10 Welsh Development Agency Act 1975 s 1(3)(g) (amended by the Government of Wales Act 1998 s 126(3)(b)); and see note 9.

11 'Land' includes buildings and other structures, land covered with water, and any estate, interest, easement, servitude or right in or over land: Interpretation Act 1978 Sch 1; Welsh Development Agency Act 1975 s 27(1) (definition substituted by the Government of Wales Act 1998 Sch 14 para 10(3)).

12 Welsh Development Act 1975 s 1(3)(h) (amended by the Government of Wales Act 1998 s 126(3)(b)). As to derelict land generally see PARA 1058.

13 Welsh Development Agency Act 1975 s 1(3)(i).

14 Welsh Development Agency Act 1975 s 1(3)(j) (added by the Industry Act 1980 s 1(3)(b); amended by the Government of Wales Act 1998 s 126(3)(d); and SI 2005/3226; and by virtue of the Government of Wales Act 2006 Sch 11 para 32).

15 Welsh Development Agency Act 1975 s 1(4) (amended by SI 2005/3226; and by virtue of the Government of Wales Act 2006 Sch 11 para 32). See AGRICULTURAL LAND.

16 Welsh Development Agency Act 1975 s 1(6) (amended by SI 2005/3226; and by virtue of the Government of Wales Act 2006 Sch 11 para 32). In particular the Welsh Ministers may acquire,

hold and dispose of securities; form bodies corporate; form partnerships; make loans; guarantee obligations arising out of loans or otherwise; make grants; act as agent; acquire and dispose of land, plant, machinery, equipment and other property; manage land, develop land, carry out works on land and maintain or assist in maintaining works; make land, plant, machinery, equipment and other property available for use by other persons; provide or assist in providing advisory or other services or facilities in relation to any of their functions; and promote or assist in promoting publicity relating to their functions under the Welsh Development Agency Act 1975: s 1(7) (amended by SI 2005/3226; and by virtue of the Government of Wales Act 2006 Sch 11 para 32).

The power to acquire land (see PARA 1053) includes power to acquire land to provide premises for the occupation of an undertaking the use of whose buildings has been interrupted by works of modernisation, adaptation or reconstruction as mentioned in note 9, or otherwise to meet the requirements of such an undertaking, and for that purpose the agency may erect buildings and carry out works on land so acquired: see the Welsh Development Agency Act 1975 s 9(2) (substituted by SI 2005/3226; and amended by virtue of the Government of Wales Act 2006 Sch 11 para 32).

17 Welsh Development Agency Act 1975 s 1(16) (amended by SI 2005/3226; and by virtue of the Government of Wales Act 2006 Sch 11 para 32).
18 As to local authorities in England and Wales see LOCAL GOVERNMENT vol 69 (2009) PARA 22 et seq.
19 As to national park authorities see OPEN SPACES AND COUNTRYSIDE vol 78 (2010) PARA 526 et seq.
20 Welsh Development Agency Act 1975 s 1(14) (substituted by SI 2005/3226; and amended by virtue of the Government of Wales Act 2006 Sch 11 para 32). This duty includes in particular a duty to prepare and submit schemes for the improvement, development or redevelopment of the environment in Wales: see PARA 1058.
21 Welsh Development Agency Act 1975 s 6(1) (s 6 substituted by SI 2005/3226; and amended by virtue of the Government of Wales Act 2006 Sch 11 para 32). The members of a committee are appointed by the Welsh Ministers and may be members of the National Assembly for Wales or persons who are not members: Welsh Development Agency Act 1975 s 6(2) (as so substituted and amended).
22 Welsh Development Agency Act 1975 s 4(a) (s 4 amended by SI 2005/3226; and by virtue of the Government of Wales Act 2006 Sch 11 para 32).
23 Welsh Development Agency Act 1975 s 4(b) (as amended: see note 22).
24 Welsh Development Agency Act 1975 s 4(c) (as amended: see note 22).

1053. Powers of the Welsh Ministers to acquire land. Certain powers of the Welsh Ministers under the Welsh Development Agency Act 1975[1] are powers to acquire land by agreement; and to acquire land compulsorily if it is in Wales or, if it is in England, compulsorily if authorised to do so by the Secretary of State[2]. Where the Welsh Ministers so acquire or have so acquired land, they have power to acquire by agreement or compulsorily (in relation to land in Wales, or, in relation to land in England, compulsorily if authorised to do so by the Secretary of State) any adjoining land which is required for the purpose of executing works for facilitating its development or use and, where the land acquired forms part of a common, an open space or a fuel or field garden allotment, any land required for the purpose of being given in exchange for it[3]. The Welsh Ministers may acquire rights over land by the creation of new rights as well as by acquiring rights already in existence[4]. Before acquiring land under these provisions for the purpose of the specified statutory function[5] the Welsh Ministers must:

(1)   consider whether the land would or would not in their opinion be made available for development if they did not act;

(2)   consider the fact that planning permission has or has not been granted in respect of the land or is likely or unlikely to be granted;

(3)   (in a case where no planning permission has been granted in respect of the land) consult every relevant local authority[6]; and

(4)   consider the needs of those engaged in building, agriculture and forestry and of the community in general[7].

Where the Welsh Ministers have acquired land for the purpose of any of their functions under the Welsh Development Agency Act 1975, they may appropriate it to the purpose of any of their other functions under that Act[8]. Where the Welsh Ministers have acquired or appropriated land for the purpose of the specified statutory function, they must, until they either dispose of the land or appropriate it to the purpose of any of their other functions under the 1975 Act, manage it and turn it to account[9].

On the completion by the Welsh Ministers of a compulsory acquisition of land under these provisions, all private rights of way, and rights of laying down, erecting, continuing or maintaining any apparatus on, under or over the land, are extinguished and any such apparatus vests in the Welsh Ministers[10]. Any person who suffers loss by the extinguishment of a right or the vesting of any apparatus is entitled to compensation from the Welsh Ministers[11].

The erection, construction or carrying out, or maintenance, of any building or work on land which has been acquired by the Welsh Ministers under these provisions, whether done by the Welsh Ministers or by a person deriving title under them, is authorised if it is done in accordance with planning permission even if it involves interference with certain interests or rights[12], or a breach of a restriction as to the user of land arising by virtue of a contract[13]. Provision is made for the payment of compensation in respect of any interference or breach[14].

Specific provision is made as to:

(a)   the use and development of consecrated ground and burial grounds[15];

(b)   the use and development of land for open spaces[16];

(c)   extinguishment of rights of way, and rights as to apparatus, of statutory undertakers[17];

(d)   rights of entry[18];

(e)   provision of information[19];

(f)   regulations as to the form of documents[20];

(g)   local inquiries[21];

(h)   Crown land[22]; and

(i)   offences by corporations[23].

If the Welsh Ministers certify, in relation to a house in Wales, or the Secretary of State certifies, in relation to a house in England, that possession of a house which has been acquired by the Welsh Ministers under these provisions, and is for the time being held by the Welsh Ministers for the purposes for which it was acquired, is immediately required for those purposes, nothing in the Rent (Agriculture) Act 1976, the Rent Act 1977 or the Housing Act 1988 may prevent the Welsh Ministers from obtaining possession of the house[24].

1   Ie under the Welsh Development Agency Act 1975 ss 1(7)(h), 16(3)(b). As to the transfer of powers under the Welsh Development Agency Act 1975 to the Welsh Ministers see PARA 1051.

2   Welsh Development Agency Act 1975 s 21A(1) (s 21A added by the Government of Wales Act 1998 s 127, Sch 13 para 2; substituted by SI 2005/3226; and amended by virtue of the Government of Wales Act 2006 s 162, Sch 11 para 32). Provisions of the Acquisition of Land Act 1981 apply, with specified modifications, to compulsory purchase under the Welsh Development Agency Act 1975 s 21A: see s 21A(8), Sch 4 paras 1, 1A, 3, 3A (s 21A(8) as so added and substituted; Sch 4 added by the Government of Wales Act 1998 Sch 13 para 3; Welsh Development Agency Act 1975 Sch 4 para 1 substituted, Sch 4 para 1A added, Sch 4 para 3 amended and Sch 4 para 3A added by SI 2005/3226; Welsh Development Agency Act 1975 Sch 4 paras 1, 1A, 3 amended by virtue of the Government of Wales Act 2006 Sch 11 para 32). Provisions of the Compulsory Purchase Act 1965 (see COMPULSORY ACQUISITION OF LAND) apply in relation to the acquisition of land by agreement under the Welsh Development Agency Act 1975 s 21A: Sch 4 paras 4, 9 (as so added). As to the Secretary of State see PARA 902.

3   Welsh Development Agency Act 1975 s 21A(2), (2A) (as added, substituted and amended: see note 2). 'Common' includes any land subject to be enclosed under the Inclosure Acts 1845 to

1882 and any town or village green; and 'fuel or field garden allotment' means any allotment set out as a fuel allotment, or a field garden allotment, under an Inclosure Act: Welsh Development Agency Act 1975 s 27(1) (definitions added by the Government of Wales Act 1998 s 128, Sch 14 para 10(2)). 'Open space' means any land laid out as a public garden or used for the purposes of public recreation or any land which is a disused burial ground: Welsh Development Agency Act 1975 s 27(1) (definition substituted by the Government of Wales Act 1998 Sch 14 para 10(3)).

4 Welsh Development Agency Act 1975 s 21A(3) (as added, substituted and amended: see note 2).
5 Ie under the Welsh Development Agency Act 1975 s 1(3)(da): see PARA 1052.
6 A 'relevant local authority' is the council of any county, county borough or district, any joint planning board, or any national park authority in whose area the land or any part of it is situated: Welsh Development Agency Act 1975 s 21A(5) (as added and substituted: see note 2). As to local authorities in England and Wales see LOCAL GOVERNMENT vol 69 (2009) PARA 22 et seq; and as to national park authorities see OPEN SPACES AND COUNTRYSIDE vol 78 (2010) PARA 526 et seq.
7 Welsh Development Agency Act 1975 s 21A(4) (as added, substituted and amended: see note 2).
8 Welsh Development Agency Act 1975 s 21A(6) (as added, substituted and amended: see note 2).
9 Welsh Development Agency Act 1975 s 21A(7) (as added, substituted and amended: see note 2). 'Dispose' includes dispose by sale or exchange or dispose by lease (whether by grant or assignment) and related expressions are to be construed accordingly: s 27(1) (definition added by the Government of Wales Act 1998 Sch 14 para 10(2)).
10 Welsh Development Agency Act 1975 Sch 4 para 5(1) (as added (see note 2); amended by SI 2005/3226; and by virtue of the Government of Wales Act 2006 Sch 11 para 32). This does not apply to any right vested in, or apparatus belonging to, statutory undertakers for the purpose of the carrying on of their undertaking: Welsh Development Agency Act 1975 Sch 4 para 5(2) (as so added). However, it does have effect in relation to any right or apparatus not falling within Sch 4 para 5(2) subject to any direction given by the Welsh Ministers before the completion of the acquisition that Sch 4 para 5(1) is not to apply, and to any agreement which may be made (whether before or after the completion of the acquisition) between the Welsh Ministers and the person in or to whom the right or apparatus is vested or belongs: Sch 4 para 5(3) (as so added and amended).
11 Welsh Development Agency Act 1975 Sch 4 para 5(4) (as added (see note 2); amended by SI 2005/3226; and by virtue of the Government of Wales Act 2006 Sch 11 para 32). Compensation is determined under the Land Compensation Act 1961: Welsh Development Agency Act 1975 Sch 4 para 5(5) (as so added).
12 Ie any easement, liberty, privilege, right or advantage annexed to land and adversely affecting other land, including any natural right to support: Welsh Development Agency Act 1975 Sch 4 para 6(3) (as added: see note 2).
13 Welsh Development Agency Act 1975 Sch 4 para 6(1) (as added (see note 2); amended by SI 2005/3226; and by virtue of the Government of Wales Act 2006 Sch 11 para 32). The use of any land which has been acquired by the Welsh Ministers under the Welsh Development Agency Act 1975 s 21A, whether the use is by the Welsh Ministers or by a person deriving title under them, is authorised by virtue of Sch 4 para 6 if it is in accordance with planning permission even if the use involves interference with an interest or right to which this paragraph applies, or a breach of a restriction as to the user of land arising by virtue of a contract: Sch 4 para 6(1A) (as added (see note 2); para 6(1A) added by SI 2013/2948).

   However, nothing in the Welsh Development Agency Act 1975 Sch 4 para 6 authorises interference with any right of way or any right of laying down, erecting, continuing or maintaining apparatus on, under or over land which is vested in or belongs to statutory undertakers for the purpose of the carrying on of their undertaking: Welsh Development Agency Act 1975 Sch 4 para 6(2) (as added: see note 2). Neither is any act or omission authorised on the part of any person which is actionable at the suit of any person on any grounds other than an interference or breach (as mentioned in Sch 4 para 6(1) or Sch 4 para 6(1A): Sch 4 para 6(7) (as added (see note 2); amended by SI 2013/2948)).
14 See the Welsh Development Agency Act 1975 Sch 4 para 6(4)–(6) (as added (see note 2); Sch 4 para 6(4) amended by SI 2013/2948; Welsh Development Agency Act 1975 Sch 4 para 6(5), (6) amended by SI 2005/3226; and by virtue of the Government of Wales Act 2006 Sch 11 para 32).
15 Welsh Development Agency Act 1975 Sch 4 paras 7, 10 (as added (see note 2); Sch 4 para 7 amended by SI 2005/3226; and by virtue of the Government of Wales Act 2006 Sch 11 para 32).
16 Welsh Development Agency Act 1975 Sch 4 paras 8, 10 (as added (see note 2); Sch 4 para 8 amended by SI 2005/3226; and by virtue of the Government of Wales Act 2006 Sch 11 para 32).
17 Welsh Development Agency Act 1975 Sch 4 paras 11–13 (as added (see note 2); amended by SI 2005/3226; and by virtue of the Government of Wales Act 2006 Sch 11 para 32).

18 Welsh Development Agency Act 1975 Sch 4 paras 14, 15 (as added (see note 2); amended by SI 2005/3226; and by virtue of the Government of Wales Act 2006 Sch 11 para 32).
19 Welsh Development Agency Act 1975 Sch 4 paras 18, 19 (as added (see note 2); amended by SI 2005/3226; and by virtue of the Government of Wales Act 2006 Sch 11 para 32).
20 Welsh Development Agency Act 1975 Sch 4 para 20 (as added (see note 2); amended by SI 2005/3226; and by virtue of the Government of Wales Act 2006 Sch 11 para 32).
21 Welsh Development Agency Act 1975 Sch 4 para 21 (as added (see note 2); amended by SI 2005/3226; and by virtue of the Government of Wales Act 2006 Sch 11 para 32).
22 Welsh Development Agency Act 1975 Sch 4 para 22 (as added (see note 2); amended by SI 2005/3226; and by virtue of the Government of Wales Act 2006 Sch 11 para 32).
23 Welsh Development Agency Act 1975 Sch 4 para 23 (as added: see note 2).
24 Welsh Development Agency Act 1975 Sch 4 para 16 (as added (see note 2); amended by SI 2005/3226; and by virtue of the Government of Wales Act 2006 Sch 11 para 32). As to the Acts mentioned in the text see further HOUSING vol 56 (2011) PARA 1 et seq; LANDLORD AND TENANT.

1054. Disposal of land by the Welsh Ministers. In exercising any power under the Welsh Development Agency Act 1975 to dispose of land[1], the Welsh Ministers[2] may not dispose of land for a consideration less than the best that can reasonably be obtained, except as provided by statute[3], or otherwise as they consider appropriate[4].

1 As to the meaning of 'dispose' see PARA 1053 note 9; and as to the meaning of 'land' see PARA 1052 note 11. As to the functions of the Welsh Ministers under the Welsh Development Agency Act 1975 see PARA 1052.
2 As to the transfer of powers under the Welsh Development Agency Act 1975 to the Welsh Ministers see PARA 1051.
3 Ie under the Welsh Development Agency Act 1975 s 16(7): see PARA 1058.
4 Welsh Development Agency Act 1975 s 21B (added by the Government of Wales Act 1998 s 127, Sch 13 para 2; amended by SI 2005/3226; and by virtue of the Government of Wales Act 2006 s 162, Sch 11 para 32).

1055. Powers of the Welsh Ministers to advise on land matters. If requested to do so by a public authority[1], the Welsh Ministers[2] may advise the authority about disposing of any of the authority's land in Wales to other persons, and assist the authority in disposing of the land[3].

The Welsh Ministers may assist:

(1) the council of a county or county borough in Wales in making an assessment of land in its area which is, in its opinion, available and suitable for development;

(2) a joint planning board[4] in Wales in making an assessment of land in its district which is, in its opinion, available and suitable for development; or

(3) a national park authority for a national park in Wales in making an assessment of land in the national park which is, in its opinion, available and suitable for development[5].

1 In this context, 'public authority' means: a government department; a county council, county borough council or community council; a national park authority; a development corporation for a new town; a local health board, special health authority or NHS trust; a body corporate established by or under an enactment for the purpose of carrying on under national ownership any industry or part of an industry; any statutory undertakers; or any other public authority, body or undertakers specified in an order made by the Welsh Ministers: Welsh Development Agency Act 1975 s 21C(2) (s 21C added by the Government of Wales Act 1998 s 127, Sch 13 para 2; amended by SI 2005/3226; SI 2007/961; and by virtue of the Government of Wales Act 2006 s 162, Sch 11 para 32). At the date at which this volume states the law no such order had been made. As to the meaning of 'statutory undertakers' see PARA 1056 note 3. A person who holds a licence under the Transport Act 2000 Pt I Ch I (ss 1–40) (air traffic services: see AIR LAW vol 2 (2008) PARA 139 et seq) is not be considered a statutory undertaker for the purposes

of the Welsh Development Agency Act 1975 s 21C: s 27(1C) (added by SI 2001/4050). As to local authorities in Wales see LOCAL GOVERNMENT vol 69 (2009) PARA 22 et seq.

2   As to the transfer of powers under the Welsh Development Agency Act 1975 to the Welsh Ministers see PARA 1051.

3   Welsh Development Agency Act 1975 s 21C(1) (s 21C as added (see note 1); amended by SI 2005/3226; and by virtue of the Government of Wales Act 2006 s 162, Sch 11 para 32). As to the meaning of 'land' see PARA 1052 note 11.

4   As to joint planning boards see PLANNING vol 81 (2010) PARA 45.

5   Welsh Development Agency Act 1975 s 21C(3) (as added and amended: see notes 1, 3). As to national park authorities see OPEN SPACES AND COUNTRYSIDE vol 78 (2010) PARA 526 et seq.

1056. Power of authorised persons to enter land. Any duly authorised person[1] may at any reasonable time enter any land[2]:

(1)   for the purposes of surveying it[3], or estimating its value, in connection with any proposal to acquire[4] that land or any other land; or

(2)   in connection with any claim for compensation in respect of any such acquisition[5]; or

(3)   for the purpose of surveying it in order to enable the Welsh Ministers to determine whether to make an application for planning permission for the carrying out of development of that land[6].

Admission as of right to occupied land may not be demanded except on 24 hours' notice to the occupier[7].

It is the duty of a person exercising a power of entry to take reasonable care to avoid damage or injury to plant, machinery, equipment, livestock, crops or enclosures, and on leaving the land to secure it as effectively against unauthorised entry as he found it[8]. Where any land is damaged in the exercise of a power of entry, compensation may be recovered by any person interested in the land from the Welsh Ministers[9].

A person who intentionally obstructs a person acting in the exercise of the powers described above is guilty of an offence[10].

If any person who is admitted into a factory, workshop or workplace in the exercise of a power of entry under these provisions discloses to any person any information obtained by him there as to any manufacturing process or trade secret, then unless the disclosure is made in the course of performing his duty in connection with the purpose for which he was authorised to enter the premises, he is guilty of an offence[11].

1   The authority must be given in writing by the Welsh Ministers: Welsh Development Agency Act 1975 s 21A(8), Sch 4 para 14(1) (s 21A and Sch 4 added by the Government of Wales Act 1998 s 127, Sch 13 paras 2, 3 respectively; Welsh Development Agency Act 1975 Sch 4 para 14(1), (2) amended by SI 2005/3226; and by virtue of the Government of Wales Act 2006 s 162, Sch 11 para 32). Evidence of the authority must be produced if required by the occupier of the land or anyone acting on his behalf: Welsh Development Agency Act 1975 Sch 4 para 15(1)(a) (as so added). As to the transfer of powers under the Welsh Development Agency Act 1975 to the Welsh Ministers see PARA 1051.

2   As to the meaning of 'land' see PARA 1052 note 11.

3   The power to survey land includes power to search and bore in order to ascertain the nature of the subsoil or the presence of minerals or contaminants in it: Welsh Development Agency Act 1975 Sch 4 para 14(3) (as added: see note 1). No works may be carried out under Sch 4 para 14(3) unless notice of the intention to do so was included in the notice required by Sch 4 para 15(1)(b) (see text and note 7): Sch 4 para 15(5)(a) (as so added). If the land in question is held by statutory undertakers who object to the proposed works on the ground that the carrying out of those works would be seriously detrimental to the carrying on of their undertakings, the works must not be carried out without the authority of the appropriate minister: Sch 4 para 15(5)(b) (as so added).

'Statutory undertakers' means:

(1)   persons authorised by virtue of any enactment to carry on any railway, light railway,

tramway, road transport, water transport, canal, inland navigation, dock, harbour, pier or lighthouse undertaking, or any undertaking for the supply of hydraulic power; and

(2) the Civil Aviation Authority, a person who holds a licence under the Transport Act 2000 Pt I Ch I (ss 1–40) (air traffic services: see AIR LAW vol 2 (2008) PARA 139 et seq) (to the extent that the person is carrying out activities authorised by the licence), any universal service provider in connection with the provision of a universal postal service, and any other authority, body or undertakers which by virtue of any enactment are to be treated as statutory undertakers for the purposes of the Town and Country Planning Act 1990 (see the Welsh Development Agency Act 1975 s 27(1) (definition amended by the Gas Act 1986 s 67(4), Sch 9 Pt I; the Electricity Act 1989 s 112(4), Sch 18; the Water Act 1989 s 190(1), Sch 25 para 51; the Planning (Consequential Provisions) Act 1990 s 4, Sch 2 para 34(3)(b); the Coal Industry Act 1994 s 67(1), (8), Sch 9 para 16, Sch 11 Pt II; SI 2001/1149; and SI 2001/4050)).

As to the Civil Aviation Authority see AIR LAW vol 2 (2008) PARA 50 et seq; and as to the provision of a universal postal service see POSTAL SERVICES vol 85 (2012) PARA 250.

'Appropriate minister', in relation to any statutory undertakers in relation to whom it is defined by the Town and Country Planning Act 1990 s 265 or any other Act, has the meaning assigned by the Act so defining it: Welsh Development Agency Act 1975 s 27(1) (definition amended by the Planning (Consequential Provisions) Act 1990 Sch 2 para 34(3)(a)).

'Universal service provider' has the same meaning as in the Postal Services Act 2011 Pt 3, and references to the provision of a universal postal service are to be construed in accordance with that Part: Welsh Development Agency Act 1975 s 27(1) (definition added by SI 2001/1149; and amended by the Postal Services Act 2011 s 91(1), (2), Sch 12 Pt 3 para 101). The undertaking of a universal service provider so far as relating to the provision of a universal postal service is to be taken to be his statutory undertaking for the purposes of the Welsh Development Agency Act 1975; and references in that Act to his undertaking are to be construed accordingly: s 27(1A) (added by SI 2001/1149). The undertaking of a person who holds a licence under the Transport Act 2000 Pt I Ch I is not to be considered to be a statutory undertaking for the purposes of the Welsh Development Agency Act 1975 except to the extent that it is the person's undertaking as licence holder; and references in that Act to the person's undertaking are to be construed accordingly: s 27(1B) (added by SI 2001/4050).

4   Ie under the Welsh Development Agency Act 1975 s 21A: see PARA 1053.

5   Welsh Development Agency Act 1975 Sch 4 para 14(1)(a), (b) (as added: see note 1).

6   Welsh Development Agency Act 1975 Sch 4 para 14(2) (as added and amended: see note 1).

7   Welsh Development Agency Act 1975 Sch 4 para 15(1)(b) (as added: see note 1).

8   Welsh Development Agency Act 1975 Sch 4 para 15(6) (as added: see note 1).

9   Welsh Development Agency Act 1975 Sch 4 para 15(3) (as added (see note 1); amended by SI 2005/3226; and by virtue of the Government of Wales Act 2006 Sch 11 para 32). Except in so far as may be otherwise provided by regulations made by the Welsh Ministers under the Welsh Development Agency Act 1975 Sch 4 para 15(4), any question of disputed compensation under Sch 4 para 15(3) must be referred to and determined by the Upper Tribunal; and the provisions of the Land Compensation Act 1961 s 4 apply to the determination of any such question, subject to any necessary modifications and to the provisions of any regulations so made: Welsh Development Agency Act 1975 Sch 4 para 15(4) (as so added; amended by SI 2005/3226; SI 2009/1307; and by virtue of the Government of Wales Act 2006 Sch 11 para 32). At the date at which this volume states the law no regulations had been made under the Welsh Development Agency Act 1975 Sch 4 para 15(4). See COMPULSORY ACQUISITION OF LAND.

10   The offence is punishable on summary conviction by a fine not exceeding level 3 on the standard scale: Welsh Development Agency Act 1975 Sch 4 para 15(2) (as added: see note 1). As to the standard scale see SENTENCING AND DISPOSITION OF OFFENDERS vol 92 (2010) PARA 142.

11   Welsh Development Agency Act 1975 Sch 4 para 15(7) (as added: see note 1). The offence is punishable on summary conviction by a fine not exceeding the statutory maximum, or on conviction on indictment by imprisonment for up to two years or a fine or both: Sch 4 para 15(8) (as so added). As to the statutory maximum see SENTENCING AND DISPOSITION OF OFFENDERS vol 92 (2010) PARA 140.

1057. Power of Welsh Ministers to obtain information. If the Welsh Ministers, with a view to performing any of their functions under the Welsh Development Agency Act 1975 relating to any land[1], consider that they ought to have information connected with that or any other land, they may serve a notice on one or more of the following:

(1)   the occupier of the land;

(2)   any person who has an interest in the land either as freeholder, mortgagee or lessee, or who directly or indirectly receives rent for the land;

(3)   any person who, in pursuance of an agreement between himself and a person interested in the land, is authorised to manage the land or to arrange for the letting of it[2].

The notice must specify the land and the function of the Welsh Ministers in question, and the provision which confers the function[3]. It must require the recipient to furnish to the Welsh Ministers within a period specified in it (which must not be less than 14 days beginning with the day on which the notice is served) the nature of his interest in the land, and the name and address of each person whom the recipient of the notice believes to be the occupier of the land and of each person whom he believes to be a person who has an interest in the land or is authorised to manage or let the land[4].

Refusal or failure without reasonable excuse to give such information, or knowingly or recklessly making a false statement in complying with the notice, is an offence[5].

The council of every county and county borough in Wales, every joint planning board for a district in Wales, and every national park authority for a national park in Wales[6] must supply the Welsh Ministers with such information as they may by regulations prescribe (being information which the Welsh Ministers may need for performing their functions under the 1975 Act), and with such certificates supporting the information as the Welsh Ministers may specify in the regulations[7]. Unless the Welsh Ministers direct otherwise[8], if a local planning authority in Wales receives an application for planning permission, it must as soon as practicable after receipt send a copy of the application to the Welsh Ministers[9], and on the grant of planning permission relating to land in Wales, the local planning authority must as soon as practicable send a copy of the notification of the planning permission to the Welsh Ministers[10].

1   As to the transfer of powers under the Welsh Development Agency Act 1975 to the Welsh Ministers see PARA 1051. As to the meaning of 'land' see PARA 1052 note 11.

2   Welsh Development Agency Act 1975 s 21A(8), Sch 4 para 18(1) (s 21A and Sch 4 added by the Government of Wales Act 1998 s 127, Sch 13 paras 2, 3 respectively; Welsh Development Agency Act 1975 Sch 4 para 18(1), (2) amended by SI 2005/3226; and by virtue of the Government of Wales Act 2006 s 162, Sch 11 para 32).

3   Welsh Development Agency Act 1975 Sch 4 para 18(1) (as added: see note 2).

4   Ie who is a person mentioned in head (2) or (3) in the text: Welsh Development Agency Act 1975 Sch 4 para 18(2) (as added and amended: see note 2).

5   The offence is punishable on summary conviction by a fine not exceeding level 4 on the standard scale: Welsh Development Agency Act 1975 Sch 4 para 18(3) (as added: see note 2). As to the standard scale see SENTENCING AND DISPOSITION OF OFFENDERS vol 92 (2010) PARA 142.

6   As to local authorities in Wales see LOCAL GOVERNMENT vol 69 (2009) PARA 37 et seq; and as to national park authorities see OPEN SPACES AND COUNTRYSIDE vol 78 (2010) PARA 526 et seq.

7   Welsh Development Agency Act 1975 Sch 4 para 19(1) (as added (see note 2); amended by SI 2005/3226; and by virtue of the Government of Wales Act 2006 Sch 11 para 32). At the date at which this volume states the law no such regulations had been made.

8   Welsh Development Agency Act 1975 Sch 4 para 19(4) (as added (see note 2); amended by SI 2005/3226; and by virtue of the Government of Wales Act 2006 Sch 11 para 32).

9   Welsh Development Agency Act 1975 Sch 4 para 19(2) (as added (see note 2); amended by SI 2005/3226; and by virtue of the Government of Wales Act 2006 Sch 11 para 32).

10   Welsh Development Agency Act 1975 Sch 4 para 19(3) (as added (see note 2); amended by SI 2005/3226; and by virtue of the Government of Wales Act 2006 Sch 11 para 32).

1058. Programmes for the improvement of the environment and for derelict land to be brought into use. The duty of the Welsh Ministers[1] to prepare and publish (after consultation with such local authorities[2], national park authorities[3] and other bodies as appear to them to have an interest) programmes for the performance of the Welsh Ministers' functions under the Welsh Development Agency Act 1975, includes in particular a duty to prepare and publish programmes for the improvement, development or redevelopment of the environment in Wales[4]. These programmes are to be implemented either by the Welsh Ministers themselves, or by the ministers acting jointly with any other authority or person, or through persons or authorities acting on behalf of the ministers[5].

Where it appears to the Welsh Ministers that steps should be taken for the purpose of reclaiming or improving land[6] which is derelict, neglected or unsightly[7], or of enabling such land to be brought into use[8], then they may[9]:

(1)   make grants to any person in respect of relevant expenditure[10] incurred by that person, of such amounts and payable at such times and subject to such conditions as the Welsh Ministers may from time to time determine[11];

(2)   after consultation with such local authorities[12] or other bodies as appear to it to have an interest, acquire that land, or any other land[13]; and

(3)   carry out any works on such land or other land[14].

After carrying out works on land so acquired, the Welsh Ministers may dispose[15] of it free of charge to a local authority or the development corporation of a new town for the purpose of its use as a public open space[16].

1   Ie under the Welsh Development Agency Act 1975 s 1(14): see PARA 1052. As to the transfer of powers under the Welsh Development Agency Act 1975 to the Welsh Ministers see PARA 1051.
2   As to local authorities in Wales see LOCAL GOVERNMENT vol 69 (2009) PARA 37 et seq.
3   As to national park authorities see OPEN SPACES AND COUNTRYSIDE vol 78 (2010) PARA 526 et seq.
4   Welsh Development Agency Act 1975 s 15(1) (s 15 substituted by SI 2005/3226; and amended by virtue of the Government of Wales Act 2006 s 162, Sch 11 para 32). The Welsh Ministers may make payments to any authority or person of such amount and in such manner as they may determine for carrying out work which the ministers consider will contribute to the purposes of such a programme: Welsh Development Agency Act 1975 s 15(2) (as so substituted).
5   Welsh Development Agency Act 1975 s 15(1) (as substituted and amended: see note 2).
6   As to the meaning of 'land' see PARA 1052 note 11.
7   Welsh Development Agency Act 1975 s 16(1)(a), (2)(a) (s 16 substituted by the Derelict Land Act 1982 s 2(1), (2), (4); and amended by SI 2005/3226; and further amended by virtue of the Government of Wales Act 2006 Sch 11 para 32). These powers also apply, except as regards the power under the Welsh Development Agency Act 1975 s 16(3)(a) (see text and notes 7–9), to land which is not actually derelict, neglected or unsightly, but which is likely to become so by reason of actual or apprehended collapse of the surface due to relevant operations which have ceased to be carried out: see s 16(2)(b) (as so substituted). 'Relevant operations' means underground mining operations other than operations for the purpose of the working and getting of coal, or of coal and other minerals worked with coal, or for the purpose of getting any product from coal in the course of working and getting coal: s 16(9) (as so substituted).
8   Welsh Development Agency Act 1975 s 16(1)(b) (as substituted: see note 5).
9   The Welsh Ministers' powers in this regard are in addition to and not in derogation from any other power conferred by the Welsh Development Agency Act 1975: s 16(3) (as substituted and amended: see note 5). Thus they have power to acquire land under s 1(7)(h), and power to survey land under Sch 4 para 14: see PARA 1053.
10   'Relevant expenditure' means expenditure incurred, with the Welsh Ministers' approval, in or in connection with:
     (1)   the carrying out, for the purpose of reclaiming or improving any land to which the Welsh Development Agency Act 1975 s 16 applies, or enabling any such land to be brought into use, of any works to which s 16(1) applies (s 16(4)(a) (as substituted and amended: see note 5));

    (2)   the carrying out of a survey of such land to determine whether such works should be undertaken (whether or not such works are carried out) (s 16(4)(b) (as so substituted and amended)); and

    (3)   the acquisition of such land by a local authority in whose area it is situated (s 16(4)(c) (as so substituted and amended)).

    As to the meaning of 'local authority' see note 10.

11 Welsh Development Agency Act 1975 s 16(1), (3)(a) (as substituted and amended: see note 5). Grants may be made in such manner as appears to the Welsh Ministers to be requisite: s 16(5) (as so substituted and amended). The maximum amount of a grant (to a person other than a local authority in whose area the land is situated) is currently 100% of the relevant expenditure, or, in the case of a periodical grant in respect of costs from time to time incurred or treated as incurred in respect of the borrowing of money to defray the relevant expenditure, 100% of the costs so incurred or treated as incurred: s 16(6) (as so substituted; and amended by virtue of SI 2004/907). The prescribed percentage was originally 80%: see the Welsh Development Agency Act 1975 s 16(6) (as originally enacted). However, the Welsh Ministers have power by order to alter this percentage and may make such transitional provision as appears to the Welsh Ministers to be necessary or expedient: ss 16(6), (8), 28(1) (s 16 as substituted (see note 5); and s 16(8) further substituted by SI 2005/3226; and amended by virtue of the Government of Wales Act 2006 Sch 11 para 32; Welsh Development Agency Act 1975 s 28(1) amended by the Government of Wales Act 1998 Sch 14 para 11). In exercise of this power the prescribed percentage of 80% was changed to 100% by the Welsh Development Agency (Derelict Land) Order 2004, SI 2004/907.

12 'Local authority' means a county council or county borough council: Welsh Development Agency Act 1975 s 16(9) (as substituted (see note 5); and amended by the Local Government (Wales) Act 1994 s 66(6), Sch 16 para 48; and the Environment Act 1995 s 120(3), Sch 24). In relation to land in a national park for which a national park authority is the local planning authority, 'local authority' includes a national park authority: Environment Act 1995 s 70, Sch 9 para 7.

13 Welsh Development Agency Act 1975 s 16(3)(b) (as substituted and amended (see note 5); and further amended by the Government of Wales Act 1998 s 152, Sch 18 Pt III).

14 Welsh Development Agency Act 1975 s 16(3)(c) (as substituted: see note 5).

15 As to the meaning of 'dispose' see PARA 1053 note 9.

16 Welsh Development Agency Act 1975 s 16(7) (as substituted and amended: see note 5). As to new town development corporations see PLANNING vol 83 (2010) PARA 1499 et seq. As to the meaning of 'open space' see PARA 1053 note 3.

B. THE WELSH INDUSTRIAL DEVELOPMENT ADVISORY BOARD

1059.   The Welsh Industrial Development Advisory Board. The Welsh Development Agency Act 1975 requires the Welsh Ministers[1] to appoint a board called the 'Welsh Industrial Development Advisory Board' ('WIDAB') to advise them with respect to the exercise of their functions relating to the giving of financial assistance to industry in assisted areas[2]. The board consists of a chairman and between four and seven other members[3]. The members must include persons who appear to the Welsh Ministers to have wide experience of, and to have shown capacity in, industry, banking, accounting, finance or the organisation or representation of workers[4]. If the board makes a recommendation with respect to any matter at the request of the Welsh Ministers but they exercise their functions contrary to it, the Welsh Ministers must, if the board so requests, publish a statement as to the matter[5].

1 As to the transfer of powers under the Welsh Development Agency Act 1975 to the Welsh Ministers see PARA 1051.

2 Welsh Development Agency Act 1975 s 13(1) (amended by the Industrial Development Act 1982 s 19(1), Sch 2 Pt II para 13; by SI 2005/3226; and by virtue of the Government of Wales Act 2006 s 162, Sch 11 para 32). The functions referred to are those under the Industrial Development Act 1982 s 7 (as to which see PARAS 1040, 1042–1043). The Welsh Ministers have power to make provision for the transfer of the functions of the board, and about the accounts and audit of the board and reports on its functions: see the Government of Wales Act 1998 ss 28, 144, Sch 4 para 12, Sch 17 para 1 (s 28 amended by the Government of Wales Act 2006

s 160(1), Sch 10 paras 41, 42; Government of Wales Act 1998 s 144 amended by the Care Standards Act 2000 s 72, Sch 2 para 18; the Learning and Skills Act 2000 s 73(1), (3)(a); the Health (Wales) Act 2003 s 7(1), Sch 3 para 11; the Public Audit (Wales) Act 2004 ss 65(1)–(3), 72, Sch 4; the Public Services Ombudsman (Wales) Act 2005 s 39(1), Sch 6 paras 61, 66, Sch 7; the Commissioner for Older People (Wales) Act 2006 s 1(2), Sch 1 para 20; the Government of Wales Act 2006 ss 160(1), 163, Sch 10 para 45, Sch 12; the Health Act 2006 s 80(1), Sch 8 para 43; by SI 2008/948; and by virtue of the National Health Service (Consequential Provisions) Act 2006 s 2, Sch 1 paras 281, 298; Government of Wales Act 1998 Sch 17 para 1 amended by the Care Standards Act 2000 ss 6, 54, 66, Sch 1 para 27(d); and the Public Audit (Wales) Act 2004 ss 65(1), (4), 72, Sch 4).

3   Welsh Development Agency Act 1975 s 13(2).
4   Welsh Development Agency Act 1975 s 13(3) (amended by SI 2005/3226; and by virtue of the Government of Wales Act 2006 Sch 11 para 32).
5   Welsh Development Agency Act 1975 s 13(4) (substituted by SI 2005/3226; and amended by virtue of the Government of Wales Act 2006 Sch 11 para 32).

C. FINANCIAL PROVISIONS

1060.   Welsh Ministers' power to borrow and guarantees. For the purpose of exercising their functions under the Welsh Development Agency Act 1975, the Welsh Ministers[1] may borrow money from any person (including their wholly owned subsidiaries[2]), but any borrowing in a currency other than sterling requires the approval of the Treasury[3].

It is the duty of the Welsh Ministers to secure that none of their wholly owned subsidiaries formed in pursuance of the exercise of the ministers' functions under the Welsh Development Agency Act 1975 borrows money otherwise than from the ministers or from another wholly owned subsidiary of the ministers, except with the ministers' consent[4].

The Treasury may guarantee the repayment of principal, the payment of interest, and the discharge of any other financial obligations in connection with any sums borrowed by the Welsh Ministers in connection with their functions under the 1975 Act[5]. Immediately after giving such a guarantee, the Treasury must lay a statement of it before each House of Parliament[6]. Where any sum is required[7] for fulfilling a guarantee, the Treasury must lay before each House of Parliament a statement as to that sum for each financial year, beginning with the year in which the sum was issued and ending with the year in which all liability in respect of the sum and interest on it is discharged[8]. If any sums are issued in fulfilment of a guarantee, the Welsh Ministers must make to the Treasury, at such time and in such manner as the Treasury directs, payments of such amounts as the Treasury so directs in or towards repayment of those sums and payments of interest at a rate directed by the Treasury, on what is outstanding in respect of those sums[9].

1   As to the transfer of powers under the Welsh Development Agency Act 1975 to the Welsh Ministers see PARA 1051.
2   'Wholly owned subsidiary' has the same meaning as in the Companies Act 2006 s 1159 (see COMPANIES vol 14 (2009) PARA 25): Welsh Development Agency Act 1975 s 27(1) (definition amended by SI 2009/1941).
3   Welsh Development Agency Act 1975 s 18(1), Sch 3 para 3 (s 18(1) substituted by the Industry Act 1979 s 1, Schedule; Welsh Development Agency Act 1975 Sch 3 para 3 substituted by SI 2005/3226; and amended by virtue of the Government of Wales Act 2006 s 162, Sch 11 para 32). As to the Treasury see CONSTITUTIONAL AND ADMINISTRATIVE LAW vol 20 (2014) PARA 262 et seq.
4   Welsh Development Agency Act 1975 Sch 3 para 5 (substituted by SI 2005/3226; and amended by virtue of the Government of Wales Act 2006 Sch 11 para 32).
5   Welsh Development Agency Act 1975 Sch 3 para 6(1) (amended by the Miscellaneous Financial Provisions Act 1983 s 4, Sch 2; by SI 2005/3226; and by virtue of the Government of Wales

Act 2006 Sch 11 para 32). The guarantee may be given in such manner and on such conditions as the Treasury thinks fit: Welsh Development Agency Act 1975 Sch 3 para 6(1).

6 Welsh Development Agency Act 1975 Sch 3 para 6(2).

7 Any sum so required must be charged on and issued out of the Consolidated Fund: Welsh Development Agency Act 1975 Sch 3 para 6(3). As to the Consolidated Fund see CONSTITUTIONAL AND ADMINISTRATIVE LAW vol 20 (2014) PARA 480.

8 Welsh Development Agency Act 1975 Sch 3 para 6(2).

9 Welsh Development Agency Act 1975 Sch 3 para 6(4) (amended by SI 2005/3226; and by virtue of the Government of Wales Act 2006 Sch 11 para 32). Any sums so received must be paid into the Consolidated Fund: Welsh Development Agency Act 1975 Sch 3 para 6(5).

(vi) Transfer of Control of Important Manufacturing Undertakings

1061. Power to prohibit the control of manufacturing undertakings passing out of the UK. The Industry Act 1975 makes provision to prohibit the passing to persons not resident in the United Kingdom of control of undertakings engaged in manufacturing industry, and gives the Secretary of State[1] power to acquire compulsorily the capital or assets of such undertakings where control has passed to such persons or where there is a probability that it will pass[2].

The powers conferred by Part II of the Industry Act 1975 have effect in relation to changes of control[3] of important manufacturing undertakings[4]. The Secretary of State may make a prohibition order if it appears to him that:

(1) there is a serious and immediate probability of a change of control of an important manufacturing undertaking[5]; and

(2) that change of control would be contrary to the interests[6] of the United Kingdom or of any substantial part of it[7].

The order must specify the undertaking, prohibit the change of control and prohibit or restrict the doing of things which would in the opinion of the Secretary of State constitute or lead to it, and may make such incidental or supplementary provision as appears to him to be necessary or expedient[8].

Nothing in a prohibition order has effect so as to apply to any person in relation to his conduct outside the United Kingdom unless he is a citizen of the United Kingdom and Colonies[9], a body corporate incorporated in the United Kingdom[10] or a person carrying on business in the United Kingdom either alone or in partnership with others[11], but in a case falling within any of these categories the order may extend to acts or omissions outside the United Kingdom[12].

No criminal proceedings lie against a person on the ground that he has committed, or aided, abetted, counselled or procured the commission of, or conspired or attempted to commit, or encouraged or assisted[13] others to commit, any contravention of a prohibition order[14]. However, this does not limit any person's right to bring civil proceedings in respect of any contravention or apprehended contravention of such an order, and, without prejudice to that right, compliance with such an order may be enforced by civil proceedings by the Crown for an injunction or any other appropriate relief[15].

1 As to the Secretary of State see PARA 902.

2 Industry Act 1975 preamble.

3 As to the meaning of 'change of control' see PARA 1062.

4 Industry Act 1975 s 11(1). 'Important manufacturing undertaking' means an undertaking which, in so far as it is carried out in the United Kingdom, is wholly or mainly engaged in manufacturing industry and appears to the Secretary of State to be of special importance to the United Kingdom or to any substantial part of it: s 11(2). As to the meaning of 'United Kingdom' see PARA 906 note 7. 'Manufacturing industry' means activities described in any of the minimum list headings in Orders III to XIX of the Standard Industrial Classification; 'industry' includes

any description of commercial activity, and any section of an industry, and 'industrial' has a corresponding meaning: Industry Act 1975 s 37(1). In determining the extent to which an undertaking is engaged in manufacturing industry, the following activities are treated as manufacturing industry so far as they relate to products manufactured or to be manufactured by the undertaking, namely: research, transport, distribution, machinery repair and maintenance, sales and marketing, storage, mining and quarrying, production and distribution of energy and heating, administration, staff training and packaging: s 37(3). 'Standard Industrial Classification' means the revised edition published by HM Stationery Office in 1968 of the publication of that name prepared by the Central Statistical Office of the Chancellor of the Exchequer: s 37(1) (definition substituted by the Co-operative Development Agency and Industrial Development Act 1984 s 5(2), Sch 1 Pt II para 1; and subsequently amended by SI 1989/992).

5   Industry Act 1975 s 13(1)(a).
6   'Interests' means interests which relate to public policy, public security or public health: Industry Act 1975 s 13(7) (definition added by SI 1998/3035).
7   Industry Act 1975 s 13(1)(b).
8   Industry Act 1975 s 13(1). The order, which must be made by statutory instrument, must be laid before Parliament after being made: see ss 15(1), (2), 38(1), (2). At the date at which this volume states the law no such order had been made.
9   Industry Act 1975 s 18(1)(a). As to categories of citizenship see BRITISH NATIONALITY vol 4 (2011) PARA 406 et seq.
10 Industry Act 1975 s 18(1)(b). A body corporate is deemed not to be resident in the United Kingdom if it is not incorporated there: s 18(2). As to incorporation by registration under the Companies Act 2006 see COMPANIES vol 14 (2009) PARA 119 et seq; and as to companies formed outside England and Wales see COMPANIES vol 15 (2009) PARA 1826 et seq.
11 Industry Act 1975 s 18(1)(c). As to partnerships see generally PARTNERSHIP.
12 Industry Act 1975 s 18(1).
13 The Industry Act 1975 s 17 includes the word 'incited'. However, the common law offence of inciting the commission of another offence was abolished by the Serious Crime Act 2007 s 59. The reference in the Industry Act 1975 s 17 to incitement now has effect as a reference to (or to conduct amounting to) the offences under the Serious Crime Act 2007 Pt 2 (ss 44–67) (ie encouraging or assisting crime: see CRIMINAL LAW vol 25 (2010) PARA 64 et seq): see s 63, Sch para 3.
14 Industry Act 1975 s 17(1).
15 Industry Act 1975 s 17(2).

1062.   Meaning of 'change of control'.   There is a change of control of an important manufacturing undertaking[1] only upon the happening of a relevant event[2]. 'Relevant event' means any event as a result of which:

(1)   the person carrying on the whole or part of the undertaking ceases to be resident in the United Kingdom[3];

(2)   a person not resident there acquires the whole or part of the undertaking[4];

(3)   a body corporate resident there but controlled[5] by a person not resident there acquires the whole or part of the undertaking[6];

(4)   a person not resident there becomes able to exercise or control the exercise of 30, 40 or 50 per cent of votes that may be cast at a general meeting of a body corporate carrying on the whole or part of the undertaking or such a percentage of votes in any other body corporate which is in control of such a body[7]; or

(5)   a person resident there and able to exercise or control the exercise of 30, 40 or 50 per cent of those votes in a body corporate carrying on the whole or part of the undertaking or in any other body corporate which is in control of such a body ceases to be resident there[8].

1   As to the meaning of 'important manufacturing undertaking' see PARA 1061 note 4.
2   Industry Act 1975 s 12(1).
3   Industry Act 1975 s 12(2)(a). As to residence of a body corporate see PARA 1061 note 10. As to the meaning of 'United Kingdom' see PARA 906 note 7.

4   Industry Act 1975 s 12(2)(b).
5   For these purposes a body corporate or an individual entitled to cast 30% or more of the votes that may be cast at a general meeting of a body corporate is in control of that body: Industry Act 1975 s 12(3)(a). Control of a body corporate which has control of another body corporate gives control of the latter body: s 12(3)(b). Any power to direct the holder of shares or stock in a body corporate as to the exercise of his votes at a general meeting of that body is treated as entitlement to cast the votes in respect of those shares or that stock: s 12(4). Two or more persons acting together in concert may be treated as a single person for the purposes of any of the provisions of Pt II (ss 11–20) as to change of control: s 12(5).
6   Industry Act 1975 s 12(2)(c).
7   Industry Act 1975 s 12(2)(d), (6).
8   Industry Act 1975 s 12(2)(e), (6).

1063. Vesting orders under the Industry Act 1975. The Secretary of State may make a vesting order[1], with the approval of the Treasury[2], if:

(1)   the conditions for the making of a prohibition order[3] are satisfied[4]; or

(2)   a prohibition order has been made in relation to an important manufacturing undertaking[5]; or

(3)   he has learnt of circumstances which appear to him to constitute a change of control[6] of such an undertaking and is satisfied that the change is contrary to the interests[7] of the United Kingdom or of any substantial part of it[8].

The vesting order (which may only be made if he is satisfied that it is necessary in the national interest[9] and that, having regard to all the circumstances, that interest cannot, or cannot appropriately, be protected in any other way[10]) directs that on a specified day certain share capital and loan capital[11], or any assets which are employed in the undertaking, are to vest in himself or in his nominees, and may contain such incidental or supplementary provision as appears to him to be necessary or expedient[12]. The order may also contain provisions by virtue of which rights, liabilities or incumbrances to which assets or capital which will vest under it are subject[13] will be extinguished in consideration of the payment of compensation[14], will be transferred to the Secretary of State[15] or will be charged on the compensation[16]. If the order provides for the vesting of assets employed in an undertaking it may prohibit or set aside any transfer of those assets or of any right in respect of them[17]. A vesting order setting aside a transfer must give a right to compensation[18].

1   The Secretary of State is in practice the Secretary of State for Business, Innovation and Skills, as to whom see PARA 902.
      A vesting order must be made by statutory instrument (see the Industry Act 1975 s 38), and may not be made unless a draft has been laid before, and approved by a resolution of, each House of Parliament (s 15(3)), and until a compensation order has also been laid before each House (see s 19(1); and PARA 1065).
      The draft may not be so laid:
      (1)   in a case under head (1) in the text, after the end of three months from the service of a notice under s 16(7) (see note 16) (s 15(4)(a));
      (2)   in a case under head (2) in the text, after the end of three months from the making of the prohibition order (unless the circumstances mentioned in head (1) or head (3) in the text exist when the draft is laid before Parliament) (s 15(4)(b));
      (3)   in a case under head (3) in the text, after the end of three months from the date when the Secretary of State learnt of circumstances there mentioned (s 15(4)(c)).
      On the expiry of 28 days from the laying of the draft in a House, the order proceeds in that House, whether or not it has been referred to a committee under Standing Orders relating to private Bills, as if its provisions would require to be enacted by a public Bill which cannot be referred to a committee: s 15(5). In reckoning these 28 days no account is taken of periods during which Parliament is dissolved or prorogued or the House is adjourned for more than four days: s 15(6). As to the procedure see STATUTES AND LEGISLATIVE PROCESS vol 96 (2012) PARA 1052 et seq. At the date at which this volume states the law no vesting order had been made.

2   As to the Treasury see CONSTITUTIONAL AND ADMINISTRATIVE LAW vol 20 (2014) PARA 262 et seq.
3   As to prohibition orders see PARA 1061. The conditions referred to are those set out in PARA 1061 heads (1) and (2).
4   Industry Act 1975 s 13(2)(a).
5   Industry Act 1975 s 13(2)(b). As to the meaning of 'important manufacturing undertaking' see PARA 1061 note 4.
6   As to the meaning of 'change of control' see PARA 1062. The change of control must have occurred on or after 1 February 1975: Industry Act 1975 s 13(2)(c).
7   As to the meaning of 'interests' see PARA 1061 note 6.
8   Industry Act 1975 s 13(2)(c). As to the meaning of 'United Kingdom' see PARA 906 note 7.
9   'National interest' means the national interest in relation to public policy, public security or public health: Industry Act 1975 s 13(8) (added by SI 1998/3035).
10 Industry Act 1975 s 13(3).
11 Ie:
    (1)   where the Secretary of State considers that the interests of the United Kingdom or of any substantial part of it cannot, or cannot appropriately, be protected unless all the share capital of the relevant body corporate vests, the share capital and so much of any of its loan capital as is specified in the order (Industry Act 1975 s 13(4)(a)); and
    (2)   in any other case, that part of the share capital of any relevant body corporate which, when the order is laid before Parliament under s 15(3), appears to him to be involved in the change of control (s 13(4)(b)).
    'Relevant body corporate' means:
    (a)   a body corporate incorporated in the United Kingdom carrying on there as the whole or a major part of its business there the whole or part of an important manufacturing undertaking (s 13(5)(a)); or
    (b)   a body corporate incorporated in the United Kingdom which is the holding company of a group of companies carrying on there as the whole or the major part of its business there the whole or part of such an undertaking, and as to which one of two conditions is satisfied (s 13(5)(b)).
    These conditions are:
    (i)   that it appears to the Secretary of State that there is a serious and immediate probability of the happening of an event in relation to the company which would constitute a change of control of the undertaking (s 13(6)(a)); or
    (ii) that he has learnt of circumstances relating to the company which appear to constitute a change of control of the undertaking on or after 1 February 1975 (s 13(6)(b)).
    'Holding company' means a holding company as defined by the Companies Act 2006 s 1159 (see COMPANIES vol 14 (2009) PARA 25): Industry Act 1975 s 37(1) (amended by SI 2009/1941).
12 Industry Act 1975 s 13(2) (amended by the British Technology Group Act 1991 s 17(2), Sch 2 Pt I). This includes provisions to safeguard any capital which is to vest and any assets of a body corporate (or of its subsidiary) whose capital is to vest, and to prohibit or set aside any transfers of it or of rights in respect of it: Industry Act 1975 s 16(3). A vesting order setting aside a transfer entitles the body corporate or subsidiary to recover any transferred assets: s 16(5). 'Subsidiary' means a subsidiary as defined by the Companies Act 2006 s 1159 (see COMPANIES vol 14 (2009) PARA 25): Industry Act 1975 s 37(1) (amended by SI 2009/1941).
13 Industry Act 1979 s 16(1).
14 Industry Act 1975 s 16(1)(a). As to compensation see s 19; and PARA 1065.
15 Industry Act 1975 s 16(1)(b) (s 16(1)(b) amended by the British Technology Group Act 1991 Sch 2 Pt I).
16 Industry Act 1975 s 16(1)(c).
17 Industry Act 1975 s 16(2). It also entitles the Secretary of State to recover any transferred capital or assets: s 16(4) (amended by the British Technology Group Act 1991 Sch 2 Pt I). The transfers to which the Industry Act 1975 s 16 applies include transfers made before a draft of the order is laid before Parliament but after the Secretary of State has served notice on the person concerned of his intention to lay the draft: s 16(7). 'Person concerned' means (in the case of an order such as is mentioned in head (a) in the text) the relevant body corporate, and (in the case of an order such as is mentioned in head (b) in the text) the person carrying on the undertaking: s 16(8). The notice must be published in the London Gazette: s 16(9).
    Any notice or other document required or authorised under the Act to be served on any person may be served either by delivering it to him or by leaving it at his proper address or by sending it by post: s 36(1). Notice is duly served on a body corporate or a firm if it is served on the secretary or clerk of the body corporate or a partner of the firm: s 36(2). For the purpose of s 36 and what is now the Interpretation Act 1978 s 7, Sch 2 para 3 (see STATUTES AND

LEGISLATIVE PROCESS vol 96 (2012) PARA 1219), the proper address of a secretary or clerk of a body corporate, is the registered or principal office of the body corporate, or of the partner of a firm, is the principal office of the firm, and the proper address of any other person, is his last known address: Industry Act 1975 s 36(3).

18 See the Industry Act 1975 s 16(6).

1064. Extension of vesting orders. Where 30 per cent or more of the share capital of a body corporate vests in the Secretary of State[1] or his nominees by virtue of a vesting order[2], the Secretary of State must serve[3] on the holders of the rest of the share capital (and on any other persons who to his knowledge have a present or prospective right to subscribe for shares in the body corporate) a notice informing them of the making of the order and of their right to require the order to extend to their share capital or rights[4]. The recipient of such a notice may within three months of its date serve on the Secretary of State a counter-notice requiring the order so to extend[5], whereupon, from the date of the counter-notice, the vesting order has effect as if the share capital or rights specified in the counter-notice had been specified in the vesting order[6].

1   As to the Secretary of State see PARA 902.
2   As to vesting orders see PARA 1063.
3   The notice must be served within 28 days of the making of the order: Industry Act 1975 s 14(1). As to the service of notices see PARA 1063 note 17.
4   Industry Act 1975 s 14(1), (4) (amended by the British Technology Group Act 1991 s 17(2), Sch 2 Pt I).
5   Industry Act 1975 s 14(2).
6   Industry Act 1975 s 14(3).

1065. Compensation orders under the Industry Act 1975. No vesting order[1] may be made until there has also been laid before both Houses of Parliament a compensation order[2] providing for the payment of compensation for the acquisition of the capital or assets and for any extinguishment or transfer of rights, liabilities or incumbrances[3]. The compensation order:

(1)   must identify the persons or descriptions of persons to be compensated and determine their rights and duties in relation to any compensation paid to them[4];

(2)   must specify the manner in which it is to be paid[5];

(3)   must provide for the payment of interest on compensation in respect of the relevant period[6];

(4)   may make different provision in relation to different descriptions of capital or assets and different rights, liabilities or incumbrances[7]; and

(5)   may contain incidental and supplementary provisions[8].

Compensation may be paid out of money provided by Parliament[9] or by the issue of government stock[10].

1   As to vesting orders see PARAS 1063–1064.
2   The order must be made by statutory instrument (see the Industry Act 1975 s 38(1), (2)) and is subject to special parliamentary procedure (s 19(2)). As to special parliamentary procedure see STATUTES AND LEGISLATIVE PROCESS vol 96 (2012) PARA 958 et seq. The Statutory Orders (Special Procedure) Act 1945 s 6(2) proviso is modified for this purpose by the Industry Act 1975 s 19(5). At the date at which this volume states the law no such order had been made.
3   Industry Act 1975 s 19(1).
4   Industry Act 1975 s 19(3)(a).
5   Industry Act 1975 s 19(3)(b). See also note 10.
6   Industry Act 1975 s 19(3)(c). 'Relevant period' means, in relation to capital or assets, the period commencing with the date of vesting and ending with the date of payment of compensation; and

in relation to rights, liabilities and incumbrances, the period commencing with the date of their extinguishment and ending on the date of payment: s 19(3) (amended by the British Technology Group Act 1991 s 17(2), Sch 2 Pt I).

7   Industry Act 1975 s 19(3)(d).

8   Industry Act 1975 s 19(3)(e).

9   Industry Act 1975 s 19(4)(a).

10   Industry Act 1975 s 19(4)(b). 'Government stock' means stock the principal of which and the interest on which is charged on the National Loans Fund with recourse to the Consolidated Fund: s 19(4)(b). The power conferred by s 19(3)(b) is a power to provide for compensation by one or both of the means specified in s 19(4): s 19(4). As to the National Loans Fund see generally CONSTITUTIONAL AND ADMINISTRATIVE LAW vol 20 (2014) PARA 500 et seq. As to the Consolidated Fund see CONSTITUTIONAL AND ADMINISTRATIVE LAW vol 20 (2014) PARA 480 et seq; PARLIAMENT vol 78 (2010) PARA 1028 et seq.

1066. Disputes as to vesting and compensation orders. A procedure is prescribed for the determination of any dispute which arises out of a vesting order[1] or compensation order[2] to which one of the parties is the Secretary of State[3] or a body corporate the whole or part of whose share capital has vested by virtue of the order in him or his nominees[4], either if the order requires it to be submitted to arbitration[5] or if one of the parties wishes it to be so submitted[6]. Where the procedure applies to a dispute arising out of an order it applies also to any dispute arising out of a related order[7].

If a party to such a dispute serves on the other party or parties to the dispute, at a time when no proceedings relating to it have been commenced in any court, a notice that he wishes it to be determined by arbitration, the Secretary of State must by order[8] establish a tribunal[9] to determine the dispute[10]. The tribunal's procedure is determined by rules to be made by the Lord Chancellor[11], although certain of the statutory arbitration provisions apply[12]. The tribunal may refer any question arising (other than a question which is primarily one of law) to a person appointed by it for the purpose, for inquiry and report[13]. The tribunal's order is enforceable as if it were an order of the High Court[14]. Appeal lies to the Court of Appeal on any question of law or fact from any determination or order of the tribunal with respect to compensation[15] on the setting aside by a vesting order of any transfer of capital or assets[16]. The tribunal may, and if so ordered by the Court of Appeal must, state in the form of a special case for determination by that court any question of law arising in the proceedings[17].

1   As to vesting orders see PARAS 1063–1064.

2   As to compensation orders see PARA 1065.

3   As to the Secretary of State see PARA 902.

4   Industry Act 1975 s 20(3) (amended by the British Technology Group Act 1991 s 17(2), Sch 2 Pt I). That amendment removed from the Industry Act 1975 s 20(3) a reference to the National Enterprise Board, but omitted to make further changes necessary in order to make sense of the provision after the removal of that reference; the provision is here treated as if those changes had been made. As to the National Enterprise Board and its abolition see PARA 1050.

5   Industry Act 1975 s 20(3)(a).

6   Industry Act 1975 s 20(3)(b).

7   Industry Act 1975 s 20(3). For this purpose a vesting order and a compensation order are related if they relate to the same capital or assets: s 20(4).

8   The order must be made by statutory instrument (see the Industry Act 1975 s 38(1), (2)). It must be laid before each House of Parliament: Industry Act 1975 s 20(1), Sch 3 para 2. See STATUTES AND LEGISLATIVE PROCESS vol 96 (2012) PARA 1032. At the date at which this volume states the law no such order had been made.

9   The tribunal is a court of record with an official seal which is judicially noticed: Industry Act 1975 Sch 3 para 3. It sits, as the Lord Chancellor, after consulting the Lord Chief Justice of England and Wales, the Lord President of the Court of Session and the Lord Chief Justice of Northern Ireland, directs either as a single tribunal or in two or more divisions, and consists of a president, who must be a person who satisfies the judicial-appointment eligibility condition on

a five-year basis or a member of the Bar of Northern Ireland or a solicitor of the Court of Judicature of Northern Ireland of at least five years standing, appointed by the Lord Chancellor, and two other members appointed by the Secretary of State, with respectively business and financial experience: Industry Act 1975 Sch 3 para 4(1) (numbered as such by the Constitutional Reform Act 2005 s 15(1), Sch 4 Pt 1 para 81(1), (2)(a); amended by the Courts and Legal Services Act 1990 s 71(2), Sch 10 para 39; the Constitutional Reform Act 2005 ss 15(1), 59(5), Sch 4 Pt 1 para 81(2)(b), Sch 11 Pt 3 para 5; and the Tribunals, Courts and Enforcement Act 2007 s 50, Sch 10 Pt 1 para 12). As to the Lord Chancellor see CONSTITUTIONAL AND ADMINISTRATIVE LAW vol 20 (2014) PARA 256 et seq; and as to the Lord Chief Justice see COURTS AND TRIBUNALS vol 24 (2010) PARA 604. As to the judicial-appointment eligibility condition see COURTS AND TRIBUNALS vol 24 (2010) PARA 645. The Lord Chief Justice of England and Wales may nominate a judicial office holder (as defined in the Constitutional Reform Act 2005 s 109(4): see COURTS AND TRIBUNALS vol 24 (2010) PARA 961) to exercise his functions under the Industry Act 1975 Sch 3 para 4: Sch 3 para 4(2) (added by the Constitutional Reform Act 2005 Sch 4 Pt 1 para 81(2)(c)). The Lord Chancellor's functions under the Industry Act 1975 Sch 3 paras 4(1)(a), 17 (see text and note 11) are protected functions for the purposes of the Constitutional Reform Act 2005 s 19: see s 19(5), Sch 7 para 4; and CONSTITUTIONAL AND ADMINISTRATIVE LAW vol 20 (2014) PARA 259. Any appointment to the office of president of the tribunal under the Industry Act 1975 Sch 3 para 4 must be made, by virtue of the Constitutional Reform Act 2005 s 85, Sch 14 Pt 3 in accordance with ss 85–93, 96: see COURTS AND TRIBUNALS vol 24 (2010) PARA 967.

The members of a tribunal hold office for such period as may be determined at the time of appointment, and are eligible for re-appointment; however, a member may resign on giving one month's written notice to the appointor, or the appointor may declare the member's office vacant on the ground of unfitness to continue, or his office may become vacant if he is the subject of a bankruptcy restrictions order or an interim bankruptcy restrictions order, or a debt relief restrictions order or interim debt relief restrictions order under the Insolvency Act 1986 Sch 4ZB (see BANKRUPTCY AND INDIVIDUAL INSOLVENCY): Industry Act 1975 Sch 3 para 6(1) (renumbered and amended by the Judicial Pensions and Retirement Act 1973 s 26(10), Sch 6 para 52; further amended by SI 2006/1722; SI 2012/2404). No appointment as president may be such as to extend beyond the appointee's 70th birthday; but this may be extended by authorisation under the Judicial Pensions and Retirement Act 1993 s 26(4)–(6): Industry Act 1975 Sch 3 para 6(2) (added by the Judicial Pensions and Retirement Act 1993 Sch 6 para 52). If a member becomes by reason of illness or other infirmity temporarily incapable of performing his duties, his appointor must appoint some other fit person in his place for any period not exceeding six months at a time: Industry Act 1975 Sch 3 para 7. A member's appointor is the Lord Chancellor or the Secretary of State, as described above: Sch 3 para 8. Where the appointor is, by virtue of Sch 3 para 8(a), the Lord Chancellor, the power conferred by Sch 3 para 6(1)(b) to declare a member's office vacant may be exercised only with the concurrence of the appropriate senior judge: Sch 3 para 8A (Sch 3 paras 8A, 8B added by the Constitutional Reform Act 2005 Sch 4 Pt 1 para 81(5)). The appropriate senior judge is the Lord Chief Justice of England and Wales, unless the member to be removed exercises functions wholly or mainly in Northern Ireland, in which case it is the Lord Chief Justice of Northern Ireland: Industry Act 1975 Sch 3 para 8B (as so added).

A tribunal may appoint such officers as it considers necessary for assisting it in the proper execution of its duties: Sch 3 para 11. Members are paid such remuneration and allowances as the Secretary of State, with the approval of the Treasury, may determine; an officer and any person to whom the dispute is referred under Sch 3 para 27 (see text and note 13) may be paid such remuneration and allowances as the Secretary of State, with the approval of the Treasury, may determine; the Secretary of State must pay any such remuneration or allowances, and must defray any other expenses out of money provided by Parliament: Sch 3 para 12; Transfer of Functions (Minister for the Civil Service and Treasury) Order 1981, SI 1981/1670. Members are disqualified for membership of the House of Commons: see the House of Commons Disqualification Act 1975 s 1(1)(f), Sch 1 Pt II (amended for this purpose by the Industry Act 1975 Sch 3 para 9); and PARLIAMENT vol 78 (2010) PARA 908. As to the Treasury see CONSTITUTIONAL AND ADMINISTRATIVE LAW vol 20 (2014) PARA 262 et seq.

10 Industry Act 1975 Sch 3 para 1. Where a dispute has been submitted to a tribunal, any other dispute of the kind described in the text must be determined by the same tribunal: s 20(2).

11 Industry Act 1975 Sch 3 para 17(1). See note 9 as to the Lord Chancellor's function under Sch 3 para 17. At the date at which this volume states the law, no such rules had been made. They must be made by statutory instrument, which is subject to annulment in pursuance of a

resolution of either House of Parliament: Sch 3 para 17(1), (2). See STATUTES AND LEGISLATIVE PROCESS vol 96 (2012) PARA 1032. Separate provision is made in relation to procedure in Scotland: see Sch 3 paras 18–25, 26(b).

12 See the Industry Act 1975 Sch 3 para 14 (amended by the Arbitration Act 1996 s 107(1), Sch 3 para 30), which provides that the provisions of the Arbitration Act 1996 Pt I (ss 1–84) with respect to oaths and affirmations, the correction of errors in awards, the summoning, attendance and examining of witnesses, the production of documents, and costs (see ARBITRATION vol 2 (2008) PARA 1201 et seq) apply with necessary modifications, but no other provisions of that Part apply.

13 See the Industry Act 1975 Sch 3 para 27. Such report may be adopted wholly or partly by the tribunal and, if adopted, may be incorporated in an order of the tribunal: Sch 3 para 27.

14 Industry Act 1975 Sch 3 para 26(a). See CIVIL PROCEDURE.

15 Ie under the Industry Act 1975 s 16(6): see PARA 1063.

16 Industry Act 1975 Sch 3 para 16.

17 Industry Act 1975 Sch 3 para 15. For the procedure see CPR Pt 52; *Practice Direction—Appeals* PD 52 para 18; and CIVIL PROCEDURE.

(vii) Utilisation of Derelict Land

1067. Power to award grants for the reclamation or improvement of derelict land in England. In relation to derelict land in England[1], the Secretary of State[2] may, with the consent of the Treasury[3], make grants[4] out of money provided by Parliament to any persons in respect of relevant expenditure[5] incurred by them, where it appears to him that steps should be taken for the purpose of reclaiming or improving any such land[6], or enabling it to be brought into use[7].

Derelict land is land which is derelict, neglected or unsightly[8] and, in relation to a local authority[9] in whose area it is situated, land which is not derelict, neglected or unsightly but is likely to become so through actual or apprehended collapse of the surface as the result of the carrying out of relevant operations[10] which have ceased to be carried out[11].

Under the Housing and Regeneration Act 2008, the Secretary of State may appoint the Homes and Communities Agency[12] to act as the agent of the Secretary of State in connection with such derelict land functions[13] as the Secretary of State may specify[14].

1 The Derelict Land Act 1982 s 1 extends only to England: s 1(13). Similar powers in respect of Wales are exercisable by the Welsh Ministers: see the Welsh Development Agency Act 1975 s 16; and PARA 1058.

2 As to the Secretary of State see PARA 902. In practice the Secretary of State here concerned is the Secretary of State for Communities and Local Government.

3 As to the Treasury see CONSTITUTIONAL AND ADMINISTRATIVE LAW vol 20 (2014) PARA 262 et seq.

4 As to grants see PARA 1069.

5 'Relevant expenditure' means expenditure incurred with the approval of the Secretary of State after 30 August 1982 (Derelict Land Act 1982 s 5(3)) in or in connection with:
   (1) the carrying out, for the purpose mentioned in the text, of any works on the derelict land or any other land (s 1(3)(a));
   (2) the carrying out of a survey of the derelict land to determine whether works for that purpose should be undertaken (whether or not such works are carried out) (s 1(3)(b)); and
   (3) in relation to a local authority in whose area the derelict land is situated, the acquisition for that purpose of the derelict land or any other land (s 1(3)(c)).

6 Derelict Land Act 1982 s 1(1)(a).

7 Derelict Land Act 1982 s 1(1)(b).

8 Derelict Land Act 1982 s 1(2)(a).

9 'Local authority' means a county, district or London borough council, or the Common Council of the City of London: Derelict Land Act 1982 s 1(11) (amended by the Local Government Act 1985 s 102(2), Sch 17; and the Environment Act 1995 s 120(3), Sch 24). As to London borough councils see LONDON GOVERNMENT vol 71 (2013) PARA 20 et seq; and as to the

Common Council of the City of London see LONDON GOVERNMENT vol 71 (2013) PARA 34 et seq. In relation to land in a national park for which a national park authority is the local planning authority, 'local authority' in the Derelict Land Act 1982 includes a national park authority: Environment Act 1995 s 70, Sch 9 para 7. 'National park' means an area designated by an order made under the National Parks and Access to the Countryside Act 1949 s 5(3) (see OPEN SPACES AND COUNTRYSIDE vol 78 (2010) PARA 636): Derelict Land Act 1982 s 1(11). The Norfolk and Suffolk Broads Authority is to be treated for the purposes of the Derelict Land Act 1982 as a national park authority, and the Broads (as defined by the Norfolk and Suffolk Broads Act 1988 s 2(3)) as a national park for which it is the local planning authority: see the Norfolk and Suffolk Broads Act 1988 s 2(6), Sch 3 Pt II para 43 (amended by the Environment Act 1995 s 78, Sch 10 para 27).

10 'Relevant operations' means underground mining operations other than operations for the purpose of the working and getting of coal, or of coal and other minerals worked with coal, or for the purpose of getting any product from coal in the course of working and getting coal: Derelict Land Act 1982 s 1(11).

11 Derelict Land Act 1982 s 1(2)(b).

12 As to the Homes and Communities Agency see the Housing and Regeneration Act 2008 s 1, Sch 1; and PLANNING vol 83 (2010) PARA 1454.

13 'Derelict land functions' means functions under the Derelict Land Act 1982 s 1 or any enactment superseded by that section, but excluding the powers to make orders under s 1(5) (see PARA 1069), s 1(7) (see PARA 1068): Housing and Regeneration Act 2008 s 27(2).

14 Housing and Regeneration Act 2008 s 27(1).

1068. Derelict land clearance areas. The Secretary of State[1] may by order[2] specify any locality in England[3] as a derelict land clearance area[4] if:

(1)   he is of the opinion that the economic situation in the locality is such that the making of the order would be particularly appropriate with a view to contributing to the development of industry in the locality[5]; or

(2)   the Treasury[6] has consented to the making of the order[7].

The effect of an area being so specified is that it is then eligible for grants[8] at the same level as those payable in relation to land in a development area[9] or intermediate area[10].

1   As to the Secretary of State see PARA 902. In practice the Secretary of State here concerned is the Secretary of State for Communities and Local Government.

2   Such an order must be made by statutory instrument which is subject to annulment in pursuance of a resolution of either House of Parliament: Derelict Land Act 1982 s 1(10). See STATUTES AND LEGISLATIVE PROCESS vol 96 (2012) PARA 1032. Localities must be specified by reference to areas created or existing for other purposes: s 1(10) (amended by the Industrial Development Act 1982 s 19(1), Sch 2 Pt II para 19 (applying s 1(4)); and the Co-operative Development Agency and Industrial Development Act 1984 s 5(2), Sch 1 Pt II para 3).

3   The Derelict Land Act 1982 s 1 extends only to England: s 1(13). Similar powers in respect of Wales are exercisable by the Welsh Ministers: see the Welsh Development Agency Act 1975 s 16; and PARA 1058.

4   Derelict Land Act 1982 s 1(7).

5   Derelict Land Act 1982 s 1(8)(a). See eg the Derelict Land Clearance Area Order 1984, SI 1984/778; and the Wakefield (Derelict Land Clearance Area) Order 1987, SI 1987/1653. These provisions replace similar provisions in the Local Employment Act 1972 s 8 (repealed) which in turn replaced the Local Employment Act 1970 s 3(1) (repealed). Under those Acts the following orders were made, which continue in force as if made under the Derelict Land Act 1982 s 1, by virtue of the Interpretation Act 1978 s 17(2)(b): the Derelict Land Clearance Areas Order 1970, SI 1970/309; the Derelict Land Clearance Areas Order 1978, SI 1978/691; the Derelict Land Clearance Areas Order 1979, SI 1979/334; the Derelict Land Clearance Areas Order 1980, SI 1980/1890; and the Derelict Land Clearance Areas Order 1982, SI 1982/935.

6   As to the Treasury see CONSTITUTIONAL AND ADMINISTRATIVE LAW vol 20 (2014) PARA 262 et seq.

7   Derelict Land Act 1982 s 1(8)(b). See also note 5.

8   As to grants see PARA 1069.

9   'Development area' means an area specified as such by an order made, or having effect as if made, under the Industrial Development Act 1982 s 1: Derelict Land Act 1982 s 1(11) (amended

by the Industrial Development Act 1982 Sch 2 Pt II para 19). As to development areas see PARA 1037. The current such order is the Assisted Areas Order 2014, SI 2014/1508.

10 Derelict Land Act 1982 s 1(7). 'Intermediate area' means an area specified as such by such an order as is mentioned in note 9: s 1(11). As to intermediate areas see PARA 1038.

1069. Grants in respect of derelict land. In England[1] the Secretary of State[2] may make grants to any person of such amounts and payable at such times and subject to such conditions as he may from time to time determine in respect of relevant expenditure[3] incurred by that person with regard to derelict land[4]. Grants may be made in such manner as appears to the Secretary of State to be requisite[5]. Grants must not exceed the prescribed percentage[6], depending on whether or not the land is situated in a development area[7], an intermediate area[8] or a derelict land clearance area[9], and on whether the applicant is a local authority[10] or other person[11]. Similar, but separate, provision is made as to the prescribed percentage[12] where the land is not situated in any such area[13]. The fact that a locality ceases to be a development area, intermediate area or derelict land clearance area, or that an area ceases to be an area of outstanding natural beauty or comprised in a national park, does not affect the amount of grant which may be made provided that the relevant expenditure was approved by the Secretary of State before the time of the cessation[14].

1 The Derelict Land Act 1982 s 1 extends only to England: s 1(13). Similar powers in respect of Wales are exercisable by the Welsh Ministers: see the Welsh Development Agency Act 1975 s 16; and PARA 1058.

2 As to the Secretary of State see PARA 902. In practice the Secretary of State here concerned is the Secretary of State for Communities and Local Government.

3 As to the meaning of 'relevant expenditure' see PARA 1067 note 5.

4 Derelict Land Act 1982 s 1(1). As to the meaning of 'derelict land' see PARA 1067. Before making any grant under s 1 where the land to which s 1(1) applies is in a national park or an area of outstanding natural beauty, the Secretary of State must consult Natural England: s 1(6A) (added by the Natural Environment and Rural Communities Act 2006 s 105(1), Sch 11 Pt 1 para 99). 'Area of outstanding natural beauty' means an area designated as such by an order made under the Countryside and Rights of Way Act 2000 s 82 (see OPEN SPACES AND COUNTRYSIDE vol 78 (2010) PARA 658): Derelict Land Act 1982 s 1(11) (amended by the Countryside and Rights of Way Act 2000 s 93, Sch 15 Pt I para 6). As to the meaning of 'national park' see PARA 1067 note 9. As to Natural England see OPEN SPACES AND COUNTRYSIDE vol 78 (2010) PARA 523.

5 Derelict Land Act 1982 s 1(4).

6 Ie the prescribed percentage of the relevant expenditure, or in the case of a periodical grant in respect of costs from time to time incurred or treated as incurred in respect of the borrowing of money to defray the relevant expenditure, the prescribed percentage of the costs so incurred or treated as so incurred: Derelict Land Act 1982 s 1(5)(a), (b). As to the amount of the prescribed percentage see note 11.

7 As to the meaning of 'development area' see PARA 1068 note 9.

8 As to the meaning of 'intermediate area' see PARA 1068 note 10.

9 The Derelict Land Act 1982 s 1(5) refers specifically only to development areas and intermediate areas, but, by virtue of s 1(7), where an area has been specified as a derelict land clearance area it is to be treated for grant purposes as if it were a development area or an intermediate area: see PARA 1068.

10 As to the meaning of 'local authority' see PARA 1067 note 9.

11 Derelict Land Act 1982 s 1(5). Where the land is situated in a development area, an intermediate area or a derelict land clearance area there is no limit to the amount of relevant expenditure which can be given by way of grant to a local authority, but in the case of any other person the prescribed percentage of relevant expenditure which may be given by grant is 80% or such other limit as may be so prescribed by order made by the Secretary of State with the consent of the Treasury: Derelict Land Act 1982 s 1(5) (definition of 'prescribed percentage' amended by the Leasehold Reform, Housing and Urban Development Act 1993 s 187(1), Sch 21 para 8). As to orders under the Derelict Land Act 1982 generally see PARA 1068 note 2. Orders under the

Derelict Land Act 1982 s 1(5) may make such transitional provision as appears necessary or expedient: s 1(10). As to the Treasury see CONSTITUTIONAL AND ADMINISTRATIVE LAW vol 20 (2014) PARA 262 et seq.

12 The prescribed percentage is described in terms similar to those set out in note 6: Derelict Land Act 1982 s 1(6)(a), (b). As to the amount of the prescribed percentage see note 13.

13 Derelict Land Act 1982 s 1(6).Where the land is in a national park or an area of outstanding natural beauty and the applicant is a local authority in whose area the land is situated, the prescribed percentage is 75%, and in any other case the prescribed percentage is 50%: see s 1(6).

14 Derelict Land Act 1982 s 1(9).

(3) DEVELOPMENT COUNCIL LEGISLATION

(i) Development Councils

1070. Establishment and purpose of development councils. A development council may be established for any industry[1] by order[2] made by the appropriate minister[3]. Before making such an order, the appropriate minister must consult any organisation appearing to him to be representative of substantial numbers of persons carrying on business in the industry and such organisations representative of persons employed in the industry as appear to him to be appropriate[4]. An order may not be made unless the appropriate minister is satisfied that the establishment of a development council for the industry is desired by a substantial number of the persons engaged in that industry[5].

The order may assign to the development council any or all of specified functions in order to increase efficiency or productivity in the industry, to improve or develop the service that it renders or could render to the community, or to enable it to render such service more economically[6]. Such functions may include:

(1) promoting:
  (a) the production and marketing of standard products[7];
  (b) the better definition of trade descriptions and consistency in their use[8];
  (c) the training of persons engaged or proposing engagement in the industry, and their education in relevant technical or artistic subjects[9];
  (d) the adoption of measures for securing safer and better working conditions, and the provision and improvement of amenities for employees, and promoting or undertaking inquiry into such measures[10];
  (e) arrangements for co-operative organisations for supplying materials and equipment, for co-ordinating production, and for marketing and distributing products[11];
  (f) the development of export trade, including promoting or undertaking arrangements for publicity overseas[12];
  (g) the improvement of accounting and costing practice and uniformity therein, including in particular the formulation of standard castings[13];
(2) undertaking:
  (a) the certification of products, the registration of certification trade marks, and the functions of proprietors of such marks[14];
  (b) arrangements for making available information obtained, and for advising, on matters with which the council is concerned in the exercise of any of its functions[15];

(3)   promoting or undertaking:
      (a)   scientific research[16];
      (b)   inquiry as to materials and equipment and as to methods of
            production, management and labour utilisation, including the
            discovery and development of new materials, equipment and
            methods and of improvements in those already in use, the
            assessment of the advantages of different alternatives, and the
            conduct of experimental establishments and of tests on a
            commercial scale[17];
      (c)   research into matters affecting industrial psychology[18];
      (d)   measures for the improvement of design, including promoting or
            undertaking the establishment and operation of design centres[19];
      (e)   research into the incidence, prevention and cure of industrial
            diseases[20];
      (f)   arrangements for encouraging entry into the industry[21];
      (g)   research for improving arrangements for marketing and
            distributing products[22];
      (h)   research into matters relating to the consumption or use of goods
            and services supplied by the industry[23];
      (i)   arrangements for better acquainting the public in the United
            Kingdom with the goods and services supplied by the industry and
            methods of using them[24];
      (j)   the collection and formulation of statistics[25];
(4)   advising on any matters relating to the industry (other than
      remuneration or conditions of employment) as to which the appropriate
      minister may request it to advise, and undertaking inquiry for the
      purpose of enabling it to do so[26].

1   The expression 'the industry' where used in relation to a development council or to an order
    under the Industrial Organisation and Development Act 1947 s 9 (levies: see PARAS 1078–1080)
    is to be construed as referring to the industry that is for the time being that for which the council
    is established or in connection with which funds are to be made available, as the case may be:
    s 14(4). A development council order must designate, in such manner as appears to the Secretary
    of State or minister concerned (see note 3) to be requisite for preventing uncertainty, the
    activities that are to be treated as constituting the industry for which the council is established,
    whether they are regarded for any other purposes as those of: a single industry, a group of
    industries, or a section or sections of an industry or industries: s 14(1). An order amending such
    an order may provide that further activities so designated are to be treated as included in the
    industry for which the council is established, or that designated activities so treated are no
    longer to be so treated: s 14(2).
2   Industrial Organisation and Development Act 1947 s 1(1). Such an order must not be made
    until a draft has been approved by a resolution of each House of Parliament: s 1(6). See
    STATUTES AND LEGISLATIVE PROCESS vol 96 (2012) PARA 1032. An order may provide for any
    incidental or supplementary matters for which it appears to the Secretary of State or minister
    concerned necessary or expedient to provide: s 1(5). At the date at which this volume states the
    law no such order was in force. See note 3.
3   Industrial Organisation and Development Act 1947 s 1(1), (2) (s 1(2) amended by SI 1955/554;
    and SI 1971/719). Formerly there were development councils for the clothing industry, the
    jewellery and silverware industry, the textile industry and the furniture industry, but these have
    all been dissolved. In 2008 the British Potato Council, the Home-Grown Cereals Authority, the
    Horticultural Development Council, the Meat and Livestock Commission and the Milk
    Development Council were all replaced by the Agriculture and Horticulture Development
    Board: see the Agriculture and Horticulture Development Board Order 2008, SI 2008/576,
    art 17; and AGRICULTURAL PRODUCTION AND MARKETING vol 1 (2008) PARA 1143.
        In this paragraph, and in PARAS 1071–1084, the expression 'the appropriate minister' is used
    to denote the person or persons who may exercise the power to make development council
    orders.

The power to make such an order was originally conferred on the Board of Trade and several different ministers, collectively referred to as 'the board or minister concerned': Industrial Organisation and Development Act 1947 s 1(2) (as originally enacted). The power is now exercisable by the Board of Trade, the Secretary of State for Business, Innovation and Skills or the Secretary of State for Environment, Food and Rural Affairs: s 1(2) (amended by SI 1955/554; and SI 1971/719). The functions of the Minister of Agriculture, Fisheries and Food were transferred in so far as they were exercisable:

(1) in relation to Wales, to the Secretary of State for Wales (Transfer of Functions (Wales) (No 1) Order 1978, SI 1978/272, art 9(1)(a));

(2) in relation to England and Wales, to that minister and that Secretary of State jointly (art 9(1)(b)); and

(3) in relation to Great Britain, to that minister, the Secretary of State for Scotland and the Secretary of State for Wales jointly (art 9(1)(c)).

The powers of the Board of Trade are in practice exercisable by the Secretary of State for Business, Innovation and Skills, who is President of the Board of Trade: see PARA 902. The power to make a development council order relating to agriculture or fisheries and extending (but not applying solely) to Scotland was vested in the Minister of Agriculture, Fisheries and Food and the Secretary of State for Scotland jointly: Industrial Organisation and Development Act 1947 s 1(2) proviso (amended by SI 1955/554). The functions previously exercised jointly by the Secretary of State, the Secretary of State for Wales and the Secretary of State were transferred to the Minister of Agriculture, Fisheries and Food: see the Transfer of Functions (Agriculture and Food) Order 1999, SI 1999/3141. All functions of the Minister of Agriculture, Fisheries and Food are transferred to the Secretary of State for Environment, Food and Rural Affairs: see ENVIRONMENTAL QUALITY AND PUBLIC HEALTH vol 45 (2010) PARA 58. Since June 2001, the functions of that minister are now exercisable as part of the remit of the Department of Environment, Food and Rural Affairs: see *Delivering Effective Government* 10 Downing Street press release, 8 June 2001. Functions of the Minister of Agriculture, Fisheries and Food, so far as exercisable in relation to Wales, were transferred to the National Assembly for Wales by the National Assembly for Wales (Transfer of Functions) Order 1999, SI 1999/672, art 2, Sch 1 and are now exercisable by the Welsh Ministers: see PARA 902 note 21. As to the meaning of 'agriculture' see AGRICULTURAL LAND vol 1 (2008) PARA 324. As to the Welsh Ministers see CONSTITUTIONAL AND ADMINISTRATIVE LAW vol 20 (2014) PARA 373 et seq.

Administrative expenses incurred by an authority listed in the Industrial Organisation and Development Act 1947 s 1(2) in the execution of that Act are defrayed out of money provided by Parliament: s 12.

4   Industrial Organisation and Development Act 1947 s 1(3).

5   Industrial Organisation and Development Act 1947 s 1(4). The persons engaged in the industry are both employers and employees, and they are not to be considered separately when assessing the degree of support for a council: *Thorneloe and Clarkson Ltd v Board of Trade* [1950] 2 All ER 245, 66 (pt 1) TLR 1117.

6   Industrial Organisation and Development Act 1947 s 1(1). For limitations under European Union law on a development council's functions, see Case 222/82 *Apple and Pear Development Council v KJ Lewis Ltd* [1983] ECR 4083, [1983] 3 CMLR 733, ECJ.

7   Industrial Organisation and Development Act 1947 Sch 1 para 5.

8   Industrial Organisation and Development Act 1947 Sch 1 para 6.

9   Industrial Organisation and Development Act 1947 Sch 1 para 8.

10 Industrial Organisation and Development Act 1947 Sch 1 para 9.

11 Industrial Organisation and Development Act 1947 Sch 1 para 14.

12 Industrial Organisation and Development Act 1947 Sch 1 para 15.

13 Industrial Organisation and Development Act 1947 Sch 1 para 17.

14 Industrial Organisation and Development Act 1947 Sch 1 para 7.

15 Industrial Organisation and Development Act 1947 Sch 1 para 20.

16 Industrial Organisation and Development Act 1947 Sch 1 para 1.

17 Industrial Organisation and Development Act 1947 Sch 1 para 2.

18 Industrial Organisation and Development Act 1947 Sch 1 para 3.

19 Industrial Organisation and Development Act 1947 Sch 1 para 4.

20 Industrial Organisation and Development Act 1947 Sch 1 para 10.

21 Industrial Organisation and Development Act 1947 Sch 1 para 11.

22 Industrial Organisation and Development Act 1947 Sch 1 para 12.

23 Industrial Organisation and Development Act 1947 Sch 1 para 13.

24 Industrial Organisation and Development Act 1947 Sch 1 para 16.

25 Industrial Organisation and Development Act 1947 Sch 1 para 18.

26 Industrial Organisation and Development Act 1947 Sch 1 para 19.

1071. Constitution and membership of development councils. A development council is a body corporate, and is to be known by the name specified in the development council order[1]. Its members are appointed by the appropriate minister[2], and must be persons of the following categories:

(1) persons capable of representing the interests of persons carrying on business in the industry[3];

(2) persons capable of representing the interests of persons employed in the industry[4];

(3) independent members[5]; and

(4) where it appears to the appropriate minister to be expedient, persons having special knowledge of matters relating to the marketing or distribution of products of the industry[6].

The development council order must specify the number or a maximum or minimum number of persons in these respective categories, and ensure that the members under heads (1) and (2) above constitute a majority of members of the council[7]. Before appointing the members under heads (1) and (2) above, the appropriate minister must consult such organisations as are required to be consulted[8] before the establishment of a development council[9]. A development council must have a chairman, who must be one of the independent members and be appointed by the appropriate minister, who may also appoint another member as deputy chairman[10].

A development council order may specify requirements as to appointment, tenure and vacation of office and as to qualification or disqualification for membership[11]. It may also provide for the payment to members of such remuneration and allowances[12] as may be determined by the appropriate minister, and for the payment on the retirement or death of any member as to whom it may be so determined, of such pensions or gratuities[13] to them or others by reference to their service as may be so determined[14].

1 Industrial Organisation and Development Act 1947 s 2(1). A development council has a common seal: s 2(9), Sch 2 para 1. As to development council orders see PARA 1070.

2 Industrial Organisation and Development Act 1947 s 2(2). As to the appropriate minister see PARA 1070 note 3.

3 Industrial Organisation and Development Act 1947 s 2(3)(a).

4 Industrial Organisation and Development Act 1947 s 2(3)(b).

5 Industrial Organisation and Development Act 1947 s 2(3)(c). Independent members are persons as to whom the appropriate minister is satisfied that they have no such financial or industrial interest as is likely to affect them in the discharge of their functions: s 2(3)(c).

6 Industrial Organisation and Development Act 1947 s 2(3).

7 Industrial Organisation and Development Act 1947 s 2(4).

8 See PARA 1070.

9 Industrial Organisation and Development Act 1947 s 2(6).

10 Industrial Organisation and Development Act 1947 s 2(7).

11 Industrial Organisation and Development Act 1947 s 2(5). Members of a development council are disqualified for membership of the House of Commons: see the House of Commons Disqualification Act 1975 s 1(1)(f), Sch 1 Pt II; and PARLIAMENT vol 78 (2010) PARA 908.

12 The remuneration and allowances are to be paid out of the money of the council: Industrial Organisation and Development Act 1947 Sch 2 para 5.

13 The pensions or gratuities are to be paid by the appropriate minister: Industrial Organisation and Development Act 1947 Sch 2 para 6(a).

14 Industrial Organisation and Development Act 1947 s 2(8).

1072. Acts, proceedings, contracts and staff of development councils. A development council order[1] may make provision with respect to:

(1) the quorum, proceedings, meetings and determinations of the council;

(2) the council accounts and accounts to be kept by the council and the audit of their accounts; and

(3) the execution of instruments and the mode of entering into contracts by and on behalf of the council and the proof of documents purporting to be executed, issued or signed by the council or a member, officer or servant of the council[2].

Subject to the provisions of the order establishing it, a development council may regulate its own proceedings[3]. It may appoint such officers, agents and servants on such terms as to remuneration[4] and other matters as it may determine, and there may be paid, on the death or retirement of any of them as to whom the council may so determine, such pensions or gratuities[5] to them or others by reference to their service as the council may determine[6].

1 As to the making of development council orders see PARA 1070.
2 Industrial Organisation and Development Act 1947 s 2(9), Sch 2 para 2.
3 Industrial Organisation and Development Act 1947 Sch 2 para 3.
4 The remuneration is to be paid out of the money of the council: Industrial Organisation and Development Act 1947 Sch 2 para 5.
5 These pensions and gratuities are to be paid either wholly by the council or partly by the council and partly by means of contributions: Industrial Organisation and Development Act 1947 Sch 2 para 6.
6 Industrial Organisation and Development Act 1947 Sch 2 para 4.

1073. Provision of information to development councils. A development council order[1] may secure that persons carrying on business in the industry[2] are to be registered by the development council in a register in which any person claiming to be a person so carrying on business is to be entitled as of right to be or remain registered, subject to any provisions of the order as to notification to the council of such claims[3]. Further, the order may enable the council to require persons carrying on business in the industry to furnish such returns and other information[4] as appears to the council to be required for the exercise of any of its functions[5]. In order to exercise these powers generally as regards the industry or any section of it, the council must have the previous consent of the appropriate minister[6] and his approval of the form in which the returns or other information are required to be furnished[7].

1 As to the making of development council orders see PARA 1070.
2 As to the meaning of 'the industry' see PARA 1070 note 1.
3 Industrial Organisation and Development Act 1947 s 3(1). The register must be kept by the development council and must be open to public inspection at all convenient hours on payment of such reasonable fee, if any, and subject to such conditions, if any, as may be specified in the order: s 3(1).
4 This includes information with respect to the productive capacity, capital assets, staff, output, orders, sales, deliveries, stocks and costs of any business: Industrial Organisation and Development Act 1947 s 3(2).
5 Industrial Organisation and Development Act 1947 s 3(2). As to the functions of development councils see PARA 1070.
6 As to the appropriate minister see PARA 1070 note 3.
7 Industrial Organisation and Development Act 1947 s 3(2) proviso.

1074. Duty of development councils to submit reports and accounts. A development council must prepare and transmit to the appropriate minister[1] annually a report setting out what has been done in the discharge of its functions during the financial year last completed[2], including a statement of the council's accounts for that year, together with any report made by the auditors or, as the case may be, the Comptroller and Auditor General, on those accounts[3]. The statement of accounts must be in the form directed by the appropriate minister, being a form conforming with the best commercial standards, and must show the total remuneration and allowances paid during the year to members of the council[4]. A copy of any report prepared by a council, or made by the auditors on its accounts or by the Comptroller and Auditor General on its statement of accounts, must be laid before Parliament by the appropriate minister[5].

1 As to the appropriate minister see PARA 1070 note 3.
2 Industrial Organisation and Development Act 1947 s 7(1). 'Financial year' means the 12 months ending with 31 March: Interpretation Act 1978 s 5, Sch 1.
3 Industrial Organisation and Development Act 1947 s 7(2) (amended by SI 2003/1326). The report must be transmitted as soon as the accounts for that financial year have been audited: Industrial Organisation and Development Act 1947 s 7(2). A person must not be appointed to audit a council's accounts unless he is eligible for appointment as a statutory auditor under the Companies Act 2006 Pt 42 (ss 1209–1264) (see COMPANIES vol 15 (2009) PARA 958): Industrial Organisation and Development Act 1947 s 7(2A) (added by SI 1991/1997; and amended by SI 2008/948). As to the office of Comptroller and Auditor General see CONSTITUTIONAL AND ADMINISTRATIVE LAW vol 20 (2014) PARA 494 et seq. Separate provision was made for the British Potato Council, the Horticultural Development Council and the Milk Development Council: see Industrial Organisation and Development Act 1947 s 7(2B), (3A)–(3C) (added by SI 2003/1326). These development councils have now been dissolved and replaced by the Agriculture and Horticulture Development Board see PARA 1070 note 3.
4 Industrial Organisation and Development Act 1947 s 7(3).
5 Industrial Organisation and Development Act 1947 s 7(4) (amended by SI 2003/1326).

1075. Continuance and dissolution of development councils. Development councils must be periodically reviewed. At a date not later than the expiration of three years from the coming into effect of a development council order[1] and at five-yearly intervals while the council continues in being after that date, the appropriate minister[2] must consult the council and such organisations as must be consulted in the setting up of the council[3] on the question whether the council should continue in being, and if so whether the development council order should be amended in any respect[4].

An order for the amendment of a development council order (whether as originally made or as previously so amended), or for the dissolution of a development council, may be made by the appropriate minister after consultation with the council and subject to the like provisions as to consultation[5] and approval by Parliament[6] as apply to the making of a development council order[7]. At the request of the council, an amending order may assign to the council functions[8] which it appears to the appropriate minister expedient for the council to exercise for any of its purposes[9].

1 As to the making of development council orders see PARA 1070.
2 As to the appropriate minister see PARA 1070 note 3.
3 As to the obligation to consult certain organisations before setting up a council see PARA 1070.
4 Industrial Organisation and Development Act 1947 s 8(3).
5 See PARA 1070.
6 See PARA 1070.
7 Industrial Organisation and Development Act 1947 s 8(1). An order for the dissolution of a development council must make provision for the winding up of the council, the imposition and recovery of charges under s 4 (see PARA 1076) if necessary to meet the liabilities and the cost of the winding up, and the application of any excess assets for specified purposes connected with the industry; and for the revocation of the development council order either with or without savings: s 8(4). See eg the Apple and Pear Development Council (Dissolution) Order 1989, SI 1989/2276.
8 Ie functions of a kind similar to those specified in the Industrial Organisation and Development Act 1947 s 1(1), Sch 1 (see PARA 1070), or such as appear to the appropriate minister to be capable of being conveniently exercised in association with functions of such a kind which have

been, or are to be, assigned to the council: s 8(2). However, functions assigned under s 8(2) may not include functions relating to remuneration or conditions of employment: s 8(2) proviso.
9   Industrial Organisation and Development Act 1947 s 8(2). As to the purposes of development councils see PARA 1070.

(ii) Levies

A. LEVIES UNDER DEVELOPMENT COUNCIL ORDERS

1076.   Charges imposed by development council orders. A development council order[1] may provide for the imposition by the development council, with the approval of the appropriate minister[2], and for the recovery by the council (in such manner and through such channels, if any, as may be specified in the order), of limited charges[3] for enabling the council to meet its expenses, to be made on and recovered from persons carrying on business in the industry or on persons carrying on any business consisting wholly or partly in the production of, or dealing in, any materials of the industry[4].

1   As to the power to make development council orders see PARA 1070.
2   As to the appropriate minister see PARA 1070 note 3.
3   The order must either provide that the charges be computed so as not to yield more than a specified amount during a specified period, or provide that they are not to be levied at more than specified maximum rates: Industrial Organisation and Development Act 1947 s 4(2).
      An order relating to agriculture providing for such charges may contain provision:
      (1)   authorising such of the persons on whom the charges are imposed as may be specified in the order to recover all or part of the charges imposed on them from such other persons carrying on business in the industry as may be so specified (s 4(2A)(a) (s 4(2A) added as a modification for this purpose by the Agriculture Act 1993 s 60(1), (3)); and
      (2)   authorising the deduction from the charges payable by the persons with such a right of recovery, or the repayment to them, of such amounts as may be determined by or under the order in respect of expenses incurred by them in exercising that right, and any sums which are, in accordance with provision made by or under that order, to be treated as irrecoverable (Industrial Organisation and Development Act 1947 s 4(2A)(b) (as so added)).
      'Agriculture' has the same meaning as in the Agriculture Act 1947 (see AGRICULTURAL LAND vol 1 (2008) PARA 324), and 'agricultural' is to be construed accordingly: Agriculture Act 1993 s 60(6). A development council order is to be taken to relate to agriculture if any of the activities that are to be treated as constituting the industry to which the order relates is an agricultural activity: s 60(5). As to the meaning of 'the industry' see PARA 1070 note 1.
      Before making the order, the appropriate minister must satisfy himself that the incidence of charges (taking into account, in the case of an order relating to agriculture, any provision made under the Industrial Organisation and Development Act 1947 s 4(2A)) as between different classes of undertakings in the industry will be in accordance with a fair principle: s 4(3) (modified in relation to orders relating to agriculture by the Agriculture Act 1993 s 60(4)). However, there is no elaboration in the statute on the phrase 'fair principle'.
4   Industrial Organisation and Development Act 1947 s 4(1). Section 4(1) is modified in relation to orders relating to agriculture by the Agriculture Act 1993 s 60(2).

1077.   Persons in industry to furnish returns and information to development councils. So far as it may appear to the appropriate minister[1] reasonably requisite for the purposes of the imposition or recovery of the charges imposed by a development council order[2], the order may empower the council to require persons carrying on business in the industry, or any business consisting wholly or partly in the production of or dealing in any materials of the industry, to furnish returns and other information, to keep records and to produce for examination on behalf of the council such records as well as books and other documents in the custody or under the control of such persons[3].

1   As to the appropriate minister see PARA 1070 note 3.
2   As to the making of development council orders see PARA 1070. As to the imposition and recovery of charges see PARA 1076.
3   Industrial Organisation and Development Act 1947 s 4(4).

B. INDUSTRIES WITHOUT DEVELOPMENT COUNCILS

1078.   Funds to be made available where there is no development council. If it appears to any of the authorities having power to set up a development council[1] to be expedient that funds should be made available for the purposes of:

(1)   scientific research;
(2)   promotion of export trade; or
(3)   improvement of design,

in connection with an industry for which there is neither a development council nor a relevant board[2], and that a body capable of carrying out that purpose satisfactorily either exists or is to be brought into being, the authority may, after such consultation as would be required prior to the making of a development council order for the industry[3], make an order providing for the imposition of charges on, and recovery from, categories of persons in relation to the industry corresponding to those who under a development council order may be liable to pay charges in connection with an industry which has a development council[4]. The order may empower the authority to require persons to furnish returns and information, to keep records and produce documents to the appropriate minister[5] in the same manner as a council may be empowered so to do under a development council order[6]. Any order imposing those charges may be amended or revoked by a further order of the authority making the original order[7].

1   See PARA 1070.
2   'Relevant board' means a board established under the Natural Environment and Rural Communities Act 2006 Pt 8 Ch 2 (ss 87–97) (see AGRICULTURAL PRODUCTION AND MARKETING vol 1 (2008) PARAS 1315–1319): Industrial Organisation and Development Act 1947 s 9(1A) (added by the Natural Environment and Rural Communities Act 2006 s 105(1), Sch 11 Pt 1 para 5(1), (3)).
3   Industrial Organisation and Development Act 1947 s 9(8). As to the organisations to be consulted see PARA 1070. As to the meaning of 'the industry' see PARA 1070 note 1.
4   Industrial Organisation and Development Act 1947 s 9(1) (amended by the Natural Environment and Rural Communities Act 2006 Sch 11 Pt 1 para 5(2)). As to the categories of persons referred to see PARA 1076. Before making an order, the appropriate minister (see PARA 1070 note 3) must be satisfied that the incidence of the charges as between different classes of undertakings in the industry will be in accordance with a fair principle: Industrial Organisation and Development Act 1947 s 9(2). An order under s 9 must specify a public fund or account into which sums recovered in respect of such charges must be paid, and sums so recovered are issued from that fund or account to the body in question to meet its expenses: s 9(3). An order may not be made unless a draft has been approved by resolution of each House of Parliament: s 9(9). See STATUTES AND LEGISLATIVE PROCESS vol 96 (2012) PARA 1032. An order was formerly in force for the promotion of export trade by the National Wool Textile Export Corporation: see the Wool Textile Industry (Export Promotion Levy) Order 1970, SI 1970/348 (amended by SI 1971/880; and SI 1982/485), but this was revoked by the Wool Textile Industry (Export Promotion Levy) (Revocation) Order 2008, SI 2008/2932 and, at the date this volume states the law, no export promotion levy order was in force. The Industrial Organisation and Development Act 1947 s 14(1), (2) (see PARA 1070) applies to orders under s 9: s 14(3).
5   As to the appropriate minister see PARA 1070 note 3.
6   Industrial Organisation and Development Act 1947 s 9(6), applying s 4(4) and s 6 in relation to s 4(4): see PARAS 1077, 1084.
7   Industrial Organisation and Development Act 1947 s 9(7).

1079.   Duties of bodies in receipt of funds to prepare accounts etc.   A body to which sums for the purposes of scientific research, promotion of export trade or improvement of design are issued[1] must prepare annually a statement[2] of its accounts for its financial year last completed and transmit it to the authority making the order[3] together with a copy of any report made by auditors on the accounts[4]. The authority must lay before Parliament a copy of each such statement and of any such report[5]. As respects each financial year, the authority making the order must prepare an account[6] of sums recovered under the order and of their disposal by the authority, and the account must be transmitted, on or before 30 November after the end of the financial year in question, to the Comptroller and Auditor General[7] who, after examining and certifying the account, must lay copies of it, together with his report on it, before Parliament[8].

1 Ie an industrial body (having no development council) which is in receipt of sums under the Industrial Organisation and Development Act 1947 s 9: see PARA 1078.
2 The statement must be in such form as the authority making the order (as to which see PARA 1078) may direct: Industrial Organisation and Development Act 1947 s 9(5).
3 Ie the order under Industrial Organisation and Development Act 1947 s 9.
4 Industrial Organisation and Development Act 1947 s 9(5). As to the meaning of 'financial year' see PARA 1074 note 2.
5 Industrial Organisation and Development Act 1947 s 9(5).
6 The account must be prepared in such form and manner as the Treasury may direct: Industrial Organisation and Development Act 1947 s 9(4). As to the Treasury see CONSTITUTIONAL AND ADMINISTRATIVE LAW vol 20 (2014) PARA 262 et seq.
7 As to the office of Comptroller and Auditor General see CONSTITUTIONAL AND ADMINISTRATIVE LAW vol 20 (2014) PARA 494 et seq. In relation to Wales, functions of the Comptroller and Auditor General under the Industrial Organisation and Development Act 1947 s 9(4) have been transferred to the Auditor General for Wales: see the National Assembly for Wales (Transfer of Functions) Order 1999, SI 1999/672, art 2(g), Sch 1.
8 Industrial Organisation and Development Act 1947 s 9(4).

1080. Excess in funds after revocation of orders. Where, after the revocation of an order applying to an industry for which there is no development council[1], there exists an excess of sums recovered under the order over the amount issued, sums not exceeding in aggregate the amount of that excess may be paid, out of the public fund or account into which the sums recovered were paid, to:

(1) any development council there may be in being for an industry comprising the whole or a substantial part of the industry in relation to which the order was made[2]; or

(2) if there is no such council, but the authority making the levy order[3] is satisfied that there exists or is to be brought into being a body which is capable of carrying out satisfactorily purposes in connection with the industry in relation to which the order was made for which the authority considers it expedient that funds should be made available, to that body but subject to such provision for securing the disposal of the sums for such purposes as it appears to the authority to be practicable and expedient to make[4].

1 See PARA 1078.
2 Industrial Organisation and Development Act 1947 s 9(10)(a). This is now unlikely to be the case: see PARA 1070 note 3.
3 Ie the authority making the levy order under the Industrial Organisation and Development Act 1947 s 9: see PARA 1078.
4 Industrial Organisation and Development Act 1947 s 9(10)(b).

(iii) Restriction on Disclosure of Information

1081. Information to be given to independent members. If a development council order[1] imposes any requirement to furnish returns or other information relating to an individual business or to produce for examination books or other documents or records², it must provide that the returns or information are to be furnished to, or the examination done by, independent members of the council³, or to or by officers of the council specially authorised in that behalf⁴.

1   As to the power to make development council orders see PARA 1070.
2   As to the power to impose such requirements see PARAS 1073, 1077.

3   Independent members are persons who have no financial or industrial interest likely to affect them in the discharge of their functions: see the Industrial Organisation and Development Act 1947 s 2(3)(c); and PARA 1071 note 5. The order may designate certain independent members only: s 5(1).

4   Industrial Organisation and Development Act 1947 s 5(1).

1082.   Protection of information regarding secret processes.   A development council order¹ must make provision for ensuring that if a person required to furnish returns or information or to produce documents² claims to use a secret process in his business that ought not to be disclosed on the ground of risk or prejudice to his business, that person will not be subject to any liability for withholding disclosure of any particulars relating to the process unless, after considering the claim, the appropriate minister³ has approved the form of the requirement and the making of it in that form⁴.

1   As to the power to make development council orders see PARA 1070.
2   As to the power to make such requirements see PARAS 1073, 1077.
3   As to the appropriate minister see PARA 1070 note 3.
4   Industrial Organisation and Development Act 1947 s 5(4).

1083.   Restriction on disclosure of information.   With certain exceptions¹, returns or information duly furnished or information duly obtained² on an examination must not, without the consent of the person carrying on the business to which the returns, information, books, or other documents or records relate, be disclosed except to specified persons³, or in the form of a summary of similar returns or information furnished by or obtained from a number of persons and so framed as not to enable particulars relating to any individual business to be ascertained from it⁴, unless such disclosure is made for the purpose of any legal proceedings⁵ pursuant to the Industrial Organisation and Development Act 1947 or of any report of such proceedings⁶. Disclosure of information in contravention of this provision is an offence⁷.

1   The Industrial Organisation and Development Act 1947 s 5(2), (3) does not apply to disclosure:
    (1)   by a development council established in relation to an industry whose activities include an agricultural activity (Industrial Organisation and Development Act 1947 s 5(3A)(a) (s 5(3A) added by the Natural Environment and Rural Communities Act 2006 s 105(1), Sch 11 Pt 1 para 4));
    (2)   to, or to an officer of, Natural England (Industrial Organisation and Development Act 1947 s 5(3A)(b) (as so added));
    (3)   to, or to an officer of, the Joint Nature Conservation Committee (s 5(3A)(d) (as so added));
    (4)   to, or to an officer of, a body specified in the Natural Environment and Rural Communities Act 2006 Sch 7 (see OPEN SPACES AND COUNTRYSIDE vol 78 (2010) PARA 520) (Industrial Organisation and Development Act 1947 s 5(3A)(e) (as so added));
    (5)   to, or to an officer of, a board established under the Natural Environment and Rural Communities Act 2006 Pt 8 Ch 2 (ss 87–97) (see AGRICULTURAL PRODUCTION AND MARKETING vol 1 (2008) PARA 1316 et seq) (Industrial Organisation and Development Act 1947 s 5(3A)(f) (as so added)).
    As to Natural England and the Joint Nature Conservation Committee see OPEN SPACES AND COUNTRYSIDE vol 78 (2010) PARAS 523, 525.

2   Ie subject to provision in the development council order under the Industrial Organisation and Development Act 1947 s 5(1): see PARA 1081. As to the power to require information etc see PARAS 1073, 1077.

3   The specified persons are:
    (1)   independent members of the development council (as to whom see PARA 1071 note 5), or such of them as are designated under the order to carry out examinations or receive information (see PARA 1081), or authorised officers of the council (Industrial Organisation and Development Act 1947 s 5(2)(b));
    (2)   the appropriate minister (see PARA 1070 note 3) or one of his officers (s 5(2)(c));
    (3)   the appropriate minister or one of his officers in connection with the execution or for the purposes of the Statistics of Trade Act 1947 (see PARA 1100) (Industrial Organisation and Development Act 1947 s 5(2)(d)).

4   Industrial Organisation and Development Act 1947 s 5(2)(a).

5   'Legal proceedings' includes civil or criminal proceedings and arbitrations: Industrial Organisation and Development Act 1947 s 5(2) proviso.

6   Industrial Organisation and Development Act 1947 s 5(2) proviso.

7   Industrial Organisation and Development Act 1947 s 5(3). An offender is liable, on summary conviction, to imprisonment for a term not exceeding three months or a fine not exceeding the prescribed sum or both, or, on conviction on indictment, to imprisonment for a term not exceeding two years or a fine or both: s 5(3) (amended by virtue of the Criminal Law Act 1977 s 32(1); and the Magistrates' Courts Act 1980 s 32(2)). As to the prescribed sum see SENTENCING AND DISPOSITION OF OFFENDERS vol 92 (2010) PARA 141.

(iv) Enforcement of Information Provisions

1084. Enforcement. A development council order[1] may provide for the enforcement of its provisions[2] as to the registration of persons carrying on business in the industry, the furnishing of returns or other information, and the production or examination of books or other documents or records or the keeping of records[3]. An order providing for levies for an industry having no development council[4] may make similar provision for the enforcement of those provisions of the order which require records to be kept, returns to be furnished and books and records to be produced for examination in connection with the imposition or recovery of charges[5].

1   As to the power to make development council orders see PARA 1070.

2   Ie the provisions requiring persons to maintain a register and to furnish information and returns see PARAS 1073, 1077.

3   Industrial Organisation and Development Act 1947 s 6. The order may provide for the imposition of time limits for the satisfaction of obligations, with or without power to the development council or other specified authority to extend limits imposed: s 6. No punishment provided may exceed those provided by s 5(3) (see PARA 1083 note 7) or, in the case of a fine for a continuing offence, £5 per day: s 6 proviso.

4   As to the imposition of charges where there is no development council see PARA 1078.

5   Industrial Organisation and Development Act 1947 s 9(6), applying s 6. The same provisions as to maximum punishments apply: see note 3.

(4) LOCAL ENTERPRISE PARTNERSHIPS

1085. Local enterprise partnerships and local enterprise zones. A local enterprise partnership is a body, designated by the Secretary of State[1], which is established for the purpose of creating or improving the conditions for economic growth in an area[2]. Local enterprise partnerships are voluntary partnerships between local authorities and businesses. They were launched in 2011 by the Department for Business, Innovation and Skills to decide what the priorities should be for investment in roads, buildings and other facilities in their area in order to promote economic growth[3]. They effectively replaced the regional development agencies which were abolished in 2012[4].

Enterprise zones comprise specific geographical areas within local enterprise partnerships' boundaries, offering a range of incentives for businesses to start up or expand[5].

1 As to the Secretary of State see PARA 902.

2 Town and Country Planning (Local Planning) (England) Regulations 2012, SI 2012/767, reg 4(3) (substituted by SI 2012/2613). At the date at which this volume states the law, there were 39 local enterprise partnerships in operation.

3 See *Supporting Economic Growth Through Local Enterprise Partnerships and Enterprise Zones* (Department for Communities and Local Government; Department for Business, Innovation & Skills and Homes and Communities Agency, 7 November 2012).

4 Regional development agencies had been established by the Regional Development Agencies Act 1998 to cover nine regions in England (ie East Midlands, Eastern, London, North East, North West, South East, South West, West Midlands and Yorkshire and the Humber): see Sch 1 (repealed). Their function was, in respect of their areas, to further the economic development and the regeneration; to promote business efficiency, investment and competitiveness; to promote employment; to enhance the development and application of skills relevant to employment; and to contribute to the achievement of sustainable development in the United Kingdom where it is relevant to do so: s 4(1) (repealed). The London Development Agency was abolished on 31 March 2012 by the Localism Act 2011 s 191; Localism Act 2011 (Commencement No 4 and Transitional, Transitory and Saving Provisions) Order 2012, SI 2012/628, art 4. The rest of the regional development agencies were abolished on 1 July 2012 by the Public Bodies Act 2011 s 30; Public Bodies Act 2011 (Commencement No 2) Order 2012, SI 2012/1662, arts 1, 2. Transfer schemes were made by order of the Secretary of State so that activities begun by a regional development agency could be continued or completed by another person: see the Public Bodies Act 2011 s 30(4)–(10); and the Public Bodies Act 2011 (Transitional Provision) Order 2012, SI 2012/1471 (which transfers functions to the Secretary of State). The only remaining provisions of the Regional Development Agencies Act 1998 which are still in force (s 14 (accounts and records), s 15 (audit), s 17 (annual report) are repealed by the Public Bodies Act 2011 s 30(3), Sch 6 as from a day to be appointed. At the date at which this volume states the law no such day had been appointed.

5 *Supporting Economic Growth Through Local Enterprise Partnerships and Enterprise Zones* (Department for Communities and Local Government; Department for Business, Innovation & Skills and Homes and Communities Agency, 7 November 2012). There are currently 24 enterprise zones. Two new zones (Blackpool and Plymouth) are planned in 2015: see Department for Communities and Local Government, Press Release (20 March 2015).

(5) ECONOMIC PROSPERITY BOARDS AND COMBINED AUTHORITIES IN ENGLAND

(i) Economic Prosperity Boards

1086. Establishment, constitution and functions of economic prosperity boards. The Local Democracy, Economic Development and Construction Act 2009 makes provision, inter alia, about local and regional development. Part 6[1] provides for the establishment of economic prosperity boards and combined authorities[2].

The Secretary of State[3] may by order[4] establish as a body corporate an economic prosperity board (an 'EPB') for an area that meets the following five conditions[5]:

(1) Condition A is that the area consists of the whole of two or more local government areas[6] in England[7];

(2) Condition B is that no part of the area is separated from the rest of it by one or more local government areas that are not within the area[8];

(3) Condition C is that there is no local government area that is surrounded by local government areas that are within the area but that is not itself within the area[9];

(4) Condition D is that no part of the area forms part of the area of another EPB, or the area of a combined authority[10];

(5) Condition E is that each local government area that forms part of the area was included in a scheme[11] for the establishment of an EPB[12].

An order establishing an EPB must specify the name by which the EPB is to be known[13].

The Secretary of State may by order make provision in relation to an EPB about its membership[14], its members' voting powers[15] and its executive arrangements[16]. Such an order may not provide for the budget of an EPB to be agreed otherwise than by the EPB[17].

The Secretary of State may by order provide for a function of a local authority[18] that is exercisable in relation to an area within an EPB's area to be exercisable by the EPB in relation to the EPB's area[19]. The Secretary of State may make such an order only if the Secretary of State considers that the function can appropriately be exercised by the EPB[20]. Such an order may make provision for the function to be exercisable by the EPB either generally or subject to such conditions or limitations as may be specified in the order[21]. An order may make provision for the function to be exercisable by the EPB instead of by the local authority, or for the function to be exercisable by the EPB concurrently with the local authority[22]. An EPB must perform the functions that are exercisable by the EPB by virtue of these provisions with a view to promoting the economic development and regeneration of its area[23].

1 Ie the Local Democracy, Economic Development and Construction Act 2009 Pt 6 (ss 88–120), which extends to England and Wales only (s 147(1)) and came into force on 17 December 2009 (ss 88–113, 118–120) and 12 January 2010 (ss 114–117) (see the Local Democracy, Economic Development and Construction Act 2009 (Commencement No 2) Order 2009, SI 2009/3318, arts 1–3).

2 As to combined authorities see PARAS 1092–1096.

3 As to the Secretary of State see PARA 902. It appears that the Secretary of State here concerned is the Secretary of State for Communities and Local Government.

4 Orders under the Local Democracy, Economic Development and Construction Act 2009 Pt 6 must be made by statutory instrument: s 117(1). A statutory instrument containing an order under s 113C(1) that is made only for the purpose mentioned in s 113C(5)(b), or an order under s 113C(2) that is made only for that purpose or for imposing conditions on the doing of things for a commercial purpose, or an order under s 116 that amends or revokes provision contained in an instrument subject to annulment by resolution of either House of Parliament, may not be made unless a draft of the instrument containing the order (whether alone or with other provisions) has been laid before, and approved by a resolution of, each House of Parliament: s 117(2), (2A) (s 117(2) substituted and s 117(2A) added by the Localism Act 2011 s 13(2)). A statutory instrument that contains an order under the Local Democracy, Economic Development and Construction Act 2009 Pt 6, and is not subject to any requirement that a draft of the instrument be laid before, and approved by a resolution of, each House of Parliament, is subject to annulment by resolution of either House of Parliament: s 117(3) (substituted by the Localism Act 2011 s 13(2)). If a draft of an order under the Local Democracy, Economic Development and Construction Act 2009 Pt 6 would otherwise be treated for the purposes of the standing orders of either House of Parliament as a hybrid instrument, it is to proceed in that House as if it were not a hybrid instrument: s 117(4). See STATUTES AND LEGISLATIVE PROCESS vol 96 (2012) PARA 1032. As to orders under Pt 6 see further PARAS 1097–1098.

5 Local Democracy, Economic Development and Construction Act 2009 ss 88(1), 120. At the date at which this volume states the law no such order had been made. As to the requirements for the making of orders see PARA 1090.

6 For these purposes, 'local government area' means the area of a county council or a district council: Local Democracy, Economic Development and Construction Act 2009 ss 88(7), 120. As to county councils and district councils in England see LOCAL GOVERNMENT vol 69 (2009) PARA 24 et seq.

7 Local Democracy, Economic Development and Construction Act 2009 s 88(2).

8 Local Democracy, Economic Development and Construction Act 2009 s 88(3).

9 Local Democracy, Economic Development and Construction Act 2009 s 88(4).

10 Local Democracy, Economic Development and Construction Act 2009 s 88(5). As to the meaning of 'combined authority' see PARA 1092 note 2.

11 Ie a scheme prepared and published under the Local Democracy, Economic Development and Construction Act 2009 s 98: see PARA 1090.

12 Local Democracy, Economic Development and Construction Act 2009 s 88(6).

13 Local Democracy, Economic Development and Construction Act 2009 s 88(8). An EPB may change its name by a resolution considered at a meeting of the EPB that is specially convened for the purpose: s 94(1), (2). Particulars of the resolution must have been included in the notice of the meeting: s 94(3). The resolution must be passed at the meeting by not less than two-thirds of the members of the EPB who vote on it: s 94(4). An EPB that changes its name under these provisions must send notice of the change to the Secretary of State, and must publish the notice in such manner as the Secretary of State may direct: s 94(5). A change of name under these provisions does not affect the rights or obligations of the EPB or any other person, or render defective any legal proceedings: s 94(6). Any legal proceedings may be commenced or continued as if there had been no change of name: s 94(7).

14 Local Democracy, Economic Development and Construction Act 2009 s 89(1)(a). The provision that may be made about membership includes provision about the number and appointment of members of the EPB and the remuneration of, and pensions or allowances payable to or in respect of, any member of the EPB: s 89(2). An order under s 89 that includes provision about the number and appointment of members of an EPB must provide for a majority of the members of the EPB to be appointed by the EPB's constituent councils; and for those members to be appointed from among the elected members of the constituent councils; and for each constituent council that is a representative council to appoint at least one of its elected members as a member of the EPB: s 90(1). For these purposes a county council is a constituent council of an EPB if the area of the county council, or part of that area, is within the EPB's area; and a district council is a constituent council of an EPB if the area of the district council is within the EPB's area: s 90(2). For the purposes of s 90 if the EPB's area coincides with or includes the whole of the area of a county council, the representative council is the county council: s 90(3)(a). If the EPB's area includes part of the area of a county council, the representative council is the county council or each district council for an area within that part, as determined by or in accordance with the order: s 90(3)(b). If the EPB's area includes the area of a unitary district council, the representative council is the district council: s 90(3)(c). For these purposes, 'unitary district council' means a district council whose area is not part of the area of a county council: ss 90(4), 120. As to county councils and district councils in England see LOCAL GOVERNMENT vol 69 (2009) PARA 24 et seq.

    If an order under s 89 provides for members of an EPB to be appointed otherwise than from among the elected members of its constituent councils, the order must provide for those members to be non-voting members: s 90(5). The voting members of an EPB may resolve that provision made in accordance with s 90(5) is not to apply in the case of the EPB: s 90(6).

15 Local Democracy, Economic Development and Construction Act 2009 s 89(1)(b). The provision that may be made about voting powers includes provision for different weight to be given to the vote of different descriptions of member: s 89(3).

16 Local Democracy, Economic Development and Construction Act 2009 s 89(1)(c). Section 89(4) provides that such executive arrangements may include provision about:
    (1) the appointment of an executive;
    (2) the functions of the EPB that are the responsibility of an executive;
    (3) the functions of the EPB that are the responsibility of an executive and that may be discharged by a committee of the EPB or by a body other than the EPB;
    (4) arrangements relating to the review and scrutiny of the discharge of functions;
    (5) access to information on the proceedings of an executive of the EPB;
    (6) the disapplication of the Local Government and Housing Act 1989 s 15 (duty to allocate seats to political groups: see LOCAL GOVERNMENT vol 69 (2009) PARA 375) in relation to an executive of the EPB or a committee of such an executive;
    (7) the keeping of a record of any arrangements relating to the EPB and falling within heads (1)–(6).
    At the date at which this volume states the law no such order had been made.

17 Local Democracy, Economic Development and Construction Act 2009 s 89(5).

18 For these purposes, 'local authority' means a county council or a district council: Local Democracy, Economic Development and Construction Act 2009 s 91(6).

19 Local Democracy, Economic Development and Construction Act 2009 s 91(1). At the date at which this volume states the law no such order had been made.

20 Local Democracy, Economic Development and Construction Act 2009 s 91(2).

21 Local Democracy, Economic Development and Construction Act 2009 s 91(3).
22 Local Democracy, Economic Development and Construction Act 2009 s 91(4).
23 Local Democracy, Economic Development and Construction Act 2009 s 91(5).

1087. General powers of economic prosperity boards. An economic prosperity board ('EPB')[1] may do:

(1) anything it considers appropriate for the purposes of the carrying-out of any of its functions (its 'functional purposes')[2];

(2) anything it considers appropriate for purposes incidental to its functional purposes[3];

(3) anything it considers appropriate for purposes indirectly incidental to its functional purposes through any number of removes[4];

(4) anything it considers to be connected with:
  (a) any of its functions; or
  (b) anything it may do under head (1), (2) or (3)[5]; and

(5) for a commercial purpose anything which it may do under any of heads (1) to (4) otherwise than for a commercial purpose[6].

However, there are limitations on the powers of an EPB[7]. An EPB is not, for example, authorised to borrow money[8], nor is it authorised under these provisions to charge a person for anything done by it otherwise than for a commercial purpose[9].

Where power is conferred[10] on an EPB to do something, the EPB has power to do it anywhere in the United Kingdom or elsewhere[11]. Any of the above powers conferred[12] on an EPB is in addition to, and is not limited by, its other powers[13].

The Secretary of State[14] may by order make provision preventing EPBs from doing specified things[15]. He may also by order provide for their power to be subject to conditions, whether generally or in relation to doing anything specified, or of a description specified, in the order[16]. Before making such an order the Secretary of State must consult such representatives of EPBs, such representatives of local government, and such other persons (if any), as the Secretary of State considers appropriate[17].

1 As to the establishment of economic prosperity boards see PARA 1086.
2 Local Democracy, Economic Development and Construction Act 2009 s 113A(1)(a) (ss 113A–113C added by the Localism Act 2011 s 13(1)). As to the functions of economic prosperity boards see PARA 1086.
3 Local Democracy, Economic Development and Construction Act 2009 s 113A(1)(b) (as added: see note 2).
4 Local Democracy, Economic Development and Construction Act 2009 s 113A(1)(c) (as added: see note 2).
5 Local Democracy, Economic Development and Construction Act 2009 s 113A(1)(d) (as added: see note 2).
6 Local Democracy, Economic Development and Construction Act 2009 s 113A(1)(e) (as added: see note 2). However, this does not authorise an EPB to do things for a commercial purpose in relation to a person if a statutory provision requires it to do those things in relation to the person: s 113B(5) (s 113B as added: see note 2). Where under s 113A(1)(e) an EPB does things for a commercial purpose, it must do them through a company (within the meaning given by the Companies Act 2006 s 1(1)), a registered society (within the meaning of the Co-operative and Community Benefit Societies Act 2014), or a society registered or deemed to be registered under the Industrial and Provident Societies Act (Northern Ireland) 1969: see the Local Democracy, Economic Development and Construction Act 2009 s 113B(6) (s 113B (as so added); s 113B(6) amended by the Co-operative and Community Benefit Societies Act 2014 s 151(1), Sch 4 Pt 2 paras 148, 154). As to such companies and societies see COMPANIES vol 14 (2009) PARA 24; and FINANCIAL SERVICES AND INSTITUTIONS vol 50 (2008) PARA 2395.
7 The Local Democracy, Economic Development and Construction Act 2009 s 113A(1) does not enable an EPB to do:

(1)   anything which it is unable to do by virtue of a pre-commencement limitation (s 113B(1)(a) (as so added)); or

(2)   anything which it is unable to do by virtue of a post-commencement limitation which is expressed to apply to its power under s 113A(1), or to all of its powers, or to all of its powers but with exceptions that do not include its power under s 113A(1) (see s 113B(1)(b) (as so added)).

'Pre-commencement limitation' means a prohibition, restriction or other limitation imposed by a statutory provision (ie a provision of an Act or of an instrument made under an Act) that is contained in an Act passed no later than the end of the Session in which the Localism Act 2011 is passed, or is contained in an instrument made under an Act and comes into force before the commencement of s 13(1) (ie 18 February 2012: see the Localism Act 2011 (Commencement No 3) Order 2012, SI 2012/411, art 2): Local Democracy, Economic Development and Construction Act 2009 s 113B(7) (as so added). 'Post-commencement limitation' means a prohibition, restriction or other limitation imposed by a statutory provision that is contained in an Act passed after the end of the Session in which the Localism Act 2011 is passed, or is contained in an instrument made under an Act and comes into force on or after the commencement of s 13(1): Local Democracy, Economic Development and Construction Act 2009 s 113B(7) (as so added). As to parliamentary sessions see PARLIAMENT vol 78 (2010) PARA 1009 et seq.

If exercise of a pre-commencement power of an EPB is subject to restrictions, those restrictions apply also to exercise of the power conferred on it by s 113A(1) so far as that power is overlapped by the pre-commencement power: s 113B(2) (as so added). 'Pre-commencement power' means power conferred by a statutory provision that is contained in an Act passed no later than the end of the Session in which the Localism Act 2011 is passed, or is contained in an instrument made under an Act and comes into force before the commencement of s 13(1): Local Democracy, Economic Development and Construction Act 2009 s 113B(7) (as so added).

8   Local Democracy, Economic Development and Construction Act 2009 s 113B(3) (as added: see note 2).

9   Local Democracy, Economic Development and Construction Act 2009 s 113B(4) (as added: see note 2). But see the Local Government Act 2003 s 93 (power of EPBs, combined authorities and other best value authorities to charge for discretionary services): see LOCAL GOVERNMENT vol 69 (2009) PARA 506.

10   Ie power conferred under the Local Democracy, Economic Development and Construction Act 2009 s 113A(1): see the text and notes 1–6.

11   Local Democracy, Economic Development and Construction Act 2009 s 113A(2) (as added: see note 2).

12   Ie conferred under the Local Democracy, Economic Development and Construction Act 2009 s 113A(1): see the text and notes 1–6.

13   Local Democracy, Economic Development and Construction Act 2009 s 113A(3) (as added: see note 2).

14   As to the Secretary of State see PARA 902. It appears that the Secretary of State here concerned is the Secretary of State for Communities and Local Government.

15   See the Local Democracy, Economic Development and Construction Act 2009 s 113C(1) (s 113C as added: see note 2). The power under s 113C(1), (2) may be exercised in relation to all EPBs, particular EPBs or to particular descriptions of EPBs: s 113C(3) (as so added). Power to make an order under s 113C includes power to make different provision for different cases, circumstances or areas, and power to make incidental, supplementary, consequential, transitional or transitory provision or savings: s 113C(6) (as so added). At the date at which this volume states the law no such order had been made.

16   Local Democracy, Economic Development and Construction Act 2009 s 113C(2) (as added: see note 2). See note 15.

17   Local Democracy, Economic Development and Construction Act 2009 s 113C(4) (s 113C as added: see note 2). Section 113C(4) does not apply to an order under s 113C(1) or s 113C(2) which is made only for the purpose of amending an earlier such order:

(1)   so as to extend the earlier order, or any provision of the earlier order, to a particular EPB or to EPBs of a particular description (s 113C(5)(a) (as so added)); or

(2)   so that the earlier order, or any provision of the earlier order, ceases to apply to a particular EPB or to EPBs of a particular description (s 113C(5)(b) (as so added)).

1088. Funding and accounts of economic prosperity boards. The Secretary of State[1] may by order make provision for the costs of an economic prosperity board ('EPB')[2] to be met by its constituent councils[3], and provision about the basis on which the amount payable by each constituent council is to be determined[4].

Each EPB must keep a fund to be known as the general fund[5] into which all receipts must be carried[6]. All liabilities falling to be discharged by the EPB must be discharged out of that fund[7]. Accounts must be kept both of receipts carried to the general fund and payments made out of the general fund[8].

1 As to the Secretary of State see PARA 902. It appears that the Secretary of State here concerned is the Secretary of State for Communities and Local Government.
2 As to the establishment and functions of EPBs see PARA 1086.
3 For these purposes:
　　(1)　a county council is a constituent council of an EPB if the area of the county council, or part of that area, is within the EPB's area (Local Democracy, Economic Development and Construction Act 2009 s 92(2)(a));
　　(2)　a district council is a constituent council of an EPB if the area of the district council is within the EPB's area (s 92(2)(b)).
　　As to county councils and district councils in England see LOCAL GOVERNMENT vol 69 (2009) PARA 24 et seq.
4 Local Democracy, Economic Development and Construction Act 2009 s 92(1). As to the area of an EPB see PARA 1086. As to the making of orders under Pt 6 (ss 88–120) see PARA 1086 note 4. At the date at which this volume states the law no such order had been made.
5 Local Democracy, Economic Development and Construction Act 2009 s 93(1).
6 Local Democracy, Economic Development and Construction Act 2009 s 93(2).
7 Local Democracy, Economic Development and Construction Act 2009 s 93(3).
8 Local Democracy, Economic Development and Construction Act 2009 s 93(4).

1089. Changes to and dissolution of an economic prosperity board's area.
The Secretary of State[1] may by order change the boundaries of the area of an economic prosperity board ('EPB')[2] by adding a local government area[3] to an existing area of an EPB, or by removing a local government area from an existing area of an EPB[4]. Such an order may be made only if the area to be created by the order meets conditions A to D for the establishment of an EPB[5], and each council to which these provisions apply[6] consents to the making of the order[7].

The Secretary of State may by order dissolve an EPB's area[8]. He may also by order abolish the EPB for the area[9]. Either such order may be made only if a majority of the councils to which these provisions apply[10] consent to the making of the order[11].

1 As to the Secretary of State see PARA 902. It appears that the Secretary of State here concerned is the Secretary of State for Communities and Local Government.
2 As to the establishment and functions of an EPB see PARA 1086. As to the area of an EPB see PARA 1086.
3 As to the meaning of 'local government area' see PARA 1086 note 6.
4 Local Democracy, Economic Development and Construction Act 2009 s 95(1). As to the making of orders under Pt 6 (ss 88–120) see PARA 1086 note 4. At the date at which this volume states the law no such order had been made.
5 Ie conditions A–D in the Local Democracy, Economic Development and Construction Act 2009 s 88: see PARA 1086.
6 Ie a county council whose area, or part of whose area, is to be added to or removed from the existing area of the EPB, or a district council whose area is to be added to or removed from the existing area of the EPB: Local Democracy, Economic Development and Construction Act 2009 s 95(3). As to county councils and district councils in England see LOCAL GOVERNMENT vol 69 (2009) PARA 24 et seq.
7 Local Democracy, Economic Development and Construction Act 2009 s 95(2).
8 Local Democracy, Economic Development and Construction Act 2009 s 96(1)(a).
9 Local Democracy, Economic Development and Construction Act 2009 s 96(1)(b).

10 Ie a county council whose area, or part of whose area, is within the EPB's area, or a unitary
    district council whose area is within the EPB's area: Local Democracy, Economic Development
    and Construction Act 2009 s 96(3). As to the meaning of 'unitary district council' see PARA 1086
    note 14.
11 Local Democracy, Economic Development and Construction Act 2009 s 96(2).

**1090. Establishment of economic prosperity board following review of the
arrangements to promote economic development and regeneration.** Any two or
more of the local authorities to which these provisions apply[1] may undertake a
review of the effectiveness and efficiency of arrangements to promote economic
development and regeneration within the area covered by the review (the 'review
area')[2]. Where the review is being undertaken by a county council, the review
area must include the areas of one or more district councils that are within the
area of the county council or, if there are no such areas, the area of the county
council[3]. Where the review is being undertaken by a district council, the review
area must include the area of the district council[4]. The review area may also
include the area of any county council or district council in England not
undertaking the review[5].

Where two or more of the authorities that have undertaken a review conclude
that the establishment of an economic prosperity board ('EPB')[6] for an area
would be likely to improve:

(1)   the exercise of statutory functions relating to economic development
       and regeneration in the area; and
(2)   economic conditions in the area,

the authorities may prepare and publish a scheme for the establishment of an
EPB for the area (the 'scheme area')[7]. The scheme area must consist of or include
the whole or any part of the review area and it may include one or more other
local government areas[8]. It must also meet conditions A to C[9] for the
establishment of an EPB[10]. The scheme area may not include a local government
area unless each appropriate authority for that area[11] either participates in the
preparation of the scheme or consents to its inclusion in the scheme area[12].

The Secretary of State[13] may make an order establishing an EPB for an area
only if, having regard to a scheme prepared and published as above, he considers
that to do so is likely to improve both the exercise of statutory functions relating
to economic development and regeneration in the area, and the economic
conditions in the area[14]. Before making the order, the Secretary of State must
consult each appropriate authority[15] and such other persons (if any) as he
considers appropriate[16]. In making the order, the Secretary of State must have
regard to the need to reflect the identities and interests of local communities and
to secure effective and convenient local government[17].

1 The Local Democracy, Economic Development and Construction Act 2009 s 97 applies to a
   county council in England, or a district council in England: s 97(2). As to county councils and
   district councils in England see LOCAL GOVERNMENT vol 69 (2009) PARA 24 et seq.
2 Local Democracy, Economic Development and Construction Act 2009 s 97(1).
3 Local Democracy, Economic Development and Construction Act 2009 s 97(3).
4 Local Democracy, Economic Development and Construction Act 2009 s 97(4).
5 Local Democracy, Economic Development and Construction Act 2009 s 97(5).
6 As to the establishment and functions of EPBs see PARA 1086.
7 Local Democracy, Economic Development and Construction Act 2009 s 98(1), (2).
8 As to the meaning of 'local government area' see PARA 1086 note 6.
9 Ie conditions A–C in the Local Democracy, Economic Development and Construction Act 2009
   s 88: see PARA 1086.
10 Local Democracy, Economic Development and Construction Act 2009 s 98(3).

11 For this purpose, a county council is an appropriate authority for a local government area that is or forms part of the area of that county council, and a district council is an appropriate authority for a local government area that is the area of that district council: Local Democracy, Economic Development and Construction Act 2009 s 98(5).

12 Local Democracy, Economic Development and Construction Act 2009 s 98(4).

13 As to the Secretary of State see PARA 902. It appears that the Secretary of State here concerned is the Secretary of State for Communities and Local Government. As to the making of an order establishing an EPB see PARA 1086.

14 Local Democracy, Economic Development and Construction Act 2009 s 99(1). As to the making of orders under Pt 6 (ss 88–120) see PARA 1086 note 4.

15 For the purposes of the Local Democracy, Economic Development and Construction Act 2009 s 99, a county council is an appropriate authority if the area of the county council, or part of that area, is within the area for which the EPB is to be established, and a district council is an appropriate authority if the area of the district council is within the area for which the EPB is to be established: s 99(3).

16 Local Democracy, Economic Development and Construction Act 2009 s 99(2).

17 Local Democracy, Economic Development and Construction Act 2009 s 99(4).

1091. Review of existing economic prosperity boards. Any one or more of the local authorities to which these provisions apply[1] may undertake, in relation to an existing economic prosperity board ('EPB'), a review of one or more EPB matters[2]. The review must relate to one or more areas of an EPB or proposed areas of an EPB[3].

Where one or more of the authorities that have undertaken a review conclude that the exercise of the power to make an order[4] would be likely to improve:

(1) the exercise of statutory functions relating to economic development and regeneration in an area of an EPB[5] or a proposed area of an EPB; or

(2) economic conditions in such an area,

the authorities may prepare and publish a scheme relating to the power or powers in question[6].

The Secretary of State[7] may make an order[8] in relation to an existing EPB only if, having regard to a scheme prepared and published as above, the Secretary of State considers that the making of the order is likely to improve either the exercise of statutory functions relating to economic development and regeneration in the area or areas to which the order relates, or economic conditions in that area or those areas[9]. Before making the order, the Secretary of State must consult such of the relevant authorities[10] and such other persons (if any) as the Secretary of State considers appropriate[11]. In making the order, the Secretary of State must have regard to the need to reflect the identities and interests of local communities, and the need to secure effective and convenient local government[12].

1 The Local Democracy, Economic Development and Construction Act 2009 s 100 applies to:
  (1) an economic prosperity board ('EPB') (s 100(2)(a));
  (2) a county council whose area, or part of whose area, is within an area of an EPB or could be within a proposed area of an EPB (s 100(2)(b));
  (3) a district council whose area is within an area of an EPB or could be within a proposed area of an EPB (s 100(2)(c)).
  As to the establishment, area and functions of EPBs see PARA 1086. In ss 100, 101, 'proposed area of an EPB' means an area of an EPB that may be created by an order under s 95 (changes to boundaries of an EPB's area: see PARA 1089): s 100(5). As to county councils and district councils in England see LOCAL GOVERNMENT vol 69 (2009) PARA 24 et seq.
2 Local Democracy, Economic Development and Construction Act 2009 s 100(1). For the purposes of s 100 an 'EPB matter' is:
  (1) a matter in relation to which an order may be made under any of ss 89, 91, 92, 95 and 96 (see PARAS 1086–1089) (s 100(3)(a));
  (2) a matter concerning the EPB that the EPB has power to determine (s 100(3)(b)).
3 Local Democracy, Economic Development and Construction Act 2009 s 100(4).

4   Ie under any one or more of the Local Democracy, Economic Development and Construction Act 2009 ss 89, 91, 92, 95 and 96. As to the making of orders under Pt 6 (ss 88–120) see PARA 1086 note 4.

5   The reference to an area of an EPB includes an area that would cease to be an area of an EPB if an order were made in relation to that area under the Local Democracy, Economic Development and Construction Act 2009 s 96 (dissolution of an EPB's area: see PARA 1089): s 101(3).

6   Local Democracy, Economic Development and Construction Act 2009 s 101(1), (2).

7   As to the Secretary of State see PARA 902. It appears that the Secretary of State here concerned is the Secretary of State for Communities and Local Government.

8   Ie under any of the Local Democracy, Economic Development and Construction Act 2009 ss 89, 91, 92, 95, 96 (see PARAS 1086–1089).

9   Local Democracy, Economic Development and Construction Act 2009 s 102(1).

10   Ie the authorities mentioned in the Local Democracy, Economic Development and Construction Act 2009 s 100(2): see note 1.

11   Local Democracy, Economic Development and Construction Act 2009 s 102(2).

12   Local Democracy, Economic Development and Construction Act 2009 s 102(3).

(ii) Combined Authorities

1092. Establishment, constitution and functions of combined authorities. The Secretary of State may by order[1] establish as a body corporate a combined authority for an area that meets the following five conditions[2].

(1)   condition A is that the area consists of the whole of two or more local government areas[3] in England[4];

(2)   condition B is that no part of the area is separated from the rest of it by one or more local government areas that are not within the area[5];

(3)   condition C is that there is no local government area that is surrounded by local government areas that are within the area but that is not itself within the area[6];

(4)   condition D is that no part of the area forms part of:
     (a)   the area of another combined authority;
     (b)   the area of an economic prosperity board ('EPB')[7]; or
     (c)   an integrated transport area[8];

(5)   condition E is that each local government area that forms part of the area was included in a scheme[9] for the establishment of a combined authority[10].

An order must specify the name by which the combined authority is to be known[11].

The Secretary of State may by order make in relation to a combined authority any provision that may be made under the Local Transport Act 2008 in relation to an Integrated Transport Authority (an 'ITA') as to constitutional arrangements[12], delegation of functions of the Secretary of State[13], delegation of local authority functions[14] and conferral of a power to give a direction[15] about the exercise of an eligible power[16]. The Secretary of State may by order transfer functions of an ITA to a combined authority[17]. Such an order may only be made in relation to functions exercisable by the ITA in relation to an area that becomes, or becomes part of, the combined authority's area by virtue of an order under Part 6 of the Local Democracy, Economic Development and Construction Act 2009[18]. The Secretary of State may by order provide for any function that is conferred or imposed on a passenger transport executive[19] by any enactment (whenever passed or made) to be exercisable by a combined authority or the executive body of a combined authority in relation to the combined authority's area[20].

The Secretary of State may by order make in relation to a combined authority any provision that may be made in relation to an EPB[21] as to the exercise of local authority functions[22]. The duty to perform functions with a view to promoting economic development and regeneration[23] applies to the exercise of functions by a combined authority as it applies to the exercise of functions by an EPB[24]. The Secretary of State may by order make in relation to a combined authority any provision that may be made as to funding[25] in relation to an EPB[26], but such an order may make such provision only in relation to the costs of a combined authority that are reasonably attributable to the exercise of its functions relating to economic development and regeneration[27].

1   As to the Secretary of State see PARA 902. It appears that the Secretary of State here concerned is the Secretary of State for Communities and Local Government. As to the making of orders under the Local Democracy, Economic Development and Construction Act 2009 Pt 6 (ss 88–120) see PARA 1086 note 4.
    In exercise of these powers, the following orders have been made: see the Greater Manchester Combined Authority Order 2011, SI 2011/908; West Yorkshire Combined Authority Order 2014, SI 2014/864.
2   Local Democracy, Economic Development and Construction Act 2009 s 103(1). 'Combined authority' means an authority established under s 103(1): s 120.
3   As to the meaning of 'local government area' see PARA 1086 note 6.
4   Local Democracy, Economic Development and Construction Act 2009 s 103(2).
5   Local Democracy, Economic Development and Construction Act 2009 s 103(3).
6   Local Democracy, Economic Development and Construction Act 2009 s 103(4).
7   As to the establishment, functions and areas of EPBs see PARA 1086.
8   Local Democracy, Economic Development and Construction Act 2009 s 103(5). As to integrated transport areas and authorities see LOCAL GOVERNMENT vol 69 (2009) PARA 49; ROAD TRAFFIC vol 89 (2011) PARA 47.
9   Ie a scheme prepared and published under the Local Democracy, Economic Development and Construction Act 2009 s 109: see PARA 1095.
10 Local Democracy, Economic Development and Construction Act 2009 s 103(6).
11 Local Democracy, Economic Development and Construction Act 2009 s 103(7). The Local Transport Act 2008 s 97 (change of name of an Integrated Transport Authority (an 'ITA'): see ROAD TRAFFIC vol 89 (2011) PARA 47) applies to a combined authority as it applies to an ITA: Local Democracy, Economic Development and Construction Act 2009 s 104(4).
12 Ie under the Local Transport Act 2008 s 84: see ROAD TRAFFIC vol 89 (2011) PARA 48. Section 85 (provision about membership of an ITA) applies to an order under the Local Democracy, Economic Development and Construction Act 2009 s 104(1) and to the combined authority to which that order applies, as it applies to an order under the Local Transport Act 2008 s 84 and the ITA to which that order applies: Local Democracy, Economic Development and Construction Act 2009 s 104(2).
13 Ie under the Local Transport Act 2008 s 86: see ROAD TRAFFIC vol 89 (2011) PARA 48.
14 Ie under the Local Transport Act 2008 s 87: see ROAD TRAFFIC vol 89 (2011) PARA 48.
15 Ie under the Local Transport Act 2008 s 88: see ROAD TRAFFIC vol 89 (2011) PARA 48. The Local Transport Act 2008 s 88(10) (provisions about directions), s 89(2), (3) (power to remedy contravention of direction) apply in relation to a combined authority on which functions of a kind described in s 88 are conferred as they apply in relation to an ITA on which such functions are conferred: see the Local Democracy, Economic Development and Construction Act 2009 s 104(3).
16 Local Democracy, Economic Development and Construction Act 2009 ss 104(1), 120. See note 1.
17 Local Democracy, Economic Development and Construction Act 2009 s 104(5).
18 Local Democracy, Economic Development and Construction Act 2009 s 104(6).
19 As to passenger transport executives see ROAD TRAFFIC vol 89 (2011) PARA 47.
20 Local Democracy, Economic Development and Construction Act 2009 s 104(7). An order under s 104(7) may make provision for any function that is conferred or imposed on an ITA by any enactment (whenever passed or made) and relates to the functions of a passenger transport executive, to be exercisable by a combined authority in relation to the combined authority's area: s 104(8).
21 Ie under the Local Democracy, Economic Development and Construction Act 2009 s 91: see PARA 1086.

22 Local Democracy, Economic Development and Construction Act 2009 s 105(1). See note 1.
23 Ie under the Local Democracy, Economic Development and Construction Act 2009 s 91(5): see PARA 1086.
24 Local Democracy, Economic Development and Construction Act 2009 s 105(2).
25 Ie under the Local Democracy, Economic Development and Construction Act 2009 s 92: see PARA 1088.
26 Local Democracy, Economic Development and Construction Act 2009 s 105(3).
27 Local Democracy, Economic Development and Construction Act 2009 s 105(4).

1093. General powers of combined authorities. A combined authority[1] may do:

(1) anything it considers appropriate for the purposes of the carrying-out of any of its functions (its 'functional purposes')[2];

(2) anything it considers appropriate for purposes incidental to its functional purposes[3];

(3) anything it considers appropriate for purposes indirectly incidental to its functional purposes through any number of removes[4];

(4) anything it considers to be connected with:
    (a) any of its functions; or
    (b) anything it may do under head (1), (2) or (3)[5]; and

(5) for a commercial purpose anything which it may do under any of heads (1) to (4) otherwise than for a commercial purpose[6].

However, there are limitations on the powers of a combined authority[7]. A combined authority is not, for example, authorised to borrow money[8], nor is it authorised under these provisions to charge a person for anything done by it otherwise than for a commercial purpose[9].

Where power is conferred[10] on a combined authority to do something, it has power to do it anywhere in the United Kingdom or elsewhere[11]. Any of the above powers conferred[12] on a combined authority is in addition to, and is not limited by, its other powers[13].

The Secretary of State[14] may by order make provision preventing combined authorities from doing specified things[15]. He may also by order provide for their power to be subject to conditions, whether generally or in relation to doing anything specified, or of a description specified, in the order[16]. Before making such an order the Secretary of State must consult such representatives of combined authorities, such representatives of local government, and such other persons (if any), as the Secretary of State considers appropriate[17].

1 As to the establishment of combined authorities see PARA 1092.
2 Local Democracy, Economic Development and Construction Act 2009 s 113A(1)(a) (ss 113A–113C added by the Localism Act 2011 s 13(1)). As to the functions of combined authorities see PARA 1092.
3 Local Democracy, Economic Development and Construction Act 2009 s 113A(1)(b) (as added: see note 2).
4 Local Democracy, Economic Development and Construction Act 2009 s 113A(1)(c) (as added: see note 2).
5 Local Democracy, Economic Development and Construction Act 2009 s 113A(1)(d) (as added: see note 2).
6 Local Democracy, Economic Development and Construction Act 2009 s 113A(1)(e) (as added: see note 2). However, this does not authorise a combined authority to do things for a commercial purpose in relation to a person if a statutory provision requires it to do those things in relation to the person: s 113B(5) (s 113B as added: see note 2). Where under s 113A(1)(e) a combined authority does things for a commercial purpose, it must do them through a company (within the meaning given by the Companies Act 2006 s 1(1)), a registered society (within the meaning of the Co-operative and Community Benefit Societies Act 2014), or a society registered or deemed to be registered under the Industrial and Provident Societies Act (Northern Ireland) 1969: Local Democracy, Economic Development and Construction Act 2009 s 113B(6) (s 113B

(as so added); s 113B(6) amended by the Co-operative and Community Benefit Societies Act 2014 s 151(1), Sch 4 Pt 2 paras 148, 154). As to such companies and societies see COMPANIES vol 14 (2009) PARA 24; and FINANCIAL SERVICES AND INSTITUTIONS vol 50 (2008) PARA 2395.

7 The Local Democracy, Economic Development and Construction Act 2009 s 113A(1) does not enable a combined authority to do:

(1) anything which it is unable to do by virtue of a pre-commencement limitation (s 113B(1)(a) (as added: see note 2)); or

(2) anything which it is unable to do by virtue of a post-commencement limitation which is expressed to apply to its power under s 113A(1), or to all of its powers, or to all of its powers but with exceptions that do not include its power under s 113A(1) (see s 113B(1)(b) (as so added)).

As to the meanings of 'pre-commencement limitation' and 'post-commencement limitation' see PARA 1087 note 7.

If exercise of a pre-commencement power of a combined authority is subject to restrictions, those restrictions apply also to exercise of the power conferred on it by s 113A(1) so far as that power is overlapped by the pre-commencement power: s 113B(2) (as so added). As to the meaning of 'pre-commencement power' see PARA 1087 note 7.

8 Local Democracy, Economic Development and Construction Act 2009 s 113B(3) (as added: see note 2).

9 Local Democracy, Economic Development and Construction Act 2009 s 113B(4) (as added: see note 2). But see the Local Government Act 2003 s 93 (power of EPBs, combined authorities and other best value authorities to charge for discretionary services): see LOCAL GOVERNMENT vol 69 (2009) PARA 506.

10 Ie power conferred under the Local Democracy, Economic Development and Construction Act 2009 s 113A(1): see the text and notes 1–6.

11 Local Democracy, Economic Development and Construction Act 2009 s 113A(2) (as added: see note 2).

12 Ie conferred under the Local Democracy, Economic Development and Construction Act 2009 s 113A(1): see the text and notes 1–6.

13 Local Democracy, Economic Development and Construction Act 2009 s 113A(3) (as added: see note 2).

14 As to the Secretary of State see PARA 902.

15 See the Local Democracy, Economic Development and Construction Act 2009 s 113C(1) (s 113C as added: see note 2). The power under s 113C(1), (2) may be exercised in relation to all combined authorities, particular combined authorities or to particular descriptions of combined authorities: s 113C(3) (as so added). Power to make an order under s 113C includes power to make different provision for different cases, circumstances or areas, and power to make incidental, supplementary, consequential, transitional or transitory provision or savings: s 113C(6) (as so added). At the date at which this volume states the law no such order had been made.

16 Local Democracy, Economic Development and Construction Act 2009 s 113C(2) (as added: see note 2). See note 15. At the date at which this volume states the law no such order had been made.

17 Local Democracy, Economic Development and Construction Act 2009 s 113C(4) (s 113C as added: see note 2). Section 113C(4) does not apply to an order under s 113C(1) or s 113C(2) which is made only for the purpose of amending an earlier such order:

(1) so as to extend the earlier order, or any provision of the earlier order, to a particular combined authority or to combined authorities of a particular description (s 113C(5)(a) (as so added)); or

(2) so that the earlier order, or any provision of the earlier order, ceases to apply to a particular combined authority or to combined authorities of a particular description (s 113C(5)(b) (as so added)).

1094. Changes to boundaries and dissolution of area of combined authority.
The Secretary of State[1] may by order change the boundaries of the area of a combined authority[2] either by adding a local government area[3] to an existing area of a combined authority, or by removing a local government area from an existing area of a combined authority[4]. Such an order may be made only if the

area to be created by the order meets conditions A to D for the establishment of a combined authority[5], and each council to which these provisions apply[6] consents to the making of the order[7].

Where by virtue of an order an area ceases to be part of the area of a combined authority, the order must make provision for designating an authority[8] to be a local transport authority for the area[9]. It may also transfer functions to that authority from the combined authority that was formerly the local transport authority[10]. Such provision may designate different authorities for different parts of the area[11].

The Secretary of State may by order dissolve a combined authority's area and abolish the combined authority for that area[12]. Such an order may be made only if a majority of the councils to which these provisions apply[13] consent to the making of the order[14]. The order must make provision for designating an authority[15] to be a local transport authority for the area that was previously the combined authority's area[16] and may transfer functions to that authority from the combined authority that was formerly the local transport authority[17]. Such provision may designate different authorities for different parts of the area[18].

1   As to the Secretary of State see PARA 902. It appears that the Secretary of State here concerned is the Secretary of State for Communities and Local Government.
2   As to the establishment of combined authorities and their areas see PARA 1092.
3   As to the meaning of 'local government area' see PARA 1086 note 6.
4   Local Democracy, Economic Development and Construction Act 2009 s 106(1). At the date at which this volume states the law no such order had been made. As to the making of orders under Pt 6 (ss 88–120) see PARA 1086 note 4.
5   Ie conditions A–D in the Local Democracy, Economic Development and Construction Act 2009 s 103: see PARA 1092.
6   The Local Democracy, Economic Development and Construction Act 2009 s 106(2) applies to a county council whose area, or part of whose area, is to be added to or removed from the existing area of the combined authority, and to a district council whose area is to be added to or removed from the existing area of the combined authority: s 106(3). As to local government authorities see LOCAL GOVERNMENT vol 69 (2009) PARA 22 et seq.
7   Local Democracy, Economic Development and Construction Act 2009 s 106(2).
8   The reference here to an authority does not include an Integrated Transport Authority ('ITA'): Local Democracy, Economic Development and Construction Act 2009 s 106(6).
9   Ie for the purposes of the Transport Act 2000 s 108(4): see ROAD TRAFFIC vol 90 (2011) PARA 954.
10 Local Democracy, Economic Development and Construction Act 2009 s 106(4). Section 106(4) does not apply if the area becomes part of the integrated transport area of an ITA by virtue of an order under the Local Transport Act 2008 s 78 or s 90 (see ROAD TRAFFIC vol 89 (2011) PARA 48): Local Democracy, Economic Development and Construction Act 2009 s 106(7).
11 Local Democracy, Economic Development and Construction Act 2009 s 106(5).
12 Local Democracy, Economic Development and Construction Act 2009 s 107(1). At the date at which this volume states the law no such order had been made.
13 Ie a county council whose area, or part of whose area, is within the combined authority's area, or a unitary district council whose area is within the combined authority's area: Local Democracy, Economic Development and Construction Act 2009 s 107(3). As to the meaning of 'unitary district council' see PARA 1086 note 14.
14 Local Democracy, Economic Development and Construction Act 2009 s 107(2).
15 The reference here to an authority does not include an ITA: Local Democracy, Economic Development and Construction Act 2009 s 107(6).
16 Ie for the purposes of the Transport Act 2000 s 108(4): see ROAD TRAFFIC vol 90 (2011) PARA 954.
17 Local Democracy, Economic Development and Construction Act 2009 s 107(4). Section 107(4) does not apply to a territory or part of a territory that becomes the integrated transport area or part of the integrated transport area of an ITA by virtue of an order under the Local Transport Act 2008 s 78 or s 90 (see ROAD TRAFFIC vol 89 (2011) PARA 48): Local Democracy, Economic Development and Construction Act 2009 s 107(7).
18 Local Democracy, Economic Development and Construction Act 2009 s 107(5).

1095. Establishment of combined authority following review of transport and arrangements to promote economic development and regeneration. Any two or more of the authorities to which these provisions apply[1] may undertake a review of:

(1)　the effectiveness and efficiency of transport within the area covered by the review (the 'review area'); and

(2)　the effectiveness and efficiency of arrangements to promote economic development and regeneration within the review area[2].

Where the review is being undertaken by a county council, the review area must include the areas of one or more district councils that are within the area of the county council or, if there are no such areas, the area of the county council[3]. Where the review is being undertaken by a district council, the review area must include the area of the district council[4]. Where the review is being undertaken by an economic prosperity board ('EPB'), the review area must include one or more local government areas[5] within the EPB's area[6]. Where the review is being undertaken by an Integrated Transport Authority ('ITA'), the review area must include one or more local government areas within the ITA's integrated transport area[7]. The review area may also include the area of any county council or district council in England that does not constitute or fall within the area of an authority undertaking the review[8].

Where two or more of the authorities that have undertaken a review conclude that the establishment of a combined authority[9] for an area would be likely to improve:

(a)　the exercise of statutory functions relating to transport in the area;

(b)　the effectiveness and efficiency of transport in the area;

(c)　the exercise of statutory functions relating to economic development and regeneration in the area; and

(d)　economic conditions in the area,

the authorities may prepare and publish a scheme for the establishment of a combined authority for the area (the 'scheme area')[10]. The scheme area must consist of or include the whole or any part of the review area, and may include one or more other local government areas. It must meet conditions A to C[11] for the establishment of a combined authority[12]. However, the scheme area may not include a local government area unless each appropriate authority[13] for that area either participates in the preparation of the scheme or consents to its inclusion in the scheme area[14].

The Secretary of State[15] may make an order establishing a combined authority for an area only if, having regard to a scheme prepared and published as above, the Secretary of State considers that to do so is likely to improve all the issues listed in heads (a) to (d) above[16]. Before making the order, the Secretary of State must consult each appropriate authority[17] and such other persons (if any) as the Secretary of State considers appropriate[18]. In making the order, the Secretary of State must have regard to the need to reflect the identities and interests of local communities and to secure effective and convenient local government[19].

1　The Local Democracy, Economic Development and Construction Act 2009 s 108 applies to a county council in England, a district council in England, an economic prosperity board ('EPB') and an integrated transport authority ('ITA'): s 108(2). As to the establishment of EPBs see PARA 1086.

2　Local Democracy, Economic Development and Construction Act 2009 s 108(1).

3　Local Democracy, Economic Development and Construction Act 2009 s 108(3).

4　Local Democracy, Economic Development and Construction Act 2009 s 108(4).

5　As to the meaning of 'local government area' see PARA 1086 note 6.

6   Local Democracy, Economic Development and Construction Act 2009 s 108(5).
7   Local Democracy, Economic Development and Construction Act 2009 s 108(6).
8   Local Democracy, Economic Development and Construction Act 2009 s 108(7).
9   As to the establishment of combined authorities and their areas see PARA 1092.
10   Local Democracy, Economic Development and Construction Act 2009 s 109(1), (2).
11   Ie conditions A–C in the Local Democracy, Economic Development and Construction Act 2009 s 103: see PARA 1092.
12   Local Democracy, Economic Development and Construction Act 2009 s 109(3).
13   For this purpose a county council is an appropriate authority for a local government area that is or forms part of the area of that county council, and a district council is an appropriate authority for a local government area that is the area of that district council: Local Democracy, Economic Development and Construction Act 2009 s 109(5). As to local government authorities see LOCAL GOVERNMENT vol 69 (2009) PARA 22 et seq.
14   Local Democracy, Economic Development and Construction Act 2009 s 109(4).
15   As to the Secretary of State see PARA 902. It appears that the Secretary of State here concerned is the Secretary of State for Communities and Local Government.
16   Local Democracy, Economic Development and Construction Act 2009 s 110(1). As to the making of orders under Pt 6 (ss 88–120) see PARA 1086 note 4. See also PARA 1092.
17   For these purposes:
    (1)   a county council is an appropriate authority if the area of the county council, or part of that area, is within the area for which the combined authority is to be established (Local Democracy, Economic Development and Construction Act 2009 s 110(3)(a));
    (2)   a district council is an appropriate authority if the area of the district council is within the area for which the combined authority is to be established (s 110(3)(b));
    (3)   an EPB is an appropriate authority if the EPB's area, or part of its area, is within the area for which the combined authority is to be established (s 110(3)(c));
    (4)   an ITA is an appropriate authority if the ITA's integrated transport area, or part of that area, is within the area for which the combined authority is to be established (s 110(3)(d)).
18   Local Democracy, Economic Development and Construction Act 2009 s 110(2).
19   Local Democracy, Economic Development and Construction Act 2009 s 110(4).

1096. Review of existing combined authorities. Any one or more of the authorities to which these provisions apply[1] may undertake, in relation to an existing combined authority, a review of one or more combined matters[2]. The review must relate to one or more areas of a combined authority or proposed areas of a combined authority[3].

Where one or more of the authorities that have undertaken a review conclude that the exercise of the power to make an order in relation to a combined authority[4] would be likely to improve:

(1)   the exercise of statutory functions relating to transport in an area of a combined authority[5] or a proposed area of a combined authority;

(2)   the effectiveness and efficiency of transport in such an area;

(3)   the exercise of statutory functions relating to economic development and regeneration in such an area; or

(4)   economic conditions in such an area, the authorities may prepare and publish a scheme relating to the exercise of the power or powers in question[6].

The Secretary of State[7] may make an order[8] in relation to an existing combined authority only if, having regard to a scheme[9], the Secretary of State considers that the making of the order is likely to improve the issues listed in heads (1) to (4) in the area or areas to which the order relates[10]. Before making the order, the Secretary of State must consult such of the relevant authorities[11], and such other persons (if any), as the Secretary of State considers appropriate[12]. In making the order, the Secretary of State must have regard to the need to reflect the identities and interests of local communities and to secure effective and convenient local government[13].

1   The Local Democracy, Economic Development and Construction Act 2009 s 111 applies to a combined authority, a county council whose area, or part of whose area, is within an area of a combined authority or could be within a proposed area of a combined authority, a district council whose area is within an area of a combined authority or could be within a proposed area of a combined authority: s 111(2). As to the establishment of combined authorities and their areas see PARA 1092. In ss 111, 112 a 'proposed area of a combined authority' means an area of a combined authority that may be created by an order under s 106 (changes to boundaries of a combined authority's area: see PARA 1094): s 111(5). As to local government authorities see LOCAL GOVERNMENT vol 69 (2009) PARA 22 et seq.

2   Local Democracy, Economic Development and Construction Act 2009 s 111(1). For the purposes of s 111 a 'combined matter' is:
    (1)   a matter in relation to which an order may be made under any of ss 104–107 (see PARAS 1092–1094) (s 111(3)(a));
    (2)   in relation to the combined authority or any executive body of the combined authority, where that body exists at the time of the review, a matter concerning the combined authority or the executive body that the combined authority has power to determine (s 111(3)(b)).

3   Local Democracy, Economic Development and Construction Act 2009 s 111(4).

4   Ie under any one or more of the Local Democracy, Economic Development and Construction Act 2009 ss 104–107 (see PARAS 1092–1094).

5   The reference here to an area of a combined authority includes an area that would cease to be an area of a combined authority if an order were made in relation to that area under s 107 (dissolution of a combined authority's area: see PARA 1094): Local Democracy, Economic Development and Construction Act 2009 s 112(3).

6   Local Democracy, Economic Development and Construction Act 2009 s 112(1), (2).

7   As to the Secretary of State see PARA 902. It appears that the Secretary of State here concerned is the Secretary of State for Communities and Local Government.

8   Ie under any of the Local Democracy, Economic Development and Construction Act 2009 ss 104–107 (see PARAS 1092–1094). As to the making of orders under Pt 6 (ss 88–120) see PARA 1086 note 4.

9   Ie a scheme prepared and published under the Local Democracy, Economic Development and Construction Act 2009 s 112.

10 Local Democracy, Economic Development and Construction Act 2009 s 113(1).

11 Ie the authorities mentioned in the Local Democracy, Economic Development and Construction Act 2009 s 111(2): see note 1.

12 Local Democracy, Economic Development and Construction Act 2009 s 113(2).

13 Local Democracy, Economic Development and Construction Act 2009 s 113(3).

(iii) Orders and Guidance

1097.   Additional provisions which may be made in orders. The Secretary of State[1] may by order[2] make incidental, consequential, transitional or supplementary provision for the purposes of, or in consequence of, an order under Part 6 of the Local Democracy, Economic Development and Construction Act 2009 or for giving full effect to such an order[3]. Such an order may include provision amending, applying (with or without modifications), disapplying, repealing or revoking any enactment, whenever passed or made[4], but such an order may not include provision amending or disapplying the statutory provisions[5] as to political balance on local authority committees etc[6].

The Secretary of State may by order make such provision as the Secretary of State considers appropriate in consequence of any provision made by Part 6 of the 2009 Act[7].

1   As to the Secretary of State see PARA 902. It appears that the Secretary of State here concerned is the Secretary of State for Communities and Local Government.

2   As to the making of orders under the Local Democracy, Economic Development and Construction Act 2009 Pt 6 (ss 88–120) see PARA 1086 note 4.

3   Local Democracy, Economic Development and Construction Act 2009 s 114(1). See the West Yorkshire Combined Authority Order 2014, SI 2014/864 (see PARA 1092); and the Combined Authorities (Consequential Amendments) Order 2014, SI 2014/866.

4   Local Democracy, Economic Development and Construction Act 2009 s 114(2). The provision
    that may be included by virtue of s 114(2) includes provision applying, with modifications, or
    disapplying any enactment amended by Sch 6: see s 114(3).
5   Ie the Local Government and Housing Act 1989 ss 15–17, Sch 1: see LOCAL GOVERNMENT
    vol 69 (2009) PARAS 375–377.
6   Local Democracy, Economic Development and Construction Act 2009 s 114(4).
7   Local Democracy, Economic Development and Construction Act 2009 s 116(1). This includes
    power to amend, repeal or revoke provision contained in an enactment passed or made before
    the day on which the Local Democracy, Economic Development and Construction Act 2009 was
    passed (ie 12 November 2009): s 116(2). See also PARA 1086 note 4.

1098.   Transfer of property rights and liabilities.   The Secretary of State[1] may
by order[2] make provision for the transfer of property, rights and liabilities for the
purposes of, or in consequence of, an order under Part 6 of the Local Democracy,
Economic Development and Construction Act 2009 or for giving full effect to
such an order[3]. Property, rights and liabilities may be transferred by the order, or
by a scheme made by the Secretary of State under the order, or by a scheme
required to be made under the order by a person other than the Secretary of
State[4]. A transfer by virtue of these provisions may have effect whether or not
the property, rights and liabilities would otherwise be capable of being
transferred, and they may have effect without any instrument or formality being
required[5]. The rights and liabilities which may be transferred include rights and
liabilities in relation to a contract of employment[6].

An order or a scheme made under it may define the property, rights and
liabilities to be transferred by specifying or describing them[7]. Provision for the
transfer of property, rights and liabilities made by virtue of these provisions may
include provision for:

(1)   the creation or imposition by the Secretary of State of new rights or
      liabilities in respect of anything transferred[8];
(2)   the shared ownership or use of any property or facilities[9];
(3)   the management or custody of transferred property[10];
(4)   bodies to make agreements with respect to any property, income, rights,
      liabilities and expenses of, and any financial relations between, the
      parties to the agreement[11];
(5)   the continuing effect of things done by the transferor in relation to
      anything transferred[12];
(6)   the continuation of things (including legal proceedings) in the process of
      being done, by or on behalf of or in relation to the transferor in relation
      to anything transferred[13];
(7)   references to the transferor in any agreement (whether written or not),
      instrument or other document in relation to anything transferred to be
      treated (so far as necessary for the purposes of or in consequence of the
      transfer) as references to the transferee[14].

1   As to the Secretary of State see PARA 902. It appears that the Secretary of State here concerned is
    the Secretary of State for Communities and Local Government.
2   As to the making of orders under the Local Democracy, Economic Development and
    Construction Act 2009 Pt 6 (ss 88–120) see PARA 1086 note 4.
3   Local Democracy, Economic Development and Construction Act 2009 s 115(1). In exercise of
    these powers, the following orders have been made: the Greater Manchester Combined
    Authority Order 2011, SI 2011/908; West Yorkshire Combined Authority Order 2014,
    SI 2014/864; the Combined Authorities (Consequential Amendments) Order 2014, SI 2014/866.
4   Local Democracy, Economic Development and Construction Act 2009 s 115(2).
5   Local Democracy, Economic Development and Construction Act 2009 s 115(3).
6   Local Democracy, Economic Development and Construction Act 2009 s 115(4). The Transfer of
    Undertakings (Protection of Employment) Regulations 2006, SI 2006/246 (see EMPLOYMENT

vol 39 (2014) PARA 111 et seq) apply to the transfer by virtue of these provisions (whether or not the transfer is a relevant transfer for the purposes of those regulations): Local Democracy, Economic Development and Construction Act 2009 s 115(5).

7   Local Democracy, Economic Development and Construction Act 2009 s 115(6).
8   Local Democracy, Economic Development and Construction Act 2009 s 115(7)(a).
9   Local Democracy, Economic Development and Construction Act 2009 s 115(7)(b).
10 Local Democracy, Economic Development and Construction Act 2009 s 115(7)(c).
11 Local Democracy, Economic Development and Construction Act 2009 s 115(7)(d).
12 Local Democracy, Economic Development and Construction Act 2009 s 115(8)(a).
13 Local Democracy, Economic Development and Construction Act 2009 s 115(8)(b).
14 Local Democracy, Economic Development and Construction Act 2009 s 115(8)(c)

1099.   Guidance by Secretary of State. The Secretary of State[1] may give guidance about anything that could be done by an authority to which these provisions apply[2] under or by virtue of Part 6[3] of the Local Democracy, Economic Development and Construction Act 2009[4]. The authority must have regard to any such guidance in exercising any function conferred or imposed by or by virtue of Part 6[5]. Any guidance must be given in writing and may be varied or revoked by further guidance in writing[6]. Any such guidance may make different provision for different cases and different provision for different areas[7].

1   As to the Secretary of State see PARA 902. It appears that the Secretary of State here concerned is the Secretary of State for Communities and Local Government.
2   The Local Democracy, Economic Development and Construction Act 2009 s 118 applies to a county council, a district council, an economic prosperity board ('EPB'), an integrated transport authority ('ITA'), a combined authority: s 118(5). As to the establishment of EPBs see PARA 1086. As to the establishment of combined authorities see PARA 1092.
3   Ie the Local Democracy, Economic Development and Construction Act 2009 Pt 6 (ss 88–120): see PARA 1086 et seq.
4   Local Democracy, Economic Development and Construction Act 2009 s 118(1).
5   Local Democracy, Economic Development and Construction Act 2009 s 118(2).
6   Local Democracy, Economic Development and Construction Act 2009 s 118(3).
7   Local Democracy, Economic Development and Construction Act 2009 s 118(4).

5. STATISTICS

(1) INFORMATION AND CENSUS

1100. Requirement to submit returns and estimates concerning trade and industry. In order to obtain information necessary to appreciate economic trends, to provide a statistical service for industry and to provide for the discharge by government departments of their functions, a competent authority[1], by notice in writing served on any person[2] carrying on an undertaking[3], may require that person to furnish, in such form and manner and within such time as may be specified in the notice, periodical or other estimates or returns about the following matters[4]:

(1)   the nature of the undertaking (including its association with other undertakings) and the date of its acquisition;

(2)   the persons employed or normally employed (including working proprietors), the nature of their employment, their remuneration and the hours worked;

(3)   the output, sales, deliveries and services provided;

(4)   the articles acquired or used, orders, stocks and work in progress;

(5)   the outgoings and costs (including work given out to contractors, depreciation, rent, rates and taxes, other than taxes on profits) and capital expenditure;

(6)   the receipts of and debts owed to the undertaking;

(7)   the power used or generated;

(8)   the fixed capital assets, the plant, including the acquisition and disposal of those assets and that plant, and the premises occupied;

(9)   assets (other than fixed capital assets) and liabilities of the undertaking, including the acquisition and disposal of those assets and the incurring and discharge of those liabilities;

(10) prices of articles and services;

(11) income (including rents, interest and investment income) received or receivable by the undertaking;

(12) dividends and interest paid or payable;

(13) profits and losses;

(14) taxes paid or chargeable on income or gains;

(15) services acquired or used[5].

The Secretary of State[6] may, by notice, require a trader[7] concerned with an essential commodity[8] to make periodical and other returns, at such times and containing such particulars as are specified in the notice, as to the stocks of the commodity held by him and as to the facilities available for storing and utilising stocks of the commodity[9]. If so required by the Secretary of State, any government department or body of persons having power by virtue of any Act to obtain information as to such matters must exercise that power for the purpose of assisting him to obtain information regarding essential commodities[10].

1   Each of the following ministers and authorities is a competent authority for these purposes: the Treasury, the Chancellor of the Exchequer, a Secretary of State, and the Board of Trade: Statistics of Trade Act 1947 s 17(3) (substituted by SI 1971/719; and amended by SI 1989/992). All functions of the Minister of Agriculture, Fisheries and Food (mentioned in the Statistics of trade Act 1947 s 17(3) as a competent authority) are transferred to the Secretary of State for Environment, Food and Rural Affairs: see ENVIRONMENTAL QUALITY AND PUBLIC HEALTH vol 45 (2010) PARA 58. As to the Secretary of State generally and the Board of Trade see PARA 902. As to the Treasury and the Chancellor of the Exchequer see CONSTITUTIONAL AND

ADMINISTRATIVE LAW vol 20 (2014) PARA 262 et seq. Functions under s 1(1), so far as exercisable by the Chancellor of the Exchequer concurrently with the Board of Trade and the Secretary of State, and concurrently with the Secretary of State as a competent authority, are delegated to the Statistics Board, by the Statistics and Registration Service Act 2007 (Delegation of Functions) (Economic Statistics) Order 2008, SI 2008/792, arts 3, 4(a), 5. For the purposes of the Statistics of Trade Act 1947, Scottish Enterprise and Highlands and Islands Enterprise are each a competent authority: Enterprise and New Towns (Scotland) Act 1990 s 12(1). As to the Statistics Board (commonly referred to as the UK Statistics Authority) see REGISTRATION CONCERNING THE INDIVIDUAL vol 88 (2012) PARA 353 et seq.

2   The notice must state that it is served under the Statistics of Trade Act 1947 s 1 and generally the purpose for which the estimates or returns are required: s 1(2). Unless the contrary intention appears, 'person' includes a body of persons corporate or unincorporate: see the Interpretation Act 1978 s 5, Sch 1.

3   'Undertaking' means any undertaking by way of trade or business, whether or not the trade or business is carried on for profit; and the exercise and performance by a local or other public authority of the powers and duties of that authority must be treated as a trade or business of that authority: Statistics of Trade Act 1947 s 17(1). Where an undertaking is wholly or partly carried on by means of branches situated at several premises, the competent authority may agree with the persons carrying on the undertaking that for the purposes of the Statistics of Trade Act 1947 a separate undertaking is to be deemed to be carried on at all or any of those branches by the branch manager or a specified person; any such agreement may contain such supplemental provisions as may be expedient for giving effect to it and continues in force for a specified term; and is subject to any provisions as to variation and revocation specified in the agreement: s 17(2).

4   Statistics of Trade Act 1947 s 1(1).

5   Statistics of Trade Act 1947 s 1(1), Schedule (amended by SI 1963/1329; 1987, SI 1987/669; and SI 1990/2597). The amendments were made by orders under the Statistics of Trade Act 1947 s 5, which gives a general power to amend the Schedule, subject to the approval of each House of Parliament. The Schedule provides that in a case where the undertaking is related to a body situated outside the United Kingdom the following information may also be required:
    (1)   the nature and the extent of the relationship;
    (2)   the nature and extent (and any changes therein) of the financial interest of the one body in the other;
    (3)   the country in which the related body is situated;
    (4)   particulars in respect of issued share capital, minority share-holders' interests, loans, reserves and provisions as recorded in the accounts of the undertaking or such particulars in respect of the related body where it is under the control of the undertaking;
    (5)   net gains or losses of the undertaking attributable to changes in exchange rates, being gains or losses arising out of the relationship;
    (6)   the profit or loss of the undertaking or related body attributable to the relationship and dividends declared by either body arising out of the relationship;
    (7)   where the body is not a company incorporated in the United Kingdom, its net value to the related body, and where the related body is not a body corporate, its net value to the undertaking.
    As to the meaning of 'United Kingdom' see PARA 906 note 7.

6   For these purposes the 'Secretary of State' is the Secretary of State for Business, Innovation and Skills, to whom the functions of the Board of Trade were transferred: see PARA 903 note 2.

7   For these purposes 'trader' in relation to any commodity means any person who for the purposes of any trade or business carried on by him, whether as a producer, merchant, broker, warehouseman or otherwise, holds from time to time a stock of that commodity: Essential Commodities Reserves Act 1938 s 6.

8   'Essential commodity' means any commodity which may be declared by order of the Secretary of State to be a commodity which, in his opinion, would be essential for the vital needs of the community in the event of war: Essential Commodities Reserves Act 1938 s 6. Any commodity which, in the opinion of the Secretary of State, may be required as food for man, forage for animals or fertiliser for land, any raw material from which any such commodity can be produced, and petroleum and any product of petroleum, may be declared to be such a commodity: s 6, Schedule. See the Essential Commodities Reserves (Declaration) Order 1938, SR & O 1938/1110.

9   Essential Commodities Reserves Act 1938 s 1(1).

10 See the Essential Commodities Reserves Act 1938 s 1(2). Any such information obtained by any government department or by any such body of persons, whether upon the requisition of the

Secretary of State or otherwise, may, notwithstanding anything in any enactment, be furnished to him: s 1(2). The Secretary of State is given the power to make payments to traders for the purpose of augmenting or maintaining stocks of essential commodities, or the improvement of storage facilities: see s 2(1). Additionally, the Secretary of State may acquire and store such stocks and take various steps in relation to them: see s 2(2), (3).

1101. Census of production and distribution. For the purpose of providing, at intervals, general surveys of the state of trade and business, the Secretary of State[1] must in each year take a census of production, and may in any year[2] prescribed by order take a census of distribution and other services[3]. Any person[4] carrying on an undertaking may be required to furnish returns[5] for the purpose of any census[6]. A census must require returns to be furnished with respect to the calendar year next preceding the date of the census[7], unless the Secretary of State permits a person for whom it would be inconvenient to furnish returns with respect to that calendar year to furnish returns with respect to some other period of 12 months[8].

1   The functions of the Secretary of State under the Statistics of Trade Act 1947 ss 2, 3, 6, 7, 8, 9(2), (3), 10, 11 and 17(2) (see text to notes 2–8; and PARA 1102 et seq) and the functions of the Secretary of State as a competent authority within the meaning of that Act (see PARA 1100 note 1) are transferred to the Chancellor of the Exchequer, so as to be exercisable concurrently with him, by the Transfer of Functions (Economic Statistics) Order 1989, SI 1989/992, art 2(1), (2). Functions under the Statistics of Trade Act 1947 ss 2(1), (4), 3(1), (2), 6(1), 7, 8(1), (2) and 17(2), so far as exercisable by the Chancellor of the Exchequer concurrently with the Board of Trade and the Secretary of State, and concurrently with the Secretary of State as a competent authority, are delegated to the Statistics Board by the Statistics and Registration Service Act 2007 (Delegation of Functions) (Economic Statistics) Order 2008, SI 2008/792, arts 3, 4(b)–(g), (c), 5, 6. As to the Statistics Board (commonly referred to as the UK Statistics Authority) see REGISTRATION CONCERNING THE INDIVIDUAL vol 88 (2012) PARA 353 et seq.

2   Ie a calendar year beginning not less than 12 months after the date of the order: see the Statistics of Trade Act 1947 s 2(1).

3   Statistics of Trade Act 1947 s 2(1). Individual orders made under s 2(1) prescribed certain years for each census: see eg the Census of Production Order 1993, SI 1993/3037, relating to the census of production to be taken in 1994 and in subsequent years and prescribing the undertaking to which the census is confined and the matters to which returns relate and providing for the exemption of certain persons. The census may either be taken to cover all undertakings in the field of production, distribution or other services, as the case may be, or it may be confined to such classes or descriptions of those undertakings respectively as may be prescribed: Statistics of Trade Act 1947 s 2(2). The Secretary of State may by order provide for exempting from the obligation to furnish returns for the purpose of a census, either wholly or to the prescribed extent, and either unconditionally or subject to prescribed conditions, any persons or any prescribed class or description of persons: 2(2). See eg the Census of Production Order 1993, SI 1993/3037, exempting persons carrying on certain activities relating to the extraction of crude petroleum and natural gas: see arts 4, 5. As to the meaning of 'undertaking' see PARA 1100 note 3. As to the making of orders under the Statistics of Trade Act 1947 generally see PARA 1114.

4   As to the meaning of 'person' see PARA 1100 note 2.

5   The matters about which a person may be required to furnish returns for the purposes of a census are such of the matters set out in the Statistics of Trade Act 1947 Schedule (see PARA 1100 note 5) as may be prescribed: s 2(3).

6   Statistics of Trade Act 1947 s 2(2).

7   Statistics of Trade Act 1947 s 2(4).

8   Statistics of Trade Act 1947 s 2(4) proviso.

1102. Census forms and instructions. The Secretary of State[1] must prepare and issue such forms and instructions as he deems necessary for the taking of a census of production or of distribution and other services[2]. A person[3] is not required to furnish returns for these purposes except in pursuance of a notice in writing from the Secretary of State requiring him to do so; and the Secretary of

State must issue, with the notice, the forms required to be filled up by that person[4]. The Secretary of State may delegate any of these functions to any other competent authority[5]. A person required to furnish returns must comply with the notice, in such manner as may be specified in the notice, on or before a day so specified being not less than two months after the service of the notice[6].

1 As to the Secretary of State see PARA 903 note 2. As to the transfer of functions to the Chancellor of the Exchequer see PARA 1101 note 1.
2 Statistics of Trade Act 1947 s 3(1).
3 As to the meaning of 'person' see PARA 1100 note 2.
4 Statistics of Trade Act 1947 s 3(2).
5 Statistics of Trade Act 1947 s 3(3). As to the meaning of 'competent authority' see PARA 1100 note 1. On delegation, references to the Secretary of State include references to any other authority to whom the functions have been delegated and a notice issued by a competent authority in pursuance of powers delegated to that authority must state that it is so issued: s 3(3).
6 Statistics of Trade Act 1947 s 3(4). In their application to a person who has been allowed to furnish returns with respect to a period ending not later than 31 October in the calendar year preceding the date on which the notice is served on him, the provisions of s 3(4) have effect as if for the reference to two months there is substituted a reference to one month: s 3(4) proviso. As to the service of notices see PARA 1115.

1103. Lists of undertakings subject to census. The Secretary of State[1] or any competent authority[2] to which he has delegated the function[3] may by advertisement in the Gazette[4] and in such newspapers as appear to him to be sufficient for notifying the persons[5] concerned, publish a list of any classes or descriptions of undertakings[6] in relation to which returns will be required for the purposes of a particular census of production or distribution and other services[7]. Upon such publication it is the duty of every person carrying on an undertaking of any specified class or description who has not received a notice requiring him to furnish returns[8], both to inform a person specified in the advertisement within a specified period (being not less than at days after the publication) that he is carrying on such an undertaking, and to give to that person such prescribed particulars of the undertaking as are so specified[9].

1 As to the Secretary of State see PARA 903 note 2. As to the transfer of functions to the Chancellor of the Exchequer see PARA 1101 note 1.
2 As to the meaning of 'competent authority' see PARA 1100 note 1.
3 The Secretary of State may delegate any of his functions under the Statistics of Trade Act 1947 s 6(1) to any other competent authority, and references in s 6(1) to the Secretary of State include references to any competent authority to whom those functions have been so delegated: s 6(2).
4 The 'Gazette' means: in relation to an advertisement concerning undertakings in England and Wales only, the London gazette; in relation to an advertisement concerning undertakings in Scotland only, the Edinburgh Gazette; and in relation to any other advertisement, the London Gazette and the Edinburgh Gazette: Statistics of Trade Act 1947 s 6(5).
5 As to the meaning of 'person' see PARA 1100 note 2.
6 As to the meaning of 'undertaking' see PARA 1100 note 3.
7 Statistics of Trade Act 1947 s 6(1).
8 Ie a notice under the Statistics of Trade Act 1947 s 3(2): see PARA 1102.
9 Statistics of Trade Act 1947 s 6(1). As to offences of failing to give such information or particulars or giving false information or particulars see s 6(3), (4); and PARA 1106.

1104. Information which may be required from air travellers. The Secretary of State[1] may by order make provision whereby any person entering or leaving the United Kingdom[2] by air may be required to give[3] particulars of his age, sex and marriage or civil partnership, of the nature of his occupation and of the country in which he last permanently resided and that in which he intends next permanently to reside[4]. If it is not reasonably practicable to require any such person to give the particulars, any other person in whose company and under whose care he is travelling may be required to give the particulars on his behalf[5].

1   As to the Secretary of State see PARA 903 note 2. As to the transfer of functions to the Chancellor of the Exchequer see PARA 1101 note 1.
2   As to the meaning of 'United Kingdom' see PARA 906 note 7.
3   Ie to give to such persons and in such form and manner as may be prescribed by order made by the Secretary of State: see the Statistics of Trade Act 1947 ss 10(1), 11.
4   Statistics of Trade Act 1947 s 10(1) (amended by the Civil Partnership Act 2004 s 261(1), Sch 27 para 12). At the date at which this volume states the law no such order had been made.
5   Statistics of Trade Act 1947 s 10(2). As to offences of failing to give such information or particulars or giving false information or particulars see s 10(3), (4); and PARA 1106.

1105.   Collection of statistics relating to trading of goods between member states.   Provision is made for the collection of statistics relating to the trading of goods between member states of the European Union. Such statistics are compiled by means of a statistical collection system known as 'Intrastat' from VAT returns and supplementary declarations made by VAT registered traders who are engaged in the trading of goods between member states[1].

1   See the Statistics of Trade (Customs and Excise) Regulations 1992, SI 1992/2790 (amended by SI 1993/541; SI 1993/3015; SI 1997/2864; SI 2000/3227; SI 2004/3284; SI 2006/3216; SI 2008/557; SI 2008/2847; SI 2009/2974; SI 2011/1043; SI 2012/532; SI 2013/3043; SI 2014/3135).

(2)   OFFENCES AND DISCLOSURE

1106.   Failure to give information, and giving false information, under the Statistics of Trade Act 1947 and the Essential Commodities Reserves Act 1938.
It is an offence for any person[1] to make a default in making any return or furnishing any information which he is duly required to make or furnish under the Essential Commodities Reserves Act 1938[2]. It is also an offence for any person knowingly or recklessly to make a false return or furnish false information or, for the purpose of obtaining any payment under that Act, knowingly or recklessly to make an untrue statement or untrue representation[3].

It is an offence for any person required to furnish estimates or returns under the Statistics of Trade Act 1947 to fail to furnish such estimates or returns unless he proves that he has reasonable excuse for the failure[4]. It is also an offence:

(1)   knowingly or recklessly to make a statement in estimates or returns which is false in a material particular[5];

(2)   for any person to fail to give any information or particulars required by the Secretary of State when he has advertised his requirements, unless the person can prove that he did not know and had reasonable cause for not knowing that he was required to give that information or those particulars[6];

(3)   knowingly or recklessly to make a statement in any such particulars which is false in a material particular[7].

Where any person is required to give information on entering or leaving the United Kingdom[8], it is an offence to fail to comply with that requirement unless he proves that he had reasonable excuse for the failure[9]. It is also an offence if any person in purported compliance with that requirement knowingly or recklessly makes any statement which is false in a material particular[10].

1   As to the meaning of 'person' see PARA 1100 note 2.

2   Essential Commodities Reserves Act 1938 s 4(1). A person guilty of such an offence is liable on
    summary conviction to a fine not exceeding level 3 on the standard scale: s 4(1) (amended by
    virtue of the Criminal Justice Act 1982 ss 38, 46). If after being so convicted a person continues
    to make the like default, he is guilty of a further offence and is liable on summary conviction to
    a fine not exceeding £50 for each day on which the default continues: Essential Commodities
    Reserves Act 1938 s 4(1). As to the standard scale see SENTENCING AND DISPOSITION OF
    OFFENDERS vol 92 (2010) PARA 142. As to the liability of officers of bodies corporate convicted
    of such offences see PARA 1107.
3   Essential Commodities Reserves Act 1938 s 4(2). It is irrelevant whether the purpose of the
    person making the statement or representation is to obtain payment for himself or any other
    person: see s 4(2). A person guilty of such an offence is, in respect of each offence, liable on
    summary conviction to a fine not exceeding level 3 on the standard scale or to imprisonment for
    a term not exceeding three months, or to both: see s 4(2) (amended by virtue of the Criminal
    Justice Act 1982 ss 38, 46; and, as from a day to be appointed, by the Criminal Justice Act 2003
    s 332, Sch 37 Pt 9, so as to remove the penalty of imprisonment; at the date at which this
    volume states the law, no such day had been appointed).
4   Statistics of Trade Act 1947 s 4(1). A person guilty of such an offence under s 4(1) is liable on
    summary conviction to a fine not exceeding level 4 on the standard scale: s 4(1) (amended by
    virtue of the Criminal Justice Act 1982 ss 38, 46). If after being so convicted a person continues
    to fail to furnish estimates or returns he is guilty of a further offence and will on summary
    conviction be punished accordingly: Statistics of Trade Act 1947 s 4(2).
5   Statistics of Trade Act 1947 s 4(3). If a person is guilty of such an offence he is liable on
    summary conviction to imprisonment for a term not exceeding three months or to a fine not
    exceeding the prescribed sum, or on conviction on indictment to imprisonment for a term not
    exceeding two years or to a fine, or in either case, to both: Statistics of Trade Act 1947 s 4(3)
    (amended by virtue of the Magistrates' Courts Act 1980 s 32(2)). As to the prescribed sum see
    SENTENCING AND DISPOSITION OF OFFENDERS vol 92 (2010) PARA 141.
6   Statistics of Trade Act 1947 s 6(3). If a person is guilty of such an offence he is liable on
    summary conviction to a fine not exceeding level 1 on the standard scale: s 6(3) (amended by
    virtue of the Criminal Justice Act 1982 s 46).
7   Statistics of Trade Act 1947 s 6(4). If a person is guilty of such an offence he is liable on
    summary conviction to imprisonment for a term not exceeding three months or to a fine not
    exceeding the prescribed sum, or on conviction on indictment to imprisonment for a term not
    exceeding two years or a to fine, or, in either case, to both: s 6(4) (amended by virtue of the
    Magistrates' Courts Act 1980 s 32(2)).
8   Ie by virtue of the Statistics of Trade Act 1947 s 10(1): see PARA 1104. As to the meaning of
    'United Kingdom' see PARA 906 note 7.
9   Statistics of Trade Act 1947 s 10(3). If a person is guilty of such an offence he is liable on
    summary conviction to a fine not exceeding level 2 on the standard scale: s 10(3) (amended by
    virtue of the Criminal Justice Act 1982 s 46).
10 Statistics of Trade Act 1947 s 10(4). If a person is guilty of such an offence he is liable on
    summary conviction to imprisonment for a term not exceeding three months or to a fine not
    exceeding the prescribed sum, or on conviction on indictment to imprisonment for a term not
    exceeding two years or to a fine of any amount, or, in either case, to both such imprisonment
    and such fine: s 10(4) (amended by virtue of the Criminal Law Act 1977 s 32(1); and the
    Magistrates' Courts Act 1980 s 32(2)).

**1107.   Offences under the Statistics of Trade Act 1947 and the Essential
Commodities Reserves Act 1938 committed by a body corporate.**   Where an
offence under the Statistics of Trade Act 1947[1] has been committed by a body
corporate, every person who at the time of the commission of the offence was a
director, general manager, secretary or other similar officer of that body, or was
purporting to act in any such capacity, is deemed to be guilty of the offence
unless he proves that it was committed without his consent or connivance and
that he exercised all such diligence to prevent its commission as he ought to have
exercised having regard to the nature of his functions in that capacity and to all
the circumstances[2].

Where an offence under the Essential Commodities Reserves Act 1938[3] has
been committed by a body corporate and it is proved to have been committed
with the consent or approval of, or to have been facilitated by any negligence on

the part of any director, manager, secretary or other officer of that body, he, as well as the body corporate, is deemed to be guilty of the offence and is liable to be proceeded against and punished accordingly[4].

1   Ie offences committed under the Statistics of Trade Act 1947 ss 4, 6(3), 9(6), 10(3), (4): see PARAS 1106, 1108. An offence committed under s 10 (see PARAS 1104, 1106) is inapplicable to a body corporate. Where a person convicted is a body corporate, such of the above provisions as limit the amount of the fine which may be imposed do not apply, and the body corporate is liable to a fine of such amount as the court thinks just: s 13(1); cf the Criminal Law Act 1977 s 32(1); and SENTENCING AND DISPOSITION OF OFFENDERS vol 92 (2010) PARA 139.
2   Statistics of Trade Act 1947 s 13(2).
3   As to these offences see PARA 1106.
4   Essential Commodities Reserves Act 1938 s 4(3).

1108. Unlawful disclosure of information under the Statistics of Trade Act 1947 and the Essential Commodities Reserves Act 1938. It is an offence to disclose information with respect to any particular undertaking obtained under or by virtue of the Essential Commodities Reserves Act 1938 without the consent of the person carrying on that undertaking otherwise than in pursuance of the performance by the Secretary of State[1] of his functions under that Act, unless such disclosure is made for the purposes of any legal proceedings which may be taken under, by virtue of or in consequence of that Act[2].

It is an offence to disclose any individual estimates, returns or any information relating to an individual undertaking[3] obtained under the Statistics of Trade Act 1947 without the previous consent in writing of the person carrying on the undertaking which is the subject of the estimates, returns or information, except either in accordance with directions given by the minister in charge of the government department in possession of the estimates, returns or information to a government department for the purposes of the exercise of its functions, or for the purposes of any proceedings for an offence under that Act or any report of those proceedings[4].

1   As to the Secretary of State and the transfer to him of the functions of the Board of Trade see PARA 902 note 1. As to the transfer of functions to the Chancellor of the Exchequer see PARA 1101 note 1. Functions under the Statistics of Trade Act 1947 ss 9(1), 9A, so far as exercisable by the Chancellor of the Exchequer for the disclosing of information obtained under that Act, are transferred to the Statistics Board by the Statistics and Registration Service Act 2007 (Delegation of Functions) (Economic Statistics) Order 2008, SI 2008/792, art 6. As to the Statistics Board (commonly referred to as the UK Statistics Authority) see REGISTRATION CONCERNING THE INDIVIDUAL vol 88 (2012) PARA 353 et seq.
2   Essential Commodities Reserves Act 1938 s 1(3). If a person is guilty of such an offence under s 1(3), he is liable on summary conviction to imprisonment for a term not exceeding three months or to a fine not exceeding the prescribed sum, or on conviction on indictment to imprisonment for a term not exceeding two years or to a fine, or in either case, to both: see s 1(3) (amended by virtue of the Criminal Law Act 1977 s 32(1); and the Magistrates' Courts Act 1980 s 32(2), (9)). As to the prescribed sum see SENTENCING AND DISPOSITION OF OFFENDERS vol 92 (2010) PARA 141.
3   As to the meaning of 'undertaking' see PARA 1100 note 3.
4   Statistics of Trade Act 1947 s 9(1), (6) (amended by the Import Duties Act 1958 s 16(4), Sch 7 (repealed); and by SI 1999/1820). If a person is guilty of such an offence he is liable on summary conviction to imprisonment for a term not exceeding three months or to a fine not exceeding the prescribed sum, or on conviction on indictment to imprisonment for a term not exceeding two years or to a fine or, in either case, to both: Statistics of Trade Act 1947 s 9(6) (amended by virtue of the Magistrates' Courts Act 1980 s 32(2); and the Criminal Law Act 1977 s 32(1)). Detailed exemptions from the duty not to disclose are enacted in respect of:
    (1)   European Union (EU) institutions (see the European Communities Act 1972 s 12);
    (2)   certain bodies performing functions under the Employment and Training Act 1973 s 4(3)–(5) (see EMPLOYMENT vol 40 (2014) PARA 564);

(3) the Health and Safety Executive (see the Health and Safety at Work etc Act 1974 s 27; and HEALTH AND SAFETY AT WORK vol 52 (2014) PARA 334);

(4) the Advisory, Conciliation and Arbitration Service ('ACAS') (see the Trade Union and Labour Relations (Consolidation) Act 1992 s 247(5); and EMPLOYMENT vol 41A (2014) PARA 1182); and

(5) the Environment Agency and the Natural Resources Body for Wales (see the Statistics of Trade Act 1947 s 9A (added by the Environment Act 1995 s 120(1), Sch 22 para 2; and amended by SI 2013/755)).

As to the Environment Agency see ENVIRONMENTAL QUALITY AND PUBLIC HEALTH vol 45 (2010) PARA 68 et seq; and as to the Natural Resources Body for Wales see FORESTRY vol 52 (2014) PARA 38. As to unauthorised disclosure of information provided by member states to the Statistical Office of the European Union ('Eurostat') see PARA 1109.

1109. Disclosure of information provided to the Statistical Office of the European Union. It is an offence for an officer or employee of the Statistical Office of the European Union ('Eurostat')[1] or any individual who, under a contract for services with Eurostat, is required to carry out duties on its premises, knowingly or recklessly to disclose within Great Britain[2] confidential statistical information without the authority of the member state who provided that information. If a person is guilty of such an offence he is liable on summary conviction to imprisonment for a term not exceeding three months or a fine not exceeding the statutory maximum, or on conviction on indictment to imprisonment for a term not exceeding two years or a fine, or in either case, to both[3].

1 The Statistical Office of the European Union was formerly referred to as the Statistical Office of the European Communities ('SOEC'), but is now known as 'Eurostat'. It is one of the directorates-general of the European Commission.

2 As to the meaning of 'Great Britain' see PARA 906 note 7.

3 Provision of Confidential Statistical Information to the Statistical Office of the European Communities (Restriction on Disclosure) Regulations 1991, SI 1991/2779, reg 3. 'Confidential statistical information' means statistical information which has been declared or classified as confidential in accordance with its law or national practice by the member state providing it, and provided to Eurostat by a member state in accordance with Euratom and Council Regulation (EC) 1588/90 on the transmission of data subject to statistical confidentiality to the Statistical Office of the European Communities (OJ L151, 15.6.1990, p 1) art 3: Provision of Confidential Statistical Information to the Statistical Office of the European Communities (Restriction on Disclosure) Regulations 1991, SI 1991/2779, reg 2. As to the statutory maximum see SENTENCING AND DISPOSITION OF OFFENDERS vol 92 (2010) PARA 140.

1110. Additional restrictions under the Statistics of Trade Act 1947 on disclosure of information. If any information to be obtained for the purposes of a census under the Statistics of Trade Act 1947[1] is also obtainable under any other enactment which restricts the disclosure of information obtained thereunder, and the Secretary of State[2] is of opinion that similar restrictions should be applied to any information to be obtained for the purposes of the census, he may provide by order[3] for those restrictions to apply, without modifications or with such adaptations or modifications as he thinks fit, to the information to be so obtained[4]. Moreover, if it appears to him that the nature of the information to be obtained for the purposes of a census, or the nature of the undertakings[5] to be covered by the census, would make it desirable to impose any other restrictions, he may by order prohibit the disclosure of information relating to particular undertakings obtained by means of the census, or any part of that information, except to specified persons or for specified purposes[6].

1 As to such a census see PARAS 1101–1103.

2 As to the Secretary of State see PARA 903 note 2. As to the transfer of functions to the Chancellor of the Exchequer see PARA 1101 note 1.

3   No order may be made under the Statistics of Trade Act 1947 s 9 unless a draft is laid before Parliament and is approved by resolution of each House of Parliament: s 9(4). See STATUTES AND LEGISLATIVE PROCESS vol 96 (2012) PARA 1032.

4   Statistics of Trade Act 1947 s 9(2). As to the making of orders under the Statistics of Trade Act 1947 generally see PARA 1114. At the date at which this volume states the law no such order had been made. If a person discloses any estimates or returns or any information contrary to s 9 he is guilty of an offence and liable on summary conviction to imprisonment for a term not exceeding three months or to a fine not exceeding the prescribed sum, or on conviction on indictment to imprisonment for a term not exceeding two years or to a fine or, in either case, to both: s 9(6) (amended by virtue of the Criminal Law Act 1977 s 32(1); and of the Magistrates' Courts Act 1980 s 32(2)). As to the prescribed sum see SENTENCING AND DISPOSITION OF OFFENDERS vol 92 (2010) PARA 141.

5   As to the meaning of 'undertaking' see PARA 1100 note 3.

6   Statistics of Trade Act 1947 s 9(3). See the Census of Distribution (1951) (Restriction on Disclosure) Order 1950, SI 1950/1245, the Census of Distribution (1958) (Restriction on Disclosure) Order 1956, SI 1956/1860, the Census of Distribution (1962) (Restriction on Disclosure) Order 1960, SI 1960/2364, and the Census of Distribution (1967) (Restriction on Disclosure) Order 1965, SI 1965/2061. As to the penalties for contravention of such an order see note 4.

1111. Disclosure in public reports under the Statistics of Trade Act 1947. No report, summary or other communication to the public of information obtained under the Statistics of Trade Act 1947 may disclose the number of returns received with respect to the production of any article[1] if that number is less than five[2]. In compiling any such report, summary or communication the competent authority[3] must prevent any particulars published in it from being identified as particularly relating to any individual person or undertaking[4], except with the previous consent in writing of that person or the person carrying on that undertaking; but the total quantity or value of any articles produced, sold or delivered may be stated, provided that prior to disclosure of such a total the competent authority has regard to any representations made to it by any person who alleges that the disclosure would enable particulars relating to him or to an undertaking carried on by him to be deduced from the total disclosed[5].

1   'Article' includes substances, plant, vehicles, vessels, animals, water, gas and electricity, and 'plant' includes any machinery, equipment or appliance: Statistics of Trade Act 1947 s 17(4).

2   Statistics of Trade Act 1947 s 9(5)(a).

3   As to the meaning of 'competent authority' see PARA 1100 note 1.

4   As to the meaning of 'undertaking' see PARA 1100 note 3.

5   Statistics of Trade Act 1947 s 9(5)(b). As to the penalties for offences under s 9 see PARA 1110 note 4.

(3) ADMINISTRATION AND NOTICES

1112. Census advisory committees. The Secretary of State[1] must arrange for the appointment of one or more committees to advise him, or any other competent authority[2] to whom functions have been delegated[3], with regard to the preparation of forms and instructions necessary for the taking of a census, the making of orders by him and to such other matters as may be referred to such a committee[4]. Committees may be appointed to advise specially about any special forms, instructions or orders, or generally about any class or description of forms, instructions or orders that may be assigned to them[5]. Every committee must include persons engaged in, or otherwise conversant with the conditions of, various trades and businesses[6].

1   As to the Secretary of State see PARA 903 note 2. As to the transfer of functions to the Chancellor of the Exchequer see PARA 1101 note 1.

2   As to the meaning of 'competent authority' see PARA 1100 note 1.
3   Ie under the Statistics of Trade Act 1947 s 3: see PARA 1102.
4   Statistics of Trade Act 1947 s 8(1).
5   Statistics of Trade Act 1947 s 8(3).
6   Statistics of Trade Act 1947 s 8(1). With the consent of the Treasury, the Secretary of State may
     determine any travelling or other allowances to be paid to the members of the committee: s 8(2).
     With Treasury approval any expenses incurred by the Secretary of State or other competent
     authority are defrayed out of money provided by Parliament: s 15.

1113.   Census report by the Secretary of State. As soon as practicable after
any census under the Statistics of Trade Act 1947[1] is complete, the Secretary of
State[2] must present to Parliament a report of his proceedings in connection with
the taking of the census and a summary of the statistics obtained[3].

1   As to such a census see PARAS 1101–1103.
2   As to the Secretary of State see PARA 903 note 2. As to the transfer of functions to the
     Chancellor of the Exchequer see PARA 1101 note 1.
3   Statistics of Trade Act 1947 s 7. If the Secretary of State thinks fit, he may include in the
     summary of statistics any statistics obtained by him or a competent authority otherwise than by
     means of a census, or statistics obtained by a Northern Ireland department and communicated
     to him for the purposes of inclusion in the report; and the summary must contain separate
     statements relating to Scotland and Wales: see s 7. As to the meaning of 'competent authority'
     see PARA 1100 note 1.

**1114.   Making of orders under the Statistics of Trade Act 1947 and the
Essential Commodities Reserve Act 1938.** The Secretary of State[1] may by order[2]
make provision for prescribing, either generally or with respect to any class or
description of persons or undertakings[3], anything which under the Statistics of
Trade Act 1947 is to be prescribed, and generally for the purposes of carrying
that Act into effect[4]. He may also make orders declaring commodities to be
essential commodities[5] for the purposes of the Essential Commodities Reserves
Act 1938[6].

1   As to the Secretary of State see PARA 903 note 2. As to the transfer of functions to the
     Chancellor of the Exchequer see PARA 1101 note 1.
2   All orders made under the Statistics of Trade Act 1947, other than orders made under s 9 must
     be laid before Parliament immediately after they are made, and if either House of Parliament,
     within 40 days, resolves that the order be annulled, the order ceases to have effect, but without
     prejudice to anything done under it or to the making of a new order: s 11(2); and see STATUTES
     AND LEGISLATIVE PROCESS vol 96 (2012) PARA 1032. In reckoning any such period of 40 days,
     no account is to be taken of any time during which Parliament is dissolved or prorogued or
     during which both Houses are adjourned for more than four days: s 11(2). Orders under s 9
     must not be made unless a draft has been laid before Parliament and approved by a resolution of
     each House: see s 9(4); PARA 1110 note 3; and STATUTES AND LEGISLATIVE PROCESS vol 96
     (2012) PARA 1032. As to orders made under the Statistics of Trade Act 1947 see PARAS 1101
     note 3, 1110 note 6.
3   As to the meaning of 'undertaking' see PARA 1100 note 3.
4   Statistics of Trade Act 1947 s 11(1). Any such order may be revoked or varied by a subsequent
     order made in like manner and subject to the like conditions as the original order: s 11(3).
5   As to the meaning of 'essential commodity' see PARA 1100 note 8.
6   See the Essential Commodities Reserves Act 1938 s 6, Schedule; and PARA 1100 note 8. All such
     orders must be laid before Parliament (s 5(2)) and may be varied or revoked by an order made
     in like manner (s 5(1)); see STATUTES AND LEGISLATIVE PROCESS vol 96 (2012) PARA 1032.

1115.   Service of notices under the Statistics of Trade Act 1947. Any notice
required or authorised by or under the Statistics of Trade Act 1947 to be served
on any person may be served by delivering it to that person, by leaving it at his
proper address[1] or by post[2]. Any notice required or authorised to be served on a
body corporate is duly served if served on its secretary or clerk[3].

Where a notice is served by post otherwise than in a registered letter or by the recorded delivery service, service is not deemed to have been effected if it is proved that the notice was not received by the person to whom it was addressed[4].

1   The proper address of any person on whom a notice under the Statistics of Trade Act 1947 is to be served is the last known address of the person to be served: s 12(3); Interpretation Act 1978 ss 7, 17(2)(a), Sch 2 para 3; and cf COMPANIES vol 14 (2009) PARA 671. Where the name of a person carrying on an undertaking at any premises is not known, then, if any such notice is sent by post in a registered letter or by the recorded delivery service so addressed as to show the name in which and the premises at which the undertaking is carried on, the letter is deemed for the purposes of s 7 to be properly addressed: s 17(2)(a); Statistics of Trade Act 1947 s 12(4); Recorded Delivery Service Act 1962 s 1(1), (2), Schedule para 1. As to the meaning of 'undertaking' see PARA 1100 note 3.
2   Statistics of Trade Act 1947 s 12(1).
3   Statistics of Trade Act 1947 s 12(2). In the case of a secretary or clerk of an incorporated company or body, the proper address for service of such a notice is that of the registered or principal office of the company or body: see s 12(3); the Interpretation Act 1978 ss 7, 17(2)(a), Sch 2 para 3; and cf COMPANIES vol 14 (2009) PARA 671.
4   Statistics of Trade Act 1947 s 12(1); Recorded Delivery Service Act 1962 s 1(1), (2), Schedule para 1. This has the effect of disapplying the Interpretation Act 1978 s 7 (which provides that a properly addressed, prepaid and posted letter is deemed to constitute proper service of a document contained in it) other than to a registered letter or a letter sent by recorded delivery.

INDEX

Telecommunications

References are to paragraph numbers; superior figures refer to notes

References are to paragraph numbers; superior figures refer to notes

References are to paragraph numbers; superior figures refer to notes

References are to paragraph numbers; superior figures refer to notes

OFFENCE
submarine cables, as to 212–214
telecommunications, as to. *See under*
COMMUNICATIONS

OFFICE OF COMMUNICATIONS
(OFCOM)
accounts and records—
duty to keep and submit 6
licence fees and penalties, as to 41
administrative charge, power to fix 83
advisory committees—
Consumer Panel, advice to 30, 31
different parts of UK, for 30
elderly and disabled persons, on 31
functions 30, 31
list of 9
membership 30, 31
annual report—
conflicting duties, summary of
resolution of 16
contents 7
preparation 7
apparatus, encouraging availability of
22
appeal against decision of—
right of 224
See also COMPETITION APPEAL
TRIBUNAL
assistance to party in proceedings,
power to give 165
body corporate, as 2
borrowing by, guarantee by Secretary of
State 37
chairman, appointment etc 3
charging for services 36
chief executive 4
code. *See* ELECTRONIC
COMMUNICATIONS CODE
Code of Practice, submission to 99n[17]
committees—
advisory committees 9
establishment 9
list of 9
nature of 9
proceedings 10
remuneration etc of members 9
role 9
competition legislation, functions under
38
Consumer Panel—
meaning 28n[5]
advisory role 28
appointment of members 29
duties and functions 29
establishment 28
maintenance 28

OFFICE OF COMMUNICATIONS
(OFCOM)—*continued*
Consumer Panel—*continued*
membership 29
consumer protection—
consumer consultation, duties as to
28
Consumer Panel. *See* Consumer Panel
above
consumer research—
nature of 26
publication 27
taking account of 27
domestic and small business
consumers 28n[6]
services and facilities, provision of
28n[8]
Content Board—
meaning 24n[3]
constitution 24
establishment 24
functions 25
maintenance 24
membership 24
payments to 24
copyright, response to online
infringement of 134
deputy chairman, appointment 3
directions from Secretary of State—
information, as to provision of 34
international purposes, for 33
networks and spectrum functions, as
to 18
disclosure of information—
Broadcasting Acts 1990 or 1996,
under 43
Communications Act 2003, under 43
Telecommunications Act 1984,
obtained under 42
disputes—
appeal—
right of 224
See also COMPETITION APPEAL
TRIBUNAL
information, power to require 223
other member states, involving 221
price control, as to 225
procedures, giving approval to 99n[18]
reference of—
action on 218
conditions for 217
legal proceedings 219
resolution—
determinations 222
powers 222
procedure for 220

References are to paragraph numbers; superior figures refer to notes

References are to paragraph numbers; superior figures refer to notes

Time

References are to paragraph numbers; superior figures refer to notes

SUNSET
local time, as reference to 316n[7]

TIME
computation. *See* COMPUTATION OF
TIME
directly: meaning 353
forthwith: meaning 352
immediately: meaning 352
local, ascertainment of 315
on or upon: meaning 353
reasonable: meaning 349
summer time—
prescription of 317
reckoning of time during 318
things done electronically, timing 319

TREASURY
financial dealings, power to suspend—
national interest, in 328
specified days, on 320

WEEK
meaning 312

WILL
period for performance of act fixed by
338

YEAR
annual finance accounts, for 303n[4]
calendar 302
child born on 29 February, completion
of anniversary 302
common year 302
contract, meaning in 304
covenant, meaning in 304n[1]
divisions 302
ecclesiastical 302
financial 303
in any one: meaning 305
income tax purposes, for 303
leap 302, 304
length of 302
period of time, as 303
quarters 306
social security benefit, for 303
statutory definitions 303

Tort

ABSOLUTE LIABILITY
meaning 523
breach of statutory duty, in cases of 523
dangerous animals, for damage by 523,
524
Rylands v Fletcher, under rule in 523

ABUSE OF PROCESS
civil proceedings, malicious 748
claim, where lying 757

ACT OF GOD
action in tort, defence to 469
breach of statutory duty, defence to 521

ACT OF STATE
defence to claim in tort, as 456

ACTION IN TORT
death, surviving 487
defences—
act of state 456
consent 465
contracting out of liability 466
ex turpi causa 467
illegality 467
inevitable accident 468
judicial acts 460
justification 461

ACTION IN TORT—*continued*
defences—*continued*
ministerial execution of decrees 460
necessity 464
protection of property 461, 463
self-defence 461, 462
self-redress, legitimate 461
statutory 458
statutory authority 457
statutory limits on liability 459
parties to—
aliens 446
assignee 442
bankrupt 441
care and welfare of child, those with
duty of 438
child 435
civil partners 433
convicted person 444
corporation 426
Crown 418
diplomats 421
disabled child, persons liable to 439
employee 429
employer 429

CONVERSION—*continued*
bailee, by. *See under* BAILEE
bank's defence to claim 661
better title, pleading 656
broker, by 649
causation of loss—
  claimant suffering loss in any event,
    where 681
  loss attributable to conversion 681
  normal causal requirements—
    application 681
    disapplication 682
  successive conversions 682
chattel—
  meaning 639
  documents 642
  human body and its parts 640
  money 641
contractual rights 643
contributory negligence no defence 658
co-owner's right to sue other co-owner
  617
co-ownership no defence 659
damages—
  causation. *See* causation of loss *above*
  consequential loss—
    heads of 683
    liability for 683
    limitations on recovery 684
  document evincing debt, measure of
    damages for 673
  effect of payment 663, 668
  less than market value of chattel—
    adjustment for improvement to
      chattel 678
    co-owner of chattel, claimant
      being 679
    lease, chattel subject to 676
    market value as starting point 674
    reduction of damages for intended
      expenditure 680
    security interest, chattel subject to
      677
    unpaid vendor, conversion by 675
  negotiable instrument, measure of
    damages for 673
  purpose 668, 673
  right to 662
  suitable replacement, cost of 669,
    683
  value of chattel—
    assessment 669, 670
    document evincing debt 673
    fall in chattel's value before
      judgment 672
    market value 669

CONVERSION—*continued*
damages—*continued*
  value of chattel—*continued*
    mitigation, claimant's duty of 671
    negotiable instrument 673
    no market value, where 669
    replacement cost 669
    rise in chattel's value before
      judgment 671
    starting point, as 668, 674
    time of assessment 670
defence—
  bailee's power of sale 661
  bankrupt's property, persons dealing
    with 661
  better title, pleading 656
  contributory negligence excluded as
    658
  co-ownership excluded as 659
  estoppel as 648
  lapse of time 660
  ministerial receipt as. *See* ministerial
    receipt as defence to *below*
  multiplicity of actions, to avoid 656
  pawnbroker 661
  purchase in good faith as. *See*
    purchase in good faith *below*
  statutory 661
deliberate interference with chattel 606
denial of title not amounting to 614
destruction of chattel 609
detention of chattel, by 613
documents 642
double liability in, avoidance of 656
double recovery, avoidance of 657
equitable title to chattel—
  examples of persons with 636
  right to sue, whether conferring 636
  trustee 637
estoppel as defence to 648
examples 605, 608–613
finder of chattel, rights of 622
general features 604
intangibles 643
internet domain name 643n[1]
joyriding as 608n[6]
land on which chattel situated, taking
  possession of 608
legal title to chattel—
  acquisition of—
    animals' offspring 626
    bailment, by 625
    chattel lease 624
    continuing possession, no need for
      621

References are to paragraph numbers; superior figures refer to notes

References are to paragraph numbers; superior figures refer to notes

Trade and Industry

References are to paragraph numbers; superior figures refer to notes

References are to paragraph numbers; superior figures refer to notes

Words and Phrases

Words in parentheses indicate the context in which the word or phrase is used

References are to paragraph numbers; superior figures refer to notes

user (public electronic communications
    service) 229n[3]
user ID 240n[8]
value added service 231n[12]
Vandepitte procedure 637n[3]
vehicle 917n[10]
vehicle company 1026n[3]
vessel—
    (Export Control Order 2008) 917n[10]
    (Submarine Telegraph Act 1885)
        212n[10]
veterinary medicinal product 1009n[10]
visitors' ground 992n[22]
visitors' premises 992n[22]
visiting team 992n[22]
waiver 484
waiver of tort 484
Wales 318n[2], 906n[7]
warehouse 939n[4]

water authority 180n[7]
water main 180n[6]
weather working days 313n[1]
week 312
Welsh Industrial Development Advisory
    Board 1059
wholly owned subsidiary 1060n[2]
wireless telegraphy 16n[9]
WMD purposes 918n[4]
work and skill rule 640
work-seeker 977n[7]
work-finding services 977n[7]
working day—
    (Export Control Order 2008) 932n[14]
    (generally) 313n[1]
works required for the public service 906
writing 168n[1]
wrongful interference with goods 603
year 303, 304n[1]